PENGUIN REFERENCE

THE COMPLETE FILM DICTIONARY

Ira Konigsberg is professor of Film and English at the University of Michigan. He directed the University's Program in Film and Video Studies from 1988–1995. He teaches film, media, and literature and has published numerous books, articles, and anthologies on these subjects. In addition, Professor Konigsberg has practical experience in film and theater production.

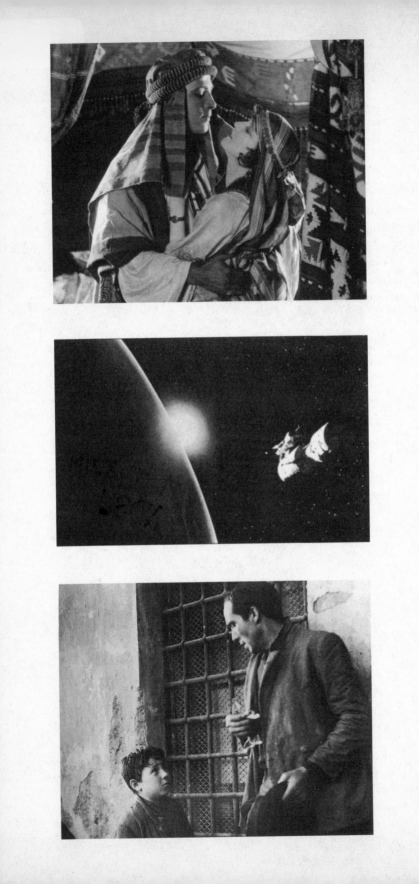

THE COMPLETE

· FILM ·

DICTIONARY

IRA KONIGSBERG

SECOND EDITION

PENGUIN REFERENCE

FOR NANCY
my companion at the movies,

AND FOR MY FATHER,
who first took me to the movies

PENGUIN REFERENCE
Published by the Penguin Group
Penguin Putnam Inc., 375 Hudson Street,
New York, New York 10014, U.S.A.
Penguin Books Ltd, 27 Wrights Lane,
London W8 5TZ, England
Penguin Books Australia Ltd, Ringwood,
Victoria, Australia
Penguin Books Canada Ltd, 10 Alcorn Avenue,
Toronto, Ontario, Canada M4V 3B2
Penguin Books (N.Z.) Ltd, 182–190 Wairau Road,
Auckland 10, New Zealand
Penguin India, 210 Chiranjiv Tower, 43 Nehru Place,
New Delhi 11009, India

Penguin Books Ltd, Registered Offices:
Harmondsworth, Middlesex, England

First published in the United States of America
in a NAL Books edition by New American Library 1987
Second edition published by Penguin Reference,
a member of Penguin Putnam Inc. 1997
This paperback edition published in Penguin Reference 1998

10 9 8 7 6 5 4 3 2 1

Still of tryptych scene from *Abel Gance's Napolean vu par Abel Gance*
copyright © Images Film Archive, Inc. 1981

THE LIBRARY OF CONGRESS HAS CATALOGUED
THE PENGUIN REFERENCE HARDCOVER AS FOLLOWS:
Konigsberg, Ira.
The complete film dictionary / Ira Konigsberg.—Sec. ed.
p.   cm.
ISBN 0-670-10009-9 (hc.)
ISBN 0 14 05.1393 0
1. Motion pictures—Dictionaries.   2. Cinematography—Dictionaries.   I. Title.
PN1993.45.K66   1997
791.43´03—dc21   96–52953

Ref.

Printed in the United States of America
Set in New Baskerville
Designed by Virginia Norey

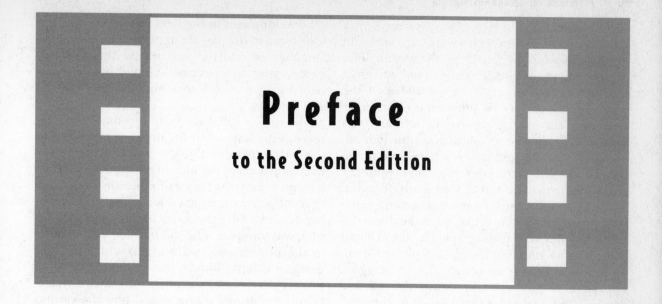

Preface
to the Second Edition

The radical and revolutionary changes in the film industry during the past decade have made the second edition of *The Complete Film Dictionary* inevitable. It is time to update the first volume and reflect the new concepts and language that have entered the world of filmmaking and film studies. In the preface to the first edition, I posed a question about the future of cinema in the United States—whether it could survive what then seemed the onslaught of change. The challenges I specified were the influences of a dominating young audience on the very content of film; the deterioration of the viewing experience with the spread of cinema complexes; the economic challenge to cinema from the home video and cable markets; and, finally and perhaps most importantly, the impact of conglomerate ownership on film. We can dismiss the first three of these issues easily.

The youthful surge has diminished and the over-forty crowd is growing as the audience matures. Especially interesting is the fact that moviegoers have more education than those who do not frequent the theaters. Although a number of the old coffinlike theaters remain from the division of larger theaters and at the complexes in shopping malls, newer multiplexes and mega-

plexes are creating viewing facilities that are both comfortable and impressive. One can sit in a flexible and plush seat, viewing a well-lit image from a wide, curved screen, while listening to digital stereophonic and surround sound. Granted that these are not the large, imposing screens of the old movie palaces, but the quality of image and sound is better than ever. And these screens keep growing in number—some 8,500 additional indoor screens appeared in the last decade alone, making the total 26,995 in 1995. Obviously the video and cable market have not hurt the movie industry—though many people now do all their movie watching at home, a great number are stimulated by such viewing to make their way to the theater. But, more significantly, such home viewing has a burgeoning role in the earning power of the large corporate organizations that own the film companies—video and cable have become significant players in the economic reality and expansion of the entertainment industry.

With all this good news, though, the present state of the cinema seems a mixed bag at best. The technology is exploding. People are making more money than ever before. But the films themselves often seem disappointing. Recent articles in the *New York Times* have stated that films have become dumber and that characters seem ever less articulate. As the technology increases and sights and sounds overwhelm us, the very qualities that once made us love films, the drama and characterization, are normally thin shadows of the past. The reason for this situation is clear. In recent years, cinema has become the software for a long list of hardware—theatrical distribution, home video, cable and network television, novelizations, musical recordings, video and computer games, theme parks, and various kinds of tie-ins. At the same time, the software has become an international commodity with foreign theatrical distribution almost equaling that in the United States in gross revenue. The motion picture, then, must be all things to all people and, in being so, must lose a good deal of its uniqueness and depth. The fourth issue that I raised in the preface to the last edition, then, has been the one that has had the greatest impact—the explosive growth of cinema into big business.

But it is hard to conceive of the technology's advancement having taken place at such a rapid rate without this economic expansion. If we are not having our minds elevated and our emotions touched, we are seeing sights that humans have never seen before. Our imaginations and minds are being developed, and our fantasies and dreams expanded. The very technology is reaching out at us, pulling us into it with new visions and new sounds. Film itself seems in the forefront of new modes of entertainment, fusing with and motivating special venues, interactive video, and virtual reality.

The two major forces in cinema I have mentioned—economics and technology—were two of the five categories that I claimed as the source of the all-inclusiveness of the first edition of *The Complete Film Dictionary*. For this volume, I claim the same five categories as the source for all my entries once again, but do so recognizing how those first two categories have impacted on the other three. In addition to those two categories, the reader will once again find all the practical terminology of filmic discourse used in the field, the basic language necessary to know what transpires when a film is made and how one can talk intelligently about what takes place on the screen; the language sufficient to understand the histori-

cal developments in the field, including what has transpired in the past changeable decade; and the language of criticism and theory that now engages a growing awareness of film dynamics, spectatorship, and the interaction between cinema and culture.

The reader will discover by examining the entire volume how much the world of business and the marketplace influence virtually everything that transpires in the industry, including what we see and hear in the theater. Before anything exists in front of the camera, a vast number of interacting contractual agreements shapes and defines what will transpire: who will play the various roles in the project and under what conditions, how the production will take place, how the finished project will make its way into a network of interrelated formats and markets, and how the various parties and individuals will share in the proceeds. It would be naive to minimize the impact of these various contractual agreements and concerns on that product we think of as "the movie." Very much connected to this web of financial concerns is the overall makeup of the industry, the vast structure of the corporations, their shifting competitions and alliances, and the men who buy, sell, and operate these various organizations—the men who are the real stars of the contemporary motion-picture industry.

But certainly what is today the most fascinating and exciting of my original five categories, the one that has fundamentally changed the most, is that of technology. All film enthusiasts know that the history of cinema is also the history of its technology, that every single technical development changes forever what we see and react to on the screen. Film, as I emphasized in the first edition, is an amalgamation of art and technology and as such is the art form of the twentieth century. As we conclude that century, we must take that insight further and say that film is already the art form of the twenty-first century as it incorporates into both its production and product the digital revolution of the new age of information and entertainment. We must also recognize the pervasiveness of film in our new world—how film, by incorporating this technology, has impacted on a host of other venues and media.

What has been most heartening about the reception of *The Complete Film Dictionary* has been its adaptation by professionals in the industry itself; by film teachers, critics, and students; and by the general reader with a love for the movies. To the before-mentioned groups, however, I add one more to my list of targeted audiences—the person in the myriad fields with some connection to cinema who has a need to understand the ways in which film interacts with other media and other businesses. I have tried to make available once again the language that will explain the various categories, their interactions, and the ways they impact on the films in a manner that is inclusive, technical, but yet readable and accessible to virtually anyone. To make the world of film available to these various readers, I have continued the practice of giving brief and, on occasion, not-so-brief essays to describe larger developments, more complicated procedures, and more general overviews as contexts for the more concise definitions that make up much of the work.

I have updated the old entries whenever necessary to bring them into accord with modern practices and developments. At the same time I have tried to recognize the ways in which older practices and technologies are still in use. Though there is tremendous glamour to the digital revolution, we would do well to remember that some of the traditional technologies can still do the job better and in a far more economical manner—the photochemical blue-screen process, rear-projection, and optical printers, for example, are still very much with us. I have also included a number of technologies that have ceased to exist because they fill an important page in the history of the medium—the history of technology is significant to the history of the films on the screen and the two are intimately related. This is a dictionary of film past, film present, and film future.

To the previous 3,500-odd entries, I have added approximately 500 new ones. Although a number of these new entries add to and refine what previously existed in this book, a number break new ground, especially as they seek to explain the impact of digital technology on the preproduction, production, and postproduction phases of filmmaking. I also have added 35 new line drawings and photographs to the previous 225. The function of this visual material is to make machinery, techniques, and film history as visible as possible (in keeping with the film medium itself). Many of the new line drawings themselves address the advancements in film technology and contribute to bringing this book up-to-date.

Once again, I have read every available piece of literature on film and the film industry; studied all the film journals, both within the industry and about it; and examined every catalogue from every major manufacturer of equipment that I could get my hands on. I have kept abreast of all the business developments by keeping my eyes glued to trade papers and financial publications. To understand and keep up with the dizzying changes in the technology, I made immediate contact with the companies and people responsible for these advancements and asked a myriad of questions, examined all the necessary documents, made on-site visits to examine the equipment, and then asked a myriad of questions once again—until I had the full and comprehensive knowledge to write the specific entries necessary for this volume.

An undertaking of this magnitude, even by a number of individuals, is, of course, fraught with great risk. I have spent many an obsessive hour checking and rechecking to get things as right as humanly possible. In this effort, I am thankful to the people who submitted letters, after the appearance of the first edition, suggesting both corrections and additional information. The spirit of these letters was always one of contributing to a noble and bold undertaking. The publication of this new volume gives me the chance to respond to these suggestions. I am especially grateful to my editors for the opportunity to change the incorrect dates or typos that caused me some distress after I discovered them in the first edition. It is my fondest hope that the new material will cause me less distress.

The Complete Film Dictionary continues its goal of being the major sourcebook in the field, both for professionals and nonprofessionals. As far as I know, there continues to be none like it in scope. Once again, though, as I did in the last volume, I wish to acknowledge those works that have also contributed to understanding the complex language of cinema, but I wish to mention how my volume differs from such works. David E. Elkins has written a Focal Handbook that is both compact and useful, *Camera Terms and Concepts* (1993), which focuses on the camera apparatus itself. Another Focal Handbook of value is Stephen E. Browne's *Film Video Terms and Concepts* (1992), which gives some very succinct and useful descriptions for corresponding technical terms in both film and video production. Michael J. McAlister, in *The Language of Visual Effects* (1993), has written a slender volume that is chock-full of useful terminology concerning the world of special effects; while John W. Cones has written a not-so-slender book, *Film Finance and Distribution: A Dictionary of Terms* (1992), that seems to include every term, with excellent cross-references, concerning that complicated and mysterious world of business underlying the making of motion pictures. Also worth noting is Richard Weiner's *Webster's New World Dictionary of Media and Communications* (1990), a very ambitious collection of terminology in all fields of communication—the entries, by the nature of the undertaking, must be quite short, but the volume has the virtue of placing a number of terms used in cinema in the context of their use by other media and systems of communication. All of these works are, of course, far more focused on a specific area of film or, in the case of the last book, far more limited in their approach to the general subject than my own volume. Most of their definitions, with the exception of those in Cone's very specialized work, are very brief and sometimes abrupt. *The Complete Film Dictionary* seeks to be as comprehensive as possible, not only in scope, but also in understanding the world of cinema from analytical, theoretical, and historical perspectives in addition to the technological and economical.

I must confess that I have the same misgiving that I did when I finished the first edition—that my field of study is so dynamic and changing that even as I put my pen to rest, new happenings and developments are transpiring. I have had the happy situation with my publisher of making additions late into production for this edition as well as the last. I have also ventured in this volume to look into the future with as many entries as possible, surveying the developments that are presently taking place and surmising where they might continue.

The fact is that with all my disappointment about so many of the dramatic products that the film industry is sending into theaters, something exciting and even astonishing remains about the cinema itself. One need only look at the latest digital images in both animation and live-action works to know that we are on the edge of something powerful and magical. One need only attend the latest IMAX 3-D film to know that we are on the edge of visual and aural experiences as yet undreamed-of—that we are to be involved in and experience a host of brave new worlds.

At this time, we can only speculate where cinema will take us. Although predictions about the demise of the wonderful chemical image have so far proven to be wrong—particularly since the film image keeps sufficiently ahead of even the latest developments in television and digital technology—specialists are predicting the time when motion pictures will be delivered digitally to motion-picture houses via (1) high-definition projection systems, (2) a fiber-optic distribution network, or (3) satellite. The savings on prints and various distribution expenses will, of course, be enormous, but also gained will be a tremendous flexibility, variety, and even quality. But one cannot think of such systems without also speculating on the effect of these technologies on the quality of home viewing, which itself must lead to speculation on the nature of HDTV, cable and satellite television, and the new DVD disc system that offers tremendous opportunities for watching motion pictures at home.

But if the parameters of viewing both in the theater and at home are expanding, the same nagging questions still remain. What will fill the images? What will these extraordinary sights and sounds deliver to us other than extraordinary sights and sounds? Is our postmodern age truly one of simulacrum, of image upon image without any reality—have we finally lost the human amidst all this technology? Is cinema ultimately to become a series of mindless spectacles that fill the eyes and ears but leave the mind and soul empty? Are we ultimately to become the cyborgs?

My answer to such questions must repeat what I said in the preface to the first edition of this book. Cinema is and remains the major art form of our time. Not since the beginning of history have we had an art form that can so impact upon us as we respond to it. In its incorporation of technology and high finance, film has become, at its worst, a reflection of the world in which we live. But it has been and can continue to be a reflection of what we are at our best. The opportunities for opening up human history and destiny with film are enormous. Amidst all the stock fare that comes out of Hollywood, good films are still made and still appear on the screen. Independently made films continue to enrich our motion-picture heritage. Good artists are born and dedicate themselves to the art of film—in narrative, documentary, and experimental works. The impulse to create art is as strong as the impulse to develop technology—film offers the opportunity to bring the two together in unparalleled ways.

I conclude this preface by offering my sincerest thanks to the people who helped me with their expertise in the preparation of the second edition of *The Complete Film Dictionary*. Ed Wicinski of Du Art Film and Video in New York City; Russell Ofria of Advanced Camera Systems in Van Nuys, California; John Ross of Digital Sound and Picture in Los Angeles; Jack Butler and Skip Farley of Butler Graphics in Troy, Michigan; Dan Kier, video specialist with Media Services at the University of Michigan in Ann Arbor; Jon Lewis, film historian at Oregon State in Corvallis, Oregon; and Russell Collins of the Michigan Theater Foundation in Ann Arbor all read portions of this book and were decent enough to stay with me until I got it right. Bob Fischer of Creative Communications Services, representing Eastman Kodak, in Carlsbad, California; David Fischer of Du Art Film and Video in New York City; Joan Graves of the Motion Picture Association of America's Classification and Rating Administration in En-

cino, California; Lynne Sauve of Ultimatte Co. in Chatsworth, California; Vince Wellman of Wayne State Law School in Detroit all talked to me and sent me important documentation. Richard Utley of Protec Film Vaults in Los Angeles, Steve Hallet of Oxberry LLC in Newark, New Jersey, Jonathan Erland, president of Composite Components in Los Angeles, Richard Glicksman, lighting expert in Burbank, California, Al Young, sound specialist and Robert Rayher, production instructor, both with the University of Michigan's Film and Video Program, Dan Breul, head of Projection Services at the same university, and Klaus-Peter Beir, research scientist in engineering, also at Michigan, were extremely forthcoming in discussions. Special thanks to Gaylyn Studlar, and William Paul, colleagues in the Film and Video Program at Michigan, for creating the kind of exciting teaching and scholarly environment that encourages works such as mine.

Jennifer Riopelle is responsible for the excellent drawings that have been added to this new edition, and Mary Corliss of the Film Stills Archive in New York City's Museum of Modern Art helped in the selection of the new photographs. The Vice-President's Office for Research and the Office of the Associate Dean for Research, Computing, and Facilities at the University of Michigan supplied funding for the drawings, photography, and final preparation of the manuscript. Finally, and with appropriate fanfare, I wish to express my gratitude to Hugh Rawson, reference editor at Penguin, who has been a calm and guiding force in seeing both editions of *The Complete Film Dictionary* to press, and to my wife, Nancy, whose help, support, and patience were instrumental in bringing this project to a happy ending.

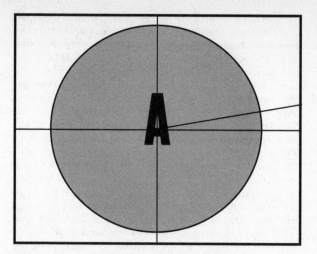

A and B printing to A-wind

wind is when the film is unwinding clockwise with the emulsion facing in and the perforations close to the viewer; B-wind is for the same conditions but with the perforations away from the viewer. Film in the camera is generally B-wind, while duplicating film for contact printing is normally A-wind. The terms have also been used for processed film with A-wind referring to film with the picture situated correctly when the emulsion faces the viewer, and B-wind for film with a properly reading image when the base faces the viewer. To avoid confusion, however, the first type of processed film is also referred to as A-type and the second as B-type. An original negative from normal or reversal film is B-type, for example, while an internegative from a reversal original is A-type.

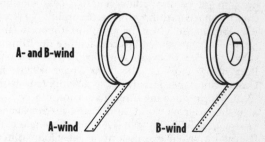

A- and B-wind

A-wind · · · · B-wind · · · ·

■ **A and B printing** A method of printing generally for 16mm film that allows multiple images, fades, dissolves, and other effects without the necessity of costly optical processes and which avoids the appearance of any splices on the screen. The shots of the negative (or sometimes positive) are staggered in alternate spaces on two rolls of film of the same length with black leader between the shots on each roll—the shots on one film correspond with black leader on the other. The odd-number shots on the A roll and then the even-number shots on the B roll are printed in consecutive order. Multiple images are achieved by printing shots together at the same point in each roll; dissolves are achieved by overlapping a fade-out on one roll with a fade-in on the other. Sometimes a C and even D roll might be incorporated for additional effects. A and B printing is sometimes used for 35mm film, for example to save the cost of creating dissolves and fades with an optical printer. *See* **checkerboard cutting** *and* **invisible splice.**

■ **A and B rolls** The rolls of film in A and B printing.

A and B rolls for A and B printing

■ **A and B roll supered titles** Titles superimposed over an image by printing together two rolls of film, one with the titles and one with the image.

■ **A- and B-type** *See* **A- and B-wind.**

■ **A- and B-wind** Terms for raw 16mm film that distinguish the positions of the single row of perforations. A-

■ **Abby Singer shot** A term used during film production that refers to the next-to-the-last shot of the day. The term originates from an individual named Abby Singer, who was an assistant director at Universal Studios during the 1950s and was constantly promising that, after the present shot, only a single shot remained before the crew would move to another part of the studio or the day's shooting would end. *See* **martini shot.**

■ **A/B'd** Running two pieces of film simultaneously, adjacent to one another, for comparison—either in an editing or projection system.

■ **aberration** An imperfection in the lens that causes a distortion in the film image.

■ **above-the-line costs** Contractual expenses agreed upon before the shooting of a film that involve the purchase of the property and salaries for such people as author, screenwriter, producer, director, and performers. *See* **below-the-line costs.**

■ **above the title** The location for the front credits that appear on the screen before the title is shown. *See* **below the title** *and* **front credits.**

■ **abrasion** Any mark or scratch on film emulsion that might be caused by the tightness of the roll or by some particle, and that generally causes an imperfection, distortion, or line in the film image.

■ **absolute film** (1) The name given to abstract films made in Germany during the 1920s. These films are composed of animated drawings of nonrepresentational lines, forms, shapes, or patterns, and emphasize the rhythmic relationship between the separate images. Well-known examples are Hans Richter's *Rhythmus 21* (1921) and Viking Eggeling's *Symphonie Diagonale* (1924). With the advent of sound, Oskar Fischinger later in the decade began making "absolute" films that integrated rhythmic visual patterns with music. (2) A term sometimes used for any abstract film that presents nonrepresentational lines, forms, shapes, or colors in rhythmic patterns. Such films are considered "absolute" cinematic performances because they emphasize the visual dimension of the image itself without any reference to external reality and because their only action and meaning is in the rhythmic movement from one image to the other. These works explore the frame's space and the film's temporality. *See* **pure cinema.** (3) The name given by the film theoretician Béla Balázs to avant-garde films that feature the filmmaker's subjective view of external reality. In *The Theory of Film,* Béla Balázs cites *De Brug (The Bridge,* 1928), by the Dutch filmmaker Joris Ivens, as an impressionistic "absolute" film, since the subjective vision can be retraced into the external world; and *Berlin, die Symphonie einer Grosstadt* (1927), by the German filmmaker Walter Ruttmann, as an expressionistic "absolute" film, since inner consciousness totally distorts external reality. (4) A term used by P. Adams Sitney in *Visionary Film* to describe the ultimate film aspired to by experimental filmmakers who seek to achieve the pure "essence of cinema" in "giant, all-inclusive forms." *See* **abstract film.**

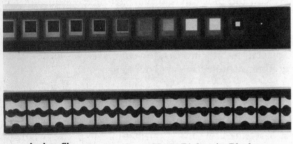

absolute film Frames from Hans Richter's *Rhythmus 21* (1921).

■ ■ ■

■ **abstract film** A general term for all experimental films that create a visual world of nonrepresentational shapes and forms or even objects with no relation to the real world. Such films create their own logic and relationships in the individual frame and in the movement from image to image. The word "abstract" means anything conceived apart from real physical objects or events, and "abstract art," from which abstract film received its impetus and name, refers to twentieth-century paintings that deal only with lines, forms, shapes, patterns, colors, and their relationships apart from any

recognizable objects or reality. Abstract film may present the same content as abstract painting, but the sequence of frames allows the artist to explore temporal relationships, rhythmic patterns, and movement as well as spatial relationships. The term "abstract film," unlike "abstract art," also includes those works that employ images of objects from the real world, but in a nonrepresentational and nonreferential way that emphasizes composition and movement. The term was used for Fernand Léger and Dudley Murphy's *Le Ballet Mécanique* (1924), which features images of faces, bodies, and kitchen implements, though purists would argue that the film is not sufficiently nonreferential to be considered "abstract." Abstract films are made by (1) animated photography, where individual drawings are photographed, as in the case of Richter's and Eggeling's "absolute films"; (2) the artist working directly on the film stock from frame to frame, as in the case of Len Lye's *Color Box* (1935); (3) computer graphics, as in Stan Vanderbeek's *Computer Art (number one)* (1966); and (4) the artist photographing reality, though in a way that makes images lose their original context and meaning, as in the case of *Le Ballet Mécanique. See* **absolute film.**

■ **academic cutting** *See* **invisible cutting.**

■ **Academy aperture** The ratio of width to height of apertures on 35mm cameras and projectors that produces the 4:3 or 1.33:1 frame standardized by the Academy of Motion Picture Arts and Sciences in 1932. *See* **aspect ratio.**

■ **Academy Awards** The awards given in the form of golden statuettes called Oscars by the Academy of Motion Picture Arts and Sciences for the best achievements in performance and filmmaking for each calendar year, and for distinguished career and technical achievements. Except for Best Picture, where nominations are voted by all the members of the Academy, specialists first vote for nominations in their own field, and then the entire Academy votes for the winner in each major category. Major categories for awards are now Best Picture, Actor, Actress, Supporting Actor, Supporting Actress, Directing, Screenplay Written Directly for the Screen, Screenplay Based on Material from Another Medium, Cinematography, Art Direction and Set Direction, Sound, Sound Effects Editing, Film Editing, Original Musical and Comedy Score, Original Dramatic Score, Original Song, Costume Design, Animated Short Film, Live-Action Short Film, Short-Subject Documentary, Feature Documentary, Foreign-Language Film, and Visual Effects. The first awards were given on May 16, 1929, for film achievements during 1927–28. Since 1934, awards have been given for each calendar year, except in the category of Foreign Film, where the year of eligibility is from November 1 to October 31. The most-honored films are *Ben-Hur* (1959; dir. William Wyler), which won eleven awards, and *West Side Story* (1961; dir. Robert Wise), which won ten. Awards are given in March or April for the previous year in a lavishly staged ceremony that has appeared on national television since 1953. Because major awards for a film mean increased publicity and revenue at the box office, as well as increased professional opportunities for the winners, a considerable amount of politicking and advertising precedes the voting. *See* **Academy of Motion Picture Arts and Sciences.**

■ **Academy leader** The piece of film attached to the beginning and end of each reel of the release print, which protects the pictures and sound, and which allows for threading before the start of the movie. The leader also supplies the projectionist with such information as the name of the work, the number of the reel, and the countdown before the picture commences. This leader, standardized by the Academy of Motion Picture Arts and Sciences, has long been replaced by the SMPTE universal leader. *See* **SMPTE universal leader.**

Academy leader

■ **Academy of Motion Picture Arts and Sciences (AMPAS)** The professional organization, with headquarters in Beverly Hills, California, for those engaged in the making of motion pictures; it has over 5,000 active members and some 850 associate members who do not vote for awards. The organization includes branches for nearly all aspects of filmmaking, and membership is by invitation only. The Academy was created in 1927 to improve the public image of the industry, handle disputes or problems between the branches, and encourage both artistic and technical improvements. After a stormy ten years, the Academy withdrew from labor negotiations in 1937 and since that time has devoted itself to supporting technical research and education in filmmaking, publishing such reference works as the *Annual Index of Motion Picture Credits,* which lists complete film credits, and the *Academy Players Directory,* and honoring distinguished achievement in performance and filmmaking each year. *See* **Academy Awards** *and* **Academy standards.**

■ **Academy Players Directory** A directory released by the Academy of Motion Picture Arts and Sciences that contains pictures and credits for 16,000 to 18,000 actors and actresses. The directory, which appears three times each year, is used for casting in the motion-picture industry.

■ **Academy roll-off, Academy curve** Standards set by the Academy of Motion Picture Arts and Sciences used in dubbing to compensate for the roll-off or loss of frequency in movie theaters. The standard, which allowed for 1,000 cycles, disappeared with the advent of Dolby sound systems in the 1970s. It was replaced by a standard called the X-curve, which allowed for 12,000 cycles and which is no longer relevant. *See* **Dolby.**

■ **Academy standards** Standards for film technology set by the Academy of Motion Picture Arts and Sciences and accepted by the film industry at large. The general use of these standards is reflected in such accepted terminology as Academy aperture and Academy leader.

■ **accelerated montage** Rapid cutting from shot to shot to increase the pacing and rhythm of action as it appears on the screen. The length of the individual shots becomes shorter as we see different views of the same action or views of different but related actions. An example of accelerated shots of the same action is the famous shower sequence in Alfred Hitchcock's *Psycho* (1960), where there are some sixty cuts in a few minutes to create for the viewer the frenzied and hysterical experience of the stabbing. Notable accelerated montages of related actions appear at the end of several films by D. W. Griffith to increase suspense as rescuer rushes to potential victim. *See* **montage.**

■ **accelerated motion** *See* **fast motion.**

■ **acceptance angle, angle of acceptance** (1) The angle formed by two lines drawn from both extremities of the view photographed to both extremities of the image received by the lens. (2) The angle formed by two lines drawn from both extremities of the lighted area to both extremities of the light that registers on the light meter. *See* **angle of view.**

■ **ace** A spotlight with a 1,000-watt bulb.

■ **ACE** *See* **American Cinema Editors.**

■ **acetate base, triacetate base** A low-combustible, slow-burning base for film. The light-sensitive photographic emulsion is attached to the base. Before acetate, nitrate was used for film base but was highly combustible and deteriorated rapidly. Acetate-base film, however, is also prone to a deterioration referred to as the vinegar syndrome. A number of films now use the stronger and longer-lasting polyester base. *See* **film** *(1),* **polyester base,** *and* **vinegar syndrome.**

■ **achromatic lens** A lens adjusted for chromatic aberrations (i.e., the dispersion of foci for different colors) so that colors are focused at the same points. This correction is often made by bringing together two lenses of different material, with one lens correcting the dispersion of the other. *See* **apochromatic lens.**

■ **Acmade numbers** Numbers thermally transferred to the workprint and magnetic sound film to allow for synchronization during editing.

■ **acoustics** (1) The science of sound. (2) The environmental factors of any area that affect the quality of sound. These are especially important in recording sound either indoors or outdoors and reproducing it in a theater or auditorium.

■ **acquisition agreement, acquisition rights** A contractual agreement by which an individual or production company acquires the rights to a property (for example, a novel, play, or song) for the purpose of making it into or using it as part of a motion picture. Such agreements normally include a date on which the rights expire should they not previously be acted upon.

■ **acting** Interpreting and pretending to be a character in a film through action, facial expression, general behavior, and, in sound movies, through speech. Unlike stage acting, where the actor directly communicates his or her interpretation of character to the audience, film acting is also communicated by means of camera, editing, and sound track, all of which may strengthen, alter, and, on occasion, even weaken a performance. Not only are scenes filmed shot by shot and some shots taken several times over, but economy and scheduling force roles to be performed out of sequence, hence destroying any continuity for the actor or actress and creating problems different from those of the stage performer. In film, performers act before a camera, frequently in close proximity, which brings before the viewer every gesture and movement, and voices are recorded through a microphone, which captures every whisper and modulation. Hence, the projection of both voice and body required of the stage performer is absent, and a more subtle and natural acting style is needed. The history of film acting can be seen as a development from the more exaggerated and theatrical performances of silent films, when actors and actresses in the new art form were still influenced by the stage and at the same time forced to project thought and feeling without the use of sound, until the present time, when performances tend to be natural and realistic, and even unskilled actors and actresses can be made to seem credible by film editing. Such a development is, of course, neither straight nor clear, and one must always recognize that different kinds of film genres make different demands on the performer.

D. W. Griffith attempted to bring greater credibility to the silent film through his casting of characters, his use of the camera, and by giving greater care to performance, though, for the modern viewer, his films still seem stylized; and, later, in the silent films of Stroheim and Murnau, great subtlety and conviction were achieved in acting. The advent of sound freed the performers from an unnatural emphasis on facial expression, gesture, and body movement, yet even in the films of the 1930s and 1940s, we can see that the "star system" and the popularity of certain "film personalities" created performances that were mannered, unvaried, and, to meet expectation, even exaggerated. It was in the late 1940s and the 1950s that film acting received its greatest impetus toward more natural and realistic performances through Italian neorealism and through the impact of the Actors Studio of New York. The acting of Marlon Brando and James Dean, both of whom had some contact with the Actors Studio, was significant in this respect, and their influence can be seen on such performers as Dustin Hoffman, Al Pacino, and Robert De Niro. But the aging of these performers and the large economic stakes of films made by the industry have tended in recent years to deemphasize realistic acting and emphasize broader visual and more youthful qualities that will appeal to an international audience. The exception has been the array of talented actors coming out of Great Britain—e.g., Anthony Hopkins, Daniel Day-Lewis, and Ralph Fiennes. There seems to be no shortage of actresses with extraordinary range and sensitivity on the screen—e.g., Meryl Streep, Michelle Pfeiffer, and Debra Winger—but good parts are not often available for actresses and they are more often forced to play conventional roles. Sometimes, however, actresses such as Jodie Foster in this country and Emma Thompson in Great Britain are able to take a more aggressive role in production and create for themselves some fine parts.

■ **acting coach** (1) A person hired to help an individual performer with his or her role in a film. (2) A teacher of acting who works independently with one or more performers.

■ **actinicity** The word "actinism" pertains to the property of radiation to cause chemical change; actinicity refers, in cinematography, to the proportion of light which actually is recorded on the emulsion of a film. For example, normal daylight would have a high actinicity for panchromatic stock which is sensitive to all the parts of the color spectrum. *See* **film** *(1)*.

■ **action** (1) The order given by the director, once the camera and sound system are operating, for the performers to start acting. (2) What the characters do during a scene: their individual acts and behaviors. (3) The general event that takes place in an individual scene or sequence (e.g., a chase). Films vary according to the amount of action in each—that is, the amount of activity in each episode and the number of general actions that make up the story. "Adventure-packed" Westerns focus more on action in both these respects and less on character than domestic dramas. (4) The general story line of the film. (5) The image on film as distinct from the sound track.

■ **action-adventure film** The term loosely applies to a number of types of films, and was very much used by the Hollywood studios to promote anything from a crime film to a swashbuckling pirate film. Such films offer the viewer excitement, suspense, and escape by involving the hero in a series of physical feats, fights, and chases—sometimes in an unusual venture and sometimes in exotic locales. In recent years Steven Spielberg's *Raiders of the Lost Ark* (1981) and *Indiana Jones and the Last Crusade* (1989) seem prime examples.

■ **action axis, axis action** *See* **imaginary line.**

■ **action cutting** Cutting from shot to shot so that action seems continuous. The viewer is normally unaware of such changes in perspective, which keep the scene from being monotonous, add excitement or drama to the scene, and bring to attention various aspects of the action or significant information. Such shots are made to seem unobtrusive and continuous by using one camera and repeating the final movements of a shot at the beginning of the next so that the action is overlapped, by filming with more than one camera at the same time and splicing the shots together at the appropriate juncture, or by precisely switching from one camera to another. The technique is also referred to as cutting on action. *See* **cutting on action, invisible cutting,** *and* **matching action.**

■ **action field** *See* **field of action.**

■ **action film** A film that features a good deal of action and minimal characterization—for example, most Westerns or gangster films.

■ **action properties, action props** Properties on the set that are used in some action (e.g., a fan or gun). Also referred to as practicals or pracs. *See* **practical.**

■ **action still** A still picture that is a blowup taken directly from the film and is often used for publicity.

■ **actor** (1) Any male who plays a role in a film. (2) Any person, male or female, who plays a role in a film. The term in relation to film has a certain resonance because of the popularity of performers, and frequently the real-life personality is as much an act as the role in a film—actors are actors even when they seem not to be acting. Sociological changes affect popular tastes, which then influence the kind of actors chosen for various roles in film (e.g., heroes, heroines, and villains), but it is also evident that movies can influence the way the public views reality and certain types of people. In general, one can distinguish the actor who brings a similar film personality from role to role; the actor who projects the individual personality of the role he or she plays; the actor who brings no particular personality to any role; and the nonprofessional who is used to bring verisimilitude to a part.

■ **Actors Studio** An actors' group in New York, founded in 1947, where performers practice and develop their art. Membership is limited to experienced or extremely promising actors. The acting style, called the "method," is naturalistic and draws inspiration from the writings of the Russian actor and director Stanislavski. The group had a significant impact on films in the 1950s, especially through the acting of Marlon Brando and James Dean, and the direction of Elia Kazan, one of the group's founders. Kazan made his widely acclaimed *On the Waterfront* starring Brando in 1954. *See* **method acting.**

■ **actress** Any female who plays a role in a film. *See* **actor** *(2).*

■ **actualités** A term given by the Lumière brothers to their short scenes of real life, which they began showing in Paris in 1895—*Arrival of a Train at a Station* is a well-known example. Edison's company and other early film production companies made these brief, straightforward filmic reproductions of scenes from the actual world, which on the screen riveted the attention of the new audiences.

actualités Frames from the Lumière brothers' *Arrival of a Train at a Station* (1895).

■ ■ ■

■ **actual sound** (1) Environmental sound recorded during the filming of a scene on location to provide authenticity. (2) Dialogue and natural sound recorded during the shooting of a scene and used in the film instead of voice-over or dubbing. (3) Any sound that derives from the action on the screen.

■ **acutance** A measure of the density change at the edge of a subject in a negative from the weakly to strongly exposed areas. The measure is done with a densitometer and gives an accurate assessment of the image's sharpness. *See* **densitometry** *and* **resolution.**

■ **AD** *See* **assistant director.**

■ **adapt** To rewrite and transform a work from one medium into another: to make, for example, a play, story, novel, or nonfiction book into a film. *See* **adaptation.**

■ **adaptation** A work in one medium that derives its impulse as well as a varying number of its elements from a work in a different medium. Film adaptations may be made from plays, stories, novels, histories, biographies, and even on occasion from poetry or song. Sometimes adaptations are loose, borrowing perhaps a general situation, an episode, a character, or even a title as the inspiration for the work; and sometimes adaptations try to be "literal," presenting the original story, characters, and even dialogue as exactly as possible. But film is a separate medium with its own aesthetics and techniques, and the original work must be transformed into what is essentially a different and unique form. Plays that are filmed directly from the stage may be of interest to a special audience, but for most viewers they are slow and often dull. A literal adaptation can be enlivened by good film technique, but this is not often enough true. The medium of fiction and nonfiction is print, and it is the filmmaker who must project his own vision of characters, action, and setting onto the screen. Film creates a fully defined and immediate physical reality that requires dramatization and exploration; it brings characters visually realized into direct relationship with their environment and in immediate proximity to the viewer. The filmmaker's concern is as much with the visual dimensions of each scene as with the drama; and the viewer's eyes require as much visual action, in the camera's presentation of character and setting, as verbal and psychological action.

Filmmakers have always been anxious to use the ready-made story lines of drama and fiction, and especially to exploit the popularity of works in other media. Some of the most popular films of all time have been based on best-sellers—for example, *Gone With the Wind* (1939; dir. Victor Fleming) and Francis Ford Coppola's *The Godfather* (1972). In both these instances, weak, though sensational, books have been given greater credibility and depth by the visual sensibility of the filmmakers. Great novels have always been more resistant to adaptation because film cannot sufficiently depict their internalization of character or the richness and suggestiveness of their language, but even here exceptions can be found, as in the case of Joseph Strick's film version of James Joyce's *Ulysses* (1967), where the director reverentially, though selectively, integrates the spirit and some of the language of the original with his sensitive visual interpretation and depiction of character, setting, and even thought. Shakespeare's plays have also received considerable adaptation in film, on occasion quite successfully when the director extends the drama into the visual medium of the film, as did Laurence Olivier in his production of *Henry V* (1944).

■ **adapter** A device that joins one piece of equipment with another—e.g., a lens adapter that attaches a lens with one type of mount to a camera that accepts another kind of mount, or a hanger adapter that attaches a luminaire with a yoke socket to a C-clamp that attaches to the overhead pipe.

■ **A/D converter, analog-to-digital connecter** A device that transforms analog signals into a digital code—e.g., the light waves from film into a binary code. *See* **digital.**

■ **added scenes** Sometimes the term refers to (1) scenes added to a script after it has been completed or during shooting; but more often it applies to (2) scenes added to the film after shooting has been finished.

■ **additional dialogue** Dialogue added to the script after it has been completed or during shooting.

■ **additive color printer, additive printer** A printer for colored film that adds together red, green, and blue light in different degrees for the desired exposure. A single lamp is divided into the three colors by dichroic mirrors. Light valves then alter the intensity of each color by means of control tapes, and the three colors are brought together by dichroic reflectors. The exposure light passing through the aperture is thus controlled to print a positive from the negative with the desired density and color balance. Sometimes three different lamps are used, the light from each individually modified and then combined with the others. *See* **subtractive color printer.**

adaptation *Ulysses* (1967; dir. Joseph Strick), with Milo O'Shea and Barbara Jefford as Leopold and Molly Bloom in this tactful version of James Joyce's celebrated novel.

■ ■ ■

■ **additive process** A method of cinematography that adds lights of the three primary colors—red, green, and blue—in controlled intensities and mixtures to the projected image. The Dufay color system employed a mosaic of tiny color particles on the film. The image was photographed through the mosaic, then developed into a positive print by a reversal process, and finally projected through the mosaic. In an early Technicolor two-strip method, two black-and-white films, originally photographed separately in a single camera, one through a red filter and the other through a green filter, were projected simultaneously through red and green filters. Hence the colors were added to the image. The additive process for color is no longer employed in cinematography. Today the subtractive method is employed for projecting color images, whereby dyes within the film subtract unwanted color from white light. A brighter and more accurately colored image is thus achieved. *See* **color film** *(2) and* **subtractive process.**

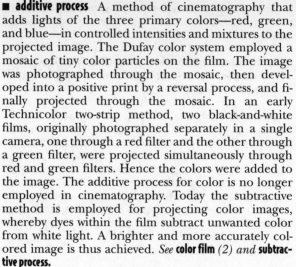

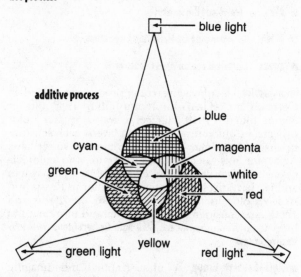

additive process

blue light

blue

cyan

magenta

green

white

red

green light

yellow

red light

■ **adjustable shutter** *See* **variable-opening shutter.**

■ **adjusted gross participation, modified gross participation** A percentage of the gross profits earned by an individual or organization after certain deductions—e.g., advertising and prints. *See* **gross profit participant.**

■ **ad-lib** To speak or act without preparation or the use of a script. To make up lines or actions on the spot. *See* **improvise.**

■ **ADR** *See* **automatic dialogue replacement.**

■ **ADR editor** The individual responsible for the recording and placement of additional dialogue for a production. During the actual shooting, dialogue may be improperly recorded, background noise may be excessive, or it may be impossible to record voices at all. For

whatever reason, the ADR editor responds to the request of the supervising sound editor by arranging for and overseeing recording sessions and then assisting, if called upon, with the alterations to the sound track. *See* **automatic dialogue replacement.**

■ **advance.** *See* **sound advance.**

■ **advertising** Selling a film through the mass media by announcing where and when the film will be shown, some details of personnel, and telling the public why they should see the film. The distribution company plans the national and regional advertising campaign, while providing publicity material to exhibitors, who place local advertising. Advertising expenses are frequently shared by the distributor and the exhibitor. Filmmaking is big business, involving a large expenditure of money that must be returned to investors or the parent corporation; a profit must be made if companies, performers, and filmmakers are to make future films. A film's financial success or failure depends as much upon the ability of advertising to entice people to see the film as the quality of the work—sometimes more. Therefore, various techniques, sometimes sensational or sexual in nature, lure people to the theater, especially through provocative images and slogans in newspaper, magazine, and television advertising. But though television can reach a wide audience all at once, it is very costly. As a result, films from the major distributors are today introduced in wide release on as many as 2,000–3,000 screens. Since total advertising averaged $15 million for a single release in 1995, and since loans are also expensive to carry, distributors are quite likely to cut short the run of a film, regardless of reviews and quality, should its early profits seem unpromising. The distributor pays for the largest share of the advertising, with the exhibitor generally paying 20 percent of the local costs. *See* **box office** *and* **marketing.**

■ **aerial-image photography, aerial-image cinematography** An optical process that allows a film image, frequently of live action, to be projected into space off a mirror positioned at a 45-degree angle and refocused by condenser lenses just below the table of an animation stand, where the image is then rephotographed with cels of artwork, titles, or animated figures placed on the table. This optical process allows for all kinds of composite shots through the running of electrically interlocked frames or through freeze-framing and frame-by-frame rephotographing without the more laborious use of bipack contact printing or traveling-matte processes. The artwork on the cels is opaque, thus acting as a matte by blocking out corresponding areas of the live-action image. Tracking and panning shots with the camera are not possible because the various components and images must be locked together for integrated focal lengths; but dissolves, fades, superimpositions, wipes, split screens, and numerous other effects may be achieved. Zoom effects are possible by

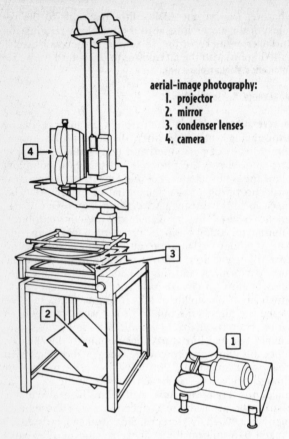

aerial-image photography:
1. projector
2. mirror
3. condenser lenses
4. camera

moving the projector along with a copying lens, thereby altering the size of the image—the projector lens with an additional field lens remain a fixed distance in front of the copying lens while the camera remains stationary above the projected image. Another process for aerial-image photography employs an optical-printer system. In this process, where the artwork becomes the aerial image and the live-action positive is photographed directly, two passes of the new film are necessary. Light passing through a glass matteboard and around the opaque artwork on the cel is focused through a lens at the same plane as the live-action film, hence exposing to the film in the camera the live action minus the area for the artwork. After the positive is removed and the film in the camera rewound, the artwork is front-lit and focused as an aerial image at the same plane, from which it is photographed into the appropriate area of the camera's film. Sometimes an actual object may be placed on an animation plate and its image projected through the lens so that it is combined with the footage. Electronically programmed motion-control systems allow precise repetition of multiple passes for a variety of effects in these systems. *See* **animation, motion control,** *and* **optical printer.**

■ **aerial mount** A special mount with an extremely secure locking system to attach a camera to an airborne

vehicle. Tyler Camera Systems is a notable manufacturer of such mounts for helicopters. *See* **gyro-stabilized camera system.**

■ **aerial perspective, atmospheric perspective** The manner in which successively distant objects in an image become smaller and less distinct.

■ **aerial shot** A shot taken from a plane or helicopter, normally by means of a special aerial mount. Aerial cinematography is necessary when an external location makes a crane impossible or when a dramatic panning shot of a terrain or location is required (e.g., at the beginning of Robert Wise's *West Side Story* [1961]). Skydiving aerial shots are achieved through special cameras attached to the divers' helmets. *See* **gyro-stabilized camera system.**

■ **aesthetics** *See* **film aesthetics.**

■ **AFI** *See* **American Film Institute.**

■ **AFMA** *See* **American Film Marketing Association.**

■ **agent** *See* **talent agency** *and* **talent agent.**

■ **Agfacolor** A subtractive color process developed in Germany by Agfa AG for 16mm film in 1936 and for 35mm film in 1940. Agfacolor was a tripack color process, in which three emulsion layers, each sensitive to one of the primary colors, were laid on a single base. Agfacolor was used by Eisenstein for the color sequence in *Ivan the Terrible, Part 2* (1958). This system and its derivatives, for example Sovcolor in Russia and Ansco Color in this country during the 1940s and 1950s, are considered to have softer and more natural hues than Eastman Color. *See* **Agfa-Gevaert Group** *and* **subtractive process.**

■ **Agfa-Gevaert Group** A photographic and imaging company with headquarters in Leverkusen, Germany and Mortsel, Belgium. The company is the result of a merger of Agfa AG of Germany and Gevaert Photo-Producten N.V. of Belgium in 1964. Gevacolor negative film made by the company was at one time popular in filmmaking.

■ **agitation, agitation pump** The motion given to film chemicals during processing so that fresh chemicals will reach the emulsion for consistent developing. This motion is created by an agitation pump. *See* **processing.**

■ **air squeegee, air squeeze** A device for blowing water free from film in processing before the film moves to the dry box.

■ **air-to-air, air-to-air cinematography** The motion-picture photography of a flying vehicle from another vehicle also in flight.

■ **aleatory technique** The adjective "aleatory" can be applied to any event that happens by chance or luck. In film, it means shooting and recording without plan; relying upon probability and chance. This is a technique often employed in documentary filmmaking to achieve unstaged and realistic behavior and actions (e.g., in the films of Frederick Wiseman).

■ **aliasing** The jagged lines and edges visible in less-developed forms of computer graphics. Such an unwanted effect is caused when the resolution is insufficient for the image's details and the electronic filtering is inadequate. The vernacular term "jaggies" is also used for this effect. "Antialiasing" is the term used to describe the various means of removing this effect. *See* **computer animation.**

aliasing

■ **Allefex** A machine capable of providing fifty different sound effects during the performance of a silent film.

■ **allegory** A term normally used in literary studies, but sometimes applicable in describing a film where the characters and events seem to suggest, in a one-to-one relationship, a situation outside the film or some universal moral situation. In the first instance, Robert Rossen's *All the King's Men* (1949) can be seen as an allegory of the rise and fall of Governor Huey Long of Louisiana; and in the second, Jean Vigo's *Zéro de Conduite* (1933), can be seen as an allegory of youth's triumph over authority and the adult world. Sometimes films are more explicitly and didactically allegorical, as Lindsay Anderson's *O Lucky Man!* (1973), which presents the adventures of an everyman hero who confronts characters representative of various aspects of western society. *See* **subtext** *and* **symbol** *(1).*

■ **Alliance of Motion Picture and Television Producers (AMPTP)** The major labor negotiator for the industry at large, this organization was originally created by the Hollywood studios in 1924 as the Association of Motion Picture Producers to handle public and government relations. In 1964, the organization merged with the Alliance of Television Film Producers and began handling labor issues for both media. Called the Association of Motion Picture and Television Producers, the organization took its present name in 1982, when two members of the alliance, Universal and Paramount, rejoined the larger group. The AMPTP, with headquarters in Encino, California, negotiates with the various unions and guilds, mediates in disputes, advises on the implementation of labor agreements, advises members on compliance with labor laws, and monitors governmental activities affecting the industry on local, state, and federal levels. The AMPTP is affiliated closely with the Motion Picture Association of America. *See* **Motion Picture Association of America.**

■ **Allied Artists Pictures Corporation** Founded in 1946 as Allied Artists Productions, a subsidiary of Monogram Pictures, the company produced a series of routine films until 1953, when both it and Monogram became Allied Artists Pictures Corporation. The producer of a series of low-budget science-fiction films, the studio produced several good ones, including Don Siegel's cult classic, *Invasion of the Body Snatchers,* in 1956. One of its most successful films was William Wyler's *Friendly Persuasion,* also released in 1956. The company later became largely involved in television production, though still sponsoring films, notably John Huston's *The Man Who Would Be King* (1975). In 1980, the company filed for bankruptcy. *See* **Monogram Picture Corporation.**

■ **allied rights** The contractual agreement to manufacture and market various items that are related to the motion picture—e.g., the recording of the soundtrack, novelization, toys, T-shirts, etc. *See* **ancillary rights.**

■ **alligator, alligator clamp, alligator clip, gator grip** *See* **gaffer grip.**

■ **all-purpose filter** A term sometimes used for camera filters that do not alter color balance (e.g., neutral density and polarizing filters). Also called universal camera filters.

■ **allusion** (1) An indirect reference by speech or image to a person, place, event, or work of art outside the film. Such allusions may be used to add greater texture and reality to a film, as do the many indirect references to future political events in Germany in Bob Fosse's *Cabaret* (1972); or may be used for contrast and irony, as the pictorial suggestion of da Vinci's fresco *The Last Supper* in the orgy scene of Luis Buñuel's *Viridiana* (1961). (2) An indirect reference, normally through image or scene, to another film. Some contemporary filmmakers employ such allusions in order to acknowledge their own debt to other directors, to enrich their work with the themes and emotions associated with the earlier work, or simply as an ironic contrast to their own characters and situations. All of these reasons explain the rich use of allusions in the films of François Truffaut and Peter Bogdanovich. *See* **homage.**

allusion A scene in Luis Buñuel's *Viridiana* (1961) sardonically suggesting da Vinci's fresco *The Last Supper.*

■ ■ ■

■ **alpha channel** The fourth channel in the composition of a computer image and the one that contains information concerning the gray scale of the image (the first three are for the primary colors). The alpha channel can be used for transparency or image mapping. *See* **computer animation.**

■ **ambient light** (1) The general, surrounding light in a scene that comes from a number of luminaires and reflective surfaces. (2) The natural light that seems to surround a character. (3) The general soft light in a theater maintained for safety and comfort after the film has begun.

■ **ambient sound** The natural environmental noise that surrounds a scene. A scene with only dialogue will seem empty and hollow without such noise, which may be recorded by a separate microphone during shooting or later added to the mix from another source. Environmental noises normally have their own sound track for mixing. *See* **mix.**

■ **ambiguity** A lack of clarity, an uncertainty, a seeming contradiction in a work's meaning or moral interpretation of its own characters and events. Such ambiguity supposedly reflects the difficulty or impossibility of understanding human nature or the world around us. Robert Altman's *Three Women* (1977) is a film that deals ambiguously with its characters to convey the enigmatic nature of identity. Richard Rush's *The Stunt Man* (1978) plays tricks with plot to convey the confusion between illusion and reality. Sometimes films are ambiguous simply because of bad writing, direction, or editing. Nicolas Roeg's *The Man Who Fell to Earth* (1976) is a film intentionally ambiguous in its content, but made more ambiguous by a badly edited and truncated version released in the United States.

■ **American Cinema Editors (ACE)** The professional society for film and television actors, which four times a year publishes *The American Cinemeditor*, a journal concerned with editing projects.

■ **American Cinematographer** *See* **American Society of Cinematographers.**

■ **American Cinematographer's Manual** *See* **American Society of Cinematographers.**

■ **American Cinemeditor** *See* **American Cinema Editors.**

■ **American Film Institute (AFI)** An organization founded in 1967 with government and private funds to preserve and catalogue films, train people in filmmaking and television, support and coordinate activities relating to the moving image, conduct research, and support young artists. Headquarters are in the John F. Kennedy Center for the Performing Arts in Washington, D.C., where the organization also has a theater that features retrospective shows. At the AFI's campus in Los Angeles, California, the Center for Advanced Film and Television Studies trains students in the various skills for film and television production while the Professional Training Division offers an AFI certificate in Multimedia Business and Production. The organization gives an annual Life Achievement Award that receives much attention, and publishes *The AFI Catalog of Feature Films.* Membership is open to anyone engaged in film studies, education, or production.

■ **American Film Marketing Association (AFMA)** An organization, with central offices in Los Angeles, that promotes the marketing of independently made motion pictures and television programs throughout the world. Such products are not produced by the major studios, though they may be distributed by them. The AFMA makes available information about film and television markets in all parts of the world, advises on licensing agreements, and seeks to identify and open new markets. The organization also offers the American Film Market meeting in Los Angeles each year, which is attended by some 5,000 people in the industry from around the world.

■ **American International Pictures (AIP)** Begun in 1954 as American Releasing Company by James H. Nicholson and Samuel Z. Arkoff and renamed American International Pictures in 1956, this company at first distributed a series of low-budget films at flat fees that ran as second features on double bills but eventually began releasing its own double features. AIP's specialty was at first the horror film, especially those made by Roger Corman and Bert Gordon. The company began a new policy of making and distributing better-quality films in color and CinemaScope, beginning with Roger Corman's *House of Usher,* a film adaptation of the Edgar Allan Poe short story, released in 1960 and starring Vincent Price. This was the first of the AIP films to be released as a single major feature and receive a percentage deal from the exhibitors. Corman then went on to make for the company a series of additional films based on Poe's works and starring Price, probably the best of which was *The Masque of the Red Death* (1964), which featured some lush photography by Nicolas Roeg. Corman also produced two popular youth-cult films, *The Wild Angels* in 1966 and *The Trip* in 1967. *Beach Party,* in 1963, began a successful series of ten teen-picture beach films. In the 1970s, the company overreached itself with some big-budget films that did poorly and in 1979 had to merge with Filmways, which, in 1982, became part of Orion.

■ **American loop** *See* **Latham loop.**

■ **American montage** A technique of editing developed in this country, especially during the 1930s and 1940s, that condenses time and space while conveying much action in a brief period through a series of jump cuts, dissolves, and superimpositions. A popular example of this technique was an image of calendar pages flipping over with brief shots of separate actions superimposed onto and dissolving into one another. The technique was also employed for dreams and hallucinatory states of mind. *See* **montage** *(5)* for a further discussion.

■ **American Museum of the Moving Image** Founded in 1988, and located in Astoria, New York, the first museum in the United States devoted to the history of the production, distribution, and exhibition of film, television, and video art. The museum is concerned with all types of work employing the moving image—fictional, documentary, avant-garde, network television, commercials, etc. Abutting the old Astoria Studios, the museum features changing exhibitions while also presenting permanent displays relating to all aspects of the industry. Especially impressive is its collection of cameras, projectors, television sets, and equipment from the entire history of both cinema and television. The museum also presents screenings of old and new films in its two theaters, often featuring the director or someone involved with the production.

■ **American Mutoscope and Biograph Company** *See* **Biograph.**

■ **American National Standards Institute (ANSI)** Formerly American Standards Association (ASA), the organization is responsible for setting standards of size, shape, and volume in the United States, which are coordinated with those in other countries. In filmmaking, the organization is responsible for such standards as those concerning film size, frame placement, and perforation, as established by the Society of Motion Picture and Television Engineers (SMPTE). The organization also gave its initials to one of the measurements for the sensitivity of film emulsion to light, which is designated as the ASA or ANSI standard. *See* **International Standards Organization** *and* **Society of Motion Picture and Television Engineers.**

■ **American shot** In French, the term is *plan américain,* which is used by French critics for a two-shot from the knees up that frequently appears in American films. *See* **two-shot.**

■ **American Society of Cinematographers (ASC)** The professional society of approximately 200 film and television directors of photography, with some 100 associated members in related fields. With headquarters in Hollywood, the society publishes *The American Cinematographer's Manual,* a professional handbook for cinematography that is updated periodically, and the monthly *American Cinematographer,* a handsome journal with a readable text on technical aspects of filming. Membership is by invitation only and members may use the initials ASC after their names in film credits. Both the society's publications are available to the public.

■ **ammeter** A meter that measures the amperage of an electric current. *See* **ampacity** *and* **amperage.**

■ **amortization** The process in accounting of charging for the cost of a film negative (i.e., for the entire production of the film) against the film's income. Negative costs are generally paid off before investors or those with a percentage of the profits receive their share. Since all types of expenses have sometimes been included in negative costs, amortization has become a much-disputed procedure.

■ **ampacity** The safe electrical capacity of cables and various equipment measured in amperes.

■ **AMPAS** *See* **Academy of Motion Picture Arts and Sciences.**

■ **amperage** The strength of an electric current measured in amperes and computed by dividing voltage into wattage.

■ **amplifier** (1) An electronic system that increases the power of an incoming signal. (2) The system that increases the volume of sound in a recording or playback system.

■ **AMPTP** *See* **Alliance of Motion Picture and Television Producers.**

■ **anaglyph process** A 3-D process by which two views of the same image, one representing the view of the right eye and the other of the left, from two cameras or a single camera with a stereoscopic lens, are superimposed upon a film in different colors, generally red and green. The superimposed images are projected on a screen and achieve a three-dimensional effect when they are seen through an anaglyphoscope, a pair of spectacles with two filters for eyepieces, each in one of the colors of the superimposed images, and each of which directs the eye looking through it to the image of the other color. This method was used to make three-dimensional short films in the 1920s and 1930s but ultimately was superseded since it could not create images in full color, as can systems employing Polaroid lenses and spectacles, and since the type of spectacles employed caused eye fatigue. *See* **stereoscopy.**

■ **analog, analogue** A method for the recording or playback of either picture or sound that uses a signal analogous to the original light or sound waves given off by the subject in terms of intensity and modulations. Such traditional methods of transmitting information are subject to deterioration in contrast to the new method of digital transmission that converts image and sound into a series of 0's and 1's (offs and ons). *See* **digital.**

■ **analog image synthesis, video synthesis** A method of creating a variety of moving and changing shapes and forms for special-effects photography (e.g., spinning globes, expanding or shrinking spheres, separating and coinciding lines). This older analog and video method has been largely replaced by digital processes. *See* **digital effects.**

■ **analog recording** Any sound recording system that creates modulations analogous to the modulations of the sound waves—for example, optical and magnetic sound recording. *See* **digital sound recording.**

■ **analytic projector** A film projector with a freeze-frame apparatus that allows the study of a single frame at a time. Such 16mm machines are often used in film-study classes and are convenient for studying the individual *mise-en-scène* of a director. *See* **projector.**

■ **anamorphic lens, anamorphic cinematography** The term "anamorphic" means "form anew" in Greek. In optics, the term means any lens that differently magnifies the horizontal and vertical axes of an image. In cinema, the term refers to the lens on the camera that compresses the horizontal axis or width of an image to half its size to fit into the width of the film's frame, and to the lens of the projector that expands the image on the film back to its normal width and appearance on the screen. In both lenses, the vertical axis is left undistorted, and the result is a wide-screen image. Instead of the normal aspect ratio of 1.33:1, projection had an aspect ratio of 2.55:1, which was later altered to 2.35:1 to allow for an optical soundtrack. The process itself was developed during the First World War by Henri Chrétien, who designed a wide-angle lens for tanks, called Hypergonar, capable of showing a field of vision of 180 degrees. This lens was used after the war for aerial photography in mapmaking. It was first used in cinema in

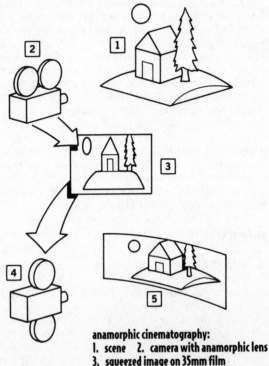

anamorphic cinematography:
1. scene 2. camera with anamorphic lens
3. squeezed image on 35mm film
4. projector with anamorphic lens
5. unsqueezed wide-screen image

1928 by Claude Autant-Lara to make the silent short film *Construire un Feu*. In 1952, Twentieth Century-Fox in this country bought the rights to the system, which was then further developed. The result was the 1953 film *The Robe* (dir. Henry Koster), released with much fanfare as having been photographed in the revolutionary process called CinemaScope. Other studios soon developed their own anamorphic systems with different names, though the process was basically the same. The term "scope" became an abbreviation for anamorphic systems because of its prevalence in these names—for example in CinemaScope, Superscope, Panascope, and Warnerscope. The anamorphic system was a much simpler method of obtaining the wide-screen image than systems that used multiple or special cameras and projectors. CinemaScope and other earlier anamorphic systems have today been superseded by the superior anamorphic lenses of Panavision, although wide-screen cinema is often achieved today through masking the apertures on cameras or, more often, on projectors. *See* **aspect ratio** *and* **wide screen.**

■ **anastigmat lens** A lens corrected for astigmatism, that is, for the failure of light rays to focus on the same point off the lens axis. *See* **astigmatism.**

■ **ancillary rights** The right of an individual, group, or company to develop other markets in relation to a film—the videocassette recording, cable and network television presentations, recording of the music, rock video, television spin-off, novelization, or merchandise such as T-shirts, children's toys, calendars, and various home objects bearing the imprint of the film's images or characters. Such rights can be a source of great revenue in addition to the film's box office. Films such as *Star Wars* (1977; dir. George Lucas) and *Batman* (1989; dir. Tim Burton) now pass into our culture as much through such parallel markets as through the films themselves. *See* **allied rights.**

■ **angle** *See* **camera angle.**

■ **angle of acceptance** *See* **acceptance angle.**

■ **angle of incidence, angle of light incidence** The angle between light rays from a source of illumination and the plane of the subject that is illuminated. Sometimes referred to as light source directionality.

■ **angle of view** The angle of the field of action recorded on the film as computed from the effective center of the lens to the extremities of the film image (the actual field of action accepted by the lens is circular, but it is masked by the camera's aperture to form the rectangular frame). Although technically relating to both the horizontal and vertical axes, in common usage the term normally relates to the horizontal axis. This angle is determined by both the film gauge (or width of the camera's aperture) and the lens's focal

length. The standard 50mm lens for 35mm film, which offers an image that corresponds to what the eye normally sees, has a horizontal view of approximately 25 degrees while a similar angle for 16mm film is obtained by a lens with a focal length of 25mm. Wide-angle lenses, which have shorter focal lengths, allow a wider angle of view, while long-focus lenses, with longer focal lengths, allow a narrower angle (e.g., a 28mm lens for a 35mm camera gives an angle of view of approximately 43 degrees and a 135mm lens gives one of approximately 9.5 degrees). Angle of view is sometimes confused with camera angle, and the camera's distance from the subject is sometimes mistakenly cited as a factor for this angle in film textbooks and glossaries. *See* **camera angle** *and* **lens.**

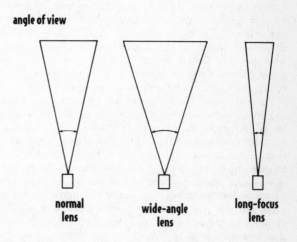

angle of view

normal lens | wide-angle lens | long-focus lens

■ **angle on** A direction, generally in a shooting script, for a different camera view of a previous shot.

■ **angle-plus-angle** A shot with the camera placed slightly to the side of the subject and also angled upward or downward so that more details are seen and a three-dimensional effect is achieved through the presentation of front, side, and underside or top.

■ **angle-reverse-angle** A series of shots showing two characters engaged in conversation, with the camera alternating between individual shots of each performer, who is facing in the reverse direction from the other. *See* **reverse angle.**

■ **angle shot** A shot of the same action as the previous shot, but from a different camera angle.

■ **Animafilm** A journal published quarterly and in several languages from Italy by the International Film Society (ASIFA). The publication has articles, many of them compiled from other journals, on past and present animated films and animation techniques throughout the world.

■ **Animascope** A system, developed in this country, that photographed live actors in such a way that outlines were prominent and specific characteristics diminished so that figures appeared like cartoon characters. Such figures were photographed against a black backdrop and their images later combined with painted backgrounds through a matting process. Actors could be dressed in any costume for the purpose of the cartoon.

■ **animation** The process of photographing drawings, puppets, silhouettes, or inanimate objects frame by frame through stop-motion photography, with each frame recording a minute progressive change in the subject. When the frames are projected onto the screen, one after the other at the standard speed of 24 frames per second, the subject seems to move or be animated (in the case of television, the speed is 25 frames per second). For ten minutes of animation, 14,400 individual drawings or setups are theoretically necessary. The speed of action is dependent on the amount of change from frame to frame; sometimes slower movements are achieved by repeating the same drawing or setup for two or three frames. In cartoon animation, most of the camera techniques that we associate with the photography of live performers—for example, cutting to different angles and panning—are actually drawn, though vertical movement of the camera and movement of the drawing are possible on the animation stand. More camera technique is possible with puppets, but the miniature size of the figures and settings curtails the positioning and movement of the camera. In cartoon animation, various parts of a scene that remain the same from frame to frame are drawn on cels (i.e., acetate sheets), which remain stationary while only the moving elements are drawn on a series of cels. Not only is an immense amount of labor saved, but with various distances of the scene drawn on different cels, perspective and depth are also achieved. Walt Disney Productions achieved perspective and depth in feature-length cartoons through the multiplane camera, which also created realistic effects through its greater capacity for movement. In model animation for recent special-effects films, animatronic puppets are controlled off-screen by rods, cables, hydraulic systems, and remote control while the go-motion process allows computerized and hence exactly repeatable movement of both camera and miniatures in stop-motion photography—the slight movement of the models during shooting gives them a blur that creates a motion more natural to the eye than the somewhat spastic motion of earlier model animation. This process also allows for a greater rate of filming. Today, computer graphics are employed in both live-action and cartoon films. The use of the computer has made the animated film once more affordable and has been responsible for the surge of such films.

Animation is used in a variety of films: in educational works, abstract experimental films, cartoons, horror or fantasy films where the animation of dolls is integrated with the action of live characters, and sometimes in musical comedies where cartoon figures and live characters perform together. Animation is also used in film credits and is especially popular for television commercials.

The first significant film cartoonist in America was Winsor McCay, whose most famous animated short, *Gertie the Dinosaur* (1914), is considered the basis of the future cinematic cartoon. A number of cartoon series followed, including Pat Sullivan's *Felix the Cat*, but the next serious development did not come until the advent of sound, with Walt Disney's *Steamboat Willie* in 1928, featuring Mickey Mouse, followed by Disney's *Silly Symphony* series in 1929, which introduced the Three Little Pigs. Disney soon added color to his films and produced his first full-length cartoon feature, *Snow White and the Seven Dwarfs*, which was released in 1937. Significant animation with dolls was achieved by Willis O'Brien in 1925 with *The Lost World* and perfected by him in the 1933 production of *King Kong*. Also significant are the "Puppetoons" of George Pal in the early 1940s. During the 1940s, such cartoon series as *Tom and Jerry* and *Bugs Bunny* competed with Disney productions, and in 1945, United Productions of America (UPA) was formed by former Disney animators. UPA reached its height of success in the early 1950s with the Mr. Magoo and the Gerald McBoing-Boing series. One of the most significant experimental and also abstract animators for many decades was the Scottish-born Norman McLaren, who created a number of impressive short works by drawing directly on film. McLaren won an Oscar in 1953 with his antiviolence film *Neighbors* (1952), for which he animated live per-

animation Winsor McCay's *Gertie the Dinosaur* (1914), the ancestor of the animated cartoon.

■■■

formers in stop-motion photography. An important animator was Ralph Bakshi, who produced such animated full-length features as *Fritz the Cat* (1971), *Heavy Traffic* (1973), and *Lord of the Rings* (1978). Another group of Disney animators broke away to form Don Bluth Productions, a company dedicated to using the best classic animation techniques along with newer techniques. The result was *The Secret of Nimh* (1982), a remarkably animated though somewhat dull feature animation film. The more energetic *American Tail* (1986) also featured animation by Don Bluth. Computer animation and technology in recent years have had a dynamic impact on the animated feature film and are responsible for the increased number of these works. *Who Framed Roger Rabbit* (1988; dir. Robert Zemeckis), an impressive blending of animation and live characters, earned Richard Williams a special Academy Award for the animation and the co-production companies of Steven Spielberg and Disney some $154 million at the box office. The Disney company's *Beauty and the Beast* (1991; dir. Gary Trousdale and Kirk Wise), *Aladdin* (1992; dir. John Musker and Ron Clements), and *The Lion King* (1994; dir. Roger Allers and Rob Minkoff), while earning the parent company a fortune both through the films and their ancillary markets, seemed on the verge of creating another golden age of the animated feature film. John Lasseter's *Toy Story* (1995), for which the images were 100 percent computer-generated, also seemed to take the animated feature cartoon a giant step into the future. The recent *Hunchback of Notre Dame* (1996; dir. Gary Trousdale and Kirk Wise) may not have made as much money as these other films, but its combination of traditional and digital animation techniques created some of the most impressive and stunning images yet to appear in the animated film. The success of these motion pictures, not to mention their lucrative outlet on home video, has sent other major studios scurrying to create their own computer-animation departments. Computer animation is having a dynamic impact on feature films in general as well as on the cartoon film (e.g., the six and one-half minutes of computer-generated dinosaurs in Steven Spielberg's *Jurassic Park* [1993]). *See* **computer animation, puppet animation,** *and* **stop motion.**

■ **animation camera, rostrum camera** A camera designed for single-frame photography of drawings, models, or anything else used for animated films as well as for photography with continuous speeds. Such a camera must have an extremely precise registration mechanism as well as a stop-frame drive for manual or automatic single-frame exposure. As part of an animation stand, the camera is supported on a column above the table on which the artwork is placed and can be moved in a vertical direction to change field size or create effects. Focusing can be changed automatically by a cam system. Computers are now used for presetting and controlling the camera's movement and operation. *See* **animation stand.**

■ **animation cycle** The repeated photographing of the same series of drawings to suggest a continuous or repetitive action in an animated film.

■ **animation disc** A circular plate generally made of aluminum and capable of turning a full circle when mounted on a drawing table. A glass or Plexiglas window is situated in the center of the disc and fits over an opening in the table through which back lighting can bring into prominence the individual drawings stacked one on top of the other. Pegs and peg bars hold the drawings in place. Also called an animation board or animation bed.

■ **animation layout** In animation work, the plan for each scene that indicates the correct size of figures, their proper spatial relationships, specific colors for the scene, and camera placement and movement. *See* **optical layout.**

■ **animation school of violence** A term used wryly to describe animated cartoons with a good deal of violence, especially the studio cartoons that came out of Hollywood during the 1940s and 1950s. Tex Avery, who worked for a number of studios, is often cited as a major influence on this school. Both the *Tom and Jerry* and *Road Runner* cartoons are good examples of this type of animation. Animation drawings allow characters to be flattened, blown out, and distorted in all sorts of ways from all sorts of physical abuse, frequently generated by another cartoon figure. The make-believe nature of the cartoon world and the fact that injury is only temporary seem to place such action beyond the realm of the possible and into the sphere of the comic and ridiculous, although the effect such violence has on young viewers is much debated.

■ **animation stand** The equipment for holding and controlling the movements of drawings and for supporting and positioning the camera that photographs these drawings one frame at a time. Various parts of the scenes are generally drawn on translucent cels and the stationary background is drawn on white paper. These picture elements are precisely held by pegs beneath the camera on a compound table; pegs on tracks allow cels to move sideways while floating pegs allow cels to move both sideways and in a north-south axis. Such pegs can also hold the cels stationary while the table top itself moves. The cels are kept flat by a glass sheet called a platen. The camera, which looks down at the drawings, can be moved vertically with great control to alter field size or achieve a zoom effect. The camera itself is run by a mechanism that permits both continuous and frame-by-frame photography, while focus is automatically adjusted when the camera moves by a cam system. The table, which itself can be moved in any direction or rotated, has an opening in the center for back-lighting transparencies and artwork or for rear projection. Normal lighting is provided by two lamps set at equal distances from the center of the table at both sides. Animation stands can achieve all types of effects—for example, transitions, distortions, matting—and are employed for titles and backgrounds as well as for animated figures. Computers are now employed for operating the animation stand itself, allowing precise and repeatable movements of the camera and artwork as well as controlled exposures of the camera. Key drawings made by the animator can be the basis of the intervening action created by a computer and photographed continuously or frame by frame. Oxberry is a notable manufacturer of such animation stands. *See* **animation, animation camera,** *and* **computer animation.**

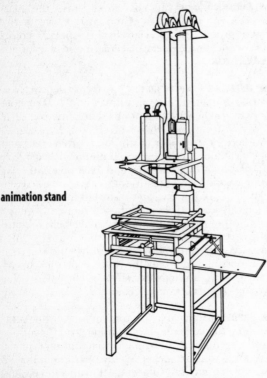

animation stand

■ **animation zoom** A zoom effect achieved in animation by altering the size of the subject photographed from drawing to drawing.

■ **animator** (1) The individual who does the drawings for an animation film. (2) The individual in charge of the general design and concept of an animated film, who may do the key drawings while others do the intermediate art work and transfer all the drawings to cels. *See* **animation.**

■ **animatronic puppets, animatronics** Puppets operated mechanically by computers or remote control while they are photographed for a motion picture. Puppets of animals or grotesque creatures are controlled by rods, cables, or hydraulic systems attached to them but oper-

ated off-screen. Attachments such as rods can later be removed from the image by a "rod articulate matte" (the puppets are normally filmed against a blue screen for later compositing) or by digitally converting the image and correcting it before it is once more recorded on film. Sometimes an individual may be inside an animatronic suit, parts of which are operated mechanically. An important integration of the old and new is go-motion animation (or go-animation) in which the various parts of puppets are connected by means of rods and cables to levers and a motorized system, all of which is operated by a go-motion animator with a joy stick. Each movement is first recorded into a computer, which then controls the actual movements of the puppet that are photographed frame by frame, giving the puppet's movements a blurred effect instead of the old staccato movements of traditional stop-motion animation. *See* **animation** *and* **go-motion.**

■ **another angle** A direction, generally in a shooting script, to photograph a previous shot from a different camera position.

■ **Ansco color** A tripack color system in the United States during the 1940s and 1950s, derived from the German Agfacolor. *See* **Agfacolor.**

■ **answer print, trial composite, trial print, approval print, first trial print, first trial composite print** The first print from the laboratory that includes synchronized image and sound in proper chronology and has been corrected for light and color. This print may be accepted but frequently further changes are required before release prints can be made.

■ **antagonist** The character in opposition to the hero or protagonist. An antagonist is frequently the villain in the film who is in conflict with the hero and instigates much of the film's action (e.g., Sydney Greenstreet in a number of Humphrey Bogart films). Sometimes the antagonist is a member of the same family, motivated less by evil than by neurotic or psychotic drives (e.g., the heroine's mother in Graeme Clifford's *Frances* [1982]). *See* **heavy.**

■ **anthology film** A full-length film made up of excerpts from other films, which are related by some theme, the appearance of the same performer(s), or because they have been made by the same studio. *That's Entertainment!* (1974), for example, is a film composed of excerpts from MGM musical comedies linked together with commentaries by former stars of these films.

■ **Anthology Film Archives (AFA)** An organization in New York City, begun in 1970 by Jonas Mekas, that collects and preserves experimental films, especially New American Cinema and European avant-garde film, and offers viewing facilities, film programs, and a research library. The AFA also supports video art.

■ **antialiasing**   *See* **aliasing.**

■ **anticipation**   A slight motion or pause by an animated figure that anticipates and hence emphasizes a main action in an animation cartoon while also creating a sense of balance and fluid movement for the figure.

■ **anticipatory camera, anticipatory setup**   A shot in which the camera focuses on a scene just before the major action takes place and hence anticipates the action.

■ **anticlimax**   A point in the film where the action should peak and the audience feel a dramatic high point, but where, instead, there is an emotional letdown as action resolves in a disappointing and ineffective manner. Sometimes an anticlimax can effectively convey the undramatic and repetitious nature of the characters' lives, as in Michelangelo Antonioni's *L'Avventura* (1960). *See* **climax.**

■ **antihalation backing, antihalation coating**   An opaque coating applied to the backside of film to absorb light and prevent reflection back through the emulsion, which would cause halation, that is, a blurred effect, around the bright parts of the image. A rem-jet backing created by the dispersion of black carbon is used for this purpose in a number of film stocks.

■ **antihalation dye**   A gray dye infused directly into the base of a film stock to deter halation and light piping. Some negative films have such a gray base but also use a black layer on the bottom of the film called a rem-jet backing. *See* **light piping.**

■ **antihalation undercoating**   An opaque coating layered between the emulsion and base of certain film stocks (e.g., reversal film) for absorbing light and preventing reflection back through the emulsion which would create halation.

■ **antihero**   The protagonist or major male figure in literature or film with whom the reader or viewer associates, but who possesses nonheroic and weak qualities not traditionally belonging to heroes. These figures tend to be alienated and isolated characters who are susceptible to human frailties, but who also manifest a private code of ethics and sometimes an individual integrity that force them to clash with society. Antiheroes in literature, who are basically a result of industrial society and a breakdown in traditional beliefs and values, tend to be weaker and more neurotic than those in film. Film tends to glamorize its antiheroes and make them seem the true heroes in a world of corrupt values. James Cagney in *The Public Enemy* (1931; dir. William Wellman) and Paul Muni in *Scarface* (1932; dir. Howard Hawks) appealed to the rebellious nature in society and the success drive during the Depression years, even though these characters were also presented for condemnation. But Humphrey Bogart in many of his

antihero   *Taxi Driver* (1976; dir. Martin Scorsese), with Robert De Niro as the highly disturbed modern hero.

■ ■ ■

films, especially in *The Maltese Falcon* (1941; dir. John Huston), *Casablanca* (1942; dir. Michael Curtiz), *To Have and Have Not* (1945; dir. Howard Hawks), and *The Big Sleep* (1946; dir. Howard Hawks), developed the persona of the antihero as a romantic rebel, a man apart from and yet superior to the world which surrounds him, a man capable of passion, anger, avarice, even weakness, but strong and tough when it really counts. In later years, films tended to sentimentalize the antihero, to make him more sinned against than sinning, and to make him likable and human: note, for example, James Dean's portrayal in *Rebel Without a Cause* (1955; dir. Nicholas Ray) and Marlon Brando's character in *The Wild Ones* (1954; dir. Laslo Benedek). This trend seems to have received further impetus with *Bonnie and Clyde* in 1967 (dir. Arthur Penn), where two real-life gangsters and murderers become romanticized figures. The protagonist played by Robert De Niro in *Taxi Driver* (1976; dir. Martin Scorsese), however, brought this type of figure closer to the neurotic antihero of literature. In recent years, actors such as Arnold Schwarzenegger and Sylvester Stallone have popularized a more simplified and visceral antihero, a physically powerful and violent figure who does not hesitate in bringing havoc and mayhem to the screen, but who is frequently justified by his position or situation. *See* **hero.**

■ **antireflection coating** The layer or layers of transparent material put on the lens of a camera to reduce the loss of light by surface reflection.

■ **aperture** (1) Lens aperture: the opening, generally controlled by the diaphragm, that regulates the amount of light to pass through the lens and reach the film. (2) Camera aperture: the opening in a camera that determines the area of each frame to be exposed. (3) Projector aperture: the opening in a projector that determines the area of each frame to be projected on the screen. (4) Printer aperture: the opening in the printer that controls the amount of light that exposes the film in the process of making a print.

■ **aperture plate** The plate in the camera, projector, and printer in which an opening controls, respectively, the image recorded, projected, or exposed. Aperture plates can be changed to accommodate different aspect ratios.

■ **A-picture** The major film in a double feature, generally distinguished from the B-picture by its larger budget and more popular performers. Such distinctions disappeared when double features passed away with the rise of television and the demise of the studio system in the 1950s. *See* **B-picture** *and* **double feature.**

■ **APO** An abbreviation for "Action Print Only," that is, for a print without sound.

■ **apochromatic lens** A lens corrected for unequal focusing of light rays or different colors. A higher order of achromatic lens. *See* **achromatic lens.**

■ **Apogee, Inc.** A special-effects organization begun by John Dykstra and others in 1978 after they left George Lucas's Industrial Light and Magic firm. Apogee did some spectacular effects for *Star Trek: The Motion Picture* (1979; dir. Robert Wise). *See* **special effects.**

■ **apple box** A box to raise performers or objects to a desired height for a shot. Sometimes such a box is used to elevate short actors. Also called a riser. *See* **pancake.**

■ **approach** (1) A camera movement from one kind of coverage of the subject to another, for example, from a medium shot to a close-up. (2) A command from the director for the camera to move closer to the character.

■ **archetype** (1) A basic character type that appears repeatedly throughout literature, drama, or film and that is an embodiment of specific human fears, needs, or desires—for example, the demonic lover (Heathcliff) in Emily Brontë's novel *Wuthering Heights* (1848) and in the 1939 film version (dir. William Wyler) as played by Laurence Olivier; or the white, virginal heroine in Hollywood motion pictures from the time of Lillian Gish's silent-film portrayals on. Such figures are not tied to any period, as are, for example, the Victorian villain of melodrama and silent film but, rather, tap in to the universal unconsciousness of all ages. (2) A basic pattern of action that appears throughout literature, drama, or film and is an embodiment of specific human fears, needs, or desires—for example, the rebirth or resurrectional pattern in Marlon Brando's moral transformation and triumphant climactic march in *On the Waterfront* (1954; dir. Elia Kazan) or in E.T.'s sudden revival, through the power of love, in Steven Spielberg's film (1982). The theory of archetypes has been much influenced by the psychology of Carl Jung, and has been especially developed for literary study by Northrop Frye in his *Anatomy of Criticism* (1956). Frye's archetypal criticism has much applicability for film study, especially since it makes no distinction between elitist and popular art. *See* **myth.**

■ **archival film** Any film made entirely of archival footage. A number of historical documentaries use such footage along with the voice-over of a commentator.

■ **archival footage, archival film** Newsreels or any film of a public event available for inclusion in a later film.

■ **archive** (1) A place that stores old films, scripts, or any production material and makes them available for study and research. (2) In computer editing, the storage of editing decisions and setups that can be recalled for further work or simply remain as back-up material.

■ **arc lamp, arc light** A high-intensity light used both for filming and in projectors. An electric current is maintained between positively and negatively charged rods and gives off an intense white light. Arc lamps with carbon rods were a standard source of lighting in studios and are still, in spite of their noise and relatively short duration, used when great luminosity is needed from a single source. The "brute" draws 225 amps, though smaller and more portable lamps of this type are available. Carbon arc lamps were employed in projectors, though xenon lamps have become more popular. Mercury arc lamps, used for silent films, are not used today. A new type of light that is very much used today is the HMI arc-enclosed, AC discharge lamp. *See* **HMI** *and* **lighting.**

■ **arc out** (1) An order given to an actor to move before the camera in a curve so that he or she will appear to be passing in a straight line and not toward or away from the camera. (2) An order given to a dolly crew to move the camera in a curve past the action sometimes for effect, sometimes for the same reason as in (1).

■ **arc shot** A shot in which the camera moves in a partial or full circle around the subject. In Brian De Palma's *Carrie* (1976), the camera continuously circles around Carrie and her escort while they dance and turn in the opposite direction, creating a dizzying and disconcerting effect.

■ **armature** The skeleton or framework upon which is placed the outer coating for a piece of sculpture. In the sophisticated models made for special-effects photography, such armatures are frequently articulated and allow for various kinds of motion. Movement of the models can be created manually, mechanically, or by stop-motion photography. *See* **miniature.**

■ **A-roll original** Original film edited together into a single roll and ready for printing.

■ **AromaRama** A process for bringing the smells of a film directly to the audience by means of air-conditioning ducts. The process was first used for the documentary *The Great Wall of China* in 1959. *See* **Smell-O-Vision.**

■ **Arriflex, Arri** Arriflex is the brand name of 65, 35, and 16mm cameras made by the Arriflex Corporation. The parent company is Arnold and Richter Cine Technic in Munich, Germany, and the trademark "Arri" is taken from the first two letters of each name. The forerunner of the lightweight and relatively small Arriflex 35 2C, with its innovative reflex viewfinder, was introduced in 1937 and since that time has been steadily improved. A later model, because of its size, weight, and portability, was instrumental in the development of the New Wave cinema and the *cinéma-vérité* documentary in France. This camera is also popular for shooting on location and in confined areas. The Academy of Motion Picture Arts and Sciences gave a special Scientific and Engineering Award to the firm of Arnold and Richter in 1966 for its Arriflex 35 2C. In 1972, the company introduced the Arriflex 35BL, a lightweight, handheld, and quiet sync camera that was given a Scientific and Engineering Award in both 1973 and 1992 by the Academy. The Arriflex 535 sync sound camera, introduced in 1991, features a swingover viewfinder, programmable variable shutter and frame rate that allows rate changes in the midst of shooting, and dual LCD information displays for everything from the time of film exposure to SMPTE Time Code. In 1993, the company introduced the 535B, the lightweight version of the 535, and in 1996 won an Academy Award for Scientific and Engineering Achievement for both 535s.

■ **Arrivision** A 3-D film process developed by Arriflex Corporation that employed only one camera either with a single-lens system (i.e., a single multifocal 3-D lens in front of a 50mm prime lens) or with a dual-lens system (i.e., individual 3-D lenses in front of the prime lens). *See* **3-D.**

■ **art card** A sheet of cardboard for mounting credits, titles, or artwork that is placed before the camera for filming.

■ **art deco** A style of setting and decor, featuring a modern and streamlined look with a lack of ornamentation and preponderance of white, that became popular in the Hollywood films of the late 1920s and 1930s. The style was first defined in film by the art director

art deco One of Cedric Gibbons's influential art-deco settings for *Our Dancing Daughters* (1928; dir. Harry Beaumont). The actress is Joan Crawford.

■ ■ ■

Cedric Gibbons, beginning with *Our Dancing Daughters* in 1928 (dir. Harry Beaumont). Associated in film with the haunts of the rich and famous, the style also became a feature of the Busby Berkeley musicals, the films of Fred Astaire, and showed up in such unlikely places as the Universal horror film *The Black Cat* (1934; dir. Edgar G. Ulmer, art dir. Charles D. Hall). Along with Cedric Gibbons, Hans Dreier is notable for creating this style of setting, especially in such films as *Monte Carlo* (1930), *One Hour with You* (1932), and *Trouble in Paradise* (1932), which were made at Paramount and directed by Ernst Lubitsch. *See* **art director.**

■ **art department** A designation sometimes used for all the personnel working together on designing, creating, and coordinating the visual elements of the film apart from the camera crew and electricians. This department is headed by the production designer and includes the various draftsmen, painters, construction personnel, and sometimes the wardrobe and make-up personnel as well as the special-effects technicians.

■ **art director** The individual who takes the production designer's vision of the film and seeks to make it into a reality on the screen. The art director may draw the plans and write the various specifications for each set or employ an assistant art director to do so. Sometimes, the art director or assistant art director constructs three-dimensional models of the sets. The art director also plays an important role in selecting the personnel and helps to run the art department in general. This person is significantly responsible for making sure the production designer's vision is carried into the very making and decorating of the sets. The art director was formerly called the set designer. *See* **production designer.**

■ **art film** (1) A type of film with serious artistic intentions as distinct from the commercial films made in Hollywood. The term came in use in the 1950s largely to describe foreign films made with smaller budgets but with great originality in technique and greater emphasis on social and psychological reality than Hollywood's traditional and escapist products. Films made by De Sica and the early Fellini, for example, played in small "art houses" for a serious film clientele. The distinction between these films and American commercial films was valid throughout the 1960s, but since that time the differences are often less apparent, and the term less useful. Foreign films now receive limited theatrical distribution because they do poorly at the box office and also are not very profitable for television and videocassette distribution. (2) Any film shown in art houses, especially during the 1950s and 1960s, for serious audiences, including small-budget but artistic foreign and domestic films, avant-garde films, and older classics. (3) Any nonfiction film that deals with the graphic arts.

■ **art house, art theater** Any film theater that features serious foreign and independent domestic films, avant-garde cinema, or classics. Such theaters are generally small and play their films for a select and discriminating clientele. These theaters began to appear in the early 1950s; by the early 1960s, there were 500 of them in the United States. Since that time, they have greatly decreased in number as the distinction between American and foreign films has become less significant, and foreign films have had a very difficult time at the box office.

■ **articulated armature** *See* **armature.**

■ **articulate matte** The hand-drawn mattes, one for each frame of movement, that prevent light from exposing film around a specific subject—another picture element will later go into the unexposed area. Rotoscoping is one means of creating such mattes. *See* **matte** *(2),* **rotoscope,** *and* **special effects.**

■ **artificial breakeven** A designated amount of money to be earned by a film before certain personnel or backers can earn some money. This contractual amount may in reality be more or less than the film's actual breakeven point.

■ **artificial light** The light created for a scene, normally from electrical sources, as opposed to light from a natural source such as the sun. *See* **available light.**

■ **art still** (1) A painting from which a slide will be made to be projected at the back of a setting or from which a plate will be made for rear or front projection. (2) A still photograph of a performer in an "arty" pose.

■ **ASA standard, ASA speed rating, ANSI standard, ANSI speed rating** A numerical rating of the sensitivity of film emulsion to light as determined by the American Standards Association, now the American National Standards Institute. ASA or ANSI numbers are sometimes given for the film speed or exposure index of motion picture film stock. Sometimes an ISO rating is given which includes both the ASA and the DIN number (the latter is a rating used in Europe). Eastman Kodak and Fuji give an exposure index number instead. *See* **DIN standard, exposure index,** *and* **ISO standard.**

■ **ASC** *See* **American Society of Cinematographers.**

■ **A scene, A side** The scene to which another is being added in the process of editing—that on the left side in reference to the B scene which is being added to it and which is on the B or right side

■ **ASCII** These letters stand for American Standard Code for Information Interchange and represent the code of binary digits (each is called a "bit") of 1's and 0's that is used in computer technology. With a specific series of bits always representing the same numbers, letters, and visuals, this code allows a standard exchange of files written in different computer languages. *See* **computer animation.**

■ **ashcan** A floodlight of 1,000 watts.

■ **aspect ratio** The ratio of width to height of the image both on film and screen. The general aspect ratio for silent film was 1.33:1 (or 4:3), the ratio first used by Thomas Edison's equipment. All kinds of reasons have been given for the persistence of this ratio—from aesthetic (it resembled the aspect ratio of classic paintings) to practical (it resulted from placing the lens in a cylinder to obtain light rays in the most efficient manner). The image appeared almost square when a sound track was added on the side of film. Since the nearly square image was less functional and pleasing, the Academy of Motion Picture Arts and Sciences, in 1932, returned the aspect ratio to 1.33:1 by masking the top and bottom of the frame. These dimensions, referred to as the Academy aperture and Movietone frame (named after the sound system), became international for making and exhibiting motion pictures. The Academy aperture was also the source of the aspect ratio standardized for television screens. A desire for innovation as well as a response to the challenge of television led to experimentation with wide-screen projection and a change in aspect ratio in the 1950s that created an image more responsive to the viewer's vision. CinemaScope at first appeared with an aspect ratio of 2.55:1, but this was later changed to 2.35:1 to allow for an optical sound track. Other anamorphic systems led to a variety of wide-screen aspect ratios, anywhere from 2:1 to 2.7:1. An unfortunate procedure was for theaters to mask the top and bottom of frames filmed at the normal aspect ratio of 1.33:1 to achieve a wide-screen image of 1.85:1 at the cost of part of the image. Today 70mm films are projected with an aspect ratio of 2:2.1, and 35mm nonanamorphic films have an aspect ratio of 1.85:1 (normally 1.66:1 in Europe). *See* **anamorphic lens** *and* **wide screen.**

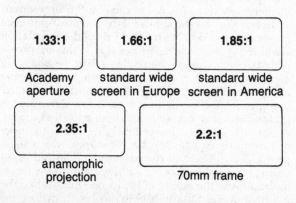

aspect ratios

■ **aspheric surface, aspheric corrector plate** A surface of a lens that is not part of the actual sphere. This type of surface is used in some zoom lenses and also in large-screen television.

■ **assemble** To begin the editing process by selecting the best takes, cutting them in rough shape, and assembling them into what should approximate the final ordering. The next stage is to make the rough cut. *See* **rough cut.**

■ **assembly** The first arrangement of usable takes into what approximates the final editing of the film. The individual takes in the assembly are also edited to some degree. *See* **rough cut.**

■ **assistant camera operator, assistant cameraman** *See* **first assistant camera operator**

■ **assistant director (AD)** The person who carries out a number of procedural duties for the director, which include scheduling shooting, arranging logistics, calling personnel to the proper location for shooting, maintaining order on the set, checking budgets, communicating with crews, rehearsing performers, and doing whatever tasks the director may find necessary. The AD is also in charge of organizing large crowd scenes. It is the assistant director who, when told by the director, gives the order for the camera and audio equipment to begin recording the scene. Often more than one assistant director is employed—there is likely to be a "second" assistant director and even a "second second" or "third" AD. *See* **second assistant director.**

■ **assistant editor, assistant film editor** Someone who, working closely with the editor of a film, keeps a record of all the pieces of film, assists in synchronically relating image and sound, splices together pieces of film, and is responsible for the maintenance of editing equipment. *See* **editing.**

■ **assistant music editor** The individual who assists the music editor. He or she helps with editing and synchronizing the music track, keeps a record of the various tracks and pieces of track, and looks after the editing room. *See* **music editor.**

■ **assistant sound editor** The individual who assists the supervising sound editor or one of the sound editors when there are several working under him or her. This person helps with the editing and synchronization of the various sound tracks and record keeping while performing various errands and tasks to help the sound editor do his or her job. *See* **sound editor** *and* **supervising sound editor.**

■ **associate producer** The term today is used rather ambiguously. Sometimes it might be a prestigious title for a production manager who is responsible for coordinating on-location shooting, handling problems that may arise on the set, and giving assistance to the producer in financial and artistic matters. The term might also be given to some other personnel such as an editor, performer, or writer as some type of compensation.

■ **associational editing, associative editing, associate editing, relational editing** Editing together shots of different actions, places, objects, or figures in order to make a thematic or emotional point through some association or relationship between the different scenes. The juxtaposing of such shots may function either to underscore a similarity or to contrast the images. *See* **relational editing.**

■ **Association of Independent Video and Filmmakers (AIVF)** Founded in 1974 and with headquarters in New York City, this organization supports the financing, production, and exhibition of independent film and video while seeking to increase the public's appreciation of such works. The organization has approximately 5,000 members and produces a number of publications, including *The Independent Film and Video Monthly.*

■ **Association of Moving Image Archivists** *See* **film preservation.**

■ **astigmatism** An aberration in a lens that prevents light rays from focusing on the same point and causes the point of an object off the lens axis to be seen as two short lines in different focal planes. Anastigmat lenses are corrected for such a defect.

■ **Astoria Studios** Opened in 1920 as the Famous Players-Lasky Studios and, after a series of mergers and changes in the company, becoming Paramount's Eastern Studios, this complex of production facilities is located in the Astoria section of the borough of Queens in New York City. One of the few studio facilities on the East Coast after the industry's migration to Hollywood, the Astoria Studios was responsible for some one hundred silent films, including all of Griffith's Paramount motion pictures. Its close proximity to New York City made the facility available to a number of Broadway personalities during the early days of sound film, and the Marx Brothers put their stage productions of *The Cocoanuts* and *Animal Crackers* on film here in 1929 and 1930 respectively. During the 1930s, the studios were used for independent productions. The Army took over the studios during the war years and it was not until 1976 that they were used once again for commercial feature films. The musicals *Hair* (1979; dir. Milos Forman) and *All That Jazz* (1979; dir. Bob Fosse) were shot here. The studios are now called the Kaufman-Astoria Studios in honor of George S. Kaufman, chairman of the board. The American Museum of the Moving Image is adjacent to the studios. *See* **American Museum of the Moving Image.**

■ **asynchronous sound** (1) Sound not directly from the image on the screen but closely related to it—for example, the distant sound of a train is heard as a character wanders aimlessly down a deserted street. (2) Sound that either anticipates or follows the action to which it belongs. The telephone, in the first case, is heard ringing at the end of the scene previous to the one in which it appears; or a lover, in the second case, is heard saying goodby after the actual parting has taken place as the other lover watches the airplane fly off into the distance. (3) Sound unintentionally out of sync with the image on the screen due to faulty editing, mixing, printing, projecting, or simply the age of the film. *See* **nonsynchronous sound** *and* **synchronous sound.**

■ **atmosphere** The mood or feeling of a scene created by any number of the following: setting, costumes, makeup, color, lighting, acting style, camera angles and movement, editing, and sound. The director Tod Browning, for example, with the help of his cinematographer, Karl Freund, was able to create an eerie and intense atmosphere during the first part of *Dracula* (1931) that evoked within the viewer a sense of terror and danger. Federico Fellini, in his film *Satyricon* (1969), created a bizarre and decadent atmosphere that to some degree is evident in many of his films.

■ **attenuated filters** Color-compensating filters that reduce the amount of blue, green, or red for changing or correcting color balance. *See* **color-compensating filter.**

■ **attenuation, attenuation loss** The reduction of electrical energy in an electrical circuit or sound wave.

■ **attenuator** A device for decreasing the electrical amplitude in a circuit.

■ **A-type** *See* **A- and B-wind.**

■ **audience** The group of people who view a film. Different films may appeal to different kinds of audiences, and advertising is sometimes directed to specific groups, but with the current high cost of filmmaking, advertising generally seeks to draw to the film the largest mass audience possible by appealing to the most universal and basic emotions. With two-thirds of the population attending at least one movie per year in this country—and more men than women—almost half the filmgoing audience is between the ages of twelve to twenty-nine and almost 70 percent is younger than thirty-nine. Although the portion of the viewers over thirty-nine is growing and now accounts for about a third of the audience, the question is whether aging will bring more mature tastes or whether the films upon which these people have been nurtured have influenced their moviegoing habits forever. Another significant factor in simplifying the nature of Hollywood films is that the industry makes almost half its profits from international audiences—a clientele so diverse in nature and

atmosphere The moody and evocative castle sequence in *Dracula* (1931; dir. Tod Browning), with Bela Lugosi as the Count and Dwight Frye as Renfield.

■ ■ ■

language that it forces the industry to emphasize action and visual delights instead of character and thought. One area of film criticism and theory deals with audience response—either individual reactions or the individual reacting as part of a group. Related to this concern is an understanding of film technique, the way the director uses his camera to make the audience respond in specific ways. Béla Balázs, in *Theory of the Film,* has said that "in the cinema the camera carries the spectator into the film picture itself. . . . Nothing like this 'identification' has ever occurred as the effect of any other system of art" (p. 48). Sigfried Kracauer, in *Theory of Film,* makes the important distinction between "trance-like immersion in a shot or a succession of shots" and "daydreaming, which increasingly disengages itself from the imagery occasioning it." For Kracauer, "the two intertwined dream processes constitute a veritable stream of consciousness. . . ."

■ **audience rating** The opinions of an audience concerning a film it has just viewed, either expressed in writing or through some form of numerical or alphabetical rating in response to specific questions. Audi-

ence ratings after previews of a film are often used for final changes before the film is released for national distribution.

■ **audio** (1) The sound portion of the film. (2) The equipment, facilities, and personnel used in creating the sound portion of a film. *See* **sound.**

■ **audio board** *See* **mixer.**

■ **audion tube** The vacuum tube invented and patented in 1906 by Lee de Forest, which allowed for the amplification of sound and was instrumental in the development of both radio and sound film.

■ **audio tape** *See* **magnetic tape.**

■ **audio-visual** A term describing the use of both sound and image—recorded sound, film, television, slides—in any presentation.

■ **audition** A live tryout for a role in a play or film, though a screen test is more traditionally used for film.

Musical scores or songs may also be auditioned both for theater and film.

■ ***auteur, auteur* theory, *auteur* criticism** The French word *auteur* means "author" and appears in a type of film criticism that sees the director as the controlling force in a film, as an artist who infuses the entire work with his or her personality and point of view and all of whose films can be related in terms of similar techniques, style, and themes. This criticism received its impetus from France, where it was first suggested in 1948 by Alexandre Astruc in his essay on *"la caméra-stylo,"* which argued for the camera itself as a pen, creating the film instead of following preconceived concepts; but it was François Truffaut, as a critic before his filmmaking career, who made the first significant and developed argument for this position in his essay "A Certain Tendency in French Cinema," which appeared in *Cahiers du cinéma* in January 1954. Truffaut argued for *"la politique des auteurs"* ("the policy of authors," later called the *"auteur* theory" by Andrew Sarris); he stood strongly against those films where a literary script was mechanically put on screen by the director and other technicians. For him, film had to be the product of the personal vision and control of the director, who himself should be the *"auteur"* of the work and not a *"metteur en scène"* (i.e., someone who merely carries out another person's concepts). Along with Truffaut, other critics writing for *Cahiers du cinéma,* such as Godard, Chabrol, and Rohmer, who also were to become filmmakers, established a canon of *auteur* directors and were especially effective in resurrecting the names of many Hollywood directors. This whole movement was the result of numerous forces, including the sudden availability of American films in France after World War II, the Cinématèque Française with its compendious showings of international films, and the desire of Truffaut and the other incipient directors to break free from the film establishment and create their own independent works.

It was Andrew Sarris who brought *auteur* criticism to this country with his article "Notes on the *Auteur* Theory in 1962," which appeared in the Winter 1962/63 issue of *Film Culture.* Sarris argued for the following three premises of the *auteur* theory: the director should have technical competence, impose his personality on his works, and give to each work an interior meaning "extrapolated from the tension between a director's personality and his material." In 1968, Sarris published *The American Cinema: Directors and Directions, 1929–1968,* in which he applied his *auteur* theory to the major directors of American sound films, both assessing and rating them.

The shortcomings of the *auteur* theory are by now obvious: such criticism sometimes fails to understand many commercial films as products of a distinct time and place; simplifies or simply ignores the influence of diverse hands in the making of a single film and also the influence of the public in shaping Hollywood studio films; ignores the impact of technical developments upon the movie itself; and tends to be a priori in its judgments, sweeping films into categories of good and bad not because of intrinsic merits or weaknesses, but because of the director to whom they belong. But the merits of the *auteur* theory are also many: such an approach promoted a seriousness and analytical method not common in film studies; developed a comparative methodology by which directors could be compared and their own works understood in relation to each other; helped sort out and distinguish films long lumped together under studio banners; helped bring attention to the accomplishments of many neglected directors; and, perhaps most significantly, supported a new direction in filmmaking, where directors had unprecedented control over their work. *See* **New Wave.**

■ **autocycler** A mechanism that automatically operates an animation camera for cel cycling, whereby cels that are to be used intermittently can be photographed on one pass of the film with the intervening frames unexposed.

■ **autofocus** (1) A cam system that automatically changes the focus of the vertically moving camera in an animation stand. *See* **animation camera.** (2) A device in a camera that automatically sets the focus by computing the distance between the lens and the subject.

■ **automatic dialogue replacement (ADR)** A type of looping session in which some of the originally recorded dialogue is repeated over and over with the corresponding picture until the performer can synchronically rerecord a better version of his or her speech. The ADR editor is the person responsible for this rerecording. *See* **ADR editor** *and* **looping.**

■ **automatic exposure** In amateur filmmaking, where only the light from the overall scene is a consideration, older, small-gauge cameras often contain a photocell that reacts to brightness and automatically opens or closes the lens diaphragm to control film exposure.

■ **automatic fade unit** A mechanism attached to a camera for controlling a variable shutter so that a fade can be automatically achieved in a select number of frames. This device can also create a dissolve. Such mechanisms are often used in animation cameras though they can operate in most cameras with a variable-opening shutter.

■ **automatic gain control (AGC), automatic level control (ALC)** A device in a recording system that maintains the same level of volume, raising lower sounds and decreasing louder ones automatically to a predetermined level.

■ **automatic slate, automatic slating, automatic clapper** A system for aligning both picture and sound without the use of a slate on a clapboard at the start of the take. A flashing light in the camera fogs a few frames at the very start of shooting while a beep-tone is sent to the magnetic sound tape by cable or radio. The editor later uses both these reference points to put picture and sound in synchronization. *See* **clapboard** *and* **synchronization.**

■ **available light** Light for a scene from normal sources as opposed to light specifically and artificially created for cinematography; for example, the sun for outdoor shots and household lamps for indoor shooting. *See* **artificial light.**

■ **avant-garde cinema** The term avant-garde in French means "advanced guard," and in cinema it refers to (1) the experimental and noncommercial films made in Europe from 1918 through the early 1930s and (2) any experimental, noncommercial films. Using *avant-garde* in its more encompassing sense, to include all experimental films, we can say that such films are considered "advanced" in that they deny the traditional narrative structure and techniques of commercial films by seeking to explore new modes of visual and emotional experience. In part as a reaction to the closed doors of commercial cinema, avant-garde filmmakers have used film as a medium of personal expression, replacing narrative structure with their own associational patterns, and often taking advantage of cheaper and more accessible modes of filmmaking to play their own sensibilities off the very nature and visual immediacy of the film image. Within both categories (1) and (2), such cinema can be divided into three very general and overlapping groups: absolute and abstract films that seek to explore the film image itself both in spatial and temporal dimensions through the use of nonrepresentational forms; surrealistic films that maintain images of the real world to express, in nonrealistic ways, emotional and psychological states of mind, and often seek to explore the unconscious through dream and fantasy; and films that are subjective impressions of the outside world itself, conveying internal visions and re-action to actual places through the flexible spatial and temporal dimension of the film image.

A history of the international avant-garde cinema would have to consider the following periods and groups: (a) the German "absolute" filmmakers of the 1920s, especially Richter and Eggeling; (b) the French experimental cinema of the 1920s and early 1930s that includes the dadaist works of René Clair, Fernand Léger, and Man Ray, and the surrealist films, the most famous of which is Salvador Dali's and Luis Buñuel's *Un Chien Andalou* (1928); (c) such impressionistic works as Alberto Cavalcanti's *Rien que les Heures* (1926) and Jean Vigo's *A Propos de Nice* (1930); (d) American avant-garde cinema, starting with the films of Maya Deren and developing into the New American Cinema that flourished from the mid-1950s through the 1970s, featuring works by Stan Brakhage, Kenneth Anger, Andy Warhol, Jonas Mekas, and Shirley Clarke; (e) what P. Adams Sitney originally called the "structural film," a type of nonrepresentational and self-reflexive work that focuses on the medium of film itself, with Michael Snow, George Landow, and Hollis Frampton as key figures; and (f) the post–structural avant-garde cinema. The avant-garde cinema has been widely diversified in the past twenty years, though one can group together films identifiable, for example, by their political nature, sensitivity to gender or sexual and ethnic orienta-

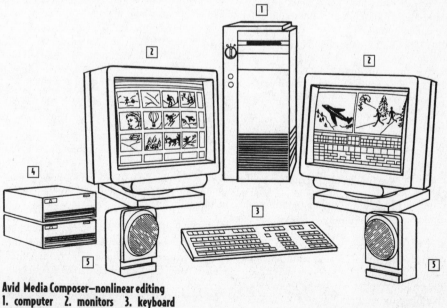

Avid Media Composer—nonlinear editing
1. computer 2. monitors 3. keyboard
4. hard drives 5. speakers

tion, or responsiveness to mass culture. A general type of recent avant-garde film, referred to as the "New Narrative," is clearly a reaction against the structural film. Included in this group are films also referred to as "new talkies" that draw their inspiration from film theory, for example, Laura Mulvey and Peter Wollen's *Riddles of the Sphinx* (1977), and the "punk" films inspired by the Hollywood B movie. Certainly the diminishment of public and private funding as well as venues for screening had a detrimental effect on this type of filmmaking. But also significant in this context was the rise of video art: the availability of video technology allowed a less-expensive and more-convenient way of both creating and showing an art of the moving image while also permitting visual effects previously employed in film only at considerable cost. *See* **absolute film, abstract film, dadaism, New American Cinema, structural film, surrealism,** *and* **underground film.**

■ **Avid Media Composer, Avid Film Composer** Made by Avid Technology, Inc., with offices in Tewksbury, Massachusetts, the Avid Media Composer is a digital nonlinear editing system that was introduced in 1989. Since that time, the Media Composer family has developed into a series of off-line, on-line, and film editing systems that incorporate the latest digital technology and operate through a Macintosh computer platform. Both sound and visuals are compressed and stored on computer hard drives. The Avid Media Composer 8000 is the top-of-the-line model that allows nonlinear off-line and on-line editing as well as film editing and 24 tracks for audio mixing. The Avid Film Composer, designed specifically for film editing, won an award for Scientific and Engineering Achievement from the Academy of Motion Picture Arts and Sciences in 1994. This Avid editor can be used for film of any gauge at 24 frames per second and allows for eighty on-line storage hours. It also allows for previewing fades, dissolves, wipes, superimpositions, and blue-screen effects. The result is a negative cut list using key numbers for negative conforming, a change list, an optical list, or an EDL list for editing a video master copy. Contributing considerable speed and efficiency to the editing process itself, the system is now being used with great frequency in the motion-picture industry. *See* **nonlinear editing.**

■ **A-wind** *See* **A- and B-wind.**

■   ■   ■

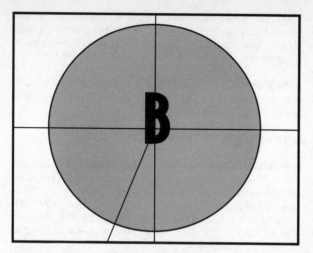

baby plate, baby wall plate to byte

■ **baby plate, baby wall plate** A metal plate with a vertical pole that attaches to a flat surface and supports a small luminaire.

■ **baby spot, baby** A small spotlight with a 1,000-watt bulb, frequently employed for close-ups, angle shots, or as a kick light. Such a fixture with a 750-watt bulb is called a *light baby* or *seven-fifty*, and with a 500-watt bulb a *weak baby* or *five hundred*. A *baby senior* has a 5,000-watt bulb while a *baby tener* a 10,000-watt bulb. A *baby baby* has a 1,000-watt bulb in a smaller housing, while a *baby junior* has a 2,000-watt bulb in the standard baby housing, which is smaller than the standard junior's housing. All these luminaires are sometimes simply referred to as *babies*.

baby spot

■ **baby tripod, baby legs** A tripod with low legs for low-angle shots.

■ **back-and-forth printing** Printing the same bit of action first forward and then in reverse (or vice versa) to achieve some complex or comic behavior on the part of the subject or, in animated cartoons, to extend the movement of the figures. *See* **reverse motion.**

■ **backdrop, drop, backing** A large painted scene either on cloth or on a series of flats, or a large photographic blowup of an actual scene used at the rear of a set as a background and often seen through a door or window. *See* **background plate.**

■ **backend** (1) Money received from a film production after production and/or distribution costs have been paid. Such money is contractually agreed upon in a backend deal. (2) The revenue earned by a film after production and/or distribution costs have been paid. *See* **contingent compensation.**

■ **back focal distance, back focus** The distance between the last glass surface of a lens and the focal plane.

■ **background (BG)** The setting, characters, and the general spatial area to the rear of the image, behind the foreground where the major action takes place. Background settings were generally built and painted in Hollywood studio productions. Today, many films are made on location with natural backgrounds. Another way of creating a background is to use a back-lit photo transparency—a large blowup of a photograph of an actual scene. *See* **background plate.**

■ **background action** Subsidiary action taking place at the same time and in the same general area as the major action. Such activity creates an environment and context for the major action and must be carefully intercut to match the central images.

■ **background artist** The individual in an animation studio who creates the scenery for the animated figures. This artist draws the foreground on cels (called overlays) and the background on separate cels or paper, between which are placed the cels with the figures. Such a technique creates a sense of depth in the image. *See* **animation.**

■ **background lighting** Lighting that illuminates the background area behind the major action. Spotlights and/or floodlights are generally used, and the background area is either lighter or darker than the performers' faces, to allow contrast for emphasizing the faces. *See* **lighting.**

■ **background music** Music that accompanies the action of the film but comes from no source within the film. Such music creates for the audience a continuity to the film's visual images and also heightens the emotional quality of the various scenes. For silent films, presupplied scores of classical or popular works were played on machines such as the Pipe-Organ Orchestra, by small musical groups, or on a piano, though sometimes orchestras played original scores for big-city performances of major films. For sound films, original scores frequently are written and recorded by large orchestras, though scores from other motion pictures or from musical libraries are also used. Popular rock music is frequently employed today as background music. *See* **music** *and* **source music.**

■ **background noise** The local and environmental noises behind the dialogue or major sounds of a scene, added to give atmosphere or added realism.

■ **background plane** *See* **plane.**

■ **background plate** A slide or film with a photographic still or drawing of a setting that is used as the background in rear or front projection. The term is also used for the film which is the source of a moving background in these processes. *See* **front projection, process plate,** *and* **rear projection.**

■ **background projection, background projector** Terms sometimes used for front or rear projection processes and the projector responsible for the background setting in either process. *See* **front projection** *and* **rear projection.**

■ **backing** (1) A backdrop. (2) The coating on the back of film stock, generally the antihalation coating.

■ **backing removal** The process of removing the antihalation backing from the underside of film during the early stages of processing. The backing is softened, washed off, and the remaining elements then scrubbed away.

■ **back light** A light placed behind and above the subject and in line with the camera. Back lighting, which is normally from a bright spotlight, outlines the subject, thus separating it from the background, giving it an appearance of depth, and highlighting the contours of its edge. Such lighting tends to give the subject a dramatic rather than realistic appearance. A back light is also sometimes called an edge, rim, or hair light. *See* **kicker light** *and* **lighting.**

■ **back lighting, bottom lighting, underlighting** Lighting from beneath the aperture of an animation table that illuminates the artwork. *See* **back-lit animation.**

■ **back-lit animation** Animation using a light beneath the aperture of an animation table to illuminate transparencies and artwork. In the Disney production *Tron* (1982; dir. Steven Lisberger), back lighting was employed for giving color and adding effects to enlarged black-and-white frames of the live action on the animation table. This technique has often been used for television commercials. Also called bottom-lit animation. *See* **animation.**

■ **back lot** The area of studio grounds where outdoor sets are built for exterior shooting and where such sets are kept for future use.

■ **back projection** *See* **rear projection.**

■ **backstage musical** A musical film that features characters who are themselves performers and a plot concerned with the problems of putting on a show. This type of musical was especially popular in the 1930s with such films as *42nd Street* (1933; dir. Lloyd Bacon), but *Kiss Me Kate* (1953; dir. George Sidney) is also a notable example. *See* **musical.**

■ **back-up camera** (1) A second camera to be employed in case of some difficulty with the primary camera. (2) A second camera shooting a scene either to cover some possible lapse with the first camera or to give an alternative perspective for editing.

■ **back-up schedule** A schedule for shooting to be followed in case the regular shooting schedule cannot be followed for such reasons as bad weather or the illness of a performer.

■ **backward motion** *See* **reverse motion.**

■ **baffle** (1) A circular shutter with a series of slots that fits over the front of a lamp and directs the light while controlling its intensity. (2) A portable wall covered with acoustical material and placed in a set to reduce reverberations during sound recording. (3) The element in a loudspeaker responsible for controlling sound vibrations.

■ **balance** (1) The arrangement of masses, space, colors, and lighting for a satisfying and dramatic composition in the image. (2) The arrangement of instruments and microphones in a sound recording so that the music is satisfactorily recorded. (3) The coordination and integration of the various sound tracks, especially in relation to the dialogue, so that the relationships, tones, and volumes are natural while the words are clear. *See* **color balance** *and* **lighting balance.**

■ **balanced print** A timed print that has been corrected for color and density. *See* **timing.**

■ **balance stripe, balancing stripe** The narrow stripe opposite the magnetic sound track that allows the film to lie flat when it goes over the magnetic heads and to roll evenly on the reel. When tracks are used on both sides of the film for multichannel stereophonic sound, such a stripe is unnecessary.

■ **balcony** The partition with seats that juts out over the main floor of a theater. When there is more than one such area, the first is called a mezzanine, the second is called the first balcony, and the third the second balcony.

■ **ballast** A device that controls and keeps constant the amount of electricity reaching a lamp.

■ **bandwidth** In digital technology, the amount of information that can be processed each second, specifically the number of bits. *See* **digital.**

■ **bank** (1) A row of lights with a single reflector for general illumination. (2) To group together a number of lights.

■ **bankroll** To finance a film.

■ **banner** A short length of film that is inserted into the film being edited to indicate a missing area. What will be placed in that area is normally written on the piece of stock—e.g., the specific scene.

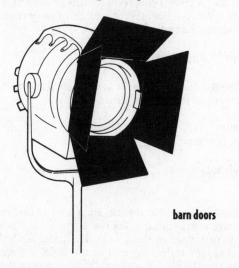

barn doors

■ **barn doors** A unit made up of two or four hinged doors that is attached to the front of a studio lamp and can be rotated. The doors are separately adjustable to direct and shape light, control spill, form shadows, and prevent illumination from shining into the camera lens. Also referred to as flippers.

■ **barney** A flexible, waterproof covering made of several layers and zipped together to cover a camera when a blimp is too restrictive or not available. The barney reduces camera noise for sound recording and sometimes contains a heating element to keep the camera warm in cold weather. The term comes from the comic strip *Barney Google,* which had a racehorse named Sparkplug who always wore a tattered blanket.

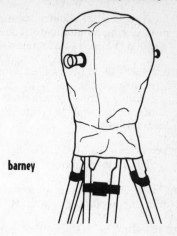

barney

■ **barrel, barrel mount** *See* **lens barrel.**

■ **barrel distortion** A lens defect that causes the sides of a square image to curve outward and the square to seem barrel-shaped.

■ **bar sheet, lead sheet** A chart that relates visual action to an already completed sound track, detailed by an animation director to guide the animator and editor. Such sheets break down action frame by frame and indicate the number of frames for each word of dialogue while also specifying camera movement, optical effects, and sound.

■ **base** The side of the film, made of cellulose acetate or polyester, upon which the light-sensitive emulsion is coated. The base of the film is shiny; the emulsion is dull. *See* **acetate base, film** *(1), and* **polyester base.**

■ **base down, base up** (1) The position of the film's base during editing. Since different generations or types of film may have a different geometry, it is especially important to be careful when cutting and intercutting film from different sources (for example, an original negative is B-type while an internegative from a reversal original is A-type). *See* **A- and B-wind.** (2) The position of certain bulbs when affixed in a luminaire.

■ **base light, foundation light, set light** The general lighting, evenly diffused throughout the set, that prevents any area from being underexposed after certain sections have been highlighted. The base light is normally established on the set before the highlighting and balancing take place. *See* **lighting.**

■ **base plate** A pedestal with a horizontal column for supporting a luminaire.

■ **base-plus-fog density** The minimum density of film without exposure that is a result of both the density inherent in the base and the density resulting from certain unexposed silver halides transforming into metallic silver during development. The same characteristics are called D-Min (i.e., minimum density).

■ **base-to-emulsion** A reversal of normal film wind in a printer to reverse the geometry of the image. This might be done to bring together two films with different geometries or simply to reverse the direction of action. *See* **A- and B-wind.**

■ **basher** A small lamp of 250 or 500 watts that can be employed as a spot or general light.

■ **bass boost** An increasing of low frequencies in the recording or rerecording of sounds.

■ **bass roll-off** The reduction of low frequencies in sound by means of a filter during recording or mixing. *See* **equalization** *and* **roll-off.**

■ **batch** (1) A single mixture for a film's emulsion. Even though great effort is taken to assure the similar composition of each batch for the same type of film, some variation is likely. For this reason, the batch number is supplied by the manufacturer with each roll of film so that the cinematographer may be assured of consistently shooting with film from the same batch and hence with the same sensitivity and qualities. (2) A chemical solution made for film processing at a single time.

■ **bath** (1) Any of the various solutions used at different times in the processing of film. (2) The containers that hold these solutions. *See* **processing.**

■ **batten** A long pole for supporting luminaires or scenery.

■ **battery belt, power belt** A belt, worn by the camera operator, which holds batteries to supply power to the portable camera. The batteries are rechargeable.

■ **battery pack** A lightweight single container that holds a number of batteries and supplies power to camera, lights, or other devices on location. The batteries can be rapidly recharged.

■ **baud** The unit representing the speed at which one piece of information is transmitted each second—for a computer, the number of bits transmitted per second. *See* **bit.**

■ **bay** (1) A separate area or room where a specific type of work takes place, e.g., an editing bay. (2) An area in a studio where scenery and sometimes property and equipment are stored.

■ **bayonet mount** A type of mount into which the camera's lens is pressed and snapped into place by a slight

twist. Such mounts are considered more stable, able to support greater weights, and easier to mount than the type that screws into place. Arriflex cameras use a notable example of this type of mount.

bayonet mount

■ **bazooka** A tubular support for an overhead lamp that is generally attached to a catwalk.

■ **BCU** Big close-up. *See* **extreme close-up.**

■ **beadboard** A foam sheet used as a reflector to create a soft, diffused bounce light.

■ **beaded screen** A screen covered with tiny glass or plastic beads that is used for daylight or front-projection process shots. *See* **front projection** *and* **screen.**

■ **beam angle** *See* **light-beam angle.**

■ **beam coverage** An area that a lamp can illuminate with 50 percent of its peak intensity.

■ **beam lumens** The amount of light within a light-beam angle. *See* **lumen.**

■ **beam projector** A spotlight with a narrow beam of light.

■ **beam splitter** An optical device, such as a prism or semireflecting mirror, that splits the light beam from the lens into two separate images. Such a device is used in (1) cameras for reflecting part of the light to form an image in the viewfinder and to allow the rest of the light to pass through and form the same image on the film; (2) special-effects cameras for forming an image on the negative and the same image on other film stock which will be made into a traveling matte (this type of camera was used in Disney studios with a rear screen illuminated by yellow-sodium vapor lamps); and (3) optical printers with two projectors on each axis, allowing, for example, separate positives and their corresponding mattes to run together to form a composite image. *See* **reflex viewfinder** *and* **traveling matte process.**

■ **bear trap** A strong clamp sometimes used for mounting lights. This clamp is also called an alligator, a gator grip, and a gaffer grip.

■ **beater mechanism** An advance mechanism used in early projectors and some narrow-gauge machines, which featured a beater roller, eccentrically mounted on a cam, pulling down the film in intermittent motion.

■ **Beaulieu** A 16mm camera made in France that is very compact and lightweight. The camera has easily accessible controls on both sides and an effective reflex-viewing system. The camera is easy to operate and adaptable for various kinds of shooting.

■ **bed** *See* green.

■ **beep tone, beep** (1) A brief noise put into a sound track to correspond with fogged frames or some visual reference in a film for synchronization of both sound and image. The automatic or electronic clapstick puts this sound into the track as soon as the recorder and camera are activated. (2) Any brief noise placed on a film or videotape to cue a performer for additional dialogue or any personnel for the addition or synchronization of sound.

■ **behind-the-lens filter** A filter inserted in a slot behind the lens of a camera. Such filters are smaller, more convenient, and less susceptible to breakage than filters in front of the lens, and, unlike the latter, are free from flare caused by unwanted light.

■ **Bell and Howell** An American company that for many years manufactured a series of dependable cameras and projectors for amateurs and professionals. This company now focuses on information access and mail processing.

■ **Bell and Howell mechanism** The intermittent movement in the camera, designed by A. S. Howell, which achieves a high degree of steadiness for the film through fixed pilot pins. *See* **pilot pins** *and* **registration** *(1).*

■ **Bell and Howell perforation (BH), negative perforation** The rectangular sprocket holes with arced ends now largely used in this country for 35mm negative and duplicating film because of their steady registration. Since BH corners are subject to tear over a period of time, the shorter Kodak standard perforation (KS) with curved corners is used in positive prints. *See* **Kodak standard perforation.**

Bell and Howell perforation

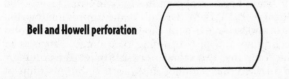

■ **bell lamp** A soft light in a brimmed dome that creates a wide beam. This luminaire lights backings or cycs while employing a variety of bulbs. It is much like the portable cinelite.

■ **bellows attachment** An accordionlike device that attaches to the camera and extends the lens, generally for extreme close-ups. The Clairmont Swing/Shift lens system employs a bellows system, but the device also permits tilts, shifts, swings, rises, and falls to achieve various effects—e.g., changing the focus plane or depth of field, distorting objects, or removing objects from the frame.

■ **belly board** A board on which the camera is mounted for low-angle shots.

■ **below-the-line costs** Expenses figured in the budget that will accrue after the film has begun—for example, expenses for shooting, editing, and all production activities. This category may also include salaries not contractually agreed upon before the shooting begins as part of the above-the-line costs. *See* **above-the-line costs.**

■ **below the title** The location for the front credits that appear on the screen after the title is shown. *See* **above the title.**

■ **bench editing, bench work** Running the film through the viewer, sound recorder, and synchronizer by turning the rewinders manually rather than mechanically for editing. Since it is almost impossible for the editor to turn the rewinders consistently, there will be some lack of clarity, especially in sound, but this method is actually faster and the film easier to control and pinpoint than in machine editing. *See* **editing.**

■ **best boy, electric best boy** The assistant to the gaffer (i.e., to the head electrician).

■ **best boy grip** The assistant to the grip (i.e., the stagehand).

■ **Beta, Betacam** *See* videotape.

■ **BG** *See* background.

■ **bias** A current applied by a sound recorder to a magnetic tape to raise the audio signal above a certain level in order to eliminate noise and distortion while recording low signals.

■ **bicycling** (1) When an actor or director runs between two productions at the same time. (2) When an actor or director becomes involved with a production right after the completion of another. (3) In silent-film years, playing the same print at more than one theater on the same day, hence rushing it from one theater to the other, often by bicycle.

■ **bid** A written request made by an exhibitor to a distribution company for the right to show a particular film starting on or about a specific date. The request often includes a guaranteed length of exhibition, financial terms, and an arrangement for advertising. *See* **bid letter.**

■ **bidirectional microphone** A microphone that picks up sound from its front and back, but not from its sides. *See* **microphone.**

■ **bid letter, bid request** A notification sent to an exhibitor by a distributor, informing the exhibitor about a film, generally some six months before its release, and requesting a bid for the right to show the film. The distributor often suggests the terms to be met or surpassed, which include both playing time and financial guarantees. This procedure is a form of blind bidding and much resented by exhibitors. *See* **blind bidding.**

■ **big caper** The big crime, generally a complicated robbery, in a big caper, caper, or heist film. The term was used more often for the films of the 1930s and 1940s, though big capers continued to be an important part of films dealing with crime, as in William Friedkin's *The Brinks Job* (1978).

■ **big close-up (BCU)** *See* **extreme close-up.**

■ **big eye** A large floodlight of 100,000 watts.

■ ***Big Reel, The*** A publication that lists 16mm and 35mm prints for sale by various dealers. This journal also lists videos, posters, and lobby cards that are for sale, advertises special meetings for dealers, and features short articles on Hollywood performers of the past.

■ **bilateral sound track** A variable area optical sound track on film in which sound modulations are symmetrically formed on both sides of the longitudinal axis. In double bilateral tracks two such patterns are formed with symmetrical sides. *See* **variable-area sound track.**

■ **billing** The way in which performers are publicized for a film, notably their ranking in screen credits and advertising. Billing is a crucial concern to performers not only because it announces their relative importance in a film and in the industry at large, but because it is also significant in terms of future hiring and salary.

■ **bin** (1) *See* **trim bin.** (2) The area in a digital nonlinear editing system for storing footage.

■ **binary** The term refers to the numbering system using the digits 0 and 1 for coding letters or visuals in any computerized system. The 1 indicates an electrical impulse and the 0 its lack—the system, therefore, indi-cates a series of "on" and "off" impulses. *See* **baud, bit,** *and* **digital.**

■ **binary opposition, binary conflict** Terms especially popular in structuralist criticism to describe two conflicting aspects of a culture, society, or narrative work, generally mediated by a third force. The anthropologist Claude Lévi-Strauss has been the main influence on this school of thought, especially in his work on primitive societies and myths. Structuralism was extremely popular in the 1960s and made its mark on a host of disciplines, including film. Structuralism seeks out the basic structures that the human mind imposes on reality and that can be found underlying both social codes and the artistic expression of any society (the aim is actually to find universal structures). Basic to these structures are binary oppositions that reflect conflicts in society—the structure is an attempt to mediate such a conflict. The concept of binary opposition, itself taken from the lectures on linguistics and semiotics by Ferdinand de Saussure, is part of Lévi-Strauss's attempt to apply the structure of language to anthropology. An example for film criticism might be the opposition between gangsters and police in a criminal film, the first representing freedom with chaos and the second representing order with restriction. In such a film, the detective might be the mediating force, embodying freedom without chaos and order without restriction. *See* **semiotics** *and* **structuralism.**

■ **binder** The substance in the film emulsion that spreads the grains of silver halide while attaching them to the film.

■ **Biograph** At first called the KMCD syndicate after the initials of its owners, Eugene Koopman, Henry Marvin, Herman Casler, and W. K. L. Dickson, then later the American Mutoscope and Biograph Company, this organization was founded in December 1895. Dickson, Edison's former associate, helped the company develop the Mutoscope, a peep-show machine that surpassed Edison's Kinetoscope, and also the Biograph camera and projector, also superior to Edison's similar machines because of better image quality from larger film. Biograph eventually had to adopt the standard-size film introduced by Edison's company so that its pictures could be shown in more theaters. The company had a studio on the roof of a building on Fourteenth Street in New York City, and in 1910 also began making films in California. From 1908 through 1913, D. W. Griffith made approximately 400 one- and two-reelers for Biograph, developing his film technique and also bringing considerable success to the company. Two years after Griffith left the company in 1913 to make longer and more ambitious films at Mutual, Biograph went out of business. Mack Sennett, Lillian and Dorothy Gish, Mary Pickford, and Mae Marsh began their careers with Biograph.

biography *The Life of Emile Zola* (1937; dir. William Dieterle), with Paul Muni in the title role.

■ ■ ■

■ **biography, biographical film, bio, biog, biopic** A film narrating the life of a well-known individual. During the 1930s and 1940s, Warner Brothers produced a number of these films, including *The Story of Louis Pasteur* (1936) and *The Life of Emile Zola* (1937), both directed by William Dieterle and featuring Paul Muni's celebrated performances. In more recent years, Ken Russell made several rather sensational and subjective film versions of the lives of famous composers.

■ **bioskop, bioscope** The camera and projector system invented by Max and Emil Skladanowsky that was responsible for the first public presentation of film in Germany on November 1, 1895, in Berlin.

■ **bipack** The employment of two pieces of film, generally in contact, in any photographing, printing, or projecting system.

■ **bipack contact matte printing, bipack printing** A matting and printing system for combining two series of images on a single film so that a composite image is formed. This is accomplished by first printing the negative, which generally contains the live action, onto a master positive. The master positive is then threaded into a process camera along with a roll of fresh stock, the first roll directly in back of the aperture and the second right below the first with the emulsion of both touching behind the aperture (hence the name bipack contact). An easel is then placed directly in front of the camera, with a white matte board on which an area is blacked out. When the camera is operating, the white area allows enough light to pass through the corresponding area on the positive and print that portion of the image on the new negative, while the black area of

the matte prevents light from passing through the positive, leaving that portion of the negative unexposed. When another matte is placed in front of the camera, with the area blacked out that corresponds with the image printed on the negative and artwork or a photograph placed in the area that was formerly blacked out, this new image will be printed in the unexposed area of the rewound negative, running by itself through the camera. This system can be used to combine live action with artwork, photographs, miniatures, or even other live action, or to combine any image with titles. This process also permits optical transitions. Bipack printing is most often used to extend or change the architecture of a setting in which live action is first filmed, thus saving on construction costs. This process has been used instead of in-the-camera matte shots because it avoids the risk of ruining the original negative with more than one exposure and the inconvenience of creating the artwork at the time of the original photographing of the live action. *See* **digital effects, matte** *(2),* **optical printer,** *and* **traveling-matte process.**

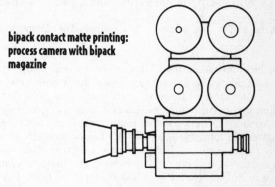

bipack contact matte printing: process camera with bipack magazine

■ **bipack double-print titles** Film titles on a picture that are the result of printing together titles and image from two separate reels in a bipack system.

■ **bipack magazine** A magazine with four chambers for feeding two pieces of film into a camera or projector and for taking up the exposed film.

■ **bipost lamp** A studio lamp with two small protrusions at the bottom that fit into two holes in the socket. After the protrusions are in the holes, the lamp is snapped into place by a slight turn.

■ **bird's-eye view, bird's-eye shot** A shot from a camera directly overhead at a distance, sometimes taken from a crane or helicopter. A shot from this angle diminishes characters and locations, while allowing the audience a wider view and more information than have the characters involved in the scene. *See* **overhead shot.**

■ **Bison Life Motion Pictures** *See* **New York Motion Picture Company.**

■ **bit** A contraction for "binary digit," the term refers to a single digit in the code of 0's and 1's employed in computerized systems. Since the 1 refers to the presence of an electronic impulse and a 0 to its lack, the bit refers to the "on" or "off" aspect of the code to which all letters and visuals are reduced. Eight bits form a byte, the smallest unit for a single letter. *See* **baud, byte,** *and* **digital.**

■ **bit depth, color depth** In computer animation and graphics, the number of bits attached to each pixel for the creation of color—e.g., 8, 16, 32, or 64 bits. *See* **bit map** *and* **palette** *(2).*

■ **bit map, bit map graphics** A type of raster computer graphics and animation in which the images are composed of tiny pixels, with each pixel assigned a specific color and quality of gray. *See* **computer animation.**

■ **bit part** A very small role in a film, generally a small speaking part as distinguished from the role of an extra, who speaks no lines and is often part of a crowd.

■ **bit player** An actor or actress who performs a bit part.

■ **black-and-white film** Film with an emulsion that when processed presents an image that transforms colors into various shades of gray. Silent-film stock was at first orthochromatic, sensitive to blue and green light waves, and then panchromatic, sensitive to all light waves. Panchromatic stock, which was normally in use by the end of the 1920s, creates a picture with more gradations of light and dark and photographs faces more naturally—but at a loss of depth of field. Black-and-white film produces images that can emphasize contrast and shadows, thus conveying a sense of stark reality, darkness, and even sinister foreboding, or images that can emphasize light to convey moods of gaiety and lightness. Such film can also create an era and mood that we associate with earlier films made in black and white. Most commercial films were made in black and white until the late 1950s, when Eastman Color made filming in color the rule, though some later films, such as Peter Bogdanovich's *The Last Picture Show* (1971) and Bob Fosse's *Lenny* (1974), used black and white to create particular environments and moods. *See* **film.**

■ **black comedy** A type of play or film that conveys a sardonic sense of humor, reacting to deadly serious subjects, such as illness, war, or death, with painful and biting laughter. Such plays or films are often satiric in nature, seeking to make us explore attitudes and behavior that hide unpleasant truths about human nature; that are, in fact, hypocritical distractions from moral action. Perhaps the most famous film of this kind is Stanley Kubrick's *Dr. Strangelove; or, How I Learned to Stop Worrying and Love the Bomb* (1963). *See* **comedy.**

■ **black level** The darkest area of a film image.

■ **black limbo** The general area of a set that is covered in black material so that characters or models photographed will be distinct and separate from the environment. Such a background can be used for making traveling mattes. When white is used for the same purpose, the area is referred to as white limbo. *See* **limbo** *and* **traveling-matte process.**

■ **blacklist** A list of people who for one reason or another are not to be hired by the various agencies or companies in an industry. In 1947 and 1951, the House Un-American Activities Committee (HUAC) carried out much-publicized investigations to discover Communists and subversives in the movie industry. In fear of both governmental regulation and losses at the box office, Hollywood supposedly developed a blacklist for those involved in the movie industry who were known to be, or even suspected of being, Communists. Although the industry denied the existence of such a list, for twenty years a large number of people were prevented from finding work in Hollywood, and many were forced to use aliases or seek work abroad. The House Committee continued its investigations until 1954. *See* **Hollywood Ten** *and* **House Committee on Un-American Activities.**

■ **Black Maria** A small studio next to the Edison laboratories in West Orange, New Jersey, designed by W. K. L.

Black Maria The small studio next to the Edison laboratories in West Orange, New Jersey, which was completed in January 1893 and in which filmstrips were made for Edison's peephole machine, the Kinetoscope.

■ ■ ■

Dickson and completed in January 1893, that was used to make filmstrips for Edison's Kinetoscopes. This small shack was called the Black Maria, a slang name for paddy wagon, because it was partly covered by black tar paper. Performers were photographed by the massive Kinetograph camera against a black background and lit by the rays of the sun, which entered through the movable roof. The entire structure could be rotated to adjust to the movement of the sun, although most of the shooting was done at noon. *See* **Edison Company.**

■ **black net** A black netting or screen placed in front of a lamp to diminish the amount of light it gives off.

■ **blackout switch** The master switch in a studio for extinguishing all lights.

■ **blacks** Any fabrics or draperies used to block out light from windows and doors. Such coverings are employed especially when shooting during the day interior scenes that are supposed to take place at night.

■ **black track print, black stripe print** An answer print with a black stripe in place of the sound track. Such prints are used for adjustments in exposure and color before the sound track is added. *See* **answer print.**

■ **black wrap, blackwrap** Black, thick, and strong aluminum foil used on lights to shape and control the beam and sometimes as a heat-resistant protection between the light and a surface.

■ **blade** A small, narrow flag generally used to block or control light falling on an area. Blades made of translucent material are used for softening illumination.

■ **blaxploitation film, blacksploitation film** A film made with black performers and aimed at a black audience, though generally made by white producers. These films were especially popular in the early 1970s and took the form of nearly every established genre, though perhaps the most prominent were the violent and sensationalistic crime films such as *Shaft* (1971; dir. Gordon Parks), which was certainly one of the best of this group. *See* **race films.**

■ **bleach** In the processing of reversal film, the bath that removes the metallic silver forming the first image and leaves the silver halides not previously exposed to be exposed or chemically treated to form the second and positive image. *See* **reversal film.**

■ **bleached out** A term applicable to any film image that is washed out and has minimal detail because of overexposure of the original film during shooting.

■ **bleeding** A dispersion of light, color, or line around the edges of a matte, titles, or an image component in

blaxploitation film *Shaft* (1971; dir. Gordon Parks), with Richard Roundtree as the black hero in the most skillful of these films.

■ ■ ■

a special-effects shot for any of several reasons, including the misalignment of a camera or poor registration of film.

■ **bleed through** Undesirable sound intruding into one theater from the motion picture playing in the next. Such an intrusion is caused by poor soundproofing between theaters but also from the highly improved sound systems now being used for motion pictures. *See* **sound.**

■ **blend** The direction to a performer to move close to another actor or group of actors.

■ **blend line** *See* **matte line.**

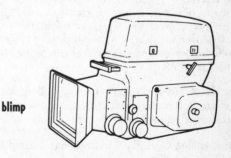

blimp

■ **blimp** A soundproof housing that surrounds the camera and prevents the noise of the motor from being recorded on the sound track. The camera shoots through a window in front of the housing, while it is fully operated from the outside. Self-blimped cameras are already encased in soundproofed housings and require no external covering.

■ **blind bidding** A film rental forced upon an exhibitor by a studio or distributor even though the exhibitor has not seen the film and may have no familiarity with it. A number of states have ruled this practice illegal.

■ **blind mix** An audio mix created with the various sound tracks but without the use of a workprint as a visual reference. Sometimes called a wild mix. *See* **interlock mix** *and* **mix.**

■ **blip sync, bleep sync, blip tone** *See* **sync beep.**

■ **block booking** A rental agreement that forces the exhibitor to book several films at once. Such an arrangement guarantees the studio or distributor a financial return on less popular or less successful films. The Supreme Court Paramount decision of 1948 ruled such a practice illegal when separating theaters from the major studios. *See* **Paramount decision.**

■ **blockbuster** (1) An extremely expensive, generally long, and lavishly made film that requires a great financial return to be profitable. A number of these films were made in the 1950s and early 1960s until the losses of *Mutiny on the Bounty* (1962; dir. Lewis Milestone) and *Cleopatra* (1963; dir. Joseph L. Mankiewicz), the first costing $18 million and the second $31 million, put an end to the production of such films for a while. Michael Cimino's *Heaven's Gate* (1980), which cost $36 million and bombed at the box office, is said to have played an important role in the downfall of United Artists. Recently, *Waterworld* (1995; dir. Kevin Reynolds) cost the extraordinary sum of somewhere between $175 million and $235 million to produce, but the film might recoup much of its costs when foreign distribution and video releases are added to the disappointing domestic box office. (2) A film that is an enormous financial success.

■ **blocking** (1) Planning the positions and movements of the performers in a particular scene. (2) Showing the performers their positions and movements in a particular scene. (3) Arranging the placement of the camera (or cameras) as well as the proper lens and focus for a shot.

■ **bloom** To apply some type of dulling spray to glass or any reflective surfaces that might cause unwanted glare during shooting.

■ **blooming** Any glare in an image caused by a highly reflective surface.

■ **bloop** (1) The noise heard in the optical sound system when a splice or some other break in the film passes the scanner. Diagonal splicing in a magnetic sound track avoids such a noise, since the area of splice passing the playback head is quite small, but a bloop can arise when the track is touched by magnetic editing tools. (2) The tape or darkened area on the positive optical-sound track or the perforation on the negative optical-sound track used in the deblooping process to make the sound of the bloop inaudible when a splice passes the sound head. *See* **deblooping.**

■ **blooper** (1) A misspoken line that inadvertently produces a comic effect. (2) The magnet or punch used for deblooping. *See* **deblooping.** (3) A small tank of water used to create the effect of exploding water. See **mechanical effects.**

■ **blooping** *See* **deblooping.**

■ **blooping ink, blooping tape, blooper patch** The various methods used to cover over a splice in an optical sound track so that a bloop will not be heard when the splice passes the sound head. *See* **deblooping.**

■ **blow up, blowup** (1) To make a larger duplicate picture from a smaller gauge. It is possible to make a 16mm film into 35mm, while still having sufficient quality and definition for public release. Since 65mm film is now rarely used to make wide-screen 70mm prints, 35mm film is blown up into the larger release print for special screenings. (2) To enlarge part of an image by means of an optical printer to remove from the frame unwanted picture elements or to give greater importance to the subject being increased in size. *See* **optical printer.** (3) The actual photograph or film that has been enlarged from a smaller gauge or picture element.

■ **blue** *See* **lavender print.**

■ **blue cometing** Tiny bluish streaks that appear in a color image and are the result of metallic particles causing contamination in the film's emulsion during development.

■ **Blue Max** *See* **blue-screen process.**

■ **blue movie** A pornographic movie; a film whose major intent is to arouse the audience sexually.

■ **blue-screen paddle** Objects of various shapes and sizes that are made from tubular neon lights, covered by translucent plastic, and that are the color of the blue-screen backing. Such objects are used during a blue-screen shot to block out unwanted elements such as wires or rods. *See* **blue-screen process.**

■ **blue-screen process** A much-used traveling-matte process that requires no special camera and eventually combines various picture elements photographed separately into a single composite image. Actors, for example, are photographed in white light against a blue background with a color negative. Because only a single roll of film is used in the camera as opposed to systems that imprint the image on two separate negatives, the process is considered a single-film traveling-matte system. By means of a series of laboratory printings of the original color negative through color filters, a matte is made in which the background area is opaque and the actors clear, and from this matte another is made in which the actors are opaque and the background is clear—the former is generally called the foreground or female matte and sometimes the matte master, or cover, action, printing, or burn-in matte; the latter is generally called the background or male matte and sometimes the hold-out matte. Because the opaque silhouettes of the actors on the background matte change from frame to frame to correspond with their movement, the entire process is considered a traveling-matte system. The combining of the actors and background images photographed separately is accomplished in an optical printer, where the background action from a positive is first printed on a fresh negative, with the background matte running in contact with the positive and blacking out an area on the negative for the foreground; and subsequently the foreground from a positive is printed in the unexposed area of the negative, with the foreground matte blocking out that positive's background area and leaving the corresponding area on the negative intact. The result is the piecing together of the foreground and background images from different shootings into a single composite image.

The blue-screen method is often advantageous to rear- or front-projection processes because it allows full movement of the camera, requires less preparation and special equipment for shooting, and permits various effects in the printing stage. Precise lighting and camera registration are necessary in the blue-screen process to avoid fringing (i.e., light bouncing off the blue backing onto the foreground objects) and visible matte lines. Shooting any blue in the foreground action has always been a problem because the blue background will print through holes in the matte, forming a blue halo around moving and often stationary objects. Sometimes a blue-spill matte drawn by hand with the use of a rotoscope is necessary to remove such contamination. Such auxiliary mattes will fill in the holes for most blues, but a better system is to create a synthetic blue color difference matte. Such a process is also more effective for recording transparent objects, reflections, and smoke. In this process, a color difference matte, which is made by bipacking the original negative with a green separation positive and printing with blue light, is used together with the green separation positive to form a synthetic blue separation matte with an opaque background. The color difference mat-

ting process was first used for the 65mm filming of *Ben-Hur* (1959; dir. William Wyler). A large number of elements—live action, animation, parts of different settings—can be combined into a single composite image by the blue-screen process, which has been effectively and frequently employed in special-effects films such as the *Star Wars* trilogy (1977–83) and the *Superman* trilogy (1978–83). The reverse blue-screen process, developed for Clint Eastwood's *Firefox* (1982) by Apogee and also used in John Badham's *Blue Thunder* (1983), is applicable only for models and not live action. In this process, many of the problems that arise from a blue-lit background are removed when the model itself becomes a source of blue illumination from phosphors in its paint being bombarded by ultraviolet radiation. Through motion control, two passes of film are made—one for the normally lit subject and the other, the matte pass, for the subject when it gives off the blue light. Apogee also developed the front-projection blue-screen method as an economical and efficient response to the high demand for blue-screen composites. Specially developed Blue Max equipment is used for this process, which creates very fine images. Rear front-projection, on the other hand, is used to omit blue spill in close-ups by increasing the distance between the front-projection camera and projector, still at 90 degrees to one another. The subject is placed between a large beam splitter and the camera, with the front-projection screen facing the projector and the camera shooting toward the beam splitter from the normal position of the projector.

Blue-screen compositing is now also accomplished digitally. Characters are shot against a blue backing and both these images and those of a separately shot background, for example, are scanned into a computer. An electric matting process called chroma key assembles the picture elements, though Ultimatte has developed such compositing for both analog video and computers with its own "additive" technology. *See* **chroma key, motion control, traveling-matte process,** and **Ultimatte.**

■ **blue spill, blue-spill matte** *See* **blue-screen process.**

■ **blur pan** *See* **swish pan.**

■ **B-negative** Original negative which is not used to make prints for editing. Such negative is catalogued and stored away in case some take might be selected for printing at a later time.

■ **body brace, body frame, body pad** A support, normally made of aluminum alloy, that attaches to the photographer's waist and shoulders and supports his hand-held camera, freeing his hands to operate the camera. Also called a shoulder brace. *See* **handheld** *and* **Steadicam.**

■ **body makeup artist** The individual in the makeup crew responsible for applying makeup to the main part of the body from the breastbone down and from the elbows up. The makeup artist is responsible for the area from the head to the breastbone and from the fingers to the elbows. *See* **makeup artist.**

■ **Bolex camera** A precision-built, lightweight, hand-held 16mm camera made in Switzerland and often used for TV news coverage, especially in Europe. Bolex makes both spring and electrically driven cameras. While most models have a bayonet mount for tele-photo and zoom lenses, the H-16 Rex 5 and H-16 SBM come with a turret for three lenses.

■ **bomb** A film that is a failure, especially with audiences and at the box office.

■ **book** (1) The nonmusical part of a musical play or film: the dialogue, action, and story. (2) Two flats that are attached by hinges so that they can be easily folded together for transportation and storage.

■ **booking** Arranging for the rental of a film from a distributor. The booker is generally the individual who works for the distributor and oversees the booking of a film in a specific area. *See* **distribution** *and* **exhibition.**

■ **boom** (1) Microphone boom: a long, mobile, tele-scopic arm with a microphone attached at one end that is held over the speaker's head, outside the camera's frame. The boom follows the characters about and per-mits synchronous sound recording of the entire scene. Also referred to as fishpole and boompole. (2) Camera boom: the sturdy, mobile camera mount, attached to a vehicle, that is capable of moving vertically and hori-zontally in space, allowing the camera operator to shoot the scene from various heights, distances, and angles. (3) Light boom: a long, extended pole that is attached to a stand and from which a light is suspended to illuminate a particular area of the set from above. *See* **crane** *and* **fishpole.**

■ **boomerang** The receptacle in front of a light that holds a filter.

■ **boom man, boom operator** The sound technician who operates the boom and the microphone attached to it.

■ **boom shot** *See* **crane shot.**

■ **boom up, boom down** (1) The vertical movement of the camera or microphone attached to a boom. (2) An order to move the boom supporting the camera either up or down.

■ **boomy, tubby** The sound quality of a location that di-minishes high frequencies and emphasizes low ones. The result is poorly defined sound and some echoing.

■ **booster** (1) A transformer that increases voltage in lamps during shooting to achieve a higher degree of

lighting than the wattage normally allows. (2) In out-door daylight photography, the artificial lights auxil-iary to the key light, which is generally the sun. (3) A filter for raising the color temperature of a light.

■ **boot** (1) A small cover that protects the head of a tripod when not in use. (2) The small light-tight com-ponent through which film from a magazine moves into the storage area during processing.

■ **border light** A strip of lights, frequently with five, ten, or twelve bulbs of 1,000 watts each. Also called a strip light.

■ **bottom-lit animation** *See* **back-lit animation.**

■ **bounce card, bounce board** A sheet made of white posterboard or Styrofoam that is used as a reflector to redirect illumination. Such sheets are normally held by stands and situated close to the subject because of their limited reflectance.

■ **bounce light** Lamps aimed at walls and ceiling to cre-ate general and diffuse lighting.

■ **box** (1) A set with four walls. (2) A computer station.

■ **box office** (1) The small booth at the front of the theater from which tickets are sold for admission. (2) The financial receipts for a particular film. (3) The suc-cess or failure of a film in the entertainment industry determined on the basis of revenues at the actual box office. Even though ancillary markets, especially the purchase and rental of films on video, are now respon-sible for a considerable portion of a film's earnings, the box office is still the determining factor, both in the amount of money it brings in and also its influence on other markets. Today, the foreign box office can earn for a film half its profits (sometimes even more), though the domestic market is still considered the hallmark of a film's success or failure. Distributors will release their big-budget blockbusters primarily during the summer months, when young people are off from school and summer vacations bring more people to the theaters and, secondarily, during the Christmas–New Year holi-day season for the same reasons. A film's best box office takes place during its opening weekend, pretty much giving an indication of how the film will do. After the first week, the box office begins to drop anywhere from 15 percent to 40 percent, depending on the film's re-views and word-of-mouth (a drop of less than 20 per-cent for the second weekend is considered a definite sign of success). The high cost of advertising and main-taining a film, as well as the competition for screens, will often force a distributor to decrease advertising for a film if it opens poorly and pull it from distribution if the box office remains low. If the film opens well, then its advertising and the number of its screens are likely to increase. Of course, reviews and word-of-mouth can also gradually build the box office for a film that opens quietly in only select theaters. The highest-grossing films at the domestic box office had been Steven Spielberg's *E.T.: The Extra-Terrestrial* (1982) and *Jurassic Park* (1993), the first earning $399,804,539 and the second $356,783,914, until the recent re-release of George Lucas's *Star Wars* (1977) sent that film plunging ahead.

■ **Box Office** A monthly magazine for film exhibitors that keeps them informed of releases, new and future productions, marketing trends, and developments in exhibition equipment.

■ **box rental, kit rental** Payment to a member of one of the technical crews for the use of his or her tools and equipment on a daily or weekly basis.

■ **B-picture** A cheaper, more quickly made, less ambitious, and less publicized film made during the 1930s and 1940s as the second film on a double bill or as one of two equally secondary films for a midweek showing. Special companies such as Monogram and Republic made only B-pictures, and major studios during this time had separate operations to make these financially profitable films. Though given small budgets and little time, such films on occasion achieved a high degree of artistry and success, as in the case of the horror films made by Val Lewton for RKO in the early 1940s. The Supreme Court Paramount decision of 1948, which freed theaters from ownership by the film studies, was instrumental in doing away with both B-films and double features. Theater owners became free to choose their own films, independents increased, and the cost of making films skyrocketed. *See* **A-picture** *and* **studio system.**

B-picture Frances Dee is awakened by something sinister in *I Walked With a Zombie* (1943; dir. Jacques Tourneur), one of Val Lewton's remarkable low-budget films for RKO.

■■■

■ **brace** A support for holding up scenery; a strut.

■ **bracketing, exposure bracketing** Shooting film at the f-stop designated by the meter and then at exposures lesser and greater to insure a good take.

■ **break** (1) The particular stage of film distribution (e.g., a first-run break at those theaters throughout the country that show a film at its first release). (2) The date on which the film is released nationally or in a particular market. (3) To release a film in some pattern of distribution.

■ **breakaway** (1) A property or part of the set made to break easily without injury to the performer, for example, a bottle or chair. (2) A miniature, such as an airplane, made to break up during a scene.

■ **breakdown** (1) An analysis of a film script in terms of costs for all aspects of production including personnel, equipment, sets, costumes, travel, etc. *See* **production board.** (2) An analysis of a film script that groups together all scenes shot in the same locations or on the same sets to allow for the most convenient and economical shooting schedule, so that each group can be shot together and an actor's shooting time be kept minimal. The individual pages of the script may be placed on individual breakdown sheets, which themselves may be used in creating the production board. *See* **production board.** (3) In the editing process, the analysis of the shots in a single roll, normally the dailies, to prepare for their arrangement in the desired sequence.

■ **breakdown board** *See* **production board.**

■ **breakdown sheets** Individual sheets for specific scenes or sequences of scenes that list the personnel, vehicles, props, and equipment needed, along with a brief synopsis of the action for each scene.

■ **breakeven** That elusive and much-controverted point at which the film has earned back all its costs and net profits thereby allowing payment to those individuals not fortunate enough to have gross profit participation. The most-significant breakeven point is figured by the distributor when the entire cost of the negative, the various gross profit participations, and the distributing and advertising costs have been paid. Because of "creative accounting," whereby all kinds of costs, including some having nothing to do with the particular film, are included, only a small percentage of films reach breakeven. "Artificial breakeven" is sometimes contractually used on the basis of gross receipts reaching three times the total cost of the negative; "cash breakeven" when the distributor has achieved negative, interest, and distribution costs and may now satisfy "gross participation" deals without losing money; "rolling breakeven" when the film has achieved "actual breakeven" on a continuing basis and profits continue to equal costs.

■ **breakout** An increase in the number of theaters screening a film after it has had a limited distribution. The increase in distribution generally occurs when a film's opening does unexpectedly well. *Il Postino* (*The Postman*; 1994; dir. Michael Radford), an Italian-French production that opened quietly and went on to earn $20 million in this country ($75 million internationally), is a recent example of such a film. *See* **distribution** *and* **platforming.**

■ **breathing** The movement of the image on the screen in and out of focus generally caused by an unsteady gate in the projector that allows the film to buckle. *See* **flutter** *and* **weave.**

■ **Breen Code** *See* **Motion Picture Production Code.**

■ **bridge music** Background music in a film that acts as a transition between two actions or locations.

■ **bridge plate** *See* **riser** *(2).*

■ **bridging shot** (1) A shot that connects two scenes in a film separated by time or place: for example, falling calendar pages in the first case or an airplane taking off in the second. (2) A shot from a different angle or distance that connects two similar shots in the same scene.

■ **briefcase dolly** A small, portable dolly that folds to suitcase size for easy transportation.

■ **brightness** The intensity of a light perceived from a light source or perceived reflecting from a surface. Since individual perceptions of light tend to be subjective, true brightness is more accurately referred to as luminance, which is the measure of light by lumens. *See* **lumen.**

■ **brightness range, brightness ratio** The range of light intensity from minimum to maximum coming from various components in a scene and measured by a light meter. Sometimes referred to as subject luminance range or overall luminance range.

■ **Brighton school** A group of filmmakers on the south coast of England, working around the turn of the century. The most notable were G. A. Smith and J. A. Williamson. Certain technical achievements ascribed to the Brighton school, for example the close-up and parallel editing, predate their use by Edwin S. Porter in this country. The most famous Brighton work is Cecil Hepworth's *Rescued by Rover* (1905), which is significant because of its editing and camera work.

Brighton school Cecil Hepworth's six-minute *Rescued by Rover* (1905) is a milestone in continuity editing.

■ ■ ■

■ **brilliance** The perceived intensity of a color or colors in a scene or image.

■ **British Academy of Film and Television Arts** Established as the British Film Academy in 1947 and joined with the Guild of Television Producers and Directors in 1958, this organization sponsors the advancement of the art of the moving image in Great Britain and is especially known for its award-granting ceremonies that appear on national television.

■ **British Film Institute (BFI)** An organization in Great Britain founded in 1933 and dedicated to supporting the production, dissemination, and study of film. With headquarters and facilities in London, the BFI exhibits films at the National Film Theater, preserves them in the National Film Archive, and distributes them through the Film Distribution Library. The organization, which is largely supported by government funds, also has an important film library and still collection. The BFI publishes the significant film journal *Sight and Sound.*

■ **broad, broadside** A floodlight that gives off a wide beam and soft, flat, even illumination. The broad is used as a fill light for general illumination. When made with one lamp, it is called a single broad or emily; when made with two, it is called a double broad. *See* **fill light.**

■ **broad release** A wide distribution of a film throughout the entire country.

■ **brute** The trade name, now applied generically, for a large, high-intensity arc spotlight of 225 amperes. This is the largest standard studio lamp and is normally

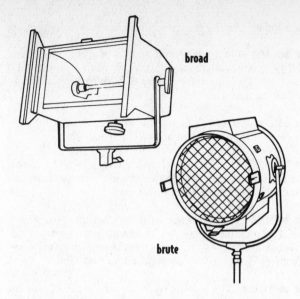

broad

brute

used for color films, especially for creating interior sunlight or lighting a sizable area. *See* **carbon arc lamps** *and* **lighting.**

■ **B scene, B side** The scene in the process of being edited to another—that on the right side in reference to the A scene to which it is being added and which is on the A or left side.

■ **B-type** *See* **A- and B-wind.**

■ **buckle switch, buckle trip** A switch in some cameras and projectors that shuts off the machine when film becomes loose or unwound.

■ **buckling** The bending, bulging, or twisting of film that is caused by stretching, shrinking, or extreme heat. Buckling is often the result of the edges of the film being shorter than the middle.

■ **buddy film** A film that features the friendship of two males as the major relationship. A number of these films were popular during the late 1960s and the 1970s, especially *Butch Cassidy and the Sundance Kid* (1969) and *The Sting* (1973), both directed by George Roy Hill and both starring Paul Newman and Robert Redford. Such films extol the virtues of male comradeship and relegate male-female relationships to a subsidiary position. Male relationships have always been a significant element in our popular culture, from the Leatherstocking Tales of James Fenimore Cooper to television beer commercials.

■ **budget** (1) The total amount of money to be spent on a film, calculated in advance by bringing together the estimates of the various units or departments. Expenses are routinely checked every day during shooting to make sure that production costs stay within the allotted money, though films frequently exceed this budget. *See* **estimate.** (2) The total amount of money spent on a film.

■ **Buena Vista Distribution Company, Inc.** Founded in 1954 by Walt Disney to distribute his own films, the organization has had a steady and growing career. The company now distributes the various films to come out of the Disney corporation. *See* **Walt Disney Company.**

■ **bug eye** *See* **fisheye lens.**

■ **build** (1) Placing the various sound effects into a single track so that sound is properly synthesized and aligned with picture. *See* **track building.** (2) Editing together various shots to build a scene or sequence. (3) Increasing action and developing plot so that dramatic intensity seems to increase for the audience.

■ **building the tracks** Editing sound. *See* **mix** *and* **sound.**

■ **buildup, build-up** (1) The use of preparatory shots and an increase in tempo to lead up dramatically to an important scene. (2) *See* **slug.** (3) Attaching the various reels of film into a single long reel for projection from a platter system with the help of the make-up table. *See* **platter system.**

■ **built-in light meter** An exposure or light meter that is part of a camera. Most 8mm cameras have built-in light meters. Such meters sometimes also control the diaphragm for automatic exposure. *See* **exposure meter.**

■ **bulk eraser** A degausser or demagnetizer; a machine that erases sound from a large amount of magnetic tape or film. *See* **degauss.**

■ **bulk-reducible composite elements** The smaller, normally background elements in a composite image that can be shot and added with less resolution.

■ **bullet hit, bullet squib** Plastic-cased detonators hidden beneath the surface of objects or clothes and electrically fired to simulate the impact of a bullet.

■ **bullet plates** Metal plates worn beneath clothes to protect performers who are to undergo one or more bullet hits.

■ **bulletproof matte** A matte for a composite shot so opaque that no light can pass through it. *See* **matte.**

■ **bump** The discordant effect when the background to the sound in two consecutive pieces of the sound track do not match. This might be the result of changing the position of the microphone for two sequential camera setups. The sound track must be separated at this point and each piece individually corrected by the sound mixer. *See* **dialogue splitting** *and* **mix.**

■ **bumper footage** A certain number of exposed frames before and after each scene of animation, allowing flexibility and safety in editing.

■ **bumper period** The time between bookings of a film studio that is allowed for the last production company to remove its sets and equipment.

■ **bump in, bump out** To cause an object or person suddenly to appear or disappear in a single frame.

■ **bump mapping** *See* **texture mapping.**

■ **burn in** (1) To change suddenly from an image to a white screen. (2) To overexpose a white area being photographed so that it appears a dense black on the negative. (3) To superimpose lettering or any picture element (such as rain) over previously exposed film. (4) To combine lettering or any graphic material with a separately shot scene in an optical printer. (5) To superimpose a time code over images normally for video or digital editing.

■ **burn-in matte** A matte on which the area of the subject is clear. When bipacked with a positive of the subject, the matte prevents the surrounding area from being photographed on the fresh negative while the subject is photographed. A hold-out matte, with the subject area opaque, is bipacked with a positive of the background and blocks out on the negative the area of the subject while the background is photographed. The burn-in matte is also called a foreground, female, cover, action, or printing matte or a matte master. *See* **matte** (2) *and* **traveling-matte process.**

■ **burn out** (1) To change from a white screen to an image. (2) In a special-effects matting process, to blacken, on an unprocessed interpositive of the live action, the area where a painting will go by means of a high-contrast matte and white light. When a dupe negative of the live action is made from the processed interpositive, the area for the painting remains unexposed and ready for the scenery to be matted into it. *See* **matte** (2) *and* **traveling-matte process.**

■ **burnt up** An overexposed film.

■ **business** (1) The general actions of a character that fill in a scene, add realism, or lead up to a specific action. (2) The financial aspects of both making and distributing a film.

■ **business manager** The person who takes care of the finances and taxes for an actor or actress.

■ **busy** (1) A scene filled with characters and action, with more happening than a viewer can perceive at once. (2) A setting filled with detail.

■ **butterfly** A large scrim of five or six feet, stretched on a frame and supported by one or more stands, that decreases, diffuses, or blocks light falling on an area beneath it. A larger version is called an overhead.

■ **butt splice** The joining by means of a piece of tape of two strips of film that do not overlap. *See* **splice.**

■ **butt-weld splice** The joining of two pieces of film by means of heat and pressure without any overlap. *See* **splice.**

■ **buzz** A general interest in a film during its production or immediately before its release that produces much talk and gossip. Such anticipation of a film among the public generally indicates a good prognosis for the initial box office. Publicity departments or agencies will attempt to create such interest, especially for costly films.

■ **buzz track** (1) A sound track without speech or sound, but with a low background noise that avoids an unnatural silence. (2) A test film used in a projector to adjust the position of the slit through which light from the exciter bulb passes on the way to the sound track.

■ **BW** *See* **black-and-white film.**

■ **B-wind** *See* **A- and B-wind.**

■ **byte** A series of 8 binary digits or "bits" necessary to encode and keep in memory a single letter, number, or visual element in a computer. *See* **bit** *and* **baud.**

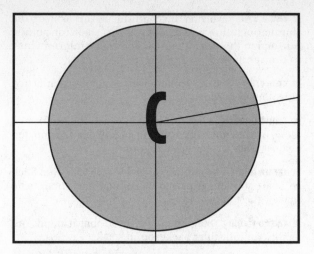

cable to cyclorama strip, cyc strip, cyclorama light

■ **cable** (1) A heavy insulated wire or a combination of separately insulated wires. (2) A heavy rope for rigging in a set.

■ **cable puller, cable handler, cable person, third man, third person** The individual who unloads and loads, sets up, and handles the cables and attachments used for sound recording during film production. This person moves the cables during a moving shot and also has the responsibility of locating and eliminating unwanted noises on the set.

■ **cable release** *See* **shutter release cable.**

■ **cable sync** A method of recording the image on film and the sound on magnetic tape in synchronization by means of a connecting cable. Crystal sync, however, which employs crystals of the same frequency in both machines, is the preferred method of synchronization today. *See* **synchronization.**

■ **cable television, cable television movie channels** Transmission of audio and visual signals for television via cable has opened up a major ancillary market for the exhibition of motion pictures previously released in theaters; films made for theatrical distribution but, for one reason or another, unable to be shown in that manner; or works made directly for television. The limitations of such exhibition, especially for films made directly for the theater, are obvious—the smaller image and, most often, reduced aspect ratio as well as colors, gray scale, and sound dependent on transmission and home equipment instead of the original film. But television viewing of motion pictures, both on cable and through the VCR, has long been a reality and also a considera-

tion in the filming of each work. With the development of HDTV, cable television will have to adopt the new digital technology and, as a result, both the quality and aspect ratio of the picture will approximate something that we see in the theater. Certainly it must be admitted that the new digital technology along with the expansion of the cable market is beginning to offer an additional opportunity for filmmakers that is likely to increase the number of motion pictures made each year. The future at this point seems unlimited in terms of numbers, especially with the development of digital and compression technologies that will allow several broadcasts to be programmed through a single channel and hundreds of channels to be available to the consumer—the goal is actually for 500 such channels. But quantity does not necessarily make quality—the mass-market appeal of television distribution seems already to be creating a blandness in films made primarily with that medium in mind.

The normal process is now for a film to move from the theater to videocassette in about six months, to cable in about a year, and to the major networks in about two years. Motion pictures are screened through cable television on stations, such as AMC (American Movie Classics), that are part of the basic service; on premium channels, such as HBO (Home Box Office) and the Movie Channel, for which one pays an additional sum each month; and on an individual basis through pay-per-view systems. HBO was established in 1972 by a small cable company belonging to Time Inc. and began beaming nationwide via satellite in 1975. In 1976, Viacom created Showtime, which began beaming via satellite in 1979, the same year that Warner Cable and American Express formed the Movie Channel. In 1980, Time Inc. formed Cinemax as a sister movie channel to HBO to appeal to a younger audience; and Showtime and the Movie Channel were merged under the control of Viacom, Warners, and American Express in 1984. By the close of the 1980s, the first two channels were pulling in about 60 percent of the premium movie channel business and the second two about 30 percent. Starting in 1985, the movie channels began to sign contracts with individual studios for exclusive rights to movies; and during the same period, HBO began its practice of "prebuying"—investing in the production of specific films for exclusive rights, and producing its own films through Silver Screen Partners, which it had created with E. F. Hutton. By 1995, 62,580,000 homes had basic cable television and 50,300,000 of them were paying for subscription services.

A nonpremier channel, TNT, began in 1988 to broadcast the MGM, RKO, and pre-1950s Warner Brothers library of films that Ted Turner had purchased from Kirk Kerkorian. In complete control of many film classics, Turner immediately ordered that one hundred such works be colorized. But the bad was mixed with the good in that a considerable number of Hollywood films were suddenly made available to television audiences (most of them in their original state).

TNT has in recent years become a more diversified station, with the new "premium channel," Turner Classic Movies, taking over the responsibility of screening a large number of these classics. Turner Broadcasting was purchased by Time Warner in 1996. *See* **DSS, HDTV,** *and* **television.**

■ *Cahiers du cinéma* An important French film journal that was founded in 1951 by André Bazin, Jacques Doniol-Valcroze, and Lo Duca, and that developed the *auteur* theory of criticism in the mid-1950s through the writings of such young critics as Truffaut, Godard, Rohmer, Chabrol, and Rivette before they began their filmmaking careers. The journal's *auteur* criticism gave serious attention to directors who had formerly been designated as merely "popular," and brought critical acclaim to Hitchcock as well as a number of other Hollywood directors. In the 1960s, *Cahiers* helped bring structuralism to film criticism by publishing Christian Metz and employing this methodology to develop its own Marxist and political approach to film. *See* **auteur** *and* **structuralism.**

■ **calculator, cine calculator, computer calculator** A calculator, especially made for the filmmaker, which allows computation for depth of field, f-stop and t-stop numbers, lens angle and picture area, shutter angle, and other important information for shooting. The Cinematographer's Computer Program is housed in a pocket-size computer calculator and allows for all kinds of calculations and information concerning, for example, color, dimensions, diopters, film, exposure, focus, lens, lighting, optics, speeds, and even the calculation of salaries. Time code calculators convert various time and time-code formats for both film and video.

■ **calendar house** A motion-picture theater that plays previously released films, each for several days. Patrons are supplied with a calendar specifying the playing dates for each film. *See* **revival house.**

■ *caligarisme* A term coined by the French from the German film, *The Cabinet of Dr. Caligari* (1919; dir. Robert Wiene) to describe (1) the chaotic and confused world after the Great War; and (2) film setting, style, and technique that resembles the expressionism of *Caligari*. *See* **expressionism.**

■ **call, call sheet, shooting call** The shooting schedule for cast and crew posted or distributed the previous day, and including times for makeup and costuming as well as technical requirements. This schedule is the responsibility of the assistant director and is approved by both the director and production manager.

■ **Callier effect** The scattering of light as it passes through optical systems.

■ **cam** The revolving mechanism in the arm of the shuttle operation in a camera or projector for putting into action the claw; it moves each frame intermittently to the aperture.

■ **camcorder** A video camera with a built-in or attached videotape recorder.

■ **cameo lighting** High-key light in which the performer, along with some surrounding objects, is illuminated against a black or gray background.

■ **cameo role** A brief but noticeable role in a film. Such roles are sometimes played by popular performers who make "guest appearances."

■ **cameo staging** Staging an action so that it stands out against an indistinct background.

■ **camera** The basic tool of all cinematography for photographing a series of progressive images on a strip of film, normally at the rate of 24 frames per second for sound motion pictures (the standard was 16 frames in silent film days though films were often shot and projected at greater speeds). When the images are made into a positive print and projected one after another onto a screen at the same speed, they create the illusion of motion. Cameras can also photograph at slower speeds to create accelerated motion and faster speeds for slow motion when the images are projected at the standard rate.

Unexposed film is stored in a magazine and drawn into the body of the camera by the engagement of teeth on a continuously rotating sprocket wheel into perforations on the sides or a single side of the film. Each frame is individually pulled down by claws that engage perforation holes. The frame is held stationary behind the shutter, often by one or two pilot pins. The shutter opens and allows the lens to form an image from light rays coming from the subject on the film (the opening in the camera is called the aperture). The shutter then closes and another frame is pulled into place by the claws, while the exposed frames are drawn into the magazine by a take-up reel. The film is moved in and out of the camera body in continuous motion by the sprocket wheels but because each frame is stopped for exposure, the operation behind the aperture is called intermittent movement. To avoid tearing film because of variations in tension as it is moved, stops, and moves again, flexible loops are formed both above and below the aperture, which is between the sprocket wheels. The entire camera is normally run by an electric motor, though some portable cameras still use a spring-wound motor.

A viewfinder is attached to the camera through which the operator can see the image being recorded on the film. Remote control systems and video monitors now allow cameras to shoot in the most difficult areas and make the most difficult moves for commercial films. The old 35mm Mitchell BNC, once the work-horse for studio shooting, is being replaced by lighter, more versatile and advanced cameras such as the Panavision Platinum Panaflex (though much of their mechanism for movement is based on that of the Mitchell); small, portable cameras, such as the classic Arriflex 35 2C, are available for fieldwork; and light-weight, handheld cameras, such as the 16mm Bolex, for action and documentary shooting. Large-format cameras, such as the Panavision System 65mm, were at one time used to create wide-screen images of high pic-ture quality, but now, because of the expense of such filming, are largely used for special-effects cinematog-raphy. Super 8mm cameras, once the tool for amateur filmmakers, have largely been replaced by camcorders and other video cameras, but a number are still in use. *See* **film** *(1) and* **viewfinder.**

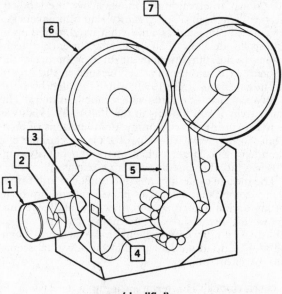

camera (simplified):
1. lens 2. diaphragm 3. variable shutter
4. aperture plate 5. film 6. feed reel
7. take-up reel

■ **camera angle, angle** The placement of the camera in relation to the subject of the image. The normal height of the camera approximates eye level, from five to six feet off the ground, and creates no discernible angle to the subject. When the camera is placed below eye level, looking up at the subject, a low-angle shot is achieved (an extreme low angle if it is far below); when it is placed above the subject, the result is a high-angle shot (an extreme high angle if it is far above). An oblique angle results when the camera tilts to the left or right, and a dutch angle when the camera tilts horizontally and vertically. Any placement of the camera away from normal eye level will affect the viewer's response to the

image on the screen. High-angle shots tend to dimin-ish a subject, making a character seem weak and vul-nerable, while low-angle shots tend to elevate and heighten the subject, making it seem strong and im-posing. Oblique angles suggest disorientation, confu-sion, impending and threatening movement or action; and both oblique and dutch-angle shots can be em-ployed subjectively to convey extreme states of mind. However, the angle of the camera is only one of many elements in a scene and can create different effects in different contexts: for example, when the high-angle shots of the two scientists in the creation scene in James Whale's *The Bride of Frankenstein* (1935) are used in con-junction with medium close-ups, bottom lighting, and rapid cuts, the images of the faces become sinister and imposing. The entire creation scene itself uses a variety of high, low, oblique, and dutch angles to help create a fantastic, disorienting, and frightening world. *See* **angle-plus-angle, reverse angle,** *and* **subjective camera angle.**

■ **camera blocking** *See* **blocking** *(3).*

■ **camera body** The major part of the camera through which the film passes and in which it is exposed to light through the aperture for the recording of a photo-graphic image. Attachable parts such as the lens and magazine are not considered part of the camera body.

■ **camera boom** The mobile but strong camera mount that is attached to a vehicle and is capable of making all types of moves in space, allowing the camera operator to shoot from a variety of distances, heights, and angles and with a variety of motions. *See* **crane** *and* **fishpole.**

■ **camera car, camera truck** A car or truck specially de-signed and fitted to carry one or more cameras and sev-eral operators for photographing fast-moving action as well as the moving background for such rear-projection shots as those taken inside a supposedly moving auto-mobile. These vehicles have a generator to run the cameras and allow shooting from a number of posi-tions.

■ **camera crew** The group of people who work under the director of photography and are responsible for photographing the film. This group generally includes the camera operator, who manages the camera during the shooting; the first assistant camera operator (called a focus puller in Great Britain), who adjusts the focus while the camera or actors move and also changes the magazines; the second assistant camera operator (also called a slateman and, in Britain, a clapper loader), who claps the board while announcing the scene and take numbers at the beginning of a shot and also loads the magazines, keeps notes on the shooting, and marks the slate; and one or more grips, whose job is to move the dolly about and perform other heavy duties in-volved in the shooting.

■ **camera department** (1) The group in the studio responsible for maintenance of cameras and other photographic equipment. This designation sometimes also includes the camera crew. (2) The camera crew.

■ **camera leading** A shot that shows the actor moving forward while the camera moves back, thus keeping an equal distance between the two.

■ **camera left** The left side of the camera from the position of the operator and hence the left side of the screen facing the audience.

■ **cameraless animation** Images drawn or painted directly on the individual frames of film so that when successively projected onto a screen, they create the illusion of movement. *See* **noncamera film.**

■ **camera log** *See* **camera report.**

■ **camera lucida** A large boxlike device with a lens that projects a scene onto a paper and allows an artist to outline the image; supposedly invented by Leone Battista Alberti in 1450.

■ **cameraman** *See* **director of photography.**

■ **camera motor** Generally an electric synchronic motor for running the camera. Wild motors are not employed for synchronic shooting of picture and sound. Synchronous motors can be interlocked with those used in sound recording so that there is simultaneous recording of both picture and sound. Such electric motors receive their power from D.C. power supplies or batteries. Spring-drive motors are still used for some portable cameras such as the Bolex H-16 Rex 5 and H-16 SBM, but these allow only thirty seconds of shooting at normal speed on one wind. *See* **spring-drive motor, synchronous motor,** *and* **wild motor.**

■ **camera mount, camera support** Any of the devices that hold a camera in place and allow for panning and tilting; these may include tripods, hi-hats, booms, hydraulic pillars, and body braces.

■ **camera movement** Any motion of the camera that makes the image seem to move, shift, or change perspective. The mobility of the camera allows the audience to stay with a character while he or she walks, follow the motion of some vehicle or object, or see the scene from the character's point of view as he or she moves. Camera movement can also lead the audience's attention to a different part of the scene or simply give the audience another perspective of the same action. Camera supports can remain in the same place, while the camera itself pans on a horizontal plane or tilts up and down by means of a moveable head. A tracking, traveling, or trucking shot that follows a character's action can be achieved by moving the camera and its support along tracks, on a mobile dolly, or on a moving vehicle. Moving vehicles also allow a camera to follow rapid action such as chases by foot or car. Shots from helicopters are especially versatile for following such action. A crane shot allows the camera great movement in both horizontal and vertical directions. Since the advent of lightweight, portable cameras it has become possible to follow action almost anywhere and achieve some striking effects by means of handheld shots. The Steadicam is a developed body brace that allows the portable camera to remain stable during a variety of mobile shots.

In the silent era, Griffith moved his camera during shots, but to a limited extent. The German expressionist filmmakers, however, used a mobile camera with dramatic effect—Murnau's *Last Laugh* (*Der Letzte Mann;* 1924) offers striking examples of this technique, especially the famous opening shot where the camera rides down an elevator and moves across the lobby to the revolving doors. The great Russian filmmakers Pudovkin and Eisenstein, on the other hand, relied upon cutting to develop their celebrated montage techniques. In the sound period, the direct influence of the German expressionist films can be seen in the American horror films of the 1930s, which blended both the Hollywood style of cutting with a mobile camera. The major style of studio films in the 1940s and 1950s was invisible cutting for continuity. Combinations of techniques were often used—Hitchcock is an example of a filmmaker who largely relied on cutting but also employed a mobile camera for striking effects.

The mobile camera moves into the scene and brings depth to the flat image, gives movement and drama to setting and architecture, and draws the audience into the world on the screen. The mobile camera also establishes a fluidity of movement on the screen that contributes to the dominant rhythm of individual scenes and the entire film.

■ **camera obscura** This term, meaning "a dark room" in Latin, was applied to a device described by Leonardo da Vinci during the Renaissance, though probably known in earlier times. A small hole at one end of a darkened room acts as a lens and focuses light rays to form an inverted image on the opposite wall. A smaller version, the size of a box, was used by artists for outlining objects.

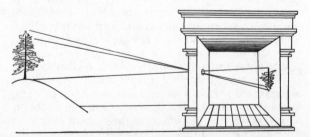

camera obscura (based on a sixteenth-century drawing)

■ **camera operator, operator, operating cameraman** The person who works under the director of photography and is directly responsible for managing the camera during shooting. He or she is responsible for viewing the scene through the viewfinder and making certain that the image is correct, for positioning the camera, and for making basic movements. The term also applies to a person using a video camera in a professional recording situation. *See* **videographer.**

■ **camera original** Film exposed in a camera as distinct from that exposed, for example, in an optical printer.

■ **camera prompting system** A device that can be run separately or attached to a camera for prompting lines. The system works by means of plastic rolls on which instructions are written or printed and a mirror placed at a 45-degree angle to the camera lens from which the performers can read the lines. The device can be operated by remote control.

■ **camera rehearsal** A rehearsal of a shot or scene with the cameras moving but without actually filming and with performers or stand-ins.

■ **camera report, camera sheet, camera log** Information concerning shooting that is sent with the film to the lab. The report informs the lab which takes should be developed and furnishes details about the film's emulsion and the type of shooting (e.g., day or night, exterior or interior). Special instructions are also given for developing, and the report includes a careful breakdown of the footage shot.

■ **camera right** The right side of the camera from the position of the operator and hence the right side of the screen facing the audience.

■ **camera speed** The rate per second of frames exposed in the camera. The rate of silent films was supposed to be 16 frames per second, though films were often shot and certainly projected at greater speeds (today projectors use 18 frames per second for silent film). Later it was necessary to speed up the camera to 24 frames per second so that the optical sound track could produce a clear sound. A variety of effects may be achieved by changing the camera speed: for example, slow-motion photography is achieved by shooting at faster speeds and projecting at the normal rate, and fast-motion by shooting at slower speeds and projecting normally.

■ **camera speed checker** *See* **tachometer.**

■ **caméra stylo** This term, meaning "camera pen" in French, was used by Alexander Astruc in his 1948 essay on *"la caméra-stylo"* in *L'Ecran français.* Astruc argues for a kind of film in which the director uses the camera personally and creatively, just as the writer does his pen. This essay anticipates the *auteur* theory developed by Truffaut and others in the mid-1950s. *See* **auteur.**

■ **camera tape** Sturdy one-inch cloth tape used for labeling film cans, magazines, and various equipment; closing cans of exposed and unexposed film seal-tight; placing focus marks on the ground; marking clapboards; and for various other tasks. Such tape is normally white or black.

■ **camera test** (1) a screen test for an actor or actress. (2) A test of the camera's various operations, which may include shooting small amounts of film.

■ **camera tracks** Tracks or metal or plywood sheets placed beneath a camera dolly to insure smoothness and straightness of movement.

■ **camera trap** A place hidden in a set or on location where a camera is positioned for shooting and is invisible to another camera when it is shooting.

■ **camera wedge** A device placed upon the tripod to support the camera and allow for greater angles of tilt than the head of the tripod normally allows. Also called a tilt plate.

■ **camp** Works of art that display an artifice and exaggeration but are compelling and pleasing. Such works may fail to meet standards of higher art, but create a style of their own that is both discernible and unique. Susan Sontag, in her essay "Camp" that appeared in her book *Against Interpretation,* claims that camp is also depolitical, androgynous, artificial, superficial, duplicitous, naïve; innocent, extravagant, unserious. According to her, "Camp asserts . . . a good taste of bad taste" and "finds success in certain passionate failures." Beginning in the eighteenth century with such cultural creations as the Gothic novel and artificial ruins, camp continued as a discernible part of popular culture and in our own century can be found readily in the cinema, especially in the musical numbers of Busby Berkeley, von Sternberg's American films that star Marlene Dietrich, and the Universal horror films of the 1930s. The word "kitsch" (from the German *kitsch,* which means "trash") is used to describe a work with no artistic value.

■ **cam-rails, camrails** Narrow rails placed on tripods to allow camera movement above ground—e.g., to shoot above water or rough terrains. The camera is placed in a trolley carriage and can be remotely operated. *See* **under-slung head.**

■ **can** A metal or plastic circular container for storing film. "In the can" means that the film is completed, in the container, and ready for release.

■ **candela** The measurement of light intensity as computed by the light given off by one-sixteenth per square centimeter of a black body at 2,042 degrees Kelvin, which is the melting temperature of platinum.

■ **candles per square foot** The measurement of light reflected from a surface by a reflected light meter.

■ **canned drama** A term sometimes applied to early silent films, since a number of such works were little more than abbreviated stage dramas put on film.

■ **canned music** Music not written and recorded for a specific film, but prerecorded and filed in a library according to type. Such recordings are generally used in a film as background music.

■ **canned theater** A term sometimes applied to early sound films. Because cameras had to be placed in soundproof booths during production, thus losing their mobility, and because the placement of microphones limited the movement of characters, early sound films seemed little more than photographed theater.

■ **canting** Angling a camera for a shot. The shot itself is called a canting or dutch-angle shot. *See* **dutch angle.**

■ **caper film, heist film** *See* **big caper.**

■ **capping shutter** An additional shutter, generally a metal blade, employed between the lens and regular shutter in an animation camera to block frames from being exposed during an animation cycle. In such a cycle, cels that are repeated at intervals are photographed at a single shooting, with the intervening cels photographed at later passes.

■ **cap sheet** *See* **dope sheet** *(4).*

■ **capstan** The shaft in a magnetic tape recorder against which the tape is pressed by a roller to give it a steady movement as it passes the various heads.

■ **capsule gun** An air gun that shoots a projectile or series of projectiles to shatter objects or glass and shoots capsules which themselves shatter on impact, spraying their content over a specific area. Capsules can spray powder to suggest dust released when a bullet hits rock or spray a dye to suggest the splattering of blood.

■ **caption** (1) A series of words on the screen that precedes a scene and announces some theme, subject, or change in time or place. (2) The series of words superimposed over the bottom of the frames to translate foreign dialogue or to communicate dialogue or commentary to the hard-of-hearing. *See* **closed captioned** *and* **open captioned.**

■ **capture board** *See* **frame grabber.**

■ **carbon arc lamps** A high-intensity, low-voltage light source employed in the production of motion pictures. An electric current maintained between carbon rods clearly illuminates objects and faithfully brings out colors. Although noisy and of relatively short duration, these lamps were once a mainstay of film production and are still useful when a great deal of light is needed from a single source. Carbon arc lamps are often used as spotlights and are manufactured in the 65-, 110-, 150-, and 225-amp categories. *See* **lighting.**

■ **card** A type of credit achieved through optical printing. The titles remain stationary but fade in and fade out.

■ **cardioid microphone** A unidirectional microphone that picks up noises from all sides, but is more responsive to sound from the front than from the rear and so highlights foreground noise from background. For this reason it is especially effective for dialogue. *See* **microphone.**

■ **carpenters** The personnel who do all the construction with wood for a film production. This group builds sets, furniture, props, and camera tracks.

■ **carpenter shop, carpenter workshop** The unit of a film production responsible for all construction with wood. This group is under the supervision of the master carpenter.

■ **car rigs** Attachments to a car or truck that support cameras and lighting: for example, a beam placed across or alongside the vehicle, a scaffold system, or a limpet mount with suction cups.

■ **carry day** A day for which payment is made but on which the performers or production people need not work.

■ **cartoon, cartoon short** A short animated film, generally made by the stop-motion photography of painted figures, puppets, or pixilated human forms. Each frame shows a minute progressive change in the subject. When the frames are successively projected onto a screen, an illusion of movement is created. Cartoons, which are almost as old as the film industry itself, often show the comic antics of humanlike animals or grotesque people. The cartoon world is a never-never land where the laws of physics are suspended and where all kinds of violent actions can take place without really hurting anyone. As a result, cartoons minimize for the viewer ever-present fears of violence and mortality by allowing a humorous and safe retreat into a semireal world of ludicrous behavior and action. Because cartoons simplify while imitating aspects of life, they have also been enjoyable devices for mild satire of human behavior. *See* **animation.**

■ **cartridge** A container or magazine into which film or tape is loaded before it is attached to the camera. The cartridge may contain both feed and take-up reels or a single reel with the film coming off the interior and returning on the exterior or vice versa. Films in these containers need not be threaded into the camera. Their reel or reels operate from the camera's drive mechanism. Such cartridges have generally been employed in regular 8mm and Super 8mm cameras.

■ **cascading** Printing several successive frames in a single frame to achieve a strobe effect.

■ **cassette** A small cartridge, normally with feed and take-up reels, that contains magnetic tape for audio and video recording or playing. Super 8mm film uses such a cassette for projection.

■ **cast** (1) The actors and actresses in a film. (2) The list of characters and their performers that is shown before or after the film. (3) To select performers for a film. This job is generally done by a casting director for all but the major performers, who are chosen for their roles independently.

■ **casting couch** The piece of furniture, generally in the producer's office, where many an actress is rumored to have begun her career in movies by granting her sexual favors. The casting couch was part of both the myth and the reality of Hollywood during its golden years.

■ **casting director** The individual who chooses and negotiates contracts for the actors and actresses playing the various roles in a film other than the leading performers who generally are already contracted.

■ **catchlight** (1) A small gleam of light coming from the performer's eyes, the source of which is one or more lamps. Also called a glint or kick. Note Bela Lugosi's eyes in Tod Browning's *Dracula* (1931), especially when he stands in the bedroom of his first female victim. (2) The lamp or lamps placed near the camera to achieve such an effect. Also called an eye light.

■ **cathode-ray tube (CRT)** A vacuum tube that generates a focused beam of electrons on a screen at its end (e.g., a television picture tube or video display tube for computer graphics).

■ **Catholic Communication Campaign** An agency of the United States Catholic Conference, this group offers a toll-free telephone number through which ratings of films are offered concerning both quality and moral content. The ratings run from A-1 for general audiences to 0 for films that are morally objectionable. *See* **Movie Rating System.**

■ **Catholic Legion of Decency** *See* **Legion of Decency** *and* **Motion Picture Production Code.**

■ **catwalk** The narrow, railed walk suspended above the stage in the studio for lighting, sound equipment, and rigging sets.

■ **CAV laser disc** The initials are from "constant angular velocity" and represent a laser disc containing a motion picture that can be stopped for a freeze frame or moved image by image—normal laser discs do not have this capacity. The CAV disc holds 30 minutes of picture and audio on each side. *See* **CLV laser disc** *and* **laser disc.**

■ **CCD** *See* **charge-coupled device.**

■ **C-clamp** A C-shaped clamp that quickly and firmly screws light fixtures to grids and pipes above the set. Such clamps come in a variety of sizes. *See* **hanger.**

■ **CD-ROM** The initials are from "compact disc read only memory" and represent a disc used for interactive computer programs because of its capacity to store a great deal of information. With video compression, the disc can store up to sixty-five minutes of images. These discs are employed for interactive entertainment that combines both digital images and spectator involvement, both the feature film and game playing. Such discs are also employed for educational programs— e.g., an interactive study of a film that uses clips from the motion picture, explanatory text, actual documents, and a menu of options. *See* **DVD.**

■ **CDS meter** An exposure or light meter that employs a cadmium sulfide photoelectric cell. Because of their extreme sensitivity, such cells are normally used in light meters employed in the film industry. *See* **exposure meter.**

■ **cel, cell** A transparent sheet on which is traced and then painted part of a scene for cel animation. When cels are superimposed upon each other, a sense of depth in the image is created; at the same time, such a process makes unnecessary the repeated drawings of stationary parts of a scene or a character. The term "cel" comes from celluloid (cellulose nitrate), the original material employed for such drawings, though cellulose acetate is now common. Along each edge of the cel are several holes through which pegs are placed to hold the various sheets together in perfect registration. Cels also are employed for titles and captions. *See* **animation** *and* **computer animation.**

■ **cel animation** The animation process that employs a number of cels, normally made of cellulose acetate, on which are drawn various parts of a scene both to create a sense of depth and to avoid drawing again and again the stationary parts of a scene or character. The general and stationary background of the scene is drawn in detail on strong white paper that remains behind the cels for the entire sequence. Parts of the background are also drawn on cels to create depth and also to allow

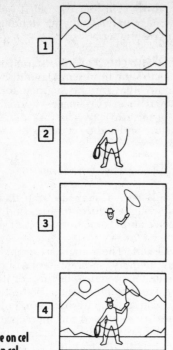

cel animation:
1. background drawing
2. stationary part of figure on cel
3. moving part of figure on cel
4. composite picture

characters to pass behind them. Individual figures may be drawn on separate cels so that their movements are operated independently, and the moving sections of their bodies may also be drawn on separate cels for flexibility and economy. Sometimes, however, it is just as efficient to draw the moving parts of different characters or objects on the same cel. *See* **animation, computer animation, full animation,** *and* **limited animation.**

■ **cel flash** A bright flash that registers on a film image from the reflection of light off the uneven surface of a cel or group of cels in cel animation or titling.

■ **cel level** The level at which a particular cel is placed and photographed on an animation table. For figures, bottom cels are composed of parts, such as the torso, that remain stationary throughout a series of frames; middle-level cels contain parts, such as hands and feet, that have some movement and are changed intermittently; and top-level cels depict features, such as eyes and mouth, that have frequent movement and need to be changed often. See **cel animation.**

■ **cell side** The base side of film as opposed to the emulsion side.

■ **celluloid** (1) The original transparent material, cellulose nitrate, used as a base for film and on which light sensitive emulsion was coated. Since cellulose nitrate proved to be highly flammable and to deteriorate

rapidly, it was replaced by cellulose acetate. (2) Any of the cellulose derivatives, including nitrate and acetate, used as a film base. (3) A colloquial term for the movies in general.

■ **cellulose acetate** *See* **acetate base.**

■ **cellulose nitrate** *See* **nitrate base.**

■ **celo, celo cuke, celo cukaloris** A cukaloris made of wire mesh with irregular patterns placed in front of a luminaire so that the light cast is diffuse with a subtle and mottled pattern. *See* **cookie.**

■ **cel sandwich** The layers of two or more cels in cel animation. *See* **cel animation.**

■ **cel-Xerox, xerography** In cartoon animation, the process of Xeroxing original drawings onto cels instead of inking them by hand. The process was introduced by Walt Disney Productions in the late 1950s.

■ **cement splice** The permanent attachment of two pieces of film by liquid cement. After the emulsion on the end of one piece has been scraped off and the cement applied, the end of the other piece of film is attached in place by the cement splicer. This method is most often used for cutting the original negative or repairing release prints. *See* **Mylar splice.**

■ **censor** The person or persons in any community or government who determine what parts of a film should not be seen or whether the film should be seen at all by the public.

■ **censorship** The act of deciding what parts of a film should not be seen or whether the film should be seen at all by the public. "Prior restraint" means forbidding a film to be released, though films are often forbidden to be played after their exhibition has begun. Censorship has been determined by various groups—by official government agencies, the judiciary, the sheriff or police, private religious or moral organizations advising the film industry or government, or by an agency of the film industry itself. The questions of what kinds of films or what subjects and actions in a film should be seen by the public and whether censorship is in the spirit of the First Amendment to the Constitution have been heatedly argued. Even today practice varies from community to community, while the Supreme Court has yet to come out with a clear decision. What is clear is that movies and community values have changed, that there is far more permissiveness than ever before in matters of sexuality and violence, and that religion and morality no longer seem to be subjects for censorship.

In 1915, in the case of Mutual vs. Ohio, the Supreme Court ruled that motion pictures were a business, and, as such, had no protection under the First Amendment. The effect of this ruling was that films were liable to censorship from all directions. In response to a public outcry against a series of scandals, the film industry founded the Motion Picture Producers and Distributors of America (MPPDA), later to be called the Motion Picture Association of America (MPAA), in order to protect itself from government intrusion and in order to save its image and box office. The organization, founded in 1922, was headed by Will H. Hays and became known as the Hays Office. The MPPDA at first fought outside censorship and sought to improve the industry's image, but in 1930 it introduced its first code for film content. In 1934, Joseph Breen joined the MPPDA to enforce the code, and censorship became a strong force in films for two decades. Breen himself had been pushed into office by the newly founded Catholic Legion of Decency, which had a strong impact on the MPPDA and film morality in general. It was not until May 26, 1952, that the Supreme Court, in the case of Burstyn vs. Wilson, announced that "sacrilege" is not a sufficient cause for banning a film. Reacting to the censorship of Roberto Rossellini's *L'Amore* (1948) by the New York State Board of Regents, the court also stated that films are "a significant medium for the communication of ideas." What the court had done, in effect, was to bring film under the protection of the First Amendment.

Since that time, the Supreme Court has removed every cause for censorship except that of obscenity and has also made it very difficult for state and local boards to censor a film. In the spirit of this movement, and in response to its own producers, the MPAA liberalized its code and finally, in 1968, gave up censoring film entirely. The organization instead instituted a rating system to advise the public about the content of films and to prevent minors from seeing certain motion pictures.

The definition of "obscenity" still has not been resolved, and the Supreme Court has gone back and forth on the issue. In 1973, in the case of Miller vs. California, the Court further confused the issue by introducing the vague factor of "contemporary community standards." But there can be no doubt that American films today are freer of censorship than ever before. Only sexuality seems to be a problem, and even here most people seem to be willing to leave others to their own predilection. *See* **Hays Office, Motion Picture Association of America, Motion Picture Production Code,** *and* **Movie Rating System.**

■ **center track** The placement of the sound track along the middle portion of magnetic film with a row of perforations along each edge. Edge track film with a single row of perforations along one edge and the sound band running along the other is the preferred film for magnetic recording in the United States.

■ **Central Casting Corporation** Established in December of 1925 by the Hollywood studios, this was the original casting organization for movie extras. The organization published a casting sheet for each feature and established a reputation for casting performers according to specific types—tough guys, cowboys, and executive types, for example. "Straight" or "right out of Central Casting" became an industry phrase to describe someone who seemed to fit one of these specific types. The studio would pay a percentage of the extra's salary for the service. In 1976, the studios ceased control over the organization and today it is run by IDC Service in Burbank, California. Other casting agencies have long been in existence, but Central Casting still seems part of the Hollywood mystique.

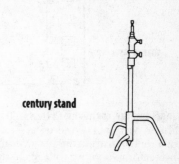

century stand

■ **century stand** A three-legged mobile stand that holds flags or other apparatus to control light or reduce its intensity. The stand also holds branches or other objects for shadow effects. Also referred to as a C stand or gobo stand.

■ **certificate of code rating** A certificate given to a producer or distributor of a film by the Classification and Rating Administration of the Motion Picture Association of America that designates what letter should be assigned to the film to advise the public about its content (e.g., PG or R). *See* **Movie Rating System.**

censorship *The Miracle* episode in *L'Amore* (1948; dir. Roberto Rossellini), with Anna Magnani.

■ ■ ■

■ **César Awards** Similar to the Academy Awards in the United States, these are awards given in France since 1976 by l'Académie des Arts et Techniques du Cinéma to outstanding French motion pictures and French film personnel. The awards are named after the person who designed the small statue given to the winners.

■ **CGI** Abbreviation for Computer Generated Imagery. *See* **computer animation.**

■ **changed-element clause** An agreement in a contract between a studio and producer that should the specific project go into turnaround and be picked up by another studio, any significant change in talent will require that the film once again be offered to the original studio. Such a clause protects a studio from giving up on a project that later acquires the involvement of a major star or director and hence becomes much more marketable. *See* **turnaround.**

■ **change-over, reel change** The immediate change from the reel on one projector to the following reel on a second projector without any loss of continuity in sound or image during a film showing. Small circles on the top right-hand corner of a series of four frames warn the projectionist to start the motor on the second projector so that it will be running at full speed; and a second series of similar circles at the end of the reel signals to the projectionist to change over to the second projector. The circles are called change-over cues or cue marks. *See* **platter system.**

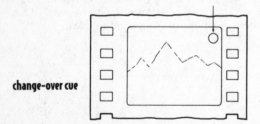

change-over cue

■ **change-over cue, cue marks** The small circles on the top right-hand corner of two series of frames coming at the end of a reel to instruct the projectionist to switch from one projector to another for the change-over from one reel to the next. The first series, also called the motor cue, indicates that the second projector should be started, and the second series indicates the actual change-over. *See* **platter system.**

■ **change pages, changes** Alterations in the script given to the performers in a film and the various personnel once production has begun. Each set of alterations is furnished on pages of a specific color to distinguish the various stages of the rewrite.

■ **changing bag** A lightproof bag with two linings, two zippers, and sleeves or elastic openings on each end through which hands may be extended to load film into, or unload it from, the magazine. The changing bag is useful on location when a darkroom is not available.

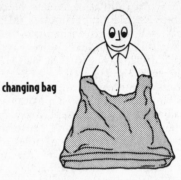

changing bag

■ **channel** In an audio system, a path for a signal that goes to a speaker. Derived channels originate from information stored within other channels; discrete channels carry only their own signal and no information for a derived channel.

■ **Channel 4** The fourth television network established in Great Britain in 1981 by an act of Parliament that continues to create programs of interest and quality beyond anything offered by Independent Television and even the two BBC channels. Channel 4 has played a significant role in motion picture production in recent years by funding such internationally successful films as *My Beautiful Laundrette* (1985; dir. Stephen Frears) and *The Crying Game* (1992; dir. Neil Jordan). Channel 4's films are originally released for theatrical distribution and later shown over the television station. Basically the major source of funding for quality films in Great Britain since its inception, Channel 4 won the Prix Rossellini at the 1987 Cannes Film festival for its contribution to British cinema. The company has recently announced that it will increase its production by funding some eighty films over the next four years with the help of co-financing.

■ **Chaplin** An international film journal published in Sweden by the Svenska Filminstitutet. This periodical keeps abreast of latest film releases, while also featuring interviews with notable figures, reviews, and essays on various film subjects.

■ **chapter play** Film jargon for a serial.

■ **character** Any one of the various fictional people that appear in a film, including heroes, heroines, villains, supporting roles, and minor and bit parts. Unlike novels, in which characters can be described internally as well as externally, film normally limits the portrayal of character to speech, appearance, and action; at the same time, film characters are seen in relation to the physical reality that surrounds them. However, much like point of view in the novel, the camera can concentrate on certain aspects of behavior, specific gestures and facial expressions; it can show a character from a variety of distances and angles; and, along with editing, it can orchestrate a series of perspectives that create a composite figure. Both the performer and the camera develop our awareness of the thoughts, feelings, and very personality of the character.

■ **character actor** A performer who specializes in secondary roles of a well-defined, often humorous nature. Such actors or actresses generally play these roles because of their own physical characteristics and individual voices. Elisha Cook, Jr., for example, played the role of small, strange, and intense crooks or deranged figures for more than forty years (e.g., in *The Maltese Falcon* [1941; dir. John Huston]), and Hattie McDaniel for some two decades played rotund, good-natured, and wise black servants, culminating with her Academy Award-winning performance in *Gone With the Wind* (1939; dir. Victor Fleming).

■ **character generator** The device on a video editing system used to create letters and numbers on a cathode-ray tube that can be recorded on the videotape both for titles and for creating time-code numbers. *See* **cathode-ray tube** *and* **time code.**

■ **characteristic curve, H and D curve, D log E curve** The curve plotted to indicate the change in density of an image as the exposure is increased. The initials in H and D curve represent the names of Hurter and Driffield because of their early work in sensitometry. *See* **gamma** *and* **sensitometry.**

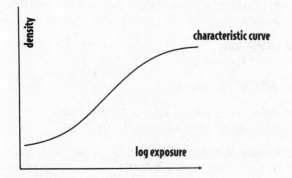

characteristic curve

density

log exposure

■ **characterization** (1) The interpretation of a character by an actor; the realization of a specific personality with particular characteristics and manners. The extent and depth of characterization differ according to the performer and film. Some productions have depended upon their leading characters maintaining an image and personality already known to the audience: it is doubtful, for example, if John Wayne changed very much from one performance to another during extensive portions of his career. But there have always been actors, such as Laurence Olivier, and actresses, such as

Joanne Woodward, who have brought novelty and imagination to a variety of roles. However, even in such instances the desire of the film industry to exploit the popularity of these leading men and ladies has resulted in an interplay between the familiar and unfamiliar from performers who entertain and engage by variety, complexity, and change in a recognizable mold. (2) The process of interpreting a character in a film.

■ **character type** A character with specific and distinct qualities who reappears frequently in films, though with different names and played by different actors: for example, the homicidal maniac; the reserved British butler; the kindhearted immigrant father with a heavy European accent; the young girl who aspires to be a ballet dancer and to devote her life to art. A good performer can, of course, breathe new life into an old form.

■ **charge-coupled device (CCD)** A solid-state image sensor that employs a silicon chip with vast rows of pixels to convert light waves into electric signals in a video camera and into a digital binary code in a scanner. *See* **digital** *and* **video camera.**

■ **chase film, chaser** A film that features the pursuit of someone or some group. From the earliest days of film, this action has been a popular staple because it exploits the very nature of the medium, which is to give images in action. Chases give the viewer actors in motion, changing backgrounds, and a great deal of suspense and anticipation. Chases have often been employed in comedies, Westerns, detective films, and war films. So popular has been the chase that entire films have been devoted to this action. In the early days of silent films, Ferdinand Zecca made a number of chase films in

chase film *The General* (1926; dir. Buster Keaton and Clyde Bruckman), with Buster Keaton as the chaser and the chased.

■ ■ ■

France for Pathé; and a chase was often a key element in many Keystone comedies made in this country during the silent period. Buster Keaton's *The General* (1926) is one of the most notable chase films from this period. More recent and serious chase films are Charles Laughton's *The Night of the Hunter* (1955) and Arthur Penn's *The Chase* (1966).

■ **chaser lights** Bulbs placed in a straight line with one lighting up after the other sequentially so that light seems to be "chasing" along the series.

■ **chatter** A trembling or movement of some object or portion of the foreground in a composite image that results from an original unsteadiness between the picture element and its matte. This unsteadiness was caused by an unstable camera or projector somewhere in the process of creating the individual parts of the image. Such an effect is sometimes discernible in earlier films using such special effects. *See* **matte.**

■ **cheat** (1) To change unnaturally the position of a subject from that in a previous shot to allow a better shot from a different angle or distance. (2) A performer cheats when he or she pretends to look at another character or some action but instead positions his or her face at a full and attractive angle for the camera. The direction for the performer to do this may be "Cheat it out" or "Cheat the look."

■ **cheat shot** A shot that fools the audience into believing that something is happening when it is not—for example, when a character pretends to leap out a window several stories high, although a mattress actually catches him a few feet below, out of the audience's view; or a character appears tall when he is actually standing on an "apple box."

■ **checker** The individual in an animation studio who "checks" all the cels and background material for each shot, making sure that they are properly ordered and that the individual drawings are properly colored. *See* **animation.**

■ **checkerboard cutting** The type of assembling used for A and B printing, generally for 16mm film. The consecutive shots of the negative are cut up and assembled alternately in two separate rolls, with black leader between the shots on each roll. Since the first shot on roll A corresponds with black leader on the second, the next shot on B corresponds with black leader on A, and so on, a checkerboard pattern is achieved between the two rolls. The shots from both rolls are printed consecutively and in order on a single film, thus preventing any splices from appearing in the printing of 16mm film. The system also allows for the easy creation of transitions and multiple exposures. *See* **A and B printing** *and* **invisible splice.**

■ **check print** A print sometimes made before the answer print to check on the various printing effects or to check on an older negative.

■ **cherry picker** A colloquial term for a crane.

■ **chewing** A disturbing trembling or movement around an object or portion of the foreground of a composite image caused by a misalignment in the artist's tracings from frame to frame in the rotoscoping process. *See* **rotoscope.**

■ **chiaroscuro** This term derives from the Italian words for "bright" (*chiaro*) and "dark" (*oscuro*). It means the arrangement of light and dark in a pictorial composition. German expressionist films achieved some remarkable effects of this sort (e.g., Paul Wegener's *Der Golem* in 1920).

■ **chicken coop** A luminaire with six 1,000-watt bulbs that is covered in the front by wire mesh and frequently used as an overhead light.

■ **child actor** A child who performs in films. Two famous children in films were Shirley Temple in the 1930s and Margaret O'Brien in the 1940s.

■ **china girl** The model in a series of frames whose skin and apparel contain all the primary and complementary colors. Her colors, along with those of various patches in the frame, are used by the grader for color correction during processing.

■ **china pencil, china marker, chinagraph** A grease pencil used in editing for marking up the work print with instructions.

■ **chinese dolly** A shot in which the camera moves back on slanted tracks while panning the scene.

■ **chip chart** *See* **color card.**

■ **choker** A tight close-up that fills the frame with the subject's head, generally from the neck up.

■ **choreographer, dance director** The person who plans and stages the dancing in a film. Busby Berkeley was the most famous dance director in the musical comedies of the 1930s. Bob Fosse achieved great success in the 1970s as a director and choreographer, notably for *Cabaret* (1972) and *All That Jazz* (1979).

■ **Christmas tree** (1) A single stand on which several luminaires are mounted. Also called a tree. (2) A small vehicle on which lighting equipment is stored.

■ **chroma** The intensity of a hue or saturation of a color; the freedom of the color from white or gray.

■ **chroma key, chromakeying** An electronic matting process for combining different picture elements into a single video image. A background image can take the place of the blue or green backing shot behind the figures—such colors are used since they do not appear in skin tones. Obviously, any part of the body clothed in such colors will disappear, an effect sometimes desired. Such a process accomplished with high-quality video is sometimes transferred to film. This process is a version of the blue-screen process. *See* **blue-screen process** *and* **Ultimatte.**

■ **chromatic aberration** The defect in the lens causing colors to be dispersed instead of focusing at the same point; the result is a color fringe around the objects of the image.

■ **chromaticity** The objective definition or measurement of color quality.

■ **chronophotographs** The multiple photography shot by Etienne-Jules Marey in the 1880s with his gunlike camera. The lens was positioned at the end of a long barrel and a glass plate revolved once per second in the chamber, taking twelve consecutive pictures. Later the plate was exchanged for paper film.

■ **cinching** Tightening a roll of film by pulling the end.

■ **cinch marks** Scratch marks on a film that are caused either by the layers of film rubbing against one another when an end is pulled to tighten a loosely wound roll or from particles between the layers.

■ **cine** The prefix that means "cinema" (e.g., in cinematographer).

■ *cinéaste* A French term meaning (1) anyone involved in the making of films; or (2) a film enthusiast.

■ *Cinéaste* A quarterly film journal, published from New York City, with a political emphasis and concern for international and noncommercial films.

■ **cine calculator** *See* **calculator.**

■ **cine camera** A motion-picture camera.

■ **Cinecolor** An early two-color film process used in place of the more expensive Technicolor process from the late 1930s until the development of tripack color systems in the 1950s. A print with emulsion on both sides, one orange-red and the other blue-green, was made from a single negative. *See* **color film** *(2).*

■ *Cinefantastique* An intelligently written and attractively illustrated bimonthly magazine that deals with fantasy films, especially the science-fiction and horror genres. Articles, interviews, and reviews are featured. The magazine is published from Oak Park, Illinois.

■ *Cinefex* Published three times a year from Riverside, California, this magazine is concerned with special effects in the movies. Each edition focuses on only a few films and presents lengthy articles and interviews that examine technical matters in depth with accompanying photographs.

■ *Cineforum* A journal published in Italy that features an international view of cinema by focusing on individual nations. This publication also gives special emphasis to emerging cinemas as well as the works of specific directors.

■ **CineFusion** An electronic compositing process created by Ultimatte that improves the blue-screen process so that transparent objects and blurred edges in the foreground can be reproduced, discoloration in the foreground caused by the blue lighting reflecting off the background can be avoided, and shadows cast on the blue-lit background can also be reproduced—the result is a composite image indistinguishable from the filming of live action. The process adapts the blue-screen color difference traveling matte system by using the difference between the blue and green components to achieve a black backing while maintaining the correct blue densities for the foreground colors. *See* **blue-screen process.**

■ **cinelight** A portable soft fill light that creates a wide beam with bulbs of anywhere from 300 to 1,000 watts. *See* **soft light.**

■ **cinema** The term comes from the Greek word *kinema,* meaning "motion," and refers to (1) motion pictures in general; or (2) motion-picture theaters (especially called so in Europe). When referring to the general world of motion pictures, the term has more aesthetic and artistic connotations than the terms "film," "movies," or "motion pictures."

■ **cinemacrography** The filming of small objects without a microscope but with normal, supplementary, or special lenses and with extension devices for the lens. This type of photography is often used for nature or biology films. Also called macrocinematography and cinephotomacrography. *See* **cinemicrography.**

■ **Cinema Digital Sound** *See* **digital sound.**

■ *Cinema Journal* The journal of the Society of Cinema Studies, published by the University of Texas Press at Austin; it features scholarly articles on commercial and noncommercial films.

■ *Cinema Nôvo* The "new cinema" that flourished in Brazil in the 1960s and sought to establish a political cinema with a bold revolutionary spirit and film technique. Important directors in this group were Glauber Rocha, Nelson Pereira dos Santos, and Ruy Guerra. By the early 1970s an oppressive government had repressed this movement. *See* **Third World cinema.**

■ **cinema of attractions** The goal of early cinema to impact on the spectator with a series of striking scenes or actions rather than the later goals of film to involve the viewer within a fictional narrative or to entice him or her to empathize with a character. This was a cinema that emphasized its own exhibitionism rather than the viewer's voyeurism. The term itself, coined and defined by the film scholar Tom Gunning, is drawn from Eisenstein's montage of attractions, the attractions of such contemporary shows as traveling circuses and carnivals from which early cinema drew some of its inspiration, and the obvious interaction of the viewer and film. The Lumière brothers' *The Arrival of a Train at a Station* (1895) and Edison's *Electrocuting an Elephant* (1903), both cited by Dunning, are examples of this type of cinema.

■ **cinéma-pur** *See* **pure cinema.**

■ **CinemaScope, scope** The anamorphic-lens system introduced by Twentieth Century-Fox in 1953 with its production of *The Robe* (dir. Henry Koster). The process was based on the work of Henri Chrétien, a Frenchman who had developed a special lens for tanks that allowed a 180-degree field of vision and was later used in aerial photography for mapmaking. The lens developed by Twentieth Century-Fox squeezed the width of the image photographed to half its size on the film and then another lens of this type on the projector unsqueezed the image when projected onto the screen. Such a system at first projected a wide-screen aspect ratio of 2.55:1, which later became 2.35:1 to allow for an optical sound track. CinemaScope 55 was a short-lived process in 1956 that anamorphically photographed on 55mm film and reduced the image to 35mm squeezed prints. A number of other film studios employed systems similar to CinemaScope, often with "scope" in the name so that the word became an abbreviation for such systems in general. Today the superior lenses of Panavision are preferred to those of CinemaScope and other earlier anamorphic systems. *See* **anamorphic lens** *and* **wide screen.**

■ **Cinémathèque Française** Now a film library, two theaters, and a museum located in Paris, this film institution was founded in 1936 by Henri Langlois along with Georges Franju and Jean Metry. Langlois and his associates were responsible for saving many silent films and also for hiding numerous films from the Germans during the occupation of France in World War II. Today the collection numbers over 50,000 films and the museum shows a wide range of exhibits covering the entire history of cinema. Its many showings, especially of Hollywood films, had an important impact both on *auteur* criticism and the New Wave cinema in France.

■ **cinematic** (1) Anything directly relating to the motion picture, for example cinematic technique or cinematic lighting. (2) Anything outside of motion pictures that has the ambience or suggestion of film: for example, a work of fiction with cinematic characters or techniques. The word "filmic" is also used in the context of the first definition, but infrequently in that of the second.

■ **Cinématographe** The camera and projector, at first in one housing, developed by the French brothers Auguste and Louis Lumière (1862–1954; 1864–1948). The machine improved upon Edison and Dickson's Kinetoscope and Kinetograph by being lighter and more portable, partly because it was hand-cranked and did not use an electric motor, and by using a claw mechanism that hooked into perforations and pulled each frame into place before the aperture. The Cinématographe was also instrumental in standardizing film width at 35mm and film speed at 16 frames per second (Edison's machine also used 35mm film but operated at 48 frames per second). On December 28, 1895, the Lumière brothers exhibited a series of short films, each only a minute or two long, before a paying public in a Paris café. In 1896, they opened a second theater and by 1898, their catalogues listed over 1,000 short films. Their most notable films were short recordings of reality (called *actualités*), for example, the workers leaving the Lumière factory and a train entering the Paris station. Because of their limited subject matter and limited technique (the camera rarely moved and simply recorded what was in front of it), the Lumière brothers were soon surpassed by other filmmakers, especially Georges Méliès with his fantasy films and trick photography. The word "Cinématographe" is responsible for later words using "cinema."

■ **cinematographer** *See* **director of photography.**

■ **Cinematographer's Computer Program** *See* **calculator.**

■ **cinematography** The word is derived from the Cinématographe of the Lumière brothers and applies to (1) the photography of moving images in the making of a motion picture. Cinematography involves such technical concerns as camera, lens, film stock, and lighting, and such techniques as camera angle, distance, and movement. Significant to each image and the relation of images are composition, form, color, light and dark, and motion. The term also applies to (2) the entire procedure for making motion pictures, which includes photography, processing, printing, and projection.

The history of cinematography, inclusive of categories (1) and (2), can be traced from such early nineteenth-century toys as the Thaumatrope, Phenakistoscope, Stroboscope, and Zoetrope, which relied upon the viewer's persistence of vision to give animation to pictures seen one after the other; and from early experiments with photography by the Frenchmen Nicéphore Niépce and Louis Daguerre, also in the early nineteenth century. Systems of projecting moving pictures date as early as the Magic Lantern in the second half of the seventeenth century; this was a device that was steadily developed as a form of popular entertainment during the next two centuries. By the end of the nineteenth century, the Frenchman Etienne-Jules Marey had developed his camera gun, which shot twelve pictures (or "Chronophotographs") a second to record the movement of humans and animals, and the American Eadweard Muybridge had learned to project consecutive photographs, also of human and animal action, to create the illusion of movement with his Zoopraxiscope. Perhaps the connecting link between these early experiments and the development of modern cinematography is Edison and Dickson's camera, the Kinetograph, and peephole machine, the Kinetoscope; and Dickson's later and improved version of the peep-hole viewer, the Mutoscope, which he developed for the Biograph Company. Modern cinematography largely begins with the first public showings of film projected from Edison's Vitascope during vaudeville shows in New York in 1896, the short film strips produced by the Lumière brothers during the final years of the nineteenth century, and the flight into fantasy and trick photography by Méliès, which overlap into this century.

Once into the twentieth century, cinematography developed with the rise of such film companies as Edison, Biograph, and Vitagraph, and the rapid growth of the Nickelodeon theaters; but the real advances came later in the silent-film era through the work of such distinct directors as Griffith, Stroheim, and Murnau, and such cameramen as Billy Bitzer, Karl Freund, Charles Rosher, Karl Struss, and William Daniels. Also of significant impact were advances in lighting and camera, and the change from orthochromatic to panchromatic film. Sound at first forced the noisy cameras to become stationary in soundproof enclosures, thus resulting in monotonous cutting from one camera to another or static frontal photography as if the film were a stage play. But once ways were found to silence the camera and resume its motion, cinematography again became flexible. The pervasive styles of each major studio should be recognized—for example, the bright, glittering images of MGM and the more dramatic and contrasty images of Warner Brothers. Also significant were the demands on cinematography by specific genres such as the gangster film and Western. At the same time, we can also find distinct cinematic styles of directors such as Rouben Mamoulian and Orson Welles, and of cameramen such as Stanley Cortez and Gregg Toland, Welles's photographer for *Citizen Kane* (1941).

Unquestionably the two most important events in cinematography after the coming of sound have been the development of color and wide-screen processes: the advent of tripack systems, especially Eastman Color in the 1950s, gradually changed most commercial films from black and white to color; and, to rejuvenate the industry in the age of television, such filming and projecting systems as CinemaScope and later Panavision created wide-screen images. These wide-screen processes themselves would not have been possible without the continuous improvement and refinement of both color stock and lighting systems. Also important are the considerable advances made in special-effects photography, especially for science-fiction films such as Stanley Kubrick's *2001: A Space Odyssey* (1968) and George Lucas's *Star Wars* (1978). The cinematographers who have learned to use new film stocks and lighting, to orchestrate colors and fill the wide screen with the director's dramatic images, cameramen such as William Fraker, Sven Nykvist, Owen Roizman, and Vilmos Zsigmond, are artists in their own right. Cinematography today, the systems of photographing, processing, printing, and projecting film, has been so refined and improved that motion pictures have truly become the art of the technological age. What remains ahead are developments in three-dimensional cinematography, which will make the image on the screen even more immediate and real, and improved technology for home viewing of motion pictures.

■ **cinematology** The study of film as a work of art with emphasis upon its internal characteristics—story elements, narrative structure, *mise-en-scène. See* **filmology.**

■ *cinéma vérité* The term means "camera truth" in French and applies to a series of documentary films which strive for immediacy, spontaneity, and authenticity through the use of portable and unobtrusive equipment and the avoidance of any preconceived narrative line or concepts concerning the material. *Cinéma-vérité* was a term used by Jean Rouch to describe the film he made with Edgar Morin, *Chronique d'un Eté (Chronicle of a Summer,* 1960), which is considered the first of these works. The theory and practice to some extent follow those of the early Russian film pioneer Dziga Vertov, who also used the term "film truth" (Kino-Pravda) for a series of newsreels; and, to a lesser extent, those of the American documentary pioneer, Robert Flaherty. A distinctive technique in *Chronique* is the filmmaker questioning and probing those interviewed, provoking the subjects to expose themselves in a spontaneous and truthful way. This is the technique which separates *cinéma-vérité* from a similar type of documentary developing in America at the same time, direct cinema, where there is no directorial intrusion and where the subjects are photographed and recorded completely on their own, exposing themselves through unprovoked though spontaneous speech and behavior. The term *cinéma-vérité* has been used to describe both movements, especially in introductory studies of film; but the distinction between the two schools of documentary is critical and the separate names are useful to keep this in mind. Other French directors who made *cinéma-vérité* documentaries are Chris Marker and Mario Ruspoli; but perhaps the most significant work to come out of this school was Marcel Ophüls's *The Sorrow and the Pity (Le Chagrin et la Pitié;* 1970), a telling and powerful exposure of France during the German occupation that is created through a remarkable series of interviews. *See* **direct cinema** *and* **documentary.**

cinéma vérité Marcel Ophüls's documentary *The Sorrow and the Pity* (1970) elicits its drama from the minds of those interviewed.

■ ■ ■

■ **cinemicrography** The filming of tiny objects or life through a microscope. This process is used both for research and for making scientific and medical films. Also called microcinematography, cinephotomicrography, and cinemicroscopy. *See* **cinemacrography.**

■ **Cineon digital film system** A system developed by Kodak that converts film images into a digital code for enhancement, alteration, or restoration, and then transfers them back onto film. The process begins with a high-resolution digital film scanner, the Lightning or Genesis Scanner, using CCD (charge-coupled device) technology and working on a Silicon Graphics Onyx platform. The monitor reproduces with great accuracy the original color of the film, allowing the image to be worked on with precision and accuracy. The Cineon Lightning film recorder, using a laser technology, transfers the new images to Kodak film in a manner that makes them indistinguishable in quality from the original. The Cinesite Digital Film Center was opened by Kodak in Los Angeles in 1992 and Cinesite (Europe) Ltd. in London in 1993 to use the new technology, but the system is available worldwide at a number of other postproduction houses. The new tabletop ver-

sions introduced in 1994, the Cineon Genesis 35 and 65 film scanners, are replacing the larger Genesis—though working at a slower scanning speed, they are more affordable and produce results of equal quality. *See* **digital, digital composite, digital effects,** *and* **digital restoration.**

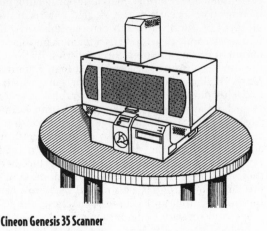

Cineon Genesis 35 Scanner

■ **Cinéorama** A wide-screen system of 360 degree that used ten separate films and projectors. The viewer, in a circular building, was surrounded by moving images of painted scenery to create the effect of traveling in a large balloon. The show was presented in Paris in 1900, but after three performances had to be closed because of the risk of fire caused by the ten projectors.

■ **cineplex** Several movie theaters in one location, generally in a single building. As large individual theaters closed down after the advent of television, these complexes of small theaters sprung up, especially at first in shopping centers or as subdivisions of large theaters. *See* **megaplex** *and* **multiplex.**

■ **Cinerama** A wide-screen process created by Fred Waller. Waller developed this process from his Vitarama show at the 1939 World's Fair, which used eleven projectors and a vast curved screen, and from his system for training antiaircraft gunners during World War II, which used five projectors beaming on a curved screen. *This Is Cinerama* appeared in a New York theater in 1952 as the first commercially successful wide-screen showing. The system employed three 35mm projectors, each in a separate booth at the rear of the theater, with the one on the right projecting onto the left third of the screen, the one in the center projecting straight ahead, and the one on the left projecting onto the right third of the screen. Images from the three 35mm films appeared on a vast wraparound screen that filled the viewer's peripheral vision and gave him or her the sense of being in the center of the scene and engaged in the action (one filmed sequence was an exciting rollercoaster ride that always produced

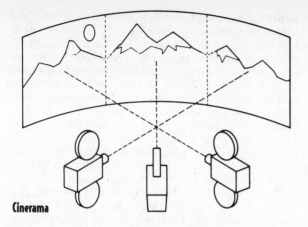

Cinerama

loud screams from the audience). The problem of joining the three images on the screen was diminished by blurring the connecting edges of the frames in the projectors themselves. For the full effect it was necessary for viewers to sit well centered in the theater, in front of the middle projector where the aspect ratio was approximately 2.5:1. Cinerama used a highly developed and impressive stereophonic sound system. Sound from seven magnetic tracks on a separate 35mm film was fed into six speakers behind the screen and others scattered round the theater. The sound of Cinerama literally followed the action on the screen, moving from one part of the theater to another.

Cinerama was an enormous success and soon played in eleven other major cities in the United States and five abroad; but the heavy expense of the system, with its three projectors, special screen, and considerable amount of film, as well as the loss of seating necessary for proper viewing, prevented Cinerama from spreading further. Another problem was the difficulty in developing subject matter and filming technique for the wraparound screen. The first productions were actually collections of travelogues, and it was not until 1962, with *The Wonderful World of the Brothers Grimm* (dir. Henry Levin and George Pal), that a fiction film was attempted. More successful on the vast screen was *How the West Was Won* (dir. Henry Hathaway, John Ford, and George Marshall) in the same year. But continuing difficulty with the overlapping images and competition from wide-screen systems with a single film forced Cinerama to become a single film process. For shooting *It's a Mad Mad Mad Mad World* (1963; dir. Stanley Kramer), UltraPanavision was used, with a 65mm anamorphically squeezed negative from which 70mm release prints were made. The name Cinerama continued to be used for the new process. *See* **wide screen.**

■ **cine-semiotics**   *See* **semiotics.**

■ **cine-structuralism**   *See* **structuralism.**

■ **cinetab**   *See* **trim tab.**

■ **Cinex-strip, Cinex**   A strip of positive film, made from a Cinex printer and included with the rushes, that shows adjacent frames in graded degrees of exposure. The strip allows the director of photography to judge the success of the shot and to see how it would appear with different printer lights.

■ **Circarama**   A system, developed for Disneyland, that projects a 360-degree image around an audience on a cylindrical screen by means of a series of projectors. At first, eleven 16mm projectors were used, but the system later used nine 35mm projectors. *See* **Circle-Vision.**

■ **circled takes**   The takes circled on a camera report for printing by the laboratory.

■ **circle of confusion**   A small circular patch formed by the lens on film that is actually the image of a specific point in the subject being photographed. Because light rays from any point nearer than infinity must converge at a point farther behind the lens than the focal plane, they will always appear as a circular patch. The smaller the circle, the less the confusion or blur and the sharper the image. Proper focusing of the lens keeps these circles to a minimum size. *See* **depth of field** *and* **depth of focus.**

■ **circle of least confusion, circle of best definition**   The circle of confusion formed by the light rays from a point on the subject acceptable for photographing.

■ **Circle-Vision**   A wraparound film and screen system developed by the Walt Disney Corporation. The system employed at the Epcot Park in Florida uses a wraparound screen of 140 feet and five 35mm projectors, run synchronically, to create 200-degree film viewing. The system at Epcot allows more than peripheral vision and creates for the viewer a sense of being immersed in the scene. The system also employs seven-track stereo sound. Films are made from five 35mm cameras, run synchronically, all of which are aimed upward at mirrors, giving them the same nodal point and avoiding difficulties with parallax. A newer version at EuroDisney in France uses nine cameras to create a 360-degree image. *See* **Circarama.**

■ **circuit theater**   A movie house or complex that is part of a chain of theaters all belonging to the same owner or corporation. Such theaters often play the same films. Circuit theaters, because of wider circulation of films and larger guaranteed audience, have been able to rent films more easily and with better financial arrangements than individually owned theaters, which, as a result, have considerably decreased over the years.

■ **circular pan, 360-degree pan**   A pan shot in which the camera rotates around a fixed axis a full 360 degrees. Ingmar Bergman positioned his camera in the middle of a circular dining table and had the camera slowly pan the faces of the guests in a full circle in *Hour of the*

Wolf (1968). This circular pan not only creates a sequence of strange babbling faces as seen by the protagonist, but also a sense of the protagonist's own separation and isolation.

■ **city symphonies** A series of nonfiction films exploring the life and physical reality of a major city, frequently in an impressionistic style. The generic name for this type of film derives from the subtitle of Walter Ruttman's *Berlin, die Symphonie einer Grosstadt* (1927).

■ **clamping disc** *See* **knuckle clamping disc head.**

■ **clapboard, sync slate, slate, clapper board, clapstick board, number board, slate board, production board, take board** A slate with a pair of boards hinged together that is photographed at the beginning of each take, both for information concerning the take and for synchronization of sound and picture. On the slate are written such data as the names of the film, director, and cameraman; the date; and the numbers of the scene and take. Such information identifies the piece of film being shot and is read onto the sound track as well as photographed. The hinged boards on top, called clapsticks, are then banged together, allowing the editor later to synchronize picture and sound by coordinating the frame of the clapsticks coming together and the first noise on the sound track. An electronic system is also used for synchronization of picture and sound. A clipboard with time-code information is called a smart slate. *See* **synchronization** *and* **time code.**

clapboard

■ **clapper/loader** *See* **second assistant camera operator.**

■ **clapsticks** The two boards in the clapboard that are hinged together and attached to a slate. Since they are both photographed and recorded when banged together at the start of a take, they serve as a synchronizing device for the picture and sound track in editing. *See* **clapboard.**

■ **Clarke process** A system, devised by Charles Clarke in the early 1950s, to photograph live action through a diapositive plate, which generally is clear at the bottom and has a still image, such as clouds, at the top. The live action and image on the plate combine on the film.

■ **classical cutting** A type of cutting for dramatic or emotional effect rather than for continuity; for example, a sudden cut from a long shot of an actor to a close-up.

■ **classic film** A work that has achieved both fame and praise because of its insightful and innovative treatment of a significant subject. The term generally applies to fictional films that have withstood the test of time, that continue to contribute to our understanding of both human behavior and the medium itself, and that still seem to contribute to the development of film. Classic films seem to sum up the state of the art at their time of production, to bring together the best techniques and insights about people, and also to advance the art and permanently change the future course of film. One need only think of such films as Stroheim's *Greed* (1923), Murnau's *Sunrise* (1927), Welles's *Citizen Kane* (1941), Resnais's *Hiroshima Mon Amour* (1959), and Kubrick's *2001: A Space Odyssey* (1968) to understand and feel the full implications of this definition.

■ **Classification and Rating Administration (CARA)** A group responsible for the classification and rating of individual motion pictures required of all films produced by members of the Motion Picture Association of America (MPAA) and permitted for nonmembers who wish to submit their films. A rating board makes its recommendation for an individual film to the administration, which then grants the film a rating certificate. Decisions may be appealed to the Classification and Rating Appeals Board. *See* **Movie Rating System.**

■ **Classification and Rating Appeals Board** A group made up of the president of the Motion Picture Association of America (MPAA), one representative designated by each member company of the MPAA, a number of representatives from the National Association of Theater Owners (NATO) equal to the number from the MPAA companies, and representatives from four independent distributors to whom a producer may appeal the rating of a film determined by the Classification and Rating Administration of the MPAA. The original rating can be overturned by a two-thirds majority of the group hearing the appeal (eleven members, of which five must be from the MPAA and five from NATO, is necessary for a quorum). *See* **Movie Rating System.**

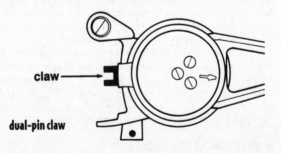

claw ⟶

dual-pin claw

■ **claw** A metal tooth in a camera's intermittent mechanism that pulls each frame of the film, one at a time, into the gate for photographing by engaging a perforation. Double claws (one on each side) are employed in many professional cameras such as the Panavision Panaflex; and two dual-pin pull-down claws (engaging four perforations) are used for fast-speed cameras such as Panavision's Panastar. In most professional cameras, after the claws disengage, registration pins hold each frame in place for exposure. *See* **intermittent movement** *and* **pilot pins.**

■ **claymation** Stop-motion animation employing clay figures. The clay figures may be remolded to change shapes from frame to frame or simply used as puppets. *See* **animation** *and* **stop motion.**

■ **clean entrance** A term used when no part or shadow of the performer or object is seen before movement into the scene. Also an order to the performer to enter in such a way.

■ **clean exit** When the performer or object moves out of the scene and completely out of sight. Also an order to the performer to exit in such a way.

■ **cleaning bath** *See* **wash.**

■ **clean shot** An uncluttered shot with the camera focusing on a single subject so that it dominates the viewer's attention.

■ **clean speech** When the performer gives his or her speech during a shot without any problems.

■ **cleanup** The process of retracing an animator's rough drawings and making them into finished artwork, a task performed in an animation studio by the cleanup artist. *See* **animation.**

■ **clear, clear yourself** An order for a performer to appear unobstructed in front of the camera, with no part hidden by some object or another performer.

■ **clearance** (1) Legal consent for the filmmaker or production company to use copyrighted material from another medium, such as music or literature, or from another film. (2) The exclusive rights obtained by a theater from a distributor to play a film in a specific geographic area for a specified time.

■ **clear the frame** An order to vacate the set in front of the camera during rehearsal.

■ **cliché** In film, like literature, the term applies to (1) hackneyed and trite language that through overuse has lost its impact and sometimes its original meaning; (2) stereotyped and trite characters of plot that have lost power and significance through overuse. In film, the term also applies to (3) any visual image or technique that has been used and imitated so much that it has lost freshness, power, or even meaning for an audience.

■ **clicks, clix, click track** A metronomic beat created digitally by punching equidistant holes on the sound track; it guides (1) the conductor of an orchestra in bringing the music in on cue and keeping a tempo for recording music after the film has been shot and edited (either the conductor alone or both he and the musicians follow the beat by earphones); (2) a composer in writing music for a film that has already been shot and edited; or (3) an animation editor in creating the rhythm and timing for a sequence of action.

■ **cliffhanger** A film of great suspense with an especially tense ending, named after early serials in which the heroine, hanging from a cliff, was rescued at the last minute. Ridley Scott's *Alien* (1979) can be considered a modern type of cliffhanger.

■ **climax** From the Greek *klimax*, meaning "ladder," the word refers to that point in any narrative art (1) of highest plot complication when action ceases to rise and begins to resolve itself and fall; or (2) of highest dramatic interest for the viewer. Both kinds of climax occur toward the end of the work, but not necessarily at the same time. *See* **anticlimax** *and* **dénouement**

■ **clip** (1) A brief selection from a film used as an illustration of the work to which it belongs or as an illustration of some point. Clips are frequently used in advertising or as parts of compilation films. (2) A brief selection from another film or any kind of film footage used in a motion picture.

■ **clip-to-clip** *See* **paper-to-paper.**

■ **closed captioned** Titles superimposed onto the bottom of a television screen and made visible by a special decoder for the hearing impaired. Such titles make available the dialogue in the program as well as describing significant sounds and music. *See* **caption** *and* **open captioned.**

■ **closed form** A film style, in contrast to open form, that seems self-contained and self-sufficient both in style and content, and that creates its own world within the frame and seems to make little reference to any reality outside the frame. Such films appear stylized and formal; the *mise-en-scène* seems more composed, controlled, artificial, and filled with detail; and action seems more choreographed and planned. Little seems accidental or natural about these films—the director is always in control; camera anticipates action; and permeating the whole is a sense of determinism. Such films tend to be more expressionistic than realistic. Fritz Lang is considered a director of films with closed form, as opposed to Renoir, who made films with open form. *See* **open form.**

■ **close down, stop down** To reduce the opening of the lens' diaphragm by turning the calibration ring on the barrel to a higher f-stop number. To open up the diaphragm requires the opposite procedure.

■ **closed set** A set, either in the studio or on location, that is not open to any visitors, including studio executives, and is open only to the director, performers, and crew. Sets are closed if a particularly intimate or controversial scene is being photographed, if the subject or treatment is to be kept secret, or if there are problems in the production itself that must be worked out.

■ **close shot (CS)** (1) A shot somewhere between a medium shot and close-up; generally one that shows a character's head and shoulders with some background. (2) Sometimes used synonymously for close-up. *See* **shot.**

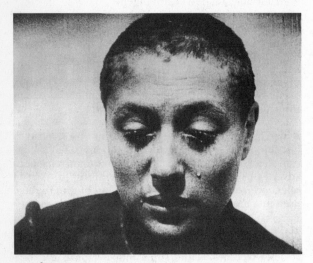

close-up Renée Falconetti's persuasive face in Carl Dreyer's *The Passion of Joan of Arc* (1928).

■■■

■ **close-up (CU)** A shot in which the camera seems to be very close to the subject. The head of a person, a small object, or part of an object fills the screen. The close-up is effective for conveying to the audience a character's emotions, reactions, and states of mind; for creating between the audience and character a greater involvement by forcing the viewer to focus on the individual and nothing else. D. W. Griffith developed the art of the facial close-up in his silent films; and Carl Dreyer, in his moving *The Passion of Joan of Arc* (1928), kept the camera for much of the film on the suffering face of his heroine. Close-ups of objects or parts of objects are effective for calling the viewer's attention to significant information and details, for building suspense by anticipating action which will use that object, and for giving symbolic value to the subject of the frame. Hitchcock created the murder scene in *Sabotage*

(1936) through a masterful blending of facial close-ups and close-ups of objects: the montage sequence moves repeatedly between the faces of Sylvia Sidney and Oscar Homolka and intrudes with images of her hands, the carving knife, the chair of her dead brother, and the cage of birds to build suspense, convey the drama between the two characters, and warn us of the coming violence. For close-ups of characters the following more specific designations are also made: medium close-up, which shows the character from somewhere between waist and shoulder to the top of the head; head and shoulders close-up (sometimes called a close shot); head close-up; and extreme, big, or tight close-up, which shows only part of the head—the area from the lips to eyes, for example. *See* **shot.**

■ **close-up lens** *See* **diopter lens.**

■ **closing credits** The names of all the performers and their roles, the complete list of technical and production personnel, the acknowledgments for various services, and the list of music and recordings that appear at the conclusion of a film. Also referred to as end titles. *See* **front credits.**

■ **clothes light** Specific lights, often kicker lights with snoots, for bringing out the texture or highlighting areas of the garment worn by a character. *See* **kicker light.**

■ **cloud wheel** A rotating wheel through which light is projected to cast a skylike effect on the rear of the set.

■ **cluster bar** A single mount for supporting more than one luminaire.

■ **CLV laser disc** The initials stand for "constant linear velocity" and represent a laserdisc on which is stored a motion picture without the capacity for freeze framing or moving the images forward one at a time. The disc holds up to sixty minutes of visuals and sound on each side. *See* **CAV laser disc** *and* **laser disc.**

■ **C-mount** The single-thread screwing device that attaches lenses to 16mm cameras. Though more common than the bayonet mount, it is not as strong and hence is less efficient in supporting such heavy lenses as the zoom lens.

■ **coated lens** A lens coated with magnesium fluoride on the surface to reduce loss of light by reflection. Coating has become a routine procedure in the manufacture of most lenses.

■ **coating** The process of laying emulsion on a film base.

■ **coaxial magazine** A film magazine with two separate chambers next to each other on the same axis for the feed and take-up reels. *See* **magazine.**

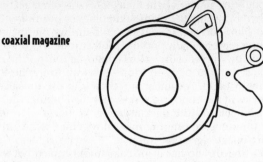

coaxial magazine

■ **cobweb gun, cobweb spinner, cobweb maker** A handheld device, composed of an electric motor, a container of latex solution, and a fan, that blows artificial cobwebs onto the set.

■ **code numbers** Consecutive and corresponding numbers printed at intervals along the edge of both the picture and sound workprints during editing to facilitate synchronization. *See* **edge numbers.**

■ **codes** *See* **semiotics** *and* **structuralism.**

■ **coding machine** *See* **edge numbering machine.**

■ **co-feature** The second feature on a double bill, generally a low-budget film or a work of lesser significance. *See* **B-picture** *and* **double feature.**

■ **collage film** An experimental film of animated collages. Stan Vanderbeek's antiwar *Breathdeath* (1963) is often cited as a prime example and features cutouts, photographs, drawings, and headlines in a powerful melange. Joseph Cornell and Bruce Conner have each made a number of collage films that assemble parts of other films in a unique manner. (See Jay Leyda, *Films Beget Films* [1964].)

■ **collective story film** *See* **composite film.**

■ **collimator** An optical device for testing a lens by magnifying the image of a test object reflected directly off moving (or stationary) film in a camera. The image is itself projected off the film and into the collimator reflex viewfinder where it can be examined for accuracy, resolution, and other qualities.

■ **collision** Sergei Eisenstein's theory of montage, based on his application of Marxist dialectics. For Eisenstein, one shot should collide with another, like a dialectical thesis and antithesis, resulting in a synthesis which is itself the start of a new collision of shots. The impact and effect of both shots result in a totality greater than the sum of the individual parts. The effect is both emotional and intellectual for the viewer; it is synchronic and immediate, not diachronic and sequential. The term "collision" brings Eisenstein's the-

ory into clear opposition with the linkage theory of montage of another great Russian film director, V. I. Pudovkin. (Eisenstein's theory of montage is developed in two collections of his essays, *Film Form* and *Film Sense.*) *See* **linkage** *and* **montage.**

■ **color** (1) The visual perception of the quality of any substance caused by the different wavelengths of reflected light and generally measured by hue, saturation, and brightness. White light is itself composed of separate wavelengths, each of which creates a different color of the spectrum. Human eyesight is basically responsive to three parts of the spectrum—blue, green, and red—the various combinations of which make the wide variety of hues we see in the world around us or in the film images projected on a screen. *See* **color film.** (2) Any details within a film—setting, objects, costumes, music, lighting, or visual color—that give the work the feel and aura of a particular time and place.

■ **color analyzer, color film analyzer** *See* **video color analyzer.**

■ **color balance** (1) The adjustment of a film emulsion either for artificial (i.e., tungsten) light, which means it is sensitive for 3,200 degrees Kelvin, or for daylight, which means it is sensitive for approximately 5,600 degrees Kelvin. (2) The emphasis upon a particular part of the color spectrum in a film image; for example, when an image focuses more upon green than blue or red, it is said to be "balanced toward green." (3) An image with all parts of the spectrum in balance is said to be "in balance" or to have a "neutral balance."

■ **color-blind film** (1) Any film insensitive to part of the color spectrum—for example, early orthochromatic film, which was insensitive to red. (2) Certain print stocks that are made insensitive to yellow light so that they can be printed and processed with safelights of such color.

■ **color card, color chart, chip chart** A card with a color scale that is photographed on a piece of film to facilitate color correction. The photographed card can be matched with the actual card to help with the timing process. *See* **timing.**

■ **color cast** An overall tint in a film image. This effect may be caused by faulty stock or printing, but sometimes such a tint is intentionally achieved to create a desired visual quality (e.g., a sepia tint to create a sense of the past as in old photographs).

■ **color Cinex-strip** *See* **Cinex-strip.**

■ **color-compensating filter, color-correction filter, color-balancing filter** A camera filter that changes, in minimal degrees, the color balance of a scene by reducing the amount of red, blue, or green. This change might correct light sources or film stock, or simply achieve a particular effect.

■ **color-conversion filter**   A camera filter that changes the color temperature of the light to suit the color balance of the film stock. For example, with a blue filter, daylight film can be used indoors with tungsten lights; with an amber filter, indoor film can be used outdoors in daylight.

■ **color correction**   (1) Altering the color of a scene's lighting by placing filters in front of the lamps or in front of or behind the camera lens. (2) Altering the quality of color for an image during printing. *See* **timing.**

■ **color depth**   *See* **bit depth.**

■ **color difference matte process**   *See* **blue-screen process.**

■ **color-difference traveling matte process, color-separation traveling matte process**   Although these terms are most applied to the blue-screen process, they also refer to traveling-matte procedures that use other colored backgrounds—green and red, for example—to separate out the subject from the background into which a separate image will ultimately be placed. This separation and compositing is caused by the difference in color between the backing and subject and the creation of male and female mattes. Because skin color is composed largely of red with some green, the blue screen is the best background for separating out characters. *See* **blue-screen process, matte,** *and* **traveling-matte process.**

■ **color duplicate negative, color dupe**   First-generation color negatives (i.e., internegatives) made directly from a color master positive (i.e., an interpositive) that may be used for making release prints. *See* **color separation** *(2)*.

■ **color enhancer**   A digital system that corrects, improves, or changes color in an image before it is transferred back to film. The da Vinci system, for example, uses a 64-bit-per-pixel primary color correction, which is supposed to track over 28 trillion colors and can be operated through an interface system that gives graphical and numerical details and control settings, setup parameters, and correction adjustments.

■ **color film, color cinematography**   (1) A motion picture in color as opposed to one in black and white. (2) The film used for making a color motion picture. Color motion pictures began as early as 1896 with the hand-painted frames of the Edison company's *Anabelle's Dance* shown in the Kinetoscope peephole machine. In France, Georges Méliès employed a similar method for his short films at the turn of the century: for such films as *A Trip to the Moon* (1902), he had the various parts of a series of frames painted by women in a production-line method. A process using stencils for the various colors was developed later, followed by a coloring machine with rollers (a method employed by Pathé Frères, also in France). Tinting was a procedure that dyed the film's base, hence allowing a single color to show

through the image's light areas. This was often accomplished by dyeing the print, sometimes by printing on a dyed film, and sometimes by hand-tinting the image. Tinting was especially popular for feature works during the 1920s, with specific colors employed for specific effects: red might be used for scenes with fire, blue for scenes at night. A similar process was to dye the silver particles in the emulsion, a process called toning, which actually colored the dark areas of the image. Tinting and toning were often employed together to give the entire image a general color.

But the development of color motion pictures was really dependent on experimentation with two photographic processes—additive and subtractive. Additive processes basically add lights of the primary colors in various proportions to the projected image. This method was popular at first because black-and-white film could still be used. Kinemacolor, a two-color system created in England by Edward R. Turner and George Albert Smith, and promoted by an American, Charles Urban, was used for a series of films culminating with the long documentary, *The Durbar at Delhi,* which played in London in 1912. Alternate frames of black-and-white film were photographed at 32 frames per second through either the red or green areas of a rotating filter, and the printed film was projected through the same filter at the same speed, with the viewer's persistence of vision combining the separate red and green images. A lenticular system developed early in the century used, on the lens of the camera, a filter with three bands of the primary colors and used film which contained minute semicylindrical lines or lenses for recording the three color bands. Dufaycolor, developed by the Frenchman Louis Dufay, used a mosaic of tiny filter elements of the primary colors between the emulsion and base of the film through which the picture was first photographed and later projected after having been printed in a reversal method. The general problem with all additive methods was that a sufficiently bright image could not be produced on the screen because of photographing and projecting through filters of the primary colors. For this reason, as well as various difficulties in the different methods, additive processes for motion pictures were abandoned about the time of the Second World War, though a variation of the system is employed for television.

The development of modern color cinematography has been based upon subtractive processes, which basically take away unwanted colors from white light through layers of subtractive colors on a single film. A subtractive color (also called a "complementary color") is what remains when one of the primary colors has been removed from the spectrum. The subtractive colors are cyan, magenta, and yellow. The emulsion of the original film is composed of three separate layers, each containing both silver halides and chemical dyes called sensitizers or couplers, which are sensitive to one of the primary colors. After exposure and during processing, the silver halides form the black-and-white image and the couplers in each layer form an image in the corresponding subtractive colors. Both the developed and undeveloped halides are washed away, leaving a negative image with colors complementary to the original colors and with light and dark reversed. The film on which the print is made is also a tripack, but after exposure and processing it offers an image with the original colors and tones in the scene. On tripack color reversal film, the exposed silver halides are first developed in each layer, then the film is either reexposed or chemically treated so that the remaining halides are developed. After all the exposed halides are bleached and washed away, a positive color image remains. When the image is projected, each of the colors acts as a filter, sending on its own color but subtracting out its complement. Variations of this process have been developed since the beginning of the century.

Herbert T. Kalmus and Donald F. Comstock began the Technicolor Motion Pictures Corporation in 1915 and ultimately developed a subtractive system with a beam splitter sending red and green light waves to two attached negatives. From these negatives two prints were made, which were then dyed and attached back to back. The most ambitious film made with this process was *The Black Pirate* (1926; dir. Albert Parker), starring Douglas Fairbanks. In 1928, Technicolor began to use the imbibition process for transferring dyes of both matrices to a single print, thus avoiding the problems of attaching both prints back to back and thus allowing multiple prints to be made from the single pair of matrices. Of great significance was the three-color process, which used three color-separation negatives with a beam splitter for all the primary colors. Developed in 1932, this method was first used in Walt Disney's animated *Flowers and Trees*. The first feature film to employ this process was Rouben Mamoulian's *Becky Sharp* in 1935; but *Gone With the Wind* (1939; dir. Victor Fleming) was the greatest achievement with the three-strip process.

In 1935, Eastman Kodak introduced Kodachrome, a tripack system for 16mm film that required only one negative, with a layer for each of the primary colors on a single base, and in 1941, Technicolor announced a 35mm monopack film, developed from Kodachrome and used effectively for *King Solomon's Mines* in 1950 (dir. Compton Bennett). Finally, in 1952, Eastman Kodak introduced Eastman Color, a 35mm tripack negative film that had color masking for developing and that could be used in a regular camera. Eastman Color has improved since its inception; it has greater sensitivity to light, allows more rapid speeds, and has less graininess. This film also photographs distant objects more distinctly and registers colors more naturally. Both Fujicolor and Gevacolor (from Agfa-Gevaert) were also negative films that created from available light an image with remarkable colors and contrasts and with minimal granularity. Technicolor's imbibition process for printing was still used until the 1970s; but the demand for the rapid production of a large number of release prints put an end to this process in the mid-1970s. The old Technicolor dye-transfer process continued in England and Italy until 1978, and today is in use only in China at the Beijing Film Lab. A significant problem with the popular Eastman Color has been the fading of colors over the years, a problem that has been partly solved by the development of low-fade stocks that use more permanent dyes. Also notable was Kodak's improvement of the Eastman stock in the mid-1980s with its T-grain emulsion that featured flatter silver halide crystals for a better distribution of light.

By the mid-1950's, less than half the commercial films were in black and white, and by now nearly all are in color. In spite of the loss of the dye-transfer process and the breakdown of colors from the earlier Eastman film, the artistic development of color in film has been significant. One need only compare, for example, the cartoonlike color in the early horror films by Hammer Studios in England during the mid-1950s with the more subtle and frightening use of color in William Friedkin's *The Exorcist* (1973).

As pointed out many times, color in a film can never be created as it exists in the everyday world; the surrounding darkness of the theater gives extra emphasis to color and the fact that color is created by light shining through film gives objects a certain luminosity. Though modern color stocks permit, with careful planning, a sufficient illusion of reality, the artificiality of the medium also allows for great artistic effects. It is not difficult to pick out landmarks in the artistic use of color, though certainly today one feels that color is often used in a pedestrian way. Certainly the three-strip Technicolor system in *Gone With the Wind* was highly successful in re-creating the pageantry and drama of America's past. Laurence Olivier's *Henry V* (1944), filmed with the Technicolor Monopack, was one of the first modern films designed in terms of color: the beginning and closing sections are photographed as a play with stage sets of unnatural and bright colors (like medieval illustrations), and the central Agincourt scenes are filmed in more natural color. Teinosuke Kinugasa's *Gates of Hell* (1953), a Japanese film in Eastman Color, had an immense impact with its remarkably evocative and beautiful color that suggested Japanese art. Michelangelo Antonioni's *Red Desert,* also filmed with Eastman Color and released in 1964, employed color in an expressive and abstract manner to create a sterile industrial landscape, while, in many of his films, Federico Fellini created a sensuous, jaded, and fantastic world of color, evoking a visual sense of his characters' decadence. The immediacy of color can create an ambience that suggests a particular time and place, as it does in Arthur Penn's *Bonnie and Clyde* (1967). The colors in John Huston's *Moulin Rouge* (1952) not only evoke a period, but also suggest French impressionist painting. A similar effect is achieved in Stanley Kubrick's *Barry Lyndon* (1975), which depicts the color of eighteenth-century England in the style of eighteenth- and nineteenth-century British painting. The contrast, tones, and emotional values of color can cause both a psychological and symbolic impact, as they do in Nicolas Roeg's *Don't Look Now* (1973), which presents a remarkable fusion of the landscape of decaying Venice with Gothicism, medieval art, and the supernatural. Color can also animate the physical world, give it not only life but poetry and drama, as it does with the changing landscape in Terrence Malick's *Days of Heaven* (1978). *See* **Colorization.**

■ **color grad filter** A camera filter containing both clear and colored areas, with a smooth transition between the two. Such filters are used for altering only part of the image—for example, a partly blue filter for deepening the sky.

■ **color internegative** *See* **internegative.**

■ **colorist** *See* **timer.**

■ **Colorization, Color Systems Technology** An early process for changing black-and-white images to color. Film images were transferred to video and then colored by means of a graphics computer. Key frames were given color values by the colorist, and the computer colored the remaining frames in the scene. This system altered some film classics for video transmission, but the results were not sufficient to return the colored images to film and project them on a screen. Today, film scanners and recorders are of sufficient quality to colorize and then return to film the altered images, but the process of colorizing black-and-white film has subsided. There had been much complaint by members of the film industry that such a process distorts and changes the original intentions and appearance of the film. Colorization was one of the reasons for the National Film Preservation Act. *See* **color film** (2) *and* **National Film Registry.**

■ **color master positive** A color positive of high quality made from a color original negative and used for making fine-grain color duplicate negatives, themselves to be used as the source of release prints.

■ **color match** The continuity, balance, and harmony of colors throughout the entire film, from shot to shot and scene to scene.

■ **color meter, color temperature meter** A device that measures the color temperature of a light source on the Kelvin scale.

■ **color rendering index (CRI)** A numerical measurement from 0 to 100 for the change in the color of an object when illuminated by a specific light source—the change is measured against an established standard for the color at the same color temperature. An acceptable measurement for rendering objects in natural colors for the purposes of photography would be between 90 and 100, with the latter figure representing normal daylight and incandescent illumination.

■ **color reversal intermediate (CRI)** A color dupe negative made directly from the original negative by means of tripack reversal film. Although such film must be printed optically for perfect orientation, the elimination of a color master positive made this an attractive process for making release prints. But because the results proved less durable and the chemicals turned out to be pollutants, the process has been largely discontinued. *See* **internegative** *and* **IP/IN.**

■ **color saturation** *See* **saturation.**

■ **color sensitivity** The degree to which a film emulsion is responsive to the various colors of the spectrum.

■ **color separation** (1) Using a separate negative for each of the three primary colors in subtractive-color cinematography processes such as Technicolor. Technicolor used a beam splitter to record on each negative: besides a negative for green, two other negatives were bipacked, emulsion to emulsion, for blue and red. *See* **Technicolor.** (2) Using three black-and-white positives (called color-separation masters), each made from the same color negative and recorded individually through a filter of a primary color, to make a record of that color. Printing through the same filters onto tripack stock creates a color duplicate negative. This procedure is employed for making a permanent record of an expensive or important color film since there are no color dyes on the positives which will fade. (3) Using three black-and-white negatives (called color-separation negatives) to record each of the primary colors for the same reason as described in (2).

■ **Color Systems Technology** *See* **Colorization.**

■ **color temperature** The measurement of the various light rays of the color spectrum coming from a light source. This measurement has been initially calculated by heating an enclosed piece of black carbon, which cannot emit incident light and is therefore a perfect source of radiant energy, and measuring the temperatures for the different colors along the spectrum from the lower blue end to the higher red. Because these temperatures are extremely high, the Kelvin scale, which measures along the centigrade scale, is used, but starting at absolute zero (or –273 Celsius). Measuring color temperature is important in balancing various light sources and adjusting them to the requirements of a film stock. The Kelvin scale is especially efficient for tungsten lamps, but judgment is required when applying it to other artificial sources and to daylight. *See* **Kelvin scale.**

■ **Columbia Pictures** A film company, begun as CBC Sales Corporation in 1920 by Harry Cohn, his brother

Jack, and Joseph Brandt, and named Columbia Pictures in 1924. The company produced a great many B-films but had its share of successful major features, especially the works directed by Frank Capra in the 1930s and the films starring Rita Hayworth in the 1940s. Columbia borrowed most of its stars, directors, and writers from other studios. It was dominated by Harry Cohn, who was both president and chief of production. In the 1950s, the company achieved considerable success, largely through its backing of independent filmmakers and foreign productions: Elia Kazan's *On the Waterfront* (1954) and David Lean's *Lawrence of Arabia* (1962) were both Columbia films. In the same period, the company started producing television programs through its subsidiary, Screen Gems. To save money, Columbia sold its own studio and moved in with Warner Brothers in 1972, making its films at the Burbank Studios. Under David Begelman, the company had a number of popular successes, including Hal Ashby's *Shampoo* (1975) and Steven Spielberg's *Close Encounters of the Third Kind* (1977). Columbia regained its impetus after Begelman's resignation because of embezzlement in 1977, and soon after sponsored such films as Robert Benton's *Kramer vs. Kramer* (1979) and James Bridges's *The China Syndrome* (1979). The organization was purchased by the Coca-Cola Company in 1982 for $750 million. Along with CBS and HBO, Columbia founded TriStar Pictures in 1982, a production company that eventually joined Columbia to form Columbia Entertainment in 1987. The Sony Corporation of Japan, which had purchased the CBS Records Group in 1987, purchased Columbia in 1989 for $3.4 billion, seeking to feed further its massive holdings in electronic hardware with expanded software holdings. Sony also purchased from Warner Brothers the distribution rights to the films made by the Guber-Peters Entertainment Company. This purchase was basically to free Jon Peters and Peter Guber to run Columbia, but the deal proved costly during the coming years and each of these men was ultimately forced to resign. Both Columbia and TriStar functioned independently as part of Sony, and then became part of Sony Pictures Entertainment Company in 1991. TriStar turned out some extremely successful films such as *When Harry Met Sally* (1989; dir. Rob Reiner) and *Terminator 2* (1991; dir. James Cameron). Columbia has been very successful in television production, especially in recent years with its two popular game shows, *Wheel of Fortune* and *Jeopardy*. But, in 1994, Columbia and TriStar drew only 9.5 percent of the domestic box office for film distribution while, in the same year, Sony took a $2.7 billion write-off for its losses in Hollywood. Columbia and TriStar did considerably better in 1995 with 12.3 percent of the box office. *See* **TriStar.**

■ **coma** A lens aberration that causes images off the optical axis to smear out; points of light form comet-shaped blurs.

■ **combination filter** Any filter composed of two different types, though one is normally a neutral-density filter. *See* **neutral-density filter.**

■ **combined dupe, composite dupe** A duplicate negative with both synchronized sound and picture ready for printing.

■ **combined move, compound move** Movement of both actor and camera at the same time: for example, a tracking shot that follows the walk of a character.

■ **combo engagement** The release of two new films to play together for a single admission price. Frequently this practice is used to promote public interest for later runs of each film, but sometimes it is a way of generating revenue for films that might not appeal to audiences if shown on their own. *See* **double feature.**

■ **combo light stand** A light stand with a 1⅛-inch receptacle for holding reflector boards or luminaires. Having three foldable legs, this stand is portable for location shooting, yet strong enough to withstand a strong breeze.

■ **comeback** A return of a performer to fame and fortune after a layoff or an unsuccessful period.

■ **comedy** A basic definition of comedy both in drama and film is a work inciting within the viewer humor and mirth and ending happily, but there are many types of comedy that inspire degrees of humor and mirth; sometimes, as in black comedy, laughter is somewhat muted by our realization of serious implications and perhaps even by an unhappy ending. Uniting all comic works is a view of the ludicrous in human behavior and affairs, and an attempt to have viewers laugh at the mistakes and misfortunes of people a little less smart and secure than themselves. Such a position allows the audience to feel superior; it also allows the audience, safely and good-naturedly, to work out its own aggressions. Even in comedies of wit, we associate with the smart talker and see the world from his or her superior position—except when he or she becomes someone else's victim. Films make us far more aware of visual reality than theater, and far more consistently integrate physical reality into comedy. With the absence of sound, early films relied on the visual dimension, and, although influenced by vaudeville, burlesque, and even the circus, largely invented their own comedy.

The Frenchman Max Linder, with his dandyish comic character, is heralded as the first major force in comic film. Linder's influence in this country is apparent in Mack Sennett's films and in the work of Charlie Chaplin. Comedy begins in this country with the world of Mack Sennett's Keystone films, a world of confusion and chaos, where machines ran wild and attacked the living, and where the living often became machines. It was a world of motion and action, of fights and chases

comedy Albert Finney plays Tom and Susannah York plays Sophia in Tony Richardson's Academy Award–winning film version of Henry Fielding's classic novel *Tom Jones* (1963).

■ ■ ■

at dizzying speeds—a world in which space and time became distorted, people became victimized by the physical world and their own physical natures, and human nature was reduced to ridiculous sight gags. It was the arrival of the great comic heroes of the silent period—Charlie Chaplin, Buster Keaton, Harry Langdon, and Harold Lloyd—that developed the comic style and created "The Golden Age of Comedy." To the chaos and confusion of the comic world was added, in counterpoint, the heroic clown. Slapstick and mime now functioned to draw out both the ridiculous and the human in a single figure. All of these figures used their bodies as physical instruments, showing the mechanical and comic in human action and behavior, but also interjecting both a befuddled and triumphant human soul.

With the advent of sound, comedy changed considerably. There were still the marvelous sight gags, the excruciating and hilarious confusion between man and reality in the films of Laurel and Hardy; but now comic performers were as aggressive and ridiculous in speech as earlier comics had been in action. The Marx brothers and W. C. Fields survived in a pretentious and silly world through a marvelous sense of the ridiculous in themselves and others, and through their own zany logic and verbal assaults. Another kind of comedy developed during the 1930s, one closer to the comedies of the theater by being more realistic, socially aware, dramatically structured, and intellectual. Such comedies, depending on dialogue for sophisticated and witty humor, were, in a sense, a compliment to movie audiences, who had become mature. These films included the slightly dry, genteel humor of the Thin Man series; the amorality and wit of Lubitsch's polished and sophisticated world, especially evident in *Trouble in Paradise* (1932); and the "screwball" comedies, which featured irresponsible, sometimes irrational behavior and a witty, energetic battle of the sexes between genuinely likable figures in films such as Frank Capra's *It Happened One Night* (1934) and Howard Hawks's *Bringing Up Baby* (1938). Although the 1940s began auspiciously with Cukor's *The Philadelphia Story*, the decade of the war years and the beginning of the Cold War seemed less receptive to witty comedy and more prone to outright farce or sentimentality. Still funny and intelligent, however, were the comedies of Preston Sturges.

A series of fine, dry, and witty comedies were produced in England, especially at the Ealing Studios, starting in 1949 with Robert Hamer's *Kind Hearts and Coronets,* which featured Alec Guinness in multiple roles. Guinness was also to work at the studio in such popular and very funny works as Alexander Mackendrick's *The Man in the White Suit* (1951) and Charles Crichton's *The Lavender Hill Mob* (1951). Also notable were a series of films with the remarkably versatile Peter Sellers, starting with Jack Arnold's *The Mouse That Roared* (featuring Sellers in multiple roles) and John Boulting's *I'm All Right Jack,* both in 1959. Not too far ahead in England was Tony Richardson's tour-de-force adaptation of Henry Fielding's classic novel *Tom Jones* (1963), which won an Academy Award in the United States as best movie of the year. One should also note the fine films made in France by Jacques Tati, who resurrected the art of mime and physical humor in such features as *Mr. Hulot's Holiday* (1953) and *Mon Oncle* (1958).

During the late 1950s and early 1960s, a series of Doris Day films in the United States, the most popular of which was *Pillow Talk* (1959; dir. Michael Gordon), took the wit and bite out of sex. Some comedies of the same period, however, seem sexually aware and realistic, if somewhat less witty and intellectual than the social comedies of the 1930s. *Some Like It Hot* (1959). which combined farce and verbal humor with a new sexual drive, and the somewhat darker *The Apartment* (1960), both directed by Billy Wilder, are among the best of these sexual comedies. The 1950s also gave rise to the films of Jerry Lewis, whose work at first seemed an energetic return to old-fashioned farce, but ultimately declined into artistic confusion.

It is difficult to sum up comedy during the recent decades. The end of the studio and star systems that allowed the development of comic talents, the juvenilization of the audience, and the influence of television have resulted in comic films that are more painful than funny. On the positive side were the farces and outrageous humor of Mel Brooks (his *The Producers* [1967] has become a cult classic) and the neurotic sensibility of Woody Allen. Allen managed to create his own subgenre, a mixture of satire, farce, and verbal wit in a contemporary post-Freudian and Marshall McLuhan world (his best film remains the Academy Award–winning *Annie Hall* [1977]). Neither has continued to have the same success, but Allen's films still remain very watchable. Also significant have been such satiric comedies as Kubrick's 1963 film, *Doctor Strangelove* (actually made in Great Britain), and Mike Nichols's *The Graduate* (1967), films with a provocative visual dimension and with low-keyed, absurd, and frightfully funny dialogue. Hal Ashby's *Harold and Maude* (1971) featured satire equally serious, but lighter in touch. In general, however, comedy in the United States has become less deft and subtle, alternating between the sit-com one-liners of Neil Simon and the schoolboy vulgarity of such films as *National Lampoon's Animal House* (1978; dir. John Landis). Great Britain, though, has given us the very uneven but sometimes very funny lunacy of the Monty Python group (their most inspired work remains the replays of their old television series). *See* **farce, genre,** *and* **slapstick.**

■ **cometing** Tiny spots of light on the film caused in the processing bath by metallic pollution.

■ **coming attractions** *See* **preview** *(1).*

■ **commentary** An explanation, normally delivered by an off-camera voice, concerning the action and characters appearing on the screen. The commentator generally speaks as an unbiased authority on the subject of the film. *See* **voice-over.**

■ **commentative sound** Sound that does not derive from any action or conversation on the screen, but in some manner comments on what is being seen: for example, spoken commentary or programmatic music.

■ **commercial distribution** The release of a film by a distributor to the mass market. The term generally designates that the film will play at a large number of theaters throughout the country at the same time and will be heavily advertised. *See* **distribution.**

■ **commissary** The studio restaurant; a place on the lot where all those involved in the making of films have their meals and which, as a result, has been glamorized in the public mind.

■ **compilation cuts** A series of cuts or shots unrelated by a continuous action or narration, but instead used in total to create the impression of a place, period of time, or a character's reactions to an event or memory of past events.

■ **compilation film** A film, generally a documentary, made by combining shots or scenes from other films and assembling them in such a way that they achieve new significance from their present context. The term was first used by Jey Leyda in *Films Beget Films* (1964). Such films often deal with past political, social, and historical events. Drawn from old newsreels, propaganda films, and official archival footage, they are often com-

piled from a specific perspective. Carol Reed and Garson Kanin's *The True Glory* (1945), a film about World War II, was a highly praised work of this type, and Frédéric Rossif's *Mourir à Madrid (To Die in Madrid,* 1962). a film about the Spanish Civil War, achieved a good deal of acclaim and popularity.

■ **complementary angles** Shots of different subjects, generally within the same scene, that are photographed with similar camera angles so that they will match together in editing. The technique normally implies the subjects' spatial proximity.

■ **complementary colors** (1) Colors opposite to the primary colors on the color wheel. When each primary color is subtracted from white, its complementary is left (when red is subtracted, a blue-green color called cyan remains; when green is removed, the result is a red-blue mixture called magenta; and the subtraction of blue leaves a combination of green and red, which forms yellow). When all three complementary colors are added together in equal amounts, a near-black or gray results. Complementary colors are used in subtractive color processes. Also called subtractive colors. (2) Both the primary color and its opposite when they are seen as related or completing each other. *See* **color film** *(2) and* **subtractive process.**

■ **complementary mattes** Although the term is most often used for the male and female mattes in the creation of composite images, especially in the traveling-matte process, it is also used in reference to any two mattes that work in conjunction in the creation of such an image. *See* **traveling-matte process.**

■ **complementary two-shots** A series of two shots alternately favoring each of two speakers. The technique is frequently employed for conversation.

■ **completion bond, completion guarantee** A contractual guarantee for those financing a film that the film will be completed by a specific time and for a specified cost. Sometimes, certain artistic requirements are included. It is normal in such an agreement to include a contingency, generally of 10 percent, to allow for cost overruns as well as an allowance for the guarantor, the party that issues the bond, to take over the production after a certain date and under certain circumstances. Such agreements were unnecessary in the days of the studio system, but now filmmakers must seek funding from banks, investors, and distributors. Such financial sources require, certainly for any film with a budget over several million dollars, that their funds should be protected against the film not being completed in a timely and professional manner. It is the responsibility of the guarantor to guarantee a return of the financing under such specified conditions. For this service, the guarantor receives a fee of anywhere from 1.5 to 6 percent of the budget.

■ **completion services** The various activities that finish a film after it has been shot—for example, processing, editing, sound mixing.

■ **component** An individual and complete image in computer graphics. Such an image may itself be composed of smaller elements (called macros) stored in the computer's memory (e.g., a figure composed of parts of the body already stored). *See* **computer animation.**

■ **composer** (1) The individual who creates original background music for a film. Sometimes composers may also adapt classical music and folk or popular tunes in a new way. (2) The individual who writes the music for songs that appear in a film. *See* **music.**

■ **composite** (1) Any film with both picture and sound in synchronization: e.g., a composite print or a composite master. (2) Any image created by the combination of two or more components from separate shots. Live action, animation, miniatures, and paintings of scenery can be combined in a number of ways—for example, with stationary mattes, front or rear projection, the blue-screen process, aerial-image photography, and now, especially, digital compositing. In Ridley Scott's *Blade Runner* (1982), ninety different composite-effects shots were achieved, some with as many as forty separate elements. The technique is sometimes referred to as "compositing" or "image compositing." *See* **aerial-image photography, blue-screen process, digital composite, front projection, matte** *(2),* **rear projection,** *and* **traveling-matte process.**

■ **composite film** A full-length film made up of two or more distinct stories. Rossellini's neorealist film *Paisan* (1946) is a celebrated example of this type of film. Also called a collective story film.

■ **composite master** A fine-grain print with both image and sound used for creating the dupe negative from which release prints are made.

■ **composite negative, composite dupe negative** The final negative with both picture and sound from which release prints are made. *See* **dupe.**

■ **composite print** A print with both picture and sound in synchronization. Sometimes called a married print.

■ **composite track, comp track, composite dub track, composite mix, comp mix** The final mix that includes all the sound (dialogue, music, sound effects) and that will join with the image to form the composite print. *See* **mix.**

■ **composite workstation** *See* **digital composite.**

■ **compositing, image compositing** *See* **composite** *(2).*

■ **composition** The arrangement of all the elements within a scene, including setting, props, lighting, characters, and movement. The frame of each particular shot must be seen both as a separate compositional unit and in the context of surrounding shots. Composition influences the way viewers read the screen, the meaning and significance they derive from each image, their emotional response to the characters and action, and their general interest throughout the film. Like a painting, the frame's composition must be seen in terms of masses, shapes, balance, lines, rhythm, color, texture, light and dark. Like a painting, the frame's composition must overcome its flat two-dimensionality and achieve an illusion of depth—the viewer's attention must be guided by the treatment of foreground, middle ground, and background. Unlike a painting, though, film offers an image constantly in change—there is movement within the individual shot and movement from shot to shot. Movement of characters and camera can increase the sense of depth and draw the viewer into the picture. The spatial composition of the frame is also crucial in directing our attention to more significant shapes or masses: the interplay of light and dark highlights and hides; the arrangement of elements creates dominating rhythmic lines that form pervasive designs, such as triangles or circles, which convey relationships and concepts. A film such as Jacques Rivette's *La Religieuse (The Nun;* 1965) can be analyzed in terms of its compositional form, the conveyance of meaning and emotion in terms of the spatial arrangement, lighting, texture, and movement of individual shots, and in the way composition interacts with composition. *See* **mise-en-scène.**

composition Anna Karina is confined to the closed spaces of the convent in Jacques Rivette's *La Religieuse* (1965).

■ ■ ■

▪ **compound move** (1) A corresponding movement of both the subject and the camera, as in a tracking shot of a character running down the street. (2) A corresponding movement of both the lens and camera, as in the famous combination zoom-in and backward dolly of the camera to suggest James Stewart's acrophobia in Alfred Hitchcock's *Vertigo* (1958).

▪ **compound table** The table of an animation stand that allows multiple arrangements and movements of the cels for photographing. *See* **animation stand.**

▪ **compression** (1) *See* **compressor.** (2) In digital technology, storing motion-picture or video information so that only the changing data and not that repeated from frame to frame are kept. The computer is able to decode the data and restore the entire image.

▪ **compression board** A device in a computer that compresses the vast amount of information available in an image for efficient digital storage. Only the moving elements and not the static setting in a motion picture need to be recorded from frame to frame; nor need one of the two interlaced fields in a video frame be digitized. Such compression is one of the ways of dealing with the vast amount of memory needed by the computer to store such images for nonlinear editing of motion pictures. *See* **digital, editing, nonlinear editing,** *and* **video editing system.**

▪ **compressor, volume compressor** A device for reducing the amplitude of sound at the time of recording or rerecording. A compressor can act as a limiter, cutting off peak areas of volume, but is more likely to be used to diminish lower levels or the entire range of sound for a more even or subtle diminishment and for a compressed volume range.

▪ **compsy** *See* **computerized multiplane system.**

▪ **computer animation, computer generated imagery (CGI), digital scene simulation (DSS), computer graphics, computer image processing** Using the computer is less expensive, faster, and more versatile than traditional methods of animation for film. Computer animation for film normally begins when objects—either two-dimensional drawings, images on film, or the three-dimensional objects themselves—are scanned into the computer's memory by means of a digital code (the computer is sometimes called a digitizer and the process digitizing). Individual images may themselves be conceived from scratch by means of a software program or drawn directly into the computer via a digitizing table and pen or some such instrument. "Modeling" begins with the use of "primitives," i.e., cubes, sphere, or cones, that are manipulated in shape and form as well as assembled together. "Texture mapping" imposes a two-dimensional surface over a three-dimensional object or frame. "Image processing" can enhance or alter image elements. Data for

a scene, including information for perspective, dimensionality, lighting, and camera movement, are also fed into the computer. "Rendering" then transforms the digital information into images. A series of images can be placed rapidly on videotape or film by means of an output device—i.e., a CRT (cathode-ray tube), lasers, or CCDs (charge-couple device). Vector graphics are composed of black-and-white lines formed between programmed coordinates for wire-frame animation—color can later be added to the forms. Raster graphics are made of pixels (for "picture elements")—that is, tiny dots of color activated by electronic line scans called rasters—which create images of striking color. Computer images are now of sufficiently high resolution and quality that they can be recorded directly on film for inclusion in a live-action motion picture.

Computer imagery was first used by Bell Labs in 1963 for designing the motion and positioning of a communication satellite. Stan Vanderbeek and John Whitney used computer animation in some abstract films back in the 1960s and 1970s. Computer graphics increased sufficiently in quality and sophistication to be incorporated with great effect in the Disney production *Tron* (1982; dir. Steven Lisberger) and in *Star Trek II* (1982; dir. Nicholas Meyer). While the graphics of *Tron* were sufficient for the film's semirealistic computer and video world, the technology then advanced to make such images sufficiently realistic to simulate actual backgrounds for live action and even to create digitally objects and figures. Certainly the twenty-five minutes of computer graphics in *The Last Starfighter* (1984; dir. Nick Castle), made with the Cray X-MP computer by Digital Productions, created images in space of greater resolution and solidarity than those in *Tron*. A new development used for the Glass Man sequence in *Young Sherlock Holmes* (1985; dir. Barry Levinson) was a laser scanner for placing the electronic image directly on film and creating an image of higher resolution than the traditional method of photographing the image off the cathode-ray tube—the stained-glass knight is also considered to be the first animated figure totally derived from the computer. Computer animation in the late 1980s and early 1990s advanced even further with James Cameron's *The Abyss* in 1989 (featuring the first three-dimensional computer-generated image in the pseudopod), *Terminator 2* (1991; dir. James Cameron), and *The Lawnmower Man* (1992; dir. Brett Leonard), certainly none dramatic masterpieces but all with some wonderful computer-generated imagery undreamed of for earlier films. For *Terminator 2,* Industrial Light and Magic considerably advanced the technique of morphing, through which a live character could undergo a series of continuous and fluid metamorphoses in human and nonhuman shapes. Notable also is the six and one-half minutes of computer-generated dinosaurs in *Jurassic Park* (1993; dir. Steven Spielberg) and the first computer-generated lead and talking figure in *Casper* (1993; dir. Brad Silberling).

computer animation The computer and video world of *Tron* (1982; dir. Steven Lisberger)

■ ■ ■

In cartoon animation, computers can color drawings, create backgrounds, and even do in-between images after the animator scans and programs in the key drawings. A programmed three-dimensional action can itself be printed onto an animation cell as a two-dimensional cartoon image. For *Who Framed Roger Rabbit* (1988; dir. Robert Zemeckis), computer-generated settings and forms were used with actual settings and characters, creating a world that integrates what appears to be traditional hand-drawn cartoon imagery into our everyday world. *Beauty and the Beast* (1991; dir. Gary Trousdale and Kirk Wise) and *Aladdin* (1992; dir. John Musker and Ron Clements) have recently returned Disney Studios to its premier status as the maker of animated features, though other major studios are now developing their own computer-animation divisions. The recently made *Hunchback of Notre Dame* (1996; dir. Gary Trousdale and Kirk Wise) features some of the most spectacular animation and computer-generated imagery yet to appear on the screen. Pixar Animation Studios, in conjunction with the Walt Disney Company, has opened up a new page in digital imagery and cartoon animation with John Lasseter's *Toy Story* (1995) by making the first film in which all the images are created entirely with computers. The question, certainly valid in light of other recent films with computerized special effects, is whether this technology will continue the dehumanization of motion pictures or, instead, expand our imaginations and sensibilities. *See* **animation.**

■ **computer-assisted animation** (1) Animation for which the artist's key drawings are scanned into the computer, and software programs are then employed to

create the in-between pictures. Also referred to as computer interpolation. (2) Animation for which the outlines of drawings are scanned into the computer, and a software program then fills them in with color. *See* **animation.**

■ **computer-based music, computer music** *See* **digital sound.**

■ **computer enhancement** *See* **image enhancement.**

■ **computer film** (1) Experimental films, generally abstract in nature, made with a computer. Such films first achieved attention in the 1960s, especially such works by Stan Vanderbeek as *Computer Art (number one)* in 1966 and by John Whitney as *Permutations* in 1968. *See* **animation, avant-garde cinema,** *and* **computer animation.**

■ **computer interpolation** In computer graphics, the technique of having the computer itself create all the in-between images from the animator's key drawings. Also referred to as computer-assisted animation. *See* **animation** *and* **computer animation.**

■ **computerized multiplane system (COMPSY)** A motion-control animation apparatus devised by Douglas Trumbull for *Star Trek: The Motion Picture* (1979; dir. Robert Wise). Like the Multiplane system developed by Walt Disney Productions, COMPSY created images in depth and with perspective by shooting through a series of planes, but the camera also moved horizontally on tracks and was controlled by a computer so that it could make any number of exactly timed passes and a variety of elaborate moves. The system was also used with great effect for Ridley Scott's *Blade Runner* (1982). *See* **motion control** *and* **multiplane.**

■ **concave lens, plano-concave lens** A lens with one surface curved and receding like the interior of a circle. A biconcave or concavo-concave lens has both sides curved and receding in the center. A concavo-convex has one side receding and the other convex or curving outward in the center, with the concave side having the greater curvature. A convexo-concave side is similar with the convex side having the greater curvature. *See* **convex lens.**

■ **concentric magazine** *See* **coaxial magazine.**

■ **concept** The basic idea for a film: a general theme, situation, or story line, sometimes with specific stars in mind, that is sufficiently provocative and financially promising to lead to the next stage of development, which is likely to be the treatment, but can even be negotiations with personnel.

■ **concert film** A film that records a live musical performance before a public audience. In commercial cinema, the form has largely been relegated to such rock documentaries as Michael Wadleigh's *Woodstock* (1970), which is as much a social commentary on its time as a musical performance, and Jonathan Demme's *Stop Making Sense* (1984), a purer record of a concert by the Talking Heads, which is also a dazzling display of moviemaking. *See* **rock documentary.**

■ **concession** The area in the motion-picture house or complex that sells refreshments, notably popcorn and soft drinks. Revenue from such concessions for the exhibitor is quite significant, and cut-rate film houses depend on such sales for the major portion of their profits.

■ **condenser lens** A lens that gathers and concentrates light rays from a wide source, thus increasing illumination. Such lenses are employed in projectors.

■ **condenser microphone, electro-static microphone** A microphone in which the vibrations of a diaphragm in relation to a fixed plate cause a variation in voltage that is the source of the amplified sound. *See* **microphone.**

■ **cone** A cone-shaped lamp that sends light rays in a wide beam to create a general, soft light.

■ **conflict** The struggle between two forces in a narrative that is frequently the motivating factor in action and plot. The first part of the work often deals with the establishment and definition of the conflict, the second with its development and intensification, and the third with its climax and resolution. Conflict may arise in a number of ways: (1) between one person and another; (2) between one person and a group; (3) between two groups; (4) between an individual or a group and external natural forces; or (5) between conflicting elements in an individual psyche (such a conflict is then psychological, and the drama emphasizes the struggle and resolution within a character). Several of these elements may be combined: for example, in Robert Redford's *Ordinary People* (1980), conflicts within the characters and between them motivate the drama. When conflicts remain unresolved or the main character has been defeated in his struggle, either internally (as in Ingmar Bergman's *Winter Light* [1962]) or externally (as in Vittorio de Sica's *The Bicycle Thief* [1948]), the work is tragic in nature.

■ **conformer** *See* **conforming** (*1*).

■ **conforming** (1) The process of matching the original film to the workprint, frame by frame, normally done by matching the edge numbers on both films. When the editing has been done on video or digitally, the negative is matched to a negative cut list. This job is done in the laboratory by someone called a conformer, negative cutter, or negative matcher. *See* **workprint.** (2) In checkerboard cutting with 16mm film, properly alternating frames between two rolls of film. *See* **checkerboard cutting.** (3) Lengthening, shortening, and synchronizing sound tracks to conform to the picture track. (4) Making the edit master videotape to follow a rough cut or the EDL (edit-decision list). In modern editing systems, the edit master video can be made automatically from the EDL. *See* **edit-decision list.**

■ **conglomerates** Large companies that own film studios as one of many holdings. Such companies have forced studios to diversify their activities and have brought a degree of financial stability, though often at some loss of artistic quality. Gulf and Western Industries, for example, purchased Paramount in 1966, changed its name to Paramount Communications in 1989, and was itself brought out by Viacom in 1994. *See* **studio system.**

■ **connotation** In literary study, the term refers to the suggestive or associative quality of a word as opposed to its explicit or denotative meaning. In film, the term can be applied to the words of dialogue, the names of characters or places, or the title of the motion picture; it can also be applied to the suggestive quality of images (e.g., a body of still water might connote peace and stability). Often an image acquires connotation from its place in the plot or simply from the genre in which it appears (e.g., a forest in a horror film connotes danger and violence). The shot itself, as well as denoting what is happening, connotes a wide range of suggestions by its technique (e.g., the high-angle shot of a character suggests, as well as makes us feel, his vulnerability, weakness, fear, or diminished social importance).

■ **consecutive action** Action of a film in the order that it is shot, which is not necessarily its chronological order or the order in which it will appear in the film. It is often more economical and expedient to shoot scenes out of order to take advantage of a star's time or a single location.

■ **consent and release** A contractual agreement signed by an individual and production company, allowing the company to use the individual as a real person in the motion picture made for either theatrical release or directly for television. The document gives the individual's consent and releases the production company from specific obligations to the person in the portrayal. Made-for-TV movies are now frequently based on events in the lives of real people, especially when they are sensational in nature.

■ **consent decrees** *See* **Paramount decrees.**

■ **console** (1) A desk, table, or board for monitoring and controlling sound recording. *See* **mixer.** (2) A flatbed editing machine. *See* **flat-bed editing machine.** (3) A Moviola with a picture head and two sound heads. *See* **Moviola.**

■ **construction coordinator, construction manager, construction foreman** The person in charge of the construction of sets. He or she generally works under the art director and is in charge of a large crew.

■ **construction crew** The group of people who, working under a construction manager or foreman, are responsible for the building of sets.

■ **contact printer** *See* **contact printing.**

■ **contact printing** Making a print by running the negative and positive together, with their emulsions touching, in front of the aperture where a light transfers the image from the first onto the second. In continuous contact printers both films move rapidly past the aperture, and the negative can move back and forth or be looped for making a large number of release prints. Intermittent (or step) contact printers transfer one image at a time and are generally used where perfect registration is needed (e.g., in making composite images through matting techniques). *See* **printer.**

■ **content curve** The period of time needed for an audience to acquire the important information of a shot. Proper cutting should be at the peak of the curve.

■ **contingent compensation** Future payment after a job is completed, normally based on certain conditions— e.g., net profits for the writer of a screenplay or additional payment to him or her when the film generates a sequel or television production. *See* **backend.**

■ **continuing zoom** A zoom shot in which the subject consistently increases in size, gradually filling the frame and then increasing beyond the frame so that only a portion of it fills the field of vision.

■ **continuity** (1) The continuous flow of a film, where shot follows shot and scene follows scene in an understandable and smooth way. An effective continuity makes us unaware of the cutting as we watch the film, of the way in which the camera and cutting control our responses. Effective continuity is dependent upon the proper matching of details, movement, and dialogue from shot to shot, and the logical and explicit development of plot from scene to scene. (2) A shooting script with all the visual and sound information specified in detail: dialogue, sound effects, shots, and even basic editing are worked out. (3) The continuity girl or clerk (see below).

■ **continuity breakdown** A listing of all the technical information for a day's shooting including scene numbers, cast, equipment, and props.

■ **continuity cutting** Editing that keeps the film moving in a straightforward, logical, and smooth way, uses time and space coherently, and develops narrative in a linear manner. The cutting is unobtrusive, with characters and objects continuing from shot to shot largely through match cuts, and scene following scene without any sudden breaks or jumps.

■ **continuity girl, continuity clerk, script clerk, script girl, script supervisor** The person responsible for maintaining continuity by keeping a record of the particulars for each completed shot. The number and duration of each take as well as dialogue, direction of movement, characters' positions, props, and furniture are all recorded in order to assure that the next shot will follow exactly, even if it should be photographed some time later. These continuity sheets also assist the editor. The position traditionally has been held by a woman.

■ **continuity notes, continuity sheets, take sheets** The log kept by the script or continuity clerk that records information concerning each take—its number, beginning and end, duration, properties, camera movement and position, the placement of characters, movement within the shot, and dialogue. *See* **continuity girl.**

■ **continuity sketches** (1) Drawings that help the production designer create the sets and also are the basis for illustrations in a shooting script. (2) Drawings of individual shots in the shooting script that assist the director. *See* **storyboard.**

■ **continuous action** Uninterrupted action within a scene, although photographed from different distances, angles, or points of view in a series of shots.

■ **continuous drive** The mechanism that continuously feeds the film from the magazine into the camera body and, after the film's intermittent movement, back into the magazine. *See* **camera.**

■ **continuous-motion prism** *See* **prism shutter.**

■ **continuous printer** A film printer in which both negative and positive run without any intermittent pauses. Continuous contact printers, where emulsions of both films are in contact as they pass the aperture, are employed for making rush and release prints. Continuous optical printers, where individual frames are projected through a lens onto the fresh film in a camera, are used to reduce motion pictures from one gauge to another. *See* **printer.**

■ **contract film** A film for which all finances have been negotiated with and underwritten by a specific studio, organization, or group.

■ **contract player** (1) An actor under contract to a particular studio. (2) An actor working under contract in a specific production and not for a regular salary.

■ **contrapuntal sound** Sound in counterpoint to the image on the screen that changes the viewer's initial perception of the image. For example, martial music might be played while people happily dance to suggest the coming war and their false hopes.

■ **contrast** The relative difference between the maximum and minimum points of light in the image. Contrast is not only determined by the relation between extremities, but also by the intermediate gray tonal scale between light and dark: the image is considered of high contrast with little gradation between the two poles and of low contrast if there is considerable gradation. A flat image has little distance between high and low points and little gradation. Contrast in the image is the result of a number of variables: (1) the reflective surface of objects; (2) lighting; (3) film stock; and (4) processing. All of these variables can be predetermined and controlled.

■ **contrast filter** Filters largely for black-and-white film that are used to separate out two colors that record with the same gray tonality. A red filter, for example, will filter out its complementary color, green, while passing its own color so that red in the image will appear brighter than green. Such filters are also used for darkening the sky and penetrating haze.

■ **contrast glass, contrast viewing glass, contrast viewing filter** An eyepiece with a dark glass or filter that is used for judging the contrast range of a scene before shooting.

■ **contrast range** The capacity of film to reproduce an image in relation to the tonal scale between light and dark. Film that is able to produce an image with both extremes and few intermediate grays is considered high contrast; film with a wide range of intermediate grays is low contrast. The range of the film's capability for contrast and the contrast of the developed image is determined by the gamma value.

■ **contrast ratio** The ratio of the highly lighted portion of the set to the less lighted—normally, the ratio of the key plus fill lights to the fill light alone. A 2:1 ratio, with a difference of a single stop on the camera, is considered standard—such a ratio seems to offer even and bright illumination with sufficient modeling. *See* **lighting.**

■ **contrasty** An image with a large degree of extreme light and dark and with minimal intermediate grays.

■ **control signal, control track** *See* **sync-pulse system.**

■ **control strip** *See* **sensitometric strip** *and* **step wedge.**

■ **convention** A widely accepted element or technique in any art form that the reader or viewer accepts without judging its artificiality or unreality. Film genres are popular because of their conventional character types and plot elements, even though they may use them in a new way. For example, characters such as the independent, fast-shooting hero, the evil owner of the gambling casino, and the school teacher heroine appear repeatedly in Westerns, as do the chase scenes and shootouts. Cinematic techniques are employed over and over: for example, the viewer accepts the convention of seeing each scene from a number of different angles even though in reality he or she would see it from the same position.

■ **convergence** The point at which the two views, one for the left eye and one for the right, converge in stereoscopy (3-D motion pictures)—the plane of convergence is called the stereo window, which should normally be at the screen or slightly behind it. Objects in front of the plane of convergence will appear to be in front of the screen and objects behind will appear to be to the rear of the screen. *See* **3-D.**

■ **convergence filter** *See* **color-conversion filter.**

■ **conversion filter selector** A slide rule with two scales that allows a desired Kelvin temperature to be set opposite to the actual temperature of a source light to find the mired shift value. On the other side of the slide rule the proper filter is designated for the mired shift value. *See* **mired.**

■ **convex lens, plano-convex lens** A lens with one surface curved outwards, like the outside of a circle. A biconvex or convexo-convex lens has both sides curved outward, while a convexo-concave has one side curved outward and the other side curved inward, with the convex side having the greater curvature. A concavo-convex lens is similar, with the concave side having the greater curvature. *See* **concave lens.**

■ **cookie, cuke, cukaloris, cookaloris** A sheet of opaque material held in a frame that either has holes cut out so that some designated pattern can be projected onto a surface when the sheet is held in front of a light, or has some pattern of perforations which allows light to pass through in a slightly mottled or shadowed way in order to break up the monotony of a flat surface.

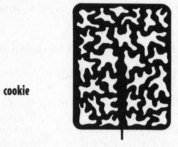

cookie

■ **cooking** Overdeveloping a film by increasing the temperature or duration of developing in order to compensate for insufficient lighting. *See* **overdevelopment.**

■ **cool image** A picture with predominantly blue tones as opposed to one with predominantly red or yellow tones, which is considered warm.

■ **coordinates** The intersecting points of horizontal and vertical lines in a grid used to place the points on a drawing board and pixels on a screen for a computer image. The joining of two such points on the grid creates a line in the drawing. X-coordinates are figured along the horizontal axis and Y-coordinates along the vertical, with the bottom left corner designated as zero. Computer animation uses two sets of coordinates, one for the entire image and the other for the individual models. *See* **computer animation.**

■ **co-production** (1) A film made by two production companies. The high cost of film production recently has generated deals between separate studios. (2) A film made jointly by filmmakers in two countries, generally to share expenses, increase audiences, and save on costs through cheaper labor or a better tax situation in one of the countries.

■ **copter mount** A camera mount for aerial shots from a helicopter that allows shooting free from the vibrations of the helicopter.

■ **copyright** The legal and exclusive right of any artist or group of individuals to control the exhibition and duplication of a literary, musical, cinematic, or any other artistic work for a limited period of time. Films are generally copyrighted under the name of the producers alone, though parts of the film, such as songs, may be separately copyrighted by the individual creator. In this country, films must be registered with the Copyright Office of the Library of Congress. Since 1978, the copyright for a motion picture made by a corporation in this country is for a seventy-five-year period from the time the film is fixed, reproducible, and offered for sale, lease, or rental—so long as it bears a notice of copyright. The copyright for a film made by an individual since that year is life plus 50 years (in the case of joint works, the life of the surviving individual plus 50 years).

■ **cording** Attaching a piece of cord or tape to the perforations at the beginning and end of a shot or scene for easy location during editing or printing.

■ **cordless sync, cableless sync** Any of the methods employed in double-system sound recording for synchronizing camera and tape recorder without the use of a sync-pulse cable—for example, a crystal sync system. *See* **synchronization** *(3).*

■ **core** A plastic hub of two or three inches in diameter on which film is stored. Raw stock is generally kept on cores to avoid abrasions caused when film is unevenly wound on reels. Short pieces of film are also wound on cores during editing.

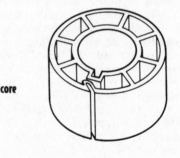

core

■ **cosine law** When illumination strikes a surface its brightness will decrease in proportion to the cosine of the light source's angle of incidence—in other words, as the light hits the surface at more of an angle, the brightness of the surface will decrease. The cosine of a right triangle is the ratio of the side adjacent to a given angle to the hypotenuse.

■ **cosmetician** *See* **makeup artist.**

■ **cost recovery** *See* **amortization.**

■ **costs** *See* **above-the-line costs, below-the-line costs,** *and* **negative cost.**

■ **costs off the top deal** A distribution agreement whereby the costs of prints and advertising are subtracted from the proceeds, which are then split by the distributor and producer. Such an arrangement is more common for the release of foreign or independent films. *See* **distribution.**

■ **costume designer** The person who designs the clothing worn by the characters in a film, whether the period of the film is past, present, or future, and oversees their production and final suitability for performers. The costume designer works in coordination with the director, art director, and later with the director of photography.

■ **costume drama, costume film** A film set in some historical period that features characters dressed in colorful and sometimes authentic costumes. Ernst Lubitsch made a number of these films in Germany during the early part of his career (e.g., *Madame du Barry* [1919]).

■ **costumer** *See* **wardrobe master.**

■ **counter** *See* **footage counter.**

■ **counterkey** A luminaire placed opposite the key light. *See* **key light.**

■ **counter matte, complementary matte** The matte with opaque and clear areas opposite to those on another matte and used in complement with it for creating a composite image during matting procedures. The counter matte blocks out the portion of the second image that corresponds with the portion of the first image that the first matte has already allowed to be printed. *See* **matte** *(2) and* **traveling-matte process.**

■ **coupler, dye coupler** Chemicals in color film that during development form color images of the subject. In the normally used tripack film, each of the three layers has certain couplers that respond to one of the primary colors. *See* **color film** *(2).*

■ **courtroom drama** Not actually a film genre, but certainly frequent enough to seem a type of subgenre, films dealing largely or significantly with trials have become a staple in cinema. Sometimes these films have been closely related to the detective film, with the lawyer playing the role of the investigator and trying, in and out of court, to clear his or her client and find the true culprit—e.g., in films such as Hitchcock's *The Paradine Case* (1948) and Billy Wilder's *Witness for the Prosecution* (1957), where both defendants turn out, however, to be guilty. On occasion, such films have stir-

ringly depicted the virtues of the judicial system by proving supposedly guilty individuals innocent, as in Elia Kazan's *Boomerang* (1947) and Sidney Lumet's *Twelve Angry Men* (1957). Courtroom dramas have been the means for exploring a host of interesting characters, including both defendants and the defense lawyers themselves, as in George Cukor's *Adam's Rib* (1949) and Otto Preminger's *Anatomy of a Murder* (1959). Trials have allowed a number of social issues to be aired in a moving and educational way, as in Robert Mulligan's *To Kill a Mockingbird* (1962) and Jonathan Demme's *Philadelphia* (1993). One should also mention such court-martial films as Edward Dmytryk's *The Caine Mutiny* (1954) and Norman Jewison's *A Soldier's Story* (1984). The list is endless, and we are not even discussing those films in which a courtroom scene brings a larger drama to a conclusion. Trials are undoubtedly a metaphor for the human condition, a way of dealing with conflicts and struggles in a succinct and impactful way. Trials are also a wonderful vehicle for exposing character and human motivations. But, most significantly, they are an immediate and powerful vehicle for creating drama and suspense.

■ **cove** A baseboard for a piece of background scenery that generally contains lights. Also called a ground row.

■ **coverage** (1) All of the individual shots, from the various distances and angles, that comprise the photographing of a particular scene. To cover a scene is to give it a wide variety of shots. Also referred to as cover. (2) A report, generally written by a reader, that summarizes and evaluates a script and makes a recommendation about whether the project should be further pursued.

■ **covering** The position of a performer when he or she blocks another performer from being seen by the camera or blocks his or her key light. The director will normally tell the culprit, "You're covering."

■ **covering power** The capacity of a lens to give sharp definition to the extremities of an image.

■ **cover set** An indoor set to be used for filming in case an outdoor set can not be used because of poor weather.

■ **cover shot, protection shot, insurance shot** (1) A shot photographed as a transition between two other shots should they not cut well together: for example, a long shot in a battle scene to bring together two separate actions. (2) A shot photographed in case an original shot is unsatisfying.

■ **cowboy shot** A term sometimes used for a shot of a performer from the knees up, derived from early cowboy movies that were obliged to show the characters' holsters and six-shooters. *See* **American shot.**

■ **crab, crab dolly** A small dolly or mobile platform that can move in any direction, including sideways and angularly like a crab, because of its four movable wheels. The camera is mounted on an arm, which can be moved up or down. The crab dolly is extremely useful for shooting in tight places.

■ **crabbing** Moving the camera sideways or in any angular direction.

■ **crab shot** A shot that shows lateral movement from the side of the scene. The camera itself may move in a lateral or angular direction like a crab.

■ **cracker smoke** A physical-effects smoke produced by vaporizing or cooking mineral or baby oil in a device called a "cracker barrel."

■ **cradle** A mount for large lenses that attaches to the camera to support the heavy weight. Also called a lens support or support mount.

■ **craft service** The group of personnel in a film production that performs such tasks as obtaining coffee and snacks for performers and crew and doing odd jobs.

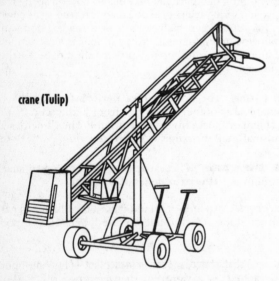

crane (Tulip)

■ **crane** A large camera trolley with a long projected arm or boom at the end of which is a platform. The platform holds the camera and seats for the camera operator, camera assistant, and sometimes the director. The crane can move forward or backward and the arm up or down (the arm can lift the camera twenty or more feet off the ground). Such machines are nor-

mally run electrically or hydraulically, though some are operated manually. They move silently and smoothly over a wide area and give enormous flexibility, movement, and coverage to shots. Smaller portable cranes, such as the Tulip, are excellent for shooting on location. The first crane was supposedly developed for the 1929 film *Broadway* (dir. Paul Fejos). Also called a cherry picker. *See* **boom** *(2)*.

■ **crane grip, crane operator** The individual responsible for running the crane on the set or on location. *See* **crane.**

■ **crane shot** A shot taken from a crane, generally when the camera moves as a result of the crane's mobility. Crane shots can follow an individual up a flight of stairs, track a character from a distance, pass over crowds of people and focus in on an individual, move over obstacles, move off from heights and into space, or give us a sudden aerial view of a scene.

■ **craning** Camera movement that results clearly from the movement of a crane (note the effective craning in the creation scene of Whale's *Bride of Frankenstein* [1935]), which gives us a dizzying and disturbing perspective on the macabre event.

■ **crash camera** A specially designed and manufactured camera for crash-camera photography. Such cameras are extremely durable and lightweight with the capacity of being easily mounted in closed-in areas. They have variable speeds and also can shoot in single-frame or time-lapse modes.

■ **crash zoom** A zoom shot that suddenly and rapidly zooms in on the subject. Such a shot, which may be used to jolt and shock the viewers, has almost become a cliché in second-rate adventure and horror films. *See* **zoom in** *and* **zoom shot.**

■ **crawl, crawl title, crawling title, creeper title, roller title, roll-up title** Titles, credits, or explanatory statements that first appear at the bottom of the frame and gradually move upward across the frame until they disappear at top.

■ **creative accounting** A pejorative term for the way in which studio/distributors do the books for a specific film so that such companies claim to be in the red while the film seems to be doing very well at the box office. Such creativity may be the result of including all kinds of overheads so that the studio can make up for films that lose money, but it may also be from the simple desire to earn more money. The victims of such a practice are people with net-profit agreements, since gross-profit participants take their cut before the magic breakeven figure is reached. *See* **breakeven, gross profit participant,** *and* **net profit participant.**

■ **Creative Artists Agency (CAA)** *See* **talent agency.**

■ **creative control** The final authority over the quality of a film; the right to make the various artistic decisions concerning story, editing, sound, and visuals. In the days of the Hollywood studios, such control normally belonged to the producer or the higher echelons of the company behind him. Today, producers or directors must negotiate for such rights and have them spelled out in their contracts. It is not unusual to see a film released with the final authority going to the producer, and some years later, if the film and director have maintained sufficient public interest, the release of the director's cut. *See* **director's cut.**

■ **creative department** A group of personnel working for a studio who are responsible for reading and evaluating various scripts and recommending which ones should be considered for production.

■ **creative geography** *See* **filmic space** *(2) and* **montage.**

■ **creature feature** *See* **monster movie.**

■ **creature shop** Any place that specializes in the manufacture and operation of models or puppets or specializes in makeup that contributes to the creation of movie monsters.

■ **credits, credit titles** The list of those responsible for the making of a film, including performers, director, producer, director of photography, art director, musical director, and all technicians; it appears at the beginning of a film (now often after an introductory scene or sequence), at the conclusion of a film, or both. *See* **closing credits** *and* **front credits.**

■ **crew** The group of people involved in some phase of the making of a film: for example, the camera crew.

■ **crew call** The call sheet for a production crew, notifying the various members of the time and place for shooting. *See* **call.**

■ **CRI, CRI print** *See* **color reversal intermediate.**

■ **cricket dolly** Made by Elemack in Italy, this collapsible unit is extremely versatile, capable of moving directionally or as a crab dolly into extremely narrow areas. The central column can rise to more than four feet by a single knob and is able to receive a camera on a jib arm. The unit operates either by electric motor or by hand pump and can be placed on tracks for movement over rough ground. *See* **spyder dolly.**

■ **criminal film** See **gangster film.**

■ **critic** *See* **film critic.**

■ **critical focus** (1) When a point in the subject being photographed appears as a point in the image recorded, it is in critical focus—all such points are in the plane of critical focus. (2) The distance between the aperture and any point in the subject when the point is in focus. Such a distance is designated in the focus band of the lens.

■ **critical fusion frequency** The point at which the individual frames on a film begin to fuse together so that the illusion of a stable, unitary world is created without any discontinuity or flicker. Such a point is determined by the sufficient number of frames per second (at least 16), the flicker frequency (i.e., 48 alternations between light and dark), and the intensity of illumination. *See* **persistence of vision** and **phi phenomenon** for two theories used to explain the individual's capacity to impose the illusion of movement and continuity on the film's frames.

■ **criticism** *See* **film criticism.**

■ **cropping** Cutting down the image either by masking it on the film or by employing a smaller projector aperture. Cropping has been used (1) to lower the height of an image for wide-screen projection; (2) to cut off the sides of a wide-screen image for general screenings; (3) to cut off the sides of a 35mm wide-screen film when reducing it to 16mm; and (4) to narrow the image for television transmission.

■ **cross-collateralization** (1) A practice in foreign distribution of films whereby profits in certain nations are offset by losses in others. The practice obviously favors the distributor. Producers would much prefer a practice called "territorial sales," which allows profits from individual nations to be earned regardless of losses elsewhere. (2) A practice whereby the profits of a producer's film released by a specific distributor are offset by losses from another or other films made by the same producer and released by the same distributor.

■ **cross-cutting** Cutting between two or more independent actions to show their relationship to one another. Frequently such actions are happening at the same time and their interplay builds suspense (an effect achieved as early as Porter's *The Great Train Robbery* in 1903) or creates an ironic counterpoint (a technique used with great power toward the end of Francis Ford Coppola's *The Godfather* in 1971, when the camera moves back and forth between the acts of violence plotted by the antihero and the baptism of his godson). Such cutting can also take place between actions of different times to show their relationship (for example, when Coppola's *The Godfather, Part Two* [1974] continuously cuts between scenes in the early life of the father and the present life of the son). The term "parallel cutting" or "parallel editing" is used synonymously, but sometimes is relegated to actions at different times, while crosscutting is then limited to actions occurring simultaneously. *See* **parallel cutting.**

■ **cross dissolve** *See* **dissolve.**

■ **cross fade** (1) A fade. (2) A type of transition where the first scene fades to a color or tone of gray instead of to black, and the new scene comes into view from the color or gray, with the two scenes sometimes overlapping. Ingmar Bergman uses red as his transitional color in *Cries and Whispers* (1972). (3) *See* **sound dissolve.**

■ **cross in, cross out** The first term refers to a performer moving into the scene from outside the frame; and the second to a performer leaving the scene and one side of the frame.

■ **crossing the line, crossing the imaginary line, crossing the proscenium** Moving the camera across an imaginary line between two or more performers so that the camera reverses its position. When shots are edited together from the different positions, the audience may lose its bearings and become confused. *See* **imaginary line.**

■ **cross light, cross lighting** Light illuminating the subject from both sides, generally in the area perpendicular to the lens axis. Also called side light.

■ **cross modulation** A sound distortion that can arise in the variable-area method of optical sound recording. This occurs because the sound-wave image extends beyond its point of focus when it is printed, resulting in low frequency components and especially a scraping noise with the sibilants. The problem can be avoided by adjusting film densities. *See* **variable-area sound track.**

■ **cross modulation test** A test to determine the proper printing densities for film that will allow minimal sound distortion in the variable-area method of optical sound recording. *See* **variable-area sound track.**

■ **crossover** The inadvertent overlap of two picture components in the creation of a composite image. In order to repair the image, some type of matting process is necessary. *See* **matte.**

■ **crossover film** A motion picture made with one specific audience in mind that manages to appeal to another or to a wider audience.

■ **cross-plot** A single-page summary that indicates the parameters and requirements of a day's shooting in terms of location, personnel, and equipment.

■ **crossplug, cross plug** (1) A trailer appearing at one theater to advertise a film in another theater. Also

called cross-plug trailer. *See* **trailer.** (2) Some type of business venture that also serves as an advertisement for a film—for example, the record of the sound track or book version of the story.

■ **cross process** A new process of creating muted and otherworldly images by developing reversal film to the negative stage and not to the normal positive stage. This process has been used in rock videos but is now making its way into motion pictures. The negative itself is unstable and must be specially treated. *See* **reversal film.**

■ **crowd shot, crowd scene** Any shot or scene that shows a great many people.

■ **CRT** *See* **cathode-ray tube.**

■ **crystal motor** A motor whose speed is accurately controlled (within .001 percent) by the vibrations of an oscillating crystal and that is frequently used in motion picture cameras and in crystal sync systems for synchronic camera and sound recording. *See* **servo motor.**

■ **crystal sync, crystal control, crystal cordless sync, crystal drive** A method for recording the image on film and the sound on magnetic tape in synchronization without connecting cables, but instead by means of oscillating crystals of the same frequency in both the camera drive and in the sync pulse generator attached to the magnetic tape recorder. This system can keep in sync a number of cameras and recorders simultaneously.

■ **C.S.** *See* **close shot.**

■ **C stand** *See* **century stand.**

■ **CU** *See* **close-up.**

■ **cue** (1) The signal given to an actor to begin a speech or action. Such a signal can be the end of a speech or action by another character in the scene, a cue light, or a sign from the director. (2) Any signal that marks the beginning or end of some speech, action, or process. (3) A tab, sticker, or bar code placed on a film during projection that signals an automation system to close or open curtains, stop the projector, start theater music, dim or increase lights, or any such activities in the theater. (4) A piece of music played within the movie. (5) To signal a performer to begin or end a speech or action. (6) To prepare a cue sheet. (7) To prepare a film with cue marks (e.g., tape or punch holes), which assist the mixer in placing sounds, music, or dialogue in proper relation to the images.

■ **cue breakdown, cue sheet** A list of cues for a composer writing a score for a film. This cue sheet is made by the sound editor and includes the time in the film (to the nearest one-third second) and the point of action for each musical interjection.

■ **cue cards, idiot cards, idiot sheet** A card with written or printed dialogue that is held outside the view of the camera to help performers deliver their lines.

■ **cue light** A small bulb, out of the view of the camera, that is switched on to signal an actor to begin some speech or action. Such a light is also used to direct narrators to resume voice-over commentary, generally in documentaries or educational films.

■ **cue marks** (1) *See* **change-over cue.** (2) Any mark in a piece of film or sound tape to signal the beginning of editing or synchronization. (3) Any tab, sticker, or bar code placed on film that triggers an automated system in a movie theater.

■ **cue patch** A small magnetic or metallic adhesive piece that is attached to the edge of a film to signal some change in the printer light or the cessation of a projector.

■ **cue print** An edited print of a film with all the cues marked for postrecording.

■ **cue sheet** (1) A log with the sound tracks in columns that indicates to the sound engineer, during mixing, where certain sounds come in and how they are to be treated when he or she is combining them into single track. Footage numbers in the cue sheet correspond to those illuminated on a counter beneath the screen during image projection. *See* **mixing cue sheet.** (2) A sheet of music arranged for playing during silent films. (3) *See* **cue breakdown.**

■ **cue track** A sound track of dialogue recorded during filming to help with the later postrecording. This track is generally used when filming is on location and there is too much noise for original sound.

■ **cukaloris, cuke** *See* **cookie.**

■ **cult film, cult movie** A film without wide popularity but that appeals primarily to a particular group or type of person. Cult films are often shown on campuses, but now are especially popular at late-night weekend performances in commercial theaters (e.g., *The Rocky Horror Picture Show* [1975]; dir. Jim Sharman).

■ **curling** A curvature along the length of the film caused by changes in the moisture content of the emulsion or base. Such a condition may be the result of changes in the air's humidity.

■ **cursor** The flashing line or marker on the computer's monitor that indicates the exact location where some operation may be performed.

■ **curvature of field** An aberration of the lens that causes the sharpest points of the image to appear on a curve instead of a flat plane.

■ **cut** (1) The instantaneous change from one shot to another by means of splicing the two shots together. (2) A piece of film containing a single shot. (3) The splice that connects two pieces of film. (4) The act of cutting a piece of film. (5) The larger and more sustained act of editing or cutting an entire film. (6) The order spoken by the director or some other personnel to stop the operation of camera and sound equipment after a shot has been taken.

Of these definitions, the first is the one most used in the discussion of film and the one that requires amplification. Perhaps the most important discovery in the earliest period of motion pictures was the realization that a film could be composed of more than a single action photographed continuously in one location from a single position, that it was possible to arrange the pieces of film in such a way that narratives could be developed more complexly and engagingly. There has been some argument about who was responsible for this realization. The Brighton school in England at the beginning of the century is supposed to have developed some cross-cutting. In this country, Edwin S. Porter in *The Life of an American Fireman* (1903) cut freely between related actions and developed this technique more skillfully in *The Great Train Robbery* (1903). Although he did use the close-up, Porter's camera remained stationary throughout each scene and he did not manipulate distance and angles. It was D. W. Griffith who developed modern film technique and left for future filmmakers the basic tools for molding a narrative. Griffith created a new kind of cinematic time and space by (1) cross-cutting between related actions taking place at the same time to tell a story or between parallel actions at different times; (2) dividing the individual scene into a series of shots from different distances and different angles; and (3) arranging the individual shots into rhythmic patterns to manipulate the audience's emotional responses. The next important stage in cutting occurred with the early Russian filmmakers Kuleshov, Pudovkin, and Eisenstein, all of whom experimented further with Griffith's techniques and developed the art of montage. In contrast to this manipulative type of film cutting was the continuous and unobtrusive style introduced by the German silent-film director G. W. Pabst and developed by the Hollywood studios during the 1930s and 1940s, a basic style of cutting that influences filmmakers to this day.

Cuts can be divided into the following general categories: (1) simple continuity cuts, which function basically to bring the narration from one scene to another; (2) cross-cuts (or parallel cuts), which alternate back and forth between related scenes; (3) match cuts, which unobtrusively alternate the distance and angles of shots in the same scene; (4) jump cuts, which obtrusively jump from different distances or angles in the same scene either for effect or from bad editing (sometimes the term also applies to sudden cuts from scene to scene); (5) thematic or montage cuts, which consecutively present shots of different characters, objects, or actions to make a significant point; (6) cutaways, which are shots that momentarily take us away from the main scene; (7) compilation cuts, which put together in rapid succession a series of shots, perhaps to establish the impression of a place, period of time, or a character's impressions of an event or series of past events.

The length of individual cuts and the interplay of their durations create a filmic time scheme that has a particular effect upon the viewer. A series of short, dynamic cuts creates a sense of excitement and rapidly builds tension; a longer series of short cuts ultimately creates a sense of time passing and much happening; longer cuts give more information and build slowly to some cumulative point; and short cuts interjected among longer ones function as commentaries and add dramatic complexity. The French critic André Bazin has distinguished two general types of film technique, that which relies on the image itself and that which relies on the assemblage of different shots of the image through cutting. But whatever the emphasis, there can be no doubt that any film relies in various extents on cutting, that without sufficient and varied cuts a film would remain little more than a photographed play. Cuts allow (1) both the condensation and extension of filmic time and space; (2) the continuous, rapid, and varied narration of story; (3) the continuous and varied depiction of a scene; (4) the depiction of a character's perspectives; (5) the dramatization of the psychological and emotional interplay of characters; (6) the manipulation of the audience's attention, intelligence, and emotions; and (7) the development of theme and moral statement. *See* **editing** *and* **montage.**

■ **cut and hold**   The director's order for shooting to end and for the characters to stop acting, but to hold their places in case the shot has to be continued or taken over.

■ **cutaway, cut-away, cutaway shot**   A shot away from the main action but used to join two shots of the main action in order to (1) designate the passage of time; (2) build suspense by extending time; (3) show the reaction of someone or some group to the major action; (4) bridge two shots that would form an unwanted jump cut perhaps because part of the action is missing; (5) remind us about some other character or action, perhaps to give added tension to the main scene; (6) allow the audience some relief from the main action.

■ **cut back, cutback**   (1) A return from a shot or action to one happening immediately before, as in the case of cross-cutting between two related events. (2) A return to the main action after an intercut.

■ **cut-in, cut-in shot**   A shot that cuts into some small portion of the main scene; one that shows, for example, an object such as a knife or gun, or part of a character, such as his eyes or hands.

■ **cutout animation**   Animation with figures cut out of some material such as wood, plastic, paper, or cardboard. The figures retain the same shape and flatness and are generally moved by jointed limbs. Each successive movement of the figures is recorded one or two frames at a time through stop-motion photography. Lotte Reiniger made a number of impressive films with silhouetted cutout figures in Germany during the 1930s. *See* **silhouette animation.**

■ **cut pix**   *See* **workprint.**

■ **cutter**   (1) The term sometimes used for the editor. (2) A person in the editing department who cuts and splices. (3) A large flag, long and narrow in shape, used for blocking light from the camera or an area of the set.

■ **cutting**   Although the term "cut" means changing from one shot to another, the term "editing" is preferred to "cutting" to describe the process of assembling the film into its final form because it suggests far more than merely cutting film into pieces and splicing them together; it is also preferred because the person who does this work is more often called the editor than cutter for the same reason. Editing suggests decision, control, and artistic sensibility as well as a larger shaping vision; it also describes the processes of integrating image and sound. *See* **editing.**

■ **cutting bench**   *See* **editing bench.**

■ **cutting continuity, cutting-continuity script, cutting script**   A film script that gives a transcript of the film substantially as it is released with shots, camera position, sound, transitions, dialogue, and action all recorded. Such scripts for notable films are often published in book form.

■ **cutting copy, cut, cut picture, cutter print, cut pix, work picture**   A workprint of the film during the various stages of editing.

■ **cutting in the camera**   Filming with sufficient setups and a sufficiently mobile camera so that minimal cutting will be necessary. The film, through the way it is shot, will have sufficient continuity and variety.

■ **cutting on action, cutting on motion, cutting on movement**   Cutting from one shot to another so that the second continues or completes an action begun by an actor in the first. The continuous movement hides the fact of the cut. This effect can be achieved either by overlapping action when filming with one camera, by shooting the complete action with two cameras and editing the pieces of action together at consecutive points, or by precisely switching from one camera to another. *See* **invisible cutting** *and* **matching action.**

■ **cutting room** The room where the film is edited and that contains such equipment as the flat-bed editing machine, editing bench, storage shelves, and film bin. Such a place may either be part of a studio or an independent establishment. *See* **flat-bed editing machine.**

■ **cutting sync, editing sync, parallel sync** Editing when the picture and sound track are still on two separate strips and the corresponding points in picture and sound are kept parallel by a synchronizer.

■ **cutting the negative** The important editing of the film's negative so that it matches the final workprint or follows the negative cut list. The cut negative is the source of a fine-grain master print from which is made the fine-grain negative that is the source of the release prints. *See* **editing** *and* **negative cutting.**

■ **cutting to continuity** Arranging shots in such a way that all the action is not shown but the continuity of narrative is maintained and the viewer is unaware of any omissions.

■ **cut to** A designation for cutting to a new scene sometimes used in film scripts but generally used in treatments that precede actual film scripts and describe only major scenes.

■ **cyan** The color blue-green that is complementary and opposite on the color wheel to red. When red is subtracted from the spectrum, the result is cyan. *See* **subtractive process.**

■ **cycle** (1) Sometimes used to designate a series of similar films, all produced in a brief period from several studios: for example, genre films such as science fiction, where successive works play off the popularity of earlier ones. (2) In animation, a series of drawings for a complete action.

■ **cycle animation** Animation that uses a series of cels, with slight movement of the subject on each, over and over to show the same action (e.g., waves of water). *See* **animation.**

■ **cyclorama, cyc** A large stretched backdrop at the rear of the set, normally made of cloth and curved like a C. Often used as the sky.

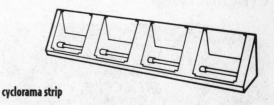

cyclorama strip

■ **cyclorama strip, cyc strip, cyclorama light** A bank of lights placed at the bottom of a cyclorama for even illumination.

■   ■   ■

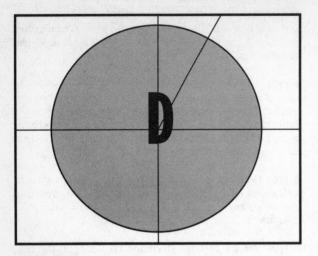

dadaism to dynamic range

dadiasm Comic nonsense in René Clair's *Entr'acte* (1924).

■■■

■ **dadaism** A cultural movement of avant-garde artists and writers in France, Germany, and Switzerland during the First World War and the 1920s that reacted against the establishment and conventional art by emphasizing instinct, spontaneity, and the irrational. The term "dada" was supposedly chosen by chance out of a dictionary (it is the child's word for hobby horse) and suggests the group's desire for the childlike and unexpected. The movement combined the visual sense of dadaist painters and the literary sensibility of dadaist writers in a few fascinating films such as Man Ray's *Le Retour à la Raison* (1923), René Clair's *Entr'acte* (1924), Fernand Léger and Dudley Murphy's *Le Ballet Mécanique* (1924), and Marcel Duchamp's *Anemic Cinema* (1925). All these films remove images of external real-ity from any rational or significant context and create new visions and perspectives of people and objects. All of them deny logic and narrative for the sake of the poetic. The dadaist movement was significant in the development of surrealism and the surrealistic film. *See* **avant-garde cinema** *and* **surrealism.**

■ **daguerreotype** A system of photography introduced by the Frenchman Louis Daguerre in 1839 and developed from the work of Nicéphore Niépce, who died six years earlier. The process, which used a silver surface on a copper plate to make a positive image, was at first very popular but was replaced because of the long period of time required for exposure and the fact that the positive could not be reprinted. Daguerre is sometimes considered to be the father of modern photography, but that accolade probably should go to the Englishman Fox Talbot who, at the same time, created a process that would allow for reproduction on sensitized paper, faster exposure, and negative-positive reproductions.

■ **dailies, rushes** The first positive prints, usually synchronized with sound, which generally are delivered by the laboratory the day after shooting. This film is used primarily for checking all facets of shooting. Printed with only a single light intensity, it also serves as the basis for making decisions for light and color corrections in future printing. Although the term "workprint" basically refers to the film worked on by the editor and already spliced into some degree of continuity, it is also employed commonly, and incorrectly, for dailies or rushes.

■ **daily production report** A full summation of the day's shooting, which is generally filled out by the assistant director and production manager. This report gives details concerning all the takes, the personnel and equipment used, the film and sound tracks used, the meals eaten, and the duration of all activities. The daily production reports allow the producer and studio's executives to follow the progress of a film.

■ *Daily Variety* An offshoot of the weekly *Variety*, this daily newspaper is published in Hollywood and keeps a constant eye on film and television as well as on other entertainment business activities. *See* **Variety.**

■ **dark end** The area for film processing where feeding, developing, and fixing take place, which must be virtually free of light to avoid spoiling the still-sensitive film emulsion. *See* **processing.**

■ **DAT** The initials stand for digital audio tape, a new system of recording sound that has made its way into film production. For location shooting, DAT offers greater sound fidelity and flexibility than standard magnetic-tape systems. *See* **digital sound recording.**

■ **database** An organized body of material stored in the computer's memory that can be drawn upon for some specified application.

■ **Dawn process** (1) A glass shot for photographing live action either before or behind scenery painted on a glass sheet, developed by Norman Dawn for still photography in 1905 and for motion pictures in 1907. The technique was much employed during the 1920s and 1930s but was later replaced by more economical and efficient matting and printing methods. (2) An in-camera matte shot also developed by Norman Dawn for cinematography and used as early as 1911. This method was much in use before the development of bipack printing. *See* **in-camera matte shot.**

■ **day and date release** The release of a film at two or more theaters in the same geographic location or at two or more geographic locations on the same day and date.

■ **day for night, day-for-night (D/N)** Shooting in daylight, but achieving the effect of night through one or more of the following: underexposure, filters, or printing. Such shooting takes place when it is difficult or too expensive to shoot at night.

■ **daylight** In cinematography, daylight is considered the illumination from both the sun and sky.

■ **daylight color film** Color film that achieves a natural balance between the three complementary colors when exposed to daylight.

■ **daylight conversion filter** A filter that allows color film balanced for indoor shooting with artificial light to be used for outdoor shooting with natural light.

■ **daylight loading spool** A carrier for film with dark sides that protects all but the outer layers from exposure. Such spools with 100, 200, and 400 feet of film for 16mm cameras and 100 for 35mm allow the loading of the magazine in general lighting situations though not in bright daylight. Some cameras with the film chamber inside the housing directly accept daylight spools with one hundred feet of film.

■ **daylight projection** Projecting film in a lighted environment either through the back of a translucent screen from a projector in a dark cabinet or frontally onto a highly reflective screen.

■ **day-out-of-days schedule** A working schedule for the individual performers during filming. It is necessary that all the scenes of expensive actors and actresses, especially if they are contracted to work only part of the production schedule, be shot as closely together as possible.

■ **day player** An actor or actress hired only one day at a time to work in a film.

■ **DCI lamp** A metal halide discharge arc lamp that operates on DC and is just being explored as a possible source of light for motion pictures. Similar to HMI lamps, these luminaires have some advantage by operating on DC current: they are smaller in size, operate with a simpler balast, are flicker free, and silent. Such bulbs with low wattage (120–1200) have so far been produced. *See* **HMI.**

■ **dead** An area in which sound has little reverberation: for example, a closed room with furniture, drapes, and carpets that absorb sound, or the great outdoors, which disperses noise.

■ **deadpan** The facial expression of a performer exhibiting absolutely no feelings or emotion. Buster Keaton's deadpan expression was his trademark in his films of the silent era.

■ **deadspot** (1) A point in an area at which reverberations from the same sound cancel each other out. (2) An area in the scene where no action takes place during the shot. (3) An area in the set not included in the camera's field of vision during a shot. (4) A place in the script with little energy, action, or intrinsic interest.

■ **dead sync, dead-head sync** *See* **editorial sync.**

■ **deal** Although the term generally means any kind of agreement made between any number of people, especially a business transaction, it has come to have specific denotations and even emotional connotations in the film industry when it refers specifically to the long and arduous series of activities that go into making the final agreement for the production of a motion picture. A small percentage of such deals are actually completed because of the highly competitive nature of the industry and the large amount of money needed to make a film, but a vast number of projects are in various stages of development, many launched by the same people in the hope that at least one will find success. The various stages can take many years and involve a changing array of personnel and even studios. A producer puts together a package of a director, star, and a story at some point of development. The producer may also be the director, or, on occasion, the writer or performer. Sometimes the producer may be one part of a package that is being promoted by an agent. A studio, if it feels attracted by the idea, will advance some developmental money (on rare occasions the project is bought outright and goes into production). The next stage calls for developing the script and negotiating with personnel. After the project is thus developed, studios often pull out of the project, deciding not to spend the great amount of money required for production and distribution. Sometimes a studio will simply become uncertain and put the project into limited turnaround, which means that any other studio can bid for it during a period of time as long as there is no "change of element" and the package remains as it is—this strategy prevents the studio from losing a project that suddenly has an important star added, but it also limits the producer from improving the package, hence placing it in limbo for a long time. All of these procedures can take years, with the project bouncing from studio to studio. Most of these properties are ultimately lost and dreams go up in smoke; but sometimes the deal is struck, contracts are signed, and the film goes into production.

■ **deal letter, deal memo** A written statement of intention, generally between a studio or production company and individual performer, director, or other personnel, to enter into negotiations and sign a contract for a particular film. Such a letter is considered binding.

■ **deblooping, blooping** (1) Reducing the bloop that can be heard when a splice or some break in the film passes the scanner in an optical sound system with blooping tape or blooping ink on the positive optical sound track, or a perforation on the negative optical sound track. (2) Erasing, with a small magnet, the sound of the bloop caused in a magnetic sound track by editing tools. *See* **bloop.**

■ **debug** To eliminate any technical problems in a piece of equipment or system; to bring its efficiency up to par.

■ **decamired** A measurement sometimes used for color temperature that is mireds divided by ten. *See* **mired.**

■ **decibel (DB)** (1) The measurement for the intensity of sound. (2) A unit that expresses the ratio of two power sources.

■ **decibel meter** A meter used to measure the volume of sound.

■ **deck** *See* **green.**

■ **decor** The type or style of decoration in a setting, either indoors or outdoors. The decor is created by furniture, ornamentation, props, costumes, and color. As well as establishing a particular time and place, the decor also establishes a general mood.

■ **découpage** The term means "to cut up" in French and has been used by some French critics to refer to the arrangement of shots in a particular scene or in a film in general. The concern here is with the particular style of editing in a film, the overall design of shots. *Découpage classique* is a term used by French critics to describe the style of cutting for narrative and dramatic

continuity that developed in the Hollywood studios. *See* **invisible cutting.**

■ **Dedolight** A relatively recent 100-watt or 150-watt light manufactured by Dedotec USA, Inc., that is small, compact, and powerful, giving an extremely even and controllable illumination with a very wide focusing range of 25:1. More efficient than a Fresnel, this lamp works as a single unit, composed of a lamp with a mirror behind it and a meniscus lens in front of it—the entire lighting unit can be moved back and forth behind a condenser lens for focusing. The luminaire is small enough to be placed on the set in some unobtrusive place.

■ **deep focus** A style of motion picture photography that has great depth of field and brings all planes of the image—foreground, middle ground, and background—into sharp focus. This type of cinematography is in contrast to the more traditional style of shallow focus that emphasizes only one plane of the image, generally the plane of action, behind which, and often in front of which, everything seems blurred. In shallow focus, the characters are set off from the background and the audience's attention is carefully guided, but in deep focus the viewer is given the entire scene and allowed to discover for himself or herself significant action and information. The French film critic André Bazin, in *What Is Cinema?*, praises the technique of deep focus because, by maintaining the continuity of dra-

deep focus Orson Welles as Kane amidst the interior space of the party scene in *Citizen Kane* (1941; dir. Orson Welles).

■ ■ ■

matic space and time, it (1) brings the viewer into a closer contact with the scene than that which he or she would experience in reality; (2) requires from the viewer more active mental participation in the scene; and (3) allows for ambiguities in the scene because the viewer's attention is not guided by extensive cutting. For Bazin, montage, and with it shallow focus, is manipulative, unreal, and less challenging. Deep focus relies on the *mise-en-scène*, the composition of individual shots, instead of the interrelationship of individual shots. The greater depth of field requires smaller apertures and hence greater exposure times; wide-angle short-focus lenses; greater distance from the subject of the image; and greater depth in lighting. Deep focus was possible in silent movies when the fast orthochromatic stock was used, but the change to the more accurate but slower panchromatic film made deep focus more difficult to achieve and less common. Renoir, however, created the illusion of deep focus by his long takes, pans, and change of focus. The improvement of filmstock in the 1930s made deep focus more accessible, but it was Gregg Toland's photography in Orson Welles's *Citizen Kane* (1941), acclaimed by Bazin, that heralded the return of deep focus. Combinations of deep and shallow focus (with less and more cutting respectively) are not uncommon today, each being used for specific dramatic purposes: note, for example, Robert Wise's gothic film *The Haunting* (1963; photographed by David Boulton), which uses deep focus to create an ambiguous and threatening sense of place and shallow focus with rapid cutting to show characters' responses and to build suspense (Wise himself edited *Citizen Kane*). *See* **depth, depth of field, long take, selective focus,** *and* **shallow focus.**

■ **deferred payment, deferment, deferral** An arrangement by which someone involved in a film production agrees to take only partial payment at first and the remainder of his or her money at a later time—e.g., as a net profit participant or, if fortunate, gross profit participant. If the film does poorly, the person may be out of luck, but should it do well, then a fortune is to be made. *See* **gross profit participant** *and* **net profit participant.**

■ **definition** The sharpness and distinction of detail in an image as (1) recorded on a specific film stock; or (2) allowed by a specific lens. Not only must there be a number of specific elements per millimeter for good definition, but black and white must not tend to fuse into gray, and tonal gradation must be precise. The term "resolution" is also used for definition.

■ **defocus** To make the plane of action in an image suddenly appear out of focus, generally by focusing on another plane.

■ **defocus transition** A transition from one scene to another by blurring the first scene and refocusing to the second. The device, no longer much used, was commonly employed to indicate a flashback, frequently at the same location, or to indicate a movement from reality to the world of dream or hallucination. *See* **ripple dissolve.**

■ **deformation** Any visible change or distortion of a model in computer animation; the alteration in form between keyframes—e.g., elongation, shrinking, inflation, deflation. *See* **morphing.**

■ **degauss** (1) To erase the recording on a magnetic tape or film; (2) to demagnetize magnetic tape, film, recording or playback heads, and editing tools. The device that does this is called a degausser or demagnetizer. (Gauss is a measurement for magnetic induction and is named after Karl Friedrich Gauss, a German mathematician.)

■ **degradation** The deterioration in an image caused by its duplication through successive stages of printing. This deterioration occurs in definition as well as in color.

■ **De Luxe Laboratories** "Color by De Luxe" in a film's credits means that the motion picture was probably shot on Eastman film but processed at De Luxe Laboratories. One of the largest film-processing houses in the world, the company was originally founded early in the century in Fort Lee, New Jersey, but later had laboratories in both New York and Los Angeles. Today, the film laboratory in Hollywood and Video by Deluxe in Los Angeles service the industry. The company is a subsidiary of Twentieth Century-Fox.

■ **demagnetize** To remove an undesired magnetic field from recording or playback heads, editing tools, or tapes; to degauss by means of a degausser or demagnetizer.

■ **denotation** The exact, literal meaning of a word. In discussions of film, the term can also be applied to the specific identities of and normal associations elicited by a person, place, object, or action as opposed to what these may suggest or connote beyond their literal meaning and significance. *See* **connotation.**

■ **dénouement** From the French word *dénouer,* "to untie," the term means that point in the plot, after the climax, when everything is unraveled and resolved. This normally occurs at the end of a dramatic work and may be the result either of external forces or some realization or change on the part of the major character. In certain realistic films, however, the director seeks to imitate life by resolving nothing and avoids an apparent dénouement; the action and characters promise to continue much as before (as for example, in De Sica's *Umberto D* [1952]). *See* **climax.**

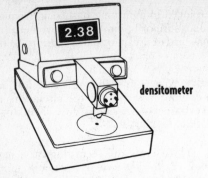

densitometer

■ **densitometer, densimeter** An instrument that measures the density of a film image, generally a photoelectric device that measures the light transmitted by the image. *See* **densitometry.**

■ **densitometry** The measurement of the density of film images. After a sensitometer places on a film emulsion a series of controlled exposures, a sensitometric strip is made and the various densities measured by a densitometer. The information from this measurement is necessary to regulate both the photographing and developing processes for the specific emulsion. *See* **sensitometer** *and* **sensitometry.**

■ **density** (1) The degree of opacity in a film image; the ability of the image to stop the reflection of light. Density is affected by film emulsion, lens, illumination, length of exposure, and the developing process itself. Specular density is measured without regard to the diffuse light transmitted by the image; diffuse density considers the transmission of all light. (2) The term also describes the amount of information in a particular image—the number of individual elements that comprise the total picture.

■ **depiction release** Contractual rights to portray an individual in a motion picture or some other dramatic presentation. Such an agreement spells out the payment to the individual as well as the degree of compliance (what type of assistance the individual will give) and extent of usage (for ancillary markets and foreign distribution). Such a release normally frees the filmmaker or film company from any possible lawsuits concerning the way in which the person is presented or the work is publicized.

■ **depth** One of the most compelling problems in cinematography is how to give the flat image on the screen an illusion of depth. The viewer makes certain mental adjustments when seeing the image because he or she is accustomed to giving depth where successive components appear in different sizes—as components grow smaller they seem to recede in space. Characters appearing in front of a background also suggests depth in a scene. But even allowing for the viewer's instinctive imposition of depth into a scene, the filmmaker must still consciously seek to create an illusion of depth or the scene will seem relatively flat and unnatural compared to the spatial dimension of external reality. Three-D photographing and projecting systems have achieved only sporadic popularity in film because of various technical difficulties and the necessity of cumbersome eye spectacles, though considerable advancement has recently been made in this area. The viewer's sense of spatial depth in a scene can be increased in a number of ways: by (1) filling up depth within the scene and emphasizing objects' differences in size due to their distances apart; (2) varying illumination so that there are distinct planes of light and shadow, and employing side lighting for characters to give them an appearance of depth; (3) varying angles and distances from shot to shot to move the viewer in and out of the scene; (4) moving the camera, especially with tracking, dolly, and boom shots, or using a zoom lens to move the viewer within the space of the scene; and (5) moving the actors in and out of the interiors of a scene. Deep focus permits the clear definition of foreground, middle ground, and background, hence creating a sense of interior space and depth for the audience. *See* **deep focus, depth of field,** *and* **3-D.**

■ **depth cueing** In computer animation, creating an illusion of depth in an image by increasing or decreasing both the sharpness of the models' edges and their clarity. Objects that are made more diffuse and less clear seem farther away in the depth of the image.

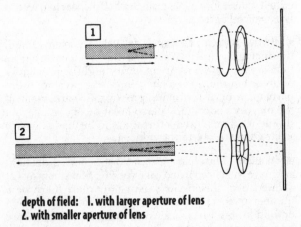

depth of field: 1. with larger aperture of lens
2. with smaller aperture of lens

■ **depth of field** The area of acceptable focus that extends both in front of and behind the primary plane of focus in a film image; that area in which the circles of confusion are still small enough to appear as points in the image. The area behind the primary plane of focus is generally more extensive than that in front of it. Greater depth of field can be achieved through wide-angle lenses, which have shorter focal lengths; larger f-stops, which require narrower apertures; greater depth in lighting; and a greater distance between the primary plane of focus and camera. Depth of field can be known in advance for lenses of specific focal lengths from a depth-of-field table that gives the figures at various apertures and at various focal distances. Some lenses for narrower gauges have a depth-of-field scale on the focus mount itself. Greater depth of field achieves deep focus; shallow depth of field requires follow focus, which means changing the focus of the scene when following a character's movements, or rack focus, which means changing the focus to change the subject of attention. *See* **circle of confusion** *and* **depth of focus.**

▪ **depth of focus** The range of focal planes behind the lens where the film emulsion will register an image in focus, with acceptable circles of confusion, in accordance with a required depth of field. This term is sometimes confused with depth of field. *See* **circle of confusion** *and* **depth of field.**

▪ **desaturation** The decrease in a color's saturation, which may be the result of a defect in the film stock, faulty processing, the age of the film, or the generation of its image. Sometimes colors are intentionally desaturated to achieve a required effect in the image. This technique, also called preflashing or prefogging, is obtained by exposing the film to a light before or after shooting the scene, or by using a beam splitter on the camera to add a fogging light to the scene as it is photographed. Desaturation is also achieved through optical printing after the negative has been developed and cut. For Alan Pakula's *Sophie's Choice* (1982), desaturation of colors for scenes in the past was achieved in the laboratory by means of A and B printing of the original negative with a black-and-white dupe negative. *See* **A and B printing.**

detective film *Chinatown* (1974; dir. Roman Polanski), with Jack Nicholson as the detective figure in an immoral and brutal world.

▪ **detail shot** Any shot that shows a very small object or very small part of an object or person. This shot is considered to be closer and more detailed than the close-up.

▪ **detective film** A genre of film that features the search for clues and culminates with the solution to a crime by either a private detective or some agent of the police force (sometimes acts of investigation are also performed by journalists, insurance investigators, and lawyers). Detective films are one type of mystery film, distinguished from other films of that group by the well-defined central figure. Detective films rely heavily on plot and plot complications; they involve the audience by establishing a mystery and then sending the protagonist forth to discover the solution—the audience both associates with the protagonist and matches wits with him or her. Anticipation and suspense give added emphasis and meaning to every detail in the film. A well-known group of detective films has featured the master British sleuth Sherlock Holmes. Detective films also offer the opportunity for a wide variety of character types, both sinister and comic, and for much action, especially fights, mayhem, and chases.

But the detective film in America has also developed certain defining characteristics and a certain ambience. Films such as Roman Polanski's *Chinatown* (1974) have featured a decadent, immoral, and brutal urban world, spanning the poor and rich, through which the protagonist must make a journey to discover the facts, but also sometimes to discover some moral truth about that world and himself. The detective figure, such as Humphrey Bogart's portrayal of Sam Spade in John Huston's *The Maltese Falcon* (1941), is a tough, morally complex, but basically sensitive figure. Although he seems independent and alone, and sometimes almost as brutal as the criminals around him, he also understands the need for law and order, the need for some kind of social contract to fight off the chaos, even though he may find society itself, and its very institutions, greedy and corrupt. Such a figure is, to some degree, an update of the hero of the Western, but denied the mythic landscape, with all its grandeur and freedom, of the West. He is an assertion of American toughness and individuality, and he takes part in a drama that condemns the decay of American values and the corruption of the modern world.

Detective figures who have worked for the police force have traditionally been more law-abiding and less morally complex figures, as in the G-Man films of the 1940s and works such as Jules Dassin's *The Naked City* (1948). In general, these figures have seemed to be bulwarks of social and moral order. But in more recent years, especially in America, the police detective and private eye have come closer together. Police organizations have seemed as corrupt or unreliable as the world outside and, like Gene Hackman's portrayal of Popeye in William Friedkin's *The French Connection* (1971) or Clint Eastwood's portrayal of the title character in Don Siegal's *Dirty Harry* (1972), the police officer has become a loner, frequently violent and complex, but ultimately with that higher sense of morality that marks most of the figures in the genre. For the past two decades, the detective narrative has fared better on network television than in the cinema, where it has decayed into violent, comedic, and mindless police detective and buddy films. Perhaps the kiss-off for the old type of private eye was Philip Marlowe (played by Eliott Gould) killing his double-crossing friend and then dancing down the road to the tune of "Hooray for Hollywood" in Robert Altman's *The Long Goodbye* (1973). *See* **mystery film** *and* **private eye film.**

■ **deuce** A 2,000-watt spotlight; also called a junior. A 1,500-watt bulb in such a fixture is called a light deuce or one-and-a-half; a 1,000-watt bulb a gutless deuce or one-key. *See* **spotlight.**

■ **developers, developing agents** The chemical solution that reacts with the silver halide crystals of the exposed emulsion to make visible the latent image in the film. In color development, the oxidized developer then reacts with couplers to form the color image. *See* **processing.**

■ **developing, development** The process of making visible the latent image in exposed film. In common usage, the term also refers to the entire processing of film, including developing, fixing, washing, and drying. In the actual development state, crystals of silver halide in the emulsion, which have been exposed to light, are converted by certain chemicals to black silver particles which form the negative image. In the development of color film, chemicals convert the crystals of silver halide to silver particles and also react with color couplers in the emulsion itself to create color dyes. After development, the silver image is bleached and washed away, leaving the color image. In tripack color film each of three separate layers in the emulsion is sensitive to one of the primary colors, and each contains a coupler which reacts with chemicals to develop a dye complementary to the primary color (yellow for the blue-sensitive layer, magenta for the green, and cyan for the red). *See* **processing.**

■ **development** Turning a concept or initial idea for a film into the screenplay ready to be put on the screen. Such a process includes negotiating the rights to material and writing the outline, treatment, and various versions of the screenplay until it is considered ready for production.

■ **development deal** A contractual agreement between a film company and an individual such as a producer, director, and sometimes screenwriter. The film company agrees to pay the individual a certain amount of money to develop a project that the film company will have first rights to produce. *See* **overall development deal.**

■ **DGA, DGA trainee** *See* **Directors Guild of America.**

■ **diachronic** A term popular in critical theory and derived from semiotics, where it means the study of language from a historical, linear perspective. Language is thus examined in the process of change, as opposed to synchronic studies, which see language structurally, at a single point of time. The term also describes the perspective that sees a work of art, including film, in terms of its linear movement in time, from one point to another, as opposed to the synchronic perspective, which sees the work all at once, with the relationship of all its parts forming a total, structural entity. *See* **semiotics.**

■ **diagonal cut, diagonal splice** The joining together, by means of an oblique cut, of two pieces of magnetic tape that avoids any obvious noise on playback.

■ **dialectic** A term important in Marxist criticism and derived by Marx from the philosopher Hegel's dialectical theory. Hegel sees the movement to truth as at first the opposition between one proposition and another—that is, between thesis and antithesis—which finally culminates in a third proposition, the synthesis, which is a higher level of truth than either proposition. Marx's dialectic belongs to his economic theory and is rooted in history and materialism. Marxist critics analyze the work of art, including film, in terms of such a dialectic and see it structured in terms of oppositions that either culminate or do not culminate in synthesis, or culminate in a synthesis that then becomes a thesis in the next opposition.

■ **dialing** Handling the dials and hence controlling the sound during sound recording for a film. A particular sound can be "dialed in" or "dialed out."

■ **dialogue** Speech between characters, generally synchronic with lip movement. Dialogue can also function nonsynchronically, with separate action as a voice-over, perhaps to suggest a character remembering or anticipating some conversation with another person. Dialogue is often recorded during the filming of a scene, but it is not uncommon, either when shooting on location or in an acoustically difficult area, or simply when sound recording has not been adequate, to record and dub in dialogue later. With the advent of sound, films in the late 1920s and early 1930s became talky and often appeared as filmed plays. It was not until filmmakers learned to control the noise of the camera, to make the instrument mobile again, and to control the placement and movement of microphones, and not until they adjusted to the new dimension in general, that sound was integrated into film and synthesized with the visuals. The films of the 1930s, 1940s, and 1950s, however, continued to rely more heavily on dialogue than recent films. Today dialogue is more integrated into the visuals and sometimes is barely articulate. The gain has been significant, but so has the loss; gone from film are the distinct voices, conversations, and hence personalities of the stars of earlier films.

■ **dialogue coach, dialogue director** The person who helps the performers learn and interpret their lines and also rehearses with them before the actual shooting of a scene.

■ **dialogue replacement** *See* **automatic dialogue replacement.**

■ **dialogue splitting** Separating a sound track of dialogue when sections do not match and background noise "bumps." This effect is often the result of changing the microphone position for different camera setups. The separated pieces of the sound track can then be corrected by the sound mixer. *See* **bump** *and* **mix.**

■ **dialogue track** A sound track on which is recorded only the dialogue of characters. Sometimes more than one dialogue track is necessary for the final sound mix. Music and sound effects are normally recorded on separate tracks. Such segregation of sound allows for better control in recording and better correction and integration of the various elements in mixing.

■ **dialogue writer** Someone who specializes in the writing of dialogue for film. Sometimes a dialogue writer is hired to help with an ailing film script.

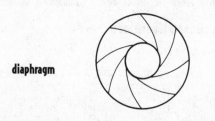

diaphragm

■ **diaphragm** Sometimes called an iris because it resembles that part of the human eye, the diaphragm controls the amount of light that passes through the lens and reaches the film. This adjustable aperture is composed of overlapping pieces of thin metal. The size of the diaphragm is controlled by the f-stop ring—the smaller the f-stop number, the larger the opening. Smaller f-stops achieve greater focus and depth of field. *See* **f-stop** *and* **t-stop.**

■ **diaphragm presetting** Setting an f-stop on the lens for desired depth of field and then lighting the scene for sufficient exposure.

■ **diapositive, diapositive plate** A glass plate on part of which is a photograph and through the clear part of which the camera photographs a particular action, combining it with the image already on the plate. This glass shot can add clouds or some scenery to the action being photographed.

■ **dichroic filter, dichroic reflector** A filter composed of a base on which dichroic substances are layered in such a way that the layers interfere with and reflect certain light waves while permitting the passage of others. Dichroic filters can be used to (1) balance the colors of quartz lights for daylight shooting; (2) determine which colors are to pass in the printing of color film; (3) reflect infrared and heat waves while passing all colors in the projection of film.

■ **diegesis** A term from semiotics applied to film criticism, especially by Christian Metz, that designates the denotative elements of a narrative—that is, all the elements of the narrative, whether shown in the film or not. Diegetic elements include all action and dialogue in their normal space and time, which rarely can be fully given in the film. *See* **semiotics.**

■ **differential focus** *See* **split focus.**

■ **differential rewind** A device that allows simultaneous winding of film on two or more reels even though the rolls of film have different diameters.

■ **diffraction** (1) The phenomenon that occurs at the edges of small opaque bodies where light waves are modulated and energy redistributed, causing tiny bands of light and dark or sometimes colored fringes. When the diaphragm of a lens is closed all the way down this phenomenon may diminish the sharpness of the image. (2) The bending of light waves and sound waves around objects in their path.

■ **diffuse density** The density of a film image measured with regard to all transmitted light, both specular and diffuse. A desenitometer is used to measure either specular or, more often, diffuse density for proper printing.

■ **diffuser** (1) Any material that is placed in front of a light source to diffuse and hence soften the light. Such material may be spun glass, netting gauze, silk, wire mesh, gelatin on a wire mesh, frosted glass, or plaster, and may also be used over part of a light source to give greater control in selecting areas for diffusion. (2) Any material, such as those listed above, that is put in front of the lens to soften the edges and details of a subject being photographed.

■ **diffuse reflectance** *See* **reflectance.**

■ **diffusion** (1) The process by which light is softened through a diffuser. (2) The process by which the details and edges of a photographed subject are softened by a diffuser in front of the lens. This last process was often used for photographing love scenes or aging actresses in the Hollywood studios. Special glass lenses with uneven surfaces and metal screening can also be employed for this effect as can jellies applied to the lens. *See* **soft focus.**

■ **diffusion lens** A special lens that fits in front of the normal camera lens to soften or diffuse the scene. Such lenses may achieve such an effect by means of an uneven surface or metal screening.

■ **diffusion screen, diffusion filter, diffusion curtain** A sheet of material for diffusion; a diffuser.

digital Woody and Buzz Lightyear, like all the characters and settings in John Lasseter's *Toy Story* (1995), were digitally created. (©The Walt Disney Company. All Rights Reserved.)

■■■

■ **digital** The term refers to an electronic coding of information through a numerical system of 0's and 1's (offs and ons), especially as it is used in computer and systems media. Digital is opposed to analog systems that record sound waves or physical imprints analogous to the original subject. Since the subject digitally recorded is, in a sense, re-created anew every time it is heard or shown, this method of storage and manifestation is superior to the analog system in which the material record must degenerate from copy to copy or degenerate on the original itself as it is copied over and

over. Each 0 or 1 is referred to as a "bit" and 8 bits form a byte, the smallest unit for a single letter or visual element. A "baud" is the term used for the rate of transmission of bits in a single second. The digital system on disc has been for some time the primary means of recording music, though digital tape has also been developed for the same purpose. The DVD (digital versatile disc), soon to be available, will record both sound and image. Digital sound is the latest development in motion-picture exhibition. Digital imagizing is heavily used for special effects and animation in the film industry. All of the characters and settings are digitally created in John Lasseter's recent *Toy Story* (1995). In the postproduction phase of filmmaking, motion pictures are now being transferred to hard drives for digital nonlinear editing. Although the image quality of digital camcorders is not equal to that of 35mm film, the resolution of their images is constantly improving. Such cameras are extremely portable and can record 90–120 minutes. Their images can be easily transmitted to a computer for editing without any loss in quality. Digital transmission of High Definition Television (HDTV) images is rapidly approaching and some experts predict that motion pictures will one day be digitally beamed into theaters. Also significant is the use of digital correction and enhancement in the restoration of older films (e.g., Walt Disney's *Snow White* [1937] by Cinesite). *See* **computer animation, DSS, DVD, editing, HDTV, sound,** *and* **special effects.**

■ **digital assemble, digital edit** *See* **nonlinear editing.**

■ **digital audio tape recorder** *See* **DAT.**

digital audio workstation (DAW)

■ **digital audio workstation (DAW), digital audio editing system** An independent editing and mixing system employed for digital sound. Because the sound is recorded on hard drive, the necessity for winding and rewinding as well as cutting and rerecording is removed, the process is simpler and quicker to use, and the digital coding prevents the loss of quality normal with analog rerecordings from generation to generation. Sounds can be enhanced, equalized, and modulated with newly created sound effects and music added. Sound and picture can also be synchronized easily. Such procedures are performed graphically, utilizing menus and diagrams on the monitor and a puck for sending instructions. Digital audio workstations are now used in large sound studios to work independently on various tracks and mixes, which can then be passed back and forth between the various workstations and ultimately sent to the mixing stage for the final mix. Although without all the equipment and capabilities of the mixing studio and more limited in memory and speed, such workstations are fast approaching the capacity to perform complete mixes on their own. *See* **digital sound recording.**

■ **digital backlog** A term used for the digital storage of old film or photograph images. Such images can be combined with recently shot footage. *See* **back lot.**

■ **digital camcorder, digital camera** A camera that records still images by transforming light rays into a digital code of binary numbers by means of a CCD (charge-coupled device). These cameras are constantly improving and now exceed Hi-8 video in resolution. The recent Sony DCR-PC7 Handycam is a small camcorder that can record up to 90 minutes in LP mode on a mini-DV cassette. Also notable is the Panasonic DVC Pro. *See* **charge-coupled device** *and* **digital.**

■ **digital capture** Feeding an image into a computer for various alterations as opposed to initial capture, which is the photographing of the image itself.

■ **digital composite** An image composed of different elements that are put together by computer at a composite workstation. The elements are first digitized into the computer, where they are assembled. The finished picture is then sent to film by a digital film recorder. The process is called compositing and sometimes image compositing. *See* **composite** *(2),* **film recorder,** *and* **film scanner.**

■ **digital computer animation, digital animation** *See* **computer animation.**

■ **digital disc recorder (DDR)** A system that records digital video on a disc. Because such discs hold only a brief duration of image and sound, they have a limited use in professional editing.

■ **Digital Domain** A company specializing in digital visual effects for motion pictures, television commercials, interactive video, and theme park entertainments, begun in 1993 by the director James Cameron along with Stan Winston, Scott Ross, and IBM.

■ **digital effects, digital effects cinematography** The most recent development in special-effects cinematography that is expanding the imagistic possibilities of cinema in a revolutionary way. The term "digital" refers to an electronic, computerized system for storing informa-

tion that is based on a process of reducing imagistic elements to a binary code of 0's and 1's (offs and ons). Computers were first used in special-effects work in motion-control systems and are now much employed in creating animation for cartoon feature films; but the term "digital effects" more specifically applies to the creation of pictures or picture elements that seem rooted in reality but could not be obtained without the employment of the computer and digital system. Computer imaging allows enormous flexibility and innovation while being able to save large sums of money. Certainly the leader in this area has been Industrial Light and Magic (ILM), begun by George Lucas in 1975 for his *Star Wars* films. Images from a film or drawing are electronically scanned into a computer where they are registered in binary figures. Such images can be converted to video pictures on a monitor. Through image-processing, painting, or morphing programs, the image elements can be altered, changed, or further developed with additional elements added. Digital compositing can put together elements from different images, combining a computer-generated background with filmed or drawn people, for example. The composite image is then recorded on film by a cathode-ray tube or laser technology. Digital effects can also correct images, removing unwanted objects or wires used in a special stunt, or even correcting defects in composite images made with an optical printer. Digital effects can merge time past with time present by combining elements from different films, including images of famous dead figures with live actors. The technology is developing so rapidly that one can expect to see motion pictures composed entirely of settings and newly created images of deceased performers created by the computer—a process giving new meaning to the word "immortality." *See* **computer animation, motion control,** *and* **special effects.**

■ **digital film workstation (DFW)** A computer area and equipment, both hardware and software, that manipulates, improves, adds to or combines film images or parts of film images that have been digitized. The film's images are first digitized by a film scanner and, when the work is done, they are returned to film by a film recorder. Scenes employing stunt work are digitized so that wires or special supports can be removed. Parts of scenes can be corrected by removing or altering objects and by improving color, lighting, and even resolution. A process equivalent to blue-screening is used for matting and combining backgrounds, live action, and model shots into single composite images. Such workstations can also create new backgrounds, settings, or picture elements and combine them with previously shot live action. *See* **computer animation, digital,** *and* **digital effects.**

■ **digital filter system** A software program that allows the colors of various filters or combinations of filters to be tried out on a preliminary image that has been scanned into the computer. Such a program also allows images to be altered in postproduction editing. The cinematographer can thus make a choice on what filters to use in shooting or what final effect to create on the images already photographed. The Tiffen Crystal Image software is used for these purposes in Kodak's Cineon digital film system. *See* **Cineon digital film system** *and* **filter.**

■ **digital head, digital reader** A sound head attached to the top of the projector system that decodes the digital sound tracks. In some projector systems, the optical sound head is capable of reading both the optical tracks and the optically recorded digital sound. *See* **sound head.**

■ **digital image** (1) Any image created by means of a computerized digital system, whether an animation picture or a picture with actual or live components that has been changed digitally or had digitally created elements added. (2) The unseen image stored in the binary code of the computer system before it is altered to a video image or placed on film.

■ **digital input device (DID)** A system first developed for *Jurassic Park* (1993; dir. Steven Spielberg) in which the movements of a stop-motion and motion-control animation armature are fed into a computer to be repeated by a computer-generated image. The process allows the image, in this case a preliminary wire-frame dinosaur, to obtain the movements of the real world. *See* **computer animation, film scanner,** *and* **input device.**

■ **digital reader** *See* **digital head.**

■ **digital restoration** Restoring an older and deteriorated film digitally. All the frames of the film are first scanned into a digital code and then each is called up on a monitor. Scratches and any other damage are repaired, as well as imperfections normally not seen in previous projections—e.g., dust, flares, and fringing. Paint workstations use software to enhance, retouch, and correct the digital images that are finally recorded onto high-resolution color intermediate film by means of a film recorder. Kodak's Cinesite used this method with the new Cineon digital film system to restore Walt Disney's *Snow White* (1937). *See* **Cineon digital film system, film recorder,** *and* **film scanner.**

■ **digital scene simulation (DSS)** Computer graphics employed for film visuals. *See* **computer animation.**

■ **digital sound** Music or sound effects created or transformed digitally by a synthesizer or computerized musical instrument. Synthesizers are capable of playing or transforming music or voices digitally recorded on a disc and also generating their own electronic sounds for digital recording. Digital musical instruments operating through keyboards, record their own scores, which can then be edited and orchestrated either in real or nonreal time. Such instruments can create any number of tracks. *See* **MIDI** *and* **synthesizer.**

■ **digital sound recording** A sound recording system that converts sound into a series of binary numbers (i.e., combinations of 0's and 1's) and stores them in a computer's memory from which they can be converted into a signal and amplified. The greater the range and amount of numbers, the greater will be the fidelity of the sound recording. Since this system converts only the numbers to sound and ignores any noisy buildup in the recording medium itself, the quality of the sound will not deteriorate no matter how many times it is rerecorded, a fact especially important when editing and mixing sound for motion pictures, which requires any number of transfers. Digital systems also allow a flexible and efficient way of equalizing and altering sounds. Digital audio tape (DAT) has made its way into film production, where it can be used in perfect sync with the camera with the help of a time code (in some systems, a separate track on the tape records a number for each frame so that image and sound can be easily edited together). Digital audio tapes have a 16-bit capacity and two tracks so that more than one source of sound can be recorded at the same time. The Nagra-D, however, using quarter-inch tape, is a four-channel reel-to-reel field unit with a 24-bit recording capability as opposed to the DAT recorders. The digital technology is used to record musical scores, sound effects, and dialogue in general, as well as for editing and mixing— for laying tracks and creating the various mixes, the sound is transferred to hard drive for easy accessibility and manipulation. The master tracks are finally placed on tape or optical disc.

Digital recording offers great opportunity to improve the quality of sound even further for motion pictures. Sound is still recorded on optical channels on release prints for analog playback; but digital sound systems are rapidly making their way into movie theaters. Seventy-mm prints of *Dick Tracy* (dir. Warren Beatty) were released in 1990 with a six-track digital sound system called Cinema Digital Sound (CDS). Today, three digital systems are in use for 35mm prints. The Dolby SR-D system places the digital code between the perforations; Digital Theater System (DTS), from MCA/Universal, places it on a disc that is in perfect synchronization with the projector by means of a time code on the film (an ironic throwback to the sound-on-disc system, Vitaphone, that was developed by Western Electric in the early days of sound film); and the third, Sony Dynamic Digital Sound (SDDS), prints the code on a track on the outside of the film and a back-up track on the other edge. While the first two systems employ six tracks, three for the left, right, and center of the screen, two for the surround sound on the left and right sides of the theater, and one for the subwoofer, the SDDS system makes available an additional two tracks for sound from the screen. Although films are still released with only analog channels, a growing number are also released with anywhere from one to all of these types of digital sound. As a result, some theaters are equipped to play all three digital sound systems, though it is likely that ultimately the industry will settle on one. Digital recording, editing, mixing, and now playback are allowing audiences to hear sound that is more clear, immediate, and real and that has a greater range of frequency than any heard before in film theaters—one need only be in a theater adjacent to another using digital sound to understand the full power and resonance on this type of sound system. *See* **analog recording** *and* **mixer.**

■ **digital sync** Synchronization in the running of both camera and audio recorder by means of a digital signal sent for each frame by the camera to the tape. This digital code allows perfect synchronization of sound and image for the editing process. *See* **synchronization.**

■ **digital table, digital tablet** An electronic drawing board with two-dimensional graphics, the key points of which are fed into a computer by means of a digital pen disturbing the table's magnetic field. The computer itself connects the various key points into an image. *See* **digitizing pen.**

■ **Digital Theater System (DTS)** *See* **digital sound.**

■ **digital versatile disc, digital video disc** *See* **DVD.**

■ **digital video effects (DVE)** Special effects and graphics achieved in a video image by means of a computerized digital coding system. The term applies to the alteration of picture elements, the compositing of elements from different images, the creation of images or picture elements, and the utilization of transitional editing techniques to move from one shot or scene to another. The Charisma Ten from Questech Ltd. in England can achieve a host of remarkable effects including page turns, rotations, wraps, bends, stretches, morphing, rolls, shatters, defocus drop shadows, and fly modes, while maintaining excellent picture quality. Technically any digital effect in a film that is photographed from a cathode-ray tube is also a video effect. *See* **digital effects.**

■ **digital videotape** *See* **videotape.**

■ **digital videotape recorder, digital VTR (DVTR)** *See* **videotape recorder.**

■ **digitizer** Any device that coverts texts, images, or objects into a digital code for storage in a computer system. *See* **digitizing pen, input device, scanner,** *and* **3-D digitizer.**

■ **digitizing** (1) The process of scanning and converting a drawing, image on a film, or object to a digital code to be stored in the memory of a computer. *See* **digitizing pen, input device, scanner, 3-D digitizer.** (2) The general process of making animated images from a computer. *See* **computer animation.** (3) The general process of altering, developing, or adding to an image or image elements by means of a computer and a digital software program. *See* **digital effects.** (4) The process of converting any analog informational system into a computerized digital code.

■ **digitizing pen, digital stylus, electric pen** A device for tracing images on a digital table so that they can be digitally stored in a computer system. In one device, the pen passes over an electronic table and creates signals by disturbing a magnetic field. The key points of a drawing or photograph are entered into the computer, which then imposes the connecting lines. The digitizing pen can also be used to transmit the information concerning the form of a three-dimensional object. *See* **digital table** *and* **mouse.**

■ **digitizing scanner, input scanner** *See* **scanner.**

■ **dimmer** A device that reduces or increases the power supply to a light, hence diminishing or increasing the illumination from that source. Such devices are effective in black-and-white photography—for example, in allowing a character to shut off lights so that they diminish smoothly without a sudden jump from light to dark—but can only be used for color photography in a limited way, since altering the power creates a change in color temperature.

■ **dimmer bank** A row of attached dimmer lights.

■ **dinky** A term sometimes used for a small, closed, incandescent lamp with a 100-watt bulb.

■ **dinky dolly** A small, compact dolly suitable for corridor and doorway maneuverability. The dolly allows four-way steering and precise turns. *See* **dolly.**

■ **dinky ink** *See* **inky dink.**

■ **DIN standard, DIN speed rating** A system of measurement which indicates the sensitivity or emulsion speed of film. The word "DIN" is derived from the initials of Deutsche Industrie Norm. *See* **ASA standard, exposure index,** *and* **ISO standard.**

■ **diopter lens, plus lens, close-up diopter, diopter** A supplementary lens, generally a simple meniscus type, placed in front of a normal lens for extreme close-ups. The power of this lens is measured in diopters: a meniscus lens that focuses at one meter has a focal length of + 1 diopter; at half meter, a focal length of + 2 diopters; etc. Split diopters cover only part of a lens and can allow two subjects, one close to the camera and one farther away, to be in focus at the same time.

■ **direct** To supervise the making of a motion picture, planning the way the film will be made as well as giving instructions to the performers and the technical personnel; to impose on the motion picture a particular control and artistic vision through such activities. *See* **director.**

■ **direct animation** *See* **direct film.**

direct cinema Frederick Wiseman's *High School* (1968), a telling example of the cinema of self-exposure.

■ ■ ■

■ **direct cinema** A type of documentary that developed in America during the 1960s and was given this name by the filmmaker Albert Maysles to suggest its direct, immediate, and authentic approach to the subject matter. A planned narrative and approach are avoided, something not true of most earlier documentaries. Events seem recorded exactly as they happened without rehearsal and with minimal editing. People are allowed to speak without guidance or interruption, inadvertently revealing their own motives, attitudes, and psychology. The camera watches objectively, not moving or shaping events, employing a zoom lens to get close to a subject without interfering in the natural flow of speech or action. The zoom lens focuses directly on subjects, waiting for them to expose themselves.

This kind of documentary was initially developed largely through the television documentary work of Robert Drew and Richard Leacock, who first made *Primary* together in 1960, a film about the primary battle between Hubert Humphrey and John F. Kennedy in Wisconsin. Drew Associates made a number of films for ABC's *Close Up!* series, and from this group Donn Pennebaker went on to make his film about Bob Dylan, *Don't Look Back* (1966), and Albert and David Maysles to make *Salesman* (1969), both of which played in commercial theaters. The techniques of direct cinema, coming from television news and documentary work,

relied upon the equipment developed for that media: small and light handheld cameras and sound equipment that could be used in sync; fast film stock employed with natural lighting; directional microphones that could pick up speech at a distance; and zoom lenses to focus in on the scene without any intrusion of the camera. Such films sometimes seem amateurish, with grainy, high-contrast images; unbalanced natural sound and rising and falling voices; or a bobbing camera indicating the cameraman's movement. However, all of this contributes to the viewer's feeling that he or she is seeing the action directly, exactly the way it happened, and not watching the product of a filmmaker.

Frederick Wiseman has made a series of impressive documentaries employing the techniques of direct cinema, including *Titicut Follies* (1967) and *High School* (1968); and later these techniques were adapted with a more dynamic editing style to a number of concert films, for example, the Maysles brothers' work based on a concert by the Rolling Stones, *Gimme Shelter* (1970). The direct approach, with its mobile equipment, has also been influential in the fictional films of John Cassavetes, for example, in *Faces* (1968) and *Husbands* (1970), which seem more immediate and spontaneous than most commercial films. Direct Cinema and *cinéma-vérité*, which developed in France at the same time and employs many of the same techniques and the same kinds of equipment, have been confused or seen as the same movement, but *cinéma-vérité* is quite distinct, with the filmmaker's voice intruding into the film, interviewing and probing the subject with questions in order to elicit the truth and create the dramatic exposure and situation. *See* **cinéma-vérité** and **documentary.**

■ **direct color print** A color print made directly from the original film. *See* **reversal film.**

■ **direct cut** An immediate cut from one scene to another without any transitional technique such as a dissolve.

■ **direct distribution costs** Costs for distributing a film. Major costs are for prints and advertising. Other costs include those for shipping and for branch-office overhead. *See* **distribution.**

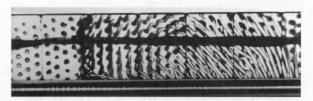

direct film Artwork was directly applied to film by Len Lye for his *Color Box* (1935).

■ ■ ■

■ **direct film** An experimental or animated film that is made by directly painting, drawing, or etching on the film stock itself. This technique may be employed for either abstract or representational images. Len Lye was significant in developing this technique, using the term "direct film" for such works as *Color Box* (1935) and influencing such filmmakers as Norman McLaren with his abstract drawings on film. *See* **noncamera film.**

■ **directional microphone, unidirectional microphone** A microphone that picks up sound largely from one direction and is, therefore, employed for dialogue and other specific sounds. *See* **microphone.**

■ **directional pattern** The pattern of sensitivity or pickup of a microphone; the direction and area from which it picks up sound. *See* **microphone.**

■ **direction of look, direction of glance** The direction in which a character looks during a scene.

■ **directions** (1) The parenthetical statements in a script instructing a performer in the general reading of a line (e.g., "angry," "happy") or giving him or her general instructions for movement. (2) The instructions the director gives to any performer or member of the production crew.

■ **direct music** *See* **source music.**

■ **director** The individual responsible for putting a work on film and sometimes for the vision and final realization of the entire motion picture. In the earliest days of filmmaking, the director was a distinct force and personality, an individual who asserted his own concepts and creativity over the entire film. Such freedom could lead to remarkable individual achievements as well as advancing the art, as it did in the works of D. W. Griffith. But almost from the start there was tension between the studios that produced the films and the director, a conflict between economics and art—Griffith had to leave Biograph and go to Mutual to make his films the way he wanted to make them. Fox Film Company brought Murnau from Germany to direct the moving and beautiful *Sunrise* (1927), but poor financial returns on the film led to interference in his future works. Stroheim is a notable example, in silent-film days, of the individualistic genius who was ultimately defeated by the studio system.

The coming of sound diminished the independence of the director even more, forcing him to rely upon elaborately prepared scripts—dialogue could not be improvised, since retakes were expensive. At the same time, greater financial investment and a greater technology provoked studios to put even more control on the director. The Hollywood director often became one of many people involved in the making of a motion picture, the person who carried out and put on film the conception and demands of others, and who at times had little to say about the final editing of the film. The star system also diminished the role of the director, making him seem the agent for putting onto film the great stars of the time. The most notable example, during the sound period, of the director of genius defeated by the studio system was undoubtedly Orson Welles.

The film criticism which came out of France in the 1950s, the *auteur* criticism as developed by Truffaut and others, forced a reconsideration of these Hollywood films and fostered a view of many, though far from all, of these directors as the controlling artist, the individual who worked amidst the demands of the studio system but triumphed in asserting his particular vision on the work (*see* **auteur**). Directors such as Howard Hawks, Nicholas Ray, and especially Alfred Hitchcock received great adulation for their film work and were themselves raised to the status of stars.

Auteur criticism had some impact on the industry's attitudes toward the director, but a greater influence was the breakdown of the Hollywood studio system. Audiences diminished with the rise of television, productions became even more expensive, and fewer films could be made—the old factory system of the studios, with all their departments and personnel, was no longer affordable. Films came to be made more independently and, over each production, a controlling vision and hand were necessary. The star system diminished with the collapse of the old studios, and directors became as important as the performers in the film—the public was going to fewer films, and those films had to offer more than just a familiar face. At the same time, the development of European film and the rise of such great foreign directors as Antonioni, Bergman, and Fellini had its impact on filmmaking in this country, especially when the works of these artists proved financially successful. American directors in the 1960s such as Arthur Penn, John Frankenheimer, and Stanley Kubrick (who actually went to England to make his films) were recognized and supported because of their independent styles and visions.

The 1970s brought a group of young, new directors, a generation of "movie brats" who had grown up with the movies and whose works showed this consciousness. A number of these directors also graduated from film schools. Peter Bogdanovich, Francis Ford Coppola, Steven Spielberg, George Lucas, and Martin Scorsese, with a variety of types of works, established the director unequivocally as the guiding intelligence and vision of the film and the individual ultimately responsible for its success or failure. In recent years the pendulum has swung back, and we are witnessing a resurgence of the producer (or producers) as the controlling influence in filmmaking, even responsible for the creative force that goes into such works. Film production has become very, very expensive, and the making of a successful motion picture is more dependent on reading the tastes of the market than on the art that goes into the motion picture itself. Certainly *auteur* filmmaking was seriously undermined by the financial debacle of Michael Cimino's *Heaven's Gate* (1980). Independent spirits, however, who have managed to withstand the tide and continue to make films that bear their own imprint, are Martin Scorsese, Robert Altman, Oliver Stone, Woody Allen, the Coen brothers, and John Sayles.

In the best of all possible filmmaking worlds, the director should be the potent force in the production of a motion picture with his vision, artistry, and knowledge of the medium controlling the film from its inception until its completion. He must, of course, make films that will find an audience, since the cost of production and distribution requires a satisfactory box office. The director is sometimes the individual who has the original idea of a film, perhaps from a novel or a scenario submitted to him, though frequently he is contracted by a producer who already has the property he wishes made into a film. From the start, the director must work closely with the screenwriter in developing the screenplay. He must always work closely with the producer to make sure that he keeps within the budget, but also to be sure that he can make the kind of film he envisions. He is involved with casting, works closely with the production designer and art director in creating sets and costumes, and helps determine which scenes will be shot on location. He helps work out the shooting schedule and plans in advance, sometimes with the help of drawings or a storyboard, how he wants each shot photographed. He works with the director of photography in planning lighting, shots, and effects, finding out what technical resources are open to him. In some cases he must have a good knowledge of special-effects photography and work with his special-effects personnel to achieve the extraordinary range of visuals that the industry now allows. He must also work with the lead performers in their interpretation of character. Since shooting must be out of sequence because of economic and locational considerations and because of the performers' schedules, he must be the one always to see the film as a whole, in its proper order, and the one to transmit this vision to those who work with him. During the shooting, he must be concerned with the actors' performances, the camera and lighting, and numerous other details at all times. He must also examine the rushes of the previous day's shooting to make decisions about timing and editing the film as well as future shooting. During the filming he must already be working with his editor; and once the shooting is over, he must be concerned with the final editing, the musical background, and the final synthesis of image, dialogue, sound, and music.

It would be foolish to underplay the importance of all those who contribute to a film. Film is a composite art, and it is often difficult to distinguish where the contribution of one person ends and that of another begins. It is also an art as much dependent on technol-ogy as the people involved. But for these very reasons, the role of the director looms large: he is the technologist and artist, the creative mind who must give to all these disparate elements unity, design, and coherence. It is his vision and sensibility that should stamp the film and infuse it with spirit and meaning.

■ **director of photography (DP), cinematographer, cameraman, first cameraman, lighting cameraman** The individual in charge of putting the scene on film; hence, the person responsible for the lighting of the set or location; the general composition of the scene; the colors of the images; the choice of cameras, lenses, filters, and film stock; the settings of the camera; the setups and movements of the camera; and the integration of any special effects. He is also involved in decisions concerning the actual printing of the film. The director of photography must be responsible for maintaining an overall style from scene to scene and keeping scenes in balance with each other in terms of lighting and color. Since he must concentrate on all these matters during shooting, the operation of the camera is handled by the camera operator, though the director of photography may sometimes handle the camera for documentaries. In addition to the camera operator, he has the first assistant camera operator (or focus puller), the second assistant camera operator (or clapper loader), and several grips working under him. He also is in charge of the gaffer (or chief electrician). The director of photography is generally involved in the planning stages of the film, consulting with the director about the kind of image desired, explaining what he himself can do and how he can do it, and contributing to the visual conception of the film. He must consult with the art director about the layout of sets (to allow for camera movement), composition, color, and costumes. He must also be in constant contact with the gaffer and work closely with the special-effects people. Though the director should be the chief intelligence of the film and the controlling force, it is the director of photography who is finally responsible for the quality of the image on the screen. The cinematographer must adapt from film to film as he works for different directors, but the best cinematographers seem to establish a certain style, a certain creativity within the confines of each work, that marks all their films.

In early films the individual in charge of photography was called the "cameraman" because his function was simply to run the camera, but as lighting developed he was called the "lighting cameraman." Later he was called the "cinematographer" to give him both recognition for the artistic quality of his work and to distinguish him from a "photographer." When sound required greater technical knowledge and, at times, the use of more than one camera, he became the "director of photography." Billy Bitzer is considered to be the first major cameraman: working with D. W. Griffith, he helped create significant techniques in camera setups and movement, lighting, and cutting. With panchromatic film, cameramen such as John F. Seitz, James Wong Howe, and Karl Struss began to break away from traditional romantic styles and achieve individual effects. Sound at first hindered the movement of the camera, but once it was again free, cinematography developed through the work of cinematographers such as Karl Freund, Stanley Cortez, and Gregg Toland. Widescreen cinematography and the developments in color stock during the 1950s and early 1960s produced new challenges and new achievements in the works of cinematographers such as Leon Shamroy and Lee Garmes. Today, cinematography advances with even more poetic and individualistic styles, with the mastery of greater technology, and with greater subtlety in color, lighting, and camera technique in the works of directors of photography such as William Fraker, Haskell Wexler, Sven Nykvist, Gordon Willis, Owen Roizman, and Vilmos Zsigmond.

■ **director's chair** The simple folding chair with director written across the back (or the director's name) has become another one of the icons that symbolize the glamour of movie-making, especially in Hollywood.

■ **director's cut** A rough cut of the film created by the director from the editor's initial assembly. This cut, normally guaranteed as part of the basic terms worked out by the Directors Guild of America, allows the director generally about six weeks and total freedom to develop what he foresees as the final version of the film. The director normally works with the editor in producing this version of the film. *See* **rough cut.**

■ **Directors Guild of America (DGA)** The professional organization and negotiating unit for directors, assistant directors, production managers, production assistants, and stage managers in both film and television.

■ **director's line** *See* **imaginary line.**

■ **director's viewfinder, director's finder** A device, often hanging by a chain from the director's neck, that aids in the selection of a lens for a shot. The finder allows the director, or the cinematographer, to see the image in different relative sizes, and a scale on the barrel allows him or her to choose the lens that will match that size. Some viewfinders allow the various lenses made by their manufacturer to be attached individually. A number of these devices also allow focusing, stopping down to check for depth of field, and zoom movements comparable to those on a zoom lens.

director's viewfinder

■ **directory** Familiar term for the Academy Players Directory, a publication of the Academy of Motion Picture Arts and Sciences, which lists actors and actresses along with their photographs and the names of their agents.

■ **direct print, direct positive** A positive print made directly from the original film without any intermediate steps. *See* **reversal film.**

■ **direct sound** (1) Indigenous sound that derives from a source in the scene. (2) Sound immediately recorded with one microphone and without interruption during each shot while filming on location. Such sound does not depend on a later mix of various tracks, but presents all the sound—voices and background—as they are recorded at the time. Direct sound is frequently used in documentaries and sometimes in fictional films for documentary effect.

■ **direct-to-video release** (1) A film that can not find a distributor for a theatrical release either in this country or abroad and that, as a result, is released directly on video cassette for rental or purchase. (2) A low-budget film made directly for a video release.

■ **dirty dupe, editing dupe** A black-and-white print of a film normally made from a workprint that is employed for sound mixing or simply as a back-up where color or quality of image is not important.

■ **disaster film** A motion picture that features great violence and injury, often caused by some natural calamity, to both a large number of people and the physical landscape. Such films generally have very little in the way of developed characters or plot and function largely to display one horrendous event after another. For the film industry, these works are a means of displaying technical wizardry through special effects. Disaster films become especially popular during periods of great national stress—perhaps, as has sometimes been suggested, because they offer a means of escape for a harried public, though more accurate reasons may be that they offer audiences a way to vent frustration and also a way to appease their own fears by seeing destructive forces both unleashed upon others and also arrested. In the Depression years, audiences spent the little money they had to see the havoc of films such as Cooper and Schoedsack's *The Last Days of Pompeii* (1935), W. S. Van Dyke's *San Francisco* (1936), and John Ford's *The Hurricane* (1937). Japan produced a number of films in the 1950s, for example Inoshiro Honda's *Godzilla* (1955) and *The Mysterians* (1957), which seem to belong less to the horror or science-fiction genre and more to the disaster type. In these works, the traumas of Hiroshima and Nagasaki are replayed when Tokyo is demolished over and over again. Also of interest are the disaster films in America during the 1970s,

disaster film A realistic scene from *San Francisco* (1936; dir. W. S. Van Dyke).

■ ■ ■

which may have been a response to the recent Vietnam war and to contemporary political and economic disenchantment. This series began with Irwin Allen's production of *The Poseidon Adventure* (1972; dir. Ronald Neame) and also included his film *The Towering Inferno* (1974; dir. John Guillermin and Irwin Allen). A recent film of this type that had great popularity was Jan De Bont's *Twister* (1996).

■ **disc, disk** (1) The storage element in a computerized system for holding large amounts of information. So-called "floppy discs," which are inserted into the computer, hold one or two megabytes of information, while hard discs that are a permanent part of the computer can hold vastly more. The floppy disc is composed of a magnetized substance in a plastic covering. (2) The storage element for both the visual and audio portions of a motion picture that is used in home playback systems in conjunction with the television set or a video monitor. Such systems give superior picture and sound than the recordings of motion pictures on videotape.

■ **disclaimer, disclaimer title** The small printed words on the screen, at the end of a film, claiming that characters in the film are not based on actual persons, living or dead, and that any resemblances are purely coincidental.

■ **discontinuity, discontinuity cutting, discontinuous editing, discontinuity shooting** Sudden and abrupt shifts from shot to shot in the editing of a film caused by the mismatching of such elements as location of characters, objects, or action; direction or speed of movement;

composition; lighting; or color. Discontinuity normally is consciously planned to achieve a sense of disharmony, disorder, confusion, or contrast and to upset the viewer. The term "jump cut" describes a similar effect, but one that may either be planned or accidental, while discontinuity generally refers to conscious intent through mismatching. *See* **jump cut.**

■ **discovery** The term, which describes a person previously unknown but suddenly recognized for great ability and potential success, perhaps even before he or she appears in a film, has great resonance in the glamorous and romantic mythology of early Hollywood.

■ **discovery shot** A continuous shot with camera movement that suddenly discovers some person, object, or action not seen at the beginning of the shot. These shots are further identified by the type of camera movement: for example, discovery pan shot; discovery tilt shot; discovery dolly shot; and discovery zoom shot (the words are sometimes reversed, as with pan discovery shot).

■ **dishing** The dropping out of the center portion of film that has been wound on a core, something that is likely to happen to the novice unless he or she keeps a hand beneath the film when holding it in a flat position.

■ **dislocation** A sense of being apart or separated from the action of the film and hence unable to be secure in any association or involvement with the characters and their world. This can be a very disturbing effect that puzzles viewers and makes them consider the reasons for their dislocation by examining the characters objectively. Such techniques are devices for an examination of the film's world and our own. Jean-Luc Godard has made dislocation a major technique ever since *Breathless* in 1959, where the viewer is kept emotionally and psychologically separate from the characters by the cynical and unsentimental treatment of them and the disorienting treatment of time, space, and continuity through jump cuts and awkward movements of the camera.

■ **dispersion** (1) The separation of light into its various colors by refraction through some kind of transparent medium such as a prism. (2) The variation of the index of refraction for the different wavelengths of light in some kind of transparent medium as a prism.

■ **displacement magazine** A single-chamber magazine in which the two rolls are sufficiently close so that the film takes up on the second roll the space that it formerly filled when unexposed on the first. *See* **magazine.**

■ **displacement mapping** *See* **texture mapping.**

■ **DISS** *See* **dissolve.**

■ **dissolve (DISS), lap dissolve, cross dissolve, mix** A transition between two scenes whereby the first gradually fades out as the second gradually fades in with some overlap between the two. This transition is normally made in an optical printer (for silent films it had to be obtained in the camera and so was not often used). Rapid dissolves suggest an immediate dramatic contrast between two scenes or a rapid change of time; slow dissolves suggest a more subtle contrast and a more gradual passing of time. Dissolves can also be employed as a transition between related actions or simply as a device to soften the change from one scene to another. When the dissolve is distorted and the images seem to ripple and blur before the second becomes clear, a flashback in a character's mind or a perspective from his distorted mind may be suggested (the technique is often called a ripple dissolve). The dissolve is less often employed today than it was in the 1930s and the 1940s because of its past overuse and because it is too obvious a signal for a change in time. The older term for this technique is lap dissolve, a diminutive of overlap dissolve. Lap dissolve, cross dissolve, and mix are all terms for this technique that suggest that the previous scene is still partly on the screen while the new one is appearing. *See* **match dissolve** *and* **ripple dissolve.**

■ **dissolve animation** In educational, scientific, and technical films, this term refers to a series of dissolves between illustrations or diagrams to suggest the progressive stages in some process.

■ **dissolve-lapse** A series of dissolves between shots of the same location that shows the progress of some action, such as the construction of a building, or the passage of time, perhaps through seasonal changes.

■ **distance** A major concern in cinematography is the distance between the audience and subject. Various distances give varying amounts of information and involve the audience in different ways. Film is able to contract and expand space, to orchestrate a series of perspectives for the viewer, allowing a far more dynamic relationship with the performers and setting than any achieved in live drama. Physical reality becomes fluid and expressive. The distance to the subject is the result of both the actual distance between camera and subject and the type of lens employed for the shot.

The apparent distances between camera and subject are designated into three broad categories—long shot (LS), medium shot (MS), and close-up (CU)—and each of these has finer designations (for example, extreme long shot (ELS), medium long shot (MLS), etc.). The long shot generally takes in an entire person or building and some of the surrounding area; a medium shot shows a view of a person from waist to head or at least half of some object or place; and a close-up brings a viewer to an intimate view of the head of a person, some small object, or a small portion of a

place. Of course, all of these are relative terms depending on the size of the subject shown—a long shot of a character would show far less area than a long shot of a building. Long shots are useful for establishing a place or setting, for giving an entire action, and, in general, for giving the viewer a good deal of information and a detached perspective. Medium shots are useful for presenting a single person performing an act or several people involved in action or conversation, allowing us both perspective and some involvement. Close-ups display the emotions and feelings of a character and involve us more deeply.

Distance can be controlled by the amount of the picture which is in focus. Shallow focus defines only one plane, marking our distance from that area of the scene while leaving the other planes a blur and not creating any sense of depth or distance within the scene. Deep focus creates a sense of depth or interior distance in the scene, making us aware of our relation to the various planes of the scene. The screen also conveys horizontal distance, which is determined by the width of the frame, the type of lens, and the distance from camera to subject (the longer the shot, the more distance we can see between the extremities of the screen). The development of wide-screen photography and projection in the 1950s brought more horizontal distance into the scene, which has been especially effective for films that emphasize outdoor locations and moving action. The camera itself, through horizontal movements such as panning and tracking shots, creates for the viewer a sense of horizontal distance and is especially effective in following action. *See* **depth** *and* **wide screen.**

■ **distortion** (1) Any misshaping or deforming of the image so that it does not have the exact proportions, clarity, or appearance of the subject in reality. Most lenses are corrected for such problems, but some are used to achieve such an effect—for example, when a fisheye lens, which makes the sides of the image curve around and overemphasizes central and close objects, suggests the vision of a deranged mind. (2) Any transformation in a sound signal that makes it lose its original clarity and quality.

■ **distortion optics** Optical devices in a camera or optical printer for achieving desired distortions in the image.

■ **distribution, distributor** The marketing of films to exhibitors, the distribution and arrangement for the transportation of films to theaters, and the promotion of the film to the public are called distribution. The people or companies that perform these tasks are distributors. For commercial theaters, distribution is by rental, though films at later stages can be rented, leased, or purchased by institutions. As well as arranging for a film's exhibition, distributors are responsible for the financial success or failure of the motion picture and undertake considerable marketing strategies and advertising to persuade people to attend it. Today, the international market also plays a significant role in the financial success of American films.

In 1909, the ten major film producers formed the Motion Picture Patents Company to consolidate control over patents, equipment, and film stock, but also to control distribution of motion pictures. These companies eventually were defeated by the "independents," which themselves became major film studios and gained control of distribution and exhibition. By the mid-1920s, chains of theaters owned individually by these major independent producers showed most of the films in this country, and it was not until 1948 that the Supreme Court, in the Paramount decision, declared such practices illegal and ordered production and distribution to be separated from exhibition. This act, along with court restrictions against block booking, freed theaters to play the best or most profitable films they could obtain. The cost of producing films increased, and by the early 1950s, the big studios had to distribute independent films as well as their own. The high cost of acquiring and distributing independent films discouraged new distributors from entering the market. Since the American market could absorb only about 400 films each year, distribution was restricted largely to the ten major companies, each of which could handle about forty films. United Artists, however, expanded significantly because it largely distributed for independent and foreign producers.

Today, the old film studios are gone; most of the major companies are parts of conglomerates. The "virtual" studios of the 1990s primarily finance "packages" put together by others and distribute such works as well as independently financed and produced works. Sony Pictures Entertainment (Columbia and TriStar), Paramount Pictures, Twentieth Century-Fox, Universal Pictures, Warner Brothers, along with Disney's Buena Vista, bring a large portion of the films that we watch to the screen. Because of the vast amount of money necessary to finance and distribute films, and the large degree of risk, the financial judgment of the major companies still determines a large part of the films that we see and the quality of motion pictures in general.

A producer and distributor often sign a domestic agreement for seven years. Distributors are responsible for selling a film to theaters, for making it known and wanted; they are responsible for the cost of prints and their circulation; and they, along with the exhibitors, are responsible for advertising costs. Distributors have their own marketing departments, which perform considerable research on potential audiences and carry out ambitious advertising campaigns. Publicists are also hired during production to keep the public aware of the film's development. Independent distributors use sub-distributors, which might even be one of the major distribution companies, to handle films in specific markets or territories. The main period for film distribution, which accounts for 40 percent of the industry's domestic business, are the months between the

Memorial Day and Labor Day weekends, when young people are home from school and adults are on vacation. The second important period, for the same reason, is during the Christmas vacation.

For the release of potential "blockbuster" films, major distributors may require up to 90 percent of the box office as a rental fee for the first week and then diminishing percentages for each succeeding week. Such percentages are computed after the theater's fixed expenses (the "house nut") have been subtracted. A percentage floor is also established for such releases, with the distributor normally guaranteed no less than 60–70 percent of the total box office and a sliding scale down to approximately 35 percent over the course of the run. The industry-wide average, however, for the exhibitor's share of box-office receipts is estimated to be approximately 60 percent for the entire run, while the other 40 percent goes to the distributor. Exhibitors must sometimes guarantee a distributor a certain fee or a percentage of box-office receipts, whichever is greater. Sometimes, especially for older films and documentaries, a flat fee is charged the exhibitor. The distributor spends approximately 28 percent of total box-office receipts for advertising, prints, and production, while keeping about 12 percent as a distribution fee. Major distribution companies frequently charge an additional percentage of production cost (for example, 25 percent at Universal) for "overhead" when the film is made within the company's studio facilities (even though such expenses are already part of production costs). The complexity and mystery of such financing have been a source of much controversy in Hollywood, especially since numerous producers of "hit" movies have had to wait a long while to see a percentage of the profits, the amount of which has often turned out to be strangely small in relation to box-office revenue. The major studios argue that the cost of prints and advertising is extraordinary, and that the fixed costs of development, production, and management must be maintained. Because of distribution and marketing costs, break-even points may be defined contractually at 2.5 times production costs. If an additional 25 percent is added to production costs for overhead, that figure increases significantly. Hence, the financial logic becomes even more precarious. Distribution fees for nontheatrical exhibition, videocassette release, television distribution, and other ancillary rights are a separate consideration.

Besides the distributors of popular commercial films, there are also distribution companies that specialize in certain kinds of films, such as foreign, experimental, educational, and pornographic. A number of distributors also specialize in 16mm films for nontheatrical bookings. Distributors of commercial films must be able to sell their films nationally and internationally and must also be concerned with cable television, regular television, and home video sales. The sale of foreign and ancillary rights, sometimes even before a film is made, form a considerable part of a film's market and often guarantee a significant return before the film is released to the theaters. Most of the major studio companies now also have separate divisions for distributing their own catalog of film classics.

International distribution has become a crucial part of the American film industry's business, now accounting for better than 40 percent of the theatrical box-office revenue (more than $3 billion annually). In 1990, American works accounted for more than three-quarters of the films shown in Europe. The potential seems even greater in newly expanding international markets—Russia, Eastern Europe, and China are markets that promise future growth for American films. At the same time, foreign films have an increasingly difficult time at the American box office because of the public's diminishing interest. Distribution abroad is largely accomplished by a small number of American-based, international organizations: e.g., Warner, Sony, United International. While the major studios have their own distribution agencies in foreign countries, the smaller studios and independent producers must strike deals with foreign distributors representing a specific country or area. If we also take into account the vast international markets for television programming, videocassettes, and music, it becomes more than clear why America's second biggest export business is the entertainment industry in spite of some attempts abroad to curtail that business and its cultural impact. *See* **exhibition** *and* **Hollywood.**

■ **distribution fee** The money paid to a distributor by an exhibitor specifically for the distributor's overhead and the cost of releasing a specific film. The fee is figured on a percentage of the rental fee, which is itself a percentage of the gross receipts of the box office. The distributor keeps some 30 percent of the rental fee, with the rest of the money going for such costs as production, prints, and advertising. The term also applies to the contractual fee for distributing a film in nontheatrical and ancillary markets. *See* **distribution.**

■ **ditty bag** A small leather bag that hangs under the tripod's head, between its legs, and contains such apparatus as tape, tools, and light meters.

■ **divergent turret, divergent lens mounting, divergent-axis turret** A mounting or turret that holds three or more lenses in divergent positions so that wide-angle lenses do not show long-focus lenses during photographing and so that several lenses with wide barrels can also be held. *See* **turret.**

■ **D log E curve** A characteristic curve showing the relationship between a film's exposure time and image density.

■ **D-max** The maximum density that an exposed film can achieve; the highest point on its characteristic curve. *See* **characteristic curve.**

■ **DME** The initials stand for dialogue, music, and effects, the three major sound tracks that go into the final mix but that may be placed separately on a single magnetic film for foreign release so that the dialogue track can be replaced with one dubbed in the foreign language for the final mix. Sometimes an M and E track is released, one with only music and effects, to which the foreign-language track can be added.

■ **D-min** The minimum density for film without exposure which is the result of both the density inherent in the base and the density that is the result of some exposed silver halides transforming to silver metal during development. The same characteristics are called base-plus-fog density.

■ **docudrama** A term employed for any dramatization that seeks to re-create actual people and events. Such a presentation uses performers and sometimes alters events, but seeks to achieve an effect of authenticity and credibility.

■ **documentary** A film that deals directly with fact and not fiction, that tries to convey reality as it is instead of some fictional version of reality. These films are concerned with actual people, places, events, or activities. The very act of putting reality on film must change that reality to some degree, must select from it and give it form and shape; and documentaries can be discussed in terms of the degree of control that the filmmaker imposes upon the reality he or she records. What is true of all of these films, however, is that they try to give us a feeling, a sense, a perspective of the reality that actually exists even if some filmmakers might use obvious cinematic techniques to achieve this or even preconceived scenes and narrative lines. Some documentaries have the purpose of persuading the audience to a particular view about some aspect of reality, as, for example, Pare Lorentz's "New Deal" films of the 1930s. When indoctrination distorts reality, however, the work must be considered a propaganda film. Other documentaries seek basically to show and explore, to educate the public about certain social situations or governmental agencies, as, for example, the films made by John Grierson's group in England, also in the 1930s.

The term "documentary" was derived from the French word *documentaire,* which means "travelogue," by Grierson in his review of Robert Flaherty's *Moana* (1926) in the *New York Sun.* Grierson later defined the term as "a creative treatment of reality." The World Union of Documentary in 1948 defined this type of work as recording on film "any aspect of reality interpreted either by factual shooting or by sincere and justifiable reconstruction, so as to appeal either to reason or emotion, for the purpose of stimulating the desire for, and the widening of human knowledge and understanding, and of truthfully posing problems and their solutions." Because the term "documentary" describes

documentary Robert Flaherty's *Nanook of the North* (1922), perhaps the most famous nonfiction film ever made.

■ ■ ■

a wide variety of films, critics and filmmakers have suggested other nomenclature. Richard Barsam argues for the term "nonfiction film" for all these works, with "documentary" reserved for films that are concerned with opinion as well as fact and that seek to persuade the audience to some point of view, and "factual film" for works concerned primarily with fact (in *Nonfiction Film*). Other terms suggested are "propaganda documentaries," "educational documentaries," "romantic" or "lyric documentaries," "avant-garde" or "experimental documentaries," and, more specifically, "newsreels," "travelogues," and "compilation films."

Many of the *actualités* that the Lumière brothers began to show in 1896 were documentaries of a sort, showing aspects of reality without any fictionalizing; but the modern documentary really begins with Robert Flaherty's *Nanook of the North,* first screened in 1922. *Nanook* inspired other films about foreign ways of life, including Cooper and Schoedsack's *Grass* (1925) and *Chang* (1927), and Flaherty's own *Moana* (1926) and *Man of Aran* (1934). Though planned and staged at times, Flaherty's films were remarkable achievements, focusing upon distant ways of life; bringing the remote into proximity with subtle artistry in his selection of scenes, camera work, and editing; and creating a visual poetry in his evocation of foreign cultures. In the Soviet Union, Dziga Vertov achieved some remarkable effects in his montage editing of newsreels in the *Kino-Pravda (Film Truth)* series, and later in the decade he applied his film techniques to documentaries about Soviet progress. Perhaps not technically documentaries, the avant-garde films about cities, the city-symphonies made on the Continent during the 1920s (e.g., Alberto Cavalcanti's *Rien que les Heures* about Paris in 1926) should also be mentioned. But after Flaherty and Vertov, John Grierson is the next significant name

in the history of the documentary, although he directed only one work himself, *The Drifters* in 1929, a film about Scottish fishermen. Grierson, as head of various government units and later sponsored by private industry, led a movement that produced some 300 films during the next decade. The films in this group educated the public about British life, government agencies, and social problems. These films generally show excellent technique, but are largely educational rather than artistic and aesthetic. However, films such as *Song of Ceylon* (1935), directed and filmed by Basil Wright, achieved a high state of art and made reality both immediate and poetic. Also significant are the films made in America during the Depression and sponsored by the government, especially two works by Pare Lorentz, *The Plow That Broke the Plains* (1936), about the Dust Bowl, and *The River* (1937), about the Mississippi Valley and the Tennessee Valley Authority. World War II evoked some fine, patriotic documentaries, for example, Humphrey Jennings's *Fires Were Started* (1943) from England and John Huston's *The Battle of San Pietro* (1944) from America.

The most significant development in the documentary since that time undoubtedly has been the *cinéma-vérité* in France and direct cinema in America in the 1960s. Both of these movements were influenced by television news and documentary work and shaped by the new lightweight, portable equipment for photography and sound. Although *cinéma-vérité* is distinguished by the technique of probing interviews, both movements sought to achieve authenticity and immediacy, a truth and directness not achieved in film before. Mobile equipment allowed filmmakers to get into their subjects with minimal technical intrusion. Their avoidance of preconceived attitudes and narrative lines, of apparent filming techniques and editing, produced films that at times seem amateurish but often seem as close to the truth of human nature as one can obtain on film. Marcel Ophüls's *The Sorrow and the Pity* (1970) is one of the most distinguished films to come out of *cinéma-vérité,* and the films of Frederick Wiseman are notable works of direct cinema. (*See* **cinéma-vérité** *and* **direct cinema**.) Also significant are such powerful political documentaries from the Third World as Fernando Solanas and Octavio Getino's *The Hour of the Furnaces* (1968), a 260-minute confrontation with political evil in Argentina and a call to arms. Sometimes a documentary can chronicle history for posterity while also leaving a document so moving and significant that it takes cinema to another level: Claude Lanzmann's *Shoah* (1985), presented in two four-and-one-half-hour parts, records the memories of the survivors of the Holocaust (both the victims' and perpetrators') through a series of *cinéma-vérité* interviews that in their force and totality give the fullest and most overwhelming picture of this dreadful event.

Although documentaries are difficult to finance because they rarely play commercial theaters—often they are made for specialized organizations, institutions, and audiences—a number of these films are so close to reality, causing us to see the world around us with such extraordinary clarity, and are so emotionally involving that they have reached the public at large (e.g., Barbara Kopple's *Harlan County, U.S.A.,* a journalistic account of a strike by miners and a moving portrait of human dignity, which won an Academy Award for 1976). Hollywood, in general, has not been responsive to the documentary film either in terms of distribution or recognition. The failure of such films as *Hoop Dreams* (dir. Steve James, Peter Gilbert, and Frederick Marx) and *Crumb* (dir. Terry Zwigoff) to win Academy Award nominations as best documentaries for 1994 created a significant stir and forced the Academy to change its rules by instituting a second nominating committee in New York City in addition to that already in Los Angeles, changing the scoring system, and requiring that nominated films, starting in 1997, play at least one week in a commercial theater in Los Angeles or New York. The public outcry and the Academy's reaction might be indications of the industry's new cognizance that the documentary offers to some of the public an important alternative to Hollywood's fictional films. *See* **propaganda film.**

documentary style *The Battle of Algiers* (1966; dir. Gillo Pontecorvo) has numerous scenes with the authenticity of a newsreel.

■ ■ ■

■ **documentary style** A style of photography, editing, and sound recording in fictional films that emulates that of the documentary in order to create a sense of reality and objectivity. For example, Henry Hathaway attempted to give a sense of immediacy and truth to the threat of Nazi spying and espionage in America during World War II, as well as a sense of confidence in American law-enforcement agencies, in *The House on 92nd Street* (1945), when he used an objective filming

style and an authoritative voice-over, both associated with the documentary and also associated with the *March of Time* series of its producer, Louis De Rochemont. Gillo Pontecorvo in *The Battle of Algiers* (1966) synthesized the look of newsreel photography with documentary technique to give credibility and force to his depiction of the Algerian struggle for independence against the French. *See* **documentary** *and* **semidocumentary.**

■ **Dolby** Trade name for a number of sound systems developed by Ray Dolby and his Dolby Laboratories, Inc. for cassettes, FM radio, film, and home theaters. Dolby developed a sound recording system during the 1970s that, by reducing background noise, allows better fidelity for magnetic tape and optical sound tracks on film. It accomplishes this by compressing the sound range during recording and decoding the signal by expansion during playback at a level greater than the level of the noise. Dolby also developed a stereo system that operates on 35mm film through two optical channels, which actually create four distinct sound tracks for left, right, and center speakers from the screen, and for surround speakers. More recently the company has introduced Dolby SR-D, one of several digital systems in use that produces sound exceeding anything heard in movie theaters before. The Dolby digital system uses six channels, optically placed between the perforations on the film, for left, right, and center speakers from behind the screen, left and right surround sound, and a subwoofer. Also worth noting is the Dolby Pro Logic, a sound system for home theaters that reproduces the stereo and surround sound heard in motion-picture houses. *See* **digital sound, home-cinema theater,** *and* **sound.**

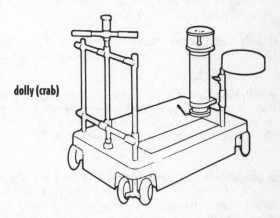

dolly (crab)

■ **dolly** A mobile platform on wheels that supports the camera, camera operator, and often the assistant cameraman, and allows the camera to make noiseless, moving shots in a relatively small area. The dolly is either driven or pushed by a person called the dolly grip or dolly pusher. It often runs on tracks for smoothness of movement. The camera itself rests on an arm which allows it to be raised, lowered, pivoted, and tilted. Normal dollies allow forward and backward movement, but crab dollies allow sideway movement as well. *See* **dolly shot.**

■ **dolly grip, dolly pusher, dolly man** The person who pushes the dolly during a shot.

■ **dolly in, dolly up, camera up** A shot that moves toward the subject by means of a wheeled support, generally a dolly.

■ **dollying** The movement of the camera during a shot by means of a wheeled support, generally a dolly.

■ **dolly out, dolly back, camera back** A shot that moves away from the subject by means of a wheeled support, generally a dolly.

■ **dolly shot, tracking shot, trucking shot, traveling shot** A shot taken by the camera while it is moving on a wheeled support, generally a dolly, though the term is often employed to designate any shot in which the camera moves through the scene. The shot is also called a trucking shot because the camera seems "trucked" from place to place. Since tracks are often used for the dolly, the shot is sometimes called a tracking shot, though this term is more specifically used for shots in which the camera follows a person or object. A dolly shot allows a smooth, even movement in a relatively small area. It can focus in on a character or an important action, object, or detail in a scene; move back and reveal something in the larger scene; suggest a character's point of view during movement; expand the viewer's sense of depth in a scene; or simply vary the viewer's perspective. *See* **dolly.**

■ **dolly tracks, camera tracks** Generally rails but also boards that allow the dolly to move smoothly and evenly during shooting.

■ **dolly zoom shot** A shot simultaneously using a zoom lens and dolly that brings the scene either closer or farther away while the camera seems to be in movement. This compound technique increases both the fluidity and sudden drama of the shot.

■ **domestic version, domestic release** A version of a film for release at home as distinct from a foreign one that might have changes for distribution abroad and dubbed in dialogue or subtitles in the foreign language.

■ **dominant, dominant contrast** That element in the visual image or single image in a montage sequence that controls the viewer's attention because of its significant contrast with other elements or images. *See* **intrinsic interest** *and* **subsidiary.**

■ **donut** A circular piece, generally made of rubber, that fits around the lens of the camera to prevent light from entering the matte box at the point of its juncture with the lens and flaring off the filters back into the camera.

■ **doorway dolly** A dolly narrow enough to pass through standard doorways.

■ **dope sheet** (1) An analysis of film stock. (2) A camera report. (3) A chart with the various camera exposures for each shot to be taken during animation photography. (4) A type of camera report generally used for documentary and news photography when no script exists. Also called a cap sheet (for caption sheet).

■ **dot** A small, circular gobo or scrim, from four to eight inches across, that blocks part of a luminaire's light from falling on a specific area of the set or the lens of the camera. Also called a target.

■ **double** A person filmed in place of a leading actor or actress when a stunt is too dangerous or demanding or for distant shots when the lead performer is not needed. *See* **stand-in.**

■ **double bill** *See* **double feature.**

■ **double broad** A large 4,000-watt floodlight with two lamps that gives a wide, diffuse light and is generally employed as a fill light. *See* **fill light.**

■ **double clod** A flat with both sides painted for scenery.

■ **double distribution fees** Two fees for the distribution of a film, one for the major distributor and another for a sub-distributor hired by the larger organization to handle the film in a specific territory or market. Such a practice can be very costly to the production company if some allowance in the fees is not made by the major distributor. *See* **distribution.**

■ **double-duping** Working with a second dupe negative derived from a previous dupe, a practice sometimes used in special-effects photography but one to be avoided because of the deterioration of the image.

■ **double 8mm film** A strip of 16mm film made up of two attached parallel rows of 8mm film. One half of the width was first exposed, then the other. After development the film was cut down the middle and then spliced together as a single piece of 8mm film. *See* **8mm film** *and* **single 8mm film.**

■ **double exposure (DX)** The superimposition of two images, one over the other, by exposing the same piece of film twice. Double exposure is a conscious technique in professional cinematography to (1) show what a person is remembering, thinking, or dreaming while he or she is still present on the screen; (2) create ghosts or other supernatural effects in an image of the real physical world; (3) comment upon the primary scene by some visual contrast or metaphor seen simultaneously with the scene; (4) suggest a change in time by dissolving from one scene to another. Exposing the same negative twice would, of course, result in an overexposed negative unless each exposure were stepped down. The primary scene should, however, be given more of an exposure. The device is not often seen today since it seems too unnatural and was often misused in the past.

▪ **double feature** A cinema presentation of two feature films for a single price of admission. This practice began in the Depression years to lure customers to the theater, and by the mid 1940s, it was a practice in two-thirds of the theaters in this country. Exhibitors, however, could afford only one first-rate feature, so it was necessary for studios to make cheaper B-pictures as well, though sometimes two B-pictures would play in a double feature during the week. The rising cost of film production and the Supreme Court's Paramount decision in 1948, which separated exhibiting from the control of the big studios, ultimately did away with the B-picture and hence the double feature for the most part: fewer films were made, the cost of exhibiting became higher, and exhibitors themselves could choose their own films and were not bound to show extra and less profitable works. Double features are still occasionally presented when new films are not doing well financially or for the reissue of popular older films. *See* **B-picture, combo engagement,** *and* **double-up day.**

▪ **double frame** A 35mm film frame that extends along eight perforations instead of the normal four. This kind of frame has been employed to obtain a wide-screen image in such systems as Vistavision because the film runs through the camera sideways. *See* **wide screen.**

▪ **double framing, double frame exposure** The process of printing each frame twice. Such double printing slows down the action but results in movement within the film that tends to be unrhythmic. *See* **skip framing** *and* **stretch framing.**

▪ **double-head projection** A type of projection and sound playback system in which the picture is on one reel and the magnetic sound on another. Both the picture and sound heads are synchronized. This system is used for screening parts of a film during production when sound and image are still separate.

▪ **double-key lighting** The illumination of a scene when two subjects or areas receive key lighting. The practice is sometimes used in conversation scenes in which the characters are separated. Also called X-lighting. *See* **key light.**

▪ **double pass system** A traveling matte process that employs two separate but precisely similar shots of the same action, painted figures on a rostrum, or miniatures. Such a process is possible now with computerized animation stands and computerized motion-control and go-control systems. A miniature of a space vehicle, for example, is first photographed against black, hence allowing a positive image, which is self-matting, to be printed. The miniature is then painted white and photographed, with the exact same shot, in bright light on high-contrast film, from which a male traveling matte is created. After the geometry of the high-contrast matte is reversed by any number of processes, the matte is used to block out the shape of the miniature in the background on a positive being photographed on a fresh negative. The empty area on the negative is then filled in from the positive image of the miniature made in the original pass. *See* **traveling-matte process.**

▪ **double perforated stock, double perforation stock, double perf stock** Film stock with perforations along both edges. Thirty-five- and 70mm films always have two rows of perforations; 16mm raw stock generally does also, though prints of this gauge with a sound track on one side may have perforations along only the other edge.

▪ **double printing** Making a composite print from two negatives in a single printing. Such a process is achieved in an optical printer.

▪ **double print titles** *See* **A and B roll supered titles.**

▪ **double system print** A work print employed in conjunction with a separate magnetic tape for sound. Both picture and sound are run synchronically for early previews of the film and for editing.

▪ **double-system projector** A machine that can play both the picture and a separate sound track on magnetic film, normally used to allow individuals to see the workprint and hear the final mixed sound track before both are joined together on a composite print.

▪ **double-system sound recording** Sound recording in most professional filming, where the sound is recorded on a separate magnetic tape and not on the film, though both are in synchronization. The sound is generally not the full or final mix. This system allows for greater fidelity in sound and greater facility in editing. *See* **single/double-system sound camera** *and* **single-system sound recording.**

▪ **double take** A repetition of the same part of an action when the action is shot from two different angles with a single camera and the overlap is printed for each or when it is shot with two different cameras and overlapped in editing. Normally a fault in editing, the effect is on occasion intentionally achieved to show the slowness or futility of a character's action.

■ **double-up** A combo engagement (i.e., a showing of two films), but generally for a single day.

■ **double-up day** A single day on which a film exhibitor shows both a new film and the film terminating its exhibition for one price of admission. Such a practice is intended to increase revenues for the day as well as encourage future patrons for the new film from good reports on the part of the present audiences. *See* **double feature.**

■ **douser, dowser** (1) The device that cuts off the beam in a projector either during a changeover to another projector for showing the next reel of film or to protect the film and gate when the projector is on but not in operation. (2) The device on a spotlight that immediately cuts off the beam of light.

■ **down** A direction in a film script to lower the volume of a particular sound, especially music.

■ **downlight** A light beamed from above a subject during shooting.

■ **download** To transfer a file or program from an outside source or from a large memory bank into the computer's own memory.

■ **down shot** A high-angle shot.

■ **downtime** (1) A period when a piece of equipment is nonfunctional. (2) A period when shooting stops because of malfunctioning equipment.

■ **DP** *See* **director of photography.**

■ **dramatic** Having the quality of the drama; a work with great conflict and strong emotions.

■ **dramatic irony** (1) Irony that results from the audience having more information than the characters and hearing them converse and watching them act in ignorance, often against their own best interests. (2) Irony that results from a dramatic situation in which the hero or heroine unwittingly acts against his or her own best interests. Irony normally suggests words that say one thing and mean another. In both (1) and (2) dramatic irony arises when what appears to happen on the surface hides some truth or reality that the characters cannot know. *See* **irony.**

■ **dramatic structure** The arrangement and relationship of a plot's elements in any narrative work, including film. The traditional manner of examining such a structure is in terms of exposition, development of action, climax, and, finally, dénouement. Many films, a number of Ingmar Bergman's works, for example, follow such an order to keep the audience involved in the work's plot and characters; but effective in a different way is Ermanno Olmi's *Tree of Wooden Clogs* (1979), which is more accumulative in nature and achieves dramatic impact from the work's totality; and films such as Michelangelo Antonioni's *L'Avventura* (1960), which make their impact from the lack of any true climax or dénouement. *See* **climax** *and* **dénouement.**

■ **dramatic unity** A dramatic structure that is tightly organized, with no divergent or peripheral plot elements that detract from the major characters and the development of their situation. In traditional dramatic criticism such a quality is also referred to as unity of action. Two other unities cited in traditional criticism are those of time and place (i.e., when all the action takes place in a single location and within a prescribed duration, generally twenty-four hours). These two unities are still sometimes cited as a requirement for dramatic unity, though with somewhat more extended space and time for modern drama and film.

■ **dramatization** Presenting in dramatic form an actual event or some literary work, particularly a novel.

■ **draper** The individual responsible for the hanging of any fabric in a set. *See* **drapery department.**

■ **drapery department** The group of people responsible for curtains, draperies, upholstery on furniture, canvas backdrops, and any fabricked object on the set.

■ **drawn-cel animation** *See* **cel animation.**

■ **dream balloon** In early silent films, a small area, like the balloon for dialogue in a comic strip, near the character's head to show his or her thoughts or dreams. Griffith seems to have introduced the convention of cutting to a separate shot to show the character's internal images. One of the earliest examples of the dream balloon appears in Edwin S. Porter's *The Life of an American Fireman* (1903), when a fireman's dream of his wife and child appears above his head.

■ **dream mode** Pictures on the screen that represent the mental images of a character's imagination, dream, daydream, or fantasy. An important plot element in Hitchcock's *Spellbound* (1945) is the visualization of Gregory Peck's dream, which was designed by Salvador Dali.

■ **Dreamworks SKG** A new film and entertainment company announced in 1994 by filmmaker Steven Spielberg; former president of Walt Disney's film studios, Jeffrey Katzenberg; and record impresario David Geffen. The studio is to focus on films, animation, television programming, records, and interactive media. In 1995, the group announced that they would build the first studio back lot created in half a century on one hundred acres north of Los Angeles airport—on land that includes the site where Howard Hughes created his famous Spruce Goose aircraft (six of the fifteen new sound studios will be built in the hangar). The studio is to be completely wired with optic fibers and include the latest computer technology. Of the $2 billion that had been raised by the company by the end of 1995, the initial $100 million had come from the three founders.

■ **dress** To prepare a set for shooting by properly arranging furniture, properties, drapes, and decorations.

■ **dresser** A costume assistant who helps the actors put on and take off their costumes.

■ **dressing** Furniture, props, curtains, drapes, paintings, statues, leaves, bushes, and even extras, all of which dress the set and add to its authenticity.

■ **dress off** A direction to an actor to position himself or herself according to an object or another person: for example, "Dress off the rear of the wicker chair."

■ **drift** (1) The slight, unintended movement of an actor out of position until the composition is ruined. (2) An order for a character to move gradually in a certain direction.

■ **drive-in movie, drive-in theater** An outdoor theater in which the audience sees the movie while seated in their automobiles. A large, elevated white screen stands in the front, with the cars facing it in long, curved rows. Small speakers are placed in each car for sound. The projection room is about two-thirds of the way back. Playgrounds for children were also a feature until insurance rates became too high. These theaters became popular in this country after the Second World War and by 1958 numbered over 4,000. They generally held about 600 or 700 cars, though a number could hold more than 2,000. Drive-in theaters became less popular, and today number approximately 850, many of them showing only exploitation films with much sex and violence. The reasons for their diminishment are varied: the novelty of the theaters wore off, and filmgoers returned to the better visuals and audio of indoor theaters; the fascination with the automobile diminished at the same time that many cars became too small for comfortable viewing; motion pictures on cable television and videotape drew audiences away from movie theaters in general; and real estate became too expensive to afford the minimal return of drive-in theaters. Such film theaters, however, still have some success in warmer climates.

■ **drive mechanism, drive system** The operating parts of a camera or projector that transport the film through the main body and are powered by the electric drive motor.

■ **drive-on, drive-on pass** A pass issued by the studio to allow an individual to drive an automobile onto the studio lot.

■ **driver** The individual responsible for driving any of the vehicles that transport equipment, scenery, and personnel for a production.

■ **drop** A large, heavy curtain, normally made of canvas, that is suspended from the fly at the rear of the set and on which background scenery is painted.

■ **dropout** The sudden absence of sound from a sound track, sometimes intentional and sometimes because of a malfunction during the recording or mixing periods. Intentional dropouts might be the result of placing blank leader in the track until the intended sound can replace it.

■ **drop shadow, dropped shadow** A method of highlighting titles, especially when they appear over live action, by shadowing the area below and to the sides of the letters. This can be achieved by employing two separate high-contrast films, one with the lettering in black and one with the lettering in white. In an optical printer, the black lettering is printed onto the background film to create the shadow, and the white lettering is then printed slightly to the side and above.

■ **drum titler, title drum** A rotating drum around which is wound a strip with printed titles or text. As the drum is rotated by an electric motor, the titles or text unwind and continuously move upward to be photographed by the camera.

■ **dry box** The drying cabinet where circulating warm, dry air removes from the film moisture obtained during processing. *See* **processing.**

■ **dry end** The final part of the processing machine, which contains the dry box.

■ **dry-ice generator** A box or container in which dry ice is released into hot water to make mist for dream sequences or fog.

■ **drying** The removal of moisture from film at the end of processing, first by a wiper and then by the circulation of dry, hot air around the film in a dry box or cabinet. *See* **processing.**

■ **dry lab** A laboratory that prints film but does not process it. Such labs are sometimes convenient for timing a film (i.e., making changes in density and color) and are also sometimes capable of turning out a large number of release prints. *See* **laboratory.**

■ **dry run** A rehearsal, generally with actors and camera, immediately before filming.

■ **DSS** (1) The initials stand for Digital Satellite System, a process of transmitting video to homes by means of an 18-inch dish picking up digital signals from a satellite in the sky. In the first two years, the system, which can beam more that 200 channels to a home, has been responsible for the sale of approximately 2 million dishes. The digital signals are transformed for viewing with standard television receivers by a converter box on top of the set. Although the picture does not have as much resolution as that which will be achieved with all digital HDTV, it is still superior to pictures from standard broadcasting and cable because the digital transmission prevents any deterioration in the signal. *See* **digital, HDTV,** *and* **television.**

■ **dual-film traveling matte process** *See* **traveling-matte process.**

■ **dual role** Two parts played by one actor in the same film; for example, Douglas Fairbanks, Jr., playing both Rupert and his stand-in in *The Prisoner of Zenda* (1937; dir. John Cromwell), and Peter Sellers playing the same roles in the 1979 comic remake of the film (dir. Richard Quine).

■ **Du Art Film and Video Laboratories** A film-processing organization begun in 1922 and centered in New York City for both 16mm and 35mm film. The company has been especially useful to independent filmmakers. Du Art uses advanced computerized technology for processing, film to video transfer, negative conforming, and blowing up to 16 and super 16mm to 35mm film.

■ **dub, dubbing, postdubbing** (1) To record dialogue and various sounds, and then integrate them into the film after it has been shot. This is done for scenes where the original recording is faulty, for scenes where it is simply more convenient to add dialogue and other sound later, and for films playing abroad which require new dialogue in the native language of the host country. Dubbing in dialogue is also called postsynching. *See* **ADR editor, automatic dialogue replacement, looping,** *and* **postsynchronization.** (2) The mixing of all the sound tracks (dialogue, natural sounds, sound effects, music) into a single track. *See* **mix.**

■ **dubb** *See* **composite track** *and* **slop mix.**

■ **dubbed version** A released version of a foreign film for which the original dialogue has been replaced by dialogue spoken in the native language of the country where the film is shown. Synchronization between the new dialogue and the moving lips of the characters on the screen is attempted, though often with limited success.

■ **dubber** (1) A sound playback unit for magnetic film that is used in conjunction with other such units for mixing the final sound track. (2) The term is sometimes used for a magnetic film recorder.

■ **dubbing mixer** *See* **mixer** *(1).*

■ **dubbing room, dubbing stage, dubbing studio, dubbing theater** A specially designed sound-proof room, with mixing console and equipment necessary for both kinds of dubbing described above under **dub.** Also called looping stage, looping studio, or looping theater when the process of looping takes place. *See* **dub** *and* **looping.**

■ **dubbing session** A period during which actors record dialogue to be dubbed into a film already shot. Also called looping session when the process of looping takes place. *See* **dub** *and* **looping.**

■ **dubbing sheet, dubbing cue sheet, dubbing log** *See* **mixing cue sheet.**

■ **dub-in** To record sound, especially dialogue, for a film that has already been shot. *See* **dub.**

■ **Dufaycolor** An additive color system, originating in France and developed during the 1930s, which used a mosaic of tiny red, blue, and green filter elements between the base and emulsion of the film through which the picture was first photographed and then projected after it had been printed in a reversal method. Because the color screen filtered out too much light in projection, the system was discarded. *See* **additive process.**

■ **dulling spray, antireflective spray** An aerosol spray put on surfaces to prevent their reflecting light into the camera.

■ **dummy** One of the playback machines that feed a reel with an individual track of sound into the mixing console to make a composite or final mix for a film. *See* **dubbing room** *and* **mix.**

■ **dummy room, machine room** A separate room with the various playback machines that feed the individual tracks of sound into the mixing console in the dubbing room to make a composite or the final mix for a film. *See* **dubbing room** *and* **mix.**

■ **dump tanks** Large tanks filled with water and placed on top of inclined channels. When water is released from the tanks and down the channels, an effect of flooding from waves or a storm is achieved. The falling water is photographed at a camera speed faster than normal so that when the image is projected at the normal twenty-four frames per second, the effect will be that of a large mass of moving water.

■ **Dunning process, Dunning-Pomeroy self-matting process** An early system of making a composite image of actors filmed in the studio with a background filmed elsewhere, developed in Hollywood in the 1920s first by C. Dodge Dunning and later by Roy J. Pomeroy. The process was used for black-and-white photography before the development of the rear-projection process. A bleached and orange-dyed positive of the background was put into a bipack camera in contact with a panchromatic raw negative. The actors were placed in front of a blank screen that was lit by blue light; they themselves were lit by orange light. With the camera operating and the two films in motion, the orange light reflecting from the actors passed through the positive and allowed them to be photographed on the negative, while the blue background around the actors provided light to print the background from the positive onto the rest of the negative. The process is sometimes called a self-matting process because the actors, by blocking out the blue light reflected behind them and hence preventing their area of the background image on the positive from being printed on the negative, acted as their own mattes. *See* **matte** *(2),* **rear projection,** *and* **traveling-matte process.**

■ **dupe, dupe negative, duplicate negative** (1) A duplicate of the original negative made from the master positive in order to preserve the original, but also made in numbers for the making of release prints. Dupes of individual scenes are sometimes made for correcting errors in exposure or printing, or for adding special effects. Optical dupes are made in different gauges for the manufacture of prints different in size from the original film (for example, when 16mm copies are to be made from an original 35mm film), or with a different aspect ratio when a format change is required (for example, when a normal wide-screen image must be made from an anamorphic image). Sometimes, especially with 16mm film, a dupe is made from a reversal print. The dupe made from the original master print is called a first-generation dupe; the dupe made from a print of the first-generation dupe is called a second-generation dupe, and so on. The quality of the picture will suffer with each successive dupe. (2) During the days of early silent movies, dupe was a term for printed duplicates of film.

■ **dupe, duplicate** (1) To make a dupe from a master positive or master reversal positive. (2) To make a duplicate of a film at any stage.

■ **dupe room** *See* **dubbing room.**

■ **duplicate color negative** *See* **internegative.**

dutch-angle shot Orson Welles's world is about to topple in *The Third Man* (1949; dir. Carol Reed).

■ ■ ■

■ **dutch angle** A camera angle that seriously deviates from the normal vertical and horizontal axis of the image to convey extreme subjective states of mind or to produce in the viewer a sense of disequilibrium and uneasiness. Dutch angles can also convey accidents (a person or vehicle turning over), violence, or extreme weather (storms or hurricanes). *See* **canting.**

■ **dutchman** A strip of canvas that is fastened over the cracks between flats and then painted as part of the set.

■ **DVD** The initials originally stood for digital video disc but now represent digital versatile disc to suggest the incorporation of both music and computer programming along with the visual in this latest technological playback system. The DVD is the same size as both an audio compact disc and a CD-ROM. Like them, it employs digital coding—i.e., the electronic recording of information through a numerical system of 0's and 1's (offs and ons)—that is read by a laser. The technology for the digital versatile disc is based upon a high storage format developed by Toshiba and a storage process developed by both Sony and Philips in competing systems—a rare example of corporate cooperation that was encouraged by IBM. This new type of disc will have the capacity to hold a 133-minute motion picture and seven times the information now stored on a CD-ROM. Both sound and picture will exceed in quality those achieved with present technologies because the playback system will be fed ten times the amount of information per second as that retrieved in present digital audio and video machines. Although the machine will not have the capacity to record sound and picture, the electronics and entertainment industries hope that it will eventually replace both the VCR and CD-ROM systems. The new DVD disc is also being considered as a possible replacement for CDs in the recording of music. The great capacity of the system is likely to be used less for greater recording time than to improve the quality of the music by recording higher frequencies and a greater range between the softest and loudest sounds. *See* **digital.**

■ **DVTR (digital videotape recorder)** *See* **videotape recorder.**

■ **DX** *See* **double exposure.**

■ **dye coupler** *See* **coupler.**

■ **dye coupling** The process of making colored film images through the interaction (i.e., "coupling") of the oxidized developer and certain chemicals (called dye couplers) in the film emulsion or sometimes in the developer itself. *See* **color film** *(2).*

■ **dye transfer** *See* **imbibition.**

■ **Dykstraflex** The motion-control system designed by John Dykstra and others at Industrial Light and Magic for George Lucas's *Star Wars* (1977). The Dykstraflex is considered the model for future systems of this kind. *See* **motion control.**

■ **Dynamation** The technique of matting live action and stop-motion animation first developed by Ray Harryhausen for his work in *The Seventh Voyage of Sinbad* (1958; dir. Nathan Juran) and employed by him in later films, such as *Clash of the Titans* (1981; dir. Desmond Davis). This dimensional technique included mounting models into actual locations and using a split screen for live action and animation. *See* **animation.**

■ **dynamic cutting, dynamic editing** Editing a series of shots of various objects, people, and details not necessarily from the same scene but that function all together to create a dramatic situation and to invoke a sense of involvement and tension in the audience. Generally there is one primary scene that is reestablished throughout the editing. Cutting seems abrupt, and the individual shots function in juxtaposition to one another, but all synthesize to form a single context. This technique is opposed to continuity cutting, which creates a sense of continuous action through a barely perceptible style of editing. Richard Lester's films—*Petulia* (1968), for example—show a bewildering display of dynamic cutting that finally reinforces his story of lives touching and separating; Nicolas Roeg employs the technique to create a sense of discontinuity and ambiguity in films such as *Performance* (1970); and, more recently, Oliver Stone, in *Natural Born Killers* (1994), assembles series of shots that border on chaos but manage to convey a world exploited and assaulted by the media.

■ **dynamic frame** A film technique, first suggested by the Russian film director Sergei Eisenstein in his essay "The Dynamic Square," whereby the size of the frame projected on the screen changes. This technique has not often been employed, both because of the expense and because the alteration of the frame's size tends to disturb an audience. It has been used infrequently and briefly in films to achieve certain effects, as at the start of Mike Todd's *Around the World in 80 Days* (1956), when the screen expands from the smaller frame of Méliès's *A Trip to the Moon* (1902), which is briefly shown, to the 70mm wide-screen image of Todd-AO. One of the few films that consistently employs the dynamic frame is the experimental work *The Door in the Wall* (1955), made by the British filmmaker Glen Alvey, Jr.

■ **dynamic microphone** A microphone that operates by means of a moving coil. A diaphragm reacts to sound waves by vibrating and causing a coil to move in a magnetic field. The coil creates voltage that corresponds to the waves and is the source of sound in a recording.

■ **dynamic range** (1) The ratio between the reflectance of 100 percent white and 100 percent black in a particular scene. *See* **reflectance.** (2) The difference in volume between an audio system's quietest and loudest points. *See* **signal-to-noise ratio.**

■ ■ ■

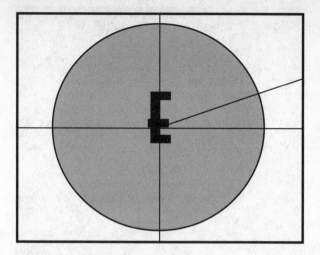

east to eye sync

■ **east** In animation work, the right side of the drawing table, animation stand, drawing, or cel as opposed to the west, or left, side.

■ **Eastman Color** An integral tripack color film used widely for motion pictures made in this country and in Western Europe. First introduced in 1952, the film was comparable in quality to and less difficult and expensive to use than Technicolor's three-strip process, and was found superior to Technicolor's monopack film. The stock has improved significantly over the years and today is a flexible and accurate color recorder. In its EXR series, Eastman's 35mm color negative film, 5245, which has a very fine grain, is today much used in motion-picture production for daylight shooting, 5293 is used for interior and night shooting, and 5298 also for such shooting, but with a faster speed to respond to less lighting. In the late 1980s, Eastman Color introduced its T-grain emulsion with flatter silver crystals, which allow for a faster film with far fewer grains and which gather light better while reducing its scatter. In 1989, the company introduced its KeyKode numbers along with a machine-readable bar code on film to facilitate editing, conforming, and transferring to video. Eastman Kodak is now introducing its Kodak Vision Color Negative Films (in gold cans), which feature thinner T-grains and a new chemical reaction to create sharper pictures with even less light scattering: the 320T, which replaces the EXR 5287 film, offers a low-contrast image with a stone-washed or pastel quality, while the 500T, which replaces the 5298, creates a high-contrast, sharp image with fine saturation. *See* **color film** *(2)*, **grain**, *and* **Key-Kode**.

■ **Eastman Kodak** The largest and most important manufacturer of film stock in the world, with headquarters and plants in Rochester, New York. The company was begun in 1880 by George Eastman, who introduced the first roll of transparent film for the camera in 1889. Kodak manufactures cameras, projectors, and all types of film equipment, but its film is its most significant and internationally used product: nearly all processing systems are designed for this kind of stock. The company recently changed the name of its Motion Picture and Television Imaging Division to that of the Professional Motion Imaging Division (which itself later became part of Entertainment Imaging) to recognize its work in newer film and digital technologies for the moving image in motion pictures, video, and interactive media.

■ **echo box, echo chamber** An enclosed space that creates reverberations for echo effects in a sound track. Today, these effects are generally achieved electronically

■ **Eclair** The brand name of cameras made by the French company, Eclair International Diffusion. Eclair Camiflex 35 is an extremely precise, light, and portable camera with a reflex-viewing system and a drive mechanism in the magazine that allows for instant changing since film can be prethreaded. The company makes the Camiflex 16/35 (also known as the Camerette or CM-3), which uses both 16 and 35mm film, and the 16mm Eclair ACL, which weighs less than eight pounds.

■ **ECU** *See* **extreme close-up**.

■ **edge detection** In computer animation and graphics, the process of creating an edge for a model when the computer responds to high contrast values between one pixel and another. *See* **computer animation**.

■ **edge fog, edge flare** Accidental exposure along the edges of film, generally at the beginning or end of a roll, caused by loosely rolled stock, a light-admitting magazine, or poor handling of film during loading and unloading.

■ **edge light** *See* **back light**.

■ **edge numbering machine** A machine for printing edge numbers on processed picture film and sound film. *See* **edge numbers**.

■ **edge numbers, key numbers, negative numbers, footage numbers, edge code** A series of numbers with key lettering printed along the edge of a 35mm negative at intervals of a foot (12 frames) before 1990 and, since, intervals of 64 perforations with mid-foot numbers between them; and on 16mm negative at intervals of one-half foot (20 frames) and one foot (40 frames). These numbers and letters are printed onto the positive with the images to facilitate editing and to allow the exact matching of the edited workprint with the negative for final editing. When sound is recorded during shooting, edge numbers on both film and magnetic sound track also help with editing. Latent-image edge numbers appear after the film is processed, while visible-ink edge numbers are already clear on raw stock, though clearer after processing. Many laboratories also print their own edge numbers in yellow after the film is processed. In 1989, Kodak introduced KeyKode edge numbers and a bar code that could be read by machine, and Fuji followed soon after with a similar coding. Such coding facilitates editing, especially when the film image is converted to video or digital coding for linear and non-linear editing. *See* **KeyKode, linear editing,** *and* **nonlinear editing.**

■ **edge stripe** A magnetic stripe on a composite print that carries sound, as opposed to an optical sound track.

■ **edge track** The sound track on magnetic film with a single row of perforations. The track is located near the edge opposite to the perforations. Edge tracks are preferred in the United States to center tracks, on which the sound band runs down the middle of the film and a row of perforations runs along each side.

■ **edgewaving** *See* **fluting.**

■ **edgewax** A lubricating substance applied to the edges of the emulsion side of release prints to permit easy passage through the projector.

■ **Edison Company** The early film company that, under the directorship of Thomas Alva Edison and through the accomplishments of W. K. L. Dickson, first photographed short films with the Kinetograph and showed these to the public in a peephole viewer called the Kinetoscope beginning in 1893. Dickson made these unedited films in a blackened shack called the Black Maria, located in West Orange, New Jersey, near the Edison Laboratories, which was considered to be the first film studio. These films ran about thirty seconds and featured all kinds of subjects, including dancers, famous personalities, and circus animals. The most famous were Fred Ott's *The Sneeze* (1891) and *The Kiss* (1896). The important technical achievement was the use of 35mm film with four perforations on each side for precise registration, which was to become standard in the film industry at large. When finally realizing, however, that projected motion pictures on a screen in front of an audience was the wave of the future, Edison manufactured and distributed the Vitascope, a projector developed by Thomas Armat and C. Francis Jenkins. The first public showing of films from the Vitascope was in New York on April 23, 1896, in a vaudeville theater, Koster and Bial's Music Hall. Edison's films, as well as those from rival companies, were first shown as part of vaudeville shows but were soon exhibited by themselves in small theaters. In 1900, Edwin S. Porter came to work for the Edison Company and in 1903 released his two famous short films, *The Life of an American Fireman* and *The Great Train Robbery.*

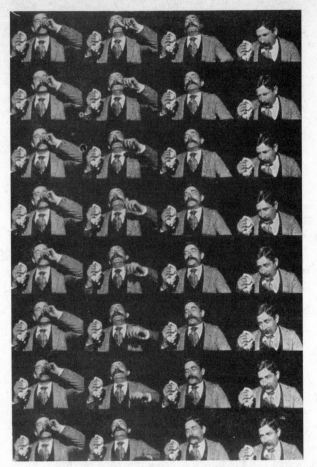

Edison Company Fred Ott's historic sneeze, photographed in 1891 for Edison's peephole machine, the Kinetoscope.

■ ■ ■

The demand for projectors and films brought many competitors into the market, and in 1908 the Edison Company, its six chief domestic rivals, and the Méliès and Pathé companies in France formed the Motion Picture Patents Company, which sought to control the manufacture and rental of all film equipment and the production, distribution, and exhibition of all films. Edison's inventions were acknowledged, and he was to receive royalties from all these companies. But the rising independents, overcoming harassment and even violence, eventually defeated the trust, which was declared illegal by the courts in 1917. Edison's film company had long been declining because of the competition, as well as its own resistance to making feature films. After the defeat of the trust, it made some feature films, but finally stopped production entirely and sold its studio in 1918. *See* **Kinetograph.**

■ **edit controller, editing control unit** A piece of equipment that includes videotape counters and various controls for running the source videotape player and videotape recorder when editing on either a single or multiple source linear system. Film is sometimes transferred to videotape to simplify the editing process. Editing on tape results in a negative cut list that is used for the actual editing of the negative. The edit controller allows synchronicity of the various machines as well as marking editing points, measuring, searching and finding, rewinding, backspacing, trying out various edits without recording them, handling picture and audio either together or separately, and adding effects. Such devices are now frequently desktop computers. *See* **editing.**

■ **edit-decision list, editing-decision list (EDL)** A list of edits resulting from linear and nonlinear editing systems that is used in making the on-line master. The list is designated in terms of tape, scene, and shot numbers, first and last frame numbers according to the time code, transitions, and sound. *See* **editing** *and* **negative cut list.**

■ **edited music** Background music edited into the film to correspond with specific actions or scenes.

■ **editing** The entire process of putting a film together into its final form, which includes the selection and shaping of shots; the arrangement of shots, scenes, and sequences; the mixing of all sound tracks; and the integrating of the final sound track with the images. The term "cutting" is sometimes used synonymously for editing, but is too limited since it conveys only a mechanical sense of snipping the film into pieces and reassembling them, without any suggestion of the technical, dramatic, and artistic skills required to make the film move effectively and form a total, coherent entity. Nor does the term give indication of the mixing and integrating of sound for which the editor is finally responsible. The independence and individual contribution of the editor will vary according to how much control the director demands over the final product. In the Hollywood studio system, the editor had more control, though sometimes the final editing was determined by the producer or another member of the studio.

Today, directors often work closely with their editors—some even plan much of the editing before production begins and edit much of the film in the shooting itself. (In certain instances, though, the producer is still a commanding influence on the film's editing.) During the shooting of the film, editing frequently begins with the editor conferring with the director about the rushes (the film shot the day before) and tentatively assembling the parts of the film. When the shooting is finished, the editor will have an assembly of what is a general continuity of all the shots and from this he will make a rough cut, which is the first completely edited workprint composed of what appears to be the best shots in the best arrangement, though without any refinements of individual shots. This cut is also frequently called the "director's cut,"

which means that it is largely the way the director sees it, without any interference from the studio or other personnel. The rough cut is in sync with the tracks of sound recorded both during and separate from the shooting. After the director and editor confer, the editor changes and refines the rough cut. Perhaps the director and editor will confer several more times and perhaps there will be several more intermediate cuts; but the editor at last makes the fine cut which includes what appears to be the final arrangements of shots, scenes, and sequences, each shot cut to exactly the right length. The fine cut includes such optical effects for transitions as fades and dissolves as well as any special-effects photography. This print in some cases may represent anywhere from one-fifth to one-tenth of the footage originally shot, though figures such as one-thirtieth are not uncommon (the ratio of footage shot to that used is called the shooting ratio). The editor will also work very closely with the mixer and supervise the final integration of all sound tracks into a master track, which includes dialogue, natural sound, sound effects, and music, and supervise the integration of this final track with the visuals. The fine cut is then used as a blueprint for cutting the original negative, which, in its final form, is sent to the laboratory along with the final sound mix, where the two are printed together on the answer print, also called the composite print or trail composite. During the processing of the answer print, the final timing, that is, adjustments in density and color quality, are made. The answer print will act as the standard for the making of all release prints. Further changes, however, may still be made in editing as a result of conferences between director and editor or audience responses to previews. To preserve the original negative, master prints are made and from these the duplicate negatives for the making of the release prints, a process which the editor may oversee.

Video and computer technology are today making important inroads in the methods of editing and are allowing greater flexibility, speed, and accuracy for the editor. Film images are transposed to either analog or digital videotape and time coded, thus allowing the editor to call up on the monitor whatever scenes he or she desires and try out a variety of edited sequences. A linear editing system works with one or more videotape players and a videotape recorder. An edit controller, frequently a desktop computer, operates the machines synchronically, handling picture and audio together or separately, allowing for the inclusion of effects, and permitting the editor to try out the cuts. Nonlinear editing utilizes a computer system that records the information digitally on hard drives, allowing the editor to call up, in random access, any shot or sequence of shots in the entire project by using a time code without having to run a tape or series of tapes linearly forward or in reverse. The digital system also allows the editor to try out a number of variations without having to record any of them until the final selection is made. Transitions may also be programmed without the necessity of two videotape players. Digital coding also allows a series of activities to take place with the same picture simultaneously. As a result of both linear and nonlinear systems, an edit-decision list (EDL) is made for the master video or a negative cut list from which the film negative can be cut or a workprint made as an intermediary step. Although dailies and rough cuts might still be edited on film with the traditional flat-bed, such early prints might also be assembled in response to a cut list from preliminary digital editing. (Most low-budget films go straight to video for all their editing.) By transferring the picture and audio of a day's shooting to digital and transmitting the information to a station located in another part of the country, editing can begin immediately. It is even possible to edit on location through the same technology. The major criticism with this kind of technology comes from editors who still like to work with the traditional hands-on method and find the electronic technology likely to provoke quick and facile decisions.

Editing can develop a narration in a continuous and fluid manner. It condenses space and time, emphasizes and brings disparate elements together, and organizes the material in such a way that patterns of meaning emerge. Editing also determines the way an audience reacts to an event: for example, a series of quick cuts can create a sense of excitement, anticipation, or bewilderment, while longer shots can create a sense of delay, emphasize the drama within a scene, and develop our involvement with the character. The way in which the sound track is integrated with the visuals also has significance for the audience: the audibility or inaudibility of dialogue, the interjection of a musical passage at a particular time, the increased or diminished volume of music, the sudden noise of the environment—all of these, in juxtaposition with a particular image, help evoke and emphasize meaning and guide our emotions.

In its early stages, the motion picture was basically an uninterrupted action filmed in one shot from an immobile camera. Although the Brighton School did innovative work with the camera and with editing in Britain at the turn of the century, much of their important work is lost. Credit for introducing basic editing techniques is, therefore, generally given to Edwin S. Porter, who made two important works for the Edison Company in 1903, *The Life of An American Fireman* and *The Great Train Robbery*. Both of these films employed simple cross-cutting between two parallel and related actions to build a single narrative and both employed some form of the close-up. But the man who significantly introduced all the basic concepts of film editing was D. W. Griffith. Griffith developed cutting for continuity, thus building and controlling the narration and emotional tempo of his film; he developed parallel cutting to integrate the elements of his narration and also build suspense; he broke down individual scenes, using a series of shots from different angles and distances,

thus controlling focus and emphasis, dramatizing point of view, and preventing boredom; and he juxtaposed shots and sequences for thematic and symbolic significance. The Russians, using Griffith as a model, went further with editing and saw the individual shot as part of a greater whole; each shot for them was incomplete without the context of other shots. They developed the theory and practice of montage, the French word "to assemble" used in France for editing but employed by the Russians to mean something much more controlled and manipulative. The film was seen as composed of fragments, of individual shots arranged in such a way that their juxtaposition created meanings realized by the audience. Pudovkin saw montage in a more linear, progressive, and narrative way than did Eisenstein, for whom montage was more analytical and dialectical, more dynamic and emotional. But the style of editing that was to be pervasive began in Germany with the silent films of G. W. Pabst and later developed in Hollywood during the 1930s and 1940s: this was "invisible cutting" or "editing for continuity," where narrative is dominant, and the audience is almost unaware of the flow of shots and manipulation of time and space. But divergent styles must also be noted: for example, the long takes and shifting focus of the French director Jean Renoir, especially in his films of the 1930s.

Various technical matters have had an impact on editing during past decades: for example, the advent of sound, the increasing practice of postrecording, and the development of sophisticated mounting systems that have increased the range of the camera's movements. Also significant has been the rise of the wide-screen format, which required directors and editors to expand traditional cutting techniques for the larger film image. Since the Second World War, individual movements have fostered changes in editing styles, for example, the diminishing of cutting and the move toward "realism" in the films of the Italian neorealists and the more idiosyncratic editing styles of French New Wave directors. Contemporary directors such as Richard Lester, Nicolas Roeg, and Bob Fosse have also created dynamic cutting techniques that strive for effect as much as continuity. A number of directors have themselves started out as editors, notably David Lean, Robert Wise, and Hal Ashby. *See* **camera movement, cut, editor,** *and* **montage.**

■ **editing bench, editing table** A work table used for editing, which holds a variety of equipment for immediate viewing of the film and cutting. The work bench normally has a pair of rewinds for finding specific shots and for rewinding the film; reels for holding the film; a viewer for finding and examining a shot; a synchronizer for keeping film and sound parallel and, if a sound head is attached, for playing the audio track; a splicer for cutting film; and assorted materials such as china pencils, scissors, tape, and gloves. *See* **editing** *and* **flat-bed editing machine.**

■ **editing in the camera** The same as "cutting in the camera," the term means using setups and camera movement in such a way that less cutting is necessary. Perhaps the most extreme example of this technique is in Alfred Hitchcock's *Rope* (1948), where one continuous shot is employed with the camera moving about a single room (the film was shot in a series of nine-minute takes to allow for the length of each reel).

■ **editing ratio** *See* **shooting ratio.**

■ **editing room** *See* **cutting room.**

■ **editing sync** When sound and picture are properly aligned together in a synchronizer for editing. *See* **synchronizer.**

■ **editing table** *See* **editing bench** *and* **flat-bed editing machine.**

■ **editor, film editor** The person responsible for putting the film together into its final form. The editor, sometimes called a cutter, is often of great significance in the success or failure of the film. It is the editor who, by shaping and arranging shots, scenes, and sequences, while also modulating and integrating sound, has considerable influence in the development, rhythm, emphasis, and final impact of the film. Today most editors work closely with the director (or sometimes producer) and are guided by his or her vision of the film and preferences in particular sequences; but the picture is still frequently dependent on the editor's skills. A number of directors began as editors, for example, Robert Wise, who edited Orson Welles's *Citizen Kane* (1941), and Hal Ashby, who won an Academy Award for editing Norman Jewison's *In the Heat of the Night* (1967). Among the many fine editors whose skill has contributed considerably to the success of the films they worked on are Ralph Dawson, who won three Academy Awards beginning with *A Midsummer Night's Dream* (1935; dir. Max Reinhardt); Daniel Mandell, who also won three such awards, including one for *The Best Years of Our Lives* (1946; dir. William Wyler); William Hornbeck, who won the Oscar for *A Place in the Sun* (1951; dir. George Stevens); Adrienne Fazan, who did a number of MGM musicals and won an Academy Award for *Gigi* (1958; dir. Vincente Minnelli); George Tomasini, who edited a number of Hitchcock's most celebrated films, including *Psycho* (1960); William Reynolds, who won an Oscar for *The Sting* (1973; dir. George Roy Hill); and Michael Kahn, who won Academy Awards for Steven Spielberg's *Raiders of the Lost Ark* (1981) and *Schindler's List* (1993). *See* **cut** *and* **editing.**

■ **editorial department** The group of people, under the supervision of the editor, who are responsible for indexing all shots, and for the assemblage of the film into its various stages and final form. The department also keeps a listing of all the shots not used and makes a record of each frame in the actual film.

■ **editorial sync, editorial synchronization, editing sync, edit-sync, editor's sync, level sync, parallel sync, dead sync, dead-head sync, printer's sync** When picture and sound are put in matching relationship by the synchronizer during the editing process.

■ **editor's cut** A term sometimes applied to the assembly of the film, the first approximation of the motion picture put together by the editor from the useable takes, to distinguish it from the director's cut, a term applied to the rough cut, the next stage of the motion picture when the director is largely responsible for the editing. *See* **director's cut** *and* **rough cut.**

■ **edit out** To remove parts of the visuals or sound during the editing process.

■ **edit video master, edited master** The fully edited videotape that results from the on-line editing—i.e., the videotape conformed to the EDL (edit-decision list) that is itself a result of the off-line editing. *See* **on-line and off-line editing** *and* **video master.**

■ **educational film** Any film made with the primary object of teaching some subject matter or skills, especially a film made for classroom viewing.

■ **effective aperture** The ratio of a lens's focal length to the width of its aperture as limited by its diaphragm. This ratio is normally given in f-stop numbers. *See* **f-stop.**

■ **effects (FX)** In general, the term means any illusory or artificial elements that are not a natural part of the scene but are added by some technical procedure. The term is more specifically employed in the following ways: (1) transitional effects achieved on film, normally through the use of an optical printer, such as dissolves, fades, or wipes; (2) special effects, either mechanical ones produced before the camera, such as exploding bullets and shells during a battle or the mad scientist's electronically pulsating laboratory in a horror film; those achieved through special photographic processes, such as the traveling-matte process; and those achieved digitally. (3) sounds added after the filming of an action, for example, gunfire, a storm, or footsteps. *See* **special effects.**

■ **effects animation** Animation not pertaining directly to characters: for example, an explosion, fire, or storm achieved through animation techniques. *See* **animation.**

■ **effects box** *See* **matte box.**

■ **effects film** A film, such as any of the *Star Wars* or *Star Trek* films, which relies heavily on special effects for its success. Such films tend to simplify character and story while emphasizing technical wizardry. *See* **special effects.**

■ **effects filter** A filter in front of the camera's lens that alters the image: for example, diffusion filters for softening the appearance of a face.

■ **effect shot** A shot that has no narrative significance but is integrated into a sequence for thematic or emotional effect: for example, a shot of a turbulent ocean or wild horses suddenly juxtaposed to the visuals of the hero and heroine making love.

■ **effects light** Lights for highlighting a specific area in a scene.

■ **effects projector** A special projector with an extremely high beam that is used for projecting film or slides in front and rear projection systems. *See* **front projection** *and* **rear projection.**

■ **effects shots** Any shots in a film achieved by means of such special effects as matting or front-projection. *See* **special effects.**

■ **effects track** The sound track that contains sound effects and is combined with voice and music during mixing.

■ **EFX** Sometimes used instead of FX as an abbreviation for either sound or special effects.

■ **eggcrate** A gridlike accessory used in front of luminaires with soft lights to control the beam.

■ **EI** (1) The initials stand for "emulsion in," which is the way film is generally placed on cores or spools for most cameras in this country. "EO" means the emulsion is out. (2) *See* **exposure index.**

■ **8mm film, regular 8, standard 8, cine 8** The narrowest-gauge film, 8 millimeters wide, was used largely for amateur photography and educational films. This gauge had 80 frames per foot and was sometimes referred to as double-eight, since it was largely manufactured in two attached parallel strips, together 16mm in size, which were split down the middle when processed. After 1966, Super 8, with smaller perforations allowing wider and higher frames and 74 frames per foot, replaced the standard 8mm film. Super 8 itself has now mostly been replaced by videotape, though one still finds such cameras in use. *See* **Super 8mm film.**

■ **eight perf** In special-effects work the term refers to the image achieved when 35mm film passes horizontally through such cameras as the VistaVision. Such images are eight perforations wide with twice the area of the normal 35mm frame. Because of their great definition, such pictures can be joined with earlier-generation images in composite pictures or with live action in front-projection shots with no disparity. *See* **flat four, front projection,** *and* **special effects.**

■ **electric department, electric crew** The group of people responsible for electrical work in a film production, especially supplying lights and current as well as maintaining all electrical equipment. The chief electrician is called the gaffer and his assistant is referred to as the best boy.

■ **electrician** *See* **electric department.**

■ **electric pen** *See* **digital pen.**

■ **Electric Theater** A small film theater opened in 1902 by Thomas L. Tally in Los Angeles and considered to be the first permanent theater for motion pictures in the United States.

■ **electronic beam recording (EBR)** A transfer process for recording a motion picture from videotape to film in a special type of flying spot telecine machine whereby an electric beam exposes the film to the information on the videotape. *See* **telecine.**

■ **electronic cinema** A term used during the 1980s for the possible cinema of the future that would employ some type of high-definition television (HDTV) for projecting the image in a theater. The ultimate electronic cinema would have the feature film itself beamed into the theater via satellite. No system has yet been developed that can electronically project an image in a theater with anywhere near the definition and resolution of the chemical image on film.

■ **electronic clapper, electronic clapstick** A synchronization mechanism in the camera used instead of the traditional clapper board for fogging the first few frames of the film and sending a signal to the corresponding part of the sound tape at the start of shooting.

■ **electronic compositing, electronic image compositing, electronic matting, video matting** Transferring images from film to videotape for electronic matting and then transferring the composite picture back to film. Electronic matting is much more rapid and economical than special-effects matting systems used only for film, but electronic images do not have the resolution and color renditions of film images. Although generally employed for special-effects films to see in advance a scene that will later be composited on film, the Ultimatte video system was considered to be of high enough quality for compositing the underwater scenes in the film *Jaws 3-D* (1983; dir. Joe Alvis). Digital technology with modern film scanners and recorders makes this process largely obsolete.

■ **electronic editing** (1) Editing a work originally shot with videotape by means of a linear or nonlinear system, i.e., either via the videotape itself in an editing suite or by means of a computer. (2) Editing a film by first transferring it to a videotape and then arranging the shots and transitions by means of a linear editing system in which the shots are selected from a source videotape player and the edited version preserved on a record videotape recorder; or by means of a nonlinear computerized system in which the information is recorded digitally on hard drives and the shots called up by random access. In both instances, the film negative might be cut by means of a negative cut list that results from the electronic editing. *See* **editing.**

■ **electronic images** (1) Images created by a computer for various types of animation work. *See* **computer animation.** (2) Images created by a video system. Video systems are now employed as monitors for rehearsing shots in advance or examining them immediately after shooting without having to wait for dailies. In electronic compositing, film images are transformed into electronic images, and the final composite picture is put back on film. *See* **electronic compositing.**

■ **electronic optical printer** *See* **optical printer.**

■ **electronic pen** *See* **digitizing pen.**

■ **electronic press kit** A press kit on videotape especially prepared for television. Such tapes might include a trailer, clips from the film, stories about the film or filmmaking, stories about the stars as well as their biographies, and other promotional material. Such kits were originally called video press kits.

■ **electronic rangefinder** *See* **rangefinder.**

■ **electronic storyboard** At first a storyboard recorded on videotape to give some sense of the development of the film and allow for guidance during the actual shooting of each shot or scene, electronic storyboards now result from sophisticated computer software, such as Story-Board Quick, that allows an individual to draw from scratch; select characters, settings, and objects from a database; and scan in images from photographs of actual places for background. Such software also allows the individual to try out a variety of layouts; camera angles, distances, and lenses; lighting effects; and colors. Sound can also be used with these images. *See* **previsualization** *and* **storyboard.**

■ **electronic viewfinder, electronic monitor viewfinder** A viewfinder system that projects the images being shot onto a small television screen, thus allowing more than one person to watch the scene—normal optical viewfinders that are part of the camera permit only the camera operator or one person to watch the scene. This device is extremely helpful to the director and director of photography, both of whom can view the scene while it is being photographed and send instructions to the camera operator or camera crew. It is possible to have a screen for each camera, if more than one is employed,

and more than one screen for a single camera. *See* **video assist.**

■ **electroprint** *See* **electroprinting.**

■ **electroprinting** (1) Printing the sound onto a film directly from a master magnetic track without the intermediate step of a master optical sound track. This process is occasionally done for 16mm film to save the expense of a master optical sound track. (2) The printing of an electronic composite. *See* **electronic compositing.**

■ **elevator** A camera support that lifts the camera and the cameraman straight up or down for shooting. Used either on the floor or on a dolly, the elevator supports a mount that permits the camera to pan and tilt.

■ **elevator shot** A shot taken from an elevator that moves the camera up or down.

■ **ellipsoidal spot** A spotlight that produces a sharp beam through an ellipsoidal lens (i.e., a lens where all the plane sections are ellipses or circles).

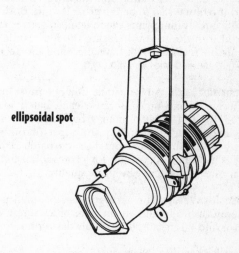

ellipsoidal spot

■ **elliptical cutting, elliptical editing** An editing style that leaves out action without including covering shots or optical transitions. Such editing results in jump cuts from action to action or place to place. A well-known example of this technique occurs in Godard's film *Breathless* (1959), which employs such elliptical cutting as part of its unemotional and "breathless" style.

■ **ELS** *See* **extreme long shot.**

■ **embossing** An irregular condition of the film when the frames are expanded and stand out in relief. This condition is generally caused by the great heat of high-intensity projector bulbs.

■ **emily** *See* **broad.**

■ **emote** To display emotion while playing a role, especially in an exaggerated manner.

■ **emulsion** The layer of light-sensitive silver salts, suspended in gelatin, which is coated on the base of film. In color film, there are normally three separate emulsion layers, each also containing a chemical coupler sensitive to a different primary color. The latent image is formed in black-and-white film when the emulsion is exposed to light and made visible when the silver salts are transformed to black metal during developing. In color film the couplers are responsible for forming the colored image, which remains after the developed silver has been removed. The picture-making quality of film stocks differs according to the varying properties and dimensions of the emulsion. The emulsion side of the film is duller than the base. Film is generally wound with the emulsion side in (EI) on spools or cores for most cameras in this country as opposed to emulsion out (EO) for many cameras in Europe. When the emulsion faces the viewer with the picture in proper geometry, the film is said to be A-type or A-wind; when the base faces the viewer with the image properly situated the film is said to be B-type or B-wind. Both 35mm prints and 16mm prints made from negatives are projected with the base side facing the lens, while 16mm prints on reversal stock have the emulsion facing the lens. *See* **A- and B-wind** *and* **film** *(1).*

■ **emulsion batch** An individual mix of emulsion manufactured at one time. Because each batch manufactured for the same film may have slightly differing qualities, some companies print a specific number on every roll of film made from the same batch. This practice is especially important for professional filming to guarantee consistency in image quality.

■ **emulsion pileup** The accumulation of small particles of emulsion normally in the gate of a camera or projector and often caused by poorly dried film.

■ **emulsion position** *See* **emulsion.**

■ **emulsion speed** *See* **film speed** *(1).*

■ **end board, end slate, end markers, end sticks** *See* **tail slate.**

■ **end sync marks** *See* **tail sync marks.**

■ **end title** Such words as "The End" or "Finis," which indicate that the film has concluded.

■ **end titles** The titles at the end of the film, which indicate production credits, the cast of characters and their performers, and such words as "The End" or "Finis." The list of personnel and performers is also referred to as closing credits.

■ **engagement** The exhibition of a film at a motion-picture theater.

■ **enlargement printing** A printing that enlarges the frame size of the original film (for example, from 16mm to 35mm for commercial release). Such a blowup is performed in an optical printer.

■ **entertainment attorney, entertainment lawyer** A lawyer who specializes in the legal aspects of the various entertainment media, especially in contract agreements, litigation, infringement, libel, copyright, and, sometimes, antitrust laws.

■ **environmental sound** The natural sounds coming from a particular location that do not necessarily originate from any action on the screen: for example, the noise of machinery in a factory or of crickets and birds in a forest.

■ **EO** The initials are for emulsion out, which designates the way the film is placed on cores or spools. Most cameras in this country require film with EI, which means emulsion in.

■ **EOR** The initials stand for "end of reel" and appear on mix sheets, during the mixing of sound tracks, to warn the mixer and projectionist from running their equipment past the end of the reel.

■ **epic, epic film, film epic** An epic is a long narrative poem that first appeared in classical times but later was imitated in European literature. Such works featured the adventures of a noble hero who represented the important virtues of his culture and underwent heroic adventures and battles of great importance to his people. The plot was generally taken from legend or tradition; the conflicts had universal moral significance; the style was dignified; and the entire work had great scope and spectacle. In film, the term "epic" generally applies to a work of great scope, spectacle, and action that features plot more than character and heroic action more than heroic virtue. The hero, like his literary prototypes, is a great figure, a noble warrior, and an intense lover; like them he is larger than life, but with a particular Hollywood simplicity, sentimentality, and unreality, and without much universal impact. There have been numerous films that fit this description, all dealing with distant cultures and times, and most reducing their backgrounds to the level of comic book presentation—for example, both the 1926 silent-film version of *Ben-Hur,* directed by Fred Niblo, and the 1959 sound production of the same story, directed by William Wyler. Cecil B. DeMille turned out a number of these epic films, borrowing material from the Bible and America's Old West, and culminating with *The Ten Commandments* in 1956. Sometimes films have achieved a rich panorama, evocative settings, a heroic narrative, and characters of complexity and significance to create a very special kind of motion-picture epic. Perhaps D. W. Griffith's *The Birth of a Nation* (1915), even with its social myopia, is the most exciting and compelling epic film made during the days of silent movies; and certainly David Lean's *Lawrence of Arabia* (1962) is one of the most heroic, dignified, and compelling epics to be produced in the days of sound motion pictures. *See* **spectacle.**

■ **episode film** A name sometimes given to a film composed of a series of short, complete episodes or stories linked together by some theme (e.g., Max Ophüls's *La Ronde* in 1950, which explores human sexuality), the identity of the author of the stories (e.g., four of Somerset Maugham's short narratives are the basis of the 1948 film *Quartet*), or the renown of the individual director or directors (in the first case, Rossellini's *L'Amore* in 1948). A number of horror films have also been made with individual gothic tales linked together only by the nature of their genre (the classic example is the British film *Dead of Night* in 1945).

■ **episodic** A dramatic structure that is largely made up of loosely related episodes. Instead of a tight dramatic plot, the work features a series of events generally related by the presence of the same character or characters and not by any cause-effect relationship. Such works as *The Nights of Cabiria* (1957) and *La Dolce Vita* (1960), both by Federico Fellini, tend to be episodic in structure, especially when compared to the tight dramatic structures of many of Ingmar Bergman's films.

■ **equalization (EQ), equalizing** Adjusting the frequencies of response by means of equalizers to improve the signal-to-noise ratio, generally in rerecording and in mixing the final composite track, though sometimes also in the recording stage. The process is important for improving the quality of sound as well as for making bass and treble changes and altering the relation of the various frequencies. Also referred to as filtering. *See* **playback equalization curve.**

■ **equalize, filter** (1) To adjust the tone and quality of sound at any point in the recording, rerecording, or mixing processes. (2) To adjust the tone and quality of sound at any point in recording, rerecording, or mixing processes specifically with the aid of an equalizer. *See* **equalizer** *and* **playback equalization curve.**

■ **equalizer, graphic equalizer** The devices inserted into the recording, rerecording, and mixing systems to adjust the frequencies of response in order to improve the signal-to-noise ratio, adjust bass and treble, and emphasize or deemphasize the various frequencies in relation to one another. *See* **playback equalization curve.**

■ **erasing** The removal of a previously recorded signal from a magnetic sound tape by an erase head in the recording equipment.

■ **erect image** An image with the correct side on top.

■ **erecting system** A system of prisms or reflecting mirrors that reverses the image and allows it to be seen with the correct side on top, especially in camera viewfinders.

■ **errors and omissions insurance** Insurance for a production that financially protects the producers and possibly others from any legal proceedings concerning such issues as copyright infringement, invasion of privacy, libel, and breach of contract.

■ **escape film** A film whose main story deals with escape from some place of entrapment. This type of narrative has been popular in motion pictures, perhaps because the very nature of watching a film (i.e., the audience's enclosure in a confined area) and the very spatial enclosure of the screen create a feeling of entrapment for the audience and a desire for freedom. There have been a large number of first-rate films of this kind, including Jean Renoir's impressive *Grand Illusion* (1937) and John Sturges's lesser but still compelling *The Great Escape* (1963).

escape film *Grand Illusion* (1937; dir. Jean Renoir), with Erich von Stroheim, Pierre Fresnay, and Jean Gabin, is as much a film about the escape from old values and a dying world as an escape from a war camp.

■ ■ ■

■ **escapist film** Any film that offers a story, characters, and setting different but yet compelling enough to remove viewers from any consciousness of their own existence and problems, involving them intensely in the world of the film. Such films avoid the struggles that we all face in our lives and deal with conflict largely in terms of simple narrative complications, focusing on characters who are uncomplex though attractive. The application of the term to various films is sometimes relative to viewers, but many adventure stories and comedies are clearly escapist in nature. John Huston's *The Man Who Would Be King* (1975) is an excellent example of the kind of escape that film can offer without any loss in quality.

■ **Essanay** An American film company organized in 1907 by George K. Spoor and G. M. Anderson. The name of the company was derived from the S and A of the founders' last names. Essanay was at first known for its Westerns, especially the 376 Bronco Billy films directed by and starring Anderson. In 1909 the company joined in the ill-fated Motion Pictures Patent Company, which attempted to control all aspects of the industry, including equipment, production, distribution, and exhibition. Essanay was also popular for its comedies, and perhaps its most significant accomplishment was luring Charlie Chaplin away from Keystone for $1,250 per week, allowing him to make fourteen short films in 1915 and 1916, including *The Tramp* (1915). In 1915, Essanay formed an alliance with Vitagraph, Lubin, and Selig, later called the VLSE Company. The next year, Essanay failed to renew Chaplin's contract and he went to Mutual. The company ceased to prosper and in 1917 was bought out by Vitagraph along with the other members of the alliance. *See* **Lubin, Motion Picture Patents Company, Selig,** *and* **Vitagraph.**

■ **establishing shot** The opening shot of a sequence, which establishes location but can also establish mood or give the viewer information concerning the time and general situation. Establishing shots generally are long shots or extreme long shots. Sometimes a series of establishing shots view the location from different angles and perspectives, or a panning or moving shot is employed for the same purpose. Reestablishing shots are also used during a sequence to remind us of location or mood, or to suggest the passage of time. *See* **orientation shot** *and* **reestablishing shot.**

■ **Estar** A polyester base film made by Kodak. Because it is tougher and more durable than acetate base, it is now frequently used for the internegatives that produce the release prints and for the release prints themselves. Because of the susceptibility of acetate base to breakdown, Estar is also being used in preservation, especially for interpositives and for black-and-white separation masters. The name Estar is sometimes used generically for polyester film in general. *See* **acetate base, film** *(1), and* **polyester base.**

■ **estimate, estimate sheet, estimate sheets** The predicted budget for a film that includes both above-the-line and below-the-line costs. A form of a single sheet is used to give a general estimate with only broader categories defined, and a longer form of several sheets is used for a more detailed and itemized breakdown. *See* **above-the-line costs** *and* **below-the-line costs.**

ethnic film *Hester Street* (1975; dir. Joan Micklin Silver) depicts Jewish immigrant life on the Lower East Side of New York City at the turn of the century.

■ ■ ■

■ **ethnic film** A film that is primarily concerned with creating the setting, character types, lifestyle, and culture of a particular social or ethnic group: for example, Shirley Clarke's 1963 *The Cool World* depicts the world of Harlem and its various characters as if she were exploring and dramatizing its ethnography and culture; the evocative *Hester Street* (1975; dir. Joan Micklin Silver) depicts the life of Jewish immigrants on the Lower East Side of New York at the turn of the century; and the recent *Once Were Warriors* (1994; dir. Lee Tamahori) is a powerful film from New Zealand about the urbanized Maori culture and one family's return to its roots.

■ **ethnographic film** (1) Ethnography is a branch of anthropology that seeks to study and describe in a scientific manner an individual culture; and the ethnographic film, in the pure sense, is an anthropological film that scientifically and analytically, through image and voice-over, seeks to present and describe a distinct culture. (2) Any documentary film that seriously attempts to reveal one society to another, for example, Robert Flaherty's *Nanook of the North* (1922). Ethnographic films are analyzed and theorized in *Visual Anthropology Review*, a journal of the Society for Visual Anthropology. *See* **documentary.**

■ **exact cut** The exact length of a shot to be used in a special-effects optical composite.

■ **exchange, film exchange** The office for a major distributor in a specific area of the country responsible for distributing films to the theaters in that region.

■ **exciter lamp** In projectors, the small bulb that beams a light on the optical sound track. The light, which is modulated either by the variable area or density of the track, causes a photocell to produce the voltage which is transformed into sound. *See* **optical sound** *and* **projector.**

■ **exclusive engagement, exclusive run, exclusive opening** The showing of a film at a single theater in one geographic area.

■ **exclusive overall development deal** *See* **overall development deal.**

■ **executive producer** (1) The individual who, working for a large studio or film company, supervises the work of individual producers on their specific films. (2) The individual in charge of the finances for a motion-picture production.

■ **exhibition** The showing of a motion picture, generally to a paying audience in a commercial theater. In this country, short movies were first shown in peephole machines in penny arcades. From 1896, they were projected onto a screen as part of vaudeville shows and soon after were also projected in small, enclosed areas of the arcades. In 1902, in Los Angeles, Thomas L. Tally converted his arcade to the Electric Theater and showed only films. His success was imitated throughout the country when numerous arcades and stores were converted to show such films. The next significant event in exhibition was the founding of the Nickelodeon in 1905 by the brothers-in-law John P. Harris and Harry Davis in Pittsburgh. In an elaborately decorated store, the brothers presented shows of short films, accompanied by piano music, from morning to late at night before large crowds. By 1908, there were nearly 10,000 such theaters across the nation, offering twenty- to sixty-minute shows for the price of a nickel. In 1909, the Motion Picture Patents Company was formed by the leading film producers to monopolize all phases of the film industry, including the rental of both projectors and films; but this attempt at monopoly soon failed because of the pressure of the independents and the rulings of the courts. While the members of the Patents Company eventually went under, the independents flourished and themselves sought to control distribution and exhibition. These companies distributed their own films and, beginning with Paramount, imposed upon exhibitors the system of "block booking," which required the rental of a specific number of films at guaranteed rates. Five major companies dominated at the start of the sound age—MGM, Paramount, Twentieth Century-Fox, Warner Brothers, and RKO—all distributing their own films to their own theater circuits, which comprised some 17 percent of the theaters in the United States, but 70 percent of those in ninety-two of the largest urban areas. New and opulent theaters were built in cities throughout the nation; the more the monopoly of these few companies flourished, the more the industry flourished—until the Great Depression took its toll.

In 1948, the Supreme Court, in the Paramount decision, ruled that such vertically integrated ownership of production, distribution, and exhibition was a violation of fair trade and therefore illegal. Exhibition was deemed a separate and free enterprise, thus making theaters independent. Today, theaters largely belong to circuits, some of them, like UA Communications with its 543 theaters and 2,517 screens, are quite large. Many independent theaters rent films together as co-operatives. But, recently, old ways seem ready to revive: some of the big distributors belong to corporations that also own movie houses and entire circuits—for example, MCA owns both Universal Pictures and the Canadian-based theater firm Cineplex Odeon, while Sony Pictures Entertainment (Columbia and TriStar) is connected to Loews Theaters (called Sony Theatres from 1994 to 1996). The significant changes in exhibiting practices since the 1950s have been the end of the double feature, the rise and decline of the drive-in theater, the end of the repertory and classic film theater, the demise of the movie palace, and the development of multiple theaters at a single location—the number of screens actually expanded from 17,590 in 1980 to 27,805 in 1995. Although the number of screens has increased, the size of the individual theaters and the actual number of seats have decreased. Gross box office receipts have increased considerably, but that is because ticket prices have escalated. But though the number of people going to films decreased after the rise of television, it has actually increased since the early 1970s. Although the growth of the multiplex theaters at first resulted in suffocating and unaesthetic viewing facilities, there has been a considerable attempt in recent years to make these kinds of picture houses more pleasing and more satisfactory in the quality of their screenings—companies like Cineplex Odeon and AMC Entertainment, for example, have created multiplex theaters in separate structures with wide screens, digital stereophonic and surround-sound systems, and comfortable seating.

Up until the 1970s, important films were released for a first or premium run at a single theater in a few major cities. This release was generally followed by a second or multiple run in several dozen medium-size cities. When the film was distributed throughout the country in cities of all sizes, it was in general release—wide release when the theaters numbered more than 500. Various types of subruns might then follow. But when the advantages of national television as a major advertising medium were discovered, exhibition practices changed, especially for major films. By the 1980s, a film might enjoy wide release on as many as 2,000 screens throughout the country, and today special blockbuster films on as many as 3,000. Sometimes distributors will seek certain exhibitors, but frequently exhibitors must bid against other circuits or theaters for a film. For important films, exhibitors may have to guarantee 90 percent of the first week's box office and diminishing percentages for succeeding weeks. These figures are computed after the exhibitor is allowed house expenses (the "house nut"). But generally a "floor" is established—i.e., a minimal percentage return of the box office to the distributor. On the average, the exhibitor ends up keeping up to 60 percent of each box-office dollar for the run. *See* **distribution, exhibitor,** *and* **movie house.**

■ **exhibitor** (1) The person or company that rents films from distributors and exhibits them at one or more theaters. (2) The theater where movies are shown. Theaters may be owned independently, but a large number belong to chains, and others have joined together to bid for films cooperatively. The major theater circuits are United Artists (UA), Carmike Cinemas, AMC Entertainment (American Multi-Cinema), Cineplex Odeon, Cinemark USA, and the General Cinema Corporation. There are close to 28,000 screens in this country at this time because of the development of the multiplex theater (and some 100,000 screens are estimated throughout the world). The exhibitor must often bid for a film, pay rental generally on some percentage basis, advertise (with the distributor) for each film, and arrange and pay for costs of exhibiting the film. Since the 1948 Paramount decision of the Supreme Court, exhibitors have been independent of the producer-distributor of films, although recently big film companies such as Sony Pictures Entertainment and Paramount have become allied with theaters once again. With almost half its proceeds now coming from overseas, the entertainment industry in this country has become involved in the building of motion-picture theaters abroad—e.g., MCA and American Multi-Cinema with their investments in Great Britain. *See* **exhibition, megaplex,** *and* **movie house, multiplex.**

■ **expanded cinema** Contemporary experimental films that employ such modern technology as the computer, laser, holograph, and synthesizer. Gene Youngblood in his book *Expanded Cinema* (1970) claims that such films must be seen as part of our environment and as a means of expanding our consciousness of contemporary existence.

■ **experimental film** A term used synonymously with avant-garde to describe any film of a noncommercial nature that avoids normal narrative lines and any realistic depiction of the world outside the cinema to present what is often a personal or subjective expression of the filmmaker's psyche through an exploration of the film medium itself. Such films may deal with taboo subjects and images or may be abstract in nature, dealing with the rhythmic interplay of lines, shapes, or forms. Such films may use images of the real world, though in ways and contexts that change them; animated drawings or cutouts; or images drawn directly on the film stock itself. Whatever the techniques, experimental films open up the medium to create new visions

through highly personal and idiosyncratic techniques. *See* **avant-garde cinema.**

■ **exploitation film** A film that exploits a subject for commercial advantage by pandering to the curiosity and prurience of the audience. Such films may exploit current violent events (as the mass suicide in Guyana) or well-known personalities in a slightly veiled way (as Jackie Kennedy and Onassis); but the term more often describes especially violent and crudely sexual films.

■ **exposed** The state of film when it has already been used in the camera so that the latent images are formed in the emulsion and ready for development.

■ **exposition** (1) That part of a narrative work, often the beginning, which establishes for the audience the general situation of characters and the premises for the action. In a play or film this may be done by characters who discuss background events and the present state of affairs that might involve them or other figures who have not yet appeared. Good exposition must seem an inherent part of the narrative structure, developing the plot at the same time as explaining it. Film can also create exposition either by a series of shots edited in such a way that they give the viewer the necessary information to understand the present situation so that the major action may start or continue (for example, the beginning of Kubrick's *2001: A Space Odyssey* [1968], which deals with the ape-men and giant monolith, is a visual exposition for the remainder of the film); or by means of flashbacks during the course of the action (for example, the scenes from the past in *Death of a Salesman* [1951; dir. Laslo Benedek], which explain the events leading to the present conflict between father and son). (2) The presentation and straightforward explanation of facts, ideas, or arguments. The term, in this sense, may apply both to the visual and audio presentation in educational and documentary films.

■ **exposure** (1) The act of exposing film in a camera or printer to light so that a latent image is formed in the emulsion. The quality of exposure in a camera is determined by the scene's lighting, the length of time that the film is exposed to the light, and the opening of the camera's lens. Overexposed film creates an image that appears very light, with details washed out, and underexposed film creates an image that appears dark and dense. Sometimes these irregular exposures may be done purposefully, in the first case to create images that seem unreal or dreamlike and in the second to create images that seem gloomy, mysterious, or foreboding. Normally it is important to have the correct exposure to create images that are clear and well defined, render colors accurately, and maintain consistency from image to image. A light meter measures either the incident light or light reflected from a subject and generally determines the f-stop number to be set. The exposure setting can also be determined by an exposure calculator or table which gives the proper number for estimated light conditions. Since f-stop numbers are often considered insufficiently accurate for professional cinematography because they do not take account of light absorption and reflection in the lens, t-stop numbers, which calculate the actual transmission of light, are also used (f-stop numbers are still needed for controlling depth of field). Camera speeds and film emulsion also determine exposure, but since most professional cameras function at a speed of 24 frames per second and the same batch of stock is used throughout each film, these are not changing factors from shot to shot or scene to scene. In a printer, exposure is determined by the emulsion of the film stock, the intensity of light, and the duration that the film is exposed to the light. *See* **f-stop** *and* **t-stop.** (2) The amount of light allowed to reach film for a latent image to be formed in the emulsion. (3) The length of time that the film is exposed to light in order to form a latent image. (4) The area on the film that is exposed to light.

■ **exposure calculator, exposure table** A small wheel or table that gives proper camera exposures for various light conditions.

■ **exposure guide** Instructions given for a particular film, suggesting exposures for different lighting situations.

■ **exposure index (EI), exposure rating** The number given by a manufacturer for a particular film stock to indicate its sensitivity, that is, its speed and latitude. Such numbers are necessary in determining exposures with a light meter. Film generally has two index numbers, one for daylight and the other for tungsten lighting. *See* **ASA standard** *and* **DIN standard.**

■ **exposure latitude** The range in which a film may be exposed and still achieve a satisfactory image.

■ **exposure meter, light meter** Either the incident light meter, which measures light falling on a subject, or the reflected light meter, held near the camera, which measures the light reflected from the scene. Incident light meters of the hemispherical type are pointed toward the camera to measure light falling on the subject from all sources, while those of the flat type are pointed at a single source of light or in a particular direction. The flat type can measure both key lights and fill lights independently, though many experienced cinematographers measure the key light only and balance fill lights and shadow by eye. Because reflected light meters, when calculating an average luminance, may be overly affected by extreme areas of light or dark, they often render key areas either under- or overexposed and measure faces improperly. For this reason they are normally not used in professional cinematography. Spot brightness meters of this type, however, with a narrow angle of acceptance, are professionally

employed to measure a small area of light from the camera's position. Exposure meters work by means of a photoelectric cell responding to light, and many have calculators that consider the film's exposure index and the camera's speed along with the intensity of illumination to suggest the proper f-stop, or diaphragm opening, for exposure. *See* **f-stop** *and* **photometer.**

■ **exposure report** A report that goes to the cinematographer along with the dailies giving information about the red, green, and blue timing lights for both designated footage and frames. This printout helps the cinematographer evaluate the exposure for the various shots on the negative and, also with the help of the workprint, decide on various changes in lighting and color for the next printing.

■ **exposure sheet** A guide for the camera operator prepared by the animator that indicates the position of each cel and the number of frames in which the cel should be photographed. The sheet also indicates the movement of the camera, transitions, and the position of the background.

■ **exposure time** The amount of time that each frame in the camera is exposed to light. This amount is calculated by the number of frames per second that pass before the lens and the shutter opening. The basic exposure time is 1/50 second per frame for the normal 24 frames per second with a 175-degree shutter. *See* **exposure.**

expressionism The distorted world of *The Cabinet of Dr. Caligari* (1919; dir. Robert Wiene).

■ ■ ■

■ **expressionism** (1) A cultural movement in Germany during the early decades of this century that sought to create art as an extension of subjective reality—distortion and exaggeration were primary means of transforming the physical world into a projection of the inner self. This movement was partly a reaction to bourgeois concepts of reality and conventional art, as well as a response to impressionism, a style of painting that depicted immediate impressions of the physical world without radically transforming that reality. The expressionistic movement was influential in painting, literature, music, and film. (2) A movement in German cinema, from 1919 to approximately 1933, that sought to present physical reality on the screen as a projection, or expression, of the subjective world, generally of a character in the film. This was accomplished through distorted and exaggerated settings, heavy and dramatic shadows, unnatural space in composition, oblique angles, curved or nonparallel lines, a mobile and subjective camera, unnatural costumes and makeup, and stylized acting. Such films create a dreamlike or nightmarish world. The most notable work of this type was Robert Wiene's *The Cabinet of Dr. Caligari* (1919), the prototype horror film with its bizarre and distorted world that seems a subjective projection of both a diseased Germany after the First World War and the madman who is the protagonist. Other significant expressionistic films were F. W. Murnau's *Nosferatu, A Symphony of Terror* (1922), Paul Leni's *Waxworks* (1924), and E. A. Dupont's *Variety* (1925). The expressionistic film in Germany gave way to other cinematic forces and was ultimately crushed by Nazi repression, but the movement had an impact in this country, especially on the settings, lighting, and camerawork of the horror films of the 1930s, through the German films themselves and through the film people who came from the German studios to work here. (3) A film technique that distorts and exaggerates the physical world so that it appears a projection of the subjective state of characters or of the filmmaker. Films may vary to the degree in which they use this technique, but settings, lighting, spatial relationships, and camera movement all express to the audience a sense of what the characters or filmmaker are feeling. There is often something dreamlike, fantastic, or nightmarish about physical reality which itself seems claustrophobic, threatening, vertiginous, tumultuous. Expressionism seeks to create an unreality that seems realer than the everyday reality that surrounds us. *See* **impressionism** *and* **UFA.**

■ **EXT** *See* **exterior.**

■ **extended scene, extended shot** A scene or shot in a workprint with a piece of leader attached—sometimes called a slug—to indicate that the scene or shot must be extended or that a part is missing. *See* **slug.**

■ **extension tube** A tube that extends the lens away from the camera and closer to the subject in order to magnify its image in sharp focus.

■ **exterior (EXT)** Any shot or entire scene that takes place at an out-of-doors location, whether actually photographed outdoors or inside the studio. *See* **interior.**

■ **exterior lighting** Both natural and artificial lighting for exterior shooting.

■ **external rhythm** A term sometimes used in critical discourse to describe the sense of a work's movement, its linear flow and development from shot to shot, scene to scene, and sequence to sequence. Such a sense of rhythm will depend upon the dominant length of individual shots, scenes, and sequences, and the dominant style of cutting, whether invisible, dynamic, or elliptical. Also significant are camera movement (whether shots are extended by a mobile camera and whether there is much panning or tracking) and the general pace of the acting. Certain filmmakers create very pervasive rhythms in their works, for example, the slow, brooding, and sometimes paralyzing rhythms of Antonioni, or the quick, elliptical, and dizzying rhythms of Godard. *See* **internal rhythm** *and* **rhythm.**

■ **extra** An actor hired to appear in a crowd scene or as an incidental figure in a film without speaking any lines. Such actors are hired from day to day and generally receive no credit for their performance (unlike bit players).

■ **extreme** A key drawing in animation cartoon work. *See* **key animator.**

■ **extreme close-up (ECU, XCU)** A shot very close to the subject so that only a small portion or detail is shown or the entirety of a small object. Such a shot of a performer would show only part of the face, such as the eyes or mouth.

■ **extreme high-angle shot** A shot from far above the subject, generally from a boom, tower, balcony, or helicopter. Such images diminish figures and give a panoramic view of the field of action or the landscape. Also called a bird's-eye shot. *See* **high-angle shot.**

■ **extreme long shot (ELS, XLS)** A shot taken at a great distance from the subject, frequently offering a wide view of a location. Such an image is often used as an establishing shot. *See* **establishing shot** *and* **long shot.**

■ **extreme low-angle shot** A shot taken from far below the subject so that characters or objects seem to tower above the camera. *See* **low-angle shot.**

■ **extreme wide-angle lens** Sometimes called a fisheye lens, this optical device gives the widest field of view, up to 180 degrees. Such a view seriously distorts the image to such an extreme that central objects receive unnatural prominence and the sides of the frame seem to curve globularly. This lens is effective in creating dreams and hallucinations or in conveying intoxication and extreme emotional states. *See* **wide-angle lens.**

■ **extrude** A procedure in computer animation or graphics of making a 2-D object into a 3-D one by pushing it along an axis perpendicular to its surface—the flat diagram is pulled and stretched until it expands and rises into a 3-D shape.

■ **eye contact** When the actor looks directly into the lens of a camera.

■ **eye-level shot, eye-level angle** A shot taken by the camera approximately five or six feet from the ground to represent the point of view of an observer of average height. This height is the point of reference for all the variable shots taken during a sequence.

■ **eye light** A small light near the camera that creates illumination in a character's eyes without affecting the exposure of the camera. Also called a catchlight.

■ **eyeline** The direction and angle of vision of a character relative to the camera. It is, of course, important that the eyelines be the same from shot to shot or logically and smoothly change from shot to shot so that a jump cut does not result. It is the role of the script supervisor to make sure that such continuity exists.

■ **eyeline match, eyeline matching cut** A cut from one shot to another in which the two shots are connected logically by a character's eyeline. For example, a character looks in a specific direction with a specific angle of view and the next shot is some object that is placed exactly where we think he or she would be looking. *See* **cut** *and* **point-of-view shot.**

eyepiece

■ **eyepiece** That part of the camera's viewfinder in which a lens is positioned and through which the camera operator views the scene before and during shooting. *See* **viewfinder.**

■ **eye sync** Synchronizing picture and sound without the use of a clapboard or sync beep. The editor tries to line up both films by some obvious point of correspondence, as when a gun is fired and a character shows physical injury. Not especially a good idea, the practice is sometimes necessary—for example, when the camera is too far from the recorder to allow for proper syncing. *See* **editing** *and* **synchronization.**

■ ■ ■

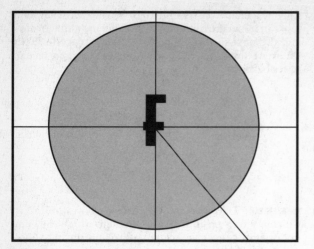

facial ratio to FX

■ **facial ratio** A term used for the subject lighting ratio when the focus of the subject is a face or faces. *See* **subject lighting ratio.**

■ **factual film** A nonfictional film that deals with actual people, events, activities, or some body of knowledge; generally a documentary film. *See* **documentary.**

■ **fade** A gradual means of closing or starting a scene, often used as a transitional device when one scene closes with the image disappearing (a fade-out) and the next scene comes into view as the image grows stronger and stronger (a fade-in). Both kinds of fades following one another indicate a significant break in action, time, or place (the viewer briefly faces a blank screen which marks this separation). Sometimes a fade-in starts and a fade-out finishes a film. A fade can be achieved in the camera by gradually opening or closing the aperture, but is more commonly and safely achieved in an optical printer when the exposure light is gradually reduced or increased. Fade-to-black occurs when the scene gradually darkens to a black screen before the new image appears and is a means of marking a significant transition in time; a fade-to-white occurs when the scene gradually bleaches out to white, a technique sometimes employed for showing a character losing consciousness. The fade, because of its strong emphasis and frequent past use, is less often employed today in a film though it is a frequent television device for opening and closing the acts of a drama.

■ **fade-in (FI), fade-out (FO)** (1) *See* **fade.** (2) The gradual increase from no sound to full sound or decrease from full sound to no sound in an audio system. Also referred to as fade up and fade down.

■ **fader** (1) The device in any optical or audio system that decreases or increases the signal. In an optical printer, the fader decreases or increases the light needed for exposure. In a mixing console, a fader lowers or increases the volume for each track and allows for the modulation and integration of all the tracks into the final composite. (2) A device in a camera or an optical printer that allows for creating a fade. Such a device generally employs a fading shutter. *See* **fade.**

■ **fail-safe** A sensing device that brings a film projector to a halt when the film breaks. In modern projector systems, a laser is employed to sense breakage when the film uses a bar-code automation system. *See* **projector.**

■ **fairing** Starting a pan with greater speed and concluding it more slowly than the general speed of the take to allow for transitions to or from a static camera.

■ **fall-off** (1) The diminishment of illumination at progressive distances from the light source. Such diminishment must be measured and considered in the lighting composition of any scene. Rapid fall-off creates sudden and stark shadows for dramatic effect. (2) The diminishment of reflected light from any object in progressive distances away from the object. Rapid fall-off creates sudden shadows that define and emphasize the edges of the object, whereas gradual fall-off smooths out and softens the edges. (3) The diminishment in brightness from the center of a screen to its edges.

■ **false reverse-angle shot, false reverse** A reverse-angle shot where the change in camera is so radical or the transition so fast that the character seems to be facing in the wrong direction when the shot is edited into the sequence. *See* **reverse-angle shot.**

■ **Famous Players** In 1912, Adolph Zukor purchased and successfully distributed the French four-reel film *Queen Elizabeth,* starring Sarah Bernhardt. Convinced that the future of motion pictures was in feature films, Zukor began his Famous Players in Famous Plays Company, with Edwin S. Porter as a director and chief of production and the popular theatrical producer Daniel Frohman as adviser. The company's first film was *The Prisoner of Zenda,* based on the theater production and starring James K. Hackett, the celebrated actor. Although Zukor filmed a series of dramas with stage performers, his company was far more successful with less prestigious works especially created for the new medium and starring screen personalities. In 1914, he hired Mary Pickford away from Biograph at the unheard-of salary of $2,000 per week, and in 1916, he guaranteed her a million dollars for the next two years in a new contract.

Zukor's Famous Players Company was one of the most successful producers of feature films. In 1916, it merged with the Jesse Lasky Feature Play Company to form the Famous Players-Lasky Corporation, with Zukor as president. In the same year Zukor was secretly responsible for the formation of the Artcraft Picture Company, which was to produce and distribute the films of Mary Pickford; and in 1918, he merged Artcraft with the Famous Players-Lasky Company while also bringing Paramount Pictures, the distributor through which he had been releasing his own films, into the new organization. The new company was enormously successful, producing and distributing films while buying up theaters all over the world. Performers such as William S. Hart, Gloria Swanson, Dorothy Gish, Richard Barthelmess, Pola Negri, and Adolphe Menjou as well as such directors as James Cruze, Victor Fleming, and Ernst Lubitsch at various times worked for the company. In 1927, when the company became Paramount Pictures, it was worth some $150 million and Zukor was considered the most important figure in motion pictures. *See* **Paramount Pictures Corporation.**

■ **fan** A devoted follower of a well-known screen personality. Especially during the days of the Hollywood studios and star system, fans were a significant consideration in the making of films and also in the mythology about the stars developed by the public relations and advertising departments of the studios. Fan clubs, which published newsletters and staged activities, were common; fan mail, delivered by the bagful to the studios, was a useful measure (along with the box office) of a star's popularity; and fan magazines, concerned with the supposedly real private lives of the stars, were numerous. Today famous performers still have their fans, a number of fan clubs and publications remain, but the star system, with all its hullabaloo, has long been dead. Successful films require more than popular stars. The adulation of celebrities has moved considerably into the arena of rock music.

■ **fan magazine** A magazine that catered to the taste and desires of an audience with a strong interest specifically in the movie stars of the film industry—in their private lives, scandals, and the fantasies that the studios and their own publicists created about them. Fan magazines were themselves extensions of the fantasies that the public saw on the screen and allowed the public to project themselves into romanticized notions of the lives of the stars. Some of the more popular fan magazines of long standing were *Photoplay* and *Modern Screen*. Today, magazines such as *Premier* seem to play something of the same role, though the stars of Hollywood no longer hold the fantasies of the American public the way they did during the days of the studio system.

■ **fantasy, fantasy film, fantastic film** A motion picture that features improbable and even impossible characters and events. Such films create a world unlike any we know outside the theater, a world where the normal laws of physics and biology are suspended. The success of such films is dependent upon the filmmaker's ca-

pacity to make such an unreality both real and believable to the audience. Because of film's capacity to alter and manipulate time and space through editing, because the medium allows for all kinds of special effects, and because film creates with immediacy a physical universe (as manufactured as it may be), motion pictures have been successful in creating this kind of work from the very earliest days of the industry when George Méliès made his imaginative films. Prose narratives may allow much room for the imagination, but film creates before us the fantasies of our imagination. Fantasy films have been seen as projections of human fears and desires, as objectified situations where both unconscious and conscious anxieties of the audience find release and satisfaction. Certainly this is true of fantasy horror films, where fears of death and injury are appeased, where needs for power and aggression are satisfied. But all fantasy films, on a more general level, satisfy the ever-present child in us with magic and wonder; they are responses to the adult world of fact and reason outside the theater and satisfy the imagination and wish for power.

The large category of fantasy films can be divided into a number of subgroups: (1) science-fiction films, such as *Star Wars* (1977; dir. George Lucas) and *Close Encounters of the Third Kind* (1977; dir. Steven Spielberg), which project us into fantastic and futuristic worlds and use science to transcend the world of reason and fact; (2) horror films, such as *Frankenstein* (1931; dir. James Whale) and *King Kong* (1933; dir. Merian C. Cooper and Ernest Schoedsack), which create fear and terror through the supernatural and bizarre; (3) adventure tales, such as *The Seventh Voyage of Sinbad* (1958; dir. Nathan Juran), which take us to strange and impossible places; and (4) romantic fairy

fantasy *Beauty and the Beast* (1946; dir. Jean Cocteau), an escape into dreams and magic with Jean Marais and Josette Day.

■■■

tales, such as Jean Cocteau's *Beauty and the Beast* (1946) and fairy tales of sheer whimsy, such as the Czechoslovakian *The Fabulous Baron Munchausen* (1962; dir. Karel Zeman), which offer us escape into a world of magic and wonder, where all our wishes can be fulfilled. *See* **horror film** *and* **science-fiction film.**

■ **farce** A comic work that features exaggerated characters in an exaggerated situation to evoke laughter. Farce has always been a significant part of the theater and was a natural form for silent films, where characters were limited to exaggerated physical action to convey the dramatic situation and to provoke from the audience some kind of response. A prime ingredient of these films was slapstick, a type of violent action largely inherited from vaudeville that was to be a frequent part of future film farces. Nearly all of the Mack Sennett comedies are farces in the broadest sense, with outrageous characters in outrageous situations, and even the works of the great comic actors—Chaplin, Keaton, Langdon, and Lloyd—are largely farcical in nature, even with their more-developed and human central figures. Sound brought more sophisticated comedy to film, but farce was to remain a central part of film comedy, which now employed absurdly funny voices and dialogue along with ridiculous plots, action, and character types. Any of the comedies of the Marx Brothers or W. C. Fields, for example, can be considered farces. Beginning in 1968 with *The Producers* and throughout the 1970s, Mel Brooks was the most successful creator of film farces in this country. Most film comedies during the past few decades have been broad farces, with some of the chief performers Bill Murray, Robin Williams, Eddie Murphy, and Jim Carrey. *See* **comedy** *and* **slapstick.**

■ **far shot** *See* **long shot.**

■ **fast cutting** Cutting rapidly between a series of brief shots, thus creating for the audience a sense of excitement. Fast cutting can also build confusion or anticipation, depending on the context. *See* **accelerated montage.**

■ **fast film, fast stock** A film stock highly sensitive to light. Such film is used when light is limited (for example, when shooting documentaries with natural lighting.) Images produced by such film tend to be more grainy than those produced by slower stock, but some new fast stocks, manufactured by Kodak in this country and Fuji in Japan, create remarkable reproductions with minimal granularity even when shot with limited lighting.

■ **fast lens** A lens with a high efficiency for transmitting light. Such lenses have a relatively large aperture, with high f-stop numbers in the 1.5 range. *See* **lens.**

■ **fast motion, accelerated motion** Motion on the screen that takes place at a more rapid speed than in the real world. This acceleration is accomplished by shooting the action at a camera speed slower than the normal 16 frames per second for silent films and 24 frames per second for sound (the technique is sometimes called "undercranking" from early film days when cameras were cranked by hand) and projecting the printed images at the normal rate. Fast motion produces unnatural, jerky, and syncopated motions which tend to dehumanize the characters and make them appear like toys or machines. Fast motion was a favorite technique in silent comedies (e.g., in the Mack Sennett comedies) and has since been used as a comic device (e.g., in Tony Richardson's *Tom Jones* [1963] and Richard Lester's *A Hard Day's Night* [1964]).

■ **fast speed** A camera speed faster than the standard 24 frames per second used to create an image in slow motion when the print is projected at the normal speed. The Image 300 35mm camera, for example, can shoot at speeds from 24 to 300 frames per second and has been used for a number of slow-motion sequences in commercial films. *See* **high-speed camera.**

■ **favor, favoring** Giving a special emphasis to a character or object by camera placement and lighting.

■ **FAY light** A sealed-beam light of 650 watts similar to the PAR light and often part of a two-, four-, six- or nine-light module for creating broad and even illumination for daytime or outdoor lighting. *See* **FCX light.**

■ **FCX light, FCX globe** A light basically the same as the FAY, but balanced for indoor shooting. *See* **FAY light.**

■ **featured part** A role secondary to the lead parts, but still significant and often played by a performer of some reputation.

■ **featured player** A performer who plays a featured part. *See* **featured part.**

■ **feature film, feature, feature-length film, full-length motion picture, multiple reeler, multiple reel film** Although the term "feature" in silent-film days derived from films that "featured" certain stars, stories, or action, it came to mean works that were the major or "featured" attraction in the showing of a series of films. Such films were feature attractions because of their greater length of five reels or more, with each reel running about fourteen minutes. In the days of sound double features, the feature film generally was an "A" production, with a higher budget, better-known performers, and a greater running time than the second feature. Today the term "feature film" applies to any full-length fictional film that plays at a commercial theater. Such films run anywhere from ninety minutes to two hours, though longer films are not uncommon.

In the early days of the film industry, the resistance to making feature films by the organizations in the Motion Picture Patents Company was one of the reasons for their ultimate demise. Although longer films were occasionally made in America, the lead in producing such films came from Italy and France. The Italian five-reeler *Dante's Inferno* was made in 1911, followed the next year by the nine-reel *Quo Vadis*, which was a great success. In 1912, two feature-length Italian productions of *The Last Days of Pompeii* also appeared. The Film d'Art company in France in 1913 produced an eight-reel version of *Germinal* and a twelve-reel version of *Les Misérables*. Adolph Zukor in America, after successfully distributing the Film d'Art's four-reel production of *Queen Elizabeth* with Sarah Bernhardt in 1912, organized his Famous Players in Famous Plays Company in the same year and began to make feature-length films. Also notable was the formation of the Jesse L. Lasky Feature Play Company and its 1914 production of the six-reel film *The Squaw Man*, directed by Cecil B. De-Mille. The growth of the feature film and the independents was rapid: it is estimated that nearly 700 feature films were made in 1917 and 850 the following year. By this time the standard show throughout the country was a feature film with one or more shorts preceding it. The double feature came into fashion during the Depression years and 1940s, but rising costs of film production as well as the end of block booking and the ownership of theaters by the large studios brought a halt to this practice during the early 1950s. Today the practice is to show a feature film without a second feature or short subject. *See* **B-picture** *and* **double feature.**

■ **featurette** A short film about the making of a film. Featurettes are intended for publicity and normally are shown on television, especially on cable-television movie channels.

■ **feed** (1) To supply film into a camera, projector, or printer. (2) Any part of the camera, projector, or printer that feeds film into the basic mechanism.

■ **feedback** The process in any electronic amplification system for sound whereby some of the output is fed back into the input to increase or improve the audio signal.

■ **feed chamber** In a two-chamber magazine, the front chamber, which feeds the unexposed film through the camera and into the take-up chamber.

■ **feed plate** A flat disc on a flat-bed editing machine that feeds film or tape in continuous motion through the machine to a take-up plate for picture or sound replay. Such editing tables have up to four feed plates. *See* **flat-bed editing machine.**

■ **feed reel** The front reel that feeds the film through the projector and to the take-up reel. Also called the supply reel. *See* **projector.**

■ **feet per minute (FPM)** The speed with which film passes through a camera or projector: 70mm sound film passes through at 112.5 feet per minute; 35mm silent film at 60 and 35mm sound film at 90 feet per minute; and 16mm silent film at 24 and 16mm sound film at 36 feet per minute.

■ **female matte** A matte for making composite images in special-effects photography that is clear in the area of the subject but opaque in the surrounding area. Also called foreground matte and sometimes matte master, cover matte, and action printing matte. *See* **matte** (2) and **traveling-matte process.**

■ **feminist criticism, feminist film theory** *See* **film theory.**

■ **festival** *See* **film festival.**

■ **FG** *See* **foreground.**

■ **FI** A fade-in. *See* **fade-in (FI), fade-out (FO).**

■ **fiber optics viewfinder** A camera viewfinder with a screen made of bundles of fine-glass rods that is able to reflect the image with great brightness. One viewfinder system uses fiber optics to relay an image with high resolution off the shutter of a camera to a video camera so that the scene can be viewed on a separate video screen. This type of system is especially used for shooting with a body-mounted camera, remote-control cameras, and on moving vehicles such as an airplane. *See* **video assist** *and* **viewfinder.**

■ **fiction film** A film with imaginary characters and events. The term generally applies to most feature and commercial films. Many fiction films use actual places; some may incorporate into the story real people and events, though their rendition is largely fictional. Some fiction films attempt to create an aura of truth and verisimilitude by employing a documentary film style, but this does not alter the fictional nature of the work. Purists would argue that even documentaries are fictional, since the very act of selecting what to film, the unnatural situation of the filming itself, and the editing of the work create a world that exists only on the screen and one that no longer resembles the reality it supposedly presents. Nevertheless, one should judge the intentions of the work and see that fictional films made primarily to entertain are very different from documentaries that employ subject matter and techniques basically to increase the viewer's understanding of some factual aspect of the world outside the theater.

■ **fidelity** (1) Accuracy in reproducing color in an image. (2) Accuracy in reproducing sound in a recording system.

■ **field** (1) The individual scannings of first the odd and then the even numbered lines that make up the individual frames of a television or video picture—there are sixty such fields for the 30 frames per second. *See* **television** *and* **video camera.** (2) *See* **field of action.**

■ **field angle** A lighted angle of 90 degrees from a spotlight.

■ **field camera** A lightweight, portable camera employed outside the studio for location work because it is easy to carry and handle (e.g., the Arriflex 35 2C).

■ **field chart, field guide** In animation work, a transparent sheet with a number of superimposed rectangles, each representing a different field size for various lenses and camera distances, which is positioned on top of the table by pegs. *See* **animation stand.**

■ **field flattener** A lens used in conjunction with other lenses to flatten the image and prevent curvature of field.

■ **field of action, field, action field, field of view** The circular area in front of the camera that is accepted by the lens and recorded as the rectangular image within the frame. Field size depends upon both the focal length of the lens and the distance between the camera and subject. In animation work, the area is measured from a twelve-field to a four-field, that is, from the largest possible area to the smallest. *See* **angle of view** *and* **animation.**

■ **field size** The area of a scene covered by a specific lens.

■ **fifty-fifty** A shot of two characters, generally talking and facing one another, who share the image equally. A two shot.

■ **fifty-fifty mirror** A special effects mirror employed with a camera to achieve a superimposition of two images directly on the film without having to achieve this effect later by bringing together two separately photographed images in an optical printer. Because the mirror is partially layered with silver or aluminum on one side, half the light reaching its surface passes through and the other half bounces back. Some action to the side of the mirror can be reflected off the layered side into the camera lens. The mirror is placed in front of the camera at a 45-degree angle so that both the scene in front of the camera and the action to the side are recorded at once, superimposed upon one another. The mirror can be employed for imposing fire, explosions, or light rays (in a laboratory) over the main scene. *See* **Schüfftan process.**

■ **fill, fill leader** Blank film that fills in the space between image sequences on a workprint or between sections of sound on a sound track. *See* **slug.**

■ **fill light, filler light, fill-in light, filler, fill** A soft light, frequently placed near the camera on the side opposite the key light, that fills in areas left unlit or softens the shadows made by the key light, thus reducing contrast. Fill lights also reduce shadows and lines on the faces of characters. These lights should neither affect the exposure of the scene nor create their own shadows. *See* **lighting** *and* **lighting ratio.**

■ **film** (1) A strip of thin, transparent, and flexible material, composed of a base supporting a layer of emulsion in which a latent image is formed upon exposure to light through a camera's lens. A series of latent images are formed on cinematographic film for a sequence of action. The entire series of frames are developed as a negative and then the pictures are transferred onto the emulsion of a separate film, which is made into a positive print (in the case of reversal film, the original stock is itself made into a positive print). When the frames of the print are projected onto a screen, one after the other at 16 or more frames per second for silent film and 24 frames per second for sound film, the images join together and an illusion of the original action, with all its movement, is reproduced.

The capacity of silver nitrate to turn black when exposed to light was commented upon as early as the seventeenth century. In the early part of the eighteenth century, experimentation was done with basic cameras, and pictures were developed on paper coated with silver bromides; but this process recorded a negative image of the subject which soon blackened when removed from the camera. In 1835, the Englishman Fox Talbot was able to fix the silver salts and achieve a permanent negative image, which was also transparent enough for light to pass through and for a positive print to be made on a second film. At the same time, in France, Louis Daguerre, continuing his earlier work with the late Nicéphore Niépce, developed a process that used a silver surface on a copper plate to make a positive image. Introduced in 1839, daguerreotypes were very popular for a while, but the lengthy time required for exposure and the fact that no duplicates could be made soon undermined the popularity of this process—the future of photography was in the type of film achieved by Talbot. Experiments continued with photography, a notable example being Muybridge's exploration of motion through a series of individual prints; but the next significant development was in the photographic process itself, with George Eastman's roll of transparent celluloid film introduced in 1889. It was with this film that Edison and Dickson developed their Kinetograph camera and Kinetoscope peep show machine, which they exhibited privately in 1891. The Kinetoscope peep show was exhibited publicly in 1893. The film used was to become standard insofar as it was 35mm wide and had four perforations on each side. The original base for motion-picture film was made of cellulose nitrate, but this was extremely flammable and also disintegrated rapidly.

From 1951, the base was generally cellulose acetate (triacetate), which is relatively flameproof but itself has proven to be vulnerable to a deterioration called the "vinegar syndrome" because of the pungent odor that results. A number of film stocks, especially internegatives for release prints and the release prints themselves, are now using polyester base, which is stronger and less susceptible to deterioration. The emulsion of film during the days of silent filmmaking was orthochromatic, which was sensitive to both blue and green light waves (the red part of the spectrum appeared as black). Panchromatic stock, a black-and-white film sensitive to all colors, became dominant after its successful use in Flaherty's *Moana* in 1926. Orthochromatic film had been fast as well as excellent for deep focus; it also had created a very sharp picture. Panchromatic stock was slower and created less depth of field; but it was more accurate in recording the gradations of color on the gray scale and was more natural in photographing faces.

Black-and-white film has a single emulsion layer that is attached to the base by a subbing layer. Color film has three emulsion layers, each with a coupler sensitive to a different primary color mixed in with the silver halides. Beneath the top blue-sensitive layer is a yellow filter that prevents blue light from reaching the next layer, which is sensitive to green and blue, and the bottom layer, which is sensitive to red and blue. Film also has an opaque antihalation backing which prevents light that passes through the emulsion from being reflected back from the base and forming an halation, that is, a blurred effect around the image. Some films also have an antiabrasion coating on the back. When each frame of the film is exposed to light, the silver halides are "tagged" and undergo a chemical change, forming a latent image which is actually bottom side up. During developing the exposed silver crystals become black silver metal, hence forming a negative image (lighted areas become black and dark areas light). In color film, the couplers in each of the three layers form an image in a color complementary to one of the primaries, after which both developed and undeveloped halides are washed away, leaving a color negative image with light, dark, and color reversed. The film is then rinsed, after which the image is chemically "fixed." In the final stages, the film is washed and dried. Positive prints can be made from the negative either in a contact printer by passing light through the negative onto fresh stock with the two emulsions touching, or in an optical printer where each image is projected and rephotographed (this method is generally used for optical and special effects as well as for changing image size). In black-and-white positives, the light and dark are reversed back to normal, and in tripack color positives the colors are also returned to their original appearance.

Reversal stock has normally been used for 8mm filmmaking and also at times for work in 16mm. In reversal processing, after the exposed silver crystals are developed into black silver metal, they are bleached out and dissolved; the remaining silver crystals are then exposed or chemically treated, after which they are developed, forming a black silver metal, but in this case the dark and light of the image correspond to the dark and light in the original subject. On tripack color reversal film, the couplers are also converted to form a color image, and the exposed halides from both stages are bleached and washed away, leaving a positive color image. Reversal film is less grainy, more sensitive, and less prone to show scratches or marks; but, at the same time, it is less forgiving of mistakes in exposure, and often expensive. An original film when developed is called the first generation; the prints made from it are second generation; and the negative made from a print is third generation (or first-generation dupe). Each new development will somewhat diminish the quality of the image.

Film stocks are made with emulsions having different degrees of sensitivity to light. The exposure index is given by the manufacturer to indicate a particular stock's speed and exposure latitude. A film with a high number is considered a fast stock and is used in situations where light is limited (for example in documentaries or on location). Slow stock, which produces less grainy and hence sharper and clearer images, is used primarily for filming indoors, in studios, where there is unlimited lighting. Film stocks also give different contrast ranges, which are measured by the gamma value. Film stocks that produce images with both extremes of black and white and a wide range of gray tonal values in between are considered to have "low contrast." "High contrast" film has a limited intermediate range between the contrasting black and white. Film emulsion in the camera faces the lens and the light coming from the subject. In projection of 70mm or 35mm film the emulsion will face away from the lens since the print has been made from the negative through contact printing and the image must be reoriented. In reversal printing, however, where the negative is made into the positive print, the emulsion will be projected facing the lens.

The standard size for professional filmmaking since the days of Edison has been 35mm, with four perforations on each side of the frame to move and position the film. The necessity of a sound track reduced only the area of the frame and not the size of the film itself. Some cameras are equipped to accept 35mm film with three perforations on each side of the frame, thus using 25 percent less film, and some shoot at 30 frames per second for direct transfer to videotape. Beginning in the 1950s, negatives of 65mm and positives of 70mm were sometimes used for wide-screen images, with five perforations on each side of the frame (in Russia and Eastern Europe, the negative was also 70mm); but today the cost of shooting with such film is considered extravagant and is done only on occasion. Images from 35mm negatives are instead sometimes blown up on 70mm prints for special films and screenings. The 16mm film employed by both professionals and amateurs has one perforation at the corners of adjoining frames either on both sides or only on one side when a sound track is on the other. Sixteen-millimeter film has generally been employed for educational films and for noncommercial showings of feature films, but is now also popular for documentary filmmaking and television. Some feature films are shot with 16mm film, which is then blown up to 35mm for commercial exhibition. Professional work is also done with Super 16, which features a wider frame on the negative for blowup to a wide-screen image on a 35mm print. Eight-millimeter film, generally made by splitting 16mm film down the middle after processing, had been popular for amateur photography. This film had a perforation at the corners of adjoining frames on one side. Super 8, which replaced regular 8mm film, has smaller perforation in the center of each frame on a single side, thus allowing a larger picture. Many television programs are now shot on 35mm film before transfer to video because of the better image achieved through this process, although 16mm and Super 16mm are growing in popularity for such shoots.

The larger the film gauge, the clearer, better defined, and less grainy will be the image on the screen. Thus, 35mm film gives a picture of excellent detail, density, and sharpness; 16mm film has to cover the same area on the screen with only one-fourth the area of film. Since both gauges contain the same kinds of emulsion, the smaller 16mm film has fewer grains in its smaller frame and amplifies them considerably more for the image on the screen. The 70mm film in professional motion pictures makes an image that is wide and sweeping in its scope, yet containing intense detail, great clarity, and rich density. Through optical printing, films made in larger gauge can be reduced for general release (e.g., 35mm to 16mm).

The original sound tracks are now recorded on magnetic tape; but the final mix is most often printed on the final composite print. The optical track is placed inside the perforations on the screen-left side of the image for 35mm film and for 16mm film is on the opposite side, which has no perforations. For stereophonic sound from 35mm film, four magnetic tracks were used, one on the inside and one on the outside of each of the two rows of perforation, though the practice is now to use two optical bands on the film which contain four separate tracks. For 70mm prints, six magnetic tracks are generally employed, two outside the perforations and one within on both sides of the film. Many 35mm films now come with a digital channel either on the outside of the film (with a back-up channel on the other side) or between perforations, though a third system places it on a disc. *See* **color film** *(2),* **digital sound, dry film, printing,** *and* **processing.**

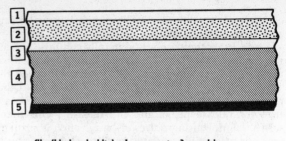

film (black and white) 1. supercoat 2. emulsion 3. subbing layer 4. base 5. antihalation backing

■ **film** (2) Any kind of motion picture, whether fictional, documentary, educational, experimental, or animated. "Film" is a general and neutral term as opposed to "cinema," which has connotations of serious art; "movie," which suggests the popular nature, entertainment value, and sometimes the economic aspects of the medium; and "motion picture," which has connotations of film either as the process of moving pictures or as a big business motivated by economics and the market place. (3) All motion pictures collectively; the entire medium. (4) The entire motion-picture industry: all the personnel, companies, productions, processes, and motion pictures. (5) To photograph a scene; to put part of a motion picture on film. (6) To make something into a film: for example, "to film" a screenplay, novel, or an actual event.

■ **film aesthetics** Aesthetics is a branch of philosophy that examines "beauty" in a work of art and seeks to develop a system of abstract principles concerning the beautiful. It is also concerned with the viewer's psychological and emotional responses to the beautiful in art. Traditional aesthetic criticism in art has fallen out of repute: it is seen as a study and love of beauty for its own sake with no concern for meaning, significance, or morality. Aesthetic criticism today has become more concerned with the impact of the work of art on its audience, how the audience responds, and how the work evokes those responses. This is the sense in which the term "film aesthetics" is used. Film aesthetics is concerned with the internal responses of the viewer—psychologically and emotionally—to the film; and how the film as a work of art, through its content, technique, and formal elements, provokes such responses in the viewer.

■ **film aperture** *See* **aperture.**

■ **film archive** Any place that preserves motion pictures and written materials concerning film and makes them available for study. Such institutions must not only select and acquire motion pictures, they must also have the facility to maintain films without any deterioration taking place. To do this an archive must be able to store motion pictures at a specific low humidity and cool temperature, in proper protective covering, depending on the kind of stock and whether the film is black and white or color. Archives must also have the facilities to catalogue films and written material and make them accessible to scholars and students. Some of the more important film archives in this country are at the Museum of Modern Art Film Study Center in New York, the International Museum of Photography at the George Eastman House in Rochester, the Motion Picture, Broadcasting and Recorded Sound Division of the Library of Congress in Washington, D.C., and the UCLA Department of Theater Arts. Some film archives, such as those at the Museum of Modern Art and the Library of Congress, also restore films. *See* **film preservation.**

■ **film base** *See* **base.**

■ **film bin** *See* **trim bin.**

■ **film buyer** (1) An individual in some organization abroad who negotiates for and licenses the distribution of a motion picture in the foreign market. (2) A term sometimes used for the person from an exhibition company who bids for and arranges terms for films that will be shown at the company's theaters or affiliated theaters. *See* **exhibition.**

■ **film can** *See* **can.**

■ **film capacity** The total footage of film that any single machine such as a camera, projector, processor, or printer is capable of using at any one operation.

■ **film censor** *See* **censor** *and* **censorship.**

■ **film chain** An early type of telecine—i.e., system of recording a film image on video—which employed a film projector beaming onto a video camera. Also called an optical multiplexer. *See* **telecine.**

■ **film checker** The person in a laboratory who examines the film for any damage.

■ **film cleaner, film cleaning machine** (1) A machine in the laboratory for cleaning film, especially the original negative that has been handled in editing, with a cleaning solution and pads or squeegees, or with an ultrasonically agitated cleaning solution. (2) A machine attached to a projector, platter, or rewind bench for cleaning release prints. Such units might contain pads moistened with a chemical solution or a dry tape web. (3) An ultrasonic film cleaner for cleaning prints or negatives. (4) Individual portions of a print may be cleaned by hand with a piece of cloth or pad containing film cleaner.

■ **film clip** *See* **clip.**

■ *Film Comment* A magazine published six times a year by the Film Society of Lincoln Center in New York City, featuring articles on American and European commercial cinema.

■ **film commission** A governmental agency with the specific functions of attracting film production to its area and helping facilitate the production itself. Most states have these commissions, as do some of the major cities such as New York and Los Angeles. The commission helps by interacting with the local communities where shooting will take place, obtaining permits, working on logistics, and putting together technical personnel.

■ **film counter** *See* **footage counter.**

■ **film critic** A person who writes about motion pictures; someone who either reviews, in a knowledgeable and detailed way, films immediately after they open, or writes analytical and retrospective essays about films and filmmakers. Although film critics often do the work of film reviewers in writing about and judging works soon after they are released for magazines and newspapers, the term should apply only to those who do more than merely review the film, who write serious and analytical examinations about the work, showing a considerable knowledge of the medium in general. *See* **film criticism** *and* **film review.**

■ **film criticism** Any writing that is primarily concerned with analyzing and judging one or more films. While a review basically describes and judges a new film to advise the public whether or not to see the work, criticism is a serious and detailed analysis of film written for people with more than a casual interest in the medium. Some writers combine the roles of reviewer and critic by writing detailed and knowledgeable essays on new films, often placing these works in the context of the entire art and manifesting a strong theoretical basis for their analysis. Such critics combine individual judgments with a solid cinematic sense.

Good film criticism, often showing an awareness of the historical development of the medium, sees the individual work in the context of traditional subjects and techniques while citing its innovative qualities. Such criticism manifests an awareness of the work's significance and meaning in terms of human values and experiences, opening up to us the film's themes and how they are developed through character and plot. But such writing also sees the film as more than a narrative or dramatic work by demonstrating a close familiarity with the technical elements of the medium, with camera, lighting, composition, editing, and sound—such criticism discusses the film as *film*. Film critics also show an awareness of the work's relationship to the social and cultural environment of the time: without minimizing the film as a self-contained work of art, such critics understand each film as a product of a particular time and place and understand the work in terms of its social and cultural impact upon the audience. Film criticism sometimes focuses on the work in terms of its emotional and psychological impact upon the viewer, showing how its various shots, scenes, and sequences, its individual techniques, and its very totality affect the audience. Some critics are also concerned with the productional aspects of a work, how it is influenced by the nature of the film industry and financial considerations. In general, film criticism should show a sensitivity to the work as a product of many artists, assessing the contributions of the director, cinematographer, editor, composer, art director, and the performers, but, at the same time, seeing the individual film in the context of the controlling sensibility, vision, and technical know-how of the director and in the context of his or her other works. Different kinds of cinema—commercial fictional films, independent features, documentaries, experimental films, and animation works, for example—will also necessitate a specific kind of film knowledge and an emphasis on different concerns.

No piece of film criticism will be able to cover all these areas in a single discussion, but certainly a number should be approached when analyzing one or more works to make the essay more than a review; and certainly a capacity to handle the other concerns must be implicit. Much early writing on film was little more than reviewing and, for the most part, a groping in the dark; but certainly the writings of the American James Agee during the 1940s as well as the Frenchman André Bazin in the 1950s and early 1960s must be acclaimed. Also significant was the criticism produced by the film journal *Cahiers du cinéma* in France during the 1950s and early 1960s. *See* **film theory.**

■ *Film Criticism* A journal begun in 1976 and published from Allegheny College that features scholarly articles on various aspects of the cinema.

■ *Film Culture* An American film journal, begun in 1955 by Jonas Mekas and published from New York City, that is largely concerned with experimental filmmaking especially in this country. *See* **Anthology Film Archives.**

■ **film cycle** A series of films, mostly within a specific genre, that are similar in both content and technique and that are produced one after the other to exploit public interest. When audiences diminish, the cycle generally ends and it is not long before a new one begins. Film cycles may be produced either by a single studio, using the same personnel, or by several studios exploiting the interest in the type of film generated by earlier works. A popular cycle of films during the 1930s were the gangster films, especially *Little Caesar* (1930; dir. Mervyn Le Roy), *Public Enemy* (1931; dir. William Wellman), and *Scarface* (1932; dir. Howard Hawks). Certainly the proliferation of special-effects science-fiction films beginning in 1977 with George Lucas's

Star Wars and Steven Spielberg's *Close Encounters of the Third Kind* can be seen as a cycle that ran for a good while and threatens to break out once again.

■ **Film d'Art** A French film company begun in 1908 to produce films of artistic merit by employing highly esteemed writers, directors, stage performers, composers, and painters. The group's first production was *The Assassination of the Duc de Guise,* which opened in the winter of 1908 with great success, and employed performers from the Comédie Française. The company drew its subjects from history, drama, and fiction, but presented them all with a fixed camera and artificial sets as if recording theatrical productions. The company's first production to appear in this country was *Queen Elizabeth* (1912), starring Sarah Bernhardt and performers from the Comédie Française. It was distributed by Adolph Zukor and influenced him to begin his Famous Players in Famous Plays Company. *See* **Famous Players.**

■ **film editor** *See* **editor.**

■ **film festival** The screening of a number of films on successive days at a single location to award prizes in various categories and publicize new productions. In addition, noncompetitive films, both old and new, may also be shown to celebrate significant achievements. Three important film festivals in Europe are held in Cannes, Venice, and Berlin. In this country, the Sundance Film Festival in Utah has become very important for launching the careers of new filmmakers, and the noncompetitive New York Film Festival has achieved prominence, while in Canada the Toronto Film Festival, also noncompetitive, shows films of great distinction. There are also festivals for specific kinds of films, for example, the Ann Arbor 16mm Film Festival and the Toronto Worldwide Short Film Festival.

■ **film gate** *See* **gate.**

■ **film gauge** *See* **gauge.**

■ **film history** A branch of film study dealing with the development of the motion picture from early experiments with image reproduction and photography until the present day. This area of study includes the development of such specific categories of motion pictures as the fictional, documentary, experimental, and animated film. Film history can be traced from the following perspectives: (1) the development of motion pictures traced through an examination of individual works and based on some aesthetic or judgmental scale that emphasizes both film technique and the treatment of specific human problems and experiences; (2) the development of the films of specific directors and the influence of such directors on motion pictures in general; (3) the development of specific genres or types within the various categories of film; (4) the develop-

Film d'Art *Queen Elizabeth* (1912), starring the world's most famous actress, Sarah Bernhardt.

■ ■ ■

ment of film in specific countries and the interrelationship of motion pictures from these various nations; (5) the history of specific movements generally in individual countries, and their influence on international cinema; (6) the impact of social history and culture on film and how the medium in turn influences society and culture; (7) the technical developments in the industry and the way these advancements have changed the nature of the medium; (8) the economic aspects of filmmaking and their impact on individual works.

International film history can also be divided into the following general periods: (1) early experimentation with optics, optical toys, photography, moving photographic pictures, and projected moving photographic pictures; (2) the early development of silent motion pictures as a commercial entertainment from about 1895 to the First World War; (3) the rise of the film industry and the establishment of the silent film as a major form of entertainment, as well as the development of early avant-garde cinema from about 1914 to the advent of sound in 1927; (4) the sound film from 1927 to the close of the Second World War (including feature, documentary, and animation works); (5) the collapse of the studio system in Hollywood and the rise of a more-independent cinema in America, the new in-

ternational cinema, the growth of experimental film, especially in America, from the postwar period into the 1960s; (6) the absorption of the motion-picture industry into entertainment conglomerates, with the resulting expansion of the video and international markets, and the new technology in color, wide-screen systems, special effects, computer animation, and sound from the 1960s until the present. *See **entries throughout this volume for discussions of specific developments and periods in film history.***

■ *Film History* A journal begun in 1987 and published by the American Museum of the Moving Image that features scholarly essays on the history of cinema both in the United Sates and abroad. Such essays are notable for their use of original documentation and exploration into the early days of cinema. *See **American Museum of the Moving Image.***

■ **filmic** Anything having to do directly and internally with a film or films—that is, anything concerned with the particulars of one or more films. The term may apply to techniques, lighting, setting, acting, characters, or plot—elements that are part of the actual works. "Filmic time," for example, describes the actual temporal ordering and manipulations that we respond to on the screen. The term "cinematic" in common usage is more general, relating both to elements within a motion picture and matters apart from specific works, but related or analogous to film.

■ **filmic space** The space created on the screen within a film as opposed to the space that exists in the real world. Filmic space can be distinguished from real space in the following ways. (1) The space that exists on the screen is two-dimensional, creating images that are flat and altering our perception of the sizes and relationships of objects. For this reason, filmmakers use the composition of the frame, specific lenses, camera movement, and editing to compensate for these distortions and create an image of the external world that suggests real space. (2) Editing shots together from different locations can create a spatially unified scene that is entirely new and unique. (Pudovkin discusses this capacity of film in *Film Technique*.) (3) Miniatures can be photographed in such a way that they appear larger, seeming to inhabit a spatially greater world than they do in actuality; and any subject can be spatially increased by means of a close-up. (4) Real and external space appears to us as continuous and unbroken; editing allows the audience to jump about in space, seeing the same scene from disparate distances and angles. Such editing also diminishes and extends spatial perspectives, creating an entirely new sense and overall perspective of space that is filmic because it can be achieved only on the screen. *See* **filmic time** *and* **space.**

■ **filmic time** The temporal ordering and arrangement of events that exists within the film as opposed to the normal flow of time in the real world. Though the audience in its own daily existence is trapped in the relentless movement of seconds, minutes, and hours, film has the capacity to create a new temporal order by (1) bringing together actions filmed at separate moments of time so that on the screen they appear to happen simultaneously or in sequence; (2) eliminating interludes of unimportant time between important scenes and sequences; (3) extending the normal time of a scene by adding together shots of the same action from different angles and distances or diminishing the time within the scene by skipping over part of the action; (4) extending or diminishing the audience's sense of time by slow or rapid cutting and camera movements; (5) moving back and forth in time, in relation to the chronological narrative sequence, through flashback or flash-forward; and (6) playing the time of a particular image against the different time of a particular portion of the sound track or superimposing images from two different times to create a sense of relatedness or counterpoint. *See* **filmic space** *and* **time.**

■ **filming** The act of putting a series of images on film for the purpose of making a motion picture. The term generally refers to the act of photographing staged actions for the making of a fictional film, but also applies to any cinematography whatsoever, whether for commercial, documentary, educational, or experimental works.

■ **filming to playback** Photographing performers as they pretend to sing a song or play music already recorded. The performers go through the motions while the master recording is played in the studio. Such a procedure takes place when (1) the musical number requires dancing or movement too difficult to permit simultaneous singing or the simultaneous playing of an instrument; (2) the sound required cannot be achieved with normal direct recording; (3) the actual singing or playing of an instrument is performed by someone else.

■ **film journal** A specialized publication, normally of a limited distribution, that deals with the subject of film. Such publications are written for readers knowledgeable in film and deal with various aspects of the subject, including specific films, the works of specific directors, the careers of individual performers, film history, film genres, film theory, motion-picture technology, and film production. Each journal has its own specific approach while some specialize in particular kinds of films (e.g., *Film Culture* specializes in experimental cinema), and some are about specific aspects of filmmaking (e.g., *American Cinematographer* is about cinematography).

■ **film laboratory, film lab** *See* **laboratory.**

■ **film leader** *See* **leader.**

■ **film library** (1) Any place that collects and catalogues films in order to make them available for circulation, private viewing, or both. Unlike a distributor, a library makes its films available for free or for a nominal fee. A film library is more limited in its functions than a film archive, since it is not also responsible for preserving and restoring films, nor for making as wide a collection of films and documents available for research. Notable film libraries in this country are the Lincoln Center Library for the Performing Arts, which is part of the New York Public Library; the Wisconsin Center for Film and Theater Research in Madison; and the Margaret Herrick Library of the Academy of Motion Picture Arts and Sciences in Beverly Hills, California. (2) *See* **stock footage library.** *See* **film archive.**

■ **film loader** *See* **assistant camera operator.**

■ **film loop** *See* **loop** *and* **loop film.**

■ **film magazine** (1) *See* **magazine.** (2) A publication dealing with film. Less professionally oriented and more popular than a film journal, these publications focus on recent commercial films and popular performers. Such publications are also more accessible at newsstands or news and magazine shops than film journals, since they are written for the broad public. A good example of such a magazine is *Premier,* which began publishing in 1987.

■ **filmmaker** The individual responsible for the making of a film. (1) In commercial cinema the term is generally applied to the director, who is often responsible for the artistic vision of the entire work. (2) The term, however, more accurately applies to an individual who is responsible not only for the artistic vision, but also the major technical operations, such as filming and editing, in what is normally a smaller-scale production, especially of a documentary or experimental film.

■ **filmmaking** The act of making any type of motion picture, including preproduction, production, and postproduction phases.

■ **film measurer** *See* **footage counter.**

■ *film noir* A French term meaning "black film," now used to describe a particular kind of film made by the Hollywood studios during the late 1940s and early 1950s that presents a dark, brutal, and violent urban world of crime and corruption, peopled by sordid and neurotic figures, and presented in a style that emphasizes bleak settings, heavy shadows, and sharp contrasts of light and dark. The term "film noir" derives from *roman noir,* which means "black novel" and was used to describe the English gothic novel of the nineteenth century. The style of this kind of film, notably its set-

film noir Barbara Stanwyck and Fred MacMurray are engaged in something unpleasant in the dark and sinister world of Billy Wilder's *Double Indemnity* (1944).

■ ■ ■

tings and lighting as well as its somber tone and tense mood, is sometimes thought to have derived in part from German expressionism of the 1920s, especially such gothic films as *The Cabinet of Dr. Caligari* (1919; dir. Robert Wiene) and *Nosferatu, a Symphony of Terror* (1922; dir. F. W. Murnau), and in part from the American horror and gangster films of the 1930s, which themselves were influenced by these German works. Certainly it is significant that Billy Wilder, who was born in Austria and worked in German cinema, Otto Preminger, who was born in Austria and began his film career in that country, and Robert Siodmak, who, though born in this country, began his film career in Germany, directed respectively *Double Indemnity* (1944), *Laura* (1944), and *The Killers* (1946).

But a more immediate influence, at least in content and attitudes, can be found in the American detective novels of Dashiell Hammett and Raymond Chandler. The popularity and proliferation of these films were also the product of the psychology of the country at the time, which found in these works the release of a negativism and nihilism evoked but repressed by the Second World War and now intensified by the Cold War—the result was a general distrust of human nature and institutions.

These films do not fit together into a sufficiently cohesive group with common themes, characters, plots and conventions to be considered an easily recognizable and specific genre. They are rather grouped together by common cynical attitudes about a corrupt and sordid human nature; a propensity for brutality and even sadism; a neurotic undertone in characters; a pervasive mood of tension and impending violence; an emphasis on dark, seamy, and unhealthy urban settings; and their dark and shadowy imagistic quality. In addition to the films already mentioned, Howard Hawks's *The Big Sleep* (1945), Edmund Goulding's *Nightmare Alley* (1947), Henry Hathaway's *Kiss of Death* (1947), and Raoul Walsh's *White Heat* (1949) are notable examples of *film noir.*

■ **filmography** A chronological list, much like a bibliography, of the films in which an individual has been involved (e.g., an actor, director, screenwriter etc.). Such a list presents the individual's entire career in films.

■ **filmology** The term was used in France by the Institute of Filmology and its journal, *The International Review of Filmology,* both begun in 1947, for the study of the physiological foundations to the impression of reality achieved by the spectator when watching a film. Cultural and social considerations were included in such studies. The term was also used by the French theoretician Christian Metz to describe the study of film from a perspective external to the mechanics of film itself—e.g., from sociological, psychological, and aesthetic perspectives. *See* **cinematology, film theory,** *and* **semiotics.**

■ **film opera, opera film** A film version of an opera. Although operas have been made into motion pictures, the practice has infrequently been successful, perhaps because sound fidelity until recent times has not kept pace with the development of film's visual dimension, and the texture, tone, and versatility of operatic singing have not been sufficiently transmitted. Perhaps also the convention of characters singing instead of talking in a dramatic situation has seemed theatrical and unreal in the physical reality of the film image. In silent-film days, the stories of operas were used as the basis of feature works, but sound was necessary for the true film opera. A number of standard operas with famous singers were made into film in Italy after the Second World War, but such performances were little more than staged operas put on film. A few film productions, however, have managed to transmit opera in an exciting visual manner, which has bridged the gap between the two arts: notable among these are Michael Powell and Emeric Pressburger's *The Tales of Hoffman* (1951) and Ingmar Bergman's *The Magic Flute* (1975).

■ **film plane** The plane where the front of the film is positioned when it is in the camera gate for proper exposure.

■ **film preservation, film restoration** Maintaining copies of films in good condition or restoring them to such condition, with all the scenes in the same order as when the film was released or as the director desired the film to be released. The loss, deterioration, and neglect of films compose the single greatest threat to the maintenance of our rich film heritage. It is estimated that anywhere from half to three-quarters of the films released in the early days of cinema have been lost, and that as much as 50 percent of all the films made before 1950 are now gone. Significant concerns are the deterioration and decomposition of motion pictures still on nitrate film, the serious fading and discoloration of films made in Eastman Color from the 1950s into the 1970s, and the vinegar syndrome that has been destroying the films made on triacetate safety base since 1951. One of the most active agencies in the preservation of film has been the American Film Institute, which has raised funds for this purpose and has played a key role in shaping policy. The AFI, in conjunction with the Academy of Motion Picture Arts and Sciences and the Library of Congress and with consultation from the Society for Cinema Studies, has been instrumental in restoring to original condition and preserving several hundred films deemed American classics. Individual film organizations have themselves contributed to this important work: the Film Study Center of the Museum of Modern Art has restored much of D. W. Griffith's *Intolerance* (1916) to the version in which the film was initially released and the National Center for Jewish Film at Brandeis University has brought back to life the powerful Yiddish classic *The Dybbuk*, made in Poland in 1938 and directed by Michal Waszynski. Although Ted

Turner has colorized a number of classics from the MGM/UA collection, he has also had new prints made for a large number of films without such alteration, preserving his own business investment and our film heritage at the same time.

The traditional way of restoring and preserving a film is to make an international search for the best available negatives or, if necessary, prints and, after cleaning and repairing the individual pieces, to assemble them into a version as close to the original as possible. From this restored version, a number of dupe negatives are made to be the source of release prints. Damaged and inferior frames can be restored optically. Cinesite recently utilized the Kodak Cineon digital system to help restore Walt Disney's *Snow White and the Seven Dwarfs* (1937). Frames that could not be restored optically were scanned into a computer, where the image was manipulated to remove original imperfections and later damage as well as to restore the original color and quality of the picture. The digital database was then transformed into an image on color intermediate film. Such digital technology expands considerably the possibilities of film preservation. Several major studios and independent production companies now preserve original negatives and other types of film in Kodak's Pro-Tek film preservation vaults. The Association of Moving Image Archivists, officially founded in 1991 and headquartered at the American Film Institute in Los Angeles, is dedicated to coordinating the preservation of films and educating the public about the need for such preservation.

■ **film production** The term applies to the three areas of activity that go into the making of a motion picture: preproduction, shooting, and postproduction.

■ ***Film Quarterly*** A film journal which studies individual films, directors, and various technical subjects from a number of critical and scholarly perspectives. The journal is published by the University of California Press.

■ ***Film Reader*** A journal published periodically from the Film Division of Northwestern University, which is concerned with contemporary film theory and its application to motion pictures. Individual issues treat at length specific theoretical concerns such as semiotics or genre.

■ **film recorder** A machine that is employed to transfer digitized images to film. Film images are first scanned and digitized by a film scanner so they can be corrected, enhanced, altered, and joined with other picture elements. Professional film scanners and recorders allow the images finally recorded on film to have the same quality as those on the original negative. Animation that is totally created in the computer can also be recorded on film with such quality that the images appear as if they were originally shot with film. The two major technologies for such recorders are laser and

CRT (cathode-ray tube). The film recorder most used in the motion-picture industry is Management Graphic's Solitaire Cine III, which employs a CRT technology along with its own Digital Geometry Control (DGC) for automatic alignment of image geometry. The Solitaire uses three passes (one for each of the primary colors) and takes from eighteen to thirty seconds to record each frame of the film. The Academy of Motion Picture Arts and Sciences gave Motion Graphics a Scientific and Engineering Achievement Award in 1992 for the Solitaire. Also worth noting is the Lightning Digital Film Recorder that employs three separate gas lasers, each with the capacity for a high degree of focus for great sharpness, to record simultaneously the red, green, and blue components of the image on film. *See* **film scanner** *and* **telecine.**

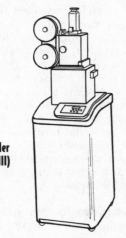

**film recorder
(Solitaire Cine III)**

■ **film register**   *See* **registration** *(1) and* **pilot pins.**

■ **film rental**   The amount of money that a theater pays to a distributor for each week's exhibition of a film. This amount is a percentage of the gross income minus the cost of showing the film (the "house nut"). *See* **distribution** *and* **exhibitor.**

■ **film review**   Any writing about a recent film with the primary objectives of informing the general public about the content of the film, the performers involved, and whether the film is worth seeing according to the reviewer's judgment. James Agee, who wrote for *Time* and the *Nation* in the 1940s, was perhaps the first writer on film who developed a national reputation by combining the roles of reviewer and critic. Reviews, however, are normally less studious and analytical than film criticism. Film reviews appear in newspapers, magazines, and, in somewhat more serious form, in film journals. When they appear in newspapers, they frequently are accompanied with specifics about the cast and the major figures involved in production. Film re-

views are also presented on radio and television. The most significant trend in film reviewing has been the appearance of the reviewer as recognizable personality on television, from the brief overviews of film critics such as Leonard Maltin on *Entertainment Tonight* to the syndicated thirty minutes of energetic debate of reviewers such as Gene Siskel and Roger Ebert. As films have become more and more a product of a marketing mentality, the judgment of film reviewers has had less and less effect on the box-office success of a film. *See* **film criticism.**

■ **film running speed, film speed, filming speed**   The speed at which film moves through the camera or projector measured at the rate of frame exposures per second or of feet per second or minute. Silent film today normally passes through the projector at a rate of 16 or 18 frames per second; the necessity of achieving sufficient speed for proper audio from a sound track requires that sound film run at a speed of 24 frames per second. Silent 35mm film at 16 frames per second passes through the camera or projector at a rate of 1 foot per second or 60 feet each minute; and 35mm sound film at 1½ feet per second, or 90 feet each minute. For 70mm wide-screen formats, which are all sound, the footage rate is 1.8 feet per second, or 112 feet per minute. At silent speed 16mm film is 24 feet per minute, and at the sound rate it is 36 feet each minute. Standard 8mm at the silent speed is 12 feet per minute and at the sound rate is 18 feet per minute. Super 8mm film at 16 frames per second is 15 feet each minute and at 24 frames per second is 20 feet each minute. *See* **camera** *and* **projector.**

■ **film scanner**   A machine that converts film images, frame by frame, from the negative into a digital code to be stored in a computer. The digitized information is then used to call up the images on a monitor so that they can be corrected, enhanced, or altered. When work on the images is complete, they can then be recorded on film by means of a film recorder. Two primary methods are employed for scanning film, one using a flying spot and the second a CCD (charge-coupled device) technology. For the first, an electronic beam creates a raster on the front of a cathode-ray tube, which then scans a moving film; the light passing through each frame is broken down into red, green, and blue by dichroic filters. The separate light waves are converted by photocells into analog electric signals, which are then digitized. In the second process, normally three trilinear CCD sensors (one for each of the primary colors) respond to a xenon light scanning the image: the vast number of pixels on the sensors react to the light waves by converting them into electric signals, which are ultimately digitized and then stored. Excellent film scanners are the Genesis 35 and 65 produced by Kodak and Rank Cintel's Klone, all of which use the trilinear CCD technology. Whereas telecines are normally employed for video transfer—e.g., for television transmission and nonlinear editing—performed in real time at 24 frames per second, film scanners, working more slowly in non-real time, store images of high resolution, at full-negative range so that they can be corrected, enhanced, altered, and finally returned to film. Also referred to as an input scanner. *See* **digital, film recorder, scanner,** *and* **telecine.**

■ **film school** A school specializing in the teaching of film production and film history. In this country some of the better-known film schools belong to such major universities as the University of California at Los Angeles, the University of Southern California, and New York University; also distinguished is the American Film Institute's Center for Advanced Film Studies in Beverly Hills, California. In Great Britain, notable examples are the London International Film School and the National Film School at Beaconsfield Film Studios.

■ **film script** *See* **script.**

■ **film shipper** An agency that transports and delivers films to various theaters: Such an organization, with offices throughout the country, works for a national distributor and is also responsible for the maintenance of each print. *See* **distribution.**

■ **film short** *See* **short.**

■ *Films in Review* A magazine published ten times a year, which reviews films and books on films, and presents articles and columns on various aspects of the industry, past and present. The magazine is associated with the National Board of Review of Motion Pictures and is published from New York City.

■ **film society** A group of people organized to promote the showing of significant films, generally on a nonprofit basis. Film societies exist in virtually every major city and are a significant part of the cultural life in most colleges and universities.

■ **Film Society of Lincoln Center** An organization headquartered at the Lincoln Center cultural complex in New York City that is responsible for publishing the film journal *Film Comment* and for presenting the New York Film Festival and New Directors/New Films series. The society also presents monthly series of films at the Walter Reade Theater, which is located in the complex.

■ **film speed** (1) A general term for the sensitivity of film emulsion to light. Fast films are more sensitive to light and have higher exposure-index numbers; slow films are less sensitive and have lower numbers. *See* **exposure index.** (2) *See* **film running speed.**

■ **film splicer** *See* **splicer.**

■ **film starts** The number of films, in the motion-picture industry, that actually go into production from the development phase each year.

■ **film stock** Raw, unexposed film. Film stocks are distinguished by gauge (70mm, 65mm, 35mm, 16mm, Super 16mm, 8mm, and Super 8mm), type (negative, positive, color, black-and-white), and exposure index (film speed and exposure latitude). For professional photography, film stock is further designated by emulsion batch. *See* **film** *(1).*

■ **film storage** The storing of film when it is not being used. Different types of film (e.g., raw stock, negative, internegative, print, nitrate base, acetate base, color, black and white) have different requirements for storage, which may also be influenced by the length of time the film is to be stored. In general, films should be kept in special facilities with a low amount of humidity and at a low temperature. Nitrate-base film is susceptible to relatively rapid deterioration and acetate-base films are falling victim to the vinegar syndrome. Since dyes in color film deteriorate in time, three black-and-white separation prints, one for each color of the tripack, are sometimes kept for long-term storage. Original negatives and internegatives of films are stored by studios in special vaults where temperature and humidity are controlled; film archives use the most stringent precautions to preserve prints in similarly controlled vaults for as long as possible. *See* **film archive** *and* **film preservation.**

■ **film strip, filmstrip** A strip of film with a series of separate images, each to be projected and viewed individually, sometimes accompanied by sound. Such strips are used for educational or business purposes.

■ **film studio** *See* **studio.**

■ **film theory** Any discourse that seeks to establish general principles concerning film as a distinct art form. Although film criticism concerning specific works and film theory are often blended together, and although most theoreticians develop their ideas from individual films, theoretical writings are more concerned with general concepts that underlie all films rather than the achievement of single works or figures. Film theory is concerned with the following areas of investigation: (1) the differences of film from drama, literature, and the graphic arts; (2) the basic nature of the medium—what exactly film is and what takes place on the screen; (3) the general techniques employed in film (e.g., cutting, montage, camera position, camera movement, lighting); (4) the nature of various components in film and their contribution to a work's entity (e.g., characters, setting, action, color, sound); (5) filmic space and time, and their relationship to real space and time; (6) film genre; (7) film and society; (8) the nature of various types of film and their differences (e.g., fictional, documentary, and experimental film); and (9) the aesthetic and psychological response of the audience to the medium.

Although film theory has been written since the earliest days of motion pictures, this type of writing took a while to achieve the quality and even abundance of theoretical pursuits for other art forms, perhaps because of the newness of the medium, its amalgamation of aspects from other art forms, its synthesis of technology and art, and its traditional acceptance as a popular art form. Film theory was also bound by the predilections of its writers, who often brought with them their training from other disciplines, especially psychology and literature.

The first major text in film theory is Hugo Münsterberg's *The Photoplay: A Psychological Study,* first published in 1916. Münsterberg claims that his work is concerned both with psychology and aesthetics, but it is in the first category that he makes some significant insights about the new art form that anticipate the concepts of Rudolf Arnheim. Münsterberg argues that film is not a "photographed drama"; the photoplay, he argues, is "freed from the physical forms of space, time, and causality" and "adjusted to the free play of our mental experiences." Rudolf Arnheim, like Münsterberg, was born in Germany, trained as a psychologist, and later taught at Harvard. Arnheim wrote a number of articles and books on film, but perhaps his most significant work is *Film as Art,* which appeared in this country in 1957 and most of which was first published in Germany in 1932. Like Münsterberg, Arnheim argues that film must be seen as an art and not a new representation of reality. The filmmaker must emphasize "the peculiarities of the medium" to give the viewer a larger and more meaningful vision than he or she can obtain in the real world. Within this context, Arnheim praises the Russian filmmakers for developing the technique of montage.

The two most distinguished Russian directors, V. I. Pudovkin and Sergei Eisenstein, in their own film studies have given both a significant explanation of their practices, but also important theoretical arguments for the use of montage, which at times penetrates into the very nature of the film medium. Pudovkin, in *Film Technique* (a series of lectures translated into English in 1929), claims that "film is not *shot,* but *built,* built up from the separate strips of celluloid that are its raw material." If his discussions of camera and editing may seem to us formalistic, we should remember, especially in light of his great film *Mother* (1926), that for Pudovkin the art of film, its very techniques, is used to heighten the human drama on the screen and to communicate both story and emotion to the viewer. Like Pudovkin, Eisenstein draws from his film experience, but goes much further, working out ingenious analyses of montage (Eisenstein's essays are available in English in two volumes, *Film Sense* [1942] and *Film Form* [1949]). Eisenstein claims, in *Film Form,* that the shot itself is only a "montage cell," and these cells undergo a trans-

formation through "collision" and "conflict." The conflicts may arise from compositional elements within each frame—camera angles and distances, lighting, movement—or from the characters themselves. The process is "dialectic" in that a synthesis is achieved by the interaction of two opposites. The effect on the viewer may be emotional, psychological, intellectual, or any combination of these.

The Hungarian-born Béla Balázs published his final and most influential film study, *The Art of Cinema,* in Russia in 1945; the book was translated into English and published in London as *The Theory of Film* in 1952. Balázs's position is midway between formalism and realism: like Arnheim and Eisenstein, he recognizes the contrivance and manipulation of the art form, of the images removed from reality, but he also places emphasis on maintaining what is inherent in the real object or scene. For Balázs, the close-up is the special technique of film that reveals what is real. Siegfried Kracauer, in *The Theory of Film: The Redemption of Physical Reality* (1960), makes what is the strongest and most learned argument for film as a reproduction of physical reality. Kracauer argues for a "'right' balance between the realistic tendency and the formative tendency," but unequivocally the latter should be subservient to the former. It is the function of film to expose, to enlarge our vision of the physical world, never to obscure or distort it.

André Bazin, the French critic and one of the founders of *Cahiers du cinéma* in 1951, is considered the most significant modern theoretician of film, even though he wrote no theoretical treatise and his general concepts are developed from a direct critical confrontation with individual works (a selection of his essays has been collected and translated into English in two volumes titled *What Is Cinema?,* published respectively in 1967 and 1971). Bazin is generally considered to belong to the "realist" school. For him "the cinema is objectivity in time." Bazin heralds "depth of focus" in the cinema, especially as it was presented in Orson Welles's *Citizen Kane* (1941), where "whole scenes are covered in one take, the camera remaining motionless." Depth of focus returns to the cinema the "unity of image in space and time" of earlier realists such as Stroheim and Murnau, while it brings the viewer closer to the image on the screen. Depth of focus "springs from a reluctance to fragment things arbitrarily and a desire to show an image that is uniformly understandable and that compels the spectator to make his own choice."

Bazin's emphasis on the achievement of individual directors was to have an impact on Truffaut and the other young critics who wrote for *Cahiers du cinéma* and developed the *auteur* theory of criticism. In the January 1954 issue, Truffaut published his essay, "A Certain Tendency in French Cinema," in which he argues for a "policy of authors." For Truffaut, the director of the film should be seen as the "auteur" of the film, the person whose vision, sensibility, and technique infuse the entire work and give it a control, order, and unique stamp, instead of as a "metteur en scène," who merely carries out the concepts of others. Truffaut, Godard, Chabrol, and Rohmer established a canon of such significant directors. In America, Andrew Sarris helped popularize auteur theory (the term was actually his) in "Notes on the *Auteur* Theory" in the 1962/63 issue of *Film Culture* and in his book *The American Cinema: Directors and Directions, 1929–1968* (1968).

If *auteur* theory stresses the accomplishment of the individual director, even amidst the pressures of the studio system, genre theory stresses the universal aspects of certain types of film, such as the Western, horror film, or gangster film, and discusses the director within the given conventions of each type. A number of essays and books have been written on individual genres (for example, John Cawelti's *The Six-Gun Mystique* [1971] on the Western), and discussions of genre permeate larger theoretical approaches (as in Leo Braudy's *The World in a Frame* [1976]). The relation of film to society has been a concern in some discussions of genre, but the subject has been more centrally confronted in political and Marxist writings (e.g., by Harry Alan Potamkin, Walter Benjamin, and later by critics in *Cahiers du cinéma*), and more broadly examined in books such as Robert Warshow's *The Immediate Experience* (1964).

In recent years, phenomenology, a branch of philosophy that investigates phenomena as observed or perceived essences, has had some impact on aesthetics in general. To some extent, Stanley Cavell's *The World Viewed: Reflections on the Ontology of Film* (1971) may be considered phenomenological in that it deals with the viewer's perceptions and experiences of film, though he does not work specifically from this philosophical school. But more central to this particular approach have been the works in France by Jean-Pierre Meunier, Amédée Ayfre, and Henri Agel, and recently in the United States by Vivian Sobchack and Allan Casabier.

A popular and significant movement in film theory, one that ushered in a new age of film theory with its broad, interdisciplinary approach and sophisticated language and concepts, was semiotics, especially as discussed by the French theoretician Christian Metz (see especially his essays in *Film Language: A Semiotics of the Cinema* [1968; trans. 1974]). Semiotics, as developed from the lectures of Ferdinand de Sausurre, the Swiss linguist, early in the century and given great notoriety by the popular French anthropologist Claude Lévi-Strauss, is the science of signs, which incorporates linguistics as only one system of communication that we confront each day. Not only are we surrounded in the real world by a myriad of distinct and overlapping systems of semiotic codes, but the work of art communicates meaning to us through such codes. For Metz, there are two general types of codes, cultural and specialized, which themselves are made up of numerous subcodes. The first type is not unique to film, though film incorporates it as part of its depiction of the real world (for example, "speech-accompanying gestures");

but the second type employs codes applicable only to film (e.g., "montage, camera movements, optical effects"). Metz spends much time working out a code for the various interrelationships of shots in a narrative sequence. Peter Wollen's book *Signs and Meaning in Cinema* (rev. 1972) offers a useful discussion of semiotics and film; and Umberto Eco has written several significant essays on the subject.

The year 1968 marks the rebellion of the students and workers in France and also a new politicization in film theory. The editors of *Cahiers du cinéma* issued an important manifesto marking the journal's disengagement from its past concern with film aesthetics and a new dedication to class conflict and Marxist ideology. Crucial to this ideology were the writings of the French Marxist Louis Althusser and the French psychoanalyst Jacques Lacan. The inclusion of semiotics in this theoretical school is partly responsible for it being referred to as "the second semiotics." A significant film theoretician who helped develop this kind of thinking was Jean-Louis Baudry, who, in his essay "Ideological Effects of the Basic Cinematic Apparatus" (1970), argues that the very machines of the cinema, the camera and projector, propagate a cultural bias in perceiving "reality." In "The Apparatus: Metapsychological Approaches to the Impression of Reality in the Cinema" (1975), Baudry relates the regressive experience of the spectator in the cinema to the child in Lacan's mirror phase first constituting a sense of self by seeing its reflection in the mirror. Not seeing himself or herself on the screen, the viewer actually constitutes a sense of self by identifying with the all-seeing eye of the camera. Baudry had a considerable influence on Metz, who further developed a Lacanian psychoanalysis of spectatorship in *The Imaginary Signifier* (1977; trans. 1982).

A vigorous and far-reaching school of film theory in recent years has been feminist theory that approaches issues of gender utilizing the political approach, as well as the Lacanian psychoanalysis of "the second semiotics," but also pushes into new and uncharted territories. The single most influential essay in this school has been Laura Mulvey's "Visual Pleasure and Narrative Cinema" (1975), which defines the dominant and most influencing gaze in the cinema as belonging to the male—classic Hollywood cinema made movies that basically diminish the male's fear of castration as elicited by the female body by treating that body sadistically in the narrative and fetishizing it in the film's visual imagery. Mulvey's essay began a long dialogue in film theory concerning the role of women as spectator, but also opened up larger issues concerning sexual differentiation, both on the screen and in the audience, and the visualization on the screen of male and female bodies. At the same time, feminist critics such as Gaylyn Studlar and Kaja Silverman, though from different perspectives, reacted to Mulvey's theory of sadistic viewing with their own theories of masochistic spectatorship.

Lacanian psychoanalysis has come under attack in recent years, but the political and cultural direction of feminist criticism has continued, not only with theoretical issues concerning gender, but also in areas dealing with ethnicity in film and national cinemas—e.g., the black, the Jew, and the Hispanic in American film and studies of film in Africa, China, Latin America, and India. A reaction against Lacanian film theory is evident in the recent application of cognitive psychology to film by writers such as David Bordwell, Edward Branigan, and, in relation to avant-garde cinema, James Peterson. The movement away from Lacan has also been emphasized by a resurgence in works on film history; but notable as well is the application of theory to history—e.g., in *The Classic Hollywood Cinema: Film Style and Mode of Production to 1960* (1985) by David Bordwell, Janet Staiger, and Kristin Thompson—and the attempt to draw theory from history—e.g., in Gilles Deleuze's *Cinema 1: The Movement Image* (1983; trans. 1986) and *Cinema 2: The Time-Image* (1985; trans. 1989).

■ **film transport** *See* **transport** *(1).*

■ **film treatment** *See* **treatment.**

■ **filter** (1) A transparent sheet of colored glass or gelatin placed in front of or behind the lens of a camera to control the transmission of the various light waves of the color spectrum. Neutral density filters, in various degrees of gray, reduce all the light waves for black-and-white as well as for color film. Dyed filters lighten their own color while blocking, to varying degrees, their complementary color, thus altering contrast as well as light and dark compositions. In addition to these changes, such filters also alter the color quality in color film. Certain color filters, yellow, for example, darken the sky and highlight clouds in black-and-white film. Conversion filters of an amber color allow color film balanced for daylight to be used with artificial lights and film balanced for artificial light to be used in daylight. Colored filters are also employed in day-for-night shooting for black-and-white as well as for color film. For both types of film, diffusion filters are employed to create soft focus, fog filters to create fog, and star filters to achieve a radiant effect. Polarized filters diminish sunlight and reflection from nonmetallic surfaces such as water and glass and also darken the sky in color film. Ultraviolet filters are effective for reducing haze. Graduated filters are clear in part and have graduated filtering material in the remaining part to alter only a section of the image. Glass filters can be screwed onto a lens; both glass and especially gelatin filters can be slid into a matte box attached to the front of a camera. In some cameras smaller filters can be inserted behind the lens, thus making them less susceptible to breakage and freeing them from flare caused by unwanted light. Since filters cut down the amount of light reaching the film, the camera exposure must be increased by a number called the filter factor to achieve a satisfactory image. (2) A transparent sheet, generally made of gelatin, that is placed before a light source

either to balance the color temperature of different types of illumination (e.g., tungsten-halogen and carbon-arc lamps) or to affect the color of a scene. (3) A device in the recording of sound that removes or reduces certain frequencies and thus highlights others. (4) To remove from an image certain unwanted elements or to alter elements in the image through the use of a filter during photography. (5) To remove from the recording of sound certain unwanted frequencies or to tone down frequencies through an audio filter; to equalize. *See* **equalizer.**

■ **filter factor** The number by which the exposure of film must be multiplied to compensate for the loss of light caused by a camera filter in the recording of an image. *See* **filter** *(1).*

■ **filter holder, filter mount** The support for a filter in front of or behind the lens in a camera or in front of the exposure light in a printer.

■ **filtering** *See* **equalization.**

■ **filter slot** A narrow opening behind the lens into which a filter may be placed so that it filters light directly in front of the film.

■ **filter wheel** A support for a filter behind the camera's lens.

■ **final cut** (1) The last edited version of the film that is ready to receive the sound mix. (2) The final mix of the sound track that is ready to be combined with the images. (3) The composite print with images and sound track. *See* **editing.**

■ **final shooting script** The script for a film after it has received its revisions and is ready for shooting. Scripts may still be revised after shooting begins. *See* **screenwriter.**

■ **final trial composite** The final film with both image and sound that has incorporated all the corrections from previous trial composites and represents the approved version of the film.

■ **financial backing** The monetary support and the group providing that support for the making of a film. For many years, the major studios, which controlled production, distribution, and exhibition, financed their own films. After exhibition was separated from production and distribution with the Paramount decision of the Supreme Court in 1948, and stars, directors, and producers more and more began to work independently, the motion-picture companies, which themselves became part of large conglomerates, took on the role of financing and distributing films made by independent "packages" of film talent. These companies are still a major source of film financing. Banks or individual lenders also remain a major source for funding a film. While newer production-distribution companies rise and fall, independent groups are formed to back films, and sometimes an individual business will finance a film. On occasion, two or more film organizations will join together. Foreign governments, which often subsidize their own national film industry, will sometimes help subsidize a large American film made in that country. In the United States, government agencies, such as the National Endowment for the Arts (NEA), film institutions, such as the American Film Institute, and various cultural organizations supply grants to independent filmmakers outside the Hollywood industry—though these sources, especially the governmental ones, are fast diminishing their support.

■ **fine cut** An edited version of a film that is considerably advanced from the rough cut and nearly ready for final approval. Sometimes the term is also used for the final cut. *See* **editing.**

■ **fine grain** A film stock that has very small silver particles in its emulsion.

■ **fine-grain duplicate negative** A negative with very small grains and high definition that is made from the fine-grain master print and employed for the making of release prints. The term usually applies to black-and-white film. Also called a master dupe negative. *See* **internegative.**

■ **fine-grain master print, fine grain master positive, master positive** A print that demonstrates a smooth picture with very small grains and high definition. The fine-grain master positive, made from the original negative, is used for making fine-grain duplicate negatives, which are themselves the source of release prints. The term usually applies to black-and-white film.

■ **finger** A long, narrow flag placed in front of a luminaire, generally on a separate stand, to block off an area of the set from illumination. Also called a cutter.

■ **fire up** To start any equipment (e.g., luminaires or the camera).

■ **first answer print, first trial print, first trial answer print, first trial composite** *See* **answer print.**

■ **first assistant** The chief assistant to the director. *See* **assistant director.**

■ **first assistant camera operator, first assistant cameraman, first camera assistant** The person in the camera crew who is responsible for proper maintenance of the camera during shooting. As well as checking that the camera works properly, this individual is responsible for changing lenses and magazines and following focus during shooting. For European films, the assistant camera operator is also called a focus puller. *See* **second assistant camera operator.**

■ **first cameraman** A term sometimes used for the director of photography. *See* **director of photography** *and* **second cameraman.**

■ **first cut** *See* **rough cut.**

■ **first dollar, first dollar gross, first money, first monies** The first money paid to a distributor for a film's release (after the cost of exhibition has been deducted from the box office gross). The money may be used to repay backers their investment, for gross profit participants, or for the distributor's own fees and costs. *See* **first position.**

■ **first feature** The major or "A-picture" in a showing of two films. *See* **double feature.**

■ **first-generation dupe, first-generation duplicate** (1) The first duplicate film made directly from an original film. (2) The first dupe negative that is either made from a master positive of the original negative or from the original negative when it is made on reversal stock. *See* **dupe.**

■ **first grip, head grip, key grip** The chief stagehand responsible for sets, properties, and various machines.

■ **first look deal** A contractual agreement between a studio and independent producer that the studio have first rights to consider a film by that producer for production and/or distribution by giving financial support during the developmental period. *See* **development deal, negative pickup deal, overall development deal,** *and* **pickup deal.**

■ **First National** Originally First National Exhibitors Circuit, the company was formed in 1917 by Thomas L. Tally and John D. Williams to fight block booking, especially by Zukor's Paramount. First National was intended to purchase pictures for its member exhibitors but soon was financing films. The company hired Charlie Chaplin to make eight short films for over a million dollars (he was to produce and pay for the films out of this money). Among the films Chaplin made for First National were *The Kid* in 1921 and *The Pilgrim* in 1923. The company also hired Mary Pickford for three films, one of which was *Daddy Long Legs* in 1919. By 1921, First National had more than three thousand theaters, including a number of the most important film houses in major cities. In that year, First National combined with a company of independent director-producers, which included Thomas Ince, Mack Sennett, and King Vidor, to form Associated First National, and in 1922 this company began to produce films in its own studios in Burbank. First National produced a number of successful films but gradually lost its major theater circuits to other companies and was finally bought out by Warner Brothers in 1929.

■ **first position, first position gross** The rights to take a specified amount of money from the gross receipts before normal distribution fees and other costs are paid. Sometimes a major performer or director may have such a deal.

■ **first property man, first prop man** *See* **prop man.**

■ **first run, premium run** The first public showing for a film in any market or area, whatever the number of theaters. *See* **exhibition.**

■ **first run theater** A theater that exhibits a film during its initial release; in a major city it may be the only theater to show the film. *See* **exhibition** *and* **movie house.**

■ **first team** The actual performers for a scene, and not their stand-ins.

■ **first trial, first trial print, first trial composite print, trial composite print** *See* **answer print.**

■ **first unit** The primary crew for a film production as opposed to the second unit, which is a smaller group.

■ **fisheye lens** An extreme wide-angle lens that takes in nearly a 180-degree field of view. Such a wide view on a flat surface distorts the image, giving prominence to central objects and rounding the image on the sides so that it resembles an elongated sphere. This distortion is especially effective in creating subjective or hallucinatory shots and in evoking an eerie or grotesque effect. *See* **wide-angle lens.**

■ **fishpole, fishing rod, fishpole boom, boompole** A long, lightweight, and easy-to-maneuver pole to which a microphone is attached for recording dialogue. *See* **microphone boom.**

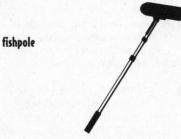

fishpole

■ **fitting fee** Pay given to a performer for his or her time in being fitted for a wardrobe.

■ **five k, five-k** A luminaire with a 5,000-watt bulb.

■ **fixed camera** A stationary camera that shoots from only one position. A fixed camera is adequate if shots

are brief enough and cutting sufficient to keep the audience involved. Sometimes a camera may effectively remain fixed on the same scene to show some gradual change in weather or time. *See* **movement** *(3).*

■ **fixed-focus lens** A lens with a set focus that cannot be changed; often a very-wide-angle lens with an extreme depth of field that can photograph action at various distances. *See* **lens.**

■ **fixed-focus viewfinder** A viewfinder on a camera that keeps the subject of the image in focus no matter what its distance. *See* **viewfinder.**

■ **fixed matte** A stationary matte with a painting or photograph that is made part of the image of a live-action scene. This picture element may be added during the photographing of the primary image by having a stationary camera shoot past it (as in *King Kong* [1933; dir. Merian C. Cooper and Ernest Schoedsack], where glass mattes with scenery painted on them were placed in front of the camera). Such matting can be done today in an optical printer: an area is first blocked from the live-action image while it is being transferred from a positive onto a negative; the stationary element is then photographed into this unexposed area from a positive of the matte. *See* **matte** *(2) and* **traveling-matte process.**

■ **fixer, fixing solution, hypo** The chemical solution that stabilizes the image during processing by removing the unexposed silver halides. *See* **processing.**

■ **fixing** The process of stabilizing the image on film after it has been developed by removing silver halides in a chemical bath. *See* **processing.**

flag

■ **flag** A square or rectangle made of wood, cardboard, or cloth, that is sometimes attached to a lamp but more often is placed on a stand in front of the lamp to shade the lens or part of the scene from illumination. A small gobo. *See* **gobo.**

■ **flagship run** One or more first-run movie theaters in a particular geographic area showing a film during its initial release. *See* **exhibition.**

■ **flagship theater** The premium first-run movie theater of a theater chain in a significant geographic area. *See* **movie house.**

■ **flame ark** A pitched frame or wire netting on which cloth is burned for high flames.

■ **flame drum** A transparent cylinder with printed shapes that is turned by a motor and through which transmitted light casts moving shadows on the set. This device is especially effective for suggesting moving flames.

■ **flaming forks** Tubes with holes or fan-shaped endings through which gas is pumped and ignited for controllable flames during a fire sequence.

■ **flange** A metal or plastic disc used with a core for evenly winding film off a reel.

■ **flapper** *See* **swinger.**

■ **flare** A fog or glow over the entire image or part of the image, generally caused by some strong light directly hitting the lens of the camera and reflecting off the various elements. Sometimes such a flare is intentionally created to suggest strong daylight or heat. Unwanted flare is minimized by the application of a coating on the lens during manufacture and by a lens hood during shooting.

■ **flash** (1) A process in sound rerecording whereby sounds originally recorded during production can be removed to a separate track, normally the sound-effects track, without the dialogue. Some type of cue such as a punched hole or piece of tape on the edge of the film initiates the portion of the track to be transferred. This procedure allows for an empty dialogue track into which foreign dialogue may later be recorded. (2) *See* **hot spot.**

■ **flashback** A shot, scene, or sequence that has taken place in the past, before the present time established in the film. Flashbacks may be employed either as part of the narrative to explain present situations or as part of character development to create visually the individual's past. They may appear either as an objective part of the film or as a subjective memory of a character. The technique was especially popular during the 1930s and 1940s. It was a favorite device in mystery films, such as Otto Preminger's *Laura* (1944), to explain events leading up to a crime and to develop various characters and their motivations. Billy Wilder's *Double Indemnity* (1944), a film-noir story of passion and murder, is narrated largely through the flashback technique. Orson Welles's *Citizen Kane* (1941) presents one of the most exciting uses of the flashback in creating the entire life of a character from the memories of the people who knew him. Also effective is Ingmar Bergman's employ-

ment of the technique in *Wild Strawberries* (1957), where the protagonist journeys back into time through memory and dream to come to some realization about himself at the same time that he is taking an actual journey. Another innovative and sophisticated use of the flashback is in Alain Resnais's *Hiroshima mon amour* (1959), where the technique explains the present political situation and the psychologies of the two lovers. Flashbacks are often subtly and briefly integrated into a narrative to suggest dramatically the impact of past events on a character's life, as in Sidney Lumet's *The Pawnbroker* (1965). In the 1930s and 1940s the technique was often introduced and concluded by a ripple dissolve or fade; today, especially to create memory, a quick cut suffices. *See* **flash-forward.**

flashback Victor Sjöström remembers a scene from his early life in *Wild Strawberries* (1957; dir. Ingmar Bergman).

■ ■ ■

■ **flash converter** A device that transfers the analog video images into the binary digital code in the computer's memory. For color images, three flash converters operate simultaneously, one for each of the primary colors. *See* **digital** *and* **digitizing** *(1).*

■ **flash cutting, flash editing** An edited sequence of very brief shots that succeed each other rapidly. The technique is effectively used toward the end of Nicolas Roeg's *Don't Look Now* (1973), when the events of recent months flash rapidly before the eyes of the dying protagonist.

■ **flash-forward, flash-ahead** A shot or action that will take place in the future, after the present time established in the film. The technique may show some subjective projection of a character, as the psychic visions of Faye Dunaway in *Eyes of Laura Mars* (1978; dir. Irvin Kershner), or objectively project a future scene to place a present action in an ambiguous or ironic context, as when the hero of Sydney Pollack's *They Shoot Horses, Don't They?* (1969) is several times seen at his trial for having murdered the heroine of the film. *See* **flashback.**

■ **flash frame** (1) The frame or few frames at the beginning and end of a shot that are overexposed because of the start up and slow down of the camera motor; or the overexposed frame or frames at the end of the shot that result when the shutter remains open for an instant after the motor has ceased. (2) A single frame, but more often a few frames, of a different image inserted into a shot for an effect: for example, the few frames of the devil's head inserted into Father Karras's dream in William Friedkin's *The Exorcist* (1973). Such a technique can also act as a flashback for a character's brief and half-developed memory of an event or as a flash-forward for a character's brief and indistinct projection into the future.

■ **flashing** (1) The process of exposing film, normally after shooting, to a controlled light in order to reduce and finely distinguish contrasts. In color photography, flashing also allows control over saturation by muting the colors. When a negative is flashed either in the camera or during development with a small amount of light, dark areas and shadows show more detail. When positives are flashed in the lab, whites are given more texture and blacks are intensified. Flashing can also be achieved chemically. *See* **VariCon.** (2) The second exposure of light given to reversal film in processing after the negative image has been bleached out. This exposure allows the remaining silver halides to be developed into the positive image. *See* **reversal film.**

■ **flash meter** An exposure or light meter used to measure a rapid flash of illumination (e.g., from a strobe light). *See* **exposure meter.**

■ **flash pan, swish pan, flick pan, zip pan** A rapid pass of the camera, which moves from one point of action to another with such rapidity that the intervening area flashes by. *See* **swish pan.**

■ **flash pot** A container with flash powder that is electrically ignited to create a flash or puff of smoke for special effects, especially in fantasy films.

■ **flash to flash** The term means to remove a part of the negative that makes up a single take, from the flash frame at its start to the flash frame at its end—i.e., from the point when the shutter opens, exposing the film as it starts to move, to the point right before the shutter closes and the film stops its movement. *See* **flash frame** *and* **neg pull.**

■ **flat** (1) A photographed image with low contrast. (2) A standard, nonanamorphic image on film (i.e., an unsqueezed image). *See* **anamorphic lens.** (3) A section of scenery made of a large flat piece of plywood or lightweight material on which a wall, landscape, or some such element of the setting is painted. Flats fit together to form the background of a shot. (4) The original quality of recorded sound, especially on the dailies, before any type of alteration or improvement.

flat-bed editing machine

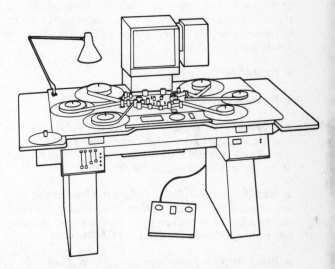

■ **flat-bed editing machine, flat-bed editor, table editing machine, editing table, tabletop editing machine, horizontal editor** A table equipped for editing which largely replaced the upright Moviola. Such editing machines are most notably made by Steenbeck and Kem. In spite of their great expense, they proved preferable to the Moviola, since they treat film more gently, allow it to be handled with greater speed and ease, create more accurate sound (though not picture), and, with as many as eight plates, allow any combination of up to four pictures and magnetic sound tracks to be run at once. The film and sound tracks run horizontally, and the picture itself is projected on a small, translucent screen. The machine also permits the use of anamorphic lenses. Some tables can be used for both 16- and 35mm film. Editing tables are manufactured that allow the transfer and mixing of sound along with the editing of both film and videotape. *See* **editing** *and* **Moviola.**

■ **flat-figure animation** Cartoon animation using jointed, two-dimensional figures with front lighting (as opposed to silhouette animation, which uses back lighting).

■ **flat four** A term used in special-effects work for a 35mm nonanamorphic film. Images in such film are flat in that they are unsqueezed, and each frame has four perforations. *See* **anamorphic lens** *and* **eight perf.**

■ **flat lighting** Lighting with low contrast that creates an even illumination for the scene. This type of lighting is effective in emphasizing daylight aspects of a scene, extreme heat, or sometimes flashbacks.

■ **flatness of field** A lens's capacity for creating an image on film with sharpness both in the middle and at the extremities.

■ **flat rental** The rental of a motion picture by a distributor to an exhibitor for a predetermined amount of money instead of a percentage of the box office. *See* **distribution** *and* **exhibition.**

■ **flat shading** *See* **shading.**

■ **flat turret** *See* **turret.**

■ **FLB filter** A filter placed before the lens of a camera when shooting under fluorescent lights with indoor film. The exposure must be increased one stop when shooting with this filter. *See* **FLD filter.**

■ **FLD filter** A filter placed before the lens of the camera when shooting under fluorescent lights with outdoor film. The exposure must be increased one stop when shooting with this filter. *See* **FLB filter.**

■ **flesh peddler** A derogatory term for an agent.

■ **flex arm** An extension arm with a number of ball joints that attaches to a century stand and permits the flexible positioning of goboes for blocking light. *See* **gobo.**

■ **flick, flicks, flicker** A colloquial term for a commercial film, which originates from early silent-film days when projectors would create a flickering effect on the screen. *See* **flicker.**

■ **flicker** The unsteady or quivering appearance of illumination on the screen caused by alternating periods of light and dark at too slow a frequency to allow for the viewer's persistence of vision. A sufficient frequency must be used, increasing as the intensity of light increases, to prevent such alternating of light and dark to the eye. For silent films, 16 frames per second allowed a continuity of movement to the action on the screen but was not a sufficient frequency of light and dark per second to avoid flicker (hence the origin of the term "flicks" for motion pictures). For this reason a three-bladed shutter that rotated in front of the film was added to the projector, allowing three black-out periods for each frame and increasing the frequency of light and dark changes to 48 per second. When the advent of sound necessitated 24 frames per second, a

shutter with two blades was used to maintain the same frequency. *See* **persistence of vision.**

■ **flicker film** A type of experimental film that explores perception through the rapid alternation of black and white or colors on the screen or by the quick succession of images, each of which may appear for the briefest instant, no more than a single frame. Various speeds of flicker and various combinations and types of images affect both the viewer's perception and cognition. *Arnulf Rainer* (1960), by the Austrian filmmaker Peter Kubelka, is a notable example of this type of film. The generic name for this type of film derives from Tony Conrad's *The Flicker* (1964).

■ **flicker frequency** The alternating periods of light and dark per second necessary for an unflickering illumination. In motion-picture projection, the critical flicker frequency is 48 alterations per second. *See* **flicker.**

■ **flies** The area above the set from which scenery is suspended and in which luminaires are supported. Also called the fly.

■ **flip, flip wipe, flipover wipe** A transition between shots, where the picture seems to turn around either vertically or horizontally and reveal another picture on its back. This transition was employed in comic sequences during silent and early sound film, but, along with the wipe, is rarely used today, although James Bridges used some horizontal flips for crisp transitions in *Perfect* (1985). The term "flipover" generally refers to horizontal flips but sometimes to vertical as well.

■ **flip cards** *See* **cue cards.**

■ **flippers** *See* **barn doors.**

■ **float** The wavering of an image, generally caused by unsteady film during exposure in the camera or projector.

■ **floating pegs, floating pegbar** *See* **animation stand.**

■ **floating track** *See* **wild track.**

■ **floating wall, wild wall** A part of a wall in a set that can be removed to allow for movement of the camera.

■ **floodlight, flood, floodlamp** A light that provides wide, diffuse, and soft illumination with little or no focus. This luminaire is employed as a general light filter. *See* **lighting.**

■ **floor** (1) The main area in the studio where shooting occurs. (2) The minimal percentage of the box office paid to the distributor of a film by the exhibitor. *See* **distribution.**

floodlight

■ **floor mixer** *See* **production sound mixer.**

■ **flopover** *See* **flip.**

■ **floppy disc** *See* **disc** *(1).*

■ **flow of-life film** A film that creates the patterns and rhythm of everyday life at the expense of a tight dramatic structure. The term is especially applicable to Italian neorealistic films and the films made in India by Satyajit Ray.

■ **flub** (1) A mistake by a performer in the recitation of his or her lines during rehearsal or actual shooting. (2) To make such a mistake.

■ **fluid camera** A filming technique that emphasizes the movement of the camera through space rather than sharp and invisible cutting. Most films employ this technique to some degree, especially with tracking and panning shots. The Steadicam permits the fluid movement of the camera to follow characters and action, with both naturalness and speed, into the most difficult or closed areas (e.g., in Stanley Kubrick's *The Shining* [1980]). The fluid camera also permits the filmmaker to overcome the two-dimensionality of the screen by moving the viewer into the inner space of the scene. The technique is effective in creating a subjective view by allowing us to see and move through the world as does the character. It must be remembered that a fluid camera, effective and dramatic as it is in many situations, slows down the pace and rhythm of the film and inevitably calls attention to the fact that the action is being filmed. Yet some major films, especially in Europe, have been successfully dominated by the technique. One of the most notable films which features the fluid camera is F. W. Murnau's German expressionist film *The Last Laugh* (1924), with its famous sequence where the camera rides down an elevator and comes sweeping into the busy lobby of a major hotel. Fluid cameras have been effective in horror films by creating mood, intensifying suspense, and creating subjective perspectives (e.g., in Mario Bava's *Black Sunday*, made in Italy in 1960). Brian De Palma has used the fluid camera with striking results in this country: his museum sequence in *Dressed to Kill* (1980) follows the movements of Angie Dickinson through the various galleries with dizzying and heightening drama, conveying her subjective point of view with a sweeping lyricism.

■ **fluid head** A camera mount that allows smooth movement for the camera through the use of liquid forced between the moving parts. Since there is no initial resistance with this type of mount, it is more suitable for slow and precise panning and tilting than the friction type of head. *See* **friction head** *and* **geared head.**

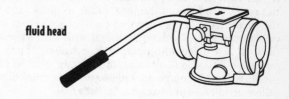

fluid head

■ **fluorescent light** A tubular light that gives off illumination when phosphers coated inside are made to glow through radiation from heated mercury vapor. Such tubes give off a cold whitish light, which can be controlled for photographing by fluorescent-light filters.

■ **fluting** The swelling and bending of a film's edges caused by excessive humidity and excessively tight winding. Either one or both edges are longer than the middle of the film. The condition is also referred to as edgewaving.

■ **flutter** (1) The fading in and fading out or general unsteadiness of a film image caused by some irregularity or movement in exposure, printing, or projection. *See* **breathing** *and* **weave.** (2) Variations in pitch or a garglelike defect in speech during sound reproduction normally caused by some irregular movement of a mechanism in recording or playback. *See* **wow.**

■ **flux** The rate of light energy measured in lumens (i.e., luminous flux). *See* **lumen.**

■ **fly** (1) The high area above a set that contains various luminaires and from which scenery is suspended; the "flies." (2) To suspend scenery in the fly area above the set.

■ **flying spot, flying spot scanner** *See* **telecine.**

■ **f-number** *See* **f-stop.**

■ **FO** A fadeout. *See* **fade-in (FI), fade-out (FO).**

■ **focal length** The distance between the center of the lens and the film, normally given in millimeters, when a far object measured at infinity comes into critical focus. A long focal length will allow a smaller area to be photographed (as in a telephoto lens) and a short focal length will allow a wider area (as in a wide-angle lens).

A focal length of 50mm is considered normal for a 35mm camera, 25mm for a 16mm camera, and 12mm for an 8mm camera.

■ **focal plane** The area behind the lens where the film is normally located and where the image comes into critical focus when the lens is focused on infinity. When the camera is focused on less than infinity, the plane is called the image plane.

■ **focal plane matte, focal plane mask** A device inserted into the camera in front of the focal plane to block part of the image from being recorded on the film so that the unexposed area can later be filled with an image or part of an image photographed separately. Such a process allows the combining of separate picture elements to form a composite image (e.g., the combining of live action and animation). *See* **matte** *(2).*

■ **focal point** The point behind the lens where a point in the image comes into critical focus when the lens is focused on infinity. When the camera is focused on less than infinity, the point is called the image point.

■ **focal spot, focus spot** A lens assembly that replaces a Fresnel lens and creates a well-defined, intense, and smooth field of light like that from an ellipsoidal spot. *See* **ellipsoidal spot.**

■ **focus** (1) The point behind the lens where the light rays from a point being photographed converge to form an image. (2) The degree of acceptable sharpness and definition to create a clear image on the film. It is possible to achieve "deep focus," where foreground to background are reasonably sharp, or "shallow focus," where only a single ground is sharply defined (*see* **deep focus** *and* **shallow focus**). (3) The degree of sharpness and definition of the image. When an image seems to have the maximum amount of sharpness and definition it is said to be in "sharp focus"; when the image intentionally is made to seem slightly blurred, it is in "soft focus." (4) The location from which a subject will record sharply on film. (5) To adjust the lens of the camera or projector so that the image photographed or projected will have the maximum clarity and definition. For a camera, the lens, which is on an adjustable barrel, is moved back and forth by means of a focus ring so that the focal length (i.e., the distance between the lens and film) is changed. This focus ring is marked with focal settings for various distances up to infinity. In a studio camera, the focus ring may also be operated by a handle, cable, or by remote control—this last method is especially useful when the camera is moving.

■ **focus drift** The shifting or loss of focus in a series of frames.

■ **focus in, focus out** (1) Directions for the camera gradually to focus on some part of the scene or to bring such an area gradually out of focus. (2) To focus a spotlight so that a sharp and narrow beam of illumination is achieved, or to spread the light so that it floods a general area.

■ **focusing** Adjusting the camera to achieve maximum sharpness and definition in the image by changing the distance between lens and film. *See* **focus** *(5).*

■ **focusing plane, focus plane** The area of primary focus in the scene being photographed. The distance between this plane and the film is measured and the lens then focused on the plane.

■ **focusing spotlight, focusing spot, variable spot-flood** A closed spotlight, often with a Fresnel lens, that emits a controllable beam of hard light as opposed to the open spotlight, which emits wider and more diffuse illumination. *See* **spotlight.**

■ **focus pull, focus shift, focus through** Changing the focus plane during a take. The focus plane goes soft while another part of the scene becomes the primary focus. Focus shifts may take place when the camera moves, pans, or tilts, when focused characters or objects move, or when a new subject for focus is desired. The member of the camera crew who makes the focus adjustments is the assistant cameraman. This effect can also be achieved in an optical printer (e.g., for dramatically bringing titles into focus). *See* **follow focus, rack focus, selective focus,** *and* **shallow focus.**

■ **focus puller** *See* **first assistant camera operator.**

■ **focus ring, focus band** The rotating part of the lens that adjusts focus and on which the distance between the lens and focal subject is calibrated.

■ **focus shift** *See* **focus pull.**

■ **fog, fogging** A haze or density over the film that is not the results of exposure but may come from unwanted light in the camera or unwanted light during loading, printing, or storage.

■ **fog filter** A camera filter that creates an appearance of fog on the image. A rotating filter will create an illusion of moving fog, though it is generally better to use a fog-making machine.

■ **fog level, fog density** (1) The amount of density on an unexposed film after it has been developed. (2) The amount of density on an exposed film emulsion after development that is not the result of exposure. The fog level in both (1) and (2) may also be the result of the chemical solution developing unexposed halides.

■ **fogmaker, fog machine, smoke machine, smoke gun** A portable device that can be carried by hand or placed on the ground to make controlled amounts of fog or smoke. The fog or smoke has normally been created by heating kerosene or mineral oil either by gas or electricity, or by vaporizing such a compound in aerosol generators, although Rosco Laboratories has developed a nontoxic and nonirritating fluid, without a petroleum base, that has been well received.

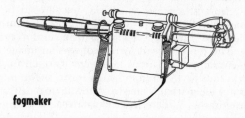

fogmaker

■ **Foley artist, Foley walker, Foley mixer** A specialist in sound effects, especially of body movements, so named after Jack Foley, the man who established modern techniques for creating sounds that are recorded to fit the pictures on the screen. Individual sound effects are sometimes referred to as Foleys, and the place where they are made as a Foley studio, Foley stage, or Foleying stages. The word "walker" in "Foley walker" comes from the specific practice of such technicians walking on boxes of gravel or starch for making the sound of a person walking outdoors on gravel or snow respectively. Such sounds are also referred to as sync FX and m and s for make and sync.

■ **follow focus** To change focus continuously in the camera in order to keep clearly defined a character or object moving toward or away from the camera or from one side of the scene to another. *See* **focus pull, rack focus, selective focus,** *and* **shallow focus.**

■ **follow focus control, follow focus mechanism, follow focus system** A device attached to the lens of the camera that allows the first assistant camera operator to change focus in order to keep a moving subject clearly defined. Panavision cameras sometimes use a speed crank or L-handle attached to the focus control to ease movement; other cameras may employ a flexible cable sometimes called a whip.

■ **follow shot** A shot in which the camera seems to pursue the subject as it moves. The recording of this movement may be achieved through a tracking shot, where the camera physically follows the character, or through a zoom lens, when the camera is immobile. With a zoom lens, the definition of the environment and relation of the subject to the environment will change.

■ **follow spot** A spotlight, normally situated on a stand, that remains focused on a moving character. Such a light has a clearly defined circular beam and is capable

of throwing its illumination a great distance. *See* **spotlight.**

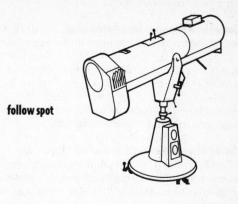

follow spot

■ **footage (FTG)** (1) The measurement of film in feet. (2) The feet of film shot for a particular take or for an entire film.

■ **footage counter** A measuring device that indicates the amount of footage of film that has passed through a camera, printer, or editing machine. The basic device is a counter attached to a sprocket that engages the film.

■ **footage numbers** *See* **edge numbers.**

■ **footcandle** A measurement for the intensity of light. Each footcandle represents the intensity of luminosity on the surface of a sphere of one-foot radius from a light source of one standard candle, which is one foot away from the center of the sphere. A footcandle is equal to one lumen per square foot. It directly measures incident light coming from external sources and illuminating the subject. The lux is a similar measurement in millimeters. *See* **lux.**

■ **footlambert** A nonmetric measurement for the brightness given off by a clear surface such as a movie screen. The measurement for a movie screen will, of course, vary according to one's viewing position, but the center of the screen should register about fifteen footlamberts in the rear third of the theater from a good 35mm projector. A footlambert equals one lumen per square foot.

■ **forced call** A required period of work when a member of the cast or crew has not had a contracted amount of time free (normally ten to twelve hours) since the previous period of work. Though the production company must pay dearly for this practice, it is sometimes necessary because of shooting schedules, location schedules, or weather conditions.

■ **forced coverage** The elimination of a mistake in shooting a scene by substituting for the cut section an additional portion shot after. The replacement may be a simple two-shot, which saves the expense and time of having to photograph the entire scene.

■ **forced development, forced processing** Additional development for a film that has been underexposed because of insufficient lighting in order to increase density and achieve a better picture. Either the time or temperature of the developing process can be increased. Sometimes film is intentionally underexposed and overdeveloped to increase contrast, a process called pushing or uprating. *See* **overdevelopment.**

■ **forced perspective** An illusion of depth and distance artificially created in sets built in limited areas or in miniature sets. Structures in the rear, for example, are unnaturally small so that they will seem a greater distance away.

■ **foreground (FG)** The front area of a scene closest to the audience, where the major action generally takes place.

■ **foreground matte** *See* **female matte.**

■ **foreground music** Music that derives from a source seen on the screen (e.g., a radio or orchestra). Also called direct music and source music.

■ **foreground plane** *See* **plane.**

■ **foreign version, foreign release** A version of a film prepared for export abroad, either by dubbing in a new sound track and putting in new titles in the language of a country where the profit will more than make up for the expense or putting in "subtitles" (a translation of dialogue and narration) at the bottom of the frames. Subtitled versions may be shown in addition to dubbed ones in a country where there is a sufficient audience wishing to hear the original dialogue of the film. Films have occasionally been made in two languages simultaneously (with separate performers) for release both in the home market and foreign countries, but the cost now makes this practice infrequent.

■ **forelengthening** The exaggerated increase of depth in an image from a wide-angle lens. Although the eyes of the viewer generally adjust to this change, such an increase may be employed to create a number of effects—for example, because such lenses exaggerate spatial distance and because objects to the front of the image are suddenly large, the movement of a character towards or away from the camera will seem very rapid. *See* **wide-angle lens.**

■ **foreshortening** The exaggerated decrease of depth in an image for a long-focus or telephoto lens. Although the eyes of the viewer gradually adjust to this change, such a decrease may be employed to create a number of effects—for example, because space is collapsed and objects at various planes are all large, a running figure to or away from the camera will seem to be getting nowhere. *See* **long-focus lens.**

■ **form** (1) The general configuration and shape of a specific area, as distinguished from its substance, texture, and color. The form of each image should not only be aesthetically satisfying, but should be functional as well, highlighting action while also conveying mood and information so that form reinforces meaning. The term "closed form" conveys an image that is self-contained and does not seem to open up to the world outside the frame; "open form" suggests a more natural image that seems to continue outside the limits of the frame. *See* **closed form** *and* **open form.** (2) The general configuration and shape of a film. This definition is more an abstract concept than an immediate reality, since the viewer sees only one part of the film at a time and must create a sense of the whole in his or her mind after viewing the film; but any competent director or editor is concerned with the way the pieces fit together, the sense of form that develops in the audience's mind as they watch the film, and the final sense of form when the film is at an end. Concepts from the drama such as "tragic" and "comic" form are sometimes applied to film; filmic genres such as Westerns and criminal films are frequently argued to have specific forms; and more general descriptive concepts such as "lyric," "expanding," or "tightening" form are on occasion used to describe a motion picture. The term "structure" generally suggests the way a work is constructed or put together or the way it can be perceived from a single spatial perspective (though today the term also has more complicated significances), while "form" suggests an appreciation of both the work's entire movement and flow as well as the final, general arrangement of its discernible elements. *See* **formalism** *and* **structure.**

■ **formal balance** A picture or, in the case of film, visual image where there is an ordered and harmonious arrangement, an equilibrium of pictorial elements. Note, for example, the visual compositions in the films by the Japanese director Akira Kurosawa. Films with closed form tend to present such self-contained and balanced arrangements, while those with open form tend to present visuals with the randomness of the world outside the theater.

■ **formal editing** Editing shots of approximately equal length. Such editing creates a dominant, slow, and formal rhythm throughout the film. The French filmmaker Robert Bresson creates a brooding and intense feeling in his works in this manner, for example in *Diary of a Country Priest* (1951).

■ **formalism** An artistic movement that emphasizes form over content, that is more concerned with the way something is presented than what is presented. For the formalist, form is an end in itself and carries its own aesthetic justification. It is difficult to point to any pure formalist tradition in the fictional film, since the medium depends so much on the replication of physical reality and the representation of human characters, but one can see certain areas of avant-garde cinema as concerned purely with form: for example, abstract films avoid any direct presentation of reality, and concern themselves with the changing arrangement of abstract forms. When the term "formalism" appears in film study, however, it generally relates to fictional works that take reality and impose upon it the formalistic elements of art in such a way that reality loses its original appearance and significance, becoming something unique to the medium—meaning derives from the formal elements employed and not the subject matter itself. The famous Russian film director Eisenstein was very concerned with form in his theoretical writings and in his films as well, especially in his discussions and creation of montage. But form for Eisenstein always had an intellectual and psychological function, and even in his later films is a means of expanding and developing the impact of the film's representation of reality. In film theory, there have been two major traditions, one featuring writers such as Balázs, who emphasize the formalistic aspects of a film, and the other featuring writers such as Kracauer, who emphasize the film's capacity to reproduce reality. *See* **film theory.**

■ **format** (1) The size of a film determined in millimeters; its gauge (e.g., 8mm, Super 8mm, 16mm, Super 16mm, 35mm, 70mm). (2) The aspect ratio of a film image; that is, the ratio of width to height. *See* **aspect ratio.** (3) The generic form of a particular work, especially for television and radio programs (e.g., "a comic format").

■ **form cut** Cutting from one shot to another when the subject of the second shot has a shape or position in the frame similar to that of the subject in the first. Such a technique both adds a continuity to the images and suggests a relationship between the subjects of both pictures. Pudovkin's famous cutting between the marching workers and flow of ice on the river at the end of *Mother* (1926) can be considered a series of form cuts. *See* **match cut.**

■ **form dissolve** The merging of two separate images with similar forms (e.g., when one character seems to merge with another or the spirit of a character reenters his body). Hitchcock uses an effective form dissolve in *Psycho* (1960), when the circular drain of the tub gradually becomes the lifeless eye of Janet Leigh. *See* **dissolve.**

■ **formula film** A film that uses story elements and character types developed in earlier, successful works. Genre films are formulaic in this way, but the term can also be applied to works that do not belong to well-established genres (e.g., domestic dramas dealing with the tribulations of marriage, or films about prizefighters). *See* **genre.**

■ **forward-backward** A system of dubbing, whereby better dialogue is recorded than that taken during actual shooting. Instead of having to loop parts of the original film and sound tape and later splice them back into the original reel, this method allows the sound technicians to run the picture and sound forward and backward as many times as necessary before a final dialogue track is made. Also referred to as rock and roll. *See* **looping.**

■ **foundation light, base light, set light** The basic, general lighting for an entire scene.

■ **found footage** Any film scene that is used in motion picture but has been shot for some other film or for some other purpose. Various pieces of found footage might be used for a compilation film; or a specific scene, a military parade, for example, might be pulled from an old newsreel for present usage. *See* **library shot** *and* **stock shot.**

■ **four-foot rule** An unwritten rule that four feet be kept free around the perimeters of a stage so that people could be free to leave in case of an accident.

■ **four-walled set** A set with four walls, instead of three, encompassing the action and camera. Some of the walls are removable to allow for camera movement during shooting. A four-walled set allows for continuous action and movement of the camera in any direction.

■ **four-walling** A type of distribution in which the distributor pays the exhibitor a flat rate for rental while handling all the arrangements for the film showing, including advertising, running the box office, and showing the film. The distributor takes in all the profits after the guaranteed payment and costs.

■ **Fox Film Corporation** A film company begun as Box Office Attractions by William Fox in 1913 and renamed after him in 1915. Fox owned a number of theaters in New York, but went into the film-production business to overcome the control of the General Film Company, which was the distributing agency of the Motion Picture Patents Company. Fox led the independents in their successful fight against the dying Patents Company and brought suit against that organization under the Sherman Anti-Trust Law in 1913. His company prospered and was engaged in all aspects of film—producing, distributing, and exhibiting. The company, under Fox, was a leader in the development of sound for motion pictures with the Movietone Sound System, and in May 1927 produced the famous Movietone newsreel of Lindburgh's historic takeoff for his cross-Atlantic flight. In 1929 Fox obtained controlling interest in the stock of Loew's, Inc., and continued to expand his theater holdings while fitting a number of his theaters for sound. Fox overextended himself and ultimately was forced out of his own company in 1931. In 1935 the Fox Film Corporation merged with Twentieth Century Pictures to become Twentieth Century-Fox. *See* **Twentieth Century-Fox.**

■ **foxhole** A perforation on CinemaScope prints with four magnetic sound tracks, so called because of the name of CinemaScope's sponsor, Twentieth Century-Fox.

■ **FPF** *See* **frames per foot.**

■ **FPS** *See* **frames per second.**

■ **fractal system** In computer animation, a process of creating a single subject that is composed of similar elements but with a degree of perturbance or variance—e.g., trees or terrain. *See* **particle system.**

■ **fractionalizing** Dividing up the rights to a film among several separate agencies—e.g., giving the distribution rights to different territorial markets or giving them to different organizations for theatrical and television distribution. Sometimes also referred to as segmentizing.

■ **frame** (1) The individual photographs on motion-picture film. A latent image is formed for each frame when new stock momentarily stops before the camera's aperture for exposure. Each frame when developed and printed as a positive will be the photograph of a single instant in a continuous action. When the frames are projected onto the screen, one after the other (sixteen or more frames per second for silent film and twenty-four for sound), the illusion of motion is created through the viewer's persistence of vision. The size of the frame is determined by the width of the film in millimeters (e.g., 8-, 16-, 35-, 65-, and 70mm) as well as the camera's aperture. *See* **film** *(1) and* **persistence of vision.** (2) The borders of the image on the screen that enclose the picture like a frame on a painting. The ratio of width to height (i.e., the aspect ratio) for silent films was 4:3, but this was virtually squared when sound films necessitated the addition of a sound track. However, the unpleasing square was changed back to the 4:3 image by masking the top and bottom of the frame on the film, and this ratio remained standard until wide-screen projections became popular in the 1950s, with aspect ratios of anywhere from 2:1 to 2.7:1. Standard 35mm nonanamorphic films today have an aspect ratio of 1.85:1 (1.66:1 in Europe) and 70mm non-anamorphic films have one of 2:2.1. *See* **aspect ratio.** (3) The entire rectangular area of the image projected on the screen. In discussions of the film image, the term "frame" is employed to suggest a single shot that is actually made up of a whole series of photographs projected from the film. The frame itself cuts off the image from the world outside the film, but the image may be conveyed in such a way that its reality seems to continue outside the frame (*see* **open form**)—this effect has been emphasized by wide-screen images. Yet often the director will emphasize the interior space of his frame and compose the image in such a way that it seems a self-contained entity, a world unto itself (*see* **closed form**). The fact that a frame is wider than high (especially in wide-screen projection) requires that the vertical dimension of important characters and objects be extended either by framing or by angling the camera. Each frame is a picture and must be composed in such a way that it takes advantage of its interior space. The center of the frame is normally the place for important action, while the rest of the frame must be so arranged that it does not draw attention unless to comment on the major action. Characters and action, however, can be distributed in the various areas of the frame to achieve certain effects. Characters on top of the frame seem to have power over those at the bottom, but, on the other hand, the bottom is the place of stability and more readily receives our attention. We tend to read a frame from left to right so that the action on the right area will naturally draw our eyes, allowing the left area to be a place for sudden surprises. In the films of the 1930s and 1940s, with their standard aspect ratio, the emphasis seemed to be on dialogue and the dramatic interplay of characters. The two-shot, which emphasized this drama, was therefore dominant. With the widening of the frame in the 1950s more emphasis was given to exteriors and locals, and the film drama, with its emphasis on dialogue, gave way to works with far more emphasis on the interplay between character and environment. As a result, open-form films became more dominant than closed-form. (4) Pictorial elements in the foreground of a picture which frame the major action—for example trees and shrubbery, a gate, a window, the backs of characters. Such frames give depth to the scene (especially if shot at an angle) while highlighting action and blocking off unused space. However, framed images must be composed so that they are not pictorially artificial. (5) The total scanning of first the odd- and then the even-numbered lines that go into the composition of a single image on television or video—each scanning is referred to as a field. There are 30 frames and 60 fields per second for each image. *See* **television** *and* **video camera.** (6) To adjust and move the camera so that action and characters being filmed are kept within the confines of the film image. (7) To adjust the projector so that frame lines are not visible and the film frames are projected individually.

■ **frame buffer** This device in the computer, created by a board with additional RAM, calls up images from the frame, still, or page store and places them as video images on the screen of a monitor to allow the artist to do further work. *See* **computer animation.**

■ **frame counter** The part of a footage counter that indicates the number of frames passing in each foot. This number is dependent on the gauge of film. *See* **frames per foot.**

■ **frame grabber**   A device in a computer that transforms images on a videotape into digital signals. Film images are normally transferred to videotape before they are digitized for editing. Also called a capture board. *See* **digital, editing,** *and* **video editing system.**

■ **frame line**   The horizontal lines that separate the frames on a piece of film (i.e., the bottom line on the top frame and the top line on the bottom frame).

■ **framer, frame puller**   The control in a projector that allows the projectionist to frame the images so that frame lines are not shown and each photograph is perfectly aligned.

■ **frame rate**   The number of frames that pass before the lens of a camera or projector per second. *See* **frames per second.**

■ **frames per foot (FPF)**   The number of frames in each foot of a particular gauge of film—8mm film has 80 frames per foot; Super 8 has 72 frames; 16mm film has 40 frames; Super 16 has 40 frames; 35mm film has 16 frames; and 70mm film has 12ᴘ frames per foot.

■ **frames per second (fps)**   The number of frames that pass before the aperture of a camera or projector per second. Silent films were standardized at 16 fps, though the speed of shooting was likely to be somewhat more and projection could be anywhere from 21 to 24 frames per second. Sound film was standardized at 24 fps because that rate achieved sufficient sound reproduction. Sometimes films are shot at 30 frames per second to allow for direct transfer to video, especially when the shooting is ultimately for video transmission.

■ **frame store**   The term technically means the storage of a single frame or image in the computer's memory, but it is now generally used to suggest the storage of several frames. The term is basically the same as still store and page store. *See* **frame buffer.**

■ **frameup**   *See* **framing** *(1) and (2).*

■ **framing**   (1) The act of fitting a subject into the frame and composing the image for photographing. (2) The act of adjusting the projector so that frame lines will not be visible on the screen and frames will be individually and fully projected. (3) Arranging a subject within an image so that it is "framed" and highlighted by objects in the foreground (e.g., shrubbery, a doorway, the backs of characters, etc.).

■ **franchise film**   A motion picture that passes through the various formats and business phases of a single corporation—originally made on film, it is then released on video, cable television, television, in novelized form, and licensed in various merchandising arrangements.

■ **free cinema**   A documentary film movement in Great Britain in the 1950s, supported by the British Film Institute. The works in this movement were a reaction to commercial films as well as traditional documentaries. They sought to portray the undramatic lives of real, everyday people, trapped by the limitations of the society rather than to analyze the institutions of that society as did previous documentaries. The directors of these films also sought to create a more personal and poetic cinema, a freer and less structured film. The first three films in this movement, shown in February 1956, were Lindsay Anderson's *O Dreamland* (1953), Karel Reisz and Tony Richardson's *Momma Don't Allow* (1955), and Lorenza Mazzetti's *Together* (1956; edited by Anderson). Several of the participants in this movement, such as Anderson, Reisz, and Richardson, later brought some of their free-cinema approaches to the making of commercial films.

■ **free lance**   Any person who works independently and is not contracted to a specific studio or production company (e.g., a director, art director, screenwriter, etc.).

■ **freeze**   (1) A freeze frame. (2) An order for actors to stop all motion and remain perfectly still.

■ **freeze frame, hold frame, stop frame, freeze**   A single frame that is repeatedly printed on a duplicate copy of the film so that the image projected on the screen seems frozen for a desired length of time. The freeze frame, which is made in an optical printer, can dramatically punctuate or emphasize some idea or concept for the audience. At the end of Truffaut's *The 400 Blows* (1959), the image of the young boy is frozen on the screen and resembles both a newspaper photograph and a mug shot to suggest his bleak future.

■ **freeze-frame printing**   The repeated printing of a single frame on a duplicate copy in an optical printer to create a freeze frame. *See* **freeze frame.**

■ **French flag**   A small flag attached to an adjustable arm which may be clamped anywhere on the set to block illumination and cause shading. *See* **gobo.**

■ **frequency**   The number of cycles per second of air compression at a given point, caused by a vibrating object in the production of sound waves. The measurement for such frequency is the hertz.

■ **frequency meter**   A type of tachometer used to read frequencies of HMI or incandescent lights by pointing the meter at the source of lumination. Such meters also measure AC frequency and camera speeds. *See* **tachometer.**

■ **frequency response** The range of frequencies that an audio system is capable of recording or reproducing. The range of such frequencies can be shown on a frequency response graph.

■ **Fresnel, Fresnel lens** A lens with stepped-down concentric circles on the convex side, which is placed in front of a bulb as a condensor. Light is flooded when the bulb is close to the lens, but when it is moved back the lens acts as a spotter, controlling the area and intensity of illumination. The Fresnel lens is especially light and easy to handle.

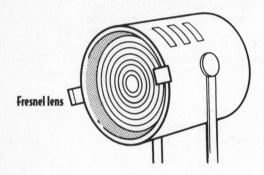

Fresnel lens

■ **friction head** A mount for the camera, generally on a tripod, that allows movement for the camera through the easy friction of two metal components. Because an initial resistance must first be overcome before a steady motion is achieved, the head is not suitable for slow and careful movements. *See* **fluid head** *and* **geared head**.

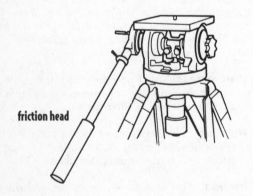

friction head

■ **frilling** The loosening of emulsion along the edges of the film's base.

■ **fringing** The breakdown of definition around the edges of an image that has been improperly matted into another image when making a composite picture. In color photography the colors at the edge disperse and do not match their original areas. *See* **matte** *(2)*.

■ **from the top** The director's command to start a scene from the beginning.

■ **front box** A small wooden box that contains various tools and accessories and is affixed to the front of the camera.

■ **front credits** The credits that appear at the beginning of the film. Such credits normally include the distribution company, the production organization, sometimes the name of the director (e.g., "a Robert Altman film"), the star performers, the various production personnel, and conclude with the producer and the director. *See* **closing credits**.

■ **front end** Costs for a film before actual production, such as advance payment for screen rights.

■ **front light/back light, front lit/back lit** A matting process in special-effects photography, much in use with motion-control systems, that requires two identical passes of the camera and model. For the first pass, the model is front lit against a black backing and appears as it will in the final image; for the second pass, from which the matte is made, a white backing is lit while the model is unlit. *See* **motion control** *and* **traveling-matte process**.

■ **front lighting** Lighting that comes from the camera area or the front of the set. Such general lighting will make the subject appear flat, though round objects will be defined by a shadow. *See* **lighting**.

■ **front-projecting blue-screen process** *See* **blue-screen process**.

■ **front projection, front-axial projection** A method of photographing live actors in a studio with a moving or still background shot elsewhere and projected on a screen behind them. While rear projection creates the background from behind the screen, this method projects the background from in front—hence the name "front projection." The projector, placed in front and to the side of the camera at a 90-degree angle, projects the moving background from a film or still background from a slide onto a semitransparent and semireflecting mirror placed at a 45-degree angle to both projector and camera. The mirror reflects the image onto a special reflex screen made of tiny glass beads that reflect back to the camera almost all the light rays. The camera shoots the scene through the mirror. Since the camera is in direct alignment with the actors, it does not record the shadows behind them caused by their blockage of the light rays from the projected background image. The actors themselves are not sufficient reflectors to show the part of the background image which falls on them. When a moving background is projected, both the projector and camera work together by synchronic interlocking motors.

Front projection has several advantages over rear projection—because the image is projected from the

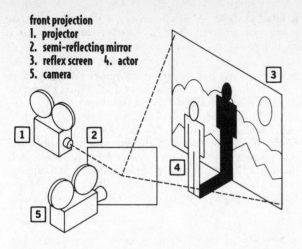

front projection
1. projector
2. semi-reflecting mirror
3. reflex screen 4. actor
5. camera

front and because of the reflex nature of the screen, the image is brighter and clearer. The reflex screen of tiny beads also creates a background image of greater depth. Less studio space is required, a larger screen can be employed, and there is more mobility in the placement of lights and performers. Since the projected background will be a generation older than the image of the live action shot in front of the screen, large-format cameras, such as the Panavision 65mm and VistaVision cameras, are used when possible to film the background, since the high quality of their images will minimize the difference. The disadvantage of this method is that actors cannot move very much and the camera must be still to avoid filming shadows on the screen caused by the performers. The method was employed in Stanley Kubrick's *2001: A Space Odyssey* (1968) with great success. Front projection was employed in the *Superman* films (1978, 1980, 1983), along with synchronized zoom lenses on the camera and projector to create the illusion of the hero flying. Both the blue-screen process and digital compositing are much in use today to achieve the same effects as front projection, though the latter process is still simpler and can be less costly. *See* **blue-screen process, digital composite, rear projection,** *and* **Zoptic front projection.**

■ **frost** A translucent white gel for diffusing light from a luminaire.

■ **frying pan** A screen placed in front of a luminaire to diffuse light.

■ **FS** *See* **full shot.**

■ **f-stop, f-stop number, f-number** The measurement for calculating the opening of the lens aperture, or diaphragm, on a camera in order to control the amount of light reaching the film. These numbers are derived by dividing the focal length of the lens by its widest effective diameter and are considered the "relative aperture" of the lens. If its focal length is 50mm and the

effective diameter 25mm, the lens is rated f-2. Smaller f-numbers represent larger apertures and hence more light reaching the film. Numbers approaching an f-1 rating indicate faster lenses. A series of numbers, or stops, is calculated from the maximum number and indicated on the lens to allow for adjustment of the diaphragm. Each successive number, which in effect halves the amount of light admitted, is calculated by multiplying the previous number by the square root of 2, or 1.4, and rounding off the result to the nearest decimal point. The f-stop series is 1, 1.4, 2, 2.8, 4, 5.6, 8, 11, 16, 22, 32. Because f-stop numbers do not account for reflection or absorption of light by the various lens elements and account only for what is considered the "relative aperture," t-stop numbers, which electronically compute the light actually at the focal plane of the film, are also employed in professional photography. The t-number is considered to be the perfect f-number of a lens. But f-numbers are still useful for calculating "object-image" relationships, reliably equating apertures for different lenses with the same focal length, and figuring depth of field. *See* **focal length** *and* **t-stop.**

■ **f-stop ring, f-stop band** The ring or band on a barrel lens, containing a series of printed f-numbers, which is turned to set the lens diaphragm at the desired number.

■ **Fujicolor** A Japanese color film introduced in 1955 for professional cinematography. Negative, positive, and reversal films are manufactured for various gauges. In 1980, Fujicolor introduced its high-speed negative film, A250 (type 8518 for 35mm and 8528 for 16mm photography), which was employed widely for interior shooting, although some cinematographers used the film for all their shots, creating remarkable color renditions and contrasts with minimal granularity. A250 film was employed in Wolfgang Petersen's *Das Boot* (1982) with striking results. The Fuji Photo Film Company received a special Academy Award in 1982 for this film. The new Negative Film Super-F series is said to achieve lifelike images with reduced granularity and exceptional sharpness. A black resin backing on such film reduces scratch, static, and camera behavior properties, while expanded exposure latitude results in a very reliable performance in the most diverse situations. The recently introduced negative film, F-500 (type 8571 for 35mm and 8671 for 16mm) is especially designed for shooting indoors or with low-light conditions. Such film has exceptionally fine grain and high speed. Like the other films in this series, the F500 is responsive to technology by having a new matting agent that allows for superior optical printing and laser scanning. The new Super F-64D, with its fine grain and capacity for accurate color, is excellent for outdoor shooting.

■ **full animation** A method for creating animated works with full drawings for each shot, which is normally no more than one or two frames. The term is used to distinguish this method from either (1) cel animation, where certain elements of a scene or even characters are repeated from shot to shot on the same cels; or (2) limited animation, where only parts of a figure are animated. *See* **animation, cel animation,** *and* **limited animation.**

■ **full aperture** (1) The maximum opening of the lens diaphragm of a camera. (2) The original aperture of camera and projector lens for 35mm film before sound, which allowed the largest possible area of the film to be used for a frame with an aspect ratio of 4:3.

■ **full coat** *See* **magnetic film.**

■ **full frame** Maximum frame size obtained on a 35mm film. *See* **full aperture** *(2).*

■ **full shot (FS), full figure shot** A long shot that takes in the entire figure of a character, with the head near the top of the frame and the feet near the bottom. *See* **long shot.**

■ **full track** An audio track that is completely filled.

■ **funnel** *See* **snoot.**

■ **furniture clamp** A small device of various sizes that clamps on to both ends of a surface and supports a small luminaire.

■ **futurism** An Italian artistic movement developed in the early decades of this century that denied the traditional while advocating the technological and industrial. Although film was seen as the modern art form to express this view, only a few works were made in the medium. The few films in the movement emphasized the visionary nature and technology of film itself by deemphasizing reality and featuring striking or novel visual concepts and special effects (e.g., Anton Giulio Bragaglia's *Perfido Incanto* [*Wicked Enchantment*]; 1916).

■ **fuzz-off** To soften matte lines so that separate picture elements blend together in a composite image without any discernible dividing lines. *See* **matte** *(2).*

■ **fuzzy** A description of an image that is unclear and out of focus.

■ **FX** Abbreviation for effects used to represent such terms as sound effects or special effects.

■   ■   ■

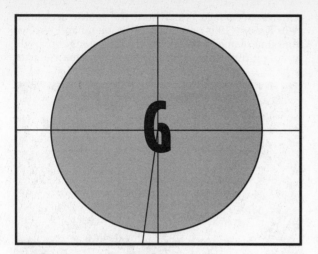

gadget bag to gyro-stabilized camera system, gyro-stabilized cinematography

■ **gadget bag** A bag belonging to the camera crew that contains small equipment and tools (e.g., scissors, tape measure, etc.).

■ **gaffer** The chief electrician in a film production, who is responsible for supplying, placing, operating, and maintaining the required lights as well as the power source for illumination both in the studio and on location. The gaffer receives instructions from the director of photography while having a number of electricians working under him or her.

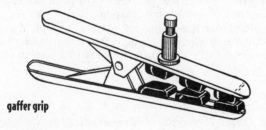

gaffer grip

■ **gaffer grip** A clamp for attaching lights to any rigging or part of a set. Also called alligator, bear trap, and gator grip.

■ **gaffer's tape** An adhesive tape used by a gaffer for such functions as fastening down stands, lights, or cables and for a variety of other functions during film production such as repairing tears in the set, fastening

film cans, or designating positions for the camera and the performers on the floor of the set.

■ **gag** (1) A specific effect achieved in special-effects photography through some kind of optical trickery (e.g., making moving smoke or water appear in sections of a scene derived from a matte painting). (2) Any kind of mechanical effect in a scene (e.g., an exploding vehicle or collapsing wall). (3) A stunt performed by a stunt man or woman for a film.

■ **gain** (1) The amplification of sound in an audio system. (2) *See* **screen gain.**

■ **gain control** The volume control on any kind of sound machine.

■ **galvanometer** A piece of equipment that transforms electrical impulses from sound into a variable-area optical sound track on film. The electrical impulses force the galvanometer coil, which is in a magnetic field, to rotate. Attached to the coil is a mirror that reflects a beam of light through a slit and onto a film. The oscillations of the coil are controlled by the variations in the signal and cause the reflected light beam to move back and forth across the slit, recording on the film an image of varying width. A print of the image can later be converted back to the original sound by an optical sound head in a projector. This variable-area method is employed primarily in recording the final sound track onto the film and is considered to be more efficient for color film than the variable-density method. It is no longer used for recording during actual shooting, since magnetic or digital systems are more efficient and cheaper. *See* **optical sound** *and* **sound.**

■ **gamma** The measurement of contrast in a film emulsion dependent on the change in development. The gamma is measured from the slope of the characteristic curve. The term "overall gamma" refers to the gamma produced from the range of films involved in creating the final image—e.g., from the negative, master positive or internegative, and release prints. *See* **characteristic curve.**

■ **gamma infinity** The maximum contrast of which a film emulsion is capable.

■ **gang** The individual sprocket wheels inside a synchronizer used in editing. Each gang is responsible for running a single piece of film, either with a picture or sound track, synchronously with other pieces of film. Synchronizers are sometimes identified by the number of sprockets and, hence, the number of pieces of film they can handle—e.g., a four-gang synchronizer.

■ **gangster film, criminal film** A distinct genre in American films that traces the rise and fall of a gangster, either fictitious or based on some well-known person.

People have always been interested in such lives because they allow vicarious thrills—we all wish to unleash hostility or aggression, and we all wish to triumph over the world around us. By associating with such criminal figures, we can feel such power for a brief period, while at the same time our moral sense can be satisfied when these wicked people are punished. Criminal stories are also appropriate for film since they offer a good deal of action, color, and suspense.

Such stories originate even before the time of Robin Hood, and during the spread of literacy they took the form of fictitious accounts or memoirs of actual figures. Criminal activities provoked by prohibition were the subject of a number of successful gangster films during the silent-film era, namely Josef von Sternberg's *Underworld* (1927) and Lewis Milestone's *The Racket* (1928). But the modern gangster film really begins with the advent of sound, specifically with Mervyn LeRoy's *Little Caesar* (1930), William Wellman's *The Public Enemy* (1931), and Howard Hawks's *Scarface* (1932), films which set the pattern for future works with their violence, urban setting, and criminal character types. Public outcry against a somewhat sympathetic and glamorous approach to such figures led to a rash of police enforcement films that simply gave the same leading men guns in the cause of justice; but it also led to far more condemning portraits of gangsters in criminal films such as *Dillinger* (1945; dir. Max Nosseck). A later development was the psychological focus on the criminal in films such as Raoul Walsh's *White Heat* (1949), where James Cagney plays the role of a psychopathic criminal with a severe oedipal complex.

The 1950s, a period that, like the war years, saw events in black and white, offered criminals who were vicious and evil, as in Don Siegel's *Baby Face Nelson* (1957). But resentment against the establishment and traditional cultural values during the next decade led to portrayals of gangsters who were more complex and attractive, who seemed as much sinned against as sinning. A good example of this type of film is Arthur Penn's *Bonnie and Clyde* (1967), a rural gangster film where the urban landscape has been exchanged for the American countryside during the Depression days—Robert Altman's *Thieves Like Us* follows the same track seven years later. A similar complexity and sympathy is evident in the portrayal of gangsters in Francis Ford Coppola's *The Godfather* (1972), but the film also reflects the public's growing resentment against organized crime and large organizations of all kinds. The parallels between the Mafia and big business are drawn frequently and even more emphatically in Coppola's 1974 sequel, *The Godfather, Part II*.

Parts I and II of *The Godfather*, especially because of the skill with which they were made and acted, influenced a number of future films, but still seem unsurpassed. Oliver Stone used the gangster-couple form explosively and satirically in *Natural Born Killers* (1994), but only to attack both the media's and public's fascination with the criminal; while Quentin Tarantino, in both *Reservoir Dogs* (1992) and the highly acclaimed *Pulp Fiction* (1994), created two violent and shrewd films that seemed to celebrate the gangster genre by divorcing it from the world outside the cinema. *See* **genre.**

gangster film Edward G. Robinson as *Little Caesar* (1930; dir. Mervyn LeRoy), the first major sound film of this genre.

■ ■ ■

■ **gang synchronizer** A mechanism with two or more sprocket wheels, employed in film editing to synchronize workprints, originals, and sound tracks. *See* **synchronizer.**

■ **garbage mattes** Animated mattes generally made of black paper and shot on an animation stand. Such mattes are used to block out unwanted areas or objects in picture elements that will go into a composite image. *See* **special effects** *and* **traveling-matte process.**

■ **gate** (1) The part of a camera or projector supporting the pressure plate that holds the film on track behind the lens. The film passes through the gate, stopping while each frame is momentarily exposed or projected. (2) The entire aperture of a camera or projector.

■ **gator grip** *See* **gaffer grip.**

■ **gauge** The width of film measured in millimeters. The standard film measurements are 8, 16, 35, 65, and 70mm. Eight-millimeter film was mostly employed for amateur photography; although less expensive and easier to use, it created a smaller picture, poorer reproduction, and less efficient sound than larger gauges. Super 8 replaced the standard 8mm film. Although both films are the same width, Super 8 allows a wider frame with almost 50 percent more picture area and a better sound track because of its smaller perforations.

In spite of its superior image, Super 8 was largely replaced in the amateur market by videotape cameras, although it is still sometimes used. Old cameras can be purchased, and at least one manufacturer still makes the camera. Sixteen-millimeter film, at first largely used by amateurs, is now being employed by professionals for documentaries, experimental works, educational films, independent fictional films, and television. The growing acceptance of 16mm film by professionals is the result of its improved quality and lower cost as well as the light and efficient camera used for this gauge. It can now be blown up to 35mm for commercial release without great loss in picture quality. A new development is Super 16, which creates a larger frame area on the standard width of 16mm negative film for blowup to a widescreen print on 35mm film—the negative area is 46 percent greater for a 1.85:1 aspect ratio and 40 percent greater for 1.66:1. The standard film width for commercial film production has been 35mm since the days of Edison, though a 65mm negative and 70mm print have sometimes been employed to achieve a better and larger picture in this country (the practice now is to blow up a 35mm original to a 70mm print for special showings of important films). *See* **film** *(1)*.

■ **gay and lesbian cinema** (1) Films about homosexuals or that include homosexuals as part of their drama. (2) Films primarily made for a homosexual audience, frequently by gays and lesbians themselves. Such films, which are often referred to as "queer cinema," have become both more apparent and more numerous as homosexuals have made claim to their place in the sun and to public acceptance. Gay and lesbian film series can now be found at universities, museums, and special theaters. Homosexuality itself was banned from the Hollywood film by the Hays Code from 1934 until the mid-1960s, but we can find numerous examples of homosexual types who were derogatorily treated throughout the history of cinema. Homosexual relationships and feelings were implicit in a wide number of films, even in Westerns such as Nicholas Ray's *Johnny Guitar* (1954) and Edward Dmytryk's *Warlock* (1959), but the issue was always avoided. When the theme does emerge in works such as William Wyler's *The Children's Hour* (1961), the film seems to trip over its own feet in backing away. William Friedkin's film version of Mark Crowley's play *The Boys in the Band* (1970) appears to be the film that opened up the possibilities for the dramatization of homosexual characters and their relationships in cinema, and John Schlesinger's British film, *Sunday, Bloody Sunday* (1971), opened up the dramatization of bisexuality. Gays, of course, continue to be stereotyped (note the rash of films with a funny, extravagant, and wise homosexual adviser to the heterosexual couple), but homosexual life has become a reality in such mainstream films as Jonathan Demme's courtroom drama about AIDS, *Philadelphia* (1993). Gays and lesbians in Hollywood cinema have recently been the subject of the documentary *The Celluloid Closet* (1995; dir. Robert Epstein and Jeffrey Friedman), based on Vito Russo's book of the same name.

Homosexuality had been dealt with more explicitly and graphically in the avant-garde or underground cinema from about 1950 on, especially in the works of Curtis Harrington, Kenneth Anger, Stan Brakhage, Andy Warhol, and Paul Morrissey. In recent years, the underground and feature film have fused in the queer cinema of the British filmmaker Derek Jarman, especially in his *Caravaggio* (1986) and *Edward II* (1991). Also notable in this respect is Gus Van Sant's *My Own Private Idaho* (1991) and Jennie Livingston's documentary about transvestism, *Paris Is Burning* (1990), both of which appealed to general audiences.

■ **G-clamp, C-clamp** A device for clamping lights to any rigging or parts of the set.

■ **geared head, gear head** A mounting for the camera on a tripod, dolly, or crane that allows smooth movements of the camera for panning or tilting by a system of gears and cranks. This system is even smoother and more precise than the fluid head and is extremely effective for heavy studio cameras. *See* **fluid head** *and* **friction head.**

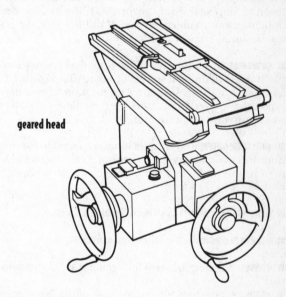

geared head

■ **gel** A colored sheet (usually gelatin) placed in front of a light source as a filter to color the illumination.

■ **gelatin** A protein substance obtained from animals and incorporated in film emulsion as the layer into which the silver halides are placed. Color or light-diffusion filters are also made from gelatin.

■ **gelatin, gelatin filter** A sheet of material (sometimes gelatin) used as a filter to diffuse and decrease the intensity of a light source.

■ **genealogy** (1) The successive stages in film duplication. *See* **generation.** (2) The changing position of the film's emulsion in relation to the screen during projection from generation to generation. For 35mm film, the emulsion of the print faces the light source, while for smaller-gauge reversal film, when the original is made into a positive, the emulsion faces the lens. However, a print made from an original reversal negative has its emulsion facing in the other direction, toward the light source.

■ **General Film Company** *See* **Motion Picture Patents Company.**

■ **general release, general showing** The distribution and exhibition of a film in numerous theaters throughout the country. The term "wide release" is used when the theaters number more than five hundred. *See* **exhibition, first run, multiple run,** *and* **wide release.**

■ **generation** The stage in film duplication. The original negative is first generation; the print is second; a negative made from this print is third. Sometimes separate generations are distinguished for negatives and positives. Generations are also specified for "dupes": for example, "first generation dupe" refers to either the first duplicate from an original film or the first dupe negative. With each stage of duplication, the image becomes grainier and less defined.

■ **generator** A motor-driven machine that creates electricity as an additional source of energy for lighting in a studio or as the major source on location where there is no other power. Generators are now silent enough to run in proximity to a shooting area.

■ **generator operator** The individual responsible for running and maintaining the generator, both the machine used in the studio and the portable one used on location.

■ **Genesis film scanner** *See* **Cineon digital film system.**

■ **Geneva movement** *See* **Maltese cross movement.**

■ **genny** A colloquial term for "generator." *See* **generator.**

■ **genre** A group of films having recognizably similar plots, character types, settings, filmic techniques, and themes. Such conventions are repeated sufficiently from film to film to make it obvious that all these works belong to a single group and that the filmmaker is relying upon the past use of these conventions and the audience's familiarity with them. The simple repetition of generic convention creates films that are dull and clichéd. The creative filmmaker relies upon conventions but also infuses his or her own vision into the work. It is the infusion of the innovative within the familiar that invokes the special pleasure we feel from a genre film. At the same time, genre films alter and develop as the culture changes, reflecting shifts in attitudes—films generically similar can still show the different attitudes of a particular era to traditional character types and values. The primary question, though, is why audiences respond so strongly to the repetition of generic film conventions. There is a great satisfaction in finding one's self in a familiar filmic world, in knowing the kinds of people and action one will confront. We go to a genre film because we already know the kind of emotional experience to be enjoyed. More significantly, genre films often evoke some aspect of our cultural heritage by presenting mythic patterns of character and action endemic to our country's history, patterns that embody the nation's moral values and moral conflicts. We can also say that genre films are popular because they repeatedly deal with universal dilemmas and appeal to universal psychic needs (note the appropriation of the American Western by Italian filmmakers). But it must be emphasized that the talented filmmaker by his or her innovative use of these conventions makes us confront the old and familiar, with all that they imply, in a new way—that the filmmaker makes us confront the traditional and universal with extended and even new responses. For financial reasons, studios have been anxious to make motion pictures that appeal to the widest audiences and, to do so, they have depended on formulas that have already been found to be successful. At the same time, the film industry, in following public tastes, has perpetuated these tastes.

In America, the most popular and discernible film genres have been the gangster, detective, war, and horror film, as well as the musical and Western (some would consider comedy as another genre, though it is composed of many disparate types). All of these films began during the days of silent films, except for the musical, which had to wait for sound. All of them have reflected, on some level, national concerns and values, and all have appealed to universal conflicts and psychological needs. The American film industry has changed, the old hard-and-fast mass audience is gone and with it the old studios that readily produced these formula films. As a result, the genre films are less apparent. But some of them still persist, especially the horror film, though it is now more violent and tasteless. The detective film has been updated because of the influence of the James Bond films. Gangster films appear on occasion, though often with a fine veneer as a result of the *Godfather* films or simply as an homage to the genre itself, as in the films of Quentin Tarantino. The musical is under relapse because of high costs and, after three decades, has still not recovered from such financially disastrous products as *Camelot* (1967; dir. Joshua Logan), though a great talent like Bob Fosse could still produce movies such as *Cabaret* (1972) or *All That Jazz* (1979). War films depend on international events and the national mood, which means that they remain popular with some consistency. After refighting and winning the Vietnamese war in a series of films dealing with missing prisoners of war, America has also gone through a period of contrition with Oliver Stone's *Platoon* (1986). Perhaps the Western, of all the genres, seems to be a victim of overexposure, but occasionally a film such as Walter Hill's *The Long Riders* (1980) or Clint Eastwood's *Unforgiven* (1992) comes along and shows that we can still respond to the traditional if it is presented with intelligence and cinematic skill.

Genre films also have undergone mutation and fusion. War films often come in the guise of science fiction or even post–James Bond detective films; the horror film sometimes has put its monster in the outer-space trappings of a science-fiction film or, by focusing on violence, revulsion, and pathology, has slipped into the shell of the gangster or criminal film; and, with rock music blaring in the background as the film's intrusive score, many comedies sound more like musicals than dramas. Discussions of various film genres appear under their appropriate headings.

■ **George Eastman House** A film museum and library in Rochester, New York, supported by the Eastman Kodak Company. This institution has an excellent collection of films, photographs, and motion-picture equipment.

■ **German expressionism** *See* **expressionism.**

■ **ghost image** A see-through image achieved through a double exposure, a superimposed printing of one image over another, or the reflection of an off-stage subject onto the primary scene by means of a two-way mirror placed before the camera. This device was commonly used in the 1940s to create the image of a spirit or a ghost, especially in comic films.

■ **ghosting** (1) Creating a ghostlike image by any of the means outlined under **ghost image.** (2) In musicals, the practice of dubbing in someone else's singing voice for a performer. The term comes from the fact that the dubbing itself as well as the singer's name is frequently undisclosed. Recordings of sound tracks became a lucrative business in the early 1950s and made this practice more difficult.

■ **gimbal** In motion-picture production, a large rig that permits entire rooms to rotate. The camera and operator are fastened down so that they move with the room, while characters and objects, by the force of gravity and sometimes with the help of wires, move across walls and ceilings. This device was used in *Royal Wedding* (1951; dir. Stanley Donen) to allow Fred Astaire to dance across the walls and ceiling of his hotel room.

■ **gimbal head, gimbal mount, gimbal head tripod, gimbal tripod** An older camera support or tripod head that allows smooth horizontal movements of the camera by means of a mobile mounting and a heavy stabilizing weight suspended between the legs of the tripod. A gimbal head tripod allows shots to be taken from slowly moving objects and is especially employed on ships. This equipment has largely been replaced by lighter and more convenient stabilizing systems.

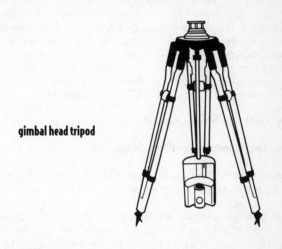

gimbal head tripod

■ **glass filter** A neutral or colored camera filter made entirely of glass or of two pieces of glass with a piece of gelatin between.

■ **glass shot** (1) A special-effects shot in which a scene in front of the camera is extended or changed by shooting through a sheet of glass on which is painted the portion of the scene to be added to the image. Photographs can be placed on the glass instead of a painting. The technique seems to have been instituted for motion pictures by Norman O. Dawn in his short film *Missing in California*, made in 1907. This technique, especially popular in the 1920s and 1930s, was notably used in Cooper and Schoedsack's *King Kong* (1933), where the miniature shots were often photographed through a series of glass sheets, which added the exotic backgrounds and created a sense of depth. Glass shots permit only a portion of a building to be constructed

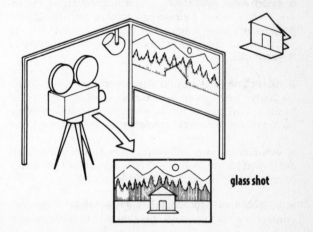

glass shot

on the set, since the remainder can be added from the painting on the glass. The technique is also practical for adding ceilings to rooms and supplying natural backgrounds and clouds. The glass shot was economical and effective. The camera could pan and tilt, although it had to remain in one place and the characters were limited in movement. Today this type of glass shot is still employed, though it is frequently more economical to use other methods. (2) A process for matting together scenery painted on a sheet of glass with another picture element such as live action (a technique used frequently in Steven Spielberg's *Close Encounters of the Third Kind* [1977]). *See* **composite**.

■ **globe** The bulb used in a lighting fixture.

■ **gloving sound** *See* **velveting sound**.

■ **glow light** Illumination for silhouetting or outlining the edge of a character or portion of the set.

■ **gobo** An opaque or black sheet, perhaps cloth on a frame, wood, or Masonite, generally held by an adjustable extension stand and positioned in front of a lamp so that it blocks the light from either the lens of the camera or a portion of the set. The gobo can be cut in patterns to form various shapes of shadow on the set or to add contrast to a background. It can also be employed to hide a light source on the set itself. Small rectangular goboes are also referred to as flags; long, narrow ones as cutters; and round ones as dots or targets.

■ **gobo stand, century stand, C stand** A stand for supporting a gobo or a similar flag that blocks or controls illumination. Such stands have three divergently placed legs so that several can be placed together.

■ **gofer, gopher** A person who does errands and menial tasks during production; someone who "goes for" things.

■ **golden frame, golden ratio** The 4:3 standard aspect ratio of films before wide-screen motion pictures. These dimensions were supposedly derived from the common ratio of width to height in Renaissance painting. *See* **aspect ratio**.

■ **golden time** The period after overtime, generally after twelve to fourteen hours of work, that, because of location and contractual agreement, pays at least double time and sometimes more for the production crew.

■ **Goldwynism** The unintentionally funny statements attributed to the Hollywood film mogul and producer Samuel Goldwyn, such as "Include me out."

■ **go-motion, go-motion animation, go-animation** A motion-control system for animation that allows both camera and models to move during stop-motion photography. Not only is the movement of both programmed and electronically controlled for numerous and exactly repeatable passes, but the models photographed in motion create a blur more natural to the eye than the strobic motion of figures in earlier animation films which were photographed motionless for each frame. This special-effects technique was first used for *Dragonslayer* (1981; dir. Matthew Robbins) and employed with great success in George Lucas's production *Return of the Jedi* (1983; dir. Richard Marquand). *See* **motion control**.

■ **good playing time** A release time for a film when large numbers of people go to the movies and profits are high. The holiday season between Christmas and New Year as well as the summer months are highly desired release times, especially since young people are off from school.

■ **goon stand** A large century stand for holding goboes or similar devices for cutting the intensity of light or for creating shadows. *See* **century stand**.

■ **gooseneck** A flexible tube that attaches to a stand or support by means of a clamp and holds a gobo before a luminaire to break up or diffuse the illumination. Such attachments are now largely replaced by flex arms. *See* **flex arm**.

■ **gothic film** (1) A film that follows the conventions of a gothic novel: that is, a film with a spooky setting, such as an old mansion or castle; mysterious events; a powerful, demonic protagonist; a chaste and threatened heroine; and sometimes elements of the supernatural. Although without any supernatural events, Hitchcock's *Rebecca* (1940) is a good example of a gothic film while Tod Browning's *Dracula* (1931) is an example of such a film that employs the supernatural. (2) An elegant term for a horror film. *See* **horror film**.

■ **Gouraud shading** *See* **shading**.

■ **governor-controlled motor, governor motor, constant-speed motor** A camera motor that runs at a single speed, normally 24 frames per second. Such motors run with sufficient constancy to allow synchronized recording of picture and sound by means of a cable which sends a reference signal from the camera to sound tape. These motors have been largely replaced by crystal motors, which do not require connecting cables. *See* **crystal motor, synchronous motor**, *and* **wild motor**.

■ **grad** A graduated filter.

■ **gradation** (1) The scale of densities or tones in a film image. (2) The extent to which a film emulsion is capable of change in an image's density or tone.

■ **grader** *See* **timer**.

■ **grading** *See* **timing.**

■ **graduated diffuser** *See* **graduated filter.**

■ **graduated filter** A filter that is clear in one area and gradually becomes denser or a single color in the remaining area. Neutral-density filters darken part of the scene, while color filters gradually change the tone or hue of an area (for example, a filter with a blue area increases the bluish quality of a sky or makes a white sky blue). Graduated diffusers are filters of this type that give a sense of distance to a portion of the scene when shooting miniatures (a technique, for example, used with great effect in Ridley Scott's *Blade Runner* [1982]).

■ **grain** The small particles of silver halide in a film's emulsion that, when exposed to light and developed, turn to metallic silver and form the image. Such grains are microscopic, but since they are unevenly distributed in gelatin and occasionally clump together, they create different densities and sometimes an appearance of graininess in the image. In the 1980s, Eastman developed a T-grain (tabular-grain) emulsion with flatter silver halide crystals that allows for a faster film with a smaller number of crystals while gathering light more efficiently and reducing its scatter. Its new Kodak Vision Color Negative Film features thinner T-grains with a new chemical structure to achieve sharper pictures with less light scattering.

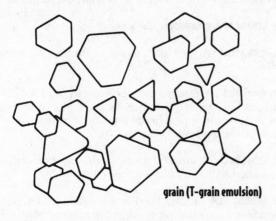

grain (T-grain emulsion)

■ **graininess** Perceptible particles in a film image caused by the clumping together of the individual silver grains in the emulsion that create the image (*see* **film**). Such clumping may be visible in high-contrast images because of overdevelopment or may be the result of a later generation of print duplication. Smaller gauges of film tend to be grainier than larger ones. Sometimes filmmakers seek to achieve a grainy quality in their image, generally to create a sense of time past or a documentary effect by imitating the texture of old newsreels. A good example of this last technique is in Gillo Pontecorvo's *The Battle of Algiers* (1965).

■ **granularity** The physical quality of an image as created by the silver granules or grains in the emulsion. Granularity is measured by a microdensitometer and considered an objective assessment of a film's graininess. High granularity means that the film stock has large grains and is therefore high-speed and very sensitive to light, as in the case of original film for shooting. Positives tend to have small granules and so are considered to have low granularity. *See* **RMS granularity.**

■ **graphic equalizer** *See* **equalizer.**

■ **graphics generator** A computer system with a good deal of storage space and special software for the creation of high-quality graphics. Such systems allow the creation of two-dimensional and three-dimensional graphics as well as the use of painting programs sometimes called a paint box.

■ **G-rated** A designation for a film that is suitable for a general audience without any restriction according to age. This is one of several ratings devised by the Motion Picture Association of America in the 1960s to replace the old Motion Picture Code. G-rated films at first made up the majority of motion pictures but are now surpassed in numbers by R-rated films, which are forbidden to anyone seventeen or younger without an accompanying adult. *See* **Movie Production Code** *and* **Movie Rating System.**

■ **graticule, graticule lines** The lines engraved on the glass of a viewfinder to form the frame of the image that the lens will accept and that will later be projected on the screen.

■ **gray base** The base of a film that has been dyed gray to minimize halation and light piping (i.e., light reflected back from the base around the image). Unlike other kinds of antihalation backing, the gray base is a permanent part of the film and need not be removed in processing. *See* **halation** *and* **light piping.**

■ **gray card, standard gray card** A card, normally eight inches by ten inches, with one side gray and the other white, which is used on occasion to read light coming from a subject with a reflected light meter. The gray side has a reflectance value of about 18 percent, which is supposed to represent an average tone. In dim light, the white side, which has a reflectance value of 90 percent, can be used, thus necessitating that the exposure indicated on the meter be increased five times. A gray card is sometimes useful for balancing studio lights or for close-ups.

■ **gray scale** A chart with gradations of gray from white to black used sometimes with a gray card and exposure meter to prepare for shooting a scene and also by a laboratory especially for establishing contrast in printing a film.

■ **grease-glass technique** The placement of some type of jelly on a lens to blur a scene.

■ **grease paint** Makeup for actors and actresses.

■ **green, greenbed, bed, deck** A wooden scaffold hung from the top of a sound stage over a set and to which luminaires are attached. Such decks normally have holes along each edge into which studs may be placed for the support of lights.

■ **green department, greenshandler, green men, greensmen** The personnel in film production responsible for both real and artificial greenery, such as foliage, trees, shrubs, and flowers.

■ **green film, green print** Recently processed film that is difficult to use in the projector because it has not completely hardened or dried. A special wax makes the film move more easily through the projector.

■ **grid** A pipe or several pipes fastened together and horizontally suspended from the ceiling above the set to function as a support for lights or pieces of scenery.

■ **grip** (1) A stagehand responsible for an assortment of jobs on the set. He or she may transport and set up equipment, props, and scenery; lay dolly tracks; and push the dolly during shooting. A grip does an assortment of hard jobs and must have a "firm grip" while carrying objects or pushing the dolly. The chief grip is called the key, first, or head grip. (2) A device for mounting cameras or lights; a grip stand.

■ **grip chain** A lightweight chain used by the grip for an assortment of jobs including fastening down pieces of scenery.

■ **grip truck** A small truck employed by grips to transport equipment or props.

■ **gross, gross receipts, gross profits, box office receipts** The full amount of money earned by a film's theatrical exhibition before expenses have been deducted. *See* **net profits.** The first three terms are now also used to refer to the total income for a film from all sources—theatrical distribution, television, video, etc.

■ **gross deal, gross participation, gross profit participation** *See* **gross profit participant.**

■ **gross profit participant** Any participant in the making of a film (e.g., a star, producer, or director) who is contracted to receive either a flat sum or percentage based on the film's gross proceeds before deduction for distribution, production, and prints. Independent producers will sometimes make a "gross deal" with a distributor whereby the producer receives a percentage of each dollar earned by the film. *See* **net profit participant.**

■ **gross rental, gross rentals** (1) A percentage of money to be paid to the distributor from the film's box office. The remainder of the money is kept by the exhibitor. (2) The total amount of money received by a film at the box office for its theatrical distribution as distinct from the gross receipts that represent moneys earned by a film from all sources—theatrical, television, video, etc. Also referred to as box office receipts. *See* **distribution** *and* **exhibitor.**

■ **ground glass viewfinder** A viewfinder, attached to or part of a camera, which uses a screen with one side ground and rough for displaying the image. The ground glass screen is either the same size as the lens or larger, with the frame area engraved upon it. An optical system magnifies the image so that the operator can see it clearly.

■ **ground noise, surface noise** The residual noise on a sound track heard when there is no talking or sound in the film. Such noise is generally the result of dirt, scratches, or particles of emulsion.

■ **ground-noise reduction** The process of reducing the ground noise, heard from the sound track during quiet parts of a film, by reducing light from the sound bulb.

■ **ground row, groundrow** *See* **cove.**

■ **group shot** A shot that contains a number of characters.

■ **guest star** A famous film personality who makes a special but brief appearance during a film, frequently to increase the appeal of the film and sometimes to add humor. *See* **cameo role.**

■ **guide track** A sound track made during shooting and intended only as a guide for later dubbing.

■ **guiding shot** A term used by Eisenstein to describe a dominant shot during a sequence around which the other shots cohere. The guiding shot helps pattern the arrangement of shots either through its repetition or by beginning or concluding the sequence.

■ **guild** One of the professional organizations for the various crafts or skills that go into the making of a motion picture. The Academy of Motion Picture Arts and Sciences is the major organization for many people who work in the industry, but the term "guild" is more normally associated with organizations representing specific occupations, for example, the Directors Guild of America or the Motion Picture Editors Guild.

■ **guillotine splicer**   *See* **splicer.**

■ **gun mike**   *See* **rifle mike.**

■ **gyro head, gyroscopic head**   An older type of camera mount, often on a tripod, with a gyroscopic device operated through a geared system to allow steady movement of the camera. The fast, smooth, and steady rotation of the flywheel in the gyroscope provides resistance to any uneven motion. *See* **head** *(3).*

■ **gyro-stabilized camera system, gyro-stabilized cinematography**   A gyroscope-based camera system that is employed to produce a stabilized frame for fast-moving or difficult shots when the camera may be attached, for example, to a helicopter, boat, or moving vehicle. SpaceCam is a much-used system of this type and was awarded a plaque for its Scientific and Engineering Achievement by the Academy of Motion Picture Arts and Sciences in 1995. Such a system allows the camera to record the horizon absolutely level as the aircraft moves forward; to take precise shots as the aircraft speeds, spins, or banks; to pan or tilt up to 120 degrees per second; or to be bracketed to the nose, side, or tail of an aircraft. As well as achieving such effects in aerial cinematography, the system can be attached to a cable or crane and operated remotely in order to achieve difficult shots in hard-to-reach places. SpaceCam's movements can now be programmed for the creation of precise background plates, which can be composited with special-effects shots and live action.

■ ■ ■

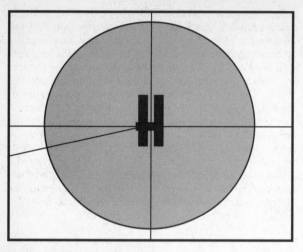

hair light to hypo

■ **hair light, hairlight** *See* **back light.**

■ **hair stylist, hairdresser** The individual who takes care of the hair of both female and male performers, setting and combing before shooting and touching up during breaks.

■ **halation** An undesired illumination around the subject of an image, normally in the form of a halo. This illumination is caused by light passing through the emulsion and reflecting off the film base. It is avoided by an antihalation backing or dye in the film base.

■ **half-apple** A box, half the height of an apple box, that elevates a performer or object to a desired position for a shot.

■ **half broad** A floodlight of one thousand watts, half the power of a full broad, used for general illumination. *See* **broad.**

■ **half-load** *See* **quarter-load.**

■ **half scrim** A circular frame half covered with wire mesh and generally used to diffuse part of the light falling on a specific area from a luminaire or all of the light falling on an area from a camera set at an angle.

■ **halftones** The tones in an image between highlight and shadow.

■ **halide** The chemical compound in film emulsion that is composed of silver and halogen. Silver halides, such as chloride, bromide, iodide, or fluoride, form a latent image in the emulsion when exposed to light. During processing the silver halides are turned to black

silver particles, which form the image, and later the unexposed halides are washed away. *See* **film** *(1)*.

■ **halogen** The nonmetallic elements chlorine, fluorine, bromine, and iodine that are combined with silver particles to form the halides in film emulsion. *See* **film** *(1)*.

■ **halogen lamp** *See* **tungsten-halogen bulb.**

■ **Hammer Film Productions** A British film company that was founded in 1948 as the production unit of Exclusive Films and named after Will Hammer, head of Exclusive. In its early years, Hammer studios produced a lackluster series of second features, but with the success of *The Quartermass Experiment (The Creeping Unknown* in the United States; 1955; dir. Val Guest), the company turned largely to making horror films. *The Curse of Frankenstein* (1957) was successful in both England and America, and *Dracula (The Horror of Dracula* in the United States; 1958) was an even greater box-office hit. Hammer Studios continued to make an onslaught of horror films, resetting many of the earlier American films of the genre in a pseudo-Victorian world and featuring in these works vivid color, female breasts, and a good deal of blood. The original Frankenstein and Dracula films were also a source of numerous sequels. Terence Fisher, who directed these two prototype films, was one of Hammer's notable directors, and Peter Cushing and Christopher Lee the studio's most popular actors. Of the more than one hundred films that Hammer Studios made during the late 1950s and the 1960s, several have become classics of the horror genre, especially the first Dracula film and Joseph Losey's black-and-white film *The Damned* (1961). Most of Hammer's films created a particular style and manner, a controlled exploitation of sex and violence, and a vivacious cartoonlike color that gave new energy to the horror genre. *See* **horror film.**

■ **hand camera, handheld camera** A small, portable camera, capable of being held by hand during shooting. Such cameras are now employed professionally for a variety of film gauges, from Panavision's Panaflex System-65 Hand-Holdable reflex camera to the 16mm Eclair ACL, which weighs less than eight pounds.

■ **hand-cranked camera** A camera operated by the manual turning of a crank. Such cameras were used in the early days of motion pictures.

■ **hand cue** A direction given to an actor in the form of a hand gesture by the director.

■ **H and D curve** *See* **characteristic curve.**

■ **hand-drawn traveling matte** A series of mattes made by rotoscoping a single frame at a time on an easel, blackening out a desired area, and photographing the silhouettes consecutively on a piece of high-contrast film from which the traveling matte and counter matte can be made. The mattes can be used in bipack printing to combine elements from two separate positives on a negative to form a composite image. The technique has effectively been used on occasion to matte falling objects, which are actually animated drawings, into a scene of live action. *See* **rotoscope** *and* **traveling-matte process.**

■ **handheld, handheld shot** A shot taken with an unmounted, portable camera held by the cameraman, sometimes with the help of a body brace, while he moves about. Such shots are necessary in documentary work and news reporting for television when it is impossible to set up a stationary camera and spontaneity and unplanned movement are desired. Handheld shots, without a support such as the Steadicam, create a discernible bouncing and wavering movement that sometimes is desired in a feature film to create a realistic or documentary effect, to communicate the excitement and motion of a crowd or fight scene, or simply to convey the point of view of a moving character. John Cassavetes made his film *Faces* (1968) with numerous handheld shots to communicate an immediacy and a sense of an intruding camera in an apparently real-life and unplanned domestic drama.

■ **handholding support** A support for a handheld camera that gives the operator some assistance and control when shooting and allows the camera a degree of balance.

■ **handlebar mount** A mount with two handles in the front, one for each hand, that allows the cameraman to control movement of the camera.

■ **handmade film** *See* **noncamera film.**

■ **hand model** An individual whose hands alone are photographed.

■ **hand props, hand properties** Small items such as pens, drinking glasses, and books used by performers during shooting.

■ **hands-on animation** The combining of animated figures, originally drawn by hand, and live action in a composite image. The animated figures, from cels photographed separately in an animation stand, are matted into the live action. The technique was effectively used for Gene Kelly's dance with Jerry Mouse in *Anchors Away* (1945; dir. George Sidney). *See* **animation.**

■ **hand test** *See* **slop test.**

■ **hanger** An adjustable mounting device that attaches to a grid or beam for supporting a luminaire. Some

hangers are available for supporting two or three luminaires. A hanger adapter allows the attachment of a double- or triple-head hanger to a C-clamp, which itself attaches to the overhead pipe.

■ **hanging miniature shot** A shot that joins a model suspended in front of the camera to a partially completed set—for example, a miniature of the top part of a building may be joined to the bottom of the structure actually built in full scale on the set so that the entire building appears in the film image. Such a technique saves a good deal of money and time. The shot is easier to light than a glass shot, though scale and perspective must be carefully worked out. The technique was employed for the fantasy world in Alexander Korda's production *The Thief of Bagdad* (1940; dir. Michael Powell). *See* **glass shot.**

■ **hard** (1) Extreme contrast in the image. (2) Lighting that creates sharply defined objects and shadows with a high degree of contrast as opposed to soft lighting.

■ **hard-edged matte** A matte with the lines sharp and clearly delineated as opposed to those on a soft-edged matte. Hard-edged mattes require perfect registration to block out areas and allow the flawless joining of different picture elements to make a composite image. *See* **matte** *(2).*

■ **hard-edge wipe** A wipe in which a sharply defined line separates the images. In a soft-edge wipe the border between the images is blurred. *See* **wipe.**

■ **harden** To make a lens's focus as sharp as possible.

■ **hardener** A chemical, such as potassium alum, in the fixing solution, which hardens the gelatin in the film emulsion. A hardener may also be employed in an early stage of the processing of reversal film because of the high temperatures that might otherwise soften the gelatin.

■ **hard-front camera** A camera with a single mount for a lens rather than a turret which holds three or four lenses. Early studio cameras allowed only one lens at a time, and special cameras today have a single lens; but most professional cameras employ turret mounts.

■ **hard light** A narrow-beamed light, generally from a spotlight, that produces strong illumination and sharp outlines. *See* **soft light.**

■ **hard ticket, hard-ticket roadshow attraction** A showing of a major first-run feature with reserved tickets at special prices. Expensive films such as David Lean's *Lawrence of Arabia* (1962) and Joseph L. Mankiewicz's *Cleopatra* (1963) were shown this way in major cities from the mid 1950s until the late 1960s. *See* **road show.**

■ **hardware** Permanent equipment such as computers (which use software such as data and programs) and projectors, video players, and television sets (which use software such as motion pictures). The equipment that creates the motion pictures (e.g., cameras and lighting) is also sometimes referred to as hardware.

■ **Hays Code** *See* **Hays Office** *and* **Motion Picture Production Code.**

■ **Hays Office** Popular designation for the Motion Picture Producers and Distributors of America (later the Motion Picture Association of America), derived from the name of its president, Will H. Hays. The MPPDA was formed in 1922 by the film industry in response to public indignation over apparent sex scandals in Hollywood (especially the Fatty Arbuckle affair, which involved the death of a young actress during a party). Hays had been Warren Harding's campaign manager and the postmaster general during Harding's presidency. He had considerable political influence and a strong moral reputation. His job, and the organization's, was mainly to prevent censorship by state and federal governments. Hays and the MPPDA did so by applying pressure on the studios to control the sexual contents of films and the private lives of their stars. Hays also worked actively to give the industry a good press. The organization encouraged producers to allow it to review summaries of screenplays and completed films. The MPPDA also performed important business matters such as instituting standard contracts and organizing the Central Casting Bureau. It was not until 1930 that renewed public pressure forced the MPPDA to draw up the Motion Picture Production Code as a guideline for the content of motion pictures; the code became mandatory in 1934. Hays served as president of the organization from 1922 to 1945. *See* **censorship, Motion Picture Producers and Distributors of America,** *and* **Motion Picture Production Code.**

■ **haze filter, ultraviolet filter, UV filter** A filter that absorbs ultraviolet rays and penetrates haze.

■ **haze lens** A lens made for shooting in soft focus either through gauze or through a jelly applied to its surface.

■ **Hazeltine** A color video analyzer, named after its manufacturer, that projects a positive image onto a screen from a negative to allow the timer to make adjustments in density and color for printing. *See* **timing** *and* **video color analyzer.**

■ **HDTV** The initials stand for high definition television and refer to the newly developing digital television systems that give a far superior image than that now available on American sets. The better image will be a result of the greater number of lines per frame—at first suggested to be 1125 lines but now probably to be 1080 in this country, more than twice the number of lines

per frame in present television sets—but also because the digital system will prevent any deterioration in image or sound during transmission or playback. Such images will also have a wider aspect ratio to create widescreen images (probably 1.78:1 instead of the present 1.33:1). *See* **digital, DSS (1), NTSC, PAL,** *and* **SECAM.**

■ **head** (1) The beginning of a film, scene, or shot. (2) The beginning of a reel of film or tape. (3) A device placed on a tripod, dolly, crane, or any kind of mounting that allows the camera free and smooth movement for panning and tilting. Friction heads operate through the easy rubbing of two metal plates; geared heads through a system of gears and cranks; and fluid heads by means of a liquid forced between moving parts. Gimbal heads permit smooth horizontal movement of the camera on a slow vehicle such as a ship by means of a movable mounting and stabilizing weight hanging between the legs of a tripod. Camera heads can be operated either by manual movement of the camera or by remote control. (4) The optical sound head in the projector that changes the variable areas of light and dark or the variable density of light recorded on the film into electrical impulses for sound reproduction. (5) In a magnetic tape recorder, the recording head that creates the magnetic field, the playback head that converts the variations in magnetic structure on the tape back into electrical impulses, and the erase head that removes the magnetic structure from the tape. *See* **magnetic recording.**

■ **head leader** The strip of film at the beginning of a reel that tells the projectionist the duration from the start of the projector until the first frame of the motion picture appearing on the screen. *See* **leader.**

■ **head of production** The senior executive in a studio responsible for selecting films to be sponsored and distributed by his company. This individual generally needs approval for such decisions from other executives in his organization.

■ **head-on, tail-away shot** A shot of a subject moving head on toward the camera until completely blocking out the frame, followed by the subject or some other character or object moving away from the camera and coming into focus. The technique is sometimes used to mark a change in time or place. It has often been used in comedy to emphasize a character's change in apparel as he or she moves toward the camera in one dress and away in another. *See* **natural wipe.**

■ **head-on shot** A shot that shows some kind of action, for example, the movement of an automobile or character coming directly at the camera.

■ **headroom, head room** (1) The space between the top of a subject and the top frame line in a shot. (2) The acceptable amplitude in sound for a magnetic tape before some type of distortion commences.

■ **head shot** A shot in which the frame is largely taken up with the head of the performer. *See* **close-up.**

■ **head slate** The slate that is photographed at the start of the take and marks the identifying details of the shot. The camera assistant reads off the important details and bangs the boards together at the top of the slate for synchronizing sound and picture later during editing. *See* **clapboard** *and* **tail slate.**

■ **heads-up, head-up, heads-out, head-out** A reel of film wound so that the first frame of the motion picture to be projected is on the outside of the reel. *See* **rail-out.**

■ **heater barney** An electrically heated padding for the camera that keeps the instrument warm and operable when shooting outdoors in extremely cold weather. *See* **barney.**

■ **heat filter, heat-absorbing filter** A filter in a projector that reduces heat striking the film from the projector lamp.

■ **heavy** The villain in a film, so named because the role was generally played by a heavy performer in early films. Such characters are immoral and sadistic figures, who seem as much motivated by an instinctual need to do bad as by a desire for personal gain. Often recognizable types by their dark and sinister appearance, such figures contrast with the handsome or personally attractive leading man. Some notable heavies have been Laird Cregar, Jack Palance, and Lee Van Cleef. The heavy, a descendant of the villain in stage melodrama, makes it easy for the audience to understand the moral issues in a film and identify with the hero. Sometimes in gangster films there is an interesting reversal when the lead criminal is portrayed attractively and some subsidiary figure takes on the role of the heavy to increase our appreciation of the main figure (e.g., in William Wellman's *The Public Enemy* [1931] and Arthur Penn's *Bonnie and Clyde* [1967]). In Martin Scorsese's *Taxi Driver* (1976), the heavy and hero merge into a single figure, a modern complex antihero played by Robert De Niro.

■ **heel** The rear bottom extremity on a film magazine, opposite to the toe.

■ **helicopter cinematography** Shots for a film taken from an airborne helicopter. Sophisticated mounts now make possible steady aerial views, which have increased the spatial perimeter of the screen. Panoramic shots of locations, battle scenes, racing vehicles, or animals can be recorded with breathtaking movement and realism.

■ **helicopter mount** A special mount for supporting a camera in a helicopter that minimizes vibration and unsteady movement of the camera. *See* **gyro-stabilized camera system.**

■ **helmer** Jargon for the person who guides the film and, figuratively, "handles the helm" of the ship. This person is most often the director, but in certain instances may be the producer.

■ **herder** Jargon for the second assistant director who must "herd" and control the extras in a film production.

■ **hero** The major male character in a novel, play, or film with whom the reader or audience sympathizes and identifies. This figure is also called the protagonist. Heroes differ according to the various nations and cultures that give birth to them, and one can also trace alterations in such figures over a span of years in any given society to account for changing attitudes and taste. Early silent films in this country were rooted in the popular melodrama of the stage, and their drama evolved around a simple conflict between the good hero and bad villain. The handsome, virtuous hero—from roles played by silent film actors such as the young Francis X. Bushman to those played by contemporary performers such as Robert Redford—has been a mainstay in American film since the cinema has become a popular art form, appealing to the fantasies and wish fulfillments of both men and women. But, at the same time, the darker and more aggressive side of our personalities has been portrayed by heroes who are less moral, and frequently less handsome, but are heroic in their struggle with society and conformity. This line can be drawn from roles played by silent film actors such as Erich von Stroheim to those acted by contemporary performers such as Robert De Niro. Certainly one must also include in this group the complex, violent, and yet sympathetic heroes of the gangster film and the isolated but powerful protagonists of the Western—both of these types, in their own maverick and independent ways, are embodiments of what America has considered "heroic" qualities. There is a line, however, beyond which one cannot pass, and a figure who seems dominantly evil or dedicated to wrongdoing, as attractive as he may be, cannot be considered a hero since the word must always denote a person we admire for heroic or, at least, admirable qualities, and who acts as some sort of ideal for us.

American films have also had a tendency to heroicize the simple, decent person, a character admirable because he possesses all the down-home virtues that the nation has traditionally glorified. Sound helped develop this strain, since such personal qualities could be further developed through a performer's mannerisms of speech (note, for example, the hesitating and homey voices of James Stewart and Gary Cooper). In later times, heroes became more like us—a little less charming, a little less tall, and more confused and complex—although they still manifested a strong sensitivity and independence (e.g., Dustin Hoffman and Al Pacino). If one were finally to draw a composite figure of the hero in American film up until recent years, he would be a person of striking and attractive, though not necessarily handsome, looks, of distinct and appealing mannerisms and voice, and of independence, will, and personal strength. He would be a loner, yet one who found it easy to draw supporters, an individual who responded to the corruption and evils of society with his own integrity and his refusal to "go along." If he finally were to fit into society, it would be because society had adjusted to him, not that he had adjusted to society. In more recent years, with the dying-off and aging of these actors and with the prominence of the high-concept film, movie heroes have been flattened to comic-book proportions, ranging from the boyish charm and athleticism of Tom Cruise and Keanu Reeves to the power and heroics of Arnold Scwarzenegger, Sylvester Stallone, and Bruce Willis. See **antihero.**

■ **heroine** The major female role in a novel, play, or film, generally a young woman of admirable character with whom the reader or audience sympathizes or identifies. The heroines of films, like the heroes, vary according to culture and periods. In American films, heroines seem too easily categorizable, perhaps because the industry has catered to a male culture and shown females largely in the guise of masculine fantasy, which even female viewers have readily accepted. Heroines in American films for many years were of two dominant types. The first was the moral and virginal figure, whose roots can be found in Victorian melodrama and who continued, through silent and sound films, to satisfy our culture's restrictive attitudes concerning female sexuality. These women, played by silent-film actresses such as the fragile Lillian Gish and girlish Mary Pickford, and by numerous sound-film actresses such as Ingrid Bergman and Audrey Hepburn, have embodied all the fresh, wholesome, and decent virtues our society has admired, while, at the same time, projecting an appealing and vulnerable attractiveness. Playing against this type, especially in the sound films from the 1930s through the 1950s, has been the more independent, aggressive, and even masculine type of heroine performed by actresses such as Joan Crawford and Barbara Stanwyck. Also sexually alluring and frequently suggesting less chaste backgrounds, these figures seem to have incorporated into themselves the individuality and power admired by their male culture.

Heroines in recent years have shown the benefits of our culture's maturation and the feminist movement. No less moral, they have certainly become less repressed and cloyingly virtuous. No less beautiful, their appearance and mannerisms have become less stereotyped and more individual. Actresses such as Jane Fonda, Sigourney Weaver, and, more recently, Michelle Pfeiffer, seem to play roles that combine the traditions

of the virginal innocent and the powerful lady without the artificiality of the first and masculinity of the second.

■ **hertz (Hz)** The measurement for cycles per second in sound frequency. A kilohertz (kHz) equals 1,000 hertz.

■ **hi-con** (1) The black-and-white image made on high-contrast film that is used in special-effects matting and titles to block out light from reaching the negative. (2) The high-contrast film stock used for such special effects as matting and titling.

■ **Hi8** See **videotape.**

■ **high-angle shot, high shot, down shot** A shot taken from above the subject, when the camera looks down at whatever is being photographed. The camera may seem to be anywhere from a few feet above (perhaps to show characters in a struggle from a top-view close-up) to several hundred feet above (perhaps a "bird's-eye view" to show the confusion of a battle or give an overall view of a landscape or location). High-angle shots reduce the height and appearance of characters and seem to reduce their speed; for this reason the shot can emphasize a character's vulnerability or diminish his or her stature. A high-angle shot of a character trekking across the desert, for example, would emphasize his precarious and weak state and make him seem engulfed and trapped by the entire desolate landscape. A remarkable high-angle shot in *The Snake Pit* (1948; dir. Anatole Litvak) shows Olivia De Havilland surrounded by other mental patients with the camera moving higher and higher until all the figures seem like snakes at the bottom of a huge pit (the final effect was

high-angle shot Someone or something seems to be looking down at Julie Harris and Claire Bloom in *The Haunting* (1963; dir. Robert Wise).

■ ■ ■

achieved by miniature rear projection on a screen behind a painting of the pit's walls).

■ **high concept**   A term used in the industry to describe a film with a subject matter, stars, and marketing possibilities put together with the major purpose of making a great deal of money. With the ever-increasing costs of making a film (at this moment approximately $60 million, including advertising and prints), studios are looking for the big blockbusters that will bring in a large profit while also paying back losses on other films and maintaining the enormous overhead for making motion pictures. The first step is to conceive of some simple, easily describable, but yet appealing story concept, one that fits into already recognizable types of film while standing out because of some unique twist, and one that will drive a narrative with a lot of exciting scenes. The next step is to think of the perfect film personality or personalities who will fit the concept and the characters, themselves based on popular film types already developed by such stars in general. In addition, such films are thought of also in terms of a highly striking and pop-art type of imagistic style, as well as a musical idiom that will undoubtedly tap into popular rock music. Such films are thought of entirely as marketable commodities, as films that must pull in a large gross profit from both domestic and foreign distribution as well as from video rentals and sales, television, and other ancillary markets. Notable recent examples of

high contrast   *Raging Bull* (1980; dir. Martin Scorsese), with Robert De Niro in the black-and-white world of the ring.

■ ■ ■

such films are the Arnold Schwarzenegger films *Total Recall* (1990; dir. Paul Verhoeven) and *Terminator 2* (1991; dir. James Cameron), Steven Spielberg's *Jurassic Park* (1993), and Jan de Bont's *Speed* (1994).

■ **high contrast**   Sharp contrast in an image between strong light and dark areas with minimal intermediary stages. Such lighting can create a powerful and sometimes assaulting effect, as it does in the fight sequences of Martin Scorsese's *Raging Bull* (1980). *See* **lighting.**

■ **high-contrast film**   A film that allows great contrast and is particularly applicable for combining titles or composite elements in a matting process.

■ **high-definition television**   *See* **HDTV.**

■ **high-intensity arc, high-intensity carbon arc, high arc light, HI arc**   Carbon arc lamps, such as the brute, which give off an intense light through carbon electrodes. *See* **arc lamp.**

high-key lighting   Greta Garbo and Robert Taylor in *Camille* (1936; dir. George Cukor), a brightly lit tragic romance from MGM.

■ ■ ■

■ **high-key lighting**   An even, bright illumination with little shadow, frequently employed for "brighter" films, such as musicals, romances, and comedies. The main source of illumination is the key light, which is normally placed in front of the scene. Fill lights soften or remove the shadows. *See* **lighting.**

■ **highlight density**   The density of the brightest area of the film image.

■ **highlighting**   Giving a special illumination to a certain part or parts of the scene being photographed. For example, a beam of light from a spotlight might highlight a gun on a table or the face in a portrait on a wall.

■ **high pass filter** A filter in an electrical audio system that diminishes frequencies below the "cut-off" point and allows the higher frequencies to pass without alteration.

■ **high roller** An overhead stand on rollers used—normally with one or more other stands—to hold an overhead, i.e., a frame with material for diffusing or blocking light from above.

■ **highs, high frequencies** Sound frequencies in the range of 15,000 hertz.

■ **high shot** *See* **high-angle shot.**

■ **high-speed camera** Cameras specially designed for shooting at a much greater rate of frames per second than normal to achieve slow-motion action of the subject when the print is projected at normal speed. There are two general types of high-speed cameras: those with regular intermittent transport mechanisms, which can expose up to 400 frames per second on 35mm film and up to 600 frames per second on 16mm film; and those with continuous transport systems which can photograph as much as 40,000 frames per second on 16mm film (the pull and stress of intermittent systems would cause the film to break at speeds much greater than 600 frames per second). Rotary prisms in the second type of camera function as optical compensators to avoid blurring and move the image along with the film. The cameras with intermittent mechanisms are for special studio work and for filming activities such as sporting events, while those with continuous systems are for scientific research. Extrasensitive film with increased perforations on 400-foot spools is often employed for high-speed cameras. Video and digital high-speed cameras are now often used for motion analysis and have achieved even higher speeds.

■ **high-speed cinematography** Cinematography at speeds far higher than normal for the following reasons: (1) to achieve slow motion; (2) to achieve a natural appearance for the motion of models or such miniature effects as water, smoke, or an explosion; (3) to record on film various phenomena for scientific research. Some standard cameras can reach speeds up to 120 frames per second, especially for effects outlined in (1) and (2) above, but for high-speed cinematography that exceeds this number two types of mechanisms are needed. Cameras with specially built intermittent transport systems can achieve up to 400 frames per second on 35mm film (miniature explosions are sometimes photographed near this rate) and up to 600 frames per second on 16mm film; cameras with continuous transport systems can achieve as many as 40,000

frames per second on 16mm film. Increased lighting and exposure are often required for high-speed cinematography, while special film, with extra sensitivity and increased perforations, is needed for extreme high speeds. *See* **high-speed camera.**

■ **high-speed duplication** Duplicating sound on a tape that is recording at a speed greater than the original tape.

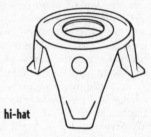

hi-hat

■ **hi-hat, high hat, top hat** A three-legged mounting approximately eight inches in height that supports a camera on a tripod head for shooting at extremely low angles, at floor level, or on the floor of a moving vehicle. The high hat can also support the camera on a high scaffolding or structure where the tripod would be inconvenient.

■ **hiss** *See* **noise.**

■ **historical film** A film purporting to deal with a historical period and the actual events of that period, though the treatment of characters may be highly fictional and great liberties might be taken with the events themselves. Historical films traditionally exploit the visual dimensions of the medium by seeking to evoke an image, albeit often romantic, of an earlier time and place. Such films often create what appears to be authentic costumes and settings and an authentic depiction of the daily life of the people. Historical films frequently focus on important political and martial events. When the production becomes expensive and sumptuous, the cost of characters great, and the narrative sweeping and panoramic, we have what has been defined earlier in this volume as an epic film.

Historical films have been produced since the days of silent motion pictures: for example, in the United States, Griffith made his epic historical film of the Civil War, *The Birth of a Nation* (1915); and in Germany, Ernst Lubitsch made the popular *Madame du Barry* (1919). One of the most striking historical works of the final days of silent films was *The Passion of Joan of Arc* (1928) by the Danish filmmaker Carl Dreyer, a work hardly epic in scope, but dramatic and moving in execution. In the 1930s, sound brought a new dimension to historical films in such works as Alexander Korda's British film *The Private Life of Henry VIII* (1933) and John Ford's American film *Mary of Scotland* (1936). One must also consider the Westerns and pirate yarns of the period as historical films of a sort. Color film gave new authenticity and opulence to the historical film, beginning especially with *Gone With the Wind* in 1939 (dir. Victor Fleming). There have been numerous epic historical films since that time, such as the unfortunate *Cleopatra* (1963; dir. Joseph L. Mankiewicz) and a number of historical films that emphasize drama rather than epic, such as the renditions of Henry II and his wife, Eleanor of Aquitaine, by Peter O'Toole and Katharine Hepburn in *The Lion in Winter* (1968; dir. Anthony Harvey). Certainly one of the most evocative and authentic historical films has been Stanley Kubrick's *Barry Lyndon* (1975), based on Thackeray's novel. Infuriatingly lethargic at times, the film still creates the setting, color, and the very feel of eighteenth-century England; this is historical painting more than filmmaking. Film's wonderful capacity to make us feel as if we had stepped into another epoch continues to seduce filmmakers to create this type of movie—e.g., Martin Scorsese's screen adaptation of Edith Wharton's turn-of-the-century drama in New York City, *The Age of Innocence* (1993), and Michael Hoffman's visually sumptuous *Restoration* (1994). *See* **epic** *and* **period film.**

historical film D. W. Griffith's *The Birth of a Nation* (1915) is a war film, spectacle, and epic as well as a historical film.

■ ■ ■

■ **hit the lights, hit the juice, hit 'em** A direction to turn on the lights for shooting. "Kill the lights" means to turn them off.

■ **hit the mark** A direction for an actor or actress to move to a previously designated mark on the floor for a particular shot.

■ **HMI** The letters represent hydragyrum (mercury), medium arc length, and iodide. Together they are a generic designation, taken from the Osram Company of Germany, for an enclosed-arc, A.C. discharge lamp.

The arc is enclosed in a low-pressure chamber with various gasses and elements that create a light spectrum suitable for both film and videotape. HMI lights are the most important recent development in film and video lighting because of their compactness and high degree of illumination from relatively small amounts of wattage, factors that far outweigh their costliness. Such lamps produce from three to four times the light of incandescent lamps from the same power: for example, the 6,000-watt HMI daylight lamp can create, from a total input of less than 7,000 watts, the same illumination and coverage as an average brute arc lamp operating with 27,000 watts. HMI lamps are now available in a variety of sizes and in a variety of luminaires. Originally employed largely as daylight lamps, they are now also produced for indoor shooting. Since HMI lights work with alternating current, creating rises and falls in illumination, flickering must be avoided during film exposure by synchronizing both light pulsation and frame rate through the use of cameras with crystal-controlled motors and stabilized generators (now also manufactured with crystal control). Lightweight ballast systems are available that also allow images without flicker. Care must be taken to measure color temperature from HMI lights, since there is some color toleration in these lamps and filters might be necessary for correction. Because HMI lights operate on high voltage (240 volts are required for single phase A.C., as opposed to 110 volts for D.C.), great care is taken with the grounding system, and special cables, distribution units, plugs, and sockets are employed.
See **DCI lamp.**

**HMI 12K light
with ballast unit**

■ **hold** (1) A take that is not developed after shooting but is kept for possible future use. Also called hold take. (2) The static frames from the start and finish of a camera's operation that are frequently helpful in editing. (3) A shot number in a film script that is reserved for possible future use during shooting.

■ **hold cel** A cel in animation that contains a stationary part of the image and is photographed for a series of frames. Other cels are changed to give the necessary movement to the scene, but one or more hold cels prevents the need for drawing the entire scene over and over.

■ **hold frame** *See* **freeze frame.**

■ **holdout matte** A matte with an opaque subject that is bipacked with a background image to block out the area into which the subject will later be placed. Also called a background or male matte. *See* **matte** *(2) and* **traveling-matte process.**

■ **holdover figure** The minimum amount of money a film must earn for one week to be held over for another week at a theater. The figure is agreed upon in advance by the distributor and exhibitor.

■ **hold takes** *See* **keep takes.**

■ **hole** Any segment of a sound track without sound. *See* **editing** *and* **mix.**

■ **Hollywood** Former movie capital of the world, center of America's dreams and fantasies, and arbiter of cultural codes and tastes, Hollywood was originally a Los Angeles suburb with barely a thousand people. The establishment of the Motion Picture Patents Company in 1908 sent a number of independent companies to southern California to escape the legal power and brute force of the eastern trust, even though some members of the Patents Company had themselves already been making films in the Los Angeles area. When such companies were followed and attacked by henchmen from the trust, the Mexican border offered escape for personnel and equipment. In the winter of 1910, Griffith, still working for Biograph, took his film company to the area. It was the Nestor Film Company, however, that first opened up shop in a suburb of Los Angeles called Hollywood, on October 27, 1911. Two years later, Cecil B. DeMille shot *The Squaw Man* for Jesse L. Lasky Feature Play Company in Hollywood. By 1911, close to twenty independents had studios in the general area. The stability of the weather and the continuous sunshine, the variety of landscape (desert, mountains, and ocean), and the cheap real estate made the area so appealing and profitable that by the time the trust was broken, the industry had been established there for good. The studios actually spread outside of Hollywood into the surrounding suburbs, but the general area of filmmaking continued to be known as Hollywood. The cheap land encouraged the building of huge studios, such as Carl Laemmle's Universal City in the San Fernando Valley. By 1920, fifty studios in and around Hollywood produced 90 percent of the films made in America. A rich, isolated, fantastic film world developed in this area, with large, elaborate studios cut off from the public, and expensive, ornate homes of the stars in nearby Beverly Hills. The movie studios became highly specialized, production-oriented worlds within themselves, and the coming of sound placed even greater demands upon their technology. Each studio carried its own group of directors, cinematographers, musicians, and performers, as well as numerous departments and crews to perform the various functions necessary for making a film. In the 1930s and 1940s, the major studios were MGM, Paramount, Twentieth Century-Fox, Universal, Warner Brothers, RKO, and Columbia, each of which produced a large number of films bearing the studio's own particular stamp. Hollywood produced approximately 400–500 films per year, both catering to and dictating American tastes.

The demise of Hollywood as the glamorous land of American dreams is attributable to the collapse of the studio system. A number of factors are responsible for the decline of the studio system: (1) the 1948 Supreme Court decision divesting film companies of their theaters; (2) the rise of television; (3) the development of European cinema; and (4) the cheaper costs of filming on location and abroad. Hollywood responded to television by developing wide-screen cinema and then, after the great success of Robert Wise's *The Sound of Music* (1965), foolishly lapsed into a bigger-is-better attitude with a number of enormously expensive failures. During this period, studios could not support their large payrolls and began to divest themselves of personnel and real estate. Soon they were renting out space for independent film production and even for television.

Today, most of the major film companies belong to large financial conglomerates, fewer films are made by them each year, and a significant number of films produced are made on location or abroad. The majors now act as producer-distributors, financing films produced by independent talents, sometimes renting out their own facilities, and distributing films either financed by themselves or by others. But the majors still pull in from 80 to 95 percent of the gross revenues of the approximately 400 new films released in this country each year, although they are responsible for roughly half of them. Movie attendance increased in the 1980s, the box office gross nearly doubling in the same decade to $5 billion, and video sales and rentals exploding to nearly the same gross. At the same time, the industry's international market grew at an even faster rate, reaching nearly $8 billion in 1993. The majors today are Disney, Paramount, Warner Brothers, MCA/Universal, Twentieth Century-Fox, and Sony Pictures Entertainment (Columbia and TriStar). Motion pictures themselves are seen as the source for numerous avenues of revenue—theatrical distribution, home video, cable movie channels, television, and various other ancillary markets—while the majors themselves, especially Time Warner and Disney, are responsible for more than half the programs we see on television.

Motion pictures have now become big business with a vengeance. Studios shift and reshift alliances. The big news is not the films being produced but the major players in the financial game, the executives who play with studios like pieces in a monopoly game and grow even more wealthy as properties change hands, the film producers who grow richer and richer even when they turn out failure after failure, and the actors who use up much of a film's budget with their salaries ranging from $10 million to $20 million. Because of the vast amounts of money involved—the average film now costs approximately $60 million to make and market—and the impossibility of predicting a winner, there is a frantic attempt to make films in the form and shape of films that have already made a profit. The eight "major" members of the Motion Picture Association of America released 212 new films in 1995 and put 153 films in wide distribution in 1995, but the financial picture remained grim. Only ten films were able to reach or surpass an international gross of $100 million that year and twelve in 1996, the figure now considered as the breakeven point for major motion pictures. The output of films by the majors is likely to be less in the coming years. The attempt is almost always to make a blockbuster, even though the products are the same and they often cater to the least discerning public tastes. Now that Hollywood's films are earning better than 40 percent of their gross from their international markets (American movies dominate 70 percent of the foreign markets, while films have become this nation's second major export), action films continue to be made in large numbers; plots, characterizations, and dialogue have become more simplified and basic; and the same few action heroes command vast salaries. New directors, supposedly with new visions and their fingers on the pulse of the younger generation that frequents the movies and rents the videos, and talented directors from abroad are absorbed into the system and leveled. Today, little is left of the old Hollywood. It remains almost a legend. A big, glamorous, vulgar world unto itself, it molded America's fantasies, creating the nation's most popular art form while giving birth to several dozen films that are among America's genuine contribution to world art. *See* **independent production, majors, Motion Picture Producers Association of America,** *and* **studio system.**

■ **Hollywood blacklist** In the late 1940s and 1950s, a large number of people who had worked in the Hollywood film industry were no longer able to obtain jobs after they were accused of being Communists, being affiliated with Communists, or being members of subversive organizations. Hollywood's boycott of these people was a product of the hunt for Communists and subversives in the movie industry by the House Committee on Un-American Activities (HUAC), especially in 1947 and 1951. The boycott was Hollywood's way of showing patriotism during the McCarthy period while protecting itself from government censorship and public disapproval. Many careers were destroyed in the movie industry as a result of the "blacklist," the existence of which Hollywood studios vigorously denied, though one had been devised by a patriotic organization called

Aware and was widely disseminated by the American Legion. A number of film people were forced to work under assumed names or to seek employment abroad. *See* **Hollywood Ten** *and* **House Committee on Un-American Activities.**

■ **Hollywood Reporter** A trade paper for the entertainment industry that is published in Hollywood and appears weekdays. This publication follows carefully the development and production of films and television programs as well as the various goings-on with personnel in the studios and agencies.

■ **Hollywood Ten** A group of members of the film industry who, in 1947, refused to answer questions posed to them by the House Committee on Un-American Activities, claiming political freedom and free speech under the Bill of Rights. The committee sought to find out whether these men were Communists. Because of their refusal to testify, they were all cited for contempt of Congress and sent to jail; later they were unable to find work in films (*see* **Hollywood blacklist**), though some did work under assumed names. The ten were directors Herbert Biberman and Edward Dmytryk, producer Adrian Scott, and screenwriters Alvah Bessie, Lester Cole, Ring Lardner, Jr., John Howard Lawson, Albert Maltz, Samuel Ornitz, and Dalton Trumbo. *See* **House Committee on Un-American Activities.**

■ **Holocaust film** A film dealing specifically with the Holocaust in Europe, especially the slaughtered 6 million Jews—from the years in the 1930s leading to its actual occurrence to the years after the Second World War, showing its repercussions. It has often been argued that such a monumental event of human suffering and destruction cannot and should not be reduced to a fictional work, that such a representation trivializes the reality, and that even a documentary cannot remotely approach the enormity of the Holocaust. Yet filmmakers have attempted to record the Holocaust through the documentary and dramatize the suffering

Holocaust film Simon Srebnik, a survivor of the Chelmno death camp, meets with Polish residents of Chelmno some forty years later in Claude Lanzmann's *Shoah* (1985).

■ ■ ■

through the fictional film. As early as 1948, a Yiddish film made in Poland, *Unzere Kinder* (dir. Natan Gross and Shaul Goskind), which featured children who were actual survivors, confronted head-on whether the Holocaust was a subject fit for art—this film was banned in Poland, exhibited in Israel in 1951, and only recently restored. Of the numerous narrative films on the Holocaust, Sidney Lumet's *The Pawnbroker* (1965) and Steven Spielberg's *Schindler's List* (1993) are the two that have come closest to conveying this human tragedy on film. Of all the documentaries on the subject, certainly Claude Lanzmann's nine-and-one-half-hour *Shoah* (1985), a film largely composed of interviews with those who survived, is the most powerful and overwhelming.

■ **hologram**   In the photographic system of holography, the pattern formed on the emulsion of a plate by two light waves from the same laser beam, one, the object beam, reflected off the subject of the image, and the second, the reference beam, sent to the emulsion without striking the subject. The hologram may be reconstructed into an image of the original subject in three dimension and with parallactic perspective in front of the emulsion by beaming onto it another light from a laser. *See* **holography.**

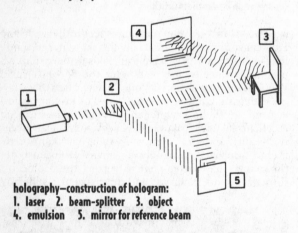

holography–construction of hologram:
1. laser   2. beam-splitter   3. object
4. emulsion   5. mirror for reference beam

■ **holography**   The term derives from the Greek word *holos,* which means "whole," and refers to a photographic system in which laser light is used to create a three-dimensional image of a subject in space that may be viewed, from a certain area, with the impression of parallax (i.e., the subject will seem displaced from different views). Such a system is also capable of creating images of great brightness and depth of field. A hologram is first formed on the emulsion of a plate by two light waves from the same laser beam; one, the reference beam, is sent to the plate without striking the subject, and the other, the object beam, is reflected off the subject and causes interference with the first on the emulsion. The interference causes a "fringe" pattern of light and dark lines to be formed; this pattern is the

source of a three-dimensional image of the subject when another laser light is beamed onto the emulsion and diffracted. At this point, laser illumination, especially for outdoor shooting, is a problem: images are limited in size and can be viewed only from a limited area, subjects are restricted in movement, and color reproduction with good resolution still has to be achieved; but work is being done to make the system applicable for the reproduction of moving pictures either through television or as a projected system on large screens.

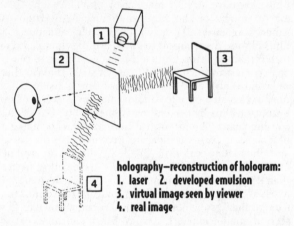

holography–reconstruction of hologram:
1. laser   2. developed emulsion
3. virtual image seen by viewer
4. real image

■ **homage**   A complimentary allusion in a film to another film or filmmaker. Such a reference may be made directly by inserting an actual clip from an original work, as when Peter Bogdanovich incorporates a sequence from Howard Hawks's *The Criminal Code* (1931) to pay tribute to that director in his own *Targets* (1967), or indirectly, as when François Truffaut imitates Hitchcock's style in *The Bride Wore Black* (1967). *See* **allusion** *(2).*

■ **home-cinema theater**   A complex of equipment in the home that plays motion pictures from a videotape in a manner that approximates the effect and quality achieved in a theater. Such a complex includes a large-screen television set of at least twenty-five inches, a videocassette recorder, a receiver, and a stereo surround sound system, such as the Dolby Pro Logic, with five speakers (three for the left, center, and right of the screen and two in the rear for the surround sound) and a separate subwoofer. The THX Sound System, developed by Lucasfilm, is an actual seal of approval given to electronics equipment and speakers that use Dolby Surround and achieve the required quality. Such a complex also sometimes includes a laser disc player. A number of electronics companies have now come out with all the appliances in a single console or "box." *See* **home video.**

■ **home video**   Videotape or laser disc recordings of motion pictures normally watched in the home. Home videos have had an enormous impact on the motion-picture industry during the past fifteen years, in terms of income but also in terms of the viewing habits of a significant portion of the American public. Although many people still attend theatrical screenings and the number of screens has actually increased in this country, such viewing is no longer a family affair, and a large portion of this public prefers to watch at home. Also significant is the impact that video viewing has had on the actual style and filming of the motion picture itself—many directors and cinematographers now plan ahead for the television screen's smaller aspect ratio by placing a good deal of the action in the center of the frame. The ready availability of motion pictures at home has also had a devastating effect on second-run and repertoire theaters, the exhibition of foreign films, and drive-in theaters.

It is estimated that three times as many people watch motion pictures on home video as go to the theater, and that 40 to 50 percent of the industry's profits for a film comes from the domestic and international market for such videos—the studios obtained $5.3 billion from video rentals and sales in 1993. It is also estimated that by 1995, some 75,800,000 homes had VCRs and 490 million videos were sold to dealers for that year. Although rentals bring in a large part of the income from such videos, actual sales for certain kinds of films are hardly negligible—Disney sold some 14 million videos of *Beauty and the Beast* by 1993. The actual distributors of such videos are now mostly companies affiliated with the large film companies, both often belonging to the same conglomerate. The retailing of such videos is controlled more and more by large companies, the most notable being Blockbuster Video, itself part of Viacom, which in 1992 had 2,100 of the 30,000 such retailers in this country. Videos are now, however, accessible for purchase in such rental stores, special stores devoted to their sale, large department and discount stores, as well as supermarkets. Film rentals also come from supermarkets as well as convenience and discount stores. Although approximately half of the videos in a typical rental store are not exhibited in theaters or on television, three-quarters of sales and rentals still apply to films originally marketed through the motion-picture houses. Home video has not, therefore, created an alternative viewing experience but a proliferation of what we are already given in the mass movie houses, only in a less-satisfying aesthetic environment. It is worth noting, however, the development of home-cinema theater with large-screen television and Dolby stereophonic surround sound that is intended to create in the home something of the experience of watching a film in a theater.

Home videos normally follow the theatrical distribution of a film by approximately six months, while screening on cable television follows by about a year, and on regular television some two years. Because video, by keeping people in their homes, has encouraged them to subscribe to cable television and watch network television, it has, ironically, pushed both these

venues into producing their own original motion pictures, which, on occasion, are superior to what is available either in the theater or through home video. *See* **home-cinema theater** *and* **made-for-TV movie.**

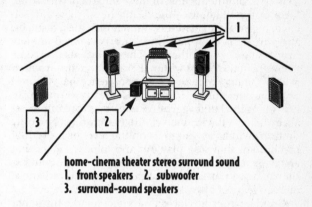

home-cinema theater stereo surround sound
1. front speakers   2. subwoofer
3. surround-sound speakers

■ **honey wagon** A portable enclosure or trailer that contains toilets and dressing rooms for personnel when shooting on location.

■ **hook** An extremely interesting and provocative opening to a film in the very first shot that immediately captures the audience's attention (e.g., the traveling shot of a statue of Jesus suspended from a helicopter at the start of Federico Fellini's *La Dolce Vita* [1960]).

■ **hookup** The interchangeable drawings employed at the conclusion of one cycle and the start of another in animation. *See* **cycle** *(2).*

■ **horizontal editor** *See* **flat-bed editing machine.**

■ **horror film** A genre of film that seeks to cause fright and even terror in the viewer. The term "horror," which is applied to all works of this genre, means an extreme feeling, almost to the point of revulsion and disgust, caused by something shocking, so that the term itself does not precisely apply to the classic works of the genre made in earlier years, though it certainly can be accurately applied to some of the more recent and violent films of the genre. The horror film offers the occasion for us to see all kinds of frightening events, to feel something of the same fear and terror as the characters on the screen, yet to enjoy these feelings because we know, sitting safely in the audience, that ultimately no harm can happen to us. A form of catharsis takes place within us, a confrontation with fears that normally exist on the preconscious and unconscious levels and a cessation, at least for a while, of the devils that haunt us. From this experiencing of fear and terror in a secure situation and from this catharsis comes a unique aesthetic pleasure that the horror film evokes—but to do this the film must be made with sufficient skill and tact so that we do not feel exploited and revolted. Horror films deal with our fears of violence and death, but they also deal with subjects beyond the pale of normal human knowledge and experience, subjects that frighten us because we know so little about them. Most of these films deal with some form of the unknown—the dead, the spirit world, science, outer space, madness—which unsettles, disturbs, and threatens us, which causes unrecognized anxiety from some region within us. These films also force us to confront the "beast within us," a subject about which religion, morality, reason, and conscience have caused us great uneasiness. Horror films do not so much satisfy our animal and aggressive nature as force us to realize and fear the instincts or drives within us. Not only do horror films appeal to us on the level of individual psychology, they also play out and appease fears that are evoked from the political and social level of our existence, fears perhaps of nuclear energy and radiation, or even fears of oppression and conformity.

Good horror films have always been made, films that do not revolt or disgust us, that do not assault our sensibilities, but that appeal to these human fears. In the era of silent film, one can find in America such fine works as John Robertson's *Dr. Jekyll and Mr. Hyde* (1920), starring John Barrymore, and Rupert Julian's *The Phantom of the Opera* (1926), starring Lon Chaney; and one can find in Germany two significant expressionist horror films, Robert Wiene's *The Cabinet of Dr.*

horror film *Frankenstein* (1931; dir. James Whale), with Boris Karloff in Jack Pierce's notorious makeup.

■■■

Caligari (1919) and F. W. Murnau's *Nosferatu, A Symphony of Terror* (1922). The great decade of American horror films in sound was the 1930s, beginning with Tod Browning's *Dracula* and James Whale's *Frankenstein* (both in 1931). In such films, German expressionism merged with American film technique and technology to create a particularly evocative and striking nightmare world, with images that still haunt the imagination. Perhaps the culmination of this period's achievement is James Whale's *The Bride of Frankenstein* (1935), but one must also commend such films as Tod Browning's *Freaks* (1932), Cooper and Schoedsack's *King Kong* (1933), and Edgar Ulmar's *The Black Cat* (1934). Though horror films began to be produced as inexpensive B-films in the 1940s, some works in the genre still achieved a level of excellence. Most notable were the low-budget horror films produced by Val Lewton for RKO. With taste and skill, he oversaw some of the most scary and poetic films of the genre, especially *Cat People* in 1942 and *I Walked With a Zombie* in 1943, both directed by Jacques Tourneur.

In the 1950s, three significant developments occurred in the horror genre: the treatment of the anxieties of the atomic age in Japanese holocaust films such as *Godzilla* (1955; dir. Inoshiro Honda) and in American mutation films such as *Them* (1954; dir. Gordon Douglas); the Communist and McCarthy paranoia films, especially Don Siegel's *Invasion of the Body Snatchers* (1956); and the color films of violence and sex by Hammer Studios in England. Hammer's best films were probably two of its earliest, *The Curse of Frankenstein* (1957) and *The Horror of Dracula* (1958), both directed by Terence Fisher.

The next decades were a more eclectic period, beginning with Hitchcock's notable *Psycho,* which took the violation of the suffering woman a step beyond earlier films and opened the door for future exploitation, and, in Italy, with Mario Bava's stunning film about witches and vampires, *Black Sunday (La Maschera del Demonio),* both in 1960. Two very successful ghost stories were Jack Clayton's *The Innocents* (1961) and Robert Wise's *The Haunting* (1963). William Friedkin's *The Exorcist* in 1973 brought demonology and Satan to a Vietnam generation anxious to put responsibility for the world's evil on some force other than human. *The Exorcist* spawned a whole series of witchcraft and satanic films, none of them as cinematically rich as their progenitor. Perhaps Brian De Palma's *Carrie* (1976) can be seen as a witchcraft film, but certainly it is much more than that: an intelligent but still terrifying film, it explores and sets loose our fears about puberty, sexuality, isolation, harassment, revenge, the dead, and telekinetic powers in a film style that is both manipulative and poetic.

A large number of recent films have been concerned with the violation of young women, a theme always prevalent in the horror film, but never before done in such an explicitly violent and revolting manner. This development has been attributed to a reaction by filmmakers and audiences to the sexual revolution and the feminist movement. Such explanations always seem glib, but the number and popularity of these films suggest some connection to social and cultural disturbances. John Carpenter's *Halloween* (1978), which gave impetus to this wave of films now seems the least offensive because it is so skillfully made. Related to these films because of its explicit connection between sex and violence is Paul Schrader's *Cat People* (1982), based on the 1942 film produced by Val Lewton. Schrader's film, however, instead of being exploitative, is one of the more visually stunning and poetic horror films of this period.

Also worthy of notice is Ridley Scott's *Alien* (1979), a film that combines both science fiction and the horror genre, and makes the first a means of dealing with the psychological fears of the second. Science fiction and horror films have generally been two separate genres, but, ever since *Frankenstein* in 1931, the two have sometimes overlapped. Pure science-fiction films seem to glamorize science; science-fiction horror films make it part of the dreaded unknown.

Although horror films seem to be plentiful in recent years, the vast majority have been poorly made and highly derivative. Both the *Friday the 13th* (1980–89) and *Nightmare on Elm Street* (1984–91) series, as well as the various spin-offs from these series, contributed to a sense of fatigue and repetition within the genre. Once fear and horror became disgust and revulsion, it was inevitable for one film to attempt to outdo the other in creating such responses with little regard for other qualities that had made the best horror films works of art. Leaving the gothicism and film technique behind, film directors were now prone to move the mayhem and sex to other types of cinema. Most significant in recent years is the breakdown in classic generic types and a new amalgamation of generic elements. Fear and revulsion have specifically moved to the mystery and gangster film, finding impetus in their new, and more realistic, surroundings. Certainly a film such as *The Silence of the Lambs* (1991; dir. Jonathan Demme) is far more disturbing and horrifying than any of the conventional horror films made in the past dozen years. *See* **fantasy, genre,** *and* **science-fiction film.**

■ **horse** A device on an editing table for holding one or more pieces of film by means of a rod through cores.

■ **horse opera, horse pic** Slang for a Western.

■ **hot** (1) Lit too brightly. The term may refer to a set, location, or the image itself. (2) Any individual or property that is much in demand.

■ **hot box** (1) The box in which lighting cables are plugged. (2) A small, portable room for loading and unloading the camera. *See* **loading closet.**

■ **hot frame, flash frame** A frame at the beginning and end of a shot that has been overexposed and is used as a marker for editing.

■ **hot lens** A lens for a luminaire that can narrow the beam while allowing a high-intensity light.

■ **hot set** A set all prepared for shooting, with scenery and props in exact position and lighting ready for use. Such a set should not be disturbed or even entered.

■ **hot splice** An overlap-cement splice in which the cement holding the pieces together is heated for rapid drying by means of electricity in the base plate of the splicer. *See* **overlap-cement splice** *and* **splice.**

■ **hot splicer** A film splicer with a base metal plate heated by electricity that shortens the drying time of the cement holding together two pieces of overlapping film. *See* **splicer.**

■ **hot spot** (1) An excessively bright area on a set. (2) An excessively bright area on a screen image.

■ **house allowance, house expense** The amount of money to be allowed for the operation of a theater during the run of a film. The sum is agreed upon by the distributor and exhibitor. Also called the house nut. *See* **exhibition.**

■ **House Committee on Un-American Activities (HUAC)** A former committee of the United States House of Representatives whose function was to discover and investigate disloyal or subversive activities in America, specifically Communist activities. In 1947, under the chairmanship of J. Parnell Thomas, a Republican from New Jersey, the committee sought to prove that Communists had infiltrated the movie industry in Hollywood, especially the Screen Writers Guild, and that films were being produced that contained propaganda for the USSR. At first, film people were outraged at this infringement on their rights and formed the Committee for the First Amendment. But the tide shifted when friendly witnesses in the industry testified before the congressional committee and supported its activities. Ten members of the industry who were suspected of being Communists refused to testify, claiming before the committee their right to political freedom and free speech (*see* **Hollywood Ten**). Fifty major film executives met at the Waldorf-Astoria Hotel in New York, and, after two days, issued a statement condemning the ten and barring them from future work in the industry. The group of fifty also dedicated themselves to the task of eliminating subversives from the industry. From that time any unfriendly witness investigated by the committee, any individual accused by a "patriotic" organization, anyone who was even suspected of being a

Communist or associating with Communists was blacklisted (*see* **Hollywood blacklist**). The committee investigated Hollywood several times afterward until 1954. It is estimated that over 300 people in the film industry were blacklisted as a result of the committee's investigations.

■ **housekeeping deal** A contractual arrangement whereby a studio, for first rights to produce and/or distribute any film projects, pays the overhead for an individual, group, or production company during the development phase. *See* **first look deal, negative pickup deal, overall development deal,** *and* **pickup deal.**

■ **house lights** (1) The general lights in the audience area of a movie theater that normally operate before and after the screening of the film. (2) The general lights in a studio exclusive of those used on the set for filming.

■ **house nut** Jargon for house expenses incurred by an exhibitor during a film showing and subtracted from box-office receipts before the distributor's percentage is calculated. Also called house allowance and house expense.

■ **house reel** A heavy metal reel that belongs to the theater and is used for projecting films because of its durability and precision and because of its smooth movement.

■ **HUAC** *See* **House Committee on Un-American Activities.**

■ **hue** (1) A particular color of the spectrum. (2) The tint or gradation of a color (pale, bright, etc.).

■ **hum.** *See* **noise.**

■ **hydro dolly** A term for a dolly that uses a hydraulic system to elevate or lower the arm that supports the camera. Such hydraulic systems may be operated by motor or, in some cases, elevated by pumping a footbar and lowered by a knob. *See* **dolly.**

■ **hype** An advertising term that describes the strong promotion of a film, perhaps by radio, television, and by personal appearances of the performers. The term probably comes from "hyper," a prefix meaning "over" in the sense of excessive.

■ **hyperfocal distance** (1) The distance at which a lens must be focused to get the greatest depth of field (i.e., when objects from infinity to half that distance will be in focus). (2) The distance between the lens and the nearest plane in focus when the camera is focused on infinity.

■ **Hypergonar** The original name for the anamorphic lens systems developed by Henri Chrétien and later developed into CinemaScope by Twentieth Century-Fox. *See* **CinemaScope.**

■ **hyphenate, hyphen** Film jargon for a person who does more than one major job in a production (e.g., a producer-director or writer-director).

■ **hypo** The chemical bath that acts as the fixing agent in film processing. The fixing agent dissolves and removes the unexposed silver halides from the emulsion. Also called fixer. *See* **processing.**

■ ■ ■

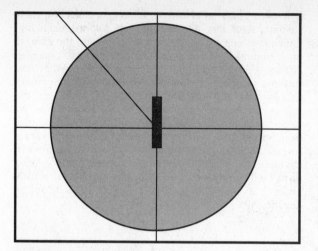

IATSE to Iwerks Entertainment

■ **IATSE** *See* **International Alliance of Theatrical Stage Employees.**

■ **IB, IB print** *See* **imbibition.**

■ **ice box** (1) Jargon for a soundproof glass compartment in which cameras were placed during the early days of sound films. Noise from the operation of the camera was thus cut off from the audio recording system; but the movement of the camera was considerably limited. The compartment itself could be moved but only with delay and effort. Cameras were soon encased in soundproofed "blimps" which permitted them mobility once again. (2) An informal name for a motion-control system designed by Douglas Trumbull and employed in such films as Steven Spielberg's *Close Encounters of the Third Kind* (1977) and Ridley Scott's *Blade Runner* (1982). The system was given this designation because of its large, squarish shape. *See* **motion control.**

■ **icon** A term, common in semiotics, which refers to a sign that resembles or looks like the object it represents (e.g., a statue or painting). The term is from the writings of the linguist C. S. Peirce, who designated other types of signs as index (a sign that represents something by being directly related to it, e.g., smoke indicating fire) or symbol (a sign that represents something other than itself, e.g., an eagle as an emblem of the United States). *See* **semiotics.**

■ **identification** An intense sense of involvement that one feels with a character in a work of art. One puts oneself into the shoes of the character in order to imagine undergoing the same experiences and emotions. Identification is a much stronger involvement than association, which occurs when one relates one's *own* feelings and experiences to those of the character, and empathy, which occurs when one feels and experiences what the character experiences and feels while still maintaining a firm hold on one's own identity. With identification one tends to become the character to a considerable extent. The nature of identification is a subject much debated by theoreticians. The French film theoretician André Bazin claims that while stage productions force us into "active individual consciousness," film, because it places us in a passive state, "encourages identification with the hero" (in *What Is Cinema?*).

■ **idiot cards, idiot sheets, idiot boards** *See* **cue cards.**

■ **idiot page** *See* **synopsis.**

■ **illumination** (1) The general lighting of a studio set or location; (2) the lighting which comes from specific light sources, both natural and artificial.

■ **image** (1) The visual representation of a scene that appears on the screen by means of the photographic process. The term, in this sense, refers to a single picture from a single distance and angle, even though it is made up of a series of frames on the film and even though it may contain movement. The individual images and the way they flow together and interrelate are the basis of cinematic art. Each individual image must be composed to convey character, action, and setting, but also to evoke within the audience a particular response to the photographed subject. At the same time, each image must contribute to the ongoing action of the film, while fitting into the general rhythmic movement and overall visual quality of the entire work. It is the director who plans each image, who prepares for it with the production designer and with the director of photography. Good directors of photography often put their own particular stamp on a visual image, their own particular lighting and texture, and a skillful director will know how to take advantage of this visual style and bring it into the context of his or her own vision. Various elements go into the making of a film image: composition, lighting, color, camera distance and angle, and the quality of the film stock itself. The technical way in which the image is formed on the film emulsion is discussed under **film.** (2) The pictorial reproduction of a photographed scene on the film itself, whether on the positive or negative. (3) The general visual quality of the entire film as opposed to the auditory. (4) The term can also be used in its rhetorical sense to apply to a character or scene that at times seems to represent something beyond itself, that seems to be a symbol or metaphor (e.g., "Cagney in many of his films of the 1930's is an image of the depression mentality, of the fear of poverty and hunger for success.").

■ **image composite** *See* **composite** *(2).*

■ **image degradation** *See* **degradation.**

■ **image distortion** *See* **distortion** *(1).*

■ **image duplication** *See* **multi-image** *and* **split screen.**

■ **image enhancement** A process that improves a digital picture by better defining the edges of objects, increasing the picture's resolution, improving color, increasing tone and contrast, and removing scratches and blemishes. The process is especially used to fix images scanned into the computer. *See* **image enhancer.**

■ **image enhancer** A piece of hardware that improves the quality of an image in a video or digital system. *See* **image enhancement.**

■ **image mapping** *See* **texture mapping.**

■ **image plane** The plane behind the lens where the image is formed when the camera is focused on less than infinity (normally the plane of the film emulsion). When the camera is focused on infinity, this plane is called the focal plane.

■ **image point** Any point of the image that comes into focus on the image plane behind the lens when the camera is focused on less than infinity. When the camera is focused on infinity, this point appears on the focal plane and is called the focal point.

■ **image processing** Performing some type of enhancements or alterations in a digital image—e.g., changing colors or tone, compositing different picture elements, altering size or shape. *See* **computer animation.**

■ **image replacement** The replacement of part of an image, or an addition to the image by any of a number of special-effects techniques: for example, scenery or parts of a building painted on a glass sheet can be added to an actual set by shooting through the glass, scenery projected onto a screen from the rear can become the permanent background to live action shot before it, or the background for live action can be projected off a beaded screen from the front. Matting techniques, which merge separate images of background and action in an optical printer, are also often employed. New digitizing processes are being used with film images scanned into the computer, altered, composited, and then recorded on film. *See* **special effects.**

■ **image size** The relative size of the subject of an image in the context of the overall area of the frame. The image size is determined both by the distance of the camera from the subject and by the focal length of the lens. *See* **focal length.**

■ **image warping** Distorting, changing, or mutating an image in computer animation or graphics. *See* **morphing.**

■ **imaginary line, line of interest, action axis, center line, screen direction, stage line, director's line** A hypothetical line drawn between two or more actors to keep the camera on a single side of the action so that if several shots with different distances or angles are edited together, the viewer's perspective remains consistent. If the camera should cross the line and turn around to record the action, the viewer's perspective would suddenly be reversed, causing a sense of disequilibrium and confusion. Sometimes crossing the line is permitted to create reverse-angle shots or depict a scene with a number of characters and actions, but such shooting and editing must be done with care so as not to bewilder the audience. The principle is also referred to as the 180-degree rule.

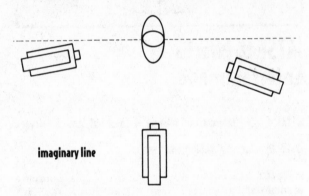

imaginary line

■ **IMAX** The name comes from "image maximization" or "maximum image" and represents a camera and projector system, first introduced in 1970, that supposedly employs the largest film frame in motion-picture history: 65mm film moving through the camera horizontally, allowing individual frames that are fifteen perforations wide and measure 71.09 by 52.63mm, ten times larger than the standard 35mm frame and three times larger than the regular 70mm frame. The print itself is on 70mm film and the sound track, composed of six channels of surround sound, is now recorded digitally on discs that run synchronically with the film. The print passes through the IMAX projector horizontally in a "rolling loop" movement. The audience sits on a series of elevated rows that are angled 30 to 45 degrees in such a way that the spectator feels merged into the picture, which is on a screen ten times the size of the average motion-picture screen and up to eight stories high. OMNIMAX (now called IMAX DOME) uses the same system plus a fisheye lens for projecting a 165-degree image on a giant dome screen surrounding the viewer with high-fidelity sound and immersing him or her even further into the created reality. IMAX theaters can be found in theme parks, museums, institutions, exhibition centers, and are now expanding into entertainment centers and movie complexes. The recently developed IMAX 3-D system, which employs an eight-story screen and special headsets with left and right liquid-crystal lenses, each of which is made clear or opaque alternately by infrared signals beamed from the front of the theater to create the dimensional effect, has been employed for a series of commercially shown films at the special IMAX Theater in the Sony Theatres Lincoln Square cineplex in New York City and at a growing number of theaters both in this country and abroad. The stereoscopic viewing experience is enhanced by IMAX PSE, a "personal sound environment" that operates from the viewer's own headset and enhances the six-channel sound in the theater. The company also introduced IMAX SOLIDO in 1992, a 3-D experience with a wide-field dome screen that creates an even greater sense of immersion in the created three-dimensional world. The IMAX Corporation is based in Toronto, Canada. *See* **3-D**.

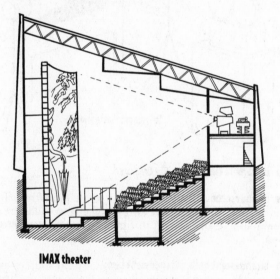

IMAX theater

■ **imbibition, imbibition transfer printing** A process of dye transfer in the making of color prints. The method was originally used with two-strip and then three-strip Technicolor negatives, but was later employed with single tripack negatives. In an optical printer, three positives, called matrices, are individually exposed to the negative, each by way of its base and through a filter for one of the three primary colors. Each of the three positives is then "imbibed" with the appropriate complementary color, yellow for blue, magenta for green, and cyan for red. Since the image on the matrix is in relief and has various thicknesses according to the density of the original negative, the amount of dye absorbed will vary according to the thickness of each area. When each of these strips in turn transfers the various densities of dye to the fresh emulsion of another film, the complementary colors will blend so that the original image with all its gradations of color can be projected. Since the same matrices can be redyed and used over and over, the method was considered economical and fast for the

making of release prints for Technicolor and later for other color systems. Such prints (also referred to as IB prints) are excellent in quality and durable. Because of the need for more rapid systems to turn out a greater number of prints, the imbibition system was no longer in use in this country after 1973 and in Britain and Italy after 1978. It is still used in China at the Beijing Film Lab. *See* **color film** *(2) and* **Technicolor.**

■ **impedance** The total opposition to alternating current in an electric circuit. Made up of resistance and reactance, impedance is measured in ohms. To avoid an impedance mismatch between microphone and circuit which would cause a deterioration in sound and loss of volume, transformers are employed either in the microphone or cable.

■ **impingement drying** Drying film during processing by means of jets of hot air blown directly at the emulsion of the moving film.

■ **impressionism** A term derived from the movement of the great French impressionist painters at the end of the nineteenth century to describe a film technique which seeks to convey a scene as it makes an immediate impression upon a viewer. This technique uses light, shadow, color, focus, the texture of the image, camera angle, and editing to move away from realistic recording and create a subjective impression. Impressionism, however, does not go as far as expressionism, which distorts reality to create the vision of a hypersensitive or even a deranged mind. The term "impressionism" has been applied to the feature narratives of the French filmmakers cited directly below and sometimes to avant-garde films such as the city symphonies (e.g., Ruttmann's 1927 work, *Berlin, die Symphonie einer Grosstadt; Berlin, Symphony of a Great City*). In a more general sense, however, impressionism can be applied to any film style that creates such an immediate subjective effect either in an entire film or part of a film. *See* **expressionism.**

■ **impressionists** A group of French filmmakers during the early 1920s—namely Germaine Dulac, Jean Epstein, Abel Gance, Marcel L'Herbier, and Louis Delluc, the last of whom was the dominant influence with his films and film theory. The term derives from French impressionist painting and denotes the attempts of these filmmakers to achieve subjective effects with the camera in their narrative works. Often their films seem to border on the expressionistic because of extreme and unnatural effects in lighting, focus, cutting, camera angles, and perspective. Delluc's *Fièvre (Fever;* 1921), Dulac's *La Souriante Madame Beudet (The Smiling Madam Beudet;* 1922), Epstein's *Coeur Fidèle (Faithful Heart;* 1923), Gance's *La Roue (The Wheel;* 1923), and L'Herbier's *L'Inhumaine (The Inhuman Woman;* 1923) are often cited as notable examples of this group's work. With the death of Delluc in 1924, the major force in the group was gone and his followers developed in their separate ways. *See* **impressionism.**

■ **improvise** To act without rehearsal or a script. Sometimes directors seek to achieve a more spontaneous and natural scene from performers by asking them to create their own lines, behavior, and feelings for a scene during the actual shooting. Improvisation is more sustained and internal than ad-libbing, which means interjecting one's own lines in an already established scene.

■ **inbetweener** An animation artist who does the drawings that fill in the action between the key drawings made by the major animator. The process is sometimes referred to as tweening. In computer animation, the computer itself is set to make the inbetween drawings.

■ **in-camera editing** Editing that is largely performed through the operation of the camera and not by the cutting and shaping of an editor. The sequence of shots and scenes remains much the same as during shooting. Individual shots and scenes are used with little pruning or alteration. Hitchcock claimed that his films were sufficiently planned in advance to allow him to do much of his editing in the camera.

■ **in-camera effects, in-the-camera-effects** Special effects made within the camera during shooting instead of those made in an optical printer or processing machine. Such effects include fast, slow, and reverse motion; image distortion by means of filters, jelly, or mirrors; day-for-night shooting; and double or multiple exposure. Time transitions such as dissolves can be made by shooting a scene, winding the film partially back, and then beginning the shooting of the next scene; and fades by gradually closing down the shutter at the end of one scene and gradually opening it at the start of the next. Such transitions were achieved this way in early filmmaking, but today are accomplished more safely and precisely through optical printing. *See* **optical printer.**

■ **in-camera matte shot, in-the-camera matte shot** A technique for joining together two or more separate components from different images into a single picture by using mattes placed before the camera or sometimes in the camera at the focal plane. This technique was found preferable to glass shots and became the common method of matting for many years in commercial films before the development of bipack matting. Light was blocked from part of the frame generally by placing in front of the camera a sheet of glass painted black in the appropriate area. After the live action was photographed through the glass, the film was wound back and exposed again, but this time with the latent image matted out by a black area on a matte-board and the previously blacked-out area on the film exposed to a painted setting or photograph on the same board.

When the film was developed, a composite image would appear in each frame. The same technique could be used to combine live action or a setting with animated miniatures. A type of in-camera matte shot is still in use today because of its excellent quality, but the chance still remains of ruining the negative with the original shooting, a danger avoided by bipack printing. *See* **glass shot, matte** *(2), and* **traveling-matte process.**

■ **in-camera pass** *See* **pass.**

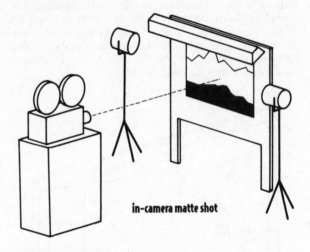

in-camera matte shot

■ **in-camera time code** *See* **time code.**

■ **incandescent** Glowing and giving off light from intense heat. Incandescent tungsten-halogen bulbs are a main source of lighting in filmmaking. *See* **incandescent bulb.**

■ **incandescent bulb, incandescent lamp** A light source that gives off illumination by glowing from intense heat caused by electricity. In cinematography, bulbs with tungsten filaments were employed at one time; these had to be discarded when their walls were blackened from the deposit of evaporated tungsten. In later years, bulbs with a small amount of halogen became popular. The halogen combines with the tungsten deposited on the walls of the bulb, forming a tungsten-halide that then decomposes on the filament, returning the tungsten to its source. Although such bulbs are more expensive, they give a greater period of light with a minimal loss of illumination. They are also smaller, more durable, and easier to use.

■ **in character** (1) The ability of a performer to stay within the confines of the personality, experiences and feelings of the character he or she is playing. (2) When dialogue, behavior, and action seem appropriate to the character.

■ **inches per second (IPS)** The measurement for the speed at which magnetic tape passes through the recorder. Most sound for film production is recorded on quarter-inch tape that passes through the recorder at seven and one-half inches per second.

■ **inching** Moving film slowly and in short lengths through a camera, projector, or editing machine for such various reasons as properly engaging the perforations of the film or locating a particular frame or scene.

■ **inching knob** The knob attached to a drive mechanism in a camera or projector that, when turned by hand, allows the slow movement of the film. Also referred to as the incher. *See* **inching.**

■ **incidental music** Background music in a film that helps create a mood for the action taking place or convey the feelings of a character. *See* **music.**

■ **incident light** The light falling on a subject from all sources of illumination as opposed to the light reflected by the subject.

incident light meter

■ **incident light meter** An exposure meter that measures light illuminating a subject rather than the light reflected by the subject. Meters of hemispherical type, when pointed toward the camera, average out the intensity of light coming from the various sources and give an f-stop setting for the diaphragm of the camera. Flat types, however, are sometimes employed to measure both key and fill lights independently. Incident light meters are normally found more efficient for professional cinematography than reflected light meters. The new Cinemeter II is both a digital and analog incident light meter that considers light intensity in the context of frames per second, film speed, shutter angle, and filter factors. The liquid crystal display can give readings in three modes: bar graph, floating zone, and dedicated zone. *See* **reflected light meter.**

■ **incoming scene** The scene that begins to appear during a dissolve, wipe, or fade-out and fade-in as opposed to the "outgoing scene."

■ **incoming shot** (1) Any shot that appears after a cut from an "outgoing shot." (2) The shot about to appear in the editing apparatus.

■ **independent** A filmmaker, not employed by a studio, who makes a film under his own authority and with his own source of financing. The term may also apply to the film made by an independent filmmaker.

■ **independent distributor** An organization that distributes motion pictures but is not part of one of the major film studios. Such an organization may distribute regionally or distribute a special type of film or low-budget, independent features.

■ **independent feature** A film of feature length, either documentary or fictional, made by independent filmmakers who are not attached to the Hollywood industry. Such films have generally been financed by private sources and/or government and philanthropic agencies. Independent features are made with much lower budgets than the normal Hollywood product, thus relying less on technique or special effects and more on subject matter and, in the case of fictional films, on dialogue. Such independent works have always been made, but a definite movement arose in the late 1960s and 1970s in response to the closed doors of a shrinking film industry. Independent features such as George Romero's *Night of the Living Dead* (1968) and David Lynch's *Eraserhead* (1978), because of their violent subject matter and professional treatment, became cult films; and Russ Meyer's soft-core pornographic films, which he both made and distributed, were singularly successful. But a significant number of independent features were serious in intent and treated a subject matter that Hollywood avoids. The more skillful of these, such as John Sayles's *The Return of the Secaucus Seven* (1980), found their audiences, though a limited national distribution. Some independent features, such as John Hanson and Rob Nilsson's *Northern Lights* (1979), found support from public television. Rare documentary features, such as Ira Wohl's *Best Boy* (1979), a film about a fifty-two-year-old retarded man which won an Academy Award, received a limited national distribution.

The more independent films, in general, have always had a rough time finding a distributor. The Sundance Film Festival has sought to be a springboard for independent filmmakers and has sent forth into the world films such as Steven Soderbergh's *sex, lies, and videotape* (1989). Independent Feature Project (IFP) and First Run Features are organizations that help in publicizing and distributing independent films; Film Forum in New York City exhibits such works. Independent feature films received a large part of their financing from federal agencies such as the National Endowment for the Humanities and the National Endowment for the Arts, and some financing from state agencies, but such funding in recent years has seriously diminished. With an increasing demand for films because of multiplex theaters, cable movie channels, and videocassettes, independent features may be facing their best years.

■ **Independent Feature Project (IFP)** An organization located in New York City that supports the making and distribution of independent feature films. This organization acts as a forum for filmmakers, offering a *Talents and Skills Directory*, newsletter, seminars, monthly screenings, and contact with creative personnel in the industry at large. The IFP presents the Independent Feature Film Market (IFFM) each year, which screens a large number of independent films and is visited by representatives of the film industry.

■ **independent film** A motion picture made by a filmmaker who has no connection with the Hollywood scene. Independent films have generally been shorts, ranging anywhere from a few minutes to less than an hour. Such works have frequently presented subjects and used techniques antithetical to standard commercial films. Because of their shorter lengths, anticommercial stance, and because they earn little money, such films have found infrequent distribution and a very small audience. A number of feature-length independent films, however, both documentary and fictional, have found a wider audience. *See* **independent feature.**

■ **independent filmmaker** (1) A term sometimes used for makers of avant-garde or noncommercial films. (2) A person who makes a commercial film, but is not associated with the Hollywood scene.

■ **independent producer** An individual who produces films independently and is not under contract to a film studio or production company.

■ **independent production** A fictional feature film made independently, outside the direct control of a Hollywood film studio, but one, unlike the "independent feature" described above, that is made by established filmmakers and performers and often receives national release by the distribution arm of one of the Hollywood studios or by a distributor unrelated to the studios. Such films have frequently been financed by a distributor, but a number have found independent backing outside the traditional establishment. When distributors finance such films, they have, of course, considerable influence on subject matter, treatment, and personnel, and the result is often a conventional product created largely for box-office appeal.

The reasons for the increase of independent productions since the 1950s are several. The antitrust Paramount decision of the Supreme Court in 1948, separating exhibition from production and distribution, forced the major studios to divest themselves of their theaters, the guaranteed outlets for their films,

and to cease the practice of block-booking in independent theaters as well. Studios now had to sell their products to exhibitors and independents found greater opportunity for showing their films. The considerable drop in film attendance during the 1950s because of the rise of television also put a great strain on the studios, which were forced to make fewer films and to cut back on personnel. It soon became more profitable to allow independent production companies to rent space and equipment for their own films, though the studios often financed these productions and had considerable influence. United Artists, which did not have its own studios, was resurrected and soon became a major financing and distributing agency for independent productions.

Roger Corman's New World Pictures, in the 1970s, though making a series of low-budget, exploitative films, was certainly not one of the majors but was instrumental in launching the careers of directors such as Peter Bogdanovich and Jonathan Demme. Although a number of firms sprang up in the 1980s to handle the distribution of independent films with commercial possibilities—Island Pictures, for example, distributed Godfrey Reggio's *Koyanisqatsi* (1983)—and a number began financing the production of small-budget independent features themselves, exhibition became a problem and advertising costs were difficult to absorb. Independent companies making these films, such as New World, Island Pictures, and Savoy Pictures, bit the dust. But "small studios" such as Miramax, Fine Line, and October Films released an impressive number of independent films. New Line Cinema has been one of the most successful independents in the history of film, releasing a number of high-box-office hits and, through its Fine Line Cinema, releasing a number of quality films; but the company, along with Castle Rock Entertainment, now belongs to the Turner Broadcasting System, which took on the status of a major when it became a member of the Motion Picture Association of America in 1995. New Line is now releasing higher-budget films, but since the Turner organization itself has recently joined Time Warner, with its Warner Brothers Pictures, New Line's future with the organization remains uncertain. Although Miramax now belongs to Disney, it has claimed its independence in releasing quality, independent features; yet the success of its own *Pulp Fiction* in 1994 (dir. Quentin Tarantino) is turning it gradually toward broader-based films. The same can be said of Fox Searchlight, owned by Rupert Murdoch's News Corporation, Sony Picture Classics, owned by the Sony Corporation, and Gramercy, owned by Polygram. A few independents, like October Films and Strand, however, have still maintained their independence, but the prognosis is that the line between films turned out by most successful independent film companies and the major studios will further erode.

Such independent productions were frequently package deals, with an independent producer generating an idea or property, then bringing together such established personnel as the director, screenwriter, and name performers, and finally selling the potential production to a studio-distributor. Whereas in 1949, 20 percent of the films released by the major distributors were independent productions, the number increased to 60 percent by the start of the 1960s. Also significant is the number of independent features now released outside of the studio distribution network. In 1995, the major studios released 234 new films and reissues, while 185 new and reissued independent films were released by organizations outside the Motion Picture Association of America. The remarkable success of independent productions during the 1996 Academy-Award competitions indicates that if such films are not more successful at the box office, they are winning the battle for quality. *See* **Paramount decision.**

■ **independents** The numerous film companies that existed between 1908 and 1914 in opposition to the Motion Picture Patents Company that had been formed in December 1908 by a group of major film companies to fight such upstart organizations. The Patents Company sought to license all film production, control the use of Edison's film equipment and Eastman Kodak's film, and regulate the showing of films by exhibitors. The trust also sought to stop the independents by roughhouse tactics, sending thugs to destroy film and equipment in studios and theaters. But the independents seemed destined to win the battle, partly through their own tenacity, partly through the mistakes of the trust, and partly through the demand for a great number of motion pictures—nearly half the Nickelodeons were not controlled by the Patents Company. The independents lured away many of the stars and personnel from the trust companies, began the star system which popularized their films, made longer films than the established companies, and produced better and more innovative films. They also were aided by their migration to Hollywood, where they generally were safe from the harassment of the trust company. The Hollywood scene also afforded the independents better weather, a variety of outdoor locations for shooting, and more centralized and efficient working conditions.

The independents flourished while the members of the trust grew weaker and weaker. Citing the Sherman Antitrust Act, William Fox instituted a suit against the Patents Company in 1913, which led to a federal court in Pennsylvania ruling the trust illegal in 1915. The Motion Picture Patents Company was legally dissolved in 1918 when its final appeal was dismissed, but the independents had actually won their battle, economically and artistically, a number of years earlier when they had already marked the path that the industry would follow for the coming decades. Some of the more important independent film companies of this period were Fox (at that time Box Office Attractions), IMP (the Independent Motion Picture Company, which consolidated with other independents to become Universal Pictures in 1912), Bison (the makers of Westerns

released by IMP-Universal and later by Mutual), Mutual (a conglomerate distributor for a number of independent film producers), and Keystone (whose comedies were distributed by Mutual). *See* **Hollywood** *and* **Motion Picture Patents Company.**

■ **index** A term defined by the American linguist C. S. Peirce and employed in semiotics to mean a sign of one thing that indicates something else by its logical relation to it. For example, an image of smoke is an icon, that is, a direct representation of smoke, but it is also an index, or indirect sign, for fire. In the film image, we are frequently called upon to make such connections when we see an index primarily as an indication of something more significant than itself. Such a process adds to our involvement in the action on the screen as we realize the bond between index and subject. The third of Peirce's signs is the symbol, which occurs when one thing represents something else through an arbitrary or cultural connection to it (e.g., red for danger). *See* **semiotics.**

■ **Indies** A colloquial abbreviation for the independent production/distribution companies as opposed to the "majors" or major Hollywood film companies. *See* **independent feature** *and* **independent production.**

■ **indigenous sound** Sound in a film for which the source is directly visible on the screen—for example, music from a piano when we actually see someone playing the instrument, or the noise of an automobile when we see it racing across the horizon. Also called direct sound.

■ **indirect voice-over** A voice that we hear from someone off-screen, giving us information not directly related to the image but rather working in counterpoint to what we are seeing. Both in documentary and fictional films the counterpoint may add to the emotional impact of the action we are witnessing by foreshadowing some future event or describing something that is going on elsewhere, thus undercutting or putting in an ironic context the image before us. *See* **voice-over.**

■ **induction motors** Motors that do not run in sync with other systems. Such motors are normally part of cameras with their own sound systems.

■ **industrial film, industrial** A film that gives information about some industry, company, or public service. Such films are frequently financed by industries or individual companies to publicize their work, brighten their image, sell their products, or educate their own workers. A number of documentaries on such subjects made by skilled filmmakers without industry's financial support can also be placed in this category. For example, the EMB (Empire Marketing Board) in Britain, under the directorship of John Grierson, made a number of films promoting British industry and services in a highly artistic way.

■ **Industrial Light and Magic (ILM)** The special-effects company organized by George Lucas in 1975 for *Star Wars*. The organization was first headed by John Dykstra, under whose supervision it built the Dykstraflex, a sophisticated motion-control system that became the model for future systems of the same type. ILM has continued to be one of the most important special-effects companies in the industry, performing its magic for the remainder of the *Star Wars* films. The company has especially been a pioneer in bringing the new digital technology into motion pictures with such films as Steven Spielberg's *Jurassic Park* (1993). *See* **computer animation, motion control,** *and* **special effects.**

■ **infinity** The normal meaning of the term is "boundless and immeasurable space or time." In photography the term has two basic meanings: (1) a distance sufficiently far from the camera so that light rays reflected from any point in that area are virtually parallel to the lens and there appears to be no definite limit to the depth of field. When the camera is focused on infinity, all the points of the scene in the action field have a satisfactory circle of confusion for image reproduction on the focal plane. (2) The setting on the camera's focusing scale whereby all points in the distance will give satisfactory circles of confusion for image reproduction on the focal plane.

■ **in-flight version** The version of a motion picture played on an airplane that is edited for family viewing, reduced in size, and difficult to see and hear.

■ **information age** The name given to this era, and those soon to come, which are highlighted by the revolutionary growth in media and their appropriate systems for the selling and exchange of information. The term "information" here applies to (1) educational ideas and data; (2) exchanges of materials between businesses and between a business and consumer; and (3) entertainment vehicles. The information age is the result of the vast and rapid growth of electronic technology, especially video and digital, and the Internet for the exchange and dissemination of such information. The motion-picture industry plays a key role in this age, but only as part of a larger business world and a vast network of activities—its own works being the source of home videos, cable and network television transmissions, video and computer games, audio records, novelizations and other books, and a host of merchandising artifacts both here and abroad. The amount of money spent in the electronic and computer sector of our economy is far vaster than anything the film industry earns. Ours is an age that has moved from an economy based on production to one that features service, entertainment, and information.

■ **informational film** Any nonfictional film that is intended to supply an audience with information about a certain subject primarily for the purpose of instruction and education. Such films are concerned with presenting factual information in a direct and immediate way, unlike many documentaries, which also seek to persuade an audience, both intellectually and emotionally, toward a particular point of view. *See* **documentary, industrial film, instructional film, nonfiction film, skill film,** *and* **training film.**

■ **information theory** The study of communication, especially the way information is transmitted. Such theory is primarily concerned with the process by which information is sent, the distortion in transmission, the process of reception, and the probability of accurate recognition. Such an approach has obvious application to film, especially in relation to the audience's response to both visual and aural information.

■ **in frame** When the image is properly aligned in the projector and the frame lines are not visible on the screen.

■ **infrared, infrared rays, infrared radiation** The invisible rays beyond the visible rays of the light spectrum that are longer and have a strong heating effect.

■ **infrared cinematography** Cinematography employing special film, either black-and-white or color, that is sensitive to infrared rays. Infrared light, when recorded on film, has the capacity to register details in shadows and in the distance not normally evident to the naked eye. Such light is also not dispersed by haze or fog. Infrared cinematography can be used to record events in sunlight as if it were a moonlit night (the film is printed somewhat darker than normal).

■ **infrared film** Black-and-white or color film sensitive to infrared rays for infrared cinematography. *See* **infrared cinematography.**

■ **infrared traveling-matte process** A traveling-matte process for the making of a composite image from different shots of background and foreground that employs infrared light for the purpose of matting. Infrared light illuminates a black or transparent backing against which an actor or actors are positioned. A prism with a dichroic filter in a beam-splitting camera permits the visible light rays from the foreground to pass onto normal film while it deflects the infrared rays from the backing onto infrared film. The result is a negative of the foreground from which a positive with the background area blacked out can be made (hence there is no need for a counter matte), and a negative of the backing from which a traveling matte can be printed with the foreground opaque and the surrounding area clear. Since infrared rays do not focus on the same focal plane as regular light, the larger matte image must be reduced to coincide with the actual foreground image by optical printing. Through bipack printing, the traveling matte can then be used to black out the appropriate foreground area in the image of the background being photographed on a fresh negative, after which the foreground action can be fitted into the unexposed area on the negative. *See* **bipack contact matte printing** *and* **traveling-matte process.**

∎ **ingenue** (1) The role of an innocent, inexperienced, and attractive young woman, normally in her late teens or very early twenties, in a play or film; (2) an actress who performs such roles. See **juvenile.**

∎ **in-house unit** A production unit that belongs to a film company rather than one specially hired for a single production.

∎ **initial capture** Capturing an image by means of traditional methods of photography as opposed to digital capture, which means feeding the image into the computer for alteration.

∎ **ink and paint** (1) The stage in animation when the rough drawings are transferred to cels, with the outlines drawn in ink and the drawings painted in the proper colors; (2) The department in an animation studio that performs this job. *See* **animation.**

∎ **inked** A slang term indicating that an individual has been contracted to a production by signing his or her name on a contract.

∎ **inker** An artist who traces the outlines from the drawings of the animator onto the cels in the animation process. *See* **animation** *and* **opaquer.**

∎ **inking** Tracing the outlines from the animator's drawings onto cels in the animation process. The job is generally performed by the inker. *See* **animation** *and* **opaquing.**

∎ **inky** A term sometimes used for an open incandescent luminaire with a 100-watt bulb and sometimes for a lensed mini or midget with a 200-watt bulb.

∎ **inky dink, dinky ink, inky, dinky** (1) A small incandescent lamp, between 100 and 250 watts, frequently employed to light a limited area. The term "inky" derives from incandescent and "dinky" suggests small. (2) The term "inky dink" is sometimes specifically used for an open incandescent lamp with a 200-watt bulb. (3) The term "inky dink" is also sometimes specifically used for a closed lamp of this type with a 100-watt bulb. (4) The term "dinky" is sometimes used for a closed incandescent luminaire with a 100-watt bulb. (5) The term "inky" is sometimes used for an open-face lamp of this type with a 100-watt bulb and sometimes for a lensed mini or midget with a 200-watt bulb. *See* **lighting.**

∎ **inner monologue** *See* **interior monologue.**

∎ **input device** Any device that converts images from one format into another; e.g., a telecine that transfers film images onto videotape or a film scanner that converts film images into a digital code for computer activities. *See* **output device.**

∎ **input scanner** *See* **film scanner** *and* **scanner.**

∎ **insert, insert shot** A shot of an object either part of a scene or external but relevant to it that is filmed separately and later inserted into the scene during editing. An example of an object in the scene might be a clock, supposedly on the wall, showing the time; an example of an object not from a scene but relevant to it might be the face of a tower clock, supposedly somewhere else in the city, also setting the time.

∎ **insert car** A vehicle equipped to carry camera, lighting, and generator as well as to tow a vehicle that is the subject of the shooting.

∎ **insert slate** A small slate with similar information to that put on clapboard, but without the clapsticks and used to give information for a shot without sound or for certain types of insert shots with long lenses. *See* **clapboard.**

∎ **insert stage** A small studio employed for photographing close-ups of objects that will be inserted into the film.

∎ **insert titles, intertitles** Printed words inserted into the body of the film instead of being placed either at the beginning or ending. In silent films, such titles gave dialogue or set time and location. In sound films such titles can set time and place or simply provide information about passing events. *See* **title.**

∎ **insert traveling matte** A traveling matte of a single area that blocks out some portion in the main image into which an action can later be inserted. For example, the area of a window in a room might first be blocked out and moving vehicles or a storm as seen through the window later inserted. The scene in the room is first photographed, then projected onto a matte board, where the window is drawn and blackened. This blackened area is photographed and a traveling matte made with an opaque area for the window. The matte is used to block out the window while the scene is rephotographed on fresh stock. By using a counter matte to block out the corresponding area surrounding the window on the background film, the proper area can be inserted into the window of the major scene on the new negative. *See* **traveling-matte process.**

∎ **in shot** Any person or object accidentally in a shot.

■ **instructional film** Any film with the primary function of teaching the audience how to perform some action or conveying information about some subject. *See* **informational film, skill film,** *and* **training film.**

■ **instrumentation camera** A special camera originally designed for scientific and engineering purposes, but which is also used for motion-picture work, generally as a high-speed camera. *See* **high-speed camera.**

■ **insurance shot** *See* **cover shot.**

■ **in sync** When picture and corresponding sound are perfectly aligned and occur at the same time.

■ **INT** *See* **interior.**

■ **integral reflex viewfinder** A reflex viewfinder that is built into the camera. *See* **reflex viewfinder.**

■ **integral screen** A screen that creates a steroscopic image, hence avoiding the need for the cumbersome glasses normally needed for three-dimensional cinema. The screen separates left and right eye images by means of lenticular strips and projects them back to the viewer. The image achieved so far is still somewhat poor and restricted to a limited area in front of the screen. Most recent work on this method was done in the Soviet Union. *See* **stereoscopy.**

■ **integral shot** A single shot that makes up an entire scene. Such a scene has no cutting.

■ **integral tripack color system** A subtractive color process employing a single film with three layers of emulsion, each recording light waves from one of the primary colors. The top layer is normally sensitive to blue. Beneath this layer is a filter that keeps blue light from penetrating to the layers sensitive to green and red. In each emulsion layer, the silver halides and chemical dyes, called couplers, are exposed and developed. When the unexposed halides are washed away and the developed halides bleached out, each layer forms an image in the appropriate subtractive (or complementary) color—that is, the color when the respective primary is removed from white light (yellow for blue, magenta for green, cyan for red)—but with the colors in concentrations opposite to those needed in the actual image. Hence the colors appear complementary to the original colors while light and dark are reversed. From this negative, a color positive is printed on another tripack film, but this time with subtractive dyes in proper concentrations so that colors appear as in the original scene with light and dark returned to normal. Positive film stock normally has the layer of the emulsion sensitive to green on top, that sensitive to red in the middle, and that sensitive to blue on the bottom. When the image is sent to the screen, each of the subtractive colors removes its primary from the light and is

itself projected. Since the early 1950s, integral tripack film has replaced the three Technicolor negatives. This development was considerably assisted by Eastman Kodak's Eastman Color, a tripack film put on the market in 1952. *See* **color film** *(2).*

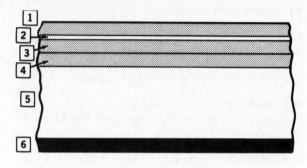

integral tripack color film 1. blue-sensitive emulsion
2. filter 3. green-sensitive emulsion
4. red-sensitive emulsion 5. base
6. antihalation backing

■ **intelligent slate** *See* **smart slate.**

■ **intensification** The process of increasing the density and hence details of an image, generally on the negative, during processing. *See* **processing.**

■ **intensity** (1) The degree of illumination in the image. (2) The degree of the volume of sound on the sound track.

■ **interactive** A system in which the viewer has some choice and asserts some control over the presentation of moving images or words offered to him or her by a medium or several media. The term originally applied to video, but in interactive video, the analog nature of the media limited the amount of choice and flexibility. With the new digital media, and the vast amount of information that can be stored with this technology, interactivity has become a much greater reality for industrial training, education, but also for entertainment. Because of the use of the computer, monitor, and CD-ROM disc for storing and sending forth both the moving image and sound, the term "multimedia" is now used more than "interactive." As well as the involvement in playing a game, this system offers the viewer the possibility of being involved in the shaping and directing of a narrative and also the opportunity to be one of the characters. *See* **analog** *and* **digital.**

■ **interaxial** The distance between the two viewpoints of a subject photographed in a 3-D film process; hence, the distance between the two axes of the lenses in a dual camera system or within a lens in a single camera system. This distance represents approximately the one-and-one-half-inch separation between the viewer's right and left eye, which is largely responsible for depth perception. *See* **convergence** *and* **stereoscopy.**

■ **interchangeable lenses** Individual lenses of specific focal lengths that can be attached to a camera with the appropriate mount. Interchangeable lenses were the rule in cinematography until the development of the turret, which can hold several lenses including a zoom lens, on the camera at once.

■ **intercut** (1) The alternation between actions taking place at two distinct locations to make one composite scene—for example, shots of a woman in her room waiting for her lover are alternated with shots of her lover rushing to meet her; or individual shots of two people carrying on a telephone conversation are alternated on the screen. Unlike cross-cutting, the technique creates an effect of a single scene rather than of two distinct actions. Sometimes intercutting is an efficient way of accelerating or slowing down a major action. An intercut can also hide the omission of an intermediate stage, thus allowing a vehicle, for example, to get from one place to another in unnaturally rapid fashion; or it can interfere with two consecutive stages, thus delaying the normal flow of time. (2) The interjection into a master scene of shots of other action for contrast or dramatic effect (when there are a sufficient number of shots of the second action, we have cross-cutting instead of intercutting). (3) The term is sometimes used synonymously with crosscut, though it is preferable to distinguish the two as in definitions (1) and (2).

■ **interdupe** A term that sometimes refers to the dupe negative made from the master positive of the original negative. Dupe negatives are the source of release prints. Also called an internegative. *See* **dupe.**

■ **interior (INT)** Any scene or setting inside a building. The interior can either be a built set at the studio or the inside of an actual building. Outside scenes are referred to as exteriors. *See* **exterior.**

■ **interior framing** *See* **framing** *(3).*

■ **interior lighting** Indoor lighting for illuminating a set or the inside of an actual building for shooting.

■ **interior monologue, inner monologue** The internal thoughts of a character presented as if the character were carrying on a continuous conversation with himself or herself. The technique is more acceptable in the novel, since we are allowed to slip into the minds of the characters as we read their thoughts; it is less natural in theater where the action has to stop while the character steps forth and recites, in soliloquy, his or her thoughts, though the convention was accepted by Shakespeare's audiences. In film, an inner monologue

can be delivered as a voice-over: as the character moves about with lips closed, we hear the individual's voice articulating his or her thoughts. This is the way Laurence Olivier handled the soliloquies in his film production of Shakespeare's *Hamlet* (1948). Eisenstein argued that montage was a way of expressing the "inner monologue," or thought process, in a visual manner (in *Film Form*).

■ **interlock** (1) A system in which two independent motors are made to run synchronically at precisely the same speed. (2) A system in which image and sound are run independently but synchronically. *See* **synchronization.**

■ **interlock mix** An audio mix for which picture and all sound tracks are utilized. Normally an interlock projector, a number of dubbers playing edited tracks, and an interlocked recorder are employed. The sound editor is able to watch a workprint at the same time that he or she hears the various tracks. *See* **blind mix.**

■ **interlock motor** Any motor that is made to run synchronically with another motor of the same type, starting and stopping at exactly the same time and running at precisely the same speed. Such motors might be employed so that two cameras film in perfect conjunction or a projector and camera work precisely together in rear-projection shots. Interlocking motors are also employed for editing and dubbing when image and sound are run independently but synchronically. *See* **synchronization.**

■ **interlock projector** A projector, generally employed for editing, that projects a picture and is, at the same time, perfectly aligned with another machine that synchronically plays back the sound from a separate tape.

■ **interlock screening** A showing of a film, before editing and mixing have been completed, with interlocked picture and sound tracks to allow the filmmaker to assess the present state of the film.

■ **intermediate** A film, other than an original negative, that is the source for duplicate copies: for example, a master positive (called an interpositive), a dupe negative made from a master positive (called an internegative or interdupe), and a dupe negative made from an original reversal color film (called an internegative). *See* **generation** *and* **printing.**

■ **intermediate-speed camera** A term sometimes applied to a high-speed camera employing an intermittent mechanism to obtain speeds higher than 24 frames per second. Such cameras have more strongly built intermittent drive systems than normal and can achieve speeds, for both 35mm and 16mm film, of several hundred feet per second. *See* **high-speed camera.**

■ **intermittent drive**   *See* **intermittent movement** *(2)*.

■ **intermittent movement**   The term "intermittent" means stopping and going with periodic pauses. In relation to cameras and projectors, the term is joined with the word "movement" to describe the following: (1) The passage of film through a camera or projector whereby each frame is put in front of the aperture and held there briefly for exposure or projection and is then moved on while the next frame takes its place. (2) The drive mechanism in a camera or projector responsible for the intermittent movement of the film. In the camera, claws engage the perforations of the frame and pull it down in front of the aperture. For 35mm film, the frame is generally held in place by registration pins and a pressure plate. When the frame is stationary, the opening in the rotating shutter passes before the aperture, allowing light to expose the frame. Meanwhile the claws have been moving upward and are now ready to bring the next frame before the aperture for exposure. The continuous movement of one or two rotating sprockets feeds the film into and withdraws it from the intermittent-movement mechanism, and a flexible loop at both entrance and departure allows the film to move in and out of the intermittent movement without tearing. In professional projectors a continuously turning shaft with a single pin engages one of four slots on a Maltese (or Geneva) cross, forcing it to turn 90 degrees at a time and intermittently turn a sprocket that places each frame individually before the projector aperture. The opening of the rotating shutter passes before the aperture at exactly the right time to allow the stationary frame to be projected by the beam from the projector lamp. To avoid flicker, the blade of a second rotating shutter cuts the exposure time in half. In simple projectors, a rotating cam moves one or two arms in shuttle fashion to engage the frame and move it into position. As in the camera, loops at both ends allow the film to pass in and out of the intermittent movement without tearing. *See* **camera** *and* **projector**.

■ **intermittent printer**   A printing machine for either contact or optical printing in which both negative and fresh stock move from continuous to intermittent and back to continuous movement. During the intermittent phase, each frame is brought to a fixed position for exposure. A rotating shutter blocks off the light when the next frame is moved into position. These machines are also called step printers. Intermittent contact printers allow perfect registration and can be employed for matting together separate picture elements or making rear-projection or front-projection plates. Optical printers of this type, because of great flexibility in moving the projector or camera elements and also because of excellent registration, can create a number of special effects, print transitions from one scene to another, change the speed of action, alter the size of various picture elements, and reduce a film from one gauge to another. *See* **printer**.

■ **intermodulation, intermodulation distortion**   A sound distortion caused by the modulation of frequencies in a complex signal fed into a nonlinear system. The output signal is out of harmony with the original basic signal.

■ **internal reflector lamp**   *See* **reflector lamp**.

■ **internal rhythm**   The flow or movement of a particular scene or sequence in a film created by such factors as the length of shots, frequency of cutting, camera angles, composition of individual shots, interplay of composition within a series of shots, and movement of action within a specific shot and series of shots. Such rhythm is also assisted by the tempo of dialogue, music, and background sound. To create a discernible rhythm there must be an established pattern interacting with opposing or varying elements. Each scene has its own particular rhythm, and the accumulative effect of such scenes creates a rhythm within a sequence. The rhythm of the sequence is itself reinforced by the length of the various scenes, the transitions from one to another, and the arrangement of these scenes. The audience is always aware of these rhythms, feeling the frenzied movement, the stately progression, or the slow languor that characterize the action and people. When the internal rhythm is not properly controlled, one may feel confusion or simply boredom. Good examples of controlled and effective internal rhythms appear in a number of classic Westerns, as in the final shoot-out sequence in John Ford's *My Darling Clementine* (1946) or George Stevens's *Shane* (1953). The rhythm predominant throughout an entire film is generally referred to as external rhythm. *See* **external rhythm** *and* **rhythm**.

■ **International Alliance of Theatrical Stage Employees (IATSE)**   An alliance of unions representing various film crafts, affiliated with the AFL-CIO. The alliance includes more than 850 locals both in the United States and Canada. It has 20 local unions in Hollywood, including those for camera personnel, electricians, editors, costumers, grips, set painters, script supervisors, make-up artists, sound technicians, laboratory technicians, and cartoonists. The IATSE negotiates many of the standard agreements with the film industry for these various locals.

■ **International Creative Management (ICM)**   *See* **talent agency**.

■ **International Standards Organization (ISO)**   This organization, centered in Paris, is responsible for setting standards of measurement. It has given its initials, ISO, to a rating system for the exposure index of films that includes both the ASA and DIN figures. This organization has been instrumental in defining computer terminology. Its affiliate in the United States is the American National Standards Institute. *See* **American National Standards Institute, ASA standard, DIN standard,** *and* **ISO**.

■ **internegative** (1) A color negative printed directly from an original negative and used for printing duplicates. *See* **color reversal intermediate.** (2) A negative made from a master positive or interpositive on the same intermediate stock which is employed for striking release prints. Also called an interdupe. (3) A dupe negative made from an original color reversal film.

■ **interpositive** A color master positive printed from the original negative for making dupe negatives. The negatives will be the source of release prints.

■ **intertitles** *See* **insert titles.**

■ **intervalometer** A device for measuring intervals between shots and operating the shutter of the camera for time-lapse photography, when single frames are shot at periods of time. The device is sometimes part of a camera for puppet animation, when each frame must be shot at set intervals.

■ **in the can** (1) Film that is already shot and ready to be put into the container that will be delivered for processing. (2) Consequently, the term also means that the shooting of the entire movie is finished, since all of the film has been processed or is ready for processing.

■ **into frame** A term in a film script indicating that someone moves into a shot that is already focused on someone or something else.

■ **into view** A term in a film script indicating that the camera moves during a shot to bring someone or something into the shot.

■ **intrinsic interest** An object or area of the image that draws an audience's attention though it is not part of the dominant interest. An object of intrinsic interest may draw our attention because it takes on significance from the major action (e.g., a gun on a table). An area of intrinsic interest may draw our attention because of some event which relates to the major action (e.g., the sudden appearance of a storm). *See* **dominant** *and* **subsidiary.**

■ **Introvision** A dual-screen process created by Introvision used safely and relatively rapidly in a studio that allows live performers to be placed in the midst of action and settings photographed elsewhere. Although such scenes could not be achieved by shooting all the action simultaneously on location, this process allows the director and cinematographer to see the final scene at once. A projector sends the images of the background plate or action plates onto a beam splitter/mirror, placed at a 45-degree angle to the camera, which then reflects part of the image or images onto a small screen on the side and part onto a larger screen behind the actors and scenery. The camera films off the beam split-ter, placing the actors and stage props in the midst of the projected setting or action.

■ **in turnaround** A property released before production by a studio and therefore available to other studios.

■ **inverse kinematics (IK)** In computer animation, a type of automatic linking system that connects groups of related objects in movement. The most obvious example is a model of the human body being animated by the movement of one joint that automatically sets off a chain of movements in the other joints.

■ **inverse square law** When the source of a light falling on a surface is a single point, the intensity of illumination falling on that area is inversely proportionate to the square of the distance between the surface and source of light.

■ **inverted telephoto lens** *See* **retrofocus lens.**

■ **invisible cutting, invisible editing** Cutting from one shot to another so unobtrusively that viewers are virtually unaware of the change in the camera's position as they watch the action. The German film director G. W. Pabst is often cited for his development in this style during the silent-film period; but invisible cutting is especially associated with Hollywood, which continued this style during the studio period, when a large number of rapidly made films emphasized no discernible or individual cutting technique but rather focused upon the action and stars. Invisible cutting contrasts with the montage style of cutting developed by Eisenstein in the Soviet Union. Eisenstein's technique evokes in the viewer intellectual, emotional, and psychological responses by the obvious cutting from shot to shot, which juxtaposes and relates a series of separate images. To a considerable extent, most contemporary films follow the invisible style of cutting, except when specific effects are intended. Such cutting, however, also seems invisible because we have become sufficiently used to such techniques to be unaware that they are even taking place.

A basic rule is to cut on action so that viewers are sufficiently involved with what is happening to be unaware of transitions from shot to shot. Normally this is done by overlapping action when one camera is employed, or using two cameras simultaneously or consecutively and joining the action in editing. Examples of cutting on action are when a character begins to move across a room to a window, and the camera suddenly focuses on him through the window itself; or a character is seen in a medium shot from the rear reaching for something on a shelf, and suddenly we see him closeup from the side taking a specific item off the shelf. Hollywood established an invisible style of cutting for conversations between two characters that focuses individually on the speaker and the reactions of the listener, alternating these shots with a master two-shot. This technique prevents the scene from becoming boring through a single long take of a two-shot. Through invisible cutting, space can be quickly condensed and the viewer moved into a new scene, for example, by an establishing shot of a building, followed by a medium shot of a specific part of the building which includes a window, and then by a shot of some character in the room behind the window. Invisible cutting, deftly accomplished, can condense time as well as space by showing us a character start to run across a field and then cutting to the other side of the field where we see the character suddenly enter a clump of trees or a house. The master scene technique was much used by Hollywood to facilitate invisible cutting—a single scene was shot in a continuous take, generally in a long shot, and then parts of the scene were photographed again in medium shots and close-ups that could be edited into the master scene. The invisible style of cutting has also been called academic cutting and continuity cutting, while French critics have called it *découpage classique*. *See* **cutting on action, dynamic cutting, master scene technique,** *and* **matching action.**

■ **invisible splice** A type of splice employed in checkerboard cutting for A and B printing. After the last frame of a shot, the film is overlapped onto the black leader, thus preventing the splice from being exposed to the positive when printing 16mm film. *See* **A and B printing** *and* **checkerboard cutting.**

■ **IP/IN** The process of making an interpositive or master positive from the original negative, and an internegative from the interpositive which will be the source of release prints.

■ **IPS** *See* **inches per second.**

■ **iris, diaphragm, iris diaphragm** A circular piece of overlapping metal leaves in the lens barrel that controls the amount of light reaching the film in the camera. The piece is called an iris because it operates like the iris of the human eye. The brighter the area, the more the iris is "stopped down," decreasing the aperture—this process also increases focus and depth of field. The iris is controlled by the f-stop ring: the larger the f-stop number, the smaller the aperture. *See* **f-stop** *and* **t-stop.**

■ **iris-in, iris-out** *See* **iris shot.**

■ **iris shot, iris** A shot with a masking generally in circular form, though rectangular, diamond, and other shapes have been employed. Especially popular during silent-film days (for example, in the works of D. W. Griffith), the iris shot today is uncommon, perhaps because it is associated with older films and now seems artificial. However, the device is sometimes found in comic films evoking the farcical spirit of earlier movies, and directors such as Truffaut occasionally employed an iris shot with arch humor (e.g., in *Small Change* [1976]). The iris shot was used for the following rea-

iris shot *The Birth of a Nation* (1915; dir. D. W. Griffith).

sons in silent films: (1) to bring a scene gradually into view by beginning with a small circle at the center of the screen and expanding the circle until the entire image is in view, or to close a scene gradually by shrinking the entire image in circular form until the screen is black—the first procedure is called an iris-in and the second an iris-out (2) to close in on a character or object while leaving the rest of the screen black in order to focus the audience's attention or achieve a dramatic effect; (3) to create a dramatic or ironic effect by focusing on a particular character or object and then expanding the image so that the entire scene becomes visible, putting the character or object into an unexpected context; (4) to create an impression of looking through a confined opening such as a keyhole.

■ **iris wipe** An iris-in or an iris-out. *See* **iris shot.**

■ **irony** An especially popular term in literary criticism that is also applicable for film study. All of the following definitions imply an incongruity between appearance and reality or between what is intended and actually occurs; all of them suggest a play of opposites and a meaning or significance that transcends the immediate; and all of them are applicable for both comic and serious effect. Irony has the following meanings helpful for film study: (1) language that says one thing while meaning another; (2) a dramatic situation about which the audience has important knowledge that is withheld from the character; (3) a dramatic situation in which the audience can see meanings or implications in a character's words or actions unknown to the character; (4) the conclusion of a plot or part of a plot where events turn out contrary to expectation. The term "dramatic irony" is also employed for the last three definitions. Film uses both verbal and dramatic irony, but it can also create (5) visual irony when an image conveys a meaning opposite to its apparent significance—the true meaning can arise from the scene's placement in the larger context of scenes, by its juxtaposition to another image or scene, or by its being undercut by the sound track (especially by music).

■ **irradiation** (1) An enlarged appearance given to any object or person from being brightly illuminated against a dark background. (2) The diffusion of light caused by the silver halides in film emulsion. Such diffusion decreases the quality of the image, especially in thick emulsions.

■ **ISO standard, ISO exposure index, ISO numbers** The initials ISO stand for International Standards Organization and are used to give the exposure index for certain films in a manner determined by that organization. The ISO numbers actually include the ASA rating for film speed, sometimes used in this country for motion picture film, and the DIN rating used in Europe. *See* **ASA standard, DIN standard,** *and* **exposure index.**

■ **Iwerks Entertainment** A company, now public, founded in 1986 by Don Iwerks and Stan Kinsey to provide large "multisensory" attractions at location-based entertainment centers and theme and amusement parks. Iwerks, with headquarters in Burbank, California, is notable for its 70mm projection onto an encompassing dome screen, 360-degree video dance theater, and ride simulations.

■ ■ ■

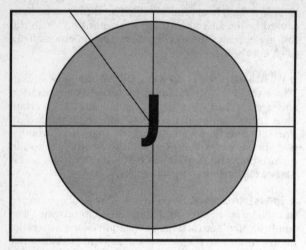

jack to juvenile

■ **jack** A connecting device for a plug-in electrical circuit.

■ **jacketed lamp** A tungsten-halogen lamp with gas between the quartz filament tube and the outer glass housing. The gas frees metal seals on the quartz from oxidation, thus giving the bulb longer life and allowing greater wattage.

■ **jaggies** *See* **aliasing.**

■ **jam** The wedging or squeezing together of loose film in the camera, camera magazine, or projector so that the machine is forced to stop.

■ **jell** *See* **gel.**

■ **jenny** Jargon for an electric generator.

■ **jib, jib arm** A projected arm of a dolly or crane to which the camera or lighting is attached. Jib arms can be placed in numerous positions and often are able to rotate a full 360 degrees.

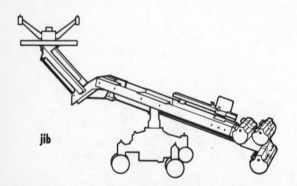

jib

■ **jitter** In animation, flickering of objects caused by poor artwork or inefficient operation of the camera.

■ **Johnston Office** Popular name for the Motion Picture Association of America (MPAA) from 1945 until 1963 under the leadership of Eric Johnston (before 1945 the organization was called the Motion Picture Producers and Distributors of America [MPPDA]). Foreign distribution of Hollywood's films, formerly a concern of the MPPDA, was made the responsibility of the new Motion Picture Export Association (MPEA), also headed by Johnston during the same period. Under his administration of both organizations, much effort was given to facing the problems caused by the Supreme Court's Paramount decision in 1948, which ended the studios' monopoly of the film industry, and to slowing the loss of audiences and revenue because of television. The MPAA kept up most of the services and activities of the MPPDA under Will Hays, but the rise of independent producers and a changing culture forced the organization to revise the Motion Picture Production Code in 1956 and ultimately to give up film censorship. *See* **Motion Picture Association of America** *and* **Motion Picture Production Code.**

■ *Journal of Film and Video* Published by the University Film and Video Association, this journal offers essays and features on the history of cinema and television as well as independent production of both film and video. The journal is geared to the teachers of film history and production.

■ *Journal of Popular Film and Television* A journal that focuses on commercial film and television from the perspective of popular culture. The journal's orientation is both social and cultural.

■ **joystick** The term is loosely applied in special effects photography to any mechanism that allows manual programming or control of the camera. The term derives from aerodynamics, where it is applied to the control stick of a plane, probably because of the joy that the pilot receives from controlling the plane.

■ **joystick zoom control** A control for a zoom lens connected by a cable and operated by a sliding thumb control that moves the lens in or out.

■ **juicer** Slang for an electrician. The head electrician in a film production is called the gaffer.

■ **jump** The undesirable vertical movement of an image projected on the screen caused by a looseness in the gate, damaged sprocket holes, or some malfunctioning part of the projector. Any vertical movement of the image should be less than .2 percent. *See* **breathing, flutter** *(1),* **Theater Alignment Program,** *and* **weave.**

■ **jump cut** A cut between two shots that seems abrupt and calls attention to itself because of some obvious jump in time or space. An undesired jump cut is caused by poor shooting or editing, but at times the cut is consciously made for some desired effect as, for example, when Godard frequently uses the technique to create the syncopated and disturbing movement of *Breathless* (1959), or, more specifically, when Hitchcock has his camera shock the audience by suddenly jumping to the gouged eyes of a victim in *The Birds* (1963). Jump cuts may be caused by the following: (1) editing out the central part of a continuous action so that the character seems to jump from one place to another; (2) switching suddenly from one action to another; (3) cutting from one time to another or from one place to another with the same camera angle and lens; (4) alternating shots between participants in a conversation with very little change in camera angle; (5) suddenly changing the angle of the camera or position of the performer in two consecutive shots of the same character; (6) cutting from a long or medium shot to a close-up of the same character or action; (7) cutting from one shot to another in the same scene with a new figure suddenly appearing in the second shot. If a jump cut is not desired to create an effect of abruptness, discontinuity, or heightened drama, efforts must be taken to overlap in shooting and match in editing two consecutive shots of the same action or to work out some transitional device between two separate actions. *See* **match cut.**

■ *Jump Cut* Published four times each year from Berkeley, California, this journal features ideological articles on film, which are concerned with such subjects as politics, sexism, homosexuality, and ethnicity.

■ **jump out** To remove unnecessary frames from a shot without any loss of continuity.

■ **junior, junior spot** A lamp with a 2,000 (or sometimes a 1,000) watt bulb for lighting a limited area or specific performer. *See* **spotlight.**

■ **junior stand, junior combo stand** A light stand for holding a 2,000-watt (or larger) luminaire. A junior combo stand holds both the lamp and reflector.

■ **justified camera movement** Any movement of the camera that has a specific purpose (e.g., following an action or bringing some person or object to the audience's attention) as opposed to movement that seems to do little more than vary perspective.

■ **justified dolly shot** A shot from a moving dolly that has a specific intention (e.g., following a moving character). *See* **dolly.**

■ **juvenile** (1) The role of a young man, normally in his late teens, in a play or film; (2) an actor who performs such roles. *See* **ingenue.**

■ ■ ■

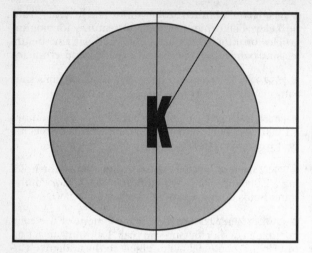

K to Kuleshov Workshop

■ **K** (1) An abbreviation for Kelvin degrees. *See* **Kelvin scale.** (2) An abbreviation for 1,000 watts; a kilowatt. This abbreviation is used more frequently than Kw in film work.

■ **Kalem** An early film production company formed in 1905. The company's name was based on the initials of its founders, George Kleine, Samuel Long, and Frank Marion. Begun with only $600, Kalem was clearing $250,000 per year by 1909 from its two weekly productions. The company has a certain renown in film history because its 1907 one-reel production of *Ben-Hur,* made with no regard for copyright, resulted in the legal decision that required all filmmakers to use copyright material only with proper consent. Some of Kalem's best films, including *Ben-Hur,* are the result of Sidney Olcott's direction. Kalem eventually had studios in Los Angeles, New York, Jacksonville, and New Orleans, and also shot several films in Ireland. Kalem was one of the forces behind the formation of the Motion Picture Patents Company in 1908, but, along with the other companies, did not inevitably meet the challenge of the independents. Kalem made only one feature film, the highly successful *From the Manger to the Cross* (1912), which was shot in Palestine and Egypt and directed by Olcott. Declining fortunes resulted in the company becoming part of Vitagraph in 1916.

■ *Kammerspielfilm* The word means "chamber-play film" in German and describes a type of silent film made in Germany during the 1920s which was both a development from Max Reinhardt's *Kammerspiel* theater and a reaction to the expressionist films of the time. These works are intimate, naturalistic, and psychological, with bleak and dark settings. A key feature is the sparse use and sometimes total lack of titles, which results in continuous narrative and greater visual impression than normal while placing more emphasis on characters' facial expressions and behavior. Sometimes this emphasis results in slow and ponderous scenes and overacting, but it also is responsible for some deeply moving images of human emotion. The most notable example of this type of film is Murnau's *The Last Laugh* (1924). *See* **UFA.**

Kammerspielfilm F. W. Murnau's *The Last Laugh* (1924) features Emil Jannings's overpowering performance and an evocatively dramatic camera.

■ ■ ■

■ **keep takes** Takes of a particular shot or scene not to be destroyed, but to be preserved for possible inclusion in the edited film.

■ **keg** A spotlight with a 500- to 1,000-watt bulb that has the shape of a beer keg.

■ **Kelvin scale** A scale for measuring the color temperature (i.e., the color quality) of a light source. The Kelvin scale is based on Centigrade degrees, but begins at the equivalent of –273°C. Normal daylight measures somewhere around 6,000°K, and a normal tungsten lamp in a studio measures about 3,200°K. Lower temperatures are in the red-to-orange scale, while higher temperatures have a greater amount of blue.

■ **Kem** Brand name of a popular flat-bed editing machine made by Kem Elektronik Mechanik GMBH in Hamburg, Germany. *See* **flat-bed editing machine.**

■ **Kem rolls** Originating from the rolls of film with either image or sound track used on a Kem flat-bed editing machine, the name now refers to such film used on any editing machine.

■ **key** (1) A specific market for film distribution: e.g., such large cities as New York and Los Angeles are major keys, middle-size cities are regular keys, and smaller cities are subkeys. (2) In electronic compositing, combining two separate images. *See* **chroma key.**

■ **key animation, keyframe animation** A type of animation for which the animator draws individual frames at key points called keys or keyframes, and other artists or a computer make the connecting frames from these key drawings (the process is sometimes called tweening).

■ **key animator** The artist who makes the key drawings in an animation film. These drawings are called keys or keyframes and represent the beginning and end of any alteration in a scene or in a figure's movement. The in-betweener is the animator who does the inbetween drawings to create the continuity of movement. In the case of computer animation, the computer itself follows instructions and creates the inbetween frames. *See* **animation.**

■ **keyframes, key frames** (1)The drawings made by the key animator that represent the beginning and end of any important alteration or movement in the sequence. The connecting drawings are made by the in-betweener. Also referred to as keys. (2) In computer animation, the beginning and concluding image for any alteration or movement in the sequence that acts as a guide for the computer automatically to create the joining frames. (3) In a digital video effect (DVE) system, the set of parameters for starting and concluding any single alteration in an effect. *See* **key animation** *and* **key animator.**

■ **key grip, head grip, first grip** The individual in charge of the stagehands, who are called the grips. *See* **grip.**

■ **keying** Listing the sequential key numbers to designate how the negative should be cut and selecting the corresponding negative for cutting by the negative cutter.

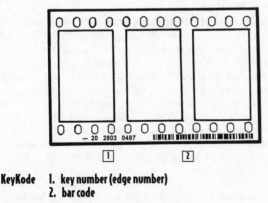

KeyKode 1. key number (edge number)
2. bar code

■ **KeyKode** A new system of numbering on film that is also coded in a machine-readable bar code introduced by Kodak for its film in 1989. The new system uses ten "key numbers" instead of the nine employed for tradi-

tional edge numbers to decrease the likelihood of repetition on rolls. The numbers appear every twenty-four perforations instead of the traditional sixty-four perforations or one foot. The bar code contains information for the key numbers, film, and manufacturer. The new KeyKode system is more convenient for transferring film to videotape and digital code, for editing in general, and for conforming the negative to the workprint or negative cut list. *See* **edge numbers.**

■ **key light** The major source of illumination for a subject or scene. The key light is normally elevated, in front of and to the side of the subject. When it is placed high to create the widest and most intense area of illumination and to minimize shadows, it is called a high key light. A particular light in the scene, such as the sun or a lamp, is sometimes made to seem the source of the key light. Other luminaires supplement the key light (e.g., filler lights and back lighting), but it is still the main source of illumination for the camera's exposure setting. *See* **lighting** *and* **lighting ratio.**

■ **key numbers** *See* **edge numbers.**

■ **keys, keyframes** The key drawing made by the key animator, which shows the beginning and end of any alteration in a scene or in a figure's movement. *See* **key animator.**

■ **Keystone** The famous silent-film company that produced a large number of popular comic films featuring some of Hollywood's greatest comic stars. In 1912, Adam Kessel and Charles O. Bauman of Mutual financed Mack Sennett, who had been working at Biograph, to organize and head the Keystone Company, which would produce films for distribution by Mutual. Sennett started out directing a reel of two short comedies each week, but success allowed a second unit to begin producing films in 1913, and by 1915 nine units were making comedies of one and two reels. Among the comic artists to work with Keystone were Charlie Chaplin, Chester Conklin, Fatty Arbuckle, and Mack Swain. After Keystone became part of Triangle in 1915, Buster Keaton, Wallace Beery, and Ben Turpin also worked with the company. Of special significance are the thirty-five Keystone films with Charlie Chaplin, especially the six-reel film *Tillie's Punctured Romance*, which appeared in 1914 and is considered the first feature-length comedy.

The approximately 500 comedies produced at Keystone under Sennett are remembered for such comic devices as the mad chases and fights with custard pies and for such figures as the zany Keystone Kops and Mack Sennett Bathing Beauties. Sennett developed the full potential of film as a visual medium for comedy. His slapstick comedies are an escape into a world of visual fantasy that seems to suspend the laws of nature. The endless sight gags, fast pacing, wild fights, farcical and preposterous characters, acrobatics machinelike human figures, animated machines and objects, and trick photography all create a world that looks like our own, but operates under laws more akin to our dream world—a dream world, however, free of anxiety and fear. Some of his films were even further removed from reality by parodying irreverently works by other filmmakers (e.g., D. W. Griffith).

Sennett left Keystone to go to Paramount in 1917. Though his career was still to be successful, his former film company could not survive his loss, no more than its parent company, Triangle, could survive the losses of Thomas Ince, D. W. Griffith, Douglas Fairbanks, William Hart, and others who also went to Paramount in the same year. By 1923, Keystone and Triangle were no more. *See* **Triangle.**

■ **Keystone Kops** A group of preposterous, funny, bungling, incompetent police officers who were part of the slapstick world of Mack Sennett's Keystone films beginning in 1912. *See* **Keystone.**

■ **keystoning** A distortion of an image caused either when a camera's lens is not at a right angle to a photographed surface (especially a surface of art work or titles), or when an image is projected from a lens axis of a projector not at a right angle to the screen. In both cases, the entire image appears in the shape of a keystone.

■ **kick** *See* **catchlight** *(1).*

■ **kicker light, kick light, rim light, cross backlight, side back light** (1) A light to the rear and side of a character that strikes him or her at an angle opposite to that of the keylight. (2) The lighting from such a lamp that outlines the subject without eliminating shadows. *See* **back light** *and* **lighting.**

■ **kill** To turn something off. The term is generally used in the imperative (e.g., "Kill the spot").

■ **kilowatt (Kw, K)** An amount of electricity equal to 1,000 watts.

■ **Kinemacolor** The first commercial color-film system, which was developed in 1906 by two Englishmen, Edward R. Turner and George Albert Smith, and financially supported by an American, Charles Urban. Urban arranged the system's first public demonstrations in England in 1908. A number of short films were made and released through Urban's company, but especially notable was the feature-length *The Durbar at Delhi*, which appeared in London in 1912. In this additive, two-color process, alternating frames of black-and-white film were exposed at 32 frames per second to either the red or green of a rotating filter. The developed film was projected through the same filter at the same speed.

■ **Kinematophone** A machine for creating sound effects during the presentation of a motion picture in the days of silent films.

■ **kinescope, kinescope recording, kine** A film recording of material originally appearing on a television tube. The television image, either live or from a videotape, appears enhanced on a monitor from which it is photographed. In a newer system an electron beam directly records on the film emulsion. For color transmission, the television image is broken down into three separations for red, blue, and green, which are then combined through dichroic mirrors or prisms onto the film. The 30 frames per second for television are converted to the 24 frames per second for film by splicing, skip-printing, or photographing with every fifth framed omitted. Sound is generally recorded on a separate tape simultaneously with the picture recording. Kinescope was originally employed for recording television programs and for delayed transmission, but ultimately was replaced for such functions by videotape.

■ **kinestasis** The use of still pictures in the making of a film. Such pictures may be photographs, paintings, drawings, collages, or a series of freeze frames from a motion picture. This term is employed variably for any of the following usages of still pictures found in both experimental and documentary films: (1) the flashing on the screen of each picture for a few frames at a time so that they hurry by, giving some type of rapid survey of a subject or creating some type of perceptual effect; (2) the moving of still pictures beneath the camera to create a sense of movement; (3) the panning of the camera itself across the picture or a zooming toward or away from the picture (works primarily using such techniques are sometimes called slide-motion films). This term is also sometimes used for (4) the appearance of a series of still pictures in any motion picture to create a sense of time and place.

■ **Kinetograph, Kinetophone, Kinetoscope** The Kinetograph was the camera developed in Edison's laboratories to make short strips of film for the Kinetoscope peephole machine. These machines were largely developed by William Kennedy Laurie Dickson. The Kinetograph itself seems to have been suggested to Edison by the Chronophotographe camera developed by the Frenchman Etienne Jules Marey. Edison and Dickson seem to have achieved a basic model of this camera in 1888, and in 1889, Dickson was able to form a picture on a screen with accompanying sound (he called the machine the Kinetophonograph). Edison had originally intended the images from film to be an accompaniment for the sound of his phonograph. Synchronization was difficult, however, and the failure of the experiment ended, for a time, attempts to link sound and picture. Edison was not interested in projecting images on an external screen from a single machine, since he believed it would be more lucrative to require separate viewers for each individual. In 1889, the East-man Company produced a durable film stock that helped Dickson considerably in the development of the Kinetograph and Kinetoscope. These machines were privately demonstrated in 1891, the same year in which Edison applied for domestic patents for both. The Kinetoscope was exhibited publicly in 1893. In 1894, the Kinetoscope Company was formed, and sixty parlors with peephole machines were opened throughout the country. Kinetoscopes were also placed in such diverse locations as hotels, department stores, taverns, and phonograph parlors.

In 1893, Dickson had a studio built for the Kinetograph in West Orange, New Jersey, next to Edison's laboratories, where he made film strips for the Kinetoscope. The small structure was called the Black Maria because it was partly covered in black tar paper (*see* **Black Maria**). The short, unedited films featured such diverse subjects as vaudeville and circus performers, trick animals, and workers. One of the most popular of these early films was *Fred Ott's Sneeze*. Edison also had developed and distributed a Kinetophone, a combination of the peephole machine and phonograph, but with nonsynchronous musical accompaniment and sound effects for the pictures (the name was also used later for a brief experiment with a projected image and synchronic sound from 1910 to 1916). In 1895, it became clear that projected pictures on a screen would be the wave of the future, and Edison was forced to move in that direction with the Vitascope, a projector actually developed by others. By the end of the century, peephole machines were out of business.

The Kinetograph, though large and unwieldy, had a number of features that were to become standard in future cameras, namely the 35mm film with four perforations on the side of each frame and the sprocket mechanism that engaged the perforations to move the film. The camera employed an intermittent movement for photographing the individual frames, and the film moved past the aperture in a horizontal motion at the fast speed of approximately 40 frames per second (anywhere from 38 to 48 have been claimed). The amount of film was limited to fifty feet because this was exactly the length that could fit around the Kinetoscope's rows of spools in a continuous band.

The Kinetoscope itself was a cabinet four feet high, with an eyepiece on top. The film was driven around the spools and pulled by sprockets over two drums, one on each side of the machine's top. An electric motor rotated one of the drums to move the film continuously. The film passed under the eyepiece, illuminated from beneath by a light and magnified from above by a glass. The intermittent effect for viewing the images was achieved by a slotted rotating shutter, also above the film, which made one turn for each frame. Sometimes customers paid in advance to have the machines run, but normally individuals inserted nickels in slots of individual machines to view each film. *See* **chronophotographs, Edison Company** *and* **Mutograph.**

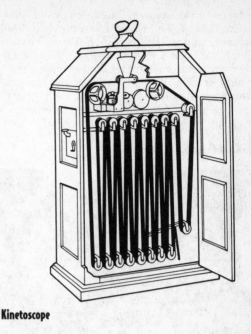

Kinetoscope

■ **Kinetophone** (1) The combination peephole machine and phonograph manufactured by the Edison Company in the mid-1890s. The music and sound effects from the wax cylinder were not synchronic with the picture. *See* **Kinetograph.** (2) The combination film projector and loud-speaking phonograph developed by the Edison Company for synchronic picture and sound which was demonstrated in 1910 and 1913. The system was used only briefly, without any great success, between 1913 and 1916.

■ **kino-eye** The film theory of Dziga Vertov (born Denis Kaufman), the maker of documentaries and newsreels in postrevolutionary Russia. "Kino-eye" means "camera eye," and for Vertov the camera was like the eyes of a person in its ability to move about and search out the important elements in any situation. But the camera eye was also more flexible than the human eye: it could see into the truth of things and make the truth more evident. It could do this by altering distances, changing angles, manipulating speeds, and reversing motion. The image itself could be frozen or broken into component parts or placed in a sequence of related images. The impulses behind all these techniques were to expose reality rather than distort it and to make the viewer examine his or her own perceptions. Vertov developed his ideas in a series of manifestos. He organized the Kino-Eye Group in 1919 and from 1922 to 1925 edited a series of newsreels called *Kino-Pravda (Film Truth)*. The film for these newsreels was shot by cameramen moving throughout all Russia and recording events of everyday life. These events were strikingly edited by Vertov to become not merely the immediate subjects of the newsreel, but an emotional and educational vista of life in Russia and a celebration of the achievements of the Revolution. Vertov's most famous film is *Man with a Movie Camera* (1929), which incorporates images from everyday life to create a remarkable demonstration of the wizardry of the camera, a dazzling exploration of printing and editing techniques, and one of the most conscious and extensive investigations into perception to appear on film.

■ *Kino-Pravda*   *See* kino-eye.

kino-eye   A scene from one of Dziga Vertov's *Kino-Pravda* newsreels (c. 1922–25).

■■■

■ **Kinothek**   A collection of scores edited by Giuseppe Becce and published in 1914 for musical accompaniment to silent films. The title is a shortened form of "Kinobibliothek," which means film library. Much of the music catalogued is by numerous composers, but Becce wrote some of the pieces himself. The collection became the most popular source of music for the last decade of silent films.

■ **kit rental**   *See* box rental.

■ **kitsch**   *See* camp.

■ **klieg light, kleig light, klieg, kliegl**   The name for a series of powerful carbon-arc lights at one time made by Kliegl Brothers. The searchlight seen moving through the sky at the time of a glamorous Hollywood film premiere was generically called a klieg light.

■ **KMCD Syndicate**   *See* Biograph.

■ **knee shot**   A medium shot of one or more characters from the knees up.

■ **knuckle clamping disc head**   Two rounded discs with grooves for holding flags.

■ **Kodak standard perforation (KS), Kodak perforation, positive standard, positive perforation**   A rectangular perforation with rounded corners on positive 35mm and 70mm film. This perforation was found to be superior for repeated projection to the earlier Bell and Howell perforation (BH), which was prone to tearing because of its sharper corners and smaller height. The Kodak standard is also found on 65mm negatives. *See* **Bell and Howell perforation** *and* **perforations.**

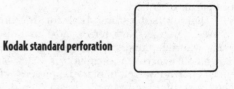

Kodak standard perforation

■ **Kodak Vision film**   *See* **Eastman Color.**

■ **Kodalith**   A high-contrast sheet of film employed in special-effects photographs and for superimposing titles on live action.

■ **Kuleshov effect**   The meaning and significance as well as the emotional impact derived from relating and juxtaposing individual shots in a context existing only from the editing itself and not inherent in any of the single pieces of film. This is the basic concept of "montage" developed by Kuleshov and his students in the State Film School in Moscow during the early 1920s. *See* **Kuleshov Workshop.**

■ **Kuleshov Workshop**   A group of students under the tutelage of Lev Kuleshov in the State Film School in Moscow. The workshop was formed in 1921 and later included among its members Vsevolod Pudovkin. Because it lacked raw stock, the group at first produced stage productions, utilizing film techniques; but the workshop is especially notable for its later experimentation with actual film and its development of montage techniques that were to influence Sergei Eisenstein as well as Pudovkin. The group edited and reedited a print of Griffith's *Intolerance* (1916), achieving a variety of effects by rearranging shots and scenes. It also assembled pieces of stock footage in a number of ways to achieve effects not latent in the individual pieces themselves. Kuleshov and his students, learning from Griffith and going beyond their master, developed a primer of cutting techniques that allowed them to manipulate filmic space in such a way that the juxtaposition of different pieces of film, even pieces shot for other purposes, could convey both action and meaning while having a specific emotional impact on the viewer. They appropriated the term *montage,* which means "editing" in French, to describe this method of filmmaking.

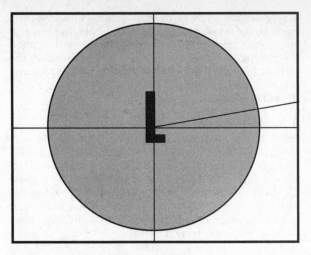

laboratory, lab to lux

■ **laboratory, lab** The place where film is developed and printed at the various stages of motion-picture production, and where various effects are achieved, sound track and image are combined, and final release prints are manufactured. Modern film laboratories are highly efficient and automated centers for the technological production of film image and sound. The laboratory first comes into play during the making of a film when it turns exposed stock from the day's shooting into rush prints or "dailies" that will be examined the next morning. The exposed film passes through a developing machine where the silver halide in the exposed emulsion is converted by certain chemicals to black silver particles that form the negative image. In the case of color film, chemicals also react to couplers in the emulsion to create dyes for a color image of the subject. The image is stabilized or "fixed" when the unexposed silver halides are removed in a chemical bath, and, in the case of color film, the black silver particles are bleached out, leaving the color dyes. Washing removes the chemical by-products, and drying removes the moisture from the film at the end of the processing. The resulting negative is "broken down," and the circled takes, specified by the camera log that has accompanied the film from the studio, are selected for printing. The scenes to be printed are then attached in the order requested by the log, and the negative is fed into a printing machine along with raw film for the making of the rush print. Both films run continuously and in contact past an aperture where a light forms a latent image from the negative onto the raw stock. In the United States, dailies are normally made with only one set of timing lights, and picture quality is dealt with at a later stage. The positive is then developed in much the same way as the negative (a dry lab performs printing but no processing). Laboratories also make available video dailies instead of, or along with, the rush

print—normally by performing a transfer by means of a telecine. Sound dailies are also made available by transferring the recorded sound from the magnetic or digital tape to mag stock.

A second area of work performed by the laboratory is the creation of transitions and special effects—e.g., fades, dissolves, wipes, freeze frames, close-ups, double exposures, split-screen pictures, as well as the printing together of separate picture elements to form a single image through a number of matting processes. Although traditionally done by an optical printer, many of these effects are now also achieved digitally: first, by transferring the film into a digital code by means of a film scanner; second, by creating these effects through image processing and manipulation; and third, by transferring the images back to film with a film recorder. Titles today are often done digitally and transferred to film.

Many laboratories are also equipped to transfer the images either to videotape for off-line editing or digitally to a computer system for nonlinear editing. When the editor has assembled the final workprint or sends to the laboratory a negative cut list generated by either video or digital editing, the negative cutter assembles the original negative to match. (The time is fast approaching when the entire digitally edited film will be directly recorded on film.) The laboratory also makes an optical sound negative from the final magnetic mix, the digitally recorded final mix, or both. The important laboratory procedure called timing alters the density and color values of each shot or scene for consistency, balance, or some desired effect during the printing of the answer or trial print, which is normally a composite of both image and sound. The edited negative is first loaded into the video analyzer and the resulting positive image is used by the timer to set the printing lights for each scene. The answer print made from this process is checked by the director and cinematographer—several answer prints may be made until a satisfactory print is achieved. The final laboratory step is the making of release copies. For large-scale distribution, these are generally made from duplicate negatives (i.e., internegatives), themselves made from a number of interpositives. Duplicate negatives insure the safety of the original negative and allow for release printing on a number of machines in separate laboratories. The high-speed, large-volume printing can be somewhere in the range of 2,000 feet per minute and the developing approximately at the rate of 700 feet per minute. Anywhere up to 1,000 release prints can be made from the internegative. The laboratory can also make prints in different gauges, generally from duplicate negatives obtained through optical printing. *See* **editing, film recorder, film scanner, printer,** *and* **processing.**

■ **laboratory effects, lab effects** Special effects achieved in the laboratory through the processing and printing of film. The term distinguishes such effects from those made either in front of the camera (i.e., mechanical effects), or in the camera (i.e., in-the-camera effects), or in a computer (i.e., digital effects). *See* **special effects.**

■ **laboratory report, lab report** A report sent from the laboratory to the director of photography with the rush print. Such a report lists various problems with the images as a result of shooting and any film damage. *See* **laboratory.**

■ **lab roll** The roll of film assembled in the laboratory from the various negatives to simplify and speed up handling and the various procedures.

■ **lace** To thread film into a projector by hand.

■ **lacquer** A clear coating put on film to protect it from scratches or abrasions.

■ **laid-in music** Background music that is not integral to or harmonized with the visual action. Such music adds a continuity to the scene or simply fills in the silence. The music may come from a source on or off the screen, such as a radio, to give a natural background.

■ **lambert** A unit of brightness equal to the luminance of a perfectly diffusing surface that reflects one lumen of light per square centimeter. *See* **lumen.**

■ **lamp** A device for providing an individual source of light. Incandescent lamps emit light when a filament, encased in a sealed glass envelope that contains an inert gas such as nitrogen, is heated by an electric current. In filmmaking, tungsten-halogen lamps are preferred to normal incandescent lamps. In the former, a tungsten filament in halogen gas burns at a much higher temperature than the filament in the normal lamp. Tungsten-halogen lamps, though more expensive, are free from blackening and thus burn at a constant temperature and give off a constant light. Carbon arc lamps are employed when a large amount of light from a single source is needed. This nonincandescent lamp creates light when an electrical current is passed between two carbon electrodes. Such lamps are cumbersome, difficult to use, and the electrodes burn out in a short period; however, they are especially useful for creating large amounts of light for color shooting. The newest type of light in motion-picture production is the HMI discharge lamp, which offers both compactness and a high degree of illumination from a small amount of power. For projectors in commercial theaters, carbon arc lamps were generally used for projecting the image on the screen, though xenon arc lamps are now in use for most theaters. *See* **lighting.**

■ **lamphouse** (1) That part of a projector that holds the lamp and emits the light to project the film image onto the screen. (2) The part of an optical printer that holds the lamp and emits the light to project the negative image onto fresh film.

■ **lamp operator** The term originally applied to technicians on the set who ran the various luminaires but who also took care of the carbon arc lamps and cleaned their rods. Since such lamps are less in use now, the term is applied to the various lighting technicians who place, set up, and focus the various lights on the set. *See* **set lighting technician.**

■ *langue* In semiotics, the science of signs, the term refers to the total language system of a particular culture. (Ferdinand de Saussure, the Swiss linguist and founder of semiotics, originated the term in his lectures, which have been published as *Course on General Linguistics.*) *Langue* has significance in conjunction with the word *parole,* which refers to the specific and particular usage of a language in an individual utterance or piece of writing. It is through the study of *parole* that one can begin to understand the *langue* that lies behind each usage. The *parole* takes on significance in its particular selection from a variety of possibilities in the *langue* itself. These concepts have been applied to other sign systems in culture (e.g., fashion, meals, traffic signals). It is possible to employ such concepts in film study, both for examining the societal codes portrayed within the film and in examining the individual film itself as a *parole,* an individual utterance or "performance" that comes out of a larger *langue,* system, or "competence" (the terms "performance" and "competence" belong to the linguist Noam Chomsky). This second approach to film might be significant in understanding genre: the genre could be examined as a particular expression from a larger system, or an individual film could be analyzed in the context of a systematic theory of the genre itself. Another possibility is to examine the various film techniques as rhetorical or communicative elements in a larger communicative system, the way Christian Metz, the most important semiotician of film, has examined particular orderings of shots (which he calls "syntagma") in *Film Language.* *See* **semiotics.**

■ **lap dissolve** An abbreviated form of "overlap dissolve." The term "dissolve," an even more abbreviated form, is now more common than either "lap dissolve" or "overlap dissolve." *See* **dissolve.**

■ **lapel microphone** A small, hidden microphone attached to a performer's clothing to pick up his or her speech.

■ **lap splice** *See* **overlap-cement splice.**

■ **large format camera** A camera that photographs a negative image larger than the normal 35mm in order to create a screen image with great picture quality and size. The cost of filming on such large stock is now considered prohibitive for commercial films, though 35mm images are sometimes blown up to 70mm prints for special screenings of special films. Exceptions are made, however, for special films such as Kenneth Branagh's recent and epic *Hamlet* (1997), which was shot with 65mm film. Two such cameras, the VistaVision 35mm camera, which creates a film frame with an aspect ratio of 1.470 to .908 inches by operating horizontally, and the 65mm Panavision, which gives a negative image of 1.912 to .870 inches, because of their picture quality are employed in special effects photography. *See* **camera** *and* **IMAX.**

■ **laser** The word is from the initials of "light amplification by stimulated emission of radiation" and signifies a device that amplifies and concentrates light waves to produce an intense beam of light (a laser beam) within or near the visible spectrum. Laser effects are sometimes used for fantasy films with the help of a laser animation stand and computer—the laser is generated, shot, stored, and then composited into the picture. *See* **holography** *and* **laser disc.**

■ **laser digitizer** *See* **3-D digitizer.**

■ **laser disc, laserdisc, laser videodisc** A disc made of durable plastic; on both sides is recorded a feature film, the pictures of which are read by a laser beam that transmits them to a television screen and audio system. Such discs are composed of more than 100 billion tiny cavities burned into each side so close together that they refract the light that makes the image visible. The CAV laserdisc (the initials represent "constant angular velocity") can be stopped for a freeze frame or be moved image by image—normal laserdiscs do not have this capacity. In spite of the fact that the laser disc offers superior picture and sound to the videotape, it has had only limited commercial success, most likely because of its inability to record picture and sound. Even though the new DVD (digital versatile disc) system will also lack a recording capacity in its first stage, the likelihood exists that it will replace the videotape and CD-ROM, as well as the laser disc, in the coming century because of its greater storage capacity and quality. *See* **DVD** *and* **videodisc.**

■ **laserdisc editing, videodisc editing** Editing systems that employ laserdisc players. Such systems are more rapid than normal editing with videotape, which require the editor to move through an entire recording to reach the desired scene (unless the unit has a large number of VCRs). Such systems use SMPTE time codes on the disc for rapid accessibility to any scene. A dual-headed videodisc player can call up two images simultaneously from the same disc, a practice especially useful for creating cuts, wipes, and dissolves. Since each disc holds about twenty-eight minutes of material, several recorders are necessary. Laserdisc editing results in an edit-decision list (EDL) for making a video master copy or a negative cut list for conforming film. Such systems are being replaced by digital nonlinear editing systems. *See* **editing, linear editing, nonlinear editing, video editing system.**

■ **laser printer** *See* **output device.**

■ **laser scanner** *See* **film scanner** *and* **scanner.**

■ **latensification** A process whereby an undeveloped latent picture, generally on underexposed stock, receives low-grade illumination over a long period of time to increase the density of the image.

■ **latent edge numbers** *See* **edge numbers.**

■ **latent image** The invisible image formed in the emulsion of a film that has been exposed to light through the camera lens. The image, which is upside down in relation to the photographed subject, remains invisible until the film is developed.

■ **latent-image matting** A technique in special-effects cinematography for joining together separate picture elements into a composite image by laying the image of one element, a matte painting, for example, into the original negative, which already contains the other part of the picture and has been only partly developed. The process thereby joins together first-generation images and avoids optical printing. *See* **matte** *(2).*

■ **lateral color** A lens aberration that causes transverse light waves to focus colors at points different from those in the subject from which they originate. As a result, color fringes appear in the image. Also called transverse chromatic aberration.

■ **lateral orientation** (1) The placement of an image so that it is seen in reverse. (2) The perception of an image from right to left.

■ **Laterna Magika** A combination live-action and film show developed in Czechoslovakia for the 1958 World's Fair in Brussels and later presented both in Europe and in the United States. This cross-media entertainment included live music and actors integrated with film, slides, and recorded music.

■ **Latham loop** The loop of film before and after the aperture in both camera and projector that prevents the film from jerking and tearing as it moves from continuous to intermittent to continuous movement. The loop, developed for the camera by Major Woodville Latham and for the projector by Thomas Armat, not only prevents tearing, but allows longer reels of film to be used. Latham's name has been given to loops in both cameras and projectors, although these are also sometimes called American loops. The term "loop," however, suffices in normal usage. *See* **loop** *(1).*

■ **latitude** (1) The range of exposure for a film that allows a satisfactory image. (2) The range of time in developing that allows a satisfactory image. (3) The range of light, from bright to dark, that a particular film emulsion can record.

■ **lavalier microphone, lavalier** A small microphone, suspended from a performer's neck and generally concealed under his or her clothes, that picks up the carrier's voice. *See* **microphone.**

■ **lavender print, lavender, blue** A master positive, printed from the original negative, which is primarily employed for making duplicate negatives. In the 1930s, such prints actually appeared lavender from the tint of the base on which the emulsion was placed (the tint prevented halation). Although fine-grain master positives today are made without a tinted base, such a film is still, on occasion, referred to as a lavender or blue.

■ **law-and order film** A film that emphasizes the triumph of law over crime, or, when the law seems incapacitated, the victory of right over wrong. These films, which generally appear during periods that seem to have an unusual amount of crime and violence, appease the public's fear from such unlawful and threatening acts. Films such as *G-Men* (1935) and *Bullets or Ballots* (1936), both directed by William Keighley, were responsive both to the times and to public uneasiness with the glorification of criminals in contemporary gangster films. More recent years have featured films such as *Dirty Harry* (1971; dir. Don Siegel) and *Death Wish* (1974; dir. Michael Winner), where an apparently liberal and ineffective legal system forces alienated individuals to fight crime in their own way. The most recent trend in this type of motion picture has been the buddy law-and-order film, where two seemingly different character types join together, with a good deal of humor and violence, to fight corruption (even though they may be a bit corrupt themselves)—e.g., *Lethal Weapon* (1987; dir. Richard Donner).

■ **lay, lay-in** To assemble a sound track so that it properly matches the film images.

■ **laydown** (1) Transferring the sound from audio tapes to a magnetic film and aligning it with the sequential ordering of the images on the workprint (e.g., for sound effects). (2) Transferring sound to a single multitrack audio tape for sweetening. *See* **sweetening.**

■ **layering** Assembling the various sound tracks in such a way that the dialogue, music, and sound effects are integrated and blend together, with the proper sounds taking dominance at the right time and the others being heard behind them in the proper order of volume and discernibility. *See* **mix.**

■ **laying tracks** Editing the various sound tracks so that they are properly aligned for mixing.

■ **layout** *See* **animation layout** *and* **optical layout.**

■ **layout artist, scene planner** The individual in an animation studio who, working from the storyboard, sketches the full drawings for each shot. The layout artist indicates the details of scenery, actions of the character, and movements of the camera. *See* **animation.**

■ **lead** (1) The main role in a film. (2) The performer who plays the main role in a film. When there are both male and female leads, the principal performers are referred to as the leading man and leading woman. (3) To compose a shot so that there is space ahead of a moving subject to prevent the audience from feeling that the subject will collide with some object off-screen. The subject is generally kept off-center. (4) To compose a shot so that there is space ahead of a performer's gaze to suggest that he or she is looking at someone or something a distance away.

■ **leader** (1) A piece of blank film attached to the head of a reel of film for threading and to both head and tail to protect the film from damage and wear. (2) A piece of film at the head and tail of each reel of a release print that follows standards set by the Academy of Motion Picture Arts and Sciences and is called the Academy leader; or, in more recent years, follows standards set by the Society of Motion Picture and Television Engineers and is called the SMPTE universal leader. While both pieces, in both instances, protect the reel, the head leader is also for threading and supplying the projectionist with information concerning the name of the work, number of the reel, and countdown numbers for changeover. (3) A piece of film used in work prints of image or sound during editing for filling in spaces.

■ **leadperson** The individual who assists the set director in obtaining, storing, and placing the various set dressings while also supervising the set dressers (also called the swing gang). *See* **set director** *and* **swing gang.**

■ **lead sheet** *See* **bar sheet.**

■ **Legion of Decency** A Catholic organization founded by a group of American bishops in 1934 for the purpose of rating films and persuading Catholics to boycott works judged objectionable. The Legion was in large part a response to the failure of the Motion Picture Producers and Distributors of America (MPPDA) to force its members to respect its own production code, which had been adopted in 1930 for regulating the content of film. The Legion drew up a rating system, thus influencing the MPPDA in 1934 to institute the Production Code Administration, under Joseph Breen, for enforcing its own code. The Legion was mostly concerned with condemning films for showing or suggesting immoral behavior. It continued to condemn films periodically on such grounds until 1968, when it changed its name to the National Catholic Office for

Motion Pictures and began to display a more enlightened attitude. *See* **Catholic Communication Campaign, censorship, Hays Office,** *and* **Motion Picture Production Code.**

■ **legs** A term applied to a film when it has had a long run and good box office at the same theaters (the film is said to have "good" or "excellent" legs).

■ **leisure-based entertainment** A term used to describe the various multisensory entertainments that represent an exciting mutual advance of technology and the moving image. For theme parks, amusement parks, and location-based entertainment centers (the last of which also contains traditional forms of entertainment such as movies, shopping, and restaurants), companies such as IMAX, Iwerks, and Showscan create special filmic entertainments by projecting large images in special theaters and creating simulated rides that bring one into the center of the Hollywood movie experience. Notable in this context are the *Back to the Future* rides at Universal Studios parks in California and Florida. *See* **special venue.**

■ **lens** A combination of transparent pieces, normally made of glass, which receive and refract light rays to form an image a prescribed distance (called the "focal length") behind the unit on the focal or image plane. Light rays, forming a cone, emanate from a single point on the subject and are bent by the lens of a camera so that they converge at a single point on the film. When the light rays from each point in the subject so converge on the film, a latent image is formed. Since light rays for different colors will not focus at the same point through a single element, several elements with different curvatures and qualities of glass are combined for them to do so. The different shapes and qualities of glass also determine whether the entire lens brings into focus objects in the distance or near to the camera as well as decide the size of the subject in focus and the depth of focus. To avoid light reflecting off the front surface of the lens, one or more coatings of a transparent and refractive material are applied. The pieces of glass are arranged and mounted in a lens barrel. The barrel includes a focusing ring (i.e., a threaded mount with calibrations) that, when turned, moves the lens toward or away from the film, thus adjusting the focus according to the lens's distance from the subject being photographed. The barrel contains an iris diaphragm, calibrated with f-stop and t-stop numbers, to control the amount of light passing through the lens aperture and reaching the film.

Each lens is designated by a focal length, which is the distance from the optical center of the lens to the plane where the various light rays are focused to form an image on the film. A lens with a focal length approximately twice the diagonal of the frame gives an image that corresponds to what the eye would normally see, with only slight distortion. Such lenses for standard 35mm film have a focal length of 50mm and a horizontal angle of view of approximately 25 degrees, while the same angle of view is achieved for 16mm film with a lens having a focal length of 25mm and for 65mm film with a lens having a focal length of 125mm. For 35mm film, a 40mm lens gives an approximation of a normal view while permitting a somewhat wider image and only minimal distortion. Lenses with shorter focal lengths are considered to be wide-angle lenses because they allow an image with a wider angle of view than the 40 or 50mm lens. For example, a lens with a focal length of 28mm gives an angle of view of approximately 43 degrees on standard 35mm film. Because lenses below a focal length of 24 degrees create a wide image with increased distortion, they are used to achieve special visual effects. For example, the fish-eye lens, an extreme wide-angle lens which can achieve virtually a 180-degree horizontal angle of view, is especially effective for creating hallucinatory effects.

Lenses with a larger focal length than 50mm are considered to be long-focus lenses. Such lenses bring a subject that is some distance away to the immediate view of the audience, but they do so while diminishing the angle of view. For example, a lens with a focal distance of 135mm has a horizontal angle of view of approximately 9½ degrees. In common usage, the term "telephoto lens" describes any long-focus lens, but, more accurately, the term should apply to those lenses with a positive front element distanced from a negative rear element so that the true focal length is greater than the distance between the lens itself and the focal plane. Such lenses are frequently employed for documentaries or for recording news and sporting events. Since long-focus lenses must focus light rays from a greater distance than short focal-length lenses, they have a much larger glass-to-air surface. Another category of lens employed in film is the anamorphic type, which helps to achieve an extreme wide-screen picture by compressing the horizontal width of each image to one-half its size to fit into the normal width of the frame; a similar lens on the projector expands the width of the image to its original size when projecting the image onto the screen.

A simple principle to remember is that horizontal angles of view vary correspondingly with focal lengths: for example, while a 50mm lens achieves for 35mm film a relatively normal angle of view of approximately 25 degrees, a wide-angle lens of 25mm gives an angle of view almost twice the area, 47½ degrees, and a long-focus lens with a focal length of 100mm gives a horizontal angle of view of virtually half the distance, or 12½ degrees. Although the desired size for the subject and the width of the entire image are prime considerations in the choice of a lens, other image qualities are a consideration. In comparison to the normal lens, wide-angle lenses have the capacity to give an increased depth of field, while long-focus lenses shrink the depth of field and focus only on a single plane. If the director and cinematographer want to place a character in a carefully defined foreground and background, they will choose the former type of lens; and if they want to focus primarily on the subject, they will choose the latter type, which will keep foreground and background in soft focus. The choice of such lenses also affects the way dramatic action appears on the screen. Because wide-angle lenses exaggerate the distances between various planes in a scene while keeping them all in focus, and because objects in the front of the image seem unnaturally large compared to those in more distant planes, the movement of a character toward or away from the camera will seem greatly accelerated. On the other hand, because long-focus lenses diminish depth and keep the size of objects in different distant planes unnaturally large, a character moving toward or away from the camera will seem to do so with exaggerated slowness—the character and the relative planes will seem to remain the same size for an extended period of time (these effects are called wide-angle and telephoto distortion respectively). Of course, the focus of the long-focus lens will have to be altered as the character moves, perhaps by a handle or by a remote-control motor that operates the focus ring. The distortion caused by different types of lenses achieves other dramatic qualities within the scene. A character's face in the extreme foreground of an image shot by a wide-angle lens will be so distorted and unnaturally large as to seem menacing, while faces tend to be rounded out and softened in an attractive manner by long-focus lenses (75mm and 100mm lenses are particularly effective for close-ups).

In recent years, the zoom lens has been much in use, especially for documentaries and for filming news and sporting events. This is a lens with a variable focal length that can focus on subjects at numerous distances from the camera or keep a moving subject in focus while smoothly changing from a wide-angle to a long-focus view. Zoom lenses at first generally had a ratio of 3:1, with the longest focal length three times greater than the shortest, but zoom lenses with a ratio of 10:1 are now frequently employed with 35mm cameras. Single lenses are attached to studio cameras when soundproofing or remote control is a factor, or on portable cameras when weight is important; but rotating turrets with three or four lenses that can individually be moved into position are now common for 35mm and 16mm cameras (most 8mm and some 16mm cameras employ only zoom lenses).

In projectors, light rays emanating from the film by means of a rear lamp must be projected and refracted by the lens so that they form a sharp image on the screen which is a distance away. For this reason, the focal length for a projector lens, anywhere from 75 to 125mm, is approximately twice the distance of that for the normal lens which shot the film. Such a focal length also allows the audience, when sitting an average distance between projector and screen, a perspective of the image similar to that of the camera.

lens
(14mm wide-angle)

■ **lens adapter**   A small device that permits a lens with a specific mount to be fitted onto a camera that accepts a different type of mount.

■ **lens angle**   *See* angle of view.

■ **lens aperture, lens stop, lens opening**   The adjustable opening at the front of the lens that is controlled by the diaphragm and regulates the amount of light to pass through the lens and reach the film. The opening is important in determining not only the amount of illumination for the image, but the depth of field as well—the more the lens is closed down, the greater is the depth of field, especially for wide-angle lenses. The focal length of the lens, which determines the magnification of the subject being photographed, is also a factor in determining the amount of light to reach the film; for this reason, the opening of the aperture is calculated by a series of f-stop numbers, which are derived by dividing the focal length by the widest effective diameter. *See* **f-stop, lens,** *and* **t-stop.**

■ **lens barrel**   The cylindrical mounting in which all the elements of the lens are contained. This barrel also contains the focusing ring and diaphragm.

■ **lens cap**   A small circular covering that fits over the outer surface of the lens to protect it from abrasion or damage when the camera is not operating.

■ **lens coating**   *See* **antireflection coating.**

■ **lens element**   One of the glass components that contributes to the magnifying and refracting powers of a lens and is generally cemented to one or more other components. *See* **lens.**

■ **lenser**   The director of photography.

■ **lens extender**   A device placed between the camera and lens that extends the lens away from the camera and closer to the subject, thereby increasing the focal length and giving a closer and more detailed image.

■ **lens filter**   *See* **filter** *(1).*

■ **lens flare**   *See* **flare.**

■ **lens hood, lens shade, sunshade**   A protective shield either mounted to or extended in front of the lens to prevent any oblique light, such as sunlight, from entering the lens or reflecting off its elements and causing flare or unwanted illumination. Circular hoods may be attached to the front of the lens, but it is more common to use an extended, rectangular type which can be adjusted in or out, in accordion fashion, to suit the particular lens. Lens hoods are generally attached to a matte box that holds filters and mattes in front of the camera's lens.

■ **lens marking**   The calibrations, numbers, and indicators on a lens that show the distance to focus area, f-stop and t-stop numbers, and depth of field.

■ **lens mount**   The device that attaches the lens to the camera. Individual lenses may be attached to a camera by a C-mount, which is a single-thread screwing device much employed for 16mm cameras. More stable is the bayonet mount, which allows the lens to be pressed into the camera and snapped into place by a slight twist. Most 35mm and a number of 16mm cameras require their own type of specific mount. Much in use are turret mounts, which can hold three or four lenses at once, each of which can be rotated in place.

■ **lens speed**   The maximum opening of the diaphragm of the lens in relation to the focal length (i.e., the maximum f-stop number) and hence the maximum capacity of the lens to pass light. *See* **f-stop** *and* **t-stop.**

■ **lens spotlight**   A spotlight with a sliding lens that controls the beam.

■ **lens stop**   Any of the series of openings for the diaphragm in the lens, calculated in f-stop numbers. *See* **f-stop.**

■ **lens support**   A support for a telephoto lens that is attached to the camera and the front end of the lens.

■ **lens turret, turret**   A rotating mount on the camera that normally contains three or four lenses with different focal lengths, each of which can be moved into place for shooting. Divergent turrets employ a wider choice of lenses placed so that none appear in the field of vision of the lens being used.

■ **lenticular process**   (1) A stereoscopic process developed for film, mostly in the USSR, which employed an integral screen with a grid of lenticular strips to separate the two images, taken with a beam-splitting camera, and send them individually to each of the viewer's eyes in order to create a three-dimensional effect. Although the process had the advantage of not requiring special glasses, it allowed viewing from only limited areas and certain positions, while still creating a disappointing image. *See* **3-D.** (2) An early additive system for color photography that employed tiny lenses in the base of black-and-white film. When light passed through a filter on the camera's lens with a band for each of the primary colors, a separate record was made in each of

the film's lenticles for the three colors. After the film was developed in a reversal process, the image was projected through a lens with the same filter so that a picture with the original colors appeared on the screen. Eastman Kodak introduced such a 16mm film in 1928, which it called Kodacolor (the same name it later used for a color film for still photographs), but the strata tended to be visible in the projected images. *See* **color film** *(2).*

■ **letterbox format**   An aspect ratio for showing a film on home video or television that is similar to the original wide-screen dimensions in theaters. Such a presentation necessitates an unused band on both the top and bottom of the screen. *See* **aspect ratio** *and* **safe-action area.**

■ **level**   The extent or measure of sound volume.

■ **level sync**   The parallel positions of image and sound in separate systems for synchronic playback, as opposed to print sync, where the sound is in advance of the image on the composite print to allow for the advanced position of the sound head in the projector.

■ **LFOA**   The letters are from "last frame of action" and refer to the very last frame of film before the leader begins.

■ **L-handle**   *See* **speed crank.**

■ **library shot**   A shot or scene already available on film (e.g., stock footage of a parade of soldiers or scenes from some exotic location). Such footage can be obtained from companies which specialize in this material and issue catalogues listing their holdings. *See* **found footage** *and* **stock shot.**

■ **library sound**   Prerecorded music and sound effects available for any film.

■ **light**   (1) Any artificial or natural source of illumination for lighting a set or location. (2) The illumination itself in a set or on location. (3) To illuminate a set or location for filming. *See* **lighting.**

■ **light-balancing filter**   A camera filter, generally some grade of amber or blue, that causes small changes in the color temperature of light coming from a subject to suit a particular film stock, to allow for varying temperatures from different sources of illumination, or to compensate for weather conditions.

■ **light-beam angle**   The angle of light given from a lighting source that is measured back to the source from the two points on each side of the beam where the intensity of illumination is half that of the peak point. Such calculations are often given by the lamp's manufacturer and are helpful in plotting the usable spread of light from the lamp. *See* **light level** *(1).*

■ **light board** *See* **lighting control console.**

■ **light boom** A long pole attached to a stand that is used for suspending a light over a particular area of the set.

■ **light box** (1) An animation desk lit from underneath. (2) An examination or editing table lit from beneath for viewing film. Also called a lighting table. (3) An internally lit box with one semitransparent side against which titles or small objects are filmed.

■ **light bridge** A catwalk above the grid holding the lights.

■ **light change** (1) Any alteration in lighting during the shooting of a scene to indicate a change in time or weather conditions. (2) Any change in the intensity of light during the printing of a film to compensate for exposure deficiencies during shooting or to alter the density of the negative in order to achieve required effects in the image. Such changes are programmed in advance on a tape that alters the lighting at various times as the film moves through the printer. The process is called timing. *See* **timing.**

■ **light-change points** The series of increases in exposure for altering the amount of light when printing a positive from a negative. These points were formerly calculated in logarithmic scales of .05 Log E but are now more commonly figured in a scale of .25 Log E. Also called printer points. *See* **light change** *(2).*

■ **light 'em out** Instructions to fade out microphone shadows by properly arranging the luminaires.

■ **light end** The drying area at the end of a film-processing machine, which is usually in a separate room and generally lit, since normal light will no longer damage the film. *See* **processing.**

■ **light flare** *See* **flare.**

■ **lighting** The illumination of performers, action, and setting in the making of a motion picture. Lighting is one of the major elements in the motion picture and is basically responsible for the fact that we see any image on the screen at all; but, in more specific ways, lighting is responsible for both the quality of the images and for much of the film's dramatic effect. The director of photography is chiefly responsible for the film's lighting, but he works out each scene's illumination with the director and often with the production designer, while his plans are put into operation by the gaffer (the chief electrician). Early films in this country were filmed outdoors with nothing more than the natural light of the sun, which created an even and hard illumination for both outdoor and supposedly indoor scenes. Some early studios had open or glass roofs so

that sunlight could be employed, but film production moved into closed studios when nonincandescent carbon-arc and mercury-vapor lamps had been developed to supply sufficient light. As a result, indoor shots eventually took on a more natural look with a greater amount of contrast and texture (one can see this development in the films made by D. W. Griffith and his cameraman Billy Bitzer). On the other hand, German filmmakers of the silent era, especially in expressionistic and semiexpressionistic films, were able to achieve a chiaroscuro style of lighting.

With the advent of sound, recording equipment necessitated a less noisy light source than the carbon-arc lamp. Fortunately, the sensitive panchromatic film stock then in use allowed incandescent lighting to become the chief source of illumination, although color films still required the large amount of light supplied by carbon-arc lamps. Incandescent lighting at first came from normal tungsten-filament lamps, but eventually this type of bulb began to be replaced by the tungsten-halogen lamp, also called the quartz-iodine lamp. Such lights have a much longer life than the normal incandescent bulb because the halogen gas in the glass envelope (which replaced nitrogen or a similar gas) prevents the bulb from blackening. At the same time, these lamps are compact and durable. Color-film stock also became more sensitive and thus permitted tungsten-halogen lighting, although carbon-arc lamps are still employed for color-film production when a great deal of light is needed from a single source. Tungsten-halogen lamps also offer a compact and easy means of on-location shooting where they are employed to supplement and correct natural lighting.

The latest development in lighting is the HMI lamp, in which an arc is enclosed in a low-pressure chamber with various gasses and elements. These lamps, though quite expensive, create illumination three to four times greater than that produced by incandescent lights. The 6,000-watt daylight HMI lamp can produce from an actual input of 7,000 watts as much light and coverage as a brute from 27,000 watts. Because HMI lights run on AC current, flicker must be avoided by snychronizing light pulse and frame rate through crystal-controlled cameras and generators or through flicker-free ballast systems. Originally employed as daylight lamps, HMI lights are now also used for indoor photography. Because of their compactness and high efficiency, HMI lights are employed with great frequency in film and television.

One can discern a dominant Hollywood lighting style that developed during the first three decades of the sound era, a style marked by carefully balanced studio lights. Although this lighting was artificial and unreal, it created unobtrusive, pleasing compositional effects and sometimes a dramatic interplay of light and shadow, especially in the early horror film and later in the *film noir*. It is also possible to discern somewhat different lighting effects for each of the major studios (e.g., MGM's brighter, more artificial, and uniform illumination as opposed to Warner Brothers' more contrasty and low-key lighting). In much of the work in color during this period, a good deal of light was needed, and the result was often an evenly lit, artificial, and cartoonlike surface. Lighting for nighttime effects was achieved by dim, overall luminosity and artificial pools of illumination from spotlights or by shooting day-for-night with filters and an underexposed camera. The development of more sensitive color film stocks since the late 1950s has resulted in images that do not rely largely on different colors for compositional effects but integrate lighting as part of the *mise-en-scène*, thus achieving a more natural image. Even nighttime scenes manage to convey both muted colors and realistic lighting (note especially Kubrick's *Barry Lyndon* [1975], photographed by John Alcott, where one scene is lit entirely by candlelight within the setting itself). Better lighting equipment and more sensitive film stock, along with a preponderance of on-location shooting, has allowed for lighting far more natural than that in earlier studio productions. But one can still discern distinct lighting effects from different directors of photography (e.g., Nestor Almendros and Owen Roizman) that at times border on the impressionistic, even though these cinematographers vary their style for the demands of different motion pictures. In *Barry Lyndon*, lighting is employed far more naturalistically than in early color films, but, at the same time, it achieves effects that bring to mind the lighting and colors in eighteenth-century English paintings. Sometimes an obvious return to artificial studio lighting is employed to suggest a world of daydream and make-believe—for example, in Herbert Ross's *Pennies From Heaven* (1981), photographed by Gordon Willis, and Francis Ford Coppola's *One From the Heart* (1982), photographed by Vittorio Storaro. In recent years, however, the capacity for shooting with lower levels of light and xenon projector bulbs that can themselves make clear images shot with the dimmest illumination have resulted in a soft and low-keyed type of lighting, a world of muted colors that seem to fade into gray and black, especially in films dealing with violence and perversion—the recent *Seven* (1995; dir. David Fincher), photographed by Darius Khondji, requires characters to use flashlights even in places lit by electricity and keeps much of its story literally in the dark.

In general, there are two basic types of luminaires for motion-picture production: the floodlight, which gives a large area of diffuse illumination, and the spotlight, from which a beam can be focused to illuminate a specific area. Floodlights are often composed of a single bulb with a reflector behind it—the distance between bulb and reflector may be adjusted to offer some control of focusing and light intensity. Examples of such luminaires are the broads, which offer nondirectional fill lighting, and sky pans, often employed to light backdrops. Some floodlights, such as banks, have two or more bulbs, each 250 watts or greater, and some

have one or more bulbs with two filaments. Sometimes a floodlight may have a lens to help diffuse and make uniform the illumination from the bulb. The range for floodlights varies anywhere from 650 watts to 10,000 watts. Spotlights contain a lamp, reflector, and condenser lens. The lens is often a lightweight and easy-to-handle Fresnel type with stepped-down concentric circles—as the lamp is moved back, the lens acts as a spotter and controls the area to be illuminated. Examples of such luminaires are the senior, with a 5,000-watt light that serves as a large key light; the junior, with a 2,000-watt bulb that serves as a key light for a smaller area; and the baby spot, which employs a bulb of 1,000 watts. The brute is a large, 225-amp carbon-arc spotlight still employed for color films especially for creating sunlight. Some spotlights, with tungsten-halogen bulbs that are small and compact, do not have a lens but are focused by a mechanism that moves the lamp toward or away from the reflector.

One must also be aware of the various ancillary equipment, which in conjunction with these luminaires helps to create the desired lighting effects. Barn doors placed in front of the lamp cut off illumination from certain areas of the set; shutters, scrims, nets, and various kinds of diffusers determine the intensity of light; cookies and gobos create shadows; filters control the color of light rays; and portable reflectors soften and diffuse light. In studio production, lights are attached to mobile riggings suspended from the ceiling, to catwalks, stands, and sometimes parts of the set. Lightweight, adjustable stands and various types of adjustable mountings for attaching the lamps to stands, structures, or sets have been devised for location shooting.

Lighting is responsible for significant effects in each scene. The composition of the *mise-en-scène* can be reinforced by the unity lighting gives certain scenic elements, by the attention it can draw to major areas of interest, and by its interplay with dark areas. At the same time, lighting can give depth to a scene, while also bringing out texture and detail in setting, decor, and clothing. Lighting also affects the appearance of a character, defining or diminishing facial characteristics and making faces appear attractive or unattractive. Finally, lighting is responsible for the mood and atmosphere of individual scenes as well as the entire film. One can basically distinguish between hard and soft light: the former, generally coming from a spotlight, clearly illuminates areas, sharply outlines and illuminates characters, brings out detail and texture, and markedly separates light and shadows; while the latter covers a wider area with a more diffuse light, diminishes outline and clarity of characters, minimizes shadow, and reduces modeling of detail and texture.

Terms commonly used in describing the dominant style of lighting for a scene are "high key" and "low key." There has been some confusion in the way these terms have been employed in film analysis, especially in recent introductory texts on film, but accuracy requires the following distinctions: high-key lighting indicates a brightly lit scene with a minimum of shadows and a key light that is bright and dominant; low-key lighting indicates a scene where the lighting is more towards the grayer and darker scale, where there is a good deal of shadow, and where the key light is less bright and does not dominate. A scene, however, with strong contrast between bright light and shadow, with a small amount of in-between gray scale, is called "high-contrast" lighting. In general, a preponderance of bright, clear, even illumination creates a sense of sunniness, joy, and security, and is therefore frequently used for comedy. More diffuse, grayer lighting can convey inclement weather and communicate the more somber and unhappy spirit of a serious drama; grayer light with more shadows is effective in mystery films, *film noir,* or horror films; while high-contrast lighting can be effective in serious drama or a mystery film.

The key light is the major luminaire that illuminates the subject of the image and is normally placed to the front and side of the subject. The fill light is generally placed on the opposite side and fills in the shadows of the subject. The third luminaire in this traditional configuration is the back light, which highlights the edges of the subject and separates it from the background (this luminaire is also called a "kicker" or "kick light" when it is to the rear and side of the subject at an angle opposite to that of the key light). There are numerous variations of this basic kind of lighting; sometimes two key lights (the "double key") may be used to highlight two subjects of interest or more than one fill light employed to illuminate shadow areas caused by one or more key lights. Frequently a foundation light is also used to give a general, diffuse illumination to the entire scene. A background or set light might also be employed to illuminate the rear part of a scene; a modeling or accent light to bring out form and texture in any part of the scene; a rim or edge light to highlight a character's outline; an eye light next to the camera to highlight a subject's eyes; a clothes light to bring out texture in clothing; and an effects light to create, in a special area, the light from a fire or lamp.

Two general schools in cinematography have been referred to as "naturalism" and "pictorialism." The first favors a key light that seems to come from a source in the scene or from a natural outside source; the second favors any placement of the key light that gives the most striking visual image. The general effect of a character's appearance is significantly determined by the angle or direction of the key light. Front lighting flattens out the face, diminishes contour and detail, and softens or even blurs the features—such lighting can diminish the appearance of aging or make a person more attractive, but it can also make the face somewhat characterless. Back lighting does not bring out details in the face, but highlights the edges of a character, creating a kind of rim or halo around the head and especially the hair while separating the individual from the background—as a result it tends to make the character

more angelic or ethereal. Top lighting bathes the character in light, as if the illumination were coming from heaven, giving him or her an angelic or spiritual appearance; while bottom lighting shadows and distorts the face, making it appear sinister, threatening, or evil. Finally, side lighting, if angled carefully, can model the face and bring out detail; but it can also highlight only half the face, leaving the other half relatively undefined or in shadow, thus suggesting a two-sided or mysterious personality.

Once the lighting for any scene has been composed, the proper exposure must be established for the camera setting. With a light meter, the director of photography might measure the illumination reflected from the subject or, more likely, measure the incident light itself which illuminates the scene. The light meter, taking into account the ASA rating (or exposure speed) for a particular film, will suggest the proper f-stop number for the diaphragm opening of the camera.

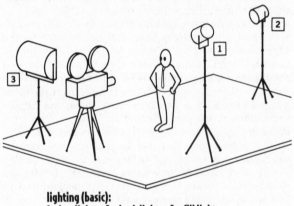

lighting (basic):
1. key light   2. back light   3. fill light

■ **lighting balance** The relationship of illuminated areas and shadows in a scene that allows (1) sufficient exposure for photographing the subject; (2) movement of the camera between areas of different illumination that will not tax the initial exposure; and (3) a satisfying compositional effect. *See* **off-balance lighting.**

■ **lighting batten** A strip of wood, long pipe, or elongated box with sockets used to accommodate individual lights; it is suspended from the ceiling over the set.

■ **lighting contrast** The degree of difference between the highest and lowest points of illumination and the extent of the intermediate gray scale in between. High-contrast lighting has considerable difference in the extremities, with little gradation between. *See* **high contrast.**

■ **lighting contrast ratio** *See* **lighting ratio.**

■ **lighting control console, lighting control board, lighting board, lighting panel** A panel or board on which are located the various switches and controls for the lights on a set. Besides turning on and off the individual luminaires or groups of luminaires, such consoles can be preset to alter brightness and focusing for each new scene or during individual scenes.

■ **lighting cradle** A structure or platform to which lights are attached and which is suspended over the set.

■ **lighting grid** A framework of parallel bars or rails to which lights are attached and which is suspended from the ceiling over the set. More advanced grid structures now allow movement of the lamps from side to side or back and forth and adjustment of lights by remote control.

■ **lighting mount** A device for supporting a lamp—for example, any stand, overhead hanger, clamp for attaching the light to a part of the grid or set itself, extension arm attached to a stand or pole, or boom.

■ **lighting plot, light plot** A diagram giving the various locations of each light on a set, the type of light, and sometimes the amount of illumination from each luminaire.

■ **lighting ratio, lighting contrast ratio** The ratio of key to fill light, frequently determined by computing the overlap of both in relation to the fill light itself or sometimes the ratio of both lights measured independently. Lighting ratio is often a factor in using a particular film stock, since the range of brightness each stock accommodates will vary. A ratio of 3:1 might be employed for a normal color image. *See* **fill light** *and* **key light.**

■ **lighting stand** Any of the stands that support one or more lights. Such stands are normally constructed of poles or pillars that are adjustable for height and are attached to a tripod. The lamps are attached to spigots or sockets on the stand itself or to an extension arm. Stands for location shooting are considerably more lightweight and compact than conventional studio stands. Special heavyweight stands for brutes can be adjusted for height, often by an electric motor, and are sometimes supported by a dolly.

■ **light level** (1) The intensity of illumination given by a light source. A standard means of calculating this level is to divide the intensity at the peak point by that distance where the illumination falls to half that intensity. In this country and in England the measurement is generally given in footcandles, though the international measurement is calculated in meters and given in lux. (2) The general intensity of illumination in an entire scene, measured either in footcandles or lux. *See* **footcandle** *and* **lux.**

■ **light lock** *See* **light trap** (1).

■ **light meter** *See* **exposure meter.**

■ **light pen** A stylus with sensitivity to light that interacts with the images or words it is creating or that already have been placed on the screen of a cathode-ray tube—in both cases, the results are digitally sent back to the computer and stored. *See* **digital** *and* **digitizing pen.**

■ **light piping** The leakage of light through the edges of the film's base, which causes fogging on the emulsion. This leakage is possible when using daylight loading spools, though a number of stocks have bases with gray dye in order to avoid this problem as well as halation. *See* **halation.**

■ **light source directionality** *See* **angle of incidence.**

■ **light-source filter, lamp filter** Any filter placed in front of a lamp to change the color of the light rays passing through or the color temperature of the light. The color temperatures of particular lamps must be changed to match those of other light sources (e.g., the color temperature of tungsten-halogen lamps must be altered to match that of the sun, or the temperature of arc lamps to match that of tungsten-halogen lamps).

■ **light-struck** Any undeveloped film emulsion accidentally exposed to light.

■ **light table** *See* **light box** (2).

■ **light-tight** Any compartment or area totally free from light (e.g., a camera or darkroom).

■ **light trap** (1) The entrance to a dark room employed for photographic processes where light is prevented from entering by interconnecting dark passages, double doors, a revolving door, or black curtains. Also called a light lock. (2) The parts of a camera that permit film to leave and reenter the magazine while blocking out light. (3) The parts of a printer that allow film to enter and leave while blocking out light. (4) Any device or covering that prevents light from entering a dark room through heating or air ducts.

■ **light valve** (1) A device that modulates the amount of light in recording an optical sound track on film. *See* **optical sound track.** (2) A device that modulates the amount of light in printing a film. *See* **printer.** In both (1) and (2) the intensity of illumination from the light source remains constant while the valve modulates the amount of illumination passing to the film.

■ **Lightworks Offline** The name of a digital nonlinear editing system made by Lighthouse U.S.A. in Hollywood. The system was introduced in 1991 and won an Academy Award in 1994 for Scientific and Engineering Achievement. This system allows the storage of visual and audio information on magnetic discs and time-line editing. Editing results in an edit-decision list (EDL) or negative cut list. *See* **Avid Media Composer** *and* **nonlinear editing.**

■ **lily** A card displaying various colors and degrees of gray that is shot at the beginning or end of a roll of film to provide the laboratory with a standard for judging the color quality and tonal values of the images on the remainder of the film.

■ **limbo, limbo background, limbo set, limbo effect** An area or set with no defining characteristics: the background seems to extend into infinity or is completely black. Such a set can sometimes be used as a background for a close-up, but it can also function for dramatic purposes, as in the undefined, unlimited, and characterless underground world in George Lucas's futuristic fantasy, *THX 1138* (1971). *See* **black limbo.**

limbo Robert Duvall and Maggie McOmie make love in the empty and sterile world of *THX 1138* (1971; dir. George Lucas).

■■■

■ **limited animation** A type of inexpensive animation where only parts of a figure are actually animated while the rest of the figure remains inanimate on a hold cel (e.g., only the legs might move to indicate running). *See* **animation, cel animation,** *and* **full animation.**

■ **limited release** A film that is exhibited in only a select number of theaters throughout the country (no more than fifty) or in only a few areas. Such films appeal to very select audiences or locations. The film might also receive a limited release to test its appeal before the distributor spends a great deal of money on a wide distribution.

■ **limiter** A component in recording or rerecording systems that prevents sound amplitude from going beyond a certain peak—this control is especially important in sound mixing when a number of tracks are combined.

■ **limpet, limpet mount, suction mount, sucker** A mount with suction cups that attaches equipment to a smooth surface. These mounts can be employed for both lighting and cameras; they are especially useful for attaching such equipment to moving vehicles.

■ **line** (1) An individual sentence or group of words from the dialogue of a play or film. (2) *See* **imaginary line.**

■ **linear distortion** Any distortion in the image caused by the refracting power of the lens. When the scene is reduced in size by the lens, the light rays cannot be bent without some change taking place in their relationships. Such distortion is not noticeable from normal lenses, but can become apparent from wide-angle lenses if the camera is improperly angled or characters move suddenly forward or backward. With extreme wide-angle lenses, such as the fish-eye lens, linear distortion is apparent at the side extremities of the image where the scene appears curved. *See* **wide-angle lens.**

■ **linear editing** The term normally applies to editing on video and derives from the fact that using videotape requires that one move sequentially though the action and sometimes change tapes to find a desired scene to make an edit. Several source tapes may be used on several videotape players with a single videotape recorder putting together the edited copy. The final edited master copy is made according to the edit-decision list (EDL) generated by the original editing process. Some linear editing systems employ an A/B roll process for making dissolves or wipes. In nonlinear editing, the digitizing of image and track on hard drives allows the random access of any scene without the necessity of having to handle an entire tape or several tapes. The terms "linear" and "nonlinear" have been used in relation to editing only since the late 1980s, when the development of digital editing made the difference between the two processes apparent. *See* **analog, editing,** *and* **nonlinear editing.**

■ **linear perspective** The perspective in depth of a scene whereby the space seems to recede deep into the background with the various lines converging into a single point. The principle is the same as that of quattrocento Renaissance painting that developed such perspective in art. Road or chase pictures tend to favor a long shot from above showing movement across the screen, but science-fiction films tend to favor linear perspective, normally from the front window of the spaceship, to emphasize the movement into the infinity of space. (See, for example, any of the *Star Trek* films [1979–96]).

■ **line of interest** *See* **imaginary line.**

■ **line producer** A producer, generally with much experience in production, who is in charge of the daily operations of a particular film. Such a person, who may be hired by the producers or even financiers of a project, supervises most facets of production as well as the work of the production manager. He or she is responsible for the financial operations of the film and for the planning, approval of costs, hiring of personnel, and maintenance of the general crew working on the production. The line producer is hired sometime during the planning stage of the film and stays with the project until the release prints are made.

■ **lines** (1) All the dialogue in a film. (2) All the dialogue of a particular character in a film. (3) Any portion of a film's dialogue.

■ **line test** *See* **pencil test.**

■ **lineup, line up** (1) Selecting and putting in proper order the various pieces of film that must go into a composite made by an optical printer. The lineup technician performs this work and prepares a lineup sheet with such information as length of shots and exposures for the operator of the printer. (2) Placing in proper order rolls of film for editing or reels for viewing. (3) Matching together separate reels in a synchronizer and any type of viewing apparatus.

■ **line-up tone** A tone of a single frequency that is recorded on a sound track for adjusting volume before rerecording the sound on the remainder of the track.

■ **lining up, lining up a shot** Choosing the proper distance and angle for a desired shot and locating the camera accordingly. The selection is made by the director, cinematographer, or both.

■ **linkage** The theory of film editing or "montage" as devised by the Russian filmmaker V. I. Pudovkin, especially as it is contrasted to the "collision" theory of montage of Sergei Eisenstein. For Pudovkin, the shots of a scene or sequence should connect naturally and logically, like the links on a chain. The sequence of shots should guide the attention of the audience, develop the narrative, establish theme, and also evoke psychological and emotional responses within the viewer; but such linking of shots must be more subtle than obtrusive, more fluid than shocking. (Pudovkin's theory of editing is described in *Film Technique and Film Acting,* a collection of his writings and talks.) Pudovkin's film *Mother* (1926) best manifests his technique of film editing. *See* **collision** *and* **montage.**

■ **lip-flap** *See* **silent lip.**

■ **lip-sync, lip sychronization** The simultaneity of a character's spoken dialogue on the sound track and lip movement in the image. If there is a separation between sound and image of more than one or two frames, the discrepancy can be noticeable.

■ **liquid gate, liquid gate printing** A gate in a printing machine where, at the time of exposure, the film moves through the liquid in a glass cell that fills any scratches, thereby preventing light refraction from forming an image of the scratches on the new film. In a wet gate printer the scratches are filled by a liquid right before exposure. *See* **printer.**

■ **liquid head** *See* **fluid head.**

■ **listening shot** A reaction shot of a character listening to someone speak who normally appears in the previous shot.

■ **literal adaptation** An adaptation to film where the dialogue and events of the original work remain almost the same. Good filming technique and acting can sometimes allow an effective literal transference of play to film, as in the case of Stanley Kramer's 1951 film adaptation of Arthur Miller's *Death of a Salesman,* but even here the motion picture was not a commercial success. In general, an original work must be significantly changed to satisfy the requirements of the film medium. *See* **adaptation.**

■ **literary acquisition agreement, literary purchase agreement** An agreement to obtain the rights to use all or part of a literary work in or as a source for a motion picture. Such an agreement will spell out all kinds of rights for both sides—e.g., whether the production company can change the work without restrictions, make sequels, and distribute the film in ancillary markets; and whether the author can use the characters again, sell the rights to his or her work for a stage play, or have some control over the film adaptation (a power rarely granted).

■ **live action** Events in a film performed by living people as distinguished from those performed by animated figures.

■ **live recording** A recording of original sound made when shooting a film, during a live performance, or in some natural environment.

■ **live sound** Sound recorded from its original source as opposed to sound derived from recordings.

■ **livestock man** The person in charge of the animals who appear in a motion picture. Also called a wrangler.

■ **load** (1) To place unexposed film in a camera or camera magazine. (2) To place an already loaded magazine on a camera for the purpose of photographing some action or scene.

■ **loader, loader boy** *See* **assistant camera operator.**

■ **loading closet** A darkroom in the studio for loading film into the camera as well as for removing exposed film. Such closets have air cans and brushes for cleaning the camera as well as cans, tape, labels, and markers for storing the film. *See* **hot box** *(2).*

■ **loading spool** *See* **daylight loading spool.**

■ **loan-out company, loan out company** A company that makes a loan-out arrangement with a production company to give the services of a member artist, normally a director, performer, or writer. Such companies are set up by the artist to decrease tax payments, but a number of these tax advantages have by now disappeared.

■ **lobby card** A scene of a film displayed in the lobby of a motion-picture house either playing the film or about to do so. Generally used to advertise the film, these small posters were popular from silent-film days through the studio system and have since become collector's items.

■ **locale** (1) The actual location or setting, whether indoors or outdoors, where some portion of a film is shot. (2) The location or setting, either indoors or outdoors, where various parts of the film are supposed to take place.

■ **local music** Music that originates directly from the scene itself and is heard by both characters and audience (e.g., music from a radio or group of musicians).

■ **location** Any place other than a studio where a film is in part or completely shot. Such a place is an actual location and not a constructed set within a studio or on its lot. Sections might be added to already existing buildings, entire structures constructed, or parts of the natural terrain changed, but the film would still be considered as shot "on location." The first silent films were shot outdoors because lighting was dependent on the sun; but with the development of artificial illumination and better film stock, motion pictures could be shot inside studios where weather was no longer a factor and where more control could be had over lighting. The advent of sound, at first recorded synchronically with the filming of the picture, made location shooting even more difficult, although films might incorporate shots of actual places for setting a location or advancing the narrative. The need for outdoor settings as well as the obligatory use of horses, especially in chase scenes, also necessitated that parts of Westerns be shot on location. The following factors eventually led to an increased number of films being shot on location from the late 1950s: the high cost of maintaining studios and making studio productions; better film stocks, especially the new tripack color film made by Eastman Kodak; lighter, more portable cameras and lighting equipment; more sophisticated sound-recording techniques that could combine on-location recordings and dubbed sound tracks; and the success of a number of significant on-location films made in Europe. The film industry also saw location shooting as a means of outdoing television, with its studio dramas. Today, audiences expect the naturalness and authenticity of location shooting, although technology makes possible, better than ever, compositing of images of performers shot in a studio and actual locations shot separately.

■ **location agreement, location release** A contractual agreement between a production company and owner of a piece of property that the company may use the property in the film. Such agreements normally spell out the terms of use and payment, as well as stipulating that the property be left in its original condition.

■ **location breakdown** (1) An itemized list of all the requirements for on-location shooting, including personnel, equipment, facilities, and transportation as well as a detailed account of the scenes to be shot. (2) A detailed accounting of the costs for an on-location shooting.

■ **location camera** A lightweight camera often for handheld shots on location and sometimes for studio shots where mobility is required. *See* **hand camera.**

■ **location cart** *See* **production cart.**

■ **location department** The group of people in film production responsible for finding suitable locations for shooting, arranging for the use of the location, and managing the transportation of equipment and personnel to these locations. *See* **location scout.**

■ **location lighting** All the lighting equipment for on-location shooting as distinguished from that employed in a studio production. Such equipment generally includes lighter, more portable luminaires and stands; special cables, plugs, and sockets; and a portable generator. *See* **lighting.**

■ **location manager** The individual who sometimes acts as a location scout, finding particular settings for a film, but also contracts for their use and arranges the details of occupancy.

■ **location picture, location film** A motion picture primarily made on location as opposed to one made in a film studio. Location pictures tend to seem less claustrophobic and confined; their ambience seems more authentic and less staged. While studio pictures emphasize the interaction of characters, films made on location focus attention on the interaction of characters and environment. *See* **location** *and* **studio picture.**

■ **location scout** An individual, frequently part of the location department, who goes in search of suitable places, either indoors or outdoors, for a film production's on-location shooting. *See* **location department.**

■ **location shooting**   Any filming at an actual place as opposed to shooting performed in a studio or on a studio lot. *See* **location.**

■ **location sound**   Any sound recorded on location as distinguished from that recorded in a studio. *See* **live recording** *and* **live sound.**

■ **locked**   The relatively completed states of the fine cut and synchronized sound track when the director and editor are satisfied. Some further refinements will undoubtedly still take place, and certainly the sound mix will require work. *See* **fine cut.**

■ **lock off**   A shot in which the camera is firmly locked in place and makes no movement at all. A lock-off shot would be taken, for example, for a special-effects composite scene in which all the picture elements must be perfectly aligned from frame to frame.

■ **lo-con, lo con**   A low-contrast stock that might be used, for example, for making another generation print from a positive.

■ **log, log sheet**   A form filled out by a technician to record some activity in the making of a film. An assistant cameraman will record on a log sheet—called a camera report, camera sheet, or camera log—all the shots taken that day, the details of shooting, which shots are to be developed, and instructions for the laboratory in the development of the film. A log is kept for the dailies and includes slate information, edge numbers, code numbers, and a description of the scene. A log called a sound log or sound report is kept for sound recording. In addition to these, a log sheet is generally made by the editor to help with sound mixing and the transference of sound to film. *See* **mixing cue sheet.**

■ **logging**   The process of filling out a log or log sheet; normally listing the shots with various specifications.

■ **logo, logotype**   A trademark that identifies the motion picture of a particular company (e.g., the roaring lion at the start of an MGM production).

■ **long-focus lens, long focal-length lens, long lens**   A lens with a longer focal length than normal, which narrows the angle of view while magnifying and bringing into focus a distant subject. For 35mm cameras, the focal length is greater than 50mm and ranges anywhere up to 300mm. These lenses decrease depth of field and flatten the image, while focusing largely on a single plane of vision (the rest of the image is in soft focus). Such lenses can, however, change focus to follow action or bring attention to another plane of action. Because these lenses keep distant objects of various planes in

relatively large size with diminished depth between the planes, a character moving toward or away from the camera will seem to move slowly and obtain little distance (this is called a telephoto effect). Such lenses, especially those of 75mm and 100mm, can be very effective for close-ups since they make the face more attractive by rounding and softening it. A long-focus lens has a much larger glass-to-air surface than a wide-angle lens (i.e., a short-focus or focal-length lens), since it must focus light rays from a greater distance. The term "telephoto" is sometimes loosely applied to these lenses; the term should apply to a specific kind of lens with a true focal length greater than the distance between the lens itself and the focal plane. *See* **lens, telephoto lens,** *and* **wide-angle lens**

■ **long pitch**   Pitch refers to the distance between perforations on film, and "long pitch" describes the slightly greater distance between such holes on print stock. Since the print stock is on the outside of the negative when they pass together over the same curved sprocket during printing, it requires a slightly greater pitch to fit over the same teeth without slippage between the two films. Most original films, in comparison, have "short pitch." Long pitch is sometimes referred to as standard pitch. *See* **printer.**

■ **long shot (LS)**   A shot that shows the subject at a distance. Characters are seen in their entirety with some area above and below them also visible. The shot takes in some of the surrounding environment as well. An extreme long shot is at a great distance from the subject and generally takes in a wide view of the location. Both long shots and extreme long shots are often used as "establishing shots" to begin a sequence. The long shot also concludes a sequence. Such a shot gives us more information about a character and his environment than the close-up or medium shot. It develops relationships between characters and allows us an objective view of a situation. Long shots, in combination with close-ups and medium shots, can either increase our awareness of the dramatic situation and hence intensify our emotions or distance us and control our involvement—which of these effects is achieved is determined by the way the shots are interrelated and what exactly is happening on the screen. *See* **close-up, establishing shot,** *and* **medium shot.**

■ **long take, sequence shot**   A lengthy shot. Early silent films were composed largely of long takes, but cutting from shot to shot soon became dominant, especially from the influence of D. W. Griffith. Early sound films, made with the camera limited to a soundproof enclosure (called an "ice box"), once more featured long takes, with the action presented much like that of a stage drama; but self-blimped, soundproofed cameras and multiple, directional, and mobile microphones allowed motion pictures to be presented again with sophisticated cutting techniques. Although long takes were still often a feature of poorly made films, creating a sense of inactivity and feeling of boredom for the viewer, they were employed consciously and effectively by a number of film directors. André Bazin, the French film critic and theoretician, has drawn attention to the related techniques of the long take and deep focus, especially in Orson Welles's *Citizen Kane* (1941), as opposed to the montage editing of early Russian filmmakers and invisible cutting of Hollywood studios (in *What Is Cinema?*). For Bazin, both the long take and deep focus opened up the image for the spectator and involved him or her more deeply in its "reality."

The French filmmaker Jean Renoir is often cited for his long takes, though he shifted the focus of his camera to different points of attention and also employed a moving camera instead of using deep focus (e.g., in *Grand Illusion* [1937]). Alfred Hitchcock, famous for his manipulative editing, made his entire film *Rope* (1948) with what appears to be one continuous take, moving the camera for dramatic effect and for guiding the audience's attention (the film was actually shot in a series of ten-minute takes, the limit for each reel of film). In a more modified version, the long take can be an effective technique when the subject is sufficiently dramatic and the performers compelling. One can cite a number of such films, from Dreyer's classic silent film *La Passion de Jeanne d'Arc* (1928) through the films mentioned above. Sometimes independent filmmakers, especially because of financial limitations, must rely on long takes; but, if the subject is interesting, the screenplay immediate, and the performers real, a refreshing honesty and candidness may be the result. *See* **camera movement** *and* **deep focus**.

■ **loop** (1) The slack, curved piece of film, above and below the aperture in a camera or projector, that allows the film to advance from continuous movement to intermittent movement and back again to continuous movement without tearing. Twenty-four frames per second must stop intermittently either to be exposed in the camera or projected from the projector; the sudden pulling, stopping, and pulling of a taut piece of film could easily cause a strain that might damage the film. Such loops were developed for the camera by Major Woodville Latham and for the projector by Thomas Armat, though the term "Latham loop" has been adopted for both of these. Such loops are also sometimes called "American loops." (2) In step printers, the slack, curved pieces of negative and fresh stock that allow these films to move in and out of intermittent movement so that frames can individually be stopped and exposed without damage. *See* **printer.** (3) A single strip of film or tape joined at both ends so that it can be continuously repeated. Such loops allow (A) a sequence of images to be projected repeatedly for a dubbing session; (B) background sounds or noises to be played continuously and dubbed into a film; (C) a sound track to be recorded on more than once during a dubbing session; (D) film in a projector to be run without rethreading as in the case of an educational strip of film in a cartridge or cassette; and (E) a negative to be run repeatedly and continuously without rethreading during the printing of a number of positives. *See* **looping.**

■ **loop film** Film joined at both ends to form a continuous band for the appropriate functions outlined above under **loop** *(3)*.

■ **looping** The process of dubbing dialogue into a motion picture by means of loop film and tape. Films are frequently dubbed in this manner if the recording made during shooting was faulty or if it was not possible to record dialogue at all. Looping is also used to dub dialogue into a foreign film. Three types of loops might be employed during this process: a loop of film of a particular scene which is projected a number of times for the performers to rehearse dialogue until sufficient lip and sound synchronization is achieved, thus allowing a final projection for the actual recording; a loop of magnetic tape for recording dialogue repeatedly on the same track, each new recording erasing the former, until a satisfactory dubbing is achieved; and perhaps a loop of the original sound track against which the performers can match their own voices. The entire process is also called postdubbing, dubbing, and postsyncing. *See* **dub** *and* **mix.**

■ **looping stage** *See* **dubbing room.**

■ **loop lines** *See* **postsynchronization.**

■ **loop printing** Printing a film from a negative whose ends have been joined together so that it can run continuously without being rewound and rethreaded. This method is employed for making prints of a short film, for producing a large number of release prints of a feature film, and for repeating exposures to achieve special effects.

■ **loop tree** A system of rollers over which loop film (i.e., film joined at both ends) is able to run continuously for purposes of dubbing and printing. *See* **loop** *(3)*.

■ **loose adaptation** Any adaptation into film of a work from another medium where characterization, plot, and dialogue are not closely followed. The characters and story line in the film may be only suggested by the original work, as in the case of Michelangelo Antonioni's *Blow-Up* (1966), which improvises on the story by Julio Cortazar. *See* **adaptation.**

■ **loose gate** A gate in a projector intentionally loosened to avoid damage to the film. *See* **tight gate.**

■ **loose shot, loosely framed shot** A shot with significant space on both sides of the subject. Such shots can allow much movement and action, distance the viewer from a character, or suggest the character either lost and overwhelmed by the environment or suddenly free within it. *See* **tight shot** *and* **tight two.**

■ **lose the light** To lose the natural lighting so that outdoor shooting has to be discontinued (e.g., when the sun sets or is hidden by clouds).

■ **lot** (1) The outdoor area of a studio where sets are constructed or stored and where shooting sometimes takes place. (2) The entire area of the studio, indoors and outdoors, where shooting takes place, as opposed to location areas for filming. *See* **studio complex.**

■ **loudspeaker** A device that converts electrical impulses into sound waves and amplifies the sound to an audible level.

■ **Louma, Louma crane** A portable, flexible, and mobile crane for a lightweight camera that sends back video pictures of the image exactly the way it will appear on the film and allows the camera to be operated from a distance by remote control. The Louma permits shots that cannot be achieved with an operator behind the camera and is capable of making a variety of difficult but fluid movements, especially when it is on a mobile crane. *See* **crane.**

■ **loupe** A small magnifying glass used by an editor to examine a single frame.

■ **louvers** The term normally applies to the openings between a series of narrow, adjustable, and overlapping slats, but in motion-picture production refers specifically to the parallel black metal strips that are placed in front of a luminaire to control spill light and the angle of light.

■ **love interest** That part of a film dealing with romantic love.

■ **low-angle prism** A device used for an extreme low-angle shot. The prism can be attached to the camera and placed only .25 inches off the ground, permitting a point of view as low as 2.5 inches. Such a device allows a shot of anything ground-level, e.g., shoes or rodents. The unit can also be inverted for extreme high-angle shots.

■ **low-angle shot, low shot** A shot from beneath eye-level, with the camera looking up at the subject. Such shots make the subject appear large, dominant, and even threatening. Background is considerably reduced while the character is dramatically played against the sky or ceiling. At the same time, figures appear to move with greater acceleration and physical violence seems more dangerous to characters and intimidating to the viewer. In two-shots, a low angle can make the relationship of the characters seem more pressing, powerful, or threatening. Low-angle shots are employed frequently in Welles's *Citizen Kane* (1941) to suggest the significance and even legendary quality of the main character, almost to the point where the action appears to take place on a raised platform.

■ **low-budget production** The making of a film with a limited amount of money. During the days of the great film studios, a large number of low-budget B-pictures were screened as second features or were presented in pairs as midweek shows; but even some A-pictures were low-budget films compared to more expensive studio motion pictures. The point is that the term is always relative: today, a low-budget film made in Hollywood can be more expensive than a work by an independent filmmaker to the extent of millions of dollars. In general, though, low-budget films are limited in equipment and film technique. Retakes are expensive and must be curtailed. Because salaries are low, expensive performers cannot be employed unless they work for less money. Such films appear to the eye to be made with a low budget. Sometimes, however, low-budget films achieve an immediacy and dramatic power absent from more expensive and technically sophisticated films.

■ **low contrast** Diminished contrast in a film image between strong light and dark areas because of a considerable range in the intermediate gray scale.

■ **low-contrast filter** A camera filter for reducing contrast in an image.

■ **low-contrast original, low-contrast positive** An original reversal film, such as 16mm Eastman Ektachrome, from which duplicate prints with excellent images can be made.

■ **low-fade positive print (LPP)** A film stock introduced in 1983 with color dyes less likely to fade or discolor than those in earlier monopack color films, especially in Eastman Color. Although such low-fade stocks are more stable than those in earlier single-film printing systems, they still do not have the durability (or quality) of those resulting from Technicolor's dye-transfer system. *See* **color** *and* **imbibition.**

■ **low-key lighting** A style of film lighting in which the key light does not predominate; instead, the general illumination is toward the grayer and darker scale. A few pools of bright light might contrast with the darkness, but the scene is underlit and has a preponderance of shadow. Such lighting is particularly effective for mysteries and horror films, since it creates a dark, uneasy, and menacing atmosphere. Low-key lighting is also effective for psychological dramas such as Edward Dmytryk's *Crossfire* (1947). It is important, though, to place and control illumination for compositional effect and to allow enough detail and modeling to keep the viewer engaged in the scene. *See* **high-key lighting** *and* **lighting.**

low-key lighting   Robert Ryan is trapped in his own dark world in *Crossfire* (1947; dir. Edward Dmytryk).

■ ■ ■

■ **low-pass filter**   A filter in an electronic system that passes frequencies only below a cut-off point. Higher frequencies are reduced.

■ **low-shrink base**   A film base with a minimal amount of shrinkage, notably acetate base as opposed to the early nitrate type, which would shrink during processing as well as after.

■ **low-speed camera**   A standard camera whose motor has been altered to operate at an extremely low speed for time-lapse photography. A mechanical or electronic device operates the motor at set intervals.

■ **LPP**   *See* **low-fade positive print.**

■ **LS**   *See* **long shot.**

■ **Lubin**   An early film company in Philadelphia begun by Sigmund ("Pop") Lubin. Lubin had previously been a merchant of eyeglasses who went on to make films for peephole machines and to sell film equipment. In 1897, Lubin made film history when he photographed for the peephole machine the Corbett-Fitzsimmons prizefight on his Philadelphia rooftop and sold the film as authentic (he did the same for the Oberammergau Passion Play). In 1909, Lubin's company became one of the founders of the Motion Picture Patents Company, but along with the other members did not prosper. In 1915, the company joined with Vitagraph, Selig, and Essenay to form the VLSE Company and was finally purchased by Vitagraph in 1917. *See* **Essanay, Motion Picture Patents Company, Selig,** *and* **Vitagraph.**

■ **lubrication**   The application of a lubricant, normally a waxy material, to film to allow its passage through machinery without friction. A lubricant is placed on the surface of prints to allow easy passage through a projector.

■ **lumen**   A measurement of luminous flux (i.e., the rate of luminous energy) in which each unit is equivalent to the amount of light per second from a point source of one candlepower intensity emitted in a unit solid angle (i.e., an angle formed at the vertex of a cone). The intensity of illumination from an electric light can be measured in lumens per watt.

■ **luminaire**   A term basically used in this country, for a lighting fixture. The fixture includes lamp, housing, reflector, lens, and cable. *See* **lighting.**

■ **luminance**   The luminous intensity, or brightness, from a surface measured according to candles per unit. The measurement is in footlamberts, each of which equals one lumen per square foot. *See* **footlambert** *and* **lumen.**

■ **luminous flux**   The rate of flux of luminous energy, which is measured in lumens. *See* **lumen.**

■ **luminous intensity**   The amount of light per second from a point source emitted in a unit solid angle (i.e., an angle formed at the vertex of a cone) and measured in candelas. *See* **candela.**

■ **lupe**   A lighting unit, containing one or more low-powered bulbs, that is attached to the camera and serves as a fill light when normal luminaires cannot be set up. Such lighting moves with the camera and is sometimes employed for close-ups or dolly shots.

■ **lux**   An international metrical measurement for the intensity of illumination. A lux equals one lumen of luminous flux striking perpendicularly a surface of one square meter; 10.764 lux equal one footcandle. *See* **footcandle** *and* **lumen.**

■ ■ ■

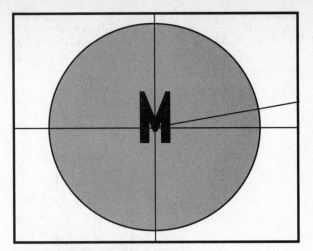

Macguffin, McGuffin, Maguffin to myth, mythic criticism

■ **Macguffin, McGuffin, Maguffin** A term devised by Alfred Hitchcock for some plot device that gets the action moving and about which the characters may care a great deal, but about which the audience may care very little. It is really the excuse to create a good deal of action and dramatic effect. Hitchcock himself liked to give the example of secret plans or stolen papers. *See* **weenie.**

■ **machine leader** A strong, durable piece of blank film attached to an undeveloped strip of film to lead it through the processing machine. *See* **processing.**

■ **macro** An image stored in the memory of a computer that can itself be called up as an element in a larger image (e.g., any of the parts of the human body that could be used as part of a figure). *See* **computer animation.**

■ **macrocinematography** The photographing of small objects without the use of a microscope but through normal, supplementary, or special lenses, sometimes with extension devices for the lenses. Such photography often uses a macro lens. Also called cinemacrography and cinephotomacrography. *See* **macro lens** *and* **microcinematography.**

■ **macro lens** A lens, used in macrocinematography (the photographing of small objects), that can focus as close as one millimeter to an object. Such lenses are generally employed with an extension tube.

■ **macro-telephoto lens** A special telephoto lens for macrocinematography, that is, for the photographing of small objects.

■ **macrozoom lens** A zoom lens that photographs small objects at very close distances (as close as one millimeter) in macrocinematography.

■ **made-for-TV movie** A motion picture made directly for television. Such films at first tended to fit the television format in their emphasis on dramatic situations, their less-complex filming techniques, and their uncontroversial or modest treatment of subject matter even when it may have been potentially controversial. But in recent years, some of these films have treated their subjects more maturely and exceeded in quality many of the films first seen in a motion-picture house. One of the first notable made-for-TV movies was *Brian's Song* in 1971, the story of a football player dying of cancer and an interracial friendship, which starred Billy Dee Williams and James Caan. Henry Fonda starred in a moving treatment of a simple man's struggle for justice that led to a landmark Supreme Court decision in *Gideon's Trumpet* (1980); and Vanessa Redgrave starred in an emotional and stirring treatment of the Holocaust and concentration camps in *Playing for Time* (1981). A major advantage of movies made for television is that they can play over a series of nights and hence offer a lengthier and more absorbing treatment of a subject than the normal two-hour span of a theatrical presentation. *Roots,* in 1977, gave considerable impetus to this form; its detailed and powerful treatment of slavery in this country captured the attention of nearly two-thirds of the television audience during its eight consecutive nights. *Lonesome Dove* wrote a new page in the history of the Western with its realistic and compelling serial presentation in 1989 (dir. Simon Wincer). Sometimes a film originally made for television also has a successful run in the theater—noteworthy was the recent theatrical distribution of *Persuasion* (1995; dir. Roger Michell), based on Jane Austen's novel and made by BBC television. Also worth noting is the movie made simultaneously to be shown in different forms for the theater and television, such as Ingmar Bergman's 1983 Academy Award–winning foreign film, *Fanny and Alexander,* which first appeared theatrically in Sweden in a 197-minute version in December 1982 and then began a four-segment, five-hour version on television a week later. Although television had a considerably adverse effect on film during its early decades, especially by drawing away a considerable portion of the audience, it has since had an interesting symbiotic relationship, especially in the making of motion pictures.

■ **mafer clamp** A popular lighting mount used for a variety of purposes on the set, including attaching luminaires to either round or flat surfaces as well as overhead grids.

■ **mag** Short for magnetic and used in relation to magnetic tapes and film as well as any of the equipment using them.

■ **magazine** (1) A lightproof container that feeds the film into the camera and takes it up after exposure. Such containers are attached to the top of the camera and often form two circular protrusions, each with a separate chamber. The film from the feed chamber is manually fed into the camera, either in a dark room or special changing bag; it is then threaded through the mechanism and attached to the spool in the takeup chamber as the camera operates. Normally the film is moved by the camera motor, though sometimes large rolls require a special motor in the magazine. Some cameras use a coaxial magazine with the two chambers side by side on the same axis; and others employ a single chamber magazine with the film on the take-up roll filling the space vacated by the film on the feed roll. *See* **camera.** (2) A container of some sort for storing or transporting pyrotechnical devices for various kinds of explosions, fires, and flashes in a motion picture. Such a magazine may be a room, structure, or a portable box or case.

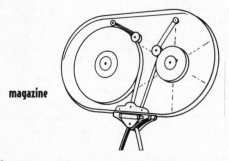

magazine

■ **magenta** The reddish-purple color that comes from the mixing of red and blue. Magenta is the complementary color of green (i.e., the color achieved when green is subtracted from light). *See* **subtractive process.**

■ **magic hour** The brief periods of dawn and dusk that allow enough light for shooting, but also create some striking effects on film.

■ **magic lantern** An early device for projecting pictures by means of a candle and lens. The concept was first written about by Athanasius Kircher in *Ars Magna Lucis et Umbrae* in 1646 and further developed in his second edition of that work in 1671. Magic lanterns were built in the latter part of the seventeenth century and became popular in the eighteenth century, both as home entertainment and traveling shows. Some illusion of movement might be achieved by using two separate slides and moving one image across the other—for example, an animal on one slide might suddenly seem to attack a man on the other. Magic lanterns developed further in the nineteenth century, especially in England where, by the last part of the century, several

lenses were employed to superimpose images and sliding panels with a number of pictures were also used to create an illusion of movement. In the mid-nineteenth century, photographs began to be used in place of drawings:

magic lantern

■ **Magliner** Tradename for a cart used by a member of the camera crew to move equipment from one place to another.

■ **Magnafilm** A short-lived wide-screen process developed by Paramount as part of Hollywood's brief flirtation with wider images during the late 1920s and early 1930s. Magnafilm used 56mm film without any special lenses, though special cameras and projectors had to be manufactured for the new film. The experiment did not last very long, and Paramount produced only two short films in 56mm. *See* **wide screen.**

■ **Magnascope** A wide-screen process, developed by Paramount in the late 1920s, that enlarged the regular 35mm image to almost four times its original size through a special magnifying lens. Because the process produced a grainy image that was not clearly visible at the rear of theaters, it was employed only for special scenes in a film. Magnascope was used in such films as Merian C. Cooper and Ernest B. Schoedsack's documentary *Chang* in 1926 and Howard Hawks's *Wings* in 1927, but its poor image quality probably caused the process's demise once its novelty was gone. *See* **wide screen.**

■ **magnetic film, mag film** Film coated in iron oxide or with one or more tracks of such material on which sound can be recorded and from which it can be played back. This film comes in sizes of 16, 17½, and 35mm, with perforations to match those on photographic film for synchronization of sound and image. *See* **magnetic recording.**

■ **magnetic film recorder, magnetic film reproducer, magnetic film recorder/reproducer, mag machine** A magnetic film recorder uses magnetic film to record sound. Original recording is done on tape through a magnetic tape recorder, and the sound is rerecorded on magnetic film for editing. A magnetic film reproducer plays back sound while a magnetic film recorder/reproducer or mag machine both records and plays back sound. *See* **digital sound recording** *and* **magnetic recording.**

magnetic film recorder/reproducer

■ **magnetic head cluster**   *See* **penthouse head.**

■ **magnetic master**   *See* **master sound track.**

■ **magnetic recording**   A recording of sound on magnetic tape or film. Sound waves are picked up by a microphone, where they are turned into electric impulses. The impulses are then amplified and sent to a magnetic recording head, where they create a magnetic field. The variations of the magnetic field alter the magnetic structure of iron oxide on the tape or film. When the tape or film is run in contact with a separate playback magnetic head, the variations in magnetic structure are reconverted into variable electric impulses that are then transformed to sound waves in a loudspeaker. Magnetic sound is employed for film production instead of optical sound because it is cheaper and easier to use, because it can be replayed immediately, because it can be erased so that the same stock can be used over again, and because of its superior quality. Since the machinery for magnetic tape recording is cheaper, more portable, and easier to handle than that for magnetic sound film and the tape itself is less expensive than film, this type of recording is employed for original sound. The recorded sound, however, is transferred to perforated magnetic film for synchronic editing of audio and image. The finally mixed sound from the master magnetic sound track must be transferred to an optical sound track for the release prints. Although the magnetic track gives better sound reproduction than the optical, the expense of preparing a single film with a magnetic sound track and optical image as well as the cost of changing theater equipment for such sound prevented the use of magnetic recording for film exhibition except for 70mm prints with stereophonic sound (35mm prints at first generally used four magnetic stripes for such sound but today use two optical bands with four tracks). In some 16mm photography, however, a single film was employed that recorded sound on a magnetic stripe at the same time that it recorded the picture. Analog sound recording on magnetic tracks is now being challenged by digital recording in all phases of sound reproduction. Digital tape is being employed to record original sound, digital audio workstations and mixing studios for preparing the final mix, and digital sound systems on film or disc for audio playback in motion-picture theaters. *See* **digital sound, magoptical print, optical sound,** *and* **stereophonic sound.**

■ **magnetic sound**   Any sound recorded on and played back from magnetic tape, film, or a magnetic stripe on the print of a motion picture. *See* **magnetic recording.**

■ **magnetic stock, mag stock**   The raw magnetic film on which sound can be recorded. *See* **magnetic film.**

■ **magnetic stripe, magnetic sound stripe, mag stripe**   A stripe of iron oxide for magnetic sound recording placed in the sound area of a film (another stripe is placed on the opposite side of the film so that it will run through the camera or projector evenly). In certain kinds of 16mm cameras, especially for documentary or news work, such film was employed since it could record sound and image simultaneously. A magnetic stripe is used for sound on 16mm prints in Europe. *See* **magnetic recording, magoptical print,** *and* **optical sound.**

■ **magnetic tape**   A quarter-inch tape coated with iron oxide on which sound can be recorded. Also called audio tape. *See* **magnetic recording.**

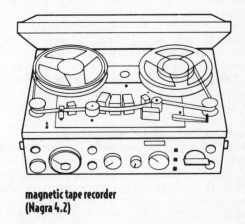

magnetic tape recorder (Nagra 4.2)

■ **magnetic tape recorder**   A recorder that uses magnetic tape to record, erase, and play back sound. Each of these actions is usually performed with a separate magnetic head, although in cheaper machines, the recording and playback heads are the same. Magnetic tape is employed for original sound recording during film production, and the sound is rerecorded on magnetic film for editing. *See* **digital sound recording** *and* **magnetic recording.**

■ **magnetic track, mag track** Any length of a film used for magnetically recording and playing back sound: (1) the magnetic stripe that runs along the edge of some 16mm film for the simultaneous recording of picture and sound; (2) the magnetic stripes on prints for stereophonic sound; (3) the stripe or stripes on magnetic film used only for sound; and (4) the entire width of a 35mm magnetic film or the width between the perforations on such film coated with iron oxide for sound recording. *See* **magnetic recording.**

■ **magnetic transfer, mag transfer** Transferring sound to magnetic film. *See* **magnetic recording.**

■ **magnification, magnification ratio, reproduction ratio** The ratio of the size of the image on the film to the actual size of the subject photographed. This ratio must always be a concern in cinematography for composition and dramatic effect. Magnification will depend both on the lens and the distance between the camera and the subject.

■ **magoptical print, mag-opt print, mag opt** A release print for a motion picture with both optical and magnetic sound tracks. Such prints were released so that they could be shown in both the majority of theaters, which were equipped only for optical sound, and those select theaters that could play back magnetic recording for stereophonic sound from several magnetic tracks on the film. *See* **magnetic recording** *and* **optical sound.**

■ **main feature** The more important and publicized feature film in a double bill. The showing of two films was the general practice in most neighborhood and second-run theaters until the late 1950s. The showings included a feature film and often a B-picture.

■ **main title, main titles** The main title is the name of the film, and the main titles are the titles that appear at the start of the film. *See* **title.**

■ **majors** (1) The large film production companies in Hollywood during the studio period. From the 1930s through 1950, these were Paramount, MGM, Twentieth Century-Fox, Warner Brothers, Columbia, Universal, and RKO. United Artists, though a film distributor for independent filmmakers, might also be included. (2) The large and influential studio/distributors today in Hollywood. The eight "major producers and distributors" who are members of the Motion Picture Association of America are Buena Vista Pictures (for the Walt Disney Company), Sony Pictures Entertainment (Columbia and TriStar), Metro-Goldwyn-Mayer (MGM and United Artists), Paramount Pictures, Turner Pictures (New Line Cinema and Castle Rock Pictures), Twentieth Century-Fox, Universal, and Warner Brothers. Al-

though these companies account for about half of the pictures released each year, they also account for roughly 80 to 90 percent of the gross profits. *See entries for each of these organizations,* **Hollywood, mini-majors,** *and* **studio system.**

■ **make and sync** *See* **Foley artist.**

■ **makeup** (1) The cosmetics applied to the face or any part of the body of performers to enhance or change their appearance, prepare them for a particular role, or make them suitable for photography. (2) The total assembly of cosmetics, wig, hair dye, costume, and anything worn or applied to a performer which prepares him or her for a role in a film. By allowing performers to appear attractive to audiences, makeup, as described in both categories (1) and (2), plays a significant role in those Hollywood films which invite viewers to escape into a world more exciting and appealing than reality and to identify with or desire the characters on the screen. Makeup artists have not only made performers seem more attractive than they normally are, but have also extended the career of many an aging actor and actress. Makeup is also significant in transforming a performer into a certain role, in making the performer appear to the audience as if he or she is actually the character. Makeup can even create figures who are not possible in our everyday world. Jack Pierce, for example, was responsible for creating at Universal the monster first played by Boris Karloff in *Frankenstein* (1931), a figure who has become a permanent part of our popular culture. The makeup artist must, of course, be knowledgeable about the medium and adapt his or her work to the lighting and color of the image as well as to the general characteristics of the film stock. It was not until 1981, with Rick Baker's makeup for *An American Werewolf in London* (dir. John Landis), that an Academy Award became an annual event for that category, although occasional citations had been made before.

Remarkable advancements have taken place in the art of makeup for motion pictures during recent years. Partly a product of the plethora of horror films, makeup technicians have developed techniques of prosthetics for replacing parts of the face and body with artificial structures. Especially popular have been foam latex and eurethane appliances for creating horrific appearances and gross transformations. Inflatable air bags, pneumatics, hydraulics, cable and remote control systems have also contributed to the creation of weird and grotesque sights. These extraordinary developments, however, have changed the nature of the field to such an extent that the Make-up and Hair Stylists Union successfully made claim that Rob Bottin's remarkable work for John Carpenter's *The Thing* (1982) should not be considered for an Academy Award since it was more in the realm of "mechanical devices, mannequins, and non-living things." The latest development in this field is digital makeup by which: (1) images of live performers scanned into a computer can be tested for a variety of makeup procedures before they are actually applied; and (2) scanned images of performers can be altered digitally, achieving astonishing makeup effects, and made part of the film itself. *See* **prosthetics.**

makeup Rick Baker's makeup won the first annual Academy Award in that category for *An American Werewolf in London* (1981; dir. John Landis).

■■■

■ **make up** To apply cosmetics to performers or to costume them in order to enhance their appearance, prepare them for a role, or make them suitable for photography. *See* **makeup.**

■ **makeup artist, makeup man, makeup person, cosmetician** The person responsible for applying makeup to the performers in a film. This individual is generally the head of a group called the makeup department. Makeup artists frequently carry out the directions of the director, cinematographer, or art director, but also, frequently, the directions of the performers. On many occasions the makeup artist has been responsible for some of a film's unique effects. While the makeup artist applies makeup from the head to the breastbone and from fingers to elbows, the body makeup artist applies it to the rest of the performer's body. *See* **makeup.**

■ **makeup call** The time that a performer is supposed to report to the makeup department to be made ready for shooting.

■ **makeup department** The group of personnel in a film production, including the makeup artist who heads the group, responsible for applying makeup to a performer.

■ **makeup effects** The term suggests the remarkable advancements in creating unusual appearances and transformations for characters, both living and dead, and other, weird animals that have been achieved in motion pictures in recent years. As well as relying on traditional techniques of makeup, such effects are achieved by advanced methods of prosthetics and the other new techniques mentioned above under makeup. *See* **makeup.**

■ **makeup reel** A reel of film that is composed of an edited sequence of shots assembled during film production.

■ **make-up table** A table used to load and unload film into and from a platter transport, which itself feeds the film into the projector system. Such a table accommodates reels with up to 6,000 feet of film. The feed and take-up are electronically operated and the speeds can be changed. One make-up table services a number of platters in a multiplex. *See* **platter system.**

■ **male matte** A matte for making composite images in special effects cinematography; it is opaque in the area of the subject but clear in the surrounding area. Also called a hold-out matte. *See* **female matte, matte** *(2), and* **traveling-matte process.**

■ **Maltese cross movement, Maltese cross mechanism** The mechanism in a professional projector that moves each frame of the film intermittently in front of the aperture for projection of the image. A single pin on a rotating shaft engages each of the four slots on a Maltese cross, causing the cross to turn ninety degrees with each engagement and thus intermittently to turn the sprocket that moves each frame before the aperture. Also called Geneva movement. *See* **intermittent movement** *and* **pull-down claw.**

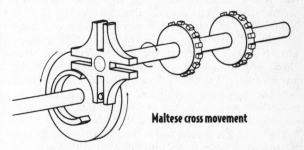

Maltese cross movement

■ **M and D, masters and dupes** *See* **fine-grain duplicate negative** *and* **fine-grain master print**

■ **M and E track** The sound track containing both music and sound effects but no dialogue. This track is made for releases in foreign countries, where the local dialogue can be mixed with the original music and sound effects. Sometimes a magnetic film with separate dialogue, music, and effects tracks, referred to as a DME, is released for the same purpose.

■ **m and s** *See* **Foley artist.**

■ **mapping** *See* **texture mapping.**

■ *March of Time, The* A series of short documentaries produced by Louis de Rochemont for the Time-Life company in this country from 1935 to 1951. These films dealt with contemporary political matters in a more liberal manner than the parent magazines. Combining newsreel footage, interviews, and staged scenes, along with a very authoritative voice-over, these films were both professional and persuasive. *See* **documentary.**

■ **marketing** Since films are consumer products and a great deal of money must be recouped to make them profitable, advertising must first convince a projected audience that they want them and then they must be made available for consumption. Distribution companies have both advertising departments and sales departments to carry on these functions respectively. A significant venue today for advertising is television, both local and network, though print still plays an important role. In the 1970s, the major distributors realized that national television was an efficient form of advertising and the venue with the greatest potential for financial return. The result of this large-scale and simultaneous type of advertising was national wide-release booking—in the 1980s, films opened simultaneously on as many as 2,000 screens and today on as many as 3,000 for special blockbusters. The days of premiere openings in select cities and road-show presentations followed by wider distribution are over. The goal now is to create a large interest in the film, normally by selling its concept and stars, especially in relation to one another. Such interest is immediately followed by a wide release throughout the country on a vast number of screens so that a large gross is achieved the very first week (actually the first weekend). It is hoped that the impetus will carry the film forward, especially with the help of word-of-mouth. The average film in 1996 from the major studio/distributors cost about $40 million, plus an additional $20 million for advertising and prints. Television reaches a wide market, but such advertising is very costly to continue for more than a week. At the same time, interest accrues on the loans borrowed to make the film. A large number of films are pulled from theaters after the first or second week when it becomes clear that they will not recoup their costs and are not worth the expense of further advertising. For certain big-budget films, the later sale and rental of the film on videocassette and screening on cable television become early concerns as do other ancillary markets—for example, toys, T-shirts, and records of the sound track. The Walt Disney Company, which wrote the book on ancillary marketing, had its own recent release of *Toy Story* (1995; dir. John Lasseter) further marketed by Frito-Lay and Burger King when these companies themselves spent an additional $125 million promoting their tie-ins to the film. Films that are considered to have a smaller audience may receive a platform release in which they first play at a limited number of theaters in the hope that such an exhibition will kindle a more general interest and result in a wider distribution. Much of what has been described above in terms of domestic marketing can also be applied to the selling of a film in foreign markets—it is important to remember that films are the United States's second largest export. The marketing of the film as product continues after its release not only on video and through ancillary markets, but also through the various theme parks, such as those attached to Disney and Universal, which make the films part of their fantasy world, and also through such stores as those using the Disney and Warner Brothers names and icons. *See* **market research.**

■ **market research** Because of the high cost of making, advertising, and distributing films, and to make the largest possible return on this investment, the major studio/distributors seek to create a product that will appeal to the widest possible audience. For this reason, the desires and interests of a potential public are first researched and then the film is shaped accordingly. It might be that the concept is conceived with the potential audience in mind and the public is then tested to see if such an interest would actually exist. In both cases, the screenplay is shaped according to the research, as is the advertising. Part of the marketing strategy is aimed at building interest in the film to create the impetus to buy the tickets before the film is released. Audience reactions from test screenings and sneak previews are used to give the film its final shape. Such screenings have been part of marketing for some decades, but market research in the larger sense, from preproduction through production, swung into full gear in the late 1970s, especially as the film companies became part of large business conglomerates and they had to follow the same business practices as their affiliates. Marketing or distribution previews allow the distributor to plan both release patterns and advertising; and exit interviews, in the early part of the film's release, are used to make adjustments in the marketing strategies. *See* **marketing.**

■ **market segmentation** Dividing the audience for a film according to characteristics such as age, sex, geography, family orientation, or gender in order to plan the advertising, marketing, and distribution strategies. Also sometimes referred to as marketing subsegmentation.

■ **mark it** An order, often given by the director of photography, to the camera assistant that he or she should clap together the hinged boards on top of the clapboard at the beginning of a take, when the camera is already operating, so that the image of the coming together of the two pieces and the bang on the sound track can later be used for the synchronization of picture and sound during editing. *See* **clapboard.**

■ **marquee** A rooflike projection over the entrance of a theater that announces the title of the film playing and sometimes the names of the stars.

■ **marquee value** The ability of a star's name "on the marquee" to draw a large number of people to see a film. Though many theaters no longer have a traditional marquee and no longer include stars' names with the listing of the films in front of the complex, the association of such a performer with a film is well known through advertising.

■ **married print** A print of the film containing both picture and sound.

■ **martini shot** The last shot of the day, right before one goes home and has a martini. *See* **Abby Singer shot.**

■ **Marxist criticism** A type of criticism based on the writings and economic theory of Karl Marx and his followers. Marxist criticism has been applied more rigorously to literature than film, but in recent years it has risen above mere polemics in film studies, especially in its relationship to linguistics, structuralism, and Freud. One might begin a study of Marxist film criticism with Eisenstein and the influence of Hegelian dialectics on his theory of montage. Eisenstein was influenced by other aspects of Marxism, and he himself was to have an influence on French film critics beginning in the 1960s, when his ideas became more available. Marxist criticism has generally had a propensity toward heavy-handedness and polemical simplification, with an antiformalist bias and simplistic application of the concept of class war to the work of art. This kind of approach was obvious in the responses that Eisenstein's own works sometimes received in the Soviet Union, and it was also evident in some of the film criticism produced in this country, especially during the 1930s. But with the influence of Saussurian semiotics, the reinterpretation of Freud by Lacan, the Marxist structuralist writings of Althusser, the films of Jean-Luc Godard, and the French publication *Tel Quel*, Marxist film criticism achieved some degree of sophistication, especially in the French film journals *Cahiers du cinéma* and *Cinéthique*. One should also note the manner in which Christian Metz incorporated Marxist thought into his own semiotic criticism. *See* **film theory.**

■ **mask, matte** (1) A partial covering placed in front of the camera lens to reduce or change the shape of the image: for example, the iris used by D. W. Griffith in his silent films to form a circular image. Such blocking devices could suggest a view through a keyhole, window, or some such opening. Griffith also employed these masks to widen or heighten the image for dramatic effect. Such masks, perhaps from overuse or simply because they are not very sophisticated devices, are no longer much employed. (2) A partial shield placed behind the lens of a camera or projector or against the

aperture of a printer to achieve a wide-screen image. (3) The partial covering placed in front of the lens of a camera to block out part of the image so that part of another image can later be added for a composite picture. Such composite printing was often performed in silent and early sound films to add background to live action, combine animation and live action, or simply to extend an already existing structure or set by means of a separate film image of a drawing. Sometimes the same original negative might pass through the camera twice to shoot both picture elements, but it was safer and more efficient to shoot the different images on separate film and later combine them on a fresh negative. (4) A device, such as another piece of film with various densities, to control light or color reaching the film in a camera or printer. *See* **iris shot** *and* **matte** (2).

mask (keyhole mask for camera)

■ **masking** (1) Applying a mask to a camera, projector, or printer for any of the reasons described above under mask. (2) A process of correcting (or sometimes distorting) color in the photographic process, often by using a black-and-white negative or positive in conjunction with the original. Such a process generally is employed to improve or alter contrast. Sometimes chemical couplers in the film emulsion itself can act as the masking agent for the couplers' absorption of color.

■ **master** (1) Any device that controls another device, itself referred to as the slave (e.g., the sync signal from a camera controlling the speed of the sound recorder). (2) A positive on which transitions or other optical effects have been added to the motion picture. (3) A final version of a work with the complete edits, e.g., a master positive or edit master tape.

■ **master dupe negative, master negative** *See* **fine-grain duplicate negative.**

■ **master-matching** *See* **matching** (2).

■ **master number** The number sometimes given to each scene in a film script. Scenes might be numbered consecutively and a letter added to the master number to indicate each shot or camera change. Sometimes consecutive numbers are used for each shot or camera change, regardless of scene.

■ **master positive, fine-grain master positive, fine-grain master print, master fine grain** A positive print of very high quality made from the original negative and used for making fine-grain duplicate negatives, themselves to be used as the source of release prints. The term "master positive" is more often applied to black-and-white film than to color film. *See* **interpositive.**

■ **master scene script, master scene screenplay** A film script that gives each scene of the film consecutively, including dialogue and action, but does not indicate shots or camera movements.

■ **master scene technique, master shot technique** A technique of filming a single scene whereby all the action is shot in a continuous take, generally in a long shot that covers all the action, and then parts of the scene are repeated for medium shots and close-ups that can later be edited into the master scene. Sometimes multiple cameras are used to film the other shots at the same time that the master scene is being photographed. This technique was employed in the Hollywood studios to allow for some choice in editing and also because it permitted Hollywood's "invisible" style of cutting. It also had the advantages of allowing the scene to be filmed with some rapidity without frequent delays for changing the position of the camera and lights. At the same time, the master shot could always be used as a "cover shot" to hide mistakes in other takes. Actors tend to prefer this technique since it allows them a continuous performance at least for the major shooting. The drawback is, of course, that the shooting ratio (the amount of film shot compared to that finally used) is higher than when each shot is photographed individually with only one camera. When middle shots or close-ups are intercut with the master scene, they are frequently made to do so on action so that the cutting seems unobtrusive. When only one camera is used for all the shooting, there must be a repetition of action at the end of each shot and the start of the next so that the movement of the characters can be matched perfectly in editing. *See* **editing** *and* **single-shot technique.**

■ **master shot, master scene** (1) The continuous shot of an entire scene, generally a long shot, used in the master-scene technique and into which middle shots and close-ups will later be intercut. *See* **master scene technique.** (2) Any of the individual shots of a scene into which other shots are cut and which function as the master shot described in (1). None of these shots are a single, long take, but they all function to orient the other shots.

■ **master sound track** The finally mixed magnetic track that contains all the sound (dialogue, music, sound effects, background noise) and is ready to be optically printed on the composite release print. Also called the final mix or magnetic master. *See* **magnetic recording** *and* **mix.**

■ **master use license** A contractual agreement that allows a film production to use a previous recording of a piece of music. Sometimes the key artist's permission may be required as well as that of the recording company. In addition to the record company being given a fee, the musician and singers are normally paid once again. *See* **performance license** *and* **synchronization license.**

■ **match cut, match-image cut** A cut from one shot to another in which the two shots are matched in action or subject by (1) a continuity of action by the same subject (*see* **matching action**); (2) a similarity in action by two different characters or perhaps by the same character at different times moving in the same direction in the same part of the image; or (3) a similarity in the two subjects' shape and form—for example, close-ups of two characters engaged in conversation, a portrait becoming a live face, or the much cited scene in Kubrick's *2001:A Space Odyssey* (1968) where the bone hurled into the air by a primitive apeman becomes a space satellite. Such cuts either allow for continuity or create an immediately recognizable similarity between the two images. *See* **form cut** *and* **jump cut.**

■ **match dissolve** A dissolve from one shot to another in which the two images are matched or related by similarities in form or action. Sometimes a series of shots or images of the same subject can dissolve one into the other to suggest the passage of time or the process of aging. Horror films frequently show their transformations of man to werewolf or Jekyll to Hyde through a series of match dissolves. *See* **dissolve.**

■ **match-frame edit** An edit in which the last frame of the first shot parallels the first frame of the second shot so that one continuous action is created.

■ **matching** (1) Editing the original negative into A and B rolls to match the similar cutting of the work print in order to make the continuous final print (generally for 16mm film). *See* **A and B printing** *and* **checkerboard cutting.** (2) Cutting any original negative to match the editing of the work print.

■ **matching action** Cutting from one shot to another of the same action so that the action seems continuous and the cut is invisible, generally accomplished by overlapping the action of the two separate shots when shooting with one camera. Camera distance or angle can thus be changed from one shot to another so long as the action continues in much the same direction within the frame and so long as relational distances within the image seem the same. *See* **cutting on action** *and* **invisible cutting.**

■ **matrix** (1) A single strip of film that transferred a colored dye to a positive print in imbibition printing. Three such matrixes were used, each transferring a complementary color for one of the primary colors. Through a subtractive process, the properly colored image was projected onto the screen. *See* **color film** *(2) and* **imbibition.** (2) Each of the three emulsion layers which combine to form modern tripack color film. Each matrix is made sensitive to a different primary color by chemical couplers that form an image on the developed negative in a color complementary to one of the primary colors. *See* **color film** *(2) and* **integral tripack color system.**

■ **matte** (1) *See* **mask.** (2) A partial covering that prevents light from reaching a certain area of the film by blocking part of the lens of the camera during shooting or part of the aperture in the printer. Part of another image will later go into the unexposed area for the creation of a composite image. Mattes for lenses were used in silent films and early sound pictures to combine live action and background, live action and animation, and to extend or change parts of sets or structures by means of filmed drawings. Mattes were often a piece of glass with part of its area blackened. A system was later developed that was less threatening to the original negative: a bipack camera was used in which the desired area of an image on a positive was printed onto a negative while both films passed the aperture in contact. The unwanted area of the positive was matted out by the blackened portion of a white board placed in front of the aperture. The same negative could then be run through the camera, and part of another image photographed into the unexposed area from another positive with its unwanted area blackened out in the same manner; or the negative could be run through the camera alone to record artwork or a photograph for background onto its unexposed area directly from the matte board with the area of the film already exposed blackened out on the board. In more advanced processes, "traveling mattes," which are strips of film with the matting area changing from frame to frame, permit movement in the foreground or background. Such mattes run in bipack with each positive in an optical printer, preventing the unwanted part of the image from being exposed to the negative. Aerial-image photography also makes composite shots: artwork can be combined with the aerial image of live action, acting at the same time as its own matte. Similar techniques of matting as those described above are employed that allow aerial-image photography to perform much the same function as a bipack camera or optical printer. Computer technology is now also employed for creating such backgrounds, which are composited with the other picture elements. (3) The matte painting or background that is matted into the composite image described in (2). *See* **aerial-image photography, bipack contact matte printing, matte painting, special effects,** *and* **traveling-matte process.**

■ **matte artist, matte painter** An individual in the special-effects department who specializes in designing or painting backgrounds on mattes for the making of composite images. Such artists now also employ computers to create electronic matte paintings that can be composited with live action. *See* **matte painting.**

■ **matte bleed** A dispersion of light and color or a line between two areas of an image that have been matted together. Such dispersion makes the matting obvious and might be caused by the misalignment of matte and film in the printer. *See* **matte** *(2).*

■ **matte-board, copy-board** A type of easel placed in front of a camera from which art work or a photograph is matted into the unexposed area of the film, forming with the image in the exposed area a composite picture. The area on the board corresponding to the already exposed part of the film is blackened. *See* **matte** *(2).*

■ **matte box** A frame mounted in front of the camera lens into which mattes (or masks) and filters can be placed and to which a sunshade is generally attached. The matte box is attached to the camera with a light-free bellows and can be made to slide along two parallel rods either toward or away from the camera and then be locked in place.

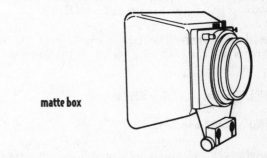

matte box

■ **matte line** (1) The line that separates the area of an image to be used in a composite picture from that area of the same image to be matted out. (2) The line that separates components matted together to form a single composite image. Such lines must be unobtrusive in the final picture and not suffer from matte bleed. For this reason perfect registration of all elements is required at each stage of the entire process. Matte lines can sometimes be slightly blurred or blended into the picture to help make them invisible. *See* **matte** *(2).*

■ **matte painting** A painting of a background that is combined with live action, an actual set, or animated models to create a composite image. The painting may be done on part of a glass sheet, with the camera shooting through the clear area at the actual scene behind; on part of a board on an easel, with the action area blacked out; or it may be photographed and projected from a slide for front or rear projection. Such backgrounds are now also created digitally on a computer and composited with the live-action image. Electronic matte painting allows the matte artist the flexibility to try out a variety of backgrounds before selecting the best version. *See* **digital effects, front projection, matte, painted matte shot,** *and* **rear projection.**

■ **matte screen** A flat projection screen that diffuses a wide angle of light so that the picture can be seen clearly at the side extremities of the theater. *See* **screen.**

■ **matte shot** (1) Any image that is the result of combining the parts of two or more separate images by means of mattes for blocking out unwanted areas and protecting previously exposed areas during photography or printing. (2) Any shot in which part of the scene is matted out so that the photographed area can at some point be joined with part of another image for a composite picture. *See* **matte** *(2).*

■ **matting** The process of integrating the parts of two or more separate images into a single composite picture by means of mattes for blocking out unwanted areas and for protecting previously exposed areas during photography and printing. *See* **matte** *(2).*

■ **maxibrute.** A term used for a nine-light with nine 1,000-watt PAR lights. See **nine-light** *and* **PAR light.**

■ **maximum aperture** The largest opening of the diaphragm in a camera's lens; consequently the lowest f-stop number.

■ **MCA/Universal** *See* **Universal Pictures.**

■ **MCU** *See* **medium close-up.**

■ **meal penalty** An amount of money due to an actor or crew member from a production company if he or she works beyond a certain number of consecutive hours without a break for eating.

■ **meat axe** A piece of black wood or cardboard attached to the end of a pole; it looks like an elongated meat axe and is used to block light from the lens of the camera or to create small areas of shadow on the set.

■ **mechanical effects, mechanical special effects** Special effects for a film that are mechanically created in front of the camera rather than optically or digitally created at a later time. Such effects would include (1) the creation of natural phenomena such as rain, snow, and storms; (2) the production of fires and explosions; (3) the use of life-size models such as apes or sharks; and (4) the creation of elaborate make-up effects. The term "physical effects" is used in Great Britain for such achievements before the camera. *See* **makeup** *and* **special effects.**

■ **mechanical makeup effects** *See* **makeup.**

■ **media server** A large hard-drive and computerized system used for storing both images and sound and making them accessible to various parties for simultaneous use.

■ **mediate** In informational theory and semiotics, to act as a medium for conveying information. Any message will itself be influenced by the medium that conveys it and the codes that are used in that medium. All the information we receive from a film is influenced by the very physical characteristics of the medium itself (which is composed of a series of flat, luminous, and moving images) as well as the various codes (social and filmic) through which the film medium operates. *See* **medium** *and* **semiotics.**

■ **medium, media** (pl.) (1) An agency for or means of transferring information. The arts are individual media—for example, film and theater. Mass media, which transfer information to large numbers of people, includes newspapers, radio, and television. (2) The material or basic elements through which an agency or artist conveys information. In this respect, paint is the medium through which a painter expresses himself or herself; words are the medium for a writer; and film images the basic medium for the filmmaker. The point frequently made, especially since Marshall McLuhan's *Understanding Media* (1964), is that "the medium is the message" in that it shapes and influences the information it transmits as well as conveying information apart from its message. Much has been said about the way the electronic image on the television screen has influenced the very information it seeks to convey at the same time that it has influenced the way we perceive and react to both that information and the world around us (a notable example would be our perceptions of and reactions to the Vietnam War). Certainly film, through its medium of visual images—their luminosity, illusory depth of field, camera perspectives, and sequences—has shaped its own world at the same time that it has had an impact on our own perceptions of the world in which we live.

■ **medium close-up (MCU), medium close shot (MCS)** A shot of a character between a medium shot and close-up that includes the area from the chest to the top of the head. Also referred to as a loose close-up. *See* **close-up** *and* **medium shot.**

■ **medium gray** The midpoint on the gray scale between white and black that is the average amount of light reflected from a surface required for a satisfactory image on film. To one side of this point the image starts to become dark and to the other it starts to become light.

■ **medium lens** A lens for a camera with a focal length that produces an image approximating what the eye normally sees. For a 35mm camera, such a lens would have a focal length somewhere in the range of 50mm; for a 16mm camera, the focal length would be about 25mm. *See* **lens.**

■ **medium long shot (MLS)** A shot somewhere between a long and medium shot that shows one or more characters from the knees up and also some of the terrain—also called a three-quarters or American shot. *See* **long shot.**

■ **medium shot (MS)** An intermediate shot between the long shot and close-up that generally shows a character from the waist up or the full figure of a seated character. Such shots can include several characters in the frame. They are effective for (1) showing the interrelationship of two or more characters while giving a sufficient amount of detail to maintain audience involvement; (2) focusing on a character in a particular surrounding without giving a large amount of the environment; and (3) bridging long shots and close-ups (or vice versa) as a transitional shot. Also sometimes called a mid-shot. *See* **close-up** *and* **long shot.**

■ **megaphone** A large funnel-shaped device for amplifying and directing the voice. Directors in silent-film days are often pictured shouting orders to crew and cast through a megaphone.

■ **megaplex** A large multiplex with sixteen or more theaters and with modern conveniences and technology. Such multiple theaters are today housed in an individual large structure with a single lobby, large concession stand, and a few box offices serving all the screenings. The AMC Grand Complex in Dallas has twenty-four screens, while the same company plans on building a twenty-five-screen complex on Forty-second Street in New York City and a thirty-screen complex in Ontario, California. Although such a large number of screens presents a wide selection of films, the megaplex does not often offer much diversity outside of the typical Hollywood product, except perhaps in certain urban areas—instead, such complexes allow hourly bookings of the same popular films in two theaters. *See* **exhibitor** *and* **multiplex.**

■ **megger** (1) A term sometimes used for the director and derived from the megaphone that early film directors are supposed to have used. (2) The person who held the megaphone through which silent-film directors were supposed to have barked their orders.

■ **Mellotron** A machine, especially popular with rock groups in the 1960s and 1970s, that contained a large number of individual tapes with music and sound effects, any of which could be dubbed into the sound track of a film during mixing.

■ **melodrama** A term originally applied to plays that focused on plot and action at the expense of character

and motivation. Such plays are uncomplicated and emotional in nature, appealing to the audience's feelings instead of minds. Moral issues are reduced to a struggle between good and evil with characters clearly representing one or the other. Such plays generally have a happy ending in which virtue is rewarded. Nineteenth- and early-twentieth-century theater in America and England featured such plays which had a marked influence on a number of early silent films. Certainly this influence can be seen in many of Griffith's films, even though some fine filmic technique and strong performances raise these works above the level of simple melodrama (note, for example, his impressive *Way Down East* in 1920, based on the stock melodrama by Lottie Blair Parker). Contemporary feminist scholars have identified and discussed a particular cinematic melodrama that focused largely on the personal and social problems of women in a highly emotional way—e.g., *Stella Dallas,* with Barbara Stanwyck as the woman who sacrifices all she has for her daughter (1937; dir. King Vidor). Such films, analyzed from the perspective of the female spectator, are seen to hide or disguise in their narratives the contradictions and stresses of women in contemporary society. *See* **woman's film.**

melodrama Lillian Gish is told never to darken the door again in D. W. Griffith's affecting *Way Down East* (1920).

■ ■ ■

■ **memorandum agreement** *See* **deal letter.**

■ **merchandising** The utilization of a film's title, logo, artwork, and characters to market a variety of products. The Walt Disney Production Company has long had a consumer products division in charge of the licensing of the Disney cartoon characters for a host of products. *Star Wars* in 1977 (dir. George Lucas) and the subsequent films in the series made other studios aware of the full economic potential of licensing its characters for such products as toys, games, dolls, books, T-shirts, clothes, and many other products. New Line Cinema created a similar financial bonanza with its Ninja turtles, beginning with the 1990 release of *Teenage Mutant Ninja Turtles*. Spielberg's production of *Jurassic Park* (1993) brought the dinosaur back from oblivion and into the home in a myriad of ways.

■ **mercury vapor lamp** A tubular type of bulb used in the early days of motion pictures. This type of lamp was suitable to orthochromatic stock because it was strong in the blue-green area of the spectrum and weak in the red area. A number of such tubes would be used in a single unit, though the light could not be easily controlled or directed. *See* **lighting.**

■ **metal halide lamp, mercury arc lamp, mercury vapor arc** *See* **HMI.**

■ **metaphor** In speech and writing, the application of a word or phrase associated with one object to another, normally unrelated, object, thus establishing an implied comparison. The object that receives the unexpected language is thus seen in a new light through the comparison (e.g., "his royal vessel sat itself down on the chair"). In film, the term "metaphor" has generally been applied to two consecutive shots when the second is a direct comparison to and hence statement on the first. The practice was used by Eisenstein in his montage sequences and is notable in his film *October (Ten Days That Shook the World;* 1928), when, for example, the entrance of the new delegates to the Congress of Soviets is related to the spinning wheels of the motorcycle battalion. Such juxtapositions are actually similes, where one object is directly compared to another. Metaphoric comparisons in film, unless they are properly integrated and poetically imaginative, can be obvious and artificial, as, for example, when the passionate lovers are compared to a pair of wild horses in heat in *Not as a Stranger* (1955; dir. Stanley Kramer). The effective metaphor in film achieves the same sudden integration of two objects as it does in language when we are surprised and delighted to discover the fitness of the comparison.

■ **method acting** A technique of acting derived from the practice and writing of the great Russian actor, director, and acting teacher Konstantin Stanislavsky (see especially his *An Actor Prepares* and *My Life in Art*). The "method" became popular in this country largely through the Actors Studio, founded in New York in 1947, and especially in film through the acting of Marlon Brando and the directing of Elia Kazan, who were important members of this group (both won Academy Awards for *On the Waterfront* [1954]). Other important method actors in the Actors Studio who worked in film were Rod Steiger, Julie Harris, James Dean, and Montgomery Clift. The "method" is an ultrarealistic style of acting that demands immense concentration and internalization on the actor's part—he or she must draw

from private experiences and feelings, actually becoming the character. This style of acting seems extremely natural; performances are often low-keyed, with pauses, hesitations, and gropings for meaning and communication. At its best, method acting was inspirational and moving; at its worst, it was mannered and dull. To some extent it has left its mark on later film actors in the realistic tradition, namely Dustin Hoffman, Al Pacino, and Robert De Niro. *See* **Actors Studio.**

method acting Marlon Brando and Rod Steiger in the famous cab scene in *On the Waterfront* (1954; dir. Elia Kazan).

■ ■ ■

■ **metonymy** In speech and writing, the application of a word or phrase belonging to one object to another object with which it is normally related (for example, when a mercenary is referred to as a "hired gun"). In film, this concept readily applies to an object that is visibly present in order to represent another object to which it is related. For example, the broken eyeglasses in Hitchcock's *Strangers on a Train* (1951) become a metonym for the slain woman who formerly wore them. In semiotics, the eyeglasses as a sign for the woman would be called an "index." Related to metonymy is synecdoche, when an actual part of an object is used as a sign for the whole or the whole is used to represent a part. *See* **index** *and* **synecdoche.**

■ **Metro-Goldwyn-Mayer, MGM** The largest and most powerful of the great film production companies of Hollywood from about 1930 until after the Second World War, which had a roaring lion as its well-known logo at the start of each film. In 1920, Marcus Loew, who owned a large theater chain, bought Metro Pictures Corporation, a production and distribution company. In 1924 he also purchased Goldwyn Picture Corporation, originally founded by Samuel Goldwyn, and then merged Metro-Goldwyn with Louis B. Mayer's production company to form Metro-Goldwyn-Mayer, or MGM as it was also known (the corporate name was actually Loew's Inc.). The company centered its film production at the Goldwyn studio in Culver City. Louis B. Mayer was made head of the studio, a position he was to hold for almost thirty years. He was helped considerably by Irving Thalberg, who had come to the Mayer Company from Universal in 1923 and at the time was only twenty-five. Between Mayer and Thalberg, MGM built one of the most efficient and skillful movie studios in the history of motion pictures, turning out as many as forty films a year in its own glossy and finished manner. While Mayer was responsible for building the lavish studios of MGM, with its stable of stars, its myriad of departments, and its company of directors and technicians, Thalberg was responsible for the high level of the product that MGM turned out, involving himself from the start to finish of each production, from the writing of the script to the final editing. MGM was especially a star's studio, and although many talented directors worked for the company, much of their work was ground down by the studio system. Among the stars who worked for MGM until the war years were John Barrymore, Joan Crawford, Mickey Rooney, Greta Garbo, Clark Gable, Jean Harlow, Spencer Tracy, and Judy Garland. Thalberg died at the age of thirty-seven in 1936, but three years later the studio was to achieve two of its greatest successes, *The Wizard of Oz* and *Gone With the Wind* (both directed by Victor Fleming).

After the war, MGM, like the other major studios, was forced to divest itself of its theaters because of the Paramount decision of the Supreme Court. The rise of television, the related decrease in audiences, and increased costs of production began to take their toll, but such films as *Ben-Hur* (1959; dir. William Wyler) and *Doctor Zhivago* (1965; dir. David Lean), though not products of the old studio system, appeared under the MGM banner and helped the ailing company. But the tide was inevitable and money losses continued. In spite of *The Dirty Dozen* in 1967 (dir. Robert Aldrich) and *2001: A Space Odyssey* in 1968 (dir. Stanley Kubrick), the company was bought by a Las Vegas businessman, Kirk Kerkorian, in 1969. While MGM produced a luxury hotel in Las Vegas, props, costumes, and studio land were sold back in Culver City. MGM became an occasional producer and distributor of films, giving up its distribution to United Artists in 1973, which it took into its own fold in 1981. The rest of MGM's history during this period is an even sorrier affair, with a brief ownership by Turner Broadcasting System leading to the sale of the Culver City studio to Lorimar Telepictures and the company's name and current productions back to Kirk Kerkorian, who had already obtained United Artists. Turner was smart enough to hold on to the MGM film library. In 1990, Giancarlo Paretti purchased MGM/UA as part of Pathé Communications Company, calling the new corporation MGM-Pathé Communications. Paretti did not have sufficient funds and lost the firm in 1992 to Crédit Lyonnais Bank Nederland in France, which had financed the original deal.

MGM/UA has recently returned to film with an upsurge of activities, releasing such hits as *Get Shorty* (1995; dir. Barry Sonnenfeld) and such quality films as *Leaving Las Vegas* (1995; dir. Mike Figgis) for a 6.3 percent share of the box office during the year 1995, and *The Birdcage* (dir. Mike Nichols) in 1996. In spite of its recent activity, and a library of United Artists films, the financial status of the company still remains strained. Its future at this point is especially unclear since Kirk Kerkorian has once more put his hands around the neck of the company, this time as the chief financial backer to MGM/UA's management group that itself recently purchased the company.

■ *metteur-en-scène* A French term for the individual, most often the director, responsible for creating the *mise-en-scène* of a film—that is, for putting everything into the image—and also for editing the film. The term is used pejoratively by French critics for directors who simply carry out orders in making a film and do not impose their own personal vision, hence failing to be an *auteur*. See **auteur.**

■ **mickey** *See* **redhead.**

■ **mickey mousing** To coordinate sound, especially music, so closely to the image that it seems to describe exactly what is taking place on the screen. In the cartoons that came from Walt Disney productions, such as those with Mickey Mouse, close synchronization may have been desirable for the simple, animated world; but in live-motion pictures, such coordination is considered too obvious and simplistic. *See* **music.**

■ **microcinematography** The photographing of very small objects by means of a microscope. Also called cinemicrography, cinephotomicrography, and cinemicroscopy. *See* **macrocinematography.**

■ **micro-major** A small production company with its own line of credit.

■ **microphone, mike** An instrument that transforms the energy produced by sound waves into an electric signal that can be recorded or transmitted and amplified. Ultimately, an electric signal is reconverted back to sound waves in a loudspeaker. There are two main methods in film production for converting sound waves into electrical energy in the microphone. In the dynamic, electrodynamic, or moving-coil microphone, a vibrating diaphragm causes a coil to move in a magnetic field, thereby creating electric voltage. In a condenser or electrostatic microphone, one of the plates of a capacitor, a device for accumulating electric energy that is fed an electric current, acts as a diaphragm—when vibrating, its changing position in relation to a fixed plate causes an alteration in the capacitance between the two plates, which can be amplified.

There are several different types and shapes of microphones for various functions in filming: the commonly used unidirectional, heart-shaped type (sometimes called a cardioid) picks up sound mostly in the direction it is aimed (sometimes two such microphones are combined so that the area of pickup can be doubled). The ultradirectional or "shot-gun" microphone, positioned at the end of a long tube, receives sound from a very narrow angle of acceptance and can pick up speech from a person a number of feet away so long as he or she is directly in front of the instrument. The omnidirectional microphone picks up sound in all directions and, though not as effective and clear as the other types, is useful for general noise from the environment or a group of people. The very small lavalier microphone, especially used in television, can be placed around the neck of a character and hidden by clothing. Wireless or radio microphones, which require no wires, have proven more effective of late when placed on characters.

Although two or more microphones are normally employed for the recording of stereophonic sound, instruments such as the stereo shotgun microphone allow for the pickup of two signals from an image source, one by means of an element aimed directly at the source and the other by means of an element positioned bidirectionally or 90 degrees to the source. *See* **sound.**

■ **microphone boom** A long pole on which a microphone is mounted so that it can be placed over a scene for sound recording. Such booms can be moved to change the location of the microphone even during a shot. On some types of boom the microphone can be extended, withdrawn, or redirected. On the perambulator type, an operator rides the vehicle and works the boom while the vehicle is pushed around by one or more members of the crew. *See* **fishpole.**

■ **microphone pickup pattern, microphone directivity pattern** The pattern of sounds from various angles that a microphone is able to pick up (e.g., unidirectional, bidirectional, and omnidirectional).

■ **microphone placement** The positioning of a microphone boom for maximum receptivity to sound.

■ **microphone presence** The immediacy of a performer's voice as picked up by a microphone. *See* **presence.**

■ **microphone shadow** The shadow of a microphone cast on part of the set. This mishap can be avoided by using some kind of flag to cast a general shadow that will absorb that of the microphone.

■ **midget** A 200-watt spotlight with a four-inch Fresnel lens. *See* **Fresnel** *and* **mini.**

■ **MIDI** The initials stand for Musical Instrument Digital Interface, an electronic system that allows the integration of digital audio from synthesizer, electronic instrument, and computer memory. MIDI can work with the SMPTE time code to match music with the images of both video and film. *See* **time code.**

■ **mighty** An open-face, variable-focus light of 2,000 watts.

■ **mike man** The individual on a set who is responsible for properly locating microphones, sometimes with the help of a boom.

■ **mimesis** A term in literary criticism that means the imitation and representation of reality. The term has applicability to film study when we decide to what degree a particular film is mimetic in aim and in the presentation of its material. Film runs the gamut from extreme mimetic representation in the newsreel and documentary to the total lack of mimesis in certain types of experimental abstract films. The degree of mimesis in fictional films is controlled by the amount of stylization in presentation and how much the film undercuts its reality by emphasizing its process as film.

■ **mini** A 200-watt spotlight with a three-inch Fresnel lens. See **Fresnel** *and* **midget.**

■ **miniature, model** A small replica, created in scale, of a vehicle, character, animal, object, or location that can be photographed and made to appear life-size or larger. Such models are painstakingly created by special-effects personnel with sufficient detail to seem realistic. A "hanging" miniature can be used in front of the camera when an actual set needs to be expanded— for example, when an elaborate ceiling has to be added—or such a miniature can be photographed and its image combined with an image of the set later in printing. Miniatures can also function as backgrounds seen through a window. Model trains, automobiles, and airplanes can be used to create spectacular crashes. When moving miniatures are photographed, the camera must operate at an accelerated speed so that at normal projection the action will be slowed down relative to the subject's increase in size within the image (the camera speed for miniature action should be the square root of the scale). The beasts and primitive animals we see in fantasy films are often miniatures that are animated through stop-motion photography, as are the human victims of such creatures during moments of violence. Shots of miniatures can either be intercut with live action or integrated with live action into a composite image through various matting techniques, rear projection or front projection, and now digitally. *See* **animation, fantasy, motion control, special effects, stop motion.**

■ **miniature rear projection** A type of rear projection in which live action is projected frame by frame onto a small screen in a scale model set. The model figures in the set are adjusted to coordinate with the human performers projected in each frame and both are photographed together through stop-motion photography—the result is an image of live and animated figures inhabiting the same world. Miniature projection was first used in *King Kong* (1933; dir. Merian C. Cooper and Ernest B. Schoedsack)—in one scene, both the hero and heroine are separately projected into a model set where a miniature Kong fights a miniature reptile. On the screen, the tiny humans seem dwarfed and threatened by these struggling monsters. *See* **rear projection.**

miniature rear projection
1. projector 2. projected image
3. model and miniature set 4. camera

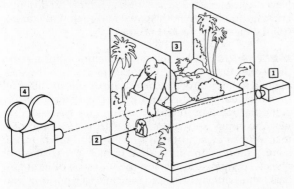

■ **miniature shot, model shot** Any shot using a miniature setting and models of vehicles, animals, or people in animation. *See* **miniature.**

■ **minibrute** A term used for a nine-light with nine FCX lamps. *See* **FCX light** *and* **nine-light.**

■ **mini-majors** The second level of film production/distribution companies, sometimes defined by their lack of studios or own foreign distribution company. In recent years, this list has been very volatile, with a number of such smaller companies as Savoy going out of business and Miramax and New Line claiming to maintain their independence while being bought up by larger companies, the first by Disney and the second by Turner (which itself then became part of Time Warner). *See* **majors** *and* **micro-major.**

■ **minimal cinema** (1) A type of avant-garde cinema that reduces to a bare minimum both subject matter and film technique. An example of this is George Landow's *Film in which there appear sprocket holes, edge lettering, dirt particles, etc.* (1966), which for four minutes presents on both the top and bottom halves of the screen identical patterns of a frame of a girl's face with a color band beside it, sprocket holes with edge letters, and half a frame of the same girl. The only "action" in the film is

the result of the girl's blinking eye in the half frame and the accumulation of dust in the sprocket holes. Since the girl's face was taken from a test strip and the laboratory was instructed not to clean Landow's film, we have an example of "found" as well as minimal art. Such works are not about filming, but are rather about the very material substance of film and screen. (2) The term is sometimes applied to certain fictional films which, in their extreme realism, minimize the use of film equipment and technique so as not to remind us that we are seeing a film. The French director Robert Bresson's *Diary of a Country Priest* (1951) is a prime example of such a film.

■ **mini-multiple** A medium distribution of a film, something less than a wide release. This release may be to test the waters or to wet the public's taste for a wide release. *See* **distribution.**

■ **minimums, minimum scale, scale** The basic amount of money to be earned by a performer or any member of a film production for a single day or week as established by the various unions, guilds, and production companies.

■ **minor character** A subsidiary character in a film who performs only a small part in the action.

■ **minus lens** A supplementary lens that extends the camera's normal lens to telephoto range. Minus lenses are normally held away from the camera by such devices as bellows or extension tubes. *See* **lens.**

■ **Miramax Films** An independent film distribution company begun in New York City in 1981 by the brothers Bob and Harvey Weinstein that also moved into production in 1989. Miramax over the years has developed a reputation for releasing independent domestic and foreign films of great quality while still achieving financial success. Miramax distributed the American films *sex, lies, and videotape* (1989; dir. Steven Soderbergh) and *Reservoir Dogs* (1993; dir. Quentin Tarantino), while making available from abroad *Like Water for Chocolate* (1992; dir. Alfonso Arau), *The Crying Game* (1992; Neil Jordan), and *The Piano* (1993; dir. Jane Campion). In 1994, the company made it big by distributing Quentin Tarantino's *Pulp Fiction.* Miramax was purchased by the Walt Disney Company in 1993 with the understanding that it would continue to act independently so long as it did not distribute unrated films. In order to meet the last commitment, the Weinsteins formed another distribution company, Shining Excalibar Films, to release Larry Clark's *Kids* in 1995.

■ **mired, mired value** The term, taken from the first letters of the words "micro reciprocal degrees," signifies a unit for measuring color temperature that is computed by dividing the Kelvin measurement into one million. Since a numerical difference in Kelvin degrees for color temperatures at the lower end of the scale is far more important than the same numerical difference for temperatures at the higher part of the scale, mireds, which convey a more accurate mathematical representation of such differences at both extremes, are used to achieve color balance and maintain color consistency for lamps and filters. *See* **Kelvin scale.**

■ **mired shift value** A measurement for indicating the effect of a filter on the color temperature of light by giving the change in Kelvin degrees in mireds. *See* **mired.**

■ **mirror shot** Any shot that uses a mirror to achieve a special effect, add an element to part of the image, or give a reflection of some performer. Although most of the shots cited below are now achieved in film laboratories or digitally, some are still realized through the methods described, especially in low-budget films. (1) A semitransparent mirror placed at a 45-degree angle in front of the camera lens will superimpose any object, action, or setting at the side of the camera over the main scene. Such a fifty-fifty mirror can therefore help create an illusion of ghosts, dreams, or hallucinations and also enlarge and superimpose flame, lightning, or an explosion onto the main image. (2) A nontransparent silvered mirror placed in part of the camera's field of view can add to the scene by reflecting a photograph, miniature set, or art work actually outside the field of view. Such a reflection can also increase the sense of space in a small set or outside a window in the set. Popular in Great Britain and Germany during the 1920s and 1930s was the Schüfftan process, which permitted the creation of a composite image by the use of a large mirror at a 45-degree angle in front of the camera lens. If all of the glass was clear except for one area in the center, the camera could record, through the glass, a model, drawing, or photograph of a setting and place within it a character who was actually to the side of the camera by photographing his reflection off the reflective center of the mirror. (3) A mirror placed beneath the lens will reverse and duplicate the subject at the bottom of the image as if he or she were reflected in water (by placing the mirror at the bottom of a pan with water, the illusion will be increased). (4) A mirror moved across the field of view in front of the lens can be used as a transitional device from one scene to another by creating the effect of a wipe with the reflected image removing the scene in front of the camera. Both scenes must, of course, be on adjacent stages. (5) Any mirror that is part of a set and employed in the action to create a reflection of a character is also called a mirror shot. In such shots the mirror, subject, and camera must be properly aligned to prevent the camera from appearing in the reflection.

■ **mirror shutter, mirror reflex shutter** A camera shutter, placed at a 45-degree angle to the lens, which has blades surfaced with silver so that when the shutter is closed it acts as a mirror, reflecting the light rays enter-

ing the lens into the viewfinder system of the camera. Hence, the cameraman can see exactly what the lens sees, and there is no distortion from parallax. *See* **reflex viewfinder.**

■ **miscast** The term describes a person who has been chosen for a role but does not possess the correct personal qualities or the talent to play the role.

■ *mise-en-cadre, mise-en-shot* The compositional arrangement of a shot, which includes the relationship of both static and moving visual elements. The terms, which are from French film criticism, signify the director "putting into a shot" all these components and are more accurately related to the film's temporal dimension than *mise-en-scène*, which derives from the theater and emphasizes the spatial dimension of a scene. Nevertheless, *mise-en-scène* is now generally used in film criticism to include both spatial and temporal compositional elements. *See* **mise-en-scène.**

■ *mise-en-scène* A French term meaning "putting into the scene" that was originally used to describe the staging of a theater director, the way he or she arranged all the visual components on the stage. The term has become fashionable in film criticism and has taken on new meanings and connotations from its filmic context. *Mise-en-scène*, in discussions of film, refers to the composition of the individual frame—the relation of objects, people, and masses; the interplay of light and dark; the pattern of color; the camera's position and angle of view—as well as the movement within the frame. Since the image we see in film, unlike our view of a live performance on stage, is two-dimensional and has no actual depth, and since it is generally larger than what we see on the stage and has its own relational sizes and perspectives, a consideration of *mise-en-scène* in film is different from that in theater. Important concerns are whether the image has deep or shallow focus and how much any distortion from the refraction of the lens may influence our perception of movement in the image. In general, directors who emphasize *mise-en-scène* are considered to rely less on montage or editing, and their style is related to the "deep-focus" technique of filming that André Bazin contrasts with montage. It is difficult, however, to claim that *mise-en-scène* directors are more realistic than those who emphasize editing, as some critics have done, since a great deal of composing in the individual frame can create a highly distinct and sometimes even artificial image. Most directors seek a balance between the individual *mise-en-scène* and its context in a sequence.

■ **mismatch** A disorienting and seemingly illogical combination of shots where characters suddenly seem to change direction or speed, where subjects unexpectedly change position, or where any compositional aspect of the image seems unexpectedly altered. Such mismatching may occur from a careless positioning of the camera from shot to shot or simply from interrupting the shooting of a scene with a long delay and not resuming the action with care. It is the editor's job to make sure that such mistakes are not included in the final version of the film and that new mismatches are not created from the editing itself.

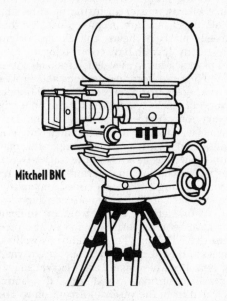

Mitchell BNC

■ **Mitchell** The brand name of cameras once made by the Mitchell Company and used as standard equipment in professional filming for over fifty years. The traditional NC (for "noiseless camera") and BNC models are still employed for film production. Both are extremely heavy, requiring two grips to move each on a dolly and both have great precision of registration in the intermittent movement. The BNC differs from the NC in several respects: it is totally soundproofed so that it can be used for indoor shooting when sound is recorded and it has a single lens mounting instead of the turret on the NC that holds four lenses. Mitchell later exchanged the rack-over viewing system for a reflex type, although the new models, designated NCR and BNCR, remained much the same. Also important is the Mitchell S35R "Mark II," a lightweight camera with a reflex viewfinder that is excellent for filming on location and can be blimped for studio work. Mitchell also made a 65mm camera, the BFC, which is much like the BNC, and a lightweight, handheld reflex camera for 65mm film, the Todd-AO AP-65. In 1990, rights to the Mitchell camera were purchased from Panavision by Flight Research, Inc., in Richmond, Virginia, basically a security camera manufacturer, which now produces only magazines for the Mitchell cameras. The camera itself is no longer produced, though many are still in use and much of its mechanism for movement appears in the Panavision cameras. A number of old Mitchells are being upgraded for use as special-effects cameras, often for shooting miniatures either

frame by frame or as part of a motion-control system. *See* **camera** *and* **special effects.**

■ **mix, mixing** (1) The process of combining all the individual sound tracks for dialogue, music, and sound effects into the single composite master sound track. This process is accomplished in a theater or studio where the images of the motion picture are projected onto a screen with a footage counter beneath. The tracks on separate magnetic films are run through playback machines (called dubbers), each of which feeds into a mixing console, and the sound from each track is adjusted for quality and volume. Special effects might be created—for example, an echo might be added for a voice or noise supposedly coming from a closed chamber. Certain sounds such as environmental noises might be played on a loop film which runs continuously. The playback machines and the mix are synchronically interlocked with the film projector, and all can be run back and forth to repeat a sequence as many times as necessary. The sound mixer knows exactly when to insert a particular sound track from the mix cue sheet which has been supplied by the editor. This sheet gives the exact foot of film when the sound should be added or stopped—film footage runs consecutively beneath the screen and on the console. Often a number of sound tacks are premixed into several tracks for the separate categories of dialogue, music, and sound effects, and these tracks are premixed into the D (dialogue), E (sound effects), and M (music) tracks. As many as fifteen, and sometimes even more, separate sound tracks may be put into the final D, M, and E tracks, which themselves will be combined into the final mix. Tracks are premixed to allow better control and balancing of the various components and also because there are not enough playback heads on the console for all the original tracks. The final track must be converted into an optical negative, which can then produce the optical print for final testing. For stereophonic sound on 35mm film, four sound tracks are printed on two optical channels that are placed on the composite print—three for the stereophonic effect from the left, center, and right of the screen, and one for surround sound. Six separate magnetic tracks are used for stereophonic and surround sound on a 70mm film.

Digital mixing is the latest advance in sound editing and will undoubtedly grow in popularity as such systems become less expensive and their capacity increases. Sound may be recorded during production either on analog or digital tape and then transferred to hard drive. Such digitized sound allows easy accessibility and tremendous flexibility in altering, improving, and combining both sounds and tracks. Sound effects and music can be borrowed from stored libraries and even created from scratch. Adjusting, improving, and combining the various dialogue, sound-effects, and music tracks are performed with great exactness, and the sound is placed with great precision in relation to the image. Much of the layering for the individual tracks can be accomplished with compact audio workstations that make the various processes quick and easy to perform, though the results are passed to the larger mixing studio with its greater amount of equipment and memory and its greater capacity for sound control and manipulation in making the final mix. ADR and Foley sound can also be piped in from their studios. Such studios are equipped to mix stereophonic sound tracks along with surround sound. The mix for the digital tracks is recorded on tape or disc and later optically recorded on the composite print along with the analog optical tracks. The entire mixing process, which began in this country in 1932, was instrumental in freeing films from the limitations of on-set and on-location recordings, while also allowing better and more complex audio than that achieved from postdubbing in the early days of sound. *See* **digital sound recording, mixer, sound,** *and* **stereophonic sound.**

(2) The final composite sound track or stereophonic tracks that result from mixing together all the sound tracks. (3) A visual transition from one scene to another in which the first scene gradually fades out as the second gradually fades in; a dissolve. *See* **dissolve.**

■ **mix down**   To combine the various sound tracks into the final sound track or mix. *See* **mix.**

■ **mixed mag, mix mag**   The final mixed sound track on either 35mm or 16mm mag stock that can be used for interlock projection with the image or transferred to video. The mixed mag has higher sound quality than the optical track on the film.

■ **mixed media**   A presentation that uses more than a single medium—e.g., film, video, slide, recorded music, and perhaps even live performers. Such presentations are frequent for business meetings or demonstrations to the public. *See* **multimedia.**

■ **mixer, sound mixer**   (1) The person in charge of mixing the various sound tracks when making the master sound track. Also called the sound editor, rerecording mixer, or dubbing mixer. *See* **mix.** (2) The person in charge of sound recording during production. His or her responsibilities include on-set or on-location coordination and mixing of sound from several microphones through a mixing panel or portable mixer. Also called the production mixer, production sound mixer, and floor mixer. (3) The person responsible for recording music for a film. Also called the music mixer.

■ **mixer, mixing console, audio board, dubbing panel, portable mixer, portable mixing console**   A mixing console is a large mixer employed for creating the final master magnetic or digitized sound track from the various individual sound tracks of dialogue, narration, music, sound effects, and environmental noises. Playback machines (called dubbers) feed the sound from the track on

each magnetic film into the console, which sometimes can handle fifteen or more signals. The channel for each track can be individually controlled to improve the quality or alter the volume of its sound, and most consoles can create echoes or similar effects for any particular sound. The original tracks can be combined into several premixed tracks (e.g., those for dialogue, sound effects, music) for further quality enhancement. Sometimes tracks are premixed because there are not enough playback heads for all the original tracks. These consoles also have controls for the film projector and playback units, as well as a footage counter for the film. They can advance, rewind, and replay sound or picture, erasing and rerecording until the desired integration of tracks is achieved for the final mix. Modern mixers now often work with digital sound: such sound permits remarkable flexibility and a wide range of possibilities in improving, altering, and manipulating sound as well as in layering the tracks. Digital sound is also not susceptible to deterioration from rerecording to rerecording since it is coded in binary numbers. Such modern consoles are connected to various digital audio workstations, where work on individual tracks may have been performed, and can also receive sound from the ADR and Foley studios as well as sound libraries and synthesizers in the process of making the final mix. Portable mixers are used during shooting to control, coordinate, and mix the sounds being recorded from the various microphones. The Sonosax SX-S portable mixing console, for example, which won for its manufacturer in Switzerland, Sonax S.A., a Scientific and Technical Achievement Award from the Academy of Motion Picture Arts and Sciences in 1995, now allows digital recording and can incorporate a film module that makes possible special feed to a video assist, remote control of Nagra audio recorders, direct communication with the boom operator, and additional outputs. *See* **mix.**

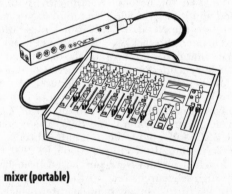

mixer (portable)

■ **mixing cue sheet, mix cue sheet, mixing sheet, mixing log**   A working chart with columns for the various sound tracks, each of which contains instructions for the integration of that sound into the final master track. This chart is drawn up by the editor or a member of his staff and designates the exact foot of film for the inclusion of each particular sound, while also giving instructions for fades, volume, and sound quality. *See* **mix.**

■ **mixing panel, fixing board, mixer, portable mixer** A small mixer used during the original recording of sound in film production to mix the sound coming from the individual microphones. The signals picked up from the microphones are fed into the panel, which has controls for volume and equalization. *See* **mixer.**

mixing studio (digital)

■ **mixing studio, mixing stage** The area for the mixing of the sound tracks. Modern mixing studios are comfortable and soundproofed areas that contain a good deal of technologically developed equipment while also being connected to other sound facilities in the building. The studio contains a series of individual machines, sometimes called dubbers, to play the individual tracks as well as a projection facility and screen for the workprint or a projection video—both tracks and picture are interlocked for synchronization so that they can be moved back and forth simultaneously. The center of the studio is the mixing console or audio board that controls the movement of the various machines while enhancing, modulating, and equalizing the sounds on the various tracks to make the final mix, which is sent to a multitrack audio recorder. The most advanced mixing studios are now completely digital. The digital console supports a vast number of inputs, is networked to a series of digital audio workstations that themselves have already worked on the various tracks, and can receive additional sound from ADR and Foley studios as well as sound libraries and synthesizers. The digitizing of the various sound elements permits remarkable speed and ease in accessing, working on, layering, and synching the sound as it is assembled into the final mix. The control surface itself is linked by means of a high-speed digital interface to the mainframe, which is normally placed in the machine room. Such digitizing allows each and every sound element to be represented graphically in an "interactive mixer's tracksheet," displayed on the monitors in front of the mixers, permitting the movement or replacement of sound to be accomplished by highlighting the elements on the monitor.

■ **MLS** *See* **medium long shot.**

■ **model** *See* **miniature.**

■ **model builder, model maker** The personnel who create the models and miniatures for special-effects shots. Models are also created for scanning into a computer for computer animation. *See* **computer animation** *and* **miniature.**

■ **modeling** (1) The detailed three-dimensional appearance of a subject that is achieved from the interplay of light and shadow. Such an effect is extremely important in giving texture and composition to an image, as well as personality and individuality to the face of a performer. *See* **relief.** (2) The process by which the models in computer animation are first created. In one method, various points are joined together by lines, forming polygons, which themselves are joined together to create the various geometric shapes called primitives. The geometric shapes are manipulated and assembled to create the model. Spline modeling, on the other hand, is composed of a series of curved lines and is more effective for rounded or curved shapes. Image mapping adds the surface to such forms. *See* **computer animation** *and* **image mapping.**

■ **modeling light** Any light specifically employed for achieving an effect of modeling on the face of a performer or any part of the set. A spotlight to the side and slightly to the front of a figure gives enough light and shadow for this detailed and three-dimensional effect on the face.

■ **model mover** The apparatus that moves a model during motion-control shots. *See* **motion control.**

■ **model sheet** A reference sheet for an animated character with the character drawn in various positions, with various expressions, and from various angles. The model sheet allows the artist to maintain consistency in all the drawings of the character to be used in the cartoon. *See* **animation.**

■ **model shot** *See* **miniature shot.**

■ **modified gross participation** *See* **adjusted gross participation.**

■ **modified wide release** *See* **mini-multiple.**

■ **modulation** (1) The regulation or adjustment of an audio signal. (2) The lowering of intensity for a voice or any audio signal. (3) The variations and changes in the light signal that are responsible for the variable area or variable density of the optical sound track—such modulation is caused by the effect of the electrical audio signal on the modulator. *See* **optical sound.** (4) The variation in the amplitude or frequency of a carrier wave caused by a single wave in the transmission of radio sound (AM is amplitude modulation and FM is frequency modulation).

■ **modulation noise**   Noise in the playback of a magnetic sound tape caused by some distortion in the tape material or by friction between the tape and playback head.

■ **modulation transfer function (MTF)**   The resolution ability of a film or lens, under the specific conditions of shooting, measured by photographing a sine-wave pattern and plotting the density of each section of the pattern's image against distance. Also called sine-wave response. MTF actually measures the contrast of a lens against its resolving power, thus designating both the sharpness and quality of the image. This comparison forms the MTF curve—normally the MTF curve for tangential lines and the curve for radial lines appear on the MTF chart.

■ **modulator**   The light valve in an optical sound system that, in response to the electrical audio signal, modulates the light so that it forms a variable-area or variable-density sound track. *See* **optical sound.**

■ **module**   (1) A component in any system that carries on a specific function and that is interchangeable. (2) An individual housing that receives a lamp. (3) An individual luminaire with its own switch that is used with other lamps of the same type as a single fixture. The lamps are worked either independently or together.

■ **modulometer**   A peak-reading meter on a Nagra sound recorder. *See* **peak-reading meter.**

■ **mogul**   The word derives from the Mongolian conquerors of India and is used to describe a powerful and autocratic person. In the film industry, the term was applied to the great studio heads such as Louis B. Mayer of MGM and Darryl F. Zanuck of Twentieth Century-Fox.

■ **Mole-Richardson Company**   Founded in 1927 by Peter Mole and located in Hollywood, this company manufactures lighting and power equipment for the visual media industry.

■ **monitor**   (1) Any device or piece of equipment used to check the quality of the picture during shooting or the quality of sound while recording. In photography, the monitor might be a small television set connected to the camera; in sound recording, it might be a loudspeaker. (2) A video screen that displays an image from a video camera or videotape player. (3) The display screen in a computer system. (4) To check the quality of picture or sound during the recording process.

■ **monitor speaker, monitor loudspeaker, sound monitor**   A loudspeaker built into a sound recording system and used during recording, dubbing, and mixing to check the quality of sound. When recording original sound, headphones attached to the speaker can be employed, though the sound can also be played aloud in a separate booth. In original recording, dubbing, and mixing, the sound is played back over the monitor speaker.

■ **monitor viewfinder, monitoring viewfinder**   A type of viewfinder with its own optical system that allows the image to be readily seen without an eyepiece and hence allows easy monitoring of the image when the camera is moving. Such a viewfinder may be mounted on the camera with the image visible on a small video screen or it might be electrically connected to the camera from a distance with the picture visible on a larger video screen. In both cases, the picture is adjusted for parallax. In some sophisticated systems for multiple cameras, the view from each of the cameras can be monitored on a console. *See* **video assist** *and* **viewfinder.**

■ **monochromatic**   (1) An image in the various tones or shades of a single color. (2) A black-and-white film image.

■ **monochromatic vision filter**   A filter that eliminates all colors and shows the eye how a scene appears in terms of light and dark.

■ **monocular finder, monocular sports finder**   *See* **sports finder.**

■ **Monogram Picture Corporation**   A commercial film production company, organized in 1930, which produced a series of low-budget films, including adventure stories with the Bowery Boys, Charlie Chan mysteries, Westerns, and some forgettable horror films. In 1946, Allied Artists was formed as a subsidiary of Monogram to produce a higher quality of film; in 1958, both companies became Allied Artists Pictures Corporation. *See* **Allied Artists Pictures Corporation.**

■ **monopack**   (1) Any film that can be used by itself in color cinematography (as opposed, for example, to the old three-strip Technicolor process). (2) Integral tripack color film where the three emulsions sensitive to the primary colors are on a single base. *See* **color film** *(2) and* **integrated tripack color system.**

■ **monopod**   A single-legged support for a camera. *See* **tripod.**

■ **monopole**   An overhead light mounting of a single pole that is suspended from a grid and can be slid from place to place and raised or lowered.

■ **monster movie** A horror film that features a monster as the agent of violence and terror. The monster may resemble a human, as in James Whale's *Frankenstein* (1931), an animal, as in Inoshiro Honda's *Godzilla* (1955), or be some unearthly creature from space, as in Ridley Scott's *Alien* (1979). Although the monster is a creature of terror because it is nonhuman, it is also, paradoxically, an embodiment of what we fear as humans (for example, the dead, violence, or alien life). *See* **horror film.**

■ **montage** The term is taken from the French *monter,* "to assemble," and has the following meanings in film. (1) In Europe, the process of editing a film, of assembling all the shots, scenes, and sequences into the final motion picture. The term, however, because of its special usage by the Russian filmmakers as described below, has connotations that suggest something more than the mechanical process of editing, that make the process itself appear to be a creative act of assembling the pieces of film, of constructing the work of art from its building blocks with consideration of a film's immediate and total effect. Sometimes, however, a simple distinction is made between both styles of editing by calling the apparently simpler kind "narrative montage" and the more artful kind "expressive montage" (see Marcel Martin, *Le Langage cinématographique*).

(2) The process of editing as it was developed specifically by the Russian filmmakers Pudovkin and Eisenstein, though even here we have two apparently distinct styles of montage. The foundation of Pudovkin's and Eisenstein's editing styles can be traced to the Kuleshov Workshop at the State Film School in Moscow. The members of the group developed the art of editing and the belief that it was the very foundation of the cinema. The montage style that Pudovkin developed (best shown in his masterpiece *Mother* [1926]) emphasized the continuity of the film where the various shots inevitably linked together like the links of a chain—for this reason his theory of montage has been called linkage. Pudovkin believed that the emotions and thoughts of the viewer could be guided through a basically nonobtrusive style of editing that did not upset the narrative line of the film while it developed certain ideas or themes, though he himself occasionally used some of the more dramatic editing that we normally associate with Eisenstein. Eisenstein's theory of montage, on the other hand, has been referred to as one of "collision" (he himself uses the terms "linkage" and "collision" in his writing), where the emphasis is on a dynamic juxtaposition of individual shots that calls attention to itself and forces the viewer consciously to come to conclusions about the interplay of images while he or she is also emotionally and psychologically affected in a less conscious way. Instead of continuity, Eisenstein emphasized conflict and contrast, arguing for a kind of Hegelian dialectic, where each shot was a cell and where a thesis could be juxtaposed to an antithesis, both achieving a synthesis or significance

which was not inherent in either shot. Eisenstein argued for the following specific kinds of montage, which could also appear together in the same sequence of shots: metric, rhythmic, tonal, overtonal, and intellectual (see "Methods of Montage" in his *Film Form*). If Eisenstein's theory of montage, and sometimes his practice, seems more intellectual and constructed than Pudovkin's, one need only compare his famous Odessa Steps sequence in *The Battleship Potemkin* (1925) with the final sequence in *Mother,* where mother and son are killed amidst the workers' demonstration, to see how much their techniques could overlap and achieve similar dynamic and emotional effects.

(3) Any editing style that seems distinct from the invisible style of cutting developed in the Hollywood studios by being more consciously constructed to achieve particular effects and to control the responses of the audience. In this sense, montage is a more artistic kind of editing where the emphasis is less on the simple progression of narration and more on the impact of the sequence of images upon the viewer. Hitchcock often referred to the editing of his films as montage, citing the particular way the pieces of film were assembled as the very foundation of his art. Certainly one could argue that a decided shift in editing took place in this country during the 1960s and 1970s as a result both of European films (for example, those of Jean-Luc Godard) and, strangely enough, television commercials. Cutting in a number of films became less invisible and more dynamic; the audience's responses and emotions were far more manipulated. This style of cutting could be seen in such action-packed films as William Friedkin's *The French Connection* (1971), but also in such offbeat romances as Richard Lester's *Petulia* (1968). This kind of montage editing has had a general effect on commercial films made since that time—one need only compare the major films from Hollywood during the 1930s with those from the present time to see that cutting is often not as invisible as it once was.

(4) The process of placing film images in a sequence so that new dimensions of space and time are created (Pudovkin, in *Film Technique*, referred to these dimensions as "filmic space" and "filmic time"). Two shots filmed in different places can be placed together so that both appear to belong to the same location (i.e., to a single space that exists nowhere but on the film). A single event can be photographed and then edited in such a way that its duration can either be shortened or lengthened, hence existing in a temporality that exists nowhere but in the film.

(5) A technique of editing developed in this country, especially during the 1930s and 1940s, that condenses time and space, conveys a great deal of information to the viewer in a short period, and may also suggest a hallucinatory state of mind, a dream, or a character's remembrance of past events. A series of jump cuts, dissolves, and superimpositions are employed in a short period of time. Pages on a calendar might flip over with short cuts of specific actions superimposed

and perhaps dissolving one into the other. In Victor Fleming's *Dr. Jekyll and Mr. Hyde* (1941), Spencer Tracy's hallucination under the power of his new drug is created by a series of dissolves and superimpositions of erotic and sadistic images involving the two women in the film. This technique is also called American montage. *See* **accelerated montage, filmic space, filmic time, Kuleshov Workshop,** *and* **relational editing.**

■ **mood lighting** Illumination employed to create a mood or atmosphere in the scene—e.g., low-keyed lighting for a mystery.

■ **mood music** Background music that creates a dramatic atmosphere appropriate to the action on the screen. Such music helps evoke in the viewer the correct emotional state for reacting to the action on the screen or appreciating the problems of the character. *See* **music.**

■ **Moog synethesizer** An electrical instrument for creating background music or musical effects. Sounds are created by turning knobs that connect modules to electric wires. *See* **synthesizer.**

■ **morphing, morfing** The term comes from metamorphosis and is used to describe a process by which one subject is visually transformed into another, gradually changing shape, color, and details until the new figure emerges from the old. Originally developed by Industrial Light and Magic and first used in *Willow* (1988; dir. Ron Howard), the technique achieved considerable attention when it was used to transform the shape of the cyborg to and from all kinds of people and objects in *Terminator 2: Judgment Day* (1991; dir. James Cameron). *See* **computer** *and* **computer animation.**

morphing

■ **mortgaging** The practice of ordering the entire amount of film needed for a single production at the beginning of photography so that all the film shot will be cut from the same emulsion, hence assuring consistency of image from scene to scene. The film manufacturer reserves all the film, placing it in a single location and delivering the required amount as ordered. Theoretically, the practice should disappear, since film is being made with extreme consistency in emulsion from roll to roll because of greater precision in sensitometry.

■ **MOS** Initials printed on a clapboard and appearing at the start of a take to indicate that the scene was shot without sound. In the early days of sound films, technical personnel were often foreign-born and these initials stand for "mit out sound," the way such an instruction might have been spoken by a German director or member of the camera crew. *See* **clapboard.**

■ **motif** A subject, idea, object, phrase, musical passage, compositional effect, film technique, or color that reappears throughout a work to form a definite pattern that imposes itself upon the viewer's awareness. Whatever keeps reappearing in this manner takes on symbolic significance because of the special attention it receives; its reappearance becomes a shorthand method of evoking within the viewer certain ideas and emotions. For example, in D. W. Griffith's *Intolerance* (1916), the image of the woman rocking the cradle is repeated throughout to form a motif that suggests the renewal or resurrection of the human spirit; in Orson Welles's *Citizen Kane* (1941), the repeated word "rosebud" forms a motif to suggest something lost in the life of the protagonist; in Federico Fellini's *La Strada* (1954), the musical passage played by the clown is heard again and again to suggest the lost innocence and happiness of the girl; in Nicolas Roeg's *Don't Look Now* (1973), the repetition of the color red suggests the impending violence and doom awaiting the hero. The concept of motif is often related to Wagner's leitmotifs, the recurring, symbolic musical passages in his great operas, and is a technique often used in novels (Thomas Mann relates his own use of the technique in his fiction to Wagner's leitmotifs). In all art forms, the motif imposes a unity and coherence upon the work as well as a symbolic significance to the repeated element. *See* **theme.**

■ **motion** *See* **movement.**

■ **motion blur** The blur caused by the motion of an object recorded on film or video. This effect is achieved when shutter and film speed are too slow. The go-motion system for film animation sometimes creates this effect when shooting the models in movement to create a natural appearance as opposed to the syncopated movement of figures in traditional stop-frame animation when the models are moved slightly between shots but photographed still. *See* **animation** *and* **go-motion.**

■ **motion capture** Feeding the data of a moving object or person into a computer. This procedure is accomplished by means of sensors on the subject. The data are later used to give motion to another object or form originating as a digital image. *See* **scanner.**

■ **motion control** An electronically programmed camera system capable of repeating the exact same movements and shots either with continuous or stop-motion photography for special-effects work. Motion-control systems are especially effective in shooting miniatures for traveling matte processes and composite pictures, since numerous passes of any duration can be made with precisely defined or exactly repeatable movements. Sometimes the models themselves are electronically programmed so that they can also make the exact same movements. These systems are capable of having numerous channels for controlling a number of possible moves of the camera and models as well as for changing lights. Two notable systems in the 1970s that had considerable influence on the future of special effects were the Dykstraflex developed at Industrial Light and Magic under the supervision of John Dykstra for George Lucas's *Star Wars* (1977) and the "Icebox" system created at Future General Corporation under the supervision of Douglas Trumbull for Steven Spielberg's *Close Encounters of the Third Kind* (1977). Also significant was the ACES system (for Automatic Camera Effects System), built by Disney Productions for *The Black Hole* (1979; dir. Gary Nelson). In spite of the remarkable advancements in this technology, it is likely that motion control systems will be seriously challenged by digital compositing. *See* **digital effects** *and* **go-motion.**

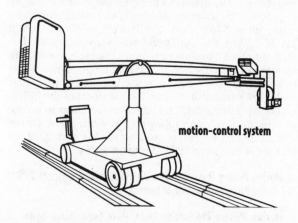

motion-control system

■ **motion picture** (1) A sequence of images, photographed one at a time in rapid succession by a motion-picture camera, that when projected onto a screen in the same sequence by a projector, creates the illusion of movement. For natural movement to appear the pictures must be photographed and projected at a rate of at least sixteen frames per second (24 frames per second have actually been used since silent-film days to allow a clear sound). The illusion of movement without any gaps between the images is created by the viewer's "persistence of vision," a phenomenon by which the eye retains an image for a brief instant after that image is gone and until the next image comes into sight. Another theory for the effect of motion from a series of separate images, called the "phi-phenomenon," explains that the brain imposes a movement upon an object when it appears in different places in consecutive images. (2) A story presented in the form of moving pictures projected on a screen. (3) The plural term, motion pictures, is also used to describe the industry at large which makes commercial films. The terms "movie" and "moving picture" are also sometimes used in the same contexts as (1), (2), and (3).

■ **Motion Picture Association of America (MPAA)** At first organized by the film producers and distributors as the Motion Picture Producers and Distributors of America (MPPDA) in 1922 and given its present name in 1945, this organization was originally created in response to public indignation over apparent sex scandals and immoral behavior among the members of the film industry. The public reacted strongly against such events as the death of a young actress at a party thrown by Fatty Arbuckle. The once-admired comedian was tried for her death and judged innocent, but the scandal ruined his career. The industry worried about the effect of such scandals on the box office and foresaw the possibility of censorship from state and local governments. Movies were a family entertainment and it was necessary to keep them free from any taint of immorality if the industry was to continue in its present lucrative state. The MPPDA was formed by the major studios and distributors to clean up the industry. Will Hays, postmaster general under President Harding, a man of impeccable credentials and high moral reputation, was named its head. Throughout the remainder of the decade, the MPPDA, informally called the Hays Office, applied pressure to the industry to encourage moral rectitude—its argument was for self-censorship, but the organization became both a place of judgment and court of appeal. The organization also formed the Central Casting Bureau for scrutinizing the backgrounds and morals of bit players and extras. It worked diligently in public relations, creating a better image of the industry in the press and warding off censorship from government institutions.

Moral indignation again began to rise at the end of the decade while new problems arose from the use of dialogue in the new sound film. The result was the Motion Picture Production Code, formulated in 1930 and made binding in 1934. No motion picture was to be released without a seal of approval, and heavy fines were established for any producer, distributor, or exhibitor who might be involved with such a film. The MPPDA set up machinery to help guide the industry from the writing of the screenplay to the final editing of the film. Revised on two occasions, the code was finally discarded in 1968, and replaced by a rating system that advised viewers about the content of films.

The MPPDA performed other functions besides

censoring the content of films and working on the industry's image in the press. The Central Casting Bureau, as well as screening out undesirables, offered an efficient means of hiring. The organization set up a Titles Registration Bureau, which kept an index on all films and arbitrated title disputes. Its Foreign Department negotiated for foreign distribution and kept itself informed about censorship abroad, while its Theater Services Department sought to improve the relationship between production, distribution, and exhibition. The MPPDA, with its Labor Committee, also became the major trade agency for the production companies.

In 1945, the Hays Office became the Johnston Office when Eric Johnston took over as head of the organization, which changed its formal name to the Motion Picture Association of America (MPAA). Under Johnston's administration, the organization confronted such problems as the studios' loss of theaters brought about by the Supreme Court's Paramount decision in 1948, the decline of movie audiences in the 1950s because of the rise of television, the need for increased foreign distribution and more foreign production facilities, and the erosion of the Production Code. To facilitate work concerning foreign distribution, a sister agency, the Motion Picture Export Association (MPEA), was formed in 1945; it also came under the leadership of Johnston. In 1966, Jack Valenti, former aide to President Lyndon Johnson, became head of the MPAA and MPEA. Valenti was instrumental in getting the 1968 rating system approved and represented the studios in negotiations with exhibitors. He was also much concerned with increasing the distribution of American films in foreign countries. Today's eight major member companies are Buena Vista Pictures (for the Walt Disney Company), Sony Pictures Entertainment (Columbia and TriStar), Metro-Goldwyn-Mayer (MGM and United Artists), Paramount Pictures, Turner Pictures (New Line Cinema and Castle Rock Pictures), Twentieth Century-Fox, Universal, and Warner Brothers. The MPAA now claims as its major functions protecting the rights of copyright owners, acting as a spokesperson to the government for the major producers and distributors, fighting censorship, directing an antipiracy program at home and abroad, and providing guidance to parents through the rating system. The Alliance of Motion Picture and Television Producers, which is closely affiliated with the MPAA, today does the actual labor negotiations with the unions and guilds and concerns itself with work-related issues. *See* **Alliance of Motion Picture and Television Producers, Hays Office, Motion Picture Production Code,** *and* **Movie Rating System.**

■ **motion-picture camera** *See* **camera.**

■ **motion-picture film** *See* **film** *(1).*

■ **Motion Picture Patents Company (MPPC)** A monopoly trust formed in December 1908 by the nine leading film companies—Edison, Biograph, Vitagraph, Essanay,

Kalem, Selig, Lubin and the French organizations Pathé and Méliès' Star-Film—along with the distributing company of George Kleine, who had suggested the trust. This consortium was organized to stop the warfare over patents among the members and to impose a monopoly over film production, distribution, and exhibition in the United States. In 1910 the organization founded the General Film Company to control the distribution of motion pictures made by its members. Edison's patents on his machinery were to be acknowledged and he was to receive a royalty from each of the other members. All members were to be exclusively licensed to manufacture films with his equipment, and Eastman Kodak would sell film only to these licensed members. Exhibitors could show films from these companies only if they used the organization's licensed projectors, showed no films made by independents, and paid the organization a stipulated royalty for each film and for the use of its machinery. The MPPC sought to impose its monopoly over the film industry in the courts and also by use of force, sending hired thugs to destroy equipment and films in the independents' studios and in theaters which showed the independents' films.

William Fox, an independent distributor and producer of films, brought the MPPC to court in 1913, and a federal court in Pennsylvania ruled the trust illegal under the Sherman Antitrust Act in 1915. In 1918 the last appeal of this decision was dismissed in court, but long before this date the organization had ceased to be effective. By the time Fox had instituted his case, the members of the MPPC were being overtaken by the independent companies. Not only did the industry require more films than the Patents Company could produce, but the independents, whose film studios were now free from harassment in the Hollywood vicinity, were producing better and also longer films. While independent film companies combined into bigger and more successful studios, the members of the MPPC gradually faded away. The last of its members to go out of business was Vitagraph, which had absorbed a number of other members and was itself absorbed by Warner Brothers in 1925. *See* **independents.**

■ **Motion Picture Producers and Distributors of America (MPPDA)** *See* **Motion Picture Association of America.**

■ **Motion Picture Production Code, Hays Code, Breen Code** A censorship code drawn up for the Motion Picture Producers and Distributors of American (MPPDA) by two Roman Catholics, Father Daniel Lord, S.J., who was a professor of dramatics at St. Louis University, and Martin Quigley, publisher of the *Motion Picture Herald*, and adopted by the organization in 1930. The code was a response to public concern with the immorality of the film industry and to the problems presented by dialogue in the new sound films. At first, the industry was asked to comply voluntarily with the code, but in 1934 it became mandatory because of growing pressure from the public and especially from the newly formed Catholic Legion of Decency. Joseph Breen, a Catholic newspaperman, joined the MPPDA to direct the enforcement of the code. His department, the Production Code Administration, reviewed screenplays and final films, while acting in an advisory capacity during production and editing. No film could be exhibited in the theaters belonging to or affiliated with the various members of the MPPDA without the organization's seal of approval. A fine of $25,000 would be the cost of doing so. The code itself laid down strictures concerning the subjects of sex, marriage, religion, crime, suicide, murder, drug addiction, child kidnapping, abortion, and prostitution. In general, films were not to be explicitly sexual or violent, they were not to condone crime or any aberrant behavior, and irreverent references to religion and even common profanity were to be avoided.

It was not until 1952 that the Supreme Court, with its decision on the "Il Miracolo" section of Rossellini's *L'Amore* (1948), freed films from censorship on religious grounds, brought motion pictures under the protection of the First Amendment, and began the collapse of the code. With the separation of exhibitors from the producer-distributors due to the Supreme Court's Paramount decision of 1948, theaters were no longer forced to show films with the seal of approval. United Artists ignored the code when it released, without the seal of approval, Otto Preminger's *The Moon Is Blue* in 1953, a rather tame film which, on occasion, explicitly discussed sexual matters, and his *The Man With the Golden Arm* in 1956, which dealt with the subject of drug addiction. In order to keep up with the liberalization of films and in an effort to control this momentum, the code was revised in 1956 as well as in 1966, and in the second instance given a rating system. Finally, in 1968, the advisory rating system presently in use was originated and the code was completely discarded. Filmmakers could produce any kind of film they desired as long as the public was informed in advance about the content and explicitness of the work. Recently, Catholicism has returned to judging motion pictures, but, in accord with the times, it makes suggestions instead of proscribing. Catholic Communication Campaign, an agency of the United States Catholic Conference, now offers a toll-free phone number through which one can obtain ratings of films concerning both quality and moral values. *See* **censorship, Hays office, Motion Picture Association of America,** *and* **Movie Rating System.**

■ **Motion Picture Relief Fund (MPRF)** A philanthropic organization, supported by the film industry, that raises money for needy persons engaged or once engaged in motion-picture work.

■ **Motion Picture Theater Owners of American (MPTO)** An organization of over ten thousand independent theater owners formed in 1920 with Sidney S. Cohen, a New York theater owner, as president and James J. Walker, a politician, as adviser. The goal of the organization was to protect the independent exhibitors from unfair booking practices by the major film producers and distributors and to stop the continuous acquisition of independent theaters by such companies, especially Adolph Zukor's Paramount Pictures. *See* **Famous Players** *and* **Paramount Pictures Corporation.**

■ **motivation lighting, motivating lighting** Lighting that seems to come directly from some source in the scene—for example, from an electric light or candle. Such lighting is normally a result of the special luminaires used to illuminate the scene.

■ **motor** *See* **camera motor.**

■ **motor cue** The set of circles in the upper right-hand corner of the picture that appear in four frames almost at the end of the reel to warn the projectionist to start up the motor of the next projector so that it is running at normal speed for the smooth transition to the next reel. The actual switch to the next projector is marked by the changeover cue right before the end of the first reel. *See* **cue marks.**

■ **mount** *See* **camera mount, lens mount,** and **lighting mount.**

■ **mountain film** A popular type of film in Germany in the 1920s and early 1930s that featured the heroic exploits of a group of characters seeking to conquer some awesome mountains by climbing up or skiing down them. The heroism and values dramatized in these films have been seen as foreshadowing the rise of the Nazi movement with its fanaticism about the *Übermensch*. The scenery in such films was especially well photographed and a fitting location for the highly noble and extremely sentimentalized action of the characters. The key maker of this type of film was Dr. Arnold Franck. Perhaps the most notable of such works was *The White Hell of Pitz Palu* (1929), which Franck directed along with G. W. Pabst and that starred Leni Riefenstahl, who had already appeared in Franck's films and was about to go on and direct her own mountain films.

■ **mouse** The small device operated by the movement and pressure of the hand that controls certain operations of computer programs by making selections on the computer's screen. The movements of the mouse on a horizontal plane are electronically followed by a cursor on the screen and pressure on the device starts and controls the various activities. Such a device with more functions and buttons is used in digitizing processes, for example with a digitizing table, and called a puck.

■ **movement** Movement is a concern of motion pictures in the following categories. (1) The movement of film through the camera to allow a series of pictures to be individually photographed, and the movement of film through the projector to allow the projection onto the screen of each of the developed images, one after the other. In both cases the film proceeds from continuous to intermittent movement, allowing each frame to stop for an instant in front of the aperture, and then back again to continuous movement. To create the illusion of movement on the screen, the frames must move and stop before the aperture at a rate of at least 16 per second. This rate was considered the norm for silent films, although a faster rate was generally used. Sound films expose 24 frames per second for the accurate reproduction of sound. The illusion of movement on the screen, without any gaps between the images, is achieved by the viewer's persistence of vision, an optical effect by which the eye maintains an image for a brief instant after it is gone until the next image comes into sight. Another explanation for this illusion is the "phi-phenomenon," an effect achieved by the brain's imposition of movement upon an object when it appears in different locations in successive images. Slow motion may be achieved on the screen by photographing action at a speed faster than that at which the images will be projected; and fast or accelerated motion by shooting at a speed slower than that of projection.

(2) The motion of characters and objects within a scene to convey specific action but also to affect the viewer's responses. Static images with little action in them may be used to present dialogue or emphasize a character's psychological state, but, in general, the medium requires that movement be exploited to keep the viewer's interest. Sometimes background movement is depicted, while the characters are stationary, to create a more visually interesting picture, for example when characters are conversing in a street or in a moving vehicle with the background flashing by, but care must be taken not to upstage the central action. Close-ups are also effective in scenes with little overt action since facial reactions are consequently magnified and become the central action. In general, the direction of movement in the image will create a specific dramatic effect. It has often been noted that we view an image on the screen much as we read, from left to right, so that an action taking place from right to left will disorient us and sometimes even take us by surprise. Movement toward or away from the camera normally will seem slower than movement across the scene because of the image's lack of depth; but, on the other hand, a wide-angle lens will accelerate such motion, sometimes in an unnatural degree—a figure moving toward the audience will become suddenly threatening. Action close to us will always seem faster than that at a distance because of the magnification of the subject as well as the motion itself and the corresponding diminishment of the area of space in which the action takes place. Movement upward or downward also conveys certain emotional effects, in the former case a sense of freedom and escape and in the latter a sense of heaviness, force, entrapment, or depression.

(3) The movement of the camera during a shot to follow a character's or object's motion, to convey a character's subjective view as he or she moves, to place a character or object in a new perspective, or to lead the viewer's attention to a new subject or to some object or character that relates to the previous subject we have been watching. Movement of the camera is achieved in a number of ways. A panning or tilting shot can be achieved when the camera is attached to a stationary tripod by means of a movable mount. A tracking or traveling shot can follow a moving subject or move us to another part of the scene by transporting the camera along tracks, on a mobile dolly (also called a dolly shot), or on a vehicle (also called a trucking shot). A crane shot can give great mobility to the camera in both horizontal and vertical directions. Helicopters are also employed now to give much lengthier tracking shots of moving subjects or give a vast panorama of a terrain. The development of cameras light enough to be held by hand now allows the camera to move into areas once too confined for shooting and permits tracking shots extremely close to characters— the recent development of the Steadicam permits the camera to remain steady during the most arduous of handheld shots. A sense of movement can also be achieved by changing focus and moving the viewer's attention to another part of the scene. A zoom lens has the capacity to change focal lengths from that of a wide-angle to that of a long-focus lens and back again; it can therefore move a subject into the distance while increasing our view of the surrounding area or move a subject which is in the distance into close view while shrinking the environment. *See* **camera movement.**

(4) A sense of movement is also achieved by cutting from shot to shot or from scene to scene. Though no actual movement takes place on the screen, the audience feels that it has been transported from one place to another. When cutting follows the line of action and individual shots are carefully matched within each scene, as in the invisible style of cutting developed by the Hollywood studios, we are generally not aware that our attention has been moved from one place to another within the scene itself, though this change of perspective is certainly responsible for our continuing involvement in the action. Our perspective of a single scene can be suddenly changed to create a dramatic effect or to give us new information by means of a jump cut that makes us aware that we have been moved from one perspective of the scene to another. Cross- or parallel cuts, which alternate between two separate actions, or cutaways, which briefly take us away from the main scene, make us aware that we have changed locations, as do continuity cuts, which simply follow the narration from scene to scene. The type of cuts, on the other hand, employed by Eisenstein in his montage sequences, seeks to minimize the sense of movement from the location of one shot to another in order to achieve an intellectual and emotional synthesis through a simultaneous juxtaposition of the two sepa-

rate shots in the viewer's mind. *See* **cutting, editing,** *and* **montage.**

■ **moveover, move-over** Transferring a film from one theater to another in the same area, generally allowing for a consecutive run. Such a transfer must be agreed-to by the distributor, and sometimes the conditions for such a change are spelled out in the contractual agreement by a moveover clause.

■ **movie** A colloquial word used for either (1) a motion picture or (2) a motion-picture theater. The plural, movies, is a colloquial word used for either (1) the motion-picture industry at large or (2) a showing of one or more motion pictures.

■ **movie brats** A term used to indicate the youth, independence, but also the cinematic knowledge of a group of filmmakers who rocked the film industry during the 1970s. A number of them were actually trained in film schools or departments—e.g., Francis Ford Coppola at UCLA, George Lucas at UCLA, Martin Scorsese at NYU, and Steven Spielberg at California State—although Peter Bogdanovich, who is sometimes included in this group, was first in the dramatic theater and then wrote film criticism.

■ **movie for television** *See* **made-for-TV movie.**

■ **moviegoer** Someone who goes to motion pictures.

■ **movie house, movie theater, cinema** A theater primarily for the showing of motion pictures. The term "cinema" is more often used in Europe. At the turn of the century in the United States, films were first viewed in peephole machines in arcades by one person at a time. When equipment had been developed to project the images on a screen, film became a novelty shown amid live entertainment in vaudeville houses. Very soon after, they were shown at the rear of arcades in blocked off and darkened areas. In rural locations, films were viewed in tents at such events as state fairs or perhaps in town halls or similar structures. As the popularity of films grew, arcades and stores in a number of cities were changed into the first permanent movie houses—notable was Thomas L. Tally's Electric Theater in Los Angeles, a reconverted arcade that began showing short films in 1902 for an admission price of 10 cents. However, the most significant development was the spread of "nickelodeons" throughout the country—reconverted stores, arcades, or halls that were highly decorated and made comfortable for viewing motion pictures. A piano accompanied the images on the screen, while continuous performances of a series of short films ran anywhere from twenty minutes to an hour—all for the price of a nickel. The first such theater was created by John P. Harris and Harry Davis in 1905 in a reconverted store in Pittsburgh. It is estimated that by 1910 there were over 10,000 nickelodeons in the United States. The next phase was the construction from scratch of better equipped, larger, and more comfortable theaters for the showing of motion pictures.

The first movie "palace," the Strand in New York City, opened in 1914, and could seat an audience of nearly three thousand. By this time, audiences were sitting for far greater lengths of time to watch "feature" films. These larger, more comfortable theaters were built for a burgeoning public not only in the big cities but also in communities throughout the country. This development reached its peak in the years after World War I with the opening of the Roxy Theater in New York City in 1927, the "cathedral of motion pictures," which could seat 6,200 viewers. By now, every city had a number of large, first-run theaters, and movie houses of significant size could also be found in virtually every suburb and town. Although it is estimated that the number of theaters in the United States at one point reached nearly 30,000, the creation of larger movie houses and the closing of many nickelodeons and small theaters dropped that number to nearly 20,000 in the early 1920s; these theaters were, however, catering to a significantly larger moviegoing public. The advent of sound in 1927 did not appreciably change the design of new theaters, though acoustics were now a consideration: existing theaters were simply furnished with the necessary equipment and alterations were sometimes made with sound-absorbent material to muffle echoes.

World War II halted the construction of new theaters, and the rise of television in the 1950s suddenly began to diminish the size of the movie audience. The result was the wholesale closing of movie houses, most of which were at first used for various businesses and then finally demolished to make way for new structures. Even drive-in theaters, which at first expanded after the war to meet the needs of an automotive society, began to close in large numbers. By the mid-1960s, the number of movie theaters had dropped almost one-third to less than 13,000; but by the mid-1970s, the number has expanded somewhat, to nearly 15,000, and by the mid 1980s to approximately 20,000, because of the creation of smaller theaters. This development was considerably bolstered by the dividing of older movie houses into two or more smaller motion-picture theaters and the new multitheater complexes at suburban shopping centers. Such multitheaters were economical to run because they had a single box office and lobby as well as a single projection booth with automatic equipment. The individual theaters normally held no more than 300 or 400 people. Such theaters may have been more intimate, but often they were depressingly close and vulnerable to unwanted sound from the film playing in the adjacent theater. Ironically, the development of wide-screen movies corresponded with the shrinking size of the motion-picture house. In recent years, the number of screens has continued to grow, and in 1995 was 26,995 (of this number the drive-in screens had shrunk to only 848 from a high of 3,801 in 1976). The good news in exhibition, however, has been the growth of superior theater complexes—multiplexes or megaplexes—sometimes in malls and sometimes as independent structures, with far better viewing facilities. The Cineplex and Odeon chains have constructed theaters in such complexes with wide screens, digital stereophonic and surround-sound systems, and comfortable seats. *See* **drive-in theater** *and* **movie palace.**

movie palace   The grand stairway in the grand hall of the Paramount Theater.

■ ■ ■

■ **movie palace**   A large, palatial movie house. The term more specifically refers to the great motion-picture theaters built in this country beginning in 1914, with the opening of the Strand Theater in New York City, which could seat almost 3,000 patrons. The Rialto opened in 1916, the Rivoli in 1917, and the Capital, which could seat more than 5,000 patrons, in 1919. The climax of this development was reached with the Paramount opening in 1926, the Roxy in 1927, which could hold an audience of 6,200 and was called "the cathedral of motion pictures," and the Radio City Music Hall in 1932. The idea for such "palaces" in New York City originated with Samuel L. Rothafel, whose nickname "Roxy" was given to the greatest of movie palaces. Large movie houses that could hold as many as 2,000 people also opened in less-populated areas throughout the country. All of these theaters were ornately decorated, spacious, and extremely comfortable. The architecture and decor ran from the gaudy to the fantastically flamboyant. Notable were Grauman's Egyptian and Chinese theaters in Hollywood, built in 1922 and 1927 respectively. Also notable were indoor theaters with star-sprinkled skies to give the impression of being outdoors, such as the Loew's Paradise in New York City's borough of the Bronx. The Paradise also featured a spacious and ornate lobby with a large goldfish pond and a curved marble stairway leading to the balcony.

■ **Movie Rating System, Motion Picture Rating System, Motion Picture Code Rating**   A system of rating films according to their content and treatment of certain subjects to inform the public whether the films are suitable as family entertainment. This rating was instituted in 1968 and supplanted the old Motion Picture Code, which had been strictly enforced as a form of censorship since 1934. Commercial filmmakers may decide not to apply for such a rating, though the vast majority do. The system allows filmmakers considerable freedom as long as the public is appropriately advised and certain prohibitions are placed on minors. The ratings are G, which stands for general audience and signifies that the film is appropriate for all ages; PG, which designates that parental guidance is recommended since some material may not be suitable for children; PG13, which asks for parental guidance for children under thirteen, normally since the film has explicit violence; R, which means that the film is restricted because of its subject and treatment, and that children seventeen or under must be accompanied by a parent or adult guardian; and NC-17, which means no children seventeen or under should be admitted and which replaced the old X rating that had come to signify pornography and was being employed in an unauthorized manner to sell such films. NC-17 applies to any film that deals with adult themes or content. When its designation was approved in 1990, the MPAA also decided to include for exhibitors and critics an explanation why a film was R-rated (though no such explanation was given for NC-17). These ratings are applied to films, both domestic and foreign, by the Classification and Rating Administration (CARA) of the Motion Picture Association of America after a recommendation by its Ratings Board. A Policy Review Committee of the Movie Rating System is comprised of six members from the MPAA and six from the National Association of Theater Owners (NATO). Producers or distributors may appeal the rating to the Classification and Rating Appeals Board or reedit the film and have it rated once again. The Classification and Rating Administration gives to either the producer or distributor a certificate of code rating (the MPAA Certificate) that designates the specific symbol to be used for the film. At first, the majority of films sought the G or PG rating so that they might appeal to the largest possible audience, but in recent years, there have been relatively few G films, and the R rating has been most sought to meet the demands of audiences for more mature or simply more explicit films. The X rating is now sometimes applied by exhibitors themselves to films that are largely pornographic. *See* **Catholic Communication Campaign, censorship,** *and* **Motion Picture Production Code.**

■ **movie star**   *See* **star.**

■ **Movietone**   An optical sound system for film developed by Theodore W. Case and Earl I. Sponable while working for Western Electric, and purchased by William Fox for Fox Film Corporation. The system, by putting on the film an optical pattern that could be converted back to sound when read by light passing from an exciter lamp to a photoelectric cell in the projector, seemed much better for synchronization and easier to use than the disc system being developed by Warner Brothers. Fox's film company first produced some shorts with the new sound in 1927, but the company's real achievement was in producing the Movietone newsreels in the same year, perhaps the most famous of which is the picture and sound recording of Lindbergh's takeoff from Long Island for his historic plane flight across the Atlantic. The next year, Fox announced that all his feature films would have sound, and he began equipping and building studios and theaters for the Movietone system. The optical type of system used by Movietone and RCA's Photophone was to become the standard method of sound reproduction in the movie industry instead of the disc method developed for Warner Brothers' Vitaphone. *See* **optical sound** *and* **sound.**

■ **Movietone frame**   The standard frame on sound film which has an aspect ratio of 4:3 or 1.33:1. This was also the aspect ratio for silent films, but in the early days of sound the frame was squared to make way for the sound track. Since the image produced was not pleasing, the area of the frame was reduced so that the dimensions could return to the 4:3 ratio (for this reason the dimensions of the aperture on camera and projector to achieve this frame are referred to as the reduced aperture). The name Movietone comes from the motion-picture sound system developed by Fox Film Corporation, which necessitated these dimensions for the 4:3 aspect ratio on its sound film. This aspect ratio was standardized by the Academy of Motion Picture Arts and Sciences in 1932, and the aperture on camera and projector to achieve these dimensions is, therefore, also referred to as the Academy aperture. *See* **aspect ratio** *and* **Movietone.**

■ **moving camera, mobile camera**   A shot in which the camera discernibly moves by such means as tracks, a dolly, or a crane. *See* **camera movement** *and* **movement** *(3).*

■ **moving matte**   *See* **traveling-matte process.**

■ **moving pictures**   A term conveying the same meaning as "motion pictures," though less frequently used. *See* **motion picture** *(3).*

■ **moving shot**   Any shot that employs a moving camera, whether the camera is held by hand or moved by means of a dolly, vehicle, or crane. *See* **camera movement** *and* **movement** *(3).*

■ **Moviola**   A trade name for an upright portable editing machine, once much in use, that is also sometimes used generically for any editing machine. The specific machine made by Moviola was run by a motor and generally equipped to handle a single reel of motion-picture film and a single sound track, though additional sound heads could be added. Both picture and sound operated individually or locked together and ran synchronically. The film ran through the machine by means of an intermittent sprocket, while the picture was viewed on a small screen. Both film and sound could be run at normal or various speeds; they could be stopped for the examination of a single frame; and they could be run backward. Since the machine was extremely versatile and easy to operate, it had been much employed in editing and also was frequently used for film study in schools, in spite of the fact that its image and sound reproduction were not especially good and the machine could behave unkindly to film. One still sees these old machines in odd corners, and they remain a symbol of the traditional filmmaking machinery of old. *See* **flat-bed editing machine.**

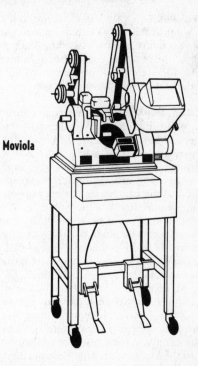

Moviola

■ **MPAA Certificate**   The certificate issued by the MPAA Rating Administration stating a certain code for a film that designates the type of audience for whom it is appropriate. *See* **Movie Rating System.**

■ **MPAA Rating Administration** *See* **Classification and Rating Administration.**

■ **MS** *See* **medium shot.**

■ **multicam, multi-cam, multi-camera, multicamera, multiple camera** A technique for shooting a scene with several cameras at once so that the shots from different angles or distances can later be edited together into a single scene. Cameras may be placed in the front and to the sides of the scene, alongside one another in front of the scene but each with a lens of a different focal length, or one or more cameras may even be hidden in the midst of the scene. Multiple cameras are generally used in television, but less often in film production. Most directors and cinematographers feel that each view of a scene must be individually lighted and are not willing to be satisfied with the general lighting that must be used for multiple cameras. Multiple cameras, however, might be used if a good deal of choice is desired when putting together the shots for a particular scene; or for scenes that can be photographed only once (e.g., a musical number, elaborate fight, or explosion of a structure). *See* **master scene technique** *and* **three-camera technique.**

■ **multi-channel sound** *See* **multitrack sound.**

■ **multihead printer** A printing machine that can make two or more prints at once from a single negative. Such a machine contains a picture head for each of the separate prints and a single sound head. Sometimes the term is used to describe a printer that makes a print from more than one negative. *See* **printer.**

■ **multi-image, multiple-image** A visual composition in which the individual frame is made up of several separate images, either the same or different, not superimposed over one another. Such compositions can be created by combining images on a single negative in an optical printer. Multi-image lenses or prisms can also be attached to the camera to achieve repeated images of the same picture in the actual shooting. It is possible to have the images move on the screen: for example, outside images can be made to rotate around a single fixed picture. As many as a dozen images can be on the screen at once. The multiple-image technique was employed as early as 1915 in D. W. Griffith's *The Birth of a Nation*, and received celebrated treatment on Abel Gance's triptych Polyvision screen for his *Napoléon vu par Abel Gance* (1927). The technique was used in sound films to show two people engaged in a phone conversation or to show a number of different people reacting to the same event. The multiple image has not often appeared in recent years, even though it seems more effective in modern wide-screen images, because most directors feel that the technique is artificial and also divides the audience's attention; but it is still used on occasion to achieve a particular effect. There was a resurgence of the technique in the late 1960s in films such as *The Thomas Crown Affair* (1968; dir. Norman Jewison), and Brian De Palma employed stationary and rotating multiple images in *Carrie* (1976) to communicate the confusion and chaos of both Carrie's consciousness and the prom scene in general. The term "split screen" is also sometimes employed for the technique, though it more accurately should apply to only two images on the screen at once. *See* **split screen.**

■ **multi-image lens** A lens employed during shooting to achieve a multiple image. Such lenses are themselves used with a 100mm lens for 35mm film or a 25mm lens for 16mm film. The images can form a number of diverse patterns. *See* **multi-image.**

■ **multi-image prism** A prism that, when used with a 50mm lens for 35mm film or a 25mm lens for 16mm film, produces a multiple image. Such images can either be in a radial pattern, with or without a central image, or in a parallel design. The prism can also be rotated while shooting so that the images will rotate on the screen. *See* **multi-image.**

■ **multilayer color film** Any color film with three layers of emulsion, each to record one of the primary colors. Also called monopack and tripack film. *See* **color film** (2) *and* **integral tripack color system.**

■ **multilight, multiple light** Any single luminaire using a number of bulbs either with separate reflectors and lenses for each bulb or a single reflector and lens for all. In most of these units, the individual bulbs can be turned on or off. Such luminaires generally function as fill lights.

■ **multimedia** (1) The term now frequently applies to any presentation on a computer, frequently from a CD-ROM disc, that utilizes still and moving images along with text and sound. Such programs are often interactive in that they require choices and involvement on the part of the viewer. *See* **interactive.** (2) Any theatrical presentation using several different media. The Czechoslovakian "Laterna Magika," for example, employed live performers, music, slides, and film when it appeared at the 1958 World's Fair in Brussels and later toured this country. *See* **mixed media.**

■ **multiplane, multiplane camera** A method of animation in which different parts of the scene are drawn on separate cels made of transparent plastic or glass, and the cels are placed a certain distance apart, in different planes beneath the camera, so that the photographed image will give an illusion of depth and three-dimensionality. The technique, developed by Ub Iwerks for Disney Studios, was first used in 1937 for the short cartoon *The Old Mill* and the first feature-length cartoon of the studio, *Snow White and the Seven Dwarfs*. Disney Studios won an Oscar for the short cartoon and

multiscreen An example of the polyvision triptych process in Abel Gance's *Napoléon vu par Abel Gance* (1927).

■ ■ ■

a special "scientific or technical" award for the multiplane camera. *See* **animation** *and* **cel animation.**

■ **multiple camera** *See* **multicam.**

■ **multiple exposure** The superimposition of several images on a film either by rewinding and then reexposing the same piece of film in the camera or by exposing the same piece of film to several images in an optical printer. Such superimposition of images might be used in a film to suggest the passage of time, to convey what has taken place over a period of time, or to show a number of simultaneous actions. When only two images are superimposed, the technique is called double exposure. Multiple exposure generally means the superimposition of three or more images, though the term is sometimes applied to double exposure as well.

■ **multiple-frame printing** The printing of a single frame more than once on the print. *See* **freeze frame.**

■ **multiple-head printer** *See* **multihead printer.**

■ **multiple-image** *See* **multi-image.**

■ **multiple pass, multiple pass photography, multiple pass cinematography, multiple pass shot** Any shot requiring two or more exposures (or passes) of different films or of the same film in the camera for a single composite image. In special-effects cinematography, models, for example, are photographed identically a number of times for traveling matte processes and compositing. *See* **motion control** *and* **special effects.**

■ **multiple printing** (1) The printing of more than one film at a time from a single negative. (2) The printing of one film from the images on two or more negatives at a single time. *See* **multihead printer.**

■ **multiple run, multiple** A distribution of a motion picture so that it is exhibited at a number of theaters. *See* **exhibition.**

■ **multiplex** Two or more theaters housed in a single structure with a single box office, concession stand, and lobby for all the theaters. Most new theaters today are housed in a multiplex, either as part of a mall or a self-standing structure. The multiplex is supposed to have been born in 1963, when Stanley H. Durwood, who founded AMC Entertainment, divided a single theater into two in Kansas City. The rapid growth of the multiplex was a response to the simple fact that not enough people would show up on most occasions to make the screening of a single film in a large theater economically worthwhile. The reaction to the uncomfortable multiplex theaters in the malls began in the late 1980s with the construction of large, attractive buildings with as many as twenty screens in wide, comfortable theaters with state-of-the-art equipment. The term "megaplex" is now used for such structures with sixteen or more screens and with modern conveniences and technology. *See* **exhibition** *and* **megaplex.**

■ **multiscreen, multiple screen** A motion-picture presentation that generally uses three or more projectors with three or more screens or with a single larger screen. This process was first used at the 1900 Paris exhibition when Cinéorama employed ten projectors to cast a circular image around the audience. A notable multiscreen process was Abel Gance's Polyvision, used for his film *Napoléon vu par Abel Gance* (1927), which employed three screens and three projectors to form a single wide-screen image or to present separate images at once, the two outside pictures often commenting on the central one. In 1952, the Cinerama process, developed by Fred Waller, opened in New York City, showing a number of travelogues on a "wrap-around screen" from three separate projectors and using a sophisticated stereo sound system. The normal problem in multiscreen presentation, the joining of the separate images to form a single picture, was partly alleviated in Cinerama by blurring the joined edges of each frame. Ultimately, Cinerama began to use a single 70mm film for the wide-screen picture rather than the multiple-screen presentation because the single-frame process was cheaper, better, and easier to use, especially for narrative films. Multiscreen presentations have also been used by large industrial companies and by governments, especially at World's Fairs. The terms "multiscreen" and "multiple screen" are also used to describe such processes that employ slides instead of film. *See* **Cinerama** *and* **wide screen.**

■ **multi-tiered audience** An audience made up of a variety of types of people. Films that appeal to blue-collar workers and professionals, men and women, black and white people, are a distributor's dream.

■ **multitrack sound, multiple-track sound, multichannel sound, multiple-channel sound** A stereophonic sound system for motion pictures that uses two or more sound tracks and speakers. Normally, the sound tracks are on the motion-picture film, though Cinerama employed a separate film with seven magnetic tracks. Four magnetic tracks were generally used on 35mm film and six on 70mm film, though the practice now is for two optical channels creating four distinct tracks on 35mm film. *See* **stereophonic sound.**

■ **Musco lights** A bank of anywhere from six to fifteen open-face HMI lights mounted on a boom, which is itself mounted on a truck. The unit is made by the Musco Light Company and its great amount of illumination can be used for lighting a vast space. The boom itself can hold the bank one hundred feet in the air. The unit comes with its own generator and a remote control that can position each light.

■ **Museum of Modern Art (MOMA)** A museum for the fine arts of the modern period in New York City; it also contains the Film Study Center, which claims to have 13,000 films and an archive with 4 million stills. Most of its films can be viewed for individual research (many are circulated for classroom or public showings at various institutions of learning). The museum publicly screens films each day and has presented numerous retrospective programs of works by individual directors. It also has played an active role in the preservation and restoration of films. The center is a significant archive for screenplays, documents, film books, journals, and newspaper clippings.

■ **music** Music was part of the motion-picture experience as early as silent films when a piano, organ, or small instrumental group accompanied the actions on the screen. The reason for the music at first may have been pragmatic—to cover up the noise of the projector—but it was almost immediately discovered that music added considerably to the emotional mood of the film and also supplied an audible continuity that helped hold together the separate images on the screen. Fairly early in the history of motion pictures, the Edison Film Company distributed suggestions for music with their films. Max Winkler formed a company that supplied cue sheets and music for various films—

the music was both taken from the classics and written directly for the films. Collections of musical scores, catalogued according to their various moods, were published, one of the most popular being Giuseppe Becce's *Kinothek* which first appeared in 1919 (the title is an abbreviated form of *Kinobibliothek*, which means "film library"). A number of machines also appeared that could play music and create sound effects for silent films. Large orchestras were sometimes used for important films at first-run theaters: for *The Birth of a Nation* (1915), D. W. Griffith had a special score, largely made up of passages from classical music and popular tunes, played by a symphony orchestra and carefully cued to the action on the screen.

The coming of sound to motion pictures was musically heralded by William Axt and David Mendoza's synchronized score for Warner Brothers' 1926 production of *Don Juan*, which starred John Barrymore. Vitaphone, a sound-on-disc process, was employed for the music and used again the following year to permit Al Jolson synchronic singing and some synchronic dialogue in *The Jazz Singer*. In the early days of sound, music was only sporadically employed or not used at all since it had to be recorded as part of the scene or played offstage while dialogue was recorded. It was not until 1932 that a sound-mixing process was developed that permitted music to be recorded separately from dialogue, thus allowing it to be edited and added at a later time. Once postdubbing and mixing sound tracks became possible, studios began to realize the benefits of musical backgrounds and formed music departments. At first musical scores seemed purely functional and were often the product of more than one person—frequently no composer was cited in the credits. But gradually the significance of a good musical score became apparent and studios began to buy the best available composers.

Because so much movie music has been pedestrian, we tend to forget that some of the best music of the past century has been written for film. The significant musical scores were largely in the Romantic tradition and highly programmatic in nature. Important composers in Hollywood from the middle of the 1930s through the 1980s were Max Steiner, Franz Waxman, Dimitri Tiomkin, Miklós Rózsa, and Erich Korngold, all from across the ocean, and the American-born Alfred Newman and Bernard Herrmann. A number of renowned composers have also on occasion contributed scores for films. As well as Prokofiev's celebrated collaboration with Eisenstein for *Alexander Nevsky* (1938), in this country Virgil Thomson has contributed scores for documentaries by Pare Lorentz and Robert Flaherty, and Aaron Copland has written scores for both documentaries and fictional films. In later years, film scores have been influenced by contemporary trends in music. Alex North is perhaps best known for his score for Elia Kazan's *A Streetcar Named Desire* (1951), which relies heavily on the idiom of New Orleans jazz. Another accomplished film composer,

Elmer Bernstein, also wrote an important score utilizing the jazz idiom for Otto Preminger's *The Man With the Golden Arm* (1955). One of the less admirable developments in sound has been the use of pop songs and rock music for all of a film's musical background—such music may convey a sense of American life, but the practice did not take long to seem limited and trite. Some rather fine musical scores, however, continue to be written by such composers as Jerry Goldsmith and John Williams.

In any discussion of film music, notice must be given to the cartoon, where music became more and more integrated until music and action seemed inseparable. At its best, the cartoon could offer a perfect synthesis of sight and sound, as it did in Disney's musical film *Fantasia* (1940); but it could also offer a naive and intrusive use of music that simply echoes the actions, a practice that came to be called "mickey mousing." *See* **dub, mix,** *and* **sound.**

musical *Gold Diggers of 1933* (1933; dir. Mervyn Le Roy) features Busby Berkeley's kaleidoscopic choreography.

■ ■ ■

■ **musical, musical comedy** A specific genre of American film that focuses on song and dance. The United States was already a musical nation with its Broadway musical (the harbinger of this type of film), radio music, and developing record industry. With the advent of sound, the Hollywood studio system was prepared to use its finances and technology to create a world of music never before seen and heard. If the Hollywood film had already established itself as a dream factory, what better way for the viewer to escape from reality and the Depression years than imagining himself or herself as the extraordinarily talented people on the screen? Many plots enforced this dream by telling stories of nobodies suddenly thrust into stardom, of a talented group of decent "kids" struggling to put on the big show.

The Jazz Singer (1927), the first feature film with sound, could be considered the first musical, since it featured a number of songs, but the film lacked the obligatory dance numbers and emphasized drama more than the music. Three types of musicals dominated the early years of sound: the Broadway musical brought from stage to film, such as *Rio Rita* (1929) and *Showboat* (1929); the revue, which presented a series of musical numbers featuring well-known singers, dancers, and comedians, such as *The Hollywood Revue of 1929* (1929) and *Paramount on Parade* (1930); and the "backstage" musical, which used a story about performers as an excuse for the song and dance—*Broadway Melody* (1929) is the film that began this tradition. Lloyd Bacon's *42nd Street* (1933), with its "backstage" plot that features the last-minute substitution of an unknown for the leading star, points the way for the development of this last type of musical. The production numbers in this film were staged by Busby Berkeley in a style impossible to present on any stage. Elaborate sets, large numbers of female dancers choreographed with precision into astonishing patterns, a mobile camera that filmed these patterns from a range of positions including the famous overhead shots—all became standard elements in a series of films that Berkeley choreographed for Warner Brothers, including the *Gold Diggers* films of 1933, 1935, and 1937. Also popular were the operetta musicals, especially those starring Jeanette MacDonald and Nelson Eddy, beginning with *Naughty Marietta* in 1935; while *The Wizard of Oz,* which appeared in 1939, has remained a popular favorite until the present time. Perhaps the most charming musicals of this period, and the ones that seem least dated, are the series of films made for RKO by Fred Astaire and Ginger Rogers, beginning with *Flying Down to Rio* in 1933.

The postwar years saw the dominance of MGM in the musical film with a series of lavish Technicolor works produced by Arthur Freed. With gusto and spirit, yet controlled by taste and intelligence, MGM produced this series of color films that encapsulated the optimism of the postwar years before the doldrums and fears of the 1950s set in. Vincente Minnelli directed for MGM such films as *Meet Me in St. Louis* (1944), *The Pirate* (1948), and *An American in Paris* (1951), the last of which featured the music of George Gershwin. The last two films starred the dancer Gene Kelly, who added considerable energy and imagination to the musical. Stanley Donen's *Seven Brides for Seven Brothers* (1954), an MGM CinemaScope production that featured Michael Kidd's brilliant choreography, remains a classic musical in spite of its rather dated attitudes about the relation of men and women.

The 1960s began with some extraordinarily successful musicals and ended with the genre's near collapse. Robert Wise's impressive and moving *West Side Story*

(1961), the very sophisticated and entertaining *My Fair Lady* (1964), directed by George Cukor, the saccharine but sometimes stirring *The Sound of Music* (1965), also directed by Robert Wise, and *Mary Poppins* (1964; dir. Robert Stevenson), from the Disney Corporation, were all so expensive and lucrative that they tempted studios to continue with lavishly financed musicals, most of which failed at the box office. Film audiences were unstable since the advent of television, and film production had become enormously expensive. Gone were the studios that could easily finance this kind of film. The musical as a film genre was much in abeyance. But since musicals exploit the full possibilities of the medium, with their exciting use of sound and picture, such films were still occasionally made and some were successful, partly because they moved in new directions. Milos Forman's intelligent and sensitive film adaptation of the stage musical *Hair* in 1979 managed to convey through music and dance the joys and frustrations of young people in the turbulent 1960s and early 1970s, and Bob Fosse offered some of the best drama and most evocative dancing yet to appear in the musical in *Cabaret* (1972) and his autobiographical *All That Jazz* (1979). One might consider such musical biographies as *Coal Miner's Daughter* (1980; dir. Michael Apted), musical dramas as *Flashdance* (1983; dir. Adrian Lyne), and Disney animated films as *Beauty and the Beast* (1991; dir. Gary Trousdale and Kirk Wise) partly musicals, but it is fair to say that since the films of Bob Fosse, no distinguished musical per se has graced the motion-picture screen. The reason for this eclipse might well be that the plethora of rock videos available on television and tape has taken away a good portion of the potential audience for such films. Much of this rock music has spilled over into the theater as the score for many motion pictures, to some extent displacing music from the center of the film by making it part of the motion picture's cultural ambiance and a running commentary on the screen's visuals.

■ **music arranger**   The person who adapts music already written for a production, rescoring and orchestrating it to suit the film's specific requirements.

■ **music contractor, musician contractor**   After helping to figure out the number and type of musicians needed for recording a film score, this individual contracts the specific musicians for a specific time and date. During the actual recording, the music contractor, who may also play an instrument, looks after the members of the orchestra while also protecting the film's budget.

■ **music cue**   *See* cue (4).

■ **music cue breakdown, music cue sheet**   *See* cue breakdown.

■ **music department**   The department of studio personnel responsible for writing or acquiring the music to be played for a film and also responsible for supervising the playing of such music whether as part of the film or as a musical background. At the beginning of sound motion pictures, the major studios formed such departments and sought to hire the best composers and personnel they could find. The departments were run by a director and included composers, arrangers, conductors, and sometimes musicians. Music was mass-produced for the numerous films that these studios turned out, often, at first, through the collaboration of composers. Nevertheless, several highly talented composers belonging to these departments wrote some very distinguished scores for motion pictures. *See* **music.**

■ **music director, music supervisor**   The person in charge of the music for a production. His or her duties include overseeing the composition of original music or selection of previously written music, as well as supervising the recording session. This individual might also compose the music and/or conduct it during the scoring session.

■ **music editor, music mixer**   The individual responsible for editing a film's music so that it properly matches the picture and fits into the mix. The music editor consults with the director, editor, and composer to figure out the timings for the music and works out a "cue breakdown" or "cue sheet" for rerecording and the final mix.

■ **music librarian**   The individual responsible for the copying and distribution of the individual instrumental parts from the film's score. This person also works out a schedule for the musicians and makes any changes necessary on the individual scores.

■ **music recording supervisor**   The person responsible for the recording of music for a film production. This individual works closely with the composer and conductor. Sometimes called a scoring mixer.

music track   One of the three final tracks, along with those for dialogue and sound effects, that go into the master sound track. Sometimes a combined music and effects track is made for foreign releases so that dialogue in another language can later be added (this is called an M and E track). *See* **M and E track** *and* **mix.**

■ **Mutograph, Mutoscope**   The Mutograph was the camera developed by the American Mutoscope Company to make photographs for the Mutoscope peephole machine, which was viewed in arcades throughout the country. Instrumental in the development of these machines was W. K. L. Dickson, who had previously helped Edison develop the Kinetograph and Kinetoscope. With Elias Koopman, Henry Marvin, and Herman Casler, Dickson formed the KMCD syndicate (the initials were from their last names), later called the American Mutoscope Company, in December 1895.

The Mutoscope differed from the Kinetoscope in that individual photographs on separate cards were used instead of a single piece of film. Attached to the machine was a crank that, when turned by hand, flipped over the cards rapidly enough so that the figures seemed to move. Since the pictures were larger than those for the Kinetoscope, they did not have to be magnified and so appeared clearer; they also cost a penny to see and not the nickel charged for the Edison machine. An outdoor stage that could be rotated to face the sun was built by Dickson on the roof of the company's building in New York City. A notable "motion picture" made for the Mutoscope in 1897 showed Joseph Jefferson performing some scenes from his successful stage play *Rip Van Winkle*. The American Mutograph Company then developed the Biograph camera and projector for screening images from motion-picture film, again in competition with the Edison Company. Once more their film was larger and its image clearer, but the 35mm film used by the Edison Company's Vitascope was to become standard. With the development of these machines, the company became the American Mutoscope and Biograph Company. *See* **Biograph** *and* **Kinetograph**.

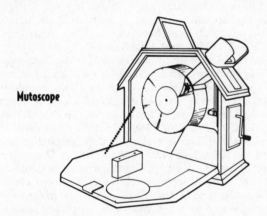

Mutoscope

■ **Mutual**   Originally organized by Harry Aitken, John R. Freuler, and Samuel S. Hutchinson to distribute films in 1912, the Mutual Film Company brought under its wing some major producers of motion pictures in the earlier silent period. Mutual was one of the independent companies that prospered during these years, distributing a large assortment of films and later moving into the distribution of feature films. The company distributed the films that Thomas Ince made for Adam Kessel and Charles Baumann's Bison Life Company and was especially successful with Ince's Westerns that starred William S. Hart. Mutual also distributed the famous comedies that Mack Sennett made for Keystone, a company set up for Mutual by Kessel and Baumann. In 1913, Griffith left Biograph because of his difficulties in making *Judith of Bethulia* (1914), and joined Harry Aitken's Reliance and Majestic film company, which distributed its films through Mutual. After

directing a number of features, Griffith began work on his monumental *The Birth of a Nation,* which Aitken and Griffith finally had to distribute themselves because of Mutual's displeasure at the film's growing costs. Even after the tremendous success of *Birth of a Nation* (1915), Aitken was dismissed by Mutual's board of directors. Aitken left Mutual along with Kessel and Baumann, and the three formed the Triangle Film Corporation, a production and distribution company, bringing into the organization Ince, Sennett, and Griffith. But Mutual seemed to recoup and in 1916 hired Charlie Chaplin, at a salary of $670,000 for one year, away from Essanay. The twelve films Chaplin made at Mutual are among his best short works and include *The Pawnshop* (1916), *The Immigrant* (1917), and *Easy Street* (1917). But in 1917, at the completion of his contract and in spite of Mutual's million-dollar offer, Chaplin accepted a better contract from First National. Without Chaplin, the company soon began to fade and by 1919 was out of business.

■ **MX**   Abbreviation for music.

■ **Mylar splice**   An editing splice that joins together two pieces of film by means of Mylar tape normally placed on both sides of the film without overlapping. Such splices are easier and faster to make than cement splices, but because the extra thickness of the tape causes a slight distortion in the image on the screen, Mylar splices are used for workprints only. *See* **splice.**

■ **mystery film**   A type of film that is sometimes considered a separate genre and focuses on the gradual and suspenseful discovery of the perpetrator of a crime or series of crimes (generally involving murder) and the reasons for such criminal acts. Movies have tended to emphasize the person who solves the mystery to such an extent that many critics prefer to place such works in the generic category of the detective film—for example, any of the *Thin Man* films of the 1930s and 1940s or tough-guy detective films such as *The Maltese Falcon* (1941; dir. John Huston) have such an emphasis. There are also a number of such works that seem equally defensible as horror films—for example, *Les Diaboliques* (1954; dir. Henri-Georges Clouzot) and *Psycho* (1960; dir. Alfred Hitchcock). Nevertheless, we can still include these works in a general category called "mystery film," which has the following characteristics: the committing of a crime or series of crimes; the search to discover the criminal and the reasons for such illegal acts; and the discovery of both the culprit and his or her motivation.

The mystery film can be traced from such silent works as Griffith's *One Exciting Night* (1922), Roland West's *The Bat* (1926), and Paul Leni's *The Cat and the Canary* (1927), the last two films based on stage plays. The detective type of mystery film is also evident in the numerous silent film versions of Sherlock Holmes both in this country and abroad. One might also want to include among silent mysteries such peripheral horror films as Griffith's version of Poe's "The Tell-Tale Heart," in *The Avenging Conscience* (1914) and Tod Browning's *London After Midnight* (1927) with Lon Chaney. The talkies began almost immediately with versions of mysteries from the stage, such as Warner Brothers' *The Terror* (1928; dir. Roy del Ruth), an adaptation of the Edgar Wallace play, and Tod Browning's *The Thirteenth Chair* (1929); detective mysteries, with such private investigators from fiction as Philo Vance in *The Bishop Murder Case* (1929) and *The Canary Murder Case* (1930); and horror-mysteries, such as *Dr. X* (1932; dir. Michael Curtiz) and James Whale's *The Old Dark House* (1932). From this point on, these three types of mystery films were made in great number: in the second category alone were films featuring detectives such as Ellery Queen, Nick Carter, Bulldog Drummond, Sam Spade, Philip Marlowe, and Hercule Poirot. Otto Preminger's *Laura* gave new impetus to the mystery film in 1944 with its intelligent blending of romance and mystery, its skillful editing, and its haunting theme song. Three important developments starting about this time were the comic-mystery film, for example those British works using idiosyncratic detective figures such as the series of films with Margaret Rutherford playing Agatha Christie's Miss Marple; the film-noir detective film, which presented a somber, dark, and disturbing vision of human nature, as in Edward Dmytryk's *Murder, My Sweet* (1944) and Robert Siodmak's *Cry of the City* (1948); and the psychological mystery, for example, Hitchcock's *Spellbound* (1945) and *Vertigo* (1958). *See* **detective film**, *film noir*, *and* **genre.**

■ **mystery thriller** A term sometimes applied to a mystery film that provokes more than the usual type of suspense and interest, but that also, because of the violence and impending threat to the major characters, creates in the audience a good deal of apprehension and even terror. Robert Siodmak's *The Spiral Staircase* (1946) is a classic example of this type of mystery film; and Alan J. Pakula's *The Pelican Brief* (1993), though also involved with politics and big business, has the requisite thrills, violence, chases, and threats to the major figures to make this an excellent recent example. *See* **mystery film.**

■ **myth, mythic criticism** The term "myth" normally applies to any of the stories that arise in a culture to explain its basic beliefs about the nature of the universe and the relation of the individual to the universe, as well as to explain certain institutions, rituals, and conventions that are part of that society's cultural heritage.

Such stories, in seeking to explain the unexplainable, employ divinities and great heroes, and, in belonging to an entire culture, come from no single individual but are the creation of numerous authors. Because so many of our psychological anxieties concerning the universe and our place within it are similar from age to age and place to place, the myths of various cultures are often similar: for example, stories concerning such divinities as the Sumerian Tammuz, the Greek Adonis, and the Egyptian Attis treat these divinities as fertility gods who are destroyed during the winter, but resurrected in the spring as harbingers of nature's renewal. Mythic criticism in literary study has sought to locate a number of universal plots and characters embedded within individual texts beneath the immediate social worlds that these works create in order to explain some underlying and basic appeal that the reader feels from these works—in this respect, Carl Jung's theories concerning our universal unconscious and universal archetypes have often been employed.

Such criticism has infrequently been used for film primarily because so much of the medium's appeal relies on its visual creation of an immediate, concrete, and particular social world; but there is no question that film, as a narrative art form dealing with recognizable human types, is open to such an approach. Rebirth myths abound in works such as John Ford's *Stagecoach* (1939) and Elia Kazan's *On the Waterfront* (1954); and archetypal figures such as the light-haired angelic maiden and the dark-haired, sensual female abound in the American films of the 1930s. Sometimes filmmakers have consciously made modern adaptations of classical myths: for example, the French directors Jean Cocteau and Marcel Camus have used the Orpheus and Eurydice myth in their respective films, *Orpheus* (1949) and *Black Orpheus* (1958). The concept of myth has also been applied to certain film genres, especially to the Western, which is seen as having created a particular kind of American myth. Though the stories or characters in these films are not based on gods (more often they are based on legend, which can be traced back to actual history), they do create national archetypal situations and figures that very much relate to our beliefs and institutions. The cowboy hero, from the Broncho Billy silent films starring G. M. Anderson to the last John Wayne films, is an embodiment of American individualism; and the conflicts between lawmen and outlaws, settlers and Indians, farmers and cattlemen, embody the ever-continuing struggle within this land between the impulses for conformity and individualism, for socialization and independence. *See* **archetype.**

■ ■ ■

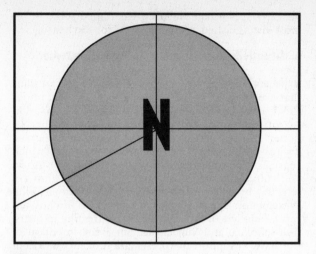

Nagra to
nuts-and-bolts film

■ **Nagra** The premier tape recorder employed in the film industry and made by Kudelski SA, a Swiss manufacturer. The machine employs a reel-to-reel mechanism and records on quarter-inch tape. For analog magnetic tape, the Nagra 4.2 remains a popular model for synchronous, mono recording, and the Nagra IV-S TC is the model for stereo and time-code recording. The Nagra-D, a four channel reel-to-reel field recorder with 24-bit recording capability (as opposed to the 16-bit capacity of other digital audio tape recorders), was an early innovation and remains state-of-the-art in digital sound recording. *See* **digital sound recording** *and* **magnetic recording.**

■ **name actor** A performer whose name is recognizable to the public and who himself or herself would draw a large number of people to the box office aside from the quality or drawing power of the film. Such an individual has name or marquee value.

■ **narration** The term specifically means the telling of a story or describing of events. In film, where we see what happens before our eyes, narration is best considered as a supplementary commentary spoken by a voice that does not synchronically originate from any of the characters on the screen. In documentaries or educational films, this voice-over generally belongs to a neutral but informed person whom we never see but who functions throughout as an expert on the subject, giving a narration that supplements the images or places them in a larger context. In fictional films, the narration frequently belongs to one of the characters and functions to expand our awareness of the characters and action, to tell us what happens during time intervals not presented on the screen, or to foreshadow future events.

The narration in fictional films also supplies a continuity and perspective to all the action. An extremely successful narration is that of the young vagabond girl in Terrence Malick's *Days of Heaven* (1978), which not only adds pathos and humor to the events we see, but also develops the girl's own wonderful character. Sometimes the narration in a fictional film does not come from any of the characters, as in the case of Tony Richardson's *Tom Jones* (1963), where the voice-over approximates the omniscient narrator of Fielding's novel, from which the film is adapted, to bring the motion picture as close to its source as possible and to create the same humorous and ironic perspective on the action as in the book; or in such fictional films as Henry Hathaway's *The House on 92nd Street* (1945), where the factual pretensions of the film are enhanced by a documentary-type narration. Film is a visual and dramatic form that communicates best through its images, dialogue, and editing unless a narration is necessary to achieve any of the effects outlined above. In Ridley Scott's *Blade Runner* (1982) the voice-over of the central figure, which follows the conventional hard-boiled, first-person narrations of detective films, was added later to give missing continuity to the action, but it seems weak and superficial in relation to the complex visual texture of the film. The voice-over was removed in the released version of the director's cut (1993).

■ **narration script** The script used by the person doing the voice-over to add the narration to a film in a recording studio after the film has already been shot and, generally, edited. Such a script will specify at what points in the motion picture the narration should be added.

■ **narrative** The term basically means any story that is narrated by someone, but also has come to mean the story in any art form, even in drama and film where, unlike literature, there is normally no narrator. *See* **story** *and* **plot.**

■ **narrative film** Any film that tells a story; also called a fiction film, a dramatic film, a theatrical film, and a feature film. Though a number of documentaries, such as those of Flaherty, have a simple narrative line embedded within them and some, such as Sidney Meyers's *The Quiet One* (1949) and Paul Dickson's British film, *David* (1951), seem to tell stories, the term "narrative film" applies to those works that emphasize the story line, are dramatic in nature, and are fictional. *See* **feature film,** *and* **fiction film**.

■ **narrator** The voice that performs the narration in a film in either a fiction or nonfiction work. Narrators in documentaries generally seem to be neutral and informed observers whom we can trust and from whom we can learn, an impression that may subtly lead us to be persuaded by the point of view of the filmmaker. It is the narrator in documentaries who gives us much of the information necessary to interpret the images on the screen and place them within some context or continuity. In certain types of recent documentaries, however, narrators in the traditional sense are not used, since the images and the speech of the people who are the subject of the work are allowed to convey to us both the necessary information and the filmmaker's point of view (*see* **cinéma-vérité** *and* **direct cinema**). In fiction films, narrators are frequently involved in the action, giving us information about themselves, the other characters, and about the story with hindsight from a later time—as in a literary narration, the narrator describes events in the past tense and gives the film something of a novelistic quality. Sometimes narrators in fiction films are not one of the characters but function to give to the film either a decidedly literary quality by sounding like an omniscient author or a credibility and authenticity by sounding like the authoritative voice-over in a documentary. *See* **narration.**

■ **narrow-gauge film** Any film narrower than the 35mm film normally used for professional cinematography—for example, Super 16mm, 16mm, Super 8mm, and 8mm. Because of better film stock and printing methods, 16mm is now employed frequently for professional work. This gauge is employed for documentary work; independently made fiction films that can later be blown up to 35mm for commercial theaters; and educational films. Films made in 35mm are reduced to 16mm prints for noncommercial distribution, and educational films originally made with 16mm stock were also, at one time, made available on Super 8 or 8mm film. Super 8mm was the most popular film gauge in this country for amateurs; though still in use, it has significantly been replaced by videotape. *See* **film** *(1).*

■ **narrow release** The initial exhibition of a film at a select number of theaters in important areas to generate interest so that a more general release may develop. The same as a platform release. *See* **exhibition** *and* **wide release.**

■ **National Association of Theater Owners (NATO)** The largest organization representing exhibitors in the United States. This organization keeps members informed about the latest developments, problems, and trends in film exhibition. It also deals with the organization representing the film producers and distributors, the Motion Picture Association of America (MPAA).

■ **National Film Board of Canada (NFB)** A government agency in Canada responsible for supporting filmmaking. The agency was founded in 1939 and first headed by the famous English documentary producer John Grierson. Although the board has been responsible for some excellent documentary work both for theater and television, it also has sponsored a number of fine feature films, such as Don Owen's *Nobody Waved Good-*

bye (1964). Norman McLaren has filmed some of his most distinguished animated works for the board.

■ **National Film Preservation Act** *See* **National Film Registry.**

■ **National Film Registry** A list of classic American films that are selected by the Librarian of Congress, under the direction of Congress's National Film Preservation Act of 1988, and made a permanent part of the National Film Collection of the Library of Congress. Twenty-five films per year, at least ten years old, "which represent an enduring part of our nation's historical and cultural heritage" may be named. Such films are selected by thirteen members of the National Film Preservation Board, who serve four-year terms and are representatives of different aspects of the film industry, film scholars, and film critics. Since the intention of the act is to support the preservation of such works in their original versions and forms, copies of the film that have been colorized or altered in any manner must be so designated. By the end of 1995, 175 films had been selected for the list, from such early silent films as Rex Ingram's *The Four Horseman of the Apocalypse* (1921) to such modern works as George Lucas's *Star Wars* (1977).

■ **National Legion of Decency** *See* **Legion of Decency.**

■ **national release** The initial exhibition of a film limited to the United States. *See* **exhibition.**

■ **NATO/Showest Convention** The major trade show for exhibitors and distributors from all over the world that takes place in Las Vegas each February. Over 5,000 people attend this showcase, sponsored by the National Association of Theater Owners, to watch films and make deals for exhibition. *See* **National Association of Theater Owners.**

■ **naturalism** The term describes a branch of philosophy that believes all natural phenomena can be explained scientifically as well as a school of fiction that developed from this belief a scientific approach to character, especially emphasizing that the individual's fate is primarily determined not by free will, but by heredity and environment. As a result, naturalist writers present the individual as a victim of natural forces, both internal and external, to such a degree that he or she sometimes resembles a brute animal. Naturalism, then, is a form of extreme realism that depicts the everyday sordid reality of people who often seem to have a narrow spiritual dimension. The novelist Emile Zola was the main proponent of this school of writing in France, and he was followed in England by novelists such as Edward Moore and George Gissing, and in America by writers such as Frank Norris and Theodore Dreiser. This type of literature has had its impact on film: Erich von Stroheim made a powerful film version of Frank Norris's *McTeague,* which he called *Greed* (1923), a landmark film because of its realism in characterization, story, and setting. A number of gangster films and film-noir works can also be considered naturalistic because of their uncompromising view of human nature in a sordid world—for example, Fritz Lang's *The Big Heat* (1953) and Samuel Fuller's *Pickup on South Street* (1953). Buñuel's *Los Olvidados* (1950) is explicit in its naturalism when it presents the corrupting influence of a sick environment on a group of Mexican juveniles. *Also see* **neorealism** *and* **realism.**

naturalism Erich von Stroheim's *Greed* (1923), which features Zasu Pitts and Gibson Gowland, is based on Frank Norris's naturalistic novel *McTeague.*

■ ■ ■

■ **natural lighting** Lighting for a scene that originates from sources other than studio luminaires. The term is most often used to describe daylight or illumination from the sun, but also applies to any illumination from actual sources in the scene such as candles, a fireplace, or lamps.

■ **natural wipe** A transition from one scene to another created by some character or object blocking out the first scene and, upon removal, allowing the second to appear. The wipe is so called because it is created by a natural element in the scene and not mechanically in the camera or an optical printer. *See* **head-on, tail-away shot,** *and* **wipe.**

■ **nature film** A nonfiction film concerned with animals, plants, or some natural habitat. Walt Disney produced a series of such works, most notably *The Living Desert* in 1953.

■ **NC-17** The newest of the film ratings of the Movie Rating System that was introduced in 1990 to replace the old X rating that itself had become an icon for advertising pornographic films, since it had not been copyrighted by the MPAA. The NC-17 rating means that no children seventeen or under may see the film because of its adult themes and content. *See* **Motion Picture Production Code** *and* **Movie Rating System.**

■ **needle drop** Jargon for the single use in a film of stock music generally already recorded and available as library sound. *See* **library sound.**

■ **negative (NEG)** (1) In black-and-white photography, a film image in which the dark and light areas are reversed, and in color photography, in which dark and light areas are reversed and colors are complementary to those in the original scene. Positive prints with dark and light areas as well as colors corresponding to the original scene are made from the negative image. (2) The film itself which contains the negative images. (3) Raw film stock intended to record negative images. (4) Film stock for negative images that has already been exposed but not yet processed. *See* **film** *(1) and* **sound negative.**

■ **negative continuity list, negative log** A list of the required cuts for conforming the negative that generally accompanies the workprint. Such a list contains shot numbers, footage, edge numbers, and sometimes descriptions and details for each cut.

■ **negative cost** The total cost up to and including the editing of the original negative. This cost includes all production expenses but not later expenses for prints, distribution, exhibition, and advertising. *See* **above-the-line costs** *and* **below-the-line costs.**

■ **negative cut list** A list of instructions for cutting and conforming the negative that results from the film's transfer to video or digital and subsequent editing. Sometimes a workprint is first made from the list to examine the editing, and the negative is cut from a final workprint. This type of editing has made considerable inroads in the film industry, since it is easier, faster, and more flexible than traditional methods of editing with flat-bed tables. The negative cut list is similar to the EDL (edit-decision list) used for making an edit master video on-line, but functions with edge numbers. *See* **editing.**

■ **negative cutter, negative matcher, conformer** *See* **negative cutting.**

■ **negative cutting** The editing of the negative so that it exactly matches the finally edited workprint of the film. Dupe negatives, derived from a master print of the original negative, are made to produce a large number of release prints, as well as to protect the originally cut negative. The cutting is performed by a negative cutter, negative matcher, or conformer in a laboratory. The cutter follows the scribe marks made on the workprint by the editor, but also uses a negative continuity list or log with footage and edge numbers for assistance. Today, with much editing performed on video or digitally, cutters work directly from a negative cut list that results from the off-line editing or from a workprint that is made from the list and that undergoes additional editing. Also called conforming. *See* **editing.**

■ **negative film, negative stock** A film stock intended to record negative images.

■ **negative image** An image in which black-and-white areas are reversed and colors are complementary to those in the original scene. Prints with proper black-and-white areas as well as the normal colors are made from negatives with these images.

■ **negative numbers** The series of numbers with key lettering along the edge of the negative that is printed onto the positive to allow for match cutting of negative and final workprint. Also called edge numbers. *See* **edge numbers.**

■ **negative perforation** The perforation on standard 35mm negatives, which is rectangular in shape and arced at each end. Such holes, referred to as BH or Bell and Howell perforations, are excellent for steady registration; but because their corners, where side and arc meet, are subject to tear over a period of time, shorter perforations, rectangular in shape with curved corners and referred to as KS or Kodak Standard perforations, are used on positive prints since these must be run a number of times. *See* **Kodak standard perforation** *and* **perforations.**

■ **negative pickup deal** A contractual agreement whereby a distributor agrees to pay a producer a certain amount of money upon completion of the film and the delivery of the final negative, completely cut and ready for printing. Producers can generally use such an agreement to finance the film or borrow from a bank, while the distributor need not worry about cost overruns or incompleted productions. *See* **completion guarantee, development deal, first look deal,** *and* **overall development deal.**

■ **negative pitch** The distance between perforations on negative film, which is shorter than that on positive film and hence also referred to as short pitch (the distance on positives is referred to as long pitch). In contact printing, the two films must pass over the same sprockets together with the positive on the outside, hence requiring the greater distance to avoid slippage.

■ **negative-positive process** Any process that develops a positive print from a separate negative as opposed to a reversal process where the positive can be processed on the original film. *See* **film** *(1).*

■ **negative pulling** *See* **negative cutting.**

■ **negative sound track** *See* **sound negative.**

■ **negative splice** The point at which two pieces of negative film are held together by cement and where the overlap is less than that for a positive splice of the same type. Such splices are less visible for narrow-gauge film and are sufficiently strong, since they are not subject to the pull and tension of a projector as are positive splices. *See* **positive splice.**

■ **neg pull, negative pull** Cutting out a specific take from the original negative—e.g., for making a new portion of the workprint or for some special photographic optical process. The practice, in general, is not a good one, since any damage to the negative loses the shot forever.

■ **neorealism** An Italian film movement that was primarily a response to the artistic limitations of the Italian film industry under the fascist government and to the social conditions of Italy during and immediately

neorealism *The Bicycle Thief* (1948, Vittorio De Sica), the most celebrated of the Italian neorealist films.

■ ■ ■

after the Second World War. Visconti's *Ossessione* (1942), based on James M. Cain's *The Postman Always Rings Twice,* is generally thought to foreshadow the neorealist film, with its realistic rural landscape and social environment, though the film was only released in a butchered version by censors during the war years and later had limited distribution because of its copyright infringement. Antonio Pietrangeli, who wrote the script for *Ossessione,* first used the term "neorealism" when discussing the film in a 1943 issue of the Italian journal *Cinema.* The movement, though, actually began with Roberto Rossellini's 1945 film, *Open City,* filming for which took place shortly after the Germans left Rome. Rossellini's film established all the elements that were to be central to the movement: realistic, authentic settings; ordinary people played by both professional and nonprofessional performers; everyday social problems; episodic plots which convey the rhythm of every day life; and unobtrusive camera and editing techniques. Rossellini's realism was aided by the film stock he had to use, which gave his images a grainy, unembellished, and documentary quality. To get on film the immediacy of actual locations, Rossellini had to forgo the synchronic recording of sound and resort to postdubbing, a practice that became permanent in the Italian film industry. *Open City* was a great international success and was followed in 1946 by Rossellini's *Paisan,* which presented six episodes concerning the Allied forces' advance in Italy, and the less successful *Germany, Year Zero* (1947), the story of a Nazified and corrupt Berlin youth.

In 1946, the first of Vittorio De Sica's three neorealist masterpieces appeared, *Shoeshine,* which told in uncompromising terms the tragic story of two impoverished boys in postwar Italy. *Shoeshine* won an Academy Award in this country as the best foreign film of the year and was followed in 1948 by *The Bicycle Thief,* a moving and beautiful film that tells, with authentic realism, the story of a poor man's struggle for survival in the harsh postwar years of Italy by focusing on both the theft of his bicycle, necessary for his work, and his moving relationship with his son. De Sica released what is considered the last of these neorealist films, *Umberto D,* in 1952, which relates in episodic fashion the plights of an impoverished old man and movingly dramatizes his tender affection for his dog. For all three films, as well as for *Miracle in Milan,* a neorealistic film with a strong comic vein that was released in 1951, De Sica's screenplays were written by Cesare Zavattini, a leading spokesman for the neorealist movement.

Two other significant films that belong to this group, both released in 1948, are Visconti's impressive *The Earth Trembles,* which relates the downfall of a family of Sicilian fishing people in a somewhat more dramatic fashion than the films already mentioned; and Giuseppe De Santis's *Bitter Rice* (1949), a film about female workers in the rice fields of Italy with a distracting erotic emphasis on Silvana Mangano. The neorealist movement ended in the early 1950s because of improving social conditions, the government's crackdown on unpatriotic films, the financial difficulties of these films (most of them were not successful in Italy and their novelty was rapidly dissipating in foreign

markets), and their directors' desire to move on to other types of film. But neorealism was to have an influence on future films: in Italy, on the works of Ermanno Olmi directly and on works by Antonioni, Fellini, Pasolini, and Petri to a lesser degree; in the United States, in a general manner, on *film-noir* works; and in India specifically on Satyajit Ray's *Apu* trilogy (1955–57) and other films. *See* **realism.**

■ **net** Cloth mesh in a holder that is attached to a stand and placed in front of a lamp to diffuse light. *See* **scrim** *(1).*

■ **net profit participant** Any participant in the making of a film (e.g., a star, producer, or director) who is contracted to receive a flat sum or percentage based upon the film's net profits. *See* **breakeven** *and* **gross profit participant.**

■ **net profits** The amount of money remaining from the gross receipts after negative costs, distribution expenses, and gross profit participations have been deducted. *See* **breakeven** *and* **gross.**

■ **neutral** A color image basically composed of black, white, and gray, with little color definition.

■ **neutral angle** A camera angle more or less at eye level with the action directly in front. *See* **camera angle.**

■ **neutral density filter** A gray camera filter of gelatin or glass that reduces the amount of light entering the camera without altering the color quality or definition of the image. Such filters are employed so that proper definition or reduced depth of field can be achieved without closing down the aperture. Graduated neutral density filters are employed to reduce light from only part of a scene (e.g., from a bright sky).

■ **New American Cinema** Avant-garde, experimental films made in America since the Second World War and through the 1970s. The name came from the New American Cinema Group, established in 1960, and had been especially propagated by Jonas Mekas and his journal *Film Culture.* The New American Cinema was a reaction to commercial film in both subject matter and technique. Its filmmakers, working independently and inexpensively outside the film industry and without the support of the industry's distribution and exhibition facilities, were free to be bold and individual in their works. Sixteen-millimeter film was mostly used, though smaller-gauge film and videotape were also employed. Anthology Film Archives, a film museum in New York City directed by Mekas, still makes the most significant works from this group available. Also important in support of these films was the New York Film-Makers' Cooperative and Canyon Cinema in San Francisco.

Technically, the New American Cinema began during the war years with the films of Maya Deren, especially her well-known *Meshes of the Afternoon* (1943; also made by Alexander Hammid), a personal dream vision that breaks down the wall between subjective and objective reality. But the movement was more closely associated with the dynamic developments that took place in experimental films during the turbulent 1960s—boldness, scorn for accepted social and aesthetic value, and extreme statements in form and content were also in part a result of the social and political events of the time. P. Adams Sitney has made the distinction between graphic films that focus on the medium of film itself (e.g., on light and dark, flicker, and the individual frame) and subjective films that deal with dream and symbol (in *Film Culture Reader*). Although he rarifies this view in *Visionary Cinema*, we can, for convenience, place in the first group films by Harry Smith, Jordan Belson, Robert Breer, and Stan Vanderbeek and in the second group works by Kenneth Anger, Stan Brakhage, and Gregory Markopoulas. Sitney, in *Visionary Cinema*, has also defined the "structural film" as a category that synthesizes both "the formalist graphic film and romantic lyrical film," that deemphasizes content and emphasizes the film's total shape, that "evokes states of consciousness . . . with the sole mediation of the camera." In this group he includes works by Michael Snow, Hollis Frampton, and Paul Sharits. *See* **avant-garde cinema** *and* **structural film.**

New American Cinema *Meshes of the Afternoon* (1943), Maya Deren's influential dream vision.

■ ■ ■

■ **new angle** A direction sometimes used in a film script to indicate a change in the camera's angle when viewing a subject. This direction indicates the need for a variation in the shot but leaves the specific angle up to the director.

■ **New Line Cinema Corporation** The most successful of the independent film distribution/production organi-

zations of the past thirty years, the company was founded in 1967 by Robert Shaye as a small distributor of foreign films. The company moved into high gear with the remarkable success of Wes Craven's *Nightmare on Elm Street* in 1984 and the subsequent series based on this film. Lightning struck a second time with *Teenage Mutant Ninja Turtles* in 1990 (dir. Stuart Gillard) and its subsequent series. The company has continued to do well through a good sense of public tastes and shrewd marketing strategies. In 1991, New Line founded Fine Line Features to make and distribute films of quality that would not do as well at the box office. Fine Line has distributed such films as Robert Altman's *The Player* (1992), and the powerful documentary *Hoop Dreams* (1994; dir. Steve James, Peter Gilbert, and Frederick Marx). In 1993, the company was purchased by Turner Broadcasting System with the guarantee of maintaining its independence and making higher-budgeted films. In 1995, Turner Broadcasting System, with the New Line and Castle Rock film units, became part of the Motion Picture Association of America. In 1996, the merger of the Turner company with Time Warner was approved by the Federal Trade Commission. New Line's share of the domestic box office in 1995 was 7.1 percent.

■ **news feature, news magazine** A short, nonfiction film that deals in reportorial fashion with some news or public event or some topic of general interest. The *March of Time* was a significant series of such films produced in America between 1935 and 1951. *See* **March of Time.**

■ **news film, newsfilm** Any film containing news events, whether newsreels or features.

■ **newsreel** A short film of anywhere from ten to twenty minutes that presents coverage of a series of news events and topics of special interest. Newsreels were an established part of film programs in movie theaters until they were replaced by television news coverage in the 1950s. Several theaters in major cities had even presented entire programs of newsreels. Film recordings of actual events were made by the Lumière brothers' cameramen as early as the last years of the nineteenth century (e.g., the coronation of Czar Nicholas II in Russia in 1896); and in the early days of silent films in this country such events were a staple of film programs (e.g., audiences could witness President McKinley's political campaign, inauguration, and funeral). Although political and military events were often staged for film, it is amazing how much authentic news film there was and what a wide expanse of America and Europe was covered. The first actual newsreel (i.e., a series of news items in a single reel) appeared in France from Pathé Frères in 1908, and soon after similar newsreels appeared in other countries. Events of the First World War were brought home to the public both in America and Europe through the newsreel; and Dziga Vertov put on film, from 1922 to 1925, the achievements of post-Revolutionary Russia in the *Kino-Pravda* newsreels.

The first sound newsreel was Fox Film Corporation's Movietone News in 1927, which became an instant success and established the newsreel pattern for coming years: important news stories with on-the-spot coverage, interviews with significant personalities, and feature stories. Each episode was introduced by a short title, shown with music and sound in the background, and accompanied by a voice-over commentary explaining the events and tying the images together. In the Second World War, the newsreel again became an important informational as well as propaganda tool for American and European governments. Television news programs eventually took the place of motion-picture newsreels after the war years and offered improvements in filming with portable equipment that permitted better on-the-spot coverage and satellite communication which immediately brought to the viewer events from the entire world. While the motion-picture newsreel had always been more for entertainment than information and more nationalistic than objective, national television news programs, especially from the time of the Vietnam War, have tended to be more analytical and skeptical.

■ **Newton's rings** A pattern of rings that appears when light passes through two surfaces a small distance apart. The phenomenon may appear on a film print if the negative and positive were not properly in contact during contact printing or if two glass filters were not properly situated in front of the camera's lens during shooting.

■ **New Wave, *Nouvelle Vague*** A movement in French cinema beginning in the late 1950s and peaking by 1962 that sought innovation in subject matter and technique. The movement itself, a response to the moribund French movie industry, received its major impetus from a small group of film enthusiasts who began their careers writing for the film journal *Cahiers du cinéma* and who were especially influenced by the film criticism of one of the journal's founders, André Bazin. These critics, François Truffaut, Claude Chabrol, Jean-Luc Godard, Eric Rohmer, and Jacques Rivette, wrote against traditional and predictable film practices and argued for a more individual style of film making under the individual inspiration and vision of the director. The first of the New Wave films is considered Chabrol's *Le Beau Serge* (*Bitter Reunion,* 1958), though 1959 marked the true rise of the movement with Truffaut's unsentimental and honest autobiographical portrait of an alienated youth, *The 400 Blows,* Resnais's brilliant narration of a love affair between a Japanese man and French woman ravaged by memories of the Second World War, *Hiroshima Mon Amour,* and Godard's irreverent, unsentimental, and comic homage to the American gangster film, *Breathless.* Because of the critical acclaim and international popularity of

New Wave *Jules and Jim* (1961; dir. François Truffaut), with Jeanne Moreau, Henri Serre, and Oskar Werner pleasantly romping together in a happier moment.

■ ■ ■

these films, the French movie industry in the next two years sponsored works by some sixty new directors, although only a small group of these filmmakers were financially successful enough to continue their careers.

Although the New Wave directors are marked by individual approaches and sensibilities, the following elements are considered central to the movement: (1) an irreverent, untraditional, and generally unsentimental treatment of character; (2) a loose, realistic, or innovative plot structure; (3) the use of lightweight, portable cameras and equipment that results in more spontaneous and realistic picture and sound; (4) much on-location and outdoor shooting; (5) elliptical cutting that draws attention to the relation between images as well as between image and sound and to the medium itself; (6) experimentation with filmic space and time; (7) allusions to earlier films to mark the continuity and discontinuity of tradition, to comment on the specific work's own self-reflexive quality as a movie, and also to pay homage to specific directors or films; and (8) a general existential attitude to an absurd universe and especially to human behavior and action. One must, of course, make distinctions between the more romantically inclined works of Truffaut, the political radicalism of Godard, the structural experimentation of Resnais, the moral sensibility of Rohmer, the theatricality of Rivette, and the eclecticism of Louis Malle.

Some other highly acclaimed films from this movement were Truffaut's *Shoot the Piano Player* (1960) and *Jules et Jim* (1961); Godard's *My Life to Live* (1962); and Resnais's *Last Year at Marienbad* (1961). Most of these directors went on to develop each in his own way; but there can be no question of the *Nouvelle Vague*'s impact on international cinema, an impact which was to help free the cinema in the United States and Germany, for example, from conventionality and tradition and contribute to the movement toward *auteur* filmmaking in these nations. *See* **auteur.**

■ **New World Cinema** Begun by Roger Corman and his brother Gene Corman in 1970, this independent production/distribution company became very successful by releasing a number of low-budget, exploitative films—its first success was *The Student Nurses* in 1960 that launched a series of subsequent "nurse" films. But New World Cinema has left a respectable paragraph in film history for two reasons: it distributed some very fine foreign films that included Ingmar Bergman's *Cries and Whispers* (1973) and Federico Fellini's *Amarcord* (1974), and also gave such directors as Peter Bogdanovich and Jonathan Demme their early opportunities in filmmaking. The company went out of business soon after Corman sold it in 1983 for $17 million.

■ **New York Motion Picture Company** Adam Kessel, Jr., and Charles O. Bauman, two former bookies who could no longer obtain films to rent from their exchange, went into the production business themselves and made their first film, the one-reel *Disinherited Son's Loyalty* in 1909, and also sent a group to Los Angeles the same year to make one-reel films. They called their production company Bison Life Motion Pictures. Although a rival to the production groups in the Motion Picture Patents Company, the New York Motion Picture Company had considerable success and should be remembered for starting the Keystone Comedies, run by Mack Sennett, and bringing Charlie Chaplin to films as well as for sending Thomas H. Ince from New York to California to direct the Bison Films. Ince formed Inceville and brought William S. Hart to the movies. The company never moved past making two- or three-reelers. In 1916, Kessler and Bauman sold their film production units for $1 million, and the company went out of business the following year.

■ **NG takes** A take which is "no good" and hence not usable. The film is thus designated because of poor quality in acting, some technical error, or because it simply does not satisfy the director.

■ **nickel cadmium battery, nicad battery** A battery used to power a camera instead of the lead-sulphuric type because it is portable, less expensive, and rechargeable.

■ **nickelodeon** An early type of motion-picture theater (frequently a converted store, arcade, or hall) with a seating capacity of approximately one hundred. Such theaters presented continuous shows of one- and two-reel films, anywhere from fifteen minutes to an hour, to the accompaniment of piano music. The term itself comes from the original "nickel" price of admission and the Greek word for theater, "odeon." The first of

these small film houses was opened in 1905 by John P. Harris and Harry Davis in a converted store in Pittsburgh. It is estimated that by 1910 there were 10,000 nickelodeons in the United States. The rise of the feature film was instrumental in ushering in the larger and more comfortable movie theaters, many of them newly built, which succeeded the nickelodeon. *See* **movie house.**

■ **night filter** A camera filter that gives a nighttime effect to a shot taken in daylight—a red filter is generally used with black-and-white film for this purpose, while a graduated neutral density filter might be used with color film, though this second process is less effective.

■ **night for day** Shooting a scene at night with sufficient lighting so that the scene appears in the film as if it were shot during the day.

■ **night for night, nite for nite** Shooting a night scene during the night on location, generally with a fast film stock and lens as well as sufficient supplementary lighting, as distinct from "night shooting," which means working in the studio at night. *See* **day for night.**

■ **night premium** Some type of increased compensation given for working during a shoot, generally after 8 P.M.

■ **nine-light** A popular multiple luminaire made of three banks of three spotlights, each lamp a module with its own switch, though the entire luminaire can work with a single switch.

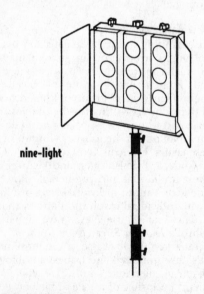

nine-light

■ **ninety/ten deal, 90/10 deal** A contractual obligation between the distributor and exhibitor whereby the exhibitor, after subtracting the house nut (the house expenses), gives the distributor 90 percent of the gross box office. During subsequent weeks the percentage for the distributor decreases, often by 10 percent. Such an arrangement is normally for the release of special films. *See* **distribution.**

■ **nit** The metric unit for the brightness or luminance of a light source. A nit is equal to one candela per square meter. *See* **footlambert.**

■ **nitrate base** A film base made of cellulose nitrate, which was generally used for commercial 35mm film until 1951. Because this base was highly flammable and prone to deterioration, it was replaced by a triacetate base starting in 1951. *See* **acetate base** *and* **film** *(1).*

■ **nitrate film** Thirty-five millimeter film made until 1951 with a nitrate base.

■ **nitrogen-burst agitation** An older method of agitating the chemical solution around the film during processing by means of releasing nitrogen bubbles into the liquid. An agitation pump is more often used today. *See* **processing.**

■ **nodal head, nodal point mount** A support used in special-effects cinematography that permits the camera to pan or tilt by turning exactly on one of the nodal points of the lens, preventing separation of hanging models or glass mattes from the background, or the subject from the background in front-projection shots. *See* **nodal points.**

■ **nodal points** The two conjugate points on the optical axis of a lens whereby a light ray entering the first will leave the second at the same angle to the axis. *See* **nodal head, principal focus,** *and* **principal points.**

■ **noise** (1) Unwanted sound in an audio system—namely, any hissing, static, popping, or flutter that is heard when the signal is amplified. *See* **noise floor.** (2) Any smoke, fog, or some such obscuring agent used to hide part of a scene in order to avoid the expense and bother of creating its details.

■ **noise floor** The hiss heard when a magnetic tape with no sound recorded is played back. *See* **dynamic range** *and* **signal-to-noise ratio**.

■ **noiseless camera** Any camera that is so encased (i.e., "blimped") that it will make a minimal amount of noise during shooting to allow for sound recording.

■ **noise reduction** The diminishment of noise in an audio system by an electronic process. *See* **Dolby.**

■ **nonabrasion layer** *See* **supercoat.**

■ **noncamera film, out-of-camera-film, cameraless animation, handmade film** A type of short motion picture for which abstract or representational forms are made directly on the emulsion by painting, drawing, or etching instead of through normal photography. Len Lye made the influential abstract film *Colour Box* in 1935 by painting on the stock and called such works "direct film." Norman McLaren, who was influenced by Lye, painted more recognizable linear forms on film in such works as *Blinkety Blank* (1955). *See* **abstract film** *and* **direct film.**

■ **nondestructive editing** The term applies to the capacity of nonlinear editing to make all kinds of changes in image and sound without affecting the source material since the editing is performed on a digital version, and also to recall, at any time, picture and sound in their originally digitized form. *See* **nonlinear editing.**

■ **nondirectional microphone** A microphone that picks up general sound from the surrounding area and not from any specific direction. Also called an omnidirectional microphone. *See* **microphone.**

■ **non-disclosure agreement** A contractual agreement in which confidentiality concerning some project is promised by one party to another—e.g., a film company promises a writer that all information concerning the plot and characters of his or her screenplay will be kept secret. *See* **submission release.**

■ **nonexclusive contract** A contract between a performer, director, or some other film person and a studio guaranteeing him or her work on a certain number of films but also permitting the individual to work outside the studio.

■ **nonfiction film** Any film that presents actual rather than fictional situations and people. Richard Barsam, in *Non-fiction Film*, includes in this category "documentary itself; factual films; travel films; educational, training, or classroom films; newsreels, and animated or cartoon films." He distinguishes the documentary from the factual film because of its "sociopolitical purpose" but includes both in the general category of nonfiction films. *See* **documentary.**

■ **nonflammable film** Film with a low flammable base, generally triacetate instead of the flammable nitrate base originally used for professional 35mm film until 1951. Polyester is now also used as a nonflammable film base.

■ **nonlinear editing** Electronic and digital editing that allows one "random access" to any scenes in any order without having to move through the motion picture sequentially and that also allows one to try out numerous edits and sequences, sometimes watching two simultaneously on the screen, before committing to a single version. Nonlinear editing is the newest development in motion picture editing and is being used for a greater number of films because it is more flexible, cheaper, and safer than traditional editing with a flat-bed. While traditional cutting on a flat-bed might still be used to create dailies and rough cuts to follow the shooting during production, nonlinear editing is also used to prepare cut lists and a video workprint for such early editing on film. Nonlinear editing is now very popular for editing the total film and creating a negative cut list for matching the negative or making a workprint from which the negative can be cut. Virtually unlimited hours of image and sound from a film can digitally be transformed and stored on hard drives by means of a telecine. The motion picture can be called up at 24 frames per second, while pictures and audio are synced by edge numbers or a burned-in time code. Fades, dissolves, wipes, superimpositions, and blue-screen effects can be tried out and previewed. Images and sound can be altered, manipulated, and auditioned in a "virtual recording," which means that the editor is not actually recording on a tape but is making a list of editing decisions—the process is referred to as "off-line" editing and the result is generally an edit-decision list (EDL) or a negative cut list. The term "nondestructive editing" is also used to describe this type of digital editing since the source material is not used and, hence, can not be affected, and since picture and sound can be recalled at any time in their originally recorded form. The EDL is used to make an edit master tape in the case of video, though some nonlinear systems have sufficient memory and storage to move into the next stage of on-line editing and produce a digital master tape. The negative cut list is used to conform the actual negative of the motion picture or, sometimes, first to assemble a workprint. Nonlinear systems, such as the Eddiflex, were introduced in the mid 1980s and employed a large number of videotape machines, allowing the separate machines to play different shots in any order for nonlinear editing (though not allowing total random access, since each tape still had to be run sequentially). Nonlinear, random-access machines that digitized both sound and picture began to be used for television postproduction work and soon made their way into the movie industry. The Avid Media Composer was introduced in 1989 and since that time has developed into a series of nonlinear editing systems that has become a staple in the video and film industries. The Avid Media Composer 8000 allows off-line, on-line, and film editing, while the Avid Film Composer is designed primarily for film editing. Also much used for motion pictures is the Lightworks Off-line editing system. The terms linear and nonlinear for editing systems have been used only since the late 1980s when the sudden rise of digital editing made the difference between the two processes apparent. See computer, editing, off-line editing, on-line editing, random access, and telecine. *See* **Avid Media Composer.**

■ **non-real time** The term is applied to the processes of transferring, recording, or rendering a series of movie images that take more or less time than the normal 24 frames per second for filming. For example, film scanners and film recorders transfer images into and from a digital code respectively at a much slower speed so that full negative resolution can be maintained. *See* **film recorder** *and* **film scanner.**

■ **nonreflexive viewfinder** *See* **side viewfinder.**

■ **nonsubstantive film** Film for which the couplers—i.e., the chemicals for producing color dyes—are in the developing solution and not in the emulsion itself. Traditional Super 8mm and 16mm Kodachrome, for example, are nonsubstantive films. *See* **film** *(1).*

■ **nonsynchronous sound, nonsync sound, wild sound** Sound that is neither matched to the image on the screen nor recorded at the time of shooting. The audience might hear some background noise or even dialogue at the conclusion of one scene that belongs to and therefore anticipates the next scene; sound that does not belong to the action on the screen might also be used as a contrast to what we see. Both Eisenstein and Pudovkin saw nonsynchronous sound as a potential element in montage, playing in counterpoint to the images. *See* **asynchronous sound** *and* **synchronous sound.**

■ **nontheatrical distribution** Distribution of films not to commercial theaters but to schools, clubs, film societies, and similar organizations that do not make a profit by exhibiting them. A number of distributors specialize in this kind of distribution and normally charge a fixed rate for exhibition.

■ **nontheatrical film** Any film, for example, an educational or industrial film, not made for theatrical distribution.

■ **nook light** A small, portable, open-faced light, made by Mole Richardson, that can be placed unobtrusively in the nooks and crannies of a set and that creates a hard, unfocused illumination.

■ **no print** An instruction on the camera report to the laboratory that a certain take should not be printed, since it is known to be deficient.

■ **normal angle** An angle of view that approximates what the eye would see, taken with what is considered a "normal lens"—for example, a lens with a focal length of 50mm for a 35mm camera. *See* **normal lens.**

■ **normal lens** A lens that gives an image approximate to what the eye would see, one with a focal length about twice the diagonal of the frame and a horizontal angle of approximately 25 degrees. A normal lens for a 35mm camera has a focal length of 50mm; for a 16mm camera a focal length of 25mm; and for a nonanamorphic 65mm camera a focal length of 125mm. *See* **focal length** *and* **lens.**

■ **north** In animation work, the top of the drawing table, animation stand, drawing, or cel as opposed to the south, or bottom.

■ **novelization** A novel that has been made from the screenplay of a motion picture to bring in additional revenue. Such an ancillary product generally has little literary value except on occasion, as when Arthur Clarke clarified, to some degree, his screenplay for Stanley Kubrick's *2001: A Space Odyssey* (1968).

■ **NTSC** The initials stand for "National Television Standards Committee," the agency that standardized a 525 scan line system at 30 frames per second in the United States for television transmission and video recording that is referred to by these letters. *See* **HDTV, PAL,** *and* **SECAM.**

■ **nudie** A film with pornographic intent that features a good deal of nudity and explicit sex. Also called a skin flick. Such films play at special theaters. *See* **pornographic film.**

■ **number board** The clapboard or slate used to mark the commencement of a shot. *See* **clapboard.**

■ **nuts-and-bolts film** A simple and generally inartistic educational film that explains how to do something or gives factual information about some topic.

■   ■   ■

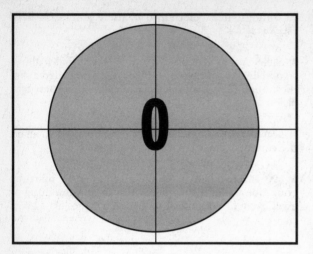

oater to oxidation

■ **oater** A Western movie. So named because horses eat oats, and Westerns have lots of horses.

■ **obie** A small spotlight of approximately 250 watts, frequently placed on top of or next to the camera to illuminate a character's face from the front in order to minimize lines and shadows. *See* **spotlight.**

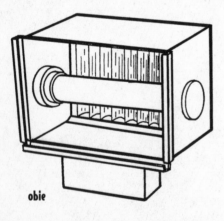

obie

■ **object animation** A technique for creating the illusion of a moving object by shooting the object a single frame at a time in stop-motion photography and altering its position or shape between shots. The term emphasizes that an actual object—for example, a model of an animal—is shot instead of artwork. *See* **animation.**

■ **objective** The lens in a camera or some other optical system that receives the light rays and forms the image of the subject on the focal plane.

■ **objective camera** Camera technique whereby the camera seems to be an objective viewer of the scene. To present such a neutral view, camera movement and editing are minimal and the camera angle is at eye level. Such a technique is more normal in the documentary, but a number of narrative films have attempted to create a factual or sometimes documentary aura by relying on the objective camera (e.g., Costa-Gavras's *Z* [1968]). *See* **subjective camera.**

■ **obligatory scene** Any scene that seems necessary and is expected by audiences in a particular type of plot. For example, the obligatory shootout between the hero and the villain in a Western or the obligatory nude love scene in a contemporary film romance.

■ **oblique angle, oblique frame** An image that is photographed with the camera tilted so that when the scene appears on the screen, characters and objects will seem to lean to a side. This shot is often used to suggest the subjective perspective of an inebriated or hallucinating character. It has also been frequently employed to create a sense of disequilibrium and tension in the audience during fight scenes or during macabre events in a horror film. In Robert Wise's *The Haunting* (1963), the camera presents an oblique angle of ninety degrees so that Julie Harris appears to be ascending the spiral staircase horizontally across the screen. In the context of the scene, the technique adds considerably to the audience's sense of fright and foreboding.

■ **observation port** The opening in the projection booth through which the projectionist is able to observe both the screen and the audience.

■ **octopus box** *See* **spider box.**

■ **off-balance lighting** Lighting in which illumination and shadows are not evenly balanced or integrated. A pool of light might dramatically illuminate a character or object against a stark black background or next to a stark black area. John Carpenter effectively uses this kind of lighting in *Halloween* (1978) when the heroine is seen several times next to or in front of a completely black closet, window, or area of the room from which the murderer suddenly emerges. *See* **lighting balance.**

■ **off-camera** That part of the scene that is not within the camera's field of view (e.g., a character whom we know to be part of the action but who is not immediately visible on the screen).

■ **off-camera turn** A turn away from the camera by a performer so that he or she is looking to the side or upstage. *See* **on-camera turn.**

■ **off-line editing** In both video and digital linear and nonlinear editing, the preliminary work of making an edit-decision list (EDL) for creating the edit video master or, in the case of film, a negative cut list for conforming the negative. Sometimes a rough cut on tape is made from video off-line, linear editing. On-line editing is the making of the actual edit video master or recording the digitally edited work onto film. *See* **linear editing** *and* **nonlinear editing.**

■ **off-microphone, off-mike** Any sound or speech not properly covered by the microphone's directional pattern, and so poorly registered.

■ **off-screen (OS)** Any character, object, or action not seen on the screen but known to be part of the scene or near the location photographed; or any sound originating from such an area. We might hear an offscreen voice or watch a character viewing an offscreen action.

■ **offset viewfinder** *See* **side viewfinder.**

■ **OK takes** Takes that are satisfactory and should be developed by the laboratory for inclusion in the workprint.

■ **omnidirectional microphone** A microphone that picks up sound from all directions. Although not very effective for a specific conversation or localized sound, this microphone is useful for picking up the general noise in an area. *See* **microphone.**

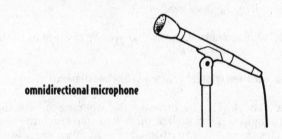

omnidirectional microphone

■ **Omnimax** *See* **IMAX.**

■ **on a bell** A term used during production either on a sound stage or on location to indicate that shooting is taking place or is about to take place, and everyone should stop activity and remain quiet.

■ **on call** When a performer or member of the crew is not actually working on the set or location but is available and ready to come if beckoned.

■ **on-camera** Any performer, object, or action visible in the camera's field of action during shooting.

■ **on-camera narration** A narration delivered by a narrator who is seen on screen while he or she speaks.

■ **on-camera turn** Any turn made by a performer so that his or her face rotates toward the camera. *See* **off-camera turn.**

■ **180-degree rule** *See* **imaginary line.**

■ **one-light dailies, one-lite dailies, best light dailies** Dailies that are timed with a single light to achieve a generally overall decent quality. *See* **timing.**

■ **one-light dupe.** A dupe negative that contains all the lighting changes so that any print made from it can be exposed at a single lighting level. *See* **one-light print** *and* **timing.**

■ **one-light print, one-line print** A print made from a dupe negative that already contains all the lighting changes, so that the entire print is exposed at a single lighting level *See* **one-light dupe, one-light workprint,** *and* **timing.**

■ **one-light workprint, one-line print** Any print made with a single exposure setting, whether the negative contains all the lighting changes or not. A one-light, untimed print is often made as a workprint for editing or for matching sound. *See* **scratchprint** *and* **timing.**

■ **one-reeler** A short film, generally about fifteen minutes in silent-film days and eleven minutes with sound. Most early silent films were one or two reelers before the rise of the feature film.

■ **ones** Frames that are exposed one at a time, in stop-motion photography, for each set of cels or movement of the model in the animation process. "Twos" refers to the shooting of two frames for each change in the drawings or model, and "threes" to three frames for each change. *See* **animation** *and* **stop motion.**

■ **one sheets** Posters for a film, generally twenty-seven by forty-one inches, which are displayed in front of a theater or in its lobby.

■ **one-shot** A shot with a single person in the frame. A medium one-shot would show a single person from the waist up or the full figure of a sitting person.

■ **one-to-one** (1) The exact transfer of sound from one monaural magnetic track to another. (2) In the use of an optical printer, the frame-by-frame exposure of fresh film to a print or negative without any omissions or duplications of frames for various effects. *See* **optical printer.**

■ **one-way set** A set made of a single flat background.

■ **on-line editing** In both video and digital editing, making the actual edit master video, or in digital editing, recording the finished work onto film. When making the master video, the time code from the edit-decision list (EDL) or the rough cut is employed to shape the various scenes and also to place them in the proper order. Corrections can also be made for lighting and color, and graphics, special effects, and sound added. The digitally edited work is transferred to film by means of a film recorder. *See* **edit controller, film recorder,** *and* **off-line editing.**

■ **on location** Shooting away from the studio, either inside a building or outdoors at an actual site. The location photographed does not necessarily have to be the place depicted in the film as long as it is real and not a studio set. Many location sites are altered for filming. *See* **location.**

■ **on ones** Animation created with the camera shooting each set of cels or position of the model one frame at a time. Such stop-motion photography creates the most fluid movement for the animated figures. "On twos" means that the artwork or model is identical for two frames at a time, "on threes" for three frames. *See* **animation.**

■ **on-screen** Any action taking place or character appearing within the frame as opposed to those supposedly "off-screen" and not appearing in the frame.

■ **on speculation, on spec** (1) Making a film independently without any prior funding from or contract with a studio, production company, or distributor with the expectation of recouping costs and making a profit through a later sale or agreement. (2) Writing a screenplay without any prior request or contract from a film company or any group or individual in the hope of later selling the work.

■ **on the nose** Shooting a scene with the lens set at the exact f-stop or t-stop number indicated by the exposure meter. *See* **exposure meter, f-stop,** *and* **t-stop.**

■ **opacity** The degree to which a material prevents light from passing through. The opacity of a film emulsion is figured by the ratio of incident light to transmitted light, though a better way of computing this quality is by measuring the emulsion's density. *See* **density.**

■ **opaque** The state of any material through which light is not transmitted. Printed photographs are opaque as opposed to printed film for motion pictures, which is transparent.

■ **opaque leader** Any piece of film used as a leader to thread a reel into a projector or printing machine which is opaque and cannot transmit light. Such film is also used in checkerboard cutting. *See* **checkerboard cutting** *and* **leader.**

■ **opaquer, painter, colorer** The individual who fills in the areas of the artwork on cels with color for animated cartoons. *See* **animation** *and* **inker.**

■ **opaquing** In cartoon work, filling in areas of the artwork on the cel with solid colors. The individual who does this job is called an opaquer or painter. *See* **animation** *and* **inking.**

■ **open captioned** Titles superimposed over the bottom of the image in a motion picture that give the dialogue and describe important sounds and music for the hearing impaired. Such prints are made available sometimes at university or institutional facilities and rarely at public theaters. *See* **caption** *and* **closed caption.**

■ **open-face light** A luminaire that has no lens and so creates a wider and more diffuse light, one more difficult to control than a light beamed through a Fresnel lens. Broads and nooks are open-face lights, for example. *See* **lighting.**

■ **open form** A film style that, in opposition to closed form, seems spontaneous and immediate, unplanned and informal, thus creating a more realistic and natural image of the physical world. The *mise-en-scène* seems to be just the way the scene was found in reality, with no formal structure and inherent composition, as if it were open and extended outside the limits of the frame. The position and movement of the camera seem spontaneous in that it follows the action; and even the action of the characters seems undetermined and free. *See* **closed form.**

■ **opening credits** Credits that appear at the start of the film. *See* **credits** *and* **title.**

■ **open-reel recorder** *See* **reel-to-reel tape recorder.**

■ **open up** (1) To increase the opening in the diaphragm of a lens so that more light can reach the film. This operation is performed by selecting a lower f-stop number on the calibration ring. Closing down the diaphragm requires the opposite procedure. (2) To develop or extend the action of a plot by adding scenes and actions that generally take place away from the central location or setting.

■ **opera film** *See* **film opera.**

■ **operator, operating cameraman** *See* **camera operator.**

■ **optical axis** In an optical system, an imaginary line passing through the focal point and actual center of a lens and extending into infinity. Such a line is the symmetrical center of the formed image.

■ **optical composite** A composite shot achieved in an optical printer. *See* **composite** *(2) and* **special effects.**

■ **optical disc** *See* **video disc.**

■ **optical effect animation** Animation achieved through optical effects: for example, a series of dissolves to progressively smaller or larger images of the same object to convey shrinking or growth. *See* **optical effects.**

■ **optical effects, opticals** Special effects generally achieved in an optical printer using already exposed film. Optical effects alter the original image by duplicating it on a second or later generation film with some alteration in lighting or exposure or with new image components added. Optical effects might be employed to create such transitions from one scene to another as dissolves, fades, or wipes; to alter the size of the image; to freeze or change the speed of the action; to combine live action and animation or characters and a new setting through matting techniques. Sometimes rear and front projection, though not dependent on optical printers, are incorrectly referred to as opticals to maintain an easy distinction between those effects dependent on photographic equipment and those achieved mechanically on the set in front of the camera. Many of the effects created with an optical printer are now also achieved digitally. *See* **digital effects, mechanical effects, optical printer,** *and* **special effects.**

■ **optical flip, optical flop** A flip (i.e., a transition in which one scene flips over, revealing another) achieved with an optical printer. *See* **flip** *and* **optical printer.**

■ **optical house** A film laboratory that specializes in optical printing. *See* **optical printer.**

■ **optical layout** In animation work, information sheets for the camera operator that specify the duration of scenes, the type of transitions between scenes, and optical effects. *See* **animation layout.**

■ **optical master** A master print made in an optical printer and used for making release prints. *See* **optical printer.**

■ **optical multiplexer** *See* **film chain.**

■ **optical print** A print made in an optical printer. *See* **optical printer.**

■ **optical printer** An optical printing system in which the images from a negative or positive are projected onto raw stock. The printer is basically composed of a projector and camera facing one another, with a light source behind the film in the projector sending the image onto a lens, which then focuses it on the raw stock in the camera. Both projector and camera are interlocked in synchronized movement so that each frame is rephotographed. There are two types of such machines, the continuous optical printer, which is largely used for reducing film formats, and the more extensively employed optical step printer, with which the re-

mainder of this essay is concerned. Optical step printers vary in complexity, some, for example, having two or more projectors and a beam splitter for combining picture elements from separate films into a single image. Since the system in general offers a considerable amount of flexibility in light intensity, lens and camera position, lens types, and film speed, and since it also allows a dupe negative to be exposed on various runs to different fine-grain master positives, numerous effects can be achieved that are impossible in normal contact printing. For this reason optical printing performs a wide variety of special functions.

A common use of the optical printer is to make transitions in the final film from one scene to another. Fade-outs are achieved by slowly closing the shutter on the camera and fade-ins by slowly opening it while the frames on the master positive are photographed. Dissolves are made by first photographing the fade-out of one scene and then photographing the fade-in of the next on the same piece of film. Though not much in use today, wipes are achieved by means of a wipe blade that moves across the image between the projector and camera, gradually matting out the picture being photographed on the new film. The blade is used again gradually to expose the second image into the matted area of the same piece of film. Variations of the wipe are achieved with the second image moving from top or bottom or expanding from the center of the frame. The capacity of the optical printer to expose the same negative to different positives in multiple runs also allows for the superimposition of two images to create hallucinatory or supernatural effects, or superimpositions of a number of images to suggest the passing of time or events occurring concurrently (*see* **montage** [5]).

Stationary mattes are employed in optical printers for various types of split-screen effects where two or more images appear simultaneously in different parts of the frame as well as for combining a foreground with a separate setting or with artwork. Traveling mattes (generally a separate reel of film run in bipack with the positive) allow the merging of separately shot image components that contain movement into a single picture—action photographed in the studio can be combined with action or scenery shot elsewhere, with animation created from stop-motion photography, or with mechanical-effects shots of fire or explosions. Any number of separately shot components can be combined into a single image by the use of mattes and multiple runs—for example, in such a "special-effects" film as *Blade Runner* (1982; dir. Ridley Scott), anywhere from thirty to forty elements were used for a number of final images (*see* **traveling-matte process**).

By altering the speed of the printer's photographing process, the speed of the action can also be altered. For example, if the projector is accelerated so that the camera only photographs alternate frames, the action will appear twice as fast as its actual occurrence (this technique is called "skip-frame printing"); and, conversely, if the camera runs faster than the projector so that each frame is photographed twice, the action will slow down to half its normal speed (this technique is called "multiple-frame printing"). A number of alterations can be made in the image itself by placing some device between the projector and camera: an optical spin attachment allows the image to rotate, as in the case of the spinning newspaper in the American montages used frequently in early sound films; lenses distort, elongate, compress, or fragmentize the image in various patterns; and diffusion filters alter the color and lighting quality of the image. Anamorphic lenses widen squeezed images or compress normal images. Altering the distance between projector and camera also achieves a number of changes in the size and distance of pictorial elements. For example, by moving the camera and lens closer to the original film, a certain area of the image will be magnified so that it fills the new frame, thus, perhaps, changing a long shot to a medium shot. By gradually moving camera and lens forward or backward, thus enlarging or distancing the subject, an "optical zoom" is achieved. By photographing from a greater distance, the original image is diminished so that it fills only a small area of the frame, hence allowing the creation of either a composite image or split-screen effect.

Optical printers can also salvage poorly shot scenes by changing the perspective, altering the position or movement of objects, eliminating unwanted camera movement, reducing the image so that unwanted areas are eliminated, and correcting color and lighting. Even scratched film can be resurrected by rephotographing the positive after it has been immersed in a special fluid. Finally, optical printers are used to reduce larger-gauge images into smaller (for example, large-format images can be reduced and squeezed to anamorphic dimensions for 35mm film and 35mm film can be reduced to 16mm for noncommercial screenings) or to blow up a smaller gauge into a larger (it is possible to shoot with 16mm film and get a reasonably good 35mm blowup for commercial release).

The once-proud warhorse of the motion-picture industry, the optical printer is now having its territory in-

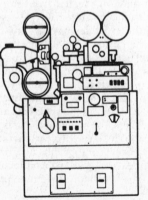

**optical step printer
(an early Acme printer)**

vaded. Digital effects are doing more easily and sometimes better the visual effects achieved by the earlier optical technology, although the optical printer in many instances is still less expensive to use and more effective for working with special effects on large-gauge film. *See* **contact printing, digital effects,** *and* **printer.**

■ **optical printing** Printing of film from another film by means of an optical printer as opposed to using a contact printer for the same process. *See* **contact printing** *and* **optical printer.**

■ **optical reader** *See* **reader** *(1).*

■ **optical reduction printing** Printing a film in a gauge smaller than the original in an optical printer. Optical reduction printers are used primarily for this function, although many other optical printers can be altered to perform this task. 35mm commercial films are generally reduced to 16mm for distribution to film societies and schools. A 16mm dupe negative made in the optical printer is used in contact printing to make release prints.

■ **opticals** *See* **optical effects.**

■ **optical sound** A system for the reproduction of sound in motion pictures that converts a photographed pattern of light into the original sound when the film passes through the projector. The original sound is picked up by a microphone and converted into electric impulses which either vary the intensity or area of a light beam photographed on a film. When this sound trace, on the composite print, passes a lamp in the projector, the variation in density or area of the optical track controls the intensity of light reaching a photoelectric cell and hence the variation in electrical impulses which the cell gives off. These impulses are then converted into the original sound and amplified. The two types of patterns formed on the film are called variable density and variable area. Although different equipment is used for recording each, both patterns can be played by any projector. In the first method, the optical pattern is composed of a series of separate striations of varying density running across the sound track, and in the second, of an oscillographic pattern with symmetrical outlines on both sides marking the variations of the sound waves. Both methods have been employed for sound reproduction in the motion picture industry, though variable-area tracks are now generally used because they are simpler to record with color stock. In the early days of sound film, optical processes were found preferable to the disc system because the sound track could be photographed along with the visuals on the same film, hence requiring only one system for playback of picture and sound and allowing more accurate synchronization. All sound reproduction was therefore optical until the 1950s, when magnetic tape was found easier and cheaper to use, allowing both instant playback and erasure while creating better sound. Magnetic recording soon became the norm in original recording, dubbing, and editing; but the finally edited magnetic sound track is still converted to an optical sound track to be photographed onto the married print, even though the sound quality in the optical system is not as good.

However, new improvements in optical sound playback systems, notably both the Dolby noise-reduction process and Dolby stereo channels, have greatly improved this type of optical sound. Such optical tracks are still largely maintained for exhibition because most projectors and theaters are designed for such systems, but release prints are now also offering optically encoded digital sound for the growing number of theaters equipped for this new audio playback system. *See* **digital sound recording, magnetic recording,** *and* **sound.**

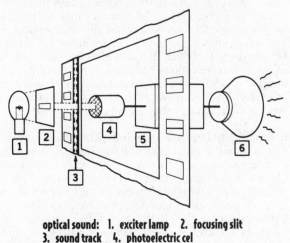

optical sound: 1. exciter lamp 2. focusing slit
3. sound track   4. photoelectric cel
5. amplifier   6. speaker

■ **optical sound head** The component in a projector or any sound playback system that converts the optical sound pattern on a film into electrical signals which are then converted into the original sound and amplified. A lamp reads the varying area or density of the photographed light pattern, and the changing intensity of its own light causes a photosensitive cell to produce the electrical impulses. A number of projectors are now also equipped with digital sound heads to read the optically encoded digital soundtrack. *See* **optical sound.**

■ **optical sound-recorder, optical sound camera** A recording machine used for sound reproduction. The sound waves are converted into electrical impulses which then control either the intensity or area of a light beam photographed on film. The varying density or area of the optical sound track will be converted back into electric impulses in the projector which will then be converted into sound. Today, magnetic recording is normally used for original recording, dubbing, and

editing, but variable-area optical recording is used for the actual playback in the theater. The finally edited master magnetic tape is converted into an optical sound track in a special optical sound recorder or camera. The sound signals from the magnetic tape control the area of light photographed from a bulb by means of a galvanometer or similar device. This sound track will generally be a negative so that it can be printed along with the picture negative onto the married print. Optical sound is often recorded as two channels for four-track stereo sound. Digital sound, which is now moving rapidly into motion-picture release, is also optically encoded on the film from a print master in a similar manner. *See* **optical sound** *and* **sound.**

■ **optical sound track, optical track** (1) The final photographed sound track that has been made from the master magnetic track and is ready to be combined with the picture on the composite print. (2) The photographed sound track that appears on a narrow band alongside the picture on the film. The area or density of photographed light is scanned by the light from a bulb in the projector, and the changing intensity of the light causes a photosensitive cell to produce various electrical impulses which are converted into the original sound and amplified. Two channels are now used for a four-track stereo playback system. (3) Any sound tracks appearing on a film that are recorded optically, whether for analog or digital sound. *See* **optical sound** *and* **projector.**

■ **optical transfer** The process of transferring the sound on a master magnetic track to an optical sound track or tracks in an optical sound recorder or camera. In the optical transfer the sound from the magnetic tape is transformed into a light pattern, which is photographed. This pattern can then be printed on the narrow sound band in the married print at the same time as the visuals. *See* **optical sound.**

■ **optical viewfinder** Any viewfinder using an optical system separate from that of the camera. Such a system has its own lens and eyepiece and produces a magnified, upright image of the subject being photographed. *See* **viewfinder.**

■ **optical zoom** A zoom effect achieved not with a camera and zoom lens but in an optical printer. A zoom-in is created by moving the camera and lens closer and closer to the film being photographed, and a zoom-out by moving them gradually further away. The advantage of this method is that the spacial distortions which come with a normal zoom shot are avoided; the disadvantage is that by enlarging the subject in a zoom-in made with an optical printer, the image becomes more grainy and less defined. *See* **optical printer.**

■ **optics** The field of physical science that deals with light and vision. Optics is especially relevant to film because it deals with the quality, intensity, and measurement of light given off from direct and reflected sources as well as the movement and refraction of light through various substances, especially lens components. *See* **lens.**

■ **option** The right to make an agreement by a specific time. The individual who takes the option pays a small amount of money, perhaps 5 or 10 percent of the final purchase price, for the right to buy the property, which may be a screenplay or book for film production. No one else can purchase the property before the agreed upon date. After the date, the individual owning the property is free to sell it to anyone else. Options allow producers time to put together a package for production and to find financial backing without losing rights to the property. An option can also be taken on a work that is not yet written, with the purchase deadline falling either on the date of completion or after a certain period of time following completion. If a screenplay is not completed at a specific time, the potential buyer can demand the return of the option fee.

■ **organ** A musical instrument with one or more keyboards that achieves a wide variety of sounds by means of compressed air passing through a series of pipes. Such organs were used in movie theaters to create music as an accompaniment to silent films. With the coming of sound films, organs became a special feature and supplied music before films. Even today, in the small number of old movie palaces that remain, such fine old instruments as those made by Wurlitzer can still be heard in concert or as accompaniment to special presentations of silent-film classics.

■ **orientable viewfinder** A flexible viewfinder that allows the camera operator to view the scene being shot no matter what his or her position or the position of the camera. This viewfinder is especially useful for shooting in confined or difficult places. *See* **viewfinder.**

■ **orientation shot** An establishing shot that communicates to the viewer information about the location, action, or situation. *See* **establishing shot.**

■ **original** (1) The direct recording of actual sound before it is rerecorded, edited, and mixed. (2) The camera-original reversal film used in the camera and made first into a negative and then into the positive. (3) *See* **original film.**

■ **original film, camera-original film, original negative** The processed film first used in the camera to photograph the production. The final editing is performed on the original negative, which is matched with the final workprint and printed along with the optical version of the master sound track on the composite or married print. Although some final adjustments in color or lighting can be made in printing the composite, the original represents the best quality of image since each following generation suffers from some degradation. For motion pictures requiring wide distribution, high-quality master positives are made from the original negative which are the source of dupe negatives used for making the release prints. Although original reversal film itself becomes the positive, this film is sometimes erroneously referred to as an "original negative" instead of, properly, as an "original." *See* **film** *(1).*

■ **original screenplay, original** A screenplay written directly for film production and not adapted from another form such as a novel or stage play. Academy Awards are today given for both the best screenplay "written directly for the screen" and the best screenplay "based on material from another medium." Original screenplays may be written in advance and then sold for a movie or they may be contracted to be written from an original idea or story line. The number of original screenplays in relation to adaptations has varied. During the years of the Hollywood studio system, when major film corporations had their own writing stables, original screenplays easily dominated. But works in other forms with already established reputations were much sought after, as they are now. *See* **screenwriter.**

■ **Orion Pictures Corporation** An independent motion picture and television production/distribution company first begun in 1978 by five former executives from United Artists (the name "Orion" was taken from a constellation mistakenly attributed with five stars). In its early years, the company produced such hits as Blake Edwards's *10* (1979) and, after merging with Filmways Pictures in 1982, went on to release such popular films as Oliver Stone's *Platoon* in 1986, Paul Verhoeven's *Robocop* in 1987, and the Academy Award–winning pictures by Kevin Costner, *Dances with Wolves* in 1990, and by Jonathan Demme, *Silence of the Lambs* in 1991. Orion also released Woody Allen's films during the 1980s. Orion's rise seemed phenomenal, the company taking in 10.4 percent and 8.5 percent of the domestic box office in 1987 and 1991 respectively—but the company unfortunately had overextended itself. With debts of more than $1 billion, it filed for bankruptcy in December of 1991. With an influx of money from John Kluge, the company came out of bankruptcy in October of 1992 and formed a production unit with Metromedia in 1993, but since that time has remained relatively quiet.

■ **orthochromatic film, ortho film** Black-and-white film sensitive to both the green and blue areas of the color spectrum but blind to the red area. Green and blue colors photograph in varying shades of gray, but reds appear as black. Orthochromatic film was normally employed during the silent-film period. Because of this film's insensitivity to the red area, the image still had a tendency to seem highly contrasted, and its quality has often been described as "soot and whitewash." Because of this limitation, heavy makeup had to be used on performers to neutralize the red tone of Caucasian skin; and shooting in studios where this color area could be eliminated from artificial lights and sets was preferred to outdoor shooting. Orthochromatic film is considered "fast film" in that its emulsion is extremely sensitive to light. Because of its speed, this film could be shot with the camera's aperture closed down when there was sufficient studio lighting, allowing the image to be photographed in "deep focus," with both background and foreground highly defined. This quality was lost when panchromatic stock became popular in 1926. The new stock was sensitive to all parts of the color spectrum and hence the image was far more natural; but because the stock was slower and the aperture had to be opened wider, the extraordinary depth of field achieved by such silent-film directors as Stroheim was largely lost until Orson Welles, with his cinematographer Gregg Toland, was able to return the technique to film with *Citizen Kane* in 1941. *See* **deep focus** *and* **panchromatic film.**

■ **OS** *See* **off-screen.**

Oscar

■ **Oscar** The gold-plated statuette given as a prize for highest achievement in the various categories of motion-picture production by the Academy of Motion Picture Arts and Sciences at the Academy Awards celebration each year. The name supposedly came from a librarian of the Academy, Margaret Herrick, who said that the statuette looked like her uncle Oscar, and was first used in 1931. *See* **Academy Awards.**

■ **out** (1) A term sometimes found in a filmscript to indicate that a specific sound, musical passage, or particular effect should be stopped by that point in the action. (2) *See* **outtake.**

■ **outboard reels** Very large reels capable of holding up to 12,000 feet of film for projection. Such reels operate independent of and to the rear of the projector. *See* **projector** *and* **projection.**

■ **outgoing scene** The scene leaving the screen during a dissolve, wipe, or fade, and which precedes the "incoming scene."

■ **outgoing shot** Any shot that precedes the cut to an "incoming shot." The term is frequently used in editing for the shot about to leave the screen of an editing machine.

■ **outline** A point-by-point synopsis or summary of a plot, normally fewer than 500 words, that gives a brief account of the story and characters and is judged as a possible source for a future film. If the outline is accepted and optioned, a "treatment" or even screenplay will follow. *See* **screenplay, screenwriter,** *and* **treatment.**

■ **out-of-camera film** *See* **noncamera film.**

■ **out of character** A phrase applied to a character in a film, play, or novel who behaves or speaks in a manner that seems out of keeping with his or her established personality and characterization.

■ **out-of-focus dissolve** A transition from one scene to another in which the first scene ends when the image grows lighter and lighter until it disappears, an effect achieved either in the camera by opening the aperture of the lens or in an optical printer by increasing the light when projecting the image from a positive onto the raw stock. *See* **dissolve.**

■ **out of frame** (1) When the image on the screen is not completely centered and part of another frame also appears. This misalignment can be corrected by turning the framing knob on the projector. (2) An object, action, or area outside the frame being photographed.

■ **out-of-sync** When the sound and its source in the image are not synchronic or simultaneous (e.g., when a character's dialogue is not properly aligned with his lip movement). *See* **sound** *and* **synchronization.**

■ **output device** (1) The recorder that transmits the digital image to film. Two technologies now employed for this transfer are cathode-ray tube and laser. *See* **film recorder.** (2) The videotape recorder that transmits the electronic signals to the tape—the monitor itself may be referred to as the output tube.

■ **outtake, out** (1) A shot not used in the final version of a film. (2) A shot eliminated from a film during editing.

■ **overact** To act with exaggeration and a display of unnatural emotion. *See* **acting.**

■ **overage** Any cost that exceeds its specified amount in the film's budget. Construction and special effects are two categories that frequently exceed their costs.

Overages are a constant nemesis in the film industry, especially today when film budgets are already astronomically high.

■ **overall development deal, overall deal** A contractual agreement by which a studio/distributor will pay the various expenses and overhead of an independent producer for first rights to any projects that the producer will develop. In an exclusive development deal, the filmmaker must distribute his or her films through the film studio only. In a first-look deal, the company can choose whether or not to do the film, and, if not, the filmmaker can go elsewhere. In a house-keeping deal, the film studio gives the filmmaker an office and development funds to get a project going normally for a first-look. *Also see* **completion bond, development deal, negative pickup deal,** *and* **pickup deal.**

■ **overall gamma** *See* **gamma.**

■ **overall luminance range** *See* **brightness range.**

■ **overcrank** To run a camera faster than the normal 24 frames per second, which results in slow motion when the printed film is projected at normal speed. The term comes from early film days when the camera was cranked by hand. To run a camera slower than normal is to "undercrank."

■ **overcranked** Referring to film that has been shot at a speed faster than the normal 24 frames per second so that when the images are projected at normal speed slow-motion action will result. Film shot slower than normal is "undercranked."

■ **overdevelopment, forced development, forced processing, pushing, uprating, cooking** Increasing the time of development or the temperature of the chemicals in order to achieve better image quality when the film has originally been exposed with poor lighting—a practice especially necessary for documentary or newsreel work. Overdevelopment is also necessary when the film itself has been exposed at a higher speed than it requires, though sometimes the process is used intentionally to increase the image's contrast. The entire process of fast exposure and overdevelopment is called pushing or uprating when it is done intentionally. The process was employed for Joseph Losey's *The Servant* (1963) to increase contrast but also to achieve deep focus through the uses of the faster film speed. It is often advisable, however, to run some tests since the process tends to increase fog level and graininess. *See* **underdevelopment.**

■ **overexposure** Too much exposure of the film to light, caused either by excessive light or too lengthy an opening of the aperture belonging to the camera or printer. The result of overexposure in a camera is a washed-out and unnaturally lit image with little gradation in lighting and little detail; and in a printer, an unnaturally dark image again with little gradation in lighting and insufficient detail. Sometimes film is intentionally overexposed in the camera to achieve a hallucinatory or dreamlike effect. The same quality can be achieved in an optical printer by using excessive light when printing from a positive. *See* **underexposure.**

■ **over frame** A term sometimes found in a film script to indicate that a particular speech or sound is to be heard even though the source does not appear in the image.

■ **overhead** (1) The costs of maintaining a film studio or film-producing business (i.e., buildings, equipment, and full-time personnel) as opposed to costs for specific productions. (2) A large scrim stretched on a frame and supported by two or more stands to decrease, diffuse, or block light descending on an area beneath it. A smaller version is called a butterfly.

■ **overhead cluster** A luminaire, generally with six 1,000-watt bulbs, used for top lighting on a set. Such a fixture gives a soft, shadowless light.

■ **overhead hanger** A device that supports a light from above and permits the luminaire to be moved up and down.

■ **overhead set** *See* **overhead** (2).

■ **overhead shot** A shot from directly above the characters or action. This is a particularly effective shot for showing a character entrapped in a small area or the general confusion and chaos of a fight. An overhead shot from a greater distance is referred to as a bird's-eye view. *See* **bird's-eye view.**

■ **overhead strip** A luminaire, generally with five 1,000-watt tungsten-halogen bulbs, used for either top or base lighting. Such a fixture gives widespread illumination.

■ **overlap** (1) The repetition of action photographed at the end of one shot and the beginning of another. This practice allows the editor to join the two shots so that there seems to be no break in the action even though the camera has changed position or distance. The continuity between two shots is most unobtrusive if the cutting takes place in the midst of an action. (2) A transition in which the action at the end of one shot is repeated at the beginning of the next. The only movement for that instant seems to be the change in the position or distance of the camera, and the character seems unable to make any progress. This type of transition is sometimes used in dream or hallucination, or in a subjectively viewed sequence. It is also an effective device to slow down action and emphasize the drama of a situation. In Eisenstein's *The Battleship Potemkin* (1925), an elaborate overlap, artificial and yet dramatically effective, takes place at the beginning of the film when the sailor is seen smashing the officer's dish, first from above his left shoulder and then from above his right. (3) The continuation of sound from one shot into another. Such an overlap of sound occurs in two shots of the same action, but may also be carried over from one scene to another, when the source of the sound is no longer present, for continuity or dramatic effect. (4) To repeat the same action at the conclusion of one shot and the beginning of another to achieve the match cut described in (1). (5) To speak at the same time that another character is talking without allowing him or her to finish.

■ **overlap-cement splice** A joining of two pieces of film by scraping off the emulsion from the end of one piece and cementing onto this portion the end of the other, hence joining the bases of the two films. This type of splice is especially convenient for 35mm film because it can be made in the space between the frames. In smaller-gauge film, where there is no such space, a frame must generally be lost and the splice is sometimes visible. For this reason checkerboard cutting is generally used for the original material of smaller gauges. The other type of splice is the butt joint, where the two ends do not overlap and are joined by a piece of tape. The overlap splice, which is easier to make and stronger, is generally made in a largely automatic splicer. Also called a lap splice. *See* **checkerboard cutting** *and* **splice.**

■ **overlap dialogue** (1) Dialogue spoken simultaneously by two or more characters, with none of the characters allowing the others to be heard, a technique used to create more natural and realistic conversation. (2) Dialogue that overlaps into another scene even though there has been an apparent jump in time or place. We might see two characters in the first scene talking as they walk along a city street and, in the next scene, continuing the same conversation in a car or in the country. Such a technique might emphasize the emotional intensity of the characters in their developing relationship. (3) Dialogue that overlaps into another shot or scene even when the characters who have been speaking are no longer visible; or dialogue heard at the conclusion of a scene which is spoken by characters who will first appear in the next scene. In the first instance, overlap dialogue might be heard in a reaction shot when the character speaking is no longer on screen and we are watching someone react to what is being said; or it might be heard from a character describing some past event as a temporal transition into the flashback we actually see on the screen. The second instance, when characters' dialogue at the end of one scene anticipates their appearance at the start of the next, is generally used as a transitional device.

■ **overlapping action** *See* **overlap** *(1) and* **matching action.**

■ **overlapping sound, overlap sound** Any sound, including dialogue, that continues from one scene into the start of another when the source of the sound is no longer present or that is heard at the conclusion of a scene and continues into the next when its source first appears. *See* **overlap dialogue** *(3).*

■ **overlap sound cut** Any cut from one shot or scene to another using overlapping dialogue or sound.

■ **overlay** In animation work, any cel, drawing, or mask placed on top of the cels which make up the main scene to create a foreground or frame and hence a sense of depth in the image. *See* **animation.**

■ **overlighting** Employing too much lighting in the illumination of a set or location. Excessive use of fill lights, for example, might diminish the type of contrast that gives mood, texture, and interest to an image. It is important to keep the various planes distinct, especially the subject plane from the background. *See* **underlit.**

■ **overload** To send too great a load through any system. In the case of an audio system specifically, to send too great a signal so that sound distortion occurs.

■ **over music** A term sometimes used in a film script to indicate that a speech or sound is to be heard with a particular musical passage in the background.

■ **overplay** To exaggerate the personality and characteristics of the character that the performer is playing. *See* **acting.**

■ **overrun lamps** Lamps used with voltage higher than normal for their type of filament in order to achieve greater light intensity and color temperature, a practice which results, though, in reduced longevity. Lightweight lamps of this type are useful for shooting on location, and standard fixtures that are part of an indoor set might be used in this fashion to achieve a higher intensity of light than normal.

■ **overs** Leftover exposed film footage, either from the camera or from the edited shot.

■ **overscale** Any salary or fee greater than the minimum set by the appropriate union and production companies.

■ **overshooting** Shooting more film than is necessary for the shot or scene in order to allow the editor a good deal of choice when selecting from the footage. *See* **undershooting.**

■ **over the line**   The cost of a film, including the salary of the high-paid star or stars. The term "under the line" is used when such salaries are not included.

■ **over-the-shoulder shot (OSS)**   A shot that is made from over the shoulder of a character, with the back of the head, neck, and shoulder generally seen at the side of the frame. The camera focuses past the character on some object or person that he or she is seeing. The shot is frequently used in conversations between two people, either showing a close-up of the speaking character from over the shoulder of the person who is listening or a close-up of the reactions of the person who is listening from over the shoulder of the person who is talking. The camera switches back and forth during the scene, giving the audience the perspectives and reactions of the characters as they engage in the conversation.

■ **over-39 light**   A term that refers to ambient light because it softens the features and hides the age of performers over thirty-nine years of age. *See* **ambient light.**

■ **Oxberry optical printer**   A once-popular optical printer for 16mm and 35mm film. Oxberry LLC still manufactures table top models and several of the larger models each year, while Oxberry Used Equipment Corporation keeps the older models running. Oxberry is meeting the digital challenge by manufacturing optical printers that incorporate digital processes and cameras for digital film recorders. *See* **optical printer.**

■ **oxidation**   A reaction between chemical compounds and oxygen in air that increases the oxygen content in the compound. Since such a reaction can seriously reduce or alter the effects of certain chemicals in the processing of film, the compounds must be used in air-free chambers. *See* **processing.**

■ ■ ■

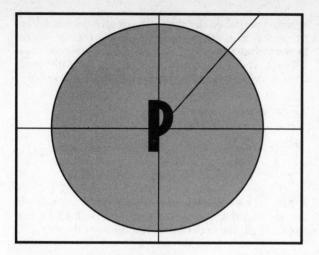

pace, pacing to pyrotechnics, pyrotechnic special effects

■ **pace, pacing** The speed or tempo with which the motion picture seems to advance. Pace depends on numerous factors: (1) the nature of the action (scenes with rapid movement will generally seem fast paced compared to scenes with little action); (2) the length of individual shots and scenes (a duration of brief shots and scenes will seem to move faster than the same period with longer shots and scenes); (3) camera position (action at a distance seems slower than events close to the camera, and low-angle shots make action seem faster than a normal eye-level view); (4) cutting (rapid change of camera angles and distances seems to accelerate action); (5) lighting (action will seem to move slower in darkened scenes, and movement from dark to light will seem sudden and rapid); (6) color (muted tones or heavy, dark colors seem to slow action, while light, bright colors seem to accelerate it); (7) composition (the lines and arrangement of masses of a scene can make action seem faster, while action played against flat or solid backgrounds will seem slower); (8) sound (a busy sound track with fast music and a good deal of environmental noise will add to the frantic nature of a scene while slow music or relative silence will add to its slowness). Different pacing is achieved, of course, for different kinds of films—Westerns and war films will generally seem faster and more action packed than domestic dramas—but even within the accepted conventions of each type considerable variation should be achieved. The pace of films also reflects the national culture and sense of time (Satyajit Ray's films originating from India seem moribund to many Americans) as well as the particular period (the Hollywood films of the 1930s seem slower and more dramatic than the rel-

atively fast-paced films of recent years which seem to deemphasize character and emphasize action and movement). *See* **rhythm.**

■ **package** A coalition of the various major elements needed for the production of a movie, generally put together by a producer in order to receive financial backing from a studio or group of investors. The package might include the property to be filmed, the screenwriter, the director, and one or more stars. Sometimes agencies that represent a number of diverse talents might put together a package. With the demise of the old studio method of production, where directors, screenwriters, and other personnel were under contract, independent packaging has become a major means of getting a film underway.

■ **pack shot lens** A lens with a short focal-ring movement that is used for sudden changes of focus from close to distant subjects. Such lenses, which are also employed for photographing small objects without microscopes, may use double- or triple-extension mounts. *See* **cinemacrography.**

■ **paddle plug** A type of flat plug often attached to motion-picture luminaries.

■ **pads** Certain items in a film's budget that are overestimated by the producer in order to allow for future contingencies, perhaps in other areas. Such a practice is normally resisted by studios and other groups which finance a film.

■ **page, page store** The term "page" in computer graphics and animation refers to the contents of a single monitor screen or frame, whether a single page of text or a single image. Page store, then, refers to the storage of such frames in the memory of the computer and is similar to frame store and still store. *See* **frame buffer.**

■ **page count** Because scenes vary in length, the amount of shooting is also designated in the number of pages from the shooting script. The fraction of a page is in eighths because it is easy to visualize a page as divided in half, then quarters, and finally eighths. Each page of shooting is estimated to run for about a minute. Therefore, a specific scene on a breakdown sheet with page designation 4/8 would run about half-a-minute. Page counts for anticipated shooting schedules are given on call sheets and shooting schedules, and for an actual day's shooting on a daily production report.

■ **painted matte shot** A special-effects shot that combines an image of live action with one of a painting to form a composite picture. The combining of such images may be done to extend a structure (e.g., a painted wing or ceiling can be added to a building) or to give a detailed background to the action (e.g., mountains or a rural landscape can be placed behind actors). Such shots were originally accomplished by in-the-camera matte work when part of the original film was matted out during shooting for the later inclusion of the second element during another pass of the film in the camera. Later, these shots were often accomplished by bipack contact matte printing, which is safer (instead of using the original negative, a positive of the action is printed on a fresh negative along with the painting) and easier. Today, such compositing can also be accomplished digitally. *See* **bipack contact matte printing, digital effects, in-camera matte shot, matte** *(2),* **matte painting,** *and* **photo matte.**

■ **painter, opaquer, colorer** The individual in an animation studio who fills in the drawings with color once they have been inked on the cel in the making of a cartoon. *See* **animation** *and* **inker.**

■ **PAL** The letters stand for "phase alternative line" and apply to the type of color television transmission and video recording used in much of Europe with a playback rate of 25 frames per second and a scan rate of 625 lines. The additional 100 scan lines create a better-defined image and richer color than the NTSC system in the United Sates. *See* **HDTV, NTSC,** *and* **SECAM.**

■ **palette** (1) The range and quality of color available to a director of photography from a specific film stock. (2) The selection of colors available to the artist in creating computer animation or graphics. The number of bits (i.e., "bit depth" or "color depth") used for each pixel will determine the number of colors available. A 32-bit palette is on the high end and offers 16.7 million colors as well as an alpha channel of 8 bits for 256 shades of gray; 24-bit color allows for the 16.7 million colors; 16-bit for 65,000 colors; and 8-bit for 256. The 8-bit palette will suffice for normal use, though obviously the high end is required for professional film work. A single bit for each pixel will allow a black-and-white image. *See* **computer animation.**

■ **pan, pan shot** A shot in which the camera moves horizontally around a fixed axis to survey an area. The term comes from "panorama," and the technique frequently functions to (1) give the audience a larger, more panoramic view of the scene than a shot from a fixed camera. The technique can also be used to (2) guide the audience's attention to a significant action or point of interest, keeping them aware of the relationships of elements in the scene (something that cutting cannot do); (3) follow the movement across the landscape of a character or vehicle; and (4) convey a subjective view of what a character sees when turning his or her head to follow an action. A swish pan occurs when the camera pans rapidly, causing the moving image to blur; a search pan when the camera seems to scan the horizon, looking for someone; a revelation pan when the camera's movement suddenly and unexpectedly reveals some action, person, or place; and a

reaction pan when the camera moves from some action or person to a character's reaction to that action or person. Sometimes the term "pan" is loosely used for a tilt shot, where the camera moves in a vertical direction from a fixed position. *See* **camera movement** *and* **tilt shot.**

pan shot

■ **pan** (1) A negative review by a critic for any work of art, including a film. (2) A flat, circular light fixture used to light the area outside a window or door.

■ **pan and scan** The method of transforming wide-screen or anamorphic films to reduced size for television presentation by focusing on important action and moving from significant point to significant point. *See* **telecine.**

■ **pan-and-tilt head, pan-tilt head** Any type of head that mounts a camera to a tripod or support and allows panning and tilting of the camera. Friction heads allow the camera to move in a relatively smooth manner by means of the sliding surfaces of two metal components, fluid heads allow smoother movement by the use of a liquid forced between the surfaces; and geared heads offer the best movement, especially for heavy studio cameras, by means of gears and cranks.

■ **Panavision** The trade name for wide-screen processes and cameras developed by Panavision, Inc. in California. Original Panavision used an anamorphic lens on the camera to squeeze the picture onto 35mm film which, when projected through the same type of lens, created an image with a 2.35:1 aspect ratio. Super Panavision photographed an unsqueezed image onto 65mm film which, when projected from a 70mm print or an anamorphically squeezed print of 35mm, had an aspect ratio of 2.2:1. Ultra Panavision used an anamorphically squeezed image on a 65mm negative and 70mm print to project a picture with a ratio of 2.7:1. Panavision makes the most-used anamorphic lenses in the industry. "Filmed in Panavision" generally means that the 35mm anamorphic process has been used for the film. Panavision also makes a series of highly esteemed cameras that use anamorphic, spherical, and specialty lenses: the 35mm Platinum Panaflex, which can be employed as both a studio and handheld camera, includes, among its features, a high magnification optical system, total crystal-controlled drive system, and internal microprocessor control for monitoring the camera's functions; while the exceptional Panavision Panaflex 16mm camera is one of the most technologically advanced models for that size film. *See* **anamorphic lens** *and* **wide-screen.**

Panavision Platinum Panaflex

■ **pancake** A box, shorter than the apple box, used to elevate a piece of equipment or object a few inches off the ground. *See* **apple box.**

■ **pancake makeup** A base makeup for performers that comes in the shape of a small cake, and is applied with a damp cloth or sponge.

■ **panchromatic film** A black-and-white film sensitive to all the colors of the spectrum, rendering them in varying shades of gray. Orthochromatic film is sensitive to both blue and green but not to red, which explains the highly contrasted "soot and whitewash" appearance of many silent films. Although Eastman Kodak had first manufactured a panchromatic film stock in 1913 for color cinematography, and the film was later, on occasion, used for black-and-white motion pictures, technical difficulties and unfamiliarity prevented its adoption until Robert Flaherty used the stock for his 1926 film *Moana,* making its more subtle shades and greater capacity for rendering realistic flesh tones apparent. Panchromatic film became the staple for all black-and-white films, but because it was less sensitive to light, the aperture had to be opened wider and depth of field was lost. Not until Orson Welles's *Citizen Kane* in 1941 (photographed by Gregg Toland) was the depth of focus achieved by silent-film directors such as Stroheim again seen on the screen. This depth in the image was possible because of the improved sensitivity of panchromatic film emulsion and greater intensity of lighting. *See* **deep focus** *and* **orthochromatic film.**

■ **pan focus** A shot in which all parts of the image, from left to right and front to back, are in focus. Such a shot has great depth of field (or deep focus) and gives us a panoramic view of a large area without having to move the camera.

■ **pan glass** A glass filter that is looked through before shooting, showing how the scene will appear on panchromatic stock.

■ **pan handle, panhandle** A handle that is attached to a pan-and-tilt head and is used for smooth movements of the camera. Such handles are necessary to keep the camera steady and balanced during pans or tilts.

■ **Panopticon** An early camera and projector, made by Major Woodville Latham and his sons, which was first used to project pictures in New York City in 1895. Although the film was 70mm and gave a larger and clearer picture than Edison's 35mm film, the projected image was unsteady and frequently flawed.

■ **panoramic shot** A shot that offers a large, panoramic view of a location, either by a pan or extreme long shot.

■ **pantheon** The group of directors with the highest level of achievement (e.g., Chaplin, Griffith, Hitchcock, Welles, etc.). The term is used in *auteur* criticism (see Andrew Sarris, *The American Cinema*). *See* **auteur.**

■ **pan title** A title that progresses across the screen in a horizontal direction.

■ **pantograph** A support that holds a lamp in a hanging position and is capable of smooth up and down movement so that the light stays balanced.

■ **papering** Putting paper markers into a reel of film to mark (1) the start and finish of a sequence to be printed by a laboratory or (2) a sequence of film to be screened by a projectionist.

■ **paper print** Prints of early motion pictures with a paper base, which were used to file copyrights and were deposited in the Library of Congress. Since no copyright law existed for motion pictures until 1907, early films had to be copyrighted as collections of still pictures. Some 3,500 collections of such stills were converted back into motion pictures on 16mm film, beginning in the 1950s.

■ **paper-to-paper, tab to tab, clip to clip** A term used in laboratories for printing a section of a negative that is marked off by paper tags, markers, or tape—as the negative passes through the printer, the tags, markers, or tape signal the start and finish of the projection of the images onto the fresh stock. This process is used for obtaining a second record of a scene that must be repeated in the film or a fresh record for one damaged in a workprint. Such a process might also be used for obtaining scenes for a preview. *Also called* **section printing.**

■ **parabolic reflector** A parabolic-shaped reflector in a luminaire that sends light out in a narrow beam. *See* **PAR light.**

■ **paradigmatic** A term in semiotics, the science of signs, which refers to a word's significance that arises from its being chosen instead of other possible words (for example, calling someone "lean" instead of "thin," "skinny," or "slender"). Semiotics also considers the syntagmatic relationships of words, that is, how they achieve significance from their relationship with other words in the sentence. Whereas syntagmatic refers to the word's place in a horizontal line (the sequence of words in the sentence), paradigmatic refers to the word's vertical significance (its relationship to a list of potential words that exist behind it or can be seen as listed beneath it). Semiotics can be applied to film, which is made up of a number of sign systems. One can discuss not only the paradigmatic significance or connotation of a word, phrase, or gesture, but also the paradigmatic implications of a particular shot—why it was used instead of other shots. *See* **semiotics** *and* **syntagmatic.**

■ **parallactic movement** Any apparent movement of objects in relation to each other caused by the movement of the camera. As the camera moves backward toward the audience, near objects at the sides of the screen seem to move past distant ones; and as the camera moves sideways, distant objects stay in sight longer as close ones pass across them. Such an effect gives the flat image on the screen an illusion of depth.

parallax 1. viewfinder 2. camera

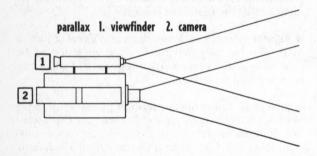

■ **parallax** The apparent displacement of an object that results from the change of perspective with which it is viewed. In cinematography, the term directly applies to the different perspectives of an object through the viewfinder and camera lens because of their slight distance apart. Such a parallax error can result in a poorly composed image or in part of the desired field of vision being omitted from the frame. To correct for this displacement and allow the scene to be seen through the lens of the camera, a reflex viewfinder is now often employed. *See* **viewfinder.**

■ **parallax error** A mistake in the image, such as part of the subject being omitted or the picture being poorly composed, that is caused by parallax (i.e., the displacement of objects as a result of the slightly different perspectives of the camera lens and viewfinder when not corrected by some kind of reflex system). *See* **parallax** *and* **viewfinder.**

■ **parallel** A platform, frequently made of sections of steel pipe, that can be set up at different heights to support the camera and its operator or luminaries. These platforms allow high-angle shots and are especially useful for exterior shooting when a crane is not possible. Parallels can be placed one on top of the other for greater height.

■ **parallel action** Action taking place at two or more locations at the same time and shown alternately on the screen with the camera parallel cutting from one location to the other. Entire films can be constructed on the basis of parallel action (for example, Robert Altman's *Nashville* [1975] continuously cuts between actions dealing with more than twenty characters over a period of five days), but the technique most often functions in parts of films to show simultaneous and related action. Parallel cutting to show such parallel action has been a major part of motion pictures since early silent-film days and was especially developed by D. W. Griffith. *See* **parallel cutting.**

■ **parallel cutting, parallel editing** Cutting between two or more related actions occurring simultaneously at different locations or occurring at different times. Although the technique was used as early as Edwin S. Porter's *The Life of an American Fireman* and *The Great Train Robbery* (both 1903), Griffith is often cited for his development of this technique (e.g., when he cuts from the endangered victim to the rescue party, a plot mechanism he first used in *The Lonely Villa* [1909]). The technique has become as basic to narrative films as it has been in fiction from the novels of Charles Dickens to the present. The term "crosscutting" is also employed for such cuts, but this term sometimes is limited to actions occurring simultaneously, while parallel cutting is then used for actions not simultaneous in time (as in Griffith's *Intolerance* [1916]). *See* **cross-cutting.**

■ **parallel sound** Nonsynchronic sound in a scene that is not played in counterpoint to the action but has a direct connection with it (for example, a voice-over narrating some past action which we see on the screen, or symphonic music playing in the background while we see the composer scribbling away the notes for the music on a sheet).

■ **Paramount decision** The decision made by the Supreme Court in 1948 that Paramount and other studios were in violation of the antitrust laws with vertical ownership of production, distribution, and exhibition. The decrees issued ruled that the five major movie studios—MGM, Paramount, RKO, Warner Brothers, and Twentieth Century-Fox—would have to divest themselves of their theaters, and the same studios as well as the three minor studios that owned no theaters—United Artists, Columbia, and Universal—would all have to stop restrictive and coercive practices in the exhibition of their films. Litigation against the studios had actually begun in 1938, but its conclusion had been delayed by the Second World War. After some futile appeals, the studios consented in 1951. The companies, however, could continue to distribute their own films and, as a result, many remained major powers in the industry, though the minor companies now became more competitive with them. With theaters free to select their own films, block booking, guaranteed exhibition, and manipulative practices were at an end for the studios. Doors were now open to independent producers and foreign films. B-pictures eventually disappeared. The studios would now have to sell each film on its merit. For these reasons, as well as the increasing costs of production, shrinking audiences at home because of television, and diminishing profits from foreign markets because of protective tariffs, the old studio system was on its way out and new ways of financing, producing, and distributing films developed. Independent production now became a reality in the film industry.

■ **Paramount decrees, Paramount consent decrees** The decrees issued by the Supreme Court in the 1948 Paramount decision divesting the major studios of their theaters and restricting them and the three minor studios from unfair practices in arranging exhibition. *See* **Paramount decision.**

■ **Paramount Pictures Corporation** A major film production company in this country that developed from the film distributor Paramount Pictures, begun by W. W. Hodkinson in 1914. Hodkinson had originated Paramount as the first national distributor of feature films and had handled films produced by such companies as Adolph Zukor's Famous Players and the Jesse L. Lasky Feature Play Company. In 1916, Zukor brought together his own company with that of Lasky and a number of smaller companies, forming the Famous Players–Lasky Corporation; he managed also to dispossess Hodkinson and bring Paramount under his control. Zukor became president of the new organization and Lasky head of production. During the silent-film period, the company became the leading force in motion pictures, with Zukor not only utilizing such directors as Cecil B. DeMille (one of the founders of the Lasky company), D. W. Griffith, and Erich von Stroheim, and stars such as Mary Pickford and Gloria Swanson, but actively gathering into the fold large numbers of exhibitors, thus achieving total integration of production, distribution, and exhibition. In 1927, the company became the Paramount Famous Lasky Corporation, but when it obtained the large theater circuit of the Publix Corporation in 1930 it became the Paramount Publix Corporation. Paramount was foremost in the development of sound, especially with the films of Ernst Lubitsch and Rouben Mamoulian, but overextension and some bad management led to financial difficulties in the 1930s and bankruptcy in 1933, at which time the company was reorganized and renamed Paramount Pictures Corporation. Paramount recouped nicely and during the sound era of the studio system was second only to MGM. Paramount was significant for its comic productions, featuring works by Lubitsch, Billy Wilder, and Preston Sturges, and stars such as Mae West, W. C. Fields, the Marx Brothers, Bob Hope, and Jerry Lewis; for its epic films by DeMille, especially his two versions of *The Ten Commandments* in 1923 and 1956 and *The Greatest Show on Earth* in 1952; and the films of Marlene Dietrich directed by Joseph von Sternberg.

In 1948, the Supreme Court ruled in the Paramount decision that vertical integration of the industry was illegal (litigation had begun in 1938 with Paramount as the test case in the antitrust proceedings). The five major companies were ordered to divest themselves of their theaters, though they could still distribute. With block booking and guaranteed exhibition at an end, and with the additional problems of increased production costs, diminishing audiences at home because of the rise of television, and shrinking revenue from foreign markets, the old studio system was ultimately to collapse. Yet Paramount remained a major producer and distributor of motion pictures, though sponsoring an increasing number of independently packaged films. Finally, in 1966, Paramount became part of the huge financial conglomerate Gulf and Western. Following the precedent set by Warner Brothers with its highly successful *The Sound of Music* in 1965 (dir. Robert Wise), Paramount, like other companies, produced several high-budget films but with dismal financial results (for example, *Paint Your Wagon* in 1969; dir. Joshua Logan); however, the company still produced a number of excellent and successful films, such as *The Godfather* in 1971 (dir. Francis Ford Coppola) and *Saturday Night Fever* (dir. John Badham) in 1978.

Paramount continued to do very well at the box office with such hits as *Raiders of the Lost Ark* (1981; dir. Steven Spielberg), *Beverly Hills Cop* (1984; dir. Martin Brest), and *Top Gun* (1986; dir. Tony Scott). The parent company, Gulf and Western, changed its name to Paramount Communications Inc. in 1989 to emphasize its specialization in film, television, and book publishing. As well as Paramount Pictures, the company owned television stations, was co-owner with MCA of USA Network on cable, owner or co-owner of more than 1,000 screens throughout the world, and owned the publisher, Simon & Schuster. In addition, Paramount owned Madison Square Garden in New York City, its cable television station, and its two sports organizations, the Rangers hockey team and the Knicks basketball team. After a remarkable corporate struggle in 1993, Viacom International, owner of MTV and Nickelodeon cable networks, Showtime and the Movie Channel, and numerous television, radio, and cable holdings, in partnership with Blockbuster Video, beat out the QVC Group, the owner of the cable shopping network, to purchase Paramount and form a vast entertainment and information conglomerate. Paramount Pictures kept up its winning ways with *Forrest Gump* in 1994 (dir. Robert Zemeckis) and 15.3 percent of the box office revenues for that year, but dropped down to a 10.3 percent in 1995. The logo for Paramount since the silent-film period has remained the snow-capped mountain and circle of stars.

■ **parent roll** The original wide rolls of manufactured film from which the various widths are cut. Manufacturers supply numbers for the parent roll, the emulsion batch from which the parent roll originates, and the strips and lengths (called "cuts") into which it is divided.

■ **PAR light, parabolic spotlight** A sealed spotlight employing a parabolic reflector to achieve either a narrow or wide beam of light. The term "PAR" is attributed to either the parabolic shape of the lamp or the initials from "parabolic aluminized reflector." Sometimes called a birdseye after its inventor, Clarence Birdseye.

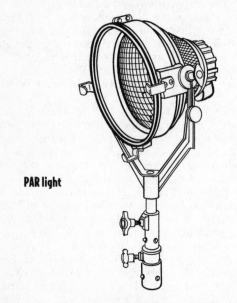

PAR light

■ **parody** A work that comically imitates another work or group of works of a more serious nature. The parody performs its humorous imitation by picking out the more pronounced and sometimes silly elements of its subject and exaggerating them, though it may do so in a good-natured as well as satiric manner. Mack Sennett's Keystone comedies offer early examples of parody in film, for example, his takeoff on Griffith's *The Lonely Villa* (1909) in *Help! Help!* (1912); and Buster Keaton parodied Griffith's *Intolerance* (1916) with his *The Three Ages* (1923). In more recent years, Woody Allen used parody as a means for his early exploratory ventures into motion pictures—for example, *Take the Money and Run* (1968) is a parody of the gangster film and *Bananas* (1971) a takeoff on films about South American politics—and Mel Brooks has continuously used parody as a vehicle for all his films, notably in the comic Western *Blazing Saddles* (1974) and his clever takeoff on the horror film, *Young Frankenstein* (1974).

Both Brooks and Allen find much humor in these forms, but neither is really satirizing them as much as affectionately using them as a springboard for their own comic visions. A film that is purer parody in that it achieves most of its humor from both satirizing and imitating an earlier group of works is *Airplane* (1980; dir. Jerry Zucker et al.), which is an irreverent treatment of the series of melodramatic and silly airport pictures starting with George Seaton's *Airport* in 1969.

parody *Young Frankenstein* (1974; dir. Mel Brooks), a respectful but zany takeoff, with Gene Wilder and Peter Boyle, on the Frankenstein films of the 1930s.

■ ■ ■

■ **parole** A term used by Ferdinand de Saussure, the Swiss linguist and founder of semiotics, the science of signs, to convey the specific and particular usage of a language in an individual utterance or piece of writing. Saussure uses the word *langue* to indicate the total language system of a particular culture to which the *parole* or particular usage belongs. Saussure's lectures have been published as *Course in General Linguistics*. For a further discussion of these two terms *see* **langue.**

■ **part** The role played by a performer.

■ **partial lighting** A lighting technique that blocks light from certain parts of the subject to achieve specific effects. For example, illumination might be blocked from a character's body to highlight his or her face, or the rear part of a set might be heavily shadowed to emphasize a lit figure or object. Such partial lighting was a hallmark of Hollywood studio productions of *film noir* and horror films. *See* **lighting.**

■ **participation** (1) A contractual agreement whereby a performer or director receives a share of the profits instead of a straight salary or in addition to a smaller salary than normal. Though always a gamble, a participation can bring the individual far greater remuneration for a successful film than only an agreed-upon sum. Participation also allows more manageable pre-production costs and makes financing a film easier. *See* gross profit participant *and* net profit participant. (2) The sharing of advertising costs for a commercial film by both distributor and exhibitor.

■ **particle system, particle group** In computer animation, a method of creating any element of an image made up of tiny moving and changing particles—e.g., fire, smoke, fog, water, blasts of light. Particle systems can give a sense of gravity, weightlessness, bounce, and randomness to the movements of such elements. Presets automatically establish the animation of each particle, a necessity since any of these picture elements can be composed of a myriad number of particles. *See* **computer animation** *and* **fractal system.**

■ **pass** The movement of film through the camera for an individual exposure. The term is frequently employed in special-effects work for the individual movements of the film and exposures when photographing miniatures, especially with motion-control systems that allow exactly repeatable shots on separate films or the same film. For example, the beauty pass is the exposure when most of the shot's information is recorded; the light pass is to record the lights emanating from the model; and the glow pass records illumination reflected off or glowing from the miniature. All of this information is combined to form a single composite image. *See* **motion control** *and* **multiple pass.**

■ **passing shot** A shot with a character or object passing before the camera, achieved either by the subject moving with the camera stationary or by the camera in motion with the subject stationary or moving more slowly. *See* **run-by.**

■ **patch** (1) A small piece of tape used to join two pieces of film. (2) A small piece of cardboard or metal with teeth used before splicing to join two pieces of film by engaging their perforations.

■ **patch cord, patch cable** A piece of cable with a plug that connects a circuit into the socket of a panel. *See* **patch panel.**

■ **patching** Connecting a circuit to a panel by means of a patch cord. *See* **patch cord.**

■ **patch panel, patch board, patch bay** The panel into which various circuits are connected by means of patch cords. *See* **patch cord.**

■ **Pathé Frères** A French film company begun by Charles Pathé and his three brothers, Émile, Jacques, and Théophile, in 1869. It was to become the largest film production company on both sides of the Atlantic before the First World War. By 1908, the company was distributing twice as many films in the United States as all this country's film companies combined. Its main studios were in Vincennes, where Ferdinand Zecca, the head of production, directed a large number of his films, beginning with his imitations of Méliès and progressing to a wide variety of types, including his famous chase films. The comedian Max Linder, who made for the company some four hundred films in which he starred, had a direct influence on Charlie Chaplin. The company is also responsible for originating the film newsreel in 1908 and introducing to America the weekly adventure serial. Pathé Frères not only controlled distribution and exhibition in France, thus achieving vertical integration, but also opened studios in a number of other European countries and in the United States. The company expanded its dominance of the film industry by manufacturing both cameras and projectors which became the most-used film equipment before the First World War, and also manufacturing and selling film. But both the war years and competition from developing film industries abroad, especially in the United States, quickly took their toll. Pathé rid itself of its foreign branches and by 1926 had conceded the manufacture of film stock to Kodak. American studios now dominated the production and distribution of motion pictures. In 1929, Charles Pathé sold the company to Bernard Natan, and in 1939 Pathé-Natan went bankrupt.

■ **pay and play** A contractual agreement that an actor, director, or producer will get paid for a project and that it will also be made. Such an agreement is essential for guaranteeing that someone who brings a project to a production company will eventually get rewarded, especially if the reward is dependent upon the film being made. *See* **pay or play.**

■ **pay or play** A contractual agreement that an actor, director, or producer will get paid for a project whether or not he or she will later be involved with the film or even whether or not it is made. Such agreements are made to obtain the support of an artist in getting a project off the ground. *See* **pay and play.**

■ **pay-per-view (PPV)** A cable television system whereby the consumer pays for individual programs—normally the showing of a recent film, athletic event, or concert. The consumer orders the event by phone.

■ **PD** *See* **public domain.**

■ **pea bulb** The tiny bulb placed inside a camera to produce a brief light to fog several frames at the start of a shot at the same instant that a beep is sent to the sound recorder. Both the fogged frames and beep are later used for synchronizing picture and sound during editing. *See* **sync beep** *(2).*

■ **peak-reading meter** A type of VU (i.e., volume unit) meter on a magnetic sound recorder that provides accurate readings of the maximum sound in decibels for even short durations. The standard VU meters are slower in response and tend to average out sound levels. *See* **VU meter.**

■ **peanut fixture** A small luminaire with a 25- to 100-watt bulb that is attached to some object to make it appear as if light were shining from the object.

■ **pedestal** (1) A mobile mount for camera or lighting with a central column that can be controlled hydraulically for height. The unit has three sets of wheels and can be easily pushed for tracking or crabbing. (2) A support for a projector and soundhead used in a projection booth. *See* **projection console.**

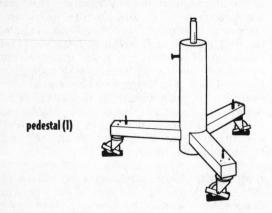

pedestal (1)

■ **peewee** A small incandescent luminaire with a 50-watt bulb.

■ **peg bar** Metal strips with three projecting pins, called register or registration pegs, that fit through punched holes in animation drawings to hold them in place or allow controlled movement. *See* **register pegs** *and* **registration** *(2).*

■ **peg board** (1) A large horizontal board on which art work and cels are registered by means of punched holes and pegs to be photographed by an overhead camera in animation, title, and matte work. (2) A large board with a series of pegs on which individual shots are hung and numbered during editing.

■ **pellicle** A thin sheet of plastic film with a reflective surface employed in such special-effects work as front-projection or mirror shots instead of a two-way mirror or optical flat. Easy to use because of its lightness, a pellicle is subject to scratches and picks up dirt easily.

■ **pencil test, line test** (1) A test for movement, continuity, and general effect in cartoon animation that uses rough pencil or line drawings recorded on film or videotape before the final artwork is drawn and painted on the cels. (2) A test for movement, continuity, and general effect in computer animation that uses wire-frame models on the monitor before the actual

images are composed and rendered. *See* **animation** *and* **computer animation.**

■ **penthouse head** The head in a reproduction system for playing magnetic stereophonic sound tracks in a projector. Such units were originally placed on top of the optical systems in projectors, but later were included as part of newly built machines. Thirty-five-millimeter film must move past the head 28 frames before the picture is projected and 70mm film 24 frames in advance because of the head's position in the projector. The part of the penthouse device that holds the multiple heads to play the various tracks (six for 70mm and four for 35mm) is referred to as the magnetic head cluster. *See* **stereophonic sound.**

■ **perambulator** The mobile platform that holds the microphone boom and its operator. The wheeled vehicle itself is pushed around by one or more members of the stage crew.

■ **perceptual film** *See* **structural film.**

■ **perforation pitch** *See* **pitch.**

■ **perforations (perfs), sprocket holes** The tiny punched holes on one or both sides of film that, perfectly duplicated and spaced, move and align the film in cameras, projectors, processors, and printers by means of the teeth on sprocket wheels. The four perforation holes on each side of the frame, devised by the Edison Company and sometimes called the American perforation, are still in use today for 35mm film. The perforations on negative 35mm film, which are rectangular in shape and arced at each end for steady registration, are referred to as Bell and Howell (BH) or negative perforations. Since the corners of such perforations tend to tear from steady use, the perforations on positives, which must be run numerous times in a projector, are slightly higher and rectangular, with curved corners. Such holes on positives are referred to as Kodak standard (KS) or positive perforations. Since the pitch (i.e., the distance between perforations) is shorter on negatives than on positives, it is called short as well as negative pitch, while that on positives is called long as well as positive pitch. The longer pitch on the positive prevents the film from slipping when it passes together with the negative, in the outside position, over the same sprockets in contact printing. Certain 35mm cameras are now equipped to accept film with three perforations for each frame, thus using 25 percent less film when shooting, and some can film at 30 frames per second, thus allowing a direct transfer to videotape. On 65mm negatives and 70mm prints, five KS perforations are used on the sides of each frame, though again the pitch is shorter on the negative. The American CinemaScope (AC) or CinemaScope (CS) perforation, a smaller hole with rounded corners, was used for CinemaScope prints to allow for the larger picture and four magnetic stereo sound tracks. All 16mm film employs a slightly rectangular perforation with curved corners, though 16mm film with a sound track has perforations only along the edge opposite from the sound track (in both cases single perforations are at the corners of adjoining frames). Since regular 8mm film was made from splitting 16mm film with perforations on both sides down the middle, it too had the same perforations on one edge. The perforations on Super 8, which are slightly vertical rectangles with curved corners, are much smaller than those on regular 8mm, to allow for a larger picture area. *See* **film** *(1).*

■ **performance license** A contractual agreement allowing a film production to use a piece of music. The agreement is between the film company and an agency representing the composer. *See* **master use license** *and* **synchronization license.**

■ **period film** Any film that seeks to evoke the reality of another time period. Since historical films deal with times distant from ours, they may be considered a type of period film; but the period film can also be less distant in time as long as it deals with an era that has its own marked appearance and style. For example, though one would not call Jack Clayton's 1974 film version of Fitzgerald's *The Great Gatsby* an historical film, it is certainly a period film in its visual recreation of this country's Jazz Age. *See* **historical film.**

■ **periodic noise** The periodic repetition of any aberrant noise in an audio system.

■ **periscope** An optical attachment to the camera for shooting at extremely low angles, above eye level, from odd angles, and for special-effects and miniature photography. *See* **snorkel.**

■ **persistence of vision** The capacity of the eye to maintain an image on the retina for a brief instant after it has disappeared, thus filling in the gaps between successive images and giving continuity from one to another. Motion pictures are actually a series of still photographs that record the successive positions of a subject in movement. Because the eye holds the image of one position after that image disappears from the screen and until the next appears and because a shutter in the camera blocks out the intermittent movement from one frame to another, the successive images seem to blend into each other, creating a continuity of movement from one position of the subject to another. With the eye holding an image for about one-third of a second, and allowing for the high intensity of illumination given by a film projector, persistence of vision will be achieved from 16 frames per second. However, the alternations between the lighted images and the dark between the frames cause an unpleasant flicker, which is reduced by increasing the speed of alternations. Such rapid alternations were achieved for silent films

by using a rotating shutter with three blades which actually blocked out each frame three times, hence giving a flicker frequency of 48 per second. When the addition of a sound track necessitated 24 frames per second, a two-blade shutter was used for the same flicker frequency. Although apparently a result of the optic nerves, the brain also is involved to some degree in the creation of persistence of vision; but there is still some vagueness concerning exactly how. *See* **phi phenomenon** for another theory concerning the illusion of movement created by motion pictures.

■ **perspective** In the field of film, the term specifically means the manner in which objects appear at a distance and in spatial relationships on the flat surface of the screen. Since three-dimensional reality is reduced to a flat image on the screen, the filmmaker must be concerned with perspective in order to create an illusion of depth and avoid distortions that are a result of the lens and the two-dimensional image (unless such distortions are desired for effect). The depth of the scene and the spatial relationship of objects are primarily the result of the distance of the camera from the scene and the type of lens employed. As we view an actual location, objects diminish in size as they recede into the distance, with the mind making some correction so that differences between objects at various planes do not appear too great to the naked eye. A "normal lens" (one with a focal length of 50mm for 35mm film) gives an image that approximates what the eye would see with very little distortion in perspective. However, wide-angle lenses tend to distort perspective by stretching out the image (objects centered in front seem larger and more menacing, while objects at the sides seem elongated) and emphasizing depth of focus (distant objects remain in focus but seem smaller and hence further away). Long-focus lenses, on the other hand, shrink depth of field, making distant objects seem larger and hence closer, while pushing objects into the background. If one desires the wider area of vision from the wide-angle lens or the magnifying power for distant objects of the long-focus lens, then one must compensate with camera angle, position, movement, composition, lighting, and color to diminish distortion. On the other hand, one can also use the distortion of perspective for effect, for example, slowing down movement of characters with a long lens or increasing it with a wide lens. A mobile camera creates a sense of depth by moving among characters and objects in the scene, as well as by constantly changing the perspective—that is, by altering the size of objects and their spatial relationships. *See* **depth** *and* **forced perspective.**

■ **perspective distortion** *See* **telephoto distortion** *and* **wide-angle distortion.**

■ **perspective matching** In computer graphics or animation, placing a 3-D model into a 2-D drawing of a background in such a way that the perspectives match and a proper composite image is achieved. Some kind of grid or system of lines can be imposed upon the background to facilitate the matching and later be removed.

■ **PG-rated** A designation for a film that advises parental guidance since some material might not be suitable for children. This is one of several ratings devised by the Motion Picture Association of America in the 1960s to replace the old Motion Picture Code. *See* **Motion Picture Production Code** *and* **Movie Rating System.**

■ **PG13** A designation for a film that advises parental guidance for children under thirteen. This rating was added to the code by the Motion Picture Association of America to warn parents about films that might be relatively free of sexual explicitness, but still contain explicit violence. *See* **Motion Picture Production Code** *and* **Movie Rating System.**

■ **phantom image** *See* **ghost image.**

■ **phase alteration line** *See* **PAL.**

■ **phasing, phase distortion, phase cancellation** An audio distortion caused by the same sound having different phases—for example, when two microphones pick up the same sound or when stereo tracks reproduce it at separate instances. Sometimes the signal might be divided into two parts, with one part slightly delayed to create a desired effect.

■ **Phenakistiscope** A toy invented by Joseph Plateau in 1832 that used the viewer's persistence of vision to create an illusion of movement within a circular series of drawings on a rotating disc. The viewer held the disc to a mirror and observed the reflection of the figures by looking through a series of slits along the circumference of the rotating disc which prevented the drawings from blurring together. *See* **Praxinoscope, Stroboscope,** *and* **Zoetrope.**

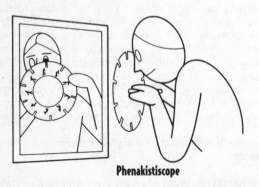

Phenakistiscope

■ **phenomenology** A branch of philosophy that deals with phenomena as observed or perceived essences (technically, all reality is intuited by the individual as intentional objects or phenomena). This branch of philosophy, developed by the German philosopher Edmund Husserl, has had a direct impact on literary critical theory and is now being explored, especially in this country, in relation to film. *See* **film theory.**

■ **phi phenomenon, phi effect** The illusion of movement created by the brain when the same object appears in different places in successive instances. Like persistence of vision, this phenomenon has been used to explain the illusion of movement created by motion pictures; but whereas the former is largely a physiological result of the optic nerves, the latter is a psychological result of the brain's operations. The term "phi leap" is sometimes used for the illusion of movement created by the distance between an object in successive images. *See* **persistence of vision.**

■ **Phong** *See* **shading.**

■ **Phonofilm** An early optical sound system invented by Lee De Forest. The system was tested in 1922 and used by De Forest for more than a thousand short films, which were shown in a large number of theaters until 1927. Although Phonofilm was much like the optical system ultimately to be employed by the film industry—and which it undoubtedly influenced—De Forest could not convince the studios to adopt his system. *See* **optical sound** *and* **sound.**

■ **photocell, photoelectric cell** A device in an electric circuit that varies operation either by its resistance to light or its conversion of light to energy. The amount of resistance or conversion depends on the intensity of light. Such a cell in a projector gives off the electrical impulses that are converted into sound. (The electrical impulses vary according to the intensity of light given off by a bulb and are controlled by the area or density of the optical sound track on the film.) In most exposure meters today, the intensity of light is measured either by the resistance of such cells to illumination or their conversion of illumination to electrical energy. *See* **exposure meter, optical sound,** *and* **projector.**

■ **photochemical process** The interaction between light and the chemicals in film emulsion during photography and printing, and also the interaction of chemicals in development solutions with those in the emulsion that have been altered by their exposure to light to create an image. *See* **film.**

■ **photoconductive cell** *See* **exposure meter.**

■ **photo-cut-out glass shot** A glass shot that uses an enlarged photograph instead of a painting. The camera shoots through a glass on which the cut photograph is attached, combining the photographed setting with the live action taking place behind it. *See* **glass shot.**

■ **photoflood** An incandescent-tungsten lamp that is run with more voltage than normal so that the filament gives off a large amount of light, although at a cost to the bulb's longevity. Such bulbs run from 250 to 1,000 watts and are frequently used for color cinematography. *See* **lighting.**

■ **photogenic** Being a suitable and attractive subject for photography; showing to best advantage when photographed.

■ **photograph** (1) Any still picture of a subject recorded by means of a chemical interaction caused by light rays hitting a sensitized surface. (2) To take either a still picture by means of photography; or to take a series of still pictures by means of cinematography for the making of a motion picture. *See* **cinematography, film** *(1), and* **photography.**

■ **photography** The process of recording images through a chemical interaction caused by light rays hitting a sensitized surface. The term "cinematography" is used for the recording of images in the making of a motion picture. The origins of modern photography begin in the early part of the nineteenth century with the experiments of Nicéphore Niépce in France, who, by 1826, managed to record an image, although of poor quality and only temporarily, on a plate with chemical emulsion by means of a type of camera obscura. It was Louis Jacques Mandé Daguerre, however, who in 1839 developed a clear and permanent image on a silvered copper plate; this was called a daguerreotype and became a popular type of photograph in the century. Daguerre's photograph was a positive and could not be reproduced. This problem was soon overcome by William Henry Fox Talbot, who invented a negative type of reproduction on paper with a silver-chloride emulsion, which could be the source of numerous prints. The last step in the origin of modern photography was replacing the paper stock with the colloidion stock developed by Frederick Scott Archer. *See* **cinematography** *and* **film** *(1).*

■ **photomacrography** *See* **macrocinematography.**

■ **photo matte** A cut-out photograph matted in with live action or another element of the final image. After the live-action image has been printed on a dupe negative with an area matted out, the cut-out photo is placed on an easel in front of the process camera with the already exposed area on the negative matted out. The dupe negative is then rerun and the photo cut-out integrated with the live action. *See* **matte** *(2) and* **painted matte shot.**

■ **photometer, photo-electric meter** A precision exposure meter that measures the intensity of light by means of a photoelectric cell. Such meters either use a photovoltaic cell to measure incident illumination by the

amount of electrical energy the cell produces in response to light rays, or a photoconductive cell that measures illumination by its resistance to light rays. *See* **exposure meter.**

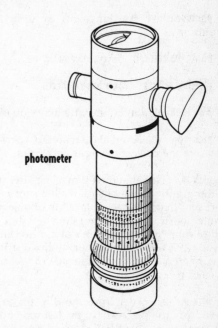

photometer

■ **photometry** The science of light measurement. Either light falling on an object from a source (called incident light) or light reflected from an object is measured. In the first instance, luminous intensity is measured by footcandles (or lux in the metric system). In the second instance, luminance is measured by footlamberts (or nits in the metric system). See these various terms in their alphabetical listing.

■ **photomicrography** *See* **microcinematography.**

■ **Photophone** An optical sound system developed by General Electric and marketed by RCA in 1928. RCA created the Radio-Keith-Orpheum Corporation (RKO), a vertically integrated film company with production studios, a distributing branch, and its own theaters to use the Photophone system. The Movietone optical sound system developed by General Electric and Marketed by Electrical Research Products Incorporated (ERPI) had already been contracted to the other major studios. *See* **Movietone, optical sound,** and **sound.**

■ **photoplay** (1) A term for a motion picture used during the silent-film period as a dignified substitute for "movies." (2) A screenplay for a motion picture.

■ **photorealistic** As real as a photograph of the real world and real people. The term is sometimes used in computer animation to judge the credibility and reality of a digitally created setting or characters. True photo-realism would mean that the digital image is indistinguishable from a photographic record of live action, a state that has not yet been achieved but is fast approaching. *See* **computer animation.**

■ **photosensitive** Anything sensitive to light (e.g., film emulsion).

■ **photo-voltaic cell** *See* **exposure meter.**

■ **physical effects** *See* **mechanical effects.**

■ **pic** A slang abbreviation for a motion picture.

■ **pick it up** (1) A verbal direction to a performer to accelerate the pace of dialogue and action. (2) *See* **pick up.**

■ **pickup** (1) A shot for a film taken after the principal photography is completed. Such a shot may be an insert shot that shows some location or object; a retake of some poorly photographed shot; or a shot necessary to fill in some gap in the film's plot. Also called a pickup shot. (2) A film obtained by a studio/distributor after it has been started or completed. (3) A microphone's area of receptivity.

■ **pick up** An order from the director to start a new take from the place where the last was ended, perhaps because some error had stopped the shooting or because additional footage is needed. Sometimes the order to "pick up" from a particular point is given. *See* **pick it up.**

■ **pickup deal** A contractual agreement by which a studio/distributor will pick up a film for distribution after it has been made by some independent group. Basically the same as a negative pickup, the agreement allows the producer a basis to find financing for making the film and removes any problems of cost overruns or incompletion of the project for the studio/distributor. *See* **completion bond** *and* **negative pickup deal.**

■ **pickup recorder** A dubber in a mixing studio that has the capacity to be stopped at any point and rolled back so that the rerecording of a segment can take place without any noticeable break from the earlier version, or new sound can be added. This process is referred to as roll back and rock and roll.

■ **pickup shot** *See* **pickup** *(1).*

■ **pick-up shot** The shot taken from a point where the previous shot has ended, frequently because of some error that has halted shooting or because more footage is needed. Sometimes the shot is taken at a later point in production or after preliminary editing.

■ **picture** (1) A colloquial term for a motion picture, frequently used in the plural, as in "Let's got to the pic-

tures." (2) The image area of film, apart from the sound-track area. (3) The film containing the images but not the sound for the motion picture.

■ **picture car** An automobile actually photographed in the film as distinct from the camera car, which is carrying the camera.

■ **picture cueing** Marking a print either by "punches" (i.e., holes) or streamers (i.e., diagonal lines scraped across a series of frames) for cueing the conductor during the recording of the score for a film. When the print is screened behind the orchestra and in front of the conductor, the cues are obvious enough for the conductor to notice without looking up from the score. The cues also allow immediate playback of both film and music to check their match.

■ **picture duplicate negative** *See* **dupe.**

■ **picture editing** Editing the picture part of a film and not the sound. *See* **editing.**

■ **picture gate** *See* **gate.**

■ **picture image** The representation of a subject on film after it has been photographed and processed.

■ **picture lock, picture freeze** The relatively finished state of the image portion of a film when the editing is complete.

■ **picture master positive** *See* **master positive.**

■ **picture negative** The negative film with the images already developed. *See* **negative.**

■ **picture palace** *See* **movie palace.**

■ **picture print** *See* **silent print.**

■ **picture release negative** The finally edited picture negative that contributes the image to the release print. Such films are generally dupe negatives made from the master print of the original negative.

■ **pilotone, pilot tone** A sync-pulse system for recording a signal along with the sound. The signal is aligned with the camera speed and is used to regulate the speed of the recorder when the sound is transferred to magnetic film to assure synchronic sound and picture. *See* **sync pulse.**

■ **pilot-pin registration, pin registration** A method of positioning each frame in exactly the same position before the aperture of a camera, projector, or printer for exposure by means of snugly fitting pins that engage the perforations. Such registration is used in most professional cameras, specialized process projectors, and for all types of special-effects work in bipack and optical printers. In most cameras, pull-down claws position each frame intermittently in front of the aperture, where it is held still by one or two registration pins. *See* **registration** *(1) and* **registration pins.**

■ **pilot pins** *See* **registration pins.**

■ **pilot print** *See* **answer print.**

■ **pincushion distortion** A fault in the lens that causes an image distortion whereby square shapes are extended at the corners so that they appear like pincushions or hourglasses.

■ **Pinewood Studios** Film studios in England that were established in 1936 and have been responsible for some of the country's most notable motion pictures. The Rank Organization produced a number of films there in the 1940s and 1950s, including David Lean's *Great Expectations* (1946) and Michael Powell and Emeric Pressburger's *The Red Shoes* (1948). Since 1960, studios have been rented out for independent films and for television production.

■ **pinhole** A tiny spot in the developed image on a film caused by some breakdown in chemicals and insufficient replenishment during processing.

■ **pin rack** A row of hooks from which film strips are hung during editing.

■ **pin screen animation, pinboard animation** An animation process, developed by Alexandre Alexeïeff in France during the 1930s, that uses a large screen with pin holes into which pins are placed at varying heights. The differing heights of the pins and their shadows caused by side lighting create a variety of forms for animation photography. Alexeïeff has made numerous short animation films with this technique and also used it to create the prologue scenes for Orson Welles's *The Trial* (1963).

■ **pipe boom** A microphone boom that is made of two sections of piping that extend or collapse together.

■ **pipe clamp** A small device for hanging lights and other equipment from steel pipes or crossbeams.

■ **pipe grid** *See* **grid.**

■ **pirated print** A print made illegally without permission of the copyright owners.

■ **pistol grip** A handle on the bottom of a hand camera or microphone for easy and firm carriage of the instrument.

■ **pitch** The presentation of a concept for a film to one or more individuals representing a film studio or some other source of funding necessary to make the film. This presentation, which is normally verbal, brief, and passionate, is an attempt to sell the concept so that it can go into development. The presentation is made at a "pitch meeting." Robert Altman's film *The Player* (1992), a satire on Hollywood filmmaking, gives an acerbic portrayal of the way pitches are made in the industry.

■ **pitch, perforation pitch** The distance between perforations on film. On positives the pitch is longer between perforations than on negatives to prevent slippage when the positive passes on the outside of the negative over the same sprocket holes during contact printing. For this reason the first distance is called long as well as positive pitch and the second is called short as well as negative pitch. On 35mm positive film, long pitch is .1866 inches and on the negative the short pitch is .1870.

■ **pitching lens** A special lens, placed at the end of an optical relay tube, that can be remotely controlled to tilt 180 degrees and rotate 360 degrees while keeping the image correctly situated in the frame. The lens has an impressive depth of field and is excellent for shooting miniatures, achieving a variety of different angles and positions as well as moving extremely close to any model.

■ **pitch meeting** *See* **pitch.**

■ **pix** A slang abbreviation for motion pictures.

■ **pixel** An abbreviation for "picture element," the term refers to the smallest dots that make up the image on a video screen. The greater the amount of pixels, the higher the degree of resolution in the image. *See* **computer animation.**

■ **pixilation, pixillation** A type of animation, generally with people as subjects, that achieves rapid, jerky movements for a cartoon effect (the term pixilated, which means comically eccentric, is a compound version of titillated pixy). This technique is achieved by (1) stop-motion photography, when characters' movements are posed like those of puppets and shot frame by frame, or (2) editing, when single frames are selected out of a regularly photographed sequence of action and run together like a series of jump cuts. A well-known short work using the first method of pixillation is the Canadian filmmaker Norman McLaren's *Neighbors* (1952). The second technique is sometimes employed for comic effect (e.g., in Tony Richardson's *Tom Jones* [1963]).

■ **plan américain (American shot)** A term used in French criticism for a type of medium long shot employed in classic American films. A character or characters are normally shown from approximately knees to head. Also called a three-quarters shot.

■ **plane** The area of a two-dimensional surface of an image. One can speak of such horizontal planes as the background, foreground, and subject. Sometimes reference is also made to the vertical planes of a picture. In deep-focus cinematography, all the horizontal planes are kept in focus. *See* **deep focus, image plane,** *and* **plane of critical focus.**

■ **plane of critical focus** The area of a subject at which all the points are in sharpest focus and will appear as points on the film. The area both in front and in back of this plane with acceptable focus is considered the image's depth of field.

■ **plano-convex spotlight** A spotlight using a plano-convex lens (i.e., a lens with one side a plane and the other convex) to focus the light into a narrow beam. *See* **spotlight.**

■ **plan-séquence** A French critical term that means, roughly, an uninterrupted sequence and is used to describe a long shot where the meaning of the scene comes from the movement and action within the frame and not the movement from shot to shot. The camera may move to follow action, but the audience discovers significance rather than having the editing discover it for them. The French director Renoir is heralded as a master of this technique. *See* **deep focus.**

■ **plate** (1) A still photograph with a glass backing. *See* **background plate.** (2) Any background shot for a composite image that may or may not include live action. (3). A shot used in making a composite image. *See* **special effects.** (4) The rewind discs on flat-bed editing machines for both picture film and sound tracks. Such machines have up to eight plates. *See* **flat-bed editing machine.**

■ **platforming** Releasing a film at first to a limited number of theaters and markets in the hope that a positive audience response will build sufficient awareness of and interest in the film among the larger public to warrant a wider distribution. *See* **distribution.**

■ **platter system, platter transport** A modern system for feeding and taking up film that runs through a projector. Three horizontal platters, each capable of holding up to four and one-half hours of film, are situated near the projector. The top platter feeds the film for an entire show into the machine, and one of the other platters receives it in such a way that the film need not be rewound. After a simple rethreading, the entire show can run again (in some machines even the rethreading is unnecessary). The third platter is normally used for the assembly of the next show. A single make-up table is used to put together and feed the film to a number

of such systems, when not in use, and also to unreel and break down the film after the screening. The film is taken up from or returned to the table electronically, and the speed of this movement can be altered. *See* **projection booth,** *and* **projector.**

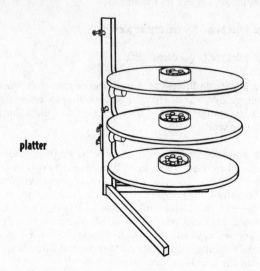

platter

■ **playback** (1) The playing of sound that has just been recorded. (2) The playing of images (and often sound) from videotape that have just been recorded at the same time the scene was photographed by a film camera. Such playback gives an immediate reproduction of the way the scene will appear on the film and tells the director whether the take needs to be repeated. (3) The playing of music and singing that have already been recorded while the actors and actresses perform the actions to the scene and mouth the words of the song for the camera. Ultimately both sound and picture will be joined. Such a technique permits optimum sound and picture as well as the dubbing of voices for performers who are not doing their own singing. (4) The playing of previously recorded music for the rehearsal of a scene.

■ **playback equalization curve** (1) A defined standard used in the making of the sound mix to equalize the various sounds and compensate for any loss. (2) A defined standard used in balancing and equalizing the sound from shot to shot in a specific scene primarily to compensate for any loss. (3) A defined standard used to equalize sound and compensate for any loss in recording, rerecording, or playback—an equalizer is also built into the amplifier of the playback system. (4) The playback equalization curve used in mixing sound for theaters, until the 1970s, to compensate for loss in the actual playback. Called the Academy curve. *See* **equalizer.**

■ **playback operator, playback engineer** The individual in a sound studio responsible for playing back the recorded music or sound for a film. Playbacks may occur to photograph a musical number or a performer lip syncing, or simply for judging the sound. The playback operator is instructed by the sound mixer.

■ **playback track**   The sound track used above in (3) and (4).

■ **playdate**   (1) The specific date on which a film is released for exhibition, either in a limited or national distribution; (2) the engagement of a film at a particular theater for a specific duration. *See* **exhibition.**

■ **playing flat**   When a film plays at a theater for a specific and single rental fee. *See* **exhibition.**

■ **playing percentage**   When a film plays at a theater for a percentage of the box-office gross. *See* **exhibition.**

■ **playoff**   (1) The duration of time that a film is contracted to play in a theater. (2) The manner of release for a film (e.g., limited, general, or wide).

■ **playtime, playing time**   (1) The uninterrupted duration of a film's run in a theater or market from the time of its release. *See* **run.** (2) A designated period for a film's release, e.g., "summer playtime."

■ **plot**   The individual events and their arrangement in a narrative work. Whereas the term "story" is concerned with the overall action of the work in chronological order and can be expressed as a general description of what occurs, "plot" refers to the specific actions, both external and psychological, and their developing relationship that results from the order and way in which they are presented in the work itself. Hence, though there may be one general story of Cinderella, there may be many treatments with different events and plot structures. E. M. Forster, in *Aspects of the Novel*, makes the well-known argument that plot is distinct from story in that its events are linked together in a causal relationship, while there is no necessary relationship between the events of a story. However, this definition does not take into account the many works whose events are linked together by some other principle than cause and effect. For example, events in the traditional picaresque novel are sometimes unrelated except for the presence of the same hero—a fact equally true of many modern novels and films. There are also those works in which events are related by a single location, historical development, or theme. Common usage, at least, prohibits us from considering these works as plotless. Some critics have distinguished plots that emphasize action, character, or ideas, but even though one can isolate such works in film as well as fiction, most often action, character, and ideas are so interrelated that it is arbitrary to argue for one emphasis instead of another. In complex narrative works, action is a result of character and character a result of action;

and what the character thinks and feels or how he or she develops is as much an action as any external event.

A popular concept in recent critical theory, though developed earlier in the century by the Russian Formalist critics, argues that plot by itself is an insufficient concept to deal with narrative structures, that there are, in fact, two kinds of plot that many works manifest—the sequence of events that we immediately confront as we read a book or witness a film, and the sequence of events that we reconstruct from this first order of events in our own mind and that is not narrated (the two types of plot are called *sujet* and *fabula*). In many works there is no distinction and the sequence of events we read or see as the work progresses is all that is important; but in other works there is another, sometimes more significant plot—one that is revealed through what characters tell us, through flashbacks, or through our own deductive capacities. For example, the mystery film often presents a plot that deals with a detective seeking to discover the reasons for a crime and the perpetrator of the crime (the *sujet*), but at the same time we piece together (along with the detective) what actually happened and join to this the present investigation as the final part of the complete action (both the events of the crime and the investigation add up to the *fabula*). In Otto Preminger's *Laura* (1944), the present plot is only a means to discover the larger overall plot of which it is a part, which began before the commencement of the film. In a number of films, past events are discovered, and sometimes shown, to make evident the effect of the past upon the present. The present is broken up with random events from the past, sometimes shown out of chronological sequence, forcing us to reassemble all the events of the *sujet*, both past and present, into the chronological sequence of the *fabula*. The most outstanding example of this is the French director Alain Resnais's *Hiroshima Mon Amour* (1959), where the love affair of the Japanese man and French woman is interrupted by scenes from their past lives that force us, as the film progresses, to reconstruct and integrate their past and present and even surmise their future. We are reminded not only of the power of the past, but also of the mind's atemporal nature which keeps the past ever-present. Plot, then, is a dynamic force that imposes both order and meaning upon the work's events. *See* **story** *and* **structure.**

■ **plug**   A device that connects an electrical cord to a current, generally by means of prongs inserted into a socket.

■ **plugging box**   *See* **spider box.**

■ **plus lens**   *See* **diopter lens.**

■ **pocket**   An outlet for electricity in a studio, which generally has a protective cover.

■ **poetic cinema** (1) A term sometimes used for American avant-garde films in the 1940s and 1950s. These films were both abstract and psychological in nature, especially showing the influence of Freud. Maya Deren's *Meshes of the Afternoon* (1943) is perhaps the best-known example. (2) The term has also been used by Jonas Mekas and others to describe New American Cinema in general. *See* **avant-garde cinema** *and* **New American Cinema.**

poetic realism *Children of Paradise* (1945; dir. Marcel Carné) features Pierre Brasseur, Arletty, and Jean-Louis Barrault in this classic film about life and art.

■ ■ ■

■ **poetic realism** A term used by Georges Sadoul (see *Histoire du cinéma mondial*) and others to describe a group of French films made from 1934 to 1940 that integrates both realism and a lyrical style of filmmaking. The subject matter of these films often deals with common, everyday life, but such concerns are infused with a lyrical treatment, a kind of moody and brooding sensitivity achieved by a strong emphasis on *mise-en-scène*—especially on composition, impressionistic lighting, and static shots. Often evident as well are suggestive symbolism and stylistic acting.

Jacques Feyder was one of the first of these filmmakers, and his two films, *The Great Game* (1934), about the Foreign Legion, and *Carnival in Flanders* (*La Kermesse héroïque;* 1935), a rich Flemish tapestry about sixteenth-century life in Flanders, are significant. Julien Duvivier also created a number of these films; perhaps the best remembered is *Pépé le Moko* (1937), a spin-off from the American gangster film with Jean Gabin as the romantic antihero of the Casbah. Marcel Carné, with the screenwriter Jacques Prévert, made several significant films of poetic realism, especially the heavy and fatalistic *Port of Shadows* (1938), also with Jean Gabin; but undoubtedly their greatest film, a land-

mark in world cinema, was *Children of Paradise* (1945), a stylish, elegant, and spectacular poetic drama dealing with theater life in nineteenth-century Paris. Although made in occupied France during the war years, this film is the culmination of French poetic realism. Also important in this group of directors is Jean Renoir, son of the great French impressionist painter, who, developing out of a career in silent films, went on to make a series of moving and powerful sound films, culminating with his antiwar *Grande Illusion* (1937), with a script by Charles Spaak and starring Jean Gabin and Erich von Stroheim, and his extraordinarily delicate, profound, and pessimistic comedy of manners about a decaying social world, *The Rules of the Game* (1939), both prime examples of poetic realism.

■ **pogo stick** *See* **polecat.**

■ **point** A percentage in a contractual agreement concerning a film—an individual or organization gets 10 percent or 10 points of a film's gross or net profits, for example.

■ **point of view** Although one sometimes talks about an author's or a director's "point of view" about certain subjects, the term, in relation to narrative form, normally applies to the eyes through which we view the action. In film, the dominant perspective belongs to the neutral camera, although there are frequent divergences from this perspective to those of various characters. Frequent shifts of point of view in a novel, however, are disturbing, perhaps because we tend to identify with the characters of fiction more than those of film by reading about their emotional lives and internalizing their thoughts. Sudden shifts in points of view jolt us out of this identification. In film, on the other hand, we are shut off from the character's inner world: since the world of sight constantly confronts us as an objective fact and since the characters themselves are a visible and concrete part of this world, we internalize and identify with them less. Because we are consistently aware of our own role as viewer and of the role of the camera as shower, we are more at ease to see things for brief moments from other possible perspectives.

The various points of view in literary narrations are often applied to film in critical discussions since both are narrative forms and since film theory has not yet worked out its own critical terminology. First-person point of view, where the literary story is narrated by a character and we are inside the character, looking out from his or her perspective, is compared to those occasions in film when we hear a voice-over from one of the characters narrating the actions that he or she has experienced and that we see (e.g., Charles Dickens's *Great Expectations* and the film version by David Lean in 1946 both use first-person narrations in this manner). Sometimes, however, what appear to be first-person narrations are employed to describe actions and points of view largely belonging to other characters, so that the technique actually resembles a third-person narration (e.g., in both Emily Brontë's *Wuthering Heights* and the film version by William Wyler in 1939). Both cases of first-person narration in film, though, are normally accompanied by a third-person camera, when we see the action and all the characters through the eyes of the camera. Sometimes we see an action the way a character sees it, through a point of view shot with the camera acting as the character's eyes, but a constantly subjective camera technique has not been successful in film and has only been tried rarely. In Robert Montgomery's *Lady in the Lake* (1946), all the action is seen as the detective sees it, but we miss seeing him as part of the action. We do not have the necessary identification with the character that we achieve in literary fiction, which would allow us to dispense with him as part of the concrete visual world that is the very medium of film. Film makes visible all the story's elements, and the absence of the protagonist's visible form leaves a gap. Film allows us the subjective or first-person point of view when the camera shows us for that instant what a character sees, but normally the camera also moves back and forth from the character's view of the scene to the camera's view of the character in the scene, and also between different subjective points of view. This switching back and forth is most obvious in film during conversations, when we move back and forth between the different perspectives of the speaking characters, looking at one person through the eyes of the other and also looking at both characters through the neutral camera.

In literary narration, two basic types of third-person point of view, when the major characters are described as he or she, not "I," are prominent. In the first, the narrator seems an omniscient person who tells us about the characters and their reactions, moving from place to place without identifying intensely with any single figure—to a large extent this is the way most films work, with the camera functioning as the omniscient narrator. In the second type, the narrator seems to disappear, and the action is described largely through the perspective of a single character for large sections of the work or for the entire work—the major character is still "he" or "she," but we are inside the character to such an extent that our involvement changes the "he" or "she" to an "I" with whom we identify. This second approach is also possible in film when we are mostly concerned with a single character for long periods; but we still sense the omniscient camera viewing the figure, viewing with the figure, and viewing others viewing the figure. The omniscience of the camera's point of view allows sufficient flexibility to incorporate within its perspective other perspectives as well.

■ **point-of-view shot (POV)** A subjective shot that shows a scene exactly the way a character would see it, hence

dramatizing his or her perspective and putting us, at least for the moment, in the character's shoes. Films integrate such shots with normal objective shots that include the character within the scene. Varying both kinds of shots can be effective in building suspense in mysteries and horror stories, since we are allowed to see more than the character while we are still involved with the character. Hitchcock is particularly adept at this kind of editing and sometimes includes subjective shots from the perspective of the criminal to intensify our fear, as he does in *Psycho* (1960). In many films, we are given point-of-view shots from several characters who appear in a scene—for example, in conversations when we watch the individual speakers talking or listening from the perspectives of the other characters. *See* **point of view.**

■ **polar diagram** A diagram showing the directivity pattern for a microphone's pickup. *See* **microphone.**

■ **polarized lens** A lens with a polarized filter for the reduction of polarized light.

■ **polarized light** Light waves "polarized" so that they vibrate on only one plane, unlike normal waves, which vibrate on all planes at right angles to their direction of movement. Such light comes from reflection or glare from nonmetallic surfaces such as water and glass when light strikes the surface at an angle or from refraction when sunlight passes through a cloudless sky. *See* **polarizing filter.**

■ **polarized projection** *See* **stereoscopy.**

■ **polarizing filter, polarizing screen, pola screen** A filter attached to a camera to eliminate unwanted reflection or glare from shiny surfaces such as water and glass, though not from metal. Such a screen is also used to darken skies, which are lit from polarized waves, to shoot through the windshield of a car, and to eliminate haze when photographing a landscape. Pola screens function by means of slits which, at right angles, stop from passing the single plane of vibrations of polarized light, while permitting nonpolarized light to pass. Such filters do not change colors in the scene, but diminish overall light, thus necessitating greater exposure for the film. *See* **polarized light.**

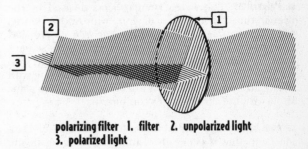

polarizing filter l. filter 2. unpolarized light
3. polarized light

■ **Polaroid fade** A fade achieved by rotating two Polaroid polarizing filters in front of the camera lens. Filters gradually moved to parallel positions result in a fade-in, and moved to cross positions result in a fade-out. *See* **polarizing filter.**

■ **polecat, pogo stick** A telescopic tube that can be extended or collapsed to fit tightly between floor and ceiling, or between two walls as a support for various types of lamps or for cross tubes that can also hold lamps. *See* **sky bar.**

■ **polish** A moderate amount of rewriting for a script—less than a revision. A polish is normally performed on a script in its final stages. A new writer might be hired at this point to "polish" the script. *See* **rewrite.**

■ **polyester base** Because of its greater strength than normal triacetate base, polyester base is now largely employed for the internegatives that have to be used in high-speed printers to make a large number of release prints. Polyester base is now also popular for the release prints themselves because it can better withstand constant usage. The recent awareness of the instability of triacetate base has made polyester the base of choice for preservation, especially for interpositives and separation masters for color images. Because polyester also creates a thinner base than triacetate, rolls can hold a larger amount of film. Triacetate base is still used for original negatives and dailies since it is easier to cut for editing. Since Kodak's Estar is a polyester base much in use, its name is often used generically for this kind of film. *See* **acetate base, film** *(1), and* **separation masters.**

■ **polygonal-based modeling, polygonal modeling** In computer animation and graphics, using an assembly of individual polygons to create a three-dimensional model. Polygons are the smallest shapes that go into the making of the primitives (i.e., cubes, cones, and spheres) that are themselves the source of the models. Since polygons have at least three straight sides, they are best used for objects with straight edges (curved edges might seem jagged, since they would be composed of a series of straight lines). Spline modeling is more effective for curved or rounded objects. *See* **computer animation** *and* **spline-based modeling.**

■ **Polyvision** The wide-screen process devised by the French director Abel Gance, along with André Debrie, for his monumental silent film, *Napoléon vu par Abel Gance* (1927). Gance used three connected screens with three projectors to create multiscreen effects with the side images complementary to or contrasting with the central image and also to create wide panoramic shots with the three images combined.

■ **pool hall lighting** Illumination for a scene from a single lamp that is generally visible and hanging in the middle of the set.

■ **pop-in, pop-out** (1) A technique in animation that allows signs such as arrows, pointing fingers, circles, or lines suddenly to appear on maps or diagrams. This effect is achieved by briefly shooting the map or diagram, stopping the camera to insert the sign, and then continuing the camera. (2) A technique in shooting a scene that allows objects or characters suddenly to appear. This effect is achieved by stopping the camera, inserting the object or character, and resuming the camera. Also referred to as pop-on, pop-off.

■ **popping** A loud popping noise that results, during recording, from a performer pronouncing the letter *p* with too much emphasis.

■ **pornographic film** Any film made solely for sexual arousement and featuring nudity and explicit sexual acts. Such films, in their crude technique and sexual exploitation, lack any "redeeming social value" (to use the Supreme Court phrase), a fact that separates them from serious films that employ sex as part of larger thematic concerns and present the human body and lovemaking with tact and imagination. Pornographic film can be roughly divided into two categories: those so brief and amateurish that they can only circulate outside film theaters (for example, films distributed or sold by sex shops) and those that are somewhat longer and more expensively made which play in theaters designated only for such film. Also referred to as porno film, adult film, X-rated film, blue movie, stag film. *See* **censorship.**

■ **portable mixer** *See* **mixer** *and* **mixing panel.**

■ **portable rig, location rig** All the equipment used for location shooting. Such equipment is lightweight, often collapsible, and easy to transport. Cameras, lighting, and their ancillary equipment make up the key portions of the portable rig.

■ **pose-to-pose animation** The technique of creating animated cartoons when the animator conceives of and draws the key poses or "extremes" and the "in-betweener" draws the connecting actions. *See* **animation.**

■ **positive (POS)** A film with developed images in which lighting values and colors correspond to those of the subject photographed. A positive is normally made from a negative, in which black and white are reversed and colors are complementary to the original colors, through contact or optical printing. In reversal film, however, the original film from the camera is made into the positive. Prints used in projectors are positive. *See* **film** *(1),* **negative,** *and* **reversal film.**

■ **positive drive** The system for moving film through a processor that uses sprockets with teeth to engage the perforations. Such a system is not used for negative film, since it sometimes damages perforations.

■ **positive perforation** The Kodak standard (KS) perforation used on positive 35mm film, which is rectangular with curved corners. Such perforations are more durable than the negative, or Bell and Howell (BH), perforation used for 35mm film, which, though better for registration, is prone to tearing because of its arced corners and shorter height. Kodak standard perforations are also used on 65mm negatives and 70mm prints. *See* **Bell and Howell perforation** *and* **perforations.**

■ **positive pitch** The distance between perforations on positive film that is longer than that on negative film and so is also referred to as long pitch. (The distance on negative film is referred to as "negative" or "short" pitch.) In contact printing, the two films must pass together over the same sprockets with the positive on the outside, hence requiring the greater distance to avoid slippage.

■ **positive sound track** The positive print of the optical sound track on which the photographed image of the light is clear (the area of light on the negative is recorded as dark). *See* **optical sound.**

■ **positive splice** The point at which two pieces of positive film are held together by cement, and where the overlap is more than that for a negative film. On small-gauge films such a splice will be visible in the frame and show on projection. For this reason A and B printing might be preferable for such film. *See* **A and B printing** *and* **negative splice.**

■ **postdubbing** *See* **dub** *and* **looping.**

■ **postflashing, postfogging** Exposing already exposed film to a constant, dim light in order to reduce contrast and mute colors. *See* **preflashing.**

■ **postmodernism** The term, which refers to the period in cultural, intellectual, and social history beginning roughly in the 1960s and continuing beyond the present, is meant to convey the radical break from the basic assumptions of "modernism," the period beginning at the end of the nineteenth century and lasting roughly until after the Second World War. Modernism was a questioning of traditional beliefs about God, the universe, morality, time and space, and art, but in the very questioning was an assumption that the earlier issues had credibility—that though the answers might change, the questions were still valid. Postmodernism assumes a definite break with the past and totally new assumptions about reality. It is significant that the pe-

postmodernism Harrison Ford is looking to do someone (or something) in as he surveys the postmodern world of Ridley Scott's *Blade Runner* (1982).

■ ■ ■

riod begins with the rise of television and the expansion of media—it is concomitant with an age dominated by media, information, and technology, all of which have changed our ways of seeing reality and ourselves.

In 1967, the French social critic Guy Debord wrote an important tract called *Society of the Spectacle* in which he proclaimed that ours was no longer an age "directly lived" but was instead an age of representation, of images detached from actuality. Our entire economic system and concept of reality is motivated by an endless succession of images of commodities—as soon as one image becomes a possessed object, another image awakens our longing. Jean Baudrillard, the French apostate of the postmodern period, divorced these images from economy and production in the present world by talking about our age as one of simulacra, of images without a reference to any reality whatsoever. The truth is that there is no truth—that images and reality have become indistinguishable. Disneyland, by pretending to be make-believe, performs the function of hiding from us the realization that the world surrounding it is one comprised of the hyperreal and simulation. Ours is a world in which the interface between media and reality breaks down, in which there finally is no separation between the images on the screen and everyday reality—we are as much part of the media as the media is part of us. Recall the striking image in David Cronenberg's *Videodrome* (1982) of the lead character literally becoming a video player, with the tapes inserted into his body.

Fredric Jameson, in his 1984 essay, "Postmodernism, Or The Cultural Logic of Late Capitalism" that appeared in the *New Left Review,* defines our new reality as one in which the individual's feelings of anxiety and alienation in the age of modernism have disappeared, in which the self has become decentered, losing the capacity for any feelings whatsoever and any sense of time. The loss of self results in the loss of individual style, producing in art the prevalence of pastiche, the accumulation of imitations of the codes of the past—a quality very much discernible in film. But Jameson also refers to our age as the latest development in the machine age, whereby the machine itself has become an agent of reproduction (creating images and simulacrum) instead of production, and space has moved from the private realm to "the circuits and networks" of some "deadly interlocking and competing information agencies"—the manifestation of "multinational capitalism."

The film that has often been cited as best manifesting the qualities of postmodernism is Ridley Scott's *Blade Runner* (1982), with its vision of a decentered, pastiche world comprised of a landscape pulling together the "futuristic" vision of Fritz Lang's 1926 film *Metropolis,* contemporary urban decay, and future technology; a world with a racially polyglot population and a breakdown in the distinction between human and machine; and a decentered, atemporal world where both space and time have lost any meaningful parameters.

■ **postproduction** That part of filmmaking that comes immediately after the shooting is completed and includes editing, the addition of special effects and optical transitions, and the mixing of all sound tracks.

■ **postproduction services, completion services** Those activities performed during postproduction. *See* **postproduction.**

■ **postproduction supervisor** The postproduction supervisor schedules, oversees, and integrates such activities as editing, sound dubbing and mixing, and special effects, keeping an eye on both the calendar and budget. For less-complicated productions, this role can be accomplished by a producer, production manager, or the editor; but for films that require a series of complicated activities, a separate individual is more likely to be assigned the job. *See* **postproduction.**

■ **postrecording** Recording dialogue and sound for a film after it has been photographed; also referred to as dubbing and postsynchronizing. *See* **dub** *and* **postsynchronization.**

■ **postscoring** Recording music for a film after it has been edited.

■ **postsynchronization, postsync** Postrecording sound, especially dialogue, after the film has been photographed and edited so that the new sound is in synchronization with the action on the screen. This technique, part of filmmaking since 1932, allows on-location shooting where recording is difficult, corrects sound recorded poorly during shooting, adds the voices of professional singers to nonsinging performers, and substitutes the audience's native language for the original dialogue of a foreign film. Most Italian films have used postsynchronization entirely since Rossellini's neorealist films. A guide track of dialogue is generally recorded during shooting and later divided into segments that are looped together and played over and over with the accompanying picture to guide the performers and allow them to rehearse for the actual postrecording. The process is also called dubbing and the dialogue recorded loop lines. *See* **dub.**

■ **pot** A rheostatic volume control on a recorder or amplifier (this word is an abbreviation of potentiometer). To "pot-up" is to increase the sound level and to "pot-down" to decrease it.

■ **POV** *See* **point-of-view shot.**

■ **powder man** Jargon for the individual responsible for fires and explosions in a film production. *See* **mechanical effects.**

■ **power belt**   *See* **battery belt.**

■ **power pack**   A small portable unit, containing batteries, that runs a lightweight camera or recording unit.

■ **power zoom**   A motor control for a zoom lens that operates the lens automatically and allows it to move smoothly at the same speed for a zoom shot. *See* **zoom lens.**

■ **practical**   The word is applied to any part of a set, such as doors, windows, and lights, that functions normally, or to the set itself when it is not used for background or decoration but is actually used by the performers. Functioning props are referred to as practicals or pracs as well as action properties or action props.

■ **practical set**   The term is used for an actual location for filming instead of a studio set and sometimes for a studio set with practical features such as real walls, doors, windows, and light fixtures.

■ **pratfall**   A slang term for a fall on the prat (i.e., buttocks), an action that has been part of comic film since the silent comedies of such filmmakers as Mack Sennett.

Praxinoscope

■ **Praxinoscope**   An early machine for viewing a series of drawings that create an illusion of motion through the viewer's persistence of vision. The machine, invented by Émile Reynaud in 1877, allowed the viewer to watch a moving strip of painted pictures, placed on the inside of a rotating drum, through their reflection in a centrally located polygonal mirror. This device was a development of the Zoetrope, but Raymond also went on to use the principle of the magic lantern and project his animated pictures, painted on translucent material, onto the rear of a screen viewed by an audience. In 1892, he began his Théâtre Optique in Paris, showing short pieces and even stories with moving figures of people and animals. These shows became quite popular and lasted until 1900, when he was put out of business by the motion pictures photographed on film. *See* **Phenakistiscope, Stroboscope,** *and* **Zoetrope.**

■ **prebreak**   To partially cut or sever a breakaway prop so that when used in the film production it will easily come apart (e.g., a chair to be broken over someone's head).

■ **prebuy**   Purchasing the rights to a film before it has actually been produced. In the industry today, such sales made especially to cable television and video cassette firms furnish producers with needed funds for making such films.

■ **predub**   *See* **premix.**

■ **preflashing, prefogging**   Exposing film not yet used for shooting to a constant, dim light in order to reduce contrast and to mute colors in the images which will later be produced. *See* **desaturation** *and* **postflashing.**

■ **prelay**   (1) Preparing the various sound tracks for the final mix: to line up the tracks. (2) To perform a preliminary mix or mixes in preparation for the final mix. *See* **mix.**

■ **prelight, prerig**   Rigging the set in advance (i.e., preparing the lighting) for the next day's shooting, perhaps while shooting is taking place elsewhere, a practice that saves a good deal of time and expense.

■ **premiere**   The first public performance of a motion picture. The term "world premiere" is sometimes employed to heighten the drama of the occasion.

■ **premix, predub**   An early mix of sound tracks which itself will later be combined with other premixes, eventually to form the final mix. Numerous tracks of dialogue, music, and sound effects are themselves premixed into several tracks for each category; these are then premixed into the dialogue (D), music (M), and effects (E) tracks, three premixes which will themselves finally combine to form the final mix. A film can have more than fifteen separate sound tracks going into the final D, M, and E tracks. Premixing allows better control and balancing of the various sound components and is also necessary because the mixing console does not have enough playback heads for all the individual tracks. Premixing the music and sound-effects tracks into the M and E track allows translated dialogue to be dubbed in later for foreign releases. *See* **M and E track** *and* **mix.**

■ **preproduction**   The early stage in making a film, preceding the actual shooting, that includes casting, contracting performers and production personnel, writing the script, designing and building sets, scheduling the shooting, and budgeting the entire enterprise.

■ **prequel**   Jargon for a sequel whose action predates that of the original film. For example, Francis Ford Coppola's *The Godfather, Part II* (1974) is as much a prequel as a sequel in that it frequently goes back in time and shows the childhood and early manhood of characters introduced in *The Godfather* (1971).

■ **prerecord, prescore** To record music or any sound for a film before the film is shot. Sound is frequently prerecorded for animation works.

■ **pre-sale, pre-sale financing** Financing a film in part by selling rights before the work has been started or finished. For example, a filmmaker may get a project off the ground by selling its cable or foreign distribution rights.

■ **prescore** To record music to be used in a film before the film is actually shot.

■ **prescore and playback** To record music and perhaps singing to be used in a film before the film has actually been shot. Musical numbers are frequently accomplished this way with the music and singing first recorded under proper conditions in a recording studio and then played back while the performers act their roles and mouth the lyrics in front of the camera.

■ **presence** (1) The immediacy and reality of recorded sound that makes the original source of the sound actually seem in the room. (2) The particular ambience and tone of sound that a location creates. (3) The sense of immediacy and the strong impact that a performer creates through his or her personality and manner.

■ **presentative blocking** Situating a character in the scene so that he or she is directly present to the camera. Sometimes a director will intentionally stage a character so that he or she is directly talking to the audience, and the distance between the two is minimized in order to create (1) a greater involvement for the viewer, as in Ingmar Bergman's *Hour of the Wolf* (1968); (2) a documentary or newsreel reality as if the character were being interviewed outside the film, as in Jean-Luc Godard's *A Married Woman* (1964); (3) and a comic effect, as in Woody Allen's *Annie Hall* (1977).

■ **preservative** A substance, such as lacquer, applied to film to prevent scratching, abrasion, or deterioration.

■ **preset** A control system that predetermines the lighting intensity for one or more luminaires and can be operated by a switch on the control panel.

■ **press agent** A less formal term for a publicist and one often used for the person who seeks to further the career of an individual, especially a performer, by acquiring for him or her publicity in any of the popular media. *See* **publicist.**

■ **press book, pressbook** A compilation of material for advertising and promoting a film sent by the production company to a distributor. Such a collection includes posters and art work of various sizes for reproduction in newspapers and other advertising media, stills from the film, photographs of the stars, information concerning personnel and the making of the film, and promotional ideas.

■ **press junket, press tour** A tour taken by the performers and director to key market areas to meet with the press, give interviews, appear on radio and television, and perform whatever activities are necessary to bring attention to a film's opening.

■ **press kit, presskit** A packet of material for advertising and promoting a film sent by the distributor to an exhibitor, an individual theater, or the press. Such a packet contains news stories and information concerning the production, stills from the film, and photographs of the stars.

■ **pressure plate** (1) A small plate behind the aperture of a camera, projector, or optical printer that applies pressure against the film base to keep the emulsion surface of the frame aligned within the focal plane of the lens. (2) A plate of glass in an animation stand that applies pressure against the cels and background artwork to keep them flat and in position. Also called a platen.

■ **prestriped stock** Film stock for cinematography with a magnetic stripe for the recording of sound. *See* **single-system sound recording.**

■ **preview** (1) A short film advertising a feature film prior to its showing. The preview is generally shown in the theater where the feature film will appear and includes brief excerpts from it. Sometimes previews, also called crossplugs, are shown at other theaters belonging to the same exhibition chain. For major films, briefer previews, sometimes called teasers and often without excerpts, are released further in advance, even in the final stages of production. Also referred to as coming attractions and trailers. *See* **trailer** *(1)*. (2) An advance showing of a film, generally soon before its release. Production previews allow the filmmakers to judge audience reactions so that they can make last-minute editing decisions. Distribution or marketing previews are used to determine release patterns and advertising strategies. Audiences normally fill out questionnaires or preview cards concerning their reactions to the film. Because these showings receive relatively little publicity, they are sometimes called sneak previews. Previews are also available to possible exhibitors of the film, film critics, and sometimes to groups with a special interest in the film's material.

■ **preview print, sample print** A print of a feature film before its release, supplied for any of the reasons listed under preview.

■ **previsualization** Any of the systems that allow the various personnel in a film production to see some estimate of how part of a film might appear before the actual shooting. Such procedures include sketches, drawings, storyboards, video composite images, and digital images. Any part of a film envisioned in advance—furniture, setting, location, costumes, makeup, shots, scenes, sequences, even casting—are part of the previsualization process. Electronic storyboarding through a number of software packages now allows the director and cinematographer to try out any number of shots with different camera angles, positions, movements, settings, and filters, as well as a variety of lighting styles and alterations in the setting. Movements of figures through the set in depth can be created as well as a whole sequence of edited actions. Characters can be photographed on film, video, or digitally and composited into a variety of settings before the costly expense of principal photography and special effects. It is now possible by digitizing image and sound to create rough cuts of a segment of shooting and view composite shots on the set.

■ **primary colors** The three colors, red, blue, and green, that mixed together form all the other colors as they appear in photographic processes. *See* **color film** *(2) and* **complementary colors.**

■ **prime fixture, prime** An open-faced luminaire with a control at the back for focusing the illumination either as a flood or spotlight—the reflector is stationary, but the bulb is moved either closer for a wider beam or farther away for a narrower light. Such lights can be used for a variety of functions—as key or back lights, for example. *See* **lighting.**

■ **prime lens** A lens for a camera with a fixed focal length that operates at a single distance from the film plane. *See* **lens.**

■ **primitives** In computer animation and graphics, such basic geometric shapes as cubes, spheres, and cones that are manipulated in shape and form, and assembled together as the basis for a model. *See* **computer animation** *and* **polygonal modeling.**

■ **principal focal plane** The plane that passes through the principal focus perpendicular to the optical axis. *See* **principal focus.**

■ **principal focus** The point at which parallel light waves refracted through a lens are imaged. *See* **nodal points** *and* **principal points.**

■ **principal photography** The main photography for a film that includes the performers, as distinguished from photography by the second unit, which normally concentrates on setting and background work. *See* **second unit.**

■ **principal planes** The planes through the principal points of the lens perpendicular to the optical axis. A light ray entering the first principal plane leaves the second the same distance from the axis.

■ **principal players, principals** The main and featured performers in a film.

■ **principal points** The points on the axis of the lens from which object and image distances are measured. Principal points are where the principal planes intersect with the optical axis. These points are formally defined as the conjugate points for which the magnification is unity. *See* **nodal points** *and* **principal focus.**

■ **principal ray, chief ray** The ray that passes through the center of the aperture of a lens and is the central ray of a bundle of rays coming from an object point.

■ **print** (1) A reel of positive film made from a negative or on original reversal film. The print contains images with the lighting and color of the actual scene. Workprints are used for editing. A print called the master positive or interpositive, which is made from the edited original, is the source of the dupe negatives used for making release prints. (2) Any duplicate, either positive or negative, made from another film. Since the dupe negative, for example, is printed from a master positive, it too is sometimes referred to as a print. In most usage, however, the term print refers to a positive. (3) To make a positive reel of film from a negative or on reversal film. (4) *See* **print it.**

■ **print and pickup** The term refers to the process of rephotographing part of a shot from a particular point. The term suggests that the first and satisfactory part of the original shot will later be printed (although the entire shot will likely be printed and the second part not used) and shooting will now pick up from the point where the shot is no longer satisfactory.

■ **printer** The machine that makes prints or duplicates of a film. Positives are normally printed from negatives, and negatives from positives. In the case of reversal film, however, negatives can be printed from negatives and positives from positives. There are basically two kinds of printers, contact and optical. In the contact printer, which operates by means of sprocket teeth engaging perforations on each film and moving them past the aperture for exposure, both negative and raw stock, for example, come in contact (emulsion to emulsion) before the aperture, where a light transfers the image of the first onto the second. There are two types of contact printers—continuous, where both films run rapidly without stop past the aperture, and intermittent or step, where each frame stops briefly before the light, which is blocked by a shutter while the next frame moves into place. Loops on both sides of the aperture permit the intermittent stop-and-go movement in the step printer without pulling on and tearing the film. Because continuous contact printers move the film so rapidly and because they are relatively easy to run, they are generally employed for making rush prints or large numbers of release prints (in the second instance, negatives can be run back and forth or looped to run without cessation). Composite negatives of both image and sound are used for the printing of black-and-white film, but color film requires that separate reels of image and sound track be printed with two separate heads onto the single composite release print. Multiple heads are also used to make several prints from a single negative in multi-head printers. The intermittent or step contact printer is employed when perfect registration of each frame is necessary, for example, in the traveling-matte processes or for making rear- or front-projection plates.

Optical printers of the intermittent variety are much employed for traveling matte processes as well as for creating transitional devices such as fades, dissolves, and wipes. These printers can also alter speed for slow and fast motion effects, change camera distance and hence alter image size, achieve split-screen images and superimpositions, correct photographic errors, and reduce image size from one gauge to another. Such versatility is possible because the printer is composed of a separate projector and camera with the images being projected, generally from an interpositive, through a special lens onto the raw stock. Since the two films are operated separately, though synchronically, flexibility is possible in the position of the lens or camera, type of lens, and film speed. Multiple runs are also possible. Continuous optical printers, the least-used of these machines, reduce film from one gauge to another.

It is frequently necessary to use a process called timing to alter density and color quality from scene to scene while printing. Such a process is used to achieve consistent density and color from scene to scene or some desired effect in individual parts of the film. For black-and-white film, the area of light may be altered by changing the size of a slit through which it beams; or the light itself may be altered by means of a valve. Video analyzers are now employed to assess color quality and compute changes. In an additive printer, the light may be divided into the three primary colors by dichroic filters, the intensity of the individual beams altered, and the three beams united again before passing through the aperture. Coded control tape, now made by the video analyzer, can regulate the valves that alter the primary colors from setting to setting so that scenes can be printed continuously, one after the other. Timing is not a simple process and may require a number of attempts and conferences between laboratory and filmmakers before the final print is achieved. When a number of dupe negatives are needed to make the larger number of release prints for exhibition, the master positive from which they are made has all the timing changes so that the negatives can be made with a single exposure level.

For 16mm film, A and B printing is generally employed: shots are alternatively distributed between two rolls, which are then successively printed on the fresh stock. Such a process avoids the appearance of splices on the final print and allows for inexpensive transitions. *See* **A and B printing, film** *(1),* **optical printer, processing,** *and* **timing.**

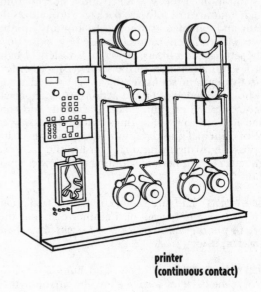

printer (continuous contact)

■ **printer fade** *See* **fade.**

■ **printer fader** *See* **fader** *(2).*

■ **printer head** The part of a printing machine where the images on one film are exposed by a printing light to the raw stock. In continuous contact printers the two films are brought together at this point, while in an intermittent optical printer each image on the developed film is individually projected through a lens onto the raw stock in a camera. Some modern continuous contact printers are multihead printers and have several heads where the negative is exposed to a number of different positive stocks at separate points, or a number of negatives are exposed to a single stock at various points. *See* **printer.**

■ **printer light** A light source in a printer, generally a tungsten-filament bulb, used to expose the images of a processed film onto raw stock so that positives can be made from negatives and negatives from positives. In a process called timing, the light is altered and its color quality changed to achieve proper density and color in the images. When a large number of release prints are to be made for commercial distribution, this process is generally performed on the master positive from which the dupe negatives are to be printed. Since the master positive is properly timed, the dupe negatives and the release prints made from these negatives can be printed with a consistent light exposure. *See* **printer** *and* **timing.**

■ **printer points**   *See* **light-change points.**

■ **printer scale**   The series of graded points for measuring the increase or decrease of light intensity in a printer. *See* **printer.**

■ **printer's sync**   *See* **editorial sync.**

■ **print film, print stock**   Film intended for a positive that will be made from a negative either through contact or optical printing. *See* **film** *(1).*

■ **printing**   The duplication of the images of one film onto another by means of a contact or optical printer: positives are printed from negatives with lighting and colors matching those in the original scene; and negatives from positives with lighting and colors reversed. Contact printers bring the films together before the aperture, while optical printers project and photograph individual frames through a lens. Continuous contact printers, where the two films move rapidly through the machinery, are used to make rush prints or large numbers of release prints, while intermittent or step contact printers are employed for special effects where perfect registration is necessary. Optical intermittent printers, which also give excellent registration and photograph each frame individually, are much employed for achieving optical effects, creating transitions, correcting images, and reducing or enlarging frames. Continuous optical printers are used for reducing film from one gauge to another. Timing allows light exposure to be altered during printing to correct or alter density and color from shot to shot. *See* **printer** *and* **timing.**

■ **printing down**   Printing a scene with less light to compensate for overexposed film.

■ **printing film, printing stock**   Any film to be made into a duplicate, either negative or positive, from another film through a printing process. *See* **film** *(1).*

■ **printing roll**   Either processed image or sound film that is ready to be used in the printer with raw stock to make a duplicate. *See* **film** *(1).*

■ **printing wind**   The position of 16mm print film so that the emulsion is in contact with the emulsion of the original film and the single row of perforations on both films are aligned during printing. The printing film is thus in A-wind. *See* **A- and B-wind.**

■ **print it, print, take it, save it**   The order given by the director when he or she is satisfied with a take, indicating that the film be sent to the laboratory and a print be made from it. The order is generally noted in the log.

■ **print pitch**   *See* **positive pitch.**

■ **prints and advertising budget, prints and ads budget, P&A budget**   The amount of money allowed by a distribution company for the release of a film, i.e., for making the prints and advertising the film. This sum may be part of the contractual agreement between the distributor and another financial group or between the distributor and production company.

■ **print sync, printing sync, printer sync, printer's sync**   The advanced position of the sound track on the married print in relation to the picture to achieve synchronic sound, necessary because the sound head is in advance of the lens in the projector. For 35mm film, the optical sound track is 21 frames in advance of the picture; for 16mm film the sound track is 26 frames in advance. *See* **sound advance.**

■ **print-through**   An unwanted noise or background on a layer of magnetic tape that comes from the sound on the next layer in tightly wound tape.

■ **print-up**   A blowup from a negative of a smaller gauge to a print of a larger gauge (e.g., a blowup of a 35mm print from a 16mm negative).

■ **prism beam splitter**   A small glass piece, generally with four sides and two equal ends, that sends separate images of the same scene to different negatives in a beam-splitter camera for making a traveling matte at the same time the picture is recorded or, in old color processes, for registering separate records of the primary colors on independent films. *See* **color film** *(2) and* **traveling-matte process.**

■ **prism lens**   *See* **multi-image prism.**

■ **prism shutter**   A small glass piece, generally with four sides and two equal ends, that rotates in high-speed cameras and film viewers when film movement is continuous in order to interrupt the path of the image and create an intermittent series of frames.

■ **prison film, prison movie**   Any movie dealing with the subject of incarceration in a prison. Such a subject has been frequently and effectively portrayed in film, perhaps because the image on the screen is entrapped within the frame and perhaps because the very sense of enclosure the audience feels in the theater suggests the feeling of entrapment experienced by the characters. There are actually two kinds of prison films, those dealing with criminals and those dealing with prisoners of war. Notable in the first group are such films as George Hill's *The Big House* (1930) and Mervyn Le Roy's *I Am a*

prison film Paul Muni is a victim of injustice in *I Am a Fugitive from a Chain Gang* (1932; Mervyn Le Roy).

■ ■ ■

Fugitive from a Chain Gang (1932), and in the second, David Lean's *The Bridge on the River Kwai* (1957) and John Sturges's *The Great Escape* (1963).

■ **private eye film** Detective films dealing specifically with the experiences of a private investigator, such as Dashiell Hammett's Sam Spade, played by Humphrey Bogart in *The Maltese Falcon* (1941; dir. John Huston), or Raymond Chandler's Philip Marlowe, also played by Humphrey Bogart in *The Big Sleep* (1946; dir. Howard Hawks). The hard-boiled, antisocial, and incorruptible private eye has become an especially popular mythic figure in American film, second perhaps only to the cowboy. Like the cowboy, the private eye represents the values of independence, toughness, and yet innocence so admired in this country. *See* **detective film.**

■ **Prizma, Prizmacolor** The name employed for two early subtractive color systems: the first, introduced in 1919, employed film dyed orange and blue-green passing through the projector at twice the normal speed, and the second, introduced in 1922, also used a two-colored print, but projected at normal speeds. Vitagraph's *The Glorious Adventure* (1921; dir. J. Stuart Blackton) is often cited as an example of Prizmacolor. *See* **color film** *(2) and* **subtractive process.**

■ **problem film** *See* **social-conscience film.**

■ **process body** The body of a vehicle such as an automobile employed in shooting foreground action before an image projected onto the back of a translucent screen in rear-projection photography. A common rear-projection shot is to photograph two characters seated in the body of an automobile with the projected image visible through the vehicle's rear window, which is generally without glass. *See* **rear projection.**

■ **process camera** A specially designed camera with the highest quality of registration and precision possible, which is used in special-effects matte shots, bipack printing, and optical printing. Each frame must be held in position in front of the aperture with perfect steadiness for combining elements of different images into a single composite picture. Pilot-pin registration, in which pins fit snugly into the film's perforations, is employed. Such cameras also have variable shutters, a variety of motors for different speeds and effects, and footage counters for stop-and-go photography. *See* **bipack contact matte printing, optical printer,** *and* **special effects.**

■ **processing** The process of developing the latent image, either positive or negative, in exposed film and treating the film so that it is washed free of all chemicals and the image is permanently fixed. Since development of the image is only an early stage in the entire process, the term "developing" is incorrectly used when it is meant to describe the entire procedure. Modern processing machines are highly complex and efficient. The film is led through the machine by a strong piece of film called a machine leader and propelled in continuous movement by rollers that either engage the film's perforations or move it by friction. Individual rolls of film are attached together by staples or tape, either overlapping or end to end. The film moves into a reservoir, which gathers enough film on both a fixed and a movable spindle to feed the continuous movement of the film as it passes through the machine while permitting the end to remain stationary long enough for the attachment of the next roll. The film passes through the various tanks in a series of long, narrow loops over the rollers in a rack. If the film contains an anti-halation backing on the base, the backing must be washed away before development of the image. In the development part of the process, the silver halides in the original film emulsion which have been exposed to various degrees of light are converted by contact with the chemical solution into black, metallic silver grains to form the negative image. In color tripack film the solution also reacts with chemicals in the emulsion called couplers to form a color image: there are three layers in the emulsion, each with couplers which react to the light waves of one of the three primary colors and produce a color complementary to the primary. Later, the light and dark areas will be reversed and the colors turned into the original colors when positive tripack film is developed after having been exposed in the printing stage to light passing through the negative.

The time of development depends both on the nature of the film stock and the temperature of the chemicals. Fresh chemicals are allowed to reach the surface of the emulsion by agitation of the solution and by replenishing the solution while withdrawing an equal amount of byproducts. After development, the film is washed to remove the developing solution and byproducts. The image is then made permanent when the unexposed grains of silver halide are washed away in a chemical process called fixing. For color film, the silver image in each layer is then reconverted to silver halides and dissolved. The film is washed once again to remove chemicals and byproducts, and finally dried in a cabinet by circulating warm air. The processing of reversal film has several additional stages: after the black silver particles form the negative image in the first developing, the film is exposed to light or chemically treated so that additional silver halides are changed to metallic silver particles which form a positive picture while the dyes create a positive color image. The image is fixed when the silver halides from both developments are bleached and washed away. *See* **color film** *(2),* **film** *(1), and* **reversal film.**

■ **process photography, process cinematography** (1) Rear-projection photography in which foreground action is shot before an image projected onto the rear of a translucent screen. This technique allows actors in a studio to appear before a setting photographed elsewhere. (2) Any photography using a process camera (e.g., bipack or optical printing). *See* **process camera** *and* **rear projection.**

■ **process plate** A background plate containing an image that is projected onto a screen from the rear and before which foreground action is photographed. *See* **background plate** *and* **rear projection.**

■ **process projection** The projection of an image onto the rear of a translucent screen before which live action is photographed in rear-projection photography. *See* **rear projection.**

■ **process projector** The projector used for sending images onto the rear of a translucent screen before which foreground action is photographed in rear-projection photography. *See* **rear projection.**

■ **process screen** The translucent screen used in rear-projection shots. The background images are projected from behind the screen while the live action is shot in front. *See* **rear projection.**

■ **process shot** (1) A shot combining a foreground of live action with an image projected from the rear onto a translucent screen in the background. *See* **rear projection.** (2) A shot in which characters are photographed against a colored background and their image is later combined with another image in a composite picture. *See* **traveling-matte process.** (3) Any shot using a process camera. *See* **process camera.**

■ **producer** The person in charge of all the financial and administrative aspects of a film production, from the very inception of the film project and its initial planning through all stages of production, distribution, and advertising. Sometimes the producer also involves himself in the artistic nature of the film and has a decided influence on the quality of the final product. Thomas Harper Ince (1882–1924) is generally heralded as the person who most significantly developed the role of the producer as the executive head of a production distinct in authority and responsibilities from the director. At his studio, called Inceville, Ince developed the studio system and the producer's role by working closely with his directors and screenwriters, budgeting and scheduling each production, and even involving himself in the editing. The major studios were soon to have a number of producers, each responsible for particular productions and each himself responsible to an executive producer or head of production such as Irving Thalberg (1899–1936) at MGM. A few producers had as much an influence on their films as the director—Val Lewton, for example, made a group of low-budget horror films for RKO in the early 1940s that strongly show his mark. Independent producers such as Samuel Goldwyn and David Selznick, who produced their own films, managed their own studios, and released through the larger companies, had an especially great amount of control over the quality of their films. A number of successful directors such as Howard Hawks, Billy Wilder, and Alfred Hitchcock were able both to direct and produce their own films while working for the major studios.

Today, producers are generally independent of film companies except for financing and distributing. The producer may be the individual who originally comes up with an idea or a property for a film. He would normally then put together the package which he would submit to a studio or some group to obtain financial backing for his production. The term executive producer is sometimes used for this individual, although such a title can also refer to anyone from an agent or manager to a financer. However, the typical producer is the person who puts together the production from inception and sees it through to distribution. He is involved with obtaining the property and assembling stars, director, screenwriter, and perhaps director of photography and production designer. Having obtained money, he involves himself, along with the director, in the writing of the screenplay by the screenwriter. He is responsible for selecting locations and studios, working out a schedule of production, and overseeing all budgetary considerations. It is the producer who manages the entire production, leaving the director free to manage the film's artistic concerns, but often having his own influence on the quality of the film. Many producers are involved with the director and editor in working out the final shape of the film. Finally, the producer makes plans for distributing the film and selling it to the public.

Obviously, the producer must be an individual knowledgeable in all aspects of filmmaking—artistic, technical, and financial. The producer is generally assisted by an associate producer, who directly oversees many of the daily concerns of shooting. In commercial filmmaking, the producer has today returned to special prominence as a force controlling all aspects of production. With a very demanding marketplace, the high cost of making and advertising a film, and especially with film as part of a large complex of business ventures, only a few directors demand the respect and have the track record to control their own projects. Producers are the individuals who take responsibility, selling projects on the basis of their own track records and bringing them into fruition on the basis of their own concepts.

■ **Producers Guild of America** The national organization for producers in motion pictures and television, with headquarters located in Beverly Hills, California. Because the National Relations Board ruled that producers are managerial, the organization cannot operate as a union and negotiate in the industry for its members.

■ **producer's rep, producer's representative** An individual or organization that acts as liaison between a producer and his distributor and that helps independent filmmakers to find a distributor.

■ **production** (1) The various stages of putting the story on film after preproduction planning and before the final editing. These stages include all the physical preparations for shooting (e.g., construction of sets, lighting, and rehearsal) and the actual shooting itself. When the film is "in production" it is actually being shot. (2) The term is sometimes used to include the various stages of editing, mixing, and special-effects photography, along with those operations listed in (1).

■ **production accountant, production auditor** The individual who keeps a record of all expenditures during production and often oversees payment of salaries and production expenses.

■ **production assistant** An individual who generally works under the director, performing a variety of tasks for the production, including distribution and posting of printed materials, preparation for rehearsals and shooting, and running errands.

■ **production audio, production sound** Sound recorded during actual production by the sound engineer as distinct from that recorded and dubbed in after.

■ **production board, production breakdown board, production strip board** A detailed breakdown of every scene to be filmed, put together early in preproduction, often by the production manager and director. The production board is itself composed of a series of panels on each of which individual breakdown strips are placed. Each scene is listed in the sequence of shooting, with the cast involved, the type of scene (interior or exterior, day or night), the location, special equipment and vehicles required all specified.

■ **production board** *See* **clapboard.**

■ **production book, production digest** An updated account of all the details of production, including both a breakdown of individual scenes and information concerning shooting, transportation, and budget. The production book is generally the source of the production board. *See* **production board.**

■ **production buyer** The individual who purchases properties for the film as well as materials for constructing sets and making costumes.

■ **production camera** A motion-picture camera employed in a studio or on location during shooting as differentiated from the process cameras employed for matte shots, bipack printing, and optical printing.

■ **production cart, location cart** A versatile, durable and easy-to-maneuver two-wheeled vehicle employed on a set or on location for moving sound, video, lighting, and other equipment.

■ **production code** *See* **Motion Picture Production Code.**

■ **Production Code Administration (PCA)** The department of the Motion Picture Producers and Distributors of America (MPPDA) that enforced the Motion Picture Production Code. The Code was adopted by the organization in 1930 in response to public criticism of the "immorality" of the film industry, and it carefully spelled out how certain subjects were to be treated in film. The code was initially voluntary, but continuing pressure, especially from the newly formed Catholic Legion of Decency, which advocated the boycotting of films it did not approve, motivated the MPPDA in 1934 to establish the Production Code Administration for enforcing the code and to hire Joseph Breen to run the department. Any film released without the Administration's seal of approval would cost the production company a fine of twenty-five thousand dollars. Breen and his office had to approve both the screenplay before shooting and the completed film. They also acted in an advisory capacity during writing, production, and editing. For twenty years Breen's office had considerable influence on the content of American film and its treatment of sex, crime, violence, domestic life, and religion. *See* **Motion Picture Producers and Distributors of America** *and* **Motion Picture Production Code.**

■ **production company** (1) An organization that makes motion pictures for commercial release. The old Hollywood studios were production companies and distributors while also owning theaters. Today the old studios are largely distributors of independent films as well as films made from their own production companies. (2) Any organization formed specifically for the making of a motion picture.

■ **production coordinator, production office coordinator** The chief administrator in the production office who is responsible for the smooth running of a number of activities and their effective coordination. This person is in charge of communication, correspondence, travel, accommodations, and making sure that the right people are at the right place to do their jobs, not to mention the payment of bills.

■ **production costs** The entire costs for making a motion picture, including the preproduction, production, and postproduction stages—everything that goes into the making of the negative. The average cost for making a film in the Hollywood industry is now about $40 million.

■ **production credits** The names of the personnel involved in the production stages of the film (e.g., director, camera personnel, gaffer, grip, etc.), which are shown either at the beginning or end of the film.

■ **production department** The personnel responsible for computing the costs of the various stages of production and for making preparations for the actual shooting of a script. The production department puts into operation the daily specifications for each day's shooting.

■ **production designer** The person responsible for the design, overall physical appearance, and entire vision of the motion picture that appears on the screen. The production designer must design and oversee the construction of settings; help select and then be in charge of adapting locations outside the studio; be satisfied that the set decorator bring to the film the proper furnishings, props, and ornamentations and that the costume designer design costumes that properly fit into the overall decor of the film; and sometimes prepare continuity sketches for actual filming. An artist in his or her own right, the production designer must also have a knowledge of all technical aspects of filmmaking, including cameras, film stock, lenses, color, and special effects, as well as a sound sense of economics. He or she supervises the art department, which has a wide variety of talents to carry out these functions. This figure was formally called the art director and the present art director was referred to as the set designer. Two notable production designers in Hollywood during the height of the studio system were Hans Dreier, supervising art director for Paramount from 1932 until 1950, who, among his vast work, designed the very elegant sets for ten of Ernst Lubitsch's comedies; and Cedric Gibbons, supervising art decorator for MGM's art department from 1924 to 1956, who designed the very impressive and striking sets for most of Josef von Sternberg's films with Marlene Dietrich—Dreier won three Academy Awards and Gibbons, who actually designed the Oscar, eleven. Also notable was William Cameron Menzies, who won the first Academy Award in this area (actually for "interior decoration") for *The*

Dove (1927; dir. Roland West) and *The Tempest* (1928; dir. Sam Taylor) and a special Academy Award for 1939's *Gone With the Wind* (dir. Victor Fleming). Among the many fine recent production designers, Dean Tavoularis stands out, especially for his work with Arthur Penn's *Bonnie and Clyde* (1967) and his production design for Francis Ford Coppola's *Godfather* films (he won an Academy Award for *Part II*, released in 1974). *See* **art director.**

■ **production digest** *See* **production book.**

■ **production dupe** *See* **dupe.**

■ **production editor** An individual who puts together the day's shooting into dailies (or rushes) and synchronizes the film with the recorded sound for playback the day after shooting. The production editor generally uses an interlock projector that shows the picture and is synchronically linked with the motor of a sound playback system. *See* **editing.**

■ **production executive** *See* **executive producer.**

■ **production, financing, and distribution agreement; production-financing/distribution agreement (PFD)** The contractual agreement that spells out the conditions for a distributor's financing of a film. This agreement will specify how the project is to be developed, the talent involved, the conditions for payment, the payments themselves, what decision-making rights the distributor has in the making of the film, and the company's rights to distribute the film in specified markets. *See* **distribution, Hollywood,** *and* **studio system.**

■ **production illustrator** The individual responsible for creating sketches, drawings, and storyboards for a film production. Sketches and drawings may be important in the early stages of planning a production, and some directors rely heavily on storyboards to plot out their shooting, even shot by shot. The production illustrator must also work closely with the special and digital effects artists in the creation of new worlds and new visions. *See* **storyboard.**

■ **production manager, unit production manager** The individual in charge of the daily business arrangements for shooting. He or she generally starts by making a breakdown for each day's shooting, calculating the most economical way to employ performers, locations, equipment, and properties. The production manager uses the breakdown for ordering equipment and props; for arranging transportation, accommodations, and meals; and for hiring extra personnel as necessary. Sometimes also called the unit manager. *See* **unit manager.**

■ **production number** (1) A number assigned to a specific film production by a studio for bookkeeping and recording procedures. (2) A lavishly staged song-and-dance performance in a stage or film musical.

■ **production overhead** Costs that are not directly related to the specific activities in making the film but rather to the general expenses of running the company and of the studio/distributor sponsoring the film. Such costs include maintenance of the offices and studio facilities, salaries and expenses of the executive staff and subsidiary personnel, and running the departments needed to perform the various activities of the studio/distributor. Such overhead is one of the areas in which creative accounting plays a significant role in figuring out the net profits for a film. *See* **creative accounting.**

■ **production report, daily production report** A report that details all the information concerning a day's shooting and includes the number of pages of the script that were shot; the shots, takes, and camera setups; the shooting time for each take; the amount of film footage used; the names of both performers and production personnel employed; and the amount of time worked by each. The report is a convenient way for both director and producer to keep informed of the production's progress, especially in relation to the production schedule.

■ **production schedule** The schedule for each day's shooting sometimes made by the production manager, which includes the order of the individual shots, their location, the actors and production personnel involved, and the equipment and properties needed. Such a schedule is necessary to utilize all personnel, equipment, and locations economically so that the production can stay within its allotted budget and planned shooting time.

■ **production script** A full script of the completed film that includes all dialogue and action. Such scripts have been published for major films and the films of major directors.

■ **production sound mixer, production mixer** The person responsible for the recording of sound during the actual shooting of a production. This person is responsible for the dialogue, environmental or ambient noise, and sound effects that are produced on the set. He or she must oversee the placement of microphones, the operation of the boom, and the proper recording of individual sounds either separately or in a mix through the use of a portable mixer. Also called the floor mixer. *See* **mixer.**

■ **production still, publicity still** A single photograph taken during production and either showing a specific action from the film or some activity related to the making of the film. These photographs are generally used for advertising.

■ **production track** A sound track recorded during the actual shooting of a film.

■ **production unit** All the personnel involved in the production stages of the film, namely the producer, director of photography, art director, gaffer, head grip, and all the members of the various crews.

■ **production values** The quality of a film production in general: its sets, costumes, properties, lighting, color, camera technique, music, and sound. High production values are readily apparent to the viewer's eyes and ears. MGM is known for the high production values of many of its films from the mid-1930s through the mid-1940s.

■ **production van** A larger tractor, with two generators on the rear, that hauls a trailer carrying equipment for on-location shooting. For small productions a single van is likely to be used, but for large films two vans, one for lighting and one for grip equipment, are employed. Cameras are normally conveyed separately for such large shoots in a five-ton carrier.

■ **product placement** Using a specific item with a brand name in a film because the manufacturer of the item has paid a fee. This practice allows the manufacturer wide publicity for the item and the film an additional source of income. What this practice basically means is that marketing has even entered the very images on the screen. *See* **marketing.**

■ **product placement agent** A person who represents certain manufacturers and their products and attempts to get the products placed noticeably in a motion picture. The placement of the candy Reese's Pieces in Steven Spielberg's *E.T. The Extra-Terrestrial* (1982) gave a big push to this kind of marketing when sales of the candy sky-rocketed. The placement of these products also earns the production company a nice bit of extra change. *See* **marketing.**

■ **profilmic** A term first used in French film theory and criticism that refers to anything in front of the camera that is photographed.

■ **program film, program picture** A feature film of roughly five reels that began to appear about 1914 as the main film in a series of motion pictures.

■ **programmer** A second-rate or B-picture of little value except to fill up a program. *See* **B-picture.**

■ **progressive angles** A series of greater angles in a sequence of shots—for example, an eye-level shot, followed by a low angle, followed by an extreme low-angle shot to emphasize the height of a building or structure as perceived by a character. In Robert Wise's *The Haunting* (1963), the vulnerable heroine confronts the ominous haunted house by a series of subjective shots with progressively higher angles. *See* **regressive angles.**

■ **progressive shots** A series of shots that progressively increase the size of an object—for example, an establishing shot of a scene, followed by a medium shot of a character within the scene, followed by a close-up of the character's face. A famous series of progressive shots takes place in James Whale's *Frankenstein* (1931) when the monster first appears and turns to face the audience: a medium shot is followed by a close-up and then an extreme close-up that shows the eyes and forehead.

■ **projection** The projecting and enlarging of a series of photographed images from a film onto a screen so that their rapid, sequential appearance creates an illusion of movement. Images for silent motion pictures were projected at a speed of approximately 16 frames per second, but the addition of a sound track required a speed of 24 frames per second for adequate sound reproduction.

■ **projection angle** The angle created by the central axis of the beam from a projector and the floor of the projection booth or some other horizontal plane.

■ **projection booth, projection room** At first a small room, generally at the rear and upper part of a theater, from which the images on a film were projected through a glass window onto a screen at the front of the theater for the showing of motion pictures. Some projection booths in older theaters still contain two projectors for playing consecutive reels, one after the other, without interruption. In more recent years, largely automatic projection systems have been developed with timers or cues on film allowing an entire show to be performed without the constant presence of a projectionist. Complete shows can be projected from a horizontal platter that holds up to four and one-half hours of film. Sometimes a series of shows can be screened automatically with time intervals programmed in between each performance. In the newer multiplex theaters, one or more long projection rooms are employed for rows of projectors beaming into the different theaters, allowing, with the platters, a minimum of human involvement. Such complexes will often use projection consoles that are fed by platters and that contain the projector, sound systems, xenon lamp, controls, and meters—everything necessary to show the film with the highest luminance and best audio. Controls for the theater's sound, lighting, screen, and curtains are also in such rooms, though most are now operated automatically, often by cues on the film. Most projection booths also contain equipment for examining and splicing film. *See* **platter system, projection console,** *and* **projector.**

■ **projection console** A single unit for showing a motion picture in a modern theater or complex. The console is fed film from a large platter system and itself contains the projector, lamphouse (normally with a high-powered xenon bulb), power supply, automation system, and sound system. Some units can show 35mm or 70mm films and most are capable of stereo, optical, and digital audio playback. *See* **platter system** *and* **projector/soundhead pedestal.**

■ **projectionist** The individual who operates the projector and sound equipment for the showing of a motion picture. He or she may also operate the lighting in the theater and play recorded music between shows, although such procedures today are themselves often automatically triggered by cues on the film. The projectionist must check the reels before performances to make sure they are properly spliced; set up the projector or projectors for showing the film without interruption; operate the changeover during the screening when older projection systems are used; and be sure that the picture is properly focused and that the sound is clear and audible. Sometimes the projectionist must properly mask the image for different aspect ratios. The projectionist normally carries on these functions in a projection booth or room. Projection has recently become largely automated in a number of modern theaters with the use of large platters capable of holding four and one-half hours of film. In this system, an entire performance comes off a single horizontal platter and is fed back onto a second platter in such a way that the film need not be rewound. Automation systems also allow cues placed on the film to perform various functions such as operating the curtains, lights, and music in the theater. An entire day's screenings can be shown in a single theater without the intrusion of a projectionist once the showings are programmed. With this new automated equipment, one or two individuals can run the shows for a large group of connected theaters in a multiplex from one or more large projection areas—a boon to exhibitors, no doubt, but not to projectionists. *See* **projector.**

■ **projection leader** The head piece of film attached to the start of a reel, which has numbers on it to permit the projectionist to begin screening the reel with the very first image. The numbers on the leader are especially important when the reel is on a second projector and must continue the motion picture from the reel on the first projector without any interruption. *See* **leader** *(2).*

■ **projection lens, projector lens** A lens made especially for a projector through which motion pictures are enlarged and projected onto a screen. Such lenses have no diaphragm for the control of light and are designed so that they attain clearest focus at the greatest opening. This lens can be focused when attached to the projector by movement of the lens barrel. An anamorphic projection lens widens a compressed image photographed through an anamorphic camera lens to its normal dimensions. *See* **lens** *and* **projector.**

■ **projection speed** The rate at which film passes through a projector, measured by the number of frames that are projected through the lens each second. Silent film was supposed to be projected at a speed of 16 frames per second, but the speed was normally faster, generally to achieve a more pleasing image, sometimes to rush the audience out of the theater. Projectionists also cranked projectors at varying speeds to achieve particular effects for different kinds of scenes. The number of frames per second was increased to 24 when sound tracks were added to achieve normal sound during playback. Today films without sound are projected at 16 or, with more recent projectors, 18 frames per second. *See* **projector.**

■ **projection synchronism, projection sync** The synchronization of picture and sound for projection which is achieved by print sync, that is, the placement of the sound track in advance of the picture on the married print due to the separate positions of the picture lens and sound head in the projector. *See* **print sync** *and* **sound advance.**

■ **projector** A machine that projects and enlarges the series of images from a reel of film onto a screen one after the other in rapid succession so that an illusion of movement is created. The illusion of movement is created by the viewer's persistence of vision, which is the capacity of the eye to maintain an image for a brief instant after it is gone until the next comes into view. Another explanation for this sense of motion is explained by the phi phenomenon, which is the brain's proclivity to impose movement upon an object when it appears successively at two different points. Originally motion pictures were viewed in peephole machines by one person at a time (*see* **Kinetograph** *and* **Mutograph**), but it was soon realized that moving pictures projected on a screen were more effective and certainly more profitable, since a large number of people could pay to see the same film at the same time.

Although there have been a number of important improvements in projectors, the basic system of projection remains the same. Film is fed into the projector and then passes into an intermittent mechanism which briefly stops each frame before the aperture. Loops of film both before and after the intermittent movement, as in a camera, allow the sudden stops and pulls to occur without tearing the film. For most commercial 70mm and 35mm projectors (many professional projectors can show both types of film), a Maltese or Geneva cross with four slots is made to turn ninety degrees at a time by the pin of a rotating shaft. The cross thus turns a sprocket intermittently, which places each frame before the aperture for an instant of exposure until it is turned again. In many smaller-gauge projectors, a rotating cam moves a single or double claw so

that it engages two perforations and places the frame before the aperture; the claw then disengages and returns to its initial position so that it can move the next frame before the aperture. A film trap employs lateral guides and bands to bring the individual frames to the correct position in front of the gate. The aperture plate in the picture gate can be changed for different aspect ratios. Once the frame is in position, the shutter opens and the image is projected from the picture gate through the lens and onto the screen by a high-intensity lamp. Carbon arc lamps were traditionally used, but these have been replaced by xenon lamps in most theaters, since they last longer and burn with less heat. Most projectors for smaller-gauge film use tungsten-halogen bulbs. For films without sound, 16 or 18 frames pass before the lens per second to allow for steady, continuous motion; but to make sound reproduction effective, prints with sound tracks pass through at 24 frames per second. To avoid flicker on the screen from the intermittent light, the shutter blocks off the illumination three times during the projection of each frame of silent film and generally twice for each frame of sound film so that there are actually 48 separate light images per second. The shutter for a silent-film projector, or one that plays both silent and sound film, has three blades and the shutter for a sound projector has two blades. Projection lenses focus best at their greatest opening. An anamorphic projection lens expands images that have been compressed on the film by being photographed in a camera also with an anamorphic lens.

After projection, the film moves continuously past the sound head. The varying area or intensity of pho-

projector
1. feed reel 2. lamp
3. condensers 4. film
5. aperture 6. shutter
7. lens 8. take-up reel

tographed light on an optical sound track (two channels for stereophonic and surround sound) is read by the light from a small lamp (called an exciter lamp), and the variations in the reading converted by a photoelectric cell into electrical impulses that themselves are changed into sound waves and amplified. Since the optical sound head is in advance of the picture lens to allow the film sufficient distance to move from intermittent to continuous movement, synchronic sound and picture is achieved by having the sound 21 frames in advance of the corresponding picture on 35mm film and 26 frames in advance on 16mm film. Seventymillimeter projectors can read six magnetic sound tracks for stereophonic and surround sound. Many 35mm projectors today have digital optical readers for transforming a binary code into stereophonic and surround sound for transmission in the theater.

Since the standard reel of 35mm motion pictures in most older and traditional projectors runs approximately twenty minutes before the film leaves the projector, it has been necessary to use two separate projectors so that the projectionist can switch from one reel to the other without an interruption in the showing of a feature film. In modern theaters, however, a platter system is now popular in which three horizontal platters, each capable of holding up to four and one-half hours of film, are situated adjacent to the projector. The top platter feeds the film into the machine and one of the other platters receives the film in such a way that rewinding is unnecessary—the completed show need only be rethreaded into the projector for the next screening. In some advanced theaters, the entire process is automatic and the next screening of the same show can start on its own. The third platter can be used to assemble the next showing at the theater. Automation systems respond to cues on the film itself as it runs through the projector to operate various activities in the theater—e.g., turning lights up or down, closing or opening the curtains, playing music in the theater, and stopping the projector.

■ **projector aperture**   The aperture plate in the picture gate of the projector, through which the projected image passes and which masks off unwanted light. The aperture plate can be changed to accommodate different aspect ratios. *See* **projector.**

■ **projector line-up leader**   A leader of film attached to each day's dailies which states the film's title and offers the projectionist both a focus chart and markers for various aspect ratios in order to obtain the proper image. *See* **dailies.**

■ **projector/soundhead pedestal**   The support platform for a projector and lamphouse used in the projection booth of a movie theater. *See* **projection console.**

■ **promotion, promo**   The various activities having to do with publicizing a film so that people will want to see it.

Promotional activities include advertising, but also events that are not paid for, though they are carefully arranged—e.g., interviews with the performers or director on television and radio, interviews for magazines and newspapers, preview screenings, public appearances of the stars, and the release of factual and not-so-factual information about the film and its performers. *See* **advertising** *and* **marketing.**

■ **promotional film**   Any nonfictional film made to promote or publicize a specific business, industry, or cause.

■ **prompter, prompter system**   Any system for aiding an individual especially in a filmed interview or documentary to remember a speech. Some of these systems employ a remote-controlled scroll or video screen that displays script or type.

■ **prop, property**   Any movable object used on a set or in a scene, whether a hand prop such as a glass or gun, a set prop such as a rocking chair or vase, or an action prop such as a fishing rod or chainsaw.

■ **propaganda film**   A film made with the intention of persuading the audience to a particular point of view concerning a subject, frequently political in nature. Although these films present a biased point of view, they sometimes employ a documentary approach to their subject, relying on the apparently real and factual nature of the images of the screen and often an authoritative voice-over to sway, unless the film is insultingly blatant, even the most adamant opponent. For this reason, films have been used as propaganda by governments to persuade the national conscience to a cause, although they have also functioned as an effective weapon to sway public opinion against established thought. Most feature films have some kind of message to import to the viewer, but the term propaganda film can only be applied to such films when their entertainment value functions almost exclusively as a vehicle for the message. Commercial films have frequently been able to incorporate propagandistic messages, often following national policy within fictional stories and characters, taking advantage of the audience's involvement and emotional responses. Sometimes such feature films themselves employ a documentary style to persuade the audience.

From the beginning, the propagandist potential of film was apparent. Newsreel films made in America, Britain, France, and Germany during the First World War used both actual and staged footage to support national pride and the military cause. Commercial films were also found to have great propagandist value: in America, for example, J. Stuart Blackton's *The Battle Cry of Peace,* starring Norma Talmadge, appeared in 1915 to arouse America to the German threat; and D. W. Griffith went to England to make *Hearts of the World*

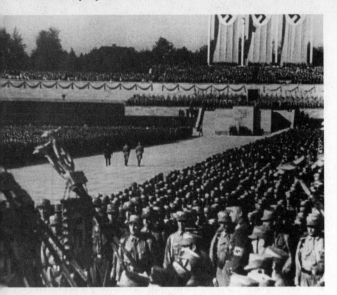

propaganda film *Triumph of the Will* (1935), Leni Riefenstahl's disturbingly powerful celebration of the Nazi's Nuremberg rally in 1934.

■ ■ ■

(1918), a documentary-style anti-German film, and *The Great Love* (1918), a fictional prowar effort, for the British government. Blatantly propagandistic were films such as *The Kaiser, The Beast of Berlin* which appeared in the United States in 1918. Propaganda films from the film division of the Committee of Public Information in this country were also widely distributed. Soviet cinema's impulse after the revolution was certainly propagandist, but these films were sometimes presented with sufficient technique and sensibility to earn reputations as significant artistic achievements. Vertov's *Kino-Pravda* newsreels and documentaries display innovative camera technique and editing, while Eisenstein's and Pudovkin's works actually rise above their nationalistic intentions and are as much propaganda for the human spirit as for the Russian Revolution.

A complex problem arises, however, when one considers the films Leni Riefenstahl made for Nazi Germany, especially *Triumph of the Will* (1935) and the two parts of *Olympia* (1938). Although blatant eulogies for Hitler, Naziism, and the Aryan race that, on an intellectual level, are an insult to most viewers, the sheer artistry of the camera work and editing in these films are still impressive and evocative. Because the brutality of the political beliefs behind these films is so well hidden, they are among the most successful propaganda films ever made. Also in Germany, Veidt Harlan's feature film *The Swiss Jew* (1940) impressed anti-Semitic European audiences during the war years, though the work today seems a symptom of a pathological national mentality. Perhaps the most impressive propaganda films to appear in America between the wars were two documentaries made by Pare Lorentz and sponsored by the government's Resettlement Administration to show the New Deal's attempts to handle national problems—*The Plow that Broke the Plains* (1936) and *The River* (1937).

During the Second World War, a number of Hollywood directors made documentaries for the armed forces. Notable in this group were the series *Why We Fight*, produced by Frank Capra (1942–1945), and such combat documentaries as John Ford's *The Battle of Midway* (1942) and John Huston's *The Battle of San Pietro* (1945). Many routine war and espionage films were made during the war years by Hollywood, but notable commercial films with strong propaganda elements were William Wyler's *Mrs. Miniver* (1942) and Herman Shumlin's *Watch on the Rhine* (1943). Michael Curtiz's *Mission to Moscow* (1943) sought to convince America of the wisdom of its new alliance with the Soviet Union against Germany, even defending the Stalinist purge trials of the 1930s—the production was to cause some of the participants significant embarrassment during the witch-hunts of the late 1940s and the 1950s. Communism was itself blatantly attacked during the postwar period in such films as *I Was a Communist for the FBI* (1951; dir. Gordon Douglas) and *My Son John* (1952; dir. Leo McCarey).

American involvement in Southeast Asia evoked a number of propaganda films. In the commercial theater, John Wayne's *The Green Berets* (1968) was a strong defense of the Vietnam War, while Hal Ashby's *Coming Home* (1978) and Michael Cimino's *The Deer Hunter* (1978) reinforced the general public sentiment that had turned against the recent war. Perhaps the most effective and bitter propaganda-documentary film to come out against the Vietnam War was Peter Davis's *Hearts and Minds* (1974). *See* **documentary.**

■ **prop box** A large container, sometimes on wheels, which contains the smaller props needed for a day's shooting.

■ **property** (1) *See* **prop.** (2) Any literary or nonliterary work that is purchased or optioned as the source for a film. The property may be a novel, short story, play, book of nonfiction, magazine article, unpublished work, song, or even an earlier film version.

■ **property department** The group of personnel in a film production responsible for obtaining and having ready all the props for a film. Property departments in studios have available to them large numbers of props used from production to production. Such personnel can alter old props or make or obtain new ones.

■ **property handler, prop handler** The individual in a film production responsible for placing the right props in the right scene at the right time.

■ **property sheet** An itemized list of props necessary for a film production, sometimes divided according to the daily shooting schedule.

■ **propmaker** An individual, generally in the property department, who makes props for a specific film.

■ **prop man, property master, props** The individual responsible for obtaining, altering, or building properties and making sure they are available when necessary during film production. The prop man is often in charge of a property department.

■ **proposal** A brief description of an idea for a film. If the proposal receives interest from a producer or studio, a somewhat fuller "treatment" might be asked for. *See* **treatment.**

■ **prop plot, property plot, prop plan, property plan** A layout for a particular set showing the specific locations for all the properties.

■ **prop truck, property truck** The vehicle that brings to the location of shooting all the necessary props.

■ **prosthetics, prosthesis** The addition of body parts, the extreme distortion of bodies and faces, visible transformations and mutations of bodies and faces, and the creation of grotesque and misshapen creatures all brought about by the use of such prosthetic makeup as foam or rubber latex, eurethane appliances, airbags, blood sacks, and a host of other devices. The person who applies these devices and creates these effects is called a prosthetic makeup artist. Starting with Rob Bottin's remarkable makeup for John Carpenter's *The Thing* (1982), cinema has become, more than ever, the place of fantasy and nightmare. *See* **makeup.**

■ **protagonist** The lead figure in a film, play, or literary work. *See* **antagonist, hero,** *and* **heroine.**

■ **protection master, protective master** The master print derived from the edited original negative for the making of future negatives so that the original negative is protected. In the case of tripack color film, the protection master might also be three separate black-and-white films, each called a matrix and each printed through a filter of one of the primary colors.

■ **protection shot** *See* **cover shot.**

■ **proximity effect, proximity presence** The low bass quality that sound may acquire when its low frequencies are picked up by a directional microphone.

■ **psychodrama** In psychotherapy, the term means an improvisational performance of psychological conflicts by a group of people as they interact with one another. In film, the term is sometimes used for a type of avant-garde work that is a direct expression of the filmmaker's own psychology. Such a film seems spontaneous and improvisational as it follows the subjective and associational pattern of the filmmaker's psyche instead of any narrative logic. Such films generally suggest a dreamlike state (many actually take place as dreams), are concerned with sexual conflict, and feature the filmmaker within the work. Notable examples of such films appeared in the United States in the 1940s and 1950s—for example, Maya Deren's *Ritual in Transfigured Time* (1946) and Kenneth Anger's *Fireworks* (1947).

■ **psychotronic films** A group of low-budget films that have a small cult following because of their bizarre, exaggerated, and compelling trashiness. Such films seem best defined by their implausible plots, one-dimensional characters, adolescent points of view, clichés, and poor production values. This group includes a large dose of cheap horror and science-fiction films but also covers a wide variety of films such as biker, women-in-prison, and drug movies. Like camp movies, these films are exaggerated, unbelievable, and border on the ludicrous, but they exceed the former category in their excessiveness, grossness, and poor quality. Perhaps the most notable of these films is Edward D. Wood, Jr.'s *Plan Nine from Outer Space* (1959), though all his films would qualify. Nor should one omit the films of Herschell Gordon Lewis, "the Godfather of Gore," especially his *Blood Feast* (1963). The term "psychotronic" seems to have first been used for the film *The Psychotronic Man* (1980; dir. Jack M. Sell). *See* **camp.**

■ **public domain (PD)** Any work of art that is not under copyright and is therefore available for use without the payment of royalty or the need for permission. The issue of public domain is significant when a film is based upon another work of art or incorporates a work such as a song and very significant in reference to its own exhibition. *See* **copyright.**

■ **publicist** The individual in charge of publicizing a film, frequently from preproduction all the way through distribution. The publicist is often in charge of a publicity department. The personnel for publicity are either part of a studio structure or hired from outside. Individual personnel, especially performers, may hire their own publicist or "press agent," as this individual is sometimes called. *See* **press agent** *and* **publicity department.**

■ **publicity department** The group of personnel either belonging to a studio or hired from outside to publicize a film from preproduction through distribution. This group writes press releases and articles for magazines which give information about the stars or technical personnel and the production. They also set up interviews for performers with journals or on television and radio, spread rumors and stories among the public, and arrange for publicity stunts.

■ **publicity still** A photograph relating to a film and taken during any stage of its production that is used for publicity; a production still. *See* **production still.**

■ **puck** A device similar to a mouse but with a greater amount of functions and controls used in a digitizing process—e.g., with a digitizing table. *See* **digital table, digitizing pen,** *and* **mouse.**

■ **pull back** An order given by the director to pull the camera back from the subject being photographed in order to enlarge the context of the scene.

■ **pull-back dolly** A pull-back shot created by moving the dolly that supports the camera back from the subject being photographed to enlarge the context of the scene.

■ **pull-back shot** Any shot that pulls back from the subject being photographed, whether by dolly, crane, or zoom lens, to enlarge the context of the scene and offer new information or suddenly and dramatically reveal some character, object, or part of the location.

■ **pulldown** When transferring a motion picture from film to video, the addition of an extra 6 frames per second so that the motion picture, originally shot at 24 frames per second, will conform to the 30 frames per second of video standard in this country. The system frequently used in this country to add the frames employs a three-two pulldown whereby each of the film's even frames utilizes three fields of the video signal and odd-numbered frames utilize the normal two fields, thus obtaining the 6 extra frames.

■ **pull-down claw** The intermittent mechanism in most cameras and in projectors for film less than 35mm. A single or double claw engages one or two perforations of each frame and pulls the frame down in front of the aperture for exposure or projection. The claw then disengages and moves back to the next frame. *See* **intermittent movement.**

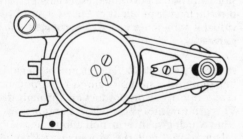

pull-down mechanism for camera

■ **pull-down mechanism** The mechanism in a camera or projector that pulls down one frame at a time, in intermittent movement, before the aperture. In most cameras and in projectors for film less than 35mm, a single or double claw engages one or two perforations and pulls each frame down before the aperture, then disengages and moves back for the next frame. In professional 70mm and 35mm projectors, a Maltese or Geneva cross mechanism is used in which the pin on a rotation shaft engages one of four slots on the crosspiece, turning it 90 degrees at a time and forcing it to turn a sprocket that places each frame individually before the aperture. In all cases, a shutter blocks the light while each frame is moved into position. *See* **intermittent movement.**

■ **pull focus** *See* **rack focus.**

■ **pulling** Locating and separating out those parts of the original film that will be used in the final edited version; also referred to as pulling negative. *See* **matching.**

■ **pulling, pull processing** Lowering the contrast and graininess of film when it has been overexposed by shortening the period of development or sometimes lowering the temperature of the chemicals. *See* **underdevelopment.**

■ **pulls** *See* **selects.**

■ **pull-up** (1) The loop of film in a projector that allows the film to pass smoothly from intermittent movement, necessary to place the individual frames in front of the aperture, to continuous movement, necessary for the film as it passes the sound head. (2) To rearrange a shot so that unnecessary environment is removed and the subject fits more tightly in the frame.

■ **pulse sync** *See* **sync pulse.**

■ **punch** A small hole in the film that acts as a signal for the conductor when the film is projected during the recording of a score.

■ **puppet animation** Animation using three-dimensional puppets instead of drawings. Stop-motion photography, shot one frame at a time, records the changed positions of the puppets. When the frames are projected consecutively onto a screen, an illusion of movement is created. The term "puppetroons" is sometimes used to describe short films that employ only such animated puppets. Puppet animation has successfully been incorporated with live performers, especially in fantasy films. The puppets are generally small models, of anywhere from a few inches to two feet, that are photographed separately and then combined with the separately photographed live action through matting techniques in bipack, optical, and aerial printing systems. Willis O'Brien pioneered this type of work in such films as *The Lost World* (1925) and especially *King Kong* (1933). A later master of this type of puppet animation was Ray Harryhausen, whose work can be seen in such films as *The Seventh Voyage of Sinbad* (1958) and *Clash of the Titans* (1981). Puppets are more expensive to use than cel drawings but can offer a convincing three-dimensional halfway point between reality and fantasy, which has been found effective in the films mentioned above as well as in the fantasies and veiled political allegories that came out of the animation studios in East Europe, with its tradition of puppet shows, after the Second World War. A celebrated creator of puppet animation was Jǐrí Trnka of Czechoslovakia who used the technique for folklore and fairly tale; his feature-length *A Midsummer Night's Dream* (1959) is justly celebrated. *See* **animation** *and* **animatronic puppets.**

■ **pure cinema,** *cinéma-pur* A term used for a number of avant-garde films made in France during the 1920s that did not create a representational reality but focused instead on form and rhythm. The term was used by Henri Chomette to define a cinema that separated itself from all normal elements of film, something he himself accomplished in his two films, *Reflets de lumière et de vitesse* (1925) and *Cinq minutes de cinéma pur* (1926), which present the pure rhythmic movement of light reflections from crystals in motion. Pure cinema was influenced by such German "absolute" filmmakers as Hans Richter and Viking Eggeling, and includes, somewhat loosely, films by such French filmmakers as Jean Grémillion, Marcel Duchamp, and Germaine Dulac. *See* **absolute film.**

■ **push in** To bring the camera closer toward the subject.

■ **pushing, uprating, push processing** Increasing the speed of film during shooting and then overdeveloping by means of a lengthier development stage or higher temperature of chemicals. The procedure is sometimes used to increase contrast in the picture, saturate colors, or achieve some desired quality in the image. Overdevelopment by itself is also employed to save film that has been shot in poor lighting conditions or at an inappropriate speed. *See* **overdevelopment** *and* **underdevelopment.**

■ **push off, pushover, push-off wipe, push-over wipe** A wipe in which one image seems to push the other off the screen, or a vertical line separating the two images seems to push one off the screen while revealing the other. Such wipes, which can be achieved in an optical printer, are not much in use today. *See* **optical printer** *and* **wipe.**

■ **pyrotechnic operator, pyrotechnist, pyrotechnic specialist** The individual in a film production responsible for pyrotechnical effects. *See* **mechanical effects** *and* **pyrotechnics.**

■ **pyrotechnics, pyrotechnic special effects** Any kind of fireworks, missiles, or flashes containing chemical powders that when ignited produce such mechanical effects as explosions, smoke, and light. These incendiaries are generally used in war and adventure films.

■ ■ ■

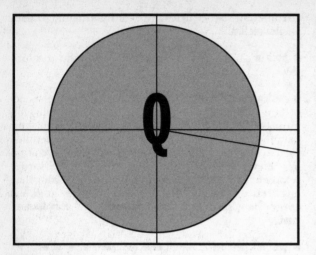

quadlite
to quick cut

■ **quadlite** A lighting unit with four 500-watt flood-lights.

■ **quantisizing** *See* **sampling.**

■ **quarter-inch tape** Standard magnetic tape used in sound recording. Generally comprised of iron oxide coated on polyester base, this tape comes in cartridges or on five-inch, seven-inch, or sometimes even larger reels. See **magnetic recording.**

■ **quarter-load** An amount of explosive powder placed in a blank cartridge to be fired from a gun. This amount produces the required noise and smoke without any danger. A half-load produces a more dramatic effect.

■ **Quarterly Review of Film and Video** A film journal that features critical and scholarly essays on both cinema and television. The publication covers commercial, experimental, and documentary works, both new and old. The journal is published by Harwood Academic Publishers.

■ **quartz bulb, tungsten-halogen bulb, halogen bulb, quartz-iodine bulb, metal-halide bulb, metal-halogen bulb** A lamp bulb of quartz glass that contains a tungsten filament in a metal halide gas such as iodine or bromine. Such bulbs, in use since 1960, have been popular in film-making because they do not blacken (the evaporated tungsten combines with the halide and is redeposited on the filament), and burn at an even color temperature. Because these bulbs are small they can be used in lightweight portable luminaires for location work. The quartz, or a special glass used in its place, will not melt at the high temperatures given off by the bulb.

quartz bulb

■ **quartz light** (1) A quartz bulb. (2) A luminaire using a quartz bulb.

■ **queer cinema** *See* **gay and lesbian cinema.**

■ **quick cut** (1) A quick change from one shot to another without any optical transition. (2) A very brief shot inserted into a scene.

■ ■ ■

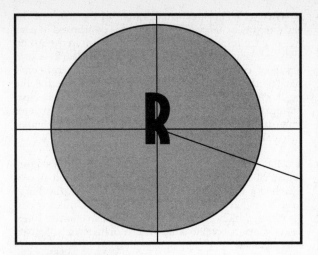

race films to rushes, dailies

■ **race films** A term used to designate films with African-American casts made specifically for African-American audiences begun in the late silent-film days and continuing until the end of the 1940s. Many of these films were imitations of the various Hollywood film genres—westerns, musicals, gangster films, mysteries, etc.—but were frequently poor in quality. Although a number were made by white filmmakers as well as black and the major figures were often light-skinned, these films were significant in offering to African-American audiences figures with whom they could identify and a sense of seeing in the cinema a world that resembled their own. One of the outstanding films of this group is *Scar of Shame* (1926), produced by the Colored Players Film Corporation and directed by a non–African American, Frank Peegini—a story that deals with social class within the black community. Perhaps the two most notable and enduring African-American film directors were Oscar Micheaux and Spencer Williams, both of whom began by making silent films and moved into the sound era. Especially notable are Micheaux's *Body and Soul* (1924), a film about religious hypocrisy with Paul Robeson playing dual roles in his film debut, and Williams's religiously inspired *The Blood of Jesus* in 1941. By the end of the 1940s, the African-American audience had lost their interest in these films and they came to an end. *See* **blaxploitation film.**

■ **rack** (1) A frame with rollers and sprockets that moves film in a series of long vertical loops through the chemical solutions in a continuous processing machine. *See* **processing.** (2) A frame of crossed strips over a bin from which pieces of film are hung by clips in an editing room. *See* **trim bin.** (3) A frame on which luminaires or other equipment is kept either on the set or in storage. (4) To align the picture correctly in the gate of a projector or any film machine. (5) To focus the lens on a camera. (6) To thread film onto a reel for editing or projection. (7) To turn the turret on a camera from one lens to another.

■ **racket cutting** The intercutting of one or two frames from two separate shots, creating an effect something like a superimposition, but one strobic and hallucinatory in effect. The technique has been used in experimental films such as Jean Mitry's *Pacific 231* (1949).

■ **rack focus, select focus, shift focus, pull focus** To change focus from one subject to another during a shot, guiding the audience's attention to a new point of interest while the previous one blurs. Such a shot maintains the spatial relationships of the scene even when changing the audience's attention, a technique effective for switching between simultaneously occurring conversations in the same location or showing a character's reaction to something that has just occurred. *See* **focus pull, follow focus, selective focus,** *and* **shallow focus.**

■ **rackover viewfinder** A viewfinder system that operates when the main camera body is racked to the side and the viewfinder takes its place behind the stationary lens. The image then appears through the optical system of the viewfinder right side up on a ground glass and can be viewed through the eyepiece exactly the way it will be photographed on the film without any parallactic displacement. The shortcoming of this system is that the viewfinder cannot be used during shooting, since the camera body must be racked back in place. For this reason a separate monitor viewfinder is attached to the camera. The rackover viewfinder was a traditional part of the Mitchell NC and BNC 35mm cameras, a number of which are still in use.

■ **rails** A grid made of rails from which luminaires are hung.

■ **rain cluster** A series of sprinklers suspended over the set from which water is dispersed to give the effect of rain in a large area.

■ **rain deflector, spinning-disc rain deflector, spinning-disc water deflector, spray deflector** A rotating glass disc placed in front of the camera to protect it from rain or spray from a body of water.

■ **rain hat** A covering for a microphone when used for outdoor shooting during a rainstorm.

■ **rain standard** A sprinkler attached to the top of a tall mobile tripod from which water is dispersed to give the effect of rain in a small area.

■ **RAM** The letters stand for random access memory, the standard type of memory in a computer system measured in K (1,024 bytes). The term refers to the fact that one can randomly call up any portion of the data in the memory without having to proceed through the other data. A normal type of computer will hold eight megabytes of such memory if it is properly equipped. *See* **byte.**

■ **random access** In computer technology, the term refers to the fact that one can retrieve from memory randomly and instantaneously any desired text or image without having to proceed through other data. The term is used in nonlinear editing, for which film images are digitized, to suggest that the editor can call up an individual scene without having to move through a series of actions to find it, as is the case of linear editing with videotape. A multiple drive system allows the large amount of storage and speed of access necessary for the immediate availability of any whole frame or shot. *See* **editing.**

■ **range** The distance between the camera and the subject being photographed.

■ **range extender** A small optical device placed between the lens and camera to extend the lens's focal distance. Such a device will increase magnification, but with reduced effective aperture and some loss of definition. A range extender is useful for telephoto and zoom lenses when extreme distances are required and when carrying large lenses would be a bother. *See* **tele-extender lens.**

■ **rangefinder, telemeter** An optical viewing system for focusing and computing distance between camera and subject by means of a split or double image, which must be properly aligned, or a microprism, which must be made clear. Such a system is employed for helicopter cinematography or for small-gauge cameras.

■ **Rank Organization** The leading film company in England during the late 1940s, with production, distribution, and exhibition facilities. Headed by J. Arthur Rank, who had begun the organization as General Film Distributors in 1935, the company became the J. Arthur Rank Organization in 1946. During its peak period, the company owned the majority of England's studios and employed the country's best directors and performers. Films such as Laurence Olivier's *Henry V* (1944) and *Hamlet* (1948), both Two-Cities productions, were made under the auspices of the Rank Organization. The company, however, overextended itself and rigid budgetary restrictions soon diminished its output. Leasing its studios to American productions, the organization eventually turned from filmmaking to other business ventures. Its well-known trademark appearing at the start of its films was a muscular, bare-chested man striking a large gong.

■ **raster** (1) The individual frame on the front of the cathode-ray or television tube that is composed of a series of parallel scan lines. The raster count in the American system is 520 such lines. *See* **NTSC** *and* **PAL.** (2) A grid made of opaque vertical slats separated by reflective slats of the same size that send to the audience the right and left eye images in a type of stereoscopic cinematography developed in the Soviet Union. In later versions of this process, the grid was made of lenticular strips. *See* **raster graphics,** *and* **stereoscopy.**

■ **raster graphics** A type of computer graphics composed of a myriad of tiny dots of color called pixels, which are activated on the screen of the cathode-ray tube by electric linescans called rasters. Unlike vector graphics, which are composed of black or white lines, raster graphics create solid and colorful visuals. *See* **computer animation.**

■ **Ratings Board** A group of eight to thirteen members who belong to the Classification and Rating Administration (CARA) of the Motion Picture Association of America (MPAA) that decides on a rating for an individual motion picture. The head of this board is chosen by the MPAA president and the members selected both for belonging to the MPAA and their parental experience. The committee, which is responsible for a vast number of films per year, and on occasion divides into two groups when many films must be viewed, decides ratings by a majority vote. *See* **Movie Rating System.**

■ **rating system** *See* **Movie Rating System.**

■ **raw stock** Unexposed motion-picture film.

■ **raytracing, ray tracing** *See* **shading.**

■ **reaction pan** A pan from some action or person to a character's reaction to that action or person. Unlike a reaction shot, the technique calls attention to itself and is used to contrast the subjects of the two shots, frequently with comic intent. *See* **pan.**

■ **reaction shot** A shot of a character, generally a close-up, reacting to someone or something seen in the preceding shot. The shot is generally a cutaway from the main action.

■ **reader** (1) A small, optical device for viewing film images attached to an editing table. Also called an optical reader. (2) A small playback device for listening to either optical or magnetic sound, which is attached to an editing table. Also called a sound reader. (3) A person in a studio's story department who reads through manuscripts and literary works to find viable properties for making a film. If the reader approves of a work, he or she submits a summary and evaluation to the story editor. Also called a story analyst.

■ **reading** (1) An audition for a part in which the performer reads from a script. (2) The light reading taken from an exposure meter, which indicates the amount of illumination in a scene; or the sound reading taken from a VU meter and indicating the volume of the sound being recorded. *See* **exposure meter** *and* **VU meter.** (3) In contemporary film theory, the process of perceiving, decoding, and analyzing a film, especially the images and their sequence, as if one were reading a written text. The implication is that both procedures are similar: one reads the signs that make up the film as one reads the signs that make up a page of print. It can also be argued that one "reads" one's surrounding reality and the physical reality that comprises the individual images in a film in the same way. *See* **semiotics.**

■ **read-through** An early rehearsal in which performers read through the script, generally for the first time, without much emotion and without any direction. This rehearsal functions to familiarize everyone with the script and with each other, and also to start discussion between performers and director.

■ **Ready-Eddy** A circular calculator used in editing for converting film footage into seconds and minutes and time into footage.

■ **realism, realist cinema** One of the most illusive yet most widely used terms in the various arts, "realism" has been much debated and defined since the early days of motion pictures. In its most uncomplicated meaning, realism in film refers to a direct and truthful view of the real world through the presentation of characters and their physical surroundings with minimal distortion from either the filmmaker's point of view or from filmic technique. In this respect film realism is related to the traditional mimetic school of criticism in literature and painting, which argues that art should be a representation of reality, heightening our consciousness about the world that surrounds us.

Ralph Stephenson and J. R. Debrix, in *The Cinema as Art* (1965), have argued that film is more conducive to creating an illusion of reality than other art forms for the following reasons: (1) cinema reproduces movement; (2) the photographic image is more objective than that in other visual arts because it is "created by a mechanical process"; (3) motion pictures give "a strong impression of . . . 'being present'"; (4) film is composed of "concrete images"; and (5) the darkened auditorium allows the figures on the screen to be accepted in their greater size because the viewer cannot see that they are disproportionate to the actual physical world that surrounds him or her. They also point out that the cinema creates a mental reality as well, dealing with the "reality of ideas, of emotions, of behavior, of character, of fundamental, universal truths." Of course, once we move into the world of ideas, emotions, and truths, realism begins to rely on individual concepts and interpretations of what is real and becomes relative and unobjective. Compounding the difficulty is the fact that each age sees both physical and mental reality differently, and what appears as realism in art to one age might seem dated and conventional to another.

Realism in film depends on both selection and art—what parts of human nature and the physical world filmmakers select to show and the techniques they select to show them. Even in the documentary, where actors are not used, the people involved are aware of the camera, while the filmmaker selects and orders the shots. Realism in the film, then, is always relative and its illusion depends on the techniques of the medium. But realist cinema attempts to play down the art, to make it invisible through medium and long shots from eye level, through long takes, and through functional, unobtrusive cutting. The French critic André Bazin, who was himself a realist in his critical bent, recognized that realism in film could only be achieved by artifice. Bazin praised Orson Welles's *Citizen Kane* (1941) for restoring continuity to the cinema through deep focus and long takes, preferring this approach to the artificiality of Hollywood's invisible editing. He also praised the works of the Italian neorealists, especially Rossellini's *Paisan* (1946), for focusing on "facts" and not shots, thus returning to cinema a "concrete density" (in *What Is Cinema?*).

The opposite of realism is expressionism, where the filmmaker expresses the character's or his or her own subjective perspective, emotions, and fantasies through the medium of film. One can see the two approaches from the start of motion pictures with the expressionistic fantasies of Méliès and the short records of reality presented by the Lumière brothers. To a considerable degree future films would move between these approaches, relying upon the image of physical reality to convince the audience of either the authenticity of its reality or the reality of its fantasy. Even in documentary work one can distinguish two general types of film, both claiming to be realistic: films about reality that clearly select, organize, and even propagandize (e.g., films by Flaherty and Pare Lorentz), and nonfiction films that attempt to get as close to reality as possible with minimal intrusion and technique (e.g., the direct cinema of Frederick Wiseman). Film theory and criticism have shown a more extreme polarity, with the disparate views of critics such as Arnheim, who emphasize the artfulness and unreality of film, and critics such as Kracauer, who see "the redemption of physical reality" as the basis of cinema.

Although realism in film frequently involves a treatment of social problems, society as a determining force upon the individual is more extensively and pessimistically treated in naturalism, an extreme view of reality in fiction and film that sees the individual primarily determined by environment and heredity, not by free will. Significant attempts to create a realist cinema, very much concerned with the individual and his or her relation to society, include the German "street" films of the 1920s, especially the work of G. W. Pabst, a few American problem films of the 1930s such as William Wellman's *Wild Boys of the Road* (1933), the Italian neo-realist films of directors such as Rossellini and De Sica after the Second World War, the British social-realist films of the 1950s such as Karel Reisz's *Saturday Night and Sunday Morning* (1960), and the films from India of Satyajit Ray, beginning with the Apu trilogy (1955–59). *See* **documentary, film theory, naturalism,** *and* **neorealism.**

■ **real time** (1) The term is applied to some process of transferring, recording, or rendering a series of moving images that takes the same amount of time as the time in which the images would normally be displayed *see* **non-real time.** (2) The normal time for displaying some action—e.g., a three-minute chase in three minutes—as opposed to slow or fast motion or some type of elliptical cutting.

■ **rear projection, back projection** The projection of either a still or moving picture onto the rear of a translucent screen in front of which live action is photographed so that both the background on the screen and the foreground action are combined into a single image on the exposed film (the camera shot itself is called a process shot). Rear projection had been used in still photography but it was applied to motion pictures by Norman O. Dawn as early as 1913 in a Western titled *The Drifter*. It was not, however, much used until the advent of sound made studio shooting necessary. Rear projection allowed an exterior scene to be projected as a background for live action filmed in the studio. It also allowed puppet animation, originally filmed in stop-motion photography, to be projected and enlarged on a screen behind live performers. Perhaps the most common use of the technique has been for shots of characters inside a vehicle with film originally shot on location in a moving vehicle projected onto the screen behind them. A single transparent slide can be projected for a still background or a series of images from a film for a moving background (both are called back-ground plates, while the first, and its actual image on the screen, is also called a stereo). If a moving background is projected, the projector must be run in sync with the camera by interlocking motors so that frames in both machines are registered precisely together and both shutters block and pass light simultaneously. A problem of this system had been the weak or uneven distribution of light, causing hot spots and falloff. To overcome this, three separate but synchronic projectors were often used either to superimpose the same image from three separate plates or to project three separate areas of the image. Although rear projection is still employed today, using one projector because of faster film stock in the camera and a better system of projection, front projection, the blue-screen process, and digital composites can often achieve a better matching of colors and more effective picture quality

when combining picture elements. *See* **blue-screen process, digital composite,** *and* **front projection.** (2) The projection of motion pictures or slides onto the rear of a translucent screen in front of which the audience sits. This process, sometimes employed in small auditoriums for educational or promotional films, permits the images to be shown when the room is lit.

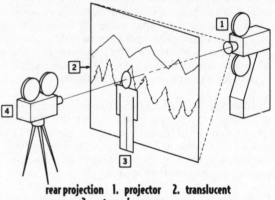

rear projection 1. projector 2. translucent screen 3. actor 4. camera

■ **rear-projection unit** A special projector for rear-projection cinematography, which is run by a motor interlocked with that of the camera. This procedure is necessary to insure that the frames for moving images projected from a film onto a screen behind the performers are registered precisely together with those exposed in the camera and that the shutters in both block and pass light at the same time.

■ **reciprocating reflex mirror** A mirror placed at a 45-degree angle behind the lens of the camera that when raised allows light to reach the film and when lowered reflects the light into the viewfinder system. *See* **reflex viewfinder.**

■ **reciprocity failure, reciprocity law failure** The failure of the reciprocity law (exposure = intensity × time) to hold for photographic emulsions at extremely long or short durations of exposure. *See* **reciprocity law.**

■ **reciprocity law** In the reaction of film emulsion to light, the degree of exposure is dependent upon the intensity of light and duration of exposure (exposure = intensity × time); hence, the exposure will remain the same if one factor increases and the other proportionately decreases. For exceptions to this law, *see* **reciprocity failure.**

■ **reconditioning** The removal of scratches, abrasions, and foreign substances from either the base or emulsion surface of negatives and prints. Various laboratories have their own secret methods, but they generally include cleaning, waxing, and chemically treating the damaged area.

■ **reconstituting, reconstituting the dailies** Putting together the images of the dailies, after they have been cut, in their proper order so that a copy can be made; and then syncing the sound to the images. *See* **editing.**

■ **recorder** (1) A machine that records sound. Original sound for film is usually registered on a magnetic recorder instead of an optical recorder because magnetic tape is easier and cheaper to use and produces better sound. Since most theaters are equipped for optical sound, however, the magnetic sound track must be made into an optical sound track in a special optical sound recorder after editing and mixing. Digital recording, mixing, and theatrical playback systems, however, are fast making their ways into the industry. Digital audio tape (DAT) recorders are starting to replace magnetic recorders. After mixing, digital sound is optically recorded on the film or played back from a disc. *See* **digital sound recording** *and* **sound.** (2) Any device that records images after they have been rendered, enhanced, or edited in a computer system, e.g., a videotape recorder or a film recorder. Also referred to as an output device. *See* **computer animation, image enhancement,** *and* **nonlinear editing.**

■ **record film** A film with the sole intention of recording in a straightforward manner a specific event or series of events without manifesting any artistic treatment or supporting any point of view. For example, the recording of an historical event for archives or of a football game for later study.

■ **recording** (1) The act of preserving sound on a magnetic tape, optical track, or disc for later playback. (2) The tape, track, or disc on which sound has been recorded for reproduction.

■ **recording engineer** An individual who works in a recording studio and assists in the recording, dubbing, and mixing of sound. *See* **dub** *and* **mix.**

■ **recording level** The volume at which a recording machine is set to record sound.

■ **recording studio** A large indoor area for the recording of sound. The sound is picked up by a microphone in a room carefully engineered for acoustics and is then piped to the recording machines, which are kept in a separate room along with the various controls. The sound can be heard either from a loudspeaker or by earphones in this room and the performers seen through a glass window. *See* **dubbing room** *and* **scoring stage.**

■ **recording system** All the components through which sound passes in a single system when being recorded (i.e., microphones, monitor, mixing console, and the recorder itself).

■ **recordist, recording supervisor, floor mixer** The individual in charge of sound recording on the set during shooting.

■ **redhead** An open-back, variable-focus 1,000-watt open-faced luminaire. The Mole-Richardson variety is called a mickey.

■ **red light** A red light bulb or beacon placed both inside the studio and outside the studio door that goes on during shooting and indicates that the studio cannot be entered and silence must be maintained.

■ **red master** A black-and-white master print, made from an original negative, with fine grain and a clear base that give the picture a reddish quality.

■ **redressing** (1) Changing the decorations and properties in a set that is designed to be used as two or more different locations in the same film. (2) Altering a set to indicate some physical change or the passage of time in the same location.

■ **reduced aperture** The aperture size on 35mm cameras and projectors that produces a frame with an aspect ratio of 4:3 (1.33:1), so called because it was necessary to reduce the frame size of silent film in order to accommodate the new sound track and still maintain the earlier conventional aspect ratio (a square image was first tried and found unsatisfactory). These dimensions are also referred to as the Academy aperture, since they were standardized by the Academy of Motion Picture Arts and Sciences in 1932, and the frame size as the Movietone frame, since the Movietone sound system necessitated such an area for the image on the film.

■ **reducers, reducing agents** *See* **developers.**

■ **reduction print** A print on a gauge smaller than that of the film from which it was printed. 16mm prints screened by film societies and educational institutions are generally derived from the original 35mm film made for commercial release.

■ **reduction printing** Printing a film on a gauge smaller than that of the film from which it is made. This process takes place in an optical printer. *See* **optical printer.**

■ **reel** (1) A metal or plastic spool, with open flanges, on which printed film is wound. Double-key reels have two square holes on each side and can be used in projectors and rewinds during editing; single-key reels, which are used for release prints, have a square on one side but a round hole on the other so that they cannot be placed on the projector backward. Projectors have both feed and take-up reels. (2) A measurement for a length of film that will play approximately ten minutes. This measurement derives from the single 35mm reel holding 1,000 feet (the same length as the camera magazine) that ran for about fifteen minutes for silent films at 16 frames per second and later about eleven minutes for sound films at 24 frames per second (or ten minutes when room is allowed for the leader). (3) A spool that holds recording tape instead of a cassette or cartridge.

■ **reel band** A thick strip of paper that fastens around a reel of a release print to hold the film in place and also to specify the name of the motion picture, the number of the print, and the number of the reel.

■ **reel change, change over** Changing from one reel to another during the performance of a motion picture. For theatrical showings, two projectors are still sometimes used to permit the change-over without interruption. To accomplish this, two series of cue marks (small circles) appear in the top right-hand corner of frames at the end of the first reel, the first set to alert the projectionist to warm up the next projector and the second series to signal the start of the new reel. *See* **projector.**

■ **reel-to-reel tape recorder, reel-reel, open-reel recorder** A tape recorder in which the tape moves from one open reel to another instead of moving within closed cassettes or cartridges. Such reels are generally five or seven inches. *See* **Nagra.**

■ **reestablishing shot** A shot, interposed during or at the conclusion of a sequence, that repeats or is similar to the establishing shot used to begin the sequence in order to emphasize once again the general location of an event. Reestablishing shots may also be employed to introduce some new element into the action, perhaps a character or vehicle; to show someone coming or going; to manifest some change in time or weather; or simply to maintain a mood. *See* **establishing shot.**

■ **reexposure** *See* **flashing** *(1) and (2).*

■ **reference print** A print of a film with optimal quality that is used as a comparison in judging the quality of future prints.

■ **reference track** A sound track shot on location not intended for actual inclusion in the final mix but rather to indicate at what point specific dialogue was spoken for future dubbing and editing.

■ **reflectance, reflectance factor, reflection factor** The ratio of light reflected from a surface to the incident light falling on it, generally expressed as a percentage. Reflectance is an important consideration in lighting a scene and setting the exposure on a camera. It is also important in measuring the quality of a screen for showing motion pictures. Also called diffuse reflectance and reflectivity. *See* **screen gain.**

■ **reflected light** The light reflected from the surface of an object as distinguished from the incident light that falls upon an object from all sources. Incident light is more often measured for professional cinematography. *See* **incident light meter** *and* **reflected light meter.**

■ **reflected light meter** An exposure (or light) meter that measures the light reflected from the subject as distinguished from the meter that measures the incident light falling on the subject from all sources. The first kind of meter is generally used at the camera position and measures the light reflected back to the lens (the meter's angle of acceptance should be close to the lens' angle of view), while the second, which is used more frequently in professional cinematography, generally measures light in the interior of the scene near the main focus of the shot. Spot meters, however, are often used in professional cinematography to measure the reflected light from a narrow angle or spot of the scene and are also useful for measuring light when a long-focal length or telephoto lens is employed. Such meters generally include an optical viewing device that allows the small area being measured to be seen in the context of the larger angle of view. A number of the old 8mm and Super 8mm cameras have built-in reflected light meters that measure the reflected light from the entire scene and, according to this measurement, control the lens diaphragm. *See* **incident light meter.**

■ **reflectivity** *See* **reflectance.**

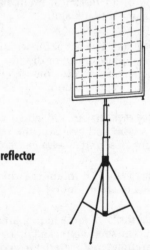

reflector

■ **reflector, reflector board** (1) A large plywood sheet, often about five feet square and covered with some kind of silver coating or foil, that reflects sunlight for outdoor shooting. Such reflectors increase and redirect sunlight as well as filling in areas of shadow. Reflectors vary from mirrorlike surfaces, which give a hard, bright light, to more textured surfaces, which give a softer and more diffuse light. (2) A curved, shiny metallic plate behind the bulb in a luminaire whose reflectance power prevents light loss, redirecting and intensifying the light forward. (3) Any surface or material used to reflect or redirect sound waves.

■ **reflector lamp, reflector light** A lamp with an internal reflector. Both spotlights and floodlights of various sizes have these curved metallic reflectors to diminish light dispersion and redirect and intensify the light coming from the lamp in a forward direction. *See* **lighting.**

■ **reflex camera** A camera with a reflex viewfinder that allows the operator to view the subject being photographed through the camera lens during filming and, hence, without parallax. *See* **reflex viewfinder.**

■ **reflex focusing** Focusing the camera by means of a reflex viewfinder. *See* **reflex viewfinder.**

■ **reflex projection** *See* **front projection.**

■ **reflex screen** A screen used in front-projection photography that is made of minute glass beads and reflects most of the light striking it directly back to its source. When camera and projector are at right angles with a semireflective mirror at a 45-degree angle between the two, the background setting from the projector will reflect off the mirror and onto the screen from which it will reflect directly back through the mirror to the camera. Hence the projected setting and live action in front of the screen will be photographed together as a single image. *See* **front projection.**

■ **reflex shutter** A mirrored shutter in the camera which, at a 45-degree angle, reflects the light entering the lens into the viewfinder system when blocking it from the film between exposures. *See* **reflex viewfinder.**

■ **reflex viewfinder** A viewfinder system in a camera that allows the operator to view the scene being photographed by means of light entering the lens of the camera and being reflected into the system by either a mirrored shutter, placed at a 45-degree angle, while the shutter blocks the light from the film, or by a rotating or oscillating semitransparent glass prism or glass membrane called a pellicle in front of the shutter. In both types, the light is reflected onto a ground-glass screen from which it is viewed through a magnifying eyepiece. Reflex viewfinders are now found in most cameras, allowing the scene to be viewed without parallax and during shooting. To prevent the rotating reflective shutter from causing flicker when it alternately passes the light to the viewfinder and film, the mirrored surface is divided by a black area, thus allowing the image to appear at the necessary 48 cycles per second. The semireflective mirror between lens and shutter avoids flicker, but reduces the clarity of the image viewed, since it only directs a small portion of the light to the viewfinder and permits the rest to pass to the film. The mirrored shutter is used largely in 35mm

cameras where there is sufficient room for its 45-degree angle, and the separate semireflectant piece is used mostly in small-gauge cameras. *See* **viewfinder.**

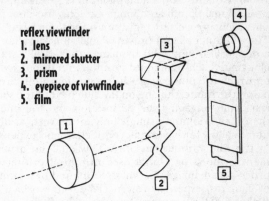

reflex viewfinder
1. lens
2. mirrored shutter
3. prism
4. eyepiece of viewfinder
5. film

■ **refraction** The directional change of a ray of light as it passes obliquely from one medium to another that is caused by the different densities of the media. Just as the eye refracts light rays so that an image of their source is formed on the retina, the lens of a camera refracts light rays to form a latent image on the film's emulsion. *See* **lens.**

■ **reframe** To move the camera slightly in order to adjust or alter the composition of the scene.

■ **regional release** A limited film release to select regions of the country to build up interest for a soon-to-follow wide release. A regional platforming of a film. *See* **platforming** *and* **distribution.**

■ **register holes, registration holes** Punched holes in drawings and cels that fit the pegs of the animation stand for precise registration beneath the camera. *See* **animation stand.**

■ **register pegs, registration pegs** Pegs inserted through the punched holes on animation drawings and cels to hold them in precise position for photography on an animation stand. Pegs are attached to several tracks that can be moved across the table to accommodate various sizes of artwork. Floating pegs attached to bars independent of the table top are employed to allow movement of top cels while bottom ones are fixed to the cel tracks. *See* **animation stand.**

■ **registration** (1) The placement of each frame in exactly the same position with perfect steadiness before the aperture of a camera, projector, or step printer. In a number of cameras each frame is pulled down and held in position by one or two claws that withdraw from the perforations only at the "dead point," when the frame is still. Steadiness is generally reinforced by the pressure plate and by a spring mechanism pressing against one edge of the film. This type of arrangement is found in many smaller gauge cameras such as the 16mm Bolex series, though some, such as the Arriflex 16BL, employ a single pilot pin and others, such as the 16mm Panaflex, use a dual pilot-pin registration. Most professional 65mm and 35mm cameras use dual pilot pins to assure perfect registration for their large film. The old Mitchell and present Panavision Panaflex use a design also employed by many other cameras: dual claws pull each frame into position and disengage, after which two pins engage the two perforations directly below the frame, the one on the side next to the sound track fully engaging the perforation and the one on the other side fitting snugly only in the vertical direction to allow for horizontal contraction and expansion of the film without buckling. This dual-pin arrangement is the same as that used in optical printers for process-plate image steadiness. Employed by a number of cameras, especially for special-effects work, is the Bell and Howell mechanism, where the frame itself is pushed onto similar pins which are attached to the aperture plate and which engage the perforations above the frame. In most projectors, the intermittent mechanism allows sufficient registration, whether it is the Maltese cross mechanism of professional 70mm, 35mm, and some 16mm projectors or the claw mechanism of the small-gauge machines; but projectors for rear projection shots must use pilot-pin registration similar to the two types described above, otherwise projected images will seem especially unsteady against the foreground action. To avoid the same problem, pilot pins must also be used in process cameras and in step-printers when making special-effects composite pictures where images are matted and combined. In such equipment the Bell and Howell mechanism is preferred as simpler and more reliable, though such mechanisms can be replaced by the Mitchell to assure that all the films and mattes have similar registrations. (2) In animation work, the precise and steady placement of drawings and cels so that they are perfectly aligned together beneath the camera for photography. Drawings and cels are punched with register holes that fit over the register peg bars attached to tracks and to floating pegs. The floating pegs secure the top cels but allow them to be moved over the artwork below. *See* **animation stand.**

■ **registration pins, pilot pins, register pins** Pins used in pilot-pin registration to hold each frame by the perforations in exactly the same position during exposure at the aperture in a camera, projector, or printer. Panavision's Panaflex cameras (the same as the Mitchell NC and BNC) use two pins to engage the two perforations directly below the frame, one engaging the opening fully and the other fitting snugly only in the vertical direction to allow for horizontal contraction and expansion of the film without buckling—such placement is considered to give process-plate image steadiness and is the same as pin registration employed in optical printers. The Bell and Howell mechanism, used by sev-

eral other cameras, employs two pins to engage snugly the perforations above the frame—this mechanism is often used for projectors engaged in special-effects shots. *See* **registration** *(1).*

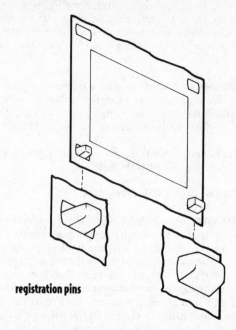

registration pins

■ **registration shot** A shot beginning with a still photograph or drawing that transforms into an image of live action. The static picture seems suddenly to come alive, since the beginning frames of movement match the still image.

■ **regressive angles** A series of diminishing angles in a sequence of shots—for example, an extreme high-angle shot, followed by a high angle, followed by an eye-level shot, all of which zero in on a character. At the start of Robert Wise's *West Side Story* (1961), a series of regressive angles, after the panoramic view of the city, brings us into the main action. *See* **progressive angles.**

■ **regressive shots** A series of shots that dramatically diminishes the size of the subject by increasing the distance of the camera. In Erich von Stroheim's great silent film *Greed* (1923), there is a dramatic series of regressive shots almost at the conclusion of the film that isolates and diminishes McTeague, who is handcuffed to the dead body of Marcus in the desert: the camera shows individual closeups of the protagonist and the bag of gold and then distances through a medium close-up, long shot, and finally an extreme long shot of McTeague. *See* **progressive shots.**

■ **regular 8** *See* **8mm film.**

■ **regular reflection** The reflection of light off a smooth surface.

■ **reissue** To release a film once again into distribution. Sometimes a film is reissued when its first run has not done well but there appears to be a growing interest in it (e.g., Brian de Palma's *Carrie* [1976]) or when the film maintains its popularity and is made available to a new generation of moviegoers (e.g., Victor Fleming's *Gone With the Wind* [1939]). The same as rerelease.

■ **relamping** Changing the bulb in a luminaire.

■ **relational editing, associational editing, associative editing, associate editing** Shaping and arranging shots to highlight some thematic, conceptual, or dramatic relationship between them. The term "relational editing" is used by Pudovkin in *Film Technique,* who claims that this type of editing offers "psychological guidance" to the spectator. He points out the following methods and examples of relational editing, citing from specific films in the third and fourth instances: (1) contrast, for example, juxtaposing scenes of a starving man with those showing the gluttony of a rich man; (2) parallelism, for example, paralleling the actions involved in a man's execution with the actions of a factory owner during the same time period; (3) symbolism, for example, intercutting the slaughter of a bull into scenes concerning the slaughter of workmen, a technique actually performed in Eisenstein's *Strike* (1925); (4) simultaneity, for example, cutting between two interrelated actions for suspense, a technique often appearing at the end of American films and specifically at the conclusion of the modern section of Griffith's *Intolerance* (1916); and (5) leitmotif, for example, a shot of a ringing church bell interspersed through a film with some trite title superimposed to emphasize the hypocrisy of the love preached by the church. *See* **montage.**

■ **relative aperture** *See* **f-stop.**

■ **relay lens** A lens in an optical printer that projects an even illumination at the film plane by projecting onto it an image of the illumination of the condenser lenses. *See* **optical printer.**

■ **release** The initial distribution and exhibition of a film. Films are later rereleased, reissued, or rerun. The release of a major film is generally preceded by a series of previews and an ambitious advertising campaign. Major releases no longer begin with an exclusive premiere, followed by a first-run showing at a first-run theater in major cities, but instead are launched with a wide release in most of the markets in the United States. The "release date" is the date on which the film first opens, the "release schedule" is the plan for its exhibition in the various theaters, and the "release pattern" the arrangement and scheduling of its exhibition for maximum profit. *See* **distribution** *and* **exhibition.**

■ **release date** The date on which a film is initially released for distribution.

■ **release form** A legal form signed by a person who has been photographed or whose voice has been recorded, giving the filmmaker all rights to use the material. The form must also be signed by a witness. There are two kinds of forms, one used when payment is given and the other when there is no payment. *See* **depiction release** *and* **submission release.**

■ **release negative** A duplicate (or dupe) negative made from an interpositive (or master positive) of the edited original negative that is used for the making of release prints. For a wide distribution of release prints, a number of release negatives are made for use at different laboratories.

■ **release pattern** The way in which a film is initially released so that it will have the largest possible box office before its initial run is complete. The strategy may be one of platforming, i.e., releasing the film to a select number of theaters—normally less than 500—and regions to build interest before a wider release; limited release to only a select number of theaters in specific regions because of the special nature of the film; or a wide release or saturation booking in the hope that the film will have an immediate national impact from advertising and public interest that will carry it forward for a number of weeks.

■ **release print** A composite print of the completed film with picture and sound that is distributed for exhibition. Such prints are made in large numbers for commercial release after a sample print made from the same release negative has been approved. Release prints are made from a release negative (or internegative) which is itself made from an interpositive (or master positive).

■ **relief** The prominence given to certain parts of the image that makes them stand out and gives to the image a three-dimensional quality. Such prominence is the result of lighting (especially the interplay of light and shadow), coloring, and the general composition of the scene. The three-dimensional effect makes the flat image on the screen seem more natural and also gives importance to certain characters and objects. *See* **depth** *and* **modeling.**

■ **relight** The process of moving and adjusting lights for each shot in a scene.

■ **religious film** A motion picture dealing with a religious subject. A number of religious organizations have hired small film companies to make such films, but few of these works have any intrinsic value. Commercial religious films have been made by the film industry since silent-film days, and such works vary in quality. Since faith is a matter of individual belief, it is best to judge these works as motion pictures and not as religious documents. A notable group of religious films has been the large epic spectaculars that use religion as an excuse for exotic backgrounds and action. An early example was Fred Niblo's *Ben-Hur* (1926), later remade into an even more spectacular eye-filler directed by William Wyler and released in 1959. Cecil B. DeMille bears considerable responsibility for America seeing the Bible in Hollywood's comic-book manner by making films such as his two versions of *The Ten Commandments,* released in 1923 and 1956. It is doubtful if heaven has forgiven him for *Samson and Delilah,* made in 1949. Hollywood treated religion with seriousness in Otto Preminger's *Saint Joan* (1957) and with taste and tact in *The Song of Bernadette* (1943; dir. Henry King). Religious figures such as priests or pastors have on occasion been seen as somewhat real people in a somewhat real world, notably in Leo McCarey's *Going My Way* (1944) and Henry Koster's *A Man Called Peter* (1955). More recent years have seen a number of films about Jesus, including George Stevens's sober and dull *The Greatest Story Ever Told* (1965). Pier Pasolini's *The Gospel According to St. Matthew* (1964), however, presents one of the most moving and evocative treatments of Jesus in the history of film. In 1973, Jesus became the hero of a rock opera in *Jesus Christ Superstar* (dir. Norman Jewison), which was not as stirring as its Broadway source.

religious film *The Gospel According to St. Matthew* (1964), Pier Pasolini's realistic presentation of Christ's ministry and crucifixion.

■ ■ ■

■ **reload** To place another film magazine in the camera or tape in the recorder. "Reload" is often shouted by the cameraman or sound recorder when they have run out of time or tape respectively, or are about to do so during a shot and require a new supply.

■ **remake** A newer version of an earlier film. Such films are made to (1) exploit the popularity of the original work; (2) exploit the popularity of a property upon which the original work was based; or (3) pay homage to, while updating, the first film. Remakes of earlier films such as Gordon Douglas's 1966 version of John Ford's *Stagecoach* (1939) and Michael Winner's 1977 version of Howard Hawks's *The Big Sleep* (1946) pale severely in comparison with their sources and cannot be justified when the originals have already been made so well. Even the remake of Frank Lloyd's *Mutiny on the Bounty* (1935), in an expensive production directed by Lewis Milestone and starring Marlon Brando in 1962, cannot come near the excellence of the original, although the 1984 version, *Bounty,* which was directed by Roger Donaldson, can be somewhat defended because of the more contemporary erotic and psychological dimensions it adds to the first film. Sometimes the property on which the original is based is so popular that it transcends any single film version and periodically warrants a new motion picture. This has certainly been true of Shakespeare's plays (e.g., the several versions of *Romeo and Juliet* or *Hamlet*), and also of a number of novels such as Dickens's *Tale of Two Cities* and Bram Stoker's *Dracula* (remade numerous times in spite of Bela Lugosi's well-known performance in the 1931 version). Robert Louis Stevenson's *Dr. Jekyll and Mr. Hyde* has inspired numerous film versions, including notable ones by Rouben Mamoulian in 1931 and Victor Fleming in 1941, only ten years apart. Homage remakes have recently been made with intelligence, in a way that recognizes the appeal of the original while developing that appeal in a modern context and for modern mores. Classic horror films have certainly been ripe for remakes that take advantage of both modern sensibilities, especially in respect to violence and sex, and modern film technologies. Two outstanding remakes and adaptations of classic horror films are Philip Kaufman's 1978 version of Don Siegel's *Invasion of the Body Snatchers* (1956), and Paul Schrader's 1981 version of the Val Lewton production of *Cat People* (1942; dir. Jacques Tourneur). Newer versions of older romantic comedies in recent years have not managed to capture the charm of the earlier films.

■ **Rembrandt lighting** A type of dramatic lighting that emphasizes shadows and highlights somewhat in the style of Rembrandt's paintings. Although used to some degree by Griffith, this style of lighting was developed by Cecil B. DeMille with the help of Wilfred Buckland, who had formerly designed sets and lighting for the Belasco theater. DeMille sought to overcome the flat lighting from the sun, which was the primary source of illumination at the time, by using black hangings and reflectors. His 1915 production of *The Warrens of Virginia* is considered a landmark in film lighting. When Samuel Goldwyn is reputed to have wired from New York that people would refuse to attend this film if they could not see it, DeMille is supposed to have responded, "Tell him it's Rembrandt lighting." *See* **lighting.**

■ **rem-jet backing** An antihalation coating on the base of film created by the dispersion of black carbon. Such a coating absorbs light and prevents it from bouncing back through the emulsion and causing halation—that is, a blurred effect around the bright areas of the image.

■ **remote-control camera** A camera operated from a distance and, as a result, capable of taking shots in difficult areas and making difficult maneuvers.

■ **remote head, remote system** The support and control system for a remote-control camera. The Cam-Remote system, one of the first such units, when hung from a Tulip crane, for example, and operated by means of a video monitor, can perform 360-degree pans as well as extreme tilts and rolls. For the digitally run Scorpio II remote-head system, which allows 360-degree continuous rolls, all movements of the camera can be programmed and repeated.

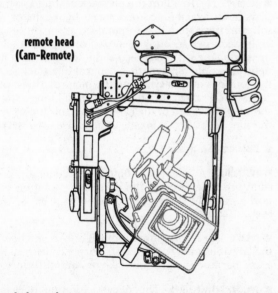

remote head (Cam-Remote)

■ **rendering an image** The process of creating the actual images from all the data in computer animation. Among the rendering algorithms available, Phong is popular, although Raytracing, in spite of being slower, creates more realistic three-dimensional images since it is especially effective with reflective and transparent surfaces. *See* **computer animation.**

■ **RenderMan** A software program produced by Pixar for rendering models with extremely rich and complex surfaces. The program also creates motion blur, depth of field, and images of film resolution. This software has been used for digital effects in a great number of films and is responsible for the dinosaurs in Steven Spielberg's *Jurassic Park* (1993) and John Casseter's all-digital *Toy Story* (1995). *See* **computer animation.**

■ **rental** The hiring of a film by an exhibitor from a distributor for public showing either for a fixed fee, a percentage of the box office, or both.

■ **replenishment** In film processing, replacing the chemical solutions either used up or decomposed in chemical reaction with the emulsion. To allow for this replacement, a portion of the old solution is removed. During the processing, the chemical solution is frequently monitored and adjusted to guarantee a high-quality image. *See* **processing.**

■ **report, report sheet** *See* **log.**

■ **representational film** Any film in which the images are a direct representation of the real physical world as opposed to those avant-garde films that either distort the image of reality or present abstract and nonrepresentational images. *See* **avant-garde cinema.**

■ **reprise shots** Shots that have appeared earlier in the film. The repetition of such shots can be an effective technique for showing a character's memory of earlier events. In Nicolas Roeg's *Don't Look Now* (1973), the protagonist remembers, at the moment of his death, a long sequence of recent events—while his life flashes by, the audience is made to see the significance and relationship of these episodes.

■ **Republic Pictures** A film corporation founded in 1935 with the merger of four smaller studios and the ascendancy of Herbert J. Yates as president. Republic was especially known for turning out in rapid and efficient fashion a number of hollow but competently made B-pictures. The company produced detective films, musicals, and serials, but is notable for its many Westerns starring John Wayne, Gene Autry, and Roy Rogers. Yates's wife, Vera Ralston, appeared in a large number of the studio's films. Republic turned out some better films in its final years, namely *The Quiet Man* in 1952, for which John Ford won an Academy Award as director, and Nicholas Ray's *Johnny Guitar* in 1953. The demise of the studio system and the B-picture in the 1950s doomed Republic, which ceased film production in 1958. *See* **B-picture.**

■ **rerecording** (1) To transfer sound from one recording to another, whether from tape to tape, from tape to magnetic film, or from a magnetic to an optical sound track. (2) The mixing of several sound tracks onto one track. *See* **mix.**

■ **rerecording log** *See* **mixing cue sheet.**

■ **rerecording mixer, rerecordist** An individual in the sound department or recording studio responsible for bringing together all the sound tracks into a single master track or mix. This individual is responsible for the synthesis of dialogue, sound effects, and music. Also called the dubbing mixer. *See* **mixer.**

■ **rerelease, rerun** A general release of a film for exhibition after its initial release. Films are rereleased if they are especially popular or if they achieve some notoriety by being nominated for or winning an Academy Award. Some films, such as Brian De Palma's *Carrie* (1976), slip through on their first release with little notice but then gain popularity by word-of-mouth and are rereleased. A number of classic films, such as Walt Disney's *Fantasia* (1940) and *Gone With the Wind* (1939; dir. Victor Fleming), have been rereleased periodically.

■ **resampling** Resampling up means increasing the number of pixels in an image and resampling down means lowering the amount. The first practice is used to maintain the resolution of an image when it is resized up and the second when it is resized down. Resampling can also be used to alter the appearance of an image without changing its size, though not necessarily for better resolution.

■ **research department** A department, belonging to a film studio, that supplies information for the production of a film concerning its time period, location, historical events, costumes, furniture, and properties. Such departments, which possess a large number of books, magazines, articles, pictures, and photographs, are especially useful for the screenwriter and art director. *See* **studio system.**

■ **reservoir** The area at the start of a continuous-processing machine in which enough film from a roll is gathered by a fixed and a moving spindle to allow the film to continue through the machine while a new roll is attached to its stationary end. *See* **processing.**

■ **resizing** In computer animation, changing the size of an image on the screen or in the frame normally maintaining the same dimensions. In order to maintain the same resolution, the image must be resampled—i.e., the pixels increased for an enlarged image and diminished for a smaller. *See* **scale.**

■ **resolution, resolving power** (1) The capacity of a lens or film to render fine detail in an image. The resolving power of a lens or film can be assessed by photographing a resolution chart and measuring the number of lines that can be distinguished in a millimeter. The greater the detail, the greater the resolution. Fine-grain emulsions have greater resolution than coarse-grain film. The resolving power of an image is also influenced by the contrast of the subject, its nearness, the intensity and length of exposure, the thickness of emulsion (thicker layers scatter light and thus decrease resolution), the nature of the developing solution, and the length of development. Because resolving power is measured on charts of high contrast that cannot account for details in areas of low contrast, and because it is not always indicative of details seen by the naked eye, acutance is now considered a better indication of an image's sharpness and clarity (i.e., the sharpness of an object's edge rendered in a photograph and measured by means of a microdensitometer). *See* **acutance.** (2) The amount of detail in a computer image, itself determined by the amount of information stored for the image. Such resolution is not the same as the monitor resolution with which the image is displayed; instead, it determines the quality of the output image on paper, videotape, or film. Image resolution is determined by the number of lines per inch (lpi) for vector graphics and the number of pixels per inch (ppi) for raster graphics. The actual work in computer animation and graphics is done with low-resolution images, since less information allows quicker procedures, while the output itself is done with high-resolution images for greater detail and a richer picture. *See* **computer animation.**

■ **resolve** (1) To adjust the playback of sound so that it plays at its exactly recorded speed by means of a resolver in the system that responds to a sync pulse (generally sixty per second) recorded on a pilot track on the same tape. (2) To rerecord the sound from a magnetic tape onto a magnetic or optical film track so that the sound is now in sync with the picture. A sync pulse (or sync signal) recorded on the initial tape with the sound at the speed of the camera controls the speed of the film recorder by means of a resolver. *See* **sync pulse.**

■ **resolver** *See* **resolve** *(1) and (2).*

■ **restrainer** A chemical compound, generally potassium bromide, used in the developing solution to retard fogging by slowing the developing process. *See* **fog level** *and* **processing.**

■ **retake** (1) A shot photographed once again because the previous take was unsatisfactory. (2) To reshoot a scene because the previous take was unsatisfactory.

■ **reticle, reticle lines** The network of fine lines seen through a viewfinder that outline or designate certain areas of the perceived subject. In a camera viewfinder these lines normally indicate the angle of view, the frame to be recorded by the camera, and the center of the frame. Modern viewfinders also designate the "safe-action area," i.e., the area for photographing major action so that it will fit within a television frame. In an animation stand a reticle on glass is moved in front of the lens after the camera has been racked over to show that part of the cels which will form the frame area. *See* **viewfinder.**

■ **reticulation** The formation of a network of wrinkles and depressions on the surface of a film's emulsion.

Such damage is generally caused by an excessive temperature change in the processing solutions.

■ **retrofocus lens, inverted telephoto lens** A lens with a front dispersive element far enough from the rear collective element to permit a back focus distance between the rear of the lens and the film plane sufficient for a mirrored shutter in a reflex viewfinder or a beam splitter in an electronic monitor viewfinder. Such lenses allow wide angles of view, a large aperture, and even illumination. *See* **lens** *and* **viewfinder.**

■ **retrospective** A special showing of a series of films belonging to a single director or performer that recapitulates his or her career.

■ **reveal** To move the camera back from a subject, hence disclosing a wider field of action and communicating more information to the audience.

■ **revelation pan** A pan shot that suddenly and unexpectedly reveals some new information in the scene, perhaps a character, vehicle, or action. *See* **pan.**

■ **reverberation** The persistence of a sound after its origin has stopped, due to the continual reflection of the sound off the surfaces in a closed area. Reverberation time is the length of time it takes the reverberations to diminish by sixty decibels.

■ **reversal film** (1) A film stock that, after exposure in the camera, is processed to form a positive image on the original base, thus eliminating the stage of printing the positive from the negative. Reversal film is first developed so that a negative image is formed, but the metallic silver forming the image is bleached and washed away. The remaining, unexposed silver halides are then exposed to light or treated chemically in such a way that they can be developed into metallic silver to form a positive image—the halides are developed in greater depth in the area where they were initially least developed and in less depth where they were most developed, hence forming a picture opposite to the negative image originally formed. In the case of tripack color reversal film, the film is reexposed to light or chemically treated after the black-and-white negative image has been developed in each of the layers; then a second development transforms the newly exposed halides into a positive image and converts the dye in each of the layers into a color complementary to one of the primary colors. The silver halides from both developments are then bleached and dissolved, leaving only the positive color image, which is the result of the combined complementary dyes. Reversal film also allows a high-quality image and diminishes the visibility of abrasions and dirt. 16mm reversal film is now being used professionally, though the necessity of making duplicate prints to protect the original diminishes the fine-grain advantage that a single-generation reversal film

has over the negative-positive process. Reversal film also has less exposure latitude in developing and tends to create more contrast in the image. But because of the elimination of the printing stage, reversal film is relatively inexpensive to use; and because the original stock can be edited and screened, it is also faster and simpler to work with than standard film. For these reasons reversal film is most often employed for smaller-gauge cameras in noncommercial filmmaking. (2) A print film that has the capacity to make a positive from a positive or a negative from another negative through a reversal process. *See* **film** *(1).*

■ **reversal intermediate** A duplicate made with reversal film that corresponds to the images on the original and is intended as an intermediate film in the making of prints. A reversal negative can be made from the original negative for such a purpose, eliminating the master-print stage and hence maintaining a relatively high quality of image. *See* **color reversal intermediate.**

■ **reversal original** *See* **reversal film** *(1).*

■ **reversal print** A print made on reversal stock, generally a positive made from an original reversal positive. *See* **reversal process.**

■ **reversal process, reversal positive process** The procedure for making a positive on original reversal film, thus skipping the printing stage necessary with regular film. The film is first developed, and exposed halides that have become metallic silver particles are next bleached and dissolved; reexposure or a chemical treatment then allows the remaining halides to form silver particles, which are developed as the positive image. In the case of color film, color dyes complementary to the primary colors form a positive image after reexposure or chemical treatment, and the silver particles from all stages of development are then removed. Positives can thus be made on the original film or on fresh stock printed in an optical printer from the original reversal positive. *See* **reversal film.**

■ **reverse angle** An angle of view opposite to that in a preceding shot. A series of reverse angles is frequently used to alternate between the points of view of two characters in a conversation (called shot/reverse-shot technique), or such a shot may be used to show a character entering a room after we have seen him leaving another room. Reverse angles have also been employed countless times to alternate points of view from victim to assaulter and back again in thrillers. *See* **angle-reverse-angle.**

■ **reverse-angle shot** A shot using a reverse angle. *See* **reverse angle.**

■ **reverse blue-screen process** *See* **blue-screen process.**

■ **reverse front-projection blue-screen process** *See* **blue-screen process.**

■ **reverse motion, reverse action** Movement in a scene opposite to the direction in which it was originally filmed. This reversal of motion is obtained in the following ways: (1) the film is run through the camera backward and the shot is ultimately projected in the normal forward direction (not all cameras, however, can photograph backward); (2) the scene is printed backward in an optical printer; (3) the camera is turned upside down with the film running normally, and later, after printing, the film is turned upside down (this method can work only for 35mm film and 16mm stock with double rows of perforations, not for Super 8mm film). Reverse motion on the screen is often used for comic effects (e.g., in silent comedies or more recently in Richard Lester's *A Hard Day's Night* [1964]), but it has also been used as an invisible technique for creating special effects from the days of Méliès. Footprints can be made to appear from nowhere, indicating the presence of an invisible being, by running film in an opposite direction on which footprints gradually disappear, an effect itself achieved by stopping the camera periodically and filling in each footprint; characters can be made to leap to incredible heights by reversing the film of a stunt man jumping down in a backward position; vehicles can be made to race toward the camera safely by turning around the film of a shot that shows the vehicle actually backing away. A number of popular spy films, such as the James Bond thrillers, employ "reverse printing" in an optical printer to achieve such effects. "Back-and-forth printing," which alternates the same action forward and backward, is employed to achieve some elaborate or comic behavior on the screen or to extend movement for cartoon figures.

■ **reverse POV** An instruction in a film script for a reverse-angle shot that shows the point of view of a character responding to someone or some action present in the preceding shot.

■ **reverse printing** Printing a sequence of film backward in an optical printer so that the action will appear reversed on the screen. *See* **reverse motion.**

■ **reverse scene** A scene which has been turned around and in which all the action has been reversed. Such an effect is achieved through reverse printing in an optical printer. *See* **reverse motion.**

■ **review** *See* **film review.**

■ **revival house** A theater that revives older motion pictures of some quality or interest. Such theaters, once common, especially in large cities, gradually disappeared with the growth of television and home video. *See* **calendar house.**

■ **rewind** (1) A geared crank with a spindle to which a reel of film is attached. Two rewinds are used, with each of the film's ends attached to one of the reels, in order to rewind the film in a projection booth or to move the film back and forth during editing. Rewinds are either operated manually or sometimes by motor. Also called a rewinder. (2) To move the film from one reel onto another, hence changing its direction either on a pair of rewinds or on a projector.

rewind

■ **rewrite, revision** An extensive alteration of a script—something more than a polish and less than a new draft. A revision might be done by the same writer who wrote the original draft or by an entirely new one. Also referred to as change pages, especially during production.

■ **rheostat** An adjustable control that changes the power and hence the speed of various camera motors.

■ **rhythm** An overall sense of movement in a film with a repeating pattern of certain elements. Whereas pace refers to the sheer tempo or speed of a film, rhythm refers to something more pronounced that gives the work both movement and coherence, that imposes some artistic ordering on the motion within the pictures and on the movement from image to image. An internal rhythm within a shot can be created by a repeated pattern of visual elements that pass before the camera or that the camera discovers as it moves, or by a repetition of camera movements. German silent-film directors such as F. W. Murnau and E. A. Dupont used a moving camera in films such as their respective *The Last Laugh* (*Der Letzte Mann;* 1924) and *Variety* (1925), both photographed by Karl Freund, and created internal rhythms within lengthy individual shots to suggest subjective points of view by repeated movements of the camera and the repeated appearance of objects. Also effective for creating internal rhythms within a sequence is the technique of "rhythmic montage," defined by the Russian film director and theoretician Sergei Eisenstein in *Film Form* as the rhythmic counterpoint of individual shots to the sequence of shots in which they appear. Eisenstein cites the Odessa Steps sequence in *The Battleship Potemkin* (1925) as an example of rhythmic montage and discusses how the repeated drum of the soldiers' feet descending the steps is "unsynchronized with the beat of the cutting" and gives way to the accelerated rhythm of the baby carriage rolling down the steps. Eisenstein's montage technique in general creates complex rhythmic patterns as the sequence moves from shot to shot, with similar or varying lengths of shots and repeated and varying visual elements playing off one another and the entire sequence within the shots.

Skillful cutting and editing techniques in film create rhythms, though ones less complex than those employed by Eisenstein. A pattern of close-ups intercut within longer shots not only conveys to us a character's reactions to the environment, but also creates within us a rhythmic expectation that sustains our interest. Brief shots of a subsidiary action intercut within longer shots of the main action not only create a parallel or counterpoint between the two events but also develop for us a rhythm of anticipation and suspense. Dramatic emphasis or even a feeling of confusion can be achieved if the duration of the shots is suddenly altered so that the rhythm is broken or changed. Sometimes we feel dominant rhythms in works of major artists—the repetition and subtle variations in reappearing visual images, symbols, and colors in works by Federico Fellini and Nicolas Roeg; the dominant patterns of long takes and close-ups in the dramatic and brooding films of Bergman and Antonioni; the repetition of fast cuts and alternating angles in films by Richard Lester, Mike Nichols, and Bob Fosse, which create a dizzying, syncopative rhythm. *See* **pace.**

■ **ride focus** To operate the focus control on a lens while the camera moves in order to keep the subject in focus (i.e., in order to "follow focus").

■ **ride gain, ride the pot, ride the needle** To monitor and control the amplitude of the audio signal during recording or playback.

■ **rifle mike, gun mike** A microphone that can be pointed in any direction like a rifle or gun to pick up the sound from a specific source. *See* **microphone.**

■ **rifle spot** A long narrow spotlight that projects a fixed beam of light. *See* **spotlight.**

■ **rig** (1) To assemble scaffolds for the support of sets, lights, various equipment, and workers. (2) To set up lights on scaffolds, rails, pipes, or towers. (3) To assemble or put in working order any structure or piece of equipment.

■ **riggers, rigging crew** The stagehands who put up the scaffolds to support sets, lighting, various equipment, and workers.

■ **rigging** (1) The narrow catwalk or scaffolding suspended from the ceiling on which lighting technicians and stagehands work and from which lighting is suspended. (2) Putting luminaires in their proper position before they are focused and set for shooting.

■ **right of first negotiation, right of last refusal** The right of a company or individual to have the first opportunity to purchase a piece of property from a seller for mutually acceptable terms—e.g., in a contract with an author to use his or her novel as the source for a film, the studio may require such rights to the subsequent book by the same author. If the studio does not make the purchase within a specified amount of time, the author may take his or her work elsewhere. The assumption is that the author will bargain in good faith and not sell the work to a third party for the same amount of money offered by the studio. Right of last refusal means that the studio also has the right to match or better any offer to an author by a third party.

■ **right reading** Any image that appears in its proper order from left to right; the opposite of "wrong reading."

■ **rim lighting** A type of lighting that illuminates only the outlines of a character or object, generally keeping the front surface dark or weakly illuminated. The character may be lit directly from the back, but more likely is lit from both sides with the lighting to the rear. Sometimes a character may have rim lighting in addition to general lighting to make him or her stand out. *See* **back light.**

■ **ripple dissolve** A transition from one scene to another with the first undulating and gradually giving way to the second. The technique was much used in the 1940s as a transition from a character recalling some past event to a flashback of the event itself. *See* **defocus transition** *and* **dissolve.**

■ **ripple effect** A wavering effect in the image achieved by shooting through a piece of moving ripple glass, e.g., at the start of a dream or a landscape seen through great heat.

■ **riser** (1) A small platform of several inches for raising a character, prop, or piece of equipment off the floor. Also called an apple box. (2) A small platform device for elevating the camera. Sometimes called a bridge plate.

■ **ritter, ritter fan** A large fan used to create the effect of a high and volatile wind or the blowing of rain and snow.

■ **Rivas splicer** *See* **splicer.**

■ **RKO Radio Pictures Incorporated** A film company organized in 1928 when the Radio Corporation of America (RCA) joined the producing and distributing company put together by Joseph P. Kennedy, which included the Keith and Orpheum theater chains—RKO were the initials for Radio-Keith-Orpheum. RCA was anxious to get into film production with its optical sound system, Photophone, in order to compete with the Movietone system marketed to other major studios by Electrical Research Products Incorporated (ERPI). The result was a vertically integrated production, distribution, and exhibition company that immediately became one of Hollywood's top five studios.

Although RKO's financial history was rarely stable, especially in 1933 when it went into receivership, the company still produced a large number of notable films. The company produced nine Fred Astaire and Ginger Rogers films, including *The Gay Divorcee* (1934) and *Top Hat* (1935), both directed by Mark Sandrich; a large number of Katharine Hepburn's early films, including *A Bill of Divorcement* (1932), with John Barrymore and directed by George Cukor, and the classic screwball comedy *Bringing Up Baby* (1938), which also starred Cary Grant and was directed by Howard Hawks; and such film classics as Cooper and Schoedsack's *King Kong* (1933), John Ford's *The Informer* (1935), Orson Welles's *Citizen Kane* (1941), and Alfred Hitchcock's *Notorious* (1946). RKO also produced a large number of B-pictures, including the masterful horror films produced by Val Lewton in the early 1940s, and distributed films by Walt Disney, Samuel Goldwyn, and David O. Selznick as well. The demise of RKO began in 1948 when Howard Hughes bought control of the company and then initiated a period of mismanagement and neglect. In 1955, he sold the company to General Tire and Rubber Company, which then sold the studios in 1957 to Desi Arnaz and Lucille Ball for Desilu television production.

■ **RMS granularity** Granularity is the objective measure of what we see as the graininess of a film's emulsion, and RMS granularity is the figure for the variation in an emulsion's density at a single exposure. RMS are the initials for "root-mean-square" and derive from the fact that the figure is achieved by multiplying the initial deviation figure by the square root of the area measured by the microdensitometer in order to compensate for the aperture of the instrument and hence the width of its beam light. *See* **granularity.**

■ **road show, roadshow** A release of a film only at select theaters in major cities with higher admission prices and reserved seating. Road shows were a popular releasing method from the mid-1950s until the late 1960s. Expensive and ambitious films such as David Lean's *Bridge on the River Kwai* (1957) and Stanley Kubrick's *2001: A Space Odyssey* (1968) were released this way, though the tendency now is to go for a wide booking to capitalize on publicity and recoup as soon as possible the large expenditures for production. *See* **distribution.**

■ **robotics** *See* **animatronic puppets.**

■ **rock and roll** Professional jargon for roll-back sound mixing in which all the sound tracks, and the picture as well, can be stopped and reversed to a certain point without loss of synchronization. This procedure can be done numerous times and portions of tracks can be rerecorded and new tracks added. Hence the systems can be rocked forward and rolled back. Also referred to as roll back and forward-backward. *See* **mix** *(1).*

■ **rock documentary** A type of concert film that presents a performance of rock music, frequently employing filmic technique to create for the audience the experience of attending such a performance while also seeming to make some kind of social statement about the music and the culture which produces it. Albert and David Maysle's *Gimme Shelter* (1970), for example, a filmed account of the Rolling Stones' notorious concert at Altamont, which includes segments from other performances as well, is a remarkable document of both society and the youth culture of the time. *See* **concert film.**

■ **role** A part in a dramatic performance played by an actor or actress, be it major or minor; the character played by the performer.

■ **roll** (1) Motion-picture film wound on a spool or core. (2) The movement of film in a camera, audio tape in a sound recorder, and videotape in a video recorder. (3) To commence or control the movement of film, audio tape, and videotape in a recording system. (4) The movement of the camera around the axis of the lens, sometimes used to suggest the point of view of an inebriated person or the perspective from a boat on unsteady water.

■ **roll-back mixing** *See* **rock and roll.**

■ **roll camera** The order from the director or assistant director to start the camera.

■ **roll 'em, roll it** The order from the director or assistant director to start the camera and sound equipment. When the camera is operating at full speed, the camera assistant may shout "rolling."

■ **roller** A pulley that rotates freely in any type of film machine to help move the film along a predetermined path.

■ **rolling spider** *See* **wheeled tee.**

■ **roll-off** A gradual diminishment in sound frequency rather than a sharp break. In sound mixing, an equalization for tracks might be the reduction of bass frequencies below 150 Hz and treble frequencies above 9,000 Hz to reduce noise and improve clarity. *See* **equalization.**

■ **rollout** A type of release in which the film gradually plays in an expanding number of theaters. The film may open in an exclusive release (i.e., a few theaters in major cities), then move to a general release (i.e., about 500 theaters), and, if the gods smile, culminate with a wide release (i.e., some 2,000 theaters).

■ **roll sound** An order to begin sound recording.

■ **roll-up titles, roller titles, rolling titles** Titles that roll up from the bottom to the top of the screen and give the names of production personnel or some introductory explanation.

■ **romance** A film that emphasizes a male-female love relationship at the expense of other story elements. The relationship itself is presented in an emotional, sentimental, and generally positive manner that glorifies the feelings of each character for the other and heralds love as the saving grace of human existence, even when environment and circumstances lead to ultimate sacrifice or unhappiness. Film has offered audiences an escape into the world of fantasy from its inception and romances have been a main staple to fill the empty lives of its viewers. Notable film romances have been Erich von Stroheim's *The Wedding March* (1928), which also included a good bit of social satire; the adventurous *The Sheik* (1921; dir. George Melford), starring Rudolph Valentino and Agnes Ayres; Frank Borzage's popular *Seventh Heaven* (1927); George Cukor's *Camille* (1936), with Greta Garbo and Robert Taylor; Henry King's *Love Is a Many Splendored Thing* (1955); Claude Lelouch's international success, *A Man and a Woman* (1966); and Arthur Hiller's popular but trite *Love Story* (1970).

■ **romantic comedy** A film dealing with the relationship of a man and a woman who, after many trials and tribulations caused by their own misunderstandings, a number of obstacle figures, or both, are finally united at the end of the film. A slight variation on this theme is the couple who start off united, are temporarily separated, but are reunited at the end of the film. In both cases, it is crucial that the attraction between the two is evident and that their trials and tribulations be treated in a comic manner. Romantic comedy has sometimes been thought of as synonymous with screwball comedy, but the second classification refers to a group of films too specific to be so all-inclusive. A number of romantic comedies have heroines less aggressive or actions less madcap so that they are distinguishable from the screwball variety (*see* **screwball comedy**). In the early days of sound, Ernst Lubitsch directed a number of charming fantasies with operatic elements, such as *Love Parade* (1929), with Jeanette MacDonald and Maurice Chevalier, that fit into this category, and certainly his nonmusical *Trouble in Paradise* (1932), with Herbert Marshall and Miriam Hopkins as the equally witty and aggressive lovers, is the very height of sophisticated romantic

romance, romantic lead *The Sheik* (1921; dir. George Melford) stars the most famous lover in film history, Rudolph Valentino.

■ ■ ■

comedy. Also equal and equally tough are Clark Gable and Jean Harlow in Victor Fleming's *Red Dust* (1932). The Fred Astaire and Ginger Rogers musicals during the 1930s can be considered romantic comedies, as can the Thin Man mystery films of the same period, with William Powell and Myrna Loy. Cary Grant and Katharine Hepburn start off George Cukor's *The Philadelphia Story* (1940) with a divorce, but come together again at the end of the film. After the war years and the post–screwball comedies of Preston Sturges, America became more middle-class and its humor somewhat less sophisticated and witty, more within the bounds of propriety as demonstrated in the romantic comedies of Doris Day. In later years, romance could still be treated with both humor and respect in films such as Billy Wilder's *Sabrina* (1954), with Audrey Hepburn and Humphry Bogart as the lovers, and Leo McCarey's *An Affair to Remember* (1957), with Deborah Kerr and Cary Grant finally straightening things out. Woody Allen began a new, and perhaps more realistic, chapter in dealing with male-female relationships with his very psychological, contemporary, and funny treatment of love in *Annie Hall* (1977).

■ **romantic lead** The leading character in a romance, normally a popular performer of great charm and attractive appearance. Popular male romantic leads of the silent-film days were Rudolph Valentino and John Gilbert; since that time, Clark Gable, Gregory Peck,

Rock Hudson, and Robert Redford have stirred many a heart.

■ **romantic team** An actor and actress who have become popular playing together as lovers in romances or any type of film. Some of the most popular performers who have appeared frequently together in romantic situations are William Powell and Myrna Loy, Fred Astaire and Ginger Rogers, Spencer Tracy and Katharine Hepburn, Nelson Eddy and Jeanette MacDonald, Humphrey Bogart and Lauren Bacall.

■ **R-190** A metal spool that holds 200 feet of 16mm film.

■ **room tone, room sound, room noise** (1) The sound quality in a specific room that is the product of the shape, size, and materials of the room and the reverberations they produce. Such factors must, of course, be a consideration in recording dialogue or music in the particular room. (2) The general ambient sound in a room or location, also called presence. Such a sound or tone is a result of the environment and may be the product of distant noise, water in the pipes, or air rushing through cracks. Ambient sound is necessary in films especially when characters are not speaking and there is no background music. Such room presence may be recorded separately or created artificially.

■ **rostrum** (1) A small platform for camera or lighting with collapsible legs of varying heights. (2) The rigid structure that supports the camera and animation board for animation work. The horizontal board holds the cels and artwork in place by means of pegs. The camera is in a vertical position, looking down on the cels and can be moved up and down the column, either by a motor or by hand, for varying distances and field of view. *See* **animation stand.**

■ **rotary movement** A spinning image created by a spin attachment in an optical printer—for example, a whirling newspaper that suddenly stops to present its headlines, an image used with some frequency in the movies of the 1940s. Also referred to as spin.

■ **rotary printer** A continuous-contact printer in which the negative and fresh stock are fed from two separate reels onto a continuously rotating sprocket that brings both films in contact to the point of exposure by means of teeth engaging their perforations. *See* **printer.**

■ **rotary shutter, rotating shutter** *See* **shutter.**

■ **rotoscope** An attachment to a process camera that projects individual frames of live action (1) onto a matte board for drawing matte lines and making mattes in order to combine elements from different film images into a composite picture in an optical

rotoscope 1. projected image 2. matte line 3. matte 4. composite picture

printer; and (2) onto an animation stand for making animated figures from live figures (as, for example, in Ralph Bakshi's *Lord of the Rings* (1978)). The attachment contains a prism or mirror that fits behind the pressure plate and a lamphouse attached to the side of the camera. Light from the lamp is reflected ninety degrees off the prism or mirror and through the individual frame of film. The light then passes through a lens that projects an enlarged image onto the matte board or animation table. *See* **animation stand** *and* **matte** *(2).*

■ **rotoscope artist, roto artist** The person who creates the rotoscope mattes for the production of composite images. *See* **rotoscope.**

■ **rough cut** An early edited version of a film that follows the general story line, but without any detailed or fine cutting. After the various takes have been put together into a rough assembly, the editor, working under the supervision of the director and with the sound tracks in interlock, selects the best takes, cuts them at appropriate points, and offers a general version of the film in conjunction with the sound. The rough cut is also called the director's cut since it is supposed to be his version of the film without any interference from the studio. *See* **editing.**

■ **rough light** *See* **foundation light.**

■ **rough mix** *See* **scratch mix.**

■ **roughs** The initial, unfinished drawings or sketches that are the basis of the detailed and finished artwork in animation.

■ **roving fill** A fill light that moves with the camera— one that is attached to the camera itself, a dolly, or one that is handheld. *See* **fill light.**

■ **R-rated** A designation for a film that is restricted because of its content or treatment of certain subjects. Children seventeen or under can see the film only if accompanied by a parent or guardian. This is one of several ratings devised by the Motion Picture Association of America in the 1960s to replace the old Motion Picture Code. The R-rating, that generally suggests a film with some sexual explicitness, profanity, and violence, is not as restrictive as the NC-17 that bans such young people entirely because of the film's adult content. *See* **Motion Picture Production Code** *and* **Movie Rating System.**

■ **rubber numbers** The numbers printed along both prints and sound track to allow for matching during editing.

■ **rub-off animation** *See* **scratch-off animation.**

■ **rumble pot** A container of boiling water into which dry ice is placed for the creation of fog.

■ **run** (1) The duration for which a film plays at a particular location. *See* **legs.** (2) To exhibit a film at a theater. (3) The operation of a piece of machinery (e.g., a camera or projector). (4) To operate a piece of machinery.

■ **runaway production** A film production made away from the Hollywood studios, frequently abroad, in order to take advantage of cheaper costs. A great number of Hollywood's films began to be made in foreign countries in the 1950s due to rising labor costs at home (the film industry is heavily unionized) as well as increasing cost of materials. Sometimes foreign armies could be hired for battle scenes in epic films, scenes that would be too expensive to mount in this country. Film companies also took advantage of tax shelters and national subsidies from the host country. *See* **subsidy.**

■ **run-by** A shot in which a vehicle, object, or character passes rapidly before the camera, which remains stationary. *See* **passing shot.**

■ **runners** The scaffolds above the set from which lights, curtains, or scenery are suspended. (2) *See* **gofer.**

■ **running shot** (1) A moving shot that follows the movements and keeps pace with a character, animal, or vehicle. *Marathon Man* (1976; dir. John Schlesinger) employed a moving camera on a vehicle to keep pace with the flight of the hero. (2) A handheld shot with a portable camera held or assisted by some sort of body brace as the cameraman runs along to follow the action. Stanley Kubrick's *The Shining* (1980) employs a number of these shots with the help of a Steadicam to follow the erratic movements of the characters.

■ **running speed** The running speed of a camera or projector, measured in the number of frames per second that film moves past the aperture and through the machine—formerly 16 and today 18 frames for projection of silent film and 24 for sound cameras and projectors. High-speed cameras, with regular intermittent mechanisms, can run at speeds as high as 600 frames per second. By slowing the running speed of the camera and later projecting the film at normal speed, accelerated motion can be achieved; and slow motion can be accomplished by accelerating the running speed of the camera and projecting at a normal rate. A tachometer is attached to cameras operating with wild or variable-speed motors to show the rate of frames per second.

■ **running time** The duration of a film run through a projector at normal speed. The normal feature film runs anywhere from ninety minutes to two hours, though longer films are not uncommon. The early silent films were anywhere from half-reelers to two-reelers, running from seven or eight to thirty minutes. Silent feature films were five reels or more, running seventy minutes or longer. Sound films, with each reel running 24 frames per second at a duration of about ten minutes, were approximately ninety minutes for the first feature and seventy for the second. *See* **double feature, feature film, reel,** *and* **silent film** (3).

■ **run of the picture** A contracted agreement for a player to be committed to a production for all the principal photography without any additional compensation after a fixed period of time.

■ **run out** (1) In animation work, to cause a line or form to develop from a single point. (2) In cinematography, to use up the film in a camera during a shot, an inexcusable error. Before the shooting begins, the assistant camera operator must judge if there is enough film in the camera for the entire shot. (3) The approximately 48 frames of opaque film at the conclusion of the pictures on a reel right before the tail leader.

■ **run through** (1) A complete rehearsal of a scene—with all the performers, extras, costumes, props, and lighting—exactly the way it will appear on film. Both camera and sound equipment also take part in the rehearsal, but without actually photographing or recording. (2) A shot in which a moving subject runs across the frame in front of the camera.

■ **run-up** The number of feet or frames necessary to pass through a camera or projector before the machine is running at normal speed.

■ **rushes, dailies** The first positive prints, generally with synchronized sound on interlocked tape or film, that are made the same night as the shooting and sent unedited to the director for viewing the next day. Such prints give some indication how the film is progressing and guide future shooting.

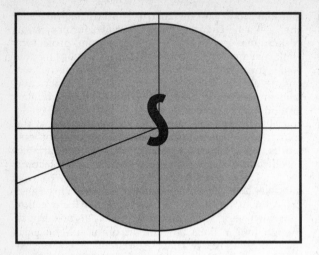

safe-action area, television safe-action area to synthetic sound

■ **safe-action area, television safe-action area** The area of action within the frame of a motion picture that will appear on a television screen during transmission. Since most films now appear with wider images than the once-standard aspect ratio in the film industry of 1.33:1, which was also adopted by the television industry, portions of the picture on both sides will be lost during television transmission. For this reason, the central action must be filmed in an area somewhat smaller than the entire frame to assure proper visibility and composition for television. Many viewfinders designate this area on the screen. The area that will assure that titles are fully visible is sometimes called the safe-title area. *See* **aspect ratio** *and* **letterbox format.**

**safe-action area
(on screen of
viewfinder)**

■ **safelight** A light used in a processing machine or darkroom where the development of black-and-white film takes place. The light must be a color that will not affect the film emulsion. Color film must be developed without any light whatsoever, a process permitted by modern daylight developers where the first part of processing takes place in light-tight tanks. *See* **processing.**

■ **safe-title area** The area of the frame that will allow titles to appear fully when the film is transmitted to a television screen. *See* **safe-action area.**

■ **safety base, safe base** Film with a base, generally made of cellulose triacetate or polyester, which is of low flammability and has a slow burning rate compared to film with the nitrate base used before 1951.

■ **safety director** The individual responsible for the safety of all individuals in and around a production, whether in the studio or on location, and in the general area of the production-company buildings. Such a person must be sure that all codes are followed and that the environment itself is respected.

■ **safety film, safe film** Any film using a safety base, generally made of cellulose triacetate or polyester. *See* **safety base.**

■ **safety shot** A second shot of a scene made either as insurance in case the previous shot might be faulty or as an alternative to offer the editor another camera angle or camera distance.

■ **SAG** *See* **Screen Actors Guild.**

■ **salad** Jargon for film that has become jammed and as a result piles up in a camera, projector, or printer.

■ **same percentage as film rental earned (SPFRE)** A contractual agreement between the exhibitor and distributor that the former will contribute to the weekly cost of advertising a film the same percentage that he or she keeps from the film's weekly box office revenue. *See* **distribution** *and* **exhibition.**

■ **sample print** (1) The final composite print that exists after all the editing, sound mixing, and picture corrections have been completed and that must be approved before release prints can be made. (2) A rush print of one or more scenes that gives an indication of picture quality without any corrections for lighting or color.

■ **sampling** The process of measuring small elements in an analog signal at a regular frequency to create a digital code. The process is also called quantisizing. *See* **analog** *and* **digital.**

■ **sandbag** A heavy canvas bag filled with sand, used as a support at the base for light stands, reflectors, and scenery.

■ **saturation**   The degree of purity of a color; its free-dom from dilution by white light and hence from gray-ness. Highly saturated colors approach 100 percent purity, and desaturated colors seem bleached out. When color films became the rule in the 1950s, colors seemed highly saturated, almost like those in comic books (note, for example, Roger Corman's and Ham-mer Film Productions' horror films).

■ **saturation booking**   Distributing a film to a large num-ber of movie houses throughout an area with a good deal of publicity. *See* **distribution, exhibition,** *and* **wide release.**

■ **save it**   Like "print it," the phrase is sometimes stated by the director to indicate that a take has been satisfac-tory and should be sent to the laboratory for printing.

■ **SC**   *See* **scene.**

■ **scale**   (1) The relative size of an object. In the frame, the size of an object is defined by its relationship to other objects. Scale, then, must be employed in allow-ing the audience to appreciate the true size of an ob-ject or in compensating for distortion caused by certain kinds of lenses—objects in the foreground, for exam-ple, may seem disproportionately large compared to those in the background when seen through a wide-angle lens. The angle of the camera and its distance from the subject are also concerns in conveying a sense of an object's size, in giving it a particular perspective within its environment. Scale can also be used to create size—for example, when individual shots of small pup-pets are matted in with shots of live performers so that the puppets appear to be colossal animals in relation to the smaller humans. *See* **animation.** (2) Minimum pay-ment generally negotiated by a union or guild with the industry for the performance of a specific job. To work for scale is to work for minimum payment.

■ **scaling**   In computer animation, the process of chang-ing the width and length of part or the whole of a model. The original ratio of height to width may be maintained or the model distorted. *See* **resizing.**

■ **scan**   To move a beam of electrons across an image, object, or page of print so that it is digitally coded and stored in the memory of a computer from which an im-age can later be accessed. *See* **scanner.**

■ **scan line, scanline**   (1) A single movement of the elec-tronic beam in a scanner across an image, object, or page of print to digitize it. *See* **digital** *and* **scanner.** (2) The individual movement of the beam of electrons across the monitor to create a television or video picture. In the Unites States, 525 lines for each frame and 30 frames are scanned onto the monitor each second. *See* **HDTV, NTSC,** *and* **PAL.**

■ **scanned print**   An older process in which a print was made from a wide-screen or anamorphically pho-tographed film by means of a scanning printer so that the action was kept within an aspect ratio of 1.33:1. This kind of print was employed for television trans-mission by means of the old film-chain system. The original wide-screen frame could not fit into the televi-sion screen, which has the standard aspect ratio origi-nally used in film of 1.33:1, and any action taking place at the edges of the frame would be lost. Scanning print-ers (normally a step optical printer) were programmed so that the lens would follow the action. *See* **pan and scan, safe-action area,** *and* **telecine.**

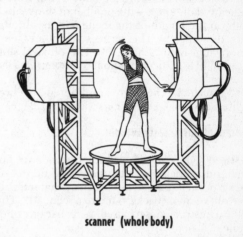

scanner (whole body)

■ **scanner**   A piece of equipment in which an electronic beam moves across a picture, page of print, or object, converting it into a digital code that is stored in the memory of a computer. The picture, print, or image of the object may then be accessed and worked upon or simply converted to another record or medium. The beam moves across the subject in a series of lines, con-verting it into a vast number of pixels, each of which is digitally coded so that the subject can be recalled as it initially appeared. Body scanners are employed to digi-tize the human form in various actions or movements; the digital information can then be used as the basis for original lifelike computerized images. Film scan-ners that digitize images directly from a negative em-ploy a flying-spot or CCD (charge-coupled device) technology. *See* **CCD, computer, computer animation, digital, film recorder, film scanner,** *and* **telecine.**

■ **scanning beam**   The narrow beam of light from the ex-citer lamp in the projector that passes through a nar-row slit to read the sound track on the film. *See* **projector.**

■ **scenario**   The term is used variably to mean any of the following: (1) a brief outline for a screenplay, which generally includes characters, actions, and sequences; (2) a narrative sketch or treatment for a screenplay, which includes characters, actions, and sequences; and

(3) the completed screenplay itself. *See* **outline, screenplay, screenwriter, script,** *and* **treatment.**

■ **scenarist** Someone who writes screenplays. *See* **screenwriter.**

■ **scene (SC)** (1) A unified action within the film's plot that normally takes place in a single location and in a single period of time. The plot itself is made up of a series of connected scenes. Sometimes a single scene may take place in more than one location—for example, when the single action of a chase moves us from place to place. A scene may be composed of a single shot or a series of shots showing the same action from various angles and distances—the number of shots will depend both on the length of the scene and the dramatic impact desired. (2) The term is sometimes employed synonymously for "shot." (3) The physical setting or location of a particular action. *See* **sequence** *and* **shot.**

■ **scene contrast** The degree of difference between the lightest and darkest elements within an image.

■ **scene planner** *See* **layout artist.**

■ **scenery** (1) The combination of elements, both natural and artificially made, that gives the out-of-doors background to a scene its particular characteristics. (2) The out-of-doors background to a scene. (3) The artificially constructed sets used as a background for a scene.

■ **scenery dock, scene dock** The place in a studio where the various parts of a set used for scenery (e.g., flats, doors, foliage) are stored. Such pieces, sometimes with alterations, can be employed for more than one scene or production.

■ **scenic artist** A member of the art department or crew responsible for painting sets or any graphics that are part of the set. *See* **art department.**

■ **scenic projection** *See* **rear projection.**

■ **Schüfftan process** A method of combining into a single shot portions of a full-scale studio set with art work or a miniature component. The process was largely developed by Eugen Schüfftan, a German cinematographer, in 1923, and was notably employed in Fritz Lang's German silent films *Die Nibelungen* (parts one and two; 1924) and *Metropolis* (1927). A mirror with a silver surface is placed at a 45-degree angle in front of the camera, reflecting into the lens a painting or miniature component from the side of the field of view. Portions of the silver are then scraped away, allowing the camera to photograph through the clear areas, thus combining the actual set behind the mirror with the reflected image. The process may be reversed with the studio set

to the side and the painting or miniature behind the mirror. In a similar manner, live-action reflected off the mirror may be placed within a painting or miniature set behind the mirror. It is also possible to use a photograph instead of a painting or a rear-projection slide instead of a normal setting. The Schüfftan process gave a good composite image because both components were shot simultaneously by the camera and it was not necessary to combine images from different generations of filming; it also allowed the combined image to be viewed at the time of shooting. Since the technique was slow, however, and the camera unable to move, the process was replaced by other methods for combining images. *See* **mirror shot** *and* **special effects.**

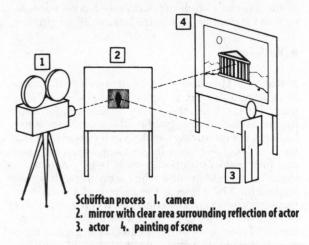

Schüfftan process 1. camera
2. mirror with clear area surrounding reflection of actor
3. actor 4. painting of scene

■ **science-fiction film, sci-fi film** Science-fiction films can be considered a subgroup of fantasy films—that is, films dealing with improbable or seemingly impossible worlds—even though this subgroup extends the possible and gives an aura of scientific authenticity to its events and created reality. Perhaps it is the fact that science is presently making actual the improbable and seemingly impossible that causes science-fiction films to be a major product of our contemporary culture. Some argue that science fiction in literature and film presents a futuristic vision based on an extrapolation from our contemporary world—for example, space-voyage films isolate modern efforts at space travel and project its possible development into the future, or films such as *Soylent Green* (1973; dir. Richard Fleischer) and *Blade Runner* (1982; dir. Ridley Scott) extrapolate from the present a deteriorating environment and show us the ultimate results of pollution and the population explosion in their fantasies about the future. However, it is just this combination of the actual and improbable, of actual propensities carried to a seemingly impossible extent, that provokes our belief in such films as well as our awe.

Film's capacity through its own technology to make visible on the screen the impossible events of our fantasies has made science-fiction films popular since the earliest silent films; interestingly, though, these films have tended to appear in spurts, as if they were suddenly produced in numbers to satisfy some immediate cultural need. For this reason, there has not been a sufficient number of these films in a consistent fashion to allow us to see them as a self-sufficient genre. On the other hand, the horror film, a type of motion picture that often seems closely akin to science fiction, has appeared more consistently and in greater numbers. A reason for this appears to be that the fantasy world of the horror film deals more directly with our inner fears and anxieties, creating a nightmare world that is an icon for the terror that lies within us, while science-fiction films provoke emotions having to do with our response to science and the wonders of external realities. Of course, these two types of film on occasion seem to overlap: horror films, as, for example, both versions of *The Thing* (1951, dir. Christian Nyby; and 1982, dir. John Carpenter), will borrow the conventions of science fiction, but only as part of the iconography of human fear and not as an end in itself; while science-fiction films, such as George Pal's *The War of the Worlds* (1953, dir. Byron Haskin) and *Forbidden Planet* (1956; dir. Fred M. Wilcox), will have their own monsters, but the focus of these films will clearly be on the futuristic fantasy and not on the human terrors these creatures represent—even the "monster of the id" in *Forbidden Planet* is given shape by electronic energy and is a product of technological wizardry.

Science fiction dates back to some of Méliès's silent fantasy excursions with the new art form in France, especially *A Trip to the Moon* (1902) and *The Impossible Voyage* (1904). Films about space voyage appeared periodically during the silent-film era: for example, the Danish film *The Sky Ship* (1917), the 1919 British film version of H. G. Wells's *The First Men in the Moon*, and, from Germany, Fritz Lang's *The Girl in the Moon* (1929). An early sound film that depicts a futuristic world in a serious manner and brings us to the threshold of space travel is *Things to Come* (1936; dir. William C. Menzies), a British production that can be considered the first authentic science fiction film to exploit with success and in a convincing manner the technology of film itself. Still a popular part of our culture are the Flash Gordon serials that were produced from 1936 to 1940 in three separate segments. Two space-travel films that were to have a decided effect on future science-fiction motion pictures were released in 1950—*Rocketship XM* (dir. Kurt Neumann) and George Pal's *Destination Moon* (dir. Irving Pichel). Of the space-travel films that followed, two are worth mentioning, Wilcox's *Forbidden Planet* and Byron Haskin's underrated *Robinson Crusoe on Mars* (1969). The watershed year for science fiction must be 1968, when Stanley Kubrick's *2001: A Space Odyssey* appeared, not only dramatically expanding for this kind of motion picture the potentials of film technology, but making science fiction a vehicle for both

poetic vision and metaphysical exploration. The next major wave of space films began with George Lucas's *Star Wars* (1977), a film building on and developing from the technology of Kubrick's film, but creating instead a comic-book and fairy-tale atmosphere that was to give the science-fiction film its greatest popularity so far.

Very much related to these space films is another group, those primarily dealing with alien invaders. Emphasis may still be given to space travel and scientific wizardry in these films but the focus is clearly on alien forms of life and their impact on our world. Creatures from other worlds had sporadically dropped into films, but in the 1950s, this theme became fully developed, perhaps because space travel was becoming more possible and we had begun to fear unwanted guests from other worlds, but more likely because nuclear warfare seemed a real possibility and invaders from space became a symbol for missiles and bombs that could fall from the sky. Since the fears dealt with were not psychological and individual, but real and social, and since the focus was still on awe-inspiring science and technology, these works were more science-fiction than horror films. In fact, it seems to have been the improbability of the science-fiction elements that allowed the audience to accept, on an unconscious level, the possibility of nuclear destruction as dimly suggested by the events of these motion pictures. The first and one of the best of these films, *The Thing* (1951) certainly seems to integrate a horror story with a science-fiction fantasy. In Robert Wise's *The Day the Earth Stood Still*

science-fiction film *Things to Come* (1936; dir. William Menzies), a British production that anticipates the science-fiction films of the present.

■ ■ ■

(1951), the tables were turned when the alien came to warn us to change our own destructive ways and to threaten us with extinction if we did not behave. Compare such a message with the hell that broke loose from the skies with the Martian invaders of *The War of the Worlds* in 1953. Similar was the devastation the Japanese unleashed upon themselves from the sky, much akin to the nuclear devastations they had experienced, in *The Mysterians* (1957; dir. Inoshiro Honda). Such films tended to diminish in the 1960s, though mention should be made of *Village of the Damned* (1960; dir. Wolf Rilla) and *The Day of the Triffids* (1962; dir. Steve Sekely), both based on novels by John Wyndham. While the Martians triumph in *The Day Mars Invaded the Earth* (1962; dir. Maury Dexter), a more kindly type of alien visitor is found in Steven Spielberg's *Close Encounters of the Third Kind* (1977) and *E.T.: The Extra-Terrestrial* (1982). But lest we be soothed into thinking that the sky has become a friendly and benevolent place, let us also remember the creature in Ridley Scott's *Alien* (1980), another film with science-fiction and horror elements.

A third significant group of science-fiction films, which occasionally may include space travel or aliens, basically portrays a futuristic society, the world the way it might become if certain tendencies in our present society are allowed to develop, but a world that fascinates because of its strangeness and differences from the reality in which we live. Certainly the most important and influential example of this type of film before sound was Fritz Lang's *Metropolis* (1927), in which the political message seems less impressive than the visual spectacle. *Things to Come* (1936), in spite of the launching of the space ship at its conclusion, certainly belongs to this group. The best of the films using time machines to bring people back and forth in history is George Pal's version of H. G. Wells's *The Time Machine* (1960). *Planet of the Apes* (1968; dir. Franklin Schaffner) also brings us into the future, although not a very futuristic one. In general, future worlds have not fared well, becoming a convenient landscape for all our fears derived from present reality. Both *THX 1138* (1970; dir. George Lucas) and *Logan's Run* (1976; dir. Michael Anderson), however, bring their heroes from sterile worlds of the future back to nature. Ridley Scott's *Blade Runner* (1982), though perhaps not totally satisfying with its hunt-and-chase narrative, has become a cult classic largely because of its striking visual dimension, creating a futuristic world that seems both prophetic and inevitable, and also because of its symbolic and provocative use of the cyborg figure, the ultimate interface between human and machine.

Like the horror film, science-fiction films seem to have lost something of their autonomy and are blending with elements from other types of film to create a contemporary amalgam. We have already seen this tendency with *Alien*, a science-fiction horror film, and *Blade Runner*, a science-fiction detective film. Films such as *RoboCop* (1987) and *Total Recall* (1990), both directed by Paul Verhoeven, take us into future worlds, but worlds that satisfy the same cravings for violence and action that have become such a mainstay of modern cinema in general. *See* **fantasy, genre,** *and* **horror film.**

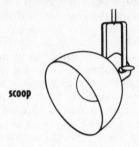

scoop

■ **scoop** A floodlight, resembling a grocer's scoop, that gives off a wide, diffuse light by means of a large reflector and a single naked bulb of 500 or 1,000 watts. This luminaire is used to illuminate backgrounds. *See* **lighting.**

■ **scope** An abbreviation for any and all of the anamorphic wide-screen processes—for example, CinemaScope; the first such process, Superscope, and Panascope. For CinemaScope, an anamorphic lens first squeezes the width of the photographed image into a normal 35mm film; and when the developed image is projected through an anamorphic lens it is unsqueezed and has an aspect ratio of approximately 2.35:1. *See* **anamorphic lens, aspect ratio,** *and* **CinemaScope.**

■ **score** (1) The musical background for a film. (2) To write the musical background for a film. *See* **music.**

■ **scoring** The session when a musical score is recorded as background music for a film. *See* **music.**

■ **scoring mixer** *See* **music recording supervisor.**

■ **scoring stage** A studio where musical scores are recorded for a film. Such places are soundproofed, with walls and ceilings acoustically padded to assure perfect sound. In the rear is a large screen where the film is projected. The musicians sit in front of the screen and facing them, and the screen behind them, is the conductor, with his music and cue sheets. The conductor may use a stopwatch to time himself and mark the duration of particular passages. Another method of keeping time is by using cues on the film itself, either punched holes, or diagonal or vertical streamers across the frames. Microphones are strategically placed throughout the studio, while the equipment and console to monitor and control the recording may be in an adjoining room, separated by a glass wall.

■ **Scotchlight process** A name for front-projection cinematography derived from the Scotchlite reflective sheeting used as the screen. *See* **front projection.**

■ **scouting** (1) Looking for suitable locations as settings for a film. (2) Looking for talented individuals or suitable performers to appear in a film.

■ **scraper** Either a separate instrument or part of a splicer that scrapes emulsion generally from the end of one piece of film so that it can be joined with the end of another in a lap splice by means of cement. *See* **splice.**

■ **scratch** A mar or cut in the form of a thin line that appears on the emulsion or base of a film. The scratch may be caused by poor handling of the film; by an improperly functioning mechanism or part in camera, projector, or printer; or by some foreign matter rubbing against the film in the reel. Most major laboratories have their own methods for filling in and making invisible such scratches. *See* **liquid gate** *and* **wet gate.**

■ **scratched print** A print that has been intentionally scratched from one end to the other so that it cannot be used again.

■ **scratch mix, slop mix, rough mix, dub** An early sound mix, sometimes made off the flat-bed editing machine, to be used in editing the film before the final mix is made. The scratch mix combines the original, uncorrected dialogue with some temporary sound effects and music, perhaps from a library or taken off records, to help with the actual editing. Such effects or music might be referred to as scratch effects or scratch music to indicate their temporary use. *See* **flat-bed editing machine** *and* **max.**

■ **scratch-off animation, wipe off animation, rub-off animation** A type of animation that allows lines or objects to appear from nowhere and is especially effective for making titles seem suddenly to write themselves. The artwork is first completed on a cel with water-soluble paint. The cel is then placed under the camera, upside down. After some initial frames are shot of the entire artwork, the camera is stopped, part of the drawing is wiped away, a series of frames is shot again, and then the camera is stopped once more to allow another part to be wiped away. This process continues until the drawing is gone. When a print is made with the sequence reversed and the images projected on a screen, the subject will seem to appear from nowhere on the screen.

■ **scratchprint, slash print, slap print, slash dupe** A print, generally black-and-white, that is made from the finished workprint without any corrections for lighting and is employed for dubbing and sound mixing. *See* **one-light workprint.**

■ **scratch track** A sync recording, made during shooting, that is intended to be used during a dubbing or looping session to help the performer prepare a better sound track *See* **dub** *and* **looping.**

■ **screen** The large reflective surface on which the audience sees the projected images of the motion picture or some other type of visual presentation. Screens vary in size according to the dimensions of the theater in which they are used. Screens have tended to be smaller in recent years to match the smaller multiplex theaters that have sprung up throughout the country. Since the 1950s, screens have been made to allow for various types of wide projection. Most theater screens are of the "matte white" variety and made of white opaque plastic that is stretched and laced to a wooden or metal frame. The screen has perforations throughout to allow for sound to be transmitted to the audience from speakers behind it. Such screens, having a gain of 1 and being less reflectant than other types, must be seen in the dark, but are the type generally used in movie theaters because they give off a widely diffuse light in all directions. It is possible to order screens with a specific gain of 1.3, 1.5, 2.0 for various kinds of presentation. The pearlescent screen gives off an image with a gain of 2 because of its coated surface, but tends to be somewhat uneven, susceptible to hot spots, and limited in its viewing angle. It is normally used with video systems. Glass beaded screens and platinum screens, also with a very high gain, are used for special daylight presentations. Silver screens, with a gain of 4 but a very narrow viewing range, are used for 3-D images. Curved screens are sometimes used, especially in AMC theaters, since they reflect light evenly, minimize loss at the sides, and also seem to direct the light directly into the theater. *See* **reflectance** *and* **screen gain.**

■ *Screen* A British journal that is the result of the merging of *Screen* and *Screen Education*. This scholarly and theoretically oriented film journal focuses on one subject per issue, especially from a political or polemical perspective.

■ **screen, the** (1) The medium of film in general, especially commercial film (sometimes referred to as the silver screen). (2) The entire motion-picture industry.

■ **Screen Actors Guild (SAG)** The trade union for screen performers and stunt personnel with offices in both New York City and Los Angeles. The SAG negotiates salaries and working conditions for those professionals who appear on the screen.

■ **screen brightness, screen luminance** The amount of light reflected by a screen. Luminance is measured in terms of candles per square meter by a photometer. Standards are established for both the center and sides of the screen to allow for maximum picture quality.

■ **screen continuity** *See* **continuity** *(1).*

■ **screen credits** (1) The list of names of performers and all personnel involved in a film production, whether published separately or appearing as titles before or after the film. (2) A list of films in which a performer has appeared or for which a production member has worked, sometimes appearing in a directory, after an article, or as part of a vita.

■ **screen direction** The direction of a subject's movement on the screen. Movement from right to left or left to right should appear constant from the perspective of the camera unless the character changes direction. The camera should not alternate shots from both sides of an imaginary line drawn through the action or the audience will be confused as to whether the subject has actually changed direction. The rule concerning constant screen direction can be ignored (1) when a character leaves one area for another (for example, when a shot of him leaving a room is followed by a reverse-angle shot of him coming through the door) and (2) when the camera shoots continuously in a tracking shot and moves from one side of the character to the other. Contrasting screen directions are properly used to show separate subjects moving toward one another. Movement toward or away from the camera is considered neutral screen direction, and the camera may show the subject coming or going or may track with the character alternatively from the front or from behind. *See* **imaginary line.**

■ **Screen Extras Guild (SEG)** The union that represents film extras and negotiates for their salaries and working conditions.

■ **screen gain** The reflectance capacity of a film screen as assessed from a specific angle and in relation to a general standard. Film screens are normally assessed at a 90-degree angle and measured against the reflectance of a matte white screen with a magnesium carbonate surface. *See* **reflectance.**

■ **screening** (1) Any showing of a motion picture. (2) A noncommercial, advanced showing of a film to various interested parties. *See* **preview** *(2).*

■ **screening room** A small room for showing motion pictures to small audiences for various purposes: a screening room might be used during production to watch workprints or it might be employed by a producer or distributor to preview the film for interested parties. Such rooms are normally comfortably furnished, and the film is shown from a projection booth in the rear.

■ **screenplay** The script for a film generally containing all the scenes, dialogue, action, and sometimes including camera position and angles (at which time it is also called a "shooting script"). The screenplay should be considered a blueprint for the final film, since many changes take place during shooting and editing. *See* **outline, screenwriter,** *and* **treatment.**

■ **screen ratio** *See* **aspect ratio.**

■ **screen test** A filmed audition for a performer, normally with full costume, makeup, setting, and lighting. Frequently the scene photographed is from a particular film for which the performer is being considered.

■ **screen time** The duration of a film's actual running time as distinct from narrative time (the duration of the story) and filmic time (the manipulation of time within the motion picture by means of cutting and editing). *See* **filmic time** *and* **time.**

■ **screenwriter, scriptwriter, scenarist** The individual responsible, in total or in part, for writing the various stages of a film script. Sometimes one person may write all the stages, but often several people have a part in developing the script. At one time each of Hollywood's major studios had its own stable of writers, with individuals specializing in certain types of subjects or even certain parts or stages of a script. Hence one can never be sure who exactly was responsible for many scripts, and until recent times the role of the screenwriter was often ignored by critics. Indeed, *auteur* criticism, which sees the director as the true creator and hence "author" of the film, has kept alive a good deal of confusion on the subject. A case in point is the critical debate over how much of the screenplay for *Citizen Kane* (1941) was the responsibility of Orson Welles and how much of his screenwriter, Herman J. Mankiewicz. In most cases, the screenwriter's lot is not completely enviable: although well paid, he or she normally works in a subservient position and must endure the criticism and rewrites of producers, directors, and even actors.

A number of major directors have insisted on writing their own scripts either alone or with others (e.g., Eisenstein, Stroheim, Renoir, Bergman, Antonioni, Huston, Wilder, Coppola, and Woody Allen). A few of the notable screenwriters who have left a decided mark on the films for which they wrote are Anita Loos, the brothers Herman and Joseph Mankiewicz, Ben Hecht, Donald Ogden Stewart, Nunnally Johnson, Robert Riskin, Ernest Lehman, Charles Brackett, Dalton Trumbo, Paddy Chayefsky, Robert Towne, and Ruth Prawer Jhabvala. Significant novelists who have written for Hollywood are William Faulkner, John Steinbeck, and F. Scott Fitzgerald. Notable playwrights have been Robert Sherwood and Neil Simon.

The long road to a finished shooting script begins with the optioning or purchasing of a property or idea described in a brief outline or synopsis. If this statement of the project seems feasible, a writer is hired who may or may not see the work to conclusion. The first step is the writing of a "treatment," which is a short summary or outline of the way the author would treat the proposed story and includes major characters and actions, specifications for location, suggestions for developing characters and plot and for putting them on film. If the studio and producer approve, the next stages might be the writing of a story line, which narrates the entire film, followed by a breakdown, which divides the story into individual scenes. With or without these stages, the process continues with the writing of the first draft of the screenplay, which includes all scenes, characters, dialogue, and action as well as more general acting and technical directions. From this point on, the screenplay is revised several times with the help of the director and perhaps the producer. Another writer may be called in to revise or help with certain difficult areas. When the final "shooting script" is finished, it will also contain directions for the camera, but the amount of camera detail will depend upon the director—a number of filmmakers prefer to work out their shots during shooting (*see* **shooting script**). Documentary scripts frequently have a separate column for camera specifications.

Since the finished script, as important as it is, must still be transposed into a film, it can only be considered a blueprint for the final product. Changes will be made to the script between shooting sessions and even on the set; and certain decisions must be made apart from the script by the director concerning the details of his actors' performances, and with his director of photography concerning the camera and lighting. When all the shooting is finished, the final version of the film will still not appear until after considerable editing. When the film is completed, a cutting-continuity script is prepared (generally not by the screenwriter, though based on his or her screenplay) that gives a transcript of the film substantially as it will be released. In this script, shots, camera positions, and transitions, as well as all the action, dialogue, and sound are specified. A number of such scripts for important films or for films by notable directors have been published.

■ **screwball comedy** A type of film comedy prominent during the 1930s and a product of the Depression period. These films were an escape from reality, offering gay and attractive characters behaving with abandon and freedom in a rich and glamorous world, one filled with eccentric though nonthreatening comic figures; but also presenting a nonvitriolic satire against the idle and not-so-idle rich, often concluded by the successful bonding of a wealthy heroine and a middle-class hero. Significant in these films was a very emancipated view of women, with the heroine behaving as independently and aggressively as the male, if not more so, and demonstrating a good deal of wit and intelligence. Breaking social taboos, such heroines demonstrated more spirit and energy in the sexual arena than their male counterparts, though without falling into promiscuity. One must especially appreciate this kind of heroine in the context of the sweet and domesticated

heroines or morally fallen women who appear in so many films of the period. The heroines of the screwball comedies certainly appealed to male tastes as well as the repressed desires of the large female audience of the time. Such heroines are very much part of the liberated spirit of these works, which itself seems a strong antidote to the heavy concerns of the Depression world. The nature of this comedy is always zany and often chaotic; the nonsense is so consistent and pervasive that it seems to operate with a logical nonlogic of its own.

The initial comedy of this group was Howard Hawks's *Twentieth Century* in 1934, but certainly Frank Capra's *It Happened One Night,* released the same year and winning four Academy Awards, set the tone for future films and helped establish many of the conventions for this type of comedy. The film considered to be the purest example of screwball comedy, however, and certainly the most insane, is Howard Hawks's *Bringing up Baby,* which appeared in 1938 and starred Katharine Hepburn and Cary Grant. By the close of the 1930s, the Depression years were giving way to a time of foreign turbulence and war, bringing into comedy more conventional behavior, situations, and morality, as if to fend off the threatening chaos from outside the country. Screwball comedy received its last statement in the broader and more mannered comedies of Preston Sturges between 1940 and 1944, films that maintained the wit and madcap humor but extended the comic net to include more aspects of American life (e.g., politics in *The Great McGinty* in 1940 and small-town life in *The Miracle of Morgan's Creek* in 1944). *See* **comedy.**

screwball comedy *Bringing Up Baby* (1938; dir. Howard Hawks), with Cary Grant and Katharine Hepburn as the off-centered romantic leads.

■■■

■ **scribe** A pointed metal tool used by the editor to scratch instructions, that is, scribe marks, into the edge of the film for cutting and assembling. *See* **editing.**

■ **scrim** (1) A flag, generally of a black color and in a circular frame, that is made of either translucent gauze or wire mesh and is placed in front of a luminaire to soften and diffuse light without altering color temperature. (2) A large piece of stretched gauze or netting, generally of a blue color, that is placed over windows or across the entire set to soften the background and give a sense of distance and aerial perspective or haze. The scrim might also be employed to suggest fog or clouds.

scrim (full)

■ **script** Any of the stages of the screenplay for a motion picture, that is, any manuscript or series of pages that includes dialogue, action, stage directions, setting, sound, and various degrees of shooting instructions. *See* **scenario, screenplay,** *and* **screenwriter.**

■ **script breakdown, production breakdown** The breakdown of a film script into groups of individual scenes and shots that are to be photographed together at the same locations and the same times, whether in narrative sequence or not. Shooting in this manner is economical and uses performers' time with maximum efficiency.

■ **script supervisor, script clerk, script girl, continuity clerk, continuity girl** The individual, male or female, responsible for maintaining perfect continuity from shot to shot by keeping a record that specifies individual takes and their details—for example, the beginning and end of the take, its duration, the properties appearing on the set, the camera's position and movement, the dialogue recorded, and the placement and movement of characters within the scene. The log (or "continuity sheets") kept by this person assists in matching to each take the next shot in a scene, which might not be photographed until later, and also helps the editor in matching cuts and assembling the film.

■ **scriptwriter** *See* **screenwriter.**

■ **scrub** (1) To remove a set, part of a set, or a property. The order is generally given to "scrub" any of these. (2) To remove some activity from a schedule of events.

■ **SD** *See* **sound.**

■ **SD EFX, SE** *See* **sound effects.**

■ **search pan** A pan shot in which the camera, from a fixed position, scans the surrounding area looking for some object or person. *See* **pan.**

■ **SECAM** The initials stand for *sequential coleur avec memoire* (sequential color with memory) and refer to a video format developed in France and Russia that employs 625 lines per frame and 25 frames per second. In this system, the color differentiation is transmitted in sequential manner on alternate lines. *See* **HDTV, NTSC,** *and* **PAL.**

■ **secondary colors** Colors formed by mixing two of the primary colors; complementary colors. *See* **complementary colors.**

■ **second assistant camera operator, second camera assistant, second assistant cameraman** The member of the camera crew who marks the slate and claps the sticks on the clapboard before each shot. This individual also is responsible for loading the magazines and keeping notes on the shooting. In Europe, this person is also called a clapper/loader. *See* **first assistant camera operator.**

■ **second assistant director** An individual who assists the first assistant director with his or her tasks. The second assistant director normally writes out the daily call sheets and gives them to the various people involved in the production. He or she also fills out the daily production report. The second assistant director helps the assistant director in running the daily operations of the set and may also oversee a second second assistant director (or third assistant director) and the assistant director trainees. Such a person may also receive instructions from the production managers. *See* **first assistant director.**

■ **second cameraman** A term sometimes used for the camera operator. *See* **camera operator** *and* **first cameraman.**

■ **second feature** The motion picture of lesser importance when two films are shown on a double bill. The other film is called the main feature. Up until the 1950s nearly two-thirds of the theaters in this country played two films, but the demise of the studio system and changing economics in the industry put an end to the practice. *See* **B-picture** *and* **double feature.**

■ **second-generation dupe, second-generation duplicate** A dupe negative made from the first-generation dupe which was itself made from the original negative. Although of inferior picture quality, second generation dupes are sometimes made for special-effects work. *See* **dupe.**

■ **second grip** *See* **best boy grip.**

■ **second run** *See* **multiple run.**

■ **second second** (1) A second assistant camera operator on the set when a second camera is being used. (2) A second assistant director, normally hired for larger productions. Such a production may have several assistant directors.

■ **second unit** A small unit of film technicians, subsidiary to the principal film unit, that photographs location, continuity, or establishing shots, and action, stunt, or mob scenes with large numbers of extras. A second unit is employed for large productions and saves time and money by shooting the scenes that do not require the stars of the film or the director and major cinematographer. The director of the film, however, will supervise the planning of such shots, which are directly supervised by a second-unit director. On occasion, large productions have had more than a single second unit. In William Wyler's *Ben-Hur* (1959) and David Lean's *Lawrence of Arabia* (1962), second units directed by Andrew Marton and André Smagghe respectively produced some notable work. Notable also is the opening Iraq sequence photographed by Billy Williams for William Friedkin's *The Exorcist* (1973). *See* **principal photography.**

■ **second-unit director** The individual who directs the second unit, generally for large film productions. Such directors must often be skilled at handling a vast number of extras for action scenes and creating credible stunt scenes. Second-unit directors, however, are often as good as the second-unit cinematographer with whom they work. A second-unit director often cited for his work is Yakima Canutt, a former stunt man, who achieved some remarkable action scenes in the films *Spartacus* (1960) and *Where Eagles Dare* (1968). *See* **second unit.**

■ **section printing** *See* **paper-to-paper.**

■ **see-through set** A set in which a door opens onto some specific scene or area.

■ **SEG** *See* **Screen Extras Guild.**

■ **segmentation** *See* **market segmentation.**

■ **segue** Pronounced "say-gway" or "se-gway," the word is derived from the Spanish word *seguida*, which means successive or following, and refers to an imperceptible change from one sound to another, generally musical, without an overlap.

■ **S-83 spool** A metal spool that holds 100 feet of 35mm film.

■ **selected take** The take of a shot chosen by the director to be processed and made part of the rush print. *See* **N G takes.**

■ **selective focus** Focusing on only a single plane or subject with the remainder of the scene blurred and out of focus. Such scenes, common in film since the introduction of panchromatic stock, have a shallow depth of field and are opposite to scenes with deep focus. *See* **deep focus** *and* **shallow focus.**

■ **selective key light** A key light that falls on only part of a character instead of illuminating his or her entire figure. Such a light might illuminate the hands of a character, while the remainder of the figure is in darkness, to suggest a threat of violence; or illuminate only one side of the face to suggest a complex or divided personality. *See* **key light.**

■ **selective sound** The highlighting of a specific sound in the mix other than the dialogue of the main characters. Such a sound might be the distant noise of footsteps to suggest a character being followed, the noise of birds and rustling trees to suggest the character's freedom in the natural world, or the clashing of machines in a nearby factory to suggest a character's sense of oppression and isolation.

■ **selects, selected takes** Scenes taken out of the dailies for inclusion in the workprint. Also referred to as pulls. *See* **circled takes.**

■ **self-blimped** A camera suitably encased so that it makes little noise when running and does not interfere with sound recording. Most studio cameras employed for sound-stage work are self-blimped. *See* **blimp.**

■ **self-matting** (1) Any matting process in the combining of elements from separate pictures in which the subject photographed acts as its own matte. For example, in the Dunning process developed in the late 1920s, the character bathed in orange light is registered on the raw stock behind the orange-dyed positive of the background in a bipack camera while blocking out the blue background behind him. *See* **Dunning process.** (2) Any matting process in the combining of elements from separate pictures in which the positive of the subject has an opaque background (perhaps by being shot against a black background), allowing the image of the character to be directly fitted into a negative on which the background scene has been printed with the subject's area matted out. *See* **matte** (2) *and* **traveling-matte process.**

■ **self-reflexive** A work of art that is concerned with its own status as art. In the case of film any motion picture that explores and exploits its own medium or that investigates its relation to reality can be considered self-reflexive. To some degree all avant-garde or experimental films are self-reflexive and call attention to their own filmic qualities: abstract films, for example, are concerned with the nature of the image, filmic space and time, and motion and rhythm created by the sequence of images; while impressionistic and surrealistic films are concerned with the relation of the film world to actual reality. *Man with a Movie Camera* (1929) is a fascinating exploration of camera and film by the notable Russian filmmaker, Dziga Vertov. In fictional films, self-reflexivity is a means of investigating the medium's capacity to deal with reality. François Truffaut's analogies to and borrowings from earlier films, Jean-Luc Godard's political assault on culture and cultural codes (of which film is one), and the phenmenological assault on both viewers' and characters' perceptions and memory by Alain Resnais are all examples of directors exploring the nature of their medium. The many films directly dealing with the motion-picture industry (e.g., Truffaut's *Day for Night* [1973]) or including a filmmaker as a subsidiary character (e.g., Bernardo Bertolucci's *Last Tango in Paris* [1972]) indicate the frequent self-consciousness of directors about their own filmmaking.

Art, in general, becomes self-reflexive in an age in which reality itself seems unpalatable or the possibility of agreeing upon any kind of objective truth seems dubious. Although critics such as Sigfried Kracauer see film as a means of preserving and rediscovering reality, the medium has become in our unsavory era an escape or diversion from, or even a denial of, reality. The very nature of film, which, on the one hand, seems to capture reality and, on the other, seems to stage and transform it, inspires the medium to be self-reflexive; and, certainly, the development of specific genres, cycles, and filmic conventions, fostered by the film industry's desire to satisfy the fantasies of its paying audience, has steeped the art in imitation and self-consciousness.

self-reflexive François Truffaut appears as a director in his own film about filmmaking, *Day for Night* (1973).

■ ■ ■

■ **Selig** An early motion-picture production organization in this country founded in 1896 by ("Colonel") William N. Selig as the Selig Polyscope Company. Selig began making films in Chicago with his Polyscope camera, an adaptation of the Lumière Cinématographe, and in 1907 his production company was one of the first to start shooting in California, where it soon set up headquarters. Tom Mix made more than one hundred short Westerns for Selig beginning in 1911; and the company is also known for its serial films, especially *The Adventures of Kathlyn* (1913). Selig was one of the organizations to form the Motion Picture Patents Company in 1908; but unlike most of the other organizations, Selig was ready to make longer films and compete with the independents. The eight-reel *The Spoilers,* directed by Colin Campbell and featuring the celebrated fight of William Franum and Tom Santschi, opened in 1914 and was an enormous success. The next year Selig joined forces with Vitagraph, Lubin, and Essanay to form the VLSE Company. When Essanay failed to renew Charlie Chaplin's contract in 1916, VLSE began to flounder and was bought out by Vitagraph in 1917. *See* **Essanay, Lubin, Motion Picture Patents Company, Vitagraph,** *and* **VLSE.**

■ **Selsyn motor** A tradename, derived from "self-synchronizing," for an interlocking system that forces two motors to run exactly together. Such a system was employed for interlocking readers, playback systems, projectors, and, then, largely for special-effects cinematography (e.g., in rear-projection shots when projector and camera must run synchronically together). The name Selsyn is sometimes used generically for any similar system. *See* **synchronous motor.**

■ **semidocumentary** A fiction film that uses the techniques of the documentary to create an authenticity for its subject. Such films employ a fairly static camera with relatively long shots, simple editing, natural locations and lighting, and frequently unknown performers. Sometimes a documentary-style voice-over is used and newsreel footage is mixed into the film. Film stock might also be employed to give the look of a newsreel. Henry Hathaway's *House on 92nd Street* (1945) and Jules Dassin's *The Naked City* (1948) are notable examples of this type of motion picture, as are the Italian neorealist films, especially Roberto Rossellini's *Open City* (1945) and *Paisan* (1946), which had a considerable impact on world cinema. In more recent years, Pontecorvo's *The Battle of Algiers* (1965) and Costa-Gavras's *Z* (1968) are important examples of this type of film. *See* **documentary** *and* **documentary style.**

■ **semiotics, semiology** The science of signs as developed from the ideas of the Swiss linguist Ferdinand de Saussure and the American linguist C. S. Peirce. Saussure's students published *Course in General Linguistics* in 1915, two years after his death; it is a systematic compilation of his theories taken from their notes. Peirce died the year after Saussure, and his papers were collected and published from 1931 to 1935. Saussure derived the term "semiology" from the Greek word for "sign," *semeion,* and Peirce employed the term "semiotics," which is more frequently used in English-speaking nations because of Peirce's nationality. When the French anthropologist Claude Lévi-Strauss made linguists and semiotics central to his own structural anthropology, the science of signs received significant notoriety and itself became an important part of contemporary intellectual thought. In film theory, the principles of semiotics were best argued and adapted by the French writer Christian Metz in *Film Language: A Semiotics of the Cinema,* and were popularized in Peter Wollen's *Signs and Meaning in the Cinema.*

Saussure argues that linguistics should be considered as only one of many sign systems that surround us, although certainly the most significant and accessible system. The very principles that apply to language, he claims, should also be used to understand these diverse social and cultural codes (the French writer Roland Barthes applied with great acumen the concepts of semiology to such diverse topics as food, clothing, and athletic events). Saussure defines *langue* as the total system that underlies any single usage, and he defines *parole* as the single usage itself. For example, a spoken sentence would be the *parole,* while the entire language system from which the sentence was chosen would be the *langue.* Through a study of individual utterances we can begin to understand the larger system that lies behind them. The individual sign of any semiotic system is called the *signifier* (e.g., an individual word), which itself refers to some idea or concept that is called the *signified.* Semiotics examines the ways in which these individual signifiers create meanings through their interrelationships both with other signifiers in a particular usage (their *syntagmatic* or horizontal relationships) and with corresponding signs in the *langue* not in that usage (their *paradigmatic* or vertical relationships). Saussure contributed a reasonably logical method of examining the various codes and systems that surround us in our daily lives and give meaning as well as order to the world we inhabit—in other words, that structure our reality.

Peirce, on the other hand, creating a semiotics less guided by linguistic principles, has not had the same extensive impact as Saussure; his popular contribution has largely been relegated to the distinctions he made between types of signs. Especially significant has been Peirce's three general categories of icon, index, and symbol: the first is a direct representation of some object (e.g., a picture of a flower); the second is a sign that indicates some object through a direct relationship to it (e.g., an image of smoke that calls to mind a fire); and the third is a signifier and signified that function primarily to suggest, through convention or association, something else (e.g., an image of a red rose, which represents passion).

The application of "cinesemiotics" to film was energetic but often overly complex, excluding the student or enthusiast of movies from any new insights or understanding. We can, however, point out some general areas where the science of signs was and can still be used with profit, even though the interest in semiotics, and related theoretical subjects, has abated to some degree. One can apply semiotics to any of the verbal levels of the film—to spoken dialogue, a voice-over, titles, or any printed words that appear in the scene—in order to understand the way information is exchanged between characters or communicated to the viewer. One can study the various visual codes within the frame (e.g., fashions, interior decorating, gestures of characters) or each *mise-en-scène* itself as part of a larger visual code that runs throughout the entire film. One can even see each film as an individual component in a larger code that is comprised of a series of related films (an approach especially useful when examining a specific genre).

As Christian Metz points out, a number of semiotic codes appear in more than one type of medium: for example, similar narrative structures appear in both film and literature, employing such conventional elements as flashbacks and parallel story lines. Metz also indicates those codes applicable only to film and not part of our general culture (e.g., montage, camera movements, and optical effects). In a particularly interesting part of *Film Language,* he outlines eight types of sequences in film that are all part of a single code: autonomous shots; nonchronological syntagmas, either comprised of two or more interwoven series of brief atemporal scenes or a string of atemporal images, each of which functions as a unit to communicate some fact, situation, or theme; descriptive syntagma, which is comprised of both single and multiple narrative lines; linear narrative syntagmas, which are continuous in time; ordinary narrative sequences, which are discontinuous in time; and episodic sequences, which are also discontinuous, but where each image is symbolic "of one stage in the fairly long evolution condensed by the total sequence." Metz's code is useful in allowing us to see the way film communicates to us both denotatively and connotatively through its basic technique, and in showing us the ways in which the content of film is structured. Metz's code also brings to our awareness the multiple levels of coding in any film, and urges us to appreciate the need for some systematic discourse that will allow us to understand the ways in which the images and sound of a film are related and structured in order to create within us our unique and shared filmic experiences. *See* **film theory** *and* **structuralism.**

■ **senior, senior spot** A 5,000-watt lamp with a Fresnel lens and parabolic mirror that gives off an intense and even light to illuminate either a particular area of the set or a specific performer. The senior is frequently employed as the key light. *See* **Fresnel** *and* **spotlight.**

■ **sensitivity** The degree to which a film emulsion is responsive to light, generally measured in terms of the exposure index (i.e., the speed rating of the film). East-man Kodak and Fuji give an exposure-index number for their motion-picture film. *See* **ASA standard, DIN standard, exposure index,** *and* **ISO standard.**

■ **sensitizer** A chemical dye added to film emulsion during manufacture to make the emulsion more sensitive to light or more responsive to the color spectrum. *See* **color film** *(2).*

■ **sensitometer** An instrument for placing on film emulsion a regulated series of exposures to light in order to study the characteristics and qualities of the film. After a test strip is exposed and then processed, its various densities can be measured by a densitometer. The resulting information is especially useful for processing the entire reel of film with optimum results. A lamp is normally employed that emanates a single density through a graduated optical wedge or filter with systematic increases in density. The series of exposures on the film is sometimes called a step wedge, and the film itself a sensitometric strip. *See* **densitometry** *and* **sensitometry.**

■ **sensitometric strip, sensitometer strip, senso strip, senso, test strip, exposure test strip** The strip of test film from a specific roll that is exposed to the sensitometer to assess the characteristics of the emulsion and to allow for satisfactory processing. The series of exposures on the strip is sometimes called a step wedge. *See* **densitometry** *and* **sensitometry.**

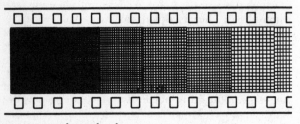

sensitometric strip

■ **sensitometry** The study of the effect of light, under various conditions and with various intensities, on photographic emulsion. Film is exposed to progressive degrees of illumination by means of a sensitometer, processed under carefully planned conditions, and the various densities of the image are then measured with a densitometer. All these steps allow the characteristics and qualities of any specific film to be known, thus permitting carefully planned photography and processing to arrive at an optimum film image. The term "densitometry" refers more specifically to the measurement of the various densities in film images. *See* **densitometry** *and* **sensitometer.**

■ **Sensurround** A special-effects system, first used for Universal's *Earthquake* (1974; dir. Mark Robson) that

created for the audience a sense of vibration and tremor. During dubbing, air vibrations were added to the sound track; these were later read by a special apparatus in the theater and amplified through anywhere from ten to twenty large speakers. Only select, first-run theaters were equipped for this effect.

■ **separation masters, separation positives** Three positive black-and-white films on which are recorded the blue, green, and red components of a color negative through yellow, magenta, and cyan filters respectively. A single color intermediate negative can be made from these positives by printing each through the same respective filter. Separation masters are generally used for long-term preservation of special or expensive color motion pictures and are sometimes employed for special-effects cinematography. *See* **color film** *(2).*

■ **separation negatives** Individual black-and-white negatives on which each of the primary colors is separately recorded. In the early Technicolor system, two separate negatives were actually employed, one for the red and the other for the green part of the spectrum. In 1932, the process began to use the three-strip camera, which was the dominant form of recording images in color until the advent of tripack film in the 1950s. *See* **color film** *(2) and* **Technicolor.**

■ **sepia effect filter** A camera filter for creating the brown tone associated with old photographs to create on the screen an image that suggests a bygone time.

■ **sepmag** A double system for showing a motion picture in which magnetic sound tracks are played from a separate film.

■ **sequel** A motion picture that continues with a character or several characters from a previous film: for example, John Frankenheimer's *The French Connection II* (1975), which continues from William Friedkin's *The French Connection* (1971).

■ **sequence** A series of related shots and scenes that form a single, coherent unit of dramatic action. Such units of action are frequently unified by a single general location and continuous chronology. The sequence has often been compared to the chapter in a book, since both have complete independent actions with apparent beginnings, middles, and ends, and both normally conclude with some type of dramatic climax. A chase sequence in a Western or adventure film is a good example of this type of dramatic structure that makes up a single component in the entire plot structure of the film. A series of shots and scenes between an actor and actress that culminate with them making love is an example of such a dramatic unit in a romantic film. Perhaps one of the most brilliantly edited sequences in the history of cinema is Sergei Eisenstein's Odessa Steps sequence in *The Battleship Potemkin*

(1925), where a series of related shots and scenes play off one another to create a rich visual montage that communicates to the viewer the horror and pathos of the massacre (*see* **montage**). Sequences at one time fre-

sequence A shot from the famous Odessa Steps sequence in *The Battleship Potemkin* (1925; dir. Sergei Eisenstein).

■ ■ ■

quently began and ended with a fade or dissolve to punctuate them as a separate unit, but the practice now is to use a straight cut for a more subtle integration of the action into the film.

Sequences need not have a single location, and sometimes the chronology might be ambiguous, so long as the effect is still one of dramatic unity. For example, cross-cutting between simultaneous scenes in two separate locations can create a sense of a single action as the hero rushes to save the heroine at the conclusion of a silent melodrama. Sometimes a whole series of scenes at different locations can form a single sequence when they are brief and tightly cut together, as in the case of the baptism and murders in Francis Ford Coppola's *The Godfather* (1971). A different type of sequence, one where brief scenes from different time periods form a single dramatic unit, takes place in Orson Welles's *Citizen Kane* (1941), when the protagonist's eroding relationship with his first wife is shown through a series of short conversations from breakfasts during their marriage: their growing separation is cleverly documented by both their dialogue during a series of close-ups and the widening distance between them at the table punctuated in the last shot of the sequence. *See* **scene** *and* **shot.**

■ **sequence shot, long take** A single shot that takes in a significant amount of action and information. The camera may change its focus intermittently to the various

planes for important action or may follow characters as they move about. *See* **long take** for a fuller discussion.

■ **serial** A single story developed in a series of individual short films, popular in earlier days of motion pictures. Each episode formed a separate unit of the larger story with its own beginning, middle, and end. Hero, heroine, sidekick, and villain appeared from week to week in a variety of parallel adventures, each running for about two reels and all contributing to the conclusion of some major action, which generally took place anywhere from the tenth to fifteenth installment, though longer serials were not uncommon. A special feature was the cliffhanger ending when hero, heroine, or both found themselves confronting a violent demise, which was mechanically and disappointingly resolved at the start of the next week's episode.

The first serial in the United States was *What Happened to Mary*, which began to appear monthly in 1912 and which starred Mary Fuller. Also significant was *The Adventures of Kathlyn*, which appeared in thirteen installments between January and May of 1913 and starred Kathlyn Williams. But probably the most famous of the silent serials was *The Perils of Pauline*, starring Pearl White, which appeared as twenty cliffhanging episodes from April to December of 1914. Pearl White went on to star in a number of similar serials, such as *The Exploits of Elaine* in 1915, and her perils spurred the making of such films both here and abroad. Also notable were the serials of Louise Feuillade in France, especially the five serials of "Fantómas" from 1911 to 1913, *Les Vampires* from 1915 to 1916, *Judex* in 1916, and *La Nouvelle Mission de Judex* in 1917.

Serials continued to be popular after the advent of sound, especially as a special feature for audiences of children during Saturday matinees. These films were made primarily by four studios—Universal, Columbia, Republic, and Mascot—and offered a wide variety of adventure stories. Westerns such as *The Lone Ranger*, science-fiction films such as *Buck Rogers* and *Flash Gordon*, jungle movies such as *Tarzan*, and detective films such as *G-Men* were a significant part of a child's culture during these years. Numerous characters, such as Dick Tracy, Superman, and Batman, made their way from newspaper comic strips to the screen as serial heroes. It has been estimated that between 1920 and 1957 approximately 375 serials were produced. Serials began to diminish in number during the early 1950s and by the middle of the decade production of these films had virtually ceased. The reasons for the serials' demise were many: such films had simply become too costly to make, especially since the old studio system which could afford to make them was disappearing; feature films were becoming lengthier; television was drawing much of the audience away and was itself offering serial programs; and the form had simply become exhausted and tiresome. Nevertheless, serial films remains one the nostalgic memories of motion-picture history. Though such films were rarely well made and were filled with clichés, they offered, especially to young audiences, an escape into fantasy and adventure, a world of heroes and villains where moral standards were simple and unambiguous. They also had their own impact on feature films and the future course of the industry—certainly the imaginations of contemporary directors such as Steven Spielberg and George Lucas were partly shaped by the fantasy world of the American serial.

serial *What Happened to Mary* (1912), with Mary Fuller, was the first American serial production.

■ ■ ■

■ **series** A group of full-length feature films, each autonomous in plot but with the same major character or characters and with similar types of plot situations and actions. Such films are generally made to cash in on the tried and true, and some of the longest series were the product of well-established studios that could churn out these works in a rapid and efficient manner. Although we can trace such films through the days of silent movies—for example, G. M. Anderson's *Bronco Billy* Westerns (1910–16) and Wallace Beery's portrayals as Sweedie (1914–15)—we normally think of these series as products of the Hollywood studio system from the 1930s on. Westerns were particularly popular, with Paramount's *Hopalong Cassidy* series, starring William Boyd, leading the way with more than sixty films. Columbia made a number of low-budget series that featured the exploits of such fictional detective figures as Ellery Queen and Boston Blackie; RKO made films about the more elegant detective figures of the Saint and the Falcon; MGM produced the very polished Thin Man series, with William Powell and Myrna Loy. Also of interest are the films with the Dead End Kids made by Warner Brothers, Paramount's six "Road" films with Bing Crosby and Bob Hope, MGM's Dr. Kildare series, and the fifteen motion pictures about Andy Hardy made by that studio between 1937 and 1947. As impressive as that last number might be, one is made

especially aware of the conventional nature of studio production and American tastes by the fact that from silent-film days there have been a total of nearly forty motion pictures each about Tarzan and Sherlock Holmes, approximately fifty features about Charlie Chan, as well as the sixty-odd Hopalong Cassidy movies already mentioned.

In the 1950s, with the demise of the studio system, the decline in the number of films produced, and the increased cost of production, series films largely disappeared from the screen, with the exception perhaps of the James Bond thrillers, which began with *Dr. No* in 1962. The practice of repeating the same characters in a series of similar stories was largely taken up by television. But in recent years the financial exigencies of moviemaking have motivated filmmakers to repeat winning formulas and the result has been a few brief series of films that almost seem carbon copies of one another, such as the four *Rocky* films with Sylvester Stallone, the *Star Wars* trilogy, itself about to become part of a series of trilogies, and the endless atrocities of the *Friday the 13th* and *Nightmare on Elm Street* films.

■ **servo mechanism** A self-regulating electronic system that is actuated and controlled by a low-energy signal and is employed when accurate and steady speed is necessary. Such mechanisms are used to operate the lens focus and diaphragm rings on motion-picture cameras with precise positioning and regulated speed as well as to control accurately the movement of zoom lenses. *See* **servo motor.**

■ **servo motor** A self-regulating motor in which the speed is carefully controlled and that is part of a servo mechanism. DC servo motors which are controlled by crystal oscillators (better known as "crystal motors") are employed in motion-picture cameras and sound-recording systems for synchronization. *See* **servo mechanism.**

■ **set** An artificially constructed place for the action of a film, which conveys some indoor or outdoor location. Although we generally associate the term with the large interiors and outdoor lots of the film studios, a set for a motion picture might be constructed anywhere. The term "set" is an abbreviation of "setting," which conveys the actual location of any scene, whether natural or artificially constructed. Although early silent films were shot outdoors for natural lighting, the development of artificial illumination soon allowed the more expeditious and controlled method of photographing indoors. The Hollywood studios developed large departments and crews dedicated only to the construction, decoration, and maintenance of sets, which themselves could easily be dismantled and used in total or in part for other films. Outdoor sets could be constructed indoors in front of large cycloramas or under the open sky on the sprawling studio lots.

Sets are normally made of lightweight and portable

materials that give an illusion of real places and buildings—the front of a house might be no more than a single wall propped from behind. Dimensions and spatial arrangements are generally different from those in the actual world in order to compensate for the limited area of the set as well as the flat screen image. Colors are also painted with some distortion or exaggeration in order to give proper densities for black-and-white cinematography or to create the specific tones and hues desired in color cinematography. To allow for movement of the camera in dolly or boom shots, rooms normally have only three walls and no ceilings. Walls, referred to as "wild," can also be moved to allow shooting in all parts of the area, while parts of a ceiling can be suspended to appear in low-angle shots. Sets must also be constructed to permit installation and placement of sound and lighting equipment. It is possible to extend the actual set that appears before the camera by photographing both the scene and an image projected behind it in front- and rear-projection processes, or by combining the image of the set with an image of a location shot elsewhere by means of a matting process in an optical printer. *See* **front projection, matte** *(2),* **rear projection,** *and* **setting.**

■ **set decorator** The individual in charge of the set-dressing department. This department is responsible for placing within the set, either in the studio or on location, the furnishings, ornamentations, and artwork required by the production designer—from the smallest to largest items that make the setting real and immediate. The set decorator is assisted by the leadperson, who is directly responsible for the various logistical problems concerning the set dressings and for the crew, which is referred to as the swing gang or set dressers. The set decorator supervises drapery, floor covering, upholstery, electrical-fixture, and floral personnel. This person must have a knowledge of the technical aspects of filmmaking, especially how a set and its properties will photograph. The set decorator works with both stunt and special-effects personnel to create for them furnishings and properties that will satisfy their needs. As well as being in charge of the rental, purchase, and manufacture of exactly the right furnishings, from floor to ceiling, the set decorator must also keep a wary eye on his department's budget. *See* **production designer** *and* **art director.**

■ **set designer** *See* **art director.**

■ **set dressers** *See* **swing gang.**

■ **set dressing** The furnishings, draperies, decorations, properties, and artwork that appear in a scene. The dressing of any scene must, of course, be appropriate to the characters who reside in the location as well as to the time and place of the film's story. The dressing must also be integrated with the action of the scene.

■ **set light, base light, foundation light** Normally placed on the set before highlighting takes place, this light gives an evenly diffused illumination over the entire location and prevents any area from being underexposed during shooting.

■ **set lighting technician** The individual in a production responsible for placing, securing, and focusing the lights. He or she works under the gaffer and best boy. Also formally called a lamp operator, this person is informally called a juicer or spark.

■ **setting** (1) The time and place in which the action of a film occurs. (2) The specific location where a scene occurs, whether natural or artificially constructed. Since the very first days of film production, filmmakers have shown a propensity for either shooting in natural locations or before sets—for example, the Lumière brothers began showing their short glimpses of the real world in France in 1895 with a scene of workers leaving their factory (*La Sortie des ouvriers de l'usine Lumière*) and Méliès, after filming similar glimpses of reality in the same country, began to make his celebrated fantasies and dramatic works in his indoor studio at Montreuil in 1897. Particular movements in motion-picture history are marked by the choice of one of these two types of settings: for example, German expressionistic films are notable for their spatially distorted and unnaturally lighted indoor sets, which convey psychological states instead of some accurate view of reality, and Italian neorealist films are significant because of their immediate recreation of contemporary society in real settings. Specific genres can also be associated with one or the other of these types of settings: for example, Westerns have often been shot out of doors to allow for external action and to recreate the natural environment, while horror films have generally been shot on indoor sets to create a claustrophobic and threatening unreality.

The American Hollywood studios filmed largely on artificially constructed indoor sets, both for exteriors and interiors, and also on sets built outside on studio lots for exteriors. Especially notable is the style of Art Deco that Cedric Gibbons brought to Hollywood cinema in the late 1920s and that flourished during the 1930s. But with the decline of the studio system in the 1950s, with its vast facilities and personnel, and with the decrease in motion-picture production, filming on location was found to be more economical, even allowing for transportation of equipment and employees, alterations of pre-existing structures or settings, and the necessity for shooting parts of films on artificially constructed indoor sets. Sometimes filmmakers, however, seek to create the semi-real and closed-off world of the studio days as, for example, in such less-than-successful films as Francis Ford Coppola's *One from the Heart* (1982) and Wim Wenders's *Hammett* (1982), both made in Coppola's former Zoetrope Studios. *See* **art deco, art director,** *and* **set.**

■ **setup, set-up** (1) The positioning of the camera for a specific shot. Such positioning involves considerations of both the camera's angle of view and distance from the action as well as the mounting of the camera and its movement by dolly or crane during the shot. (2) The positioning of the camera and luminaires for a specific shot. Because of the difficulty and expense in rearranging heavy studio cameras and lighting equipment, careful consideration must be given in advance to such setups. The same setups for different actions are frequently shot consecutively and intervening shots photographed later for this reason. (3) The arrangement of camera, lights, setting, and props for a specific shot. (4) In animation cinematography, the field of the drawing viewed by the camera from a determined distance.

■ **70mm film** The widest gauge of film used for release prints of large and ambitious feature films. In the United States and in Western Europe, 70mm film has been employed for prints made from 65mm film negatives, the extra width necessitated by stereophonic tracks. In recent years, however, the practice of blowing up images from 35mm negatives into 70mm prints has become more popular for special showings of important films because of the high expense and somewhat limited mobility of shooting with 65mm film, though the gauge is sometimes used for shooting special films (e.g., Kenneth Branagh's *Hamlet* [1997]). With twice the width of the standard 35mm film and projecting an aspect ratio 2.2:1 for its wide-screen image, 70mm film creates a picture with excellent definition, clarity, and brightness. This gauge, running thirteen frames per foot and with two rows of perforations, has wide margins along both edges for the four magnetic sound tracks. A number of special 70mm systems, some with multiple cameras and projectors and some with the film moving horizontally, have been created for extreme wide-screen, wraparound, and 3-D shows at museums, trade shows, expositions, and theme parks.

■ **sexploitation film** Jargon for any film made primarily for the purpose of sexually arousing its audience. The term may apply to (1) any of the hardcore pornographic films that play in special movie houses for a specific clientele; (2) any soft-core films that feature a more limited array and specificity of sexual practices and play the same theaters as well as normal motion-picture houses at midnight showings, drive-in theaters, and sometimes cable television; and (3) the better-made, though still exploitive, films, with performers such as Bo Derek. All three types of sexploitation films have found an increased market in the form of videotapes for home viewing. *See* **censorship.**

■ **SFX** *See* **sound effects.**

■ **shading** In computer graphics or animation, the process of imposing qualities of color, shade, shadows, and reflectance on a model's surface. There are a number of rendering algorithms for this process. Flat shading is the most preliminary of these, emphasizing the separate polygons. Gouraud is somewhat better, though the surface is muddy and the edges not smooth. Phong shading is the most used because it creates surfaces with convincing shadows and reflectance in real time (24 frames per second). But ray tracing is certainly the high end of these processes and the one most used professionally, since it creates surfaces that are extremely realistic in color, shading, shadows, transparency, and reflectance. This last shading process, however, is quite expensive because the model must be rendered in non-real time, with each frame requiring up to several hours for rendering. *See* **computer animation.**

■ **shallow focus, shallow depth of field** A narrow area of sharp definition in the film image, with the surrounding area out of focus or blurred. Such an image allows the director to focus the viewer's attention on a specific character or action without distraction from other planes in the frame. Hence, the technique of shallow focus is more controlling of the viewer's attention than the technique of deep focus where the viewer is allowed to discover independently points of interest in the greater depth of field. Shallow focus is also less concerned with a character's relationship to the surrounding area or physical environment. With the change from orthochromatic to the slower, though more accurate, panchromatic film stock in 1926, the film image generally had less depth of field since it was necessary to shoot with a wider aperture—the result was that motion-picture technique in general relied on shallow focus. More sensitive panchromatic stock and the greater intensity of lighting ultimately allowed the option of deep focus. *See* **deep focus, focus pull, follow focus, rack focus,** *and* **selective focus.**

■ **sharp** (1) Pertaining to an image in which the edges of the subject are clearly defined and details are distinctly visible. (2) Pertaining to a lens capable of creating the image described in (1).

■ **sharp focus** The appearance of an image in which the edges of the subject are clearly demarked and details are clearly defined.

■ **sharpness** The degree of definition in a film image, determined by the preciseness of the subject's edges and clarity of detail. Sharpness is influenced by the gauge and type of film, quality of lens, and intensity of lighting. Other factors are the efficiency of processing, generation of print, and quality of projection system. To obtain a picture with sufficient sharpness, the camera must be set at the correct f-stop with the subject fully in focus.

■ **shock cut, smash cut** A sudden cut from one shot to another. *See* **dynamic cutting.**

■ **shoot** To photograph a subject with a motion-picture camera. The term, along with "shooting," seems to derive from Etienne-Jules Marey's experiments in photographing motion with a camera shaped like a rifle. Marey's camera, first used in France in 1882, had a long barrel that held a lens and a round chamber in which a circular glass disk spun around once per second, allowing a circle of twelve separate exposures.

■ **shoot around** To continue shooting a scene without one of the performers, whose shots will later be edited into the scene. The process sometimes requires much ingenuity but can save a good deal of money by allowing shooting to continue in spite of the absence of an important actor or actress.

■ **shooting** The entire process of putting on film the action of a motion picture.

■ **shooting call** The instructions to all personnel concerning the place and time for the next day's shooting. These instructions might be located somewhere in the studio or at the location of the present day's shooting. *See* **call.**

■ **shooting date** The specific day on which parts of a film are to be photographed.

■ **shooting log** *See* **camera report.**

■ **shooting on playback, shooting to playback** Photographing a performer while he or she acts to dialogue or music recorded earlier and now played back over a sound system. Such a practice allows the performer to record sound earlier in a relaxed manner and under optimum conditions while later acting before the camera unrestricted by the placement of the microphone and the acoustics of the location. The actor or actress mouths the words or perhaps pretends to play an instrument while sound system and camera operate synchronically.

■ **shooting on speculation** *See* **on speculation** *(1)*.

■ **shooting ratio** The ratio of footage shot to that used in the actual motion picture. Anywhere between 5:1 to 10:1 is considered acceptable for a feature film, though the ratio is generally much higher for a documentary.

■ **shooting schedule, production schedule** The plan for shooting on a single day or series of days, which includes scenes and shots to be photographed, time and place of shooting, and required performers, personnel, equipment, and properties. Scenes frequently are shot out of sequence for reasons of economy and convenience. *See* **production board.**

■ **shooting script** The final written version of a film used by the director during shooting. This script,

which includes instructions for the camera as well as dialogue and action, is broken down according to individual scenes, with shots numbered consecutively in chronological order from the start of the script. The shooting script is itself broken into the individual shooting schedules, which determine which shots and scenes are to be photographed on what specific day or days and in what order. *See* **screenwriter.**

■ **shooting upside down** Photographing with the camera upside down so that when the images are developed and the print run right side up in reverse order, the action seems to move backward.

■ **shooting wild** Photographing a scene without sound. *See* **wild shooting.**

■ **short, short subject** Any film of three reels or less that runs no more than thirty minutes. Earliest silent films were only a few minutes in length, but the duration of motion pictures soon stretched to one reel, which ran about fifteen minutes, and sometimes to two reels. The early nickelodeons in the United States, starting in 1905, played shows of short films that ran anywhere from fifteen minutes to an hour; but within a decade feature films began to push their way into the industry, and the practice was soon established of showing a full-length film with several shorts preceding it. Starting in the Depression and during the 1940s, double features became the rule, but often such films were still accompanied with a short subject. When the double feature virtually disappeared during the 1950s, a single feature film, now normally running almost two full hours, was frequently accompanied by a short subject such as a cartoon, but in more recent years that practice has ceased and few shorts are to be seen on the commercial screen.

The term "short" or "short subject" actually applies to individual action films with live performers, serial episodes, cartoons, newsreels, documentaries, and avant-garde films, though the term is often used specifically to apply to the first category only. During the heyday of the Hollywood studios, individual units operated within the major production companies to turn out in rapid fashion such live films, a large number of which were broad farces, following in the tradition of the great slapstick comedies of the silent era: for example, the Three Stooges appeared in nearly 200 shorts for Columbia between 1934 and 1958. Laurel and Hardy, beginning in the final years of the silent period and continuing well into the 1930s, starred for the Hal Roach studios in some seventy shorts which were distributed by MGM. Also notable were the "Pete Smith Specialties," produced for MGM by "a Smith named Pete" from 1936 until the 1950s, and winning for their producer a special Academy Award in 1955 (two of his approximately 300 films, *Penny Wisdom* in 1937 and *Quicker'n a Wink* in 1940, won Academy Awards in the short subject categories). Today, live-action shorts are for the most part independently made and rarely appear in commercial theaters.

■ **short end** The unexposed film that remains in the magazine of the camera after shooting because it is too short to use for another complete shot.

■ **short focal-length lens, short-focus length lens** A lens with a wider angle of view than normal and hence commonly called a wide-angle lens. For a 35mm camera, any lens with a focal length less than 40 or 50mm. *See* **wide-angle lens.**

■ **short pitch** The slightly shorter distance between perforations on negative film stock compared to that between such holes on print stock, which is referred to as long pitch. Print stock requires the slightly longer space to avoid slippage during printing, since it must pass in contact with the negative over the same curved sprocket while on the outside.

■ **shot** The term is sometimes defined as (1) the single uninterrupted operation of the camera that results in a continuous action we see on the screen and sometimes as (2) the continuous action on the screen resulting from what appears to be a single run of the camera. Since the film resulting from a single run of the camera, however, might itself be edited before appearing as a continuous action on the screen or perhaps even broken up into two segments by means of an insert, it is best to refer to (1) as a "take" and only (2) as a "shot" to preserve the sense of continuity and completeness we associate with the term. A shot might itself include a changing focus or a movement of the camera so long as it appears to be the result of a single take of the camera. A shot is considered the basic building block of a film, much like a single word in language—shots are edited together to form scenes, and scenes to form sequences.

Shots may vary in length from a few frames, a technique that creates a fleeting impression or a subliminal effect and is often found in avant-garde cinema, to ten minutes, the duration of a full reel of film in a professional camera. Hitchcock sought to make *Rope* (1948) give the impression of being comprised of one continuous shot, though in fact the movie had to be photographed in ten-minute segments to allow for the duration of each load of film in the camera. Most shots in commercial films vary in length from thirty seconds to two minutes, and the total number of shots is frequently well above 300. One can discern a polarity in the dominant length of shots, with, on the one hand, the short, rapid shots of the Russian filmmakers, especially Eisenstein and Pudovkin, exploding off one another in their montage technique to create a totality larger than the sum of the parts; and, on the other hand, the long takes or sequence shots found in what André Bazin, in *What Is Cinema?*, identifies as the

"depth of focus" technique, used by directors such as Orson Welles to emphasize the relationship of characters in the various planes of action within the frame. Somewhere in between this polarity Hollywood established its "invisible" style of cutting, which was to have a general influence on the making of feature films and emphasized the dramatic function of the shot—cutting was on action and each shot was to have an integral role in the development of the film's narration. The dominant length of shots throughout a film often reinforces a director's approach to his subject and sometimes creates a particular rhythm that helps convey the work's intention. For example, the long brooding shots in Carl Dreyer's films help gradually to strip away the characters' facades, exposing their emotional and psychological states; the relatively long shots in the films of the Italian neorealists help to explore the characters' interrelationship with their physical environment, a technique especially effective in Luchino Visconti's *La Terra Trema* (*The Earth Trembles;* 1948), where the long, evocative shots of the peasants in the Sicilian landscape create a spiritual and universal dimension to their social drama; and the short, rapid shots in the earlier films of Richard Lester, especially in his *Petulia* (1968), create a staccato rhythm that conveys the fragmented world of his characters. Jim Jarmusch's independent film *Stranger Than Paradise* (1984) is structured as a series of individual scenes composed of a single shot of long duration that contributes to what Pauline Kael refers to as the "dead space" of the characters' world, while Oliver Stone's recent *Natural Born Killers* (1994) evokes a dizzying variety and combination of shots to convey the world as both driven by and perceived through the violent and exploitative media.

D. W. Griffith is generally heralded as the man responsible for shaping the motion picture into its present form by composing each scene of a series of related shots of different perspectives. Griffith was not the first to use these perspectives, but before him the motion picture was comprised dominantly of "full shots," with characters photographed from slightly below their feet to slightly above their head, much as they would appear on a stage, with different distances used only occasionally for a specific effect. Griffith was the first to move his camera both toward and away from his characters, using each shot for its emotional and psychological value and for developing the drama of the scene. He was the first to have a series of shots interact to create and manipulate tempo and to affect the total impact of the scene. He was also significant in making the camera's movement, with the panning and traveling shot, part of the director's arsenal of techniques.

Shots are generally categorized by (1) the apparent distance from camera to subject; (2) the angle of the camera in viewing the subject; (3) the movement of the camera during a shot; and (4) the number of characters within the frame. In the early days of cinema, when cameras had a single fixed lens, the only consideration in distance was the actual space between camera and subject, but today the nature of the lens being used for the specific shot is also a factor. Also important is the relative size of the subject—for example, a close-up of a character and one of a flower will require different distances between camera and subject or different focal lengths of the lens.

The terms for the apparent distance between camera and subject are defined in the following manner: (1) the extreme long shot (ELS, XLS), which shows the landscape or a specific setting from a considerable distance and is sometimes used as an "establishing shot" to set the location or background for the following scene; (2) the long shot (LS), which shows characters somewhat distant, especially in the context of their physical environment, and is also sometimes used as an "establishing shot"; (3) The medium long shot (MLS), which presents characters closer to the camera, from the knees up, but still as part of the setting, and is also called a three-quarters or American shot; (4) the medium shot (MS), which shows a character or characters from the waist up and is also sometimes called a mid-shot; (5) the medium close-up (MCU) or medium close shot (MCS), which shows a character from the mid-point of the chest to the top of the head; (6) the close-up (CU), which presents the full head and shoulders of a character or some important part of a subject in close detail; and (7) the extreme close-up (ECU, XCU), which brings to immediate view a small object or some portion of a face or object.

Shots that are defined by the angle of the camera to the subject have the following designations: (1) the eye-level shot, which is the standard against which the other shots in this category are measured; (2) the low-angle shot, which views the character or characters from below, making them seem taller and more imposing; (3) the extreme low-angle shot, which makes them seem even stronger and more imposing and buildings seem towering and threatening; (4) the high-angle shot, which looks down at characters, diminishing them and making them seem somewhat vulnerable; (5) the extreme high-angle shot, which dwarfs them even more and makes them seem insignificant; (6) the aerial shot, when the camera is photographing from some moving aircraft, creating a wide-sweeping panoramic shot of the terrain; (7) the oblique-angle shot, when the camera is leaning left or right, creating a disconcerting sense of imbalance; and (8) the dutch-angle shot, when the camera is tilted both horizontally and vertically, creating a disorienting, subjective, or hallucinatory effect.

Moving shots have the following designations: (1) the tracking, traveling, or trucking shot, when the camera and its support move along the ground, following action or taking us to some particular place; (2) the dolly shot, which designates specifically that the camera is being moved by a dolly to achieve the previously mentioned effects; (3) the crane shot, when camera

shots

1. extreme long shot

2. long shot

3. medium long shot

4. medium shot

5. medium close-up

6. close-up

7. extreme close-up

and support are moved by a crane for both horizontal and vertical movement and to approach and withdraw from the subject in a more sweeping and dramatic manner; (4) the follow shot, which merely designates that the camera is following action; (5) the handheld shot, when the operator holds the camera by hand, perhaps with the aid of a body brace, to follow action or bring us to some inner recess of the scene, often creating a more naturalistic and immediate sense of location and action; (6) the pan shot, when the camera from a fixed point sweeps along the horizon, either tracing a particular action or giving a panoramic view of the location; (7) the swish pan, when the camera, from a fixed point, suddenly turns right or left, blurring the intervening space and focusing us suddenly on some new point of action; and (8) the tilt shot, when the camera from a fixed point looks up or down, following, perhaps, the ascent or descent of a character or the perspective of a character.

Shots that are termed according to the number of characters within the frame are self-explanatory and generally are designated as follows: the one-, two-, or three-shot. The term "tight shot" designates that the characters are tightly bound by the frame, or we might have the word "tight" used in conjunction with any of the previous shots that specify numbers of characters (e.g., a tight two-shot). The "fifty-fifty" shot is a term sometimes applied to an image where two characters face one another, sharing the screen equally.

The following terms, which designate a number of shots of a miscellaneous variety, should also be noted: the bridging shot, which forms a transition between two shots or scenes separate in action or separated by time or space; the insert shot, which is an image of some detail photographed out of sequence but inserted into the scene during editing; the point-of-view shot, which presents some action or setting as viewed from the eyes of a particular character; the reaction shot, which shows a character's facial response to something that has just taken place on the screen; the over-the-shoulder shot, which shows some action or setting as viewed from the perspective of a character by photographing with part of the character's head and shoulder framing the scene; the reverse-angle shot, which presents some action from the direction exactly opposite to that of the last shot; the zoom shot, which moves smoothly in to or away from the subject generally by means of a zoom lens; and, finally, the stock shot, which simply means any shot of scenery or action previously photographed and stored, and now used in the present film. *See* **camera angle, camera movement,** *and* **distance.**

■ **shot analysis** A shot-by-shot breakdown for a critical study of a film. Each shot is described in detail with complete visual and aural information. Sometimes sketches of individual frames or a series of frames are included.

■ **Shot Box** A device that works with the camera's video assist to assemble both the live action and images already stored to create an instant composite picture so that the director and cinematographer can see the way the finished scene would appear. Such a practice allows the best shot selection for the final image and also saves the significant costs of putting together a composite image that might not be satisfactory. *See* **video assist.**

■ **shot breakdown** (1) A list of all the shots to be used in a film presented in proper order and including the location for each shot as well as the performers, personnel, and equipment necessary. (2) A list of all shots for a particular scene that clearly indicates the camera position for each shot.

■ **shotgun microphone** A long microphone with a narrow acceptance range that can isolate sounds. This instrument is especially effective in picking up dialogue when there is considerable noise from the background or in picking up the voice of a particular performer when several characters are talking. *See* **microphone.**

■ **shot list, shot sheet** (1) A list of all the shots in the order in which they were photographed during filming. (2) A list of all the shots included in the final edited version of the film.

■ **shot plot** A plan for a specific set, with camera angles drawn at appropriate places for each shot and required focal lengths of the lens indicated.

■ **shot/reverse-shot technique** A technique of cutting developed by the Hollywood studios in which the camera switches between two conversant or interacting individuals. The technique was already prevalent in film as early as 1915. *See* **invisible cutting.**

■ **shot-sequence editing** Editing together a scene in a rather rigid and conventional manner by following the progression of triple-take shooting: the camera moves from an establishing long shot, to one or more medium shots, to one or more close-ups. *See* **triple-take** *(1)*.

■ **shoulder** The highest portion of the characteristic curve drawn to indicate the change in density of an image as exposure is increased. At this area change will be minimal and will cease entirely at the leveling-off point. *See* **densitometry** *and* **sensitometry.**

■ **shoulder brace, shoulder pod** A support for the camera in handheld shots that generally fits over the operator's shoulders and under his or her armpits. The brace is frequently a chrome-metal framework with sufficient flexibility to allow for some movement of the camera. Also called a body brace. *See* **handheld** *and* **Steadicam.**

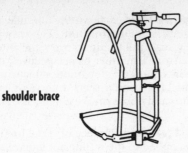

shoulder brace

■ **showcase** A screening of a film in a number of select theaters.

■ **shower curtain** A translucent sheet, generally made of white or light vinyl, that is attached to a frame and placed in front of a luminaire to diffuse illumination.

■ **show print** The final positive print. The term is most often used in animation cinematography.

■ **Showscan** A large-screen film system created by Douglas Trumbull that uses a 65mm negative for shooting and a 70mm film, which contains both image and sound tracks, for projecting at a rate of 60 frames per second. The Showscan image is remarkably clear and bright, with far more presence than the standard film image because of the larger picture, but especially because the faster rate of projection removes the necessity for showing each frame twice to avoid flicker (as must be done with the 24 frames per second of 35mm film), hence allowing us 60 individual frames of information per second, and also allowing a much-brighter light in the projector to send forth richer and more saturated colors without melting the fast-moving film. Trumball and Richard Yuricich formed Showscan Entertainment in 1984 to develop the process. Showscan has been shown at world's fairs, theme parks, and select theaters, but so far the industry has not jumped on the bandwagon because of the considerable expense in using so much film but also in retooling to make the films and then screening them. Trumbull himself came to the conclusion that the technology is better suited as a special-venue presentation than for full-length films. He left Showscan in 1989.

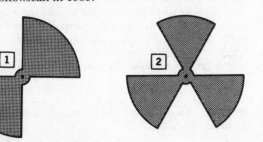

shutter (projector):
1. two-bladed for sound speed
2. three-bladed for silent speed

■ **shrinkage.** A reduction in the width and thickness of film, which may result in developing but is more likely to happen during drying. Film may also shrink while being stored over a long period of time. Film will normally lose a certain amount of solvent and plasticizer from the base after a relatively long duration and for this reason must be carefully stored under set temperatures. See film storage.

■ **shutter** (1) A device in the camera, normally placed between the aperture and film, that prevents light from entering the camera while each frame is pulled down into the film gate for exposure. Shutters are generally rotating discs with an opening that allows the light to reach the film during exposure. In professional cameras, a "variable shutter" is used in which a second moving blade controls the size of the opening and hence the amount of light reaching the film during exposure. When the opening on the shutter is reduced to half, the decrease in exposure is equal to one full stop of the lens aperture. Shutter openings can be reduced when wider lens apertures, controlled by the iris diaphragm, are employed for reduced depth of field. Shutters with a silver surface are placed at a 45-degree angle to reflect incoming light into an optical system as part of a reflex viewfinder. (2) A device in the projector that prevents the light beam from reaching the screen while the next frame is pulled into place. During the early days of silent film, the projection of images at a rate less than 48 per second caused a discernible flicker. For this reason a three-bladed disc with three openings was used as a shutter and made to rotate during the projection of each of the approximately 16 frames per second. With the advent of sound and the projection of 24 frames per second, a two-bladed disc with two openings became necessary to achieve the 48 exposures per second, although a number of cameras still use the three-bladed shutter to accommodate both types of film. (3) An adjustable device, much like a venetian blind, that reduces the intensity of illumination from a luminaire. *See* **camera, reflex viewfinder,** *and* **variable-opening shutter.**

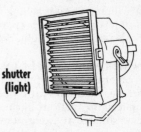

shutter (light)

■ **shutter angle, shutter opening** The angle in degrees of the opening in the camera shutter which permits light to reach the film. The largest opening on most camera shutters is 170 to 180 degrees. In variable shutters, a second blade can reduce this opening to any desired angle. *See* **shutter** (1).

■ **shutter control, variable shutter control** The device on the camera that increases or decreases the opening in the shutter for more or less exposure.

■ **shutter ghost, travel ghost** An unwanted streak or blur in the film image on the screen because of a vertical movement of the film in the projector's gate when the shutter opens.

■ **shutter release cable, shutter release, cable release** A cable attached to a camera that allows the operator to start and stop filming without causing any vibration or movement of the camera. The device is especially useful in stop-motion photography.

■ **shutter speed, shutter open time** The length of time that the shutter is opened to allow the exposure of a single frame of film.

■ **shuttle** That part of the intermittent mechanism in a camera or projector that moves the claw to engage the perforations on the film and position the next frame for exposure. *See* **intermittent movement.**

■ **shuttle pins** *See* **pilot pins.**

■ **sibilance** The hissing noise made by a voice when recorded through a microphone, generally caused by undue emphasis on the "s" sound or by speaking too close to the microphone.

■ **side-drift** A flaw in a zoom lens that causes the subject in the frame to shift to the side when zooming in or zooming out.

■ **sidekick** The trusty friend to the major figure in a film. A notable example is George "Gabby" Hayes, who was the rambunctious, toothless, spouting friend of such Western heroes as William Boyd (Hopalong Cassidy) and Roy Rogers.

■ **side light** Illumination reaching the subject from either right or left at an angle perpendicular to the camera's axis. Also called cross light. *See* **cross light.**

■ **side viewfinder, offset viewfinder, nonreflex viewfinder, side finder** An older type of viewfinder, attached to the side of the camera, that allows the operator or someone else to watch the action during filming. Such a viewfinder is situated at the center of the side, parallel to the lens, and can be adjusted to compensate for the parallax between its own view of the scene and the scene as photographed; but such a correction is not possible to make when the camera is close to the subject. Side viewfinders were sometimes more convenient to use for the camera operator during fast moving or difficult shots than through-the-lens viewfinders. *See* **video assist** *and* **viewfinder.**

■ *Sight and Sound* A quarterly film magazine published by the British Film Institute. This very prestigious and widely read publication covers the international film scene from a number of perspectives, offering articles on works in production, motion-picture history, and individual films and careers. Interviews as well as reviews of films and books on the cinema are also featured.

■ **sight gag** A small piece of visual humor. The term is aptly applied to the wonderful moments of physical lunacy that appear in the great comic films of the silent era, especially in the works of Charlie Chaplin and Buster Keaton.

■ **sight line** The line of vision from any seat in the audience to the screen or stage.

■ **sign** Both the vehicle and the idea that the vehicle represents in any communicative system. Signs are the smallest elements of meaning in any such system and the building blocks from which all communication proceeds. In speech, the sign would be both the uttered sound and what is communicated to the listener by the sound—for example, the vocal articulation of the word "tree" and the image of the natural object it conjures up in our minds. In semiotics, the science of signs, the former is referred to as the "signifier" and the latter as the "signified." In writing, the sign is made up of the printed word we see on the page (the signifier) and the idea it communicates to us (the signified). We are surrounded by all kinds of sign systems, or codes, in our everyday world, each one with its own array of separate signs and its own system of interrelationships between signs—for example, traffic signals, clothing fashions, and even architecture. In film, we are confronted with a barrage of separate sign systems (1) from our everyday world (e.g., speech, writing, characters' gestures and movements); (2) from the world of film (e.g., the conventions of traditional genres); and (3) from film technique itself (e.g., lighting, shots, and editing). C. S. Peirce, the American linguist, designated three types of signs, the icon, index, and symbol: the first is a direct representation of an object (e.g., a picture of a person); the second indicates something connected to it (e.g., a marquee indicating a theater); and the third is a signifier and signified that suggest, through connection or association, something else (e.g., a skull and crossbones representing death). *See* **semiotics.**

■ **signal** Electrical impulses that are converted into pictures or sound.

■ **signal-to-noise ratio (S/N)** The ratio of amplitude in decibels between a transmitted signal and the noise in the transmitting system without the signal. *See* **dynamic range.**

■ **signification** The process by which signs in a semiotic system convey meaning; the transmission of the "signified" by the "signifier." *See* **semiotics** *and* **sign.**

■ **signified** The idea or concept conveyed by a sign. In semiotics, the science of signs, the vehicle that conveys the idea or concept is referred to as the "signifier." For example, the articulated sound of the word "tree" is the signifier, while the concept of the natural object it conveys is the signified. Both together form the sign. *See* **semiotics** *and* **sign.**

■ **signifier** That part of a sign that is the actual vehicle conveying the meaning or "signified." The spoken word, for example, would be the signifier and the meaning it transmits the signified. *See* **semiotics** *and* **sign.**

■ **silent bit** A bit part in a film for which the performer speaks no lines.

■ **silent film** (1) Any motion picture without sound. (2) Any individual film from the start of motion pictures to the advent of sound pictures. (3) The entire corpus of motion pictures during the period when there was no sound, starting about 1895 until 1927. The films of this period should be understood in terms of their historical development as well as the special characteristics which separate them from sound films.

There is some dispute regarding when the era of the silent film began. Edison's Black Maria, the first movie studio, was built in East Orange, New Jersey, in 1893, and his first Kinetoscope peep-show opened in New York City in 1894; Major Woodville Latham demonstrated some brief films with his Eidoloscope in Chicago at the Model Variety Theatre on August 26, 1895; Max and Emil Skladanowsky employed their Bioscope to show motion pictures during a variety show in Berlin on November 1, 1895; the Lumière brothers showed films with their Cinématographe before a paying audience of thirty-three in a café in Paris on December 28, 1895; and the first projection of Edison's short films was at Koster and Bial's Music Hall in New York City on April 23, 1896.

Any history of the silent film would have to consider the following important stages. (1) The short films of a minute or less made for Edison's peephole machines at the Black Maria studio by W. K. L. Dickson starting in 1893; the short *actualité* films made and projected by Auguste and Louis Lumière with their Cinématographe machine in France starting in 1895; and the short narratives also made in France by Georges Méliès, beginning in 1897. (2) The development of the film companies that later became the Motion Picture Patents Company in 1908—namely, Edison, Vitagraph, Biograph, Essanay, Selig, Kalem, and Lubin in the United States, and Pathé and Méliès's Star Film company in France. (3) The cinematic career of Edwin S. Porter, beginning with The *Life of an American Fireman*

and *The Great Train Robbery,* both made for Edison in 1903; and the 450 films made by D. W. Griffith, during the first part of his career, with Biograph until 1913. (4) The development of the feature film; the rise of the "independents" and demise of the studios in the Patents Company; the advent of the star system; and the elevation of Hollywood as center of the world's film industry. (5) The cinematic climax of D. W. Griffith's career with his monumental *Birth of a Nation* in 1915 and *Intolerance* in 1916. (6) "The Golden Age of Comedy," beginning with Mack Sennett's Keystone company in 1912 and featuring films by Charlie Chaplin, Buster Keaton, Harry Langdon, and Harold Lloyd. (7) The sometimes neglected but nevertheless powerful Scandinavian silent film, especially the works of Victor Söström in Sweden and Carl Dreyer in Denmark. (8) The accomplishments of the German filmmakers, notably the expressionistic cinema and Kammerspielfilm (i.e., "the chamber play film"). (9) The post-Revolution Soviet cinema, especially the works of Sergei Eisenstein, V. I. Pudovkin, and Alexander Dovzhenko. (10) The French avant-garde film. (11) The solidification of the major studios and the studio system in Hollywood, with special attention to the popular cinema of Cecil B. DeMille, the controversial accomplishments of Erich von Stroheim, and the sophisticated comedies of Ernst Lubitsch. All these categories suggest in only the briefest outline the richness and fullness of the silent era.

Silent film did not merely lay the foundation for the sound film, but was itself a separate, autonomous art with significant achievements that were never to be equaled. Films during the period were not actually watched in silence, since musical accompaniment filled the audio vacuum, giving a continuity to the images on the screen and guiding the audience's emotions; sometimes live actors actually read dialogue from behind or from the sides of the screen. But the normal absence of words and natural sounds resulted in a visual dimension that compensated for this absence. The wonderful sight gags of Chaplin and Keaton, the dynamic and dramatic montages of Eisenstein and Pudovkin, and the astonishing pictorial beauty of films such as Murnau's *Sunrise* (1927) could not survive in a cinematic world made real by the advent of sound. *See* **film history.**

■ **silent frame** The frame size with an aspect ratio of 4.3 or 1:33.1 used on 35mm film before sound. Without sound tracks, the full area between perforations could be used. The aperture on cameras and projectors that produced such a frame was referred to as full aperture.

■ **silent lip** A term applied to the technique of splicing together two pieces of film with a portion of the sound track on one piece of film removed to allow for the jointure—the result is that for a brief instant a character is seen on the screen moving his or her lips but making no sound. Also called lip-flap. *See* **splice.**

■ **silent print** A positive print of a film with no sound tracks. Also called a picture print.

■ **silent speed** The rate at which film passes through the camera for recording visual images that will be seen with no accompanying sound from a track on the film. During the silent-film period, hand-cranked cameras might record a scene at a rate of 12 to 20 frames per second, with the speed depending upon the nature of the scene—for example, a chase might be photographed at a slower speed and projected normally for accelerated motion. The standard rate for filming and projecting was supposed to be 16 frames per second, the minimal and most economical speed at which movement seemed normal—at this rate, and with a rotating three-bladed shutter which came into use about 1909, the necessary 48 images per second were projected to avoid flickering. Projection, though, was also thought to be better at 20 or 21 frames per second. The truth is that there was much variation at greater speeds for both cameras and projectors. Today projectors operate at 16 or, more recently, 18 frames per second for silent film.

■ **silhouette animation, silhouette film** A type of animation that uses the shadowed form of flat figures in stop-motion photography. These figures are back lit, unlike the forms of flat-figure animation, which are front lit and fully visible. The most distinguished practitioner of this type of animation has been Lotte Reiniger, who began making short films of this nature in Germany in 1919 and in 1926 made *The Adventures of Prince Ahmed*, a popular success considered to be the first feature-length animation film. *See* **animation.**

silhouette animation Lotte Reiniger's *The Adventures of Prince Ahmed* (1926) was the first feature-length animation film.

■ ■ ■

■ **silk** A diffuser, made of a stretched piece of white material on a frame, that generalizes the illumination and makes it less intense.

■ **silver halide** The small crystals of silver bromide, chloride, or iodide in the film's emulsion which, when exposed to light, form a latent image on the surface made of tiny specks of silver. When the film is placed in developing agents, the tiny specks act as catalysts in converting the halide into black metallic silver, which forms the image. The undeveloped silver halides are removed in the fixing bath. *See* **film** *(1) and* **processing.**

■ **silver track** An optical sound track on a color film that has been treated with a viscous fluid to prevent silver from being bleached out during the developing of the picture. Such a track produces better sound than a dyed track. *See* **optical sound** *and* **sulphide track.**

■ **sine wave response** *See* **modulation transfer function.**

■ **single** A shot of only one person, generally referred to as a one-shot.

■ **single broad** *See* **broad.**

■ **single/double-system sound camera** A camera capable of recording image and sound on the same film or photographing the scene while the sound is recorded on a separate though synchronic system. *See* **double-system sound recording** *and* **single-system sound recording.**

■ **single 8mm film, single 8** Film 8 millimeters in width that was used in the camera and processed as a single strip instead of the "double-8mm" film, which was shot and processed as two rows on a single film 16 millimeters wide. *See* **double 8mm film, 8mm film,** *and* **Super 8mm film.**

■ **single feature** A film program in which only one feature film is presented. Screenings of only one film have been the general practice since the demise of the double feature during the 1950s. *See* **double feature.**

■ **single-frame camera** A camera equipped to take a single picture at a time for time-lapse photography, accelerated action, pixillation, or animation.

■ **single-frame exposure, single-frame cinematography, single-frame shooting, single framing** Shooting one frame at a time with a specially equipped camera. This technique is used for (1) time-lapse photography; (2) accelerated or pixillated action; or (3) animation. Also called stop-motion or stop-action cinematography. *See* **stop motion.**

■ **single-frame motor** A special motor, used in animation work, that functions continuously and brings each frame in the camera individually to exposure by means of a rotating shaft when the camera operator employs the single-frame release. *See* **animation.**

■ **single-frame release** A button or release on a single-frame camera that allows each frame to be exposed one at a time. A cable attached to the camera might also be used to avoid vibration. *See* **single-frame camera.**

■ **single-perforation film** Film with sprocket holes along one edge. Sixteen-millimeter film has perforations along one side when a sound track is required on the other side. Super 8mm film also has single rows of perforations. *See* **perforations.**

■ **single scrim** *See* **scrim.**

■ **single-shot technique** Filming a scene with a series of sequential shots instead of using the master-scene technique by which the same action might be photographed first with a master shot and then a series of shots of the same action or part of the action with different camera distances or angles. More economical, the single-shot technique requires overlapping and some careful planning beforehand to allow for unobtrusive editing of the continuous action. *See* **master scene technique.**

■ **single-strand printing** Making a print or an intermediate dupe from a single composite film passing through the printer once as opposed to using the separate A and B rolls, which must pass through the printer independently. Though a cheaper laboratory procedure, single-strand passes for both Super 8 and 16mm films allow the splices to be visible. The frame line on 35mm film, however, is sufficiently wide to make such jointures invisible. This procedure also makes such effects as dissolves, fades, and superimpositions impossible, since overlapping shots from and A and B rolls are not possible. *See* **A and B printing.**

■ **single stripe, single-stripe film** A film with a single magnetic track for recording. Such films normally have a second oxide stripe to balance the first and guarantee even movement. *See* **balance stripe** *and* **three stripe.**

■ **single-system sound camera** A camera that records both image and sound on film simultaneously. Such cameras of the 16mm variety were used in television news work before the development of portable videotape recorders. Examples of this type of camera were the Cinema Products CP-16A and the Mitchell SS-R16. Such cameras are no longer made and the film is available only on special order.

■ **single-system sound recording** Recording sound on the same film that is photographing the scene. Originally recorded on an optical track, sound was then registered on a magnetic track. This process was used in 16mm cameras for news work, but is not used much today. *See* **double-system sound recording** *and* **single/double-system sound camera.**

■ **sit into the shot** Direction for a performer to be ready to sit down as soon as the word "action" is spoken and the camera begins shooting.

■ **situation comedy, sitcom** (1) A comic film dependent on the interaction of a small group of characters, often including the members of the same family—for example, any of the fifteen Andy Hardy films made between 1937 and 1947 and starring Mickey Rooney. The term is commonly used now for the dreary stuff that appears on television. (2) A term sometimes employed to describe a film dependent on some uncommon and amusing situation, for example, Preston Sturges's *The Miracle of Morgan's Creek* (1943), in which Betty Hutton must legitimize her mysterious pregnancy in small-town America during the war years.

■ **16mm film** Introduced in 1923 for the amateur cinematographer, film 16 millimeters wide became the major gauge for training films made by the United States Army during World War II, since it was cheaper and easier to use than 35mm film. Sixteen-millimeter film also became popular for making industrial, governmental, and educational films after the war. Lightweight 16mm cameras became the primary means of filming television news until they were replaced by portable video cameras. Sixteen-millimeter film also became and has remained a popular film size for documentaries, experimental films, and independent filmmakers. The Ann Arbor 16mm Film Festival highlights works made in this gauge each March. Sixteen-millimeter film has become so sensitive and accurate that it is now sometimes used for shooting feature films, after which it is blown up into 35mm film for release in commercial theaters—Robert Altman, for example, has shot a number of feature films with 16mm film. Super-16, a film with a 40 percent greater frame area than standard 16mm film, was introduced in 1971, offering a wide-screen image on a negative for blowup to a 35mm print; yet in spite of the excellence of its image, this type of film has been more successful in Europe than in the United States. Sixteen-millimeter film comes with two rows of perforations when used in silent cameras or with only one row when used in single-system sound cameras so that the other side of the frame can carry a sound track.

■ **65mm film** Wide film stock used for original cinematography, which is later printed on 70mm film to allow for stereophonic sound tracks. The 65mm negative has a 1.85:1 frame with an area 4½ times that of a 35mm frame and more than 2½ times that of a 35mm anamorphic frame, thus creating an image of extreme resolution and quality. The expense of this large format, however, and the difficulties in shooting with it have limited the film's use today, though 35mm pictures are at times blown up to 70mm for important motion pictures. Large-format cameras are now sometimes used for special-effects work because of their high-quality image or for special venues at such locations as theme parks. *See* **70mm film.**

■ **skid** *See* **wheeled tee.**

■ **skill film** A short film that demonstrates in a methodical fashion how to perform some task or learn some skill. *See* **informational film, instructional film,** *and* **training film.**

■ **skin flick** A film that features a large amount of nudity, generally female, and not necessarily a good deal of sex. Since the main object of such films is sexually to arouse the audience, they are often considered pornographic. Also called nudie. *See* **pornographic film.**

■ **skip-frame printing, skip framing, skip printing, skip out** Omitting frames at regular intervals while making a print from a negative. This process will accelerate the action photographed when it is projected on the screen—for example, skipping ever second frame will double the speed of the action. *See* **double framing** *and* **stretch framing.**

■ **skipping, strobing** The seemingly jerky and disconnected effect between images of the same object when the camera pans rapidly across the scene or the subject moves rapidly in front of the camera. *See* **strobing.**

■ **skivings** Threads or slivers of a film print scraped off when running through a projector with some type of impediment or misalignment.

■ **skull shot** A close-up; generally a reaction shot.

■ **sky bar** An extendable bar fitting between two walls near the ceiling and used to support lamps or tubes from which lamps are supported. *See* **polecat.**

■ **sky filter** (1) A graduated filter used in black-and-white cinematography to darken the sky. (2) A largely colorless filter employed in color cinematography to absorb ultraviolet rays and penetrate haze.

■ **sky light** Natural light from the sky, but not directly from the sun.

■ **sky pan** A luminaire for filling a wide area with general lighting, made of a reflecting aluminum dish with an uncovered bulb of 5 or 10 kilowatts and a cage.

■ **slapstick, slapstick comedy** Any comic drama or film with a good deal of aggressive or violent action as the source of its humor. The term "slapstick" derives from the object comprised of two pieces of wood hinged together that was used by clowns to make a loud clapping noise when they apparently struck one another. The term is especially applicable to the comedy of silent

film days, for example, the Mack Sennett films of the Keystone Studio. Both the silent and sound films of Laurel and Hardy are also notable for their slapstick humor. The Three Stooges are later, though more vulgar, practitioners of this type of comedy. *See* **comedy** *and* **farce.**

■ **slash dupe, slash print** *See* **scratchprint.**

■ **slasher film** A general category for horror films that focuses upon the mutilation and killing of women, generally by a psychotic killer—e.g., Alfred Hitchcock's *Psycho* and Michael Powell's *Peeping Tom*, both 1960, would be two early examples of this type of film. But *see* **slice-and-dice, splatter,** *and* **stalker films** *for related designations.*

■ **slate** (1) That part of a clapboard on which is marked such information as production number, director, director of photography, date, and the numbers of the scene and take to identify each piece of film for editing. The slate is photographed at the start of each take while the camera assistant announces the scene and take and then bangs together a pair of hinged boards, the "clapsticks," on top of the slate, allowing the editor later to synchronize picture and sound by matching the frame of the sticks coming together and the first noise on the soundtrack. An electronic device is also employed today for such synchronization. (2) The term is sometimes used for the entire clapboard. Both (1) and (2) are also sometimes called a production slate or number board. (3) The photographed take that has been marked with a slate. (4) To mark a take at the start of shooting with a clapboard. (8) An order by the director for the camera assistant to operate the clapboard and state the numbers of the scene and take. *See* **clapboard.**

■ **slate board** *See* **clapboard.**

■ **slate light** A slating device, attached to a sound recorder, that produces an audible beep and flash of light for synchronizing sound and picture during editing.

■ **slateman** The second assistant camera operator who holds the slate in front of the camera and claps the boards at the start of each shot. *See* **slate.**

■ **slate number** *See* **take number.**

■ **slave** (1) Any mechanism controlled from a distance. (2) Any mechanism controlled by another device, which is referred to as the master.

■ **sleaze** The horrendous group of low-budget films that began to be made in the 1960s with no purpose but to make money by exploiting sex and violence. This group includes horror, martial arts, and motorcycle films.

■ **sled** A metal frame with a socket used to support a luminaire from a wall. Sleds can also be suspended from hand rails by rope.

■ **sleeper** A film that first appears with little publicity and notoriety but becomes an artistic or financial success. An example might be Richard Rush's film *The Stunt Man* (1978), which almost failed to receive a national distribution—although not a financial success, the film did finally reach an appreciative audience.

■ **slice-and-dice film, slice-'n'-dice film** Any one of a group of horror films in recent years that features the butchering of human beings, often attractive young females. All of the *Friday the 13th* films would fit this category. *See* **splatter, slasher,** *and* **stalker films** for related designations of this kind of horror film.

■ **slice-of-life film** A film that gives the illusion of dealing with everyday people and events in a realistic and untheatrical way—as if the camera just happened to be present to record and disclose the events that transpire before the lens. For the neorealist screenwriter Cesare Zavatini, the ultimate film was the screening of a continuous hour and one-half in an individual's life—no plot, no actors, no extraordinary events. For Zavatini, the dignity of common life was sufficiently compelling. The neorealist film that he wrote with the director Vittorio de Sica, *Umberto D* (1952), comes as close to that standard as a fictional feature film can. Like *Umberto D* and the other neorealist films, most slice-of-life films deal with the lives of common and unexceptional people. This impulse toward realism, to allow the camera to give us the illusion of eavesdropping on reality, has been part of cinema from the start, from the first *actualité* films of the Lumière brothers. A noteworthy series of films of this type, influenced by neorealism is Satyajit Ray's *Apu* trilogy (1955–59), a natural and compelling depiction of life in a Bengali village. *See* **realism** *and* **neorealism.**

■ **slide** An individually mounted transparency used to project a picture. Such a slide might be a source of the background in a rear- or front-projection shot.

■ **slide-motion film** A film, generally a documentary, that uses a series of still pictures like a filmograph, but in which the camera seems to move among the pictures' elements by means of panning or a zoom lens. *See* **photokineses.**

■ **slit-scan** A type of streak photography used by the experimental filmmaker John Whitney, Sr., and later developed by Douglas Trumbull for the "Stargate Corridor" sequence in Stanley Kubrick's *2001: A Space Odyssey* (1968). The technique employs a camera photographing planes of illuminated artwork through a slit in a screen with long single-frame exposures while the camera, artwork, and sometimes the slit are in motion.

The camera tracks in and out, keeping the artwork, which itself is altered or moved, constantly in focus during the exposure. The effect is such that the camera seems to be rushing into or out of the scene. *See* **streak photography.**

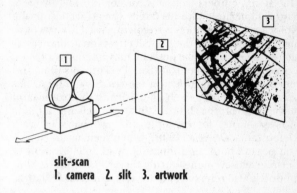

slit-scan
1. camera   2. slit   3. artwork

■ **slomo** Jargon for slow motion. *See* **slow motion.**

■ **slop print** (1) An unedited print made directly off a negative to check printing results. (2) A print made off a workprint to allow the sound mixer to work with a splice-free copy while preparing the final mix and also to allow the negative cutter to conform the negative to the final workprint while the mix is being prepared.

■ **slop test, hand test, dip test** Examining a short piece of exposed film for quality and results by processing it in portable equipment.

■ **slow cutting** A type of editing with shots of fairly long duration. *See* **rhythm** *and* **shot.**

■ **slow film, slow stock** Film less sensitive to light, with a lower exposure-index number. Such stock requires more exposure or considerable illumination, but is capable of achieving pictures with great sharpness and detail.

■ **slow in/slow out** The technique of slowly beginning any panning or traveling shot, gradually building up movement, and then slowing down to conclude in order to avoid any sudden motion that might jolt the viewer. *See* **pan** *and* **traveling shot.**

■ **slow lens** A lens with a relatively low efficiency for transmitting light. Such lenses have smaller apertures, with a maximum f-stop number of 2.8. *See* **lens.**

■ **slow motion** Action on the screen at a rate slower than normal, achieved by shooting a scene at a speed faster than the standard 24 frames per second and projecting it at 24 frames per second. A scene photographed at 48 frames per second, when projected at 24, will move at half its original speed, since each frame is now shown for twice the length of its original exposure. While fast motion is generally used in a comic context, slow motion is employed for more serious effects. It is particularly effective in evoking a mood of nostalgia or lyricism for scenes from the past, as when the protagonist in Sidney Lumet's *The Pawnbroker* (1965) remembers from his former life in Europe a pastoral interlude with his family, long since lost in the Holocaust. Slow motion is frequently used for acts of violence, diminishing their harsh effects on audiences by making them seem like graceful movements in a ballet, a practice given impetus by Sam Peckinpah's films and repeated endlessly in action movies. Slow motion has been used less offensively in glorifying the beauty and movement of the human body in acts of athletic prowess—note, for example, the two parts of Leni Riefenstahl's *Olympia* (1938), which seem as much a visual poem about the human body as a celebration of German achievements during the 1936 Olympics. Slow motion is also referred to as overcranking. *See* **fast motion.**

■ **slow speed** A camera speed slower than the standard 24 frames per second, used for achieving fast-motion when the picture is projected at the standard speed. Many cameras can shoot at a variety of speeds.

■ **slug** A strip of film leader spliced into a picture or sound workprint to replace missing or damaged film. Also called buildup, extended scene, or spacing.

■ **slug in** To insert into a picture or sound workprint a strip of leader to replace missing or damaged film.

■ **smart slate, time-code slate, intelligent slate** A clapboard that also includes time-code information. The camera photographs the clapboard at the start of the shot, and the time-code numbers later help in synchronizing the film with the sound record that also has time-code information. *See* **slate.**

■ **smart sync** Synchronizing picture and sound by means of a smart slate. *See* **smart slate.**

■ **smash cut, shock cut** A sudden cut from one shot to another. *See* **dynamic cutting.**

■ **smellies** Any of the systems that release aromas into the air of a movie house to accompany the motion picture. *See* **AromaRama** *and* **Smell-O-Vision.**

■ **Smell-O-Vision** A process for releasing odors that correspond to the particular events of a film through tub-

ing that runs to each seat in the movie house. The various odors, contained in vials on a rotating drum, are released by signals on the film. The system was sponsored by Michael Todd, Jr., and used for a single feature film, *Scent of Mystery* in 1960. *See* **AromaRama.**

■ **smoke machine, smoke gun** *See* **fog maker.**

■ **smoke pot** A small container that produces smoke for mechanical effects. The container holds some chemical, such as naphthalene or bitumen, which is fired either by electricity or a burning fuse.

■ **smooth** Leveling and balancing the background sound recorded during shooting from shot to shot and scene to scene, especially for constancy in volume.

■ **SMPTE** *See* **Society of Motion Picture and Television Engineers.**

■ **SMPTE test film** Any of the pieces of film devised by the Society of Motion Picture and Television Engineers for testing film equipment.

■ **SMPTE time code, SMPTE/EBU time code** *See* **time code.**

■ **SMPTE universal leader** The leader designed by the Society of Motion Picture and Television Engineers to be attached to the head and tail of each reel of film. The leader placed at the start of each reel of the release print has information concerning the film and the countdown numbers that enable projectionists to focus and change from one reel to another without interrupting the motion picture. Sometimes called society leader. *See* **Academy leader** *and* **projector.**

■ **sneak preview** A showing of a film before its general release, sometimes to assess audience reaction for making last-minute changes, sometimes to furnish information for distribution and publicity, and sometimes to provoke interest in the local area where the film will play.

■ **snoot** A metal mask with a cylinder that fits over a spotlight and restricts the illumination to a fixed circular area. Snoots are in various sizes, though some allow different openings to control the size of the beam.

■ **snorkel** A camera attachment that permits greater depth of field than the similar periscope attachment and is especially functional for photographing miniatures. *See* **periscope.**

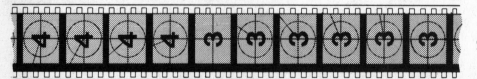

SMPTE universal leader

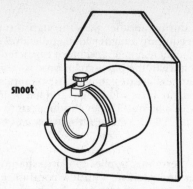

snoot

■ **snorkel camera** Any of the remote-control cameras that can be operated by boom or cables in difficult-to-reach areas and that are capable of making complex maneuvers. *See* **remote-control camera.**

■ **snow effects** An appearance of snow in a scene created by such artificial means as rock salt on the ground, plastic chips or chopped feathers blown by a fan, gypsum for heavy snow, and regular salt on the garments of the characters.

■ **snuff film** A film, other than a newsreel or documentary, in which a human life is actually taken. Such films are supposedly made for the purpose of providing pleasure. Although none of these films have publicly surfaced, their very concept offers the next step beyond the present state of violence and mayhem in the cinema.

■ **soap opera** A term originally from radio and also now applicable to television afternoon serials that feature a good deal of sentimental, romantic, melodramatic, and escapist events among a group of related individuals. Each character has his or her own erotic and tragic story, with the various stories getting extremely tangled as the action continues from day to day. The term derives from the fact that the radio programs were largely sponsored by soap or detergent manufacturers. One occasionally hears the term applied to certain sentimental and melodramatic films, such as the 1934 and 1959 versions of *Imitation of Life,* directed by John Stahl and Douglas Sirk respectively.

■ **social-conscience film, social consciousness film, problem film** A film that deals with some social problem from a moralistic perspective, exposing injustice and suggesting some type of ameliorative action. Such films are often quite simplistic, presenting complex social issues in a manner that will offend few and not interfere with box office receipts, but will still stir the social conscience of its audiences, making viewers feel good about themselves for condemning the injustices they see on the screen. The injustices attacked are those most audiences would condemn in the first place. The United States in the 1930s produced a number of such films, with a few achieving excellence because of their sheer dramatic power, notably Mervyn Le Roy's exposé of prison life in the South, *I Am a Fugitive from a Chain Gang* (1932) and Fritz Lang's *Fury* (1936), an indictment of lynching. The social-conscience films of the post-war years tended to be glossy and superficial, though once again a few were outstanding: two of the many race-relations films that stand out are *Lost Boundaries* (1949; dir. Alfred Werker) and *Edge of the City* (1957; dir. Martin Ritt). Stanley Kramer made a number of problem films throughout the 1950s and 1960s that managed to offend few and make a good deal of money. In 1979, *The China Syndrome* (dir. James Bridges) attacked the potential dangers of nuclear power plants in an engrossing manner. For a brief period in more recent years, Hollywood found an audience for films dealing with urban life in the black ghetto. The two most outstanding of these films, depicting the struggles and trauma of young people trying to survive in a world of poverty and violence, were *Boyz N the Hood* (1991; dir. John Singleton) and *Menace II Society* (1993; dir. Allen and Albert Hughes). Although foreign film industries have also largely ignored social concerns in their drive for profit, notable examples of films dealing centrally with social problems have come forth, such as the Italian neorealist films made during the years immediately after the Second World War, and, more recently, the politically conscious films of Third World cinema. *See* **neorealism** *and* **Third World cinema.**

social-conscience film *Fury* (1936; dir. Fritz Lang), a film about lynching in America.

■ ■ ■

■ **social drama** (1) A play or film dealing with social relationships and conflicts between characters. Ibsen's *A Doll's House* would be such a stage play and Paul Mazursky's *An Unmarried Woman* (1977) an example of such a film, although the term is not often used for the cinema. (2) The term is sometimes used for a social-conscience film (see above).

■ **socialist realism** The doctrine and dogma for art in the Soviet Union, beginning in the 1930s and lasting into the 1950s, which pronounced that all art must be historically true and concrete, while ideologically educating the workers in the cause of Communism. The contradiction in these goals is evident—art could not be both truthful and propagandistic. Subjectivism and individualism were not to have any role in art, and formalism was directly attacked. These principles were strongly advocated by Joseph Stalin from the time he took the reins of Soviet leadership in 1927; and socialist realism was actually pronounced the officially sanctioned form of art at the Twentieth Party Congress in 1932. At the First Congress of Soviet Writers in 1934, the principles of socialist realism were spelled out. The pressure was especially felt in cinema, where the formalism and experimentation of such artists as Eisenstein, Pudovkin, and Vertov were decried. As a result, the greatest period in the history of Russian cinema, and one of the great achievements in world cinema, was brought to an end. Ironically, during their period of freedom, the Russian filmmakers had created the most socially relevant and persuasively pro-Soviet art ever achieved in that country. The demand for socialist realism virtually put an end to any viable artistic achievement by filmmakers in the Soviet Union for some time, with the exception, perhaps, of Eisenstein's sound films.

■ **Society leader** *See* **SMPTE universal leader.**

■ **Society of Motion Picture and Television Engineers (SMPTE)** The organization of engineers in both the film and television industries, which establishes standards for film and film equipment for the American National Standards Institute (ANSI). The organization publishes *The Journal of the Society of Motion Picture and Television Engineers (JSMPTE)*, an important technological periodical.

■ **sodium vapor traveling matte process, sodium light process, sodium process** A multifilm traveling matte method of combining foreground action with a background shot separately. A yellow screen is lit by sodium vapor lamps and the characters before it by incandescent lamps. A beam-splitting prism in the camera sends the yellow light from the backing around the characters to one of the films so that a negative is formed, with the background opaque and foreground clear, from which a positive male matte can be struck with the performers opaque and the background clear. The prism also sends the light reflected from the characters onto the other film, which is insensitive to the yellow light and leaves the surrounding area clear on the negative, from which a self-matting positive can be struck with the background opaque. When the background positive is run in bipack with the male matte through an optical printer, space is left on the negative into which the foreground action can be fitted from the self-matting

positive during another pass through the printer. Although requiring a higher footcandle level of lighting, using a smaller screen, and more restricted in camera movement than the blue-screen process, this traveling-matte process creates some sharp composite images without matte lines and fringes and has been used with great success by Walt Disney Productions (e.g., in *Mary Poppins* in 1964). *See* **blue-screen process** *and* **traveling-matte process.**

■ **soft** A term that applies to (1) unsharp images; (2) negatives and positives with low contrast; and (3) diffuse lighting, as opposed to hard, which does not sharply define objects or shadows and creates minimal contrast.

■ **soft box** A large box containing several lamps and covered by some material that is used to create a soft, diffuse light devoid of any shadows.

■ **soft-core pornography, soft porn film** A pornographic film with the sole purpose of sexually arousing the audience and with sexual acts either simulated or not fully demonstrated. *See* **pornographic film.**

■ **soft cut** A dissolve that is extremely short.

■ **soft-edge** A diffuse or slightly blurred boundary to the perimeters of an image.

■ **soft-edge wipe** A wipe in which the border between the two images is blurred. A hard-edge wipe has a sharply defined line between the two images. *See* **wipe.**

■ **soft focus** (1) A visual effect in which the image seems somewhat hazy and not sharply defined, achieved by shooting with the lens slightly out of focus or shooting through a special lens, filter, gauze, or substance such as petroleum jelly. Soft focus has often been employed from the days of silent film to the present to create a romantic mood, as in F. W. Murnau's *Sunrise* (1927), or a feeling of nostalgia and idealism, as in the picnic scene with Bonnie's family in Arthur Penn's *Bonnie and Clyde* (1967). The effect has also been used to introduce flashbacks, create subjective or hallucinatory points of view, and, especially in studio days, to soften the features of aging actresses. *See* **diffusion.** (2) The somewhat undefined and hazy part of an image, which highlights that part of the picture in sharp focus—the background might be hazy to focus our attention on what takes place in the foreground or the foreground unclear to bring our attention to some action in the rear and to emphasize the image's depth.

■ **soft light, softlight, softlite** An open-faced lamp that creates a diffuse and soft illumination with subtle shadows from a distance and with no shadows when it is placed close to the subject. *See* **lighting.**

soft light

■ **software** Although the term is now commonly associated with the programs and data used to run a computer, it is also applied to the motion pictures themselves that are displayed through such permanent "hardware" as projectors and home-video systems.

■ **solarization** (1) A partial reversal that takes place during development with positive or negative elements and is caused accidentally by rehalogenation or brought about intentionally by the laboratory. Accidental solarization is generally the result of overexposure, especially when photographing a light source such as the sun. (2) A fog or flare effect in an image caused by accidental exposure to light during developing.

■ **solenoid** An electromagnetic piece of equipment used as part of a remote control system to allow limited movement to such a device as an armature in a model figure. *See* **armature.**

■ **Sony Dynamic Digital Sound (SDDS)** *See* **digital sound, sound,** *and* **stereophonic sound.**

■ **Sony Pictures Entertainment** *See* **Columbia Pictures** *and* **TriStar Pictures.**

■ **Sony Pictures Imageworks** One of the premier houses for digital special effects, animation, and previsualization. SPI is under the supervision of Ken Ralston.

■ **soubrette** The term was originally used to describe an intriguing and flirtatious maid servant in a stage drama, but is also sometimes used to describe any coquettish role or the actress playing such a role in the theater or on the screen.

■ **sound (SD)** Experimentation with synchronic sound and image began at virtually the inception of the motion picture. Edison initially conceived of moving pictures as accompaniments to the sound from his new phonograph; and W. K. L. Dickson, Edison's assistant developed a Kinetophonograph, a device capable of projecting images from film while playing synchronic sound from a phonograph, which he demonstrated to his employer in 1889. Synchronization, however, presented great difficulties, and Edison's company went

forward with his peephole machine, the Kinetescope, though he did build and deploy in 1895 at least fifty peephole machines with nonsynchronic music and sound effects, supplied by a phonograph, which he called Kinetophones. Once projected motion pictures were established, Edison made a further try between 1910 and 1916 to develop synchronic sound for such images with a louder phonograph and longer cylinder record (the system was also called the Kinetophone), but the attempt was finally unsuccessful. Although the problem of amplifying sound was solved by Lee De Forest with his invention of the audion (patented in 1907 and actually used by De Forest for amplification in 1912), the only further significant attempt to use the phonograph for synchronic sound and film was the sound-on-disc system developed by Western Electric Company and Bell Telephone Laboratories, and employed by Warner Brothers as the Vitaphone system in 1926.

A parallel development toward sound motion-pictures involved photographing an optical sound track on the film itself. Although experimentation in photographing sound had been carried on since the 1880s, the first major attempt to put such optical recording on the same film as the image seems to have been performed by Eugene Augustin Lauste, a Frenchman who began working for Edison in 1887 and started experimenting with the project about 1900. Lauste continued working on the project both in the United States and in England, and in 1911 is supposed to have demonstrated the first sound-on-film motion picture in this country. A considerable advance in this technology was made by Josef Engl, Joseph Massole, and Hans Vogt in Germany, who began developing in 1918 the Tri-Ergon ("the work of three") process, and, simultaneously and independently in the United States, by Lee De Forest, inventor of the audion tube, who developed the Phonofilm process. De Forest actually used his Phonofilm process to make more than a thousand short films between 1923 and 1927, but could not convince the Hollywood studios that his sound system was anything more than a costly novelty. From 1922 until 1925, De Forest had shared some of his procedures with Theodore W. Case and E. I. Sponable, and, at the end of their working agreement, the Case laboratory continued its experimentation with sound, selling a system very much dependent on De Forest's work to the Fox Film Corporation in 1926. While Western Electric Company and Bell Telephone Laboratories had been developing the sound-on-disc system that was to become Vitaphone, they had also been working on a sound-on-film process, with both systems employing the same microphones, amplifiers, and loudspeakers. Also to prove significant was the work done on optical sound recording by General Electric Company and Westinghouse, both of which worked cooperatively with RCA as their distributor. In 1928, RCA Photophone Inc., a subsidiary of RCA, was formed to advance commercially this work with sound-on-film.

Having established all the main contributors to the new technology, we can now trace the sudden rise of sound in the motion-picture industry. On August 6, 1926, in New York City, Warner Brothers presented *Don Juan,* directed by Alan Crosland and starring John Barrymore, with a full musical score played by the New York Philharmonic and recorded on disc with the Vitaphone system. Before viewing this filmic extravaganza, the audience had watched a number of musical sound shorts and a brief synchronic speech by Will Hays, head of the Motion Picture Producers and Distributors of America (MPPDA), welcoming the new sound era. Warner Brothers, a one-time secondary studio now flushed with the possibility of undreamed-of success, went on to make synchronic scores for all its films, wired theaters throughout the country for sound, and built a sound studio for film production. Its production of *The Jazz Singer,* directed by Alan Crosland and starring Al Jolson, opened on October 5, 1927, and exploded the film industry. For the most part a film with synchronic music, and with conversation still largely conveyed by titles, *The Jazz Singer* had a few scenes of sound dialogue that gave screen characters a new dimension and suddenly brought the world on the screen closer to reality. Parallel to this development was Fox Film Corporation's development of the system purchased from Theodore W. Case and Earl I. Sponable and now called Fox Movietone. Fox had presented some sound shorts and a film with synchronized music, *Seventh Heaven* (dir. Frank Borzage), in the earlier months of 1927, but more significant, in the same year, were its sound films of Charles Lindbergh's takeoff for his historic flight across the Atlantic and his later reception by President Coolidge at the White House in the company's Movietone News, the first sound newsreel. Warner Brothers followed next with the first completely sound commercial film, *Lights of New York* (dir. Brian Foy) in 1928. The conversion to sound was then rapid and total for the entire industry. The box office had been sagging because of the rapid development of radio but also because of a general decline in the quality of film production and an increase in the price of admission.

Sound cinema was the needed impetus to bring people back to the theaters and it became the financial salvation of the motion-picture industry during the Depression. By 1930, almost two-thirds of the theaters in the United States, more than 13,000 movie houses in all, were equipped for sound. In the same year, only 5 percent of the films produced in Hollywood were silent. The cost of this conversion was considerable both for the theaters, which spent anywhere from $8,000 to $20,000 to install sound equipment, depending on the system and size of the theater, and for the studios, which had to borrow considerable sums of money from Wall Street to create sound stages and hire the personnel to run the new technology. Warner Brothers became a major film company, the fortunes of

Fox Film Corporation soared, and all the Hollywood studios reaped the benefits of the new technology as people flocked to the theaters. In April and May of 1928, five Hollywood studios—MGM, Paramount, United Artists, First National, and Universal—contracted for sound with Electrical Research Products Inc. (ERPI), the commercial distributor for Western Electric's sound equipment. In the same year, RCA joined the Film Booking Company, which owned the Keith and Orpheum theater chains, to form Radio-Keith-Orpheum (RKO), an organization intended to make films with the Photophone sound-on-film system. Pathé and Mack Sennett studios also contracted to use the Photophone system, and later, between 1933 and 1936, Disney, Republic Pictures, Warner Brothers, and Columbia Pictures did the same.

Many theaters were at first equipped to use both sound on disc and on film, but it soon became clear that the latter system was more efficient and its sound of better quality. When Warner Brothers itself switched to optical sound, the type of disc system that had begun with Edison's early version was no longer employed for sound film. Optical sound recording used both the variable-density and variable-area methods: in the first instance light modulated by sound waves is recorded on film in various intensities, and in the second light is recorded in varying widths (modern variable-area systems actually record the light bilaterally with symmetrical outlines on both sides of the horizontal band). Optical sound is reproduced in the projector when the track passes between a lamp and a photoelectric cell: the electrical output from the cell which is converted into soundwaves is determined by the amount of light which the soundtrack allows to pass. Projectors were equipped to play either kind of optical track. Since variable-density and variable-area methods soon produced equally good results, they were both used by the major studios (e.g., MGM recorded with variable density and released with variable area). In later years, variable-area tracks came into favor because they could be more expeditiously printed in color systems.

The coming of sound radically changed the film industry and the movies that came out of Hollywood. Numerous silent-film stars soon found their careers at an end because their voices did not have the necessary quality or did not correspond to their film image. Stage performers with good voices, script writers who could write dialogue, and Broadway plays were imported in large numbers. The canned theater that Hollywood produced in the early days of sound was as much the result of necessity as of the industry's inexperience with the new cinematic dimension. Studios were ruled by the new sound technicians and the placement of the immobile microphone, which managed to pick up every unwanted noise on the set. Because of their noise, cameras had to be placed in soundproof booths with glass fronts, where they had to remain without movement—to move the camera and booth required enormous time and effort. Sometimes three or four separate cameras and booths might be used to achieve a variety of shots, but the practice was also costly and time consuming. Any kind of elaborate editing of the film was also impossible, since picture and sound were recorded simultaneously and continuously, and since complex editing could not be performed with a sound track or with sound on a disc.

The films from this period seem inert, dull, and often silly; but it was not long before creative minds triumphed over the limitations of this early technology. Rouben Mamoulian, for his initial film with sound, *Applause* (1929), is credited with first using two microphones for one scene and coordinating their sound with a mixer. For the same film, he also shot several scenes silently and added sound later. King Vidor for *Hallelujah* (1929), Ernst Lubitsch for *The Love Parade* (1929), and Lewis Milestone for *All Quiet on the Western Front* (1930) also dubbed sound later to scenes shot silently. Both Eddie Mannix, a sound technician for MGM, and Lionel Barrymore, the actor and director, are credited with thinking up the "boom," a long pole with the microphone attached to follow the movement of the actors yet remain above their heads and outside the view of the camera. Also significant was the development of the blimp, a soundproof encasement in which the camera was placed to deaden the noise of the motor. As early as 1929, *In Old Arizona* (dir. Raoul Walsh and Irving Cummings) could lay claim to being the first film with sound recorded largely out of doors; and, in the same year, the musical, a natural product of sound cinema, advanced beyond *The Jazz Singer* with *Broadway Melody* (dir. Harry Beaumont), the first sound

sound *The Jazz Singer* (1927; dir. Alan Crosland), with Al Jolson's voice heralding in the sound era.

■ ■ ■

film to win an Academy Award. In 1932, dialogue and music recorded on separate tracks began to be mixed, allowing for more subtle and integrative uses of musical scores. In 1933, Cooper and Schoedsack's *King Kong* demonstrated the full possibilities of synthesizing dialogue, sound effects, and music.

The advent of sound also brought an end to certain types of cinema: the golden age of comedy, the wonderful physical antics and silent genius that had flourished from the Sennett studios and risen to its heights with Chaplin and Keaton, came to a sudden end; and the kind of melodrama that had reached such heights with Griffith no longer seemed acceptable with the realism of sound. But if comedy lost something of its wonderful physical dimension, it also gained from the addition of a verbal dimension that could appeal to both the audience's intelligence and sense of the irrational—certainly the Marx brothers and W. C. Fields appealed to both. The comedies of Ernst Lubitsch achieved a wonderful sophistication and subtlety, especially films such as *Trouble in Paradise* (1932) and *The Shop Around the Corner* (1940), through the use of both language and sound. And the wonderful screwball comedies of the 1930s are the products of captivating stars and their dizzying use of language. The wonderful visual achievement of the silent camera might be at an end, but film could now approach social and psychological problems, reach depths of human experience that had previously been cut off by silence.

Sound technology did not advance significantly until the 1950s, when magnetic tape became the principal means of recording sound for film, and stereophonic sound using magnetic tracks and multiple speakers became an attraction for wide-screen cinema. Although Walt Disney's *Fantasia* (1940) had already used a stereophonic system with three optical tracks and a control track on a separate film for a limited number of screenings, stereophonic sound had to await the advent of the wide-screen image, which supported a wider distribution of sound, in the 1950s before it became a more integral part of motion pictures. In 1952, Cinerama, a three-projector system, employed seven magnetic sound tracks on a separate piece of film for stereophonic sound; and in 1953, CinemaScope, an anamorphic system, used four magnetic tracks, with two on each side of the picture, for 35mm film, and six tracks, with three on each side, for 70mm film to create stereophonic sound for special productions and in theaters specially equipped. Most of the CinemaScope prints were actually magoptical, containing both the stereophonic magnetic tracks and a monaural optical track. First used for wide-screen stereophonic sound, magnetic tape was discovered to be cheaper and more flexible to use than optical systems, producing a higher quality of sound and permitting the easy mixing of numerous tracks. Magnetic tape became the general rule for recording, dubbing, and mixing in the industry at large, with sound transferred to an optical track on the general release print since it was too expensive for theaters throughout the country to convert to magnetic sound. The result was still an important improvement over previous sound reproduction in theaters. Today more than fifteen separate tracks for dialogue, sound effects, and music, themselves perhaps premixes of other tracks, might be mixed in a sophisticated dubbing theater where they are eventually made into a final master magnetic track, which can then be converted into the optical track on the release print. Although postdubbing is an efficient way of recording sound for various types of scenes or simply for improving the sound where an original recording was deficient, sound is still often recorded synchronically with the picture.

A more recent advance in sound playback has been the Dolby System, which reduces background noise and thus allows better fidelity for both magnetic and optical tracks. The expense of placing magnetic sound tracks on film and equipping theaters to play such sound led to further developments in optical stereo sound, especially by Dolby—converting a projector with a silicon solar cell to play such sound was not expensive. Dolby Stereophonic Sound, with its two optical bands and four sound tracks, has replaced magnetic stereophonic systems for 35mm film; and Dolby-Surround Sound now makes possible a theater filled with sound effects and music from a separate track and speakers to the sides and rear of the audience. The THX Sound System, introduced by Lucasfilm in 1983, made it possible for sound systems in the theater to put forward the full stereo range of Dolby Stereophonic sound by employing left, right, and center speakers along with a subwoofer and some twenty-two surround speakers (the company actually licenses manufacturers to make the equipment that meets its system's standards). Home THX, developed for living-room use, requires only two surround speakers.

Also significant is the new technology for digital sound, which is making its way into the recording and mixing of sound as well as the exhibition of motion pictures. Digital recording, which converts sound into a series of binary numbers and stores them in a computer's memory from which they can be converted into a signal and amplified, ignores noise in the recording medium, thus allowing any number of rerecordings without deterioration, and also offers a greater range, and hence fidelity, for sound. The digitizing of sound allows for manipulation, reorchestration, and integration into new aural settings as well as the creation of new sounds by means of synthesizers and computer instruments. Digitizing all recorded sound especially allows for simpler and more versatile postproduction editing and mixing. Digital systems are now creating sound of great clarity, resonance, range, and fidelity in a growing number of theaters. Dolby SR-D places the digital code between the perforations of the 35mm film; Digital Theater System (DTS) from MCA/Universal, the most popular format so far, places it on a disc and operates the sound by means of a time code on the film (note the old Vitaphone system at the birth of sound film, discussed earlier in this essay, that also placed the sound on a separate recording); and Sony Dynamic Digital Sound (SDDS) places the code on a track on the outside of the film with a back-up track along the opposite edge. Although the industry is likely eventually to settle on one of these systems, a number of theaters are equipped to play all three. While films are still released with only an analog sound track, an increasing number are also released for digital audio systems. *See* **asynchronous sound, digital sound, dub, magnetic recording, mix, nonsynchronous sound, optical sound,** *and* **synchronization.**

■ **sound advance** The distance on film between a frame and the point in the sound track with the matching synchronic sound. Since film must move intermittently before the aperture and continuously before the sound head in the projector, a sufficient distance must be allowed for the film to pass smoothly from one movement to the other without being pulled or torn. On 16mm film, sound on an optical track is 26 frames in advance of its image; on 35mm film, 21 frames in advance; but on 70mm film, magnetic sound is 24 frames behind.

■ **sound band** *See* **sound track.**

■ **sound camera** A self-blimped camera that runs noiselessly so that it can be used while sound is recorded. Sound cameras and sound recorders are often run synchronically at identical speeds by means of crystal-drive motors. *See* **camera, sound,** *and* **synchronization.**

■ **sound console** *See* **mixer.**

■ **sound crew** The group of personnel responsible for recording sound during the shooting of a film. This group must maintain and use the sound equipment so that the sound recording is clear, accurate, and balanced. The sound crew must also carry out its duties in a manner that does not interfere with the actual shooting. The head of this group is the sound mixer, who is also sometimes referred to as the production or floor mixer. He or she works the portable mixer, coordinating sounds from different microphones. The sound mixer is a highly trained and skilled individual with a knowledge of recording equipment and acoustics. He or she must know how to record dialogue for optimum effect both on sets and on location. The sound mixer works closely with the director of the film and is generally assisted by a sound recorder or sound camera operator; a boom operator, who manages the microphone boom; and perhaps several additional operators and cable pullers. (The individual who later mixes the various sound tracks for the final edited version of the film is also called the sound mixer as well as the dubbing mixer.)

■ **sound cutter** The person who places the sound track or tracks in proper relation to the picture during editing. Also called the track layer.

■ **sound designer** A person who designs sounds for a motion picture. Such a person records natural sounds or specially created sounds and then lays the tracks to create a mix that evokes specific effects and moods. *See* **sound.**

■ **sound displacement** The difference between the places on a film for the image and corresponding sound. *See* **sound advance.**

■ **sound dissolve, cross-fade** A brief overlapping of two sounds, originally from two separate tracks, with one fading out while the other fades in. The technique is frequently used to anticipate the change to a new scene: a close-up of a character might be accompanied by the present sound giving way to dialogue that is part of the next scene.

■ **sound editor** (1) The individual who works under a supervising sound editor, assisting that person while, perhaps, being in charge of editing the sound for a specific portion of the film. (2) The supervising sound editor for a smaller production. (3) The sound-effects or music editor. *See* **mixer.**

■ **sound effects (SFX, SD EFX, SE)** All the sound in a film other than dialogue, voice-over, and music; this sound is normally added at a time after shooting. Sound effects are frequently combined into a separate E (effects) track, which is then combined with the M (music) and D (dialogue) tracks. Normal environmental sound is difficult to control and unreal when recorded. Sound effects can create what seems to be the accurate sound of a place in such a manner that such noises also contribute to the dramatic impact of a scene. Synchronic sounds of characters' actions can also be integrated into the scene with accuracy and impact. Sound-effects libraries, which may be independent or part of a studio, have a large number of tapes, discs, and optical tracks that include a vast variety of noises, from the rifle shots, exploding shells, and screams of battle to the rustling trees, blowing wind, and thundering storms of the great outdoors. While some noises are recorded specifically for a motion picture, some studios have elaborate sound-effects consoles that store a great many sounds that can be directly added to the effects track. Computerized sound effects and sound-editing systems are now being employed, the most advanced with digital computerized sound. Such systems allow easy and creative manipulation of programmed sounds and countless rerecordings without any loss of quality. Electronic instruments, especially the synthesizer, have recently opened up a new area of sound effects for the motion picture. The personnel responsible for sound effects, especially those of body movements, are called Foley artists, Foley walkers, or Foley mixers after Jack Foley, the man responsible for establishing the modern system of creating such sound effects for film. The sound editor or sound-effects editor is the individual responsible for putting these sounds together and synchronizing them. *See* **sound.**

■ **sound-effects editor** An individual who works primarily on assembling and synchronizing special effects and sometimes the music track (the editor of the film works with the dialogue and voice-over while a music editor generally edits the score).

■ **sound-effects library** A catalogued collection of discs, tapes, and optical tracks with a wide variety of recorded sounds, both natural and artificial, for sound effects in motion pictures. Such a library may be part of a studio or an independent enterprise.

■ **sound engineer** (1) A specialized technician who works with the sound tracks and helps create the final mix. *See* **mix.** (2) The individual operating the sound control board during a shoot. *See* **mixer** *(2).*

■ **sound film** Any motion picture with synchronized sound, whether optical, magnetic, or digital. Some very early sound films used a sound-on-disc system. *See* **sound.**

■ **sound head** (1) That part of the projector that initiates the sound signal either from optical, magnetic, or digital tracks on the film. Variable-area or variable density optical tracks are read by a photoelectric cell when the film passes a lamp, while magnetic tracks are read by a magnetic head. A digital sound head or reader is sometimes attached to the top of the projector system. *See* **sound.** (2) The magnetic heads used for sound recording, replaying, and erasing in magnetic tape recorders. All three functions are performed by separate heads in professional machines, while one head performs the first two operations and a second the erasing in domestic versions of the machine. *See* **magnetic recording.**

■ **sound log, sound report** (1) A form on which the recordist lists the various takes for each shot and makes some comment on the general quality of the recording for each take. Sync and wild recordings are distinguished, and identifying elements for wild recordings might be specified. This document, along with the camera log or report, is used in synchronizing rushes. (2) A form filled out by the editor for the sound mixer which details the various tracks and marks footage and cues for mixing. *See* **mix.**

■ **sound loop** A piece of sound-track film or magnetic tape that is attached at both ends to form a loop so that it can be repeatedly played to add continuous sound effects (e.g., the dashing of waves against the shore) to the sound mix.

■ **sound mixer, mixer** (1) The individual responsible for the final mixing of all the sound tracks into the composite track. This person is also sometimes called the sound editor, rerecording mixer, or dubbing mixer. *See* **mix** *and* **mixer.** (2) The individual in charge of recording sound during the actual shooting of a film. This person is also called the production mixer, production sound mixer, or floor mixer. *See* **sound crew.** (3) The person in charge of recording music for the film. This individual is also called the music mixer. (4) Equipment used to mix sound from various sources during recording or rerecording: in the first instance, the portable mixing panel that combines the sound from several microphones during actual shooting; in the second instance, any type of sound-mixing equipment, including a mixing console, that brings together the various sound tracks. *See* **mix** *and* **mixer.**

■ **sound monitor** *See* **monitor speaker.**

■ **sound negative** An optical negative made from the master sound track in a special camera. This negative and the final edited picture negative together make the married print.

■ **sound-on-film (SOF)** (1) A term referring to a camera that records sound on the film at the same time as photographing the image. The term was generally used for a variety of lightweight and mobile 16mm cameras that were first developed for recording news events for television, but later largely replaced in such work by video cameras. A number of these cameras could record sound optically, although recording on a prestriped magnetic track was the preferred method. The Cinema Products CP-16A and Mitchell SS-R16 were examples of such single-system cameras. *See* **single-system sound camera.** (2) A term referring to film that photographs the image at the same time as it records the sound, either optically or magnetically. *See* **single-system sound camera.** (3) A term referring to picture film with a sound track. (4) A term referring to the process of putting sound tracks, whether optical, magnetic, or digital, on film.

■ **sound overlap** *See* **overlapping sound.**

■ **sound perspective, aural perspective** The sense of appropriate distance between the sound heard by the audience and its origin in the image: a sound must seem to come from its source in the depth of the scene.

■ **sound presence** *See* **presence.**

■ **sound reader** *See* **reader** *(2).*

■ **sound recorder** *See* **recorder.**

■ **sound recording** (1) The act of copying sound on film, tape, or disc. (2) The record itself on which sound is copied.

■ **sound recording studio** *See* **recording studio.**

■ **sound recordist** A term sometimes used to describe the individual in charge of sound during shooting; also called the sound mixer and floor mixer. *See* **sound crew.**

■ **sound release negative** The negative of the final mix of the sound track from which the sound track is printed onto the release print.

■ **sound report** *See* **sound log.**

■ **sound roll number** The number given to each roll of magnetic tape or film on which sound has been recorded. The numbers allow the rolls to be matched to the appropriate takes during editing.

■ **sound separation** The distinct audibility of specific sounds in a mix from other sounds. This quality is extremely important so that dialogue can be clearly heard and is not confused with environmental noises or background music. Some directors, however, try at times to achieve a more natural effect by having the audience strain to hear the characters' words amid all the sound in the mix.

■ **sound speed** The standard rate of speed at which film passes through the camera and projector so that sound may be clearly and audibly played back from a track on the film. The standard speed for silent film was generally 16 frames per second, though films were shot and certainly projected at greater speeds. The addition of a sound track to film necessitated that the speed be standardized at 24 frames per second, which allowed sufficient speed for audible sound. *See* **film running speed.**

■ **sound stage** A special studio for shooting a film and recording sound. The studio is both soundproof and acoustically engineered so that maximum results can be achieved when recording dialogue.

■ **sound stock** Film used primarily for sound tracks.

■ **sound stripe** *See* **stripe.**

■ **sound take** Any shot photographed while sound is being recorded synchronically.

■ **sound tape** Magnetic tape, normally a quarter-inch wide, that is made of plastic and covered with a coating of iron oxide for recording sound. Also referred to as audio tape. *See* **magnetic recording.**

■ **sound track, track** (1) The narrow band on film that is located by the side of the image and on which the sound is recorded. Release prints can use variable-density or variable-area optical tracks that are read and converted to sound when the track passes between a lamp and a photoelectric cell in the projector, although variable-area tracks are now preferred because they are easier to print in color processes. The optical track on 35mm film is located within the perforations on the side of the image which appears on the left part of the screen. Some prints released in foreign countries have two tracks, one for music and sound effects and one for dialogue dubbed in the native tongue. Sometimes a magnetic track of iron oxide is used for recording sound. On 70mm film six magnetic tracks are employed for stereophonic sound, two in each of the wide bands on the outsides of the perforations and one in each of the narrower bands on the insides. For stereophonic sound 35mm film with smaller perforations than normal at one time held four magnetic tracks, two on the outsides of the perforations and two on the insides, and 35mm film with standard perforations sometimes held three magnetic tracks, a central one with a narrower track along each of its edges where the optical track normally appears. The practice today is to use two optical bands with four tracks on 35mm prints for stereophonic sound. A film with four magnetic tracks and an optical track in its regular position was called a magoptical print or mag-opt print. Films now also feature digital sound tracks: the Dolby SR-D system places the digital code between the perforations; Digital Theater System (DTS) places it on a disc; and Sony Dynamic Digital Sound (SDDS) prints the code on a channel on the outside of the film and a back-up channel on the other edge. While the first two systems use six tracks, three for the screen, two for the surround sound on both sides of the theater, and one for the subwoofer, the SDDS system makes available an additional two tracks for sound from the screen. (2) Any film used primarily to carry a sound track, whether optical, magnetic, or digital. Magnetic tape is still most often used for recording, but the sound is transferred to a magnetic stripe on film for editing. The final mix is converted into a single optical track on a film from which it is transferred along with the picture to a composite print unless stereophonic sound is required when two channels are used for four tracks. Recording on digital tape during production is growing in popularity, with the sound transferred to a computerized system for mixing, ultimately finding its way optically coded on the composite print (in one system, however, the digital sound tracks are played from a disc). *See* **digital sound, magnetic recording,** *and* **optical sound.**

■ **sound track applicator, sound track solution applicator** A rotating wheel that reapplies developer to the sound track of a colored positive, after bleaching but before fixing, so that the top layer is silver for producing optimum sound. *See* **processing.**

■ **sound transfer, stripe transfer, transfer** (1) The process of rerecording sound from one type of recording material to another. (2) The rerecording of sound from magnetic tape onto film with a magnetic track for purposes of editing.

■ **sound truck** A mobile van that contains the equipment necessary for recording sound during shooting, including a separate power system and sometimes an area for changing film.

■ **sound workprint** A sound track on film, whether containing dialogue, music, or special effects, which is used for editing.

■ **soup** Jargon for the chemical solutions used in developing film.

■ **source lighting** Any illumination in a scene that seems to come from some source in the set—for example, from a table lamp or from the sun.

■ **source music** Music in a film for which the source is visible on the screen—for example, the sounds of a symphony when we see the orchestra performing. Also called direct music and foreground music. *See* **background music** *and* **indigenous sound.**

■ **south** In animation work, the bottom of the drawing, drawing table, animation stand, or cel as opposed to their top, which is referred to as north.

■ **space** While painting and architecture are basically spatial art forms, since they exist all at once in space and are unchanging from moment to moment, and music is basically temporal, since it is dependent on sequentiality and change in time, film, because it creates a series of spatial though changing pictures, is dependent on both dimensions. Rudolf Arnheim, in *Film as Art*, has argued that because film works without depth and because sizes and shapes are distorted in proportions and perspective, "the spectator's attention is drawn to the two-dimensional pattern of lines and shadow masses." He further points out that since the three dimensions of bodies are projected onto a plane, they all become "elements of the surface composition." The film image, then, attracts our attention to its formal compositional elements more than does the world we see outside us, although we see the image as a representation of three-dimensional reality at the same time.

The arrangement of lines, masses, sizes, shapes, and spatial relationships, while creating aesthetically satisfying pictures as well as an image of reality for us, also reinforces dramatic situations, psychological states, and thematic concepts. Characters' spatial relationships with each other and with their environment contribute to our understanding of and responses to what is taking place. The amount of space characters take up, their area of the screen, their relative size and location in relation to other people and to objects must all be worked out in advance by the director. Since space is never static in the continuum of changing images, new camera positions and angles are employed to create not only a variety of dynamic perspectives but also to communicate information through changing spatial relationships from one shot to another. When the camera cuts from one scene to another, spatial relationships become important, either creating a smooth transition or a jump cut that jolts the viewer, either emphasizing relationships or contrasts between the scenes. The image's representation of spatial reality creates for us not only an impression of the real world, but also a sense of involvement, as if we ourselves were moving through the interior of the scene. This sense of realistic space and depth is created within the flat, two-dimensional image by composing the scene in such a way that various distances are separated and emphasized: camera angles and the distances of each shot are varied while both the camera and performers move within each location so that the viewer also seems to move within the space of the scene.

The term "filmic space" is sometime used to refer to the unique and separate space that film creates as distinguished from the real space that surrounds us. Filmic space is unique because of its two-dimensionality and visible discontinuity from surrounding space; it is also unique because of its malleability, a product of the cutting and editing that allow us to see the same action in the same location from a series of different perspectives, and because of its newness and originality, the fact that the space we see is created only by the technology of film (e.g., when two shots photographed in separate places are edited together so that their spatial locations seem the same, or when close-ups of miniatures create on the screen objects or figures that seem large and imposing). *See* **depth, filmic space,** *and* **time.**

■ **space blanket** A lightweight reflective sheet, often made of plastic, that is taped to a wall to soften the light which bounces off it.

■ **spacecam** *See* **gyro-stabilized camera system.**

■ **space opera** A humorous term for a science-fiction film, suggested, undoubtedly, by the term "soap opera," and so called because of such films' unreality, exaggeration, and melodrama.

■ **spacer** (1) Blank leader or scrap film used to fill in spaces on sound film during editing. (2) A hub located between the reels of a rewind to keep them properly aligned for feeding film into and taking it up from the synchronizer.

■ **spacing** *See* **slug.**

■ **spaghetti Western** A Western produced primarily in Italy, though sometimes also filmed in Yugoslavia or Spain, and often starring American performers. This type of film received great impetus from the works directed by Sergio Leone, especially his films starring Clint Eastwood as the "Man with No Name" in the 1960s, beginning with *For a Fistful of Dollars* in 1964, a reworking of Kurosawa's *Yojimbo* (1961). Leone's Westerns reached a high point with the flamboyant, though impressive, *Once Upon a Time in the West* (1967).

■ **spark** Jargon for an electrician.

■ **spec** An abbreviation and jargon for "on speculation," which means that a director or performer, for example, is working on a film for later payment, which may be a percentage of the film's profits.

■ **special effects (SP-EFX)** (1) Any image or element within an image achieved by unusual technical means. This general definition includes both effects achieved through special photographic techniques or processes and those specially created before the camera when it is shooting normally. Both types of special effects are employed when the desired result is too expensive or unsafe, or is simply impossible to achieve by normal means. The first category is sometimes also referred to as "visual" or "photographic" effects. Although "optical effects" more accurately refers to pictorial elements achieved through an optical printer, and "process cinematography" to effects created through specially designed process cameras, these terms also are sometimes used for this category of special effects. Such visual effects were informally referred to as "trick photography" throughout the silent era. The second category is also called "mechanical effects" and refers to various kinds of phenomena that are created mechanically on the set before the camera. This group would include the creation of natural phenomena such as rain, snow, and fog, and the production of fire and explosions of any sort or size. Life-size models, such as the twenty-five-foot-long shark in Steven Spielberg's *Jaws* (1975), and elaborate makeup effects are often included in this second category. Another type of special effects sometimes designated as mechanical is when a centrifuge or wires are used to give the impression of weightlessness. Sometimes both visual and mechanical effects are used together, for example when makeup and stop-motion photography are employed for the many transformations in early werewolf films.

The term "special effects" appears to have been employed first by Fox Film Corporation as a credit for mechanical effects in Raoul Walsh's *What Price Glory* (1926); the first film to win an Academy Award for "special effects" was *The Rains Came* (1939; dir. Clarence Brown), which featured an impressive monsoon, largely created before the camera. Such mechanical effects have recently been the subject of Robert Mandel's suspense and adventure film, *F/X* (1986). *See* **FX, mechanical effects, optical effects,** *and* **process photography.**

(2) The term "special effects" is now often used with specific application to effects achieved through photographic processes, partly because recent books on these techniques have limited the term to this context (note especially the seminal book by Raymond Fielding, *The Technique of Special Effects Cinematography*) and partly because the term has been so popularized in relation to the extraordinary developments with these various processes in recent fantasy films. An extended variation of this term, "special photographic effects" is frequently found in film credits for this type of visual achievement. Such special effects are almost as old as cinematography itself.

The first such effect in cinema is thought to have taken place in a brief film made at the Edison studio in West Orange, New Jersey, by Alfred Clark in 1895 for the Kinetoscope peephole machine. In this film, *The Execution of Mary, Queen of Scots,* the queen seems actually to be decapitated—the image was created by stopping the camera and replacing the actress with a dummy whose head was sliced off in the next shot. Also significant are some of the films made in England by G. A. Smith of Brighton, who used double exposures for creating visions and ghosts in such films as *The Corsican Brothers* (1897) and *Photographing a Ghost* (1898); and Robert W. Paul, who explored a number of techniques that were later to become central to special-effects cinematography—for example, the miniature shot, double exposure, and composite printing—in such films as *The Magic Sword* (1902) and *The Motorist* (1906). But the accolades generally go to the Frenchman Georges Méliès for being the founder of special-effects cinematography. Although he may have been predated in some of his effects by Smith and Paul, a far larger number of his films survive (approximately ninety) and his reputation has been far greater. In a movie career that lasted from 1896 until 1912, Méliès produced some 500 short films, the most notable being his fantasy films, especially *A Trip to the Moon* (1902) and *The Conquest of the Pole* (1911). Méliès photographed a number of his trick films at the Théâtre Robert-Houdin, utilizing the stage trickery of the magician Houdini, but he also achieved a number of effects only possible through such photographic techniques as stop-motion cinematography, animation, miniature cinematography, multiple exposure, matting, and the dissolve. In the United States, Edwin S. Porter used miniatures, stop-motion cinematography, and mattes to fine effect in some of his films. Notable are the scenes in *The Great Train Robbery* (1903) when a passing train is seen through the window of the telegraph office and the passing landscape through the open door of a baggage car, both effects achieved through double exposure with an in-the-camera matte.

Throughout the silent-film period, such basic visual effects as slow or fast motion; fades, dissolves, or superimposures; and distorted or altered images were achieved through direct use of the camera. Norman A. Dawn, who brought to cinematography his expertise from still photography, helped develop both the glass and matte shots in American films during the early part of the century—in the glass shot, the camera photographs through glass from which painted elements are added to the actual scene, and in the matte shot, an actual set and a painted scene are combined by reexposing the same film twice with mattes blocking out appropriate areas on the negative. Bipack cameras were developed that allowed composite printing: a blackened section on an illuminated board acted as a matte, preventing a corresponding area on a positive of live-action from being printed on a negative with which it ran emulsion to emulsion past the aperture of the camera; when another matte was placed in front of the camera with artwork in the previously blackened area and an area now blackened corresponding to that part of the live action printed on the negative, the artwork would be printed into the unexposed area of the rewound negative, running by itself through the camera. Shooting past a hanging miniature could have the same effect as a glass shot by adding the hanging component to an actual set.

Also significant in the silent-film period were the animation techniques that enlarged and gave life to small models (e.g., Willis O'Brien's work in *The Lost World* [1925]). It was during this period that traveling-matte processes were also developed: unlike procedures using a single matte to block out a stationary area of an image in order to fit in the new picture element, traveling mattes, so called because the matte changed from frame to frame, allowed moving subjects to be combined with separately photographed backgrounds. Frank Williams patented such a system in 1918: in this "black-backing system," silhouetted mattes were made from performers photographed in front of a black or white screen, which could then be used to block out the appropriate area of a scene on a film as it was exposed to a fresh negative in a bipack camera. The live action could then be fitted into the unexposed area of the negative from its separate film. Such "Williams Shots" were used with great effect in the 1926 production of *Ben-Hur* (dir. Fred Niblo). The German film industry during the silent period achieved a high degree of sophistication in special effects, especially in both parts of Fritz Lang's *Die Nibelungen* (1924) and in his *Metropolis* (1927)—animation, miniatures, glass shots, and stationary and traveling mattes were among the techniques used. Eugen Schüfftan developed the "Schüfftan process," which shot live-action through the clear portion of a mirror placed at a 45-degree angle in front of the camera and combined it on the negative with the image of a miniature setting, which was reflected off the silvered part of the mirror into the camera; or the process combined live action reflected off the silvered part with a miniature or painting shot through the glass—this type of "mirror shot" achieved some convincing and powerful effects in Lang's *Metropolis*.

The advent of sound made new demands on special-effects departments since films now had to be photographed largely in the studios where dialogue could be properly recorded, necessitating that external settings be added to the action through photographic trickery. A popular traveling matte system during this period was the Dunning-Pomeroy process. An orange-dyed positive of a setting and a fresh negative were run through a bipack camera while actors lit by an orange light performed in front of a blank screen, which was lit by a blue light. The orange light reflected from the actors passed through the positive and allowed them to be registered on the negative while the blue light from the area on the screen surrounding them provided light to print the comparable area from the setting on the positive around their image on the negative. The rear-projection process allowed a separately photographed background to be projected onto the rear of a translucent screen and combined with live-action photographed before the screen.

The optical printer, which had also been introduced during silent-film days, now became a major piece of equipment for all kinds of special effects. Such a device is basically a projector and camera facing one another with a light behind the positive in the projector sending the image onto a lens which then focuses it onto the negative in the camera. The optical printer became the key tool for creating transitions such as fades, dissolves, and wipes; for combining in the frame elements from separate images in superimposition, split-screen pictures, and composite pictures made through stationary or traveling mattes; for altering action through skip-frame printing, multiple-frame printing, and freeze-framing; and for altering the image by using lenses to elongate, compress, or fragmentize the picture into various patterns. Another method for creating composite images that began to be developed during this period was aerial-image photography, a process in which a film image of live action is projected into space off a mirror and refocused by condenser lenses below the table of an animation stand to be rephotographed with artwork, titles, or models placed on the table.

Willis O'Brien and a host of technicians, using almost every effect available and perfecting many to a point that still has not been surpassed, made Cooper and Schoedsack's *King Kong* (1933) into one of the greatest adventure-fantasies of all time. In the same year, John Fulton was responsible for the remarkable effects in James Whale's *The Invisible Man*. The British film industry also achieved a high degree of excellence with special effects, notably in Alexander Korda's production of *Things to Come* (1936; dir. William Cameron Menzies) and later in his production of *Thief of Bagdad* (1940; dir. Ludwig Berger, Michael Powell, and Tim Whelan), which was completed in Hollywood.

Two important developments that occurred in film during the 1950s and that had a direct impact on special-effects cinematography were wide-screen cinema and tripack color film. The first development allowed a larger picture, which made the assembly of various elements into a composite picture easier to achieve. The better image from larger film stock or from a larger frame area also permitted the joining of image components from films of different generations without an apparent loss of quality in any part of the composite. Such improvement was also evident when the composites were reduced from 70mm to 35mm film for normal distribution. Color film permitted new and better traveling-matte processes, especially the blue-screen process in which actors illuminated in white light against a blue backing are photographed on a color negative from which mattes can be derived by means of color-separated positives. The foreground action of the actors can then be combined with a background shot separately by means of these mattes in an optical printer. The blue-screen process was very popular during the 1950s and was used in the most impressive effects film of the decade, Cecile B. DeMille's *The Ten Commandments* (1956), for which John Fulton was in charge of special effects. The process later came into favor again because of the development of a synthetic blue color-difference matte, which has removed the problem of photographing any blue in the foreground action against the blue screen. The development of beam-splitting cameras, also during this period, gave rise to several successful traveling-matte processes. In the sodium vapor process, a beam-splitting prism in the camera sends the yellow light surrounding the actors, who are in front of a screen lit by a sodium vapor lamp, to one of the films so that a negative is formed with the background opaque and the characters clear, from which a positive male matte can be struck with the performers opaque and the surrounding area clear. At the same time, the characters, who are lit by normal incandescent lamps, are pho-

special effects *2001: A Space Odyssey* (1968; dir. Stanley Kubrick) revitalized film technology and set the course for future effects films.

■ ■ ■

tographed with their surrounding area clear on a negative insensitive to the yellow light, from which a self-matting positive of the characters can be struck with the background opaque. Actors and a separately photographed background are combined through a series of steps in an optical printer. The sodium vapor process was used with much success by Walt Disney Productions, notably in its production of *Mary Poppins* (1964; dir. Robert Stevenson).

In 1968, Stanley Kubrick's *2001: A Space Odyssey* was released, revitalizing the entire field of special effects, as well as the science-fiction genre, and pointing the way to the future of film as well as the future of the human race. As much visual poetry as drama, the film expertly advanced a number of special effects. Notable are Douglas Trumbull's development of the slit-scan, a streak photography process used to record the "Stargate Corridor" sequence toward the end of the film; and front projection, which was significantly improved and popularized by the film. Using a highly reflective material developed by the 3M corporation for a screen ninety feet long and forty feet high, the front-projection system sends directly back to the camera a far clearer background image than that achieved with rear projection—the technique is employed with great success in the opening "Dawn-of-Man" sequence.

The next important step in special-effects films was the development of motion control by Douglas Trumbull for *The Andromeda Strain* (1970; dir. Robert Wise), a system later advanced by John Dykstra with his creation of the "Dykstraflex" for George Lucas's *Star Wars* (1977). Motion-control systems are electronically programmed to control with absolute precision the motion of the camera as well as models for repeated exposures in various types of effect shots. Related to motion control was Stuart Ziff's development of go-control for *Dragonslayer* (1981), a system electronically programmed to control precisely the motion of both camera and models during stop-motion cinematography so that a blur is created and the model's movements look more natural than the strobic effect of a figure's motion in earlier animation films. This technique was employed with great success in Lucas's *Return of the Jedi* (1983; dir. Richard Marquand). Mention should also be made of Steven Spielberg's *Close Encounters of the Third Kind* (1977) which achieved some stunning results with models, front projection, motion control, and matting. Animatronics and the art of cinematic puppetry in general has advanced considerably because of these new computerized processes.

The latest and most rapid development in the field of special effects, however, is computer graphics and animation, first used with impressive results in the Disney production of *Tron* (1982; dir. Steven Lisberger), *Star Trek* (1982; dir. Nicholas Meyer), and especially in *The Last Starfighter* (1984; dir. Nick Castle). Advances in this area, in recent years, have been remarkable: especially notable are the six and one-half minutes of prehistoric creatures created digitally for Steven

Spielberg's *Jurassic Park* (1993) and John Lasseter's totally digitized children's film, *Toy Story* (1995). Morphing, used so impressively in *Terminator 2* (1991; dir. James Cameron), has added new flexibility and mutability to the fantastic forms and shapes of the film image, while *Who Framed Roger Rabbit* (1988; dir. Robert Zemeckis) has taken the integration of cartoon and live characters, of the totally created and the totally real worlds, to a new level of credibility. Woody Allen's *Zelig* (1983) integrated the lead character into the newsreel world of the past, into a world of real people now dead and gone; this technique of breaking down the separation of past and present, of overcoming time through the magic of the computer, was used with even more visual credibility and impressiveness in Robert Zemeckis's *Forrest Gump* (1994). At this time, there seem no boundaries to the physical world of space and time that the computer cannot overcome for the film image. We are rushing toward the era when the computer will be able to generate film images that seem as realistic—if not more real—as the world in which we live. The computer will be able to create not only new images and worlds, but also to resurrect dead worlds and even actors to give them new life on the motion-picture screen.

Special-effects cinematography, in general, has advanced further than any other branch of film during the past two decades. Such advance has been a visual delight, bringing sights never before seen in the history of the human race to the modern spectator, expanding both our visual sense and our imagination. The question that arises is "To what end?" Film after film has arrived in recent years with special effects that dazzle our eyes but do not increase our understanding. The human dramas that once engaged our minds and our sensibilities now seem occasional and special. An exception such as *2001* seems to suggest how special effects can be used to create works of great beauty and power, but what has come our way have been comic-book fantasies that appeal to the child and not the adult within us. The potential effect of special effects still remains before us.

See the entries under the names of the various processes and equipment mentioned above for fuller descriptions.

■ **special-effects coordinator, special-effects supervisor** The individual in charge of the special-effects department and responsible for all the special effects created for an individual film—for their planning, performance, and readiness to be integrated into the final film. This person is responsible for both the special effects created in-house and those commissioned out to independent special-effects companies. Also referred to as visual effects coordinator or supervisor and sometimes special effects or visual effects producer. *See* **special effects.**

■ **special-effects department** The personnel of a studio involved in the creation of special effects, both mechanical and photographic. Throughout much of the silent-film period such effects were the responsibility of various members of the film crew, but eventually special-effects departments began to take shape, though not necessarily concerning themselves with all aspects of the field. With the advent of sound, special-effects departments grew in importance and responsibility when they were called upon to bring, through photographic trickery, external locations to the main action, which had to be filmed inside the studio so that dialogue could be properly recorded; with the collapse of the studio system in the 1950s, most of these departments were closed down. Although special-effects units are still put together for individual features, independent groups of special-effects specialists began to proliferate, especially in the 1970s, the most important of which were George Lucas's Industrial Light and Magic (ILM) and John Dykstra's Apogee companies. *See* **special effects.**

■ **special-effects makeup artist** Because of the extraordinary developments in cinematic makeup in the past few decades, especially the use of prosthetics and mechanical means to create new faces and shapes, this type of technician has developed to assist the makeup artists and take the appearance of characters and monsters into a new realm of visual fantasy. Rob Bottin is certainly the individual who launched this kind of specialization, especially with his work for John Carpenter's *The Thing* (1982). *See* **makeup.**

■ **specialized distribution** The release of a film in only select theaters in select markets for a limited and specialized audience. The advertising for such films is both limited and directed toward a specific audience. Such films might be considered specialized because of their subject matter, ethnic orientation, or intellectual depth. *See* **distribution.**

■ **specialized lights** Any light with a specific function that adds to the general lighting of the set—e.g., an eye light or rim light.

■ **special venue** A type of filmic exhibition at a location that features a large format and creates an immersive motion-picture experience. Such presentations normally play at theme parks, museums, expositions, and entertainment centers. Such works are brief sojourns into natural terrains and faraway places that make viewers feel as if they are totally immersed in and traveling through the replicated world that seems to surround them. Such effects are achieved by shooting with such wide-gauge film as 65mm, projecting on a wraparound or curved screen, and using digital sound. Notable examples are Doug Trumbull's *Back to the Future—the Ride* at Universal Studio's theme parks in Hollywood and Florida, which was shot with his Showscan system and any of the Imax 3-D films shown at the Sony Theater Lincoln Center cineplex in New York City and other such theaters. *See* **IMAX, leisure-based entertainment,** *and* **Showscan.**

■ **special visual effects** *See* **special effects.**

■ **spec script** A screenplay written by a writer, on speculation, without any prior contract or agreement for production as opposed to a script "written for hire." The writer or writer's agent must seek to sell a spec script.

■ **spectacle, spectacle film, spectacular, spex** A feature film made with great expense and offering an opulent visual display of colorful scenery, crowds of performers, and exciting action. Cecil B. DeMille made a number of these films, including his two versions of *The Ten Commandments* (1923 and 1956). Although such films frequently emphasize the glamour or exoticness of past times and the excitement of historical events, sometimes a sufficient amount of spectacle is achieved in contemporary settings, as evidenced by DeMille's circus film, *The Greatest Show on Earth,* which won an Academy Award as best picture of the year for 1952. *See* **epic.**

■ **spectral response** The capacity of a film's emulsion to register the various wavelengths (i.e., colors) of light.

■ **spectrum** The band of color produced when light passes through a prism, which contains red, orange, yellow, green, blue, indigo, and violet, and which also contains at the extremities the effects of radiant energy not visible but capable of registering on film—that is, infrared wavelengths beyond the red area and ultraviolet wavelengths beyond the violet.

■ **specular, specular reflection** (1) Normal reflection as distinct from diffuse. (2) Sometimes used to describe reflected light from a performer's eyes or teeth.

■ **specular density** The density of a film image measured without regard to diffuse light transmitted by the emulsion. A reading of either specular or diffuse density may be achieved with a densitometer for assuring proper printing, though the second type of reading is more common. *See* **densitometry.**

■ **speculation film, spec film** A film made "on speculation"—that is, without any financial support from an outside source. Costs and profits must be obtained from future distribution, sales, or rentals. *See* **on speculation.**

■ **speech breakdown** The precise relationship of each syllable of dialogue to the appropriate frame in animation work.

■ **speech chart** A form used by the animator which gives the speech breakdown.

■ **speed** (1) The relative sensitivity of film emulsion to light, designated in this country by the ASA rating (the higher the number, the faster the film). See **exposure index.** (2) The maximum capacity of a lens's diaphragm to allow light into the camera, generally designated as the maximum f-stop number. See **lens speed.** (3) The rate at which the frames of film pass through the camera, at 16 or more frames per second for silent film or 24 for sound. Cameras also have the capacity for slower or faster speeds for accelerated or slow motion respectively. See **camera speed.** (4) The rate at which the frames of film pass through the projector for normal projection, at 16 or more frames per second for silent film or 24 frames for sound. (5) The word spoken by the sound recordist to let the director know that the tape recorder is working at the same speed as the camera, generally spoken after the director's order to cameraman and recordist to "Roll 'em" and right before he or she says "Action."

■ **speed crank, L-handle** An attachment to the knob of the follow-focus control on a camera that allows easy rotational movement especially during a long follow-focus shot. The crank is in the shape of an "L" and is normally operated by the assistant camera operator or focus puller. See **follow focus, follow focus control,** and **whip.**

■ **speed lines** Lines drawn behind figures in animation to indicate their rapid motion.

■ **SPFRE** The letters stand for "same percentage as film rental earned" and refer to a contractual agreement made between an exhibitor and distributor by which the former shares in the expense of advertising a film at the same percentage used to compute the money retained by the exhibitor after the film rental has been paid to the distributor.

■ **spherical aberration, spherical distortion** A fault in a spherical lens caused by its spherical shape, which allows light rays from a point to pass through its extremities and focus closer to the lens than the light rays from a point passing through its center. The result is an image somewhat out of focus with square shapes rounded. This type of fault can be avoided by joining two or more spherical lenses with different capacities of refraction to correct one another, or by using a non-spherical lens or floating element with the spherical lens.

■ **spherical optics** The term in cinematography refers to spherical lenses with curved surfaces used for both cameras and lighting as distinct from anamorphic lenses, for example, with cylindrical shapes. See **anamorphic lens.**

■ **spider** A device with three arms that when extended act as supports for the legs of a tripod to prevent them from moving or scratching the floor. Such a device with wheels is referred to as a rolling spider or wheeled tie. The spider is also called a spreader, triangle, or tee.

■ **spider box, distribution box, junction box, plugging box, tie-in box, octopus box** A small receptacle with several outlets into which electrical lights or equipment can easily be plugged on sets or on location.

■ **spill light, spill** (1) Undesirable illumination that scatters outside the beam of light from a lamp. (2) Undesirable illumination on a set in general.

■ **spin** A rotating image, such as a whirling newspaper that suddenly stops to show the audience a headline, created by a spinning attachment in an optical printer. Also referred to as rotary movement.

■ **spindle** The rotating shaft in a film rewind mechanism.

■ **spinning-disc rain deflector, spinning-disc water deflector** See **rain deflector.**

■ **spin-off** A film project that results from the success of another film.

■ **spin transition** A transition from one shot to another in which the first suddenly rotates rapidly on the screen until it blurs, and the second emerges, rotating from the blur.

■ **splash box** See **water box.**

■ **splatter film** A film with a good deal of violence and a large amount of blood (e.g., *Theatre of Blood* [1973; dir. Douglas Hickox]). See **slice-and-dice film** and **stalker film.**

■ **splice** (1) Joining together the ends of two pieces of film so that they form one continuous strip. (2) The point at which the separate ends of two pieces of film have been joined together to form one continuous strip. There are two basic ways of joining together the pieces of film, either by scraping the emulsion from the end of one piece and cementing the two overlapping strips together (an overlap-cement or lap splice) or by placing the two pieces end to end so that they abut one another and attaching them by a piece of transparent tape (the butt splice). Since a cement splice is permanent and can only be cut away and since the taping method is easier to do, butt splices are normally employed for workprints. But since the butt splice is less strong and causes optical blurring, lap splices are employed in most other situations for professional cinematography. Since there is no space between frames on 16mm film and since cement splices will thus show briefly during projection, checkerboard cutting for A and B printing is often employed especially for professional work. For both 35 and 16mm film, a hot splicer, which dries the cement and strengthens the joint, might be employed. For amateur cinematography with smaller-gauge film, the butt splice is often used because it is easier to make and because it is far less visible than the lap splice. Butt splices, with tape only on one side and a diagonal cut, are employed for joining two strips of magnetic film since a cement splice causes a drop in sound. A less common type of joint is the butt-weld splice, which attaches the two ends of film by means of heat and pressure. Polyester bases cannot be joined by cement and must be spliced either with tape or by an ultrasonic splicer which welds the pieces together. *See* **A and B printing** *and* **checkerboard cutting.**

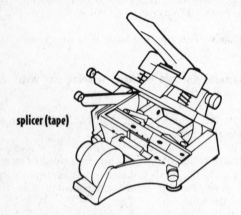

splicer (tape)

■ **splicer, film splicer, splicing machine** A small device for joining the ends of two pieces of film together to form a single strip. Two such devices in common use are the cement splicer, which attaches overlap splices with cement, and the tape splicer, which attaches two abutting ends of film with transparent tape so that they form a butt splice. Professional cement splicers are durably built and offer ease and precision in use. Film ends are carefully registered by means of pins in their perforations, and their edges are exactly aligned. The clamps that hold the films may be operated by hand, foot pedals, or knobs, depending on the degree of sophistication of the machine, while both the scraper and cement applicator may also be automatically operated. Such a machine is often a "hot splicer" with an electrical heating element for faster drying of the cement and a stronger bond. Since this type of splice is durable and permanent, it is mostly used for preparing negatives for printing or used for permanent prints. There are two standard tape splicers: the Rivas, popular in the film industry in this country, that requires one movement of the film and uses a strong perforated tape (the Hollywood film splicer is similar); and the guillotine, which uses a thinner tape that the machine itself must perforate. The guillotine splicer requires two movements of the film, one for cutting and the other for splicing; the machine also tends to be less durable and

leaves a residue from the film's perforations. Splicers that cut straight along the frame line are used to join two pieces of film with picture or picture and track, while slash-cut or diagonal splicers are used for sound tracks alone. The relatively new polyester bases, such as Estar, cannot be joined by cement but must be welded together by an ultrasonic splicer or spliced together by tape.

■ **splicing block** A simple device for splicing together two pieces of film with tape. A channel and registering pins hold the two pieces, while a vertical groove guides the razor when cutting picture film and a diagonal groove guides it for cutting magnetic sound film.

■ **splicing tape** *See* **tape** *(2) and* **Mylar splice.**

■ **spline-based modeling** In computer animation or graphics, creating three-dimensional primitives or models by using a series of spline curves. This type of modeling is especially effective for creating round or curved objects with smooth lines and permits a good deal of easy manipulation of shape and form. *See* **computer animation** *and* **polygonal-based modeling.**

■ **split bill** A double feature. *See* **double feature.**

■ **split-field lens, split-focus lens, split diopter lens, split-field diopter lens** A lens that can be positioned to cover the principal lens on the camera so that two different planes are in focus. Frequently, half of the split-field lens is a close-up diopter and the other half is clear glass; sometimes only half a lens is used. Such lenses are employed when the depth of field of a single lens cannot keep in focus a plane of action near the camera and one in the distance. *See* **diopter lens.**

■ **split focus** Focusing the lens between two widely separated planes of action so that both receive equally sharp definition.

■ **split-focus rangefinder, split-image rangefinder** *See* **rangefinder.**

■ **split-focus shot** A shot in which the area of sharp definition is changed from one plane to another.

■ **split reel** (1) A special type of reel, generally employed in editing, that can be separated into two parts so that film on a core can be inserted or removed without winding or unwinding. (2) A term used in silent-film days for a short motion picture taking up less than a full reel.

■ **split screen, split-screen shot, split-screen effect, split frame** A visual composition in which the frame is divided into two separate images not superimposed over one another. The term is also commonly employed to describe frames divided into more than two components, but "multi-image" or "multiple-image" are more accurate designations for such frames. Split-screen effects are achieved by matting part of the negative when it is exposed to an image in an optical printer and then photographing into the matted side another image while the previously exposed portion is protected by a matte. This technique is often employed to show two people engaged in a phone conversation (e.g., in *Pillow Talk* [1959; dir. Michael Gordon]). *See* **multi-image.**

■ **splitting tracks** Dividing the sound track into individual tracks for mixing. The dialogue track, for example, might be split to allow the mixer to equalize the sound for the various shots. Dividing the dialogue into A and B tracks with filler between the sound on each allows for proper cueing or segueing from the sound in one scene to that in another.

■ **spoking** The irregular and wavy appearance of the sides of loosely wound film when the film is already distorted by curling. *See* **curling.**

■ **spool** A plastic or metal cylindrical device on which film is wound with flanges on the sides of the spool protecting the edges of the film. Daylight loading spools for cameras have closed flanges to protect the film from light, allowing it to be put into the camera during daylight. Such spools generally come with one hundred or two hundred feet of film. Spools with open flanges are also called "reels" and are normally employed for projection. *See* **reel.**

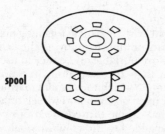

spool

■ **spool box** Enclosures on a professional projector, one from which film is fed into the main mechanism and the other into which it passes after projection. First used as a safety device to prevent fire from passing up flammable nitrate stock into the reels of film, these enclosures are still employed to keep dirt from modern, nonflammable stock. *See* **projector.**

■ **sports finder, sports viewfinder** An auxiliary viewfinder attached to a camera for spotting small objects like golf balls or animals when filming sporting events or action at a distance. The finder is looked through with one eye, like a telescope, and can magnify objects approximately six times. The normal viewfinder is still used with the other eye for framing the subject. Also referred to as a monocular finder or sports finder.

■ **spot** (1) *See* **spotlight.** (2) The circle of light cast by a spotlight.

■ **spot coding** Coding a specific area of the film image or sound track. For example, sometimes a piece of the image or sound track might be damaged, so it is necessary to use a new portion and code the new piece as close to the original code or edge numbers as possible.

■ **spot effects** Specific sound effects such as a car screeching or a door slamming, which must be precisely placed (or "spotted") in a sound track or mix.

■ **spotlamp** (1) A bulb for a spotlight. (2) The spotlight itself.

spotlight

■ **spotlight, spot, spotlamp** A luminaire that projects a beam of light capable of being narrowed so that it can precisely focus in a circular pattern on a specific subject or area. Such luminaires are made of a cylindrical housing with a reflector behind the lamp and a lens in front. Focus of the light can be controlled by moving the lamp or, on some fixtures, by adjusting the lens. "Open-faced" spotlights have no lens and produce a wider beam of light. Spots are generally attached to a Y- or U-shaped yoke with a clamp or spud, allowing them to be tilted and fastened to stands or overhead grids. Spotlights vary in size from the 100-watt dinky to the 10,000-watt tener. *See* **floodlight** *and* **lighting.**

■ **spotlighting** Illuminating a particular person or small area in a round circle of light by means of a spot.

■ **spot meter, spot brightness meter, spot exposure meter** An exposure meter with a narrow angle of acceptance for measuring, normally from the camera's position, light reflected from a small area. Such meters are useful for measuring light from subjects that are extremely small or far away. The viewer aims the meter at the area of reflection, looks through the eyepiece, presses a button, and reads the measurement or the suggested lens aperture while also seeing the designated area against the general background. *See* **exposure meter.**

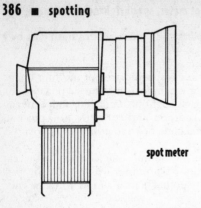

spot meter

■ **spotting** (1) Determining the locations of specific dialogue or sounds on the sound track in relation to the images during editing. (2) Determining where the individual sections of a musical score should go in the motion picture. Such determinations are normally made by the composer and director during a spotting session with the editor and the music editor. The music editor makes "spotting notes" during this session. (3) Marking locations on the dialogue track as designations for titles in a foreign-language release. (4) Stains or blemishes in a developed film image caused by poor processing.

■ **spray deflector** *See* **rain deflector.**

■ **spray processing** A type of processing whereby the film passes through a fine spray of chemicals rather than being emerged in tanks of chemicals.

■ **spread** (1) The width of a beam of light from a luminaire. The usable portion of the spread is considered to lie between the midpoints on each side of center where the illumination is half the intensity of center. (2) To diffuse the beam from a luminaire.

■ **spreader** A device with three extended arms in a T or Y shape, which is attached to the legs of a tripod for support and to keep it from sliding or marring a floor. Also called a tee, triangle, or spider.

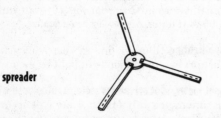

spreader

■ **spring-drive camera** A camera run by means of a spring-drive motor. *See* **spring-drive motor.**

■ **spring-drive motor, spring-driven motor, spring drive, spring motor** A camera motor operated by a spring drive and controlled by a governor, which is wound by hand and achieves speeds from 8 to 64 frames per second and

shots of approximately thirty to forty-five seconds. Such motors were generally found in narrow-gauge, amateur cameras, but can also be found now in Bolex 16mm cameras. *See* **camera motor.**

■ **sprocket, sprocket wheel, sprocket roller** A wheel with regularly positioned teeth that engage the perforations on film to move the film through a camera, projector, or printer.

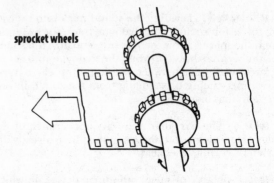

sprocket wheels

■ **sprocket holes** The perforations along the edge or edges of film that are engaged by the teeth of sprocket wheels to move the film through a camera, projector, or printer.

■ **spud** A support for a luminaire, often attached to the Y- or U-shaped yoke around the fixture's housing.

■ **spun** Gauze used as a diffuser in front of a camera to break up the definition of a scene

■ **spyder dolly** A vehicle formerly made by the Elemack company in Italy for moving the camera during shooting. More portable and easier to use on sets and on location than the crab dolly, the unit has a hydraulic column on which the camera may be raised or lowered into a fixed position and wheels attached to projecting legs that can be turned to various positions. A jib arm can be added to the column to allow for movement of the camera during shooting. The company now manufactures the cricket dolly instead, although the spyder is still much in use. *See* **cricket dolly.**

■ **spy film** A type of film emphasizing the espionage activities of foreign agents and their discovery. In part a subgenre of the detective film, the spy film is distinct in this larger group because of its political emphasis and greater reflection of world situations. Spy films in general increase our involvement and anxiety by suggesting threats to our nation's security. Sometimes such films are based on true events and presented in a semi-documentary style—for example, Louis de Rochemont's *The House on 92nd Street* (1945; dir. Henry Hathaway), which uses some of Rochemont's *March of Time* techniques—but spy thrillers are also an excuse for fantasy and entertainment. Hitchcock directed some pleasant romances in this vein, namely *The Thirty-Nine Steps* (1935) and *The Lady Vanishes* (1938), although he could also strike more serious and somber notes amidst romance in works such as *Sabotage* (1936) and *Notorious* (1946).

After the Second World War and the plethora of Nazi-spy films, with Hollywood's heroes fighting the foreign menace on home shores, the villains changed to Communists in such broad propaganda films as *I Was a Communist for the FBI* (1951; dir. Gordon Douglas). The fantasy element in such films erupted into blatant escapism with the very polished but violent and sexual James Bond thrillers, the best of which starred Sean Connery and began with *Dr. No* in 1962 (dir. Terence Young). A number of good spin-offs emerged from this series, some far more subtle and sophisticated than the originals, notably *The Ipcress File* in 1965, starring Michael Caine and directed by Sidney J. Furie. But virtually at the same time a series of films began to appear lacking any glamour and giving evidence of a public frightened by the inhumanity of both sides in the Cold War—the very first of these films, *The Spy Who Came in from the Cold* (1966; dir. Martin Ritt), still remains one of the most impressive. With the end of the Cold War, spy films seem to have become totally escapist entertainment—e.g., *True Lies* (1994; dir. James Cameron).

■ **squash and stretch** The technique of drawing animated figures in cartoons so that their bodies seem to compress as they stop their rapid movement and extend as they begin such a motion. Although certainly a comic device, reminding us of the make-believe nature of these figures and their freedom from physical injury, the technique, when not too exaggerated, seems to give a more natural appearance to their bodies when they stop and start their movement. *See* **animation** *and* **cartoon.**

■ **squawk box** Slang for a speaker in an amplifying system.

■ **squeegee** A wiper blade of plastic or rubber, sometimes attached to a vacuum suction, or a roller of rubber or sponge used to remove liquid from film as it passes through processing. An air squeegee is less prone to scratch the film and is frequently employed when the film moves at fast speeds. *See* **processing.**

■ **squeeze** The term is used to describe the compression or act of compressing an image horizontally onto film through an anamorphic lens on the camera. The picture is unsqueezed when it is projected through an anamorphic lens onto the screen as a wide-screen image. *See* **anamorphic lens.**

■ **squeeze ratio** The horizontal compression of an image on film when photographed through an anamorphic lens. When such a lens produces an image with a 2:1 squeeze ratio, a scene twice as wide as that shot with a normal lens of the same focal length is fitted into the 35mm frame. *See* **anamorphic lens.**

■ **squib** A small, smokeless explosive mounted to a thin metal plate, which is attached to a performer or part of a set and can be detonated by battery, wire, or remote control to suggest the impact of a bullet.

■ **SS** *See* **stock shot.**

■ **stability** (1) The capacity of a camera or projector to record or project respectively a picture without undesirable movement of the image. (2) The capacity of a recorder or player to register or play back sound without undesirable fluctuation in frequency.

■ **stabilization** The stage during the film's processing of making the image permanent and preventing any aftereffects from chemical residues in the emulsion by employing a stabilizer right before drying.

■ **stabilizer** (1) A chemical solution used right before drying in the processing of film to remove chemical residues from the emulsion and make the image permanent. (2) A mount that stabilizes the camera and is especially useful for shooting from a moving carrier, during a handheld shot, and with a long focal-length lens.

■ **stack ads** The organization of the advertisements for a chain of motion-picture houses into lists of showings, one theater above the other, or into a similar arrangement in a newspaper or other publication.

■ **stage** That part of a studio where sets are erected and shooting takes place. Since most modern stages are soundproofed and equipped for recording, they are also referred to as sound stages.

■ **stage brace** A support and stabilizer for scenery which is attached to the floor and the rear of a flat or constructed piece. Such a brace might be a metal pole or piece of wood with flat ends, or a triangular wooden frame.

■ **stagehand** *See* **grip.**

■ **stage plug** An electric connector capable of supporting a greater amount of power than normal plugs for distributing electricity to one or more luminaires.

■ **stag film** A pornographic film intended to appeal to male viewers.

■ **staging** The way a film or part of a film is "staged"—that is, the way in which action and setting are arranged and integrated. The term obviously comes from the theater and suggests the visual impact of performers, action, scenery, costuming, and lighting; it can be used in reference to a shot, scene, sequence, or the general impression of the film as a whole. The term is less formal and less concerned with the compositional and aesthetic qualities of the individual frame than *mise-en-scène*. *See* **mise-en-scène.**

∎ **stalker film, stalk-and-slash film** A film that features a knife-wielding maniac tracking and dispatching a series of victims, generally women (e.g., any of the Jack the Ripper films). *See* **slasher, slice-and-dice,** *and* **splatter films.**

∎ **stand** (1) A support for a luminaire. Such supports vary in size and weight, from the heavy stands for brutes, which can be automatically elevated or lowered, to the lightweight type used on location, which can be conveniently folded or collapsed. Luminaires are normally attached to stands by spigots and sometimes, when light enough, by sockets. (2) A support for any of the ancillary equipment used in lighting—for example, a reflector or gobo.

∎ **standard pitch** *See* **long pitch.**

∎ **standards** Specifications established in the industry for film and other equipment. *See* **American National Standards Institute.**

∎ **standee** A large promotional item that stands in a theater lobby, either advertising the present or a coming feature—perhaps a cutout or a mounted poster.

∎ **stand-in** An individual with the same physical characteristics as a major performer who replaces the actor or actress while the lights are set and camera position and movement are established. The stand-in permits the lead performer to rest, rehearse, or go about other business. *See* **double.**

∎ **standing set** A set that has been constructed and assembled.

∎ **star** A performer with a national or international reputation who appears in major roles and has great box-office appeal. Such performers tend to dominate the roles they play to such an extent that audiences come to see the specific actor or actress, film after film, rather than the dramas in which they appear. A star is a public figure, someone whose personal qualities have been developed and exploited to offer audiences a recognizable type, someone with whom audiences can identify, but through whom, at the same time, they can escape their own everyday reality. *See* **star system.**

∎ **star filter, star screen** A filter, engraved with lines, that when placed in front of the camera lens causes highlights to break up into streaks of light in the same directions as the lines. Such a filter with lines in the form of a square creates the effect of a four-pointed star; one

with lines at 45-degree angles would create an eight-pointed star.

∎ **starlet** A young woman, generally in her early twenties, who was developed by one of the Hollywood studios as a future star. Such women received training and appeared in small roles, but they mainly functioned as publicity for the studios, feeding the imaginations of countless moviegoers who fantasized about becoming stars.

∎ **star system** The method and manner of exploiting the on- and off-screen existence of specific performers to sell motion pictures to the public. The very presence of such a performer in a film transcends any other aspects of the work. Stars are made to have recognizable characteristics that appeal to the public and lure people into the theater no matter what role the actor or actress performs. The star system, through magazines, newspapers, and other publicity vehicles, as well as through the movies themselves, creates identifiable types of luminaries with whom the public can identify and through whom they can escape the limitations of their own personalities and realities. At first production companies kept their performers anonymous, minimizing their importance so that they could minimize their salaries—performers might be known by the names of the characters they played or given some nickname by the public. Carl Laemmle, recognizing the public's great interest in these figures and realizing their drawing power to the movie house, hired Florence Lawrence, who was already known to the public as "the Biograph girl," away from Biograph to his own Independent Motion Picture Company (IMP) in 1910 and announced her actual name for IMP's next film. Other companies followed suit, celebrating the names and personalities of their stars, and by 1919 the star system was established, with the individual performer as the major force in motion pictures. Mary Pickford, "little Mary" as she was first known to audiences, became "America's sweetheart," the most popular figure in films and the first quintessential star, moving from Biograph to one studio after another, raising her salary to extraordinary heights even by modern standards. Pickford was followed by Charlie Chaplin, with the two moving rapidly toward million-dollar salaries.

Edgar Morin, in his book *The Stars,* has identified some general categories for the stars of the silent period: the "innocent or roguish virgin," such as Pickford and Lillian Gish; the vamp, notably Theda Bara; the suffering and mysterious "divine," especially Greta Garbo; the adventurous hero, such as Douglas Fairbanks and William S. Hart; the lover, for example, John Gilbert; and the adventurous lover, notably Rudolph Valentino. These figures are largely archetypes, broad characterizations that represent general human characteristics and fantasies. The nature of the star changed with the advent of sound and with the changing realities of the Depression and prewar years. The

star The "divine" Greta Garbo.

■■■

star figure became more complex, more socially oriented, and more like us—but like us at our very best. The homespun qualities of men such as Henry Fonda, James Stewart, and Gary Cooper endeared them to us all. James Cagney and Humphrey Bogart became antiheroes, mixing the good and the bad, the sensitive and the tough, the glamorous and the real. Of course, adventurous heroes such as John Wayne, Burt Lancaster, and Kirk Douglas, continued to thrill us after the war years, but Marlon Brando and James Dean burst on the scene to mark the advent of the rebel as hero. Female stars also underwent metamorphosis in sound films, with the innocent virgin becoming smarter and perkier, like Claudette Colbert and Rosalind Russell, or less virginal, like Joan Crawford and Barbara Stanwyk. Vamps such as Marlene Dietrich may have remained sultry and mysterious, but the full-scale sex goddess emerged to give us a more complex and human sense of beauty and eroticism, with the vulgar brashness and sensitivity of Jean Harlow, the innocence and childishness of Brigitte Bardot, and the vulnerability of Marilyn Monroe. With all their human characteristics, stars were public luminaries who shone with glitter and glamour, who were the centers of America's fantasies. They were cultural heroes and heroines, divinities who lived outside the motion-picture house in regal estates and in a colorful, exciting world about which we could only dream. Stars were dependent on the studio system, on constant exposure through a steady flow of films as well as through the elaborate publicity that these production companies could put forth.

When the studio system collapsed in the 1950s, the star system deflated. A number of the old stars continued making films and a number of new luminaries arose in the heavens; but the number of stars dwindled and Hollywood ceased to exist as a dream world. Directors took on new importance, a number with greater reputations and more box-office appeal than the performers with whom they worked. The fewer stars who appeared in fewer films seemed less glamorous and special. The major performers in Hollywood today are known primarily for their box-office clout and the high salaries they command, but little is made of their private lives (both mythical and real); nor do they command the worshipful interest and adoration of the public. As movies have become more geared for both younger and international audiences, the appeal of the performers who have won the approval of such viewers has become broader, simpler, more basic and generic. Rock musicians and some television personalities have in part made up for the deficit left by the demise of the motion-picture star system; but much of America at this point seems denied the stuff upon which dreams are made—it may be that ours is an age without the capacity to believe in stars. *See* **hero, heroine,** *and* **studio system.**

■ **start mark** A mark at the very beginning of a piece of film to indicate at what point some process should begin—for example, printing, synchronizing with a similarly marked magnetic track, or projecting. On the leader of release prints the start mark indicates a specific amount of footage to the first frame.

■ **star vehicle** A film that is made largely for showing off the physical features and talents of a specific star.

■ **static** Interference in an audio system caused by an electrical disturbance.

■ **static camera shot, stationary camera shot** A shot in which the camera does not move. Many shots are stationary when there is sufficient cutting to different camera positions to give a variety of perspectives and movement to the scene. Longer shots of this type are used when deep focus is employed and the viewer's eyes move to the different planes of action, or when the camera shifts focus for the audience. Prolonged stationary shots with a single plane of action can be used with great effect to show some dramatic or subtle interaction (the Japanese director, Yasujiro Ozu, for example, in films such as *Tokyo Story* [1953], consistently uses such a shot with a camera angle from several feet off the floor to represent the point of view of a Japanese person sitting on a mat). However, long stationary shots can frequently evoke boredom and inattention on the part of the viewer, as they did during the early days of sound, when cameras had to be kept in soundproof enclosures. *See* **deep focus.**

■ **static marks, static electricity marks** Exposed portions on undeveloped film that later show up as dark streaks or branches, produced by static electricity especially in dry and cool air and especially on black-and-white film. The static electricity can also result from friction as the film passes through the camera or from rapid rewinding.

■ **stay with the money** A direction to shoot a scene so that the camera will focus on the star or on some particular action that will also have sufficient box-office appeal to generate the income for the film.

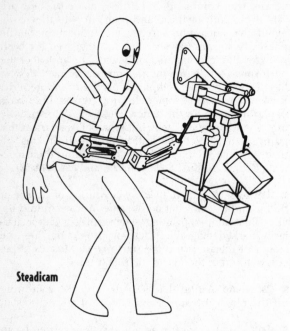

Steadicam

■ **Steadicam** The trade name for a now much-employed device that allows the operator to keep the camera steady during handheld shots. The articulated arm extends from a vest, which fits around the operator's body and counterbalances the camera it supports by means of spring force, while a free-floating gimbal attaches the arm to the camera mounting. A video viewfinder and monitor allow the operator to perceive his shots with relative ease. The Steadicam permits the operator to move about freely over rough terrain and into areas where tracks cannot be placed for a dolly. The device was employed with some striking visual results in Stanley Kubrick's *The Shining* (1980).

■ **steadiness test** A test for evaluating the registration of film within a camera, normally accomplished by photographing a black cross on white, rewinding the film, shooting the cross from a slightly different angle, and then projecting the developed image to see the steadiness of the two crosses in relation to one another.

■ **Steenbeck** A well-known brand of flat-bed editing machine manufactured by the Steenbeck Company located in Chatsworth, California. *See* **flat-bed editing machine.**

■ **step-boosting transformer** A device that raises the voltage of some tungsten lamps for greater intensity and color temperature without any significant increase in amperage.

■ **step contact printer** Another name for an intermittent contact printer, a machine that brings both a negative or positive and fresh stock together, emulsion to emulsion and a frame at a time, in front of the aperture, where a shutter exposes the frame to the printing light. Such printers are used when precise registration is needed in traveling-matte processes, for example, or for making rear-projection or front-projection plates. *See* **printer.**

■ **step deal** A contractual agreement between a film company and a producer, writer, director, or performer that the film company has a right to back out of the project and make no further payments at any of the specified stages of development (e.g., at the completion of the treatment or the first draft of the screenplay).

■ **step lens** A condenser lens with the plano side in graduated steps to focus a beam of light from a lamp.

■ **step optical printer** Another name for an intermittent optical printer, a machine that sends an image from a negative or positive in a projector onto fresh stock in a camera through a special lens, one frame at a time, when both films remain briefly stationary and are exposed by the shutter to the printing light. Since the pieces of film are not in contact and can be operated separately, and since great flexibility is possible with the camera's position, speed, and type of lens, optical printers are employed for a number of effects. Such printers are used for creating transitional devices between scenes (e.g., fades, dissolves, and wipes); altering speeds of action for slow and fast motion; manipulating the image by moving the camera's distance; achieving split-screen effects and superimpositions; employing traveling mattes to create composite pictures from different images; and for changing a motion picture from one gauge of film to another. Today, however, much of this work is being done digitally. *See* **digital effects** *and* **printer.**

■ **step printer** Any printer that brings a negative or positive and fresh stock one frame at a time to a stationary position in front of the aperture where they are exposed by the shutter to the printing light—that is, either a step contact printer, in which the emulsions touch before the aperture; or a step optical printer, where the image is projected onto the fresh stock through a special lens. Such printers are too slow to produce release prints, which require printers with continuous movement, but are employed by the laboratory for other important work in the preparation of the images. Also called an intermittent printer. *See* **printer.**

■ **step printing** Any printing procedure that uses an intermittent printer. *See* **step printer.**

■ **step prism, stepped prism** A prismatic device with its surface in steps for focusing a beam from a light source—for example, a Fresnel lens.

■ **step wedge, step table** A series of precisely measured increasing densities on a strip of film made from a series of graduated exposures and used for testing processing machines, printers, or specific film stocks. The film itself is called a sensitometric strip. *See* **densitometry** *and* **sensitometry.**

■ **stereo, stereo transparency** In rear-projection cinematography, when the background to the action being photographed comes from a projector behind a screen, the term "stereo" is sometimes used to describe either (1) the background image on the screen or (2) the transparency from which it emanates. *See* **rear projection.**

■ **stereophonic sound** Sound recorded on two or more separate tracks and played back through two or more corresponding loudspeakers to create the impression that the sound is coming from several areas on the screen or in the theater. Such systems also produce sound of great fidelity and range. Abel Gance used a primitive form of stereophonic sound, which he called "Pictographe" and which used notches on the film to send sound effects and speech to various loudspeakers behind the screen and around the audience, in Paris in 1934 for a version of his epic film *Napoléon vu par Abel Gance* (1927). Walt Disney's "Fantasound" had three optical, variable-area sound tracks along with a control track on a film separate from the picture to create stereophonic music for his *Fantasia* in 1940. But stereophonic sound became a more significant part of film with the rise of wide-screen motion pictures, when the greater scope of the picture logically called for a distribution of sound along the screen, especially from the extremities. Cinerama, a three-projector system with overlapping pictures, which appeared in 1952, employed seven magnetic sound tracks on a separate film running synchronically with the picture to produce sound through six speakers behind the screen and others scattered about the auditorium. CinemaScope, the first successful wide-screen process on one film, which employed an anamorphic lens on both the camera and projector, first appeared in 1953, with four magnetic tracks on the same piece of film as the picture, three for speakers behind the screen and one for speakers in the auditorium. Wide-screen systems in this country and Britain employed a 65mm negative printed on 70mm stock to allow for six magnetic sound tracks; 35mm wide-screen prints generally used four such tracks on film with smaller perforations and sometimes three tracks on film with normal perforations. But placing magnetic striping on the film as well as equipping theaters for such a system was costly and inconvenient.

The next step was optical stereophonic sound (especially since the conversion of a projector with a silicon solar cell to play the optical tracks proved not expensive). Today, two optical channels with four sound tracks are printed on the same 35mm film as the picture for sound from the left, center, and right of the screen, as well as surround sound. The latest development in stereophonic sound is the digital systems, with their sound of great quality, that are being used in a growing number of theaters. Three systems are now in use: the Dolby SR-D that places the digital code between the perforations of the film; Digital Theater System (DTS) from MCA/Universal that places it on a disc and operates the sound by means of a time code on the film; and Sony Dynamic Digital Sound (SDDS) that places the code on a track on the outside of the film and a back-up track along the other edge. The digital coding in the first two systems contains the three stereophonic tracks for the right, left, and center of the screen, two surround sound tracks, one for each side of the theater, and a sixth track for a subwoofer for the bass sound; while the SDDS system offers an additional two tracks for sound emanating from the screen. Although the DTS system is now most in use, a number of theaters are equipped to play all three digital processes in addition to the analog optical stereo system. *See* **sound** *and* **wide screen.**

■ **stereophonic variable-area track, stereo variable-area track** A single optical variable-area track on film which is able to feed sound to separate speakers for stereophonic effect. MGM and Paramount flirted with such a system, called "Perspecta Sound," in the 1950s. Dolby stereophonic sound today uses two optical bands that create four separate tracks on 35mm film for stereophonic and surround sound. *See* **stereophonic sound.**

■ **stereoscopy, stereoscopic cinematography, stereographic cinematography** *See* **3-D.**

■ **stereotype** A character in a film, drama, or novel obviously derived from similar characters in other works. A stereotypical character offers little that is new and appears to be a repetition of the physical appearance, manners, and personality of the earlier figures. Familiar to the audience, this character type already seems a cliché on his or her first appearance—for example, the long-suffering mother of the criminal in the gangster film, the attractive female schoolteacher in the Western, and the mad scientist's hunchbacked helper in the horror film. *See* **stock character.**

■ **stereo window** In stereoscopy (i.e., 3-D motion pictures), the plane at which the two views, representing the left and right eyes, converge, which is often the screen plane or right behind it. Objects in front of the plane of convergence will appear to be before the screen, and objects behind will seem to the rear of the screen. *See* **stereoscopy.**

■ **stick it, sticks, sticks in, slate it** The order to the assistant camera operator to clap the sticks together on the clapboard in front of the camera to mark the beginning of a take. *See* **clapboard.**

■ **sticks** (1) An abbreviated form of the word "clapsticks." (2) A tripod with wooden legs.

■ **still** A single photograph taken with a still camera or blown up from a frame of a motion picture. The still man assigned to a film production takes pictures of action supposedly in the film that are often separately staged for him, as well as behind-the-scene photographs for publicity, advertising, and archives. Such stills are also used for books or articles about motion. pictures.

■ **still background, static background** Any background to a scene which is totally void of movement.

■ **still frame** *See* **freeze frame.**

■ **still photographer** A photographer assigned to a film production for taking still pictures of actions supposedly in the film that are often specially staged, and pictures of behind-the-scenes activities. Such photographs are taken for publicity and advertising as well as for film archives. The still photographer may also take photographs at events related to the film and at premiers.

■ **still store** The term basically has the same meaning as a frame store and page store and refers to the keeping of one or more images in the computer's memory. *See* **frame buffer.**

■ **sting** (1) *See* **stinger.** (2) To add a stinger to a scene or soundtrack for punctuation, for example, to add a musical chord or a loud but brief noise such as a shout.

■ **stinger, sting** (1) A sudden musical note, chord, or phrase that punctuates or concludes a musical background or scene. (2) A sudden noise, such as a shout, that punctuates the dramatic action or increases tension in a scene.

■ **stirrup, stirrup hanger** A device for suspending luminaires.

■ **stock** (1) Unexposed film; also referred to as raw stock. (2) Footage of actions, events, or settings previously shot and now available for purchase or rental from a film library or laboratory. Such stock is used to save on present shooting expenses.

■ **stock character** A standard figure who frequently appears in certain kinds of movies—for example, the butler in murder mysteries or the younger brother in teenage romances. The term refers to the general type of character and his or her general situation, leaving considerable leeway for interpretation—stock characters need not be turned into stereotypes. *See* **stereotype.**

■ **stock footage library** (1) A location where stock footage is kept and made available for rental or purchase. (2) The collection itself of stock footage. *See* **stock shot.**

■ **stock part, stock role** A part in a film based upon a stock character. *See* **stock character.**

■ **stock shot (SS), stock footage** (1) Standard shots of actions, events, or settings previously photographed for newsreels, documentaries, or even for feature films and presently stored in a stock footage library or laboratory from which they can be purchased or rented, frequently by the foot, for insertion in a present film—for example, footage of a military parade or hurricane. Such shots are employed to save on production costs. *See* **found footage** *and* **library shot.** (2) The term is also sometimes used to describe a shot photographed for a film that seems sufficiently unoriginal to be from a film library.

■ **stop** *See* **lens stop.**

■ **stop bath** (1) Any chemical solution employed in the processing of film to end the activity of the previous solution. (2) The term is used more specifically to refer to the acid bath that terminates the activity of the developing solution. *See* **processing.**

■ **stop date** The contractually agreed-upon date on which a performer will no longer be responsible to a particular film production whether or not it is completed. Sometimes a clause might specify extra compensation for passing a particular date and name a later date for a closure to the performer's commitment. Such agreements will also nullify such dates if the performer is responsible for any delay in the film's completion.

■ **stop down, close down** To decrease the aperture of the lens by closing down the diaphragm in order to diminish the amount of light entering the lens. The lens opening is normally calculated in f-stops—the higher the number, the smaller the aperture. The opposite is to "open up" the diaphragm. *See* **f-stop, lens stop,** *and* **t-stop.**

■ **stop frame** *See* **freeze frame.**

■ **stop motion, stop-motion cinematography, stop-action, stop-action cinematography, single-frame cinematography** Any cinematographic technique that utilizes the constant stopping and starting of the camera to allow for a change in the subject during the interval that the camera is not shooting which will produce some effect when the printed film is projected continuously. Stop-motion cinematography can be broken down into the following categories. (1) A type of photography that shoots a single frame at a time, with a lengthy duration between each shot, to show some process or development taking place over a long duration—for example, the growth of a flower. Also called time-lapse cinematography. (2) A cinematographic technique in which the camera is stopped during a shot, an alteration is made in the scene, and then the camera resumes shooting in order to achieve some trick effect in the projected scene. (3) A cinematographic technique for speeding up a scene by intermittently stopping the camera, advancing the action, and then continuing shooting. (4) A cinematographic technique employed to achieve a pixillated effect for live figures. In a continuing procedure, characters are photographed in a still position for a frame or more and then moved slightly while the camera is stopped. (5) A basic technique in all animation work which gives movement to drawings or models. In both cases, special cameras are employed that can shoot one frame at a time. In the first instance, individual drawings, each with a slight change in the position of the subject, are individually shot; in the second, models are photographed a frame at a time, and their positions slightly altered between frames. When the photographs are consecutively projected, the drawn figures or models seem to move with continuous motion. *See* **animation** *and* **cartoon.**

■ **stopwatch** A large timepiece that can be started and stopped to measure the length of a take, an individual action, or the duration of a voice-over. Such timepieces can frequently measure in film footage and frames as well as in minutes and seconds.

■ **store theaters** A term used for the first theaters in this country devoted to screening motion pictures, undoubtedly derived from the original business sites that were converted into these theaters.

■ **story** The overall pattern of events in a narrative that includes the major actions of the central figures in chronological order. The story is a general overview of what happens, as distinct from the plot, which is composed of all the individual events, both external and psychological, in the order in which they appear in the work itself. *See* **plot** *and* **structure.**

■ **story analyst** Also called a reader, this individual works in the story department of a production company and reads submitted scripts or other materials as sources for possible film productions. The reader may return the work or submit a synopsis and evaluation to the story editor. *See* **story department.**

■ **storyboard, story board** A series of sketches or sometimes photographs that represents the individual shots to be taken for a film production. The individual shots are arranged in the normal sequence of action and represent a visual blueprint of the entire film (or sometimes only parts of the film). Dialogue, sound effects, music, and camera movement are also frequently noted. The sketches might be hung in order on a wall or assembled together in script form. Essential in planning animation works, they are also frequently used in the making of feature films to allow the director and the director of photography to prepare for and carry out various setups and camera movements. With its series of illustrations and captions, the storyboard resembles a cartoon strip. Electronic storyboards have also become popular in recent years, at first using video to demonstrate a pictorial development of the film and now employing computer software either to create or assemble a series of detached pictures that previsualize an entire film. Also called continuity sketches. *See* **electronic storyboard.**

■ **storyboard artist, story sketch artist** The individual in an animation studio who draws the individual sketches for each shot, that when assembled together into a storyboard give the animator a sense of the continuity and overall design of the cartoon. *See* **animation.**

■ **story conference** A meeting between the writer (or writers) of a screenplay and personnel involved in the making of a film to discuss the writing or revising of a script. Initial story conferences may take place between the writer and the story editor who works for the production company, and may eventually include production executives. Later meetings, when the script is nearly in finished form, will include the director and producer along with the writer and story editor. *See* **story department** *and* **story editor.**

■ **story department** The personnel attached to a film production company who read material, both submitted and found, as possible sources for film productions. The group generally reads film scripts and sometimes synopses and treatments submitted by agents or writers, but also examines novels, plays, and short stories that might be made into films. The preliminary examination is by a reader or story analyst in the department, who either returns the material or submits a summary and evaluation to the story editor. The story editor then decides whether to recommend the work to an executive or producer. *See* **story editor.**

■ **story editor** The individual in the story department who is responsible for acting on the story analyst's synopsis and evaluation of a screenplay or some other material, and either turns the project down or submits it to an executive producer for serious consideration as a film production. Once the project has been accepted, the story editor will generally have one or more story conferences with the screenwriter, advising him or her in the writing or revisions of the script, and may also take part in later meetings between the writer, director, and producer. *See* **story department.**

■ **story line** A simple, general description of the sequence of major actions in a narrative.

■ **story script** A script of a film that presents the story according to the proper arrangement of its master scenes without any breakdown for camera setups, shots, or movements. The story script presents locations, actions, and dialogue and must eventually be developed into a shooting script. *See* **shooting script.**

■ **straight cut** An immediate change from one shot to another without an optical transition such as a fade or dissolve. This type of immediate change is the staple cut of most film narratives and normally occurs imperceptibly within individual scenes to allow us different views of the action. A straight cut might also be used in a scene to create a reaction shot, which shows us what a character perceives immediately after we see the character perceiving. A straight cut is now frequently employed to move the audience from one scene to another regardless of the separation in time and place. A straight cut, either within a scene or from one scene to another, with the two images clashing discordantly is also called a jump cut. *See* **cut.**

■ **straight man** The actor who functions as a foil for a comedian and elicits his jokes—for example, Dean Martin early in his career when he appeared with Jerry Lewis.

■ **straight part, straight role** A normal dramatic role for a performer without any stereotypical or unusual features.

■ **streak photography** A streaking effect achieved for moving objects normally with an animation stand for objects in drawings or with a motion-control system for models. The technique generally involves long exposures with the camera or subject moving. It has often been employed for moving words or logos in television and has become a staple for special-effects work in fantasy films (e.g., the "Worm Hole" sequence in *Star Trek: The Motion Picture* [1979; dir. Robert Wise]). *See* **slit-scan.**

■ **streamer** A diagonal or lateral mark scratched or made by a wax pencil on a film, which will appear during projection for editing or cueing purposes. A diagonal scratch on the film is projected onto the screen to warn the conductor to watch for a bright flash, made by a punched hole at the end of the scratch, which acts as his cue for a specific musical effect.

■ **street film** A type of silent motion picture made in Germany during the 1920s that emphasized the depressing and dehumanizing aspects of urban life for the lower-middle class. Such films, showing the brutalization of human life caused by the establishment and bourgeoisie, featured sensitive individuals seeking to rise above the limitations of their environment. Al-

though showing signs of the expressionism developed in the German film industry, especially in lighting and sometimes in setting, these films sought to achieve a high degree of realism in the sets of city streets constructed in the UFA studios. The first of these films was Carl Grune's *The Street* (1923), and perhaps the most notable is G. W. Pabst's *Joyless Street* (1925). *See* **expressionism** *and* **UFA.**

street film *Joyless Street* (1925; G. W. Pabst), the best-known of the German silent films dealing with the poverty and struggles of urban life.

■ ■ ■

■ **stretch framing, stretch-frame printing, stretch-printing, stretching frames** Slowing down the action of a shot by repeating the individual frames two or three times each. The result is a jerky movement on the screen with the subject alternating between stasis and motion. *See* **double framing** *and* **skip framing.**

■ **stretch out** To make a spoken speech or commentary longer by slowing the pace and taking greater pauses.

■ **stretch-out** A limousine that holds six passengers and is used for transporting studio personnel.

■ **strike** (1) To take down and put away a set. (2) To remove any prop or part of a set.

■ **stringout** A section of the film that is made off the workprint as a black-and-white dirty dupe at some point during the editing to allow the editor to get on with his or her work while the various sound technicians can get on with their own. A stringout may be used for additional dialogue replacement, sound effects, or recording music. *See* **dirty dupe** *and* **editing.**

■ **strip** (1) A striplight. See below. (2) A separate piece of film taken from the manufacturer's original wide roll. A single wide roll of film may be the source of some forty individual strips of 35mm film, which are individually marked in their cans according to the number of their parent roll and sometimes with their own number in the series. (3) Removing the packing insulation from any piece of machinery.

■ **stripe, sound stripe, sound stripping** A band of magnetic iron oxide on a film for recording sound and from which sound can be played. A narrower balancing stripe is placed along the other edge of the film so that it will move evenly past the magnetic head and roll evenly on the reel. *See* **magnetic recording.**

■ **striping** Applying a narrow band of magnetic iron oxide to a roll of a film for recording sound. *See* **magnetic recording.**

■ **striplight** A single narrow lighting unit that is open on one side and generally contains a row of five, ten, or twelve individual 1,000-watt bulbs. With only one connector, such units have more than one circuit in case a bulb burns out—for example, a cyclorama strip. Also called a border light. *See* **cyclorama strip.**

■ **stripping** Eliminating extraneous noise from a sound track with dialogue to allow a clean mix. *See* **mix.**

■ **strip-title** One or more lines of text arranged horizontally across the screen—for example, subtitles giving dialogue at the bottom of a foreign film.

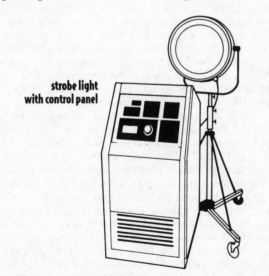

strobe light with control panel

■ **strobe light, stroboscopic light** A lamp pulsating anywhere from forty-eight to two thousand pulses per second (pps), employed either at the lower rates to create blinking light (perhaps for a musical number) or at higher speeds, above sixty pulses per second when the light appears without blinking, to give sharp detail to a subject in fast motion (e.g., cascading water). Strobe

lights must be operated in sync with the camera, and care must be taken not to use a rate much less than thirty pulses per second, which is capable of bringing about ill effects to a viewer and even seizures in epileptics.

■ **strobing, strobe effect** A seemingly disconnected and jerky effect between images of the same object on the screen. This effect is sometimes noticeable when the camera pans too rapidly across static objects or the subject moves too rapidly in front of a static camera, but in neither case fast enough to blur the image. In the first case, for example, pillars or a picket fence will appear to flicker and jump; in the second, a rotating wheel might even appear to move backward. There are several theories which explain this phenomenon, one claiming that such an effect is achieved when an image is so rapidly displaced from frame to frame that it fails to register on certain viewing cells because of the angle of the eye's retina; another arguing that the intervals between exposures, which make up half of each second when the image is blocked from projection, cause too significant a displacement of a fast-moving object to allow for the illusion of continuity—for example, if the image of a rotating wheel is photographed with the spokes at a slightly regressive position for each frame, and the intervening forward positions blocked out, the wheel will even seem to rotate backward in the projected image. Skipping can be avoided by slowing the motion of camera or subject, opening the camera's shutter, increasing its speed, or decreasing the brightness of the screen.

■ **Stroboscope** An early persistence-of-vision device for creating moving images invented by Simon Ritter Von Stampfer in Vienna and exhibited in 1833. Much like the Phenakistiscope, simultaneously developed by the Belgian Joseph Antione Ferdinand Plateau, the Stroboscope created the illusion of movement by having the viewer spin a round disc on the inside of which was placed a series of drawings and observing the reflected image of these drawings in a mirror through slots in the disc. Stampfer later developed this device to have two rotating discs, one with the slots through which the viewer looked and the other with the drawings. *See* **Phenakistiscope, Praxinoscope,** and **Zoetrope.**

■ **structural film** A term first used by P. Adams Sitney in the Summer and Winter 1969 issues of *Film Culture* to describe a specific type of American experimental film that emerged in the mid-1960s and that suggests a predetermined and simplified shape as "the primal impression of the film." George Maciunas, in a retort to Sitney that appeared in the same Winter issue of the journal, argued that images and generalizations are drawn from the particulars of such films, and that "the material is [these films'] concepts." Sitney had stated that the four characteristics of structural films are a fixed camera position, the flicker effect, loop printing (for repeated shots without variation), and rephotography off a screen. Peter Gidal later developed these ideas in his "Theory and Definition of Structuralist/Materialist Film" (in *Structural Film Anthology,* published by the British Film Institute in 1976) when he stated that this type of film, which is "non-illusionist" and does not represent anything, creates a tension between "materialist flatness, grain, light, movement, and the supposed reality that is represented." For Gidal, "the root concern" of these films is "the structuring aspects and the attempt to decipher the structure and anticipate/recorrect it, to clarify and analyze the production process of the specific image at any specific moment."

Such works are also sometimes referred to as perceptional films since they explore the interaction of perception and cognition through the medium of film. Michael Snow, George Landow, Hollis Frampton, and Paul Sharits are among the filmmakers who have created structural films. A notable example is Snow's *Wavelength* (1967), which features a zoom shot of forty-five minutes with a fixed camera. The film begins by focusing on a row of windows and finally ends by focusing on a photograph of waves on a wall between the windows, with only a few actions interspersed. The dominant sound is an electrical sine wave, gradually increasing in cycles and interspersed with some speech, music, and natural noises. *See* **avant-garde cinema.**

structural film   The setting for Michael Snow's forty-five-minute zoom shot in *Wavelength* (1967).

■ ■ ■

■ **structuralism, cine-structuralism** A school of thought that sees our perception of reality comprised not of individual objects but of the relationship between objects. The mind imposes upon the world around us a variety of structures that give order to the raw stuff of reality. By understanding such structures, we can understand the operations of the human mind and the structures of our psyche. Because modern concepts of structuralism have been influenced by semiotics, the

science of signs, these structures are also referred to as codes and can be read as separate systems of signs. The Swiss linguist Ferdinand de Saussure, whose lectures on semiotics were published as *Course in General Linguistics* in 1915, claims that any language has to be studied synchronically, as a total immediate entity, and not only diachronically, as it developed in time. Language should be viewed as a complete system, a total structure, which can best be understood by examining the relationships of its individual components. In *Structural Anthropology,* the French anthropologist, Claude Lévi-Strauss suggests that Saussure's linguistic concepts can be employed to understand the various structures that underlie the existence of a society, including its mythologies and art. In his structural analysis of the Oedipus myth in the same book, he uses the various treatments of the story as individual usages from which collectively we can understand the basic structure that underlies the myth in general. Categorizing elements from the various versions of the myth and placing them in binary oppositions, Lévi-Strauss then presents what he sees as the structure that embodies, for the myth's culture, a basic conflict concerning the origins of man.

Structuralism had a fashionable currency in literary criticism for a while, and works by such Continental critics as A. J. Greimas and Tzvetan Todorov, who sought to work out the structures of surface narrative in various literary forms by using linguistic principles as opposed to the deep structures that Lévi-Strauss found hidden beneath versions of the same myth, were read in America and England with much interest during the late 1960s and early 1970s. Structuralism, or cine-structuralism as it is called in film study, has been applied to some degree and with various amounts of success to the works of specific directors and genres. In England, Geoffrey Nowell-Smith, in *Luchino Visconti* (1967), and Peter Wollen, in his discussions of Howard Hawks and John Ford in *Signs and Meaning in the Cinema* (1969; rev. 1972), utilize what is sometimes referred to as auteur-structuralism in searching out thematic structures and tensions in the films of their respective directors. In *Horizons West,* published in England in 1969, Jim Kitses uses a similar approach when he establishes a basic structural and thematic dialectic in the Western and traces its development in the works of specific directors. Semiotics itself has had more of a direct impact on film studies than structuralism, perhaps because sign codes are easier to devise and discern and seem less reductive than the structural binary oppositions that have been employed by film structuralists; and perhaps because structuralism has been undermined in literary study by poststructuralism, a school of thought that argues against the possibility of monolithic and fixed structures in texts because of the very unfixed nature of language. *See* **semiotics.**

■ **structure** The arrangement of the various parts and total organization of a work of art. The term should not be confused with structuralism, a specific cultural movement and analytical approach described above. Structure is a critical term for various forms of art; it came into fashion during the decades preceding structuralism. The type of structure discussed depends very much on the art form and also the perspective taken by the critic. In film studies, it is possible to discuss (1) narrative structure, the arrangement and total organization of characters, actions, and story lines; (2) thematic structure, the way in which specific concepts or ideas are developed through the relationships between the various elements of the story and between the film's images; and (3) filmic structure, the interaction and total effect of specific types of shots and editing techniques. *See* **plot** *and* **story.**

■ **Struss lens, Struss pictorial lens** A soft-focus lens developed by the cinematographer Karl Struss during his early period as a still photographer and first adopted for cinematography in 1914.

■ **strut** A support for holding up scenery; a brace.

■ **studio, film studio** (1) The stage or sound where sets are assembled and filming and sound recording take place for the production of a motion picture. Film companies normally have a number of soundproofed stages, specially equipped for assembling scenery, setting up lights, positioning and moving cameras, and recording dialogue. (2) The entire physical plant, including all the buildings, stages, and lots, owned by a film company. *See* **studio complex.** (3) The company or corporation itself that produces films.

■ **studio camera** A camera too large and heavy to be used anywhere but inside a studio. Supported by a strong tripod, such cameras are mounted directly to a head which permits easy turning or tilting. For mobile shots, a studio camera might be attached to a column on a dolly or the boom of a crane. *See* **camera.**

■ **studio complex** All the buildings, lots, services, and equipment that make up a film company. The complex includes actual stages where films are shot; workshops where sets are built; storerooms where sets, properties, furniture, and costumes are kept; areas for maintaining and storing cameras, lights, and related equipment; dressing and makeup rooms; editing facilities; sound-recording and dubbing studios; facilities for special effects; screening theaters; all the administrative and executive offices and buildings; and all the machinery and personnel involved in the plant's operation and the making of movies.

■ **studio exterior** (1) Any outdoor scenery constructed and set up within a studio. (2) Any shot of an exterior that is an actual set within the studio.

■ **studio lighting** Lighting equipment heavier and less portable than that used for location shooting. *See* **lighting.**

■ **studio lot** A studio complex with a company's major facilities for both administration and production. *See* **studio complex.**

■ **studio manager, plant manager** The individual who supervises the entire operation of a studio, including all departments and personnel, but who is not directly involved in the making of a film.

■ **studio picture, studio film** A film made primarily in a studio as opposed to one made on location. Studio pictures tend to have a more controlled and artificial *mise-en-scène* no matter how elaborate and detailed the setting. The lighting is, after all, unnatural, space is confined, and locations are constructed. The emphasis is more on the interaction of characters and less on the interaction of character and environment. The world of studio films seems both intensely close to the viewer and yet dreamlike and escapist. *See* **location picture** *and* **studio system.**

■ **studio system** The large-scale method of making motion pictures used by the Hollywood studios from the 1920s through the early 1950s. The figure generally cited as initiating this type of production and establishing the prototype for future film studios was Thomas H. Ince, who built Inceville in the Hollywood area in 1912 while working for the New York Motion Picture Company. Here Ince directed numerous films while also evolving into a producer and production manager, supervising the making of numerous films which he did not specifically direct, but over which he had complete control. A number of films were made simultaneously on different studio lots, with directors working from carefully and specifically drawn scripts that Ince himself approved and that laid out the entire film. The complete production was carefully scheduled, and Ince himself had the final word on editing. Mass production of films, division of labor, shooting scenes out of order to save on costs, supervision of films by a production head, and the manufacture of formula films, which were cheaper to make in number and had a sure market, all became part of the movie scene for more than thirty years and allowed Hollywood to turn out enough films to satisfy a vast movie public both in its own country and abroad.

Also significant in the development of the studio system was the control of distribution by film companies, a practice begun in 1917 when Adolph Zukor acquired Paramount Film Corporation and Artcraft Pictures Corporation as distributors for the recently formed Famous-Players-Lasky Corporation. Distribution not only became an important money-making business for studios, helping them to finance their films, it also allowed them to force theater owners to block-book all their offerings. The next logical step was for the studios to acquire the theaters so that they would have total control over all aspects of the industry and guaranteed markets for their products. With vertical control of production, distribution, and exhibition, the studios had a virtual monopoly in the industry. Although profits were enormous, so were costs, and the studios themselves fell more under the control of bankers and businessmen, with production supervisors making the decisions, practical as well as artistic, instead of directors. In order to make films rapidly and efficiently, decisions were made from above, and the tasks of production assigned to various specialists and departments. The director often became just another one of these specialists whose task it was to put a predetermined script on film and then send it off to allow other specialists to put it into final form. The film itself was a product that had to make money, and to do so it had to follow certain criteria that had already proven successful at the box office; similar types of films following conventional story-lines with common backgrounds were also more economical to make.

The coming of sound increased the expense of production, putting studios further under the control of Wall Street bankers and increasing the departmentalization of film production. By the middle of the 1930s the major film studios were MGM, Paramount, Twentieth Century-Fox, Warner Brothers, Columbia, Universal, RKO, and United Artists, the last largely a distributor for independent film productions. By the end of the decade these companies were responsible for more than three-fourths of the films released in this country, each turning out more than 50 films a year. Hollywood was producing some 400–500 films per year for an audience buying approximately 80 million tickets each week. Monogram and Republic were smaller studios producing low-budget B-pictures, especially Westerns, in rapid fashion, while Walt Disney turned out his own specialized animation films. Double features were the rule in most local theaters, with the major studios having special production units to turn out low-budget B-pictures as second features. Each studio generally had one figure in charge of total production (e.g., Irving Thalberg as vice-president for MGM), and working under him were numerous producers or associate producers in charge of specific films. Each studio had its stable of stars, directors, writers, and designers as well as its various departments of technicians. Individual talent was not suppressed, and stars developed in their own ways; but even here a certain consistency in manner and role was expected from film to film. Directors such as John Ford or Billy Wilder were allowed to leave their own indelible mark on each film while working within the system—so long as their films were profitable. Hollywood managed to turn out some remarkable films during these years in spite of the studio system and partly because of it; but it also produced hundreds and hundreds of mediocre works cast in conventional molds.

Although Hollywood developed a slick and easy style with which to make most of its motion pictures, individual studios managed to focus on specific types of films and create their own looks. MGM, for example,

studio system   Metro-Goldwyn-Mayer Studios in 1933.

■ ■ ■

with its popular stars, ambitious sets, high fashions, and high-key lighting, was the studio of glamor which created family entertainment. Warner Brothers, on the other hand, created less glamorous and more contrasty images to deal with its less escapist fare, creating gangster movies, social dramas, and even musicals closer to the world outside the theater. Paramount created a glittering and bright world of sophisticated entertainment and, after financial difficulty in 1933 and reorganization in 1935, became the center for light entertainment and comedy for many years. Universal specialized in the dark, low-contrast world of the horror film, virtually creating a film genre on its own.

The demise of the studio system began with the 1948 Supreme Court Paramount decision, which ordered the companies to divest themselves of their theater holdings, thus ending their control of all levels of the industry and taking from them their guaranteed market. The studios were still in control of distribution and might have struggled along, but the rise of television cut seriously into audiences and sent film companies scurrying for new ways to draw people back to the theaters. Color cinematography, a brief flirtation with 3-D, and especially wide-screen processes had some impact, but not enough. While independent and European films were making inroads into the industry, American film producers and directors were finding it cheaper to make films abroad, where labor was inexpensive and governments were willing to subsidize filmmaking—by 1960 almost 30 percent of the films made by the major studios were filmed abroad. Studios began to rent out space to television companies and then began producing shows for the new medium themselves—the RKO studios were acquired by Desilu in 1953 for the sole purpose of making television programs. Production companies found themselves with large overheads they could no longer afford—numerous departments and personnel, expensive sound stages and equipment, high-salaried stars and technicians on permanent contract were adding 30 percent in costs for each film that was made. The time had come to cut back and eliminate departments, fire personnel, and sell the large studio lots that were now desirable real estate in a flourishing area of California. The last stage in the demise of this once immense and wealthy system of making motion pictures was the purchase of the film companies themselves by large conglomerates, in which film became one of many business ventures, the software for a server of hardware venues.

The film studios now release fewer films each year than they did during the studio-system days—234 new films and reissues in 1995 instead of the 400 to 500 of the late 1930s and early 1940s. Independent organizations released 185 films outside the major studios in 1995. As well as films germinating directly from the studios themselves, a number now originate individually and often independently, with a producer or sometimes talent agency "packaging" a production by bringing together perhaps a property, star, and director, and selling the package to either a studio or an independent group. The production group might rent facilities from a studio that does or does not finance the film, though, in either case, it is still likely to distribute the film through the same studio. Studios have become production/distribution houses—the central points for much of the industry's major activity (even with their smaller number of productions and distributions, they still account for 80 to 90 percent of the industry's income), but no longer the centers of film creativity and action. Although many projects bounce around the film industry for long periods of time, fewer films are made and these are produced at greater and greater costs—the result has been movies designed largely in terms of the marketplace and studio heads and stars with box-office attraction drawing astronomical salaries. Moviemaking in Hollywood has become big business with a vengeance. The high cost of filmmaking has now resulted in studios joining together—the 1995 Academy Award–winning *Braveheart* (dir. Mel Gibson) was credited to Paramount, which only put up 40 percent of the picture's money and got domestic distribution, while 20th Century-Fox put up the other 60 percent for international distribution. The studio system was concerned with producing films for money, but somehow, amidst all the mass production, there was room to make films for prestige; and somehow, in spite of all the hands involved in putting together a motion picture, the pieces occasionally fell together in a magical way. *See* **Hollywood.**

■ **studio tank** A large vessel for holding water that is up to fifty feet in diameter and fifteen feet deep and is placed either inside a film studio or on a studio lot for shooting scenes that take place on or beneath a body of water. Painted backdrops can be used to fill out the scene, while ports on the sides of the tank permit underwater filming. Various types of actions can be filmed with such tanks, but they are most often employed for shooting model boats. *See* **tank shot.**

■ **studio zone** An area within a thirty-mile radius of a shooting area (e.g., within the radius of a studio). Personnel must be paid for mileage outside this area during the period of production and certain working regulations also apply when outside the studio zone.

■ **stunt coordinator** The individual in charge of all the stunts for a film production—planning, arranging, and supervising them, as well as selecting and overseeing the stunt people who will do these actions.

■ **stunt man, stunt woman, stunt double** An individual who substitutes for an actor or actress to perform some difficult or dangerous action. This person must, of course, have some resemblance to the original performer and be dressed in an identical manner. Shots of such action are taken so that the identity of the stunt person is hidden. Stunt personnel are especially adept at taking falls, surviving crashes, or performing demanding athletic feats. When a film requires a group of such people performing a number of these actions, a stunt coordinator is hired.

■ **Stuntmen's Association of Motion Pictures** An organization made up of stunt men and women for the purpose of keeping the members informed of new stunt techniques and for exchanging information. Stunt people also belong to the Screen Actors Guild. *See* **Screen Actors Guild.**

■ **style** The general form and specific characteristics associated with a work of art either as it belongs to a group of works with similar qualities or as an individual creation. Style is more concerned with appearance than with content, the way something is presented rather than what is presented, although the two can be properly understood only in relation to one another. The concept of style may be applied to (1) a cultural movement, such as neoclassicism or expressionism; (2) a historical period, such as the Regency in Britain or the 1920s in the United States; (3) a period in an art form's development, for example, sound film in the 1930s; (4) a type of performing, for example, the somewhat melodramatic acting associated with silent films or the extreme realism of performers associated with the Actors Studio; and (5) a specific film artist, especially a director or cinematographer. The concept of style can be used to discuss film in the context of all the above categories: a film may be influenced by a specific cultural movement, such as expressionism; depict historically a particular period by imitating its style in settings and dress; be the stylistic product of a particular age in film history; feature a specific type of acting; and be analyzed largely as the stylistic creation of the filmmakers. Most often in film studies the concept is used to define the special characteristics of a specific director's works—the type of plot, camera technique, *mise-en-scène*, editing, sound, and acting that occur in individual works and from work to work. In this respect, style is ultimately the personal stamp and vision of the director imposed upon the subject of the film. As Béla Balázs states in *Theory of Film*, style "is always a deviation from authentic, objective reality."

■ **subbing layer, sub coat** The thin coating put on the base of film as an adhesion for the emulsion. Also called the substratum. *See* **emulsion** *and* **film** *(1)*.

■ **subdistributor** An organization which distributes films in a specific market or territory for an independent distributor. *See* **distribution.**

■ **subject-background ratio, subject/background ratio** The ratio of lighting intensity between the subject and background planes of a set.

subjective camera Robert Montgomery looks in the mirror at himself and at Audrey Totter in *Lady in the Lake* (1946; dir. Robert Montgomery).

■ ■ ■

■ **subjective camera** A technique for employing the camera in such a way that the point of view of a specific character is suggested. The camera might be angled or tilted to suggest the character's perspective; a panning shot might suggest his or her examination of a scene;

or a trucking shot suggest the character's movement. A handheld camera is a convenient means of conveying the ambulatory motion of a character. A transition is generally made between a close-up of the character and a point-of-view shot to lead us into the sustained perspective of the subjective camera. Such a technique should not be employed at too great a length lest both the orientation and interest of the audience be lost: we generally need a sufficient physical presence of the character on the screen in order to sustain our involvement with him or her. Robert Montgomery's *Lady in the Lake* (1946) forces the viewer into such a general displacement by using a subjective camera to convey the point of view of Philip Marlowe, the private eye, for the entire film. Delmer Daves used the subjective camera for the first part of *Dark Passage* the following year, until the plot brought Humphry Bogart to plastic surgery and his own face. The technique is best employed occasionally for dramatic effect, to increase our involvement with a character at an important point in the film. *See* **objective camera.**

■ **subjective camera angle, subjective angle** An angled perspective of the camera that suggests a specific character's point of view (e.g., an extreme high-angle shot suggesting a character's view from the top of a building).

■ **subject lighting ratio** The lighting ratio, i.e., the ratio of key to fill light, as it affects the subject of a shot. *See* **lighting ratio.**

■ **subject luminance range** *See* **brightness range.**

■ **subject plane** *See* **plane.**

■ **sublatent image** Specks of a latent image in exposed film emulsion that are too minute to change the surrounding halide to metallic silver during processing. *See* **film** *(1) and* **processing.**

■ **subliminal cut, sublim** A very brief shot meant to register on the viewer's mind almost imperceptibly and certainly ambiguously to suggest, anticipate, or remind the audience of some action or to create an underlying mood. In William Friedkin's *The Exorcist* (1973), Father Karras's dream is made even more disturbing by a subliminal shot of a satanic figure.

■ **submission release, submission agreement** A document freeing a studio or producer from liability to an author submitting a screenplay should the studio or producer use any "similar or identical" material. Such a document is required if the manuscript is directly submitted by the author and not through an agent. The document also frees the studio or producer from liability should the submitted work itself be subject to litigation. *See* **non-disclosure agreement.**

■ **subplot** A secondary sequence of action in a narrative concerning important but subsidiary characters.

■ **subrun, subsequent run** A release that follows the original distribution of a film. *See* **exhibition.**

■ **subsidiary, subsidiary contrast** An element in the visual image or a single visual image in a montage sequence that plays a subordinate role while contrasting with or highlighting the dominant contrast. *See* **dominant** *and* **intrinsic interest.**

■ **subsidy** A financial incentive made by a nation to a film company to produce a motion picture in that country. Many countries totally subsidize their national film industry, but a number of other countries have sought to encourage local filmmaking through some form of financial aid. American companies have been able to meet the requirements established by such countries to qualify as local producers, often entering into coproduction with domestic film personnel. Subsidies have come in the form of outright cash grants, low-interest loans, guarantees against financial loss both locally and abroad, or payments from taxes imposed on tickets in the host country. American film producers have been able to enter into coproductions in the past in Britain, France, and Italy, for example, with favorable financial assistance.

■ **substanative film** Film in which the couplers—that is, chemicals for producing color dyes—are already in the emulsion as opposed to nonsubstanative film, for which the couplers are in the developing solution. Eastman Color, for example, is a substanative film.

■ **substandard film** An older term for narrow-gauge film—that is, for 8mm, Super 8, and 16mm film.

■ **substratum** *See* **subbing layer.**

■ **subtext** The meanings or ideas that reside beneath the surface text (i.e., beneath the language, plot, character, and images) of a literary work, drama, or film. Such themes are suggested in film perhaps by the images or elements within the images, by the juxtaposition of scenes, or by background sound or music. The subtext is implicit and not explicit; it adds both depth and resonance to the work. The text of Ingmar Bergman's *The Virgin Spring* (1959), for example, deals with the rape of a young girl and the revenge of her father, while the subtext subtly and movingly elicits our realization about the struggle of Christianity to overcome paganism and about the need for faith. *See* **allegory** *and* **symbol** *(1).*

■ **subtitles** Words that appear at the bottom of the frame, normally to translate foreign dialogue. *See* **title.**

■ **subtractive color printer, subtractive printer** A printer for color film in which the white printing light is changed to the desired color by means of transparent colored filters covering various size holes in control bands. Density is controlled by neutral density filters or by altering the aperture. Additive printers, which add together the primary colors in different degrees for the required light, are now generally employed. *See* **additive color printer** *and* **printer.**

■ **subtractive colors, subtractive primaries** The color that remains when one of the primary colors is subtracted from white light and that is opposite to that primary on the color wheel: the blue-green color cyan remains when red is subtracted; the red-blue color magenta when green is eliminated; and yellow, a combination of green and red, remains when blue is removed. Both the subtractive color and the primary opposite to it on the wheel are referred to as complementary colors in that they complete one another. *See* **complementary colors** *and* **subtractive process.**

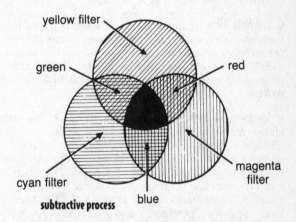

subtractive process

■ **subtractive process** A method of projecting color images by filtering out undesired parts of the spectrum from white light. This process is the one employed in film today as opposed to the additive process which creates the image by adding together the primary colors and which is the basis of color television. An early process used with great success was Technicolor, in which a beam-splitting prism in the camera sent light-waves to three separate negatives, two in bipack, for individual recording of each of the primary colors. The necessity for the large and cumbersome camera and the complicated processing system for the three negatives was eliminated when integral tripack film became available in the early 1950s. In the tripack method three separate emulsions, one for each of the primary colors, are combined in layers on a single base, the first sensitive to blue light, the second to green, and the third to red. When the negative is developed, chemical couplers in each later produce a dye in the corresponding subtractive or complementary color—that is, the color that remains when the primary has been subtracted from the spectrum. The three layers are yellow, magenta, and cyan respectively, but their concentrations are in reverse amounts to those needed for the original colors and tones. Hence colors appear complementary while light and dark are reversed. The image is then printed onto a tripack positive, generally with the magenta couplers on top, the cyan immediately below, and the yellow at the bottom, to form an image with dyes in sufficient concentrations to create the scene's original colors with normal light and dark. On reversal film the positive image is printed on the original film. When the picture is projected, each of the colors subtracts its own complementary (in this case primary) color from the light of the projector bulb and is itself sent to the screen. *See* **additive process, color film** *(2), and* **Technicolor.**

■ **suction mount** *See* **limpet.**

■ **suitcase** A small scrim, generally two or three feet in size, that is placed on a stand in front of a luminaire to control the intensity of light. *See* **scrim.**

■ **sulphide track** A sound track on some color reversal film in which the silver halide has been converted to silver sulfide, which will not wash out when the silver halide is removed from the image area. A silver area is necessary for the sound recording. *See* **reversal film** *and* **silver track.**

■ **Sundance Institute** This institute, founded in 1980 largely through the efforts of the actor Robert Redford and supported by contributions from the industry, is dedicated to developing new talent in filmmaking and raising the quality of the art in general. The institute has an especially noteworthy training program for young screenwriters but also brings to its facilities, in Utah, directors, producers, and performers for workshops. It also makes available limited funding for film projects and sponsors the now-celebrated festival each year for independent films, which is well attended by members of the industry.

sun gun

■ **sun gun, sungun** A lightweight luminaire with an extremely high-intensity light that can be held by hand or attached to a portable camera for filming news events. Such a light can be run by a thirty-volt battery belt.

■ **sunk up** Jargon for sound which is synchronized with the image.

■ **sunlight** Light directly from the sun. Daylight is considered sunlight plus light from the sky.

■ **sunshade, lens hood, lens shade** A device mounted on the camera to prevent stray light from entering the lens and generally attached to a matte box that holds filters or mattes in front of the lens. Sunshades are sometimes circular in shape, but a rectangular type, which can be bellowed in or out, is more efficient.

■ **supercoat** A thin layer of gelatin placed on top of the film to protect the emulsion from scratching or abrasion. Also called a nonabrasion layer. *See* **emulsion** *and* **film** *(1).*

■ **Super 8mm film, Super 8** A narrow-gauge film that began to replace standard 8mm film in 1966. Super 8 has a 50 percent larger image area than original 8mm film, since the perforations are reduced, allowing a wider frame, with its height proportionately increased. Super 8 has one perforation outside the middle of each frame and runs 72 frames to the foot. Both optical and magnetic sound tracks can be used on this film. The larger picture area produces images of greater definition and higher color quality than the standard 8mm film. Super 8 was very popular at one time for amateur photography and was even employed for educational and industrial films; but the new videotape, proving much easier and cheaper to use, considerably replaced this film in the marketplace. The 7008 Pro Beaulieu, from France, is the only Super 8mm camera made today, though one finds a number of the older cameras still in use. Super 8 has been used recently in both commercials and music videos to achieve certain visual effects. Super 8 Sound, with offices in both Cambridge, Massachusetts, and Burbank, California, is the center in the United States for this kind of filmmaking. Because of the limited types and amount of Super 8 film available, the company itself perforates and slits rolls of Eastman and Fuji 35mm film, and reloads the stock in traditional Super 8 cartridges—the product is called Pro-8. *See* **gauge.**

■ **superimpose, super** To place two or more images over each other in the same frame. Such a technique can be accomplished in the camera by reexposing the same piece of film, but is normally accomplished in an optical printer, where separate images are printed on the same film, one over the other. Not much used today, the technique has frequently been employed to show both a character and his or her thoughts or memories at the same time; actions taking place at different locations but simultaneously; the passage of time by overlapping a series of sequential actions; supernatural events such as the appearance of ghosts; and an analogy or contrast to the main image by placing on top of it the corresponding or contrasting image. Superimpositions take place in a dissolve when the initial scene and the following scene briefly overlap on the screen.

The process is also referred to as double exposure when only two images are superimposed over one another.

■ **superimposed titles, supers, supered titles, burn-ins** Titles that appear on top of a still or action image, sometimes used for credits at the start or conclusion of a film or for subtitles translating foreign dialogue at the bottom of the frame. Superimposed titles are normally made in an optical printer by printing together the titles and images from their respective films on fresh stock. *See* **title.**

■ **superimposition** The simultaneous appearance of two or more images over one another in the same frame. Also called double exposure when only two images are employed. *See* **superimpose.**

■ **Superscope** An early wide-screen process in which an image that extended the full width of the 35mm film between the perforations was shot with a regular lens and cropped on top and bottom for a 2:1 aspect ratio. The image was then horizontally compressed and vertically enlarged to fit into an anamorphic frame by means of an optical printer. When the image was projected through an anamorphic lens, a wide-scope picture was achieved. The system was first employed for *Vera Cruz* (1953; dir. Robert Aldrich). *See* **wide screen.**

■ **Super 16mm film, Super 16** Sixteen-millimeter negative film with an increased picture area from which the picture is blown up to a wide-screen image on a 35mm print. Super 16 has an image area 40 percent larger than regular 16mm masked for a 1.66:1 aspect ratio and 46 percent larger than such film masked for a 1.85:1 ratio. Introduced in 1971, the film has had moderate popularity. Robert Altman's *Come Back to the Five and Dime, Jimmy Dean, Jimmy Dean* (1983) and Peter Greenway's British film *The Draughtsman's Contract* (1983) employed this type of film.

■ **super speed lens** A wide-aperture lens that obtains acceptable exposure for film generally in areas of low light. *See* **lens.**

■ **Super 35** A wide-screen format that results from shooting with a spherical lens on 35mm film and employing an optical printer for creating the dupe negative used for making the release prints. Such a process is used for achieving a 1.85 aspect ratio (Super 1.85) or a 2.35 ratio (Super 2.35). For the 2.35 ratio, the frame is slightly widened into the space for the soundtrack on the negative. The Panavision Super R-200° 35mm camera is accessible to such film. *See* **wide screen.**

■ **supervising editor** The individual in charge of the editing operation. The supervising editor works directly with the producers and director, applying their concepts and ideas to the actual editing of the film while also creatively contributing to the process. In charge of the various editing personnel, he or she oversees the digital editing, preparation of workprints, and then works on the more-developed versions of the motion picture right up until the time of the release prints. *See* **editing.**

■ **supervising sound editor** The individual in charge of all the mixing and editing that goes into the final sound track. This person supervises the mixer, ADR editor, sound editor, and music editor among others. He or she normally prepares a temporary track and, in response to the director and perhaps the editor or producer, may ask for the recording of additional dialogue, sound effects, and music. The supervising sound editor will normally prepare the cue sheet for the making of the final mix.

■ **supply reel** The reel that feeds the film into the projector. Also called a feed reel.

■ **supply roll** The roll of fresh stock which is fed into the camera for exposure.

■ **supply spool** The cylindrical device on which fresh stock is wound and that feeds the film into the camera for exposure.

■ **supporting role** The term generally means a character in a film who is of secondary but significant importance to the lead roles. Academy awards are given to both an actor and an actress for playing such roles, even though the designation sometimes becomes dubious when a performer who has played a lead role is nominated for such an award.

■ **surface noise** Extraneous noise in any sound reproduction system, whether optical, magnetic, or disc. *See* **Dolby.**

■ **surrealism** A cultural movement in France that arose in the mid-1920s in painting, literature, and film. Related to the dadaist movement, surrealism had a similar anticonventional and absurdist bias, but also sought to recreate the poetry of the mind, especially with the help of Freud, and make a more pronounced and political attack on the establishment, with some help also from Marx. The French poet and writer André Breton, in his two manifestos on surrealism (1924 and 1929), argued for an art that expressed the mind without hindrance of reason, morality, or preconceived notions about art. For him, dream, hallucination, the free play of the mind, and the unconscious itself were the true real—even the super-real. Such a reality was created in art through the uncontrolled and unmediated process of "psychic automatism." The surrealist film as it developed in this movement collapsed the distinction between inner and outer reality, destroyed normal expectations about cause and effect, emphasized chance and the unexpected, presented strange and shocking relationships, and expressed the irrational, neurotic, and even grotesque recesses of the mind. It was an art form of strange and compelling images, where objects were dislocated from any natural or logical context, taking on abstract and even symbolic quality—but a symbolic quality that one interpreted only at great risk.

The most notable of the surrealist films were Man Ray's *L'Etoile de Mer* (1928) and Luis Buñuel and Salvator Dali's *Un Chien Andalou* (*An Andalusian Dog;* 1928). In 1930, Buñuel made *L'Age d'Or* (*The Golden Age*), with some early help from Dali on the script, a film in which the surrealism did not hide the vehement attack against the Church and middle-class morality. Buñuel went on to direct feature films that were considerably influenced by his early surrealistic avant-garde films, still with the same biting ridicule of conventional society, for example, *The Discreet Charm of the Bourgeoisie* (1972) and *The Phantom of Liberty* (1974). Jean Cocteau, French poet, writer, artist, and filmmaker, is also credited with making some important surrealist films, though both he and the surrealists would deny any affinities. His first film, *The Blood of a Poet* (1930), which creates the world of a poet where imagination and reality fuse, presents striking surrealist imagery. Also significant in this respect are his two further studies of the poet's mind, *Orpheus* (1950) and *The Testament of Orpheus* (1960). *See* **avant-garde cinema.**

surrealism The most famous of the shocking and irrational images in Salvador Dali and Luis Buñuel's *Un Chien Andalou* (1928).

■ ■ ■

■ **surround sound** A term applied to both music and sound effects that come from a separate track (the "surround channel") and are played from speakers at the sides and rear of a theater in a stereo system. Surround sound has added considerably to the effect of music and sound effects, placing the viewer's hearing in the midst of the screen's action. On 35mm film, two analog optical channels actually hold four tracks, three for the stereophonic effect coming from the screen

(right, center, and left) and one for the surround sound. The new digital systems, Dolby SR-D and Digital Theater Systems (DDS), have six channels with two for distinct left and right surround sound, while the Sony Dynamic Digital Sound (SDDS) has eight tracks, also with two for surround sound on each side of the theater.

■ **suspense** A state of uncertainty and delay that builds up anxiety as one awaits the outcome of a situation. Suspense seems to elongate time and delay the inevitable, but without decreasing our interest or tension. All plots must have some degree of suspense to maintain our interest, but certain types of films exploit this effect to create for the viewer a consistently tense and even exciting experience. Horror films use suspense to bring us to a state of expectation and dread as we await the fate of a potential victim; and adventure films make us fear for the life of the hero as he faces one threatening event after another. So called "suspense thrillers," such as Robert Siodmak's *The Spiral Staircase* (1945), are adept at bringing the audience to a paralytic state of near hysteria. *See* **thriller.**

■ **suture** A term used in psychoanalytic film theory to suggest the complex process whereby the spectator is stitched into the multitude of shots and spaces on the screen, thus becoming formulated as a subject while imposing a coherent unity upon the complex images on the screen. The concept of "suture" originates in the psychoanalytic thought of Lacan and was first applied to film in 1969 by Jean-Pierre Oudart, who argued that the shot/reverse-shot technique is the primary means of erasing the absences and closing the differences on the screen while suturing the spectator into the chain of meaning. *See* **film theory.**

■ **Svensk Filmindustri** The Swedish film production company that achieved significance during the silent era from films directed by Victor Sjöström and Mauritz Stiller. Svensk returned to its earlier glory after the Second World War with films by Alf Sjöberg and Ingmar Bergman.

■ **S-VHS** *See* **videotape.**

■ **swashbuckler** The term means a swaggering swordsman or adventurer and is also used to describe a film that features the exploits of such a figure. Films such as *The Black Pirate* with Douglas Fairbanks (1926; dir. Albert Parker) and *Captain Blood* with Errol Flynn (1935; dir. Michael Curtiz) feature a good deal of robust athletics and exciting swordplay.

■ **sweetening** Adding new sound to an already existing track, often additional sound effects.

■ **sweetening session** The final session for mixing sound, in which any additional sounds might be added. *See* **mix.**

▪ **swinger** A flat that can be swung out of the way to allow for the movement of the camera. Also referred to as a flapper.

▪ **swing gang, set dressers** The personnel who ready the set and sound stage for filming or who strike the set when it is no longer needed. Working under the leadperson, the swing crew dresses each set with the appropriate furnishings and properties. *See* **set decorator** *and* **leadperson.**

▪ **swish pan, flash pan, blur pan, flick pan, whip pan, zip pan** A transition between scenes made by the camera appearing to pan so rapidly that the intervening area passes by in a blur. Although taking longer than a direct cut, the technique is frequently employed to suggest that two actions are happening simultaneously. The sudden movement of the camera juxtaposes the actions in an immediate and dramatic manner. A particularly effective example of the swish pan occurs in Billy Wilder's *Some Like It Hot* (1959), when scenes of lovemaking between Marilyn Monroe and Tony Curtis are comically juxtaposed with the dancing of Jack Lemmon, who is disguised as a woman, and Joe E. Brown. *See* **pan.**

▪ **switchback** (1) A cut back to an original action after a cutaway to the present action. (2) The cuts back and forth between two parallel actions. (3) A flashback.

symbol The various symbols in Ingmar Bergman's *The Seventh Seal* (1957) weave together to form a rich allegory about the struggle between life and death.

▪ ▪ ▪

▪ **symbol** (1) Any object, setting, person, or action having a significance or meaning beyond that achieved from its immediate dramatic function. As well as having a denotative meaning, a symbol has an implicit and connotative significance that may arise from some universal association already implanted in the perceiver or from its context in the work of art. In Griffith's *Intolerance* (1916), the image of the mother (played by Lillian Gish) rocking the cradle, which ties together the four

stories, is clearly a symbol of life's continuity, which we understand from our own experience and knowledge; while "Rosebud," the famous sled in Orson Welles's *Citizen Kane* (1941), takes on its full significance as a symbol of Kane's lost childhood and innocence only from the context of the entire film. Symbols are a way of enriching a work's meaning, of giving it a subtext which extends the significance of the dramatic events taking place on the screen. When a work is replete with such symbols, especially characters who represent more than themselves, and the major action itself takes on a symbolic value, we have an "allegory" (e.g., Ingmar Bergman's *The Seventh Seal* [1957], which weaves plot and characters like a medieval tapestry that represents the universal struggle between the forces of death and life). *See* **allegory** *and* **subtext.**

(2) In semiotics, one of the three types of signs defined by C. S. Peirce. A symbol is made up of a signifier that is attached to what it signifies only by association or convention and not because it is a direct representation of the signified, as in the case of an icon, or is directly related to it, as in the case of an index. For example, the American eagle has become a symbol of the United States. *See* **semiotics.** (3) In computer graphics, a basic shape, such as a circle or square, that is stored permanently in a computer's memory and can later be employed as part of a drawing. *See* **computer animation.**

▪ **sync** An abbreviation for "synchronization," commonly used in film terms related to synchronized sound and picture—for example, sync beep or sync mark.

▪ **sync beep, sync pop, sync plop, sync tone** (1) A noise produced by a prerecorded tone of 1,000 Hz on a quarter-inch piece of magnetic tape with an adhesive backing that is attached to the leader of a magnetic sound track. The noise corresponds to several marked frames on the picture workprint and is employed for synchronization of sound and picture. Such noises are also used for synchronizing the various sound tracks during mixing. On an optical sound track, the beep creates a signal for synchronization with the edited original film in making the married print. (2) The noise at the beginning of a sound tape used in conjunction with several fogged frames at the start of the picture film to begin synchronization during editing. The sound is itself produced by a signal sent from the camera through a cable or by radio at the same instant that the frames are fogged by a light in the camera when the film begins to move. This process is called automatic slating. *See* **clapboard, editing,** *and* **synchronization.**

▪ **sync bench** *See* **editing bench.**

▪ **synchronic** The term comes from linguistics and semiotics to describe any language or code of signs as it exists all at once, as a single system, and is used in opposition to "diachronic," which refers to such a system as it develops through time. Both terms are now sometimes employed in critical discourse, synchronic in relation to any work of art as it is perceived spatially as a total entity, and diachronic as the work is perceived temporally as a changing and developing form. *See di-achronic and semiotics.*

■ **synchronism** The alignment of sound and picture so that the sound seems to originate directly from some action within the image.

■ **synchronization** (1) The placement of sound so that it seems to come directly from some action on the screen. (2) The alignment of both sound and picture so that the two are directly related. (3) The alignment of both camera and sound recorder in double-system filming so that both picture and sound will be perfectly matched. Several methods have been used at the beginning of shooting to mark the corresponding starts of both picture and sound. In the first, a clapboard with information relevant to the shooting is photographed to mark the take while the information is read into the sound recorder onto the quarter-inch magnetic tape. The clapsticks attached to the board are then slapped together, allowing the editor later to start synchronization by aligning the frame in which the clapsticks come together with the exact point on the tape when the clap is first heard. Time-code numbers on a clapboard, called a smart slate, and also registered on the audio tape allow for matching as well. In another method, called automatic slating, a flashing light in the camera fogs a few frames just as the film begins to move, while a beep tone is sent to the magnetic tape—the editor later uses both these reference points to start synchronization of picture and sound. An older method of recording both picture and sound so that they could later run in continuous synchronization employed a sync-pulse generator in the camera that sent a signal at the same frequency as the speed of the camera through a cable or by radio to the magnetic tape, where it was recorded on a separate track along with the sound. When the sound from the tape was transferred to magnetic film, the pulse signal could control the speed of the recorder so that the track was perfectly aligned with the picture. A more efficient way of achieving continuous synchronization of picture and sound is by means of a crystal oscillator in the camera that controls the machine's speed and a matching oscillator in the sound recorder that leaves a record on the tape identical to the camera's speed. The record on the tape can later be used when transferring the sound from tape to film to control the speed of the recorder so that the sound is in synchronization with the picture. Time-code technology is further used to allow for synchronization of picture and sound when a generator in the camera, synchronized with the audio recorder, prints the time-code numbers on the edge of the film at the same time that they are recorded on the audiotape. *See* **editing.**

■ **synchronization license** (1) Permission for using previously written or recorded music as part of the sound background to a film in synchronization with the images. This permission is normally given with the performance license for a single fee. The film company obtains contractual rights from an agency representing the composer. *See* **master use license** *and* **performance license.** (2) Permission for using recorded music as background for an animation film.

■ **synchronize** (1) To align both sound and picture so that the former seems to originate from the latter. (2) To bring both sound and picture into proper correspondence during editing by means of a synchronizer, that is, into "editing sync." (3) To bring sound into direct relation with the picture by advancing the sound track a certain distance ahead of the corresponding image on the married print (21 frames on 35mm film and 26 frames on 16mm film) to allow for the different positions in the projector of the sound head and lens; that is, to bring sound and picture into "print sync." (4) To interlock in proper relationship a combination of cameras, projectors, or dubbers for any of a number of processes (e.g., a rear projection shot or a dubbing session). *See* **sound advance** *and* **synchronization.**

■ **synchronized sound** *See* **synchronous sound.**

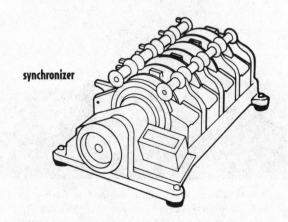

synchronizer

■ **synchronizer** A machine used in editing to place both picture and sound film in proper relationship to one another and also to measure feet and frames. Such a device consists of two or more pairs of sprocket wheels mounted on a single rotating shaft and allows one or more combinations of picture and sound to be played and aligned. The sprockets on the wheels engage the film's perforations, holding them in sync, while the films are moved either backward or forward by rewinds. A sound head mounted on a wheel can pick up the sound signal and send it to an amplifier and speaker. When sound and picture are properly aligned in the machine, they are considered to be in "editing sync."

■ **synchronous drive** *See* **synchronous motor.**

■ **synchronous motor** The term specifically refers to a motor that runs a camera at a precisely constant speed for recording the picture synchronically with the recording of sound and derives its energy and consistency from the sixty-cycle pulse of alternating current. The selsyn interlocking system was at one time used to guarantee that both camera and recorder motors would run in tandem. D.C. governor-controlled motors, which were smaller and more portable, were then employed in place of the A.C. synchronic motors. Crystal motors are most often used today for running movie cameras. Oscillating crystals of the same frequency in both the camera drive and sync pulse generator attached to the tape recorder keep both machines in tandem without the need for connecting cables. *See* **wild motor.**

■ **synchronous sound, sync sound** Sound that is heard in direct alignment with its source in the picture or its apparent source outside the image—for example, when dialogue seems to come directly from the character's mouth and "lip sync" is achieved. *See* **asynchronous sound** *and* **nonsynchronous sound.**

■ **synchronous speed** (1) The same precise rate of operation employed by camera and sound system for synchronic photographing and recording. (2) The standard 24 frames per second used by cameras and projectors for synchronous sound.

■ **syncing dailies** The process of arranging workprints of the day's shooting and sound recording for synchronized projection and playback.

■ **syncing tip** Coordinating the picture and sound films and attaching leader so that both will always start and remain in synchronization during editing.

■ **syncing up** Synchronizing picture and sound, especially during editing. *See* **synchronization.**

■ **sync loop** A piece of sound track looped together with a sync mark that allows the sound to be rerecorded at a specific point in the picture and for as long a time as required.

■ **sync mark** (1) A mark placed on the working leader of a piece of film that acts as a reference point for synchronizing the film with one or more sound tracks or with other pieces of film during editing. (2) A mark placed on the frame in which the clapsticks come together to act as a reference point for the start of syn-

chronization with the sound track when the clap of the sticks is first heard. (3) A marked frame on the leader of a release print that allows the projectionist to thread the film so that it is properly aligned between the projector's lamp and sound head.

■ **sync pop** *See* **sync beep.**

■ **sync pulse** An electrical pulse (generally sixty per second) from a generator in the camera or one attached to the audio recorder that is recorded on the sync (or pilotone) track on the audiotape. When the sound from the tape is transferred to magnetic film, the pulse controls the speed of the recorder so that the new track will be at exactly the same speed as the camera. *See* **synchronous motor.**

■ **sync-pulse cable** *See* **sync-pulse system.**

■ **sync-pulse generator** *See* **sync-pulse system.**

■ **sync-pulse system, pulse sync system** An older process for guaranteeing continuous synchronization of picture and sound in a double-recording system when magnetic sound recording is employed. A sync-pulse generator in the camera creates a sync pulse that acts as a reference point for the speed of the camera and is sent by cable or radio to the sound tape, where it is recorded, on a separate track, along with the sound. When the sound is rerecorded on perforated film with a magnetic track, the sync-pulse track from the original tape controls the speed of the recorder, thereby creating a sound track in precise synchronization with the picture. *See* **crystal sync** *and* **synchronous motor.**

■ **sync punch** (1) A hole punched on the working leader of a piece of film that acts as a sync mark for synchronizing this piece with other strips of film. (2) A hole punched on a sound track, either at the start or later on, that acts as an audible cue for synchronizing the sound with the picture or with other sound tracks.

■ **sync reference** The time-based signal that locks together the speed of one machine to that of one or more other machines. In film and sound synchronization, the signal is generally a sync pulse sent by a crystal oscillator. *See* **time code.**

■ **sync slate** *See* **slate.**

■ **sync-tone oscillator** A device in the camera that sends an audible signal to the sound tape, at the very instance that the first frames of film are fogged by a light. The fogged frames and sync beep are used as starting points for synchronization between sound and picture. *See* **synchronous motor.**

■ **sync track** The separate track on the sound tape that records the pulse signal from the camera for controlling the speed of the recording machine when the sound is transferred to film so that both sound and picture will be in continuous synchronization.

■ **synecdoche** A figure of speech in which a part represents the whole (e.g., when employees are referred to as hired "hands") or a whole represents a part (e.g., when athletes are referred to by the name of their country in Olympic competition). In film, these concepts and terms can be applied, in the first instance, to a close-up of the turning wheels of a train, which suggests to us the entire vehicle or, in the second, to a shot of a marching army, which represents for us the movements of an individual soldier. In semiotics, all of these are examples of an index, since each represents something else to which it has a direct connection. Related to synecdoche is metonymy, when one object is used to represent another with which it is normally associated (e.g., when a pair of wings indicates a pilot). *See* **index** *and* **metonymy.**

■ **synergy** The term means combined action, especially the working together of various parts in coordination and cooperation, and is now used to describe the synergistic activities of the various parts of a large conglomerate that derive from the making of a film. A single motion picture is employed in a series of distinct media—film, videotape, laser disc, cable television, regular television, CD-ROM, CD musical recordings of the sound track, novelization, and manufactured objects. The principle is that the sum of the activities produces action and revenue greater than any single part. The concept suggests the full marketing strategies that go into the making of a single film. *See* **Hollywood.**

■ **synopsis** A brief summary of a film or potential film written in a few paragraphs and including only a general outline of events. A synopsis might be used as a convenient way of first interesting a story editor or producer in a film project. Sometimes referred to as an idiot page. *See* **screenwriter.**

■ **syntagmatic** A term in semiotics used to describe a word's linear or "horizontal" relationship to other words in a sentence. A single word accrues meaning only in relationship to the words that have gone before and come after it in the sentence. The term "paradigmatic" is used in reference to the word's capacity to accrue meaning through its associative or "vertical" relationship with similar words in the language system, the fact that it is specifically chosen instead of another of those words. Signs in other sign systems can be studied in the same ways. Christian Metz, in *Film Language:*

A Semiotics of the Cinema, has categorized various kinds of shots and sequences in film as syntagmatic units, parts of his "grand syntagmatique," which are autonomous segments deriving their "final meaning in relation to the film as a whole." *See* **paradigmatic** *and* **semiotics.**

■ **syntax** In the study of language, the term refers to the structure of word order in a grammatical sentence or phrase. In film study, the term has sometimes been applied to the way in which shots are put together to convey meaning or create a specific effect, or the way in which the various elements of a *mise-en-scène* are ordered within the space of the frame to create meaning or affect the viewer. *See* **syntagmatic.**

■ **synthesizer** An electronic instrument sometimes used in a film to create striking or unusual music or sounds, and also sometimes employed for entire musical scores. Giorgio Moroder used the synthesizer to create some effective background music that matches the rather bold and assaultive images of Alan Parker's *Midnight Express* (1978) and Paul Schrader's *Cat People* (1982). Digital technology has now become part of the synthesizer with this electronic instrument replaying all kinds of instrumental and voice sounds digitally stored and with the synthesizer itself feeding sounds into a computer for manipulation and alteration. Sounds generated by a synthesizer can be digitally altered and integrated with other digital audio by means of Musical Instrumental Digital Interface (MIDI) and then matched through SMPTE time code to either film or video. Synthesizers can also produce printouts of scores and logs.

■ **Synthespians** A term now part of the lexicon of computer animation that refers to artificial characters created by means of digital magic. The term is also sometimes used for possible characters in the future who might be digital extensions of actual performers of the past. *See* **computer animation.**

■ **synthetic sound** Noises that have no direct origin in reality but are created specially for a film. Murray Spivack employed a number of unique procedures to create the noises of the prehistoric world in Cooper and Schoedsack's *King Kong* (1933), such as using bellows for the heavy breathing of the animals or running backward recordings of actual animals' cries for the sounds of the animated models. Electronic equipment and instruments are employed today to create unusual noises as well as musical scores for films. *See* **synthesizer.**

■   ■   ■

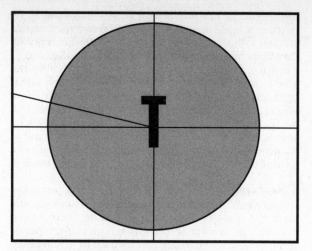

table editing machine, tabletop editing machine to typecasting

■ **table editing machine, tabletop editing machine** *See* **flat-bed editing machine.**

■ **table-top photography** The shooting of close-ups of small objects, sometimes on the top of a table.

■ **tab-to-tab** *See* **paper-to-paper.**

■ **tachometer** A device attached to a camera to indicate its speed in frames per second. Although important for cameras with wild or variable-speed motors, a tachometer is also useful to indicate when, after starting, a studio camera with a synchronic motor has obtained its fixed speed of 24 frames per second. *See* **frequency meter.**

■ **tag** The final scene in a film, immediately after the climax, that ties up all the action, offers a happy resolution, or puts some ironic touch to the conclusion of the work; the denouement.

■ **tag line** The concluding statement to a joke or routine that, culminating what has gone before, has some emotional impact upon the audience. The punchline.

■ **tail** (1) The end of a shot, scene, or entire film. (2) The end of a piece of film or entire reel of film. Also called tail end or foot. *See* **head.**

■ **tail-away shot** A shot of a character moving directly away from the camera.

■ **tailgate** The projector in an optical printer. *See* **optical printer.**

■ **tail leader** A strip of blank film attached to the end of a piece or reel of film that allows the proper projection of the final frames and protects the film. *See* **leader.**

■ **tail-out, tails out, tail up, tails up** The term refers to a reel of film with the end on the outside—for example, the film on the take-up reel of a projector that must be rewound. The terms "head out" or "head up" are used to describe a reel with the beginning of the film on the outside.

■ **tail slate** The slate that marks the identifying details of a shot when it appears at the end of a take instead of the beginning, generally in an upside-down position. Also called upside-down slate, endboard, and end slate. *See* **clapboard.**

■ **tail sync marks, end sync marks** Sync marks at the end of both picture and sound films that generally allow printing in reverse as well as in a forward direction.

■ **take** (1) A single uninterrupted recording of a shot. Normally several takes are photographed for each shot and the best is used in the edited film. The individual takes are numbered sequentially and marked on the slateboard, which is photographed at the start of each shooting; at the same time, the take number is read onto the sound track. Each shooting after the first is called a retake. *See* **shot.** (2) The continuous operation of the camera in recording a single version of a shot.

■ **take board** The clapboard or slateboard photographed at the start of each take that provides information concerning the take. Also called the number board. *See* **clapboard.**

■ **take camera** (1) A direction from the director for a performer to turn toward the camera, sometimes at the end of a shot so that the audience can see the character's reaction to the previous action. (2) A direction from the director, when he or she is showing on the set how some action should be performed, for the actor or actress to stand by the camera and see the way the action will appear to the audience.

■ **take it** *See* **print it.**

■ **take number, slate number** (1) The consecutive numbers assigned to both scenes and takes on the slateboard. Consecutive letters of the alphabet are attached to the number of the scene for each sequential segment (e.g., Scene 3A, Take 2). (2) The consecutive numbers for the individual takes of each shot marked on the slateboard along with a number and letter for the scene. *See* **clapboard.**

■ **take sheets** *See* **continuity notes.**

■ **take-up** That part of any film machinery, normally a reel or spool, on which film is wound after it has been exposed for photographing, printing, editing, or projecting.

■ **take-up chamber** That part of the magazine attached to the camera into which the film passes after it has been exposed in the camera. The film enters the camera from the feed chamber. *See* **magazine.**

■ **take-up plate** The reel on which film is wound after it passes through a flat-bed editing machine. The film enters the machine from the feed plate. Such an editing table may have two or more pairs of such plates *See* **flat-bed editing machine.**

■ **take-up reel** The reel on a projector that receives the film after it has passed through the machine and been projected. The film enters the projector from the feed reel.

■ **take-up spool** The spool in a camera on which film is wound after it has been exposed. The film enters the camera from the feed spool.

■ **taking lens** The lens on a turret that is placed in front of the aperture and through which the light passes on the way to the film; the lens used for the actual take. Such turrets hold three or more lenses, any of which can be rotated in front of the aperture to become the taking lens. *See* **turret.**

■ **talent** (1) Professional performers. (2) The personnel employed as performers in a specific film production.

■ **talent agency** An organization that represents various kinds of entertainment personnel in seeking employment and in business negotiations. Although writers are frequently represented by literary agencies, especially those based in New York City, some larger agencies in Los Angeles represent such individuals engaged in the entertainment field as well as representing performers, directors, producers, and cinematographers. Talent agencies with important motion-picture departments are Creative Artists Agency, International Creative Management, the William Morris Agency, and United Talent Agency. It is essential for these agencies to keep abreast of all activities in the industry, especially plans for future productions, and vigorously to seek work for their clients. It is also the responsibility of the agency, now that the Hollywood studios are no longer able to perform this job, to promote and develop the career of its talent. Such talent agencies, and the many smaller organizations that perform the same functions, are franchised by the numerous motion-picture and television guilds to negotiate for their members' financial terms and working conditions that meet certain basic requirements. For these services the agencies receive 10 percent of their clients' gross pay. In recent years, some agencies have engaged in the practice of "packaging," which means putting together a potential film production with several of its own talents (e.g., a major star, producer, and director) and selling the project to a studio or group of investors. Such talent agencies have also been responsible for the astronomical rise in salaries for stars and thus partly responsible for the economic struggles of the industry. Agencies have become so much a part of the film industry and so involved in preproduction planning that a number of successful agents have gone on to run major studios.

■ **talent agent** An individual who represents a particular talent in the entertainment field in seeking employment and in business negotiations. Performers, directors, producers, screenwriters, cinematographers, and even set designers are represented in this manner. The agent will frequently work for a large talent agency and have behind him or her the vast resources of the organization; but often a client might prefer the closer attention that comes with an agent who belongs to a small group or works independently. (The independent agent or the agency for which the agent works normally receives 10 percent of the client's gross pay). In all cases, the relationship between client and agent is of paramount importance for both the career and the psychological well-being of the client. *See* **talent agency.**

■ **talent scout** An individual who travels about discovering unknown talent and future stars; generally thought of as working for one of the major Hollywood studios during the days of the studio system.

■ **talent union** A labor organization to which performers belong (e.g., the Screen Actors Guild).

■ **talkies** A colloquial term for sound motion pictures, especially used during the years immediately after the advent of sound in 1927.

■ **talking heads** One or more shots composed largely of medium close-ups of characters engaged in conversation with little action taking place. The result is generally static and undramatic.

■ **tank** *See* **studio tank.**

■ **tank shot** A shot employing a studio tank holding water, generally to suggest some action taking place on a body of water. A mockup of part of a boat might be placed in such a pool on rockers which create the pitching movement of the vessel, while a wave machine might be employed to make the water seem storm-tossed. Such tanks are frequently employed for photographing miniatures of boats. Some studio tanks have ports on the side to permit underwater filming. *See* **studio tank.**

■ **TAP** *See* **Theater Alignment Program.**

■ **tape** (1) The quarter-inch magnetic tape on which iron oxide has been coated for the recording and playback of sound; also called audio tape. *See* **magnetic recording.** (2) Audio tape that records sound digitally. Such recording is now being employed during film production. Sony introduced its Digital Audio Tape cassettes (DAT) less than a decade ago. Nagra has produced a recorder, the Nagra-D that, employing quarter-inch digital tape, looks and functions much like its magnetic tape models. (3) Transparent and adhesive splicing tape either with perforations or perforated by the tape splicer for joining two pieces of film in a butt splice. *See* **splicer.** (4) Any adhesive tape employed in film work (e.g., for marking camera or luminaire positions on the floor of the set, sealing film cans, or attaching objects together). Such tape is generally called gaffer or camera tape. (5) To measure the distance from the camera lens to the plane of action in order to set the camera's focus. (6) To record sound on magnetic tape. *See* **magnetic recording.**

■ **tape deck** A magnetic tape recorder without speakers. *See* **magnetic recording.**

■ **tape hook** The hook to which the tape is attached when measuring the distance from the camera lens to the plane of action for setting focus.

■ **tape recorder** *See* **magnetic recording** *and* **magnetic tape recorder.**

■ **tape speed** The rate at which magnetic tape passes the recording and playback heads in a magnetic tape recorder for good sound reproduction, normally computed in inches per second. Speeds of 15 and 7½ inches per second are employed for professional work in most instances, while 3¾ and 1⅞ are sufficient for home use. *See* **magnetic tape recorder.**

■ **tape splice** A connection of two pieces of film made by a transparent piece of adhesive tape; a butt splice. *See* **splice.**

■ **tape splicer, tape joiner** A small machine that attaches two abutting pieces of film with transparent tape so that they form a butt splice. The tape may already have perforations or be perforated by the machine itself, which is then called a guillotine splicer. *See* **splicer.**

■ **tapping the track, tapping the tape** Marking a sound track or magnetic tape to indicate musical beats in order to facilitate the mixing of other sounds during editing.

■ **target** A small round flag, generally three to nine inches across and made of opaque material, which is often placed in front of the camera to block light from

entering the lens or placed on the set to create a shadow. Also called a dot.

target

■ **target audience, target market** A specific audience for whom a film is intended—for example, the young teenage audience for whom a broad farce about high-school life is primarily made.

■ **T core** A plastic centerpiece for holding up to 400 feet of 16mm film.

■ **tearjerker** A film, play, or literary work with much pathos and suffering that seeks to elicit an emotional and heartfelt response from the audience—for example, *Dark Victory* (1939; dir. Edmund Goulding), in which Bette Davis plays a well-to-do young woman dying of a brain tumor. Also referred to as a weepie.

■ **teaser** (1) An opening scene in a film that appears before the credits and arouses the audience's attention in an immediate way while building anticipation for future action (e.g., the colorful, violent, and sometimes lengthy beginnings to the James Bond movies). Such a scene is sometimes referred to in the trade as a pre-credits grabber. (2) A short preview that appears before the regular trailer and advertises a film that will not be appearing until a later time. *See* **trailer.**

■ **teaser campaign** The advertising program on radio, television, and in publications that is carried on before the release of a film to arouse the public's curiosity about the motion picture and lure them to the theater.

■ **tea-wagon** Jargon for a mixing console. *See* **mixer.**

■ **technical adviser** An individual with a specific expertise hired for a film from outside the motion-picture industry to furnish advice—for example, a doctor to advise on medical procedures in a hospital film. Sometimes a specialized group that appears in a film might assign one of its own members to act as such a consultant.

■ **Technicolor** A series of color processes originating with the work of Herbert T. Kalmus and Donald F. Comstock, who formed the Technicolor Motion Picture Corporation in 1915. The earliest system was an additive process that exposed two negatives in the camera by means of a beam splitter to the red and green components of light respectively, and then projected the separate prints through the corresponding red or green filter in a single projector. The process was employed for *The Gulf Between*, a feature film made by the company in 1917. A general problem in aligning the two images on the screen, however, led to the development of a subtractive process, again using a beam-splitting camera to make two color records, but this time on a single film from which two separate relief images were made and glued together, each side then dyed in its appropriate complementary color, either magenta or cyan. Metro used the system for *Toll of the Sea* in 1922, but perhaps the most notable film made with this process was *The Black Pirate* (1926), starring Douglas Fairbanks. In 1928, Technicolor introduced its imbibition method of printing, employing two matrices with relief images, made from the color records on the black-and-white negatives, that were dyed in their appropriate complementary colors and their dyes then transferred to a single print.

In 1932, the company at last introduced full-color cinematography, now using a camera with a beam splitter to make three color-separation black-and-white negatives, the blue and red lightwaves generally recorded on two films in bipack and the green on a separate film. Three separate matrices were made from the three negatives, each matrix employed in the imbibition printing process to transfer a dye in its appropriate complementary color to the single print. Walt Disney first used this three-color subtractive process to make his animated short *Flowers and Trees* in 1932; the first feature film to employ this color system was Rouben Mamoulian's *Becky Sharp* in 1935. The Technicolor company always supervised the use of its process, supplying both the equipment and personnel; the cost was high but the results generally were worth it—one need only think of the bold picturebook colors of *Gone With the Wind* (1939; dir. Victor Fleming).

The company also introduced a "tripack" negative that could be used in a standard camera: developed from Eastman Kodak's 16mm Kodachrome, this film had three separate emulsions for each of the primary colors. This tripack film, first employed for some sequences in *Dive Bomber* (dir. Michael Curtiz) in 1941, was splendidly used for *King Solomon's Mines* (dir. Compton Bennett) in 1950. Technicolor's tripack film, however, was replaced after 1952 by Eastman Kodak's Eastman Color, a less expensive and faster film that could also be employed in normal cameras and developed as a single negative, while the imbibition process for printing developed by the Technicolor company was maintained in this country until the 1970s, when a large number of release prints was required. "Color by Technicolor" still appeared in titles after the demise of the tripack film and imbibition process, but the quality of the Eastman Color was not the same. Most significantly, the durability of the old Technicolor systems was gone, at least until 1983, when the problem was partly

rectified with low-fade stock. The old Technicolor dye-transfer process continued in England and Italy until 1978; and today only in China at the Beijing Film Lab can one find it still in use. *See* **color, imbibition, integral tripack color system, Technirama,** *and* **Techniscope.**

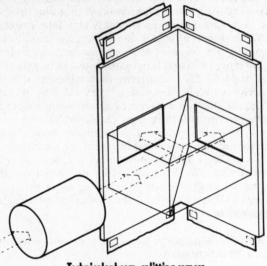

Technicolor beam-splitting camera

■ **technique** (1) The manner in which the various methods or procedures for creating a work of art are employed. In film the term would apply to the way in which camera, lighting, color, *mise-en-scène*, cutting, or sound are employed or the way in which performers act their roles. The better directors have a discernible manner of employing these elements of film which creates a specific style. *See* **style.** (2) The special methods or procedures that are employed in creating a work of art; in film, the methods listed in (1) as well as all the technical procedures employed in creating a film. (3) The technical capacity of an individual to perform the requisite skills in carrying out a specific function—for example, an actor has "good technique" when he or she performs a role with intelligence and competence.

■ **Technirama** A wide screen film process developed by the Technicolor Motion Picture Corporation that used 35mm film moving horizontally through the camera while exposing a frame of eight perforations behind an optical system which compressed the image. The frame was printed with further horizontal compression on a 35mm film so that it could be projected through a CinemaScope lens with an aspect ratio of 2.35:1 (unsqueezed prints could also be made on 35mm film). The increased size of the frame on the negative resulted in a picture of excellent definition and clarity. For special showings a contact print could be made directly from the original negative and projected through a horizontal projector. Super Technirama 70 used the same double-size, compressed frame on the negative, but unsqueezed it on a 70mm print in order to project a wide-screen image of 2.2:1 through a normal lens. Technirama was used from 1956 through the mid-1960s in films such as *The Music Man* (1962; dir. Morton de Costa). *See* **wide screen.**

■ **Techniscope** A wide-screen process, introduced by Technicolor Italia in 1963, that employs a camera with a two-perforation pulldown to make a frame only half the normal height, but with a 2.35:1 ratio, and compresses the image into the normal anamorphic frame of a 35mm print for projection through an anamorphic lens so that it will have the 2.35.1 ratio on the screen. The process is economical, saving half the cost of the negative, and though the size of the frame on the negative is small, the regular size frame with the squeezed image on the 35mm print creates a picture with satisfactory definition. This system was used for such films as Sergio Leone's *Once Upon a Time in the West* (1969) and George Lucas's *American Graffiti* (1973). *See* **wide screen.**

■ **tee** A device with three extended arms in a T or Y shape that acts as a support for the legs of a tripod and keeps the tripod from slipping or marring the floor. Also called a spreader, spider, or triangle.

■ **teenie** A small open-faced luminaire with a 650-watt bulb.

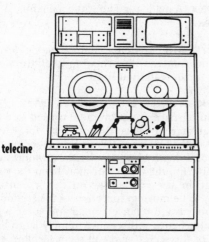

telecine

■ **telecine** The word derives from "television cinematography" and originally referred to a machine that converts pictures on motion-picture film into a signal that can be converted into television images via videotape. This device is still employed for transmitting over television via videotape anything intended for that medium but originally shot on film (e.g., news segments or made-for-television movies) or for transmitting motion pictures. But today telecines also change film images to video pictures for off-line editing or convert the film image directly into a digital code for nonlinear editing. An early type of telecine, called a film chain, employed a television camera looking into the

lens of a projector and scanning the individual frames, with the light broken down into its blue, green, and red components, each of which was converted into a signal by a separate tube in the camera. The most common type of telecine since the late 1970s has been the flying spot scanner, which employs a flying spot raster from a cathode-ray tube to scan the film. The light passing through each frame is then broken down by dichroic mirrors into the three primary colors, each of which is converted by a separate photocell into a signal. The signals are next preamplified and corrected before they are recorded onto videotape or digitized for storage. A recent technology employs three trilinear CCD (charge-coupled device) sensors, one for each of the primary colors, responding to a xenon light source: the vast number of pixels on the CCDs convert the light energy into analog electric signals that ultimately record the image on the videotape.

Older motion pictures with a standard aspect ratio of 4.3 can be transmitted in full, since television screens have the same dimensions, but flying spot systems pan across images from films with wide-screen ratios to pick out the areas of major action while zooming into the film image. Fixed wide-screen blanking in some systems allows a number of aspect ratios when a letter-box image is sought to convey the original widescreen image. Largely used in postproduction, the Rank digital URSA telecine, with its flying spot and digital technology, has the capacity to perform horizontal and vertical pans as well as zooms, create a variety of effects, properly align the images, and also correct color. Kodak and Philips have just put on the market the Spirit DataCine, a state-of-the-art telecine that creates a high-resolution image by using a 2K file with a resolution of 2,000 lines. Telecine machines might also rerecord the sound from optical tracks, but more often the sound is generated from an interlocked magnetic film or later added.

Much television is shot on film and transferred to videotape because the dynamic range of the film image will ultimately create a better video image. Modern telecine machines have been much improved, creating reproductions that are now much closer to the film image. Original negative films are used to create television images with great fidelity in shadows and color; master positives and dupe negatives create nearly as good an image; and print film, creating an image with a certain loss of density information and increase in contrast, is rarely used. To match up the 24 frames per second of film with the 30 frames in NTSC video used in the United States, a 2:3 pulldown is used; i.e., one frame of film is transferred into two fields of the video, while the next frame of film is transferred into three fields. Film telecines record at real time the 24 frames per second for any type of video transmission, while film scanners digitize pictures at a much slower rate of 5-24 seconds per frame so that the image can ultimately be returned to film with its original resolution. *See* **film scanner** *and* **film recorder.**

■ **telecine timer, telecine colorist** Someone who is in charge of maintaining the quality of the image in transferring film images to video by means of a telecine. Such a person seeks to obtain the same quality of color, dark and light, sharpness, and motion. *See* **timer.**

■ **tele-extender lens** A range extender used with a long-focus or zoom lens to increase the focal length by factors of 1.5, 2, or 3. Such lenses, placed between the lens and the camera, increase magnification, but with reduced effective aperture and some loss of definition. *See* **range extender.**

■ **telefilm** (1) A television program originally photographed on film. (2) *See* **made-for-TV movie.** Also called a telepix.

■ **tele-lens** *See* **telephoto lens** *(1).*

■ **telemeter** *See* **rangefinder.**

■ **telephoni bianchi** The term is Italian for white telephone and refers to a group of escapist films made in fascist Italy during the 1930s and 1940s that featured characters belonging to the wealthy class in opulent, sterile settings that included white telephones. Such films were light romantic comedies that gave an upbeat and positive depiction of life in Italy.

telephoto distortion This still from Stanley Kubrick's *Barry Lyndon* (1975) shows the long-focus effect of a special zoom lens designed for the film.

■ ■ ■

■ **telephoto distortion, telephoto effect** The diminishment of depth and flattening of background created by a telephoto or long-focus lens that causes characters and objects at the various distant planes to seem unnaturally large and a character moving toward or away from the camera to do so with extreme slowness, as if hardly moving at all—both the character and the relative

planes will seem to remain the same size for a long period of time. *See* **lens, long-focus lens, telephoto lens,** *and* **telescopic effect.**

■ **telephoto lens, tele-lens** (1) A lens, ranging anywhere from 150 to 1,000mm, with a positive front element distanced from a negative rear element so that the true focal length is greater than the distance between the lens itself and the focal plane. Also called a true telephoto lens to distinguish it from the types of lens described in (2) and (3) below as "telephoto." Since these lenses can function as a telescope, magnifying and bringing into focus a subject in the distance while tending to blur other planes of action, they are much used for news and sporting events as well as for documentary filmmaking. Because such lenses also keep distant objects relatively large while flattening depth between planes, they are employed in motion pictures for creating a sense of the compactness of urban life (e.g., rows of automobiles can be compressed into and on top of one another) and also for making a character running toward or away from the camera hardly seem to move at all. (2) Any lens with the capacity of magnifying a subject 50 percent more than a normal lens. (3) The term is loosely applied to any lens with a focal length larger than normal, including long-focus lenses. *See* **lens, long-focus lens,** *and* **telephoto distortion.**

■ **telepix** A made-for-TV movie; a telefilm. *See* **made-for-TV movie.**

■ **telePrompTer** Trade name for a cueing device placed near the camera with a rotating scroll from which performers can read their lines.

■ **telescopic effect** (1) *See* **telephoto distortion.** (2) The distortion of space and movement caused by a lens of either greater or lesser than normal focal length: for lenses of the first type, distant objects are kept relatively large and depth between planes is compressed so that a figure running toward or away from the camera will change in size very slowly on the screen and seem hardly to be moving; for lenses of the second type, distant objects are relatively small and space is extended so that a figure will seem extremely large toward the front of the screen and will seem to move excessively fast either away from or toward the camera.

■ **television** The transmission of electrical signals that, when received by an appropriate piece of equipment, form a visual image with accompanying sound. The electrical signals may themselves depict some live action in a studio or at some location; be transmitted from a videotape at a studio; or come directly from a videotape in a videocassette recorder attached to the television set. In a color television set three electronic guns individually emit beams for each of the primary colors that scan the television set, from left to right and from top to bottom, illuminating appropriately colored red, blue, and green dots on the screen of the tube with varying intensity . These beams scan a total of 525 lines in the American NTSC system, first the odd- and then the even-numbered lines—each of the scans is called a field and both the fields interlace to form a frame. The field frequency is 60 per second while the frame frequency is 30. DSS (Digital Satellite System), with the use of an 18-inch dish picking up digital signals from a satellite and a set-top converter box transforming them for a standard analog television receiver, creates images of laser-disc quality and sound as if it were from a CD. High Definition Television (HDTV) is about to improve the quality of images and sound even further. With an all-digital system that will prevent any deterioration in picture and sound; 1080 scan lines, more than twice the number now in use; and an aspect ratio of 16:9 to accommodate wide-screen films, HDTV will certainly bring home television into the twenty-first century. The term "video" is sometimes used synonymously with television, though it more often refers either to the entire technology or to its nonbroadcasting portion (e.g., videotape, video art, video assist). *See* **video.**

■ **television cutoff, television cropping** The reduction of a film frame when transmitted over television.

■ **television mask, TV mask** A mask used in a viewfinder or in preparing animation or titles on a film to indicate the safe-action area that will appear on a television screen. *See* **safe-action area.**

■ **television safe-action area** *See* **safe-action area.**

■ **temp dub** An early mix of dialogue, music, and sound effects on a separate track that is used in proper sync with a temporary version of the film. Such playback is useful for making judgments and then changes in the edited film.

■ **template** An opaque sheet with portions cut away so that a patterned shadow is formed when the sheet is placed within a spotlight.

■ **tempo** *See* **pace.**

■ **temp track, temp music track** A temporary sound track with music from various sources that is played during early previews or screenings of a film before its own music is composed and recorded.

■ **tendency drive** The mechanism for passing film through a continuous processing machine by means of friction from a series of rotating rollers instead of by sprocket teeth engaging the film's perforations. Because such a mechanism puts little strain on the film or its perforations, it is especially employed for processing original negatives. Such a mechanism is sometimes called a sprocketless drive. Processing machines with both these rollers as well as sprockets are said to operate by a semi-tendency drive. *See* **processing.**

■ **tener, tenner, ten-K, 10-K** A 10,000-watt spotlight with a Fresnel lens. *See* **Fresnel.**

■ **tenlight** A lighting unit with ten bulbs in a rectangular housing that gives off a diffuse, soft light.

■ **terminal.** (1) The device through which an electrical connection is made to a piece of equipment. (2) The point at which an electrical connection is made to a piece of equipment.

■ **terms** The stipulations agreed upon by the distributor and exhibitor for the public showing of a film in the exhibitor's theater or theaters. These terms would include rental fee, the duration of the exhibition, and the sharing of the advertising costs. *See* **distribution** *and* **exhibition.**

■ **territorial sales** A method of foreign distribution for a film whereby a producer receives profits from individual nations without having them offset by losses in other locations. If profits are offset by losses elsewhere, the method is called cross-collateralization.

■ **test, test strip** A piece of film that is exposed in the camera and then processed to see if equipment, shooting conditions, or the processing itself is adequate, or under what conditions the remainder of a roll to which the piece belongs should be processed.

■ **test booking, test marketing** Releasing a film in only a select market or to only a select number of theaters to see how the audience reacts to both the advertising and the film in order to plan the future advertising and publicity campaign for the wide release. Changes in the film might sometimes be made in response to the audience's reactions. *See* **preview** *(2).*

■ **test camera** A basic camera and rostum used in animation only for line testing.

■ **test film** A film especially made to assure that a piece of equipment (e.g., a projector) is running properly. Subjective test films allow the evaluation of a projector from watching and listening while quantitative test films require various measuring devices to give a precise and scientific reading.

■ **text** In literature the term refers to the actual written words of the author that are the basic substance of the work of art. In film studies the term refers to (1) the surface of the work as made up of numerous semiotic codes that must be read independently and dependently as they form the meaning and create the impact of the work—language, sound, settings, dress, gesture, images, shots, editing, and generic conventions, for example, all operate as the separate codes which form the work's text; and (2) the characters, plot, dialogue and images that make up the surface of the work and are clearly discernible—that is, their immediate denotative meaning—as opposed to the work's subtext, which is connotated and suggested, residing beneath the work's surface. *See* **semiotics** *and* **subtext**.

■ **texture** The visual tactile structure of a surface. This characteristic is significant in relation to the grain of an image—for example, the graininess we associate with newsreel and documentary films can be employed in a feature film to suggest an actual event and a factual approach. Texture also is important when considering the various elements within an image—for example, the porosity of skin or surface of garments. In the Japanese film *Woman in the Dunes* (1964), Hiroshi Teshigahara, with his cinematographer, Hiroshi Segawa, creates a wonderfully textured interplay between sand and human flesh in creating a sexual drama about human loneliness and dependency.

■ **texture mapping** Wrapping a two-dimensional surface around a three-dimensional model in computer graphics or animation to create a recognizable or realistic object. Texture mapping refers to a variety of surface types, not all of which we think of in the context of "texture." The following types of mapping belong to this general category: bump mapping, which results in a bumpy or uneven surface; environment (sometimes also referred to as reflection or reflectivity) mapping, which creates the illusion of a reflected environment off an object; specular mapping, which creates a specular reflection; transparency mapping, which creates both a surface and the appearance of seeing through it; and color or surface color mapping, which is perhaps the most used. The surface itself may be created by the artist or removed from another digitized object to be placed on the model. Displacement mapping, a different procedure, creates the illusion of jagged peaks or a series of high and low points or areas, for example, by actually changing the geometry of the surface. *See* **computer animation.**

■ **T-grain emulsion** *See* **grain.**

■ **Thaumatrope** An early persistence-of-vision toy, so named by Dr. J. A. Paris of London from the Greek for "magical turning" and commercially developed by him in the 1820s. Two objects drawn on opposite sides of a disc could be merged into a single image when the disc was spun by means of cords attached to each of its sides.

■ **theater** *See* **movie house.**

■ **Theater Alignment Program (TAP)** A program instituted by Lucasfilm in cooperation with film distributors and

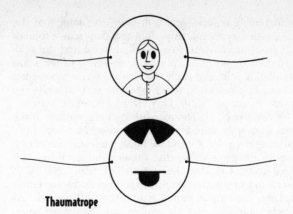

Thaumatrope

exhibitors, including the National Association of Theater Owners (NATO), establishing goals for the quality of 35 and 70mm film screenings in indoor motion-picture houses. The standards are divided into three categories: print condition, technical aspects of presentation (viewing conditions/image quality and sound quality), and theater maintenance and operations.

■ **theater sig, theater signature, theater logo** The name, address, and phone number of a theater as it is presented independently at the bottom of a printed advertisement for a film or uniformly with a list of other theaters belonging to the same circuit and playing the same film.

■ **theatrical circuit, theater chain** (1) A number of film theaters, generally in a particular area, owned by a single organization. (2) All the film theaters, generally in a particular area, in which a motion picture circulates. (3) The term is sometimes loosely used for all the movie houses in the nation which show films for profit.

■ **theatrical distribution** The commercial distribution of a film to movie houses as distinct from nontheatrical distribution to colleges and private groups. *See* **distribution.**

■ **theatrical documentary** A term sometimes used for a documentary that, though based on real life and people, uses some of the techniques of a fictional film—for example, dialogue, plot, dramatic climax, staged or reshot scenes. Sidney Meyer's *The Quiet One* (1949), the story of a disturbed black youth in Harlem, is a notable example of such a film. *See* **documentary.**

■ **theatrical exhibitors** The individuals or organizations that show motion pictures in commercial theaters for profit.

■ **theatrical film** A motion picture produced for commercial distribution to movie houses; generally a feature film.

■ **Theatrograph** A projector, devised in England in 1896 by R. W. Paul, that ultimately stems from Edison's Kinetescope and Paul's earlier work with Birt Acres in the development of a camera. In 1896, Méliès purchased such a machine from Paul when he was unable to obtain a Cinématographe from the Lumière brothers, and from it designed his own camera. Paul, who himself was an important pioneer filmmaker, later changed the name of his machine to the Animatographe.

■ **thematic montage** A type of editing that links shots together by means of some idea or theme rather than by narrative development. Such editing operates without regard to temporal or spatial relationships, but instead creates for the viewer some intellectual concept that unifies the montage. Eisenstein classifies a related type of editing as "intellectual montage" in his essay, "Methods of Montage" in *Film Form. See* **montage.**

■ **theme** A general subject, topic, message, concept, social attitude, or mood that runs throughout a work of art. In a narrative work, such as film, the term applies to some pervasive element that seems both a product of the work's plot and its manner of presenting the plot as well as a unifying factor to its various actions and characters. The theme of a work is commonly thought of as its "message" or idea, but many works are not sufficiently didactic or reductive to satisfy such a limited definition, while they do seem unified by certain connecting strands that run from their beginning to end. More complex works of art have a number of themes working together to create a rich experience for the audience. *See* **motif.**

■ **theme music** A recurrent musical melody or passage that runs throughout a film. Sometimes films have separate themes relating to specific characters, as in Franz Waxman's effective score for *Bride of Frankenstein* (1935; dir. James Whale), with its individual melodic lines for both the monster and the bride, and for specific places, as in Max Steiner's celebrated score for *Gone With the Wind* (1939; dir. Victor Fleming), with its lyrical "Tara's Theme."

■ **theme park** *See* **leisure-based entertainment.**

■ **theme song** A song sung at the start of a film, at some key point, or at intervals, that becomes associated with the film—for example, the title song to *High Noon* (1952; dir., Fred Zinnemann), with music by Dmitri Tiomkin and lyrics by Ned Washington. *See* **title song.**

■ **theory** *See* **film theory.**

■ **thesis film** Generally a pejorative term for a film that clearly presents some message at the expense of character and complexity.

■ **thin** (1) A term used to describe a negative insufficiently exposed to produce a well-defined image. (2) A term used to describe an image with shallow density.

■ **third man, third person** *See* **cable puller.**

■ **Third World cinema** Films made by countries not belonging to developed industrial societies—generally films from the postcolonial countries of Latin America, Africa, and Asia, often with a decidedly revolutionary or leftist political bent. Our closest neighbor, Mexico, has had the most-developed film industry in Latin America, but its film history has been varied. The 1940s and 1950s are considered a high point of Mexican cinema, especially with the films directed by Emilio "El Indio" Fernández and photographed by Gabriel Figuero. Luis Buñuel made most of his films in Mexico from 1947 through 1965, including *Los Olvidados* (1950; *The Young and the Damned*), his powerful study of the lost youths of Mexico City, which was itself photographed by Figuero. The 1970s was also a high point for Mexican cinema, beginning with Paul Leduc's film about John Reed, the American journalist, *Reed: Insurgent Mexico* (1970). Economic instability and governmental withdrawal hurt the industry in the late 1970s and early 1980s, but a renewal of government support and better conditions have produced a revival, especially with such internationally respected films as Paul Leduc's *Frida* (1983) and the very popular *Like Water for Chocolate* (1992), directed by Alfonso Arau. Brazil's Cinema Novo movement, a politically oriented cooperative, produced significant works in the 1960s, especially by Glauber Rocha, before the group gave way to military and political pressure. But Brazil went on to have an international audience for a number of its nonpolitical films—Bruno Barreto's *Dona Flor and Her Two Husbands* (1976) and Carlos Diegues's *Bye Bye Brazil* (1980) were especially popular. Hector Babenco, a Chilean who took up residence in Brazil, emerged with his *Pixote* (1982) and *Kiss of the Spider Woman* (1985). Argentina's Leopoldo Torre Nilsson directed a number of implicitly political films that received some attention, but Fernando Solanas and Octavio Getino's impressive anticolonial and antigovernment documentary, *The Hour of the Furnaces* (1969), has had much impact. With the improved political situation in Argentina, Luis Puenzo's *The Official Story* (1985) achieved international notice with its dramatic treatment of life under that country's recent military junta. Also of interest has been the work of the Argentinean Maria Luisa Bemberg, who reached a wide international audience with her polemical *Camila* in 1984 and compelling *I Don't Want to Talk About It* in 1993. In Chile, Miguel Littín had a brief but notable career (e.g., *The Jackal of Nahueltoro,* 1969) before Allende's murder but after that time had to work abroad. The defeat of the Pinochet regime in Chile in 1988 instituted a resurgence of cinematic energy marked by Ricardo Larrain's stunning drama about the recent political

Third World cinema *YOL* (1982), a Turkish film directed by Yilmaz Güney while in prison.

■ ■ ■

oppression, *La Frontera* (1991), and Raul Ruiz's return to complete his *White Dove* (1992). Also receiving much attention has been Victor Gaviria's Colombian film about the bleak and violent lives of young people in Medellín, *Rodrigo D.—No Futuro* (1990). In general, Latin American cinema has been under great strain in recent years because of the domination of home markets by American films and the extreme difficulty of finding foreign distribution, especially in the United States. Before we leave this hemisphere, though, Cuba must be mentioned for its solid contribution to world cinema, with the short nonfiction films of Santiago Alvarez and fiction films of Tomas Gutierrez Alea and Humberto Solas. Alea's antibourgeois *Memories of Underdevelopment* (1968) and his recent *Strawberry and Chocolate* (1993), which was banned in Cuba because of the film's attack against the "revolutionary" government's homophobia, have both achieved international reputations.

India maintains a vast film industry that produces more films than any other nation in the world, some 900 each year for a weekly audience of approximately 100 million people. The center for films in the Hindi language is Bombay, which produces about one-quarter of India's motion pictures. The center for Bengali films is Calcutta. Most of India's films are extremely conventional musical romances with very popular and highly paid stars. The Bengali filmmaker Satyajit Ray, however, was India's cinematic contribution to world art, especially with his *Apu* trilogy (1955–58). What has been called a "parallel cinema" began in the late 1960s with support from the country's Film Finance Corporation; notable in this movement was the work of Mrinal Sen. In recent years, this "parallel cinema" has produced the important work of Aparna Sen, one of the country's few women directors, and the diverse films of Ketan Mehta.

Economic and political conditions have restricted the growth of cinema in Africa, but still the continent has produced two notable national cinemas, one in Algiers, where Mohamed Lakhdar-Hamina made *Chronicle of the Years of Embers,* which won the Grand Prix at the Cannes festival in 1975; and one in Senegal, where Ousmane Sembene has directed a number of impressive films, most notably *Black Girl* (1960) and his bitingly satiric *Xala* (1974). A number of remarkable filmmakers have appeared from other African countries. Souleymane Cisse from Mali has received much praise for his remarkable *Yeelen* (1987), a film that seems to take us into another culture and physical universe entirely; Désiré Ecaré, from the Ivory Coast, took twelve years to complete *Faces of Women* (1985), which then received considerable attention and popularity; and two films by Burkina Faso's Ouedraogo Idrissa have been especially admired, his *Yaaba* (1989) and *Tilai* (1990), the latter winning the Special Jury Prize at the Cannes festival.

In the Middle East, Iran has a long and conflicted film history. Before the revolution that brought the Ayatollah Khomeini to power in 1979, a popular commercial cinema existed. Darius Mehrjui's *The Cow* (1969) announced a new socially realistic and independent cinema, and his *The Cycle* won the Critic's Prize at the 1978 Berlin Film Festival. After the revolution, in spite of both government support and controls, Iran still turned out some powerful films—Abbas Kiarostami is a recent film artist whose interest in children has resulted in such notable works as *Where Is My Friend's Home?* (1987) and *And Life Goes On . . .* (1991). Though Turkey has largely produced a commercial cinema of only local interest, Yilmaz Güney and the filmmakers he influenced created a significant political motion-picture movement. Güney, who died in 1984, wrote and directed *Herd* (1978) and the magnificent *Yol* (1982) while a political prisoner in Turkey. After his escape and while in exile, he wrote and directed *Le Mur* (1983).

■ **thirty by forty (30 x 40)** A poster for a motion picture thirty inches wide and forty inches high that is displayed in front of or in the lobby of a theater to advertise the present film or a feature to be shown at a later date.

■ **thirty-degree rule, 30-degree rule** An informal rule for continuity editing that the camera placement in the second of any two shots of the same subject change by at least 30 degrees in order to avoid the impression of a jump cut. *See* **continuity cutting** *and* **editing.**

■ **35mm blowup** An enlargement of a film to 35mm film from a smaller gauge, generally 16mm. Professional films are sometimes shot in the less expensive 16mm gauge and enlarged to 35mm by means of an optical printer.

■ **35mm film** The standard gauge for professional film-making. 35 millimeters in width and with four perforations along both sides of each frame, this gauge runs sixteen frames to the foot. (Sometimes three perforations are used to save 25 percent of the footage during shooting.) This type of film was originally introduced by the Edison laboratory and Eastman Kodak in 1899, and because of the popularity of Edison's equipment soon became standard for making motion pictures. The 35mm gauge in general creates images that can be projected to a sufficient size for audience viewing and that offer a well-defined, ungrainy, and accurate representation of reality. The advent of sound in 1929 at first necessitated the squaring of the frame to allow room for the sound track, but the aspect ratio was soon returned to the more pleasing dimension of 1.33:1 of silent film by a reduction of the frame's size. Anamorphic lenses in the later 1950s squeezed a wider field of vision into the 35mm frame and then unsqueezed it into a wide-screen image during projection. Although such lenses are still employed to create wide images from 35mm stock, the less expensive and easier process of masking the frame is often employed for creating "flat" images on 35mm stock that can be projected into wide-screen cinema because of the availability today of superior standard lenses and film stock. *See* **film** *(1),* **perforations,** *and* **wide screen.**

■ **thread, thread up** To position film so that it will run properly in its path through a piece of film machinery.

■ **threading path** The proper route for a film to pass through a piece of film machinery.

■ **three-camera technique** Shooting a scene with three cameras, each photographing from a different distance or angle (e.g., for long, medium, and close-up shots). This method gives the editor a wide range of shots to choose from when putting together a film and also avoids the reshooting of a difficult or expensive scene necessary with the single-camera technique when the original shot is faulty—but it is a costly way of making a film. Television production normally operates by employing such multiple cameras.

■ **three-color process** Any system that employs all three primary colors—red, green, and blue—in photographing and reproducing images. *See* **color film** *(2).*

■ **3-D, 3-D cinematography, 3-D stereoscopy, stereoscopy, stereoscopic cinematography, stereographic cinematography** A motion-picture photographic process that creates the illusion of actual depth in the image so that the foreground seems to stand out in relief and the various planes of the image seem spatially distinct and separate. By using the distance between left and right viewpoints of the image, called the "interaxial," stereoscopy creates the same sense of depth and perspective as that created by normal binocular vision when the approxi-

mately two-and-one-half-inch separation between the eyes produces two different retinal images, the left eye perceiving somewhat more around the left side of the subject and the other eye around the right side. The point at which the two views of the image meet is referred to as the "convergence" and the plane of convergence as the "stereo window," which normally should be at the screen or slightly behind the screen. Objects in front of the plane of convergence will appear before the screen, and objects behind will appear at the rear of the screen.

Stereoscopic vision was achieved early with still pictures: the stereoscope was a popular parlor item at the end of the nineteenth century, and projectors were also employed at the time to achieve three-dimensional images. But projecting stereoscopic moving pictures to a wide audience presented great challenge, which until this day has not been fully met. The anaglyph process was an early attempt, in which two views of the same scene were simultaneously shot and then printed in different colors, generally red and green, on a single reel of two-layered film. The projected image was viewed through spectacles, with each eyepiece in one of the two colors guiding the eye to the image of the opposite color and blocking out the image in its own. A presentation of some scenes in the anaglyphic 3-D process made by Edwin S. Porter and William E. Wadded is supposed to have taken place in New York City on June 10, 1925; and the first feature film in this process, *The Power of Love* (dir. Harry K. Fairoll), was shown in Los Angeles on September 27, 1922. Paramount released some shorts in this method, called "Plastigrams," in the early 1920s, and MGM released a series of Pete Smith's "Audioscopiks" with the same process in 1935. But the anaglyph process was ultimately found unsatisfactory

3-D
1. **camera lens with two optical axes**
2. **convergence at figure situated between fence and building**
3. **projector** 4. **stereo window (plane of convergence) at screen with fence appearing before figure and building behind**

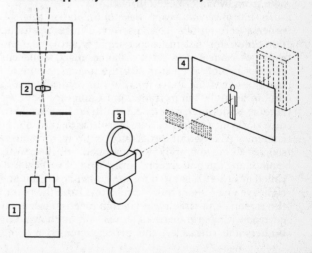

because it could not create images in full color, because the picture was itself somewhat indistinct, and because the glasses caused headaches.

More promising was a system that used two Polaroid lenses on one or two cameras to shoot the scene, one lens passing light waves vibrating on only a single plane and the other passing waves vibrating in a perpendicular plane. When the two images were projected simultaneously through separate projectors and viewed through spectacles with polarized eyepieces, each with a filter set to pass light at one or the other plane, an effect of binocular vision was achieved, with the picture seen in depth. Polaroid 3-D allowed a better picture and could create color images, although the spectacles were still a nuisance and the binocular effect unstable. First employed for the Italian black-and-white film *Beggar's Wedding* in 1936 and the German film *You Can Nearly Touch It* in the same year, this process was ultimately developed and used as one of Hollywood's innovations to draw people back to the theater from the television screens in the early 1950s: Arch Obler's *Bwana Devil*, in color, met with commercial success in 1952 because of the novelty of its three-dimensional cinematography, as did the more exciting *House of Wax*, also in color, the next year (dir. André de Toth). Other films employed this process, but the novelty was soon gone, audiences diminished, and the expense and problems with achieving the three-dimensional picture no longer seemed worth the effort—*Kiss Me Kate* (1953; dir. George Sidney) and Hitchcock's *Dial M for Murder* (1954) were both released with flat images, though originally shot in 3-D. Variations of this process were still employed on occasion, generally as a novelty for films that were themselves somewhat off the beaten path—e.g., for Andy Warhol's *Frankenstein* (1974; dir. Paul Morrissey). Most of the 3-D films during this period employed two cameras, sometimes positioned at right angles and shooting off a half-silvered mirror and sometimes facing one another and shooting off two mirrors situated 45 degrees to the lenses' axes, to create the image for each eye; and then projected the images from two interlocked projectors.

In more recent years, developments of this 3-D process were employed in a series of unsuccessful action films. Most systems used a single camera and a lens with two optical axes set a distance apart, while employing a single projector with the images for the left and right eyes one above the other or vertically side by side in a single 35mm frame. Jim Cameron, however, recently shot his *Terminator 2 3-D* ride for Universal Studios parks in California and Florida with twin 65mm cameras. A different procedure entirely for stereoscopic cinematography was pursued in the Soviet Union; an "integral screen" with a grid of vertical slats called a "raster" separated for the audience the left and right eye images sent by two projectors from the rear of the screen. The screen was later changed to a lenticular type with a grid made of lenses. Although avoiding bothersome spectacles, this process created a somewhat unsatisfying image, which could only be seen in a limited portion of an auditorium and from restricted positions of the viewer's head. More recently, the SteroKino Group of Moscow has employed a single-camera system using 70mm film for 3-D cinema in a series of theaters throughout Russia.

But certainly the most important recent development in three-dimensional cinematography has been the IMAX 3-D system: the viewer wears a headset with liquid crystal lenses, each of which is made clear and opaque alternately by infrared signals beamed from the front of the theater. The camera itself employs two lenses, 2.85 inches apart to approximate the 2.75 inch separation of human eyes in order to record the slightly different perspectives of the subject on two individual films. Prints of the two separate films are simultaneously projected in the theater with the right and left crystal lenses alternately opening for 1/96th of a second. The brain's capacity to retain each image creates the illusion of seeing a single image, and the combination of the two perspectives creates the three-dimensional effect. IMAX has a growing number of these special 3-D theaters throughout the world. The image that appears on the eight-story screen at the IMAX Theater in the Sony Theatres Lincoln Square cineplex in New York City, for example, is certainly the most dramatic and continuously three-dimensional yet to appear in the cinema. The stereoscopic effect is enhanced by 3-D sound created by the IMAX PSE (personal sound environment) system, which is incorporated into the headset and enhances the theater's six-channel digital sound system. IMAX SOLIDO, which was introduced in 1992, employs a wide-field dome screen that creates an even greater sense of immersion in the three-dimensional world. Holography, which creates an image of an object as if it were in real space by first having laser light record directly on film emulsion and then having such light deflect off it, also offers possibilities for future developments in three-dimensional cinematography. *See* **depth** *and* **holography**.

■ **3-D computer graphics, three-dimensional computer graphics** *See* **computer animation.**

■ **3-D digitizer** A scanner that transmits the coordinates for shape and color of an actual object into a computer system in digital form for the creation of a three-dimensional model. Such systems play an important role in the creation of computer animation because the resulting model is based on the actual dimensions of a real object. In addition, such a model is easier to create than one originating from scratch in a software program. Once the subject is scanned in any of these systems, the three-dimensional model can be changed, distorted, morphed, or combined with other picture elements. The type of digitizer now most often used in the film industry is the laser scanner that can transmit details concerning form and shape as well as color. In the Cyberware 3-D color digitizer, a high-quality video sensor captures and digitizes the object's profile from two perspectives after it is lighted by the laser, and a second video sensor captures the color information. Smaller scanners can transmit the necessary information for any type of object, while more ambitious body scanners can feed into the computer the details for creating realistic human models in action. The Cyberware Whole Body Scanner can digitize the entire body with four scanners moving in one pass from the person's head to feet. *See* **computer animation** *and* **scanner.**

■ **threefold**   A term referring to a flat that is employed in creating scenery and is constructed of three pieces hinged together.

■ **three o'clock**   The call sheet generally posted at three o'clock that announces the next day's shooting schedule for cast and crew while also specifying the required equipment. *See* **call.**

■ **three-perf, three-perforation**   Film and filming processes that employ three perforations on each side of the 35mm frame instead of the normal four in order to use 25 percent less film for each shoot. *See* **film** *(1) and* **perforations.**

■ **three-point lighting**   The standard lighting setup, employing the key light, fill light, and back light. The term sometimes refers more specifically to a three-quarter front key light as well as the fill and kicker light.

■ **three-quarter angle, three-quarter view**   The position of the camera so that it faces 75 percent of the subject being photographed, giving it a more dimensional and modeled appearance than a shot fully from the front.

■ **three-quarter front key**   A key light at an angle 45 degrees to the camera axis and somewhat higher than the camera, frequently used for portrait lighting along with the fill and back light. *See* **key light** *and* **lighting.**

■ **three-shot**   A shot of three people, normally at medium range or in a medium close-up.

■ **360-degree pan; 360**   A panning shot that makes a complete circle from a fixed point, taking in the entire circumference of a scene. Also called a circular pan. *See* **circular pan.**

■ **three-strip camera**   A motion-picture camera that utilizes three separate films for recording light waves of each of the primary colors. In 1932, the Technicolor Motion Picture Company introduced their famous camera of this type, which employed a beam-splitting prism to make separate color records of blue and red on two films in bipack and of green on a third film. *See* **color film** *(2) and* **Technicolor.**

■ **three stripe, three-stripe film, three head, 3 H master, triple track, triple stripe**   A single film with three magnetic tracks on which are normally located the three major premix sound tracks—dialogue (D), music (M), and effects (E). *See* **mix, premix,** *and* **single stripe.**

■ **three track**   Magnetic film for recording sound with three discrete tracks, normally a premix with separate tracks for dialogue, music, and effects. *See* **magnetic film** *and* **mix.**

■ **three-track stereo**   Sound recorded in three tracks on a normal positive print with standard perforations. The tracks allow distribution to the left, middle, and right areas behind the screen without a fourth track for auditorium sound. *See* **stereophonic sound.**

■ **three-wall set**   A set containing the two sides and back wall of a location without the front wall.

■ **threshold**   The point of exposure at which film emulsion begins to produce a density distinct from fog level when processed. *See* **fog level.**

■ **thriller**   Any film that creates excitement and suspense, especially a mystery or crime film, though the term is also employed on occasion for spy or adventure works. *See* **suspense.**

■ **through-the-lens**   The term refers to a reflex viewfinder that receives light waves through the lens of the camera so that an image of the scene to be photographed can be viewed without parallax. The initials TTL are also employed in reference to such viewfinders. *See* **reflex viewfinder** *and* **TTL.**

■ **throw**   (1) The distance from the projector to the screen. (2) The distance from a luminaire to its place of illumination in a set or location. (3) To place illumination from a luminaire in a chosen area in a set or location.

■ **thunderflash**   A sealed cardboard tube, containing a pyrotechnic mixture, that is buried beneath sand or a thin layer of dirt to give the effect of an exploding shell or high-powered bullet when it is set off.

■ **THX Sound System**   *See* **sound.**

■ **tie-down**   (1) A device composed of a piece of chain attached to a "bridle" of three smaller pieces of chain that prevents a tripod from being upset on an unstable or precarious surface (e.g., on a moving vehicle). The three pieces of the bridle fasten to the bottom of the top casting of the tripod, while the long piece of chain is attached directly below to a stage screw by means of an adjustable turnbuckle. (2) A term loosely applied to a spreader. *See* **spreader.**

■ **tie-ins** A promotional campaign involving products that are spin-offs from a specific motion picture, but ones that also bring in additional revenue—e.g., a novelization of the film's story, toys or games employing the characters from the film, T-shirts referring to the film, or any household objects that have some reference to the film. Such business relationships can sometimes gross a production company as much as $40 million.

■ **tighten, pull up** To rearrange the shot so that much of the environment is eliminated and the subject fits more closely in the entire frame.

■ **tight gate** A gate, normally in a special-effects camera, that holds the frame precisely in position during exposure with heavy pressure. *See* **loose gate.**

■ **tight shot, tightly framed shot** A shot in which the characters are closely confined by the perimeters of the frame with little surrounding space. Such shots close the distance between viewer and characters, creating a greater sense of involvement. *See* **loose shot.**

■ **tight two** A tight shot of two characters that generally shows little more than their shoulders and heads. *See* **tight shot.**

■ **tight wind, tight winder** A rewind that winds film onto a plastic core by means of a roller mechanism.

■ **tilt** A movement of the camera up or down along a vertical axis from a fixed position. *See* **tilt shot.**

■ **tilt-focus lens** A device attached to the camera and lens that allows a 360-degree rotation and an 8-degree tilt in any direction. Tilting the lens results, for example, in changing the plane of focus and allowing the camera operator to bring some person into focus while excluding another.

■ **tilt plate** *See* **camera wedge.**

tilt shot

■ **tilt shot** A shot in which the camera moves up or down along a vertical axis from a fixed position by means of a special tripod head that permits such movement. A tilt shot may be employed to suggest the subjective view of a character looking up at some location or down from a height. Such a shot can also follow the movement of a subject for the audience, expand our awareness of the environment, or show us the relationship between two areas of action. The directions of the camera are referred to as tilt up and tilt down. The tilt shot is the opposite of a pan, in which the camera moves from a fixed position along a horizontal axis. *See* **dutch angle** *and* **pan.**

■ **time** As well as presenting a spatial world on the screen, film also creates a world of time through the sequential continuity of both its actions and images. Film actually develops for us a number of temporal levels—physical, dramatic, psychological, affective, cultural, historical, and filmic—all of which work together and influence our reactions to the individual work. Physical time is the actual duration in which the entire film takes place, the approximately two hours in which we watch the movie and of which we are always vaguely aware, while dramatic time is the fictional duration in which the events transpire. On rare occasions both of these time levels are the same—e.g., in Alfred Hitchcock's *Rope* (1948) and Fred Zinnemann's *High Noon* (1952)—but normally film, like most narrative art, creates a dramatic temporal dimension that far exceeds our viewing time, taking advantage of our willingness to see only what is significant and to be transported in time. Dramatic time allows us, within our brief sojourn in the theater, to view action that takes place in a duration anywhere from a few days to a lifetime—sometimes a flashback might be employed to take us back to some incident before the narrative's present or a flashforward to what is clearly anticipated as future time. A dissolve was often the technique for suggesting to the viewer that unimportant periods of time had been omitted from shot to shot, but in more recent years a simple cut suffices, as long as the transition in time is made clear.

Psychological time, the way in which a character experiences the passing of time, might be quite distinct from the dramatic duration of the action. A series of brief cuts, with intervening moments of action omitted, can convey to us the hurried and excited way in which a character experiences an event; a series of long takes with minimal cutting and gradual camera movement can create the slow way in which he or she feels during a scene. In narrative fiction, the time in which the narrator lives is sometimes clearly distinguished from the time of the action he or she describes—in such cases the relationship between the two time levels may make up the story, especially when the earlier events are used to explain the present situation or psychological state of the narrator. In such narratives, dramatic and psychological time may also combine as the narrator remembers and experiences time past while living in the present. Such an effect can be achieved in film through the use of a narrative frame in which the character appears and from which the flashback technique psychologically returns him or her to time past—an excellent example of such a film is Ingmar Bergman's *Wild Strawberries* (1957), where an elderly man fuses in his mind present and past, dream and reality, while undergoing a spiritual rebirth.

Affective time is the sense of time passing that we feel as we watch the film, a temporal feeling that is often quite distinct from the actual physical time in which the film takes place. Often we may share a character's psychological sense of time through the way in which the film is edited, but frequently our sense of time is affected, our involvement in the film manipulated, in a separate way—for example, the remarkable conclusion to Michelangelo Antonioni's *The Eclipse* (1962), with its fifty-eight shots of Rome now vacant of the two lovers, creates for us a sense of the slow and empty passage of time distinct from what any character is experiencing at that instant; and the nine shots that repeat the sailor's movement when he breaks the officer's plate against the table in Sergei Eisenstein's *The Battleship Potemkin* (1925) create for us a dramatic and extended experience distinct from what the character is feeling.

Cultural time is the way in which a particular society or civilization experiences the passing of time and the way in which it lives in the context of time. Satyajit Ray, for example, creates his world of India in the context of a temporal dimension, with its unique flow and significance, distinct from that created in western films, especially in his remarkable Apu trilogy, *Pather Panchali* (1955), *Aparajito* (1956), and *The World of Apu* (Apu Sansar; 1959). And, finally, historical time is a temporal dimension created by films that seek to present dramatic time within a larger temporal scheme, one that transcends the lives and fates of individual characters. Behind the dramatic events that unite the characters of D. W. Griffith's *The Birth of a Nation* (1915) is the director's vision of the entire Civil War.

The Russian film director V. I. Pudovkin, in *Film Technique*, has defined filmic time as that temporal dimension created by the medium of film and distinct from that which operates in the real world in front of the camera. In this sense, all the temporal dimensions described above, except for physical time, belong to this category. But we can make Pudovkin's category more exclusive and use it to describe that sense of time created by film's technology that is unique to the medium and nonimitative of any sense of time we may have in the real world. For example, film can create slow and accelerated motion for various reasons, but neither of these temporal phenomena belong to the normal world of time. In a much grander way, a film such as David Jones's *Betrayal* (1983) can regress in time, starting with the termination of a love affair and taking us backward through the various stages of the relationship to its first hopeful moments, thus conveying to us a sense of pathos and loss. Especially in avant-garde cinema, however, filmmakers such as Stan Brakhage and Bruce Baillie have created through various techniques a world free from external and real time, a self-enclosed cinema that achieves its own temporality by ignoring the temporal requirements of story and character and the demands of a commercial audience. Such a cinema actually develops the mind's capacity to escape the limitations of a time-bound world. *See* **avant-garde cinema** *and* **space**.

■ **time and policy** The specifications of playing times and prices of admission for a particular film in a specific theater that appear in an advertisement for the film.

■ **time base signal** An electronic signal simultaneously recorded along the edge of the film and on a track on the sound tape during shooting that will be employed for synchronic playback of picture and sound.

■ **time code, SMPTE time code, SMPTE/EBU time code** An electronic synchronizing system, standardized by the Society of Motion Picture and Television Engineers and the European Broadcasting Union that has been employed for editing video images and sound but is now also being used for editing motion pictures. Time code records on both film and sound tape a series of 80 pulses for each frame that is used to document individual frame numbers as well as hours, minutes, and seconds and can also be used for recording such information as scene, take, camera, and roll number. In film production, the time code is employed for synchronizing picture and sound from a day's shooting, shots from multiple cameras, and multiple sound tracks. The system is also used for slating the start of each take and for transferring sound from tape to magnetic film. In-camera time codes are now especially useful for transferring the film image to video and to digital systems for nonlinear editing. In electronic editing in general, each coded frame can be read and brought to the monitor, and the correspondingly coded elements of sound can be brought to the speaker. The time code in an EDL (edit-decision list) that is the result of nonlinear digital editing can be matched to KeyKode numbers on the film to create a negative cut list for editing the negative (or first creating a workprint). For double system video, a time code generator applies the time code both to a videotape recorder and audiotape recorder; while a time code reader will display the code (on the monitor, itself, or both) and keep both picture and sound synchronized for editing. *See* **editing**.

■ **time-code calculator** A device that calculates for NTSC, PAL, and SECAM video time codes and for 16mm and

35mm feet-frames. The calculator also converts from one format to the other and allows for quick edit calculations. *See* **NTSC, PAL,** *and* **SECAM.**

■ **time code generator, time code reader** *See* **time code.**

■ **timed print** A print for which all the shots and scenes have been evaluated and corrected during printing to achieve the desired color quality and density. *See* **timing.**

■ **timed workprint** A workprint for which all the shots or scenes have been evaluated and corrected during printing to achieve the desired color quality and density. *See* **timing.**

■ **time-gamma-temperature curve** A characteristic curve that shows the relationship between the duration of developing and the contrast (i.e., the gamma value) achieved in an image for a specific developer and emulsion. *See* **characteristic curve.**

■ **time lapse, time-lapse cinematography** A method of filming some process, frequently unnoticeable to the eye, over a lengthy duration by shooting one frame at a time at predetermined intervals. When the positive is projected at normal speed, the process will seem to speed up and can be viewed during a brief period. This method can allow us to view the blooming of a flower, the changing pattern of weather, or even the growth of a man-made edifice in an instant. Time-lapse cinematography can also be employed in scientific investigation, where it might be used for recording chemical change through a microscope. A camera capable of shooting one frame at a time must be employed along with a timing device, called an intervalometer, which can operate the shutter and sometimes illumination for the photography. Also called stop-motion cinematography, stop-action cinematography, and single-frame cinematography. *See* **stop motion.**

■ **time-lapse camera** A camera specially equipped with a single-frame shooting mechanism and a timer for automatically photographing some process a frame at a time at exact intervals during a designated period for time-lapse cinematography. *See* **time lapse.**

■ **time-lapse cutaway, time-lapse cutaway shot** A cutaway shot primarily used to distract the audience while the main action is advanced in time. When the audience's attention is returned to the main scene, such "cheating" goes unrecognized and the sequence seems to move rapidly along. *See* **cutaway.**

■ **time-lapse motor** The motor attached to a camera for taking single-frame shots at timed intervals for time-lapse cinematography. *See* **time lapse.**

■ **timer** The individual in the laboratory who first examines the negative to determine what shots or scenes are overexposed, underexposed, or improperly colored and then adjusts the intensity and color of the printing light to achieve a print that is consistent and balanced. The timer is sometimes called a colorist for color films and is also called the grader in Great Britain. *See* **timing.**

■ **time scale exposure** A step wedge film with the series of greater densities determined by the increasing length of exposure while the intensity of illumination remains constant. *See* **step wedge.**

■ **timing** The process of altering the density and color values of a film from shot to shot or scene to scene during printing in order to achieve constancy, balance, or some effect. Decisions for such changes may be the result of consultations between the laboratory, the director of photography, and the director. Test prints made up of select frames or a series of continuous frames from each scene can be employed for such consultation. The person responsible for this process during the printing is the timer. For routine printing of film, the timer alone may make changes to achieve balance of density and color. A video color analyzer, such as the Hazeltine, can project a positive image onto a screen from a negative and allow the timer to make such adjustments. Black-and-white film can be timed by altering the size of the slit through which the printer light shines or with a valve. For color film, in an additive printing process, the light is divided into the three primary colors by dichroic filters, the intensity of the individual beams altered, and the three combined again before they enter the aperture. Coded timing tape, made by the video analyzer, changes each valve that controls one of the primary colors from setting to setting as all the scenes run continuously through the printer. In more recent and computerized versions of this technology, the timer types in the information to the system that produces the tape. The tape, which contains the cues for the various light beams according to the footage of the film itself, is fed into the printer, programming it in advance for the actual timing. When the negative and fresh film are run through the printer, the three light valves (for the primary colors) are automatically adjusted for the various changes necessary to correct or alter the images' color and lighting. One new system analyzes the film automatically and stores instructions in a database that are to be used later in the creation of the answer print—the color corrections stored in the database are referenced to the key numbers on the negative. (2) The process of precisely fitting a voice-over to the images in a motion picture so that the two correspond moment by moment—for example, in a documentary film. (3) Determining the exact duration of a shot or scene. (4) Determining the speed of an action or sound for an animation film.

■ **timing notes** The notes written by the music editor after the spotting session which specify the timings for the various musical passages in the film. These notes are given to the composer who then uses them to write and score the various musical passages so that they fit precisely and effectively into the film's narrative. *See* **spotting.**

■ **timing tape** A tape on which information for timing is recorded and that controls changes in the light's intensity and color during printing. *See* **timing.**

■ **tinseltown** A formerly popular name for Hollywood, implying its glitter, pretense, and unreality. *See* **Hollywood.**

■ **tinted base** A print of a motion picture with the black-and-white image on a colored base. Used during the silent-film period, this type of film imposed on the image a color related to its specific action, mood, time, or place by coloring the light areas. Tinting was often used with "toning," a process that dyed the silver particles in the emulsion, thereby coloring the darker areas of the image. *See* **tinting** *and* **toning.**

■ **tinting** (1) A method of creating a color image during the silent-film era by dyeing the base of the film and thus coloring the light areas. The process was achieved by dyeing the base of the print, printing on an already dyed base, or hand-tinting. Specific colors would be used to convey the action, mood, time, or place of a scene—for example, red for a battle, blue for melancholy or a nighttime episode, and sepia for an interior. Tinting was distinct from "toning," which specifically meant coloring the opaque areas by dyeing the silver particles in the emulsion. Films might be released with both tinting and toning. *See* **color film** *(2)*. (2) The term is sometimes loosely used for any of the processes that gave an overall color to the images of silent films, whether tinting as described above, toning, or both.

■ **titan arc** A 350-ampere carbon arc lamp, the most powerful of this type of luminaire. *See* **arc lamp.**

■ **title, titles** Any words that appear on the screen not as part of the scene but as a means of conveying information to the audience. (1) "Credit titles" appear at the start and conclusion of a film to cite the various personnel responsible for the motion picture; (2) the "main title" gives the name of the film, and the "main titles" are all those that appear at the start of the film; (3) the "end title" tells us that the film is concluded and the "end titles" give us the credits; (4) "insert titles" or "intertitles," placed in the body of the film, were used in silent films to give dialogue, comment on action, or set time and location, and are used in sound film to set time and place or provide information; and

(5) "subtitles" are placed at the bottom of the screen to translate foreign dialogue. Titles may appear separately on the screen, be superimposed over a scene, crawl or roll up the screen, or seem to be panned by the camera. In recent years, the main title and credits are frequently given after an opening scene that is called a teaser.

■ **title background** The scene that appears behind titles. *See* **title card.**

■ **title card, title board** A card or cel with printed material that is photographed and made part of the motion picture to supply information to the audience. See-through cels are used when the background is to show through the titling. During the silent-film period, title cards inserted throughout the film gave dialogue, commented on action, and also established time and place.

■ **title drum** *See* **drum titler.**

■ **title music** Music that is played with the credit titles at the start and conclusion of a film.

■ **title song** (1) A song that is sung with the credit titles at the start and conclusion of a film. (2) A song with the same title as the film that is sung during the motion picture.

■ **title stand, titler** A stand for photographing titles that supports both the camera and the title card placed in front of the lens.

■ **Todd-AO** A wide screen process developed for Michael Todd by Dr. Brian O'Brien and the American Optical Company (the source of the "AO" in the name of the process). Todd is reported to have asked O'Brien to create for him a wide-screen process in which "everything comes out of one hole," a request made in response to the three projectors used by Cinerama. Shooting on 65mm film, which allowed a frame with a 2.2:1 aspect ratio, also removed the necessity of employing anamorphic lenses for the wide image. The picture was actually printed on 70mm film to allow for six stereophonic sound tracks on four magnetic strips. Because the system photographed at thirty frames per second, Todd-AO films could only be shown with special projectors. Todd-AO was actually the first of the 70mm film processes during the early years of widescreen cinema when it was used for *Oklahoma!* (dir. Fred Zinnemann) in 1955 and the extremely popular *Around the World in Eighty Days* (dir. Michael Anderson) the following year. Both films were also shot simultaneously at 24 frames per second, the first with 35mm CinemaScope and the second on 65mm film for reduction to 35mm prints. *See* **anamorphic lens, Cinerama,** *and* **wide screen.**

■ **toe** (1) The bottom part of a characteristic curve showing the increase of an emulsion's density just above fog level in relation to the increase in log exposure. *See* **characteristic curve.** (2) The forward extremity of the bottom of a film magazine, opposite to the heel.

■ **tone** (1) A shade or tint of a color in a photographic image. *See* **toning.** (2) The contrast or brightness range in a photographic image. (3) A continuous audio signal of a single frequency. (4) The quality or characteristics of a sound. (5) The mood or emotional atmosphere of a film.

■ **tone track** A sound track with environmental noises that goes into the final mix.

■ **tongue** To move the boom of a dolly to the left or right. The command is "tongue left" or "tongue right."

■ **toning** (1) A method of staining an image to a general color by chemical means during processing. (2) A method of coloring the opaque parts of an image to a general color during silent-film days by means of dyeing the silver particles in the emulsion, a process distinct from tinting, which dyes the base and hence clear parts. Toning and tinting were often used together to give a general color to the entire image. *See* **tinting.**

■ **top billing** The highest place for a performer's name, either in credits or in media advertising for a film, generally before the title of the film. Much sought-after and normally agreed upon in the contract, top billing is frequently shared by two and sometimes by three performers, at which point the spacing for the names must be negotiated. Top billing can also be a concern for a director or a producer.

■ **top hat** *See* **hi-hat.**

■ **top lighting, toplight** Lighting that comes from a source directly above the subject. Such illumination, which seems to come from heaven, can give a character a spiritual and angelic appearance. *See* **lighting.**

■ **topsheet** A page outlining and summarizing all the accounts for a film and appearing as the first page to the detailed budget, which might itself run more than one hundred pages.

■ **torque motor** A type of motor that produces torsion or rotation and is used to rotate the spindles in a camera, projector, printer, or sound recorder.

■ **total running time** The full length of a film normally designated by the number of minutes. Total running times for a film may vary, since films are often shortened during their different releases or when they are used for television transmission. Sometimes the producer will shorten the length of the director's cut for the initial release. Restored films have total running

times either as they were first released or as the director wanted them to be released. *See* **director's cut.**

■ **Touchstone Pictures** *See* **Walt Disney Company.**

■ **traced matte** Mattes made by rotoscoping a single frame of a film on an easel, tracing the matte line on translucent paper, tracing the line from the first sheet onto another by means of an animation light box, and then blackening the first matte on one side of the line and the second on the other. The two mattes are used for blocking out the respective parts of two images when they are individually transferred to a negative in a printer to form a composite picture. The same method can be employed for combining any number of elements from separate images. *See* **matte** (2), **photoscope, special effects,** *and* **traveling-matte process.**

■ **track** (1) A sound track on film or tape. (2) The rails or planks of wood sometimes employed to move a dolly in a steady and easy manner. (3) To make a tracking shot by moving the camera. *See* **tracking shot.** (4) To keep a subject in steady focus when moving toward or away from it with a zoom lens.

■ **track building** Putting all the sound effects in their proper place in the sound-effects track. This process was originally done by splicing specific sounds and fill into individual rolls and operating the tracks synchronously so that they could be properly mixed. Today, the process is often done for both magnetic and digital tracks through the SMPTE time code. *See* **time code.**

■ **tracking** Putting music into a motion picture that has not been composed directly for the film but is from a prerecorded library.

■ **tracking, trucking, traveling, dollying** Moving the camera during a shot, generally by means of a wheeled support. *See* **tracking shot.**

■ **tracking platforms** Platforms attached to the roof, front, or rear of a vehicle to support the camera and camera operator during a tracking shot.

■ **tracking shot, trucking shot, traveling shot, dollying shot** All these terms are employed for any shot in which the camera moves, generally by means of a wheeled support. A tracking shot, so called because it is sometimes photographed from a dolly that moves on tracks, also refers particularly to a shot in which the camera follows the movement of a subject; a trucking shot sometimes specifically refers to a shot from a moving vehicle; and a dolly shot to any shot taken from a moving dolly. Such designation as "forward" or "horizontal" might be attached to the term "tracking shot" when it refers, in a general manner, to any moving shot, or such directions as "track in" or "track out" might be given. *See* **camera movement** *and* **movement** (3).

■ **tracking vehicle** *See* **insert car.**

■ **track laying** (1) Placing the sound track or tracks in proper relation to the picture during editing, a job performed by the sound cutter, who is also sometimes referred to as the track layer. (2) Placing tracks on the ground so that the dolly can move easily and steadily.

■ **trades** The newspapers and journals published specifically for the members of the film and entertainment industry. *Variety,* the most popular trade journal for the industry, appears weekly from New York City, and the *Daily Variety* appears each weekday from Hollywood. Also important is the daily *Hollywood Reporter.* An example of the more specialized trade journals that appear for specific groups is the monthly *Box Office,* which is directed toward exhibitors.

■ **trade screening** An advanced screening by a distributor for exhibitors in a specific market area to interest them in exhibiting the film.

■ **trafficking** In marketing, the term refers to the movement of film prints or any advertising materials from one place to another.

■ **trailer** (1) A short film of two or three minutes that advertises a feature motion picture prior to its showing, generally in the theater where the feature will appear; it normally includes brief excerpts from the motion picture. So called because this brief film originally was shown after (i.e., "trailed") the feature film. A shorter trailer that appears before the regular trailer and briefly advertises a film that will appear at a later date is sometimes referred to as a teaser, and a trailer that advertises a film shown at another theater is sometimes referred to as a crossplug. The trailer is also referred to as a preview and coming attractions. It is normally made by the distributor of the film. (2) The term is sometimes used to describe the tail leader, a piece of blank film that is attached to the end of the film to protect the motion picture and allow it to finish moving through the projector in a smooth and proper manner.

■ **trailer crossplug** *See* **crossplug** *(1).*

■ **training film** A film that instructs some group in the performance of a specific skill, task, or occupation—for example, a military training film. *See* **informational film, instructional film,** *and* **skill film.**

■ **transducer** A device that changes energy from one form to another—for example, a microphone that changes mechanical energy to electric is considered a mechanical-electro transducer.

■ **transfer** (1) To duplicate sound from one recording to another—for example, to rerecord sound from mag-netic tape to film. (2) The sound rerecorded from another tape or film.

■ **transfer function** *See* **modulation transfer function.**

■ **transfer room** The room in a sound studio in which the sound transfers take place—e.g., from magnetic tape to an optical track or tracks on film.

■ **transistor** A semiconductor used in sound reproduction that is much smaller and more efficient than the old vacuum tubes.

■ **transit case** A packaging made of metal and lined with wood that is used for shipping 35mm film.

■ **transition** (1) Any technique used for changing from one scene to another, generally indicating a movement in space and time. A straight cut might be employed for such a movement, but it would also have to be a match cut with picture elements sufficiently harmonized in order to avoid a jump cut, which might jolt the audience, unless such an effect was desired. When a cut is employed for this type of transition some visual or auditory clue must be given to inform the audience of the change in location and time (e.g., a distinct alteration in the setting or a musical theme suggesting the new place or time). Sometimes a bridging shot might be employed to connect two distinct scenes (e.g., the turning wheels of a train or the takeoff of a plane indicating the change from one geographic area to another). A fade is a common device for emphasizing such a change, allowing the present scene to fade out gradually and then the new one to fade in—when the two scenes overlap during this same process, we have a dissolve, a transitional device that is less often employed today. Other transitional devices popular during earlier film days, and occasionally employed today to evoke the mood of these earlier films, are the wipe, when one scene appears to be wiped off the screen by the new scene, generally in a vertical direction; a flip or flipover wipe, when the picture appears to turn around either vertically or horizontally to reveal the new scene on its back; and the iris-out and iris-in, when a scene is concluded by a gradual shrinking of the entire image in circular form until the screen is black and the new scene is then expanded from a small circle in the center of the screen to its full size. Although these transitional devices were at one time achieved only with the camera, they are all, with the obvious exception of the cut, today accomplished in an optical printer. (2) Any connection between two shots of the same scene, for example, a cutaway shot to some spectator of the scene or to another action entirely to avoid a jump cut from one part of the main action to another.

■ **transition focus** A technique for indicating a transition in time by gradually bringing the scene out of focus and then gradually focusing in on the same scene.

Such a transition is also sometimes employed for a transition from one location to another.

■ **translight backing, translite backing, translight screen, translite screen** A background to a set composed of a photograph rear-projected on to a screen. Such a photograph often depicts a landscape or urban skyline, sometimes viewed from a balcony or through a window.

■ **translucent** Referring to any material that allows light waves to pass through while diffusing them. Objects on the other side of the material will appear indistinctly.

■ **translucent screen** A semitransparent screen with one layer of sufficiently diffused material on which a projected picture can be formed. Such a screen is employed in rear-projection cinematography. *See* **rear projection.**

■ **transmission, transmittance, transmission factor** The ratio of light passing through a medium to the incident light falling upon it. *See* **sensitometry.**

■ **transparency** A still image printed on a transparent medium such as glass or celluloid and projected as a background in a process shot. *See* **process shot.**

■ **transport** (1) The various parts for pulling film through a film machine, including both the continuous drive and intermittent mechanism of a camera, projector, or printer. (2) The mechanism that pulls magnetic tape from the feed to take-up spool, past the various heads in a tape recorder.

■ **transportation captain, transportation coordinator** The individual in charge of the transportation department. *See* **transportation department.**

■ **transportation department** The group of personnel in a studio in charge of maintaining and operating all vehicles, including large trucks and trailers for transporting equipment, tracking vehicles, limousines, and cars used in the film. The transportation captain is the individual in charge of the department.

■ **transverse chromatic aberration** *See* **lateral color.**

■ **trapeze** A metal pole or structure running across the length of the stage, from which luminaires can be suspended above the set.

■ **travel ghost** *See* **shutter ghost.**

■ **traveling-matte process** A special-effects process by which elements from different images are matted together to form a composite picture. In simple matting procedures, stationary mattes are employed to block out part of an image during printing and then to fit a new picture element into the unexposed area of the negative. In more advanced systems, the mattes change shape from frame to frame (hence the term "traveling"), thus allowing moving action to be combined with other picture elements. The process allows the bringing together of live-action shot in the studio with backgrounds photographed elsewhere or with animated models. In recent fantasy films, various types of picture elements, sometimes a large number of them, have been combined to form single images that could only be created through the technology of the medium.

There are two basic traveling-matte procedures: those which use a single film and a normal camera to record the live action, and those which employ two films in a special camera with a beam splitter when recording such action. The most popular of the single-film systems is the blue-screen process, in which foreground action is lit in normal fashion and photographed against a blue backing, which leaves the green and red layers surrounding the action virtually unexposed on the film. When the color negative is step-printed in the laboratory with filters, mattes can be created by means of color-separated positives. When the "male" matte, with the action an opaque silhouette and the surrounding area clear, is bipacked with a positive of the background in an optical printer, the result is a negative with the area unexposed in the background from frame to frame where the live action will fit. During a second pass of the negative through the printer, the live action can be fitted into the unexposed area when its positive is run in bipack with a "female" matte, in which the action area is clear and the background completely opaque. A variation of this procedure called the "color difference" traveling-matte process removes the blue halo found around moving and sometimes stationary figures, permits the reproduction of translucent and blue objects shot in the foreground against the blue backing, allows the performers in the foreground to move behind objects in the background, and also creates a self-matting image of the foreground, which eliminates the need for the female matte in the final pass through the printer. Computerized motion-control systems have been extremely helpful in using the blue-screen system to make composites involving models for fantasy films when several passes of film are necessary. A recent development is the front-projection blue-screen system created by Apogee for making a large number of blue-screen composites of high quality.

The advantage of the dual-film system is that the traveling matte is created at the same time that the principle action is photographed. Although dual-film processes with infrared and ultraviolet light waves making the traveling matte have been employed in motion-picture work, a more successful process was the sodium vapor process. This process, used with much success by Walt Disney Productions, employs a beam-splitting prism in the camera to send the yellow light from the area of a screen lit by sodium vapor lamps and surrounding the performers to one of the negatives so that a traveling matte with the foreground action clear and the surrounding area opaque is formed from which a positive male matte can be struck with the performers opaque and the surroundings clear. At the same time, the characters, who are lit by normal incandescent lamps, are photographed with their surrounding area clear on a negative insensitive to the yellow light, from which a self-matting positive can be struck with the background opaque. When the background positive is run with the male matte in bipack through an optical printer, space is left on the negative into which the foreground action can be fitted from the self-matting positive during another pass through the printer. *See* **digital effects, matte** *(2)*, **motion control,** *and* **special effects.**

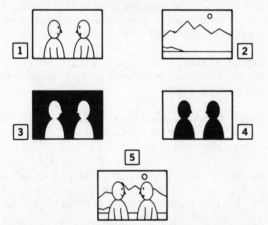

traveling matte 1. foreground action
2. background 3. female matte of foreground action
4. male matte made from female matte 5. composite image.

When the male matte is bipacked with a positive of the background in an optical printer, a negative is achieved with the area unexposed from frame to frame where the foreground will be printed when its positive is bipacked with the female matte during a second run of the negative.

■ **traveling shot** *See* **tracking shot.**

■ **travelogue, travelog, travel film** A film showing and describing the sights and everyday life of foreign places. Such films were a staple of early silent cinema before the advent of the feature film and later became popular "selected short subjects" that accompanied feature films in local theaters. Travelogues, whether made by Hollywood or independently produced for foreign agencies, seemed to have the sole purpose of increasing tourism: the result was often a glamorized, vulgarized, and stereotyped view of life in the "exotic" country. Films such as Robert Flaherty's *Nanook of the North* (1922), Cooper and Schoedsack's *Grass* (1925),

and, later, Chris Marker's *Dimanche à Pékin* (*Sunday in Peking;* 1955) should be distinguished from the travelogue as serious documentaries. *See* **documentary.**

■ **treatment, treatment outline** A stage in the writing of a film that comes immediately after the outline and right before the first version of the screenplay itself. The treatment, either written in simple descriptive prose or in outline form, generally employs the present tense to give a full account of the story with all the characters, actions, and scenes, but often without dialogue and normally without individual shots. This early version of the film, normally from ten to forty pages, shows how the writer would "treat" the story in a screenplay. *See* **outline, screenplay** *and* **screenwriter.**

■ **treble roll-off** The reduction of high frequencies by means of a filter during recording or mixing. *See* **equalization** *and* **roll-off.**

■ **tree, Christmas tree** A stand with horizontal bars for supporting luminaires.

■ **trench, trenching** A hole in the ground in which performers or objects may be situated to make them seem shorter or into which the camera may be placed for a shot at a desired height.

■ **triacetate base, acetate base** Film base made from cellulose triacetate on which the light-sensitive emulsion is layered. This "safety" base replaced the cellulose nitrate used before 1951 because it is far less combustible and is supposed to deteriorate far more slowly. But since triacetate base has itself proven unstable, a number of film stocks now use polyester base, which is stronger and less susceptible to degradation. *See* **film** *(1)*, **polyester base,** *and* **vinegar syndrome.**

■ **triacetate film** Film that uses triacetate base. *See* **triacetate base.**

■ **trial print, trial composite print** *See* **answer print.**

■ **triangle** (1) A device with three extended arms in triangular shape; the arms are used to hold the legs of a camera tripod to prevent them from slipping or spreading apart. This collapsible and portable device is also called a spreader, spider, or tee. (2) Relating to the three sources of illumination in standard film lighting—the key, back, and fill lights. *See* **lighting.**

■ **Triangle** A film company formed in 1915 by Harry Aitken along with Adam Kessel and Charles D. Bauman, all of whom had distributed their films through Mutual. Aitken, the sole force in Mutual to back *The Birth of a Nation* (1915), was motivated by the success of D. W. Griffith's film to start the new company, which would make films by a "triangle" of great directors,

Griffith, Thomas Ince, and Mack Sennett, while featuring notable stars of the stage. Douglas Fairbanks left the stage to achieve stardom with Triangle, and William S. Hart, who had already left the stage in 1914 to make films with Ince, contributed a number of successful Westerns to the new company. The aim of the company was to distribute shows made up of two five-reel films, one from Ince's unit and one from Griffith's, along with a comic short from Sennett's group, for which the viewer would pay the high figure of two dollars at a Triangle theater. Griffith, Ince, and Sennett actually supervised, instead of directed, the large number of films made by their groups, and Griffith soon began to give most of his attention to his own production of *Intolerance* (1916). The high salaries paid to its stars and especially the failure of audiences to flock to its films, even at reduced prices, were significant reasons for the company's ultimate failure. In 1917, Griffith, Ince, and Sennett, along with Fairbanks, went to work for Adolph Zukor at Artcraft and Paramount. Triangle leased its new facilities to Samuel Goldwyn in 1918 and virtually ceased to exist as a force in the industry.

■ **trick film** A motion picture that features trick photography. The term is applicable to many of the short works of the early film pioneer Georges Méliès, for example. In recent years the term "effects film" has been used for motion pictures that feature the more elaborate trickery of special-effects cinematography. *See* **special effects.**

■ **Tri-Ergon Process** An early sound-on-film process developed in Germany. The name "Tri-Ergon" means "the work of three" in German, and the company is so named after its three inventors, Josef Engl, Joseph Massole, and Hans Vogt. Patented in 1919, the process photographed the varying density of light modulated by sound waves and then converted the optical track back to sound when it passed between a lamp and a photo-electric cell in the projector. Tri-Ergon was adapted by Tobis-Klangfilm in Germany and soon became the major sound system in Europe. *See* **sound.**

■ **trigger film** A short film made for the sole purpose of stimulating discussion about some controversial or important issue such as drug-taking or foreign affairs. Generally composed of some inconclusive dramatic situation, the film provokes the audience into working out solutions.

■ **trim** (1) To cut off a portion of a shot or scene during editing so that it fits properly into its sequence. (2) To diminish the brightness from a luminaire with a scrim.

■ **trim bin, bin** A container, generally made of metal or metal lined with canvas, on which pieces of film are hung. This container is generally found in an editing room or other places where film is handled. The bin in an editing room has a rack from which trims are hung immediately after they are cut from a film during the editing process. *See* **trims.**

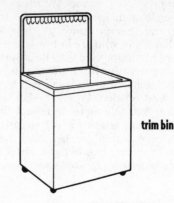

trim bin

■ **trims** The pieces of film cut from the various shots during editing. Such pieces must be registered and retained during the various stages of editing in case they are later needed to be reincorporated into the film. Also called outtakes and outs.

■ **trim tab, cinetab** A cardboard marker attached to each roll of film and sound track for identification during editing. *See* **editing.**

■ **tripack** Film with three layers in the emulsion, each for recording one of the primary colors. *See* **color film** (2) *and* **integral tripack color system**.

■ **trip gear** A device in animation or time-lapse cinematography that permits the camera to expose automatically a single frame or series of frames by means of a clutch and electric motor.

■ **triple-head optical printer** An optical printer with three projectors that permit the printing of several strips of film at once on a single film, thereby saving much time while greatly increasing the precision of the operation. The triple printing heads allow complex traveling-matte shots as well as other optical effects. *See* **optical printer.**

■ **triple-head process projector** A system with three projecting mechanisms for rear-projection cinematography developed by Farciot Edouart and used in the 1940s especially for Technicolor films, which required a brighter background image than that obtained with single-image projectors. A single projector sent the image straight ahead through the rear of the screen while images from two perfectly synchronized projectors, situated on either side and facing inward, were reflected off mirrors and onto the screen. The integrated triple images gave a sufficiently lit picture to match the live-action photographed in front of the screen. *See* **rear projection.**

■ **triple take** (1) Photographing the same action three consecutive times from the perspectives of a long shot, medium shot, and close-up. The action must be repeated identically to allow for match cutting, but the technique permits a good deal of choice for the editor when putting the film together. *See* **shot-sequence editing.** (2) The term is sometimes used to describe the planning and photographing of three consecutive shots so that the end of the first and beginning of the second and the end of the second and beginning of the third overlap with repeated action to permit the editor to create what appears to be a continuous action when putting the shots together.

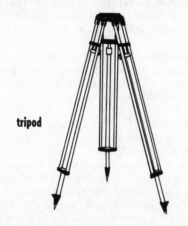

tripod

■ **tripod** A three-legged support for the camera made of hardwood or stainless steel. A mounting plate on top of the dolly permits the attachment of a head for panning or tilting the camera. The legs of the tripod are adjustable to change the height of the camera or allow for a level shot on uneven ground. The three basic types of tripods are the standard, with a height of approximately four to seven feet; the sawed-off, which is operable from approximately three to five feet; and the baby, which works from roughly two to three feet. The hi-hat, which is not technically a tripod but is a metal casting without adjustable legs, allows the camera to shoot approximately eight inches off the ground or a surface. Each leg of a tripod generally has a point that penetrates into the ground; sometimes it has a rubber covering to avoid scratching the floor. A spreader, with three extended arms, each of which supports one of the legs, might be employed to keep the legs from spreading or marring the floor. A tie-down, which is a length of chain attached from the topcasting to the floor, prevents the tripod from being upset on a precarious or moving surface. A tripod with wheels, sometimes called a tripod dolly, is employed for mobility; or a spider with wheels, called a wheeled tee or rolling spider, might be attached to the dolly to allow movement. *See* **tripod head.**

■ **tripod dolly** (1) A tripod with wheels. *See* **tripod.** (2) *See* **wheeled tee.**

■ **tripod head** A mount attached to the tripod that permits the camera to move freely for panning and tilting. Friction heads operate through the easy rubbing of two metal plates and, because of the plates' initial resistance, are normally employed for shots not requiring precise movements. The geared head, which operates through a system of gears and cranks turning a flywheel, creates an extremely smooth and easy movement, but its large size limits its use to a studio camera. Fluid heads, which function by means of liquid forced between moving parts, are often employed because of their fine and easy movement. The gimbal head, part of a unit called a gimbal tripod, is a movable mounting that, along with a stabilizing weight between the legs of the tripod, permits level shots and easy movement from a slow moving vehicle such as a ship. *See* **tripod.**

■ **triptych screen** A three-panel screen with three separate images, the side images generally commenting on or playing off the central picture. Abel Gance used such a technique, which he called Polyvision, for his *Napoleon vu par Abel Gance* (1927).

■ **TriStar Pictures** A production company begun in 1982 by Columbia Pictures, which was to distribute the films of the new organization; HBO, which was to show its films on cable; and CBS, which was to show them on network television. The new company began releasing in 1984, grossing almost 5 percent of the domestic box office. In 1986, TriStar purchased the Loew's theaters and was granted freedom from the Paramount Consent Decree by the courts in 1987. CBS soon sold its interest in the company and HBO gradually pulled away until, in 1987, TriStar joined Columbia, then owned by the Coca-Cola Company, to become part of Columbia Entertainment. When Sony purchased Columbia in 1989, both TriStar and Columbia functioned independently and then became part of Sony Pictures Entertainment in 1991. TriStar has done extremely well over the years with such films as *The Natural* (1984; dir. Barry Levinson), *Total Recall* (1990; dir. Paul Verhoeven), and *Sleepless in Seattle* (1993; dir. Nora Ephron). *See* **Columbia Pictures.**

■ **trombone** An extendible hanger that can be attached to the wall of a set and from which a luminaire is hung.

■ **trucking shot** The term generally means the same as a tracking shot, but is sometimes used more specifically to mean a shot taken from a truck or moving vehicle. *See* **tracking shot.**

■ **true telephoto lens** *See* **telephoto lens** (1).

■ **t-stop, t-number** The *t* stands for transmission, and these terms refer to the measurement of the exact transmission of light through a lens. While the f-stop number really tells the amount of light reaching the lens and does not take into account reflection and absorption by the lens elements as the light passes through, the t-number actually designates the amount of light to reach the focal point of the film—for this reason it is consulted for controlling the light reaching the film. T-stop numbers run the same as f-stop numbers, with each successive figure halving the amount of light admitted. T-numbers are calculated by electronically measuring the light reaching the focal plane and are printed along with f-numbers on most professional lenses. Although the distinction between both calibrations has lessened with the improvement of modern lenses, the difference is an important consideration with older lenses and especially with zoom lenses, where the multiple elements cause considerable loss of light. *See* **f-stop.**

■ **TTL** The abbreviation for "through-the-lens." The letters are applied to (1) exposure meters that read light from behind the lenses of smaller-gauge cameras for automatic control of the diaphragm opening; and (2) reflex viewfinders that show the camera operator the scene to be photographed from the perspective of the lens without parallax. *See* **through-the-lens.**

■ **tub thumper** Jargon for a publicity agent or publicist. The term is from the beating of a tub or drum, which beckoned people to a medicine show in former days. To "tub thump" is to publicize a person, property, or film.

■ **tuchel connecter, tuchel plug** A small connector with a tubular piece surrounding the female part that attaches to the threads of the male part; frequently used in audio systems. *See* **XLR connector.**

■ **tulip crane** A small, portable crane that is excellent for shooting on location. The crane folds to eight feet for easy transport and extends to sixteen and one-half feet. *See* **crane.**

■ **tuner** Jargon for the composer who writes music for a film.

■ **tungsten bulb** A normal incandescent bulb with a tungsten filament. Since these lamps blacken from the deposit of evaporated tungsten on the envelope and the filament gives way in time, they were replaced in filmmaking by tungsten-halogen lamps. *See* **tungsten-halogen bulb.**

■ **tungsten-halogen bulb** A quartz lamp with a tungsten filament in a metal halide gas such as iodine or bromine. Since the evaporated tungsten reacts with the gas and is redeposited on the filament, such bulbs do not blacken and the filament lasts much longer than those in normal bulbs. These lamps are also extremely compact and hence suitable for location work. The high temperature of these bulbs at one time required a

quartz jacket, but now an extremely strong glass is also used. *See* **quartz bulb.**

■ **tungsten print** A print balanced at 3200 K so that it can be projected from a projector using a tungsten bulb. *See* **xenon print.**

■ **tungsten rating, tungsten index, tungsten speed** The measurement of the sensitivity of film to photographic lights as opposed to its sensitivity to daylight, generally given in Kelvin degrees. Sometimes these terms are used for the measurement of the lights themselves.

■ **tungsten-to-daylight** Changing the color temperature of tungsten light by means of filters so that it is compatible with daylight.

■ **turbulation** The motion given to chemicals during processing to carry away by-products and bring fresh solution to the emulsion for consistent developing. Also called agitation.

■ **turnaround** (1) The term refers to a project that has been dropped by one film studio and is free to be picked up by another. A project is "in turnaround" when it has been terminated by one studio and is in search of another. *See* **changed-element clause.** (2) The duration necessary for one set to be struck and another assembled on a sound stage. (3) The contractually agreed duration between the close of one day's shooting and the start of the next. If such an agreement is not met, personnel are given extra compensation.

■ **turn over** An order given to the cameraman to switch on the power for the camera.

■ **turn-over prism, dove prism** A prism that can turn an image upside down or reverse it from left to right.

■ **turret, lens turret** A rotating mount, attached to the camera's aperture, that contains several different lenses, any of which can be moved into place for shooting. Flat turrets have two more parallel lenses, while divergent turrets may have three or four of various sizes that are so placed that none will appear in the line of vision of the lens in use. Such turrets can be operated electrically from the rear of the camera or by remote control.

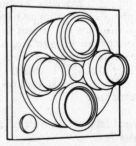

turret

■ **turtle** A three-legged stand for mounting luminaires close to the ground.

■ **TV cutoff** *See* **television cutoff.**

■ **TV print** *See* **xenon print.**

■ **tweenie** A spotlight with a six-hundred-watt bulb. *See* **spotlight.**

■ **tweening** *See* **inbetweener.**

■ **tweeter** (1) A loudspeaker with the capacity of producing high frequencies. (2) That part of a loudspeaker that carries high frequencies. *See* **woofer.**

■ **Twentieth Century-Fox** A major Hollywood studio formed in 1935 from the merger of the old Fox Film Corporation and Twentieth Century Pictures, which had recently been founded in 1933 by Joseph M. Schenck and Darryl F. Zanuck. Schenck became president of the company and Zanuck vice-president in charge of production, a position he was to hold for more than twenty years and from which he supervised the details of individual productions. The company was not at first especially strong in big stars, although it had inherited Shirley Temple from Fox. It was especially adept at making popular musicals with such performers as Alice Faye, Carmen Miranda, and later Betty Grable. Its major performers also eventually included Henry Fonda, Tyrone Power, Gregory Peck, and Marilyn Monroe. Some of its notable directors were John Ford, Joseph Mankiewicz, and Elia Kazan. Among its best films during the 1940s were Ford's *The Grapes of Wrath* (1940), Henry King's *The Song of Bernadette* (1943), and Elia Kazan's *Gentleman's Agreement* (1947). In 1953, the company led the way in the development of wide-screen cinema with *The Robe* (dir. Henry Koster), which featured the anamorphic-lens process, CinemaScope.

But the company fell on bad days with its expensive and disastrous production of *Cleopatra* in 1962, a $40 million dud that removed from the presidency Spyros Skouras, a position he had held since 1942. Zanuck, who had been working independently since 1956, returned to the organization as the new president. Robert Wise's *The Sound of Music* made the studio wealthy again in 1965. In 1969, Zanuck was made chairman of the board and his son, Richard, who had been chief of production, was made president, a position he was to lose two years later because of a series of tasteless films, such as *Myra Breckinridge* in 1970, even though the company had delivered Franklin Schaffner's *Patton* and Robert Altman's *M*A*S*H* in the same year.

Although still untouched by the conglomerates, Twentieth Century-Fox was purchased by oil millionaire Martin Davis in 1981, when the company's fortunes appeared to be in decline. But in 1985 the company was purchased by Australian media tycoon Rupert Murdoch's News Corporation and became part of Fox Corporation, which also included the Fox Broadcasting Company and Fox Television Stations. In spite of the thriving ways of its parent corporation and big blockbusters such as *Die Hard 2* (1990; dir. Renny Harlin), *Home Alone* (1990; dir. Chris Columbus), and *Mrs. Doubtfire* (1993; dir. Chris Columbus), the motion-picture company has had a less than enviable record in the market share of films released domestically in recent years. Even with such hits as James Cameron's *True Lies* and Jan DeBont's *Speed* in 1994, the company earned only 9 percent of the box-office market for that year. In 1995, its earnings dropped to 8 percent. *See* **CinemaScope** *and* **Fox Film Corporation.**

■ **twisting** A distortion in film caused by the loose winding of new prints with the emulsion side in.

■ **two-bladed shutter** *See* **shutter.**

■ **two-color process** Early color systems for cinematography that responded to only two of the primary colors, for example, Technicolor's subtractive process in the 1920s, which was sensitive to red and green. *See* **color film** *(2) and* **Technicolor.**

■ **two-headed nail** A nail, used in set construction with a second head below the first that prevents the nail from being driven all the way into the wood and allows it to be easily removed with the claw of a hammer.

■ **Two K** A 2-kilowatt light, either open-faced or with a Fresnel lens.

■ **two-reeler** A short film, especially in silent-film days, of approximately twenty to thirty minutes. Charlie Chaplin's memorable films for Mutual in 1916 and 1917 were two-reelers.

■ **twos** In animation work, the term refers to the exposure of two frames for each change in the drawings or for each movement of the models instead of single frame exposure. *See* **animation.**

■ **two-shot** Generally a medium or close shot in which two people fill the frame. This is the basic shot for most scenes of conversation in a film, showing the characters talking and responding to one another in profile or in a variety of stances and from a variety of angles. So popular was this shot in Hollywood movies that it was called the "American shot" in a number of European countries.

■ **two step** A box with two levels that is used for a number of purposes on a set—perhaps as a stand for a lamp in the scene, as a short step-ladder, or as a seat for a performer in a close-up.

■ **two-wall set** A constructed part of a room with two walls meeting at a corner for photographing characters in a limited space.

■ **Tyler helicopter mount** A sturdy camera mount that eliminates vibrations when taking aerial shots from a helicopter.

■ **typage** The term used by the Soviet film director Sergei Eisenstein in reference to his use of nonprofessional performers in his films who fit certain human types easily identified by the audience, a practice he traces back to the theater (see his essay "Through Theater to Cinema" in *Film Form*).

■ **typecasting** Choosing a performer to play a particular role that fits his or her appearance, mannerisms, personality, and often the general impression that the audience already has of the performer. Casting against type is to choose a role for a performer that he or she would not normally play and that requires a development of the performer's abilities.

■ ■ ■

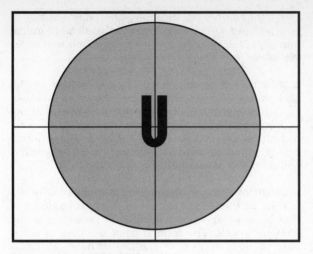

U core to UV filter

■ **U core** A plastic center piece for holding various types of 35 mm film.

■ **UFA, Universum Film A.G., Universum Film Aktien Gesellschaft** A major and internationally influential film company organized in Germany in 1917 when a number of smaller production companies were brought together, with the government supplying one-third of the financial support for the new organization. The initial aim of the new company was to uplift the spirit of the German people at home and increase the reputation of the nation abroad through a national cinema with the highest standards of production. The company built its impressive studios at Neubabelsberg, near Berlin, and began to put together a staff of performers, directors, and production personnel that was equaled only by the staffs of the major studios in Hollywood; it also began to develop its distribution capacity and accumulate a large number of theaters, becoming the most important force in Germany's film industry. In 1918, after Germany's defeat in World War I, the government sold its shares in the company to the Deutsche Bank and several private corporations, thus making UFA into a private organization dependent upon its financial success in the international market place. UFA, seeking to produce lavish costume spectacles similar to those coming out of Italy such as *Cabiria* (1914), produced Joe May's *Veritas Vincit* in 1918 and a number of lavish historical dramas directed by Ernst Lubitsch, most notably his international success *Madame Dubarry* (entitled *Passion* in America) in 1919, which starred Pola Negri. In the same year the company released *The Cabinet of Dr. Caligari*, directed by Robert Wiene. The first of its great expressionist works, this motion picture also marked the start of Germany's "Golden Age of Film." The three most significant directors to work for UFA were Fritz Lang, among whose films were his visually evocative two-part version of the Siegfried legend, *Die Nibelungen* (1924), and his futuristic fantasy, *Metropolis* (1927); F. W. Murnau, whose classic horror film *Nosferatu* (1922) remains one of the best treatments of the vampire story and whose 1924 film, *The Last Laugh* (*Der Letzte Mann,* in German), is the best of the Kammerspiel (i.e., "intimate theater") films made by UFA; and G. W. Pabst, a stunning realist and film stylist who directed the "street" film, *Joyless Street* in 1925 and *Pandora's Box* in 1929.

In spite of Erich Pommer's excellent administration as chief of production beginning in 1923 and the many fine films produced by the company, UFA's financial fortunes progressively worsened during the decade because of the high cost of its productions and American competition. An agreement signed with Paramount and MGM in 1926 brought UFA a desperately needed loan, but at the cost of opening its theaters, at disadvantageous terms, to films from the American companies and making available to Hollywood its best personnel. The very next year the American interest was bought out by Dr. Alfred Hugenberg, a National Socialist supporter who became chairman of the board and moved the company in a decidedly political direction, especially by having UFA newsreels give prominent attention to Nazi rallies. With the coming of sound, UFA produced a number of musical films, but moved further in a political direction once the National Socialists came into power in 1933 by making blatantly pro-Nazi movies. In 1937, the government actually took over the company, which, after a dismal period, was to expire with Nazi Germany at the end of the war in 1945. The UFA company founded in West Germany in 1956 did not long survive. *See* **expressionism, Kammerspielfilm,** *and* **street film.**

■ **Ultimatte** The Ultimatte 300 is an analog video system that allows the director and cinematographer to see how a scene will ultimately be composited together right before the shooting of the action. With a video cassette in a player supplying the background and a video camera shooting the scene or action, a composite image appears on a small monitor. Ultimatte has developed a number of compositing processes for analog video and for the computer that much resemble the color-difference blue-screen process used in filmmaking. Instead of using the chroma-key technology, the company employs an additive procedure that first processes foreground and background separately and then brings them together (chroma key is non-additive in that it switches back and forth). In 1995, Ultimatte was given a Technical Achievement Award by the Academy of Motion Picture Arts and Sciences for its CineFusion software that works directly with a Silicon Graphics workstation. The company is headquartered in Chatsworth, California. *See* **blue-screen process, chroma key,** *and* **video assist.**

■ **ultrasonic** Sound waves of a frequency higher than those within the audible range.

■ **ultrasonic cleaner, ultrasonic film cleaner** A system for cleaning film that employs a solution agitated by ultrasonic soundwaves. This method of cleaning is especially efficient for removing dirt from release prints.

■ **ultrasonic splicer** A splicer that uses ultrasonic power to join together two pieces of film with a polyester base such as Estar. Such bases cannot be spliced with cement and must be connected by either an ultrasonic weld or tape.

■ **ultraviolet** Light waves beyond the violet part of the color spectrum, which, though invisible, affect a film's emulsion.

■ **ultraviolet filter, UV filter, haze filter** A filter that absorbs ultraviolet rays and also penetrates haze.

■ **ultraviolet traveling-matte process** A dual-film system for making mattes that allows the combining of different picture elements into a single image. Livé action is photographed in front of a translucent screen illuminated from the rear by ultraviolet light. A beam-splitting prism in the camera sends the ultraviolet rays to one film so that a traveling matte is formed with the foreground action clear and the surrounding area opaque. From this female matte a male matte is made with the performers opaque and the surroundings clear. At the same time, the normal incandescent light that illuminates the performers is sent to the other film, which forms a negative with a clear area surrounding the characters. From this negative a self-matting positive can be made with the background opaque. *See* **special effects** *and* **traveling-matte process.**

■ **umbrella** A device in the shape of an umbrella made of a material that reflects light onto a certain area and creates a soft, diffuse light.

umbrella

■ **unbalanced** The term refers to an emulsion on color film not balanced for the color temperature of a spe-

cific light source. For example, when daylight film is used without a correcting filter for artificial illumination the result is an image with a red or yellow tint. *See* **color balance.**

■ **under** (1) Referring to any sound played in the background of a scene at a volume lower than the major sound (e.g., music or environmental noises that can be heard behind the performers' dialogue). (2) A direction during recording or editing to modulate a particular sound so that it is heard as a background behind the major sound.

■ **undercrank** To run a camera at a rate slower than the normal 24 frames per second so that accelerated motion is achieved when the image is projected at the standard speed. The term is from the days of silent films when cameras were cranked by hand. To run a camera faster than normal is to "overcrank."

■ **undercranked** Referring to film that has been shot at a speed slower than the normal 24 frames per second so that when the images are projected at normal speed fast-motion action will result. Film shot faster than normal is "overcranked."

■ **underdeveloped** Referring to a film that has been developed at too short a length of time or in a solution of incorrect temperature so that the resulting image is not sufficiently defined or detailed but appears light and washed out.

■ **underdevelopment** Processing a film for a shorter length of time or at a lesser temperature than the stock normally requires to decrease contrast or graininess or to compensate for overexposure. The technique is rarely used because of the loss in picture quality. Also called pulling. *See* **overdevelopment.**

■ **underexposure** The exposure of film either in a camera or printer with an insufficient intensity of light or for an insufficient time. The resulting image from film that has been underexposed in a camera is too dark, with insufficient details in the shadows; the image that results from improper exposure in the printer appears washed out, with insufficient definition and detail. *See* **overexposure.**

■ **underground film** Another name for the avant-garde or experimental cinema in the United States starting in the 1950s. The name New American Cinema also covers these films for roughly the same period, but specifically derives from the New American Cinema Group, which was established in 1960. The term "underground film" originates from the artistic revolt and experimentation of the Beat Generation in the 1950s, which was taking place especially in San Francisco and New York City. Experimental film in the United States came into its own as part of the social and artistic explosion of the turbulent 1960s. The term "underground film" suggests the noncommercial and radical aspects of these films; it also suggests that these works were made privately, independent of the film industry. The underground film emphasizes the private, subjective vision of the filmmaker, while reacting against accepted social and aesthetic values. It also explores the medium of film itself in a way that may at first seem crude or amateurish, but actually demonstrates great innovation and technical insight about the nature of film and perception. Among the makers of underground film, the names of Stan Vanderbeek, who coined the term, Jordan Belson, Kenneth Anger, and Stan Brackhage stand out. *See* **avant-garde cinema** *and* **New American Cinema.**

■ **underlit** Any set or location so deficient in lighting that the entire image or parts of it are indistinct or do not have sufficient details. *See* **overlighting.**

■ **underplay** To perform a role in a low-key manner with subtlety and restraint.

■ **undershooting** Shooting a scene or entire film with insufficient shots and setups for adequate editing. *See* **overshooting.**

■ **under-slung head, underslung head** A special fluid head that holds the camera from above. Such a head is useful for shooting with the camera a short distance from the ground. Cameras can be placed beneath cam-rails and can also be operated and moved by remote. *See* **cam-rail.**

■ **understudy** A performer who learns a role and is prepared to substitute for the actor or actress playing that role in case of some emergency or special circumstance.

■ **under the line** The cost of a film excluding the amount paid to the highly compensated star or stars. When such costs are included, the term "over the line" is employed.

■ **underwater cinematography** The photography of moving pictures beneath the surface of water, whether beneath the surface of a studio tank or a large body of water such as an ocean. To accomplish this type of cinematography specially trained personnel are required as well as cameras in waterproof housings or specially built cameras that require no shell. Artificial lighting, which is especially required at depths farther away from the surface of the water, may be obtained either from individual units with a lamp and battery, which are specifically employed for close-ups or from a number of lamps attached to cables and powered by one or more generators from above the water. Since objects photographed underwater appear to the camera lens,

as they do to the eye, one-quarter closer than they actually are because of refraction, the distance between the lens and subject must be multiplied by a factor of 1.33. Wide-angle lenses are normally employed to compensate for this shrinking of distance and to minimize the amount of water between the camera and the subject. Filters can be employed on the camera to compensate, up to a point, for the absorption of red light by the water, although it is also possible to improve color balance and density with filters during printing. Underwater cinematography, which has been a staple of Hollywood's commercial films since Cecil B. DeMille's *Reap the Wild Wind* in 1942, achieved some fine visual effects for the Disney production *20,000 Leagues Under the Sea* in 1954 (dir. Richard Fleischer). This type of photography was especially advanced by the United States Navy and also developed for scientific films and documentaries, notably for the Jacques-Yves Cousteau films, which have appeared on television. The most outstanding underwater cinematography in recent years appears in James Cameron's *The Abyss* (1989), a considerable portion of which was shot in a huge tank in an unfinished nuclear power plant in South Carolina and lit by specially designed HMI lights. *See* **underwater housing.**

underwater cinematography John Cameron achieved some of the best underwater cinematography in recent years in *The Abyss* (1989).

■ ■ ■

■ **underwater housing, underwater blimp** A specially built waterproof shell for protecting a camera while shooting underwater. Such covers must be able to withstand the pressure caused by the weight of the water while being balanced for equilibrium and designed for rapid movement. Special waterproof and pressure-resistant cameras, such as Eclair's Aquaflex, do not require an underwater housing. *See* **underwater cinematography.**

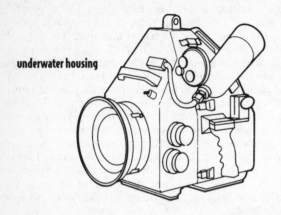

underwater housing

■ **undeveloped** (1) Exposed film that has not yet been processed. (2) Film being processed that has not yet reached the developing stage.

■ **unexposed** Film that has not yet been exposed to light either in a camera or printer and that remains raw.

■ **unidirectional microphone** A commonly used heart-shaped microphone that picks up sound mostly from the direction in which it is aimed. Also called a cardioid microphone. *See* **microphone.**

■ **unilateral track** A variable-area sound track in which the changes in width representing the various frequencies are recorded along only one side. This track, used during the earlier days of sound films, was changed to a bilateral track in which the changes are symmetrically recorded on both sides and which gives a better sound. *See* **variable-area sound track.**

■ **unintentional, unintentional cut** A cut made in the workprint and then respliced without any change in the film. When such a workprint will be used for conforming the negative, two horizontal marks are made over the splice to indicate that it is unintentional and should be ignored (vertical lines are used to mark intentional cuts).

■ **unit** An individual crew for a specific film. Sometimes commercial films may have a smaller second unit for location shooting while the first unit photographs the performers in the main action. *See* **second unit.**

■ **United Artists Agency (UAA)** *See* **talent agency.**

■ **United Artists Corporation** A film company organized in 1919 by Charlie Chaplin, Mary Pickford, Douglas Fairbanks, and D. W. Griffith with the sole purpose of distributing the films made by these luminaries as independent producers. Through such an arrangement, these figures would have full control over their productions while receiving profits formerly shared with the studios. During its early years, the company released some fine works, beginning with Fairbanks's *His Majesty, the American* and Griffith's *Broken Blossoms* in 1919; and Fairbanks's *The Mark of Zorro*, Griffith's *Way Down East*, and Pickford's *Pollyanna* in 1920. Chaplin gave to the company *A Woman of Paris* in 1923, which he directed and in which he did not appear, and in 1925 his remarkable *The Gold Rush*. But in spite of these and other fine works, the company had difficulty finding sufficient films to release and sufficient theaters at which to exhibit. Under the presidency of Joseph Schenk, United Artists began to distribute the films of Gloria Swanson in 1925 and films produced by Samuel Goldwyn in 1927. Schenk also distributed films from his own Art Cinema Corporation and began to put together the United Artists Theater Circuit. United Artists released Charlie Chaplin's *City Lights* in 1931 and *Modern Times* in 1936. The company also released Alexander Korda's *The Private Life of Henry VIII* in 1933 and then entered into contract to release a series of films made by Korda's London Film Corporation. In 1937 both Goldwyn and Korda failed in an attempt to take over the company, which then went through a rather lackluster period, changing leadership a number of times.

The Paramount decrees of 1948, however, which ultimately forced the major studios to divest themselves of their theaters, were to prove a great asset to United. Without its own studios and free from any vast overhead, the company was unencumbered and was able to adjust to the new period in film history. Since theaters could now bid for the best pictures, regardless of who distributed them, and since the demand for more films increased due to the rapid decline in productions from the major studios, United Artists achieved a new attractiveness for the burgeoning crew of independent producers. The company distributed some very fine films in the 1950s under the presidency of Arthur Krim, including Stanley Kramer's *High Noon* in 1952 (dir. Fred Zinnemann) and *Marty* in 1955 (dir. Delbert Mann). In 1967, United Artists became part of the conglomerate Transamerica, and David Picker became the company's president two years later. United did surprisingly well in the 1970s, with three films in a row that won Academy Awards for best picture of the year: *One Flew Over the Cuckoo's Nest* in 1975 (dir. Milos Forman); *Rocky* in 1976 (dir. John Avildsen); and *Annie Hall* in 1977 (dir. Woody Allen). The company also continued to do well distributing films made abroad, notably the James Bond series, which it had begun to distribute in the early part of the previous decade. But United ran into considerable difficulty at the end of the 1970s when it overextended itself supporting Michael Cimino's *Heaven's Gate* (1980). Transamerica sold the company to MGM in 1981, and MGM/UA began to finance and distribute a number of films each year—but the old United Artists was very much a thing of the past.

MGM/UA was purchased in 1986 by Ted Turner who then sold the production and distribution part to Kirk Kerkorian. The UA banner disappeared entirely when the company was bought by Giancarlo Paretti in 1990 as part of Pathé Communications Company, which itself became MGM-Pathé Communications. The name Metro-Goldwyn-Mayer, Inc., was returned to the film organization in 1992, when it was taken over by Crédit Lyonnais Bank Nederland in France because Paretti did not have the funds to pay the debt. MGM/UA once more got into the film business in 1993 and since that time has had some success. At this point, however, the organization's future remains unclear, especially since Kirk Kerkorian has once again become involved with the film organization, this time as the chief backer to MGM/UA's own management group that has recently purchased the company. *See* **Metro-Goldwyn-Mayer.**

■ **unit manager** (1) A person responsible for the daily management of a film company on location: for example, for transportation, housing, food, and equipment. (2) A person who works under the production manager and is directly involved with preparation for a day's shooting and acquiring accommodations for personnel. (3) The production manager. *See* **production manager.**

■ **unit photographer** *See* **still man.**

■ **unit production manager** *See* **production manager.**

■ **unit publicist** *See* **publicist.**

■ **unit set** A set made up of parts that can be arranged in a number of ways to create a variety of scenes.

■ **universal camera filter** A term sometimes used for "all-purpose" camera filters that do not alter color balance (e.g., neutral density and polarizing filters). *See* **filter** *(1).*

■ **universal leader, SMPTE universal leader** A piece of film attached to both the beginning and end of release prints that permits the reel to be properly threaded and on which specific signs permit the projectionist to change from one reel to another without interruption during the screening. Similar in function to the Academy leader, the universal leader has been designed by the SMPTE (the Society of Motion Picture and Television Engineers). Also called society leader. *See* **Academy leader** *and* **leader.**

■ **Universal Pictures** A film-production company formed in 1912 by Carl Laemmle when he amalgamated his Independent Motion Picture Company (IMP) with several other organizations. Universal was one of the independents that withstood the pressures of the film companies of the Motion Picture Patents Company to become a major Hollywood studio, building the famed Universal City in the San Fernando Valley in 1915. Erich von Stroheim made his early films at Universal before he was forced out by his conflicts with chief of production Irving Thalberg. Two of the company's stars during the silent period were Rudolph Valentino and Lon Chaney. Universal turned out a large number of modest films during this period, a practice it continued into the 1930s. In that decade the company also produced a series of classic horror films, beginning with Tod Browning's *Dracula* and James Whale's *Frankenstein,* both in 1931, and several distinguished motion pictures, such as Lewis Milestone's *All Quiet on the Western Front* (1930) and the classic screwball comedy *My Man Godfrey* (1936), directed by Gregory La Cava. The company's ailing financial situation forced Laemmle, along with his son, to relinquish management in 1936; but Universal was kept afloat in the 1940s with the films of Deanna Durbin, Abbott and Costello, W. C. Fields, and some Technicolor fantasies with Maria Montez.

In 1946, the company joined with International Pictures, and the new organization was known as Universal-International until 1952, when it reverted to the old Universal name immediately before its takeover by Decca Records. In 1962, Universal, along with Decca, became part of the Music Corporation of America (MCA), the former talent agency that was then heavily into television production. Universal had success in the 1960s with the titillation comedies of Doris Day and was especially fortunate in its television productions. In the 1970s Universal achieved considerable financial and artistic success with such films as George Lucas's *American Graffiti* (1973), Steven Spielberg's *Jaws* (1975), and Michael Cimino's *The Deer Hunter* (1978). The company moved into the 1980s with a big bang when it released Spielberg's *E.T.: The Extra-Terrestrial* (1982) and continued to do well with such films as *Back to the Future* (1985; dir. Robert Zemeckis) and Steven Spielberg's *Jurassic Park* (1993). Films of distinction during this period were Spielberg's *Schindler's List* and Jim Sheridan's *In the Name of the Father,* both in 1993. In 1990, MCA/Universal was purchased by Matsushita Electric Industrial Company of Japan for the remarkable price of $6.9 billion. Like Sony, with its purchase of the CBS Records Group in 1987 and Columbia in 1989, Matsushita sought to purchase a software venue for its own electronic hardware, while also becoming an international powerhouse in the world of media. Like Sony, once again, Matsushita came to regret its intrusion into Hollywood and the American entertainment industry. The company sold 80 percent of MCA to the Seagram Company and its CEO, Edgar Bronfman, Jr., in 1995, for $5.7 billion in cash (both MCA and Seagram already owned 80 percent of the Cineplex Odeon theater chain). Two months later, MCA and Dreamworks SKG (the new studio of Steven Spielberg, Jeffrey Katzenberg, and David Geffen) announced an arrangement by which Universal would distribute the motion pictures, home videos, and music of Dreamworks outside the United States, Canada, and Korea. The studio's market share of film distribution in 1994 was 13.6 percent and in 1995 was 13.2 percent. Adding to the mystique of the classic age of film is Universal's notable theme parks, Universal Studios Hollywood and Universal Studios Florida (in Orlando).

■ **unmodulated track, unmod track** A sound track without any audio signal that is used to fill in the gaps between sounds on a synchronized track.

■ **unsqueeze** To project an image that has been horizontally compressed on film by an anamorphic lens on the camera through the same type of lens on the projector so that the scene appears normal, though with a wide-screen aspect ratio. *See* **anamorphic lens, aspect ratio** *and* **wide screen.**

■ **unsqueezed print** A release print with normal images not requiring projection through an anamorphic lens that has been made from a negative with anamorphically squeezed images in an optical printer. *See* **anamorphic lens.**

■ **untimed print** *See* **one-light print.**

■ **up** (1) A direction to increase the volume of a sound or the intensity of some piece of equipment such as a light. (2) A term used to describe a performer who is nervous and forgets lines.

■ **UPA (United Production of America)** An animation studio formed in 1943 by a group of animators who had defected from Walt Disney Productions sometime after a strike in 1941. The group, headed by Stephen Bosustow, sought creative independence and more contemporary styles of animation. At its best, UPA created a leaner and less lush style than the Disney Studios, witty and even surrealistic: objects and parts of locations appeared as needed, suspended in space; and characters were sharper, flatter, more suggestive, and less mobile.

At its best, the group also exchanged Disney's sentimentalism and romanticism for realism and clever satire. Mr. Magoo first appeared in John Hubley's *Ragtime Bear* in 1949 and became a popular character in future cartoons, especially those by Pete Burness; and Bob Cannon created another UPA star with the title figure of *Gerald McBoing Boing* in 1951, bringing him back on occasion in another popular series. The company created its best works in the 1950s, but in 1958 had to close its New York studio and concentrate more on commercials and cartoons for television from its Burbank studio. *See* **animation** *and* **cartoon.**

■ **upfront exposure** The money put forward by a distribution/production company or other group to get a project launched or developed whether or not it is actually filmed.

■ **uprating** *See* **overdevelopment** *and* **pushing.**

■ **up shot** A low-angle shot with the camera tilting up at the subject.

■ **upside-down slate** A clapboard held upside down with the clapsticks banged together at the bottom of the frame to indicate the conclusion of a shot. Sometimes it is necessary to start photographing the scene immediately without holding the clapboard right side up at the start of the shot. Also called tail slate and endboard. *See* **clapboard.**

■ **upstage** (1) The rear part of the stage. (2) To draw the audience's attention away from a performer—sometimes caused by the action of another performer or some business in the scene. (3) To force a performer to face upstage—sometimes caused by another performer or some action to the rear of the scene. (4) An order for a performer to look away from the camera or to look to the rear of the scene.

■ **utility department** The group of personnel, belonging to a studio or film organization, that performs routine jobs and janitorial services.

■ **utility man** A laborer working for a film production who performs routine jobs.

■ **UV filter** *See* **haze filter.**

■ ■ ■

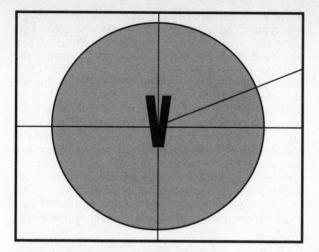

vacuum tube to VU meter, volume units meter, VU indicator, VI meter, volume indicator meter

■ **vacuum tube** An electronic device with an evacuated envelope formerly used as a semiconductor in sound reproduction and now replaced by transistors.

■ **vamp** A term derived from "vampire," which was used, especially in silent-film days, to describe a *femme fatale*, a beautiful and seductive woman who lures men to their doom. Theodosia Goodman took on the acting name of Theda Bara, supposedly an anagram of "Arab Death," and became known as the "Vamp" after she appeared in *A Fool There Was* in 1914, a film based on Rudyard Kipling's poem, *The Vampire*.

■ **variable-area sound track, variable-area recording** An optical sound track for audio playback that is comprised of an oscillographic pattern with symmetrical outlines on both sides marking the variations of the sound waves. The track is itself the photograph of a light beam, the area of which has been varied by the sound waves picked up by a microphone and converted to electric impulses. The track controls the intensity of light reaching a photoelectric cell from a lamp in the projector and hence the variation in electric impulses that are given off by the cell and converted into sound. Both variable-area and variable-density tracks have been employed for sound, though the area method is now generally employed since it is easier to use with color film. *See* **optical sound, sound,** *and* **variable-density sound track.**

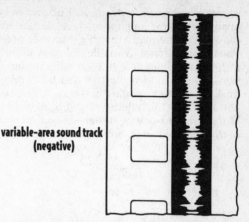

variable-area sound track
(negative)

■ **variable-density sound track, variable-density recording** An optical sound track for audio playback that is comprised of a series of separate striations of varying density across the width of the track. The spacing between the striations is the result of the frequency of the sound recorded while their density is controlled by the volume. Both variable-area and variable-density tracks can be converted to sound by the same equipment in the projector, though the former is now the preferred method of sound recording since it is easier to use with color film. *See* **optical sound, sound,** *and* **variable-area sound track.**

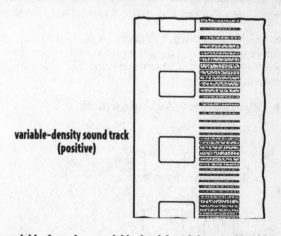

variable-density sound track
(positive)

■ **variable-focus lens, variable-focal-length lens, varifocal lens** *See* **zoom lens.**

■ **variable-opening shutter, variable shutter** A shutter in professional cameras with a second rotating blade controlling the size of the opening in the primary blade and hence the amount of light reaching the film. The shutter's opening, which can be fully extended to between 170 and 180 degrees and closed down to zero, is controlled by a calibrated knob or lever at the rear of a camera. In some cameras the opening may be closed and enlarged automatically to produce a fade-out and fade-in or a dissolve, although such effects are more normally achieved in an optical printer in which the process camera contains such a shutter. Animation cameras also contain a variable shutter to produce such transitional effects. Variable shutters allow shooting with the same depth of field in different lighting situations. The second blade can also be employed to reduce the shutter opening and thus necessitate a wider lens aperture for reduced depth of field (a reduction of the shutter opening to half is equal to one full stop of the lens aperture). *See* **shutter** *(1)*.

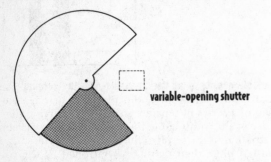

variable-opening shutter

■ **variable shutter control** The calibrated knob or lever on the rear of a camera that controls the opening in a variable shutter. *See* **variable-opening shutter**.

■ **variable speed control** Any device in the camera or its motor that changes the operating speed of the camera.

■ **variable-speed motor, wild motor** A camera motor with the capacity for operating at a variety of speeds through the adjustment of a rheostat that controls the amount of current.

■ **variable spot-flood** *See* **focusing spotlight**.

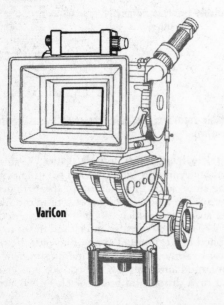

VariCon

■ **VariCon** A device that controls contrast by emitting a low and even light before the lens to permit greater detail in shadowed areas and reduce the image's grain without diminishing its resolution or disturbing the more illuminated areas. The device can also act as a filler light in close-ups, put color into shadowed areas, and alter color tone with special filter packs. The controls and light sit on top of the camera illuminating the twin filters below. Manufactured by the Arriflex Corporation, the VariCon is smaller and less bulky than the company's earlier Lightflex, which was used for much the same effects. The VariCon performs something of the same function as flashing the film in the laboratory, except that the cinematographer has more control over the contrast and can test the various effects in advance by looking through the viewfinder. *See* **flashing** *(1)*.

■ *Variety* A weekly newspaper published in New York City that is the major trade journal of the entertainment industry. The publication offers news items and feature articles about all aspects of the film industry as well as reviews and box-office results for current motion pictures. The *Daily Variety* is published in Hollywood and maintains a running commentary on the television and film industry as well as on other entertainment activities.

■ **varifocal lens** *See* **zoom lens**.

■ **vault** A fireproof place for the long-term storage of motion pictures with constant temperature and humidity control to prevent deterioration of the film. Special precaution is taken when motion pictures on nitrate base, which was commonly used before the safer acetate base, are stored. Film studios, archives, and laboratories have such vaults. Film studios store original negatives as well as final prints.

■ **vector graphics** An older type of computer graphics composed of black and white lines formed between the programmed coordinates on the screen of the cathode-ray tube. *See* **computer animation** *and* **raster graphics**.

■ **vehicle** A term in media for any specific medium such as television, newspaper, or film itself.

■ **velocitator** A mobile carrier for a camera that is larger than a dolly and contains a small crane that can elevate the camera up to six feet. The velocitator, which contains seats for the camera operator and camera assistant, is either pushed by hand or run by motor.

■ **velveting sound, gloving sound** The process of cleaning a sound track by moving it between two pieces of soft cloth.

■ *The Velvet Light Trap* A scholarly journal from the Wisconsin Center for Film and Theater Research that focuses on the history of cinema. Issues are frequently devoted to a specific subject (e.g., film comedy) from both critical and theoretical perspectives.

∎ **vertical control** A term applied to the major Hollywood studio's ownership of production, distribution, and exhibition components of the film industry beginning in the days of silent films and ending in the early 1950s after the Supreme Court's Paramount decrees of 1948 declared such practice in violation of the antitrust laws. The studios were required to divest themselves of their theaters, thus leaving exhibition an open market and encouraging the rapid increase in independent productions. The end of vertical control also marked the beginning of the end for the Hollywood studio system, which was further undermined by the dramatic decrease in audiences due to the rise of television and the decrease in foreign markets due to protective tariffs. Vertical control, however, has returned in recent years with the courts becoming more permissive about production/distribution companies purchasing theaters—e.g., both Universal Pictures and the Canadian-based theater circuit, Cineplex Odeon, are owned by MCA, while Sony owns Columbia and TriStar as well as the Loews Theatres. Another modern form of vertical control, or vertical integration, is the ownership of film production/distribution companies and cable movie channels at the same time—e.g., Time Warner owns both Warner Brothers and HBO, not to mention the film and television holdings that the Turner Broadcasting System brought to the organization. *See* **Paramount decrees** *and* **studio system.**

∎ **vertical pan** *See* **tilt shot.**

∎ **vertical wipe** *See* **wipe.**

∎ **video** The term comes from the Latin word *videre,* which means "to see," and describes (1) both the picture and audio elements transmitted by a television system; (2) the picture element as distinct from the audio in a television system; (3) the picture element of any medium, including motion pictures, as distinct from the audio; (4) any performance, production, or demonstration recorded on videotape (e.g., a rock video performance); and (5) the videotape or video-cassette itself used for recording image and sound.

In recent years video, as defined in (1) and (2), has come to play a greater role in the making of motion pictures and has even begun to rival film in such markets as home, educational, instructional, and experimental movies because of the improved quality, greater availability, and decreased price of videotape and equipment. Although the picture quality of videotape has improved remarkably, its images still cannot be viewed with anything near the brightness, contrast, definitions, color, and immediacy of images projected by film, nor are they of sufficient quality to be transferred

to film for projection (even though such a process was actually used by Frank Zappa for *200 Motels* [1971]). A better result was achieved when HDTV (high definition television), which offers a sharper and richer picture than normal television systems, was initially used and the image then transferred to film for *Julia and Julia* (1987; dir. Peter Del Monte). But though the picture quality of video systems has improved remarkably, such images still cannot be projected with the quality of images shot with film, nor are the video images of sufficient quality to be transferred to film and projected with comparable effect. Video, however, is now incorporated into the production of commercial films in a number of significant ways.

Video recordings may be used in preproduction for casting, selecting locations, and viewing storyboards. A "video assist" attached to the motion-picture camera sends images to one or more monitors so that the director and other personnel can view the scene during shooting along with the camera operator; in some instances, especially during difficult shots, the film camera itself can be operated from a distance by remote control in response to such video images (the Louma Crane, for example, sends back video images directly from the viewfinder for such operation). The video assist also allows the director, cinematographer, and other key personnel to view the scene from videotape immediately after it is shot, thus allowing them to decide if another take is needed and to make decisions concerning future shots.

Video is also making important inroads in the editing procedures for motion-picture film, especially with the development of sophisticated video-editing desks that, employing both video and computer technology, are far more flexible and easy to use then the more cumbersome film-editing equipment. The film images can be transposed to videotape and editing can proceed from electronic images on monitors with decisions made by the simple operation of pushing buttons, without the need for making and handling workprints. Editing is simplified by coding the video images with numbers by means of a computer, thus allowing the editor to call up on the monitor, or monitors, various frames and try out, in rapid fashion, an edited sequence before recording it. The procedure also allows the editor to record several versions of the same sequence and compare them before making a final decision. Logging the frames in this manner not only makes it easy to call up any image in an instant, but also offers an efficient method for cutting the original negative. But as rapidly as video has offered a fast and efficient means of editing motion pictures, it is already being replaced by newer technology. Computerized nonlinear editing systems that digitally encode both picture and sound are now being employed since they allow random access of scenes as well as greater speed and flexibility in trying out a variety of possibilities and performing the final editing.

Electronic techniques for altering images, called "videographics," also permit a rapid and easy way of achieving such various effects as transitions between scenes and composite images, which are normally achieved on film through slow and expensive methods and normally require optical printing. Although such video images are not generally suitable for incorporation into a film, they do offer a means of testing various possibilities for the motion picture and they sometimes can be used when a finely defined picture is not necessary (e.g., for composite pictures in underwater sequences).

Video color analyzers, such as the Hazeltine, are now used for timing both rush and answer prints. In both cases the negative is run through the machine and a positive image appears on the screen of the video system. The picture is then altered for density and color. Reference pictures from a print can be sent to an adjoining screen from a still projector. Many such analyzers are also capable of producing the control band that will control the printer for making the alterations in the print.

Video plays a more obvious role in bringing to home viewers motion pictures either though television transmission or by means of a videocassette played on a video recorder. It has been estimated that by 1995 close to 76 million homes had VCRs—almost 80 percent of the households in this country with television sets—and that the gross for rentals and purchases of tapes was nearly that for theatrical distribution. Undoubtedly, films on videotape keep many people away from the motion-picture theater, but they also seem to keep alive a general interest in the cinema that sends people back to the theaters for new releases. *See* **nonlinear editing** *and* **timing.**

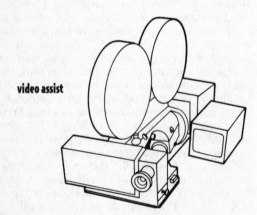

video assist

■ **video assist** A video system attached to a film camera for creating "instant dailies" so that a shot just taken can be immediately judged. Such systems allow a scene to be viewed on a monitor during shooting and on videotape immediately after. Video viewfinders are often tied into the film camera's reflex viewfinder. Also called a video tap. *See* **video.**

■ **video camera** A camera used to record or transmit images electronically. The imaging device was formerly a photoconductive tube, but is now more often a CCD (charge-coupled device), a solid-state image sensor that uses a silicon chip with a myriad of rows of pixels to convert the light waves to electronic signals, which must then be amplified. In the photoconductive tube, an electric gun twice scans the image on the faceplate line by line, creating two fields that are transmitted sequentially and that together form a single frame on the television or video screen, while a memory area in the CCD's chip stores the same line-by-line signal and sends it out in a manner similar to the two fields scanned in the tube. Video cameras normally contain three CCDs, one for each of the primary colors.

■ **video cassette, videocassette** A cartridge containing a videotape for recording or playing back both picture and sound. The tape runs between feed and take-up spools in the cartridge so that the cassette is a self-contained unit that may be inserted into the recorder without the tape having to be threaded.

■ **videocassette recorder (VCR)** A machine that attaches to a television set to record on tape in a videocassette both image and sound or to play previously recorded picture and audio. *See* **home video** *and* **videotape.**

■ **video color analyzer, video analyzer** A video system, such as the Hazeltine, for assessing both the density and color of a film image during the timing process. The negative is run through the apparatus and the image transmitted to the video screen in its positive form. The timer then adjusts the density and color of the image. Part of the system is a still projector, which is sometimes used to project frames of a print on an adjoining screen for comparison. A number of analyzers create the control band that makes the changes in the image during printing. In some analyzers the negative can be run with the control band to check the alterations on the video screen before they are actually made during printing. *See* **laboratory** *and* **timing.**

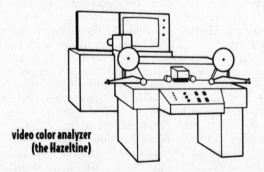

**video color analyzer
(the Hazeltine)**

■ **videodisc, video disc, laser disc, laserdisc** A disc on which video images and sound are recorded and from which they may be played back on a television screen or video monitor. The older form of videodisc, which used a stylus for recording and playing back the image and sound, had proved unpopular and was phased out; but the laser or "optical" recording and playback system for discs is now employed because of its higher quality of reproduction and more numerous programmable functions. Although the present laser system has not proved as popular as the normal VCR, both the electronics and entertainment industries have high hopes for the new DVD (digital video or versatile disc) system. *See* **DVD** *and* **laser disc editing.**

■ **videodisc editing** *See* **laserdisc editing.**

■ **video editing system** A system that edits images by selecting them from a source videotape player and copying them in a desired order onto a videotape recorder. Two or more videotape players are used for eliminating a change of reels, but also for creating more sophisticated transitions than simple cuts (e.g., dissolves and fades). An edit controller runs the various operations of the machines synchronically and also marks editing points. Such editing systems are called linear, since specific scenes can be accessed only by sequentially moving through the entire work instead of calling them up randomly. Motion pictures are sometimes transferred to videotape, allowing the editor to edit the film rapidly and efficiently without having to cut and splice a workprint. The images are time-coded by means of a computer and can be quickly called to one or more monitors along with the appropriate sound. This system allows the editor to try out various sequences and to record several versions before assembling the final version from which an edit-decision list (EDL) is made for the creation of a master video copy or a negative cut list for conforming the actual negative of the film. Nonlinear digital systems, however, are fast replacing linear video editing systems. Several nonlinear video systems were introduced in the early 1980s (e.g., the Eddiflex, with eight separate VCRs feeding the process), but these are being replaced by digital nonlinear systems that allow total random access. *See* **edit controller, editing, linear editing, nonlinear editing,** *and* **video.**

■ **video format** The various types of television transmission that differ in lines per frame and frames per second. *See* **HDTV, PAL, NTSC,** *and* **SECAM.**

■ **videographer** An individual who uses a video camera to record some action, whether it be actual or dramatized. The term "camera operator" is used more often for the person employing a video camera in a studio situation.

■ **videographics** *See* **video.**

■ **video master** The videotape that is the source of a video workprint—e.g., the videotape that results from a film-to-tape transfer in a telecine. *See* **edit video master.**

■ **video matchback** An editing procedure in which a video workprint and EDL (edit-decision list) are used to match and cut the camera negative. The EDL is itself converted to a negative cut list with key numbers. This system is used for editing 35mm film and also 16mm film with A and B rolls. Filmmakers can thus shoot with film and finish with film while taking advantage of the flexibility and ease of editing on video. *See* **KeyKode** *and* **telecine.**

■ **videomatics** An estimate of the way a scene might appear by first filming it on video. Sometimes the scene might be incorporated into the workprint to allow for continuity in the editing. This process is extremely useful for planning or trying out a difficult shot or previsualizing one that may require physical or special effects for a final composite.

■ **video matting, video composite** *See* **electronic compositing.**

■ **video recorder** Any machine using film, tape, or disc to record and play back images and sound from television transmission.

■ **video tap** *See* **video assist.**

■ **videotape, video tape, digital video tape** A tape with a coating of magnetized iron oxide on which images and sound can be recorded for playback on a television system, either by means of a video recorder or directly from a television transmission. In analog systems, two-inch tape was originally used for professional television recording and transmission, but was replaced by one-inch tape, which gave an equally good picture. Three-quarter-inch tape was then used for recording news events and shooting documentaries and video production, although the recording was transferred to 1 inch tape for transmission. Sony's half-inch Betacam and advanced Betacam SP, however, have replaced the three-quarter-inch system and become the industry standard for news recording, documentaries and video programming. Today, a variety of sources of transmission are used as the technology changes—one-inch in older stations, NBC's one-half inch Mz, Betacam SP, Betacam digital. Newly equipped stations are now transferring programs from a variety of tape sources to a digital file server on hard drive for transmission. Half-inch tape has been the most popular format for home use, although systems with two-, one-, three-quarter-, and one-quarter-inch tape have also been on the market. The two formats using one-half-inch tape for home use were originally the Betamax or Beta system, manufactured primarily by Sony, and the VHS system—both employed a similar cassette but had different ways of feeding the tape into the recorder. The Beta system has now become largely obsolete for home viewing. Much heralded at its inception, though slow in gaining adherents, the S-VHS (Super VHS) system creates a far better picture with greater resolution than the normal

VHS tape. Also creating images of high quality is the Hi8, a tape 8mm or slightly more than one-quarter inch wide.

Because digital videotapes employed in video and computerized systems encode picture and sound information in binary figures of 0 and 1, instead of the analog information stored on the videotapes described above, they are able to produce generations of copies that come close to maintaining the quality of the original recording. D-1 uses a one-inch tape, D-2 a 19mm or approximately three-quarter-inch tape, and D-3, D-5, and digital betacam all use one-half-inch tapes, though with different systems. *See* **digital** *and* **videotape recorder.**

▪ **videotape recorder (VTR), video recorder, digital video tape recorder (DVTR)** A machine that records image and sound on tape coated with magnetized iron oxide for playback on a video system. The signals may come from a video camera, a television receiver, another videotape, or may be transferred from a film. Videotapes normally have a track for the image, two or four for sound, and a control track for synchronization. Today, there are two types of videotape recorders, analog and digital, the first recording variable patterns analogous to the intensity and fluctuations in light and sound waves, and the second encoding such signals in binary numbers of 0 and 1. The digital recorders are the more recent type used in professional computerized video systems both for recording and editing.

▪ **video toaster** A relatively inexpensive desktop video and digital workstation that can create all types of visual effects either directly for video or for testing out in advance composite and other special-effects shots for a motion picture.

▪ **video viewfinder** *See* **video assist.**

▪ **vidicon telecine** An older telecine machine for converting images from motion-picture film into a signal for television transmission in which a vidicon tube is employed in a television camera for scanning and transmitting the individual frames of film in a projector. *See* **telecine.**

▪ **viewer** A small machine through which film can rapidly be run in either direction by motor or manually by rewinds and which permits individual shots or scenes to be found and examined on a small screen. A small lamp illuminates the frames while a rotating prism creates the intermittency for viewing the images in motion. A viewer is normally found on an editing bench. *See* **editing.**

▪ **viewfinder** An optical device that is attached to or part of the camera and is used for viewing the field of action recorded through the camera's lens. The most common type employed today is the reflex viewfinder, which permits the scene to be viewed without parallax by the camera operator during shooting. The scene is viewed through the camera's lens either by means of a mirrored shutter, which is situated at a 45-degree angle behind the lens and sends the light to the ground-glass screen while blocking it from the film; or a rotating or oscillating semitransparent glass prism or membrane called a pellicle, which is placed before the shutter and directs a small portion of the light to the viewfinder and the remainder to the film. The first type of viewfinder is employed mostly in 35mm cameras where there is sufficient room for the 45-degree angle of the shutter; the second type, which gives a less visible image since the semi-reflective mirror directs only a small portion of the light to the viewing screen, is employed in cameras for films of a smaller gauge.

The side or offset viewfinder, still used on a number of older cameras, is attached to the side of the camera and does not permit viewing the scene through the camera's lens while shooting. Adjustable mattes, either part of the viewfinder or inserted into it, are moved to focal-length markings so that the action field on the viewfinder's screen is close to that of the camera lens. Even though the lenses of the viewfinder and camera are kept as close as possible, parallax is still a factor and is sometimes corrected in the optics of the viewfinder or by pivoting the device itself. In some viewfinders a cam system adjusts the image as the focus changes in the camera. A few older cameras, notably the Mitchell NC and BNC, employ a rackover system in which the shooting lens remains stationary while the rear part of the camera, which contains the film, is shifted to the side and the viewfinder comes into position directly behind the lens. Since this system cannot be employed while the camera is shooting, a separate monitor viewfinder is generally attached. Viewfinders attached to the side of a camera are sometimes used in addition to the reflex type to allow the director or cinematographer to view the shot at the same time as the camera operator or to allow the operator to view the image when the camera's position or movement makes it difficult to look through the eyepiece of the reflex system. Many Arriflex cameras use a swingover reflex viewfinder that allows the camera operator to position himself or herself on either side of the camera or to view the scene from any angle. An electronic viewfinder called a video assist is often part of professional cinematography today: such systems employ a "video tap" into the reflex viewfinder to deflect light rays to a small, attached television camera, which then converts them to an image on a monitor, also attached to the film camera. Such units allow the scene to be viewed easily while it is shot and also to be recorded on videotape for later examination. The scene can also be sent back to one or more monitors at a distance from the actual shooting. Not only can various personnel see the scene exactly as it is photographed, but the camera can be operated by remote control for difficult or fast-moving shots.

■ **viewfinder mismatch** When the objective lens or matte employed in the viewfinder is incompatible with the camera's lens. Such a problem may arise when switching the lenses on a turret attached to the camera. *See* **viewfinder.**

■ **viewfinder objective lens** The front lens of an optical viewfinder on which the image is formed. *See* **viewfinder.**

■ **viewing glass, viewing filter, contrast glass** A filter or glass through which a cinematographer may view a scene before shooting with either black-and-white or color film to assess how the scene will appear, especially in reference to the contrast range of the lighting.

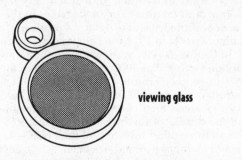

viewing glass

■ **vignette** (1) An image clearly focused in the center with the borders blurred or fading away. Such an image resembles an old photograph portraiture and was first employed in the films of D. W. Griffith. Although Orson Welles had vaseline smeared around the circumference of the camera lens for *The Magnificent Ambersons* (1942) to achieve the effect of old photographs, the technique has also been achieved by employing a mask in the camera or in an optical printer. (2) To make an image with the borders blurred or fading away to highlight a character or create the effect of an old photograph.

■ **vignetting** The technique of making a vignette. *See* **vignette.**

■ **villain** *See* **antagonist** *and* **heavy.**

■ **VI meter** *See* **VU meter.**

■ **vinegar syndrome** A malady that affects cellulose-acetate (or triacetate) base film when stored in relatively high humidity and temperature. The breakdown that takes place in the base of the film causes buckling and shrinkage. The process of hydrolysis and the breakdown of the acetate result in the creation of acetic acid which gives off a gas with the odor of vinegar and with the capacity to start the same process in neighboring films. Although various theories for retarding this process have been put forward—e.g., keeping the films in a well-ventilated area, storing them in special containers with spongelike molecular sieves, or storing them in reduced temperature—this deterioration seems impossible to stop once it has started. Since this "safety" film has been used for commercial cinema since 1951 (the previous cellulose-nitrate film was thought more flammable and likely to deteriorate), a considerable part of our film heritage is threatened. One hope for film preservation is to make digital copies of as many films as fast as possible. *See* **film preservation.**

■ **virgin loop** A sound film of excellent quality that is looped for recording, especially during a dubbing session. *See* **dub** *and* **loop** *(3).*

■ **virtual photography** A term sometimes used for the image-making capacity of the computer—its capacity both to add elements to and change an already-existing image, as well as to create forms and even entire pictures from the start. *See* **digital.**

■ **virtual reality** An illusion of reality derived from technological means that gives the spectator the sense that he or she is immersed in and interacting with the created world. Virtual reality goes beyond what Bazin calls "total cinema"—"a total and complete representation of reality"—by creating a fully dimensional and surrounding world that responds to one's presence. Unlike viewing a two-dimensional film on a screen in front of the theater and sitting passively while one identifies with the characters in a plot, the spectator of virtual reality definitely feels that he or she is moving through a created world while also manipulating the various objects that fill the world. The fully dimensional and surrounding world is created through the use of a type of head set that contains a liquid-crystal display monitor in front of each eye with the difference in the two images creating the stereophonic impression. The monitors are connected to a computer that alters the images with the movement of the head, giving one the impression of moving through the actual space of this world; while a specially designed glove or control system connected to a computer by means of fiber-optic cables allows one to handle the various objects in that world. Omni-directional sound that also alters as one moves through this illusion of reality is transmitted by means of earphones in the head set. Virtual reality has great potential in industrial designing, military training, education, interactive video/computer games, and for a new and powerful type of interactive entertainment. *See* **holography** *and* **3-D.**

■ **virtual tape** The digitally recorded edited version of a motion picture, referred to by this name because no actual tape exists, even though the film may be viewed from start to finish on a monitor.

■ **visc** A condensed and abbreviated form of video disc. *See* **video disc.**

■ **visible spectrum** That part of the spectrum between the ultraviolet and infrared portions with colors visible to the naked eye.

■ **VistaVision** A wide-screen film process developed by Paramount in the 1950s in response to Twentieth Century-Fox's CinemaScope, but without anamorphic lenses for the camera and projector. VistaVision employed 35mm film running through a camera horizontally rather than vertically, thereby creating a frame eight perforations across with an area twice the normal size and an aspect ratio approximately 1.85:1. Paramount wanted the print run through a special projector in the same manner, but was unable to persuade many exhibitors to purchase the new and costly machine. The general practice instead was to reduce and print the images on normal 35mm film, a practice that still resulted in a much sharper picture than that achieved with a standard camera or with anamorphic lenses, because of the size of the frame on the original negative. Films using this system were generally shot with action in the center of the frame so that the image could be projected to suit screens of various sizes. Paramount first used VistaVision for *White Christmas* (dir. Michael Curtiz) in 1954 and employed the system for several of Alfred Hitchcock's films, including *Vertigo* in 1958. VistaVision was no longer used after 1961 because of its expense and the development of simpler wide-screen systems, but the original camera is still sometimes employed in special-effects cinematography because its high-resolution image can be matched with earlier-generation images in composite pictures or with live-action in front-projection shots. *See* **CinemaScope** *and* **wide screen.**

■ **visual anthropology** *See* **ethnographic film.**

■ **visual device** Any technique or method for achieving a special visual effect, for example, front or rear projection. *See* **special effects.**

■ **visual effects** Special effects achieved in cinematography through photographic techniques or processes, as distinct from those achieved before the camera with normal shooting, which are sometimes called mechanical effects. *See* **special effects.**

■ **visual effects coordinator, visual effects supervisor, visual effects producer** *See* **special-effects coordinator.**

■ **visual primary** An image with the picture element dominant to the sound.

■ **visuals** The pictures or picture elements of a film as distinct from the sound.

■ **Vitagraph** An early film studio established in 1899 by J. Stuart Blackton and Albert E. Smith in New York City.

The two had purchased a Vitascope projector along with some films from Edison in 1896, and Smith developed the Vitagraph projector soon after. In order to keep up with the demand for the films they were showing at a vaudeville house, Smith developed a camera and he and Blackton began to produce motion pictures on the roof of a building on Nassau Street that housed their new office on the top floor; the first film made at this location was *Burglar on the Roof* in 1897. In addition to such fictional works, the organization also made "actuality films," which were supposedly of real events but which were often feigned. Vitagraph prospered because of the demand for such works and because their films were compatible with Edison's projectors from which their own machinery was derived. Vitagraph eventually opened studios in the Flatbush area of Brooklyn and by 1908 was producing eight short films a week; in 1911 the company also opened a studio in California. Vitagraph was the only member of the Motion Picture Patents Company (MPPC), formed in 1909 to protect Edison's patents and monopolize the industry, to meet the challenge of the independents with feature-length films and the only member to survive the demise of that organization. In 1915, Vitagraph and three other members of the MPPC—Lubin, Selig, and Essanay—joined together to strengthen their positions by forming the VLSE company, which Vitagraph eventually took over. In 1925, after a long and prosperous career, Vitagraph was itself taken over by Warner Brothers. Among the notable figures who appeared for Vitagraph were Florence Turner, the "Vitagraph girl"; her co-star, Maurice Costello; John Bunny, the first comic star of film; Rudolph Valentino; and Norma Talmadge, who first achieved stardom at the age of fourteen in the company's 1911 production of *A Tale of Two Cities,* which also starred Costello. *See* **Motion Picture Patents Company.**

■ **Vitaphone** A sound-on-disc system for motion pictures developed by Western Electric, the research facility of Bell Telephone. In 1926, Western Electric formed the Vitaphone Company with Warner Brothers, a floundering film company seeking to make its fortune by applying the system to motion pictures. At Warner's Theater in New York City on August 6, 1926, *Don Juan,* starring John Barrymore, was presented with a synchronized symphonic score recorded on the Vitaphone system. Before the film, Will Hays, head of the Motion Pictures Producers and Distributors of America (MPPDA), appeared on the screen to herald the new sound era, and a series of short entertainment features with synchronized sound was presented. Warner Brothers created two similar programs with sound as theaters began to equip for the new type of motion picture; but it was the presentation of Al Jolson in *The Jazz Singer* on October 6, 1927, that rocked the industry and began the inevitable changeover to sound film. Since only the musical numbers and four brief scenes of dialogue had synchronized sound, *The Lights of New York,* which Warner's released in July of the next year, has been called the "first 100 percent talkie." Vitaphone employed seventeen-inch discs played on a turntable at 33⅓ rpm in synchronization with the picture, a system that proved too difficult and uncertain compared to the optical sound-on-film process that was developed simultaneously and soon superseded it. *See* **optical sound** *and* **sound.**

■ **Vitarama** A wide-screen process employing eleven interlocked projectors developed by Fred Waller and demonstrated with great success at the 1939 World's Fair in New York. Vitarama led to Waller's development of Cinerama. *See* **Cinerama.**

■ **Vitascope** A projector developed by Thomas Armat and C. Francis Jenkins that was purchased by Edison to meet the challenge of the new projecting systems abroad, especially the Lumière brothers' Cinématographe, as well as the challenge of the Mutoscope to his own peephole machine, the Kinetoscope. Since Edison had the capacity to manufacture and distribute the machine, Armat, who now owned the projector independently, gave up his rights to the invention for a handsome settlement. The projector, which used the Latham loop to avoid the tearing of the film when it moved into and out of the intermittent movement, projected some of Edison's own Kinetoscope films for the first commercial screening of film in this country on April 23, 1896, at Koster and Bial's Music Hall in New York City as part of a vaudeville show. *See* **Edison Company** *and* **Latham loop.**

■ **Vitasound** A sound system, briefly employed by Warner Brothers in the 1950s, that used three speakers behind the screen, the two side ones to give a sense of expansiveness and a stereophonic effect to the music and the middle speaker to supply both dialogue and sound effects.

■ **VLSE** A consortium organized in 1915 by Vitagraph, Lubin, Selig, and Essanay, four of the organizations in the Motion Picture Patents Company, which at the time was in its waning days, with each studio still producing its own films. Vitagraph eventually took over all the other members of the group and was itself finally purchased by Warner Brothers in 1925. *See* **Vitagraph.**

■ **VO** *See* **voice-over.**

■ **VOD** The initials stand for Video-On-Demand, a type of digital transmission to consumers of individually selected and purchased programs. Proposed by both the cable and telephone industries, with some early testing already performed, the system works on the principle that large computers can hold a sufficient number of digitized programs to supply consumers any selection immediately upon demand.

■ **voice artist** The performer who creates the voices for the characters in an animated cartoon. Certainly the most celebrated of such artists was Mel Blanc, who began working for Warner Brothers in 1937 and created the voices for such characters as Bugs Bunny, Porky Pig, and Daffy Duck. *See* **cartoon.**

■ **voice cue** A verbal signal given by the director or an assistant for a performer to make an entrance or begin some action. Such a cue may also be given by another performer as part of the dialogue.

■ **voice-over (VO)** A voice heard concurrently with a scene but not synchronically belonging to any character talking on the screen. The voice heard over the action may be that of (1) a commentator in a documentary; (2) an objective narrator in a fictional film bringing us forward in time, preparing us for an event, or commenting on the action; (3) a first-person narrator who participates in the film and now gives us a subjective commentary on a scene in which he or she appears, or performs the narrative functions described in (2) during part of the film in which he or she does not appear; (4) a character on the screen whose thoughts we overhear; (5) a character in the film whose voice is heard in the imagination of another character (e.g., while reading that person's letter); (6) a character or characters talking inside some building or vehicle when only the outside of the building or vehicle is seen on the screen; (7) a character or characters whose talk overlaps from the previous scene into the one now on the screen or whose voices anticipate their appearance in the next scene. Voice-overs as defined in categories (2) through (5) tend to be literary in nature and are not often employed today in fictional films since directors prefer to rely more on the visual and dramatic nature of their works to convey information and move the story along, though striking exceptions can be found (e.g., the first-person voice-over narrations in Terrence Malick's *Badlands* [1973] and *Days of Heaven* [1978]). Even the documentary is less prone to use a voiceover because of the development of direct-cinema and *cinéma-vérité* styles of exposition. The voiceover techniques defined in (6) and (7), which are decidedly nonliterary since a literary text cannot maintain separate visual and spoken actions at the same time, have become convenient ways of moving a narrative film along by simultaneously presenting separate picture and sound. The term "off-screen voice" should not be confused with voice-over, since the speaker in the first case is understood as actually talking at the present moment in a space contiguous to the scene on the screen and gives us the impression that he or she could be photographed doing so by a movement of the camera. *See* **cinéma-vérité, direct cinema, indirect voice-over,** *and* **sound.**

■ **voice test**   Either a live audition or a test recording to see if the voice of a performer or narrator is satisfactory for a film.

■ **volt**   The unit for measuring electromotive force; that is, the potential difference that will force a current of one ampere through a conductor with a resistance of one ohm.

■ **voltage**   Electromotive force expressed in volts.

■ **voltage drop**   The loss of voltage passing through a cable because of resistance. Such a loss can alter a light's color temperature and intensity.

■ **volume**   The intensity and amplitude of sound; its audibility and loudness.

■ **volume compressor**   *See* **compressor.**

■ **volume control**   *See* **fader** *and* **gain control.**

■ **VTR**   *See* **videotape recorder.**

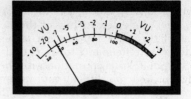

VU meter

■ **VU meter, volume units meter, VU indicator, VI meter, volume indicator meter**   A device attached to a recorder or playback system for indicating the amplitude of sound, generally by decibels, above or below an average point. Such a meter is important when recording to make sure that the sound is neither too low with insufficient range nor too high and distorted. VU meters tend to give average readings of sound levels and are not fast enough to respond to high volumes of short duration. Peak-reading meters are more precise for registering such volume peaks. Some VU meters and peak-reading meters employ a series of small lights instead of a dial and printed scale. *See* **peak-reading meter.**

■ ■ ■

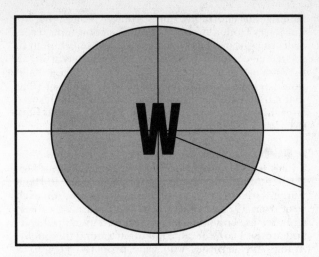

wagon-wheel effect to Wurlitzer

■ **wagon-wheel effect** An illusion of wheels with spokes rotating backwards, caused by the spokes being in a slightly regressive position each time the camera shutter opens and the forward-moving positions being blocked out when the shutter is closed. *See* **strobing.**

■ **Waldorf statement** *See* **House Committee on Un-American Activities.**

■ **walk-on** (1) A small part in a film without any lines of dialogue, less developed or significant than a bit part. (2) The performer who plays such a small part. (3) A person playing a small part in a film who is not previously contracted or hired but is spontaneously selected to appear before the camera at the time of shooting.

■ **walk-through** A rehearsal without the camera operating and the characters speaking their dialogue, but with the performers going through their motions.

■ **walla** A sound effect that creates the murmur of a crowd with no distinct voices for the background to a scene. It is reported that in the early days of sound cinema, groups of extras would recite the word "walla" over and over into a microphone to create the noise of a crowd.

■ **wall bracket** A support attached to a wall or flat for holding a luminaire.

■ **wall plate** A metal plate with a socket that is attached to a wall or flat for supporting a luminaire and comes in a baby or junior size.

■ **wall rack** A bin attached to a wall for temporarily holding or storing film during editing.

■ **wall sled** A metal support for a luminaire that looks like a sled and can be hung over the top of a wall or flat.

■ **wallspreader** *See* **spreader.**

■ **Walt Disney Company, The** When Walt Disney began his career as a commercial artist in Kansas City in 1919, he met another artist named Ub Iwerks who was to become a close partner in Disney's future achievements. Both men joined the Kansas City Film Ad Company, which produced animated advertisements for local movie houses. Disney and Iwerks were soon producing a series of cartoons called *Laugh-O-Grams,* which were basically comic treatments of fairytales. In 1923, Disney, along with Iwerks and under the business management of his brother Roy, began making in Hollywood the *Alice in Cartoonland* films, a series of shorts featuring a live girl and animated figures. Disney was soon supervising the films without actually participating in the art work. *Oswald the Lucky Rabbit,* a new series begun in 1927, demonstrated the fast-improving animation techniques of the Disney group, but the character was soon taken away from the company by its distributor.

The turning point for the group was in 1928, when it released *Steamboat Willie,* a cartoon introducing Mickey Mouse and featuring the new synchronized sound dimension of motion pictures. From this cartoon, Disney learned to design his films to a particular musical meter. The group began producing the *Silly Symphony* series, which featured the first Technicolor cartoon, *Flowers and Trees,* in 1932; *The Three Little Pigs,* in 1933, a revelation in cartoon characterization; and *The Old Mill,* in 1937, the first animated cartoon to use the multiplane camera. During this period such characters as Donald Duck, Goofy, and Pluto were also introduced. By this time the Disney company was the most efficient, ambitious, and artistic animation studio ever to be assembled. Its next high point was the creation of its first feature-length cartoon, *Snow White and the Seven Dwarfs,* in 1937. Even more impressive was the full-length *Pinocchio* in 1940. In the same year Disney released *Fantasia,* an exciting and sometimes breathtaking amalgamation of animation and classical music. Mention should also be made of the last two feature-length cartoons from the company's golden period, *Dumbo* in 1941 and *Bambi* in 1943.

Future years showed a diversity in the efforts of Walt Disney Productions. Family live-action films began with *Treasure Island* in 1950 and featured such relative high points as *20,000 Leagues Under the Sea* (1954), *The Absent Minded Professor* (1960), and *Mary Poppins* (1964). In the early 1950s, a group of nature documentaries were produced, notably *The Living Desert* (1953). In 1954, Disney formed the Buena Vista Distribution Company to distribute his own films and free him from the costs and inconvenience of using the major studios. In 1955, he created the fantasy world of Disneyland, an amusement park in Anaheim, California. Although Disney died in 1966, his organization continued to prosper, opening the second park, Disney World in Orlando, Florida, in 1971 and one in Tokyo in 1983. In 1983, the company also formed a pay-cable television station, the Disney Channel. Because of a series of lackluster films beginning in the 1970s and weak management, control of the company was finally wrested away by a group of financiers under the instigation of Walt Disney's nephew, Roy, in 1984. In the same year, Touchstone Films was organized to produce films for mature audiences and began successfully by releasing *Splash* (dir. Ron Howard).

After Michael Eisner, former president of Paramount, was made chief executive, Walt Disney Studios, under the directorship of Jeffrey Katzenberg, produced a series of successful films and the company moved even more aggressively into television, elevating its stock to new heights. Hollywood Pictures was formed in 1990, and in 1993, Disney purchased the Miramax Company, a production/distribution organization distinguished for the quality of the domestic and foreign films it released in this country—Miramax so far has continued as an independent and autonomous unit. The Disney Company has been remarkably successful in recycling its classic films in the theaters, on videocassette, and also on the Disney Channel. Its Consumer Products Division continues to exploit the Disney name and properties with ubiquitous success. The Disney-MGM Studio Theme Park opened in Orlando in 1990 (Disney had managed to work out a 20-year rental from MGM for most of its films and its logo), continuing the company' s remarkable success in the area of entertainment parks; and even the Euro Disney Theme Park in France, which was not at first successful after its opening in 1992, has become a major tourist attraction in Europe.

In recent years, the company has regained its great prestige and success in animation films, especially by developing the capacities of computer animation. *Beauty and the Beast* (1991; dir. Gary Trousdale and Kirk Wise), *Aladdin* (1992; dir. John Musker and Ron Clements), and *The Lion King* (1994; dir. Roger Allers and Rob Minkoff) have been conspicuous successes, while the company also sponsored Pixar's *Toy Story* in 1995 (dir. John Lasseter), a film totally composed of computer-generated images and animation. The Disney Company earned $10 billion with 19.4 percent of the domestic box office for film distribution in 1994 and 18.2 percent of the box office in 1995. In the same year, Frank G. Wells, president of Disney, died in a helicopter crash, and Jeffrey Katzenberg resigned when he was not offered the presidency. Earlier in the year, Disney had purchased Capital Cities/ABC Incorporated, obtaining its successful television network and such enterprises as its ESPN sports cable network. Disney now had a national outlet for its programs, while also becoming an enormous entertainment conglomerate. But losses from a number of its live-action films, especially in light of what appears to be a diminishment in the teenage audience, have resulted in a downsizing in the area of film production—Disney announced that it would release in 1997 only half the number of films that it did in 1996, even though it still turned out some large hits in the earlier year. *See* **animation, Miramax Films, multiplane,** *and* **UPA.**

■ **WAMPAS baby stars** The first word is derived from the initials for Western Association of Motion Picture Advertisers and the second two words refer to the thirteen young starlets who were cited by this organization each year, from 1922 to 1934, for having promising careers as actresses. The undertaking received much publicity and aroused considerable attention among the public. Among the actresses who were properly recognized were Clara Bow in 1924; Mary Astor, Joan Crawford, Janet Gaynor, and Fay Wray in 1926; Jean Arthur and Loretta Young in 1929; Joan Blondell in 1931; and Ginger Rogers in 1932.

■ **warbler** Jargon for a singer.

■ **wardrobe** (1) The clothing, costumes, and accessories worn by performers in a film. (2) The department in a studio responsible for making, acquiring, maintaining, and storing clothing, costumes, and accessories for the studio's film productions. Such garments may be already owned by the studio, designed and made specially for the film, acquired from the performer's own wardrobes, or rented from outside sources.

■ **wardrobe box** A large mobile box with wheels used for transporting clothes, costumes, and accessories to a set or location where shooting is taking place and also for storing such materials.

■ **wardrobe call** An appointment made at a specific time and place for a costume fitting.

■ **wardrobe department** *See* **wardrobe** (2).

■ **wardrobe supervisor** An individual responsible for procuring clothing, costumes, and accessories for a film production before the actual shooting begins and for maintaining them during the actual filming. There may be as many as two men and women carrying out such duties, who also are responsible for fitting the various secondary performers in a film and who often assist the major performers in dressing for the day's shooting. Also called a costumer. *See* **costume designer.**

■ **wardrobe truck** A special truck equipped to transport clothing to the location of shooting and also equipped for repairing garments.

■ **war film** A motion picture dealing with war either as the major action of the film or the background to the film's action. Although war films are generally thought of as combat films that focus primarily on preparation for fighting and the actual armed conflict, the genre also includes other types of situations that are directly related to or the result of war: for example, prisoner-of-war stories, often focusing on escape; the struggles and activities of the underground in occupied countries; spy adventures at home or abroad; and stories that use war as a context for dramatic situations and interactions among characters who are generally not taking an immediate role in the fighting. War films can also be categorized according to the general attitude to war demonstrated by the individual work: there are films basically propropagandistic in nature that motivate audiences to the virtues of the cause supported by their nation especially by showing the heroism of their own countrymen and the evils of the enemy; films that show that "war is hell" and demonstrate that there are no winners in such a conflict; films basically escapist in nature that use war as a context for exciting adventure and heroics; and films that use war as the context for satire or comedy.

War films have been part of the cinema from the early days of silent film, when the first studios pretended to shoot actual battles in real wars but actually staged them on the fields of New Jersey or the rooftops of New York City. Griffith made *The Battle* in 1911, a one-reeler with an extraordinarily staged combat scene out of the bloody days of the Civil War, and *Massacre* in 1912, a two-reel version of Custer's Last Stand. In the same year that Griffith's monumental *Birth of A Nation* (1915), as much a war film as a historic epic, appeared, J. Stuart Blackton's fictional invasion of New York, *The Battle Cry of Peace*, was calling America to prepare for the coming war with Germany. Thomas H. Ince's *Civilization, or He Who Returned* (1916), a pacifist war film, could not prevent the inevitable conflict between these two powers. America's involvement in the war abroad produced few memorable war films, though Griffith's *Hearts of the World* (1918), sponsored by the British government and using actual footage from the battle front in France, is certainly worth citing.

Wars are generally followed by films that may still appeal to our sense of the dramatic, but which also show the miseries of such conflicts: two notable examples after the First World War were King Vidor's *The Big Parade* in 1925 and Raoul Walsh's *What Price Glory* in 1926. Perhaps the most powerful of the antiwar combat films in this period was Lewis Milestone's *All Quiet on the Western Front* (1930), a moving adaptation of Erich Maria Remarque's novel, which showed the hell of the First World War from the German point of view. Also significant was Jean Renoir's inspired prisoner-of-war and escape film, *Grand Illusion*, which appeared in 1937. But high adventure could still be gotten from wartime situations, especially by playing down the ferocity and reality of the enemy. *Wings* (1927; dir. William Wellman), for example, is one of many aviation films, an extremely popular subgroup of the combat film, to excite and dazzle audiences before the real guns of war echoed across both oceans.

The Second World War brought forth in the film industry a multitude of anti-German and anti-Japanese war films, not to mention the fine nonfiction films mentioned under **documentary** elsewhere in this volume. Certainly Lewis Milestone's *A Walk in the Sun* (1946), a probing study of the hearts and minds of a patrol during a single day of the Salerno invasion, and Lewis Seiler's *Guadalcanal Diary* (1944), gritty and realistic as well as patriotic, are among the best of the combat films from the two campaigns. A significant number of films during the war dealt with life in occupied countries, notably Renoir's *This Land is Mine* (1943), which takes place in France, and Lewis Milestone's *Edge of Darkness* (1943), which dramatizes wartime Norway. Alfred Hitchcock's *Foreign Correspondent* (1940) was certainly one of the best spy and espionage films to result from that period, while the Selznick production of *Since You Went Away* (1944), directed by John Cromwell, was the most stirring and expert of the sentimental life on-the-home-front films. The Korean War was too far away, too small, and too little-understood to produce many significant war films at that time, though it was responsible for an exciting yet thoughtful film about that struggle and war in general, Mark Robson's *The Bridges at Toko-Ri* (1954). But war at this point could be as much a source of comedy as tragedy as evidenced by Billy Wilder's World War II prisoner-of-war romp, *Stalag 17* (1953).

war film *All Quiet on the Western Front* (1930; dir. Lewis Milestone), which stars Lew Ayres, graphically demonstrates the horrors of war.

■ ■ ■

The years after these wars produced the distance necessary to eschew nationalism and condemn war in general, especially in light of the Cold War and the apparent madness of both world forces. The result of such attitudes were three classic antiwar films, David Lean's *The Bridge on the River Kwai* and Stanley Kubrick's *Paths of Glory*, both in 1957, and Kubrick's devastating satire six years later, *Dr. Strangelove; or, How I Learned to Stop Worrying and Love the Bomb.* But war was still a good subject for spectacle, especially if the treatment seemed historical and antiseptic, as was the case with the Darryl F. Zanuck production of *The Longest Day* (1962). At the same time, John Sturges's *The Great Escape* (1963) showed that prisoner-of-war films could still excite for reasons having nothing to do with politics. The unpopularity of the Vietnam War did not hamper films such as Robert Aldrich's Second World War adventure, *The Dirty Dozen* (1967) from having great success so long as they had nothing to do with the war in which we were presently engaged; but when John Wayne sought to rally the country around the flag for the Vietnam War with *The Green Berets* (1968), the result was an unmitigated disaster. The Vietnam War and its impact on this country had to be confronted when the conflict was finished, at first through the pain and suffering of Hal Ashby's *Coming Home* and Michael Cimino's *The Deer Hunter*, both in 1978. Later, the superheroes of Hollywood cinema refought and won the Vietnam War for us, although Oliver Stone's *Platoon* (1986) returned us to a more somber examination of that conflict. Unfortunately, both politics and the taste of audiences will always keep the war film a popular genre even when no apparent conflict confronts our nation, sometimes to reaffirm human values (e.g., *Glory* [1989; dir. Edward Zwick]), sometimes to create entertaining suspense and drama (e.g., *The Crimson Tide* [1995; dir. Tony Scott]), and sometimes to appeal to the primitive aggression within us. *See* **genre.**

■ **warm image** An image with predominantly red and yellow colors as opposed to a cool image with a predominantly blue color.

■ **Warner Brothers** A motion-picture production company organized in 1923 by the four Warner brothers, with Harry president of the firm, Albert treasurer, Sam chief executive, and Jack chief of production at the Burbank studios. In 1925 the company purchased Vitagraph, acquiring its national exchange system for distribution, and in 1926 joined with Western Electric to form the Vitaphone Company in order to develop a sound-on-disc system that could be synchronized with pictures. The system was employed at the Warner's Theater in New York on August 6, 1926, for synchronic music to *Don Juan*, starring John Barrymore, before which the audience had viewed on the screen Will Hays praising the new achievement of sound motion pictures and a series of musical "preludes." But it was *The Jazz Singer* on October 6, 1927, with its synchronic mu-sical numbers and four scenes of dialogue, that rocked the industry and made Warner Brothers into a major production company. In 1928 the organization purchased the Stanley Company with its three hundred theaters and also obtained one-third interest in First National, which it completely took over in 1930.

Warner Brothers in the 1930s made films that seemed close to the world of the Depression years, even allowing for their escapist qualities. This was partly a result of economics: the company was run tightly and tautly with films about ninety minutes long, with lighting low-key, flat, and starkly black and white to disguise the minimal settings. This might not have been the opulent and bright style of MGM, but it was immediate and real enough for presenting some of the more dramatic and socially aware films of the period. Warner Brothers gave to the screen two classic gangster films, Mervyn Le Roy's *Little Caesar* (1930) and William Wellman's *The Public Enemy* (1931); powerful works of social realism such as *I Am a Fugitive from a Chain Gang* (1932) and *Wild Boys of the Road* (1933), by the same two directors respectively; and a series of backstage musicals with Busby Berkeley's elaborate choreography, for example, *42nd Street* (1933; dir. Lloyd Bacon) and *Gold Diggers of 1933* (1933; dir. Mervyn Le Roy), which had the Depression world at least in the background. Warner Brothers also produced a number of distinguished biographical films such as William Dieterle's *The Story of Louis Pasteur* (1936) and *The Life of Emile Zola* (1937), both starring Paul Muni. In the 1940s, the company produced a series of fine films with Humphrey Bogart, notably *The Maltese Falcon* (1941; dir. John Huston), *Casablanca* (1942; dir. Michael Curtiz), and *The Treasure of the Sierra Madre* (1948; dir. John Huston). Other stars who added impact to Warner's films of the thirties and forties were James Cagney, Edward G. Robinson, Errol Flynn, Bette Davis, Joan Crawford, and Barbara Stanwyck.

Along with the other major studios, Warner Brothers eventually lost its theaters because of the Supreme Court's Paramount decrees of 1948, but it met this challenge, as well as that offered by the new medium of television, by turning out a number of impressive films, such as George Cukor's *A Star is Born* (1954), with Judy Garland, and Nicholas Ray's *Rebel Without a Cause* (1955), with James Dean, while itself becoming a successful producer of television entertainment. Warner Brothers sponsored a number of impressive musicals during the 1960s, notably Morton da Costa's *The Music Man* in 1962, George Cukor's *My Fair Lady* in 1964, and Joshua Logan's *Camelot* in 1967. In 1967, the company became Warner Brothers-Seven Arts when it was purchased by Seven Arts, a distributor and dealer of old films. Kinney National Services, a vast financial enterprise, purchased the film company in 1969 and itself became Warner Communications in 1971. In 1967, the film company distributed Arthur Penn's *Bonnie and Clyde* reluctantly, but earned a good deal of money as a result. *All the President's Men* in 1976 (dir. Alan J.

Pakula) linked the Warner name again with films of social and political relevance. Notable also are the very successful films derived from comic book figures, *Superman* in 1978 (dir. Richard Donner) and *Batman* in 1989 (dir. Tim Burton).

In 1990, Warner Communications was purchased by Time Incorporated which then became Time Warner Incorporated, a vast communications, information, entertainment, and media conglomerate with major interests in publication, music, television, cable television, videocassettes, and, of course, film. Time Warner owns a considerable share of Cinamerica Theaters and also owns motion-picture houses throughout the world. In 1994, Warner Brothers studios earned 14.5 percent of the market share for film distribution and in 1995 shot up to 16.3 percent. During these years, the company released Martin Scorsese's *Goodfellas* and Barbet Schroeder's *Reversal of Fortune*, both in 1990, Clint Eastwood's *Unforgiven* in 1992, and Oliver Stone's *Natural Born Killers* in 1994. In 1996, the merger of Time Warner with Turner Broadcasting was approved by the Federal Trade Commission, thus creating the largest media conglomerate in the world and bringing under the same flag as Warner Brothers the film studios of New Line Cinema and Castle Rock Entertainment, while joining Turner's library of pre-1948 Warner Brothers films to Time Warner's library of the same studio's post-1948 films.

■ **Warnercolor** A color system employed by Warner Brothers using Eastman Color film stock and the production company's own processing.

■ **warning bell** The bell or horn that sounds on a studio set, warning that a shot is about to start and quiet should reign. The end of the shot is normally announced by two chimes or blasts.

■ **wash** (1) Any of a series of brief stages in film processing when chemicals just used are removed so as not to contaminate chemicals in the next action. (2) The stage in processing when film already developed and fixed is run through a cascade of water to remove any remaining fixing solution and byproducts. *See* **processing.**

■ **washout** A transition in which the first scene gradually whitens out or dissolves into a single color before the next scene follows.

■ **water bag** A rubber container with water employed as a weight to keep a piece of equipment with legs firmly implanted on the ground.

■ **water box, splash box** A wooden box with a glass or plastic front in which the camera is placed to protect it against water when shooting on or near a body of water.

■ **waterspots** Stains or splotches on the film that are the result of faulty drying during processing in the laboratory.

■ **water tank** *See* **studio tank.**

■ **watt** A unit of electrical power equal to the rate of work of one ampere of current under the pressure of one volt.

■ **wattage** (1) Electrical power measured in watts. (2) The number of watts necessary to run an electrical device.

■ **wavelength** The distance between two points traversed by any form of energy at the same phase of oscillation; the distance covered by a single cycle of that energy.

■ **wave machine, wave generator** A device generally run by an electric motor and placed at the side of a studio tank that rhythmically submerges and removes some variably shaped object to create waves of any desired size. Such a device may employ a sealed drum, wedge-shaped plunger, or revolving rollers to create the waves.

■ **wax** (1) To apply a substance along the edge of a release print that will insure the steady movement of the film through the projector without drag or pile-up. (2) The substance applied to a release print for the process defined in (1).

■ **weave** The undesirable movement of film from side to side in the gate of a camera or projector caused by faulty threading or some improperly fitted or functioning part in the machine. *See* **breathing** *and* **flutter.**

■ **wedge exposure test strip** A strip of negative film that progressively gets darker from frame to frame and is used by the laboratory for testing; a sensitometric strip. *See* **sensitometer** *and* **sensitometric strip.**

■ **wedge spectrogram** A colored strip submitted by a film manufacturer with a particular stock to show the color sensitivity of the film to each wavelength of the spectrum. The wavelengths of the spectrum progress in length from left to right along the strip.

■ **weekly** A contractual agreement between a performer and production company that is based on a weekly arrangement.

■ **weenie** Some object that motivates the action of a plot, normally in a film serial, though the term is occasionally used for other types of motion pictures. The weenie might be a stolen idol or a missing map. *See* **Macguffin.**

■ **weepie** *See* **tearjerker.**

■ **west** In animation work, the left side of the drawing table, animation stand, drawing, or cel as opposed to the east or right side.

■ **Western** A film genre popular since the earliest days of motion pictures that derives from the history and legends of the western part of this country, especially during the last half of the nineteenth century. Although the West has been fictionalized in countless novels, such works have themselves been influenced by the motion picture, which has largely developed the conventions, themes, and iconography for this world. The Western, more than any other film genre and more than any other creative form, has both embodied America's cultural history and helped shape the nation's image of itself. The Western has consistently created a world of expansiveness and expectation, where the vast, untamed landscape is indicative of the independence and potentiality of its inhabitants. Although such a location is far from the stifling reality and social restrictions of the civilized East, the people who live there—and struggle against the wildness of the terrain, its indigenous inhabitants, and the outlaws with their rampant individualism—have created a code of personal ethics that affirm their own dignity and independence without denying their responsibility to others.

But even within such a liberating world, elements of civilization—the farmer, the town, the encroaching system of law and order—are already being felt; indeed, the eventual demise of this type of life is an inherent part of the very films which celebrate it. Although the Western has established its code of conventions—its character types, such as the independent hero, black-clad outlaw, and attractive female schoolteacher; its plot elements, such as the chase or shootout; its images, such as the saloon or majestic landscape—this type of film has also shown remarkable adaptability to the changing times of its audience, manifesting certain enduring qualities while also showing them in the context of the very forces challenging the world outside the theater.

Edwin S. Porter's *The Great Train Robbery,* made for the Edison Company in 1903 and filmed in New Jersey, is notable not only for its early use of parallel cutting and the close-up, but for first presenting to American audiences such perennial ingredients of the Western as the potent six-shooter, train holdup, and chase on horses. Appearing in this film was G. M. Anderson, born Max Aronson, who later played Broncho Billy in *The Bandit Makes Good* for his own Essanay company in 1908 with such success that he was to become the first cowboy star, playing the same role in some four hundred films. Thomas H. Ince, the pioneer director and producer, made a number of authentic-looking and ex-

Western John Ford's *Stagecoach* (1939), starring John Wayne and the vast landscape of the West

■ ■ ■

citing Westerns (he used the cast of a Wild West show for *The War on the Plains* in 1912), but is especially notable for bringing to the screen in 1914 the second major star of the Western, William S. Hart in *The Bargain*. *Hell's Hinges* (1916) is a good example of the many films directed by and starring Hart, with their morally complex protagonist, dramatic focus, and authentic locals. Hart's last film, *Tumbleweeds*, which he made for Paramount in 1925, has more spectacle and humor than his previous works and also contains a classic land-rush sequence. Tom Mix, coming directly from a Wild West Show, appeared in over a hundred films for Selig between 1911 and 1917 and then went on to Fox, where his daredevil horsemanship in excitement-filled films ultimately made him America's number one cowboy. In 1923, James Cruze's *The Covered Wagon* opened up America's landscape to the Western in spectacular fashion; and in 1924, John Ford, who had already made a number of Westerns, directed *The Iron Horse*, the story of the building of the transcontinental railroad and the first of his popular epic Westerns.

The 1930s were not a propitious decade for the Western, perhaps because the national spirit was not in the mood for any celebrations of America's past and American individualism, although the decade did begin with Wesley Ruggles's *Cimarron* (1931), the first Western to win an Academy Award as the year's best picture. The decade instead featured such low-budget "B" Westerns as the Hopalong Cassidy series, starring William Boyd, and introduced in its second half the mild-mannered films of the singing cowboys, Gene Autry and Roy Rogers. But, 1939 gave new impetus to the Western with the Cecil B. DeMille railway epic *Union Pacific*, John Ford's skillful and dramatic *Stagecoach*, the first of his Westerns to star John Wayne, and George Marshall's classic comic Western, *Destry Rides Again*. A type of anomaly, the anti-Western appeared in 1943 with William Wellman's attack against lynching in his dark but moving *The Ox-Bow Incident*. In the same year, Howard Hughes's *The Outlaw* brought sex to the genre, also something of an anomaly in the Western world of independent masculinity. Sex was to be exploited again in David O. Selznick's pretentious production of *Duel in the Sun* (1946; dir. King Vidor), but was not to become a staple of the genre.

The postwar years at first brought a feeling of relief and pride to the nation along with a resurgence of the Western: John Ford's *My Darling Clementine* (1946), the best of the OK Corral shoot-out movies, Howard Hawks's splendid *Red River* (1948), and Ford's action-packed cavalry film *She Wore a Yellow Ribbon* (1949) are all classics of the genre. The Westerns of the 1950s, however, reflect the complex social and political issues of the decade. Henry King's *The Gunfighter* (1950), with Gregory Peck, and Fred Zinnemann's *High Noon* (1952), with Gary Cooper, explore the Western hero more introspectively and show him in confrontation with the values of society; while Delmer Daves's *Broken Arrow* (1950) begins a tradition of sympathetic Indians

who are also victimized by the values of white society. George Stevens's *Shane* in 1953 uses all the stock elements of the Western with great beauty and expertise, but the hero, played by Alan Ladd, seems part of a vanishing breed, a nostalgic vision of values that are disappearing from the bold but tamed landscape. John Wayne appears in John Ford's 1956 production of *The Searchers*, brutalized and victimized by the Indians and their culture; but reappears three years later in Howard Hawks's *Rio Bravo* as an indomitable and spirited presence in a Western world that has become more comic book than real.

There seem to have been two general traditions of Westerns in the 1960s and early years of the 1970s, the first showing the demise of both the values and landscape of the Old West in films such as David Miller's very touching *Lonely Are the Brave*, John Ford's *The Man Who Shot Liberty Valance*, and Sam Peckinpah's *Ride the High Country*, all in 1962; and the second group offering violence and brutality to feed the jaded appetites of a culture itself feeling brutalized by domestic violence and its country's foreign policy, especially in such films as the "spaghetti Westerns" made by the Italian Sergio Leone and starring Clint Eastwood, beginning with *A Fistful of Dollars* in 1967, and Sam Peckinpah's *The Wild Bunch* in 1969, rightfully judged the bloodiest Western made to that time. George Roy Hill's *Butch Cassidy and the Sundance Kid* in 1969 brought a sizable amount of humor and charm to the Western, while Robert Altman's *McCabe and Mrs. Miller* in 1971 brought a fresh though unheroic vision to the disappearing frontier. In recent years, however, the Western has been unable to flourish. Perhaps the Western has been exhausted as a film genre; perhaps we have lost faith in the simple heroics of time past because of our own disillusion with the time in which we live; perhaps the population that makes up so much of today's film audience has become detached from our nation's heritage—whatever the reasons, the Western itself seems to have become as much a part of our history as the world which it explored and glorified. The few good Westerns still produced seem in many ways to continue the attack against the values expounded in the earlier genre. Kevin Costner's *Dances with Wolves* (1990) presents one of the most sympathetic and human portrayals of Native Americans and Native American culture, much at the expense of white civilization, yet to appear in the genre; while Clint Eastwood's stunning and explosive *Unforgiven* (1992) gives us the very dark and violent side of the Western ethos. The most impressive, human, but still self-critical Western in recent years has not been made for the movie screen, but was made for television—the four-part series *Lonesome Dove* (1989; dir. Simon Wincer). *See* **genre.**

■ **western dolly** A transport for a camera during shooting that can carry a heavy load and, with its heavy wheels, is also capable of moving over rough terrain. *See* **dolly.**

■ **wet gate, wet gate printing, wet printing** A method of printing in which the original film passes through a solution, just before exposure, so that scratches and abrasions are filled on both sides to prevent light refraction from printing them on the fresh stock. In "liquid gate" printing, the scratches are filled by a fluid in a glass cel through which the film moves at the time of exposure.

■ **wetting agent** An agent sometimes added to the chemical baths and water used for washing during film processing that causes an even application of the solutions to the film and uniform drying so that blotches or waterspots will not be formed.

■ **WGA** *See* **Writers Guild of America.**

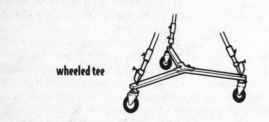

wheeled tee

■ **wheeled tee, wheelies, wheeled spreader, wheeled triangle, wheeled tie-down, rolling spider, tripod dolly, skid** A spreader that keeps in place the three legs of a camera tripod and to which wheels are attached for mobility. Such a device is useful for moving the camera from place to place for different camera positions, but is rarely suitable for a moving shot.

■ **whip** A device composed of a cable with a knob at the end that is attached to the follow-focus control on a camera. This attachment allows the assistant camera operator or "focus puller" to perform the follow-focus shot more easily and at a slight distance from the camera. *See* **follow focus, follow focus control,** *and* **speed crank.**

■ **whip pan, whip shot, whip** A rapid movement of the camera, while it is in a fixed position, from one point to another so that the intervening territory is blurred. Also called a swish pan. *See* **swish pan.**

■ **white limbo** *See* **black limbo.**

■ **whodunit** A popular term for a mystery film in which a crime is committed, and the audience tries to figure out the identity of the criminal (e.g., Sidney Lumet's *Murder on the Orient Express* [1974]). *See* **mystery film.**

■ **Whole Body Scanner** *See* **3-D digitizer.**

■ **whoofer** A device that scatters particles and powder when compressed air is released in order to create the illusion of an explosion. A cylinder with compressed air is attached to a funnel-shaped hopper into which and on top of which the material is piled.

■ *Wide Angle* A film journal published four times each year from Ohio University, featuring critical assessments of directors and films, often from recent theoretical perspectives, and theoretical discussions of the medium in general.

■ **wide-angle converter, wide-angle adapter lens** A lens attached to the camera's lens in order to reduce its focal length and widen the image registered on the film. Not much in use today, this converter was at one time often employed with a zoom lens. A fisheye variety is still sometimes attached to a normal lens to achieve an extremely wide and distorted image. *See* **fisheye lens** *and* **zoom lens.**

■ **wide-angle distortion, wide-angle effect, wide-angle lens distortion** An unnatural and sometimes dramatic effect achieved by using a wider-angle lens, especially at a distance close to the scene. Since objects in the rear are abnormally small and those close to the camera are abnormally large, the area between the various planes seems exaggerated and action to or away from the camera appears accelerated. Objects or faces close to the camera may seem distorted and manacing; the horizontal plane may sometimes seem distorted or stretched out at the extremities of the image, with objects appearing warped. Also called perspective distortion. *See* **telephoto distortion** *and* **wide-angle lens.**

■ **wide-angle lens** The common name for a short focal-length or short-focus length lens. Such a lens for a 35mm camera has a focal length shorter than that of a 40mm or 50mm lens and hence a wider angle of view than normal. A wide-angle lens creates an increased depth of field, thus keeping in focus both foreground and background. For this reason this type of lens is especially effective in showing simultaneous planes of action or playing a character in the foreground against his or her environment or against less prominent but still clearly defined characters in other parts of the image. Because objects in the foreground seem disproportionately large in relation to those toward the rear of the image and because the distance between planes seems exaggerated, the motion of a character toward or away from the camera will seem unnaturally fast. A character in the extreme foreground of the image will also appear sufficiently exaggerated as to seem menacing. A wide-angle lens of 25mm gives an angle of view of 47½ degrees, almost twice that of a 50mm lens. Since lenses with focal lengths less than 24 degrees give an image with increased distortion, they are used to achieve specific visual effects—the fish-eye lens, for example, with almost a 180-degree angle of view, is extremely effective in suggesting the distorted perspective of a hallucinating mind. *See* **lens, long-focus lens,** *and* **telephoto lens.**

■ **wide-angle shot** A shot made with a wide-angle lens that presents an image with both a greater horizontal

wide-angle shot One of the impressive wide-angle and deep-focus shots in Orson Welles's *The Magnificent Ambersons* (1942).

■ ■ ■

plane of action and a greater depth of field than that obtained with a normal lens. Such shots are effective for giving a wider panorama of a location and for placing a character in the context of an area. They are also effective for giving an image in depth with several defined planes of action so that on event may be seen immediately in the context of other actions and so that the viewer may be enticed to seek out important points of interest. *See* **lens** *and* **wide-angle lens.**

■ **widen** To widen the field of vision by moving the camera back from the action or zooming out with a zoom lens.

■ **wide open** A term applied to a lens when the iris is at its maximum opening, hence allowing the greatest amount of light to pass through the aperture. To achieve such a maximum opening, the camera lens is set at its smallest f-number. *See* **f-number.**

■ **wider angle** An instruction in a script to change the perspective of the scene to one with a wider horizontal plane of action. This wider perspective is generally employed to show a character in relation to other characters or in the spatial and environmental context of the scene.

■ **wide release** The distribution of a commercial film throughout the country to a large number of commercial theaters. The number has altered as screens have multiplied and distribution practices have changed—while 1,000 screens were considered a wide release in the 1980s, the figure has increased to about 2,000 in the 1990s and even hit 3,000 recently. *See* **exhibition** *and* **general release.**

■ **Widescope** An early wide-screen film process introduced in 1921 that employed two projectors, each sending an image from a 35mm film that was half the original 70mm film. The system was briefly tried again as Thrillerama in 1956.

■ **wide screen** Any film presentation employing an image on the screen with an aspect ratio wider than 4:3 or 1.33:1, which was the standard ratio in the film industry from the days of silent film until the early 1950s. The 1.33:1 aspect ratio became standardized in the industry because of the popularity of Edison's equipment which used these dimensions. The image was temporarily squared during the early days of sound films to allow for an optical sound track on the film, but since the new picture was less pleasing and functional, the Academy of Motion Picture Arts and Sciences in 1932 returned the image to the earlier ratio by masking the top and bottom of the frame. The 1.33:1 image, which remained standard in the industry for another twenty years and later became the source for the dimensions of the television screen, was referred to as the "Movietone frame," after the sound system necessitating the change in the frame's size, while the opening on cameras and projectors that produced this ratio was referred to as the "Academy aperture" and "reduced aperture."

Several systems that widened the image and gave audiences a more extensive and encompassing picture, however, were tried during this period. Starting in the 1920s Paramount used a process called Magnascope, which enlarged the image four times by means of a special magnifying lens on the projector, but the resulting picture was not of high quality and the system could be employed for only special scenes in a film. A number of film companies experimented in the late 1920s with wider-gauge film—anywhere from 56mm to 70mm—which gave a much better wide-screen image. A few motion pictures, most of which had also been photographed in standard 35mm, were actually shown in these wide-screen formats in a few cities between 1929 and 1931—for example, *Fox Follies of 1929* (1929) and *The Big Trial* (1930) were both shown in a 70mm process called Fox Grandeur; Warner Brothers used a 65mm film process called Vitascope for *Kismet* (1930); and Roland West did a version of his *The Bat Whispers* (1930) for United Artists in a process he called "70mm Wide Film" that likely used the same type of Mitchell camera as Fox Grandeur—but poor economic conditions in the country, as well as the costs for the recent conversion to sound, made theater owners refuse the expense of the new wide-screen equipment.

A different approach had been taken in France when Abel Gance and Claude Autant-Lara developed a triptych process called Polyvision, which employed a screen of three panels to show three 35mm films and was used with great impact in Gance's *Napoléon vu par Abel Gance* in 1927. This type of process was further developed with Fred Waller's Cinerama, introduced in the United States with great success in 1952. Cinerama employed three 35mm projectors to create an image three times the normal width and also twice the standard height on a wraparound, three-screen triptych. Although most of the major cities presented Cinerama spectacles for a number of years, equipping local theaters was too costly an undertaking and producing regular dramatic works too expensive and difficult, nor did the vast screen seem to adapt itself to fictional films.

But it was clear at the time that wide-screen cinema could offer audiences a visual experience not available from the quickly expanding medium of television, which was now keeping an alarming number of people away from the movie houses. Twentieth Century-Fox met the challenge by purchasing and adapting for motion pictures an anamorphic system developed by Henri Chrétien, which was originally called Hypergonar and which was first used by Claude Autant-Lara in 1927 for the silent short *Construire en Feu*. In 1953 Fox released *The Robe* (dir. Henry Koster) in the revolutionary wide-screen process CinemaScope, which employed an anamorphic lens on the camera to squeeze a wide image to one-half its width on 35mm film and the same type of lens on the projector to unsqueeze it. The process was so successful that other companies were soon using similar systems with similar names such as Superscope, Panascope, and Warnerscope, while the term "scope" was commonly employed for any such anamorphic process. The anamorphic lens was at first used for an image with an aspect ratio of 2.55:1, later altered to 2.35:1 to allow for an optical sound track and standard perforations.

Wide-screen cinema became so much in demand that films shot with the once-standard aspect ratio of 1.33:1 were actually cropped at the bottom and top of the image during projection, creating some awkward compositions or at times eliminating important elements; while a number of films were actually shot with the camera's aperture masked at top and bottom. In 1954, Paramount introduced its VistaVision process with *White Christmas* (dir. Michael Curtiz), a nonanamorphic system that passed normal 35mm film through the camera horizontally instead of vertically, thus creating a frame eight perforations across with an aspect ratio approximately 1.85:1. Although a corresponding print was sometimes run through a projector horizontally for special showings, the general practice was to reduce and print the image on normal 35mm film, a practice that resulted in a fine wide-screen image because of the large, well-defined picture on the negative. Technirama, a system popular from 1956 to the mid-1960s, also used a horizontal camera, but with the 35mm film moving behind an optical system which squeezed the image. The image was further compressed in the printing stage so that when projected through a CinemaScope lens, a picture with an aspect ratio of 2.35:1 was achieved. Super Technirama used the same double-size, compressed image on the negative, but unsqueezed it on a 70mm print.

Todd-AO, however, introduced in 1955 with *Oklahoma!* (dir. Fred Zinnemann) and later used for the immensely popular *Around the World in Eighty Days* (1956; dir. Michael Anderson), employed 65mm film in the camera and projected from a 70mm print to achieve an aspect ratio of 2.2:1 without any anamorphic squeezing and unsqueezing, the extra width on the print containing the six stereophonic sound tracks. Twentieth Century-Fox took over this system in the 1960s, producing a number of ambitious films, including the very successful *The Sound of Music* (dir. Robert Wise) in 1965. Other similar wide-film systems were developed, such as Super Panavision, which also used a 65mm unsqueezed negative, and Ultra-Panavision 70, which used the same size negative with an anamorphically squeezed image to produce a 70mm anamorphic print that could project a picture with an aspect ratio of 2.75:1 (this last process was employed for David Lean's spectacular *Lawrence of Arabia* in 1962).

Since wide-film processes were expensive and difficult to use and also required theaters of sufficient size with suitable projectors, they normally were employed for large-scale films that were shown in roadshow distributions at special theaters in larger cities. For general release, such motion pictures were optically reduced to 35mm film, either in a squeezed format, necessitating an anamorphic lens in projection, or as a flat print, in both cases still allowing a fine picture because of the size and quality of the image on the original negative. Today the 65mm negative is rarely employed for shooting a film because of its expense and the restrictions in employing its larger camera; instead films shot on 35mm film are blown up to 70mm prints for special showings. Panavision, for example, has developed an anamorphic lens for a 35mm camera as well as a deanamorphasizing lens for an optical printer of such quality that a number of films shot anamorphically with the smaller-gauge film are printed flat on 70mm film for special screenings. The Panavision lens is today employed for most anamorphic shooting. Also of interest is the Techniscope process introduced by Technicolor Italia in 1963, which employed a camera with a two-perforation pull-down to make frames half the normal height, thus saving on the cost of the negative while producing an image with an aspect ratio of 2.35:1. Such images could be squeezed to one-half their width into the normal anamorphic frame of a 35mm print for projection through an anamorphic lens.

With all the variability in the size of the image produced by these different processes, the aspect ratio of 1.85:1 became standard for wide-screen presentation in this country, especially when the image was projected from flat 35mm film, while 1.66:1 became the norm in Europe. These ratios are achieved by masking the 35mm frame, a practice that still leaves a fine image because of the high quality of film emulsion used today. Since most commercial films ultimately find their way to a television screen, with its 1.33:1 aspect ratio, directors generally place their major action in that part of the frame called the safe-action area, which corresponds to the dimensions of the television screen. For wide-screen motion pictures produced without such regard, a film for television can be transferred to video by a telecine machine that scans each frame of the original to find the central action. Films are also sometimes transferred to video in the "letterbox" format, with the top and bottom parts of the screen blacked out, to maintain a wide-screen image—though something close to the image's original dimensions are maintained, the result is less than imposing.

Obviously the wide screen was a gift for filming historical and epic dramas, for photographing wide panoramas and rapid or extended action, but it also was an important visual tool for the creation of human drama. The compositional tightness of the older aspect ratio and the pictorial unity of the closed frame might now be difficult to achieve, but the new wide screen could have its own compositional aesthetics. Traditional invisible cutting on narration would still be employed, but now the emphasis would be more on the single shot, on the *mise-en-scène* in which a good deal of visual information and a number of actions could be presented simultaneously. Close-ups and scenes of dialogue were still effective, but at the same time characters could be seen in the context of their environment. The wide screen not only extended the horizontal space of the image, surrounding the viewer's focus on the center of the picture with more peripheral vision, it also horizontally extended the sense of depth in the scene, an effect especially evident when depth of field was increased. The result was an image that involved the audience in its spaces, that brought the viewer into the image with an immediacy greater than that achieved with the older and more limited space of the Academy aperture.

See the various processes described above under their individual names as well as **IMAX** *and* **special venue.**

■ **wide-screen release print** A print made for commercial exhibition on which the frame has been reduced or shaped so that it will appear on the screen with an aspect ratio greater than 1.33:1 for wide-screen presentation. In this country the standard wide-screen image has an aspect ratio of 1.85:1, in Europe the ratio is generally 1.66:1. *See* **wide screen.**

■ **wigwag** The red light outside the door to a sound stage that flashes on and off to indicate that shooting is in progress and no one should enter.

■ **wild** (1) Any device not precisely controlled, for example, a variable-speed motor in a camera not sufficiently accurate for recording synchronic sound. (2) Any procedure accomplished independently and not in tandem with some other controlling procedure or device, for example, nonsynchronous sound recorded independently of the picture. (3) Any part of a set that

is not precisely fixed and that can be moved, for example, wild walls.

■ **wild lines** Lines of dialogue not recorded synchronically while shooting, but recorded later to be used during editing and added to the mix. The term generally refers to lines added without lip-sync. *See* **wild track.**

■ **wild mix** *See* **blind mix.**

■ **wild motor** A variable-speed motor for a camera that can operate at a range of speeds and is not employed when synchronically recording sound. Such a motor can be adjusted to allow the camera to shoot at slower or faster speeds than the normal twenty-four frames per second to achieve fast or slow motion respectively. *See* **governor-controlled motor** *and* **synchronous motor.**

**wild motor
(variable-speed motor)**

■ **wild picture** Film or the images on such film shot without synchronous sound. *See* **MOS.**

■ **wild recording** Any recording of sound not made while synchronously shooting the picture. Such recording is most often employed for sound effects, environmental noises, music, and voice-overs. *See* **dub, synchronization, wild sound,** *and* **wild track.**

■ **wild shooting** Photographing a scene without simultaneously recording synchronic sound. Such shooting may be necessary for outdoor scenes, noisy locations, or when it is simply too difficult to acquire a sufficient calibre of sound. Sometimes an entire film may be shot wild with dialogue dubbed in after and other sound later added to the mix, as is generally the case with films made in Italy.

■ **wild sound, nonsynchronous sound, nonsync sound** Any sound recorded without the simultaneous synchronized photographing of the image to which it will later be joined. Such sound might be environmental noises or sound effects. *See* **nonsynchronous sound, wild recording,** *and* **wild track.**

■ **wild track** A sound track not recorded in synchronization with the shooting of a scene. Such a track may be recorded at the time the scene is shot or independently for background noises, sound effects, or even lines of dialogue. Sometimes referred to as a floating track. *See* **wild recording** *and* **wild sound.**

■ **wild wall** A wall of a set that can be moved to allow for the placement of a camera. Also called a floating wall.

■ **William Morris Agency** *See* **talent agency.**

■ **Williams shot** An early special-effects matting process patented by Frank Williams in 1918. A matte was made from the negative of performers photographed in front of a black or white screen, which was then bipacked with the background in either a bipack camera or contact printer. The technique was employed for such films as *The Lost World* (1925; dir. Harry D. Hoyt). *See* **matte** *(2).*

■ **wind** (1) To roll film on a core, spool, or reel. (2) To transfer film or tape from a core, spool, or reel to a similar or other type of holder. (3) To tighten the spring motor drive in a camera by rotating a key or crank so that the camera will operate. Spring mechanisms are generally found in narrow-gauge cameras. (4) The position of the emulsion and perforations for 16mm film. With the base side out and the film rotating clockwise, A-wind is when the perforations are toward the viewer and B-wind when they are away. *See* **A- and B-wind.**

■ **wind gag** A screen or cover that fits around a microphone to muffle the noise of the wind.

■ **windhowler** A machine that creates a variety of wind sounds by using a fan with numerous resonators. *See* **wind machine.**

■ **wind machine** A large fan specially designed to create the effect of wind during shooting. The standard device has a large propeller surrounded by a grid, although smaller fans are employed when only a light breeze is required, and aircraft engines are used when hurricane type winds are needed especially for outdoor shooting. Normally several of the standard types are sufficient for creating a storm within the studio. A material such as polystyrene can be dropped in front of the rotating blades to create a snow storm and a wind howler employed to create the sound of wind. *See* **windhowler.**

■ **window** (1) The length of time in which a film is available for a specific kind of release. The first such duration is domestic theatrical release, for which the window is normally not fixed but dependent on the box office. Sometimes films are directly released on video for a time period, which also has an unfixed duration. Fixed durations apply, for example, to the length of time a film is available to a particular network for television viewing or to a particular cable channel. (2) The term is sometimes used to designate for a film the length of time between the end of one type of a release and the start of another—e.g., between domestic theatrical release and pay television.

■ **window filter, window gel** A color-conversion filter placed over a window generally to convert the daylight to 3200° Kelvin for indoor shooting. Such a filter comes in four-foot rolls and has either an acetate or a gel base. Panels made of thick acrylic are used when the exterior must be seen distinctly through the window.

■ **winds** A shortened form of "wind up" in the sense of completing something—for example, "Shooting winds today."

■ **windscreen, windshield, windsleeve** *See* **zeppelin.**

■ **wind up** The same as (1), (2), and (3) under **wind.** (4) To end or complete a procedure such as the day's shooting or the entire shooting of the film.

■ **wing it** To act or perform without rehearsal; to improvise.

■ **wipe** A transition from one scene to another in which the new scene gradually appears while pushing or "wiping" off the old. A line between the two seems to act as a wiper as it moves across the screen: when the line is out of focus, we have a "soft-edge wipe"; when it is sharp, we have a "hard-edge wipe." As well as the standard vertical type, horizontal, diagonal, iris, spiral, and a variety of other wipes have been used. The term "burst" or "explosive" wipe is sometimes employed for an asymmetrically shaped wipe opening up on the screen. The wipe is created in an optical printer by means of wipe blades or, for complicated effects, by a traveling mate. This type of transition was popular in the 1930s and 1940s when it seems to have run its course, but it has occasionally been brought back to give a period feeling to films (e.g., in George Roy Hill's *The Sting* [1973]).

■ **wipe-off animation** *See* **scratch-off animation.**

■ **wipe to black** A transition in which a partial wipe is achieved when a scene is erased and a black screen follows. The darkened screen may then be followed by a wipe or fade-in to the new scene. Such a transition is also an emphatic form of punctuation to separate the two sequential scenes.

■ **wired for sound** An extra who is permitted to speak some dialogue because he or she is a member of the Screen Actors Guild as well as the Screen Extras Guild.

■ **wire-frame model, wire-frame graphics, wire-frame animation** (1) An early stage in computer graphics or animation in which a basic form of a three-dimensional object is designed by attaching designated points with lines. *See* **animation** *and* **computer animation.** (2) Animation using only the contour lines of characters and objects (e.g., vector graphics).

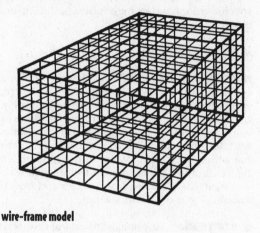

wire-frame model

■ **wireless microphone, radio microphone** A small transmitter worn on the person of a performer that sends sound to a receiver a short distance away for recording when either a cable to the microphone or a mike boom is impractical. *See* **microphone.**

■ **wire-tripping** A method for causing horses to fall, especially in Westerns, by means of a taut wire.

■ **wire work, wirework** Allowing characters to fly through the air by means of wires, a very old and still much-used technique. A very popular film that used wire work with great skill was *Mary Poppins* (1964; dir. Robert Stevenson). When wires cannot be hidden, it is possible to matte them out in special-effects shots. It is now also possible for the image to be digitized and the wires digitally removed, after which the scene is recorded back on film—a much easier process.

■ **WI/wind** Raw film with the emulsion wound in. Certain cameras require emulsion wound in and not facing the lens during exposure. The opposite is WO/wind, which refers to film with the emulsion wound out and facing the lens.

■ **woman's film, woman's picture** A film produced by Hollywood, especially in the 1930s and 1940s, and directed largely toward a female audience. Such films, which featured a well-known actress, were normally melodramas with a plot dealing with romance, family, or some kind of conflict between self-assertion and self-sacrifice that led to much suffering. Molly Haskell, in *From Reverence to Rape: The Treatment of Women in the Movies*

(1974), distinguishes categories of women's films that focus on (1) the woman's sacrifice (e.g., King Vidor's *Stella Dallas* [1938]); (2) her affliction (e.g., Edmund Goulding's *Dark Victory* [1939]); (3) her difficult choice (e.g., Otto Preminger's *Daisy Kenyon* [1947]); and (4) her competition, often with another woman, for a man (e.g., Vincent Sherman's *Old Acquaintance* [1943]). Mary Ann Doane, in *The Desire to Desire: The Woman's Film of the 1940s,* claims that the "seeing and desiring female subject" provokes a violence and attempted repression that culminate in such "gothic paranoid films" as Alfred Hitchcock's *Rebecca* (1940) and George Cukor's *Gaslight* (1944). Such films offer an interesting study in the context of Laura Mulvey's influential essay, "Visual Pleasure and Narrative Cinema" (1975), which argues for a Hollywood cinema dominated by films created for a male gaze. Scholars such as Doane investigate the complex nature of what is supposed to be the dominant and "authentic" female subjectivity of these films and the corresponding supposedly "male appropriation of the gaze."

■ **woofer** (1) A loudspeaker with the capacity for reproducing low frequencies. (2) That part of a loudspeaker that carries low frequencies. *See* **tweeter.**

■ **work book** A breakdown of the action and its timing for an animation film.

■ **working distance** The maximum area in which a performer's speech will be clearly picked up by a microphone.

■ **working leader** A piece of blank film, generally with identification and sync marks, that is attached to the start of a picture or sound workprint for threading into editing equipment.

■ **working title** A tentative name given to a film for identification during production. The final title is chosen later.

■ **work light** The normal light in a studio as distinct from the lighting employed for actual shooting.

■ **work picture** *See* **cutting copy.**

■ **workprint, work print, cutting copy** (1) A print, made from the original negative, that is used by the editor for the various stages of cutting, hence protecting the negative from any damage. The print is first composed of the best takes in the general sequence of events intended for the final version (this stage is called an assembly). The workprint is generally made with a single printer light and is not of high quality. Edited in synchronization with the sound workprint, the picture workprint is eventually made into a rough cut and then a fine cut. The original negative is cut to conform to the final workprint. *See* **editing.** (2) A print composed of all the sound tracks, with the general exception of the musical score, which is edited in synchronization with the various stages of the picture workprint. Also called a work track. *See* **mix.**

■ **workstation** An area that utilizes computer technology for some operation—e.g., a digital audio workstation (DAW) or digital film workstation (DFW).

■ **work track, worktrack** A sound workprint. *See* **workprint** *(2).*

■ **wow** A distortion in the pitch of sound caused by the slowing down of the recording or playback mechanism. This effect is sometimes apparent at the starting or stopping of the mechanism or is sometimes caused by an improperly rotating reel of tape or disc. The term signifies a low rate of flutter. *See* **flutter.**

■ **WO/wind** Raw film with the emulsion wound out. Certain cameras require emulsion wound out and facing the lens during exposure. The opposite is WI/wind, which refers to emulsion wound in and not facing the lens.

■ **wrangler** Another term for "livestock man," the person responsible for the animals appearing in a film.

■ **wrap** (1) The completion of a film's shooting or some part of the shooting (e.g., a shot or scene). (2) To complete a film's shooting or some part of the shooting. (3) A command spoken by the director or assistant director to indicate that shooting for the day, part of the day, or for some particular part of the film is concluded. (4) To place dust covers on the set's furniture and put away the various properties when the day's shooting is complete.

■ **wrap party** A party for all those involved in the making of a film which is given when the principal shooting is concluded.

■ **wratten filter** A gel filter manufactured by Eastman Kodak that is used in a camera, often behind the lens itself in a special holder. Employed instead of a glass filter (or sometimes with one), this gel filter eliminates a specific color band or highlights another through such elimination.

■ **writer** *See* **screenwriter.**

■ **Writers Guild of America (WGA)** The professional union for screenwriters, which negotiates with production companies the minimum wage for a screenplay and for the various stages of writing, credits for the writing, and working conditions. The guild also represents writers for television and radio. Writers Guild of America, East, has offices in New York City and negotiates for members east of the Mississippi, and Writers Guild of America, West, has offices in Los Angeles and negotiates for members west of the Mississippi.

■ **wrong reading** Any image appearing reversed from its natural order; the opposite of "right reading."

■ **wrong set** A term indicating that a set is no longer needed for shooting, and that it is time to start shooting on the next set.

■ **Wurlitzer** The brand name of an organ popular in motion-picture houses during the 1930s and 1940s, when it would suddenly rise up from the pit of the theater along with its instrumentalist to entertain audiences during intermissions. The Wurlitzer filled in the silence left by the conclusion of the sound film.

■   ■   ■

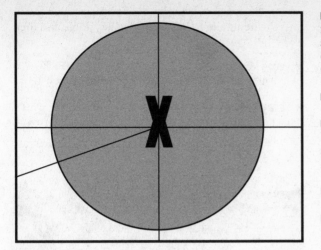

X to
X-sheet

■ **X** (1) An abbreviation for a single exposure of film in a camera or for a single frame on a film. (2) One of a series of such marks written on a page of the playscript to indicate the movement of a character. *See* **X-rated.**

■ **XCU** *See* **extreme close-up.**

■ **X-curve** *See* **Academy roll-off.**

■ **x-dissolve, (XD)** An abbreviation for cross-dissolve. *See* **dissolve.**

■ **xenon lamp** A high-intensity discharge lamp that employs an arc between two tungsten electrodes in an envelope with inert xenon gas. Such lamps have replaced the carbon arc lamp for most professional projectors. Because of the intensity of the light and the narrow and circular nature of its beam, xenon luminaires are sometimes used to create sunlight or a searchlight in a film. *See* **projector.**

■ **xenon print** A print balanced at 5400k so that it can be run in a projector with a xenon bulb. *See* **tungsten print.**

■ **xenon projector, xenon arc projector** A projector that uses a xenon lamp. *See* **xenon lamp.**

■ **xerography, cel-Xerox** An electrophotographic copying process used to transfer drawings to cels in cartoon animation in place of inking. Such a process was developed by Walt Disney Productions along with the Xerox Corporation. *See* **animation.**

■ **X-lighting** *See* **double-key lighting.**

■ **XLR connector, XLR plug** A small connector with a tubular piece surrounding the pins on the male plug that snaps into the female receptacle; generally used in audio systems. *See* **tuchel connector.**

■ **XLS** *See* **extreme long shot.**

■ **X-rated** (1) A film formerly rated X by the Classification and Rating Administration (CARA) of the Motion Picture Association of America (MPAA). The designation meant that the film was restricted and that no one under the age of seventeen or eighteen (depending on the state) could see it. With such a rating, a commercial film would not do well at the box office and in some instances would not be advertised in local media. For such reasons, filmmakers in most instances were coerced into making cuts so that the Classification and Rating Administration would reconsider their film. The Motion Picture Association of America changed the X-rating to NC-17 in 1990, when it had finally lost any significance, largely because of its unauthorized use for advertising pornographic films. *See* **Motion Picture Association of America** *and* **Movie Rating System.** (2) A label associated with a pornographic film in the public's mind because of the past use of such a designation by the Classification and Rating Administration of the MPAA and one frequently used for advertising such a film by distributors and exhibitors to entice the appropriate audience into the theater.

■ **x-ray** A strip of lights suspended above a set.

■ **X rays** A type of electromagnetic energy with wavelengths shorter than those of light and with the capacity of penetrating solids. Such rays are used in cineradiography to create medical photographs and films of the body's internal state and operations.

■ **X-sheet** Abbreviation for exposure sheet, a guide prepared by the animator for the camera operator.

■ ■ ■

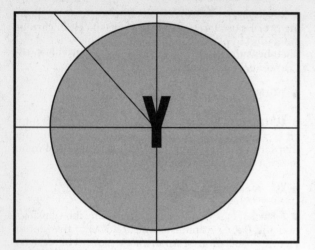

Y core to youth-culture film

■ **Y core** A plastic centerpiece used for holding 35mm film over 1,000 feet in length.

yoke

■ **yoke** The *Y-* or *U-*shaped bracket into which the housing of a luminaire fits and to which a clamp is generally attached in the center for fixing the luminaire to a stand or support. A knob on either arm of the yoke al-

lows the luminaire to be adjusted to any angle and then locked in place.

■ **young leading man** A general designation for a male performer in the twenty to twenty-five age bracket.

■ **young leading woman** A general description for a female performer in the twenty to twenty-five age bracket.

youth-culture film *Easy Rider* (1969; dir. Dennis Hopper) stars Hopper, Peter Fonda, Jack Nicholson, and two impressive motorcycles.

■ ■ ■

■ **youth-culture film** A term sometimes applied to a film dealing with young people struggling against the mores of a corrupt and deadening adult society while trying to live their own lives in their own ways. The term is more specifically applied to a group of such films released in 1969 and 1970 that resulted from the impact of the Vietnam War on American society and the development of a counterculture among young people in response to that war especially on and around the campuses of universities. *Easy Rider* (1969; dir. Dennis Hopper) and *Alice's Restaurant* (1969; dir. Arthur Penn) are the best of these films. Although the first film is more acerbic and angry than the second, both show the hopelessness of their characters' rebellion.

■ ■ ■

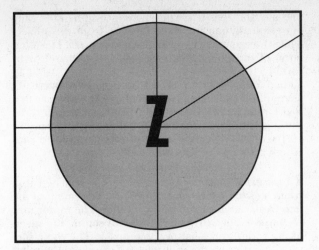

Zagreb Film Studio to Zoptic front projection, Zoptic system

the cut and a shutter blocks out the unwanted frames on each roll during printing. Such a method has the advantage of keeping shots unedited and in their original state so that they can be used again. *See* **A and B printing.**

■ **zero out** To set a footage counter to zero on any editing apparatus such as a synchronizer. *See* **editing.**

■ **ZI** *See* **zoom in.**

■ **zinger** A directional light used to add some brightness to a set with predominantly soft illumination.

■ **zip pan** An extremely fast motion of the camera from one point to another while it is in a fixed position so that intervening space flashes by. Also called a swish pan. *See* **swish pan.**

■ **zits** Jargon for any problems or errors in a digital image.

■ **ZO** *See* **zoom out.**

Zoetrope

■ **Zagreb Film Studio** An animation studio, founded in Yugoslavia in 1956 with government support, that produced a number of celebrated cartoons. The studio was especially known for the satire, parody, and political commentary of its works, and for the sparse, pointed style of its drawings, which were somewhat in the fashion of the UPA studio in the United States. Dušan Vukotić, the studio's founder and first supervisor, directed a number of the group's best works, including *Concerto for Sub-Machine Gun* (1959); *Piccolo* (1960); and *Ersatz* (1961), the last of which was the first foreign-made cartoon to win an Academy Award in the United States. *See* **animation** *and* **UPA.**

■ **Z core** A plastic center on which a roll of raw 16mm film stock, four hundred feet in length or more, is wound.

■ **zeppelin, zeppelin windscreen** A long tube with holes that is placed over a shotgun microphone to avoid noise from the wind.

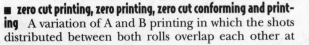

zeppelin windscreen

■ **zero cut printing, zero printing, zero cut conforming and printing** A variation of A and B printing in which the shots distributed between both rolls overlap each other at

■ **Zoetrope** A device, invented by William George Horner in England in 1834 and originally called the Daedaleum, that used the viewer's persistence of vision to create an illusion of movement within a series of drawings on a strip of paper wrapped around the inside of a rotating drum. The viewer looked at such images as jugglers and jumping horses through slits in the drum opposite to the drawings and located above the strip. *See* **Phenakistiscope, Praxinoscope,** *and* **Stroboscope.**

■ **zoom** (1) The apparent movement either toward or away from a subject due to the use of a zoom lens (also called a varifocal lens). Although the term should technically be limited to the use of such a lens, it is also sometimes employed to describe similar effects achieved in film without the use of a varifocal lens—e.g., by means of rapid movement of the camera on wheeled supports (*see* **dolly shot**) or the quick cut from a long shot to close-up. Of course, the actual zoom shot flattens out the space between the camera and subject, while the dolly shot moves the viewer through space, and the quick cut eliminates spatial continuity entirely. Optical zooms are created by moving the camera and lens either toward or away from the film being photographed in an optical printer, while zooms are created in animated films by the rapid movement of the camera up or down the animation stand. (2) A shot in which the camera seems to move either toward or away from a subject because of the use of a zoom lens. (3) To make the camera appear to move toward a subject or away from it by means of a zoom lens. (4) A zoom lens. *See* **zoom lens** *and* **zoom shot.**

■ **zoom back (ZB)** *See* **zoom out.**

■ **zoom director's viewfinder** A director's viewfinder with zoom movement patterned after a zoom lens. Such a device, often with a zoom range of 10:1, is adjustable for 16mm, 35mm, or anamorphic formats, and also has a series of adjustable aspect ratios. *See* **director's viewfinder.**

■ **zoom drive** *See* **zoom motor.**

■ **zoom-freeze** A zoom shot that concludes with a static image of the subject: for example, when a film ends with the camera seeming to move in to a close-up of a character's face, which is then frozen before our eyes, permanently to remain that way in our memory.

■ **zoom in (ZI)** To increase the focal length of a zoom lens in the process of a shot so that the camera seems to move in to the subject as it is continuously magnified. To "zoom out" achieves the opposite effect. *See* **crash zoom** *and* **zoom shot.**

■ **zooming** The process of changing the size of a subject and the field of view with a zoom lens during shooting so that the camera seems to move in to or away from the subject. *See* **zoom shot.**

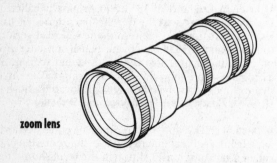

zoom lens

■ **zoom lens, varifocal lens, variable-focal-length lens** A lens with a variable focal length that can be progressively changed from wide-angle to long focus, or the reverse, in the process of shooting without changing the focus or aperture setting. Such a unit, made of both fixed and movable lenses, creates the impression of the camera gradually moving in to or away from the subject while the camera actually remains stationary. The alteration of focal length may be achieved by hand or by turning the barrel with a crank, handle, or cable attached to the lens or by an electric motor which creates a smoother movement. Although zoom lenses at first had a ratio of 3:1, with the longest focal length three times greater than the shortest, lenses with a ratio of 10:1 (e.g., 24–240mm) are now often employed with 35mm cameras. *See* **zoom shot.**

■ **zoom motor** An electric motor that is attached to a zoom lens to operate and control the movement of the lens from one focal length to another. The motor unit is composed of a drive, a rheostat for setting the speed of the zoom, and a battery power-pack. The zoom motor allows a smoother movement of the zoom than that achieved manually.

■ **zoom out (ZO), zoom back (ZB)** To decrease the focal length of a zoom lens in the process of a shot so that the camera seems to move away from the subject as it is continuously decreased in size. To "zoom in" achieves the opposite effect. *See* **zoom shot.**

■ **zoom range** The extent of the focal length of a zoom lens from its longest to shortest points. Zoom lenses used in motion picture work vary anywhere from 3:1 to 20:1, that is, with the longest focal length anywhere from three to twenty times greater than the shortest. *See* **zoom lens.**

■ **zoom shot** A shot taken with a zoom lens in which the focal length of the lens changes from wide angle to long focus or the reverse so that the camera seems to move in to (i.e., "zoom in" to) or away from (i.e., "zoom out" from) the subject while the camera actually remains stationary. Such a shot is much less difficult to obtain than a dolly or traveling shot, since a separate vehicle is not necessary to move the camera nor does the focus or aperture setting have to be changed, because the camera stays in one place and the distance between lens and subject remains the same. The effects of both types of shot are also somewhat different: a shot with the camera actually moving toward the subject takes the viewer through the space of the scene with the perspective constantly changing because of parallax and also because objects in the foreground increase in size more rapidly than those in the background while objects rush past the camera; a shot with a zoom lens maintains the same distance between camera and subject and hence the same perspective, with the scene becoming two-dimensional as the background grows rapidly in size and seems to flatten out behind the subject as it approaches the camera. Zoom shots, then, can be quite effective for rapidly and dramatically bringing us into or out of a scene; for bringing our attention suddenly to some person or object previously in the distance; for suddenly pulling us back from a scene so that we can see a character in the context of the environment; and for following the movement of a character or vehicle. Stanley Kubrick achieved some striking shots in *Barry Lyndon* (1975) through a special zoom lens with a 20:1 ratio which, for example, could smoothly move the audience from its close involvement in a parade of British soldiers to the distant perspective of characters watching the parade. Zoom lenses have also been effective in documentary and news filming when cumbersome equipment and changes of lenses would be difficult, and they have been especially useful in such filming to focus on people in the distance when immediate accessibility is difficult or when it is desirable to photograph such figures so that they are unaware of the camera. *See* **zoom lens.**

■ **zoom stand** An informal term for an animation stand because of the capacity of its camera to create zoom effects by moving rapidly up or down the column and hence away from or toward the drawing. *See* **animation stand.**

■ **Zoopraxiscope** A type of projector invented by Eadweard James Muybridge at the end of the nineteenth century, which was comprised of an enlarged Phenakistiscope wheel with glass-plate photographs and a magic lantern for the actual projection. Muybridge completed his invention in 1879, calling it a Zoogyroscope, but changed the name of his device to a Zoopraxiscope in 1881. An Englishman who performed most of his photographic experiments in the United States, Muybridge originally performed a series of exercises photographing moving forms with twelve or more cameras operating in rapid succession; his most famous series was of a running race horse, photographed in 1878, to discover for Governor Leland Stanford of California, who had bet on the matter, whether the animal at any one point lifted all four feet from the ground. *See* **magic lantern** *and* **Phenakistiscope.**

■ **Zoptic front projection, Zoptic system** A front-projection system developed by Zoran Perisic for creating the illusion that the subject is actually moving in the depth of the scene while, in fact, remaining the same relative distance from both the screen and front-projection equipment. To achieve this effect, zoom lenses on both the projector sending the background image and the camera are electronically controlled to work in tandem: for example, the subject seems to move away from the camera and into a scene when the lens on the projector zooms out to a wide-angle view and the lens on the camera makes a corresponding move to encompass the extended scene—in this instance, the background seems to remain the same size while the subject grows smaller. The Zoptic system was employed with great effect to make the hero appear to fly in the three Superman films (1978, 1980, and 1983). Similar effects can be achieved by employing a tracking front-projection unit with a fixed lens and an autofocus system for both the projector and camera, but this method is less flexible and the apparent speed of the subject is more restricted. *See* **front projection.**

■ ■ ■